Dear Student:

You have chosen to begin a career as a business professional by majoring in a business discipline. If your experience is anything like mine, you will not regret your choice. Working in business leads to fulfilling and enjoyable experiences and relationships with interesting, quality people. Working in a company you admire that sells products or services in which you believe will enable you to feel positive about yourself, your contributions, and your professional life.

Do you want to be more than just another department manager? Do you see yourself as a future business leader? If so, the MIS course is THE most important course in the business curriculum. Are you surprised to read that? If you view the MIS course as the "Excel class" or the "Access course," that opinion is preposterous. As you will learn in Chapter 1, learning software is not the major goal of this class. Instead, you will learn how businesses use information systems and technology to accomplish their goals, objectives, and competitive strategy.

Think about any modern organization. How does Amazon.com ship millions of items per second, 24/7, worldwide? How does YouTube store and deliver thousands of hours of video every day? How do Facebook and MySpace connect you to your friends? They use information systems! And, those organizations have succeeded primarily because they found innovative ways to apply emerging information technology.

Maybe you're thinking, "Not me! I'll leave that stuff to someone else." Well, you might leave the technical details of information systems to someone else, but if you leave the thinking about innovative applications of information systems to someone else, you're in trouble. In the twenty-first century, every business professional must be able to envision ways to gain competitive advantage using information systems and know how to collaborate with professionals to develop and maintain those systems.

To help you gain this critical knowledge, we have included three unique features in this book. First, every chapter and every chapter extension is organized around a set of questions. Use these questions to manage your study time. Read until you can answer the questions. Second, every part and every chapter begins with a real-life scenario of a business professional who needs knowledge of information systems. Use those scenarios to understand how you can apply the knowledge of information systems to gain a personal competitive advantage. Finally, read the two-page boxed inserts, called "Guides." If possible, discuss the questions in these guides with other students. Such discussions will give you a chance to practice your listening skills and to learn to assert your own opinions in an effective manner.

Like all worthwhile endeavors, this course is work. That's just the way it is. No one succeeds in business without sustained focus, attention, desire, motivation, and hard work. It won't always be easy, it won't always be fun. However, you will learn concepts, skills, and behaviors that are essential for success in business in the twenty-first century.

I wish you, as an emerging business professional, the very best success!

Sincerely,

David Kroenke

Whidbey Island, Washington

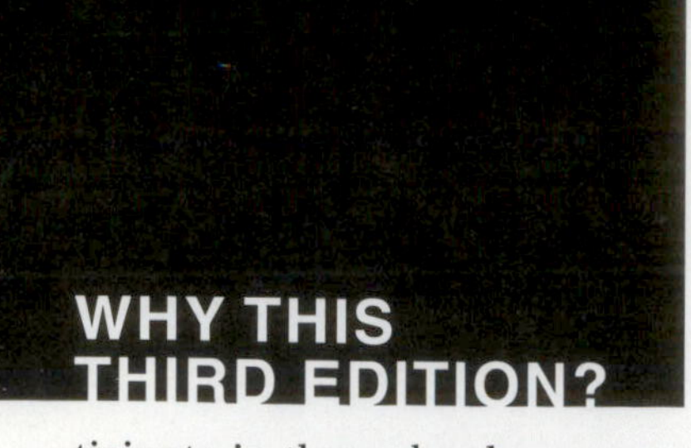

WHY THIS THIRD EDITION?

MIS is changing faster today than at any time since the invention of the personal computer. It is incredibly fascinating to observe and participate in these developments. Not a day goes by that we don't hear of some business doing something innovative with new technology. Apple leads that movement with the iSomethings, but other organizations that don't have Apple's scope are innovating new products and services that are just as important within their own markets.

Accordingly, this third edition of *Experiencing MIS* is a major revision from the second edition. Table 1 lists new and nearly new features in this edition, as well as topics that were deleted from the second edition. Two themes emerge. First, nearly free data communications and data storage enable businesses to reach out to customers and suppliers in dramatically new ways. Second, business processes, rather than isolated IS requirements, drive the use and success of new technology.

Hence, this edition includes new chapters and chapter extensions on remote computing and geographic information systems and on business process management and enterprise resource planning (ERP). Also, a new chapter extension on international IS replaces the international dimension in the second edition. This edition also includes a new feature, Experiencing MIS InClass, which is designed to help students apply their knowledge in class exercises, and new opening cases for all 12 chapters as well. Two new cases introduce the chapters. FlexTime, a workout studio, introduces Chapters 1–6 and Fox Lake Country Club, an organization that has just started a new business unit for wedding events, introduces Chapters 7–12.

Nearly new features include a new presentation of business processes in Chapter 2 that better conforms with the BPM and ERP chapter extensions that follow. Also, Office 2010 and SharePoint 2010 have markedly changed the collaboration systems environment. Data communication in Chapter 6 has been simplified and consolidated to make room for the addition of new social networking computing material. Chapter 7 has been reworked to conform to the new BPM and ERP material.

Students don't need to know how to use Facebook and Twitter, and they don't need many examples of how businesses use them either. What they do need to know, I believe, are the economic underpinnings of social networks. Hence, both Chapter 8 and Chapter Extension 14 include discussions on the theory of social capital and how that theory can be used to evaluate social networking as well as Enterprise 2.0.

This text includes 40 different exercises for applying Microsoft Office and other applications to the solution of business problems. Further, all the examples, as well as Chapter Extensions 5–9, use Office 2010.

Table 1 also shows major deletions. Good-bye Dee! You had a great run, but your blog problem is trivial today. MRV is out as well; Fox Lake Country Club replaces it with a new emphasis on the problems of information silos. The discussion of TCP/IP was deleted primarily because the opportunity cost of teaching it is too high. Innov8 and small-scale systems development were deleted for similar reasons.

Table 1 Changes in *Experiencing MIS*, 3rd Edition

New	Chapter Extension 10, Remote, Nomadic, and Mobile Systems Chapter Extension 18, Business Process Management Chapter Extension 12, Enterprise Resource Planning (ERP) Systems Chapter Extension 17, Geographic Information Systems Chapter Extension 21, International MIS Experiencing MIS InClass Exercises FlexTime Case for Chapters 1–6 (with six new videos) Fox Lake Case for Chapters 7–12 (with six new videos)
Nearly new	Chapter 2, Business Processes, Information, and Information Systems Chapter Extension 2, Using Collaboration Information Systems Chapter 6, Data Communication Chapter 7, Enterprise Systems Chapter 8, E-Commerce, Web 2.0, and Social Networking Chapter Extension 14, Processing Social Capital: Facebook, Twitter, and User-Generated Content (UGC) Application Exercises Office 2010 Throughout
Deleted from Second Edition	Emerson and MRV cases Chapter Extension 10, How the Internet Works Chapter Extension 12, Cross-Functional, Processes, Applications, and Systems Chapter Extension 14, Innov8 Chapter Extension 18, Systems Development for Small Businesses Part Closing Sections

The Guides

Each chapter includes two unique guides that focus on current issues in information systems. In each chapter, one of the guides focuses on an ethical issue in business. The other guide focuses on the application of the chapter's contents to other business aspects. The content of each guide is designed to simulate thought, discussion, and active participation to help YOU develop your problem-solving skills and become a better business professional.

LEARNING AIDS FOR STUDENTS

We have structured this book so you can maximize the benefit from the time you spend reading it. As shown in the table below, each chapter includes a series of learning aids to help you succeed in this course.

Resource	Description	Benefit	Example
Question-Driven Chapter Learning Objectives	These queries, and the subsequent chapter sections written around them, focus your attention and make your reading more efficient.	Identifies the main point of the section. When you can answer each question, you've learned the main point of the section.	p. 5
Guides	Each chapter includes two guides that focus on current issues relating to information systems. One of the two deals with an ethical issue.	Stimulates thought and discussion. Helps develop your problem-solving skills. Helps you learn to respond to ethical dilemmas in business.	p. 16
Experiencing MIS InClass Exercise	Each chapter of this text includes an exercise called *Experiencing MIS InClass*. This feature contains exercises, projects, and questions for you and a group of your fellow students to perform in class. Some of those exercises can be done in a single class period; others span several class sections with out-of-class activities in between. For example, see the first Experiencing MIS InClass Exercise on online dating, page 11.	These exercises help you relate the knowledge you are learning in the chapter to your everyday life.	p. 11
How Does the Knowledge in This Chapter Help . . . and You? (near the end of each chapter)	This section revisits the opening scenario and discusses what the chapter taught you about it.	Summarizes the "takeaway" points from the chapter as they apply to the company or person in the story, and to you.	p. 15
Active Review	Each chapter concludes with a summary-and-review section, organized around the chapter's study questions.	Offers a review of important points in the chapter. If you can answer the questions posed, you will understand the material.	p. 20
Key Terms and Concepts	Highlights the major terms and concepts with their appropriate page reference.	Provides a summary of key terms for review before exams.	p. 19
Using Your Knowledge	These exercises ask you to take your new knowledge to the next step by applying it to a practice problem.	Tests your critical-thinking skills and keeps reminding you that you are learning material that applies to the real world.	p. 19
Collaboration Exercise	A team exercise that focuses on the chapter's topic.	Use Google Docs, Microsoft Windows Live SkyDrive, Microsoft SharePoint, or some other tool to collaborate on collective answers.	p. 21

Resource	Description	Benefit	Example
Case Study	A case study closes each chapter. You will reflect on the use in real organizations of the technology or systems presented in the chapter and recommend solutions to business problems.	Requires you to apply newly acquired knowledge to real situations.	p. 22
Application Exercises (at the end of the book)	These exercises ask you to solve business situations using spreadsheet (Excel) database (Access) applications, and other Office applications.	Helps develop your computer skills.	p. 602
Videos	All chapter-opening scenarios are depicted in a series of short dramatizations that emphasize the importance of the chapter content.	Brings to life the opening scenarios and puts you right in the action.	These accompany each part opening and chapter opening.
myMISlab	myMISlab contains a Microsoft Office 2010 simulation environment with tutorials, SharePoint collaboration tools and assignments, student assessments, and classroom videos.	Expands the classroom experience with valuable hands-on activities and tools.	**www.mymislab.com**
SharePoint Hosting	Pearson will host Microsoft SharePoint site collections for your university. Students need only a browser to participate.	Enables students to collaborate using the world's most popular collaboration software.	**www.pearsonhighered.com/kroenke**

THIRD EDITION

EXPERIENCING MIS

David M. Kroenke

Prentice Hall

Boston Columbus Indianapolis New York San Francisco Upper Saddle River
Amsterdam Cape Town Dubai London Madrid Milan Munich Paris Montreal Toronto
Delhi Mexico City Sao Paulo Sydney Hong Kong Seoul Singapore Taipei Tokyo

Editorial Director: Sally Yagan
Editor in Chief: Eric Svendsen
Executive Editor: Bob Horan
Director of Development: Steve Deitmer
Development Editor: Laura Town
Senior Editorial Project Manager: Kelly Loftus
Director of Marketing: Patrice Lumumba Jones
Senior Marketing Manager: Anne Fahlgren
Senior Managing Editor: Judy Leale
Senior Production Project Manager: Ann Pulido
Senior Operations Supervisor: Arnold Vila
Operations Specialist: Arnold Vila
Creative Director: Christy Mahon
Senior Art Director/Design Supervisor: Janet Slowik
Interior and Cover Designer: Karen Quigley
Interior and Cover Illustrations: Simon Alicea
Lead Media Project Manager: Lisa Rinaldi
Editorial Media Project Manager: Denise Vaughn
Full-Service Project Management: Jen Welsch/BookMasters, Inc.
Composition: Integra
Printer/Bindery: Banta dba RRD - Menasha
Cover Printer: Lehigh-Phoenix Color/Hagerstown
Text Font: 10/13, Utopia

Credits and acknowledgments borrowed from other sources and reproduced, with permission, in this textbook appear on appropriate page within text or on page 633.

Library of Congress Cataloging-in-Publication Data

Kroenke, David.
Experiencing MIS / David M. Kroenke.—3rd ed.
p. cm.
Includes bibliographical references and index.
ISBN 978-0-13-215794-0 (pbk. : alk. paper)
1. Management information systems. 2. Business—Data processing. I. Title.
T58.6.K767 2011
658.4'038011—dc22

2010032136

10 9 8 7 6 5 4 3 2 1

Prentice Hall
is an imprint of

www.pearsonhighered.com

ISBN 10: 0-13-215794-2
ISBN 13: 978-0-13-215794-0

CONTENTS OVERVIEW

Experiencing MIS offers basic topic coverage of MIS in its 12 chapters and more in-depth, expanded coverage in its chapter extensions. This modular organization allows you to pick and choose among those topics. Here, chapter extensions are shown below the chapters to which they are related. You will preserve continuity if you use each of the 12 chapters in sequence. In most cases, a chapter extension can be covered *any time* in the course after its related chapter. You need not use any of the chapter extensions if time is short.

CONTENTS

Part 2: Information Technology

Chapter 4: Hardware and Software p. 72

Chapter 5: Database Processing p. 98

CHAPTER EXTENSIONS

Chapter Extension 6: Preparing a Computer Budget Using Excel p. 367

Chapter Extension 7: Database Design p. 383

Chapter Extension 8: Using Microsoft Access 2010 p. 398

Chapter Extension 9: Using Excel and Access Together p. 418

Chapter Extension 10: Remote, Nomadic, and Mobile Systems p. 445

TO THE STUDENT

If you were to walk into my office today and ask me for advice about how to use this book, here's what I'd say:

1. This class may be the most important course in the business school. Don't blow it off. See the first few pages of Chapter 1.
2. This class is much broader than you think. It's not just about Excel or Web pages or computer programs. It's about business and how businesses can be more successful with computer-based systems.
3. The design of this book is based on research into how you learn. Every chapter or extension starts with a list of questions. Read the material until you can answer the questions. Then, go to the Active Review and do the tasks there. If you're successful with those tasks, you're done. If it takes you 5 minutes to do that, you're done. If it takes you 5 hours to do that, you're done. But you aren't done until you can complete the Active Review tasks.
4. Pay attention to the issues raised by the opening cases and the videos. Those cases are based on real people and real companies and real stories. I changed the names to protect the innocent, the guilty, the publisher, and me.
5. Read the guides. Those stories are what my own students tell me teach them the most.
6. To make it easy to pick up and read, this book includes a lot of colorful and interesting art. However, don't forget to read.
7. I have worked in the computer industry for more than 40 years. There isn't anything in this text that a business professional might never use. It's all relevant, depending on what you decide to do.
8. However, this book contains more than you can learn in one semester. All of the content in this book will be needed by someone; but it may not be needed by you. Pay attention to what your professor says you should learn. He or she knows the job requirements in your local area.
9. With the national unemployment rate near 10 percent, your primary task in college is to learn something that will get you a job. Many exercises ask you to prepare something for a future job interview. Do those exercises!
10. Technology will create wonderfully interesting opportunities in the next 10 years. Get involved, be successful, and have fun!

David Kroenke
Whidbey Island, Washington

MIS and You

Knowledge of information systems will be critical to your success in business. If you major in accounting, marketing, management, or in another, less technical, major, you may not yet know how important such knowledge will be to you. The purpose of Part 1 is to demonstrate why this subject is so important to every business professional. We begin with a real-life case.

This could happen to you

FlexTime is a hip, urban, sophisticated workout studio located in downtown Indianapolis. Kelly Summers started FlexTime 20 years ago after teaching aerobics at another firm. She began modestly, teaching a few classes a week at a small facility in the back of an office building. Over time, she hired other instructors to help. Within a few months, she expanded her business by finding new clients and hiring other, "star" instructors to teach most of the classes. She paid those instructors a percent of the class revenue and worked hard to make their lives easier and to make them feel appreciated, and they, in turn, took care of the clients.

The formula worked. Over the years, FlexTime expanded from the small backroom to a full floor, then two floors, and, by 2005, FlexTime occupied all four stories of its building. Today, FlexTime clients make more than 15,000 visits a month. During prime time, the building is packed, the tempo is fast paced, and the atmosphere is intense; loud music and well-dressed urban professionals flow through the hallways.

About the time that Kelly started FlexTime, Neil West was ranked as the number one amateur surfer in Southern California. Neil finished college at San Diego State and took a job in telemarketing sales for a small software company. He excelled at his job, and within a few years was selling large enterprise solutions for Siebel Systems, then a leading vendor of customer relationships management software (discussed in Chapter 7). Neil sold software through the

heyday of the dot-com explosion and by 2005 was in a financial position to retire. His last major client was located in Indianapolis, where he enrolled in a kickboxing class taught by Kelly.

At that point, FlexTime was a screaming success in every aspect save one—the back office was a disorganized mess. Kelly and her staff were running the business out of several file cabinets with temporary record storage in an orange crate. Neil experienced numerous delays when attempting to pay for goods and services at the front desk, and he noticed the inefficiency of FlexTime's business processes. When Neil mentioned that he was about to leave Siebel, Kelly asked if he'd be willing to help her organize FlexTime's office records.

Up to that point, Neil had planned on returning to California, but he agreed to help Kelly redesign FlexTime's accounting, customer management, operations, and related processes in what he thought would be a 6-month consulting job. He led several projects to install information systems, convert FlexTime from manual to electronic records, and train personnel on the use of the new systems. As he got into the project, he saw great potential for FlexTime and bought out Kelly's financial partners to become a co-owner and partner of FlexTime. In 2008, they were married.

With Kelly running the client/trainer side of the business and Neil managing the back-office system, today FlexTime is an unqualified success. However, that does not mean that it does not have problems and challenges, as you are about to learn.

CHAPTER 1

The Importance of MIS

This could happen to you

"Fired? You're firing me?"

"Well, *fired* is a harsh word, but . . . well, FlexTime has no further need for your services."

"But, Kelly, I don't get it. I really don't. I worked hard, and I did everything you told me to do."

"Jennifer, that's just it. You did everything *I* told you to do."

"I put in so many hours. How could you fire me????"

"Your job was to find ways we can generate additional revenue from our existing club members."

"Right! And I did that."

"No, you didn't. You followed up on ideas *that I gave you.* But we don't need someone who can follow up on my plans. We need someone who can figure out what we need to do, create her own plans, and bring them back to me . . . . And others."

"How could you expect me to do that? I've only been here 4 months!!!"

"It's called teamwork. Sure, you're just learning our business, but I made sure all of our senior staff would be available to you . . . "

"I didn't want to bother them."

"Well, you succeeded. I asked Jason what he thought of the plans you're working on. 'Who's Jennifer?' he asked."

"But, doesn't he work at night?"

"Right. He's the night staff manager . . . and 37 percent of our weekday business occurs after 7 P.M. Probably worth talking to him."

"I'll go do that!"

"Jennifer, do you see what just happened? I gave you an idea and you said you'll do it. That's not what I need. I need you to find solutions on your own."

"I worked really hard. I put in a lot of hours. I've got all these reports written."

STUDY QUESTIONS

Q1 Why is Introduction to MIS the most important class in the business school?

Q2 What is an information system?

Q3 What is MIS?

Q4 Why is the difference between information technology and information systems important to you?

Q5 What is your role in IS security?

How does the **knowledge** in this chapter help ***Jennifer*** and **you?**

"Has anyone seen them?"

"I talked to you about some of them. But, I was waiting until I was satisfied with them."

"Right. That's not how we do things here. We develop ideas and then kick them around with each other. Nobody has all the smarts. Our plans get better when we comment and rework them . . . I think I told you that."

"BUT TODAY, THEY'RE NOT ENOUGH."

"Maybe you did. But I'm just not comfortable with that."

"Well, it's a key skill here."

"I know I can do this job."

"Jennifer, you've been here almost 4 months; you have a degree in business. Several weeks ago, I asked you for your first idea about how to upsell our customers. Do you remember what you said?"

"Yes, I wasn't sure how to proceed. I didn't want to just throw something out that might not work."

"But how would you find out if it would work?"

"I don't want to waste money . . . "

"No, you don't. So, when you didn't get very far with that task, I backed up and asked you to send me a diagram of the life cycle for one of our clients . . . how we get them in the door, how we enroll them in their first classes, how we continue to sell to them . . . "

"Yes, I sent you that diagram."

"Jennifer, it made no sense. Your diagram had people talking to Neil in accounts receivable before they were even customers."

"I know that process, I just couldn't put it down on paper. But, I'll try again!"

"Well, I appreciate that attitude, but times are tight. We don't have room for trainees. When the economy was strong, I'd have been able to look for a spot for you, see if we can bring you along. But we can't afford to do that now."

"What about my references?"

"I'll be happy to tell anyone that you're reliable, that you work 40 to 45 hours a week, and that you're honest and have integrity."

"Those are important!"

"Yes, they are. But today, they're not enough."

Optional Extensions for this chapter are • CE1: Improving Your Collaboration Skills 310 • CE2: Using Collaboration Information Systems 319

Q1 Why Is Introduction to MIS the Most Important Class in the Business School?

Introduction to MIS is the most important class in the business school. That statement was not true in 2005, and it may not be true in 2020. But it is true in 2011.

Why?

The ultimate reason lies in a principle known as **Moore's Law**. In 1965, Gordon Moore, cofounder of Intel Corporation, stated that because of technology improvements in electronic chip design and manufacturing, "The number of transistors per square inch on an integrated chip doubles every 18 months." His statement has been commonly misunderstood to be, "The speed of a computer doubles every 18 months," which is incorrect, but captures the sense of his principle.

Because of Moore's Law, the ratio of price to performance of computers has fallen from something like $4,000 for a standard computing device to something around a penny for that same computing device.[1] See Figure 1-1.

As a future business professional, however, you needn't care how fast a computer your company can buy for $100. That's not the point. Here's the point:

Because of Moore's Law, the cost of data communications and data storage is essentially zero.

Think about that statement before you hurry to the next paragraph. What happens when those costs are essentially zero? Here are some consequences:

- YouTube
- Facebook
- Pandora
- LinkedIn
- iPhone
- Second Life
- Twitter

None of these was prominent in 2005, and, in fact, most didn't exist in 2005.

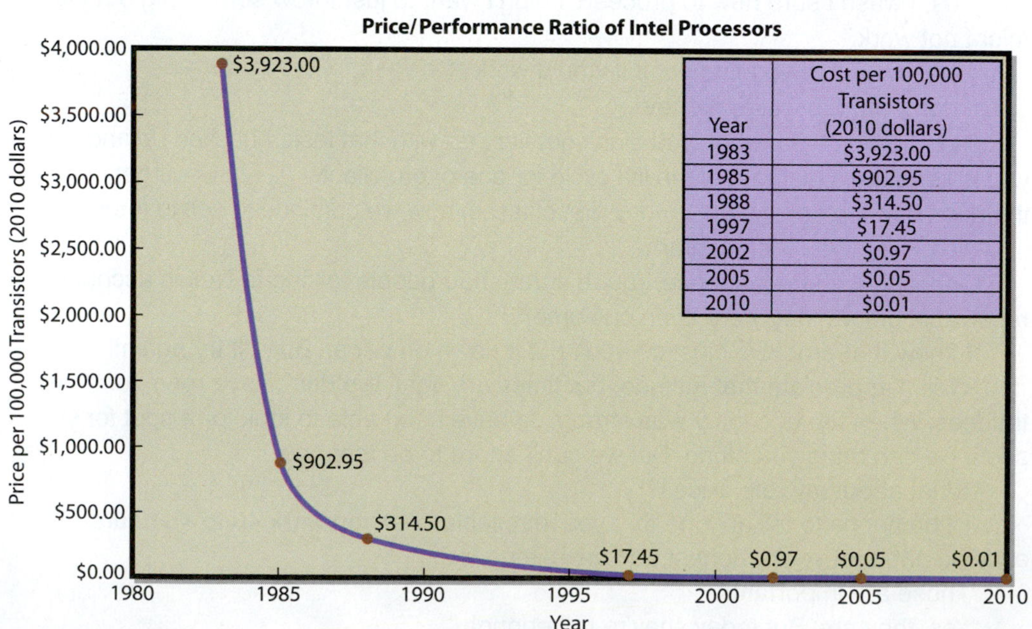

Year	Cost per 100,000 Transistors (2010 dollars)
1983	$3,923.00
1985	$902.95
1988	$314.50
1997	$17.45
2002	$0.97
2005	$0.05
2010	$0.01

Figure 1-1 Computer Price/Performance Ratio Decreases

[1] These figures represent the cost of 100,000 transistors, which can roughly be translated into a unit of a computing device. For our purposes, the details don't matter. If you doubt any of this, just look at your $199 iPhone and realize that you pay $40 a month to use it.

Are There Cost-Effective Business Applications of Facebook and Twitter?

Of course. FlexTime is profitably using them today. Fitness instructors post announcements via Twitter. FlexTime collects those tweets and posts them on its Facebook page. Total cost to FlexTime? Zero.

But ask another question: Are there wasteful, harmful, useless business applications of Facebook and Twitter? Of course. Do I care to follow the tweets of the mechanic who changes the oil in my car? I don't think so.

But there's the point. Maybe I'm not being creative enough. Maybe there are great reasons for the mechanic to tweet customers and I'm just not able to think of them. Which leads us to the first reason Introduction to MIS is the most important course in the business school today:

Future business professionals need to be able to assess, evaluate, and apply emerging information technology to business.

You need the knowledge of this course to attain that skill, and having that skill will lead to greater job security.

How Can I Attain Job Security?

Many years ago I had a wise and experienced mentor. One day I asked him about job security, and he told me that the only job security that exists is "a marketable skill and the courage to use it." He continued, "There is no security in our company, there is no security in any government program, there is no security in your investments, and there is no security in Social Security." Alas, how right he turned out to be.

So what is a marketable skill? It used to be that one could name particular skills, such as computer programming, tax accounting, or marketing. But today, because of Moore's Law, because the cost of data storage and data communications is essentially zero, any routine skill can and will be outsourced to the lowest bidder. And if you live in the United States, Canada, Australia, Europe, and so on, that is unlikely to be you. Numerous organizations and experts have studied the question of what skills will be marketable during your career. Consider two of them. First, the RAND Corporation, a think tank located in Santa Monica, California, has published innovative and groundbreaking ideas for more than 60 years, including the initial design for the Internet. In 2004, RAND published a description of the skills that workers in the twenty-first century will need:

> Rapid technological change and increased international competition place the spotlight on the skills and preparation of the workforce, particularly the ability to adapt to changing technology and shifting demand. Shifts in the nature of organizations . . . favor strong nonroutine cognitive skills.[2]

Whether you're majoring in accounting or marketing or finance or information systems, you need to develop strong nonroutine cognitive skills.

What are such skills? Robert Reich, former Secretary of Labor, enumerates four components:[3]

- Abstract reasoning
- Collaboration
- Systems thinking
- Ability to experiment

Figure 1-2 shows an example of each. Reread the FlexTime case that started this chapter, and you'll see that Jennifer lost her job because of her inability to practice these skills.

2. Lynn A. Kaoly and Constantijn W. A. Panis, *The 21st Century at Work* (Santa Monica, CA: RAND Corporation, 2004), p. xiv.
3. Robert B. Reich, *The Work of Nations* (New York: Alfred A. Knopf, 1991), p. 229.

Figure 1-2
Examples of Critical Skills for Nonroutine Cognition

Skill	Example	Jennifer's Problem
Abstraction	Construct a model or representation.	Inability to model the customer life cycle.
Systems thinking	Model system components and show how components' inputs and outputs relate to one another.	Confusion about when/how customers contact accounts payable.
Collaboration	Develop ideas and plans with others. Provide and receive critical feedback.	Unwilling to work with others with work-in-progress.
Experimentation	Create and test promising new alternatives, consistent with available resources.	Fear of failure prohibited discussion of new ideas.

How Can Intro to MIS Help You Learn Nonroutine Skills?

Introduction to MIS is the best course in the business school for learning these four key skills, because every topic will require you to apply and practice them. Here's how.

Abstract Reasoning

Abstract reasoning is the ability to make and manipulate models. You will work with one or more models in every course topic and book chapter. For example, later in this chapter you will learn about a *model* of the five components of an information system. Chapter 2 will describe how to use this model to assess the scope of any new information system project; other chapters will build upon this model.

In this course, you will not just manipulate models that your instructor or I have developed, you will also be asked to construct models of your own. In Chapter 5, for example, you'll learn how to create data models, and in Chapter 7 you'll learn to make process models.

Systems Thinking

Can you go down to a grocery store, look at a can of green beans, and connect that can to U.S. immigration policy? Can you watch tractors dig up a forest of pulpwood trees and connect that woody trash to Moore's Law? Do you know why one of the major beneficiaries of YouTube is Cisco Systems?

Answers to all of these questions require systems thinking. **Systems thinking** is the ability to model the components of the system, to connect the inputs and outputs among those components into a sensible whole that reflects the structure and dynamics of the phenomenon observed.

As you are about to learn, this class is about information *systems*. We will discuss and illustrate systems; you will be asked to critique systems; you will be asked to compare alternative systems; you will be asked to apply different systems to different situations. All of those tasks will prepare you for systems thinking as a professional.

Collaboration

Collaboration is the activity of two or more people working together to achieve a common goal, result, or work product. Chapter Extensions 1 and 2 will teach you collaboration skills and illustrate several sample collaboration information systems.

Every chapter of this book includes collaboration exercises that you may be assigned in class or as homework.

Here's a fact that surprises many students: Effective collaboration isn't about being nice. In fact, surveys indicate the single most important skill for effective collaboration is to give and receive critical feedback. Advance a proposal in business that challenges the cherished program of the VP of marketing, and you'll quickly learn that effective collaboration skills differ from party manners at the neighborhood barbeque. So, how do you advance your idea in the face of the VP's resistance? And without losing your job? In this course, you can learn both skills and information systems for such collaboration. Even better, you will have many opportunities to practice them.

Ability to Experiment

"I've never done this before."

"I don't know how to do it."

"But will it work?"

"Is it too weird for the market?"

Fear of failure paralyzes many good people and many good ideas. In the days when business was stable, when new ideas were just different verses of the same song, professionals could allow themselves to be limited by fear of failure.

But think again about the application of social networking to the oil change business. Is there a legitimate application of social networking there? If so, has anyone ever done it? Is there anyone in the world who can tell you what to do? How to proceed? No. As Reich says, professionals in the twenty-first century need to be able to experiment.

Successful experimentation is not throwing buckets of money at every crazy idea that enters your head. Instead, **experimentation** is making a reasoned analysis of an opportunity, envisioning potential solutions, evaluating those possibilities, and developing the most promising ones, consistent with the resources you have.

In this course, you will be asked to use products with which you have no familiarity. Those products might be Microsoft Excel or Access, or they might be features and functions of Blackboard that you've not used. Or, you may be asked to collaborate using Microsoft SharePoint or Google Docs. Will your instructor explain and show every feature of those products that you'll need? You should hope not. You should hope your instructor will leave it up to you to experiment, to envision new possibilities on your own, and experiment with those possibilities, consistent with the time you have available.

The bottom line? This course is the most important course in the business school because

1. **It will give you the background you need to assess, evaluate, and apply emerging information systems technology to business.**
2. **It can give you the ultimate in job security—marketable skills—by helping you learn abstraction, systems thinking, collaboration, and experimentation.**

Finally, throughout your career you may from time to time be faced with ethical issues involving your use of information systems. To help you prepare for those challenges, in every chapter of this book we have included an *Ethics Guide.* These Guides will get you to start thinking about ethical dilemmas, which will help you clarify your values and make you ready to respond authentically to future ethical challenges.

With that introduction, let's get started!

The first Ethics Guide, on pages 16–17, considers what to do with the information that comes your way but that was not intended for you.

Q2 What Is an Information System?

A **system** is a group of components that interact to achieve some purpose. As you might guess, an **information system (IS)** is a group of components that interact to produce information. That sentence, although true, raises another question: What are these components that interact to produce information?

Figure 1-3 shows the **five-component framework** of computer hardware, software, data, procedures, and people. These five components are present in every information system—from the most simple to the most complex. For example, when you use a computer to write a class report, you are using hardware (the computer, storage disk, keyboard, and monitor), software (Word, WordPerfect, or some other word-processing program), data (the words, sentences, and paragraphs in your report), procedures (the methods you use to start the program, enter your report, print it, and save and back up your file), and people (you).

Consider a more complex example, say, an airline reservation system. It, too, consists of these five components, even though each one is far more complicated. The hardware consists of dozens or more computers linked together by telecommunications hardware. Further, hundreds of different programs coordinate communications among the computers, and still other programs perform the reservations and related services. Additionally, the system must store millions upon millions of characters of data about flights, customers, reservations, and other facts. Hundreds of different procedures are followed by airline personnel, travel agents, and customers. Finally, the information system includes people, not only the users of the system, but also those who operate and service the computers, those who maintain the data, and those who support the networks of computers.

These five components also mean that building information systems requires many different skills besides those of hardware technicians or computer programmers. People are needed who can design the databases that hold the data and who can develop procedures for people to follow. Managers are needed to train and staff the personnel for using and operating the system. We will return to this five-component framework many times throughout this book.

Before we move forward, note that we have defined an information system to include a computer. Some people would say that such a system is a **computer-based information system**. They would note that there are information systems that do not include computers, such as a calendar hanging on the wall outside of a conference room that is used to schedule the room's use. Such systems have been used by businesses for centuries. Although this point is true, in this book we focus on *computer-based* information systems. To simplify and shorten the book, we will use the term *information system* as a synonym for *computer-based information system*.

Q3 What Is MIS?

Today, there are thousands, even millions, of information systems in the world. Not all relate to business. In this textbook, we are concerned with **MIS**, or **management information systems**. MIS is the development and use of information systems that help businesses achieve their goals and objectives. This definition has three key elements: *development and use*, *information systems*, and *business goals and*

Figure 1-3
Five Components of an Information System

Five-Component Framework

Hardware	Software	Data	Procedures	People

Experiencing MIS InClass Exercise 1

Information Systems and Online Dating

"Why should I go to a bar and take the risk that nobody I'm interested in will be there during the 2 hours I'm there, when I can spend half an hour searching online for people that I *am* likely to be interested in? At worst, I've wasted half an hour. And at least I didn't have to blow-dry my hair."

Lori Gottlieb, *The Atlantic*, February 7, 2006, www.theatlantic.com/doc/200602u/online-dating

Some online dating services match couples using a proprietary algorithm (method) based on a theory of relationships:

- **Chemistry (*www.chemistry.com*).** Matches are made on the basis of a personality test developed by Dr. Helen Fisher.
- **eHarmony (*www.eHarmony.com*).** Matches are made on the basis of a test entitled the "Compatibility Matching System" by Dr. Neil Clark Warren.
- **PerfectMatch (*www.PerfectMatch.com*).** Matches made on the basis of a test based on Duet, a system developed by Dr. Pepper Schwartz.

Other sites match people by limiting members to particular groups or interests:

Political interests:

- **Conservative Dates (*www.conservativedates.com*)**—"Sweethearts, not bleeding hearts."
- **Liberal Hearts (*www.liberalhearts.com*)**—"Uniting Democrats, Greens, animal lovers & environmentalists who are like in mind and liberal in love."

Common social/economic interests:

- **Good Genes (*www.goodgenes.com*)**—"[Helping] Ivy Leaguers and similarly well-educated graduates and faculty find others with matching credentials."
- **MillionaireMatch (*www.millionairematch.com*)**—"Where you can add a touch of romance to success and achievement!"

Common activity interests:

- **Golfmates (*www.golfmates.com*)**—"The world's premier online dating service designed specifically for the golfing community."
- **EquestrianCupid (*www.equestriancupid.com*)**—"The best dating site in the world for friends and singles who are horse lovers."
- **CowboyCowgirl (*www.cowboycowgirl.com*)**—"Join thousands of singles that share your love for the country way of life."
- **Single FireFighters (*www.singlefirefighters.com*)**— "The ONLY place to meet firefighters without calling 911!"
- **Asexual Pals (*www.asexualpals.com*)**—"Because there is so much more to life!"

InClass Group Exercise:

1. Visit one of the proprietary method sites and one of the common interest sites.
2. Summarize the matching process that is used by each site.
3. Describe the revenue model of each site.
4. Using general terms, describe the need these sites have for:
   a. Hardware
   b. Software
   c. Data
   d. Procedures
   e. People
5. People sometimes stretch the truth, or even lie, on matching sites. Describe one innovative way that one of the two companies your team chose could use information systems to reduce the impact of this tendency. As you prepare your team's answer, keep the availability of nearly free data communications and data storage in mind.
6. Suppose that the company in your answer to step 5 has requested your team to implement your idea on reducing the impact of lying. Explain how having strong personal skills for each of Reich's four abilities (i.e., abstract thinking, systems thinking, experimentation, and collaboration) would enable each of you to be a better contributor to that team.
7. Working as a team, prepare a 3-minute verbal description of your answers to steps 5 and 6 that all of you could use in a job interview. Structure your presentation to illustrate that you have the four skills in step 6.
8. Deliver your answer to step 7 to the rest of the class.

objectives. We just discussed *information systems.* Now consider *development and use* and *business goals and objectives.*

Development and Use of Information Systems

Information systems do not pop up like mushrooms after a hard rain; they must be constructed. You might be saying, "Wait a minute. I'm a finance (or accounting, or management) major, not an information systems major. I don't need to know how to build information systems."

If you are saying that, you are like a lamb headed for fleecing. Like Jennifer, throughout your career, in whatever field you choose, you will need new information systems. To have an information system that meets your needs, you need to take an *active role* in that system's development. Even if you are not a programmer or a database designer or some other IS professional, you must take an active role in specifying the system's requirements and in helping manage the development project. Without active involvement on your part, it will only be good luck that causes the new system to meet your needs.

To that end, throughout this text we will discuss your role in the development of information systems. In addition, we devote all of Chapter 10 to this important topic. As you read this text and think about information systems, you should ask yourself questions like, "How was that system constructed?" and "What roles did the users play during its development?" If you start asking yourself these questions now, you will be better prepared to answer them once you start a job, when financial, career, and other consequences will depend on your answers.

In addition to development tasks, you will also have important roles to play in the *use* of information systems. Of course, you will need to learn how to employ the system to accomplish your goals. But you will also have important ancillary functions as well. For example, when using an information system, you will have responsibilities for protecting the security of the system and its data. You may also have tasks for backing up data. When the system fails (most do, at some point), you will have tasks to perform while the system is down as well as tasks to accomplish to help recover the system correctly and quickly.

Achieving Business Goals and Objectives

The last part of the definition of MIS is that information systems exist to help businesses achieve their *goals and objectives.* First, realize that this statement hides an important fact: Businesses themselves do not "do" anything. A business is not alive, and it cannot act. It is the people within a business who sell, buy, design, produce, finance, market, account, and manage. So information systems exist to help people who work in a business to achieve the goals and objectives of that business.

Information systems are not created for the sheer joy of exploring technology. They are not created so that the company can be "modern" or so that the company can claim to be a "Web 2.0 company." They are not created because the IS department thinks it needs to be created or because the company is "falling behind the technology curve."

This point may seem so obvious that you wonder why we mention it. Every day, however, some business somewhere is developing an information system for the wrong reasons. Right now, somewhere in the world, a company is deciding to create a social networking site for the sole reason that "every other business has one." This company is not asking questions like, "What is the purpose of the social networking site?" or, "What is it going to do for us?" or, "Are the costs of the site sufficiently offset by the benefits?"—but it should be!

Even more serious, somewhere right now an IS manager has been convinced by some vendor's sales team or by an article in a business magazine that his or her company must upgrade to the latest, greatest high-tech gizmo. This IS manager is attempting to convince his or her manager that this expensive upgrade is a good idea. We hope that someone somewhere in the company is asking questions like, "What business goal or objective will be served by the investment in the gizmo?"

As a future business professional, you need to learn to look at information systems and technologies only through the lens of *business need*. Learn to ask, "All of this technology may be great, in and of itself, but what will it do for us? What will it do for our business and our particular goals?"

Again, MIS is the development and use of information systems that help businesses achieve their goals and objectives. Already, you should be realizing that there is much more to this class than buying a computer, writing a program, or working with a spreadsheet.

Q4 Why Is the Difference Between Information Technology and Information Systems Important to You?

Information technology and information systems are two closely related terms, but they are different. **Information technology (IT)** refers to the products, methods, inventions, and standards that are used for the purpose of producing information. IT pertains to the hardware, software, and data components. As stated in the previous section, an *information system (IS)* is an assembly of hardware, software, data, procedures, and people that produces information.

Information technology drives the development of new information systems. Advances in information technology have taken the computer industry from the days of punched cards to the Internet, and such advances will continue to take the industry to the next stages and beyond.

Why does this difference matter to you? Knowing the difference between IT and IS can help you avoid a common mistake: Do not try to buy an IS; you cannot do it.

You can buy IT; you can buy or lease hardware, you can license programs and databases, and you can even obtain predesigned procedures. Ultimately, however, it is *your* people who execute those procedures to employ that new IT.

For any new system, you will always have training tasks (and costs), you will always have the need to overcome employees' resistance to change, and you will always need to manage the employees as they utilize the new system. Hence, you can buy IT, but you cannot buy IS.

Consider a simple example. Suppose your organization decides to develop a Facebook page. Facebook provides the hardware and programs, the database structures, and standard procedures. You, however, provide the data to fill your portion of the Facebook database, and you must extend Facebook's standard procedures with your own procedures for keeping that data current. Those procedures need to provide, for example, a means to review your page's content regularly and a means to remove content that is judged inappropriate. Furthermore, you need to train employees on how to follow those procedures and manage those employees to ensure that they do.

Managing your own Facebook page is as simple an IS as exists. Larger, more comprehensive information systems that involve many, even dozens, of departments and thousands of employees require considerable work. Again, you can buy IT, but you can never buy an IS!

Q5 What Is Your Role in IS Security?

As you have learned, information systems create value. However, they also create risk. For example, Amazon.com maintains credit card data on millions of customers and has the responsibility to protect that data. If Amazon.com's security system were breached and that credit card data stolen, Amazon.com would incur serious losses—not only lost business, but also potentially staggering liability losses. Because of the importance of information security, we will consider it throughout this textbook. Additionally, Chapter 12 is devoted to security.

However, you have a role in security that is too important for us to wait until you read that chapter. Like all information systems, security systems have the five components, including people. Thus, every security system ultimately depends on the behavior of its users. If the users do not take security seriously, if they do not follow security procedures, then the hardware, software, and data components of the security system are wasted expense. So, before we proceed further, we will address how you should create and use a strong password, which is an essential component of computer security.

Almost all security systems use user names and passwords. As a user of information systems in a business organization, you will be instructed to create a strong password and to protect it. *It is vitally important for you to do so.* You should already be using such passwords at your university. (According to a recent article in the *New York Times*,[4] 20% of people use an easily guessed password like 12345. Don't be part of that 20%!)

Strong Passwords

So what is a strong password, and how do you create one? Microsoft, a company that has many reasons to promote effective security, defines a **strong password** as one with the following characteristics:

- Has seven or more characters
- Does not contain your user name, real name, or company name
- Does not contain a complete dictionary word in any language
- Is different from previous passwords you have used
- Contains both upper- and lowercase letters, numbers, and special characters (such as ~ ! @; # $ % ^; &; * ( ) _ +; – =; { } | [ ] \ : " ; ' <; >;? , . /)

Examples of good passwords are:

- Qw37^T1bb?at
- 3B47qq<3>5!7b

The problem with such passwords is that they are nearly impossible to remember. And the last thing you want to do is write your password on a piece of paper and keep it near the workstation where you use it. Never do that!

One technique for creating memorable, strong passwords is to base them on the first letter of the words in a phrase. The phrase could be the title of a song or the first line of a poem or one based on some fact about your life. For example, you might take the phrase, "I was born in Rome, New York, before 1990." Using the first letters from that phrase and substituting the character < for the word *before*, you create the password *IwbiR,NY<1990*. That's an acceptable password, but it would be better if all of the numbers were not placed on the end. So, you might try the phrase, "I was born

[4] Ashley Vance, "If Your Password Is 123456, Just Make It HackMe," *New York Times*, January 21, 2010, p. A1. Available at *www.nytimes.com/2010/01/21/technology/21password.html?hp.*

at 3:00 A.M. in Rome, New York." That phrase yields the password *Iwba3:00AMiR,NY,* which is a strong password that is easily remembered.

Password Etiquette

Once you have created a strong password, you need to protect it with proper behavior. Proper password etiquette is one of the marks of a business professional. Never write down your password, and do not share it with others. Never ask others for their passwords, and never give your password to someone else.

But what if you need someone else's password? Suppose, for example, you ask someone to help you with a problem on your computer. You sign on to an information system, and for some reason you need to enter that other person's password. In this case, say to the other person, "We need your password," and then get out of your chair, offer your keyboard to the other person, and look away while he or she enters the password. Among professionals working in organizations that take security seriously, this little "do-si-do" move—one person getting out of the way so that another person can enter a password—is common and accepted.

If someone asks for your password, do not give it out. Instead, get up, go over to that person's machine, and enter your password yourself. Stay present while your password is in use, and ensure that your account is logged out at the end of the activity. No one should mind or be offended in any way when you do this. It is the mark of a professional.

How does the knowledge in this chapter help Jennifer and you?

It's too late for Jennifer, at least at FlexTime. However, it's not too late for you, and it's not too late for Jennifer at her next job. So, what are the takeaways from this chapter?

The Guide on pages 18–19 shares my personal opinion about why you should overcome any preconceived negative notions you had about this class.

First, learn Reich's four key skills: abstract thinking, systems thinking, experimentation, and collaboration. And practice, practice, practice them. This class is the best one in the b-school for teaching those skills, so engage in it. As you study and perform assignments, ask yourself how your activity relates to those four abilities and endeavor to improve your proficiency at them.

Second, realize that the future belongs to businesspeople who can creatively envision new applications of information systems and technology. You don't have to be an IS major (though it is a very good major with excellent job prospects), but you should be able to innovate the use of MIS into the discipline in which you do major. How can management, marketing, accounting, production, and so on take advantage of the benefits of Moore's Law?

Next, learn the components of an IS and understand that every business professional needs to take an active role in new information systems development. Such systems are created for your needs and require your involvement. Know the difference between IT and IS. Finally, learn, now, how to create a strong password and begin using such passwords and proper password etiquette.

We're just getting started; there's lots more to come that can benefit Jennifer (in her next job) and you!

Ethics Guide

Ethics of Misdirected Information Use

Consider the following situations:

Situation A: Suppose you are buying a condo and you know that at least one other party is bidding against you. While agonizing over your best strategy, you stop at a local Starbucks. As you sip your latte, you overhear a conversation at the table next to yours. Three people are talking so loudly that it is difficult to ignore them, and you soon realize that they are the real estate agent and the couple who is competing for the condo you want. They are preparing their offer. Should you listen to their conversation? If you do, do you use the information you hear to your advantage?

Situation B: Consider the same situation from a different perspective—instead of overhearing the conversation, suppose you receive that same information in an email. Perhaps an administrative assistant at the agent's office confuses you and the other customer and mistakenly sends you the terms of the other party's offer. Do you read that email? If so, do you use the information that you read to your advantage?

Situation C: Suppose that you sell computer software. In the midst of a sensitive price negotiation, your customer accidentally sends you an internal email that contains the maximum amount that the customer can pay for your software. Do you read that email? Do you use that information to guide your negotiating strategy? What do you do if your customer discovers that the email may have reached you and asks, "Did you read my email?" How do you answer?

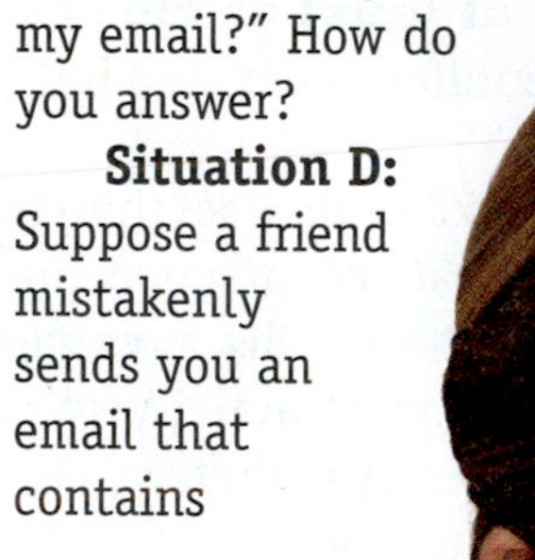

Situation D: Suppose a friend mistakenly sends you an email that contains

sensitive personal medical data. Further, suppose you read the email before you know what you're reading and you're embarrassed to learn something very personal that truly is none of your business. Your friend asks you, "Did you read that email?" How do you respond?

Situation E: Finally, suppose that you work as a network administrator and your position allows you unrestricted access to the mailing lists for your company. Assume that you have the skill to insert your email address into any company mailing list without anyone knowing about it. You insert your address into several lists and, consequently, begin to receive confidential email that no one intended for you to see. One of those emails indicates that your best friend's department is about to be eliminated and all of its personnel fired. Do you forewarn your friend?

Discussion Questions

1. Consider the questions in situations A and B. Do your answers differ? Does the medium by which the information is obtained make a difference? Is it easier to avoid reading an email than it is to avoid hearing a conversation? If so, does that difference matter?
2. Consider the questions in situations B and C. Do your answers differ? In situation B, the information is for your personal gain; in C, the information is for both your personal and your organization's gain. Does this difference matter? How do you respond when asked if you have read the email?
3. Consider the questions in situations C and D. Do your answers differ? Would you lie in one case and not in the other? Why or why not?
4. Consider the question in situation E. What is the essential difference between situations A through D and situation E? Suppose you had to justify your behavior in situation E. How would you argue? Do you believe your own argument?
5. In situations A through D, if you access the information you have done nothing illegal. You were the passive recipient. Even for item E, although you undoubtedly violated your company's employment policies, you most likely did not violate the law. So for this discussion, assume that all of these actions are legal.
   a. What is the difference between legal and ethical? Look up both words in a dictionary, and explain how they differ.
   b. Make the argument that business is competitive and that if something is legal, then it is acceptable to do it if it helps to further your goals.
   c. Make the argument that it is never appropriate to do something unethical.
6. Summarize your beliefs about proper conduct when you receive misdirected information.

Guide

Duller Than Dirt?

Yes, you read that title correctly: This subject can seem duller than dirt. Take the phrase, "development and use of IS in organizations." Read just that phrase, and you start to yawn, wondering, "How am I going to absorb hundreds of pages of this?"

Stop and think: Why are you reading this book? Right now in the Sea of Cortez, the water is clear and warm, and the swimming and diving are wonderful. You could be kayaking to Isla San Francisco this minute. Or, somewhere in the world people are skiing. Whether in Aspen, Colorado, or Portillo, Chile, people are blasting through the powder somewhere. You could be one of them, living in a small house with a group of friends, having good times at night. Whatever it is that you like to do, you could be doing it right now. So why are you here, where you are, reading this book? Why aren't you there?

Waking up should be one of your goals while in college. I mean waking up to your life. Ceasing to live according to someone else's plan and beginning to live your own plan. Doing that requires you to become conscious of the choices you make and the consequences they have.

Suppose you take an hour to read your assignment in this book tonight. For a typical person, that is 4,320 heartbeats (72 beats times 60 minutes) that you have used to read this book—heartbeats that you will never have again. Despite the evidence of your current budget, the critical resource for humans is not money but time. No matter what we do, we cannot get more of it. Was your reading today worth those 4,320 heartbeats?

For some reason, you chose to major in business. For some reason, you are taking this class, and, for some reason, you have been instructed to read this textbook. Now, given that you made a good decision to major in business (and not to kayak in Baja), and given that someone is requiring you to read this text, the question then becomes, "How can you maximize the return on the 4,320 heartbeats you are investing per hour?"

The secret is to personalize the material. At every page, learn to ask yourself, "How does this pertain to me?" and "How can I use this material to further my goals?" If you find some topic irrelevant, ask your professor or your classmates what they think. What's this topic for? Why are we reading this? What am I going to do with it later in my career? Why is this worth 1,000 (or whatever) heartbeats?

MIS is all-encompassing. To me, that's one of its beauties. Consider the components: hardware, software, data, procedures, and people. Do you want to be an engineer? Then work with the hardware component. Do you want to be a programmer? Write software. Do you want to be a practicing philosopher, an applied epistemologist? Learn data modeling. Do you like social systems and sociology? Learn how to design effective group and organizational procedures. Do you like people?

Become an IS trainer or a computer systems salesperson. Do you enjoy management? Learn how to bring all of those disparate elements together.

I've worked in this industry for almost 40 years. The breadth of MIS and the rapid change of technology have kept me fascinated for every one of those years. Further, the beauty of working with intellectual property is that it doesn't weigh very much—moving symbols around won't wear you out. And you do it indoors in a temperature-controlled office. They may even put your name on the door.

So wake up. Why are you reading this? How can you make it relevant? Jump onto Google, and search for "MIS careers" or use some other phrase from this chapter and see what you get. Challenge yourself to find something that is important to you personally in every chapter.

You just invested 780 heartbeats in reading this editorial. Was it worth it? Keep asking!

Discussion Questions

1. Explain what it means to "wake up to your life."
2. Are you awake to your life? How do you know? What can you do once a week to ensure that you are awake to your life?
3. What are your professional goals? Are they yours, or are they someone else's? How do you know?
4. How does this class pertain to your professional goals?
5. How are you going to make the material in this class interesting?

ACTIVE REVIEW

Use this Active Review to verify that you understand the material in the chapter. You can read the entire chapter and then perform the tasks in this review, or you can read the text material for just one question and perform the tasks in this review for that question before moving on to the next one.

Q1 Why is Introduction to MIS the most important class in the business school?

Define *Moore's Law* and explain why its consequences are important to business professionals today. State how business professionals should relate to emerging information technology. Give the text's definition of *job security* and use Reich's enumeration to explain how this course will help you attain that security.

Q2 What is an information system?

List the components of an information system. Explain how knowledge of these components guides business professionals (not just techies) as they build information systems.

Q3 What is MIS?

List the three elements of MIS. Why does a nontechnical business professional need to understand all three? Why are information systems developed? Why is part of this definition misleading?

Q4 Why is the difference between information technology and information systems important to you?

Define *IS*. Define *IT*. Does IT include IS, or does IS include IT? Why does technology, by itself, not constitute an information system?

Q5 What is your role in IS security?

Summarize the importance of security to corporations like Amazon.com. Define *strong password*. Explain an easy way to create and remember a strong password. Under what circumstances should you give someone else your password?

KEY TERMS AND CONCEPTS

USING YOUR KNOWLEDGE

1. Do you agree that this course is the most important course in the business school? Isn't accounting more important? No business can exist without accounting. Or, isn't management more important? After all, if you can manage people why do you need to know how to innovate with technology? You can hire others to think innovatively for you.

   On the other hand, what single factor will impact all business more than IS? And, isn't knowledge and proficiency with IS and IT key to future employment and success?

   Give serious thought to this question and write a single page argument as to why you agree or disagree.

2. Describe three to five personal goals for this class. None of these goals should include anything about your GPA. Be as specific as possible, and make the goals personal to your major, interests, and career aspirations. Assume that you are going to evaluate yourself on these goals at the end of the quarter or semester. The more specific you make these goals, the easier it will be to perform the evaluation.

3. Consider costs of a system in light of the five components: costs to buy and maintain the hardware; costs to develop or acquire licenses to the software programs and costs to maintain them; costs to design databases and fill them with data; costs of developing procedures and keeping them current; and finally, human costs both to develop and use the system.
   a. Over the lifetime of a system, many experts believe that the single most expensive component is people. Does this belief seem logical to you? Explain why you agree or disagree.
   b. Consider a poorly developed system that does not meet its defined requirements. The needs of the business do not go away, but they do not conform themselves to the characteristics of the poorly built system. Therefore, something must give. Which component picks up the slack when the hardware and software programs do not work correctly? What does this say about the cost of a poorly designed system? Consider both direct money costs as well as intangible personnel costs.
   c. What implications do you, as a future business manager, recognize after answering parts a and b? What does this say about the need for your involvement in requirements and other aspects of systems development? Who eventually will pay the costs of a poorly developed system? Against which budget will those costs accrue?

COLLABORATION EXERCISE 1

Before you start this exercise, read Chapter Extensions 1 and 2, which describe collaboration techniques as well as tools for managing collaboration tasks. In particular, consider using Google Docs, Windows Live SkyDrive, Microsoft SharePoint, or some other collaboration tool.

Collaborate with a group of fellow students to answer the following questions. For this exercise do not meet face to face. Coordinate all of your work using email and email attachments, only. Your answers should reflect the thinking of the entire group, and not just one or two individuals.

1. Abstract reasoning.
   a. Define *abstract reasoning*, and explain why it is an important skill for business professionals.
   b. Explain how a list of items in inventory and their quantity on hand is an abstraction of a physical inventory.
   c. Give three other examples of abstractions commonly used in business.
   d. Explain how Jennifer failed to demonstrate effective abstract-reasoning skills.
   e. Can people increase their abstract-reasoning skills? If so, how? If not, why not?
2. Systems thinking.
   a. Define *systems thinking*, and explain why it is an important skill for business professionals.
   b. Explain how you would use systems thinking to explain why Moore's Law caused a farmer to dig up a field of pulpwood trees. Name each of the elements in the system, and explain their relationships to each other.
   c. Give three other examples of the use of systems thinking with regard to consequences of Moore's Law.
   d. Explain how Jennifer failed to demonstrate effective systems-thinking skills.
   e. Can people improve their systems-thinking skills? If so, how? If not, why not?
3. Collaboration.
   a. Define *collaboration*, and explain why it is an important skill for business professionals.
   b. Explain how you are using collaboration to answer these questions. Describe what is working with regards to your group's process and what is not working.
   c. Is the work product of your team better than any one of you could have done separately? If not, your collaboration is ineffective. If that is the case, explain why.
   d. Does the fact that you cannot meet face to face hamper your ability to collaborate? If so, how?
   e. Explain how Jennifer failed to demonstrate effective collaboration skills.
   f. Can people increase their collaboration skills? If so, how? If not, why not?
4. Experimentation.
   a. Define *experimentation*, and explain why it is an important skill for business professionals.

b. Explain several creative ways you could use experimentation to answer this question.
c. How does the fear of failure influence your willingness to engage in any of the ideas you identified in part b?
d. Explain how Jennifer failed to demonstrate effective experimentation skills.
e. Can people increase their willingness to take risks? If so, how? If not, why not?

5. Job security.
a. State the text's definition of *job security*.
b. Evaluate the text's definition of job security. Is it effective? If you think not, offer a better definition of job security.
c. As a team, do you agree that improving your skills on the four dimensions in Collaboration Exercises 1 through 4 will increase your job security?
d. Do you think technical skills (accounting proficiency, financial analysis proficiency, etc.) provide job security? Why or why not? Do you think you would have answered this question differently in 1980? Why or why not?

CASE STUDY 1

Getty Images Serves Up Profit and YouTube Grows Exponentially

Chapter 1 stated that near-free data communication and data storage have created unprecedented opportunities for highly profitable businesses. Here we will consider two: Getty Images and YouTube.

Getty Images was founded in 1995 with the goal of consolidating the fragmented photography market by acquiring many small companies, applying business discipline to the merged entity, and developing modern information systems. The advent of the Web drove the company to e-commerce and in the process enabled Getty to change the workflow and business practices of the professional visual-content industry. Getty Images had grown from a start-up to become, by 2004, a global, $600 million plus, publicly traded, very profitable company. By 2007, Getty had increased its revenue to more than $880 million. More recent financial information is unavailable, because in July 2008 Getty was purchased by the private equity firm Hellman & Friedman, LLC for $2.4 billion.

Getty Images obtains its imagery (still, video, and audio) from photographers and other artists under contract, and it owns the world's largest private archive of imagery. Getty also employs staff photographers to shoot the world's news, sport, and entertainment events. In the case of photography and film that it does not own, it provides a share of the revenue generated to the content owner. Getty Images is both a producer and a distributor of imagery, and all of its products are sold via e-commerce on the Web.

Getty Images employs three licensing models: The first is *subscription*, by which customers contract to use as many images as they want as often as they want (this applies to the news, sport, and entertainment imagery). The second model is *royalty-free*. In this model, customers pay a fee based on the file size of the image and can use the image any way they want and as many times as they want. However, under this model, customers have no exclusivity or ability to prevent a competitor from using the same image at the same time.

The third model, *rights managed*, also licenses creative imagery. In this model, which is the largest in revenue terms, users pay fees according to the rights that they wish to use—size, industry, geography, prominence, frequency, exclusivity, and so forth.

According to its Web site:

> **Getty Images has been credited with the introduction of royalty-free photography and was the first company to license imagery via the Web, subsequently moving the entire industry online. The company was also the first to employ creative researchers to anticipate the visual content needs of the world's communicators (*http://corporate.gettyimages.com/source/company.html, accessed December 2007*).**

Because Getty Images licenses photos in digital format, its variable cost of production is essentially zero. Once the company has obtained a photo and placed it in the commerce server database, the cost of sending it to a customer is zero. Getty Images does have the overhead costs of setting up and operating the e-commerce site, and it does pay some costs for its images—either the cost of employing the photographer or the cost of setting up and maintaining the relationship with out-of-house photographers. For some images, it also pays a royalty to the owner. Once these costs are paid, however, the cost of producing a photo is nil. This means that Getty Images' profitability increases substantially with increased volume.

Why did Hellman & Friedman purchase Getty Images? According to its Web site, Hellman & Friedman, "focuses on investing in businesses with strong, defensible franchises and predictable revenue and earnings growth and which generate high levels of free cash flow or attractive returns on the capital reinvested in the business." With a near-zero cost of production, it is likely that Getty Images does indeed generate high levels of free cash flow!

At the same time that Getty Images was achieving its peak as a public company, another team of entrepreneurs found a different way to take advantage of near-free data communications and data storage. On February 15, 2005, Chad Hurley, Steve Chen, and Jawed Karim registered the domain "YouTube" and by April 23 had posted their first video. By November 2005, YouTube had 200,000 registered users and was showing 2 million videos per day. In 9 months, YouTube had grown from nothing to 200,000 users.

By January 2006, YouTube was showing 25 million videos per day. By May 2006, YouTube was showing 43 percent of all videos viewed over the Internet. By July 2006, users were viewing 100 million videos and uploading 65,000 new videos per day. YouTube had a total of 30 employees. Think about that: 30 employees were serving 100 million videos per day. That's 3.33 million videos *per employee*, all accomplished in just over 1 year.

That phenomenal success was capped by Google's $1.65 billion acquisition of YouTube in October 2006. In just 20 months, YouTube's founders had turned nothing but an idea into $1.65 billion. That's a rate of $2,750,000 of equity per day.

What's the point of these examples? The opportunities were there in 1995, in 2005, and they are still there today. Although it is unlikely that you, too, will have such success, think about it: How can you use free data communications and data storage in your business? Or, in a job interview, how might you suggest that your prospective employer use such resources?

Sources: www.gettyimages.com (accessed December 2004, May 2007, June 2009); *www.hf.com* (accessed June 2009); and *www.youtube.com/watch?v=x2NQiVcdZRY* (accessed June 2009).

Questions

1. Visit *www.gettyimages.com*, and select "Images/Creative/Search royalty-free." Search for an image of a major city of interest to you. Select a photo and determine its default price. Follow the link on the photographer's name to find other images by that photographer.
2. Explain how Getty Images' business model takes advantage of the opportunities created by IT as described in Chapter 1.
3. Do you think Getty Images' marginal cost is sustainable? Are its prices sustainable? What is the key to its continued success?
4. What seems to be Getty Images' competitive strategy?
5. Explain how Getty Images' use of information systems contributed to the company's value when it was acquired.
6. How did the availability of near-free data communication and data storage facilitate YouTube's success? Would YouTube have been possible without them?
7. Even though the cost of data communication and data storage is very low, for the volume at which YouTube operates they are still substantial expenses. How did YouTube fund these expenses? (Search the Internet for "History of YouTube" to find information to answer this question.)
8. How does YouTube (now owned by Google) earn revenue?

Using the cases of Getty Images and YouTube as a guide, answer the following questions:

9. Choose a corporation located in the geographic vicinity of your college or university. In what ways is it already taking advantage of the low cost of data communication and data storage?
10. Using the corporation you identified in question 9, identify three innovative ways that the corporation could take advantage of the low cost of data communication and storage.
11. Create an outline of a statement about this importance of near–zero-cost data storage and data communication that you could use in a job interview. Assume you wish to demonstrate that you have knowledge of the power of emerging technology as well as the capacity to think innovatively. Incorporate the example you used in your answer to questions 9 and 10 in your answer.

CHAPTER 2

Business Processes, Information, and Information Systems

This could happen to you

"No, Felix! Not again! Over, and over, and over! We decide something one meeting and then go over it again the next meeting and again the next. What a waste!"

"What do you mean, Tara? I think it's important we get this right."

"Well, Felix, if that's the case, why don't you come to the meetings?"

"I just missed a couple."

"Right. Last week we met here for, oh, 2, maybe 3, hours and we decided to look for ways to save costs without changing who we are as a studio."

"But Tara, if we could raise revenue, we wouldn't have to save costs. I have a great idea: Sportswear! Our clients love to shop!"

"Felix! Last week we discussed raising revenue and decided it was too risky . . . we wouldn't see results in time. Plus, that's not what Kelly asked us to do."

"Look, Tara, Kelly just wants the studio to be profitable. Sales are down and costs aren't. I'm guaranteeing you we could sell a ton of this stuff! Sportswear!"

STUDY QUESTIONS

Q1 Why does the FlexTime team need to understand business processes?

Q2 What is a business process?

Q3 How do information systems support business processes?

Q4 What is information?

Q5 Where is the information in business processes?

How does the knowledge in this chapter help *FlexTime* and you?

"Right. But how do you do it? And what's the cost of raising sales? Come on, Felix, you're driving me nuts. We discussed revenue options *ad nauseam* last week. Let's make some progress. Why don't some of you other guys help me! Jan, what do you think?"

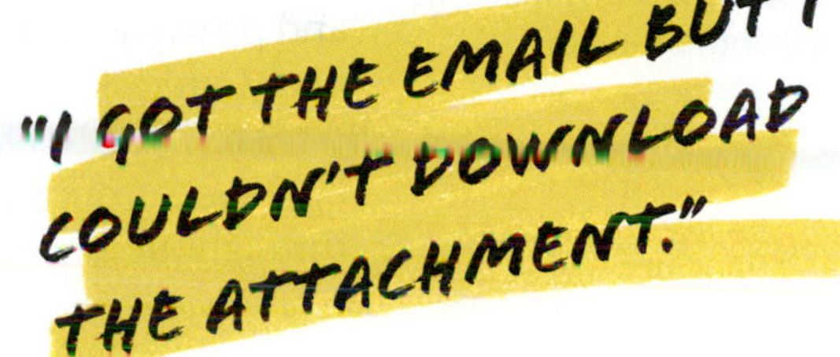

"Felix, Tara is right. We did have a long discussion on sales opportunities—and we did agree to focus on saving money."

"Well, Jan, I think it's a mistake. Why didn't anyone tell me? I put a lot of time into developing my sportswear sales plan."

"Did you read the email?" Jan asks tentatively.

"What email?"

"The meeting summary email that Jan sends out each week."

"I got the email but I couldn't download the attachment. Something weird about a virus checker couldn't access a gizmo or something like that . . . "

Tara can't stand that excuse. "Here, Felix, take a look at mine. I'll underline the part where we concluded that we'd focus on sales so you can be sure to see it."

"Tara, there's no reason to get snippy about this. I thought I had a good idea."

"OK, so we're agreed—*again this week*—that we're going to look for ways of reducing costs. Now, we've wasted enough time covering old ground. Let's get some new thinking going."

Felix slumps back into his chair and looks down at his cell phone.

"Oh, no, I missed a call from Mapplethorpe. Ahhhh."

"Felix, what are you talking about?"

"Mapplethorpe, my best client. Wants to change his PT appointment this afternoon. I'm sorry, but I've got to call him. I'll be back in a few minutes."

Felix leaves the room.

Tara looks at the three team members who are left. "Now what?" she asks. "If we go forward we'll have to rediscuss everything we did when Felix comes back. Maybe we should just take a break?"

Jan shakes her head. "Tara, let's not. It's tough for me to get to these meetings. I don't have a class until tonight, so I drove down here just for this. I've got to pick up Simone from day care. We haven't done anything yet. Let's just ignore Felix."

"OK, Jan, but it isn't easy to ignore Felix."

The door opens and Kelly, FlexTime's co-owner, walks in.

"Hi everyone! How's it going? OK if I sit in on your meeting?"

Optional Extension for this chapter is • CE3: Information Systems and Decision Making 335

Q1 Why Does the FlexTime Team Need to Understand Business Processes?

Tara, Jan, Felix, and the rest of the team at FlexTime need to understand business processes, and, even more important, they need to know how to improve business processes. Judging from their frustration and anger in this meeting, they need a better process for collaboration, including a better means of establishing team ground rules such as what their objective is and when they'll meet. They also need better processes for sharing work product. You can learn about collaboration processes and the role of information systems for collaboration in Chapter Extensions 1 and 2.

Equally important, to accomplish the task they were assigned, this team needs to understand FlexTime's business processes. Kelly asked the team to find innovative ways of saving costs without losing FlexTime's character as an organization. Faced with this question, Felix takes a beginner's approach. He has no idea how to save costs, so he proposes an off-the-wall idea for increasing sales. Tara corrects him.

In all meetings, it is important to demonstrate empathetic thinking. The Ethics Guide on pages 36–37 discusses the difference between empathetic and egocentric thinking.

But, how will that team know where and how to save costs? One of the best ways is to study FlexTime's business processes and look for inefficiencies. For example, FlexTime has processes for obtaining new clients, processes for scheduling classes, and processes for hiring and firing instructors. Can any of those processes be simplified? Can tasks be reordered or reorganized to eliminate tasks and save labor hours?

And, finally, can FlexTime reduce process costs by applying information technology? We'll examine this possibility later in this chapter and other similar examples throughout this text.

Q2 What Is a Business Process?

A **business process** is a network of activities, roles, resources, repositories, and data flows that interact to accomplish a business function. In this question, we will define and illustrate each of these terms. We begin with example business processes.

Figure 2-1 shows the relationships among three important FlexTime business processes: Solicit Memberships, Schedule Classes, and Register Participants. Notice that each of these processes takes some kind of input and produces some kind of output. Solicit Memberships, for example, takes Prospects as input and produces Club Members as output. We cannot tell from this diagram, but presumably some activity within the Solicit Memberships process collects money from prospects and enrolls them into the Member Records list.

These business processes overlap. The Register Participants process uses the Member Records list produced by Solicit Memberships and the list of scheduled classes and instructors produced by the Schedule Class process.

Every business, including FlexTime, has dozens of processes. FlexTime has a process for hiring new trainers; a process for terminating trainers; a process for de-enrolling customers; and a process for paying trainers, suppliers, taxes, and so forth. You can model any organization as a complex maze of interacting business processes.

FlexTime's Register Participants Process

Figure 2-2 shows FlexTime's Register Participants process in more detail. The process begins when a member makes a Class Request. The Desk Clerk checks that person's membership status in Member Records, and, if the membership is valid, proceeds to Check Class Availability. If the member status is invalid, the Desk Clerk initiates a Membership Request that is input into the Solicit Memberships process.

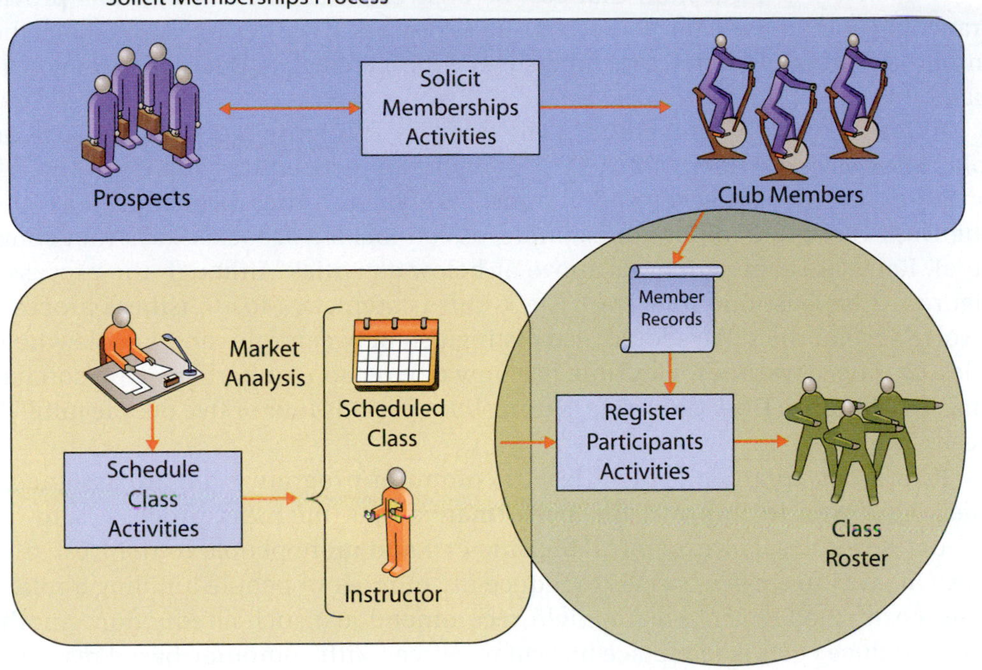

Figure 2-1 Three Business Processes at FlexTime

In the Check Class Availability activity, the Desk Clerk accesses the Class Roster records to determine if the class is full. If not, the Desk Clerk enrolls the customer in the Add Member to Class activity and, in that activity, updates the Class Roster records. If the class is not available, the Desk Clerk notifies someone in the Schedule Class process about the need for more spaces.

Components of a Business Process

Consider each of the elements in Figure 2-2: activities, decisions, roles, resources, repository, and data flow. **Activities** are collections of related tasks that receive inputs and process those inputs to produce outputs. The Check Membership Status activity takes Class Request and Member Records inputs, processes those inputs by determining if the person making the request is a valid member, and produces one of two outputs depending on the results of a decision. Activities can be manual (people following procedures), automated (hardware directed by software), or a combination of manual and automated. Activities are shown in rectangles.

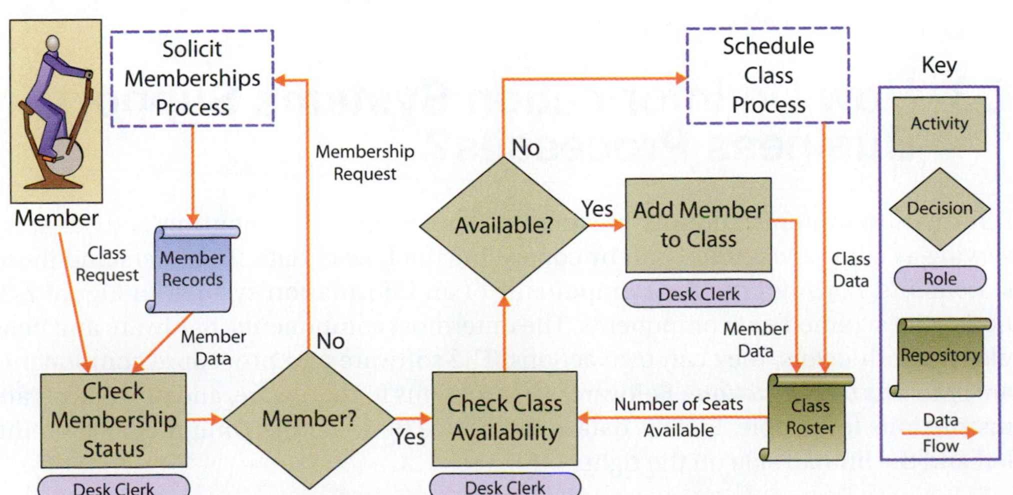

Figure 2-2 Register Participants Process

A **decision** is a question that can be answered Yes or No. Decisions provide branching points within the flow of a business process. If the person is a Member, then enrollment proceeds. If not, a Membership Request is created. Decisions are shown in diamonds.

Roles are sets of procedures. The process in Figure 2-2 involves just one role, Desk Clerk. The Desk Clerk role includes procedures for executing the activities in this process, and it most likely has other procedures as well. The Desk Clerk role might, for example, assign lockers or locker keys (not shown here). Roles are shown in ovals above or below activities. Although the process in Figure 2-2 has just one role, Desk Clerk, this is atypical. Most business processes involve several roles. We should also distinguish between roles and people who fill roles. During slow times, FlexTime has only one person, or perhaps a person half-time, fulfilling the Desk Clerk role. During busy periods four or five people fulfill the Desk Clerk role.

Resources are not typically shown on a process diagram, but are documented in other ways that you will learn about in Chapter Extension 11.

Resources are people, facilities, or computer programs that are assigned to roles. One way to improve the performance of a business process is to add resources to roles. For example, FlexTime can add more people to the Desk Clerk role. One way to reduce costs is to reduce the number of people fulfilling a role. To saves costs, the FlexTime team might recommend just such a reduction. Another way to reduce costs is to replace human resources with computer-based resources, as you will see.

A **repository** is a collection of business records. A repository can be a cardboard box, a notebook, a list, an Excel spreadsheet, a database, or even a collection of databases. Repositories hold the collective memory of the organization. One of the major considerations in the design of information systems is determining how many repositories should exist, or, equivalently, how much data should be stored in particular repositories. In the process in Figure 2-2, for example, should the Member Records and the Class Roster records exist in the same repository, or in a different one? In Figure 2-2, repositories are shown as scrolls.

Reread the introduction to FlexTime on pages 2–3. Neil knew that FlexTime needed help when he saw that records were being kept in cardboard boxes (the repository). That, in itself, was not the major problem (though it involves opportunity costs, as you'll learn in Q5). The major problem was the long line of customers as desk clerks fumbled through records in the cardboard boxes.

Finally, business processes include data flows. A **data flow** is the movement of a data item from one activity to another activity or to a repository. Data can be a simple item like a Membership Number, or it can be a complex document like a Member History. We will explore the relationship of data and information in Q5. Data flows are shown as directed arrows, labeled with the name of the data.

Q3 How Do Information Systems Support Business Processes?

Information systems support business processes by implementing activities, by serving as data repositories, and by controlling the flow of data. To understand those statements, consider the five components of an information system. In Figure 2-3, notice the symmetry of components. The outermost components, hardware and people, are both *actors*; they can take actions. The software and procedure components are both sets of *instructions*: Software is instructions for hardware, and procedures are instructions for people. Finally, data is the bridge between the computer side on the left and the human side on the right.

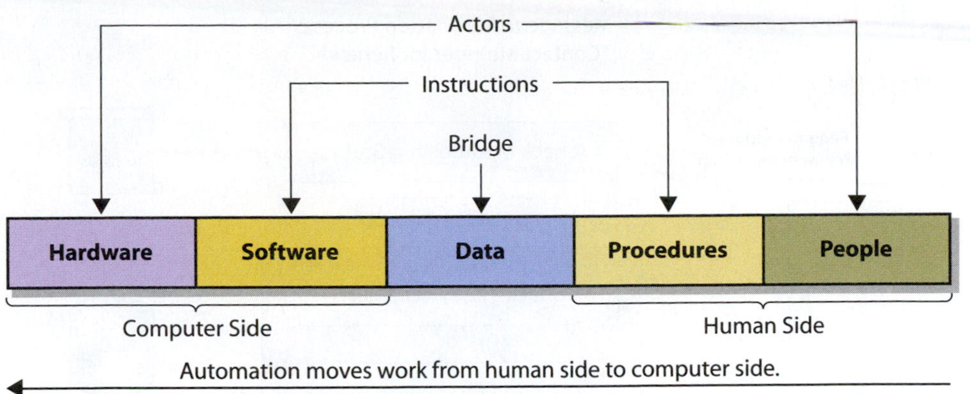

Figure 2-3
Characteristics of the Five Components

When a business process activity is automated, work formerly done by people following procedures has been moved to computers that perform the work by following instructions in software. Thus, the automation of a process activity consists of moving work from the right-hand side of Figure 2-3 to the left.

Examine Figure 2-2 again. If we assume that the Desk Clerk role is fulfilled by humans, then this is an entirely manual process. Member Records and Class Roster data is stored somewhere, maybe in one of those cardboard boxes! The flow of data is determined by the people who work as Desk Clerks. They write data into repositories, and they send data to other processes, such as Solicit Memberships, as shown in Figure 2-2.

Now examine Figure 2-4, which shows an automated process. The Register Participants application (a computer program) fulfills all of the Desk Clerk roles in Figure 2-2. Further, in this diagram, data is stored in two different databases, which are structured repositories of data, as you will learn in Chapter 5. Finally, flow of data within the business process is controlled by the application. Note the small arrows within the application rectangle. The disk drive symbol in Figure 2-4 is standard notation for a database.

FlexTime can potentially save money by implementing the system in Figure 2-4. Removing Class Scheduling work from the Desk Clerk role means that FlexTime can apply fewer resources to that role. However, FlexTime must pay for the development and use of the automated system, so the net savings may or may not be positive.

Figures 2-2 and 2-4 represent the extremes of the continuum. Figure 2-2 is entirely manual, and Figure 2-4 is entirely automated. It is possible, of course, to have systems that have both manual and automated elements. Figure 2-5, for example, shows the Register Participants process in which the Check Membership activity

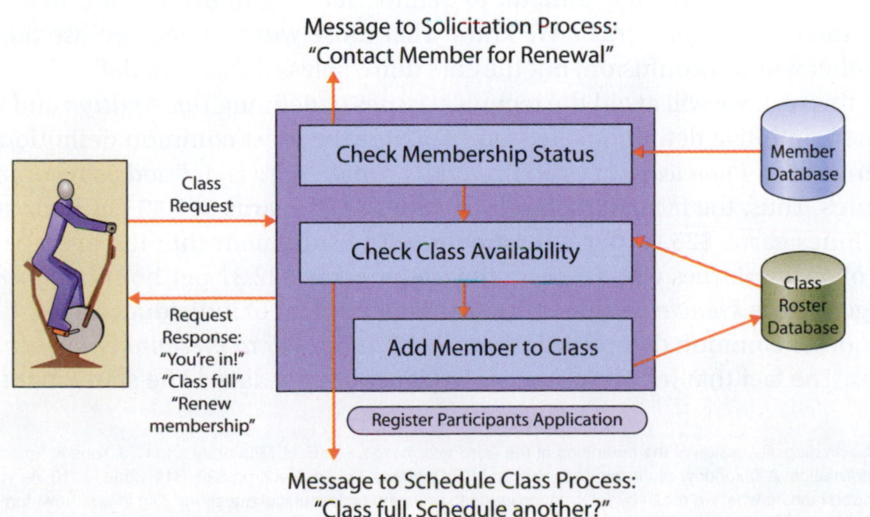

Figure 2-4
Automated Register Participants Process

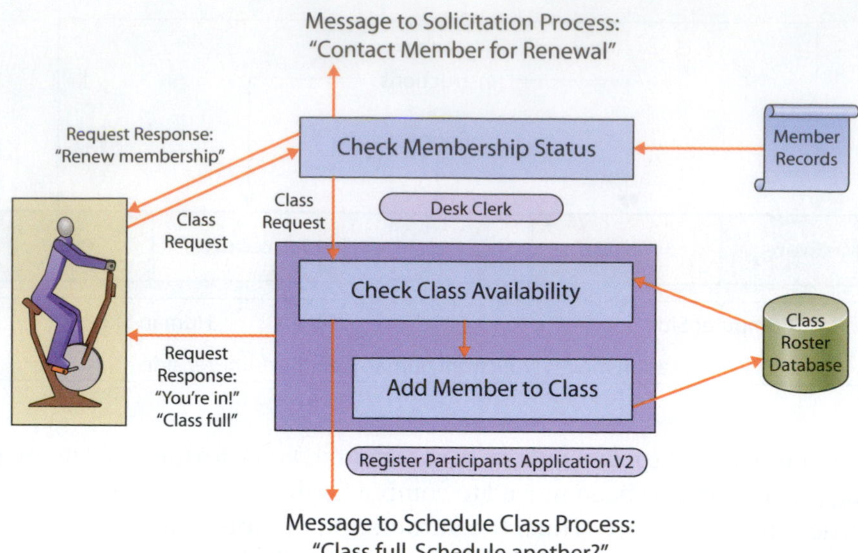

Figure 2-5
Manual and Automated Register Participants Process

is manual but the Check Class Availability and Add Member to Class activities are automated.

As you study these alternatives, you might wonder, which of them is the best? Or, in terms of the FlexTime team's assignment, could FlexTime save costs by using information systems to implement either of the alternatives in Figures 2-4 or 2-5? They might, depending on the costs and benefits of those alternatives.

Businesses ask questions like these every day. Can we reduce costs or improve service by using information systems? Two simple possibilities are shown in Figures 2-4 and 2-5; we will consider dozens more as we progress. Maybe, too, you can see why business professionals cannot leave the answers to such questions only in the hands of technical personnel.

Q4 What Is Information?

So far, we have been using the terms *data* and *information* rather loosely. Before we go further, it is important to explore the meaning and relationship between those two terms.

Information is one of those fundamental terms that we use every day but that turns out to be surprisingly difficult to define. Defining *information* is like defining words such as *alive* and *truth*. We know what those words mean, we use them with each other without confusion, but they are nonetheless difficult to define.[1]

In this text, we will avoid the technical issues of defining *information* and will use common, intuitive definitions instead. Probably the most common definition is that **information** is *knowledge derived from data*, where *data* is defined as recorded facts or figures. Thus, the facts that employee James Smith earns $17.50 per hour and that Mary Jones earns $25.00 per hour are *data*. The statement that the average hourly wage of all employees who work on the front desk is $22.37 per hour is *information*. Average wage is *knowledge* that is derived from the data of individual wages.

Yet a fourth definition of *information* is presented in the Guide on pages 38–39. There, *information* is defined as "a difference that makes a difference."

Another common definition is that *information is data presented in a meaningful context*. The fact that Jeff Parks earns $10.00 per hour is data.[2] The statement that Jeff

[1] For a fascinating discussion of the meanings of the word *information*, see E. H. McKinney and C. J. Yoos II, "Information About Information: A Taxonomy of Views." Available at: *MIS Quarterly*, Vol 34, No 2, pp 329–344, June, 2010. As you'll learn there, understanding what we mean by *information* leads to profound philosophical questions. Dig in and have fun!

[2] Actually, the word *data* is plural; to be correct, we should use the singular form *datum* and say, "The fact that Jeff Parks earns $10.00 per hour is a datum." The word *datum*, however, sounds pedantic and fussy, and we will avoid it in this text.

Experiencing MIS InClass Exercise 2

Woot.com

Woot (*www.woot.com*) is a Web site that offers a featured item for sale each day. Starting at midnight (U.S. Central time), a featured item is posted for sale at a deep discount. When the inventory of that item is gone, the selling stops. The next day Woot offers a different product. Rinse and repeat.

1. Go to *www.woot.com* and click around the site. See what today's item is. Click "What is woot?" and read the FAQs (frequently asked questions). Discuss the site with your team and, as a team, write a one-paragraph summary of this business. (Ignore any of the specialty Woots, such as Kids.woot or Shirt.woot.)
2. Identify five business processes that Woot needs to run this site. Name the processes and briefly describe them. Select processes that are critical to the operation of the site (avoid generic processes such as Hire Employees or Pay Taxes).
3. Woot's business model is considerably more simple than the typical online retailer's. Name and describe three business processes that typical online retailers need that Woot avoids.
4. Diagram the key processes involved in each day's sales. Use the same level of detail as in Figure 2-2. You can draw that process by hand, but a better solution is to go to *www.pearsonhighered.com/kroenke/*, select this text, and download the Application Exercise files. Find the files for Chapter 2, and select the file Chapter2_Figures.pptx. The last slide in the file contains symbol pieces you can use to create your own diagram. (If you don't know how to use PowerPoint, now is the time to learn. It's not difficult, and, in 2011 and beyond, you cannot be a successful business professional without PowerPoint skills.)
5. Describe (in generic terms) the contents of what you think is the most important repository in your answer in step 4.
6. List five types of information that Woot can obtain from the repository in your answer to step 5.
7. Present your business process (from step 4) and your answers to steps 5 and 6 to the rest of the class.

Parks earns less than half the average hourly wage front desk clerks, however, is information. It is data presented in a meaningful context.

Another definition of *information* that you will hear is that *information is processed data*, or, sometimes, *information is data processed by summing, ordering, averaging, grouping, comparing, or other similar operations.* The fundamental idea of this definition is that we do something to data to produce information.

All of these definitions are used in business. Some are better than others for particular purposes. We will explore the relationship of data, information, and business processes further in Q5.

Characteristics of Good Information

All information is not equal: Some information is better than other information. Figure 2-6 lists the characteristics of good information.

- Accurate
- Timely
- Relevant
  - To context
  - To subject
- Just sufficient
- Worth its cost

Figure 2-6
Characteristics of Good Information

Accurate

First, good information is **accurate information**, which is information that is based on correct and complete data, and it has been processed correctly as expected. Accuracy is crucial; managers must be able to rely on the results of their information systems. The IS function can develop a bad reputation in the organization if a system is known to produce inaccurate information. In such a case, the information system becomes a waste of time and money as users develop work-arounds to avoid the inaccurate data.

A corollary to this discussion is that you, a future user of information systems, ought not to rely on information just because it appears in the context of a Web page, a well-formatted report, or a fancy query. It is sometimes hard to be skeptical of information delivered with beautiful, active graphics. Do not be misled. When you begin to use an information system, be skeptical. Cross-check the information you are receiving. After weeks or months of using a system, you may relax. Begin, however, with skepticism.

Timely

Timely information is information that is produced in time for its intended use. A monthly report that arrives 6 weeks late is most likely useless. The information arrives long after the decisions have been made that needed that information. An information system that tells you not to extend credit to a customer after you have shipped the goods is unhelpful and frustrating. Notice that timeliness can be measured against a calendar (6 weeks late) or against events (before we ship).

When you participate in the development of an information system, timeliness will be part of the requirements you will request. You need to give appropriate and realistic timeliness needs. In some cases, developing systems that provide information in near real time is much more difficult and expensive than producing information a few hours later. If you can get by with information that is a few hours old, say so during the requirements specification phase.

Consider an example. Suppose you work in marketing and you need to be able to assess the effectiveness of new online ad programs. You want an information system that will not only deliver ads over the Web, but one that will also enable you to determine how frequently customers click on those ads. Determining click ratios in near real time will be very expensive; saving the data in a batch and processing it some hours later will be much easier and cheaper. If you can live with information that is a day or two old, the system will be easier and cheaper to implement.

Relevant

Relevant information is information that directly pertains to both the context and to the subject it references. Considering context, you, the CEO, need information that is summarized to an appropriate level for your job. A list of the hourly wage of every employee in the company is unlikely to be useful. More likely, you need average wage information by department or division. A list of all employee wages is irrelevant in your context.

Information should also be relevant to the subject at hand. If you want information about short-term interest rates for a possible line of credit, then a report that shows 15-year mortgage interest rates is irrelevant. Similarly, a report that buries the information you need in pages and pages of results is also irrelevant to your purposes.

Just Barely Sufficient

Just barely sufficient information is information that is sufficient for the purpose for which it is generated, but only so. We live in an information age; one of the critical decisions that each of us has to make each day is what information to ignore. The higher you rise into management, the more information you will be given, and because there is only so much time, the more information you will need to ignore. So information should be sufficient, but just barely.

Worth Its Cost

Information is not free. There are costs for developing an information system, costs of operating and maintaining that system, and costs of your time and salary for reading and processing the information the system produces. For information to be **worth its cost**, an appropriate relationship must exist between the cost of information and its value.

Consider an example. What is the value of a daily report of the names of the occupants of a full graveyard? Zero, unless grave robbery is a problem for the cemetery. The report is not worth the time required to read it. It is easy to see the importance of information economics from this silly example. It will be more difficult, however, when someone proposes some new system to you. You need to be ready to ask, "What's the value of the information?" or "What is the cost?" or "Is there an appropriate relationship between value and cost?" Information systems should be subject to the same financial analyses to which other assets are subjected.

Q5 Where Is the Information in Business Processes?

If you use any of the definitions of information in the last question and look for information in the business process in Figure 2-2, you won't find any. At least not on the surface. Where is knowledge derived from data? Where is a difference that makes a difference? Where is data presented in a meaningful context? None of these appear. Instead, what we find are *data* items flowing among activities.

But let's look deeper. In Figure 2-2, the Check Membership Status activity reads Member Data from Member Records. Most of that data is just data. Name, Email, Address, all of those items are just data to the person performing the Desk Clerk role. However, when that person reads MemberStatus (a value that indicates if the person's membership is current), he or she responds depending on the value. So the Desk Clerk considers the value of MemberStatus to be information; it is a difference that makes a difference. Depending on the value of MemberStatus, the person can enroll in a class or not. In this sense, any value that is used for the basis of a decision is a data item that induces information.

Information in Repositories

But there is more to this story. Consider the data that accumulates in the Member Records and Class Roster repositories. If, as Neil first found at FlexTime, that data is stored in cardboard boxes, then it remains data; it is not information. It will be very difficult for anyone at FlexTime to obtain any information from data forms in a box.

However, consider the Member and Class Roster databases in Figure 2-4. Here is some of the data they contain:

Customer data: Name, Email, Address, Phone(s), DateOfBirth

Membership data: DateOfMembership, MembershipType, FeePaid, ExpirationDate

Course data: Name, Description, StandardFee, PromotionalTerms

Class data: CourseName, StartDate, EndDate, Instructor, AvailableSeats

As data accumulates in those repositories, more and more information can be obtained from them. We can obtain, for example, information about the number of repeat memberships or information about the relationship of renewals and membership fees. We can determine the relative popularity of classes given at different times of the day, or the average number of available seats per class, or the popularity of different courses, and so forth.

Chapter Extension 8 discusses how to use Microsoft Access, a program for processing databases to create information in the form of reports and queries.

If, as shown in Figure 2-4, this data is stored in a database, then it will be quite easy to produce the information just described. You will see how in Chapter 5. From this example, you can see that although storing records in a cardboard box (or other non–computer-sensible format) may not be an operational problem, it has opportunity costs in lost information.

The discussion in Q3 implied that the major benefit of computer-based systems is labor savings. When FlexTime fulfills all or a portion of the Desk Clerk role with computer programs, it saves labor hours assigned to the Desk Clerk role. Although such labor savings are indeed a benefit of automation, often they are not the major benefit.

Instead, the major benefit of automating a process is that the data stored in databases and other repositories can readily be processed to produce information. So, the two major benefits of an information system are:

- Labor savings
- More data that can be processed for more information

Before we conclude this chapter, we need to address one important, but subtle, fact that we have been dancing around: Data is a stimulus; information is a response to that stimulus. To understand this, we need to consider a process that is less structured than those processes shown in Figures 2-2 through 2-4.

Information for Unstructured Processes

Not all processes are formally structured like the one shown in Figure 2-2. Consider, for example, the process you used in selecting your college or university. You gathered data about alternatives and created information for your decision; you constructed differences among those alternatives that made a difference to you. Then you employed some process to make your decision using that information. Your process was not structured like that in Figure 2-2; it was fluid and unstructured. You are enrolled where you are today because of that information—because of the differences you constructed—and that process.

Consider another example of an unstructured process. Suppose you have a perfect information system that can predict the future. No such information systems exist, but assume one does. Now suppose that on December 14, 1966, your perfect information system tells you that the next day, Walt Disney will die. Say you have $50,000 to invest; you can either buy Disney stock or you can short it (an investment technique that will net you a positive return if the stock value decreases). Given your perfect information system, how do you invest?

Before you read on, think about this question. If Walt Disney is going to die the next day, will the stock go up or down? Most students assume that the stock will go down, so they "short it" on the theory that the loss of a company's founder will mean a dramatic drop in the share price.

In fact, the day after Walt Disney's death the value of Disney stock increased substantially. Why? The market viewed Walt Disney as an artist; once he died he would no longer be able to create more art. Thus, the value of the existing art would increase because of scarcity, and the value of the corporation that owned that art would increase as well.

Now, ask the question, where was the information? The data was the prediction of his death. The information was a response you construed as a result of that data, with the aim of increasing your net worth. In a strict sense, data did not become information. Instead, data was a stimulus that caused *you* to create information—in your mind. So, we can query, report, and reformat data, but it is still data. It does not become information until you or others in the organization construe that data in the context of some goal.

You had perfect data, but you used that data to construct information that led you astray. Even if you have perfect data about the future, if you do not know what to do with that data, you are wasting your time and money. The *quality of your thinking* is a large part of the quality of the information system you use, especially for unstructured processes.

So, in an information system, the hardware and software components can produce accurate data, but unless the process is highly structured, as in Figure 2-2, the quality of the resulting information is determined by people and the procedures they use to interpret that data.

Information is used for transaction processing, day-to-day management, and strategic decision making. See Chapter Extension 3 for more.

How does the knowledge in this chapter help *FlexTime* and you?

Business processes provide a structure that the FlexTime team can use to investigate possible cost savings. The team can model important business processes and identify processes that could be simplified, or processes for which fewer resources could be allocated, or processes that could be partly or fully automated.

Considering costs from a process perspective will help the team understand how changes in one activity (or process) will impact other activities and processes. That understanding will enable the team to avoid costly mistakes. Finally, business processes will provide a guiding framework for the team's conversations, discussions, and decisions. The FlexTime team also knows that automating business processes not only can result in cost savings, but also make more information available from repositories.

Ethics Guide

Egocentric Versus Empathetic Thinking

According to one definition of the term, a *problem* is a perceived difference between what is and what ought to be. When developing information systems, it is critical for the development team to have a common definition and understanding of the problem. This common understanding, however, can be difficult to achieve.

Cognitive scientists distinguish between egocentric and empathetic thinking. Egocentric thinking centers on the self; someone who engages in egocentric thinking considers his or her view as "the real view" or "what really is." In contrast, those who engage in empathetic thinking consider their view as one possible interpretation of the situation and actively work to learn what other people are thinking.

Different experts recommend empathetic thinking for different reasons. Religious leaders say that such thinking is morally superior; psychologists say that empathetic thinking leads to richer, more fulfilling relationships. In business, empathetic thinking is recommended because it's smart. Business is a social endeavor, and those who can understand others' points of view are always more effective. Even if you do not agree with others' perspectives, you will be much better able to work with them if you understand their views.

Consider an example. Suppose you say to your MIS professor, "Professor Jones, I couldn't come to class last Monday. Did we do anything important?" Such a statement is a prime example of egocentric thinking. It takes no account of your professor's point of view and implies that your professor talked about nothing important. As a professor, it's tempting to say, "No, when I noticed you weren't there, I took out all the important material."

To engage in empathetic thinking, consider this situation from the professor's point of view. Students who do not come to class cause extra work for their professors. It doesn't matter how valid your reason for not coming to class was; you may actually have been contagious with a fever of 102°. But no matter what, your absence is more work for your professor. He or she must do something extra to help you recover from the lost class time.

Using empathetic thinking, you would do all you can to minimize the impact of your absence on your professor. For example, you could say, "I couldn't come to class, but I got the class notes from Mary. I read through them, and I have a question about business processes and how they relate to information. . . . Oh, by the way, I'm sorry to trouble you with my problem."

Before we go on, let's consider a corollary to this scenario: Never, ever, send an email to your boss that says, "I couldn't come to the staff meeting on Wednesday. Did we do anything important?" Avoid this for the same reasons as those for missing class. Instead, find a way to minimize the impact of your absence on your boss.

Now what does this have to do with MIS? Suppose that you buy a new laptop computer and within a few days, it fails. Repeated calls to customer support produce short-term fixes, but no one remembers who you are or what has been suggested to you in the past. Assume the keyboard continues to lock up every few days. In this scenario, there are a few views of the problem: (1) Customer support reps do not have data about prior customer contacts; (2) the customer support rep recommended a solution that did not work; and (3) the company is shipping too many defective laptops. The solution to each of these problem definitions requires a different information system.

Now imagine yourself in a meeting about this situation, and suppose that different people in the meeting hold the three problem views. If everyone engages in egocentric thinking, what will happen? The meeting will be argumentative and likely will end with nothing having been accomplished.

Suppose, instead, that the attendees think empathetically. In this case, people will make a concerted effort to understand the different points of view, and the outcome will be much more positive—possibly a definition of all three problems ranked in order of priority. In both scenarios, the attendees have the same information; the difference in outcomes results from the attendees' thinking style.

Empathetic thinking is an important skill in all business activities. Skilled negotiators always know what the other side wants; effective salespeople understand their customers' needs. Buyers who understand the problems of their vendors get better service. And students who understand the perspective of their professors get better . . . .

Discussion Questions

1. In your own words, explain the difference between egocentric and empathetic thinking.
2. Suppose you and another person differ substantially on a problem definition. Suppose she says to you, "No, the real problem is that . . . ," followed by her definition of the problem. How do you respond?
3. Again, suppose you and another person differ substantially on a problem definition. Assume you understand his definition. How can you make that fact clear?
4. Explain the statement, "In business, empathetic thinking is smart." Do you agree?

Guide

Understanding Perspectives and Points of View

Every human being speaks and acts from the perspective of a personal point of view. Everything we say or do is based on—or biased by—that point of view. Thus, everything you read in any textbook, including this one, is biased by the author's point of view. Authors may think that they are writing unbiased accounts of neutral subject material. But no one can write an unbiased account of anything, because we all write from a particular perspective.

Similarly, your professors speak to you from their points of view. They have experience, goals, objectives, hopes, and fears, and, like all of us, they use those elements to provide a framework from which they think and speak.

Sometimes, when you read or hear an editorial or opinion-oriented material, it is easy to recognize a strongly held point of view. It does not surprise you to think that such opinions might contain personal biases. But what about statements that do not appear to be opinions? For example, consider the following definition of *information*: "Information is a difference that makes a difference." By this definition, there are many differences, but only those that make a difference qualify as information.

This definition is obviously not an opinion, but it nevertheless was written from a biased perspective. The perspective is just less evident because the statement appears as a definition, not an opinion. But, in fact, it is the definition of information in the opinion of the well-known psychologist Gregory Bateson.

I find his definition informative and useful. It is imprecise, but it is a pretty good guideline, and I have used it to advantage when designing reports and queries for end users. I ask myself, "Does this report show people a difference that makes a difference to them?" So I find it to be a useful and helpful definition.

My colleagues who specialize in quantitative methods, however, find Bateson's definition vapid and useless. They ask, "What does it say?" or "How could I possibly use that definition to formalize anything?" or "A difference that makes a difference to what or whom?" Or they say, "I couldn't quantify anything about that definition; it's a waste of time."

And they are right, but so am I, and so was Gregory Bateson. The difference is a matter of perspective, and surprisingly, conflicting perspectives can all be true at the same time.

One last point: Whether it is apparent or not, authors write and professors teach not only from personal perspectives, but also with personal goals. I write this textbook in the hope that you will find the material useful and important and that you will tell your professor that it is a great book so that he or she will use it again. Whether you (or I) are aware of that fact, it and my other hopes and goals bias every sentence in this book.

Similarly, your professors have hopes and goals that influence what and how they teach. Your professors may want to see light bulbs of recognition on your face, they may want to win the Professor of the Year award, or they may want to gain tenure status in order to be able to do some advanced research in the field. Whatever the case, they, too, have hopes and goals that bias everything they say.

So, as you read this book and as you listen to your professor, ask yourself, "What is her perspective?" and "What are his goals?" Then compare those perspectives and goals to your own. Learn to do this not just with your textbooks and your professors, but with your colleagues as well. When you enter the business world, being able to discern and adapt to the perspectives and goals of those with whom you work will make you much more effective.

Discussion Questions

1. Consider the following statement: "The quality of your thinking is the most important component of an information system." Do you agree with this statement? Do you think it is even possible to say that one component is the most important one?

2. Although it does not appear to be so, the statement "There are five components of an information system: hardware, software, data, procedures, and people" is an opinion based on a perspective. Suppose you stated this opinion to a computer engineer who said, "Rubbish. That's not true at all. The only components that count are hardware and maybe software." Contrast the perspective of the engineer with that of your MIS professor. How do those perspectives influence their opinions about the five-component framework? Which is correct?

3. Consider Bateson's definition, "Information is a difference that makes a difference." How can this definition be used to advantage when designing a Web page? Explain why someone who specializes in quantitative methods might consider this definition to be useless. How can the same definition be both useful and useless?

4. Some students hate open-ended questions. They want questions that have one correct answer, like "7.3 miles per hour." When given a question like that in question 3, a question that has multiple, equally valid answers, some students get angry or frustrated. They want the book or the professor to give them the answer. How do you feel about this matter?

5. Do you think individuals can improve the quality of their thinking by learning to hold multiple, contradictory ideas in their minds at the same time? Or do you think that doing so just leads to indecisive and ineffective thinking? Discuss this question with some of your friends. What do they think? What are their perspectives?

ACTIVE REVIEW

Use this Active Review to verify that you understand the ideas and concepts that answer the chapter's study questions.

Q1 Why does the FlexTime team need to understand business processes?

Name and describe the two major reasons that the FlexTime team needs to understand business processes. State the objective of the FlexTime team, and explain why knowledge of business processes will help the team to accomplish that objective.

Q2 What is a business process?

Define *business process.* Explain the purpose of each of the processes in Figure 2-1. Explain the interaction of the elements in Figure 2-2. Define *activity, decision, role, resource, repository,* and *data flow.* Show the graphical symbol for all but resource. Explain the difference between a role and a resource.

Q3 How do information systems support business processes?

Name and explain three ways that information systems support business processes. Describe the symmetry in the five component model, and use that model to differentiate manual, automated, and mixed manual/automated systems. Explain the interaction of the elements in Figures 2-4 and 2-5.

Q4 What is information?

Give four definitions of *information.* Rank those definitions in the order of usefulness in business. Justify your ranking. Name and describe characteristics of good information.

Q5 Where is the information in business processes?

Explain why Member Name and Email are data in Figure 2-2, but MemberStatus can be considered both data and information. Use the example of Member and Class Roster databases in Figure 2-4 to show how repositories can lead to the creation of information. Name and describe two benefits of process automation. In your own words, explain the difference between a structured and unstructured process. Use the example of Disney's death to show that data is a stimulus for the creation of information, but that data is not information itself. Explain the role of your thinking in the creation of information.

How does the knowledge in this chapter help *FlexTime* and you?

Summarize how knowledge and consideration of business processes will enable the FlexTime team to accomplish its goal.

KEY TERMS AND CONCEPTS

Accurate information 32
Activities 27
Business process 26
Data flow 28
Decisions 28
Information 30
Just barely sufficient information 32
Relevant information 32
Repository 28
Resources 28
Roles 28
Timely information 32
Worth-its-cost information 33

USING YOUR KNOWLEDGE

1. Consider the four definitions of *information* presented in this chapter. The problem with the first definition, "knowledge derived from data," is that it merely substitutes one word we don't know the meaning of (*information*) for a second word we don't know the meaning of (*knowledge*). The problem with the second definition, "data presented in a meaningful context," is that it is too subjective. Whose context? What makes a context meaningful? The third definition, "data processed by summing, ordering, averaging, etc.," is too mechanical. It tells us what to do, but it doesn't tell us what information is. The fourth definition, "a difference that makes a difference," is vague and unhelpful.

   Also, none of these definitions helps us to quantify the amount of information we receive. What is the information content of the statement that every human being has a navel? Zero—you already know that. However, the statement that someone has just deposited $50,000 into your checking account is chock-full of information. So, good information has an element of surprise.

   Considering these points and the discussion of information in unstructured processes in Q5, answer the following questions:
   - **a.** What is information made of?
   - **b.** If you have more information, do you weigh more? Why or why not?
   - **c.** If you give a copy of your transcript to a prospective employer, is that information? If you show that same transcript to your dog, is it still information? Where is the information?
   - **d.** Give your own best definition of *information.*
   - **e.** Explain how you think it is possible that we have an industry called the *information technology industry,* but we have great difficulty defining the word *information.*

2. The text states that information should be worth its cost. Both cost and value can be broken into tangible and intangible factors. *Tangible* factors can be measured directly; *intangible* ones arise indirectly and are difficult to measure. For example, a tangible cost is the cost of a computer monitor; an intangible cost is the lost productivity of a poorly trained employee.

   Give five important tangible and five important intangible costs of an information system. Give five important tangible and five important intangible measures of the value of an information system. If it helps to focus your thinking, use the example of the class scheduling system at your university or some other university information system. When determining whether an information system is worth its cost, how do you think the tangible and intangible factors should be considered?

3. Suppose you manage the Purchasing activities at FlexTime and that you have been asked to help determine the requirements for a new purchasing information system. As you think about those requirements, you wonder how much autonomy you want your employees to have in selecting the supplier for each purchase. You can develop a system that will make the supplier selection automatically, or you can build one that allows employees to make that selection. Explain how this characteristic will impact:
   - **a.** The skill level required for your employees
   - **b.** The number of employees you will need
   - **c.** Your criteria for hiring employees
   - **d.** Your management practices
   - **e.** The degree of autonomy for your employees
   - **f.** Your flexibility in managing your department

   Suppose management has left you out of the requirements-definition process. Explain how you could use the knowledge you developed in answering this question to justify your need to be involved in the requirements definition.

COLLABORATION EXERCISE 2

Before you start this exercise, read Chapter Extensions 1 and 2, which describe collaboration techniques as well as tools for managing collaboration tasks. In particular, consider using Google Docs, Windows Live SkyDrive, Microsoft SharePoint, or some other collaboration tool.

Many students, especially those with limited business experience, have difficulty understanding how important business processes are and how complex even simple processes can become. The following business situation and exercises will help you understand the need for business processes, the importance of process design, and the role that information systems play in support of such processes.

Suppose you work for a supplier of electric and plumbing supplies, equipment, and tools. Your customers are home builders and construction companies that are accustomed to buying on credit. When you receive an order, you need to evaluate it and approve any special terms before you start removing items from inventory and packaging them for shipment. Accordingly, you have developed the order-approval process shown in Figure 2-7.

As you can see, your order-approval process consists of three stages: Check Credit, Check Inventory, and Approve Special Terms. You check credit and inventory on every order, but you need to approve special terms only if the customer asks for something special, such as free shipping, an extra discount, or unusually fast service and delivery.

As you will see, even a business process this simple has unexpected complexity. For one, are the checks in the proper order? This business process checks credit before it checks inventory levels. Does it make sense to take the time to evaluate credit if there is some possibility that you won't have the items in inventory? Should you check inventory before you check credit? And, if it turns out that you are going to reject the special terms of an order, would it make sense to check them first, before evaluating credit and inventory?

Notice that the arrows between Check Credit and Customer Credit Database flow both ways. The arrow from Credit Check to the Customer Credit Database means that once you have approved the credit for a customer, you update something about the customer's credit. Commonly, when an order is approved the amount of the order is removed from the total available credit for that customer.

Updating the Customer Credit Database makes sense, but what if it turns out that you have insufficient inventory? In that case, you will reject the order, but the credit has already been allocated. So you or one of your employees will need to remember to return the credit not used to the customer's credit record. Of course, you might have sufficient inventory to process part of the order, in which case you will need to return just part of the credit reserved to the customer.

Other problems occur because you are most likely processing many orders at the same time. Suppose two orders include one Kohler Supreme kitchen sink, but you have just one in inventory. You want to sell the sink to the first customer, but that means you must allocate that sink to it. Otherwise, both orders will be processed for the same sink. But suppose that the special terms of the order to which you've allocated the sink are disapproved. You would like to reassign the sink to the second order if it is still around to be processed. How can you accomplish that?

This scenario ignores another possibility. Suppose you have two order requests for the same sink; one is from a retail customer who wants it for her mountain home, and the second is from Big Sky Construction, a customer that buys 500 sinks a year from you. To which customer do you want to allocate that single sink? And how do you know how to do that?

Working with your team, answer the following questions:

1. Based on Figure 2-7, explain the business consequences if you debit customer credit in step 1, but then in steps 2 or 3 do not return credit for orders that you cannot process.
2. Recommend a process for adjusting credit for orders that are not approved. Who, in particular, should make the adjustment, and how do they receive the data they need to do so?
3. In Figure 2-7, explain why inventory must be allocated to orders in step 2. What is the business consequence if these allocations are not adjusted when special terms are not approved?
4. Recommend a process for adjusting inventory for orders for which the special terms are not approved. Who, in particular, should make the adjustment, and how do they receive the data they need to do so?
5. There are six different sequences for the three approval tasks in Figure 2-7. Name each and select what your team considers to be the most promising three.
6. Evaluate each of the three sequences that you selected in question 5. Identify which sequence you think is best.

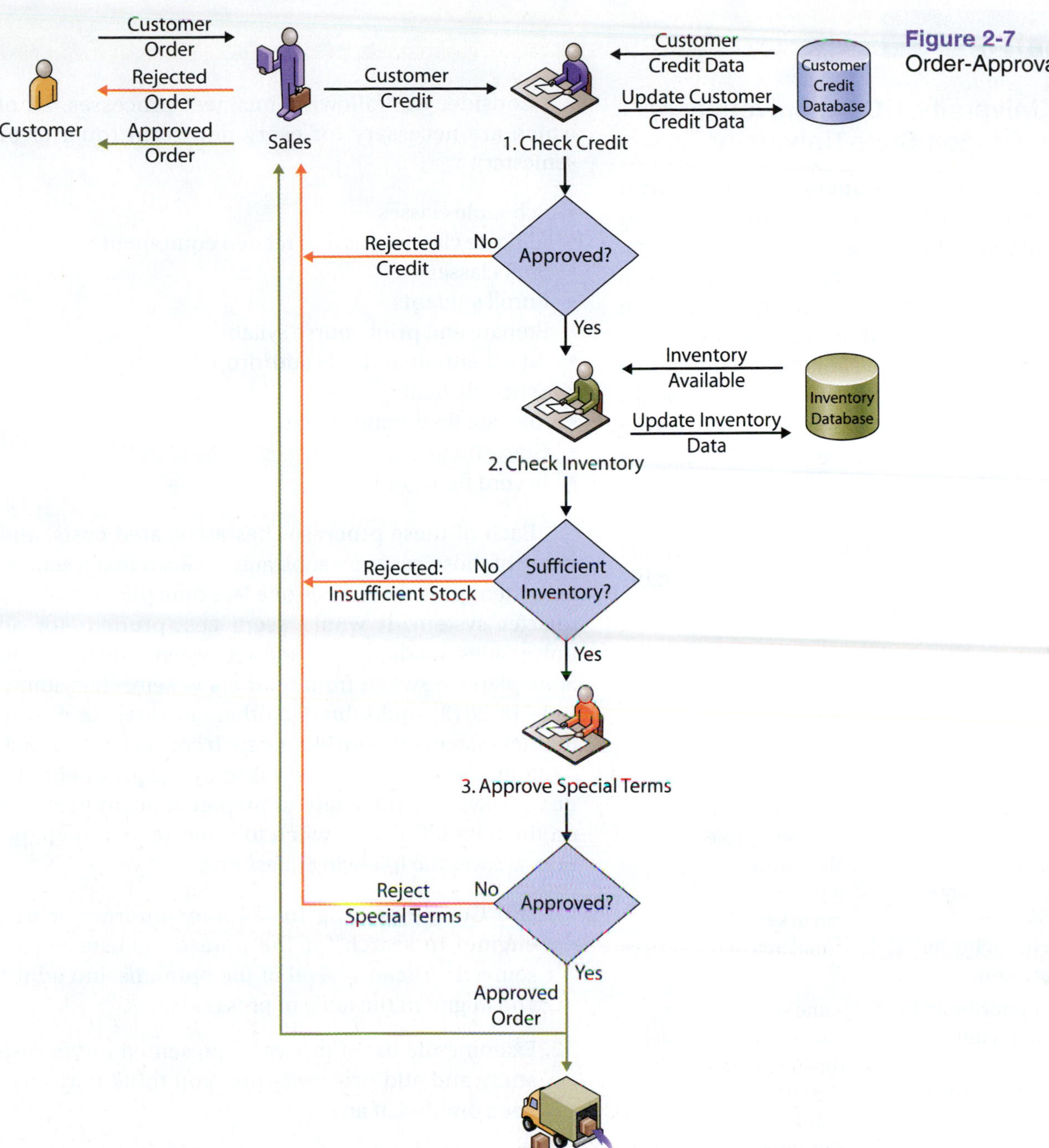

Figure 2-7
Order-Approval Process

7. State the criteria that you used for making your selections in questions 5 and 6.

8. So far, we haven't considered the impact of this process on the salesperson. What information do salespeople need to maintain good relationships with their customers?

9. *Optional extension.* Download the Visio diagram version of Figure 2-7 from this book's Web site, *www.pearsonhighered.com/kroenke*. Modify the diagram to illustrate the sequence of tasks you chose as best in your answer to question 6.

CASE STUDY 2

Ohio State University, UCLA, University of Washington, Oregon State University . . .

All three of these universities operate on the quarter system, in which the academic year is broken into four terms (including summer) of about 10 weeks each. Most students at these schools attend three quarters a year: Fall, Winter, and Spring. Other universities (in fact the majority in the United States) operate on the semester system, whereby the year is broken into three terms (Fall, Spring, and Summer) of about 15 weeks each. Most students attend only the Fall and Spring semesters. One unit of credit in the quarter systems is worth two-thirds a unit of credit in the semester system.

Students and faculty have different opinions on the relative merits of the two systems. The following table summarizes most of these arguments.

	Pros	Cons
Quarters	Can take more classes Opportunity cost of a frivolous class (ballroom dancing) lower Bad class experience shorter Exposure to more professors More flexibility for professors	Too fast paced Exams too frequent Don't get ill for a week! Not enough time for serious projects More work for professors Out of sync with majority of universities
Semester	More opportunity to focus on difficult subjects Less frenetic course pace More time for serious projects More time to meet fellow students	Some subjects don't need a full semester Too long to remember course content for final Bad class lasts forever

Few of the arguments that you'll find on the Web focus on costs. In a time of burgeoning educational expense, this omission seems odd. Perhaps costs are too pragmatic for proper consideration within ivy-covered walls. We in the College of Business, however, need not be so constrained.

Consider the following business processes, all of which are necessary for every new term (quarter or semester):

- Schedule classes
- Allocate classrooms and related equipment
- Staff classes
- Enroll students
- Prepare and print course syllabi
- Adjust enrollments via add/drop
- Schedule finals
- Allocate final exam rooms
- Grade finals
- Record final grades

Each of these processes has associated costs, and many of those costs are substantial. Given that a semester system pays these costs one less time per year than a quarter system, it would seem cost-prudent for all universities to adopt the semester system. Indeed, Ohio State plans to switch from quarters to semesters sometime in 2012; undoubtedly, other universities on the quarter system are considering such conversions as well.

Suppose you have been asked by the president of a quarter-system university to prepare a position report on the possibility of a switch to semesters. In preparation, answer the following questions:

1. Use Google or Bing (or another Internet search engine) to search for the phrase "quarter versus semester." Read several of the opinions and adjust and augment the table of pros and cons.

2. Examine the list of processes presented in the case study and add processes that you think may have been omitted, if any.

3. Choose two of the processes in the augmented list in your answer to step 2. Diagram those processes to the same level of detail as the process in Figure 2-2. (If you go to *www.pearsonhighered.com/kroenke* and download the supplements to this text, you can find a PowerPoint file named Chapter2_Figures.pptx that has the symbols used in Figures 2-1 through 2-4. Modify that file to document your answer to this question.)

4. List the sources of costs for each of the two processes you chose in your answer to step 3.

5. Considering just the College of Business at your university, estimate each of the costs in step 4. Make and justify assumptions about labor rates and other factors.

6. Assuming that costs for other colleges are the same as for the College of Business (an unrealistic assumption; law and medicine probably have higher costs), what is the total cost for the two processes you selected for your university, in total?

7. List and describe five factors that you think could be keeping a university that is on a quarter system from converting to a semester system.

CHAPTER 3

Organizational Strategy, Information Systems, and Competitive Advantage

This could happen to you

"Hey, look who's here! . . . Felix, you made it!"

"Yes, I did. I could come to a lot more 'meetings' once we stopped trying to meet in person and all at once. It was just such a drag to get everyone together at the same time."

"I'll say. Kelly, this is the first time we've met in person in a month, and we're doing it now just so we can show you and Neil what we've got so far." As Jan makes this statement, she's thinking about the time and money she saved not having to arrange for child care for multiple meetings.

"Great. What have you got?" Kelly asks, excited to hear what the team has developed.

"Well," Tara says, clearly struggling with her words, "well, we found that we really didn't know who we are . . . No, that's not right. I mean, we know who we are, but we had trouble expressing it in words."

Felix jumps in, "Kelly, it's like this. We think we succeed because we offer the best workout in the city. But, what does *best* really mean? It isn't because of our great juice bar, even though it is great. We decided we're best because of our *intensity.* People come here, it's all business; we get to it and provide a fast-paced, to-the-max cardio workout. People leave here pumped and upbeat!"

STUDY QUESTIONS

Q1 **How does organizational strategy determine information systems structure?**

Q2 **What five forces determine industry structure?**

Q3 **What is competitive strategy?**

Q4 **How does competitive strategy determine value chain structure?**

Q5 **How do value chains determine business processes and information systems?**

Q6 **How do information systems provide competitive advantages?**

How does the knowledge in this chapter help *FlexTime* and you?

"OK, that makes sense to me. Go on."

"So, in an effort to reduce costs, we can't lose that," Felix says, wistfully.

Tara jumps back into the conversation. "So, in our discussion board, we wrote about ways to reduce costs. We had a long thread going and we weren't getting very far until Jan pointed out that the size of the class doesn't seem to impact intensity . . . but, in fact, packing her spinning classes actually adds to the intensity."

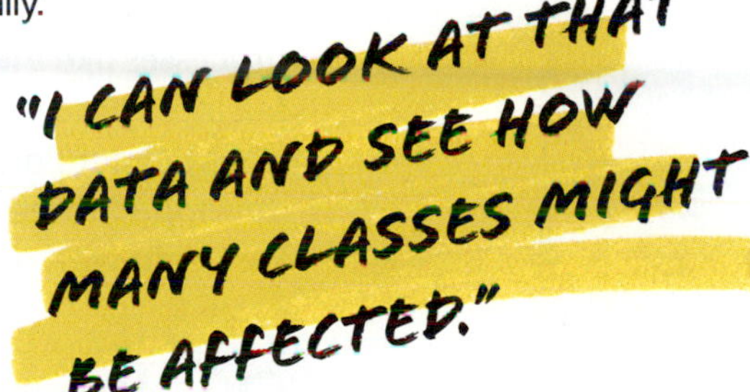
"I CAN LOOK AT THAT DATA AND SEE HOW MANY CLASSES MIGHT BE AFFECTED."

"Yeah, I did," admits Jan. "But I'm not crazy about where this goes. Because, if we pack our classes more, well, we'll save FlexTime money, but . . . well, I may as well say it, fewer classes means less money to us. If we're not teaching we're not getting paid . . ."

An awkward pause fills the room.

Felix jumps in, "We love FlexTime and we're willing to take a hit in the short run. But, how much of a hit will it be? And for how long? We don't know. And we're worried, too."

"Maybe I can help there." Neil speaks for the first time. Everyone turns to listen. "I've got a couple of thoughts. But, first, thanks for taking this so seriously and for bringing this issue to light. Now, as you know, we record all of our class registration data into our database. We've got records going back several years. I can look at that data and see how many classes might be affected. We can look for classes that have lower enrollments, but also at the differences between average class size and maximum class size."

"And then what?" Kelly looks at Neil . . . wondering where he's going with this.

"That will tell us how many classes we might want to cancel, what the benefit would be. And, if there is substantial cost savings to be had, it will help to answer Felix's question about how much of a hit we'll have to take."

Later, Kelly and Neil are talking alone in Neil's office.

"This is risky, Neil. If we start cancelling classes, it will look like we're in trouble. We don't want the staff to start communicating that to our customers."

"Yeah, you're right. And we might lose some staff. But, we haven't decided anything yet. I need to look at the data and see the impact. It's not worth doing if it doesn't help our bottom line, and I'm not sure it will."

"Neil, isn't it great that they get what makes FlexTime special? I was really proud of them for coming up with this idea. These jobs mean a lot to them."

Optional Extension for this chapter is • CE4: Knowledge Management and Expert Systems 341

CE

"If we do make classes larger, maybe I can come up with some bonus program . . . maybe we take the average maximum number of students for each class in each time slot and then provide a bonus for each student they enroll over that number . . . or . . ." Neil looks over Kelly's shoulder, deep in thought.

"I don't mean to be negative, but this sounds complicated. Anyway, I've got a class to teach."

"OK, Kelly, I'll get back to you with what I find out."

Q1 How Does Organizational Strategy Determine Information Systems Structure?

Kelly assigned the FlexTime team the task of finding ways of reducing costs without "losing who we are as a company." That is a sensible and appropriate task, but it starts in the middle of the story. In this chapter, we will back up to understand how Kelly and Neil arrived at that assignment.

Figure 3-1 summarizes a planning process used by many organizations. In short, organizations examine the structure of their industry and, from that, develop a competitive strategy. That strategy determines value chains, which, in turn, determine business processes like those we discussed in Chapter 2. As you saw in that chapter, the nature of business processes determines the requirements and functions of information systems.

Michael Porter, one of the key researchers and thinkers in competitive analysis, developed three different models that help us understand the elements of Figure 3-1. We begin with his five forces model.

Q2 What Five Forces Determine Industry Structure?

Porter developed the **five forces model**[1] as a model for determining the potential profitability of an industry. Over the years, this model has been applied for another purpose, as a way of understanding organizations' competitive environments. That understanding is then used to formulate a competitive strategy, as you will see.

Porter's five competitive forces can be grouped into two types: forces related to competition and forces related to supply chain bargaining power.

Competitive Forces

- **Competition from vendors of substitutes**
- **Competition from new competitors**
- **Competition from existing rivals**

Figure 3-1
Organizational Strategy Determines Information Systems

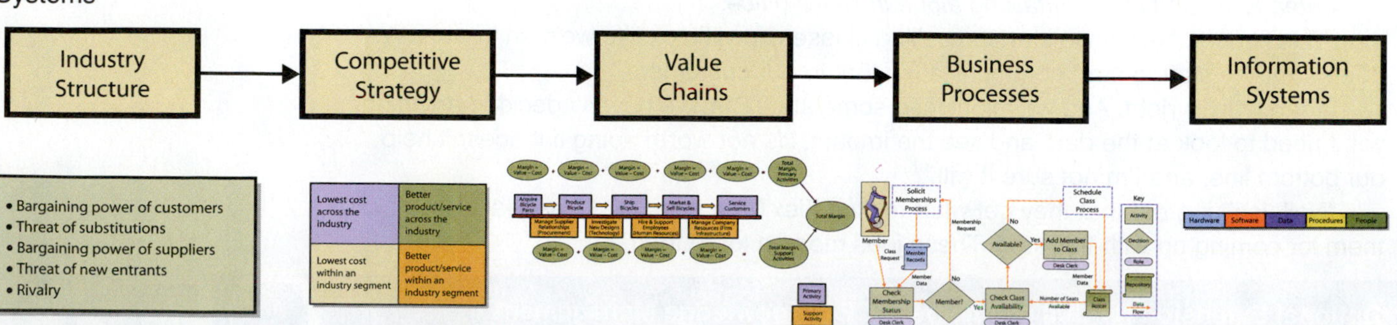

1. Michael Porter, *Competitive Strategy: Techniques for Analyzing Industries and Competitors* (New York: Free Press, 1980).

Bargaining Power Forces

- **Bargaining power of suppliers**
- **Bargaining power of customers**

Porter assesses these five forces to determine the characteristics of an industry, how profitable it is, and how sustainable that profitability will be. Here, we will use this model for a different purpose: to identify sources of strong competition and use that knowledge to create a competitive strategy to combat those strong forces. We will apply this technique to FlexTime and see, in the process, that Kelly's assignment to the team was exactly right.

Each of the three competitive forces concerns the danger of customers taking their business elsewhere. As shown in the first column of Figure 3-2, two strength factors that relate to all three of these forces are switching costs and customer loyalty. If the costs of switching to another vendor are high, then the strength of the competitive forces is low. Similarly, if customers are loyal to the company or brand, then the strength of the competitive forces is low.

Now consider each of the three competitive forces individually. The threat of a substitute is stronger if the substitute's price is lower and if the perceived benefits of the substitute are similar. As shown in Figure 3-2, FlexTime views home workouts and exclusive, members-only athletic and country clubs as substitution threats.

FlexTime judges the threat from home workouts to be medium, because, although switching costs are low and working out at home is cheap, the experience of a home workout is not as motivating as a FlexTime workout. To manage this threat, FlexTime needs to ensure that members have a vastly superior workout experience compared to the one that they can have at home.

Figure 3-2
Five Forces and FlexTime

Type (Strength Factors)	Competitive Force (Strength Factors)	FlexTime Threat (Factors Assessment)	FlexTime's Strength Assessment
Competitve (Switching costs, customer loyalty)	**Substitutes** (Lower price and perceived benefits the same)	**Home workouts** (Low switching costs, cheap, but not the same experience at all) **Athletic clubs** (Expensive, high switching costs, substitute not as familiar)	**Home workouts threat:** medium **Athletic club threat:** weak
	New Entrants (Barriers to entry, capital requirements, noncapital resources)	**New copycats** (Medium switching costs, customers loyal to FlexTime, capital requirements medium, customer database is barrier to entry)	**New copycat threat:** weak
	Rivalry (Price, quality, innovation, marketing)	**Rivals** (Medium switching costs, customers loyal to FlexTime, customers influenced by price/quality/innovation/marketing)	**Rivals threat:** strong
Supply chain bargaining power (Availabilty of substitutes, relative size)	**Supplier**	**Landlord** (Few suitable buildings with parking, FlexTime switching costs high, multiyear contract) **Equipment & supply vendors** (Many subtitutes, low switching costs, brand not important)	**Landlord bargaining power threat:** strong **Equipment & supply vendors bargaining power threat:** weak
	Customer	**Club members** (Relative size: bargaining power of a single customer is weak)	**Club member bargaining power:** weak

The threat from athletic and country clubs is weak, because the initial membership fee is expensive, the switching costs are high (people have to apply for membership and pay annual fees), and the experience is less familial. To manage this threat, FlexTime needs to keep its familial atmosphere.

Figure 3-2 also shows how FlexTime views threats from new entrants and industry rivals (called copycats). FlexTime judges the competitive threat of new entrants to be weak for the reasons shown. Note that the cost of developing a large database of active customers is high and that it requires months or years to compile. Thus, FlexTime's customer database is a barrier to new entrants.

FlexTime judges the threat to rivals as strong, the strongest of all the competitive threats. FlexTime needs to ensure that it develops a competitive strategy to combat such rivals. Felix's comments about intensity at the start of this chapter are exactly the factors that FlexTime needs to consider.

The last two rows of Figure 3-2 concern bargaining power forces from suppliers or from customers. As shown, the strength of these forces depends on the availability of substitutes and the relative size of the firm (here FlexTime) compared to the size of suppliers or customers. A Nobel–prize-winning scientist has strong bargaining supplier power at your university because such scientists are rare. In contrast, a temporary part-time instructor has little bargaining power, because many people can fill that role. If such instructors were to form a union, however, then that union would have greater bargaining power because of its relative size.

Similarly, you, as an individual, have little bargaining power as a customer to your university. Your application can be readily replaced with another, and you are an individual attempting to bargain with a large organization. In contrast, a large organization such as Oracle, Microsoft, or Google would have much stronger bargaining power for its employees at your university.

Examine Figure 3-2 to learn why FlexTime views the bargaining power of its landlord to be strong, but the power of equipment and supply vendors as weak. It also views the bargaining power of any single customer to be weak as well.

To summarize, FlexTime concludes that, whatever it does to save costs, it needs to proceed in such a way that it does not weaken its ability to combat the threats from rivals or further reduce its bargaining power with the owner of the building it occupies.

Q3 What Is Competitive Strategy?

An organization responds to the structure of its industry by choosing a competitive strategy. As shown in Figure 3-3, Porter defined four fundamental competitive strategies.[2] An organization can be the cost leader and provide products at the lowest prices, or it can focus on adding value to its products to differentiate them those of the competition. Further, the organization can employ the cost or differentiation strategy across an

Figure 3-3
Porter's Four Competitive Strategies

	Cost	Differentiation
Industry-wide	Lowest cost across the industry	Better product/service across the industry
Focus	Lowest cost within an industry segment	Better product/service within an industry segment

2. Michael Porter, *Competitive Strategy* (New York: Free Press, 1980).

industry, or it can focus its strategy on a particular industry segment. In this text, we define **competitive strategy** to be one of the four alternatives shown in Figure 3-3.

Consider the car rental industry, for example. According to the first column of Figure 3-3, a car rental company can strive to provide the lowest-cost car rentals across the industry, or it can seek to provide the lowest-cost car rentals to a "focused" industry segment—say, U.S. domestic business travelers.

As shown in the second column, a car rental company can seek to differentiate its products from the competition. It can do so in various ways—for example, by providing a wide range of high-quality cars, by providing the best reservation system, by having the cleanest cars or the fastest check-in, or by some other means. The company can strive to provide product differentiation across the industry or within particular segments of the industry, such as U.S. domestic business travelers.

According to Porter, to be effective the organization's goals, objectives, culture, and activities must be consistent with the organization's strategy. To those in the MIS field, this means that all information systems in the organization must facilitate the organization's competitive strategy.

Consider competitive strategy at FlexTime. Its primary competitive threat is from rivals. FlexTime can meet that threat by having the lowest prices or by adding something to the workout experience that differentiates it from the competition. As Felix says in the opening vignette, FlexTime differentiates on the intensity of its workouts. As he says, "People leave here pumped and upbeat!"

FlexTime is not as profitable as its owners want it to be. To increase profitability, it seeks ways to save costs. But whatever cost savings FlexTime implements, it cannot lose workout intensity, its competitive advantage over rivals. We will see how FlexTime uses its database to guide its decisions in this regard in Chapter 5.

Q4 How Does Competitive Strategy Determine Value Chain Structure?

Organizations analyze the structure of their industry, and, using that analysis, they formulate a competitive strategy. They then need to organize and structure the organization to implement that strategy. If, for example, the competitive strategy is to be a *cost leader*, then business activities need to be developed to provide essential functions at the lowest possible cost.

A business that selects a *differentiation* strategy would not necessarily structure itself around least-cost activities. Instead, such a business might choose to develop more costly systems, but it would do so only if those systems provided benefits that outweighed their risks. Porter defined **value** as the amount of money that a customer is willing to pay for a resource, product, or service. The difference between the value that an activity generates and the cost of the activity is called the **margin**. A business with a differentiation strategy will add cost to an activity only as long as the activity has a positive margin.

A **value chain** is a network of value-creating activities. That generic chain consists of five primary activities and four support activities. **Primary activities** are business functions that relate directly to the production of the organization's products or services. **Support activities** are business functions that assist and facilitate the primary activities. Value chain analysis is most easily understood in the context of manufacturing, so we will leave the FlexTime case for now and switch to the example of a bicycle manufacturer.

Primary Activities in the Value Chain

To understand the essence of the value chain, consider a small a bicycle manufacturer (see Figure 3-4). First, the manufacturer acquires raw materials using the inbound logistics activity. This activity concerns the receiving and handling of raw materials

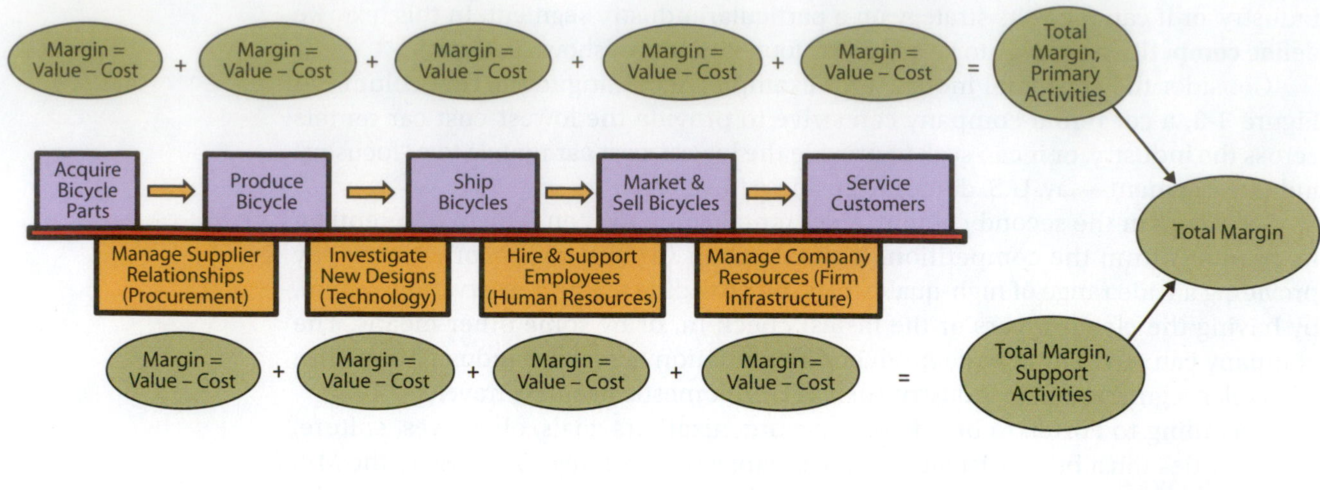

Figure 3-4
Bicycle Maker's Value Chain

and other inputs. The accumulation of those materials adds value in the sense that even a pile of unassembled parts is worth something to some customer. A collection of the parts needed to build a bicycle is worth more than an empty space on a shelf. The value is not only the parts themselves, but also the time required to contact vendors for those parts, to maintain business relationships with those vendors, to order the parts, to receive the shipment, and so forth.

In the operations activity, the bicycle maker transforms raw materials into a finished bicycle, a process that adds more value. Next, the company uses the outbound logistics activity to deliver the finished bicycle to a customer. Of course, there is no customer to send the bicycle to without the marketing and sales value activity. Finally, the service activity provides customer support to the bicycle users.

Each stage of this generic chain accumulates costs and adds value to the product. The net result is the total margin of the chain, which is the difference between the total value added and the total costs incurred. Figure 3-5 summarizes the primary activities of the value chain.

Support Activities in the Value Chain

The support activities in the generic value chain facilitate the primary activities and contribute only indirectly to the production, sale, and service of the product. They

Figure 3-5
Task Descriptions for Primary Activities of the Value Chain

Primary Activity	Description
Inbound Logistics	Receiving, storing, and disseminating inputs to the product
Operations/Manufacturing	Transforming inputs into the final product
Outbound Logistics	Collecting, storing, and physically distributing the product to buyers
Sales and Marketing	Inducing buyers to purchase the product and providing a means for them to do so
Customer Service	Assisting customer's use of the product and thus maintaining and enhancing the product's value

include procurement, which consists of the processes of finding vendors, setting up contractual arrangements, and negotiating prices. (This differs from inbound logistics, which is concerned with ordering and receiving in accordance with agreements set up by procurement.)

Porter defined technology broadly. It includes research and development, but it also includes other activities within the firm for developing new techniques, methods, and procedures. He defined human resources as recruiting, compensation, evaluation, and training of full-time and part-time employees. Finally, firm infrastructure includes general management, finance, accounting, legal, and government affairs.

Supporting functions add value, albeit indirectly, and they also have costs. Hence, as shown in Figure 3-4, supporting activities contribute to a margin. In the case of supporting activities, it would be difficult to calculate the margin because the specific value added of, say, the manufacturer's lobbyists in Washington, D.C., is difficult to know. But there is a value added, there are costs, and there is a margin, even if it is only in concept.

Value Chain Linkages

Porter's model of business activities includes **linkages**, which are interactions across value activities. For example, manufacturing systems use linkages to reduce inventory costs. Such a system uses sales forecasts to plan production; it then uses the production plan to determine raw materials needs and then uses the material needs to schedule purchases. The end result is just-in-time inventory, which reduces inventory sizes and costs.

Value chain analysis has a direct application to manufacturing businesses like the bicycle manufacturer. However, value chains also exist in service-oriented companies like FlexTime. The difference is that most of the value in a service company is generated by the operations, marketing and sales, and service activities. Inbound and outbound logistics are not typically as important.

Before leaving the topic of competitive strategy, consider the issues raised in the Ethics Guide on pages 60–61. This guide discusses a company's competitive strategy and its possible impact on employees.

Q5 How Do Value Chains Determine Business Processes and Information Systems?

As you learned in the last chapter, a business process is a network of activities, resources, facilities, and information that accomplish a business function. Now we can be more specific and say that business processes implement value chains or portions of value chains. Thus, each value chain is supported by one or more business processes.

For example, Figure 3-6 shows a portion of a bike rental value chain for a bicycle rental company. The top part of this figure shows how a company having a competitive strategy of providing low-cost rentals to college students might implement this portion of its operations value chain. The bottom part shows how a company with a competitive strategy of providing high-quality rentals to business executives at a conference resort might implement this portion of that same value chain.

Note that the value chain activities are the same for both companies. Both greet the customer, determine the customers' needs, rent a bike, and return the bike. However, each company implements these activities in ways that are consistent with its competitive strategy.

The low-cost vendor has created barebones, minimum processes to support its value chain. The high-service vendor has created more elaborate business processes (supported by information systems) that are necessary to differentiate its service from that of other vendors. As Porter says, however, these processes and systems must create sufficient value that they will more than cover their costs. If not, the margin of those systems will be negative.

	Value Chain Activity	Greet Customer	Determine Needs	Rent Bike	Return Bike & Pay
Low-Cost Rental to Students	Message that implements competitive strategy	"You wanna bike?"	"Bikes are over there. Help yourself."	"Fill out this form, and bring it to me over here when you're done."	"Show me the bike." "OK, you owe $23.50. Pay up."
	Supporting business process	None.	Physical controls and procedures to prevent bike theft.	Printed forms and a shoe box to store them in.	Shoe box with rental form. Minimal credit card and cash receipt system.
High-Service Rental to Business Executives at Conference Resort	Message that implements competitive strategy	"Hello, Ms. Henry. Wonderful to see you again. Would you like to rent the WonderBike 4.5 that you rented last time?"	"You know, I think the WonderBike Supreme would be a better choice for you. It has ..."	"Let me just scan the bike's number into our system, and then I'll adjust the seat for you."	"How was your ride?" "Here, let me help you. I'll just scan the bike's tag again and have your paperwork in just a second." "Would you like a beverage?" "Would you like me to put this on your hotel bill, or would you prefer to pay now?"
	Supporting business process	Customer tracking and past sales activity system.	Employee training and information system to match customer and bikes, biased to "up-sell" customer.	Automated inventory system to check bike out of inventory.	Automated inventory system to place bike back in inventory. Prepare payment documents. Integrate with resort's billing system.

Figure 3-6
Operations Value Chains for Bicycle Rental Companies

If a value chain's margin is negative, the company must make some change. Either the value must be increased, or the costs of the value chain need to be reduced. To investigate this principle further, consider Collaboration Exercise 3 on pages 65–66.

Before we continue, review Figure 3-1 again. The material in these first three chapters is presented from the right to the left in this figure. We began with the components of an information system in Chapter 1. We then considered business processes in Chapter 2. In this chapter, we have considered value chains, competitive strategy, and industry structure.

Q6 How Do Information Systems Provide Competitive Advantages?

In your business strategy class, you will study the Porter models in greater detail than we have discussed here. When you do so, you will learn numerous ways that organizations respond to the five competitive forces. For our purposes, we can distill those

Experiencing MIS InClass Exercise 3

Industry Structure → Competitive Strategy → Value Chains → Business Processes → Information Systems

As shown in Figure 3-1, information systems are a logical consequence of an organization's analysis of industry structure via the chain of models shown in the title of this feature. Consequently, you should be able to combine your knowledge of an organization's market, together with observations of the structure and content of its Web storefront, to infer the organization's competitive strategy and possibly make inferences about its value chains and business processes. The process you use here can be useful in preparing for job interviews, as well.

Form a three-person team (or as directed by your professor) and perform the following exercises. Divide work as appropriate, but create common answers for the team.

1. The following pairs of Web storefronts have market segments that overlap in some way. Briefly visit each site of each pair:
   - *www.sportsauthority.com* vs. *www.soccer.com*
   - *www.target.com* vs. *www.sephora.com*
   - *www.woot.com* vs. *www.amazon.com*
   - *www.petco.com* vs. *www.healthyfoodforpets.com*
   - *www.llbean.com* vs. *www.rei.com*
2. Select two pairs from the list. For each pair of companies, answer the following questions:
   a. How do the companies' market segments differ?
   b. How do their competitive pressures differ?
   c. How do their competitive strategies differ?
   d. How is the "feel" of the content of their Web sites different?
   e. How is the "feel" of the user interface of their Web sites different?
   f. How could either company change its Web site to better accomplish its competitive strategy?
   g. Would the change you recommended in step f necessitate a change in one or more of the company's value chains? Explain.
3. Use your answers in step 2 to explain the following statement: "The structure of an organization's information system (here a Web storefront) is determined by its competitive strategy." Structure your answer so that you could use it in a job interview to demonstrate your overall knowledge of business planning.
4. Present your team's answers to the rest of the class.

ways into the list of principles shown in Figure 3-7. Keep in mind that we are applying these principles in the context of the organization's competitive strategy.

Some of these competitive techniques are created via products and services, and some are created via the development of business processes. Consider each.

Competitive Advantage via Products

The first three principles in Figure 3-7 concern products or services. Organizations gain a competitive advantage by creating *new* products or services, by *enhancing* existing products or services, and by *differentiating* their products and services from those of their competitors. As you think about these three principles, realize that an

Figure 3-7
Principles of Competitive Advantage

Product Implementations
1. Create a new product or service
2. Enhance products or services
3. Differentiate products or services

Process Implementations
4. Lock in customers and buyers
5. Lock in suppliers
6. Raise barriers to market entry
7. Establish alliances
8. Reduce costs

information system can be part of a product or it can provide support for a product or service.

Consider, for example, a car rental agency like Hertz or Avis. An information system that produces information about the car's location and provides driving instructions to destinations is part of the car rental, and thus is part of the product itself (see Figure 3-8a). In contrast, an information system that schedules car maintenance is not part of the product, but instead supports the product (Figure 3-8b). Either way, information systems can achieve the first three objectives in Figure 3-7.

The remaining five principles in Figure 3-7 concern competitive advantage created by the implementation of business processes.

Competitive Advantage via Business Processes

Organizations can *lock in customers* by making it difficult or expensive for customers to switch to another product. This strategy is sometimes called establishing high **switching costs**. Organizations can *lock in suppliers* by making it difficult to switch to another organization, or, stated positively, by making it easy to connect to and work with the organization. Competitive advantage can be gained by *creating entry barriers* that make it difficult and expensive for new competition to enter the market.

Another means to gain competitive advantage is to *establish alliances* with other organizations. Such alliances establish standards, promote product awareness and needs, develop market size, reduce purchasing costs, and provide other benefits. Finally, by creating better business processes, organizations can gain competitive

Figure 3-8
Two Roles for Information Systems Regarding Products

a. Information System as Part of a Car Rental Product

b. Information System That Supports a Car Rental Product

Daily Service Schedule—November 17, 2010

StationID 22
StationName Lubrication

ServiceDate	ServiceTime	VehicleID	Make	Model	Mileage	ServiceDescription
11/17/2010	12:00 AM	155890	Ford	Explorer	2244	Std. Lube
11/17/2010	11:00 AM	12448	Toyota	Taccoma	7558	Std. Lube

StationID 26
StationName Alignment

ServiceDate	ServiceTime	VehicleID	Make	Model	Mileage	ServiceDescription
11/17/2010	9:00 AM	12448	Toyota	Taccoma	7558	Front end alignment inspect

StationID 28
StationName Transmission

ServiceDate	ServiceTime	VehicleID	Make	Model	Mileage	ServiceDescription
11/17/2010	11:00 AM	155890	Ford	Explorer	2244	Transmission oil change

advantage by *reducing costs*. Such reductions enable the organization to reduce prices and/or to increase profitability. Increased profitability means not just greater shareholder value, but also more cash, which can fund further infrastructure development for even greater competitive advantage.

All of these principles of competitive advantage make sense, but the question you may be asking is, "How do information systems help to create competitive advantage?" To answer that question, consider a sample information system.

How Does an Actual Company Use IS to Create Competitive Advantages?

ABC, Inc.,[3] is a worldwide shipper with sales well in excess of $1 billion. From its inception, ABC invested heavily in information technology and led the shipping industry in the application of information systems for competitive advantage. Here we consider one example of an information system that illustrates how ABC successfully uses information technology to gain competitive advantage.

ABC maintains customer account data that include not only the customer's name, address, and billing information, but also data about the identity of that customer and the locations to which the customer ships. Figure 3-9 shows a Web form that an ABC customer is using to schedule a shipment. When the ABC system creates the form, it fills the Company name drop-down list with the names of companies that the customer has shipped to in the past. Here, the user is selecting Prentice Hall.

When the user clicks the Company name, the underlying ABC information system reads the customer's contact data from a database. The data consist of names, addresses, and phone numbers of recipients from past shipments. The user then selects a Contact name, and the system inserts that contact's address and other data into the form using data from the database, as shown in Figure 3-10. Thus, the system saves customers from having to reenter data for people to whom they have shipped in the past. Providing the data in this way also reduces data-entry errors

Figure 3-11 shows another feature of this system. On the right-hand side of this form, the customer can request that ABC send email messages to the sender (the customer), the recipient, and others as well. The customer can choose for ABC to send an email when the shipment is created and when it has been delivered. In Figure 3-11, the user has provided three email addresses. The customer wants all three addresses to receive delivery notification, but only the sender will receive shipment notification.

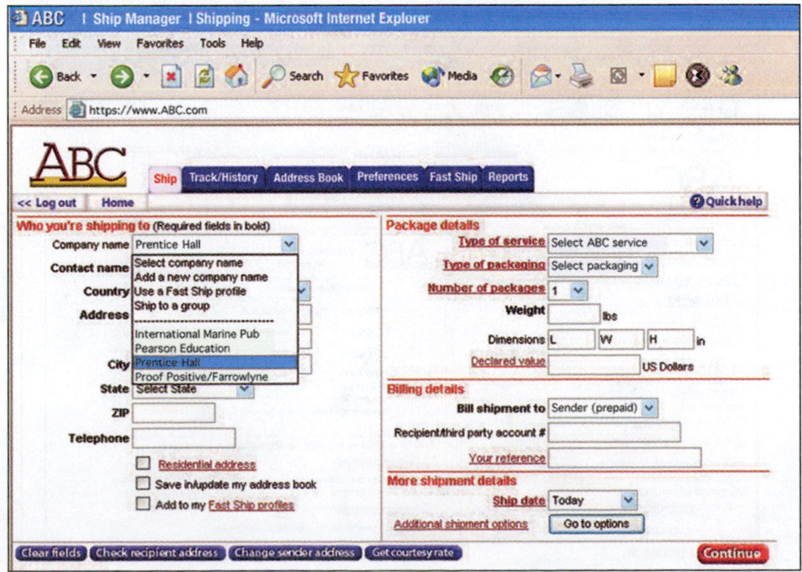

Figure 3-9
ABC, Inc., Web Page to Select a Recipient from the Customer's Records

3. The information system described here is actually used by a major transportation company.

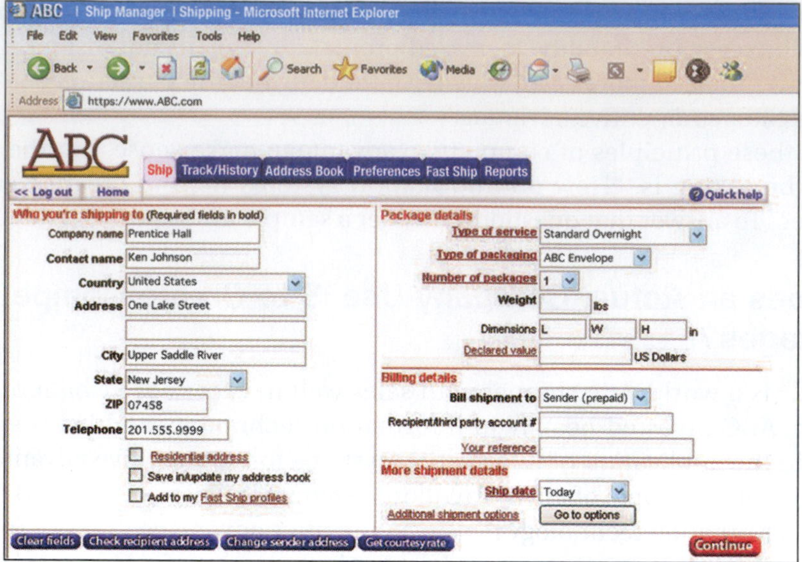

Figure 3-10
ABC, Inc., Web Page to Select a Contact from the Customer's Records

The customer can add a personal message as well. By adding this capability to the shipment-scheduling system, ABC has extended its product from a package-delivery service to a package- *and* information-delivery service.

Figure 3-12 shows one other capability of this information system. It has generated a shipping label, complete with bar code, for the user to print. By doing this, the company not only reduces errors in the preparation of shipping labels, but it also causes the customer to provide the paper and ink for document printing! Millions of such documents are printed every day, resulting in a considerable savings to the company.

How Does This System Create a Competitive Advantage?

Now consider the ABC shipping information system in light of the competitive advantage factors in Figure 3-7. This information system *enhances* an existing product because it eases the effort of creating a shipment to the customer while reducing errors. The information system also helps to *differentiate* the ABC package delivery product from competitors that do not have a similar system. Further, the generation of email messages when ABC picks up and delivers a package could be considered to be a *new* product.

Because this information system captures and stores data about recipients, it reduces the amount of customer work when scheduling a shipment. Customers will

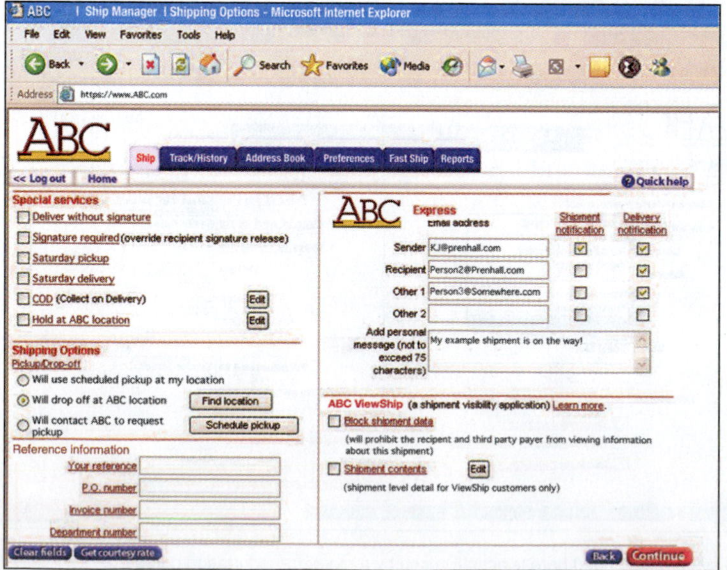

Figure 3-11
ABC, Inc., Web Page to Specify Email Notification

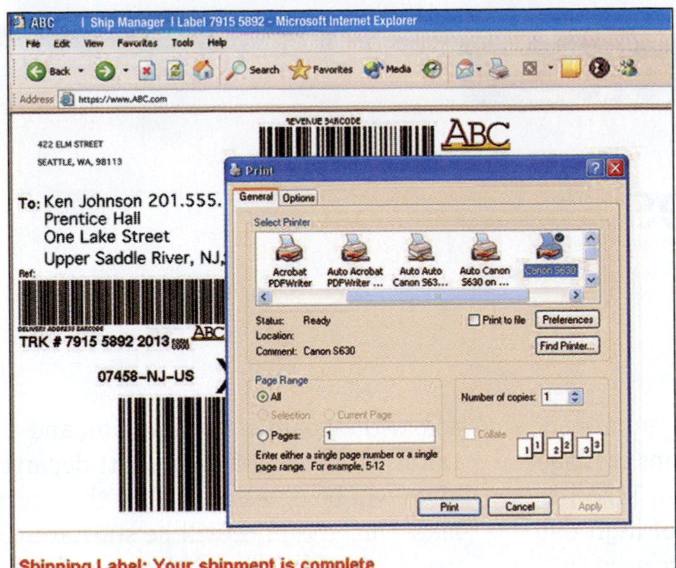

Figure 3-12
ABC, Inc., Web Page to Print a Shipping Label

be *locked in* by this system: If a customer wants to change to a different shipper, he or she will need to rekey recipient data for that new shipper. The disadvantage of rekeying data may well outweigh any advantage of switching to another shipper.

This system achieves a competitive advantage in two other ways as well: First, it raises the barriers to market entry. If another company wants to develop a shipping service, it will not only have to be able to ship packages, but it will also need to have a similar information system. In addition, the system reduces costs. It reduces errors in shipping documents, and it saves ABC paper, ink, and printing costs. (Of course, to determine if this system delivers a *net savings* in cost the cost of developing and operating the information system will need to be offset against the gains in reduced errors and paper, ink, and printing costs. It may be that the system costs more than the savings. Even still, it may be a sound investment if the value of intangible benefits, such as locking in customers and raising entry barriers, exceeds the net cost.)

Before continuing, review Figure 3-7. Make sure that you understand each of the principles of competitive advantage and how information systems can help achieve them. In fact, the list in Figure 3-7 probably is important enough to memorize, because you can also use it for non-IS applications. You can consider any business project or initiative in light of competitive advantage.

How does the knowledge in this chapter help *FlexTime* and you?

Based on the knowledge presented in this chapter, FlexTime is on the right track. They are seeking ways to save costs without compromising who they are, or, put in the terms of this chapter, without compromising FlexTime's competitive strengths over its rivals—the major competitive threat. Given the knowledge of this chapter, we could state FlexTime's goal differently: FlexTime wants to examine all of its value-generating activities and determine if there isn't some way to reduce costs without reducing the value generated.

The principal value to you of this chapter is summarized in Figure 3-1. You now know a process for tracing the line of development from analysis of industry structure all the way through to requirements for information systems. And, to underline an important point, all activities in the firm need to facilitate the organization's competitive strategy. This principle is important for MIS (the development and use of information systems) as well as for all other business activities. Keeping all of this in mind will help you be a more informed and effective consumer of the services of IS professionals!

The Guide on pages 62–63 helps you understand how to use the principles of competitive advantage in a personal way.

Ethics Guide

Yikes! Bikes

Suppose you are an operations manager for Yikes! Bikes, a manufacturer of high-end mountain bicycles with $20 million in annual sales. Yikes! has been in business over 25 years, and the founder and sole owner recently sold the business to an investment group, Major Capital. You know nothing about the sale until your boss introduces you to Andrea Parks, a partner at Major Capital, who is in charge of the acquisition. Parks explains to you that Yikes! has been sold to Major Capital and that she will be the temporary general manager. She explains that the new owners see great potential in you, and they want to enlist your cooperation during the transition. She hints that if your potential is what she thinks it is, you will be made general manager of Yikes!

Parks explains that the new owners decided there are too many players in the high-end mountain bike business, and they plan to change the competitive strategy of Yikes! from high-end differentiation to lowest-cost vendor. Accordingly, they will eliminate local manufacturing, fire most of the manufacturing department, and import bikes from China. Further, Major Capital sees a need to reduce expenses and plans a 10 percent across-the-board staff reduction and a cut of two-thirds of the customer support department. The new bikes will be of lesser quality than current Yikes! bikes, but the price will be substantially less. The new ownership group believes it will take a few years for the market to realize that Yikes! bikes are not the same quality as they were. Finally, Parks asks you to attend an all-employee meeting with the founder and her.

At the meeting, the founder explains that due to his age and personal situation, he decided to sell Yikes! to Major Capital and that starting today Andrea Parks is the general manager. He thanks the employees for their many years of service, wishes them well, and leaves the building. Parks introduces herself to the employees and states that Major Capital is very excited to own such a great company with a strong, quality brand. She says she will take a few weeks to orient herself to the business and its environment and plans no major changes to the company.

You are reeling from all this news when Parks calls you into her office and explains that she needs you to prepare two reports. In one, she wants a list of all the employees in the manufacturing department, sorted by their salary (or wage for hourly employees). She explains that she intends to cut the most costly employees first. "I don't want to be inflexible about this, though," she says. "If there is someone whom you think we should keep, let me know, and we can talk about it."

She also wants a list of the employees in the customer support department, sorted by the average amount of time each support rep spends with customers. She explains, "I'm not so concerned with payroll expense in customer support. It's not how much we're paying someone; it's how much time they're wasting with customers. We're going to have a barebones support department, and we want to get rid of the gabby chatters first."

You are, understandably, shocked and surprised . . . not only at the speed with which the transaction has occurred, but also because you wouldn't think the founder would do this to the employees. You call him at home and tell him what is going on.

"Look," he explains, "when I sold the company, I asked them to be sure to take care of the employees. They said they would. I'll call Andrea, but there's really nothing I can do at this point; they own the show."

In a black mood of depression, you realize that you no longer want to work for Yikes!, but your wife is 6 months pregnant with your first child. You need medical insurance for her at least until the baby is born. But what miserable tasks are you going to be asked to do before then? And you suspect that if you balk at any task Parks won't hesitate to fire you, too.

As you leave that night you run into Lori, the most popular customer support representative and one of your favorite employees. "Hey," Lori asks you, "what did you think of that meeting? Do you believe Andrea? Do you think they'll let us continue to make great bikes?"

Discussion Questions

1. In your opinion, did the new owners take any illegal action? Is there evidence of crime in this scenario?
2. Was the statement that Parks made to all of the employees unethical? Why or why not? If you questioned her about the ethics of her statement, how do you think she would justify herself?
3. What do you think Parks will tell the founder if he calls as a result of your conversation with him? Does he have any legal recourse? Is Major Capital's behavior toward him unethical? Why or why not?
4. Parks is going to use information to perform staff cuts. What do you think about her rationale? Ethically, should she consider other factors, such as number of years of service, past employee reviews, or other criteria?
5. How do you respond to Lori? What are the consequences if you tell her what you know? What are the consequences of lying to her? What are the consequences of saying something noncommittal?
6. If you actually were in this situation, would you leave the company? Why or why not?
7. In business school, we talk of principles like competitive strategy as interesting academic topics. But, as you can see from the Yikes! case, competitive strategy decisions have human consequences. How do you plan to resolve conflicts between human needs and tough business decisions?
8. How do you define *job security*?

Guide

Your Personal Competitive Advantage

Consider the following possibility: After working hard to earn your degree in business, you graduate, only to discover that you cannot find a job in your area of study. You look for 6 weeks or so, but then you run out of money. In desperation, you take a job waiting tables at a local restaurant. Two years go by, the economy picks up, and the jobs you had been looking for become available. Unfortunately, your degree is now 2 years old; you are competing with students who have just graduated with fresh degrees (and fresh knowledge). Two years of waiting tables, good as you are at it, does not appear to be good experience for the job you want. You're stuck in a nightmare that will be hard to get out of—and one that you cannot allow to happen.

Examine Figure 3-7 again, but this time consider those elements of competitive advantage as they apply to you personally. As an employee, the skills and abilities you offer are your personal product. Examine the first three items in the list, and ask yourself, "How can I use my time in school—and in this MIS class, in particular—to create new skills, to enhance those I already have, and to differentiate my skills from the competition?" (By the way, you will enter a national/international market. Your competition is not just the students in your class; it's also students in classes in Ohio, California, British Columbia, Florida, New York, and everywhere else they're teaching MIS today.)

Suppose you are interested in a sales job. Perhaps you want to sell in the pharmaceutical industry. What skills can you learn from your MIS class that will make you more competitive as a future salesperson? Ask yourself, "How does the pharmaceutical industry use MIS to gain competitive advantage?" Use the Internet to find examples of the use of information systems in the pharmaceutical industry. How does Pfizer, for example, use a customer information system to sell to doctors? How can your knowledge of such systems differentiate you from your competition for a job there? How does Pfizer use a knowledge management system? How does the firm keep track of drugs that have an adverse effect on each other?

The fourth and fifth items in Figure 3-7 concern locking in customers, buyers, and suppliers. How can you interpret those elements in terms of your personal competitive advantage? Well, to lock in, you first have to have a relationship to lock in. So do you have an internship? If not, can you get one? And once you have an internship, how can you use your knowledge of MIS to lock in your job so that you get a job offer? Does the company you are interning for have an information systems for managing customers (or any other information system that is important to the company)? If users are happy with the system, what characteristics make it worthwhile? Can you lock in a job by becoming an expert user of this system? Becoming an expert user not only locks you into your job, but it also raises barriers to entry for others who might be competing for the job. Also, can you suggest ways to improve the system, thus using your knowledge of the company and the system to lock in an extension of your job?

Human resources personnel say that networking is one of the most effective ways of finding a job. How can you use this class to establish alliances with other students? Does your class have a Web site? Is there an email list server for the students in your class? How about a Facebook group? How can you use these to develop job-seeking alliances with other students? Who in your class already has a job or an internship? Can any of those people provide hints or opportunities for finding a job?

Don't restrict your job search to your local area. Are there regions of your country where jobs are more plentiful? How can you find out about student organizations in those regions? Search the Web for MIS classes in other cities, and make contact with students there. Find out what the hot opportunities are in other cities.

Finally, as you study MIS, think about how the knowledge you gain can help you save costs for your employers. Even more, see if you can build a case that an employer would actually save money by hiring you. The line of reasoning might be that because of your knowledge of IS, you will be able to facilitate cost savings that more than compensate for your salary.

In truth, few of the ideas that you generate for a potential employer will be feasible or pragmatically useful. The fact that you are thinking creatively, however, will indicate to a potential employer that you have initiative and are grappling with the problems that real businesses have. As this course progresses, keep thinking about competitive advantage, and strive to understand how the topics you study can help you to accomplish, personally, one or more of the principles in Figure 3-7.

Discussion Questions

1. Summarize the efforts you have taken thus far to build an employment record that will lead to job offers after graduation.
2. Considering the first three principles in Figure 3-7, describe one way in which you have a competitive advantage over your classmates. If you do not have such competitive advantage, describe actions you can take to obtain one.
3. In order to build your network, you can use your status as a student to approach business professionals. Namely, you can contact them for help with an assignment or for career guidance. For example, suppose you want to work in banking and you know that your local bank has a customer information system. You could call the manager of that bank and ask him or her how that system creates a competitive advantage for the bank. You also could ask to interview other employees and go armed with the list in Figure 3-7. Describe two specific ways in which you can use your status as a student and the list in Figure 3-7 to build your network in this way.
4. Describe two ways that you can use student alliances to obtain a job. How can you use information systems to build, maintain, and operate such alliances?

ACTIVE REVIEW

Use this Active Review to verify that you understand the ideas and concepts that answer the chapters's study questions.

Q1 How does organizational strategy determine information systems structure?

Diagram and explain the relationship among industry structure, competitive strategy, value chains, business processes, and information systems. Working from the bottom up, explain how the knowledge you've gained in these first three chapters pertains to that diagram.

Q2 What five forces determine industry structure?

Describe the original purpose of the five forces model and the different purpose for which it is used in this chapter. Name two types of forces and describe the strength factors for each. Name three competitive forces and describe the strength factors for each. Name two supply chain forces. Summarize the strong forces operating on FlexTime.

Q3 What is competitive strategy?

Describe four different strategies, as defined by Porter. For each strategy, offer an example of a company that uses that strategy.

Q4 How does competitive strategy determine value chain structure?

Define the terms *value, margin,* and *value chain.* Explain why organizations that choose a differentiation strategy can use value to determine a limit on the amount of extra cost to pay for differentiation. Name the primary and support activities in the value chain and explain the purpose of each. Explain the concept of linkages.

Q5 How do value chains determine business processes and information systems?

What is the relationship between a value chain and a business process? How do business processes relate to competitive strategy? How do information systems relate to competitive strategy? Justify the comments in the two rows labeled "Supporting business process" in Figure 3-6.

Q6 How do information systems provide competitive advantages?

List and briefly describe eight principles of competitive advantage. Consider your college bookstore, and list one application of each of the eight principles. Strive to include examples that involve information systems.

How does the knowledge of this chapter help FlexTime and you?

Summarize why the knowledge in this chapter indicates that FlexTime is on the right track in its search for cost savings. Explain the importance of Figure 3-1. Discuss how the principles of competitive advantage apply to you personally.

KEY TERMS AND CONCEPTS

Competitive strategy 51
Five forces model 48
Linkages 53
Margin 51
Primary activities 51
Support activities 51
Switching costs 56
Value 51
Value chain 51

USING YOUR KNOWLEDGE

1. Suppose you decide to start a business that recruits students for summer jobs. You will match available students with available jobs. You need to learn what positions are available and which students are available for filling those positions. In starting your business, you know you will be competing with local

newspapers, Craig's List (*www.craigslist.org*), and with your college. You will probably have other local competitors as well.

a. Analyze the structure of this industry according to Porter's five forces model.
b. Given your analysis in part a, recommend a competitive strategy.
c. Describe the primary value chain activities as they apply to this business.
d. Describe a business process for recruiting students.
e. Describe information systems that could be used to support the business process in part d.
f. Explain how the process you described in part d and the system you described in part e reflect your competitive strategy.

2. Consider the two different bike rental companies in Figure 3-6. Think about the bikes that they rent. Clearly, the student bikes will be just about anything that can be ridden out of the shop. The bikes for the business executives, however, must be new, shiny, clean, and in tip-top shape.
   a. Compare and contrast the operations value chains of these two businesses as they pertain to the management of bicycles.
   b. Describe a business process for maintaining bicycles for both businesses.
   c. Describe a business process for acquiring bicycles for both businesses.
   d. Describe a business process for disposing of bicycles for both businesses.
   e. What roles do you see for information systems in your answers to the earlier questions? The information systems can be those you develop within your company or they can be those developed by others, such as Craig's List.

3. Samantha Green owns and operates Twigs Tree Trimming Service. Samantha graduated from the forestry program of a nearby university and worked for a large landscape design firm, performing tree trimming and removal. After several years of experience, she bought her own truck, stump grinder, and other equipment and opened her own business in St. Louis, Missouri.

   Although many of her jobs are one-time operations to remove a tree or stump, others are recurring, such as trimming a tree or groups of trees every year or every other year. When business is slow, she calls former clients to remind them of her services and of the need to trim their trees on a regular basis.

   Samantha has never heard of Michael Porter or any of his theories. She operates her business "by the seat of her pants."
   a. Explain how an analysis of the five competitive forces could help Samantha.
   b. Do you think Samantha has a competitive strategy? What competitive strategy would seem to make sense for her?
   c. How would knowledge of her competitive strategy help her sales and marketing efforts?
   d. Describe, in general terms, the kind of information system that she needs to support sales and marketing efforts.

4. FiredUp, Inc., is a small business owned by Curt and Julie Robards. Based in Brisbane, Australia, FiredUp manufactures and sells a lightweight camping stove called the FiredNow. Curt, who previously worked as an aerospace engineer, invented and patented a burning nozzle that enables the stove to stay lit in very high winds—up to 90 miles per hour. Julie, an industrial designer by training, developed an elegant folding design that is small, lightweight, easy to set up, and very stable. Curt and Julie manufacture the stove in their garage, and they sell it directly to their customers over the Internet and via phone.
   a. Explain how an analysis of the five competitive forces could help FiredUp.
   b. What does FiredUp's competitive strategy seem to be?
   c. Briefly summarize how the primary value chain activities pertain to FiredUp. How should the company design these value chains to conform to its competitive strategy?
   d. Describe business processes that FiredUp needs in order to implement its marketing and sales and also its service value chain activities.
   e. Describe, in general terms, information systems to support your answer to part d.

COLLABORATION EXERCISE 3

Before you start this exercise, read Chapter Extensions 1 and 2, which describe collaboration techniques as well as tools for managing collaboration tasks. In particular, consider using Google Docs, Windows Live SkyDrive, Microsoft SharePoint, or some other collaboration tool.

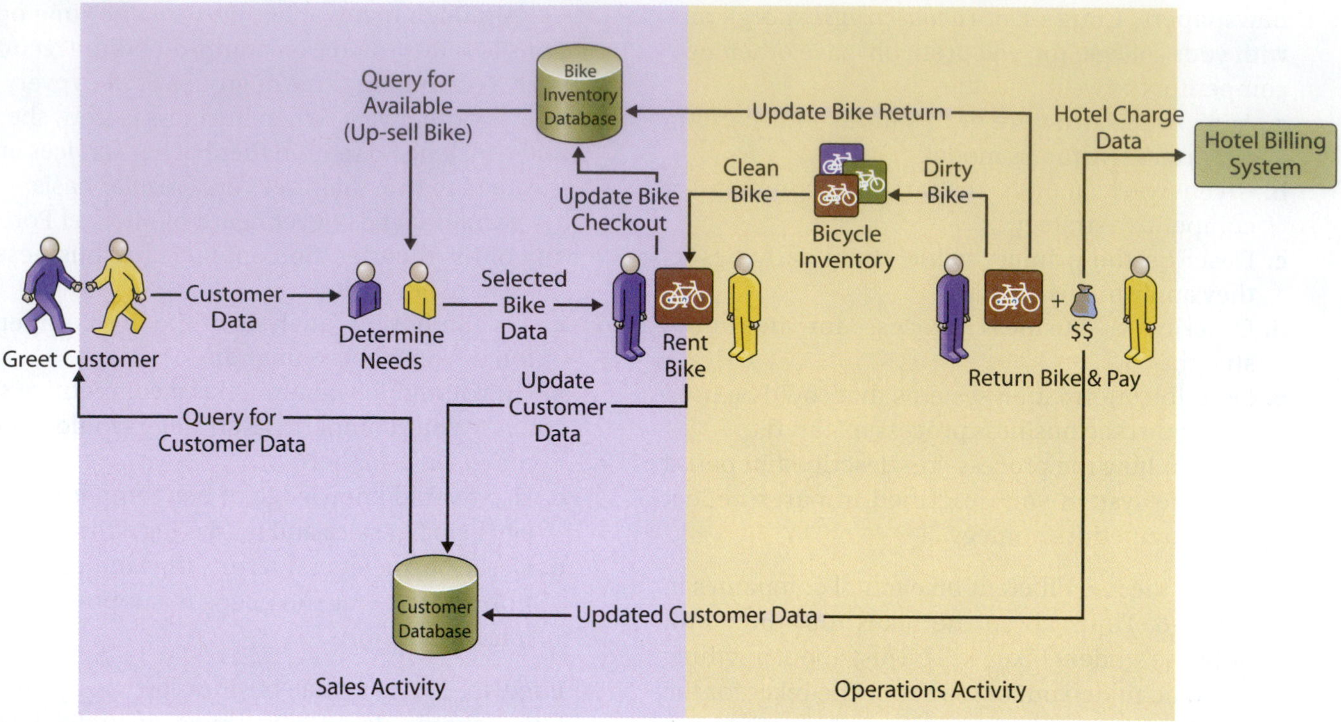

Figure 3-13
Rental Process for High-Value Bike Rental

Figure 3-13 shows the business process and related information systems for the high-value bike rental company described in Figure 3-6. In terms of Porter's value chain model, this process involves both the sales and operations activities. The bike rental company uses information systems to maintain customer data in the Customer database and bike inventory data in the Bike Inventory database and to transmit hotel charge data to the Hotel Billing system.

Each information system consists of all five IS components. Consider, for example, the information system for processing the Bike Inventory database. With regard to hardware, the database itself will be stored on a computer, and it will be accessed from other computers or computing devices, such as cash registers or handheld scanning devices (possibly used to check bikes in). Computer programs will provide forms for the system users to query and update the database. Other computer programs will be used to manage the database. (You will learn about such programs in Chapter 5.) Data, the third component of an information system, will be stored in the database. Each employee will be trained on procedures for using the system. For example, the sales clerk will learn how to query the database to determine what bikes are available and how to determine promising up-sell candidates. Finally, the people component will consist of the clerks in the rental shop as well as any support personnel for maintaining the inventory system.

Information systems that support the Customer database and those that interface with the Hotel Billing system will also have the five IS components. (By the way, whenever you consider the development or use of an information system, it is good practice to think about these five components.)

As stated in this chapter, business processes must generate more value than their cost. If they do not—if the margin of a business process is negative—then either costs must be reduced or the value increased. Considering the business process in Figure 3-13, one possibility for reducing costs is to eliminate rental personnel. Bicycles could be placed on racks having locks that customers can open with their hotel room keys; the bike would be rented until the customer places the bike back on the rack. Another possibility is to increase the value of the process. The rental agency could decide to rent additional types of equipment or perhaps to sell clothing or food and beverages.

Collaborate with your team to answer the following questions.

1. Explain the relationship between value and cost according to the Porter model. When does it make sense to add cost to a business process?

2. Suppose you are told that the business process in Figure 3-13 has a negative margin. Explain what that means. Suppose the margin of some business process is a negative $1 million. If costs are reduced by $1.2 million, will the margin necessarily be positive? Explain why or why not.

3. Consider the alternative of replacing the rental personnel from the business process in Figure 3-13.
   a. Describe changes that will need to be made to the process documented in Figure 3-13. One way to answer is to scan a copy of this diagram and annotate the changes on that copy. Or, if the annotations are too extensive, make another version of the diagram entirely.
   b. Would eliminating the rental personnel change the competitive strategy of this company? Is it possible to be a high-value company with no rental personnel? Explain why or why not.
   c. Would eliminating the rental personnel necessarily reduce costs? What costs would increase as a result of this change?

4. Consider the alternative of increasing the value delivered by existing rental personnel. The text suggests possibly renting more kinds of equipment or selling items of use to guests who are renting bicycles, but consider other options as well.
   a. Describe five ways that you think the existing personnel could increase the value of this business process.
   b. For the five alternatives you developed in part a, name and describe criteria for selecting among them.
   c. Using your criteria in part b, evaluate the alternative you identified in part a and select the best one. Explain your selection.
   d. Redraw Figure 3-13 for the alternative you selected in part c.

CASE STUDY 3

Bosu Balance Trainer

The Bosu balance trainer is a device for developing balance, strength, and aerobic conditioning. Invented in 1999, Bosu has become popular in leading health clubs, in athletic departments, and in homes. Bosu stands for "both sides up," because either side of the equipment can be used for training. Figure 3-14 shows a Bosu in use.

Bosu is not only a training device; it also reflects a new philosophy in athletic conditioning that focuses on balance. According to the Bosu inventor, David Weck, "The Bosu Balance Trainer was born of passion to improve my balance. In my lifelong pursuit of enhanced athleticism, I have come to understand that balance is the foundation on which all other performance components are built." In order to obtain broad market acceptance both for his philosophy as well as for the Bosu product, Weck licensed the sales and marketing of Bosu to Fitness Quest in 2001.

The Bosu has been very successful, and that success has attracted copycat products. Fitness Quest has successfully defeated such products using a number of techniques, but primarily by leveraging its alliances with professional trainers.

According to Dustin Schnabel, Bosu product manager,

> **We have developed strong and effective relationships with more than 10,000 professional trainers. We do all we can to make sure those trainers succeed with Bosu and they in turn encourage their clients to purchase our product rather than some cheap imitation.**
>
> **It's all about quality. We build a quality product, we create quality relationships with the trainers, and we make sure those trainers have everything they need from us to provide a quality experience to their clients.**

That strategy has worked well. In the fall of 2004, Fitness Quest had a serious challenge to the Bosu from a large sports equipment vendor that had preexisting

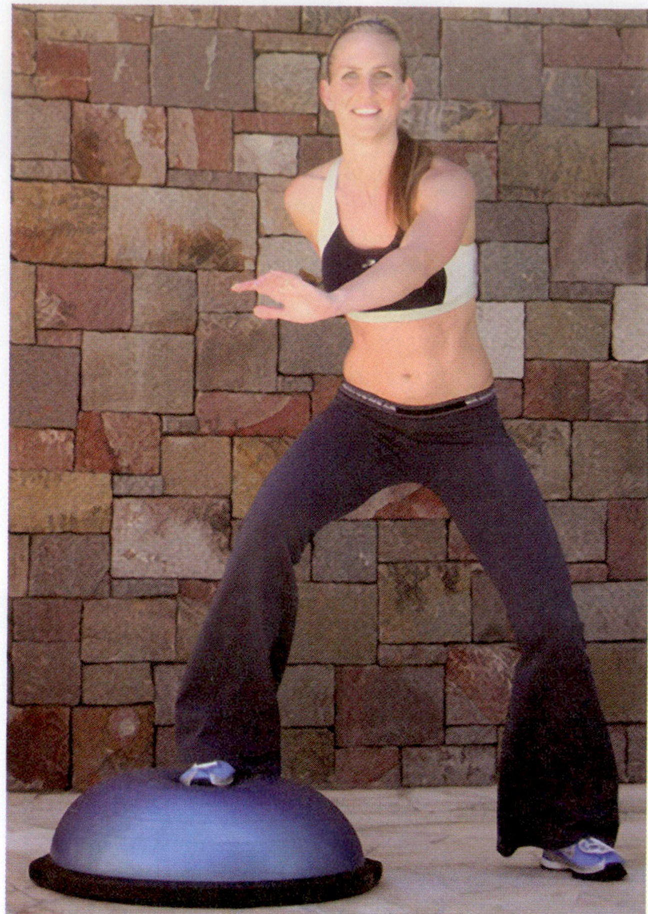

Figure 3-14
The Bosu Balance Trainer

alliances with major chains such as Target and Wal-Mart. The competitor introduced a Bosu copycat at a slightly lower price. Within a few months, in an effort to gain sales the competitor reduced the copycat's price, eventually several times, until the copycat was less than half the price of the Bosu. Today, that copycat product is not to be seen. According to Schnabel, "They couldn't give that product away. Why? Because customers were coming in the store to buy the Bosu product that their trainers recommended."

Fitness Quest maintains a database of trainer data. It uses that database for email and postal correspondence, as well as for other marketing purposes. For example, after a marketing message has been sent, Schnabel and others watch the database for changes in trainer registration. Registrations increase after a well-received message, and they fall off when messages are off-target.

Fitness Quest and Schnabel are in the process of introducing a new piece of cardio-training equipment called the Indo-Row (shown in Figure 3-15) for which they intend to use the same marketing strategy. First, they will leverage their relationships with trainers to obtain trainer buy-in for the new concept. Then, when that buy-in occurs, they will use it to sell Indo-Row to individuals.

Go to *www.indorow.com* and watch the video. As you'll see, Indo-Row competes directly with other equipment-based forms of group exercise, such as Spinning. Schnabel states that many clubs and workout studios are looking for a new, fun, and innovative group training medium, and Indo-Row meets that need.

You can learn more about Bosu devices at *www.bosu.com*, more about Indo-Row at *www.indorow.com*, and more about Fitness Quest at *www.fitnessquest.com*.

Sources: Bosu, *www.bosu.com* (accessed June 2010); Indo-Row, *www.indorow.com* (accessed June 2010); and conversation with Dustin Schnabel, July 2009.

Questions

1. Review the principles of competitive advantage in Figure 3-7. Which types of competitive advantage has Bosu used to defeat copycat products?
2. What role did information systems play in your answer to question 1?
3. What additional information systems could Fitness Quest develop to create barriers to entry to the competition and to lock in customers?
4. In 2004, Fitness Quest had alliances with trainers and its main competitor had alliances with major

Figure 3-15
The Indo-Row

retailers. Thus, both companies were competing on the basis of their alliances. Why do you think Fitness Quest won this competition? To what extent did its success in leveraging relationships with trainers depend on information systems? On other factors?

5. The case does not state all of the ways that Fitness Quest uses its trainer database. List five applications of the trainer database that would increase Fitness Quest's competitive position.

6. Describe major differences between the Bosu product and the Indo-Row product. Consider product use, product price, customer resistance, competition, competitive threats, and other factors related to market acceptance.

7. Describe information systems that Fitness Quest could use to strengthen its strategy for bringing Indo-Row to market. Consider the factors you identified in your answer to question 6 in your response.

Part 2

Information Technology

The next three chapters address the technology that underlies information systems. You may think that such technology is unimportant to you as a business professional. However, as you will see at FlexTime, today's managers and business professionals work with information technology all the time, at least as consumers, if not in a more involved way.

This could happen to you

Chapter 4 discusses hardware and software and defines basic terms and fundamental computing concepts. You will see that Neil and Kelly have important decisions to make about the next version of software that they will use to run their business.

Chapter 5 addresses the data component of information technology by describing database processing. You will learn essential database terminology and be introduced to techniques for processing databases. We will also introduce data modeling, because you may be required to evaluate data models for databases that others develop for you. At FlexTime, Neil will use a database to analyze the cost-saving alternatives the team identified in Chapter 3.

Chapter 6 continues the discussion of computing devices begun in Chapter 4 and describes data communications and Internet technologies. FlexTime is responding to the threat of its landlord (a supplier) by buying its own building. FlexTime needs to save costs, but it also needs to wire the building for data communications in the next 10 years. What capabilities does FlexTime need?

The purpose of these three chapters is to teach you technology sufficient for you to be an effective IT consumer, like Neil at FlexTime. You will learn basic terms, fundamental concepts, and useful

frameworks so that you will have the knowledge to ask good questions and make appropriate requests of the information systems professionals who will serve you. Those concepts and frameworks will be far more useful to you than the latest technology trend, which may be outdated by the time you graduate!

CHAPTER 4

Hardware and Software

This could happen to you

"Neil, I hate to interrupt our night out together, but I'm confused about the software problem at work. Why didn't we upgrade the program?"

"Let me back up, Kelly. Four years ago, we paid $35,000 for Version 2 of the Studio Management software."

"OK, I've got that."

"Since then, we've paid a support fee of $5,000 a year. That fee enables us to call their tech support when something goes wrong, like when we installed the three new printers last year. They help us in other ways, too."

"So, Neil, that means we've paid them $55,000 so far?"

"Right. Now, 2 years ago they came out with Version 3 of their software. I looked at it and didn't see any reason to upgrade, and they wanted another $25,000 license fee. So, I passed on it."

"OK, that seems logical. So what's the problem?"

"When I was at Siebel, we called it *strangle and cram.* Actually, I think the term came from IBM in the 1960s, but it doesn't matter. The idea is that you cut off support to an older version of the product (that's the *strangle*) and tell your customers that to get support they have to upgrade to the new version (that's the *cram*)."

"Wow. Can we sue them or something?"

"Do we want to mess up our lives with a lawsuit?"

"No."

"Besides, the contracts say they can do this."

STUDY QUESTIONS

Q1 What do business professionals need to know about computer hardware?

Q2 What is the difference between a client and a server?

Q3 What do business professionals need to know about software?

Q4 Why are thin clients preferred over thick clients?

Q5 Is open source software a viable alternative?

How does the knowledge in this chapter help *Kelly* and you?

"So we upgrade?"

"Maybe, Kelly. The thing is, though, their architecture is old. Even with the new version they're still using thick clients and I just don't think we want to stay there."

"Neil, I have absolutely no idea what you're talking about. And I'm hungry. Let's order."

They order.

"Kelly, you know that computer that sits in the corner of my office? That's our server. It's a computer that receives requests from the other computers and processes them. All the other computers at FlexTime are client computers; they call the server to do things like store data in our database. But, to make that work, we had to install a special computer program on each client."

> "WHEN I WAS AT SIEBEL, WE CALLED IT STRANGLE AND CRAM."

"So what are you telling me?"

"Thick clients are out; they're based on 1980s' technology. The new way is to use Internet technology and substitute a browser for the thick client. There are lots of reasons to do that, but one is that nobody needs a special program installed on their computer to access our systems. They can do it from a browser. So, I don't have to keep installing and uninstalling software on our trainers' computers. People can also access the system from their iPhones, or whatever they're using. They just use their browsers."

"So this upgrade that they're cramming is based on older technology?"

"Right. I've been looking at other options. Problem is we'd have to train everyone to use the new system . . . and that would be ugly . . . and costly."

"Well, if we have to do it, we have to do it."

"Yeah. We could wait until we have the new building, but I hate to put that much change on everyone at once."

"OK, so what's holding you back?"

"Cost. They want $65,000 up front and 10 percent, $6,500, a year for support."

"Ouch."

"There's another option: open source. There's a group that's created a version that might do the job, and it's free."

"How can it be free?"

"Well, I should say license free. We won't have to pay the upfront cost but we would pay the company that supports it."

Optional Extensions for this chapter are • CE5: Introduction to Microsoft Excel 2010 349 • CE6: Preparing a Computer Budget Using Excel 2010 367

"But why no upfront cost?"

"Because the programmers who build it are unpaid volunteers."

"Neil, are you saying we're going to run our business on a program created by a bunch of amateurs?"

"No, not amateurs. Think Wikipedia. It's done by volunteers, and the quality of the information there is high. The Wikipedia community sees to that. It's the same for good open source software. Linux was built that way."

"Linux? Oh no, another term. That's enough. Let's eat." "How do other small businesses do it? I mean you spent all those years selling software, you know the game. How does the average club owner make these decisions?"

"They waste a lot of money."

"And time."

Q1 What Do Business Professionals Need to Know About Computer Hardware?

Like Neil, you might go into the computer industry and then transition to some other business. If so, you'll know "how the game is played." However, you might not. You might become a department manager, or own your own small business, or be appointed to your law firm's technology committee. Whatever direction your career takes, you don't want to be one of those professionals who "waste a lot of money . . . and time." The knowledge from this chapter can help.

You don't need to be an expert. You don't need to be a hardware engineer or a computer programmer. You do need to know enough, however, to be an effective consumer. You need the knowledge and skills to ask important, relevant questions and understand the answers.

Basic Components

As discussed in the five-component framework, **hardware** consists of electronic components and related gadgetry that input, process, output, and store data according to instructions encoded in computer programs or software. Figure 4-1 shows the components of a generic computer.

Typical **input hardware** devices are the keyboard, mouse, document scanners, and bar-code (Universal Product Code) scanners like those used in grocery stores. Microphones also are input devices; with tablet PCs, human handwriting can be input as well. Older input devices include magnetic ink readers (used for reading the ink on the bottom of checks) and scanners such as the Scantron test scanner shown in Figure 4-2.

Figure 4-1
Input, Process, Output, and Storage Hardware

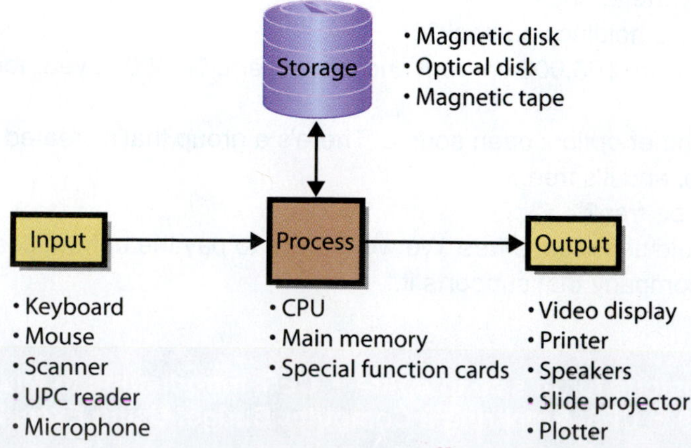

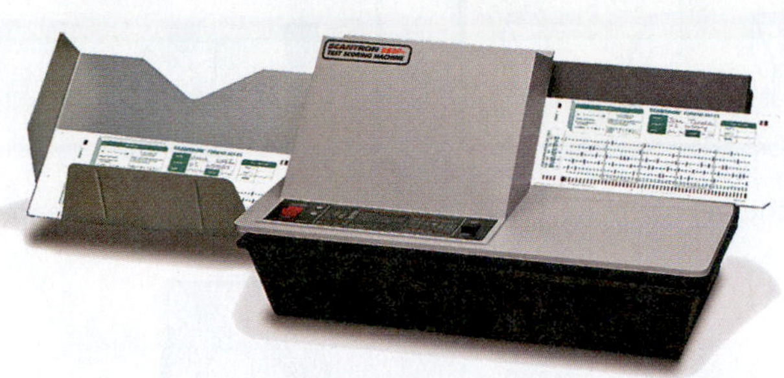

Figure 4-2
Scantron Scanner

Source: Courtesy of Harrison Public Relations Group, Scantron Corporation.

Processing devices include the **central processing unit (CPU)**, which is sometimes called "the brain" of the computer. Although the design of the CPU has nothing in common with the anatomy of animal brains, this description is helpful, because the CPU does have the "smarts" of the machine. The CPU selects instructions, processes them, performs arithmetic and logical comparisons, and stores results of operations in memory. Some computers have two or more CPUs. A computer with two CPUs is called a **dual-processor** computer. **Quad-processor** computers have four CPUs. Some high-end computers have 16 or more CPUs.

CPUs vary in speed, function, and cost. Hardware vendors such as Intel, Advanced Micro Devices, and National Semiconductor continually improve CPU speed and capabilities while reducing CPU costs (as discussed under Moore's Law in Chapter 1). Whether you or your department needs the latest, greatest CPU depends on the nature of your work, as you will learn.

Main memory consists of circuitry for storing data and instructions that are acted upon by the CPU. The CPU reads data and instructions from memory, and it stores results of computations in main memory. We will describe the relationship between the CPU and main memory later in the chapter. Main memory is sometimes called **RAM**, for *random access memory*.

Finally, computers also can have **special function cards** (see Figure 4-3), which are electronic components on thin fiberglass backing that can be added to the computer to augment its basic capabilities. A common example is a card that provides enhanced clarity and refresh speed for the computer's video display.

Output hardware consists of video displays, printers, audio speakers, overhead projectors, and other special-purpose devices, such as large flatbed plotters.

Storage hardware saves data and programs. Magnetic disk is by far the most common storage device, although optical disks such as CDs and DVDs also are popular. In large corporate data centers, data is sometimes stored on magnetic tape.

Computer Data

Before we can further describe hardware, we need to define several important terms. We begin with binary digits.

Figure 4-3
Special Function Card

Source: Photo Courtesy of Creative Labs, Inc. Sound Blaster and Audigy are registered trademarks of Creative Technology Ltd. in the United States and other countries.

Figure 4-4
Bits Are Easy to Represent Physically

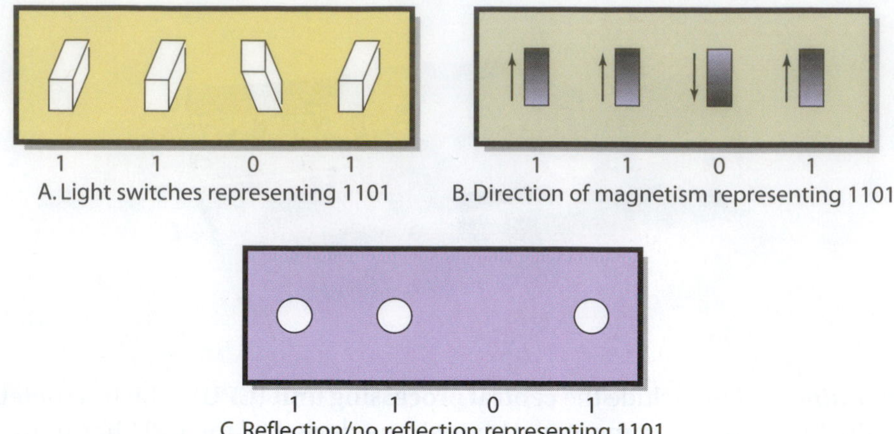

Binary Digits

Computers represent data using **binary digits**, called **bits**. A bit is either a zero or a one. Bits are used for computer data because they are easy to represent electronically, as illustrated in Figure 4-4. A switch can be either closed or open. A computer can be designed so that an open switch represents zero and a closed switch represents one. Or the orientation of a magnetic field can represent a bit; magnetism in one direction represents a zero, magnetism in the opposite direction represents a one. Or, for optical media, small pits are burned onto the surface of the disk so that they will reflect light. In a given spot, a reflection means a one; no reflection means a zero.

Sizing Computer Data

All computer data are represented by bits. The data can be numbers, characters, currency amounts, photos, recordings, or whatever. All are simply a string of bits.

For reasons that interest many but are irrelevant for future managers, bits are grouped into 8-bit chunks called **bytes**. For character data, such as the letters in a person's name, one character will fit into one byte. Thus, when you read a specification that a computing device has 100 million bytes of memory, you know that the device can hold up to 100 million characters.

Bytes are used to measure sizes of noncharacter data as well. Someone might say, for example, that a given picture is 100,000 bytes in size. This statement means the length of the bit string that represents the picture is 100,000 bytes or 800,000 bits (because there are 8 bits per byte).

The specifications for the size of main memory, disk, and other computer devices are expressed in bytes. Figure 4-5 shows the set of abbreviations that are used to represent data-storage capacity. A **kilobyte**, abbreviated **K**, is a collection of 1,024 bytes. A **megabyte**, or **MB**, is 1,024 kilobytes. A **gigabyte**, or **GB**, is 1,024 megabytes, and a **terabyte**, or **TB**, is 1,024 gigabytes.

Figure 4-5
Important Storage-Capacity Terminology

Term	Definition	Abbreviation
Byte	Number of bits to represent one character	
Kilobyte	1,024 bytes	K
Megabyte	1,024 K = 1,048,576 bytes	MB
Gigabyte	1,024 MB = 1,073,741,824 bytes	GB
Terabyte	1,024 GB = 1,099,511,627,776 bytes	TB

Sometimes you will see these definitions simplified as 1K equals 1,000 bytes and 1MB equals 1,000K. Such simplifications are incorrect, but they do ease the math. Also, disk and computer manufacturers have an incentive to propagate this misconception. If a disk maker defines 1MB to be 1 million bytes—and not the correct 1,024K—the manufacturer can use its own definition of MB when specifying drive capacities. A buyer may think that a disk advertised as 100MB has space for 100 × 1,024K bytes, but in truth the drive will have space for only 100 × 1,000,000 bytes. Normally, the distinction is not too important, but be aware of the two possible interpretations of these abbreviations.

In Fewer Than 300 Words, How Does a Computer Work?

Figure 4-6 shows a snapshot of a computer in use. The CPU is the major actor. To run a program or process data, the computer first transfers the program or data from disk to *main memory*. Then, to execute an instruction, it moves the instruction from main memory into the CPU via the **data channel** or **bus**. The CPU has a small amount of very fast memory called a **cache**. The CPU keeps frequently used instructions in the cache. Having a large cache makes the computer faster, but cache is expensive.

Main memory of the computer in Figure 4-6 contains program instructions for Microsoft Excel, Adobe Acrobat, and a browser (Microsoft Internet Explorer or Mozilla Firefox). It also contains a block of data and instructions for the **operating system (OS)**, which is a program that controls the computer's resources.

Main memory is too small to hold all of the programs and data that a user might want to process. For example, no personal computer has enough memory to hold all of the code in Microsoft Word, Excel, and Access. Consequently, the CPU loads programs into memory in chunks. In Figure 4-6, one portion of Excel was loaded into memory. When the user requested additional processing (say, to sort the spreadsheet), the CPU loaded another piece of Excel.

If the user opens another program (say, Word) or needs to load more data (say, a picture), the operating system will direct the CPU to attempt to place the new program or data into unused memory. If there is not enough memory, it will remove something, perhaps the block of memory labeled "More Excel," and then it will place the just-requested program or data into the vacated space. This process is called **memory swapping**.

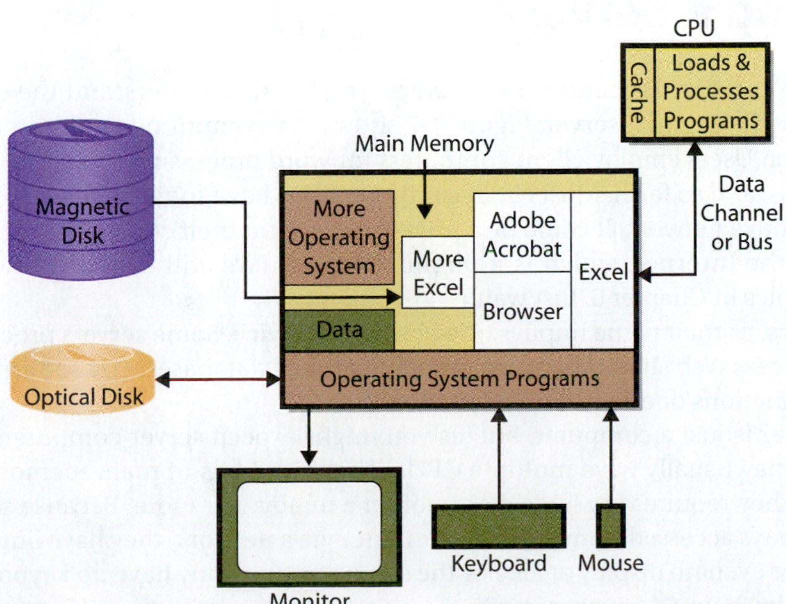

Figure 4-6
Computer Components, in Use

Why Does a Manager Care How a Computer Works?

You can order computers with varying sizes of main memory. An employee who runs only one program at a time and who processes small amounts of data requires very little memory—1GB will be adequate. However, an employee who processes many programs at the same time (say, Word, Excel, Firefox, Access, Acrobat, and other programs) or an employee who processes very large files (pictures, movies, or sound files) needs lots of main memory, perhaps 3GB or more. If that employee's computer has too little memory, then the computer will constantly be swapping memory, and it will be slow. (This means, by the way, that if your computer is slow and if you have many programs open you likely can improve performance by closing one or more programs. Depending on your computer and the amount of memory it has, you might also improve performance by adding more memory.)

How much hardware do you need? The Ethics Guide on pages 90–91 features a contrarian who sees consumers as being trapped by a conspiracy between hardware and software vendors.

You can also order computers with CPUs of different speeds. CPU speed is expressed in cycles called *hertz*. In 2010, a slow personal computer has a speed of 1.5 Gigahertz. A fast personal computer has a speed of 3+ Gigahertz, with dual processing. As predicted by Moore's Law, CPU speeds continually increase.

Additionally, CPUs today are classified as 32-bit or 64-bit. Without delving into the particulars, a **32-bit CPU** is a processor that can effectively utilize up to 4GB of main memory. A **64-bit CPU** is a processor that can use, by today's standards, an almost unlimited amount of main memory; 64-bit processors have speed advantages as well. As you would expect, 64-bit processors are more expensive than 32-bit processors.

An employee who does only simple tasks such as word processing does not need a fast CPU; a 32-bit, 1.5-Gigahertz CPU will be fine. However, an employee who processes large, complicated spreadsheets or who manipulates large database files or edits large picture, sound, or movie files needs a fast computer like a 64-bit, dual processor with 3.5 Gigahertz or more.

One last comment: The cache and main memory are **volatile**, meaning that their contents are lost when the power is off. Magnetic and optical disks are **nonvolatile**, meaning that their contents survive when the power is off. If you suddenly lose power, the contents of unsaved memory—say, documents that have been altered—will be lost. Therefore, get into the habit of frequently (every few minutes or so) saving documents or files that you are changing. Save your documents before your roommate trips over the power cord.

Q2 What Is the Difference Between a Client and a Server?

Before we can discuss computer software, you need to understand the difference between a client and a server. Figure 4-7 shows the computing environment of the typical user. Users employ **client** computers for word processing, spreadsheets, database access, and so forth. Most client computers also have software that enables them to connect to a network. It could be a private network at their company or school, or it could be the Internet, which is a public network. (We will discuss networks and related topics in Chapter 6. Just wait!)

Servers, as their name implies, provide some service. Some servers process email; others process Web sites; others process large, shared databases; and some provide all of these functions or other, similar functions.

A server is just a computer, but, as you might expect, server computers must be fast, and they usually have multiple CPUs. They need lots of main memory, at least 4GB, and they require very large disks—often a terabyte or more. Because servers are almost always accessed from another computer via a network, they have limited video displays, or even no display at all. For the same reason, many have no keyboard. Most servers today have 64-bit processors.

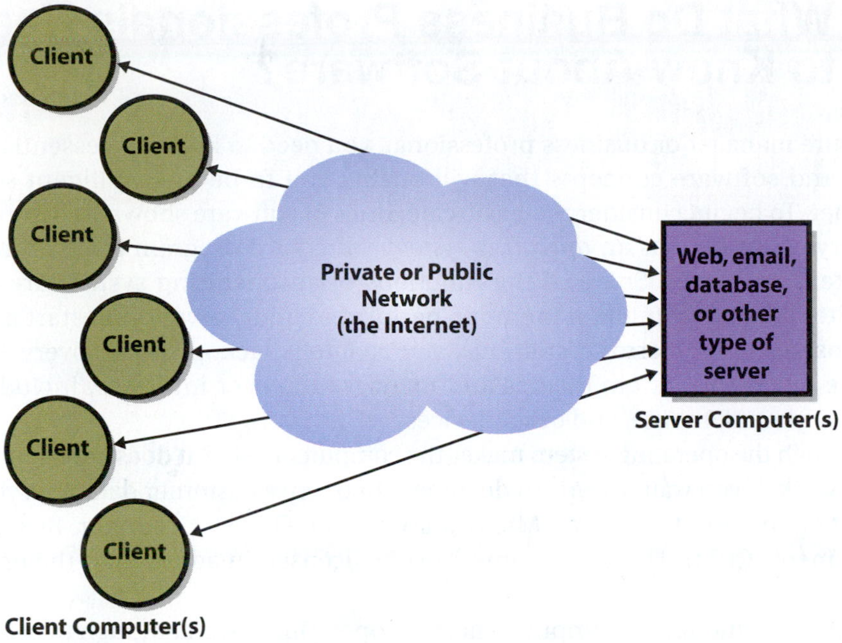

Client
Client
Client
Client
Client
Client
Private or Public Network (the Internet)
Web, email, database, or other type of server
Server Computer(s)
Client Computer(s)

Figure 4-7
Client and Server Computers

For sites with large numbers of users (e.g., Amazon.com), servers are organized into a collection of servers called a **server farm** like the one shown in Figure 4-8. Servers in a farm coordinate their activities in an incredibly sophisticated and fascinating technology dance. They receive and process hundreds, possibly thousands, of service requests per minute. For example, in December, 2009, Amazon.com processed an average of 110 order items per second for 24 hours straight![1] In such a dance, computers hand off partially processed requests to each other while keeping track of the current status of each request. They can pick up the pieces when a computer in the farm fails. All of this is done in the blink of an eye, with the user never knowing any part of the miracle underway. It is absolutely gorgeous engineering!

Figure 4-8
A Server Farm

Source: Lucidio Studios, Inc., The Stock Connection.

1. *BusinessWire*, "Amazon Kindle Is the Most Gifted Item Ever on Amazon.com," December 26, 2009. Available at *www.businesswire.com/portal/site/home/permalink/?ndmViewId=news_view&newsId=20091226005004&newsLang=en* (accessed April 2010).

Q3 What Do Business Professionals Need to Know About Software?

As a future manager or business professional, you need to know the essential terminology and software concepts that will enable you to be an intelligent software consumer. To begin, consider the basic categories of software shown in Figure 4-9.

Every computer has an *operating system,* which is a program that controls that computer's resources. Some of the functions of an operating system are to read and write data, allocate main memory, perform memory swapping, start and stop programs, respond to error conditions, and facilitate backup and recovery. In addition, the operating system creates and manages the user interface, including the display, keyboard, mouse, and other devices.

Although the operating system makes the computer usable, it does little application-specific work. If you want to write a document or query a customer database, you need *application programs* such as Microsoft Word or Oracle Customer Relationship Management (CRM). These programs must be licensed in addition to the operating system.

Both client and server computers need an operating system, though they need not be the same. Further, both clients and servers can process application programs. The application's design determines whether the client, the server, or both, process it.

You need to understand two important software constraints. First, a particular version of an operating system is written for a particular type of hardware. For example, Microsoft Windows works only on processors from Intel and companies that make processors that conform to the Intel **instruction set** (the commands that a CPU can process). Furthermore, the 32-bit version of Windows runs only on Intel computers with 32-bit CPUs, and the 64-bit version of Windows runs only on Intel computers with 64-bit CPUs. In other cases, such as Linux, many versions exist for many different instruction sets and for both 32- and 64-bit computers.

Second, application programs are written to use a particular operating system. Microsoft Access, for example, will run only on the Windows operating system. Some applications come in multiple versions. There are, for example, Windows and Macintosh versions of Microsoft Word. But unless informed otherwise, assume that a particular application runs on just one operating system.

We will next consider the operating system and application program categories of software.

What Are the Four Major Operating Systems?

The four major operating systems are listed in Figure 4-10. Consider each.

Windows

For business users, the most important operating system is Microsoft **Windows**. Some version of Windows resides on more than 85 percent of the world's desktops, and, considering just business users, the figure is more than 95 percent. Many different

Figure 4-9
Categories of Computer Software

	Operating System	Application Programs
Client	Programs that control the client computer's resources	Applications that are processed on client computers
Server	Programs that control the server computer's resources	Applications that are processed on server computers

Category	Operating System (OS)	Instruction Set	Common Applications	Typical User
Client	Windows	Intel	Microsoft Office: Word, Excel, Access, PowerPoint, many other applications	Business Home
	Mac OS (pre–2006)	Power PC	Macintosh applications plus Word and Excel	Graphic artists Arts community
	Mac OS (post–2006)	Intel	Macintosh applications plus Word and Excel Can also run Windows on Macintosh hardware	Graphic artists Arts community
	Unix	Sun and others	Engineering, computer-assisted design, architecture	Difficult for the typical client, but popular with some engineers and computer scientists
	Linux	Just about anything	Open Office (Microsoft Office look-alike)	Rare—used where budget is very limited
Server	Windows Server	Intel	Windows server-type applications	Business with commitment to Microsoft
	Unix	Sun and others	Unix server applications	Fading . . . Linux taking its market
	Linux	Just about anything	Linux & Unix server applications	Very popular—promulgated by IBM

Figure 4-10
What a Manager Needs to Know About Software

versions of Windows are available: Windows 7, Windows Vista, and Windows XP run on user computers. Windows Server is a version of Windows designed for servers. As stated, Windows runs the Intel instruction set on both 32- and 64-bit computers.

Mac OS

Apple Computer, Inc., developed its own operating system for the Macintosh, **Mac OS**. The current version is Mac OS X. Macintosh computers are used primarily by graphic artists and workers in the arts community. Mac OS was designed originally to run the line of CPU processors from Motorola. In 1994, Mac OS switched to the PowerPC processor line from IBM. As of 2006, Macintosh computers are available for both PowerPC and Intel CPUs. A Macintosh with an Intel processor is able to run both Windows and the Mac OS.

Most people would agree that Apple has led the way in developing easy-to-use interfaces. Certainly, many innovative ideas have first appeared in a Macintosh and then later been added, in one form or another, to Windows.

Unix

Unix is an operating system that was developed at Bell Labs in the 1970s. It has been the workhorse of the scientific and engineering communities since then. Unix is generally regarded as being more difficult to use than either Windows or the Macintosh. Many Unix users know and employ an arcane language for manipulating files and data. However, once they surmount the rather steep learning curve most Unix users become fanatic supporters of the system. Sun Microsystems and other vendors of computers for scientific and engineering applications are the major proponents of Unix. In general, Unix is not for the business user.

Linux

Linux is a version of Unix that was developed by the **open source community** (see Q5, page 86). This community is a loosely coupled group of programmers who mostly volunteer their time to contribute code to develop and maintain Linux. The open source community owns Linux, and there is no fee to use it. Linux can run on client computers, but it is most frequently used for servers, particularly Web servers.

IBM is the primary proponent of Linux. Although IBM does not own Linux, IBM has developed many business systems solutions that use Linux. By using Linux, IBM does not have to pay a license fee to Microsoft or another OS vendor.

Own Versus License

When you buy a computer program, you are not actually buying that program. Instead, you are buying a **license**, which is the right to use a certain number of copies of that program subject to limits on the vendor's liability. Typically, when you buy a Windows license, Microsoft sells you the right to use Windows on a single computer, subject to pages of legalese that limit Microsoft's liabilities. Microsoft continues to own the Windows program.

Large organizations do not buy a license for each computer user. Instead, they negotiate a **site license**, which is a flat fee payment for the right to install the product (operating system or application) on all of that company's computers or on all of the computers at a specific site.

In the case of Linux, no company can sell you a license to use it. It is owned by the open source community, which states that Linux has no license fee (with certain reasonable restrictions). Large companies, such as IBM, and smaller companies, such as Red Hat, can make money by supporting Linux, but no company makes money selling Linux licenses.

Cloud Computing and Virtualization

You may hear two new terms that have become popular with regard to server computer hardware and software: cloud computing and virtualization. **Cloud computing** is a form of hardware/software leasing in which organizations obtain server resources from vendors that specialize in server processing.[2] The amount of server time and the resources leased is flexible and can change dynamically (and dramatically). Customers pay only for resources used. Major companies that offer cloud computing products include Amazon.com, IBM, Microsoft, and Oracle.

Your university is a prime candidate to use cloud computing for systems such as class registration. If you are on a semester program, registration occurs only three times a year, so any servers that are dedicated solely to registration will be idle most of the year. With cloud computing, your university could lease server resources when it needs them from a cloud vendor such as IBM. Your university will use substantial computing resources to support registration in August, January, and June, but nearly none in other months. It will pay just for the services that it uses.

Cloud computing allows multiple organizations to use the same computing infrastructure. Tax preparation firms can use the same IBM computers in April that your university uses in August, January, and June. In a sense, cloud computing is a form of CPU-cycle inventory consolidation.

Cloud computing is feasible because cloud vendors harness the power of virtualization. **Virtualization** is the process whereby multiple operating systems share the

2. See, for example, *www-03.ibm.com/cloud.*

same hardware. Thus, with virtualization one server can support, say, two instances of Windows Server, one instance of Linux, and three instances of Windows 7. Because these instances are isolated, it will appear to each that it has exclusive control over the server computer.

Because of virtualization, it is quite easy for cloud vendors to reconfigure servers to support changes in workload. If your university needs another 100 servers in August, IBM needs only to add 100 instances of your university's server environment to its virtual computers. If, 2 days later, your school needs another 100 instances, IBM allocates another 100. Behind the scenes, IBM is likely moving these instances among servers, balancing its workload on the computers that run the virtual operating systems. None of that activity is visible to your university or to the students who are registering for class.

What Types of Applications Exist, and How Do Organizations Obtain Them?

Application software performs a service or function. Some application programs are general purpose, such as Microsoft Excel or Word. Other application programs provide specific functions. QuickBooks, for example, is an application program that provides general ledger and other accounting functions. We begin by describing categories of application programs and then describe sources for them.

What Categories of Application Programs Exist?

Horizontal-market application software provides capabilities common across all organizations and industries. Word processors, graphics programs, spreadsheets, and presentation programs are all horizontal-market application software.

Examples of such software are Microsoft Word, Excel, and PowerPoint. Examples from other vendors are Adobe's Acrobat, Photoshop, and PageMaker and Jasc Corporation's Paint Shop Pro. These applications are used in a wide variety of businesses, across all industries. They are purchased off-the-shelf, and little customization of features is necessary (or possible).

Vertical-market application software serves the needs of a specific industry. Examples of such programs are those used by dental offices to schedule appointments and bill patients, those used by auto mechanics to keep track of customer data and customers' automobile repairs, and those used by parts warehouses to track inventory, purchases, and sales.

Vertical applications usually can be altered or customized. Typically, the company that sold the application software will provide such services or offer referrals to qualified consultants who can provide this service.

One-of-a-kind application software is developed for a specific, unique need. The IRS develops such software, for example, because it has needs that no other organization has.

How Do Organizations Acquire Application Software?

You can acquire application software in exactly the same ways that you can buy a new suit. The quickest and least risky option is to buy your suit off-the-rack. With this method, you get your suit immediately, and you know exactly what it will cost. You may not, however, get a good fit. Alternately, you can buy your suit off-the-rack and have it altered. This will take more time, it may cost more, and there's some possibility that the alteration will result in a poor fit. Most likely, however, an altered suit will fit better than an off-the-rack one.

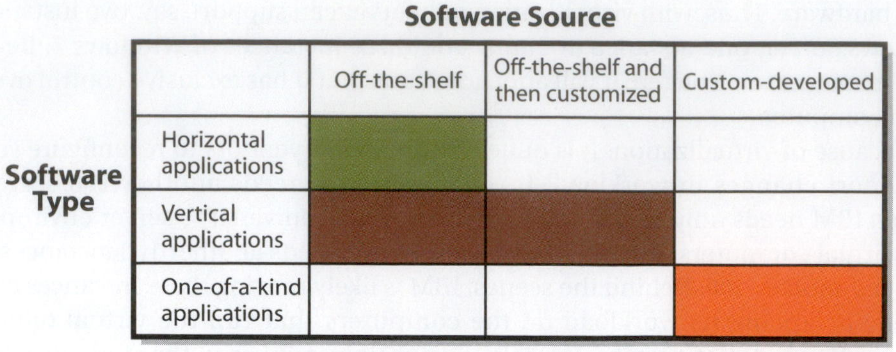

Figure 4-11
Software Sources and Types

Software Type	Software Source: Off-the-shelf	Off-the-shelf and then customized	Custom-developed
Horizontal applications			
Vertical applications			
One-of-a-kind applications			

Finally, you can hire a tailor to make a custom suit. In this case, you will have to describe what you want, be available for multiple fittings, and be willing to pay considerably more. Although there is an excellent chance of a great fit, there is also the possibility of a disaster. Still, if you want a yellow and orange polka-dot silk suit with a hissing rattlesnake on the back, tailor-made is the only way to go. You can buy computer software in exactly the same ways: **off-the-shelf software**, **off-the-shelf with alterations software**, or tailor-made. Tailor-made software is called **custom-developed software**.

Organizations develop custom application software themselves or hire a development vendor. Like buying the yellow and orange polka-dot suit, such development is done in situations in which the needs of the organization are so unique that no horizontal or vertical applications are available. By developing custom software, the organization can tailor its application to fit its requirements.

Custom development is difficult and risky. Staffing and managing teams of software developers is challenging. Managing software projects can be daunting. Many organizations have embarked on application development projects only to find that the projects take twice as long—or longer—to finish as planned. Cost overruns of 200 and 300 percent are not uncommon. We will discuss such risks further in Chapter 10.

In addition, every application program needs to be adapted to changing needs and changing technologies. The adaptation costs of horizontal and vertical software are amortized over all of the users of that software, perhaps thousands or millions of customers. For custom software developed in-house, however, the developing company must pay all of the adaptation costs itself. Over time, this cost burden is heavy.

Because of the risk and expense, in-house development is the last-choice alternative and is used only when there is no other option. Figure 4-11 summarizes software sources and types.

What Is Firmware?

Firmware is computer software that is installed into devices such as printers, print servers, and various types of communication devices. The software is coded just like other software, but it is installed into special, read-only memory of the printer or other device. In this way, the program becomes part of the device's memory; it is as if the program's logic is designed into the device's circuitry. Users do not need to load firmware into the device's memory.

Firmware can be changed or upgraded, but this is normally a task for IS professionals. The task is easy, but it requires knowledge of special programs and techniques that most business users choose not to learn.

Experiencing MIS InClass Exercise 4

Purchasing a Computer

In this exercise, you will form a team with other students and compete against other teams to identify the most appropriate computer for three different scenarios. For each scenario, you need to determine hardware and software requirements. Such requirements include the size and type of computer, the processor speed, the sizes of main memory and disk, the operating system, application programs, maintenance and support agreements, and any other factors you deem appropriate. Given those requirements, search the Web for the best system and price that you can find.

You are competing with other student groups, so think and search carefully. The following Web sites may be useful in completing this activity:

- *www.dell.com*
- *www.hp.com*
- *www.lenovo.com*
- *www.cnet.com*

Do not constrain yourselves to this list, however.
Evaluate each of the following scenarios:

1. Your roommate, a political science major, asks you to help her purchase a new laptop computer. She wants to use the computer for email, Internet access, and for note-taking in class. She wants to spend less than $1,000.
   a. What CPU, memory, and disk specifications would you recommend?
   b. What software does she need?
   c. Search online for the best computer deal for her.
   d. Which computer would you recommend, and why?
   e. Present your answer to the rest of the class. May the best team win!

2. Your father asks you to help him purchase a new computer. He wants to use his computer for email, Internet access, downloading pictures from his digital camera, uploading those pictures to a shared photo service, and creating documents for members of his antique auto club.
   a. What CPU, memory, and disk specifications would you recommend?
   b. What software does he need?
   c. Shop online for the best computer deal.
   d. Which computer would you recommend, and why?
   e. Present your answer to the rest of the class. May the best team win!

3. Due to cuts in the university's budget, your campus newspaper has lost its funding, and you and a group of five students have decided to replace it with your own newspaper. To do so, your group decides that it needs three computers. At least two of them need to be laptops. One can be either a laptop or a desktop.

   The university offers to sell you three Dell laptops for $2,100. Each laptop has 3G of main memory, a 250GB disk, and a dual 1.7-MHz, 32-bit CPU. The laptops include Windows Vista and Office 2007 Ultimate (Access, Excel, Groove, InfoPath, OneNote, PowerPoint, Publisher, and Word).
   a. What CPU, memory, and disk specifications do you need? Justify your assumptions.
   b. What software do you need? Justify assumptions.
   c. Shop online for the best deal you can find.
   d. Should you buy the university's computers? Explain your answer.
   e. Present your answer to the rest of the class. Again, may the best team win!

Q4 Why Are Thin Clients Preferred Over Thick Clients?

When you use client applications such as Word, Excel, or Acrobat, those programs run only on your computer. They need not connect to any server to run. Such programs are called **desktop programs** and are not considered clients, of any type.

Applications that process code on both the client and the server are called **client-server applications**. A **thick-client** application is an application program that must be preinstalled on the client. FlexTime's current system is a thick-client application, because every computer that accesses the FlexTime class schedule must have a client application program installed. Neil or another staff member must install the thick-client application before it can be used on a particular computer. Microsoft Outlook is an example of a thick-client application.

A **thin-client** application is one that runs within a browser (Internet Explorer, Firefox, Safari, or Chrome) and need not be preinstalled. When the user of a thin-client application starts that application, if any code is needed the browser loads that code dynamically from the server. It is not necessary to preinstall any client code. If FlexTime were to implement a thin-client solution, Neil wouldn't have to spend his time installing application software on FlexTime's computers.

To summarize, the relationship of user application types is as follows:

- Desktop application
- Client-server application
    - Thick-client application
    - Thin-client application

To see a thin-client application in action, open a browser and go to *www.LearningMIS.com*. When you do so, the browser starts by downloading needed code from the server that hosts that site.

All other things being equal, thin-client applications are preferred over thick-client applications because they require only a browser; no special client software needs to be installed. This also means that when a new version of a thin-client application is created, the browser automatically downloads that new code. With a thick-client application, a system administrator must install the new version on each user computer. Additionally, thin clients make it easier for people to access systems from remote locations and from special-purpose devices such as cell phones.

You can learn about a third type of client software, the mobile client, in Chapter Extension 10, "Mobile Computing."

As stated, client and server computers can run different operating systems. Many organizations have standardized on Windows XP or Windows 7 for their clients but use Windows Server or Linux for their servers. Figure 4-12 shows an example. Two thin clients are connecting via browsers to a Web server that is running Windows Server. Two thick clients are connecting via an email client (like Microsoft Outlook) to an email server that is running Linux. Those two clients are thick because Microsoft Outlook is preinstalled on them.

Q5 Is Open Source Software a Viable Alternative?

To answer this question, you first need to know a bit about the open source movement and process. Most computer historians would agree that Richard Matthew Stallman is the father of the movement. In 1983, he developed a set of tools called **GNU** (a self-referential acronym meaning *GNU Not Unix)* for creating a free Unix-like operating system. Stallman made many other contributions to open source, including the **GNU general public license (GPL) agreement**, one of the standard license agreements for open source software. Stallman was unable to attract enough developers to finish the free Unix system, but continued making other contributions to the open source movement.

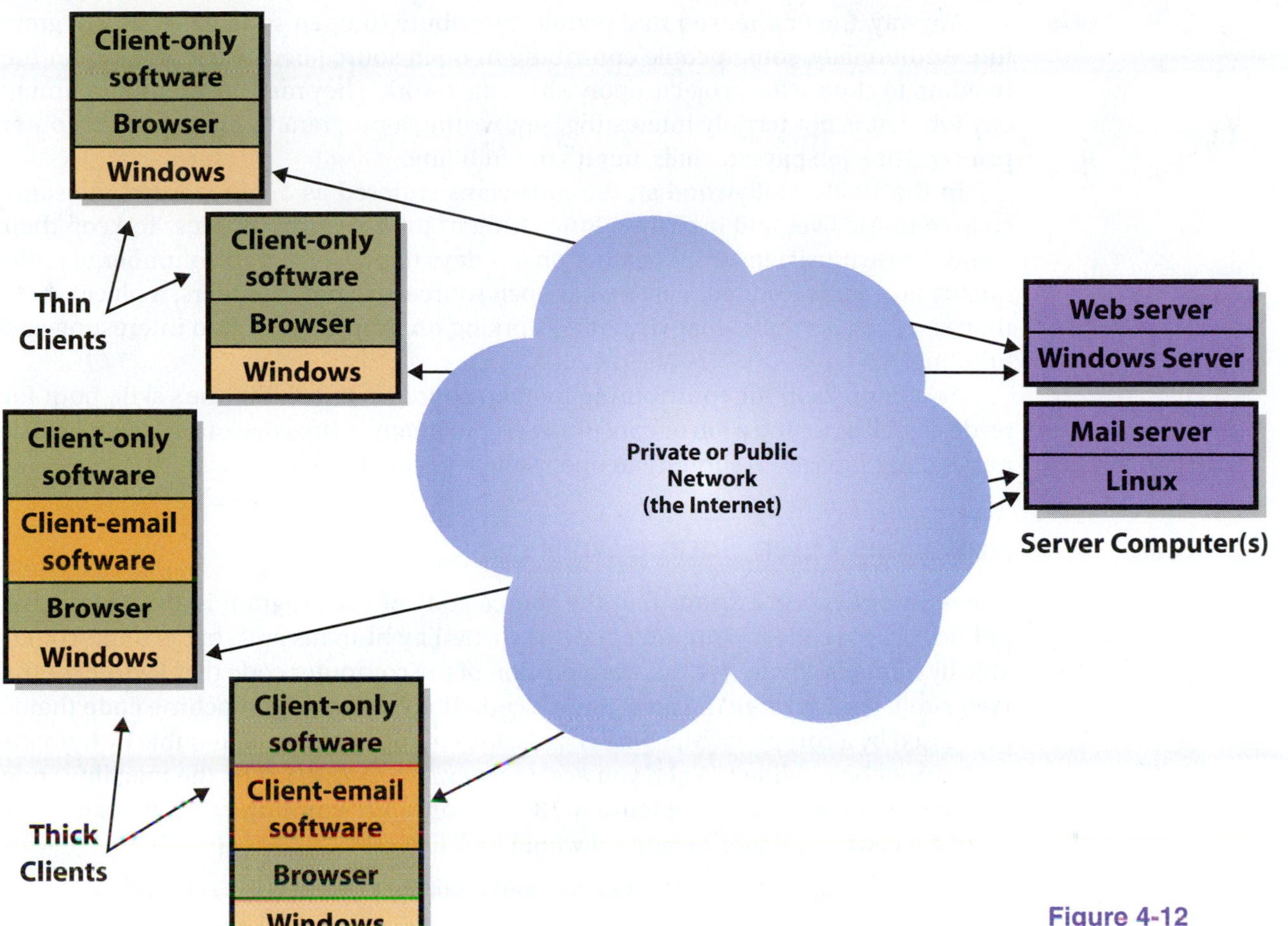

Figure 4-12
Thin and Thick Clients

In 1991, Linus Torvalds, working in Helsinki, began work on another version of Unix, using some of Stallman's tools. That version eventually became Linux, the high-quality and very popular operating system discussed previously.

The Internet proved to be a great asset for open source, and many open source projects have become quite successful, including:

- Open Office (a Microsoft Office look-alike)
- Firefox (a browser)
- MySQL (a DBMS, see Chapter 5)
- Apache (a Web server, see Chapter 8)
- Ubuntu (a Windows-like desktop operating system)
- Android (a mobile-device operating system)

Why Do Programmers Volunteer Their Services?

To anyone who has never enjoyed writing computer programs, it is difficult to understand why anyone would donate their time and skills to contribute to open source projects. Programming is, however, an intense combination of art and logic, and designing and writing a complicated computer program is exceedingly pleasurable (and addictive). Like many programmers, at times in my life I have gleefully devoted 16 hours a day to writing computer programs—day after day—and the days would fly by. If you have an artistic and logical mind, you ought to try it.

Anyway, the first reason that people contribute to open source is that it is great fun! Additionally, some people contribute to open source because it gives them the freedom to choose the projects upon which they work. They may have a programming day job that is not terribly interesting, say, writing a program to manage a computer printer. Their job pays the bills, but it's not fulfilling.

In the 1950s, Hollywood studio musicians suffered as they recorded the same style of music over and over for a long string of uninteresting movies. To keep their sanity, those musicians would gather on Sundays to play jazz, and a number of high-quality jazz clubs resulted. That's what open source is to programmers. A place where they can exercise their creativity while working on projects they find interesting and fulfilling.

Another reason for contributing to open source is to exhibit one's skill, both for pride as well as to find a job or consulting employment. A final reason is to start a business selling services to support an open source product.

How Does Open Source Work?

The term *open source* means that the source code of the program is available to the public. **Source code** is computer code as written by humans and that is understandable by humans. Figure 4-13 shows a portion of the computer code that I wrote for the Web site *www.LearningMIS.com.* Source code is compiled into **machine code** that is processed by a computer. Machine code is, in general, not understandable by humans and cannot be modified. When you access *www.LearningMIS.com,* the machine code version of the program in Figure 4-13 runs on your computer. We do not show machine code in a figure, because it would look like this:

1101001010010111111100111011110010001110000011111101110111110011 . . .

In a **closed source** project, say Microsoft Office, the source code is highly protected and only available to trusted employees and carefully vetted contractors. The source code is protected like gold in a vault. Only those trusted programmers can make changes to a closed source project.

With open source, anyone can obtain the source code from the open source project's Web site. Programmers alter or add to this code depending on their interests and goals. In most cases, programmers can incorporate code they find into their own

Figure 4-13
Source Code Sample

```
#region Dependency Properties

public static readonly DependencyProperty
    LessonIDProperty = DependencyProperty.Register(
        "LessonID",
        typeof(int),
        typeof(Lesson),
        new PropertyMetadata(new PropertyChangedCallback(Lesson.OnLessonDataChanged)));

public int LessonID
{
    get { return (int)GetValue(LessonIDProperty); }
    set { SetValue(LessonIDProperty, value); }
}

private static void OnLessonDataChanged(DependencyObject d, DependencyPropertyChangedEventArgs e)
{

    // reload the stage for the new TopicID property
    Lesson thisLesson = d as Lesson;

    lessonObject = thisLesson; // there is only one lesson object ... this is a static ref to it

    thisLesson.LoadLessonData(); // get data from xml file on server
    //call to thisLesson.CreateLessonForm(); must be done after load b/c of asynchronous read
}

#endregion
```

projects. They may be able to resell those projects depending on the type of license agreement the project uses.

Open source succeeds because of collaboration. A programmer examines the source code and identifies a need or project that seems interesting. He or she then creates a new feature, redesigns or reprograms an existing feature, or fixes a known problem. That code is then sent to others in the open source project. These people then evaluate the quality and merits of the work and add it to the product, if appropriate.

Typically, there is a lot of give and take. As with any effective collaboration, there are many cycles of iteration and feedback. Because of this iteration, a well-managed project with strong peer reviews can result in very high-quality code, like that in Linux.

So, Is Open Source Viable?

The answer depends on to whom and for what. Open source has certainly become legitimate. According to *The Economist,* "It is now generally accepted that the future will involve a blend of both proprietary and open-source software."[3] During your career, open source will likely take a greater and greater role in software. However, whether open source works for a particular situation depends on the requirements and constraints of that situation. You will learn more about matching requirements and programs in Chapter 10.

By the way, Neil at FlexTime eventually decided not to use the open source software he had identified. In some cases, companies choose open source software because it is "free." It turns out that this advantage may be less important than you'd think, because in many cases support and operational costs swamp the initial licensing fee.

How does the knowledge in this chapter help *Kelly* and you?

Kelly needs the knowledge in this chapter to be a better partner in the FlexTime business. Because of strangle and cram, FlexTime must upgrade its firm management software to a new version of something. But what? Should it upgrade to the next thick-client application? Should it change to a vendor that offers a thin-client application? Should it choose open source software? Without the knowledge of this chapter, Kelly cannot participate in any meaningful way in that decision.

You need the knowledge of this chapter because you might be in Kelly's shoes someday. You might work for a similar small business that has such decisions. Or, if you work in a large business, you might be asked to participate in such discussions as a manager of a department. And, of course, you might need to make selections like those in MIS InClass Exercise 4 on page 85.

Over the course of your career, application software, hardware, and firmware will change, sometimes rapidly. The Guide on pages 92–93 challenges you to choose a strategy for addressing this change.

3. "Unlocking the Cloud," *The Economist,* May 28, 2009. Available at *www.economist.com/opinion/displaystory.cfm?story_id=13740181* (accessed June 2009).

Ethics Guide

Churn and Burn

An anonymous source, whom we'll call Mark, made the following statements about computing devices:

"I never upgrade my system. At least, I try not to. Look, I don't do anything at work but write memos and access email. I use Microsoft Word, but I don't use any features that weren't available in Word 3.0, 20 years ago. This whole industry is based on 'churn and burn': They churn their products so we'll burn our cash.

"All this hype about 3.0GHz processors and 500GB disks—who needs them? I'm sure I don't. And if Microsoft hadn't put so much junk into Windows, we could all be happy on an Intel 486 processor like the one I had in 1993. We're suckers for falling into the 'you gotta have this' trap.

"Frankly, I think there's a conspiracy between hardware and software vendors. They both want to sell new products, so the hardware people come up with these incredibly fast and huge computers. Then, given all that power, the software types develop monster products bloated with features and functions that nobody uses. It would take me months to learn all of the features in Word, only to find out that I don't need those features.

"To see what I mean, open Microsoft Word, click on View, then select Toolbars. In my version of Word, there are 19 toolbars to select, plus one more to customize my own toolbar. Now what in the world do I need with 19 toolbars? I write all the time, and I have two selected: Standard and Formatting. Two out of 19! Could I pay Microsoft 2/19 of the price of Word, because that's all I want or use?

"Here's how they get you, though. Because we live in a connected world, they don't have to get all of us to use those 19 toolbars, just one of us. Take Bridgette, over in Legal, for example. Bridgette likes to use the redlining features, and she likes me to use them when I change draft contracts she sends me. So if I want to work on her documents, I have to turn on the Reviewing toolbar. You get the idea; just get someone to use a feature and, because it is a connected world, then all of us have to have that feature.

"Viruses are one of their best ploys. They say you better buy the latest and greatest in software—and then apply all the patches that follow so that you'll be protected from the latest zinger from the computer 'bad guys.' Think about that for a minute. If vendors had built the products correctly the first time, then there would be no holes for the baddies to find, would there? So they have a defect in their products that they turn to a sales advantage. You see, they get us to focus on the virus and not on the hole in their product. In truth, they should be saying, 'Buy our latest product to protect yourself from the defective junk we sold you last year.' But truth in advertising hasn't come that far.

"Besides that, users are their own worst enemies as far as viruses are concerned. If I'm down on 17th Street at 4 in the morning, half drunk and with a bundle of cash hanging out of my pocket, what's likely to happen to me? I'm gonna get mugged. So if I'm out in some weirdo chat room—you know, out where you get pictures of weird sex acts and whatnot—and download and run a file, then of course I'm gonna get a virus. Viruses are brought on by user stupidity, that's all.

"One of these days, users are going to rise up and say, 'That's enough. I don't need any more. I'll stay with what I have, thank you very much.' In fact, maybe that's happening right now. Maybe that's why software sales aren't growing like they were. Maybe people have finally said, 'No more toolbars!'"

Discussion Questions

1. Summarize Mark's view of the computer industry. Is there merit to his argument? Why or why not?
2. What holes do you see in the logic of his argument?
3. Someone could take the position that these statements are just empty rantings—that Mark can say all he wants, but the computer industry is going to keep on doing as it has been. Is there any point in Mark sharing his criticisms?
4. Comment on Mark's statement—"Viruses are brought on by user stupidity, that's all."
5. All software products ship with known problems. Microsoft, Adobe, and Apple all ship software that they know has failures. Is it unethical for them to do so? Do software vendors have an ethical responsibility to openly publish the problems in their software? How do these organizations protect themselves from lawsuits for damages caused by known problems in software?
6. Suppose a vendor licenses and ships a software product that has both known and unknown failures. As the vendor learns of the unknown failures, does it have an ethical responsibility to inform the users about them? Does the vendor have an ethical responsibility to fix the problems? Is it ethical for the vendor to require users to pay an upgrade fee for a new version of software that fixes problems in an existing version?

Guide

Keeping Up to Speed

Have you ever been to a cafeteria where you put your lunch tray on a conveyor belt that carries the dirty dishes into the kitchen? That conveyor belt reminds me of technology. Like the conveyor, technology just moves along, and all of us run on top of the technology conveyor, trying to keep up. We hope to keep up with the relentless change of technology for an entire career without ending up in the techno-trash.

Technology change is a fact, and the only appropriate question is, "What am I going to do about it?" One strategy you can take is to bury your head in the sand: "Look, I'm not a technology person. I'll leave it to the pros. As long as I can send email and use the Internet, I'm happy. If I have a problem, I'll call someone to fix it."

That strategy is fine, as far as it goes, and many businesspeople use it. Following that strategy won't give you a competitive advantage over anyone, and it will give someone else a competitive advantage over you, but as long as you develop your advantage elsewhere, you'll be OK—at least for yourself.

What about your department, though? If an expert says, "Every computer needs a 500GB disk," are you going to nod your head and say, "Great. Sell 'em to me!" Or are you going to know enough to realize that's a big disk (by 2010 standards, anyway) and ask why everyone needs such a large amount of storage. Maybe then you'll be told, "Well, it's only another $150 per machine from the 120GB disk." At that point, you can make a decision, using your own decision-making skills, and not rely solely on the IS expert. Thus, the prudent business professional in the twenty-first century has a number of reasons not to bury his or her head in the technology sand.

At the other end of the spectrum are those who love technology. You'll find them everywhere—they may be accountants, marketing professionals, or production-line supervisors who not only know their field, but also enjoy information technology. Maybe they were IS majors or had double majors that combined IS with another area of expertise (e.g., IS with accounting). These people read CNET News and ZDNet most days, and they can tell you the latest on IPv6 addresses. Those people are sprinting along the technology conveyor belt; they will never end up in the techno-trash, and they will use their knowledge of IT to gain competitive advantage throughout their careers.

Many business professionals fall in between these extremes. They don't want to bury their heads, but they don't have the desire or interest to become technophiles (lovers of technology) either. What to do? There are a couple of strategies. For one, don't allow yourself to ignore technology. When you see a technology article in the *Wall Street Journal*, read it. Don't just skip it because it's about technology. Read the technology ads, too. Many vendors invest heavily in ads that instruct without seeming to. Another option is to take a seminar or pay attention to professional events that combine your specialty with technology. For example, when you go to the banker's convention, attend a session or two on "Technology Trends for Bankers." There are always sessions like that, and you might make a contact with similar problems and concerns in another company.

Probably the best option, if you have the time for it, is to get involved as a user representative in technology committees in your organization. If your company is doing a review of its CRM system, for instance, see if you can get on the review committee. When there's a need for a representative from your department to discuss needs for the next-generation help-line system, sign up. Or, later in your career, become a member of the business practice technology committee, or whatever they call it at your organization.

Just working with such groups will add to your knowledge of technology. Presentations made to such groups, discussions about uses of technology, and ideas about using IT for competitive advantage will all add to your IT knowledge. You'll gain important contacts and exposure to leaders in your organization as well.

It's up to you. You get to choose how you relate to technology. But be sure you choose; don't let your head fall into the sand without thinking about it.

Discussion Questions

1. Do you agree that the change of technology is relentless? What do you think that means to most business professionals? To most organizations?
2. Think about the three postures toward technology presented here. Which camp will you join? Why?
3. Write a two-paragraph memo to yourself justifying your choice in question 2. If you chose to ignore technology, explain how you will compensate for the loss of competitive advantage. If you're going to join one of the other two groups, explain why, and describe how you're going to accomplish your goal.
4. Given your answer to question 2, assume that you're in a job interview and the interviewer asks about your knowledge of technology. Write a three-sentence response to the interviewer's question.

ACTIVE REVIEW

Use this Active Review to verify that you understand the ideas and concepts that answer the chapter's study questions.

Q1 What do business professionals need to know about computer hardware?

List categories of hardware and explain the purpose of each. Define *bit* and *byte*. Explain why bits are used to represent computer data. Define the units of bytes used to size memory. In general terms, explain how a computer works. Explain how a manager can use this knowledge. Explain why you should save your work from time to time while you are using your computer.

Q2 What is the difference between a client and a server?

Explain the functions of client and server computers. Describe how the hardware requirements vary between the two types. Define *server farm* and describe the technology dance that occurs on a server farm.

Q3 What do business professionals need to know about software?

Review Figure 4-10 and explain the meaning of each cell in this table. Explain the difference between software ownership and software licenses. Explain the differences among horizontal-market, vertical-market, and one-of-a-kind applications. Describe the three ways that organizations can acquire software.

Q4 Why are thin clients preferred over thick clients?

Define *client-server application* and differentiate it from, say, Microsoft Excel. Explain the difference between thin and thick clients. Describe two advantages of thin clients.

Q5 Is open source software a viable alternative?

Define *GNU* and *GPL*. Name three successful open source projects. Describe four reasons programmers contribute to open source projects. Define *open source, closed source, source code,* and *machine code.* In your own words, explain why open source is a legitimate alternative but may or may not be appropriate for a given application.

How does the knowledge in this chapter help Kelly and you?

Explain how Kelly was hampered by a lack of the knowledge in this chapter. Describe three ways that you might use the knowledge you've gained here.

KEY TERMS AND CONCEPTS

32-bit CPU 78
64-bit CPU 78
Application software 83
Binary digit 76
Bits 76
Bus 77
Bytes 76
Cache 77
Central processing unit (CPU) 75
Client 78
Client-server applications 86
Closed source 88
Cloud computing 82
Custom-developed software 84
Data channel 77
Desktop program 85
Dual processor 75
Firmware 84
Gigabyte (GB) 76
GNU 86
General Public License (GPL) agreement 86
Hardware 74
Horizontal-market application 83
Input hardware 74
Instruction set 80
Kilobyte (K) 76
License 82
Linux 82
Mac OS 81
Machine code 88
Main memory 75
Megabyte (MB) 76
Memory swapping 77
Nonvolatile 78
Off-the-shelf software 84
Off-the-shelf with alterations software 84
One-of-a-kind application 83
Open source community 82
Operating system (OS) 77
Output hardware 75
Quad processor 75
RAM 75
Server farm 79
Servers 78
Site license 82
Source code 88
Special function cards 75
Storage hardware 75
Surface 95
Terabyte (TB) 76
Thick client 86
Thin client 86
Unix 81
Vertical-market application 83
Virtualization 82
Volatile 78
Windows 80

USING YOUR KNOWLEDGE

1. Microsoft offers free licenses of certain software products to students at colleges and universities that participate in the Microsoft Developer Network (MSDN) Academic Alliance (AA). If your college or university participates in this program, you have the opportunity to obtain hundreds of dollars of software, for free. Here is a partial list of the software you can obtain:
   - Microsoft Access 2010
   - OneNote
   - Expression Studio
   - Windows 2008 Server
   - Microsoft Project 2010
   - Visual Studio Developer
   - SQL Server 2008
   - Visio

   a. Search *www.microsoft.com*, *www.google.com*, or *www.bing.com* and determine the function of each of these software products.

   b. Which of these software products are operating systems and which are application programs?

   c. Which of these programs are DBMS products (the subject of the next chapter)?

   d. Which of these programs should you download and install tonight?

   e. Either (1) download and install the programs in your answer to part d, or (2) explain why you would not choose to do so.

   f. Does the MSDN AA provide an unfair advantage to Microsoft? Why or why not?

2. Suppose you work at FlexTime and Neil has asked you to help analyze the software situation. He wants to compute the total costs of three alternatives: (1) upgrading to Version 3 of the current software, (2) licensing the open source software, and (3) licensing another vendor's thin-client software. He has asked you to identify all of the costs that should be considered. Note that he is not asking you to determine those costs, nor even to know how to determine those costs. He simply wants a list of costs to consider (Figure 4-14).

   a. Using Figure 4-14 as a guide, identify potential costs for each component for development and operation of the new system.

   b. Using your intuition, do you think the list of costs that you identified in part a is likely to swamp the costs of the software license fee? Why or why not?

COLLABORATION EXERCISE 4

Before you start this exercise, read Chapter Extensions 1 and 2, which describe collaboration techniques as well as tools for managing collaboration tasks. In particular, consider using Google Docs, Windows Live SkyDrive, Microsoft SharePoint, or some other collaboration tool.

In the past few years, Microsoft has been promoting **Surface**, a new hardware–software product that enables people to interact with data on the surface of a table. Surface initiates a new product category, and the best way to understand it is to view one of Microsoft's promotional videos at *www.microsoft.com/surface.*

Surface paints the surface of the 30-inch table with invisible, near-infrared light to detect the presence of objects. It can respond to up to 52 different touches at the same time. According to Microsoft, this means that four people sitting around the Surface table could use all 10 of their fingers to manipulate up to 12 objects, simultaneously.

Surface uses wireless and other communications technologies to connect to devices that are placed on it, such as cameras or cell phones. When a camera is placed on Surface, pictures "spill" out of it, and users can manipulate

	Development	Operational
Hardware	Hardware purchases	Hardware maintenance fees
Software	Software licenses Project costs for custom software	Software maintenance and support fees and costs
Data	Data conversion costs	Data acquisition costs
Procedures	Design, development, and documentation	Procedure maintenance costs
People	Initial training costs	Labor costs of using system

Figure 4-14
Sources of System Costs

those pictures with their hands. Products can be placed on Surface, and their product specifications are displayed. Credit cards can be placed on Surface, and items to be purchased can be dragged or dropped onto the credit card.

Currently, Microsoft Surface is marketed and sold to large-scale commercial organizations in the financial services, health care, hospitality, retail, and public service business sectors. As of June 2010, Microsoft Surface is not available for individual purchase or for purchase by small organizations. At present, Microsoft negotiates the price of Surface with each company.

One of the first implementers of Surface was the iBar lounge at Harrah's Rio All-Suite Hotel and Casino in Las Vegas, Nevada. The subtitle for the press release announcing iBar's system read, "Harrah's Reinvents Flirting and Offers New Uninhibited Fun and Play to iBar Patrons."[4]

The potential uses for Surface are staggering. Maps can display local events, and consumers can purchase tickets to those events by just using their fingers. Surface can also be used for new computer games and gambling devices. Children can paint on Surface with virtual paintbrushes. Numerous other applications are possible. At the product's announcement, Steve Ballmer, CEO of Microsoft, said "We see this as a multibillion dollar category, and we envision a time when surface computing technologies will be pervasive, from tabletops and counters to the hallway mirror. Surface is the first step in realizing that vision."[5]

As you can see at the Surface Web site, this product can be used for many different purposes in many different places, such as restaurants, retail kiosks, and eventually at home. Probably most of the eventual applications for Surface have not yet been envisioned. One clear application, however, is in the gambling and gaming industry. Imagine placing your credit card on a Surface gambling device and gambling the night away. Every time you lose, a charge is made against your credit card. Soon, before you know it, you've run up $15,000 in debt, which you learn when Surface tells you you've reached the maximum credit limit on your card.

Recall the RAND Study cited in Chapter 1 that stated there will be increased worldwide demand for workers who can apply new technology and products to solve business problems in innovative ways. Surface is an excellent example of a new technology that will be applied innovatively.

1. Consider uses for Surface at your university. How might Surface be used in architecture, chemistry, law, medicine, business, geography, political science, art, music, or any other discipline in which your team has interest? Describe one potential application for Surface for five different disciplines.
2. List specific features and benefits for each of the five applications you selected in question 1.
3. Describe, in general terms, the work that needs to be accomplished to create the applications you identified in question 1.
4. Using the five-component framework, describe the tools, documentation, and facilities that Microsoft or one of its partners must provide to enable widespread development of Surface applications.
5. Suppose you and your teammates want to start a consulting firm. Describe the opportunity for your firm that exists in your answer to question 4. Describe specific services that you could provide to help others create Surface applications.
6. Suppose you and your teammates want to start a consulting firm. Describe the opportunity that exists as a developer of complete and finished Surface applications.
7. You will sometimes hear the expression, "Emerging technology is constantly leveling the playing field," meaning that technology eliminates competitive advantages of existing companies and enables opportunities for new companies. How does this statement pertain to your answers to questions 5 and 6?

CASE STUDY 4

Dell Leverages the Internet, Directly, but for How Long?

When Michael Dell started Dell Computer in 1984, personal computers were sold only in retail stores. Manufacturers shipped to wholesalers, who shipped to retail stores, which sold to end users. Companies maintained expensive inventories at each stage of this supply chain. Dell thought that he could eliminate the retail channel by selling computers directly to consumers:

> **I was inspired by how I saw computers being sold. It seemed to me that it was very expensive and it was**

[4] "Harrah's Entertainment Launches Microsoft Surface at Rio iBar, Providing Guests with Innovative and Immersive New Entertainment Experiences." Microsoft Press Release, *www.microsoft.com/presspass/press/2008/jun08/06-11HETSurfacePR.mspx* (accessed June 2010).

[5] Microsoft Press Release, May 29, 2007.

> **inefficient. A computer cost at the time about $3,000 but there were only about $600 worth of parts inside the computer. And so I figured, hey, what if you sold the computer for $800? You don't need to sell it for $3,000. And so we changed the whole way computers were being sold by lowering the cost of distribution and sales and taking out this extra cost that was inefficient.**
>
> **Now, what I didn't know was that the Internet would come along and now people can go on the Internet and they can go to *Dell.com* and buy a computer and that makes it a lot easier.**
>
> **I'd say the most important thing we did was listen very carefully to our customers. We asked, what do they want, what do they need and how can we meet their needs and provide something that's really valuable to them? Because if we could take care of our customers, they'll want to buy more products from us, and they have.[6]**

Eliminating retail stores not only reduced costs, but it also brought Dell closer to the customer, enabling it to listen better than the competition. It also eliminated sales channel inventories, which allowed Dell to rapidly bring new computers with new technology to the customer. This eliminates the need to recycle or sell off existing pipeline inventory whenever a new model is announced.

Additionally, Dell focused on its suppliers and now has one of the most efficient supply chains in the industry. Dell pays close attention to its suppliers and shares information with them on product quality, inventory, and related subjects via its secure Web site *https://valuechain.dell.com*. According to its Web site, the first two qualities Dell looks for in suppliers are (1) cost competitiveness and (2) an understanding of Dell's business.

In addition to computer hardware, Dell provides a variety of services. It provides basic technical support with every computer, and customers can upgrade this basic support by purchasing one of four higher levels of support. Additionally, Dell offers deployment services to organizations to configure and deploy Dell systems, both hardware and preinstalled software, into customers' user environments. Dell offers additional services to maintain and manage Dell systems once they have been deployed.

Dell enjoyed unprecedented success until the recent economic downturn. In May 2009, Dell reported that first-quarter earnings had fallen 63 percent compared to a year earlier, and sales had dropped 23 percent. This report was on top of prior quarter losses, in which earnings had dropped 48 percent from the same quarter a year before.

The problem is not only Dell's, however. Sales were down in 2009 for other hardware vendors as well. The economy was responsible for some of this decline, but some of it was also due to the fact that customers were waiting to buy PCs until the release of Windows 7 in late 2010.

However, another financial result had to have been troubling to Dell. In 2009, Intel reported that sales were returning to "normal patterns," and Cisco (maker of routers and other communication devices) reported that sales seemed to have bottomed out. So, the components of PCs seem to be selling, but not the PCs themselves. What might this mean?

In September 2009, Dell tipped its hand as to how it views the future. On September 21 of that year, it bought Perot Systems for $3.9 billion. Perot was a provider of information systems services to health care and governmental customers. Clearly, Dell plans on making some changes to its corporate strategy.

Source: "Dell: No Relief in Sight," *BusinessWeek*, May 28, 2009. Available at *www.businessweek.com/technology/content/may2009/tc20090528_130058.htm* (accessed June 2009).

Questions

1. Explain how selling direct has given Dell a competitive advantage.
2. What information systems does Dell need to have to sell directly to the consumer? Visit *www.dell.com* for inspiration and ideas.
3. Besides selling direct, what other programs has Dell created that give it a competitive advantage?
4. Consider Dell's recent financial troubles.
   a. What are the implications of the company's tactics when revenue falls 63 percent but sales fall only 23 percent?
   b. Intel sells CPUs and memory, and its sales have stabilized. Dell and HP make computers, and their sales continue to decline. Assume the sales of other PC manufacturers are similar to those for Dell and HP. What do you conclude?
   c. Go to *http://news.cnet.com/8301-1001_3-10357598-92.html*. Summarize what you believe the Perot purchase means about Dell's future direction. Is this a smart move for Dell? Why or why not?

[6] Michael Dell, speech before the Miami Springs Middle School, September 1, 2004. Available at *www.dell.com*, under Michael/Speeches (accessed January 2005).

CHAPTER 5

Database Processing

This could happen to you

"Nope. It doesn't make any sense. I looked at the data and found we can't pack customers into classes. We don't have enough capacity."

"But, Neil, look at that Sunday night spinning class . . . it's half full. We could put another 25 people into that class."

"It's not what it seems. I queried the database, and at first glance you'd think we have plenty of opportunity to fill unoccupied seats. According to our database, we have a 9.7 percent vacancy rate in our classes."

"That's a lot."

"Yes, but looking more closely I found that all of those empty seats occur in awkward time slots. The database shows that all of Monday–Saturday primetime class slots are full—99.8 percent occupancy."

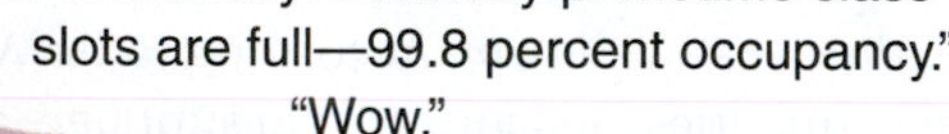

"Wow."

"It's the Sunday and the mid-day classes that have the vacancies."

"Well, let's try to consolidate those classes."

"Not a good idea, for two reasons. One, we'd only be able to cancel two, maybe three classes, and that doesn't save us much. But, the stronger reason it won't work is that people are inflexible in the time slots they choose."

"How do you know that?"

"Felix, I was amazed, but 93 percent

STUDY QUESTIONS

Q1 What is the purpose of a database?

Q2 What does a database contain?

Q3 What is a DBMS, and what does it do?

Q4 What is a database application?

Q5 What is the difference between an enterprise DBMS and a personal DBMS?

How does the knowledge in this chapter help *FlexTime* and you?

of our customers always take a class on the same day and time. Even if they take a different class, they always pick one on the same date and time."

"I guess that makes sense, Neil. They've got their lives set up to come here at a particular time on particular days and, well, they don't want to change that."

"That's true for more than 9 out of 10 customers."

"Hey, Neil, it's great that our software lets you query the data like that."

"Actually, it's not so flexible. I have about 25 standard queries that I can make against the database, selecting customers who've taken particular classes, etc. Those standard queries don't give me all the data I need. If I were a programmer type, I could write my own queries against the database, but I'm not."

"THE DATABASE SHOWS THAT ALL OF MONDAY–SATURDAY PRIMETIME CLASS SLOTS ARE FULL—99.8 PERCENT OCCUPANCY."

"So what do you do?"

"Felix, I'm a whiz at Excel! I run a database query that's as close as possible to what I want and then bring the results into Excel. I move and sort and sum and average the data around in Excel until I get the information I want."

"That seems like a pain."

"Yeah, maybe, but it works."

"Neil, that leaves us where we started, doesn't it? If we can't save money by packing customers into classes, what are we going to do?"

"I'm looking at the juice bar right now. Seems like our inventory costs are too high and we may need to reduce its operating hours. But don't say anything to anyone about that. I haven't looked at the data yet."

"The trainers will be glad we aren't cancelling classes."

"Yes, why don't you tell them on your team site? And not cancelling classes saves us possible public relations problems with our customers. Anyway, we avoided a train wreck on this one. Hey, I'm gonna go for a run. Cheers!"

Optional Extensions for this chapter are • CE7: Database Design 383 • CE8: Using Microsoft Access 2010 398 • CE9: Using Excel and Access Together 418

Q1 What Is the Purpose of a Database?

The purpose of a database is to keep track of things. When most students learn that, they wonder why we need a special technology for such a simple task. Why not just use a list? If the list is long, they think, put it into a spreadsheet.

Many professionals do keep track of things using spreadsheets. If the structure of the list is simple enough, there is no need to use database technology. The list of student grades in Figure 5-1, for example, works perfectly well in a spreadsheet.

Suppose, however, that the professor wants to track more than just grades. The professor may want to record email messages as well. Or perhaps the professor wants to record both email messages and office visits. There is no place in Figure 5-1 to record that additional data. Of course, the professor could set up a separate spreadsheet for email messages and another one for office visits, but that awkward solution would be difficult to use because it does not provide all of the data in one place.

Instead, the professor wants a form like that in Figure 5-2. With it, the professor can record student grades, emails, and office visits all in one place. A form like the one in Figure 5-2 is difficult, if not impossible, to produce from a spreadsheet. Such a form is easily produced, however, from a database.

The key distinction between Figures 5-1 and 5-2 is that the list in Figure 5-1 is about a single theme or concept. It is about student grades only. The list in Figure 5-2

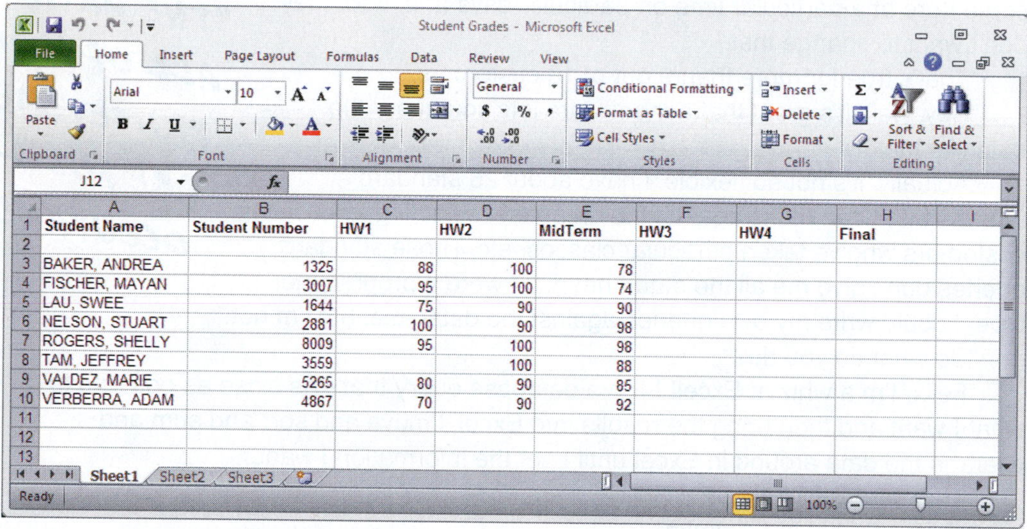

Student Name	Student Number	HW1	HW2	MidTerm	HW3	HW4	Final
BAKER, ANDREA	1325	88	100	78			
FISCHER, MAYAN	3007	95	100	74			
LAU, SWEE	1644	75	90	90			
NELSON, STUART	2881	100	90	98			
ROGERS, SHELLY	8009	95	100	98			
TAM, JEFFREY	3559		100	88			
VALDEZ, MARIE	5265	80	90	85			
VERBERRA, ADAM	4867	70	90	92			

Figure 5-1
A List of Student Grades Presented in a Spreadsheet

STUDENT

Student Name: BAKER, ANDREA
Student Number: 1325
HW1: 88
HW2: 100
MidTerm: 78

EMAIL

Date	Message
2/1/2010	For homework 1, do you want us to provide notes on our references?
3/15/2010	My group consists of Swee Lau and Stuart Nelson.
3/5/2010	

Record: 3 of 3 No Filter Search

OFFICE VISITS

Date	Notes
2/13/2010	Andrea had questions about using IS for raising barriers to entry.

Record: 2 of 2 No Filter Search

Record: 1 of 8 No Filter Search

Figure 5-2
Student Data Shown in a Form from a Databse

has multiple themes; it shows student grades, student emails, and student office visits. We can make a general rule from these examples: Lists that involve a single theme can be stored in a spreadsheet;[1] lists that involve multiple themes require a database. We will learn more about this general rule as this chapter proceeds.

To summarize, the purpose of a database is to keep track of things that involve more than one theme.

Q2 What Does a Database Contain?

A **database** is a self-describing collection of integrated records. To understand this definition, you first need to understand the terms illustrated in Figure 5-3. As you learned in Chapter 4, a **byte** is a character of data. Bytes are grouped into **columns**, such as *Student Number* and *Student Name*. Columns are also called **fields**. Columns or fields, in turn, are grouped into **rows**, which are also called **records**. In Figure 5-3, the collection of data for all columns (*Student Name, Student Number, HW1, HW2*, and *MidTerm*) is called a row or a record. Finally, a group of similar rows or records is called a **table** or a **file**. From these definitions, you can see that there is a hierarchy of data elements, as shown in Figure 5-4.

It is tempting to continue this grouping process by saying that a database is a group of tables or files. This statement, although true, does not go far enough. As shown in Figure 5-5, a database is a collection of tables *plus* relationships among the rows in those tables, *plus* special data, called *metadata*, that describes the structure of the database. By the way, the cylindrical symbol represents a computer disk drive. It is used in diagrams like that in Figure 5-5 because databases are normally stored on magnetic disks.

Relationships Among Records

Consider the terms on the left-hand side of Figure 5-5. You know what tables are. To understand what is meant by *relationships among rows in tables*, examine Figure 5-6.

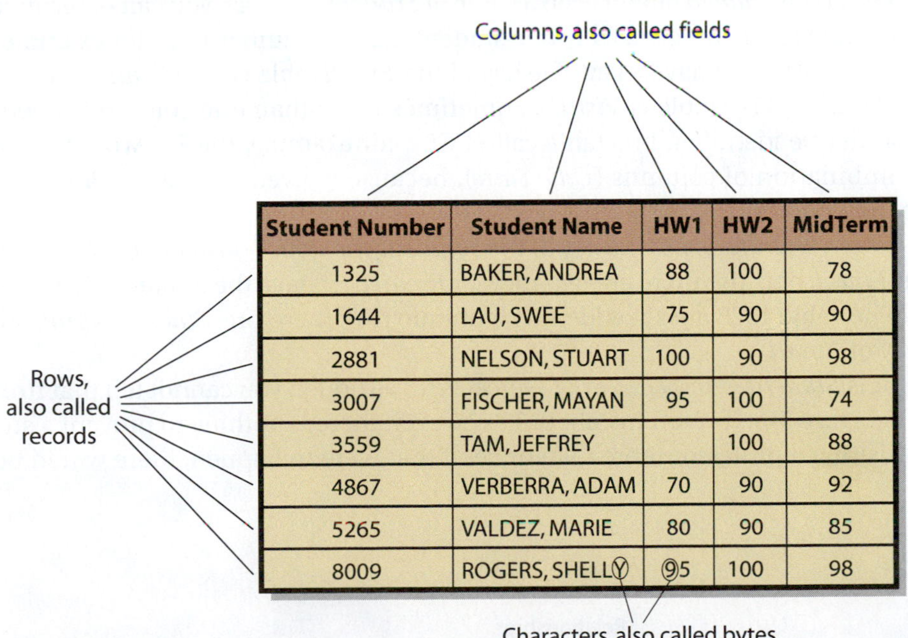

Student Number	Student Name	HW1	HW2	MidTerm
1325	BAKER, ANDREA	88	100	78
1644	LAU, SWEE	75	90	90
2881	NELSON, STUART	100	90	98
3007	FISCHER, MAYAN	95	100	74
3559	TAM, JEFFREY		100	88
4867	VERBERRA, ADAM	70	90	92
5265	VALDEZ, MARIE	80	90	85
8009	ROGERS, SHELLY	95	100	98

Figure 5-3
Student Table (also Called a File)

1. This doesn't mean, however, that any list with a single theme *should* be stored in a spreadsheet. If there is a lot of data, and if you want to query, sort, and filter that data, you probably should use a database, even for data having just one theme.

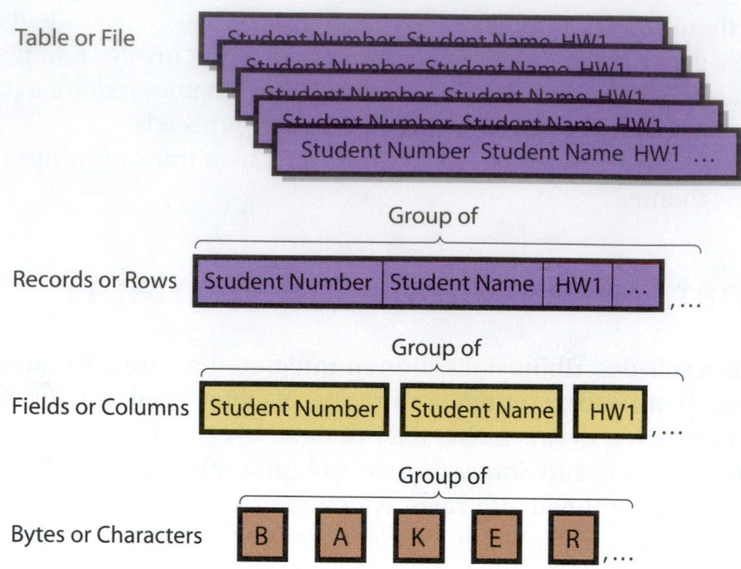

Figure 5-4
Hierarchy of Data Elements

It shows sample data from the three tables *Email, Student,* and *Office_Visit.* Notice the column named *Student Number* in the *Email* table. That column indicates the row in *Student* to which a row of *Email* is connected. In the first row of *Email,* the *Student Number* value is 1325. This indicates that this particular email was received from the student whose *Student Number* is 1325. If you examine the *Student* table, you will see that the row for Andrea Baker has this value. Thus, the first row of the *Email* table is related to Andrea Baker.

Now consider the last row of the *Office_Visit* table at the bottom of the figure. The value of *Student Number* in that row is 4867. This value indicates that the last row in *Office_Visit* belongs to Adam Verberra.

From these examples, you can see that values in one table relate rows of that table to rows in a second table. Several special terms are used to express these ideas. A **key** is a column or group of columns that identifies a unique row in a table. *Student Number* is the key of the *Student* table. Given a value of *Student Number,* you can determine one and only one row in *Student.* Only one student has the number 1325, for example.

Every table must have a key. The key of the *Email* table is *EmailNum,* and the key of the *Student_Visit* table is *VisitID.* Sometimes more than one column is needed to form a unique identifier. In a table called *City,* for example, the key would consist of the combination of columns (*City, State*), because a given city name can appear in more than one state.

Student Number is not the key of the *Email* or the *Office_Visit* tables. We know that about *Email,* because there are two rows in *Email* that have the *Student Number* value 1325. The value 1325 does not identify a unique row; therefore, *Student Number* is not the key of *Email.*

Nor is *Student Number* a key of *Office_Visit,* although you cannot tell that from the data in Figure 5-6. If you think about it, however, there is nothing to prevent a student from visiting a professor more than once. If that were to happen, there would be two

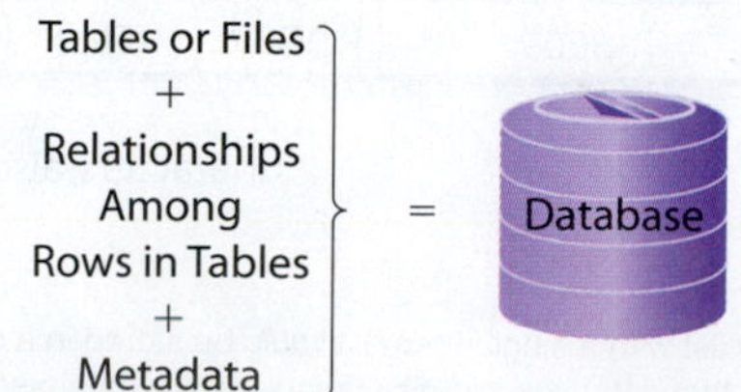

Figure 5-5
Components of a Database

Email Table

EmailNum	Date	Message	Student Number
1	2/1/2011	For homework 1, do you want us to provide notes on our references?	1325
2	3/15/2011	My group consists of Swee Lau and Stuart Nelson.	1325
3	3/15/2011	Could you please assign me to a group?	1644

Student Table

Student Number	Student Name	HW1	HW2	MidTerm
1325	BAKER, ANDREA	88	100	78
1644	LAU, SWEE	75	90	90
2881	NELSON, STUART	100	90	98
3007	FISCHER, MAYAN	95	100	74
3559	TAM, JEFFREY		100	88
4867	VERBERRA, ADAM	70	90	92
5265	VALDEZ, MARIE	80	90	85
8009	ROGERS, SHELLY	95	100	98

Office_Visit Table

VisitID	Date	Notes	Student Number
2	2/13/2011	Andrea had questions about using IS for raising barriers to entry.	1325
3	2/17/2011	Jeffrey is considering an IS major. Wanted to talk about career opportunities.	3559
4	2/17/2011	Will miss class Friday due to job conflict.	4867

Figure 5-6
Example of Relationships Among Rows

rows in *Office_Visit* with the same value of *Student Number.* It just happens that no student has visited twice in the limited data in Figure 5-6.

Columns that fulfill a role like that of *Student Number* in the *Email* and *Office_Visit* tables are called **foreign keys**. This term is used because such columns are keys, but they are keys of a different (foreign) table than the one in which they reside.

Before we go on, databases that carry their data in the form of tables and that represent relationships using foreign keys are called **relational databases**. (The term *relational* is used because another, more formal name for a table is **relation**.) In the past, there were databases that were not relational in format, but such databases have nearly disappeared. Chances are you will never encounter one, and we will not consider them further.[2]

Metadata

Recall the definition of database again: A *database* is a self-describing collection of integrated records. The records are integrated because, as you just learned, relationships among rows are represented in the database. But what does *self-describing* mean?

It means that a database contains, within itself, a description of its contents. Think of a library. A library is a self-describing collection of books and other materials. It is self-describing because the library contains a catalog that describes the library's

2. Another type of database, the **object-relational database**, is rarely used in commercial applications. Search the Web if you are interested in learning more about object-relational databases. In this book, we will consider only relational databases.

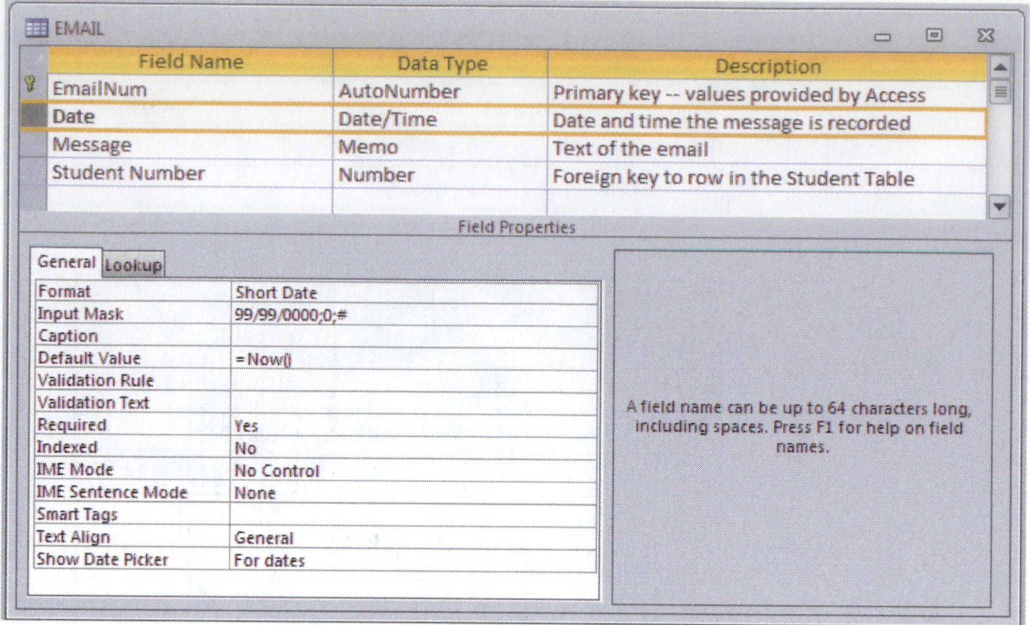

Figure 5-7
Sample Metadata (in Access)

contents. The same idea also pertains to a database. Databases are self-describing because they contain not only data, but also data about the data in the database.

Metadata are data that describe data. Figure 5-7 shows metadata for the *Email* table. The format of metadata depends on the software product that is processing the database. Figure 5-7 shows the metadata as they appear in Microsoft Access 2010. Each row of the top part of this form describes a column of the *Email* table. The columns of these descriptions are *Field Name, Data Type,* and *Description. Field Name* contains the name of the column, *Data Type* shows the type of data the column may hold, and *Description* contains notes that explain the source or use of the column. As you can see, there is one row of metadata for each of the four columns of the *Email* table: *EmailNum, Date, Message,* and *Student Number.*

The bottom part of this form provides more metadata, which Access calls *Field Properties,* for each column. In Figure 5-7, the focus is on the *Date* column (the row surrounded by a tan line). Because the focus is on *Date* in the top pane, the details in the bottom pane pertain to the *Date* column. The *Field Properties* describe formats, a default value for Access to supply when a new row is created, and the constraint that a value is required for this column. It is not important for you to remember these details. Instead, just understand that metadata are data about data and that such metadata are always a part of a database.

For a view on using Excel as a spreadsheet, read the Guide on pages 114–115.

The presence of metadata makes databases much more useful than spreadsheets or data in other lists. Because of metadata, no one needs to guess, remember, or even record what is in the database. To find out what a database contains, we just look at the metadata inside the database.

Q3 What Is a DBMS, and What Does It Do?

A database, all by itself, is not very useful. The tables in Figure 5-6 have all of the data the professor wants, but the format is unwieldy. The professor wants to see the data in a form like that in Figure 5-2 and also as a formatted report. Pure database data are correct, but in raw form they are not pertinent or useful.

Figure 5-8 on page 106 shows the components of a **database application system**, which is an assembly of forms, reports, queries, and application programs that process a database. Such applications make database data more accessible and useful.

Experiencing MIS InClass Exercise 5

How Much Is a Database Worth?

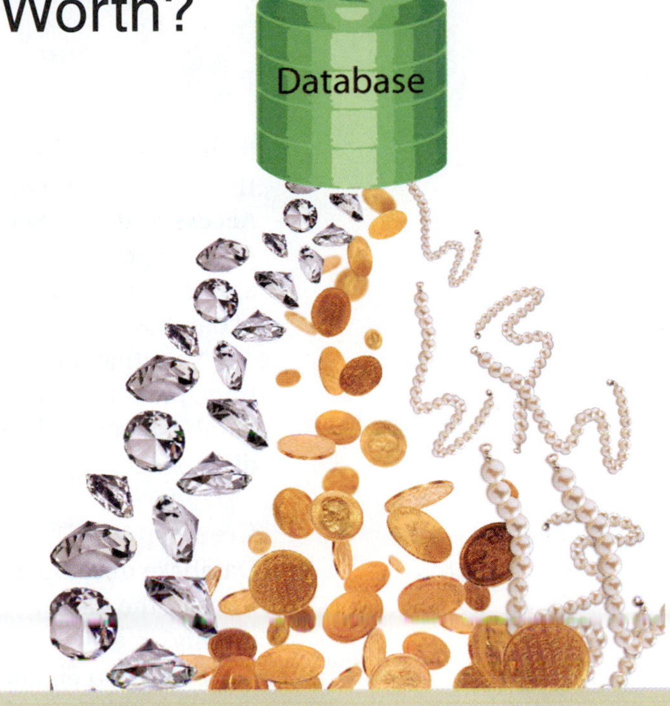

FlexTime realizes over 15,000 person-visits a year, an average of 500 visits per day. We've seen how important their database was in assessing the possibility of packing more clients into classes. In fact, Neil believes that the database is FlexTime's single most important asset. According to Neil:

> **Take away anything else—the building, the equipment, the inventory—anything else, and we'd be back in business 6 months or less. Take away our customer database, however, and we'd have to start all over. It would take us another 8 years to get back where we are.**

Why is the database so crucial? It records everything the company's customers do. If FlexTime decides to offer an early morning kickboxing class featuring a particular trainer, it can use its customer database to offer that class to everyone who ever took an early morning class, a kickboxing class, or a class by that trainer. Customers receive targeted solicitations for offerings they care about and, maybe equally important, they *don't* receive solicitations for those they don't care about. Clearly, the FlexTime database has value and, if it wanted to, FlexTime could sell that data.

In this exercise, you and a group of your fellow students will be asked to consider the value of a database to organizations other than FlexTime.

1. Many small business owners have found it financially advantageous to purchase their own building. As one owner remarked upon his retirement, "We did well with the business, but we made our real money by buying the building." Explain why this might be so.
2. To what extent does the dynamic you identified in your answer to step 1 pertain to databases? Do you think it likely that, in 2050, some small business owners will retire and make statements like, "We did well with the business, but we made our real money from the database we generated?" Why or why not? In what ways is real estate different from database data? Are these differences significant to your answer?
3. Suppose you had a national database of student data. Assume your database includes the name, email address, university, grade level, and major for each student. Name five companies that would find that data valuable, and explain how they might use it. (For example, Pizza Hut could solicit orders from students during finals week.)
4. Describe a product or service that you could develop that would induce students to provide the data in step 3.
5. Considering your answers to steps 1 through 4, identify two organizations in your community that could generate a database that would potentially be more valuable than the organization itself. Consider businesses, but also think about social organizations and government offices.

   For each organization, describe the content of the database and how you could entice customers or clients to provide that data. Also, explain why the data would be valuable and who might use it.
6. Prepare a 1-minute statement of what you have learned from this exercise that you could use in a job interview to illustrate your ability to innovate the use of technology in business.
7. Present your responses to steps 1 through 6 to the rest of the class.

The forms, reports, queries, and application programs call on the database management system (DBMS) to process database tables. We will first describe DBMS characteristics and then discuss database application components.

Database Management Systems

A **database management system (DBMS)** is a program used to create, process, and administer a database. As with operating systems, almost no organization develops

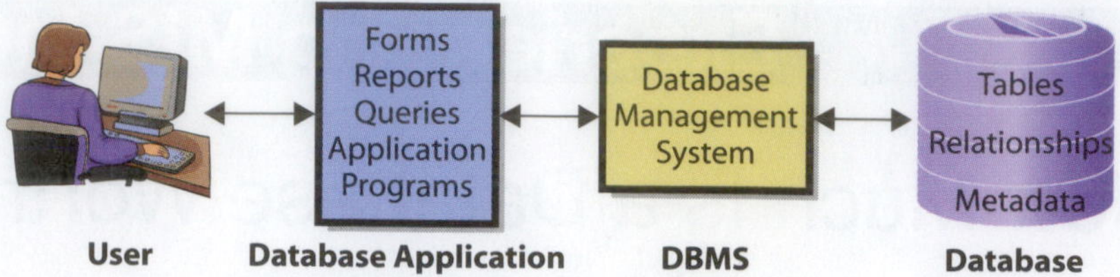

Figure 5-8
Components of a Database Application System

its own DBMS. Instead, companies license DBMS products from vendors such as IBM, Microsoft, Oracle, and others. Popular DBMS products are **DB2** from IBM, **Access** and **SQL Server** from Microsoft, and **Oracle** from the Oracle Corporation. Another popular DBMS is **MySQL**, an open source DBMS product that is free for most applications. Other DBMS products are available, but these five process the great bulk of databases today.

Note that a DBMS and a database are two different things. For some reason, the trade press and even some books confuse the two. A DBMS is a software program; a database is a collection of tables, relationships, and metadata. The two are very different concepts.

Creating the Database and Its Structures

Database developers use the DBMS to create tables, relationships, and other structures in the database. The form in Figure 5-7 can be used to define a new table or to modify an existing one. To create a new table, the developer just fills out a new form like the one in Figure 5-7.

To modify an existing table—for example, to add a new column—the developer opens the metadata form for that table and adds a new row of metadata. For example, in Figure 5-9 the developer has added a new column called *Response?* This new column has the data type *Yes/No*, which means that the column can contain only one of the values—Yes or No. The professor will use this column to indicate whether he has responded to the student's email. Other database structures are defined in similar ways.

Processing the Database

The second function of the DBMS is to process the database. Applications use the DBMS for four operations: to *read, insert, modify,* or *delete* data. The applications call upon the DBMS in different ways. From a form, when the user enters new or changed

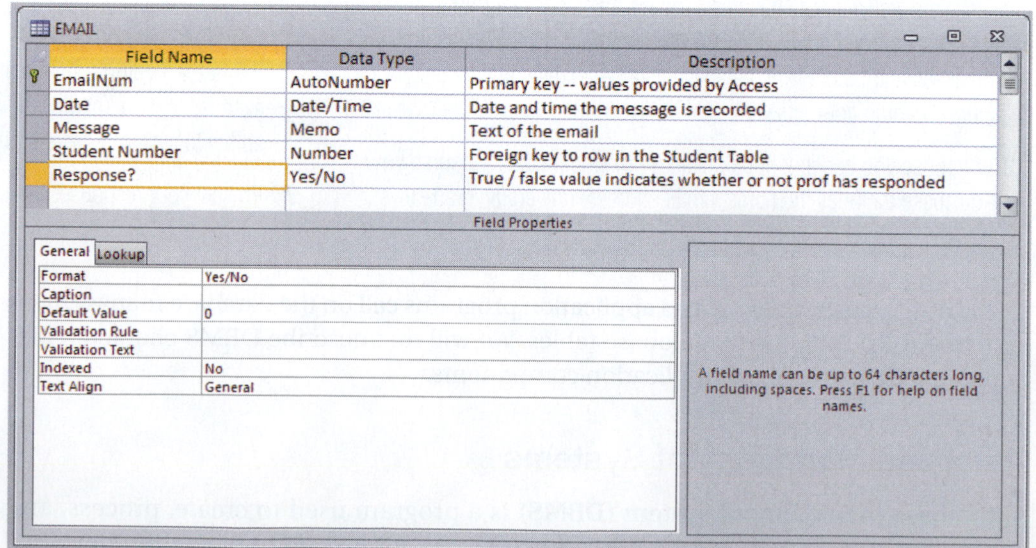
EMAIL

Field Name	Data Type	Description
EmailNum	AutoNumber	Primary key -- values provided by Access
Date	Date/Time	Date and time the message is recorded
Message	Memo	Text of the email
Student Number	Number	Foreign key to row in the Student Table
Response?	Yes/No	True / false value indicates whether or not prof has responded

Field Properties

General | Lookup

Format	Yes/No
Caption	
Default Value	0
Validation Rule	
Validation Text	
Indexed	No
Text Align	General

A field name can be up to 64 characters long, including spaces. Press F1 for help on field names.

Figure 5-9
Adding a New Column to a Table (in Access)

data, a computer program that processes the form calls the DBMS to make the necessary database changes. From an application program, the program calls the DBMS directly to make the change.

Structured Query Language (SQL) is an international standard language for processing a database. All five of the DBMS products mentioned earlier accept and process SQL (pronounced "see-quell") statements. As an example, the following SQL statement inserts a new row into the *Student* table:

```
INSERT INTO Student
([Student Number], [Student Name], HW1, HW2,
MidTerm) VALUES (1000, 'Franklin, Benjamin', 90, 95, 100)
```

Statements like this one are issued "behind the scenes" by programs that process forms. Alternatively, they can also be issued directly to the DBMS by an application program.

You do not need to understand or remember SQL language syntax. Instead, just realize that SQL is an international standard for processing a database. Also, SQL can be used to create databases and database structures. You will learn more about SQL if you take a database management class.

Queries at FlexTime

The FlexTime client application provides a set of fixed, predefined queries. Those predefined queries do not provide the exact data that Neil needs to determine the availability of empty class slots and of members' willingness to take classes at different times. As he says, however, he's a whiz at Excel. So he imports the results of the queries into Excel and then manipulates the data to obtain the data he needs. This is a common strategy for business users.

If Neil knew SQL, he could formulate his own queries against the database. In truth, almost no business manager knows SQL sufficiently to do this. (And, for security reasons, it is probably not a good idea for them to do, anyway.) However, business analysts working in data warehouses often do know SQL and use it for such purposes, as you will learn in Chapter 9.

To understand the power and problems of end users who can use SQL, see the Ethics Guide on pages 112–113.

Administering the Database

A third DBMS function is to provide tools to assist in the administration of the database. Database administration involves a wide variety of activities. For example, the DBMS can be used to set up a security system involving user accounts, passwords, permissions, and limits for processing the database. To provide database security, a user must sign on using a valid user account before he or she can process the database.

Permissions can be limited in very specific ways. In the *Student* database example, it is possible to limit a particular user to reading only *Student Name* from the *Student* table. A different user could be given permission to read all of the *Student* table, but only be able to update the *HW1*, *HW2*, and *MidTerm* columns. Other users can be given still other permissions.

In addition to security, DBMS administrative functions include backing up database data, adding structures to improve the performance of database applications, removing data that are no longer wanted or needed, and similar tasks.

Q4 What Is a Database Application?

A **database application** is a collection of forms, reports, queries, and application programs that process a database. A database may have one or more applications, and each application may have one or more users. Figure 5-10 shows three

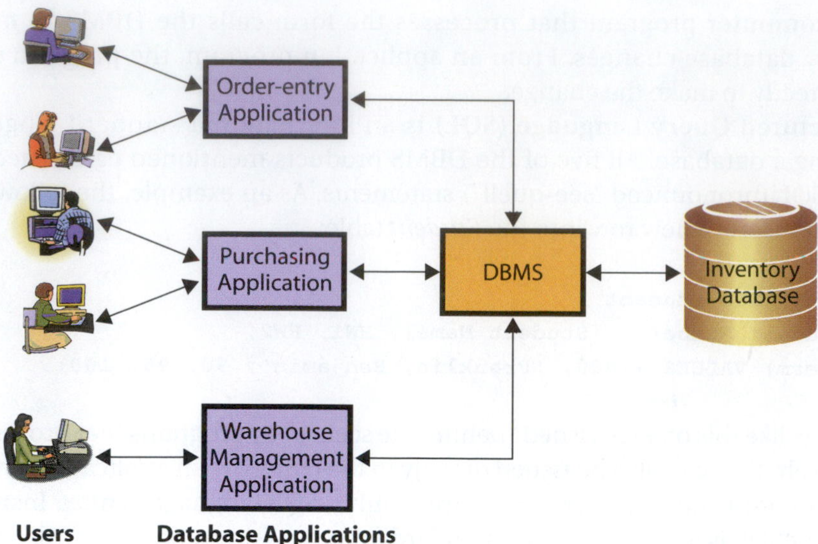

Figure 5-10
Use of Multiple Database Applications

applications; the top two have multiple users. These applications have different purposes, features, and functions, but they all process the same inventory data stored in a common database.

Forms, Reports, and Queries

Figure 5-2 (page 100) shows a typical database application data entry **form**, and Figure 5-11 shows a typical **report**. Data entry forms are used to read, insert, modify, and delete data. Reports show data in a structured context.

Some reports, like the one in Figure 5-11, also compute values as they present the data. An example is the computation of *Mid Term Total* in Figure 5-11. Recall from Chapter 1 that one of the definitions of *information* is "data presented in a meaningful context." The structure of this report creates information because it shows the student data in a context that will be meaningful to the professor.

DBMS programs provide comprehensive and robust features for querying database data. For example, suppose the professor who uses the Student database remembers that one of the students referred to the topic "barriers to entry" in an office visit, but cannot remember which student or when. If there are hundreds of students and visits recorded in the database, it will take some effort and time for the professor to search through all office visit records to find that event. The DBMS, however, can find any such record quickly. Figure 5-12(a) (page 109) shows a **query** form in which the professor types in the keyword for which she is looking. Figure 5-12(b) shows the results of the query.

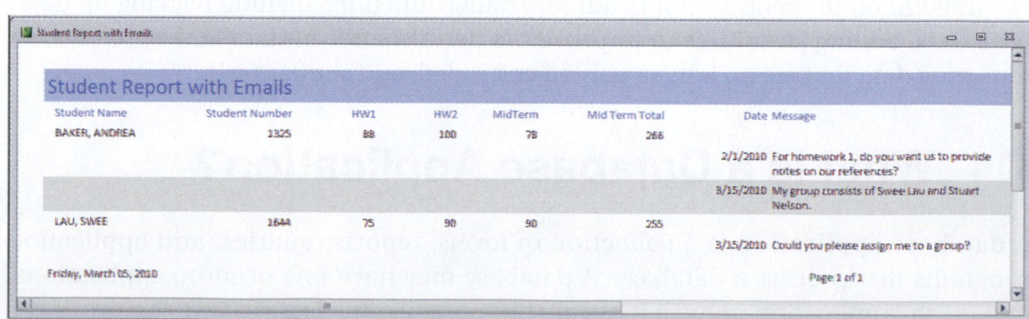

Student Report with Emails

Student Name	Student Number	HW1	HW2	MidTerm	Mid Term Total	Date	Message
BAKER, ANDREA	1325	88	100	78	266		
						2/1/2010	For homework 1, do you want us to provide notes on our references?
						3/15/2010	My group consists of Swee Lau and Stuart Nelson.
LAU, SWEE	1644	75	90	90	255		
						3/15/2010	Could you please assign me to a group?

Friday, March 05, 2010 Page 1 of 1

Figure 5-11
Example of a Student Report

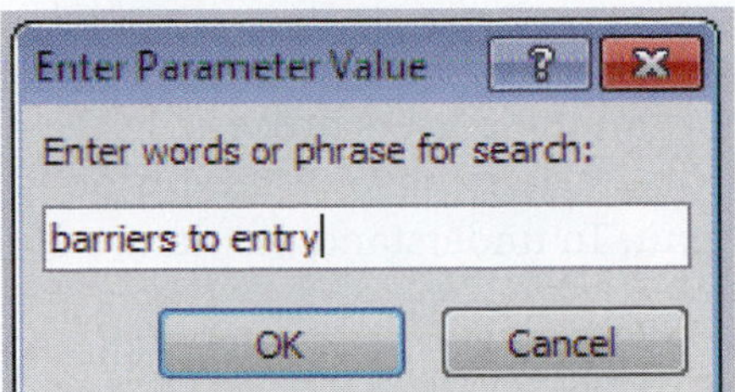

Figure 5-12(a)
Sample Query—Form Used to Enter Phrase for Search

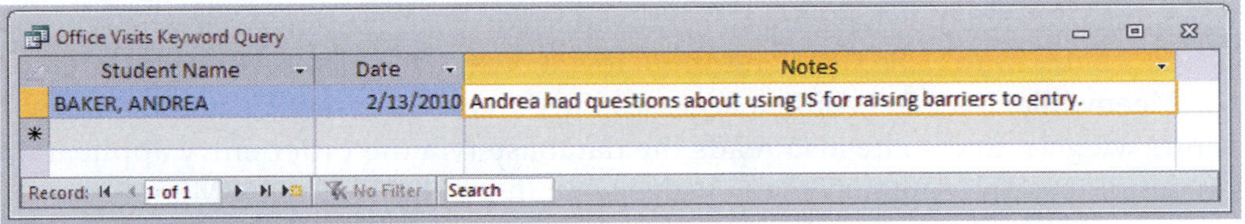

Figure 5-12(b)
Sample Query—Results of Query Operation

Database Application Programs

Forms, reports, and queries work well for standard functions. However, most applications have unique requirements that a simple form, report, or query cannot meet. For example, in the order entry application in Figure 5-10, what should be done if only a portion of a customer's request can be met? If someone wants 10 widgets and only 3 are in stock, should a back order for 7 more be generated automatically? Or should some other action be taken?

Application programs process logic that is specific to a given business need. In the Student database, an example application is one that assigns grades at the end of the term. If the professor grades on a curve, the application reads the break points for each grade from a form, and then processes each row in the *Student* table, allocating a grade based on the break points and the total number of points earned.

Another important use of application programs is to enable database processing over the Internet. For this use, the application program serves as an intermediary between the Web server and the database. The application program responds to events, such as when a user presses a submit button; it also reads, inserts, modifies, and deletes database data.

Figure 5-13 shows four different database application programs running on a Web server computer. Users with browsers connect to the Web server via the Internet. The Web server directs user requests to the appropriate application program. Each program then processes the database as necessary. You will learn more about Web-enabled databases in Chapter 8.

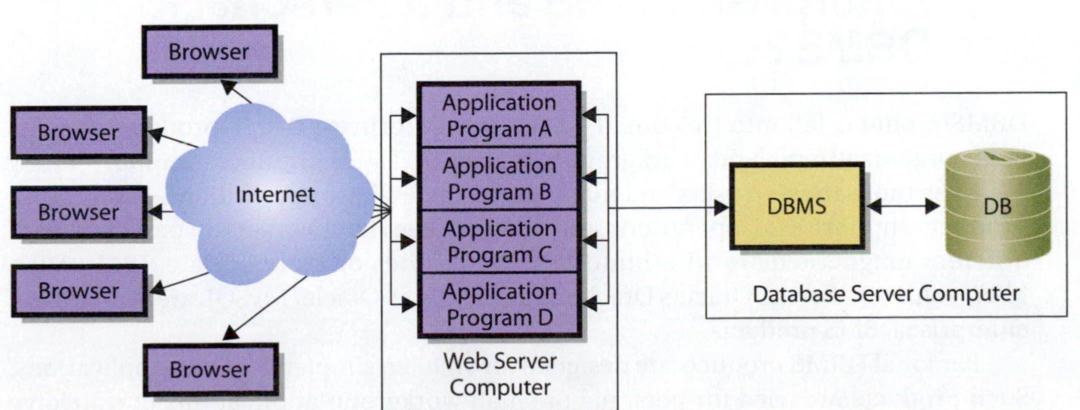

Figure 5-13
Four Application Programs on a Web Server Computer

Multiuser Processing Considerations

Figures 5-10 and 5-13 show multiple users processing the database. Such **multiuser processing** is common, but it does pose unique problems that you, as a future manager, should know about. To understand the nature of those problems, consider the following scenario.

Two users, Andrea and Jeffrey, are clerks using the order entry application in Figure 5-10. Andrea is on the phone with her customer, who wants to purchase five widgets. At the same time, Jeffrey is talking with his customer, who wants to purchase three widgets. Andrea reads the database to determine how many widgets are in inventory. (She unknowingly invokes the order entry application when she types in her data entry form.) The DBMS returns a row showing 10 widgets in inventory.

Meanwhile, just after Andrea accesses the database, Jeffrey's customer says she wants widgets, and so he also reads the database (via the order entry application program) to determine how many widgets are in inventory. The DBMS returns the same row to him, indicating that 10 widgets are available.

Andrea's customer now says that he'll take five widgets, and Andrea records this fact in her form. The application rewrites the widget row back to the database, indicating that there are five widgets in inventory.

Meanwhile, Jeffrey's customer says that he'll take three widgets. Jeffrey records this fact in his form, and the application rewrites the widget row back to the database. However, Jeffrey's application knows nothing about Andrea's work and subtracts three from the original count of 10, thus storing an incorrect count of seven widgets in inventory. Clearly, there is a problem. We began with 10 widgets, Andrea took five and Jeffrey took three, but the database says there are seven widgets in inventory. It should show two, not seven.

This problem, known as the **lost-update problem**, exemplifies one of the special characteristics of multiuser database processing. To prevent this problem, some type of locking must be used to coordinate the activities of users who know nothing about one another. Locking brings its own set of problems, however, and those problems must be addressed as well. We will not delve further into this topic here, however.

Realize from this example that converting a single-user database to a multiuser database requires more than simply connecting another user's computer. The logic of the underlying application processing needs to be adjusted as well.

Be aware of possible data conflicts when you manage business activities that involve multiuser processing. If you find inaccurate results that seem not to have a cause, you may be experiencing multiuser data conflicts. Contact your MIS department for assistance.

Q5 What Is the Difference Between an Enterprise DBMS and a Personal DBMS?

DBMS products fall into two broad categories. **Enterprise DBMS** products process large organizational and workgroup databases. These products support many (perhaps thousands) of users and many different database applications. Such DBMS products support 24/7 operations and can manage databases that span dozens of different magnetic disks with hundreds of gigabytes or more of data. IBM's DB2, Microsoft's SQL Server, Oracle's Oracle, and Sun's (now Oracle) MySQL are examples of enterprise DBMS products.

Personal DBMS products are designed for smaller, simpler database applications. Such products are used for personal or small workgroup applications that involve

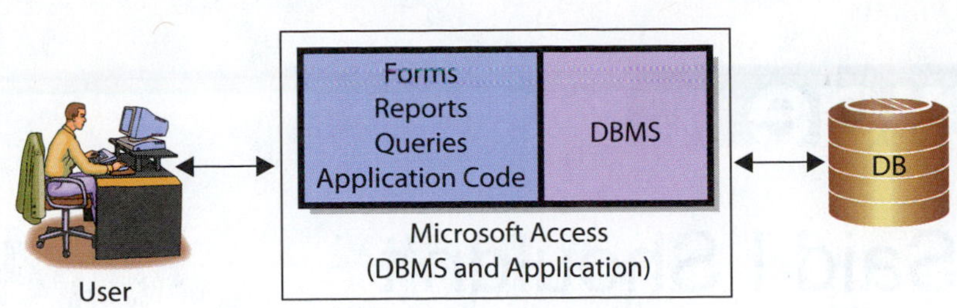

Figure 5-14
Personal Databse System

fewer than 100 users, and normally fewer than 15. In fact, the great bulk of databases in this category have only a single user. The professor's Student database is an example of a database that is processed by a personal DBMS product.

In the past, there were many personal DBMS products—Paradox, dBase, R:base, and FoxPro. Microsoft put these products out of business when it developed Access and included it in the Microsoft Office suite. Today, the only remaining personal DBMS of significance is Microsoft Access.

To avoid one point of confusion for you in the future, the separation of application programs and the DBMS shown in Figure 5-10 is true only for enterprise DBMS products. Microsoft Access includes features and functions for application processing along with the DBMS itself. For example, Access has a form generator and a report generator. Thus, as shown in Figure 5-14, Access is both a DBMS and an application development product.

How does the knowledge of this chapter help *FlexTime* and you?

Neil has sufficient knowledge of database processing to know to import query results into Excel and to rework the data in Excel to obtain the knowledge he needs. Kelly, Felix, Tara, and other FlexTime employees would benefit personally if they had such knowledge as well.

Neil also has sufficient knowledge of this material that, when he interviews vendors of new studio management software (discussed in Chapter 4), he is not fazed when they use the terms of this chapter. He can participate in the conversation with those vendors.

You, too, can obtain these benefits if you remember Neil's query strategy: If you find yourself working with an application with fixed queries that are close to what you want, import those queries into Excel and use your knowledge of Excel to obtain the exact data that you need. Also, you can participate in the conversation with your vendors or IT professionals. With the knowledge of this chapter, you need not hide when you hear terms like *Oracle, DBMS, query,* or *metadata.*

Ethics Guide

Nobody Said I Shouldn't

My name is Chris, and I do systems support for our group. I configure the new computers, set up the network, make sure the servers are operating, and so forth. I also do all of the database backups. I've always liked computers. After high school, I worked odd jobs to make some money, then I got an associate degree in information technology from our local community college.

"Anyway, as I said, I make backup copies of our databases. One weekend, I didn't have much going on, so I copied one of the database backups to a thumb drive and took it home. I had taken a class on database processing as part of my associate degree, and we used SQL Server (our database management system) in my class. In fact, I suppose that's part of the reason I got the job. Anyway, it was easy to restore the database on my computer at home, and I did.

"Of course, as they'll tell you in your database class, one of the big advantages of database processing is that databases have metadata, or data that describe the content of the database. So, although I didn't know what tables were in our database, I did know how to access the SQL Server metadata. I just queried a table called *sysTables* to learn the names of our tables. From there it was easy to find out what columns each table had.

"I found tables with data about orders, customers, salespeople, and so forth, and just to amuse myself and to see how much of the query language SQL that I could remember, I started playing around with the data. I was curious to know which order entry clerk was the best, so I started querying each clerk's order data, the total number of orders, total order amounts, things like that. It was easy to do and fun.

"I know one of the order-entry clerks, Jason, pretty well, so I started looking at the data for his orders. I was just curious, and it was very simple SQL. I was just playing around with the data when I noticed something odd. All of his biggest orders were with one company, Valley Appliances, and even stranger, every one of its orders had a huge discount. I thought, well, maybe that's typical. Out of curiosity, I started looking at data for the other clerks, and very few of them had an order with Valley Appliances. But, when they did, Valley didn't get a big discount. Then I looked at the rest of Jason's orders, and none of them had much in the way of discounts, either.

"The next Friday, a bunch of us went out for a beer after work. I happened to see Jason, so I asked him about Valley Appliances and made a joke about the discounts. He asked me what I meant, and then I told him that I'd been looking at the data for fun and that I saw this odd pattern. He just laughed, said he just 'did his job,' and then changed the subject.

"Well, to make a long story short, when I got to work on Monday morning, my office was cleaned out. There was nothing there except a note telling me to go see my boss. The bottom line was, I was fired. The company also threatened that if I didn't return all of its data, I'd be in court for the next 5 years . . . things like that. I was so mad I didn't even tell them about Jason. Now my problem is that I'm out of a job, and I can't exactly use my last company for a reference."

Discussion Questions

1. Where did Chris go wrong?
2. Do you think it was illegal, unethical, or neither for Chris to take the database home and query the data?
3. Does the company share culpability with Chris?
4. What do you think Chris should have done upon discovering the odd pattern in Jason's orders?
5. What should the company have done before firing Chris?
6. Is it possible that someone other than Jason is involved in the arrangement with Valley Appliances? What should Chris have done in light of that possibility?
7. What should Chris do now?
8. "Metadata make databases easy to use—for both authorized and unauthorized purposes." Explain what organizations should do in light of this fact.

Guide

No, Thanks, I'll Use a Spreadsheet

"I'm not buying all this stuff about databases. I've tried them and they're a pain—way too complicated to set up, and most of the time, a spreadsheet works just as well. We had one project at the car dealership that seemed pretty simple to me: We wanted to keep track of customers and the models of used cars they were interested in. Then, when we got a car on the lot, we could query the database to see who wanted a car of that type and generate a letter to them.

"It took forever to build that system, and it never did work right. We hired three different consultants, and the last one finally did get it to work. But it was so complicated to produce the letters. You had to query the data in Access to generate some kind of file, then open Word, then go through some mumbo jumbo using mail/merge to cause Word to find the letter and put all the Access data in the right spot. I once printed over 200 letters and had the name in the address spot and the address in the name spot and no date. And it took me over an hour to do even that. I just wanted to do the query and push a button to get my letters generated. I gave up. Some of the salespeople are still trying to use it, but not me.

"No, unless you are General Motors or Toyota, I wouldn't mess with a database. You have to have professional IS people to create it and keep it running. Besides, I don't really want to share my data with anyone. I work pretty hard to develop my client list. Why would I want to give it away?

"My motto is, 'Keep it simple.' I use an Excel spreadsheet with four columns: Name, Phone Number, Car Interests, and Notes. When I get a new customer, I enter the name and phone number, and then I put the make and model of cars they like in the Car Interests column. Anything else that I think is important I put in the Notes column—extra phone numbers, address data if I have it, email addresses, spouse names, last time I called them, etc. The system isn't fancy, but it works fine.

"When I want to find something, I use Excel's Data Filter. I can usually get what I need. Of course, I still can't send form letters, but it really doesn't matter. I get most of my sales using the phone, anyway."

Discussion Questions

1. To what extent do you agree with the opinions presented here? To what extent are the concerns expressed here justified? To what extent might they be due to other factors?
2. What problems do you see with the way that the car salesperson stores address data? What will he have to do if he ever does want to send a letter or an email to all of his customers?
3. From his comments, how many different themes are there in his data? What does this imply about his ability to keep his data in a spreadsheet?
4. Does the concern about not sharing data relate to whether he uses a database?
5. Apparently, management at the car dealership allows the salespeople to keep their contact data in whatever format they want. If you were management, how would you justify this policy? What disadvantages are there to this policy?
6. Suppose you manage the sales representatives, and you decide to require all of them to use a database to keep track of customers and customer car interest data. How would you sell your decision to this salesperson?
7. Given the limited information in this scenario, do you think a database or a spreadsheet is a better solution?

ACTIVE REVIEW

Use this Active Review to verify that you understand the ideas and concepts that answer the chapter's study questions.

Q1 What is the purpose of a database?

Describe the purpose of a database. Explain when to use a spreadsheet and when to use a database.

Q2 What does a database contain?

Explain the hierarchy of data from bytes to tables. Show how a database stores the relationships among rows. Define *key* and *foreign key*. Define *metadata*, and explain how metadata makes databases more useful.

Q3 What is a DBMS, and what does it do?

Describe a database application system. Define *DBMS*. Name three prominent DBMS products. Describe the difference between a database and a DBMS. Explain the three major functions of a DBMS. What is SQL used for?

Q4 What is a database application?

Name and describe the components of a database application. Describe the circumstances that require a special logic for database applications. Describe the lost-update problem. Explain, in general terms, how this problem is prevented.

Q5 What is the difference between an enterprise DBMS and a personal DBMS?

Explain the function of an enterprise DBMS and describe its characteristics. Explain the function of a personal DBMS and describe its characteristics. Name the only surviving personal DBMS. Explain the differences between Figures 5-10 and Figure 5-15.

How does the knowledge in this chapter help *FlexTime* and you?

Explain two ways that Neil benefits from having the knowledge of this chapter. Describe how those same benefits can apply to you.

KEY TERMS AND CONCEPTS

USING YOUR KNOWLEDGE

1. Suppose you are a marketing assistant for a consumer electronics company and are in charge of setting up your company's booth at trade shows. Weeks before the shows, you meet with the marketing managers and determine what displays and equipment they want to display. Then, you identify each of the components that need to be shipped and schedule a shipper to deliver them to the trade-show site. You then supervise convention personnel as they set up the booths and equipment. Once the show is over, you supervise the packing of the booth and all equipment as well as schedule its shipment back to your home office. When the equipment arrives, you check it into your warehouse to ensure that all pieces

of the booth and all equipment are returned. If there are problems due to shipping damage or loss, you handle those problems. Your job is important; at a typical show, you are responsible for more than a quarter of a million dollars of equipment.

a. You will need to track data about booth components, equipment, shippers, and shipments. List typical fields for each type of data.

b. Could you use a spreadsheet to keep track of this data? What would be the advantages and disadvantages of doing so?

c. Using your answer to part a, give an example of two relationships that you need to track. Show the keys and foreign keys for each.

d. Which of the following components of a database application are you likely to need: data entry forms, reports, queries, or application program? Explain one use for each that you will need.

e. Will your application be for one user or for multiple users? Will you need a personal DBMS or an enterprise DBMS? If a personal DBMS, which product will you use?

2. Samantha Green (the same Samantha we met at the end of Chapter 3, p. 65) owns and operates Twigs Tree Trimming Service. Recall that Samantha has a degree from a forestry program and recently opened her business in St. Louis, Missouri. Her business consists of many one-time operations (e.g., remove a tree or stump), as well as recurring services (e.g., trimming customers' trees every year or two). When business is slow, Samantha calls former clients to remind them of her services and of the need to trim their trees on a regular basis.

a. Name and describe tables of data that Samantha will need to run her business. Indicate possible fields for each table.

b. Could Samantha use a spreadsheet to keep track of this data? What would be the advantages and disadvantages of doing so?

c. Using your answer to question a, give an example of two relationships that Samantha needs to track. Show the keys and foreign keys for each.

d. Which of the following components of a database application is Samantha likely to need: data entry forms, reports, queries, or application program? Explain one use for each that she needs.

e. Will this application be for one user or for multiple users? Will she need a personal DBMS or an enterprise DBMS? If a personal DBMS, which product will she use?

3. FiredUp, Inc., (the same FiredUp we met at the end of Chapter 3, p. 65) is a small business owned by Curt and Julie Robards. Based in Brisbane, Australia, FiredUp manufactures and sells FiredNow, a lightweight camping stove. Recall that Curt used his previous experience as an aerospace engineer to invent a burning nozzle that enables the stove to stay lit in very high winds. Using her industrial design training, Julie designed the stove so that it is small, lightweight, easy to set up, and very stable. Curt and Julie sell the stove directly to their customers over the Internet and via phone. The warranty on the stove covers 5 years of cost-free repair for stoves used for recreational purposes.

FiredUp wants to track every stove and the customer who purchased it. They want to know which customers own which stoves in case they need to notify customers of safety problems or need to order a stove recall. Curt and Julie also want to keep track of any repairs they have performed.

a. Name and describe tables of data that FiredUp will need. Indicate possible fields for each table.

b. Could FiredUp use a spreadsheet to keep track of this data? What would be the advantages and disadvantages of doing so?

c. Using your answer to question a, give an example of two relationships that FiredUp needs to track. Show the keys and foreign keys for each.

d. Which of the following components of a database application is FiredUp likely to need: data entry forms, reports, queries, or application program? Explain one use for each needed component.

e. Will this application be for one user or for multiple users? Will FiredUp need a personal DBMS or an enterprise DBMS? If a personal DBMS, which product will it use? If an enterprise DBMS, which product can it obtain license-free?

COLLABORATION EXERCISE 5

Before you start this exercise, read Chapter Extensions 1 and 2, which describe collaboration techniques as well as tools for managing collaboration tasks. In particular, consider using Google Docs, Windows Live SkyDrive, Microsoft SharePoint, or some other collaboration tool.

Figure 5-15 shows a spreadsheet that is used to track the assignment of sheet music to a choir—it could be a church choir or school or community choir. The type of choir does not matter, because the problem is universal. Sheet music is expensive, choir members need to be

Figure 5-15
Spreadsheet Used for Assignment of Sheet Music

	A	B	C	D	E
1	Last Name	First Name	Email	Phone	Part
2	Ashley	Jane	JA@somewhere.com	703.555.1234	Soprano
3	Davidson	Kaye	KD@somewhere.com	703.555.2236	Soprano
4	Ching	Kam Hoong	KHC@overhere.com	703.555.2236	Soprano
5	Menstell	Lori Lee	LLM@somewhere.com	703.555.1237	Soprano
6	Corning	Sandra	SC2@overhere.com	703.555.1234	Soprano
7		B-minor mass	J.S. Bach	Soprano Copy 7	
8		Requiem	Mozart	Soprano Copy 17	
9		9th Symphony Chorus	Beethoven	Soprano Copy 9	
10	Wei	Guang	GW1@somewhere.com	703.555.9936	Soprano
11	Dixon	Eleanor	ED@thisplace.com	703.555.12379	Soprano
12		B-minor mass	J.S. Bach	Soprano Copy 11	
13	Duong	Linda	LD2@overhere.com	703.555.8736	Soprano
14		B-minor mass	J.S. Bach	Soprano Copy 7	
15		Requiem	J.S. Bach	Soprano Copy 19	
16	Lunden	Haley	HL@somewhere.com	703.555.0836	Soprano
17	Utran	Diem Thi	DTU@somewhere.com	703.555.1089	Soprano

able to take sheet music away for practice at home, and not all of the music gets back to the inventory. (Sheet music can be purchased or rented, but either way, lost music is an expense.)

Look closely at this data and you will see some data integrity problems—or at least some possible data integrity problems. For one, do Sandra Corning and Linda Duong really have the same copy of music checked out? Second, did Mozart and J. S. Bach both write a Requiem, or in row 15 should J. S. Bach actually be Mozart? Also, there is a problem with Eleanor Dixon's phone number; several phone numbers are the same as well, which seems suspicious.

Additionally, this spreadsheet is confusing and hard to use. The column labeled *First Name* includes both people names and the names of choruses. *Email* has both email addresses and composer names, and *Phone* has both phone numbers and copy identifiers. Furthermore, to record a checkout of music the user must first add a new row and then reenter the name of the work, the composer's name, and the copy to be checked out. Finally, consider what happens when the user wants to find all copies of a particular work: The user will have to examine the rows in each of four spreadsheets for the four voice parts.

In fact, a spreadsheet is ill-suited for this application. A database would be a far better tool, and situations like this are obvious candidates for innovation.

1. Analyze the spreadsheet shown in Figure 5-15 and list all of the problems that occur when trying to track the assignment of sheet music using this spreadsheet.

2. The following two tables could be used to store the data in Figure 5-15 in a database:

   ChoirMember (*LastName, FirstName, Email, Phone, Part*)
   MusicalWork (*NameOfWork, Composer, Part, CopyNumber*)

   Note: This notation means there are two tables, one named *ChoirMember* and a second named *MusicalWork*. The *ChoirMember* table has five columns: *LastName, FirstName, Email, Phone,* and *Part*; *MusicalWork* has four columns: *NameOfWork, Composer, Part, CopyNumber.*

   a. Redraw the data in Figure 5-15 into this two-table format.
   b. Select primary keys for the *ChoirMember* and *MusicalWork* tables.
   c. The two tables are not integrated; they do not show who has checked out which music. Add foreign key columns to one of the tables to integrate the data.
   d. This two-table design does not eliminate the potential for data integrity problems that occur in the spreadsheet. Explain why not.

3. A three-table database design for the data in the spreadsheet in Figure 5-15 is as follows:

   ChoirMember (*LastName, FirstName, Email, Phone, Part*)
   MusicalWork (*NameOfWork*)
   CheckOut (*LastName, FirstName, NameOfWork, Part, CopyNumber, DateOut, DateIn*)

   a. Redraw the data in Figure 5-15 into this three-table format.
   b. Identify which columns are primary keys for each of these tables.
   c. The foreign keys are already in place; identify which columns are foreign keys and which relationships they represent.

d. Does this design eliminate the potential for data integrity problems that occur in the spreadsheet? Why or why not?

4. Assume you manage the choir and you foresee two possibilities:
   - Keep the spreadsheet, but create procedures to reduce the likelihood of data integrity problems.
   - Create an Access database and database application for the three-table design.

Describe the advantages and disadvantages of each of these possibilities. Recommend one of these two possibilities and justify your recommendation.

CASE STUDY 5

Aviation Safety Network

The mission of the Aviation Safety Network (ASN) is to provide up-to-date, complete, and reliable information on airliner accidents and safety issues to those with a professional interest in aviation. ASN defines an *airliner* as an aircraft capable of carrying 14 or more passengers. ASN data include information on commercial, military, and corporate airplanes.

ASN gathers data from a variety of sources, including the International Civil Aviation Board, the National Transportation Safety Board, and the Civil Aviation Authority. Data are also taken from magazines, such as *Air Safety Week* and *Aviation Week & Space Technology*; from a variety of books; and from prominent individuals in the aviation safety industry.

ASN compiles the source data into a Microsoft Access database. The core table contains over 10,000 rows of data concerning incident and accident descriptions. This table is linked to several other tables that store data about airports, airlines, aircraft types, countries, and so forth. Periodically, the Access data are reformatted and exported to a MySQL database, which is used by programs that support queries on ASN's Web site (*http://aviation-safety.net/database*).

On that site, incident and accident data can be accessed by year, by airline, by aircraft, by nation, and in other ways. For example, Figure 5-16 shows a list of incidents and accidents that involved the Airbus 320. When the user clicks on a particular accident, such as the one

date	type	registration	operator	fat.	location		pic	
26-JUN-1988	Airbus A320-111	F-GFKC	Air France	3	Mulhouse-Hab...			A1
14-FEB-1990	Airbus A320-231	VT-EPN	Indian Airlines	92	near Bangalore-Hi...			A1
20-JAN-1992	Airbus A320-111	F-GGED	Air Inter	87	near Strasbourg-E...			A1
14-SEP-1993	Airbus A320-211	D-AIPN	Lufthansa	2	Warszawa-Oke...			A1
10-MAR-1997	Airbus A320-212	A4O-EM	Gulf Air	0	Abu Dhabi In...			A1
22-MAR-1998	Airbus A320-214	RP-C3222	Philippine Air Lines	0+ 3	Bacolod Airp...			A1
11-APR-2000	Airbus A320-231	F-OHMD	Mexicana	0	Minatitlan A...			O1
23-AUG-2000	Airbus A320-212	A4O-EK	Gulf Air	143	near Bahrain Inte...			A1
07-FEB-2001	Airbus A320-214	EC-HKJ	Iberia	0	Bilbao Airpo...			A1
24-JUL-2001	Airbus A320-231	4R-ABA	SriLankan Airlines	0	Colombo-Band...			C1
28-AUG-2002	Airbus A320-231	N635AW	America West	0	Phoenix-Sky ...			A1
03-MAY-2006	Airbus A320-211	EK-32009	Armavia	113	near Adler/Sochi ...			A1
05-MAY-2006	Airbus A320-211	EK-32010	Armavia	0	Brussel-Zave...			O1
05-MAY-2006	Airbus A320-211	EK-32001	Armenian International Airways, opf. Air Arabia	0	Brussel-Zave...			O1
05-MAY-2006	Airbus A320-232	SX-BVB	HellasJet, opf. Volare Airlines	0	Brussel-Zave...			O1
17-JUL-2007	Airbus A320-233	PR-MBK	TAM Brasil	187+ 12	São Paulo-Co...			A1
30-MAY-2008	Airbus A320-233	EI-TAF	TACA	3+ 2	Tegucigalpa-...			A1
27-NOV-2008	Airbus A320-232	D-AXLA	Air New Zealand, opf. XL Airways Germany	7	near Canet-Plage			A1
15-JAN-2009	Airbus A320-214	N106US	US Airways	0	Hudson River...			A1

Figure 5-16
Incidents and Accidents Involving the Airbus 320 from the ASN Aviation Safety Database

Source: Reprinted by permission of Aviation Safety Network, ©2009 ASN. *www.aviation-safety.net*.

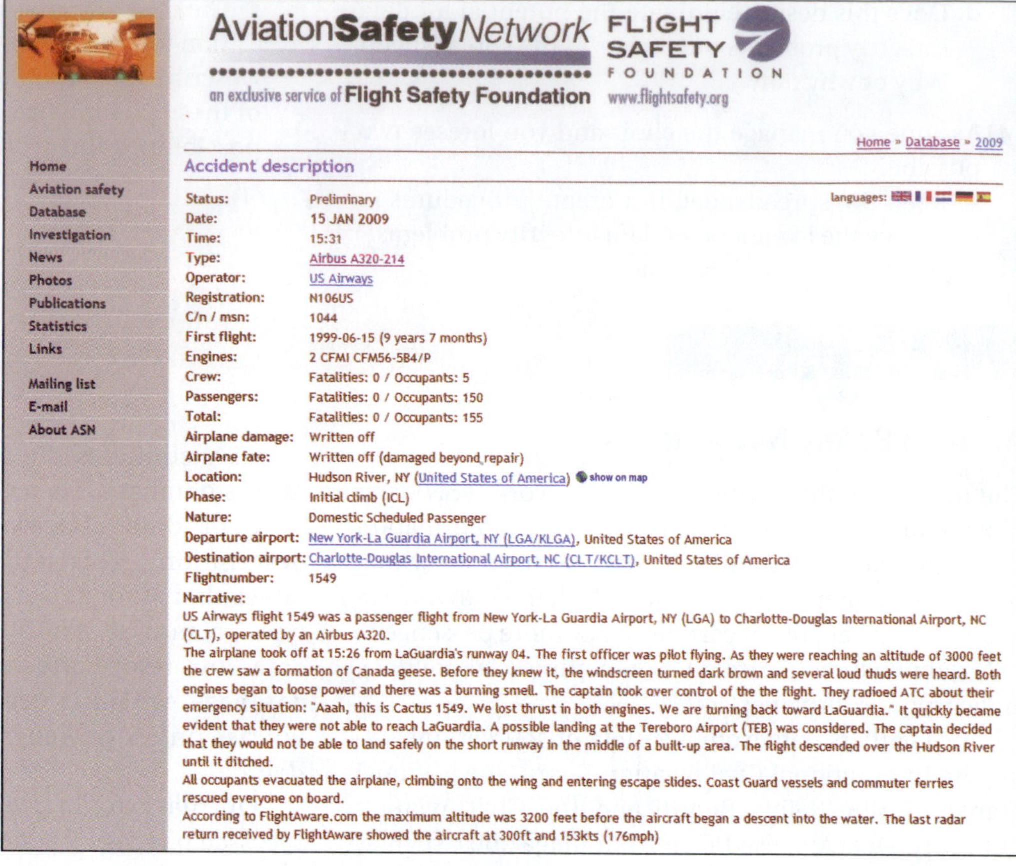

Figure 5-17
Incidents Description Summary from the ASN Aviation Safety Database

Source: Reprinted by permission of Aviation Safety Network, ©2009 ASN. *www.aviation-safety.net.*

on January 15, 2009, a summary of the incident is presented, as shown in Figure 5-17.

In addition to descriptions of incidents and accidents, ASN also summarizes the data to help its users determine airliner accident trends. For example, Figure 5-18 shows the geographic locations of fatal accidents for 2007. Notice that there were almost no such accidents in Australia, Russia, or China. Either these countries are particularly vigilant about aircraft safety, were lucky, or not all accidents were reported.

Hugo Ranter of the Netherlands started the ASN Web site in 1995. Fabian I. Lujan of Argentina has maintained the site since 1998. ASN has nearly 10,000 email subscribers in 170 countries, and the site receives over 50,000 visits per week. For more information about this site, go to *http://aviation-safety.net/about.*

Questions

1. All of the data included in this database is available in public documents. Thus, what is the value of the Aviation Safety Network? Why don't users just consult the online version of the underlying references? In your answer, consider the difference between data and information.

2. What was the cause of the incident shown in Figure 5-17? That incident, in which no one was fatally injured, was caused by geese that stuck an Airbus 320 that was flown by US Airways out of La Guardia Airport in New York. It would be illogical to conclude from this one incident that it is dangerous to fly where there are geese or when flying Airbus 320s, US Airways, or out of La Guardia. Or, would it? Suppose that you wanted to determine whether there is a systematic pattern of flights downed by geese or with the Airbus 320, US Airways, or La Guardia. How would you proceed? How would you use the resources of *http://aviation-safety.net* to make this determination?

3. The ASN database and Web site were created and are maintained by two individuals. The database might be complete and accurate, or it might not be. To what extent should you rely on these data? What can you do to decide whether you should rely on the data at this site?

4. Consider the data in Figure 5-18. Do you notice anything that indicates that this figure might not include all accident data? If you believe that not all data is included, what value does this figure have to

Figure 5-18
Fatal Accidents, Worldwide, 2007

Source: Reprinted by permission of Aviation Safety Network, ©2009 ASN. *www.aviation-safety.net.*

you? What would be legitimate uses for this data, and what uses are likely to be erroneous?

5. Suppose you work in the marketing department for an airline. Can you use these data in your marketing efforts? If so, how? What are the dangers of basing a marketing campaign on safety?

6. Suppose you are a maintenance manager for a major airline. How can you use these data? Would it be wise to develop your own, similar database? Why or why not?

CHAPTER 6

Data Communication

This could happen to you

"Neil, I don't want to put up the condo."

"Kelly, you were there. We heard him together: Our house valuation came in too low, and they want more collateral. It's either the condo or take another $150,000 out of the building infrastructure."

"If this economy doesn't improve, and if FlexTime can't support the new mortgage, we could lose it all. The business, our house, everything. The condo would be all we have left."

"OK, Kelly, let's look again at the costs."

Neil opens his laptop computer on his desk. They look at it together.

"The land, the basic building construction, the parking lots . . . I don't see how we get those costs down, but I'll talk to the contractor again. What about the locker rooms? Can we do anything to bring the locker room costs down?"

"Neil, I've been thinking about that. Maybe we go to a warehouse look. Of course we have to have showers and toilets and sinks and

STUDY QUESTIONS

Q1 What is a computer network?

Q2 What are the components of a LAN?

Q3 What are the alternatives for connecting to a WAN?

Q4 What are the fundamental concepts you should know about the Internet?

Q5 What happens on a typical Web server?

Q6 How do organizations benefit from VPNs?

How does the knowledge in this chapter help *FlexTime* and you?

mirrors . . . and the lockers, but what if we go radical industrial? We could save on tile and fixtures."

"OK, Kelly, that's a start. What else?"

"Hey, Neil, what's this $175,000 for network infrastructure? What do we need that for?"

"$175,000 TO HOOK UP A COMPUTER?"

"Hooking up all the computers."

"$175,000 to hook up a computer? Come on, Neil, get real."

"Kelly, it's not just one computer, it's all of our computers. Plus all the new gear."

"Speaking of new gear!" Felix sticks his head into Neil's office, "Check out my new shoes. They talk to my wristband and, if I have a wireless network nearby, the wristband talks to the network and stores my workout data on my workout Web site. Cool! Is this going to work in the new building?"

Felix heads down the hall.

"See what I mean, Kelly? Plus all the new machines have network adapters—either wired or wireless. And this is just the tip of the iceberg. Everybody wants to have their workout data collected and stored and processed. We're going to have to store more and more personal workout data. And it's got to get from the spinning machine, or the shoes, or the whatever, to the network somehow."

"Neil, I can understand spending money on wires; they're made of something and they have to be installed. But wireless? How come the air costs $175,000?"

"That's not fair, Kelly. The $175,000 includes wires installed in the walls, but actually, that's not a big expense. The major expenses are equipment items like switches and routers and other equipment that can give us the performance we need."

"Neil, this stuff is expensive. Cisco router??? Why do we need four of them? Or, hey, what is a VPN/firewall appliance? Appliance? Like a toaster? Pricey little number. Can we get by without it? There must be some fat in here we can remove."

Neil grimaces.

"Neil, why don't we just use iPhones? They talk to shoes, too."

"You mean have our clients use an iPhone app?"

"Yeah. I tried one last week, Neil, and it was great. I didn't have a wireless network anywhere near me so it used a satellite or something. Anyway, when I got

Optional Extension for this chapter is • CE10: Remote, Nomadic, and Mobile Systems 445

CE

back here I used the app to download the data to our computer. Why don't our clients do that?"

"Kelly, where is FlexTime in that transaction?"

"FlexTime? Nowhere. It was just me and shoes and the iPhone and the app and, ah Neil, I get the picture. Why would they need us?"

"Plus we have to do all we can to support whatever devices are coming down the road in the next 10 years."

"Neil, I'm in over my head on this. I don't even know the difference between a LAN and a WAN. But, I'll talk to our architect and try to get the locker room costs down. Meanwhile, can you take a look at this $175,000? Do we need all of it? Do we need all of it now? Can we shave even $20,000 off?"

Q1 What Is a Computer Network?

If you go into business for yourself, there's an excellent chance you'll have a problem just like FlexTime's. How much do you really have to pay for a network infrastructure? You'll need the knowledge of this chapter to understand the conversations you'll have to make that assessment. Of course, you can just rely on outside experts, but that probably doesn't work in the twenty-first century. Many of your competitors will be able to ask and understand those questions—and use the money their knowledge saves them for other facilities they need, like locker rooms and parking lots.

Or, what if you work in product management for a large company? Does your product "talk" to some network? If not, could it? Should it? Does it require a LAN or a WAN? We'll begin with that question.

A computer **network** is a collection of computers that communicate with one another over transmission lines or wirelessly. As shown in Figure 6-1, the three basic types of networks are local area networks, wide area networks, and internets.

A **local area network (LAN)** connects computers that reside in a single geographic location on the premises of the company that operates the LAN. The number of connected computers can range from two to several hundred. The distinguishing characteristic of a LAN is *a single location.* **Wide area networks (WANs)** connect computers at different geographic locations. The computers in two separated company sites must be connected using a WAN. To illustrate, the computers for a College of Business located on a single campus can be connected via a LAN. The computers for a College of Business located on multiple campuses must be connected via a WAN.

The single- versus multiple-site distinction is important. With a LAN, an organization can place communications lines wherever it wants, because all lines reside on its premises. The same is not true for a WAN. A company with offices in Chicago and Atlanta cannot run a wire down the freeway to connect computers in the two cities. Instead, the company contracts with a communications vendor that is licensed by the government and that already has lines or has the authority to run new lines between the two cities.

An **internet** is a network of networks. Internets connect LANs, WANs, and other internets. The most famous internet is **"the Internet"** (with an uppercase letter *I*), the

Figure 6-1
Major Network Types

Type	Characteristic
Local area network (LAN)	Computers connected at a single physical site
Wide area network (WAN)	Computers connected between two or more separated sites
The Internet and internets	Networks of networks

collection of networks that you use when you send email or access a Web site. In addition to the Internet, private networks of networks, called *internets*, also exist.

The networks that comprise an internet use a large variety of communication methods and conventions, and data must flow seamlessly across them. To provide seamless flow, an elaborate scheme called a *layered protocol* is used. The details of protocols are beyond the scope of this text. Just understand that a **protocol** is a set of rules that two communicating devices follow. There are many different protocols; some are used for LANs, some are used for WANs, some are used for internets and the Internet, and some are used for all of these. We will identify several common protocols in this chapter.

Q2 What Are the Components of a LAN?

A LAN is a group of computers connected together on a single site. Usually the computers are located within a half mile or so of each other. The key distinction, however, is that all of the computers are located on property controlled by the organization that operates the LAN. This means that the organization can run cables wherever needed to connect the computers.

A Typical SOHO LAN

Figure 6-2 shows a LAN that is typical of those in a **small office or a home office (SOHO)**. Typically, such LANs have fewer than a dozen or so computers and printers. Many businesses, of course, operate LANs that are much larger than this one. The principles are the same for a larger LAN, but the additional complexity is beyond the scope of this text.

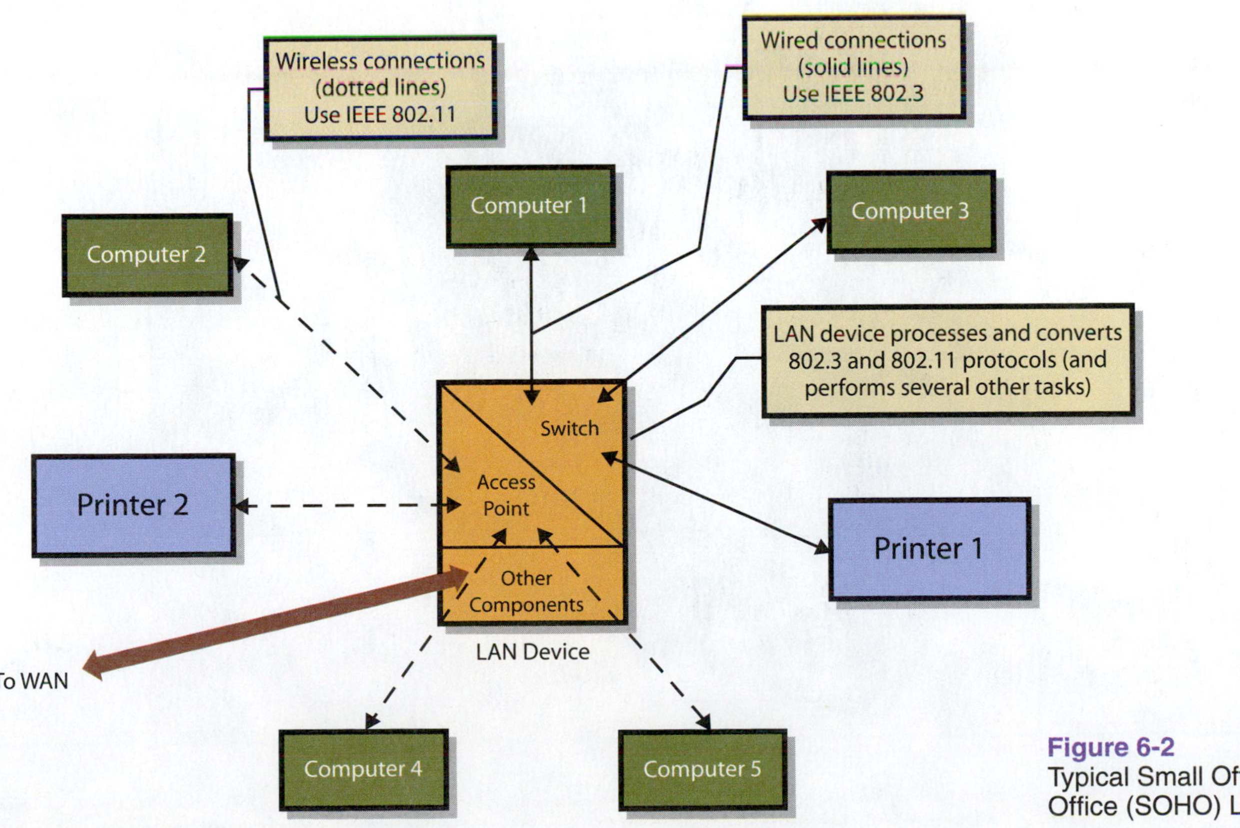

Figure 6-2
Typical Small Office/Home Office (SOHO) LAN

The computers and printers in Figure 6-2 communicate via a mixture of wired and wireless connections. Computers 1 and 3 and Printer 1 use wired connections; Computers 2, 4, and 5 as well as Printer 2 use wireless connections. The devices and protocols used differ for wired and wireless connectivity.

Wired Connectivity

Computers 1 and 3 and Printer 1 are connected to a **switch**, which is a special-purpose computer that receives and transmits wired traffic on the LAN. In Figure 6-2, the switch is contained within the box labeled "LAN Device." When Computer 1 or Computer 3 communicate with each other or with Printer 1, they do so by sending the traffic to the switch, which then redirects the traffic to the other computer or Printer 1.

The **LAN device** contains several important networking components. It has a switch, as just described; it also has a device for wireless communication, as you are about to learn. In most cases, it has devices for connecting to a WAN and via the WAN to the Internet and to numerous other elements (discussed in Q3). For SOHO applications, LAN devices are usually provided by the phone or cable provider. They have many different names, depending on their brand. The example device in Figure 6-3 is called a gateway. It was manufactured by the 2Wire Corporation and was provided to the user by Qwest.

Each wired computer or printer on the LAN has a **network interface card (NIC)**, which is a device that connects the computer's or printer's circuitry to the network cables. The NIC works with programs in each device to implement the protocols necessary for communication. Most computers today ship from the factory with an **onboard NIC**, which is a NIC built into the computer's circuitry.

The computers, printers, and switch on a wired LAN are connected using one of two wired media. Most LAN connections are made using **unshielded twisted pair (UTP) cable**. This cable contains sets of wires that are twisted together to improve signal quality. However, if the connection carries a lot of traffic, the UTP cable may

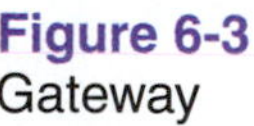

Figure 6-3
Gateway

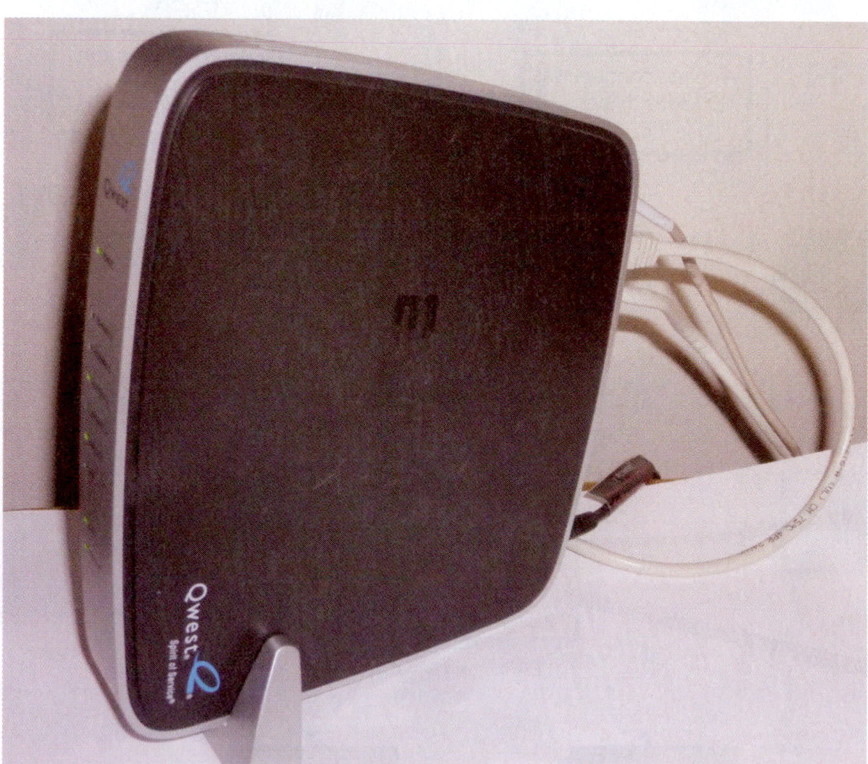

be replaced by **optical fiber cables**. The signals on such cables are light rays, and they are reflected inside the glass core of the optical fiber cable.

LANs that are larger than the one in Figure 6-2 use more than one switch. Typically, in a building with several floors a switch is placed on each floor, and the computers on that floor are connected to the switch with UTP cable. The switches on each floor connect to each other via the faster-speed optical cable.

Wireless Connections

In Figure 6-2, three of the computers and one printer are connected to the LAN using wireless technology. In the wireless computers and printer, a **wireless NIC (WNIC)** is used instead of a NIC. Today, nearly all personal computers ship from the factory with an onboard WNIC. (By the way, in almost all cases a NIC or WNIC can be added to a computer that does not have one.)

As shown in Figure 6-2, the WNIC devices connect to an **access point**, which is the component of the LAN device that processes wireless traffic and communicates with the wired switch. Thus, with this design every device on the LAN, whether wired or wireless, can communicate with every other device. Wireless devices communicate to each other via the access point. If wireless devices need to connect to a wired device, they do so via the access point, then to the switch, and then to the wired devices. Similarly, wired devices communicate to each other via the switch. If the wired devices need to connect to wireless ones, they do so via the switch, then to the access point, and then to the wireless devices.

LAN Protocols

For two devices to communicate, they must use the same protocol. The Institute for Electrical and Electronics Engineers (IEEE, pronounced "I triple E") sponsors committees that create and publish protocols and other standards. The committee that addresses LAN standards is called the *IEEE 802 Committee*. Thus, IEEE LAN protocols always start with the numbers 802.

The **IEEE 802.3 protocol** is used for wired LAN connections. This protocol standard, also called **Ethernet**, specifies hardware characteristics, such as which wires carry which signals. It also describes how messages are to be packaged and processed for wired transmission over the LAN.

The NIC in most personal computers today supports what is called **10/100/1000 Ethernet**. These products conform to the 802.3 specification and allow for transmission at a rate of 10, 100, or 1,000 Mbps (megabits per second). Switches detect the speed that a given device can handle and communicate with it at that speed. If you check computer listings at Dell, HP, Lenovo, and other manufacturers, you will see PCs advertised as having 10/100/1000 Ethernet.

By the way, the abbreviations used for communications speeds differ from those used for computer memory. For communications equipment, *k* stands for 1,000, not 1,024 as it does for memory. Similarly, *M* stands for 1,000,000, not 1,024 × 1,024; *G* stands for 1,000,000,000, not 1,024 × 1,024 × 1,024. Thus, 100 Mbps is 100,000,000 bits per second. Also, communications speeds are expressed in *bits*, whereas memory sizes are expressed in *bytes*.

Wireless LAN connections use the **IEEE 802.11 protocol**. Several versions of 802.11 exist, and as of 2010 the most popular is IEEE 802.11g. The differences among the variations are beyond the scope of this discussion. Just note that the current standard, 802.11g, allows speeds of up to 54 Mbps.

Observe that the LAN in Figure 6-2 uses both the 802.3 and 802.11 protocols. The NICs operate according to the 802.3 protocol and connect directly to the switch, which also operates on the 802.3 standard. The WNICs operate according to the 802.11

Type	Topology	Transmission Line	Transmission Speed	Equipment Used	Protocol Commonly Used	Remarks
Local area network	Local area network	UTP or optical fiber	10,100, or 1,000 Mbps	Switch NIC UTP or optical	IEEE 802.3 (Ethernet)	Switches connect devices, multiple switches on all but small LANs.
	Local area network with wireless	UTP or optical for non-wireless connections	Up to 54 Mbps	Wireless access point Wireless NIC	IEEE 802.11g	Access point transforms wired LAN (802.3) to wireless LAN (802.11).
Wide area network connections	DSL modem to ISP	DSL telephone	Upstream to 256 kbps Downstream to 1.544 Mbps	DSL modem DSL-capable telephone line	DSL	Can have computer and phone use simultaneously. Always connected.
	Cable modem to ISP	Cable TV lines to optical cable	Upstream to 256 kbps Downstream 300–600 kbps (10 Mbps in theory)	Cable modem Cable TV cable	Cable	Capacity is shared with other sites; performance varies depending on others' use.
	WAN wireless	Wireless connection to WAN	500 kbps to 1 Mbps	Wireless WAN modem	EVDO, HSDPA, WiMax	Sophisticated protocol enables several devices to use the same wireless frequency.

Figure 6-4
Summary of LAN and WAN Networks

protocol and connect to the wireless access point. The access point must process messages using both the 802.3 and 802.11 standards; it sends and receives wireless traffic using the 802.11 protocol and then communicates with the switch using the 802.3 protocol. Characteristics of LANs are summarized in the top two rows of Figure 6-4.

Bluetooth is another common wireless protocol. It is designed for transmitting data over short distances, replacing cables. Some devices, such as wireless mice and keyboards, use Bluetooth to connect to the computer. Cell phones use Bluetooth to connect to automobile entertainment systems.

FlexTime has a LAN that connects computer workstations to one another and to the server. The network also makes Internet connections using a DSL modem (defined on page 129). Desktop computers and some of the stationary workout equipment use wires and Ethernet. Laptops and some of the other workout equipment are wireless and use a version of IEEE 802.11. Some of the devices used by clients at FlexTime, such as Felix's talking shoes, connect using Bluetooth.

Q3 What Are the Alternatives for Connecting to a WAN?

A WAN connects computers located at physically separated sites. A company with offices in Detroit and Atlanta uses a WAN to connect the offices' computers together. Because the sites are physically separated, the company cannot string wire from one site to another. Rather, it must obtain connection capabilities from another company (or companies) licensed by the government to provide communications.

Although you may not have realized it, when you connect your personal computer, iPhone, iPad, or Kindle to the Internet you are connecting to a WAN. You are connecting to computers owned and operated by an **Internet service provider (ISP)** that are not physically located at your site.

An ISP has three important functions. First, it provides you with a legitimate Internet address. Second, it serves as your gateway to the Internet. The ISP receives the communications from your computer and passes them on to the Internet, and it receives communications from the Internet and passes them on to you. Finally, ISPs pay for the Internet. They collect money from their customers and pay access fees and other charges on your behalf.

Many employees use computers to send and receive personal emails at work. Is this ethical? We consider this question in the Ethics Guide on pages 144–145.

Figure 6-4 shows the three common WAN alternatives for connecting to the Internet. Notice that we are discussing how your computer connects to a WAN; we are not discussing the structure of the WAN itself. WAN architectures and their protocols are beyond the scope of this discussion. Search the Web for *leased lines* or *PSDN* if you want to learn more about WAN architectures.

SOHO LANs (like that in Figure 6-2) and individual home and office computers are commonly connected to an ISP in one of three ways: a special telephone line called a DSL line, a cable TV line, or a cell-phone-like connection. All three of these alternatives require that the *digital data* in the computer be converted to a wavy, or **analog**, signal. A device called a **modem**, or *modulator/demodulator,* performs this conversion. Figure 6-5 shows one way of converting the digital byte 01000001 to an analog signal.

(By the way, because LAN devices like the one shown in Figure 6-3 almost always contain a modem, they are sometimes called *modems.* As you have learned, however, they contain much more than just a modem, so we do not use that term in this text.)

As shown in Figure 6-6, once the modem converts your computer's digital data to analog, that analog signal is then sent over the telephone line, TV cable, or air. If sent by telephone line, the first telephone switch that your signal reaches converts the signal into the form used by the international telephone system.

DSL Modems

DSL stands for **digital subscriber line. DSL modems** operate on the same lines as voice telephones, but their signals do not interfere with voice telephone service. Because DSL signals do not interfere with telephone signals, DSL data transmission and telephone conversations can occur simultaneously. A device at the telephone company separates the phone signals from the computer signals and sends the latter signal to the ISP. DSL modems use their own protocols for data transmission.

There are gradations of DSL service and speed. Most home DSL lines can download data at speeds ranging from 256 kbps to 6.544 Mbps and can upload data at slower speeds—for example, 512 kbps. DSL lines that have different upload and download speeds are called **asymmetric digital subscriber lines (ADSL)**. Most homes and small businesses can use ADSL because they receive more data than they transmit (e.g., pictures in news stories), and hence they do not need to transmit as fast as they receive.

Some users and larger businesses, however, need DSL lines that have the same receiving and transmitting speeds. They also need performance-level guarantees. **Symmetrical digital subscriber lines (SDSL)** meet this need by offering the same fast speed in both directions.

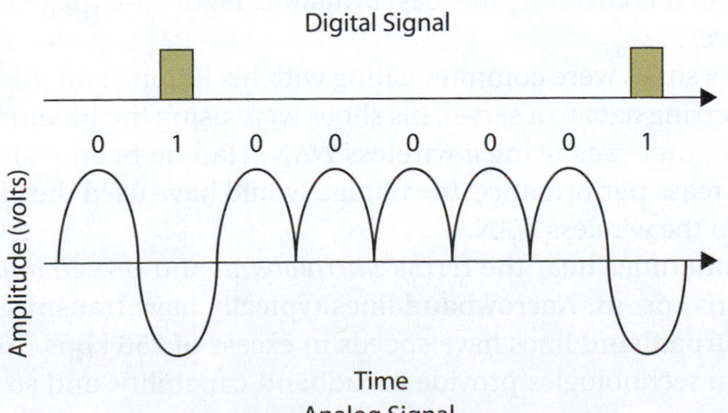

Figure 6-5
Analog Versus Digital Signals

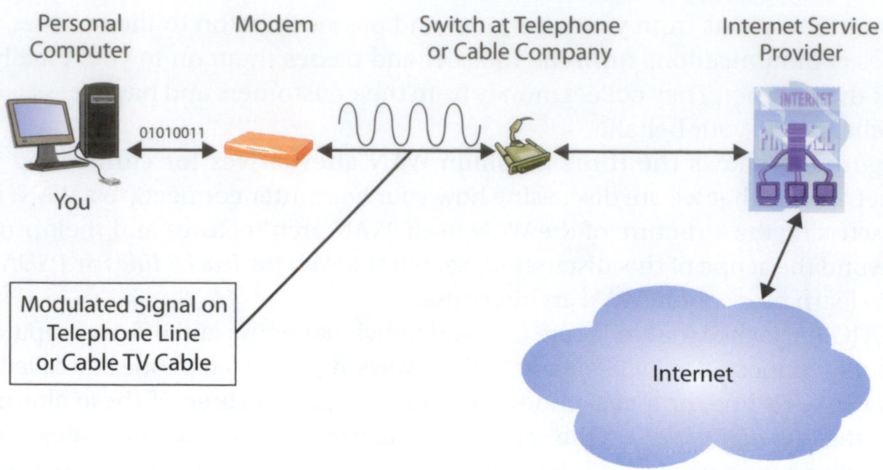

Figure 6-6
DSL and Cable Internet Access

Cable Modems

Cable modems provide high-speed data transmission using cable television lines. The cable company installs a fast, high-capacity optical fiber cable to a distribution center in each neighborhood that it serves. At the distribution center, the optical fiber cable connects to regular cable-television cables that run to subscribers' homes or businesses. Cable modems modulate in such a way that their signals do not interfere with TV signals.

Because up to 500 user sites can share these facilities, performance varies depending on how many other users are sending and receiving data. At the maximum, users can download data up to 50 Mbps and can upload data at 512 kbps. Typically, performance is much slower than this. In most cases, the speed of cable modems and DSL modems is about the same. Cable modems use their own protocols.

WAN Wireless Connection

Another way that you can connect your computer, iPhone, Kindle, iPad or other communicating device to the Internet is via a **WAN wireless** connection. Amazon's Kindle, for example, uses a Sprint wireless network to provide wireless data connections. The iPhone uses a LAN-based wireless network if one is available and a WAN wireless network if one is not. The LAN-based network is preferred, because performance is considerably higher. As of 2010, WAN wireless provides average performance of 500 kbps, with peaks of up to 1.7 Mbps, as opposed to the typical 50 Mbps for LAN wireless.

A variety of WAN wireless protocols exist. Sprint and Verizon use a protocol called **EVDO**; AT&T, which supports the iPhone, and T-Mobile use one called **HSDPA**. Another protocol, **WiMax**, has been implemented by Clearwire and is available on Sprint's XOHM network (see Case 6 on page 150). The meaning of these acronyms and their particulars are unimportant to us; just realize that a marketing and technology battle is underway for WAN wireless. WiMax has the greatest potential for speed, but it is currently the least available. Figure 6-4 (page 128) summarizes these alternatives.

We have appliances that communicate with each other, but is this always a good thing, or even necessary? See the Guide on pages 146–147 for a discussion of the interpretation of exponential phenomena.

When Felix's shoes were communicating with his iPhone and the iPhone application was transferring data to a server, his shoes were using the Bluetooth wireless protocol and the iPhone was using a wireless WAN. Had he been inside the FlexTime building, to increase performance, the iPhone would have used the FlexTime wireless LAN rather than the wireless WAN.

You will sometimes hear the terms *narrowband* and *broadband* with regard to communications speeds. **Narrowband** lines typically have transmission speeds less than 56 kbps. **Broadband** lines have speeds in excess of 256 kbps. Today, all popular communication technologies provide broadband capability, and so these terms are likely to fade from use.

Q4 What Are the Fundamental Concepts You Should Know About the Internet?

As discussed in Q1, the Internet is an *internet*, meaning that it is a network of networks. As you might guess, the technology that underlies the Internet is complicated and beyond the scope of this text. However, because of the popularity of the Internet, certain terms have become ubiquitous in twenty-first-century business society. In this question, we will define and explain terms that you need to know to be an informed business professional and consumer of Internet services.

An Internet Example

Figure 6-7 illustrates one use of the Internet. Suppose that you are sitting in snow-bound Minneapolis and you want to communicate with a hotel in sunny, tropical, northern New Zealand. Maybe you are making a reservation using the hotel's Web site, or maybe you are sending an email to a reservation clerk inquiring about facilities or services.

To begin, note that this example is an internet because it is a network of networks. It consists of two LANs (yours and the hotel's) and four WANs. (In truth, the real Internet consists of tens of thousands of WANs and LANs, but to conserve paper we don't show all of them here.)

Your communication to the hotel involves nearly unimaginable complexity. Somehow, your computer communicates with a server in the New Zealand hotel, a computer that it has never "met" before and knows nothing about. Further, your transmission, which is too big to travel in one piece, is broken up into parts and each part passed along from WAN to WAN in such a way that it arrives intact. Then your original message is reassembled, any parts that were lost or damaged (this happens) are resent, and the reconstructed message is delivered to the server for processing. All

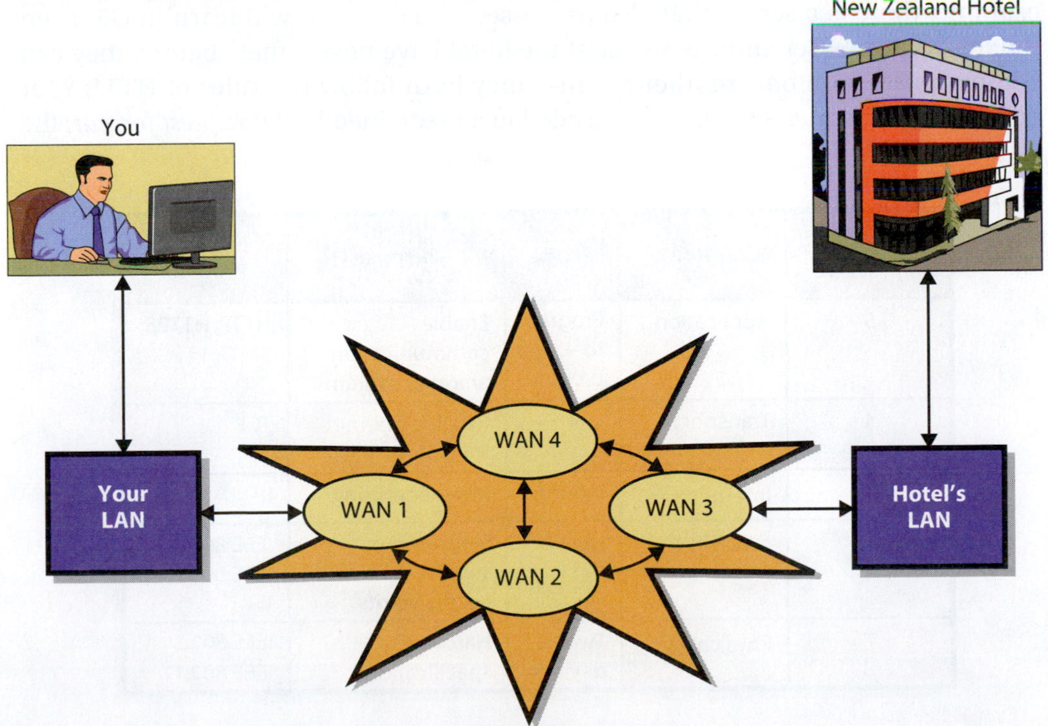

Figure 6-7
Using the Internet for a Hotel Reservation

of this is accomplished by computers and data communications devices that most likely have not interacted before.

What all these devices do know, however, is that they process the same set of protocols. Thus, we need to begin with Internet protocols.

The TCP/IP Protocol Architecture

The protocols used on the Internet are arranged according to a structure known as the **TCP/IP Protocol (TCP/IP) architecture**, which is a scheme of five protocol types arranged in layers. As shown in Figure 6-8, the top layer concerns protocols for applications such as browsers and Web servers. The next two layers concern protocols about data communications across any internet (note the small *i*; this means any network of networks), including the Internet. The bottom two layers involve protocols that concern data transmission within a network. For example, the IEEE 802.3 and 802.11 LAN protocols operate at the bottom two layers.

As stated, a protocol is a set of rules and data structures for organizing communication. One or more protocols is defined at each layer. Data communications and software vendors write computer programs that implement the rules of a particular protocol. (For protocols at the bottom layer, the physical layer, they build hardware devices that implement the protocol.)

You are probably wondering, "Why should I know about this?" The reason for knowing about this is to understand terms you will hear and products you will use, buy, or possibly invest in that relate to each other via this architecture.

Application Layer Protocols

You will directly encounter at least three application layer protocols in your professional life. (In fact, you have used two of them already). **Hypertext Transport Protocol (HTTP)** is the protocol used between browsers and Web servers. When you use a browser such as Internet Explorer, Firefox, Safari, or Chrome, you are using a program that implements the HTTP protocol. At the other end, at the New Zealand Hotel for example, there is a server that also processes HTTP, as you will learn in Q5. Even though your browser and the server at the hotel have never "met" before, they can communicate with one another because they both follow the rules of HTTP. Your browser sends requests for service encoded in a predefined HTTP *request format;* the

Figure 6-8
TCP/IP Protocol Architecture

Layer	Name	Scope	Purpose	Example Protocol
5	Application	Program to program	Enable communication among programs	HTTP; HTTPS; SMTP; FTP
4	Transport	internets	Reliable internet transport	TCP
3	Internet	internets	internet routing	IP
2	Data Link	Network	Flow among switches and access points	IEEE 802.3 IEEE 802.11
1	Physical	Two devices	Hardware specifications	IEEE 802.3 IEEE 802.11

server receives that request, does something, and formats a response in a predefined HTTP *response format.*

As you will learn in Chapter 12, there is a secure version of HTTP called **HTTPS**. Whenever you see *https* in your browser's address bar, you have a secure transmission, and you can safely send sensitive data such as credit card numbers. However, when you are on the Internet, unless you see *https* in the address bar, you should assume that all of your communication is open and could be published on the front page of your campus newspaper tomorrow morning.

Hence, when you are using HTTP, email, text messaging, chat, videoconferencing, or anything other than HTTPS, know that whatever you are typing or saying could be known by anyone else. In your classroom, when you send a text message to a fellow student that message can be intercepted and read by anyone in your class, including your professor. The same is true of people at a coffee shop, an airport, or anywhere else.

Two additional TCP/IP application layer protocols are common. **SMTP**, or **Simple Mail Transfer Protocol**, is used for email transmissions (along with other protocols as well). And **FTP**, or **File Transfer Protocol**, is used to move files over the Internet. One very common use for FTP is to maintain Web sites. When a Web site administrator wishes to post a new picture or story on a Web server, the administrator will often use FTP to move the picture or other item to the server. Like HTTP, FTP has a secure version as well, but do not assume you are using it.

With this knowledge, we can clear up one common misconception. You are using the Internet when you use any of these protocols. However, you are using the Web only when you use either HTTP or HTTPS. Thus, the **Web** is the Internet-based network of browsers and servers that process HTTP or HTTPS. When you use FTP or SMTP, you are using the Internet, but not the Web.

TCP and IP Protocols

You have some idea of the protocols used at the application (top) layer in Figure 6-8, and from the discussion in Q2 you have some idea of the LAN protocols used at the bottom two layers. But what is the purpose of the layers in between, the transport and internet layers? You know these two layers must be important because the architecture is named after their protocols.

These protocols manage traffic as it passes across an internet (including the Internet) from one network to another. The most important protocol in the transport layer is **TCP**, or **Transmission Control Protocol**. As a transport protocol, TCP has many functions, most of which are beyond the scope of our discussion. One easily understood function, however, is that TCP programs break your traffic up into pieces and send each piece along its way. It then works with TCP programs on other devices on the internet to ensure that all of the pieces arrive at their destination. If one or more pieces is lost or damaged, TCP programs detect that condition and cause retransmission of that piece. Hence, the TCP layer is said to provide *reliable internet transport.*

The primary protocol of the internet layer is the **IP (Internet Protocol)**, which is a protocol that specifies the routing of the pieces of your data communication through the networks that comprise any internet (including the Internet). In Figure 6-7, programs on devices at each of the networks (the two LANs and the four WANs) receive a portion of your message and route it to another computer in its network, or to another network altogether. A **packet** is a piece of a message that is handled by programs that implement IP. A **router** is a special purpose computer that moves packet traffic according to the rules of IP.

Your message is broken into packets (for simplicity, we're leaving a LOT out here), and each packet is sent out onto the internet. The packet contains the address of where it is supposed to go. Routers along the way receive the packet, examine the destination IP address, and send it either to the desired destination, or to another router that is closer to the desired destination.

When your message starts on its way to the New Zealand hotel, no device knows what route the pieces will take. Until the last hop, a router just sends the packet to another router that it determines to be closer to the final destination. In fact, the packets that make up your message may take different pathways through the Internet (this is rare, but it does occur). Because of this routing scheme, the Internet is very robust. In Figure 6-7, for example, either WAN 2 or WAN 4 could fail and your packets will still get to the hotel.

To summarize, TCP provides reliable internet transport and IP provides internet routing.

IP Addressing

An **IP address** is a number that identifies a particular device. **Public IP addresses** identify a particular device on the public Internet. Because public IP addresses must be unique, worldwide, their assignment is controlled by a public agency known as **ICANN (Internet Corporation for Assigned Names and Numbers)**.

Private IP addresses identify a particular device on a private network, usually on a LAN. Their assignment is controlled within the LAN, usually by the device labeled "LAN Device" in Figure 6-2. When you sign on to a LAN at a coffee shop, for example, the LAN device loans you a private IP address to use while you are connected to the LAN. When you leave the LAN, it reuses that address.

Use of Private IP Addresses

When your computer uses TCP/IP within a LAN, say to access a private Web server within the LAN, it uses a private IP address. However, and this is far more common, when you access a public site, say *www.LearningMIS.com*, from within the LAN, your traffic uses your internal IP address until it gets to the LAN device. At that point, the LAN device substitutes your private IP address for its public IP address and sends your traffic out onto the Internet.

This private/public IP address scheme has two major benefits. First, public IP addresses are conserved. All of the computers on the LAN use only one public IP address. Second, by using private IP addresses, you need not register a public IP address for your computer with ICANN-approved agencies. Furthermore, if you had a public IP address for your computer, every time you moved it, say from home to school, the Internet would have to update its addressing mechanisms to route traffic to your new location. Such updating would be a massive burden (and a mess)!

Public IP Addresses and Domain Names

IP addresses have two formats. The most common format, called **IPv4**, has a four-decimal dotted notation like 165.193.123.253; the second, called **IPv6**, has a longer format and will not concern us here. In your browser, if you enter *http://165.193.123.253*, your browser will connect with the device on the public Internet that has been assigned to this address. Try it to find out who has this address.

Nobody wants to type IP addresses like *http://165.193.123.253* to find a particular site. Instead, we want to enter names like *www.Pandora.com* or *www.Woot.com* or *www.MyMISTutor.com*. To facilitate that desire, ICANN administers a system for assigning names to IP addresses. First, a **domain name** is a unique name that is affiliated with a public IP address. When an organization or individual wants to register a domain

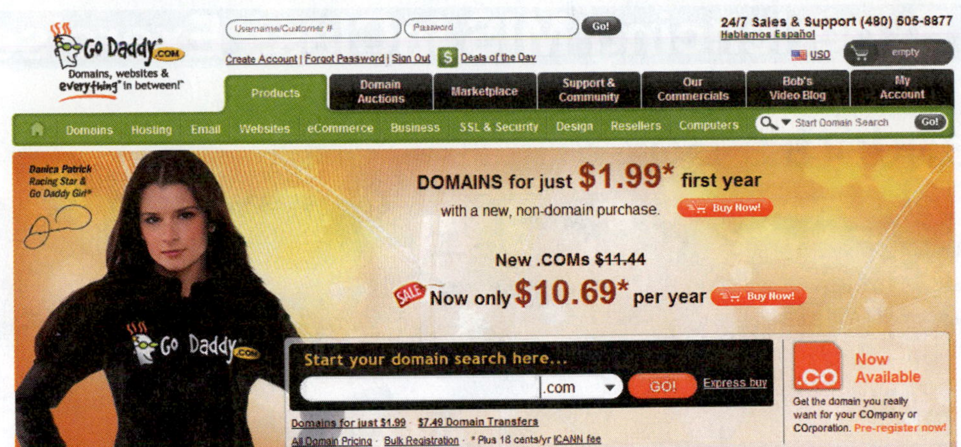

Figure 6-9
GoDaddy.com Welcome Page

Source:

name, it goes to a company that applies to an ICANN-approved agency to do so. An example of a company that registers domain names with ICANN is GoDaddy.com (*www.GoDaddy.com*; Figure 6-9).

GoDaddy.com (or other, similar company) will first determine if the desired name is unique, worldwide. If so, then it will apply to register that name to the applicant. Once the registration is completed, the applicant can affiliate a public IP address with the domain name. From that point onward, traffic for the new domain name will be routed to the affiliated IP address.

Note two important points: First, several (or many) domain names can point to the same IP address. Right now, *www.MyMISProf.com* and *www.MyMISTutor.com* both point to the same public IP address. Second, the affiliation of domain names with IP addresses is dynamic. The owner of the domain name can change the affiliated IP addresses at its discretion.

Before we leave the Internet, you need to know one more term. A **URL (Uniform Resource Locator)** is an address on the Internet. Commonly, it consists of a protocol (like *http://* or *http://*) followed by a domain name or public IP address. A URL is actually quite a bit more complicated than this description, but that detailed knowledge won't get you a good date, so we'll hurry along. The preferred pronunciation of URL is the sound of the letters U, R, L.

Q5 What Happens on a Typical Web Server?

In this question, we will apply the knowledge of this chapter to investigate what happens on a typical Web server. We will use the example of a Web storefront, which is a server on the Web from which you can buy products. Web storefronts are one type of e-commerce, which we'll discuss in Chapter 8. Here, just consider the Web storefront as an example Web server.

Suppose you want to buy climbing equipment from REI, a co-op that sells outdoor clothing and equipment. To do so, you go to *www.REI.com* and navigate to the product(s) that you want to buy (see Figure 6-10, page 137). When you find something you want, you add it to your shopping cart and keep shopping. At some point, you check out by supplying your credit card data.

In Q4, we discussed how your traffic crosses over the Internet to arrive at the REI server. The next question is: What happens at that server when it arrives? Or, from another perspective, if you want to set up a Web storefront for your company, what facilities do you need?

Experiencing MIS InClass Exercise 6

Opening Pandora's Box

Nearly free data communications and data storage have created unprecedented opportunities for businesses, as we have described numerous times. Inevitably, such technology will have a revolutionary impact in the home as well. The Guide on pages 146–147 discusses why you should be wary of toasters and microwaves that talk to each other, but home entertainment is another matter.

Sonos is a good example of a company leveraging technology to provide entertainment. Sonos uses emerging technologies, especially wireless technologies, to develop easily installed, high-quality wireless audio systems. Customers hook one of several different Sonos devices into their home LAN device using a wired Ethernet connection. That device then connects wirelessly to up to 32 other Sonos audio devices around the home. Each device can play its own music or other audio, all independently; some can play the same program; or all can be forced to play the same audio program.

Some Sonos devices provide wireless audio to existing stereo systems. Others provide the wireless receiver and an amplifier, with the customer providing the speakers. Still other Sonos devices package the wireless receiver, an amplifier, and the speakers into one unit.

Each Sonos device includes a small computer running Linux. Those computers communicate wirelessly using a proprietary Sonos protocol. Because every device communicates with every other device, Sonos refers to its network of equipment as a *wireless mesh*. The benefit of this mesh to the consumer is flexibility and ease of installation. The devices find each other and determine their own data communications pathways (akin to, but different from, IP routing on the Internet).

Sonos works with any Internet radio source and with music services such as Pandora (*www.Pandora.com*). With Pandora (and similar services), you establish a personal radio station by selecting a favorite song or musical work. Pandora then plays music based on your selection. You can vote thumbs up or thumbs down on music that is played. Based on your ratings and a proprietary algorithm, Pandora then selects additional music you may like.

Form a group of students and answer the following questions.

1. Imagine that you have graduated, have the job of your dreams, and want to install a wireless stereo system in your new condo. Assume that the spare bedroom that you use as an office has a LAN device connected to the Internet. You have an existing stereo system in your living room, a pair of unused speakers, but no other stereo equipment. Assume you want to play audio and music in your office, your living room, and your bedroom.
   a. Go to *www.Sonos.com* and select and price the equipment you will need.
   b. Go to Sonos' competitors at *www.LogitechSqueezeBox.com* and *http://Soundbridge.Roku.com* and select and price equipment you will need.
   c. Recommend one of the selections you identified in your answers to parts a and b and justify your selection.
   d. Report your findings to the rest of the class.
2. Visit *www.Pandora.com*. Using the free trial membership, build a radio station for your group. Base your station on whatever song or music your group chooses.
3. The Sonos equipment does not have an on-off switch. Apparently it is designed to be permanently on, like your LAN device. You can mute each station, but to turn a station off, you must unplug it, an action few people take. Suppose you have tuned a Sonos device to a Pandora station, and you mute that device. Because the Sonos equipment is still on, it will continue downloading packets over the Internet to a device that no one is listening to.
   a. Describe the consequences of this situation on the Internet.
   b. You pay a flat fee for your Internet connection. In what ways does such a fee arrangement discourage efficiency?
   c. It turns out that if you pause the music, rather than mute the device, the Sonos device will stop downloading packets. Do you think this design is appropriate? If not, how would you change it?
4. Using your group's imagination and curiosity, describe the consequences of Internet-based audio on:
   a. Existing radio stations
   b. Vendors of traditional audio receivers
   c. Audio entertainment
   d. Cisco (a vendor of Internet routers)
   e. Your local ISP
   f. Any other companies or entities you believe will be impacted by wireless audio systems

5. Report your conclusions to the rest of the class.
6. Using history as a guide, we can assume that audio leads the way for video.
   a. Explain how you could use a wireless video system in your new condo.
   b. In the opinion of your group, is having multiple wireless video players in your condo more or less desirable than wireless audio? Explain your response.
   c. Answer parts a through f in step 4, but use wireless video rather than audio as the driving factor. Report your answers to the rest of the class.
7. Considering all of your answers to steps 1 through 5:
   a. What industries are the winners and losers?
   b. What companies are the winners and losers?
   c. How does your answer to parts a and b guide your job search?
8. Use the knowledge you have gained in answering steps 1 through 6 to prepare a 1-minute statement that you could make in a job interview about the emerging opportunities in Internet-based audio and video. Assume that with this statement you want to demonstrate your ability to think innovatively. Deliver your statement to the rest of the class.

Three-Tier Architecture

Almost all e-commerce applications use the **three-tier architecture**, which is an arrangement of user computers and servers into three categories, or tiers, as shown in Figure 6-11. The **user tier** consists of computers, phones, and other devices that have browsers that request and process Web pages. The **server tier** consists of computers that run Web servers and process application programs. The **database tier** consists of computers that run a DBMS that processes SQL requests to retrieve and store data. Figure 6-11 shows only one computer at the database tier. Some sites have multicomputer database tiers as well.

When you enter *http://www.REI.com* in your browser, the browser sends a request that travels over the Internet to a computer in the server tier at the REI site. That request is formatted and processed according to the rules of HTTP. (Notice, by the

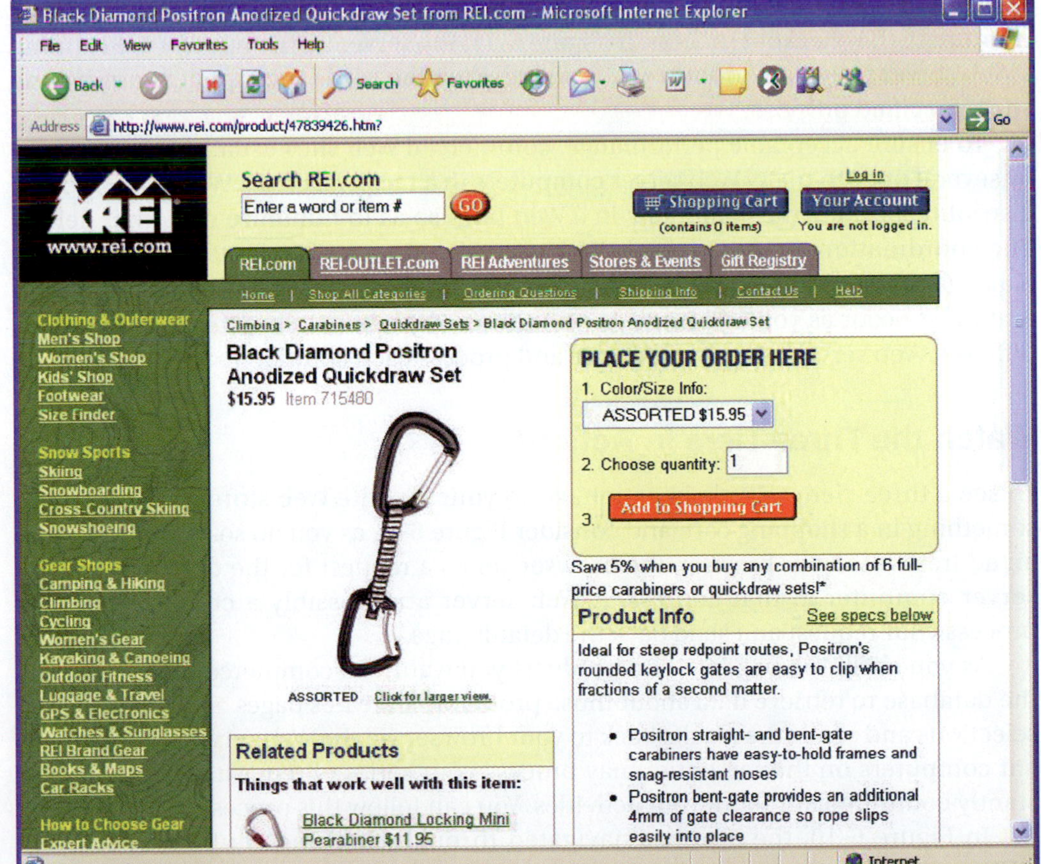

Figure 6-10
Sample of Commerce Server Pages: Product Offer Page

Source: Used with permission of REI and Black Diamond.

Figure 6-11
Three-Tier Architecture

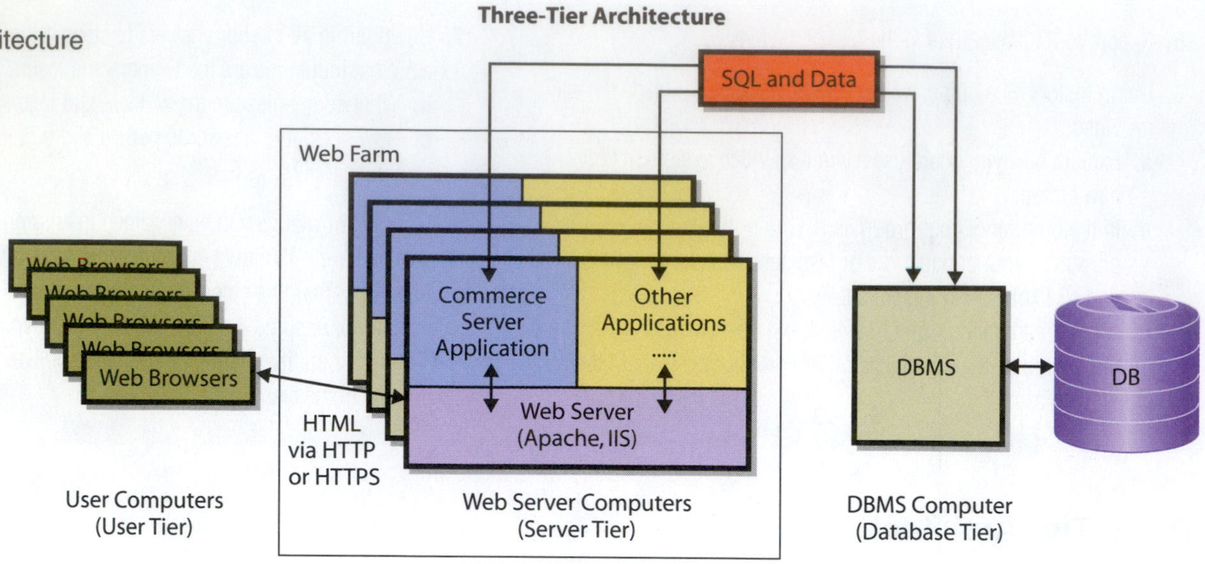

way, that if you just type *www.REI.com*, your browser will add the *http://* to signify that it is using HTTP.) In response to your request, a server tier computer sends back a **Web page**, which is a document that is coded in one of the standard page markup languages. The most popular page markup language is the *Hypertext Markup Language (HTML)*, which is described later in this section.

Web servers are programs that run on a server tier computer and that manage HTTP traffic by sending and receiving Web pages to and from clients. A **commerce server** is an application program that runs on a server tier computer. A commerce server receives requests from users via the Web server, takes some action, and returns a response to the users via the Web server. Typical commerce server functions are to obtain product data from a database, manage the items in a shopping cart, and coordinate the checkout process. In Figure 6-11, the server tier computers are running a Web server program, a commerce server application, and other applications having an unspecified purpose.

To ensure acceptable performance, commercial Web sites usually are supported by several or even many Web server computers in a facility called a **Web farm**. Work is distributed among the computers in a Web farm so as to minimize customer delays. The coordination among multiple Web server computers is a fantastic dance, but, alas, we do not have space to tell that story here. Just imagine the coordination that must occur as you add items to an online order when, to improve performance, different Web server computers receive and process each addition to your order.

Watch the Three Tiers in Action!

To see a three-tier example in action, go to your favorite Web storefront site, place something in a shopping cart, and consider Figure 6-11 as you do so. When you enter an address into your browser, the browser sends a request for the default page to a server computer at that address. A Web server and possibly a commerce server process your request and send back the default page.

As you click Web pages to find products you want, the commerce server accesses the database to retrieve data about those products. It creates pages according to your selections and sends the results back to your browser via the Web server. Again, different computers on the server tier may process your series of requests and must constantly communicate about your activities. You can follow this process in Figure 6-11.

In Figure 6-10, the user has navigated through climbing equipment at *www.REI.com* to find a particular item. To produce this page, the commerce server accessed

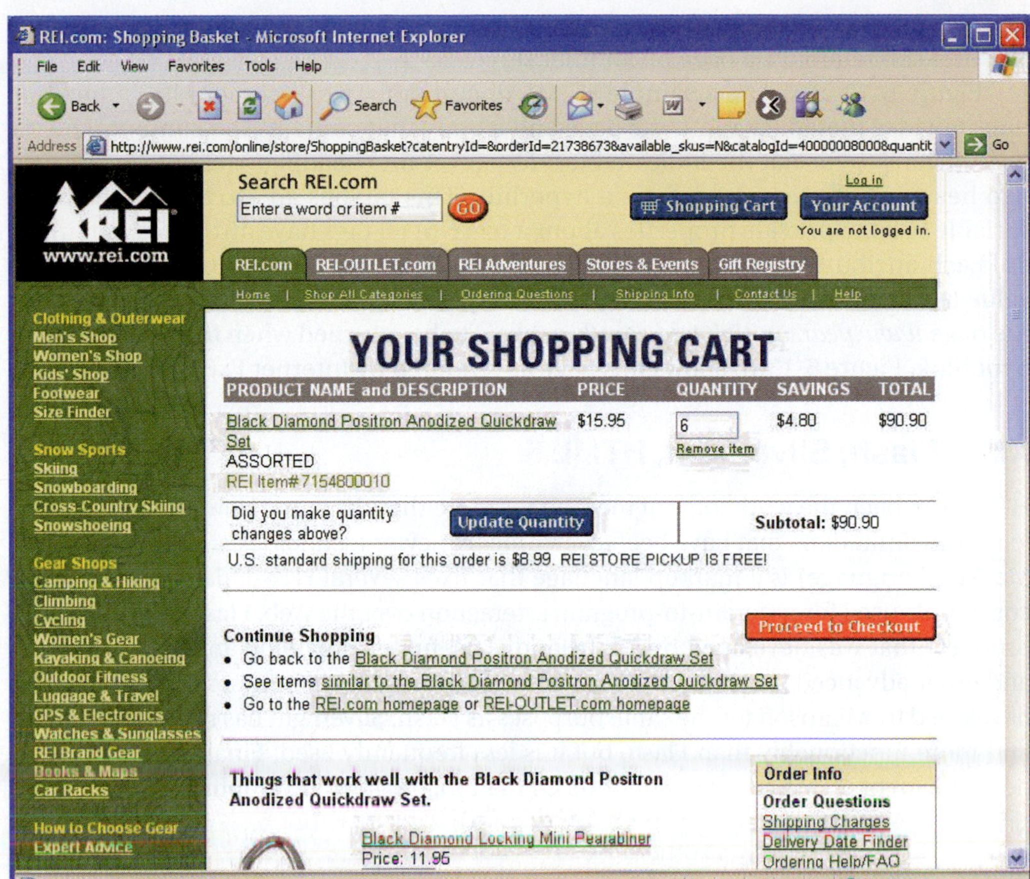

Figure 6-12
Shopping-Cart Page

Source: Used with permission of REI.

a database to obtain the product picture, price, special terms (a 5% discount for buying six or more), product information, and related products.

The user placed six items in her basket, and you can see the response in Figure 6-12. Again, trace the action in Figure 6-11 and imagine what occurred to produce the second page. Notice that the discount was applied correctly.

When the customer checks out, the commerce server program will be called to process payment, schedule inventory processing, and arrange for shipping. Most likely the commerce server interfaces with enterprise applications like those you will learn about in Chapter 7. Truly this is an amazing capability!

Hypertext Markup Language (HTML)

Hypertext Markup Language (HTML) is the most common language for defining the structure and layout of Web pages. An HTML **tag** is a notation used to define a data element for display or other purposes. The following HTML is a typical heading tag:

```
<h2>Price of Item</h2>
```

Notice that tags are enclosed in < > (called *angle brackets*) and that they occur in pairs. The start of this tag is indicated by <h2>, and the end of the tag is indicated by</h2>. The words between the tags are the value of the tag. This HTML tag means to place the words "Price of Item" on a Web page in the style of a level-two heading. The creator of the Web page will define the style (font size, color, and so forth) for h2 headings and the other tags to be used.

Web pages include **hyperlinks**, which are pointers to other Web pages. A hyperlink contains the URL of the Web page to find when the user clicks the hyperlink. The

URL can reference a page on the server that generated the page containing the hyperlink or it can reference a page on another server.

Figure 6-13(a) shows a sample HTML document. The document has a heading that provides metadata about the page and a body that contains the content. The tag <h1> means to format the indicated text as a level-one heading; <h2> means a level-two heading. The tag <a> defines a hyperlink. This tag has an **attribute**, which is a variable used to provide properties about a tag. Not all tags have attributes, but many do. Each attribute has a standard name. The attribute for a hyperlink is *href*, and its value indicates which Web page is to be displayed when the user clicks the link. Here, the page *www.pearsonhighered.com/kroenke* is to be returned when the user clicks the hyperlink. Figure 6-13(b) shows this page as rendered by Internet Explorer.

XML, Flash, Silverlight, HTML 5

HTML has been the workhorse of the Web for more than 15 years. However, it has problems and limitations that have been overcome by newer technologies. **XML (eXtensible Markup Language)** is a markup language that fixes several HTML deficiencies and is commonly used for program-to-program interaction over the Web. **Flash** is an add-on to browsers that was developed by Adobe and is useful for providing animation, movies, and other advanced graphics inside a browser. **Silverlight** is a browser add-on that was developed by Microsoft for the same purposes as Flash. Silverlight has newer technology and more functionality than Flash, but it is less frequently used. Finally, HTML 5.0 is a new version of HTML that also supports animation, movies, and graphics.

See "Service-Oriented Architecture" in Chapter Extension 18

Figure 6-13a
Sample HTML Code Snippet

```
<title>UMIS Example HTML</title>
<style type="text/css">
.style1 {
    font-size: xx-large;
    text-align: center;
    font-family: Arial, Helvetica, sans-serif;
}
.style2 {
    color: #FF00FF;
}
.style3 {
    font-size: medium;
    text-align: center;
    font-family: Arial, Helvetica, sans-serif;
}
.style5 {
    font-size: medium;
    text-align: left;
    font-family: Arial, Helvetica, sans-serif;
}
</style>
</head>

<body>

<p class="style1">
    <span class="style2"><strong>Using</strong></span>
    <strong>MIS</strong></p>
<p class="style1"> </p>
<p class="style3"><em>Fourth Edition</em></p>
<p class="style3"> </p>
<p class="style5">Example HTML Document</p>
<p class="style5"> </p>
<p class="style5"> </p>
<p class="style5">Click <a href="http://www.PearsonHigherEd.com/kroenke">here</a>
for the textbook&#39;s web site at Pearson Education.</p>

</body>
```

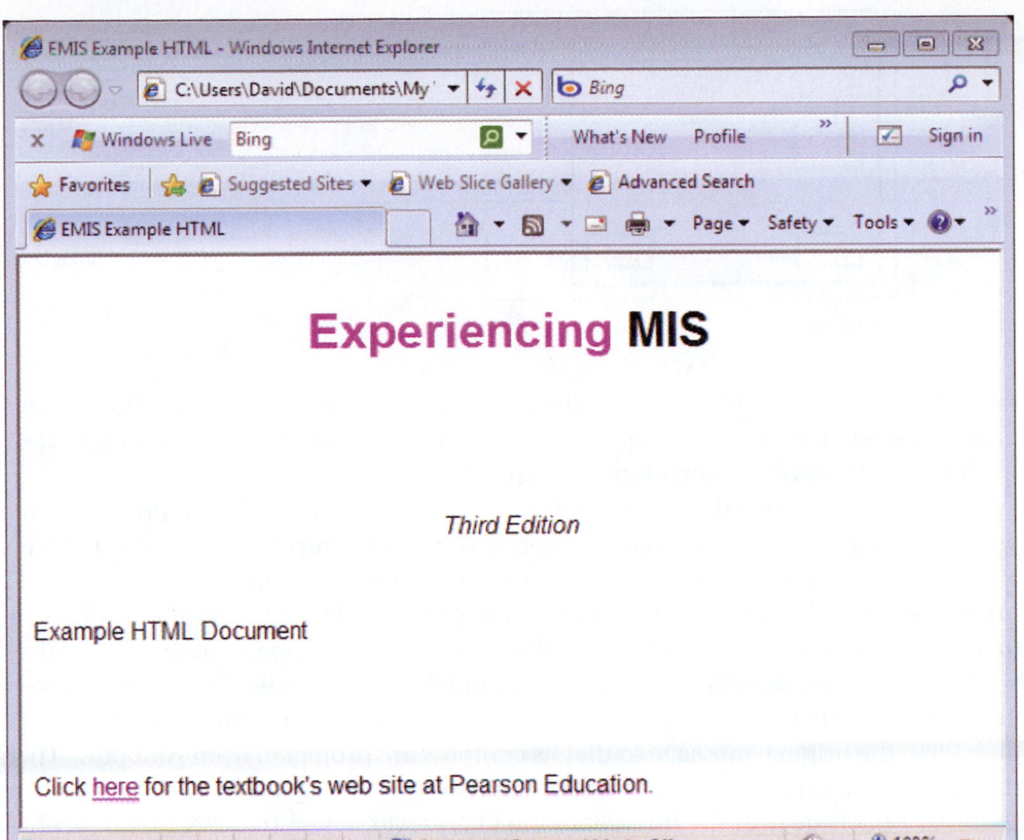

Figure 6-13b
Document Created from HTML Code in Figure 6-13a

Source: Microsoft product screenshot reprinted with permission from Microsoft Corporation.

Almost all experts agree that XML will continue to be most the most important language for interprogram communication on the Web. Some experts think that HTML 5.0 will replace standard HTML and Flash, and possibly Silverlight as well.

Q6 How Do Organizations Benefit from VPNs?

A **virtual private network (VPN)** uses the Internet to create the appearance of private point-to-point connections. In the IT world, the term *virtual* means something that appears to exist that does not in fact exist. Here, a VPN uses the public Internet to create the appearance of a private connection.

A Typical VPN

Figure 6-14 shows one way to create a VPN to connect a remote computer, perhaps an employee working at a hotel in Miami, to a LAN at a Chicago site. The remote user is

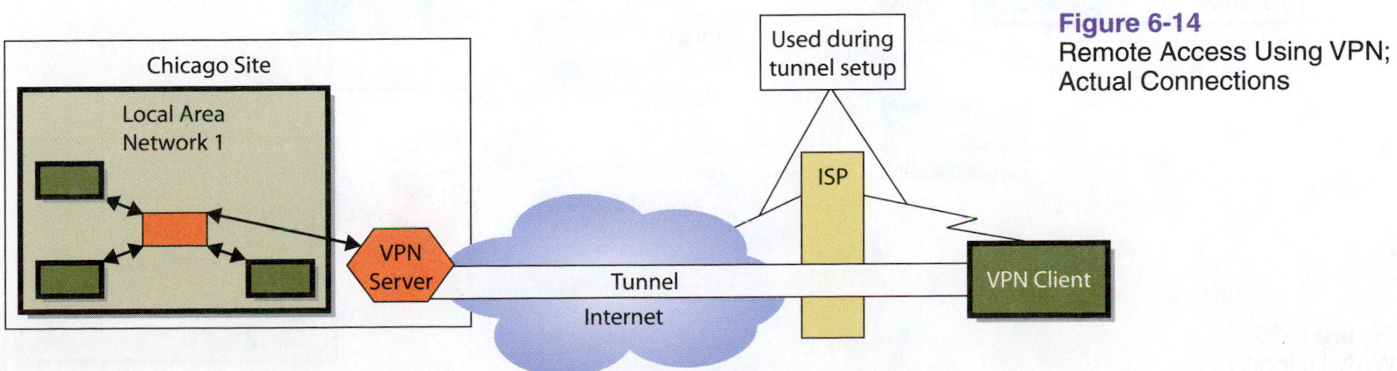

Figure 6-14
Remote Access Using VPN; Actual Connections

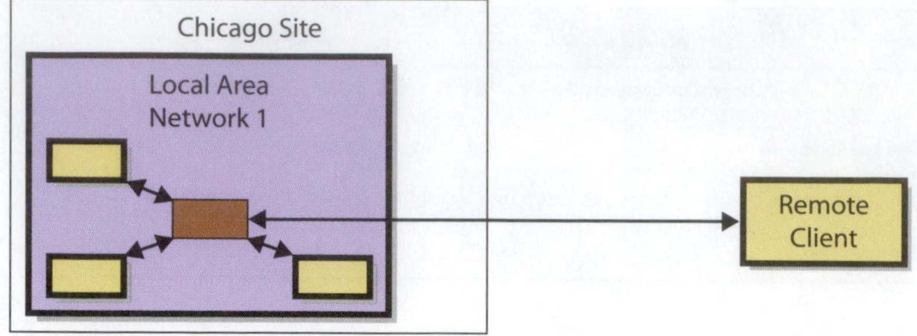

Figure 6-15
Remote Access Using VPN; Apparent Connection

the VPN client. That client first establishes a connection to the Internet. The connection can be obtained by accessing a local ISP, as shown in the figure; or, in some hotels, the hotel itself provides a direct Internet connection.

In either case, once the Internet connection is made VPN software on the remote user's computer establishes a connection with the VPN server in Chicago. The VPN client and VPN server then have a point-to-point connection. That connection, called a **tunnel**, is a virtual, private pathway over a public or shared network from the VPN client to the VPN server. Figure 6-15 illustrates the connection as it appears to the remote user.

VPN communications are secure, even though they are transmitted over the public Internet. To ensure security, VPN client software *encrypts*, or codes (see Chapter 12, page 289), the original message so that its contents are protected from snooping. Then the VPN client appends the Internet address of the VPN server to the message and sends that package over the Internet to the VPN server. When the VPN server receives the message, it strips its address off the front of the message, *decrypts* the coded message, and sends the plain text message to the original address on the LAN. In this way, secure private messages are delivered over the public Internet.

VPNs offer the benefit of point-to-point leased lines, and they enable remote access, both by employees and by any others who have been registered with the VPN server. For example, if customers or vendors are registered with the VPN server, they can use the VPN from their own sites. Figure 6-16 shows three tunnels: one supports a point-to-point connection between the Atlanta and Chicago sites and the other two support remote connections.

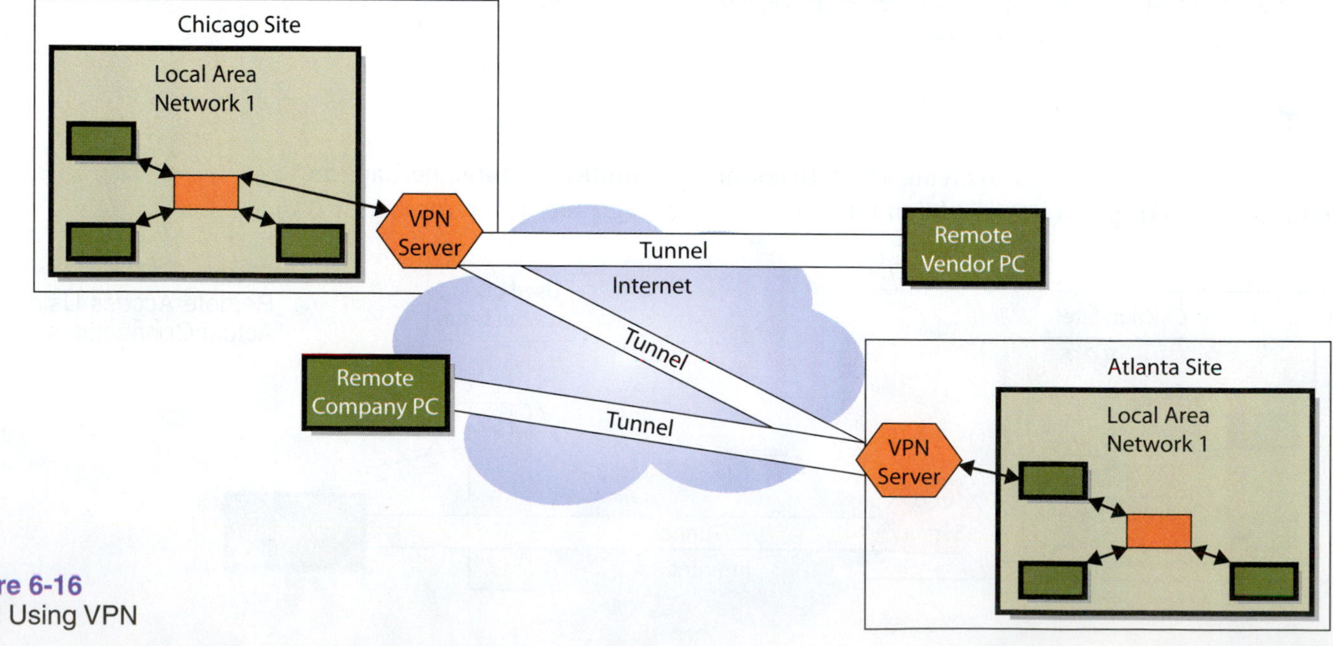

Figure 6-16
WAN Using VPN

Microsoft has fostered the popularity of VPNs by including VPN support in Windows. All versions of Microsoft Windows have the capability of working as VPN clients. Computers running Windows Server can operate as VPN servers.

FlexTime uses a VPN. Currently, Version 2 of its software can only be accessed via a LAN. But Kelly, Neil, and key employees need to be able to access that software from home or from another remote location. Accordingly, FlexTime has set up a VPN. Remote users sign on to the VPN, and then they can work as if they were using a computer that is directly connected to FlexTime's LAN.

FlexTime could continue using the VPN in this way and not move to a thin-client application. However, it would still have the burden of installing and maintaining thick clients on user computers, and Neil wants to eliminate that burden. Furthermore, if it moved to a thin-client application, customers could access the FlexTime system using their browsers.

How does the knowledge in this chapter help *FlexTime* and you?

The owners at FlexTime have to make decisions about what data communications equipment to install in their new building. It's not an option; they have to do it. Any decisions they make are fraught with risk. However, with knowledge, they have a better chance of making a good decision. And, as Kelly says in the accompanying video, because she has no data communications knowledge, she cannot be a good partner.

The same might happen to you. With the knowledge of this chapter, you're on the road to having knowledge like Neil, and not being a passive bystander, like Kelly.

Ethics Guide

Personal Work at Work?

Let's suppose you go on your vacation to New Zealand and you decide to email pictures of your amazing surfing skills to a friend who works at, say, some company in Ohio. Your email does not concern your friend's work or his company's business. It is not an emergency email, nor is it even a request for a ride to your house from the airport. Your email concerns your surfing skills! Even worse, your email is not just a few sentences that would consume a little file space. Rather, your email contains a dozen pictures, and, without noticing it, you sent very high-quality pictures that was 6.2 megabytes in size, each.

"Come on," you're saying, "give me a break! What's the matter with an email and some pictures? It's me surfing, it's not some weird pornographic material."

Maybe you're right; maybe it's not a big deal. But consider the resources you've consumed by sending that email: Your message, over 60 megabytes of it, traveled over the Internet to your friend's company's ISP. The packets of the email and picture were then transmitted to the Ohio company router and from that router to its email server. Your message consumed processing cycles on the router and on the email server computer. A copy of your picture was then stored on that email server until your friend deleted it, perhaps weeks later. Additionally, your friend will use his computer and the company LAN to download the pictures to his desktop computer, where they will be stored. In fact, the entire computing infrastructure, from the ISP to your friend's desk, is owned, operated, and paid for by your friend's employer. Finally, if your friend reads his email during his working hours, he will be consuming company resources—his time and attention, which the company has paid for while he is at work.

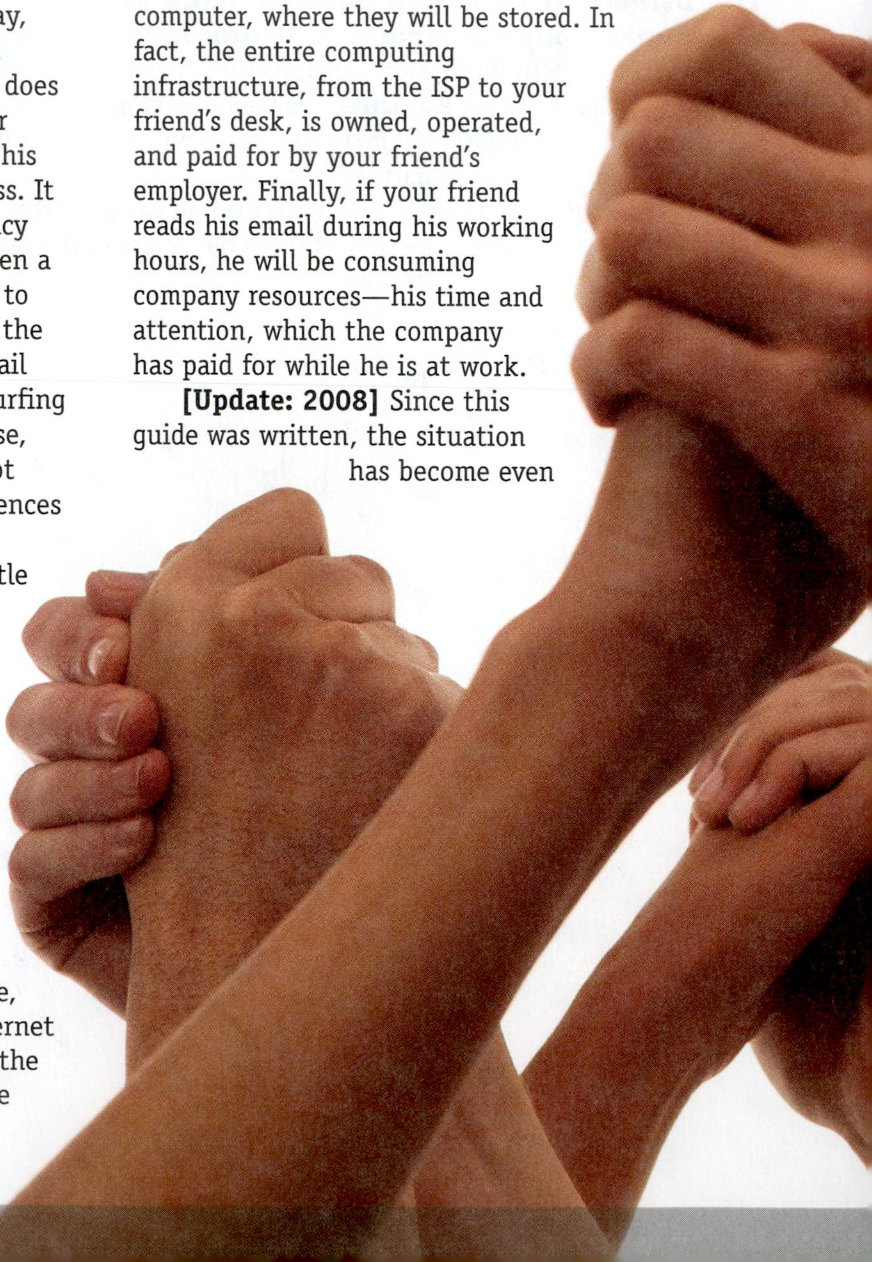

[Update: 2008] Since this guide was written, the situation has become even more complicated. Now, in addition to (or instead of) emailing pictures, you're likely to be updating your Facebook page with the photos, and your friend is likely using his computer to view those photos and to comment on your page, and to update his. Now, the pictures are no longer stored on the Ohio company's servers, but they are still being transmitted over that company's data communications network.

[Update: 2010] Since the 2008 update was written, personal, intelligent devices such as the iPhone, the iPad, and Windows 7 Series phones, not to mention BlackBerry phones, have become affordable and popular. Consequently, your friend can choose to read your Facebook updates, tweets, and so on from his phone or iPad. If his device connects to his company's LAN, then he is still using the company's data communications network. However, if that phone makes a WAN wireless connection, then he is no longer using any of his company's data communications network. He is, however, using company time to do so.

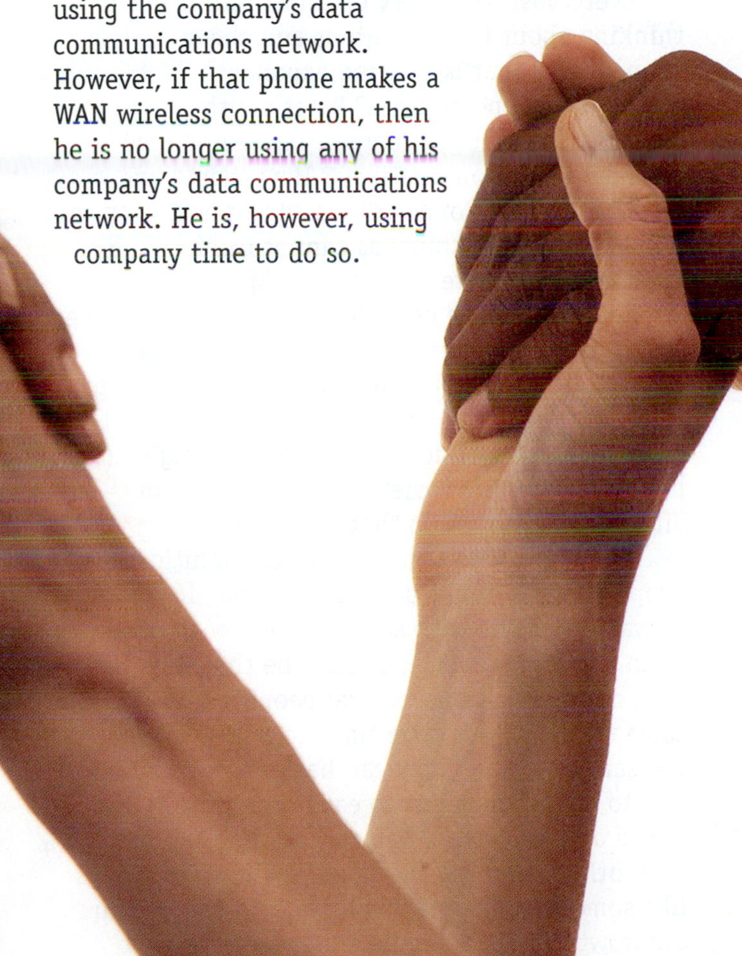

Discussion Questions

Questions 1–4 concern the original scenario, before the 2008 and 2010 update.

1. Is it ethical for you to send the email and picture to your friend at work?
2. Does your answer to question 1 change depending on the size of the pictures? Does your answer change if you send 100 pictures? If you send 1,000 pictures? If your answer does change, where do you draw the line?
3. Once the pictures are stored on the Ohio company's email server, who owns the pictures? Who controls those pictures? Does the company have the right to inspect the contents of its employees' mailboxes? If so, what should managers do when they find your picture that has absolutely nothing to do with the company's business?
4. What do you think is the greater cost to your friend's company: the cost of the infrastructure to transmit and store the email or the cost of the time your friend takes at work to read and view your pictures? Does this consideration change any of your answers above?
5. How does the 2008 update change the ethics of the situation? Explain. Is it ethical for your friend to read and update Facebook using the company's computers?
6. How does the 2010 update change the ethics of the situation? Is it any of the company's business what your friend does with his iPhone or other device at work?
7. Describe a reasonable policy for computer/phone/communicating device use at work. Consider email, Facebook, and Twitter, as well as the 2008 and 2010 updates. Endeavor to develop a policy that will be robust in the face of likely data communication changes in the future.

Guide

Thinking Exponentially Is Not Possible, but . . .

Nathan Myhrvold, the chief scientist at Microsoft Corporation during the 1990s, once said that humans are incapable of thinking exponentially. Instead, when something changes exponentially, we think of the fastest linear change we can imagine and extrapolate from there, as illustrated in the figure on the next page. Myhrvold was writing about the exponential growth of magnetic storage. His point was that no one could then imagine how much growth there would be in magnetic storage and what we would do with it.

This limitation pertains equally well to the growth of computer network phenomena. We have witnessed exponential growth in a number of areas: the number of Internet connections, the number of Web pages, and the amount of data accessible on the Internet. And, all signs are that this exponential growth isn't over.

What, you might ask, does this have to do with me? Well, suppose you are a product manager for home appliances. When most homes have a wireless network, it will be cheap and easy for appliances to talk to one another. When that day arrives, what happens to your existing product line? Will the competition's talking appliances take away your market share? However, talking appliances may not satisfy a real need. If a toaster and a coffee pot have nothing to say to each other, you'll be wasting money to create them.

Every business, every organization, needs to be thinking about the ubiquitous and cheap connectivity that is growing exponentially. What are the new opportunities? What are the new threats? How will our competition react? How should we position ourselves? How should we respond? As you consider these questions, keep in mind that because humans cannot think exponentially, we're all just guessing.

So what can we do to better anticipate changes brought by exponential phenomena? For one, understand that technology does not drive people to do things they've never done before, no matter how much the technologists suggest it might. (Just because we *can do* something does not mean anyone will *want to do* that something.)

Social progress occurs in small, evolutionary, adaptive steps. Right now, for example, if you want to watch a movie with someone, you both need to be in the same room. It needn't be that way. Using data communications, several people can watch the same movie, at the same time, together, but not in the same location. They can have an open audio line to make comments to each other during the movie or even have a Web cam so they can see each other watching the same movie. That sounds like something people might want to do—it's an outgrowth of what people are already doing.

However, emerging network technology enables my dry cleaner to notify me the minute my clothes are ready. Do I want to know? How much do I care to know that my clothes are ready Monday at 1:45 rather than sometime after 4:00 on Tuesday? In truth, I don't care. Such technology does not solve a problem that I have.

So, even if technology enables a capability, that possibility doesn't mean anyone wants that capability. People want to do what they're already doing, but more easily; they want to solve problems that they already have.

Another response to exponential growth is to hedge your bets. If you can't know the outcome of an exponential phenomenon, don't commit to one direction. Position yourself to move as soon as the direction is clear. Develop a few talking appliances, position your organization to develop more, but wait for a clear sign of market acceptance before going all out.

Finally, notice in the exponential curve that the larger the distance between Now and the Future, the larger the error. In fact, the error increases exponentially with the length of the prediction. So, if you hear that the market for talking kitchen appliances will reach $1 billion in 1 year, assign that statement a certain level of doubt. However, if you hear that it will reach $1 billion in 5 years, assign that statement an exponentially greater level of doubt.

Discussion Questions

1. In your own words, explain the meaning of the claim that no one can think exponentially. Do you agree with this claim?
2. Describe a phenomenon besides connectivity or magnetic memory that you believe is increasing exponentially. Explain why it is difficult to predict the consequences of this phenomenon in 3 years.
3. To what extent do you think technology is responsible for the growth in the number of news sources? On balance, do you think having many news sources of varying quality is better than having a few with high quality control?
4. List three products or services, such as group movie viewing, that could dramatically change because of increased connectivity. Do not include movie viewing.
5. Rate your answers to question 4 in terms of how closely they fit with problems that people have today.

ACTIVE REVIEW

Use this Active Review to verify that you understand the ideas and concepts that answer the chapter's study questions.

Q1 What is a computer network?

Define *computer network*. Explain the differences among LANs, WANs, internets, and the Internet. Describe the purpose of a protocol.

Q2 What are the components of a LAN?

Explain the key distinction of a LAN. Describe the purpose of each component in Figure 6-2. Describe the placement of switches in a multistory building. Explain when optical fiber cables are used for a LAN. Define *IEEE 802.3* and *802.11* and differentiate between them. Name the functions of the LAN device.

Q3 What are the alternatives for connecting to a WAN?

Explain why your connection to an ISP is a WAN and not a LAN. Name three functions of an ISP. Describe the purpose of a modem. Identify and describe three ways you can connect to the Internet. Describe the differences among DSL, cable, and WAN wireless alternatives.

Q4 What are the fundamental concepts you should know about the Internet?

Explain the statement, "The Internet is an internet." Define *TCP/IP,* and name its layers. Explain, in general terms, the purpose of each layer. Explain the purpose of HTTP, HTTPS, SMTP, and FTP. Explain why TCP is said to provide *reliable internet transport.* Define *IP, packet,* and *router*. Explain why IP is said to provide internet routing. Describe the advantages of private and public IP addresses. Explain, in general terms, how you would obtain a domain name. Describe the relationship between domain names and public IP addresses. Define *URL.*

Q5 What happens on a typical Web server?

Explain what a Web storefront is. Define *three-tier architecture,* and name and describe each tier. Explain the function of a Web page, a Web server, and a commerce server. Explain the purpose of a Web farm. Explain the function of each tier in Figure 6-10 as the pages in Figures 6-9 and 6-11 are processed. Define *HTML,* and explain its purpose. Define *href* and *attribute.* Explain the purpose of XML, Flash, Silverlight, and HTML 5.

Q6 How do organizations benefit from VPNs?

Describe the problem that a VPN solves. Use Figure 6-15 to explain one way that a VPN is set up and used. Define *tunnel.* Describe how encryption is used in a VPN. Explain why a Windows user does not need to license or install other software to use a VPN.

How does the **knowledge** in this chapter help *FlexTime* and **you?**

Summarize Kelly's need for the knowledge of this chapter. Explain how her role in her partnership would be different if she knew this material. Explain how Kelly's situation pertains to you.

KEY TERMS AND CONCEPTS

USING YOUR KNOWLEDGE

1. Suppose you manage a group of seven employees in a small business. Each of your employees wants to be connected to the Internet. Consider two alternatives:
   - Alternative A: Each employee has his or her own modem and connects individually to the Internet.
   - Alternative B: The employees' computers are connected using a LAN, and the network uses a single modem to connect.

   a. Sketch the equipment and lines required for each alternative.
   b. Explain the actions you need to take to create each alternative.
   c. Which of these two alternatives do you recommend?

2. Suppose that you have a consulting practice implementing LANs for fraternities and sororities on your campus.

   a. Consider a fraternity house. Explain how a LAN could be used to connect all of the computers in the house. Would you recommend an Ethernet LAN, an 802.11 LAN, or a combination of the two? Justify your answer.
   b. This chapter did not provide enough information for you to determine how many switches the fraternity house might need. However, in general terms, describe how the fraternity could use a multiple-switch system.
   c. Considering the connection to the Internet, would you recommend that the fraternity house use a DSL modem, a cable modem, or a WAN wireless alternative? Although you can rule out at least one of these alternatives with the knowledge you already have, what additional information do you need in order to make a specific recommendation?
   d. Should you develop a standard package solution for each of your customers? What advantages accrue from a standard solution? What are the disadvantages?

3. Consider Neil's problem at FlexTime. He wants to carefully review the $175,000 network infrastructure proposal and eliminate any equipment or services that he can. At the same time, as the building is being remodeled the walls will be open, so this will be the best possible time to add cabling and any other equipment that FlexTime may eventually need.

   Assume that you have Neil's task. How would you proceed? We don't have enough information to analyze that proposal in detail. Instead, answer the following questions that concern how Neil might go about making this analysis.

   a. Describe FlexTime equipment that is likely to have a wired connection to a LAN.
   b. Describe FlexTime equipment that is likely to have a wireless connection to a LAN.

c. Describe customer equipment that is likely to have a wireless connection to a FlexTime LAN.
d. Neil (and you) need to plan for the future. How are your answers to parts a–c likely to change in the next 5 years? In the next 10 years?
e. Describe a process for determining the total wireless demand for a room that contains 50 spinning bicycles.
f. Using the knowledge you have gained from this chapter, list all of the equipment and cabling that FlexTime will need for the new building. Just list equipment categories; you do not have sufficient information to specify particular brands or models of equipment.
g. Suppose Neil receives three different bids for the network infrastructure. Does he necessarily choose the lowest-cost one? Why or why not? What process should Neil use to analyze the three proposals?

COLLABORATION EXERCISE 6

Before you start this exercise, read Chapter Extensions 1 and 2, which describe collaboration techniques as well as tools for managing collaboration tasks. In particular, consider using Google Docs, Windows Live SkyDrive, Microsoft SharePoint, or some other collaboration tool.

Consider the information technology skills and needs of your parents, relatives, family friends, and others in the Baby Boomer generation. Though you may not know it, you possess many skills that generation wants but does not have. You know how to text chat, how to download music from iTunes, how to buy and sell items on eBay, how to use Craig's List how to customize and use your cell phone, how to download an iPad application, and so forth. You probably can even run the navigation system in your parents' car.

a. Thinking about Baby Boomers whom you know, brainstorm with your team on the skills that you possess that they do not. Consider all of the items just described and others that come to mind. If you have not read MIS InClass Exercise 6 (page 136), do so now. Make a list of all those skills that members of your team possess that Baby Boomers do not.
b. Interview, survey, or informally discuss the items on your list in part a with your parents and other Baby Boomers. As a team, determine the five most important skills that these people do not possess.
c. The Baby Boomer market has both money and time, but not as much information technology capability as they need, and they do not like it.

   With your team, brainstorm products that you could sell to this market that would address the Baby Boomers' techno-ignorance. For example, you might create a video of necessary skills, or you might provide a consulting service setting up Microsoft Home Server computers. Consider other ideas and describe them as specifically as you can. You should consider at least five different product concepts.
d. Develop sales material that describes your services, the benefits they provide, and why your target market should buy those products. Try your sales pitch on friends and family.
e. How viable is your concept? Do you think you can make money with these products? If so, summarize an implementation plan. If not, explain why not.

CASE STUDY 6

Keeping Up with Wireless

Data communications technology is one of the fastest-changing technologies, if not *the* fastest changing, in all of IT. Substantial portions of the knowledge you gain from this chapter will be obsolete within the first 5 years of your career. Unfortunately, we do not know which portions those will be.

Consider the example of WAN wireless technology. Three protocol standards are in competition: EVDO, HSDPA, and WiMax. Because WiMax has the greatest potential performance, we will consider it further in this case.

Craig McCaw built one of the world's first cellular networks in the early 1980s and brought cell phones to the masses. In the 1990s, he sold his company to AT&T for $11.5 billion. In 2003, McCaw started a new venture, Clearwire, by buying rights to technology based on WiMax, to address what is called the "problem of the last mile." Will WiMax defeat the other WAN wireless technologies? We do not know. But, when someone with McCaw's knowledge, experience, and wealth starts a new venture based on that new technology, we should pay attention.

To begin, what is the **problem of the last mile**? The bottleneck on data communications into homes, and into smaller businesses, is the last mile. Fast optical fiber transmission lines are buried under the street in front of your apartment or office; the problem is getting that capacity into the building and to your computer or TV. Digging up the street and backyard of every residence and small business to install optical fiber is not an affordable proposition. Even if that could be done, such infrastructure cannot be used by mobile devices. You cannot watch a downloaded movie on a commuter train using an optical fiber line.

The WiMax standard, **IEEE 802.16**, could be implemented by many companies, but only if those companies own wireless frequencies for data transmission. Hence the interest by people like McCaw and other cellular players such as Sprint. The WiMax standard includes two usage models: *fixed* and *mobile*. The former is akin to LAN wireless in existence today; mobile access allows users to move around, as they do with cell phones, staying connected.

On December 1, 2008, Clearwire merged with Sprint Nextel and received a $3.2 billion outside investment. In the process, Clearwire gained access to Sprint Nextel's spectrum holdings (authority to use certain frequencies for cellular signals). The merged company is called Clearwire, and the products are marketed as Sprint Xohm.

Clearwire already provides fixed use in many cities. As of June 2010, mobile WiMax services were available only in selected cities, but roll out to many more cities is planned in the near future.

Questions

1. Read the "Thinking Exponentially" Guide on pages 146–147. Keeping the principles of that Guide in mind, list five possible commercial applications for mobile WiMax. Consider applications that necessitate mobility.

2. Evaluate each of the possible applications in your answer to question 1. Select the three most promising applications and justify your selection.

3. Clearwire went public in March 2007 at an initial price of $27.25. As of April, 2010, the price was $8.00. Go online and research the company to find out what happened to its share price. Explain why its share price has dropped.

4. AT&T and T-Mobile have endorsed HSDPA, but it does not have the same potential maximum transmission rates. Rather than jump on the WiMax bandwagon, those companies plan to deploy a different technology called Long Term Evolution (LTE). Search the Web for LTE versus WiMax comparisons and compare and contrast these two technologies.

5. Where will this end? On which of these technologies would you be willing to invest $100 million? Why?

Part 3

Using IS for Competitive Strategy

This could happen to you

Fox Lake Country Club is a private golf and tennis club located in the suburbs of Hartford, Connecticut. Founded in 1982, the club features two 18-hole golf courses, 14 tennis courts, a swimming pool, a restaurant, meeting rooms, and a pro shop that sells golf and tennis gear and clothing. The golf courses, designed by a leading golf professional, are beautiful and challenging. Indeed, all of the Fox Lake grounds are picturesque and meticulously maintained by the groundskeeping staff.

All this beauty is not cheap; memberships cost $125,000 in initiation fees and a monthly fee of $425. The club's bylaws allow for up to 1,500 club memberships. Like most such organizations, member initiation fees are invested and the proceeds pay mortgages on the club's facilities as well as maintenance expenses on capital equipment. Monthly membership charges pay operational expenses, including salaries for Fox Lake's 35 full-time employees and hourly wages for about 100 seasonal workers. The restaurant and pro shop are intended to be profit-generating centers for the club.

Fox Lake employs golf and tennis professionals as subcontractors. These professionals staff the pro shop and activity centers for a few hours each week. They spend the bulk of their time, however, teaching club members.

The problems in the U.S. financial industry hit Fox Lake hard. For the first time in 30 years, in December 2008, the club had open memberships. Since then, as of 2010, all memberships are sold. However, the waiting list is only months long for prospective members, whereas at the end of 2008 it was years long. Furthermore, both the pro shop and the restaurant lost money in 2009 and 2010.

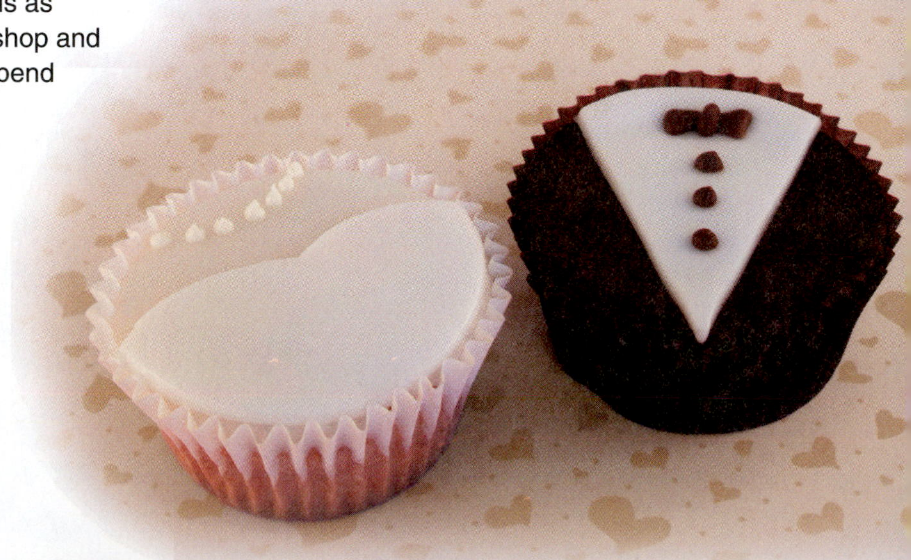

In response to these financial challenges, the club's board of directors asked the club's general manager, Jeff Lloyd, to seek additional sources of revenue. Because of the beauty of its grounds, Fox Lake had been used as the site of several weddings, and Lloyd developed a business plan to expand such one-off events into a wedding-hosting business. Fox Lake is gorgeous in the summer, of course, but even in the winter, when the grounds are covered with snow, the scene is lovely, and he reasoned that weddings and receptions could provide year-round revenue.

With the board's approval, Lloyd hired Anne Foster to develop this new business. At the time, Foster was working as a successful independent wedding planner, and she wanted an opportunity to expand her business. It seemed to be a good match; Fox Lake provided her a beautiful venue and greater opportunity for more events, and her knowledge of the industry as well her contacts with vendors and potential clients jumpstarted Fox Lake into the wedding event business.

We will use the Fox Lake Country Club as an example for Chapters 7 through 12. To avoid unnecessary complication, we will ignore tennis and swimming activities at the club, as well as the pro shop. The golf course, wedding events, restaurant, and facility maintenance business units will provide more than enough fodder for our investigation into organizational information systems.

CHAPTER 7

Enterprise Systems

This could happen to you

"Mike, what are you telling me?" Anne Foster struggles to keep her voice down as she talks with Mike Stone, the facilities manager.

"I'm saying that we've got to do the earthquake retro-fit on the Oak Room."

"That's fine, Mike. Do it next winter. I'll work around it."

"Anne, that won't work. It's got to be done by November 1. The insurance company said so."

"Look, I'm a wedding planner—I plan weddings, in fact I've already got four of them for the first two weeks of October. The good news is that I only need the Oak Room for one."

STUDY QUESTIONS

Q1 How do information systems vary by scope?

Q2 When are information silos a problem?

Q3 How do enterprise information systems eliminate silos?

Q4 How do CRM, ERP, and EAI support enterprise systems?

Q5 What are the challenges when implementing new enterprise systems?

How does the knowledge in this chapter help *Fox Lake* and you?

"I'm sorry, Anne. I really am. I thought you knew."

"Knew? Would I plan a wedding that we can't do? What am I supposed to do, go back to the bride and say, 'Hey, change of plans, you'll have to do your wedding reception elsewhere!'"

"Sorry, but that's the way it is."

"Oh, no, Mike. You might be a good facilities manager; but you don't know anything about brides!" Anger and desperation fill her voice.

"Well, we can get 150 people into the Maple Suite, if we open the walls and set tables outside."

"Oh, great!!! Wonderful!!!! I've got two problems with that, Mike: One, what if the weather is bad? What if it's too cold to open the walls? But that's nothing compared to my second problem."

"Let's hear it."

"How old is your daughter, Mike?"

"Three."

"OK, I'll accept that you just don't get it. Our bride is having her special day. She and her betrothed have sent out their save-the-date cards. In fact, they've even sent out their invitations. To 185 people, Mike! That's 185, not 150 if the weather is good."

"Anne, I scheduled this REQUIRED maintenance 6 months ago."

"Maybe so, Mike, but nobody told ME."

"OK, Anne. Imagine this: Let's say we put off this maintenance and, God forbid, we have an earthquake. You know what the lawyers would say if we knew we needed the work, but didn't do it just for the revenue of another 35 people?"

"Lawyers!!!" Anne shouts, "You want to see lawyers???? Her father is the partner in the biggest firm in Hartford, founding member of Fox Lake Country Club, past president of the board."

"Then I'm sure he'll understand."

"Mike, you're an idiot."

"Let's go talk to Jeff."

"MAYBE SO, MIKE, BUT NOBODY TOLD ME."

Optional Extensions for this chapter are • CE11: Functional Processes, Applications, and Systems 455 • CE12: Enterprise Resource Planning (ERP) Systems 466

Q1 How Do Information Systems Vary by Scope?

Something is amiss at Fox Lake Country Club. Months ago, the facilities department scheduled needed maintenance on the club's buildings. The wedding events group, unaware of this scheduled maintenance, planned a wedding and reception that conflicts with the maintenance activity. The facilities department claims that the maintenance cannot be delayed because of a directive from the insurance company. Eventually, Fox Lake will solve this problem. However, Fox Lake management will be in turmoil before a solution is found and implemented, and the solution will be so expensive that it exceeds the profit of wedding events for the second half of that year.

Fundamentally, this problem was caused by the existence of **information silos**, a condition that exists when data are isolated in separated information systems. (Isolated systems are referred to as *silos,* because when drawn in diagrams they appear as long vertical columns—like grain silos.) In this chapter, we will discuss the problems of such silos and the role of enterprise information systems in eliminating them.

To begin that discussion, consider the scope of information systems summarized in Figure 7-1. As you move from the top to the bottom in this figure, the scope of information systems widens to include more people and organizations.

Personal Information Systems

Personal information systems are information systems used by a single individual. The contact manager in your iPhone or in your email account is an example of a personal information system. Because such systems have only one user, procedures are simple and probably not documented or formalized in any way.

You and the other members of your organization may duplicate data; many of you may have phone numbers and email addresses for the same people, but such data duplication is normally not important. When phone numbers change, for example, you all make that change in your own way in your own time without any real problem.

It is easy to manage change to personal information systems. If you switch email from, say MSN to Google, you'll have to move your contact list from one vendor to the

Figure 7-1
Scope of Information Systems

Scope	Fox Lake Example	Characteristics
Personal	Contact manager	Single user; procedures informal; problems isolated; data duplication among employees; easy to manage change
Workgroup	Scheduling of groundskeeping	10 to 100 users; procedures understood within group; problem solutions within group; data duplication among departments; somewhat difficult to change
Enterprise	Charging of membership fees	100 to 1000s of users; procedures formalized; problems solutions affect enterprise; data duplication minimized; very difficult to change
Interenterprise	Ordering of restaurant supplies from suppliers	1000s of users; procedures formalized; problems solutions affect multiple organizations; controlled data duplication; difficult to change; interorganization IS required

other, and you'll have to inform your correspondents of your new address, but you control the timing of that change. Because you will be the sole user of the new system, if new procedures are required, only you need to adapt. And, if there are problems, you can solve them yourself.

Workgroup Information Systems

A **workgroup information system** is an information system that is shared by a group of people for a particular purpose. At Fox Lake, the groundskeepers (personnel who maintain the golf courses and club lawns and gardens) share a workgroup information system for scheduling tasks and employees to accomplish those tasks.

Workgroup information systems that support a particular department are sometimes called **departmental information systems**. An example is the accounts payable system that is used by the accounts payable department. Other workgroup information systems support a particular business function and are called **functional information systems**. An example of a functional system is a Web storefront like the one discussed in Chapter 6. Finally, the collaboration information systems discussed in Chapter Extension 2 are also workgroup information systems.

Workgroup information systems, whether departmental, functional, or collaborative, share the characteristics shown in Figure 7-1. Typically workgroup systems support 10 to 100 users. The procedures for using them must be understood by all members of the group. Often, procedures are formalized in documentation, and users are sometimes trained in the use of those procedures.

When problems occur, they almost always can be solved within the group. If accounts payable duplicates the record for a particular supplier, the accounts payable group can make the fix. If the Web storefront has the wrong number of widgets in the inventory database, that count can be fixed within the storefront group.

(Notice, by the way, that the *consequences* of a problem are not isolated to the group. Because the workgroup exists to provide a service to the rest of the organization, its problems have consequences throughout the organization. The *fix* to the problem can be usually obtained within the group, however.)

Two or more workgroups within an organization can duplicate data, and such duplication can be very problematic to the organization, as we discuss in Q2. Finally, because many people use workgroup information systems, changing them is more difficult than changing personal information systems. All the members of the workgroup need to be informed and trained on the changes to procedures when the system is altered.

Enterprise Information Systems

Enterprise information systems are information systems that span an organization and support activities in multiple departments. At Fox Lake, all customer charges are recorded against membership accounts; no cash or credit card transactions are allowed. The restaurant, the golf course, the pro shop, and the wedding events departments all use the same enterprise information system to record sales.

Enterprise information systems typically have hundreds to thousands of users. Procedures are formalized and extensively documented; users undergo formal procedure training. Sometimes enterprise systems include categories of procedures, and users are defined according to levels of expertise with the system as well as by levels of security authorization.

The solutions to problems in an enterprise system usually involve more than one department. Because enterprise systems span many departments and involve potentially thousands of users, they are very difficult to change. Changes must be carefully planned, cautiously implemented, and users given considerable training. Sometimes users are given incentives and other inducements to motivate them to change. As you will learn in this chapter, a major advantage of enterprise systems is that data duplication is either eliminated altogether or it is allowed to exist, but changes to duplicated data are carefully managed to maintain consistency.

We will discuss the most common examples of enterprise information systems in Q4 and the problems of implementing and changing enterprise systems in Q5.

Interenterprise Information Systems

Interenterprise information systems are information systems that are shared by two or more independent organizations. At Fox Lake, the information system that the restaurant uses to order supplies and ingredients from its suppliers is an interorganizational system. Because such systems are used by employees of different organizations, procedures are formalized and user training is mandatory.

Such systems typically involve thousands of users, and solutions to problems require cooperation among different, usually independently owned, organizations. Problems are resolved by meeting, contract, and sometimes by litigation.

Data are often duplicated between organizations, but such duplication is carefully managed. Because of the wide span, complexity, and multiple companies involved, such systems can be exceedingly difficult to change. The interaction of independently owned and operated information systems is required.

We will discuss interorganizational information systems in Chapter 8.

Q2 When Are Information Silos a Problem?

As stated, information silos exist when data are isolated in separated information systems. Information silos are created over time, as information systems are implemented to support personal and workgroup applications. As organizations grow, however, at some point such silos will duplicate data and become a source of potentially serious problems.

How Do Information Silos Arise?

No organization plans to create information silos. They arise as a consequence of an organization's growth and increasing use of information systems.

Consider the example of Fox Lake in Figure 7-2. The wedding events department is new and Anne, the manager, has been given incentives to grow the business. At the

Figure 7-2
Fox Lake Country Club Departmental Goals

Wedding Events	Golf Operations	Facilities

• Increase business • Develop high-quality reputation • Manage complicated details • One-off customers	• Satisfy golfers • Keep golf pros busy • Extend season • Manage proshop profitably • Repeat customers	• Maintain top-level club appearance • Protect and conserve club physical assets • Resolve problems quickly • Stay within budget

same time, both she and Fox Lake have a reputation to protect, so she wants to grow the business so that Fox Lake weddings and receptions have a superior reputation.

The golf operations department has a very different set of goals. Golfing is the primary concern of club members, and the club must provide golfers with accurate tee times (starting times) and with a pleasant golfing experience. The club contracts with professional golfers to teach golf lessons. The pros make most of their income from lessons, and to attract and keep quality pros the course needs to give them plenty of business. Other concerns of golf course operations are listed in Figure 7-2.

The goals of the facilities department are completely different from the other two groups. The facilities department is concerned with maintenance for top-level appearance, protecting club assets, solving problems, and so forth. Unlike wedding events or golf operations, the facilities department generates no revenue; it is all cost. So, the facilities manager is incentivized to carefully manage the facilities budget.

Before continuing, consider the different needs for information systems among these groups. Wedding events is concerned with growth of one-time events. Golf operations is concerned with customer satisfaction and with maintaining golf pro instruction. Facilities is concerned with accomplishing needed maintenance tasks on time and within budget and with solving problems quickly and efficiently.

Because of these different orientations, each group will develop information systems of a different character, as shown in Figure 7-3. Because these systems have nearly nothing to do with each other, they can operate as isolated entities for a long time, without problem. In fact, **islands of automation** is another term for information silo; it just means groups of information systems that operate in isolation from one other.

Information silos (or, equivalently, islands of automation) are not a problem until they begin to share data about the same entities. Or, stated differently, until they duplicate data. At that point, they can become quite problematic, as Fox Lake learned, and as many other businesses have learned over time.

What Are Common Departmental Applications?

Before we address the problems caused by information silos, realize that many, many departmental applications and information systems have been developed and are still in use today. Figure 7-4 lists common departmental applications. Like

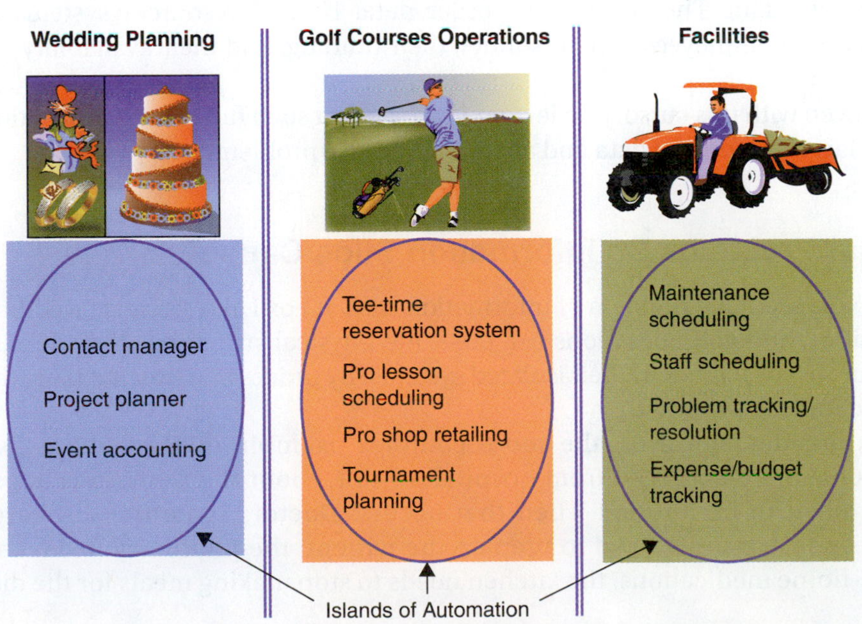

Figure 7-3
Fox Lake Country Club Departmental Information Systems

Figure 7-4
Common Departmental Information Systems

Department	Application
Sales and marketing	• Lead generation • Lead tracking • Customer management • Sales forecasting • Product and brand management
Operations	• Order entry • Order management • Finished-goods inventory management
Manufacturing	• Inventory (raw materials, goods-in-process) • Planning • Scheduling • Operations
Customer service	• Order tracking • Account tracking • Customer support and training
Human resources	• Recruiting • Compensation • Assessment • HR Planning
Accounting	• General ledger • Financial reporting • Cost accounting • Accounts receivable • Accounts payable • Cash management • Budgeting • Treasury management

the departmental systems at Fox Lake, each of those systems was created to support a given department's information processing needs. They work fine for those departments.

However, even a quick glance at this list indicates that these activities are likely to duplicate data. For example, many of these applications concern customers. Information systems for sales and marketing, operations, manufacturing, and customer service all process their own customer data. At least the first three of those process finished-goods inventory data. They all process order data. Human resources systems duplicate data about employees and personnel, their training, and their availability with other departments.

Even with this cursory review, you can see that such functional applications duplicate large amounts of data and are likely to cause problems.

What Problems Do Information Silos Cause?

We have seen one problem of information silos at Fox Lake. Because wedding events, facilities, and golf operations use the same physical structures, they duplicate data about those facilities in their isolated systems. By processing isolated data, their plans can conflict, as they did.

Consider, however, the more complex example in Figure 7-5. Every day, patients are discharged from hospitals. Think about the numerous departments that need to be notified when that occurs. Doctors issue the discharge order. In response, nurses need to prepare the patient, the pharmacy needs to prepare take-home medications, the kitchen needs to stop making meals for the discharged

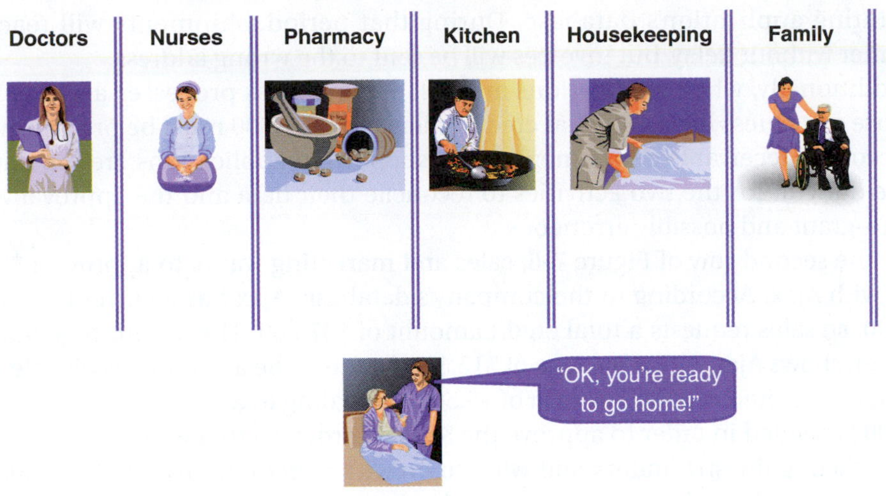

Figure 7-5
Some of the Departments Involved in Patient Discharge

patient, housekeeping needs to clean the vacated room, and the family needs to be notified to ensure someone is available to take the patient home. If each of these departments maintains its own island of automation, disaster will ensue. We will consider some of those problems and their solution in Q3.

Figure 7-6 summarizes the problems of the information silos created by isolated information systems. First, data are duplicated because each application has its own database. If accounting and sales/marketing applications are separated, customer data will be duplicated and may become inconsistent. Changes to customer data made in the sales/marketing application may take days or weeks to reach the

Figure 7-6
Problems Created by Information Silos

Problem	Sales and Marketing		Accounting
Data duplication, data inconsistency	Ajax Construction Ship to: Reno, NV Bill to: Reno, NV		Ajax Construction Ship to: Reno, NV Bill to: Buffalo, NY
Disjointed processes	Get Credit Approval	Request $37,800 Approve $32,300	Approve Customer Credit
Limited information and lack of integrated information	Order Data Is IndyMac a preferred customer?	??	Payment Data
Isolated decisions lead to organizational inefficiencies	Order Data Redouble sales efforts at IndyMac.		Payment Data OneWest has been slow to pay.
Increased expense	Σ of problems above.		

accounting application's database. During that period, shipments will reach the customer without delay, but invoices will be sent to the wrong address.

Additionally, when applications are isolated, business processes are disjointed. Suppose a business has a rule that credit orders over $20,000 must be preapproved by the accounts receivable department. If the supporting applications are separated, it will be difficult for the two activities to reconcile their data and the approval will be slow-to-grant and possibly erroneous.

In the second row of Figure 7-6, sales and marketing wants to approve a $20,000 order with Ajax. According to the company's database, Ajax has a current balance of $17,800, so sales requests a total credit amount of $37,800. The accounting database, however, shows Ajax with a balance of $12,300, because the accounts receivable application has credited Ajax for a return of $5,500. According to accounting's records, only $32,300 is needed in order to approve the $20,000 order, so that is all they grant. Sales and marketing doesn't understand what to do with a credit approval of $32,300. Was only $14,700 of the order approved? And why that amount? Both departments want to approve the order. It will take numerous emails and phone calls, however, to sort this out. The interacting business processes are disjointed.

A consequence of such disjointed systems is the lack of integrated enterprise information. For example, suppose sales and marketing wants to know if IndyMac is still a preferred customer. Suppose that determining whether this is so requires a comparison of order history and payment history data. However, with information silos, that data will reside in two different databases and, in one of them, IndyMac is known by the name of the company that acquired it, OneWest Bank. Data integration will be difficult. Making the determination will require manual processes and days, when it should be readily answered in seconds.

This leads to the fourth consequence: inefficiency. When using isolated functional applications, decisions are made in isolation. As shown in the fourth row of Figure 7-6, sales and marketing decided to redouble its sales effort with IndyMac. However, accounting knows that IndyMac was foreclosed by the FDIC and sold to OneWest and has been slow to pay. There are far better prospects for increased sales attention. Without integration, the left hand of the organization doesn't know what the right hand of the organization is doing.

Finally, information silos can result in increased cost for the organization. Duplicated data, disjointed systems, limited information, and inefficiencies all mean higher costs.

These problems are solved by enterprise information systems, and we consider them for the rest of this chapter.

Q3 How Do Enterprise Information Systems Eliminate Silos?

The fundamental problem of information silos is data that are duplicated and stored in isolated systems. The most obvious fix is to eliminate that duplicated data by storing a single copy of data in a shared database and revising business processes (and applications) to use that database. Another remedy is to allow the duplication, but to manage it to avoid problems.

An Enterprise System at Fox Lake

Figure 7-7 shows how the first remedy is applied at Fox Lake. First, a database is created that contains reservations for club facilities. Then each department alters its business processes (and applications) to use the shared database. In this simple

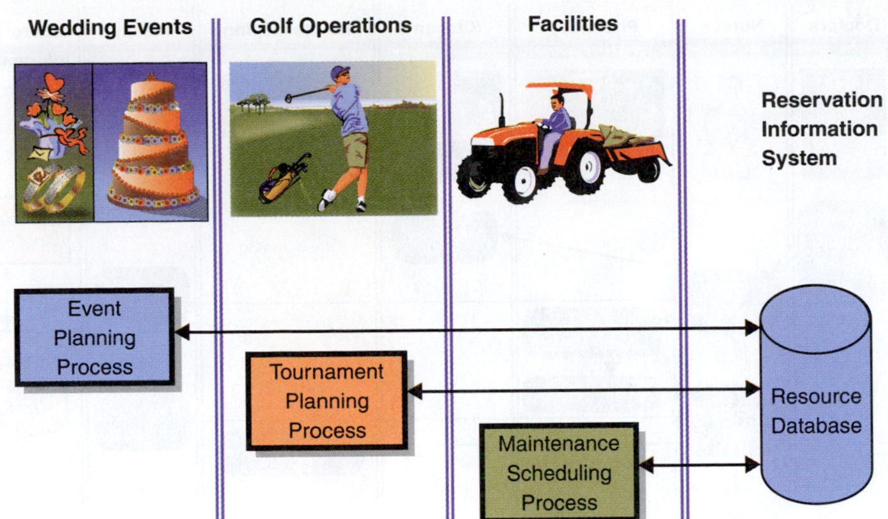

Figure 7-7
Fox Lake Country Club Enterprise Reservation System

example, the only change needed is to develop procedures to check availability before scheduling activities and to record any intended use for shared resources in the database. One or more database applications may need to be developed to enable availability checking.

However, with this solution, each department must be mindful that they are processing a shared resource. For example, prior to the shared database, the facilities department would block out weeks of time on its calendar for building maintenance, much more time than it actually needed. It would then work in maintenance activities during that block in accordance with its own tasks and priorities. If the facilities department continues this practice, it will needlessly block out wedding events and reduce potential club revenue. With the shared database, the facilities department needs to schedule specific activities against specific buildings for the minimum necessary blocks of time.

Before we go on, this simple example illustrates a phenomenon that creates difficult management challenges. When an enterprise system is implemented, all the departments that use it must change their business processes. People do not like to change; in fact, unless the benefit of the change is easily recognized, people resist change. However, in some cases new enterprise systems require departments to change without any obvious benefit *to that department.* In the Fox Lake example, when moving to the system in Figure 7-7, the facilities department will need to change its processes for the benefit of the wedding events department (and for Fox Lake as an enterprise), but for no benefit to itself. Facilities personnel may perceive the new system as a lot of trouble for nothing.

The system in Figure 7-7 is an enterprise information system in that different departments do share data. However, notice that the business processes do not overlap departments; they are still isolated. This is not the case in most organizations. Usually, enterprise business processes span departments. When they do so, the development of enterprise systems is considerably more difficult but potentially more beneficial. Consider the hospital example previously introduced.

An Enterprise System for Patient Discharge

Figure 7-8 shows some of the hospital departments and processes involved in discharging a patient at a hospital. A doctor initiates the process by issuing a discharge patient order. That order is delivered to the appropriate nursing staff, who initiates

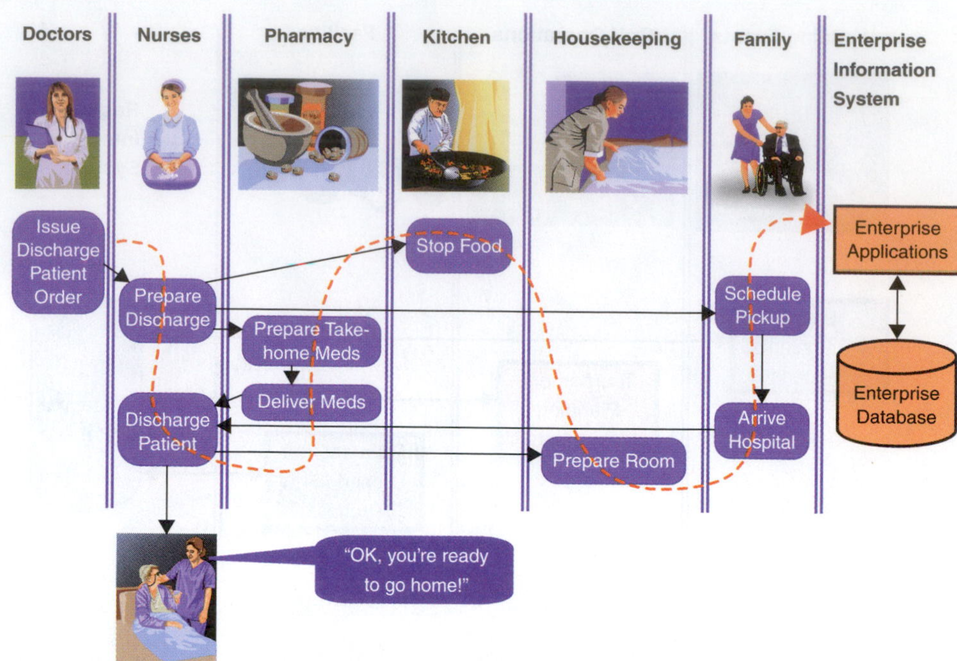

Figure 7-8
Example Enterprise Process and IS

activities at the pharmacy, the patient's family, and kitchen. Some of those activities initiate activities back at the nursing staff. In this figure, the enterprise information system is represented by a dotted red line.

Prior to the enterprise system, the hospital had developed procedures for using a paper-based system and informal messaging via the telephone. Each department kept its own records. When the new enterprise information system was implemented, not only was the data integrated into a database, but new computer-based forms and reports were created. The staff needed to transition from the paper-based system to the computer-based system. They also needed to stop making phone calls and let the new information system make notifications across departments. These measures involved substantial change, and most organizations experience considerable anguish when undergoing such transitions.

Business Process Reengineering

Enterprise systems like the one in Figure 7-8 were not feasible until network, data communication, and database technologies reached a sufficient level of capability and maturity in the late 1980s and early 1990s. At that point, many organizations began to develop enterprise systems.

As they did so, organizations realized that their existing business processes needed to change—partly to utilize the shared databases and partly to utilize new computer-based forms and reports. An even more important reason for changing business processes was that integrated data and enterprise systems offered the potential of substantial operational efficiencies. It became possible to do things that had been impossible before. Using Porter's language (Chapter 3, page 49), enterprise systems enabled the creation of stronger, faster, more effective linkages among value chains.

For example, when the hospital used a paper-based system, the kitchen would prepare meals for everyone who was a patient at the hospital as of midnight the night before. It was not possible to obtain data about discharges until the next midnight. Consequently, considerable food was wasted at substantial cost.

With the enterprise system, the kitchen can be notified about patient discharges as they occur throughout the day, resulting in substantial reductions in wasted food. But, when should the kitchen be notified? Immediately? And what if the discharge is cancelled before completion? Who will notify the kitchen of the cancelled discharge? Many possibilities and alternatives exist. So, to design its new enterprise system, the hospital needed to determine how best to change its processes to take advantage of the new capability. Such projects came to be known as **business process reengineering**, which is the activity of altering and designing business processes to take advantage of new information systems.

Unfortunately, business process reengineering is difficult, slow, and exceedingly expensive. Systems analysts need to interview key personnel throughout the organization to determine how best to use the new technology. Because of the complexity involved, such projects require high-level and expensive skills and considerable time. Many early projects stalled when the enormity of the project became apparent. This left some organizations with partially implemented systems that had disastrous consequences. Personnel didn't know if they were using the new system, the old system, or some hacked-up version of both.

The stage was set for the emergence of enterprise application vendors, which we discuss next.

Q4 How do CRM, ERP, and EAI Support Enterprise Systems?

When the need for business process reengineering emerged, most organizations were still developing their applications in-house. At the time, organizations perceived their needs as being "too unique" to be satisfied by off-the-shelf or altered applications. However, as applications became more and more complex, in-house development costs became infeasible. As stated in Chapter 4, systems built in-house are expensive not only because of their initial development, but also because of the continuing need to adapt those systems to changing requirements.

In the early 1990s, as the costs of business process reengineering were coupled with the costs of in-house development, organizations began to look more favorably on the idea of licensing preexisting applications. "Maybe we're not so unique, after all."

Some of the vendors who took advantage of this change in attitude were PeopleSoft, which licensed payroll and limited-capability human resources systems; Siebel, which licensed a sales lead tracking and management system; and SAP, which licensed something new, a system called *enterprise resource management*.

These three companies, and ultimately dozens of others like them, offered not just software and database designs. They also offered standardized business processes. These **inherent processes**, which are predesigned procedures for using the software products, saved organizations from expensive and time-consuming business process reengineering. Instead, organizations could license the software and obtain, as part of the deal, prebuilt procedures, which the vendors assured them were based upon "industry best practices."

Some parts of that deal were too good to be true, because, as you'll learn in Q5, inherent processes are almost never a perfect fit. But, the offer was too much for many organizations to resist. Over time, three categories of enterprise applications emerged: customer relationship management; enterprise resource planning, and enterprise application integration. Consider each.

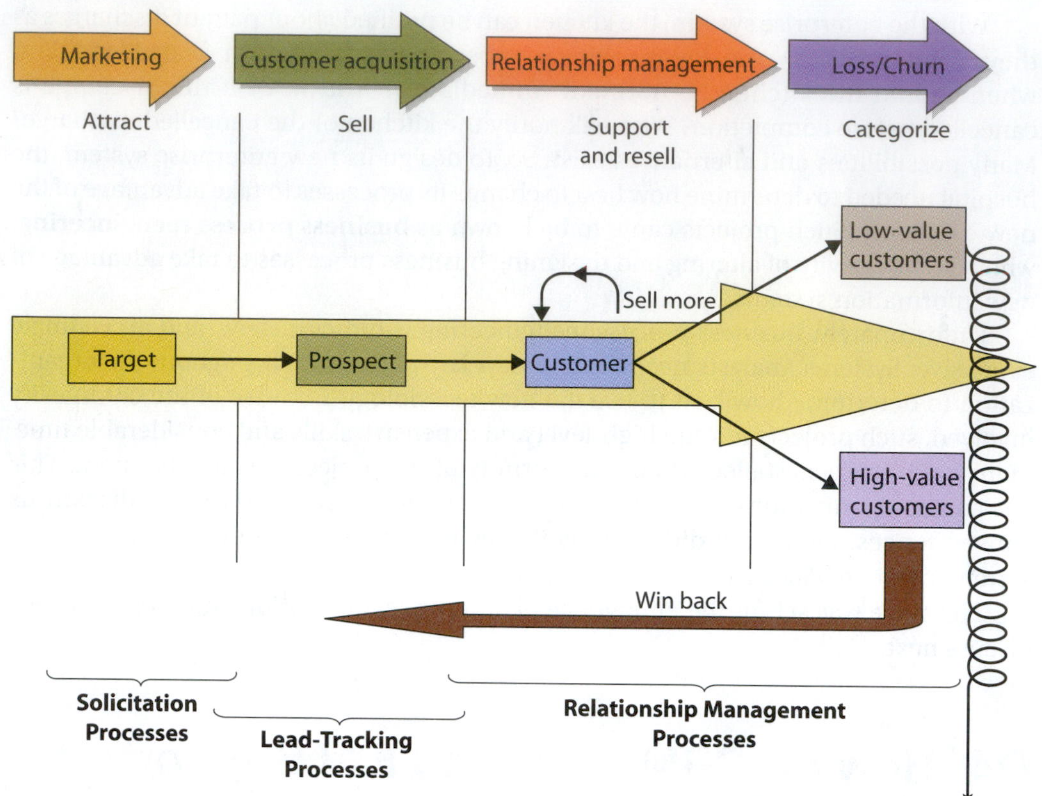

Figure 7-9
The Customer Life Cycle

Source: The Customer Life Cycle. Used with permission from Professor Douglas Maclachian, University of Washington Business School, University of Washington, Seattle, Washington.

Customer Relationship Management (CRM)

A **customer relationship management system (CRM)** is a suite of applications, a database, and a set of inherent processes for managing all the interactions with the customer, from lead generation to customer service. Every contact and transaction with the customer is recorded in the CRM database. Vendors of CRM software claim using their products makes the organization *customer-centric*. Though that term reeks of sales hyperbole, it does indicate the nature and intent of CRM packages.

Figure 7-9 shows four phases of the **customer life cycle**: marketing, customer acquisition, relationship management, and loss/churn. Marketing sends messages to the target market to attract customer prospects. When prospects order, they become customers who need to be supported. Additionally, relationship management processes increase the value of existing customers by selling them more product. Inevitably, over time the organization loses customers. When this occurs, win-back processes categorize customers according to value and attempt to win back high-value customers.

Figure 7-10 illustrates the major components of a CRM application. Notice that components exist for each stage of the customer life cycle. As shown, all

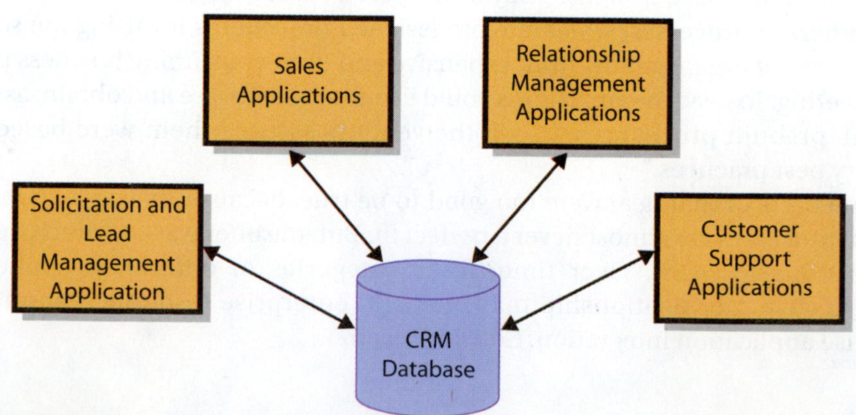

Figure 7-10
CRM Applications

Experiencing MIS InClass Exercise 7

Choosing a CRM Product

Choosing a CRM product is complicated. Dozens of CRM products exist, and it's difficult to determine their different features and functions, let alone how easy they are to learn and use, how difficult they are to implement, and so forth. Choosing a CRM requires knowing the organization's requirements as well, and often those requirements aren't fully known, or, if they are known, they are changing as the organization grows.

This exercise is designed to give you a sense of the challenges involved when choosing a CRM product. Form a team of students, fire up your browsers, and answer the following questions:

1. Act! and GoldMine are two of the lower-end CRM products. They began as sales lead tracking tools for individuals and small offices but have evolved since then.
   a. To learn about those products, visit *www.act.com* and *www.frontrange.com/goldmine.aspx.*
   b. As you can see, it is difficult to know how these products compare based just on the information on those sites. To learn more, Google or Bing the phrase "Act vs. Goldmine." Read several comparisons.
   c. Summarize your findings in a 2-minute presentation to the rest of the class. Include in your summary the intended market for these products, their costs, and their relative strengths and weaknesses.
2. Salesforce.com and Sugar are CRM products that are intended for use by larger organizations than Act! and GoldMine.
   a. To learn about these products, visit *www.salesforce.com* and *www.sugarcrm.com.*
   b. These two products seem to differ in orientation. To learn how others view these differences, Google or Bing the phrase "Salesforce vs. Sugar CRM." Read several comparisons.
   c. Summarize your findings in a 2-minute presentation to the rest of the class. Include in your summary the intended market for these products, their costs, and their relative strengths and weaknesses.
3. Of course, the major software vendors have CRM offerings as well. Using a combination of acquisition and internal development, Microsoft created the Dynamics CRM product. Oracle, meanwhile, through acquisition of Siebel Systems in 2005 and other acquisitions, has developed a suite of CRM applications.
   a. To learn about these products, visit *http://crm.dynamics.com/en-us/Default.aspx* and *www.oracle.com/us/solutions/crm/index.htm.*
   b. Oracle offers a suite of products. List and briefly describe Oracle's offerings. Briefly describe Microsoft's CRM offering. To learn more, Google or Bing "Microsoft CRM vs. Oracle CRM."
   c. Summarize your findings in a 2-minute presentation to the rest of the class. Include in your summary the intended market for those products, their costs, and their relative strengths and weaknesses.
4. Given your answers to parts 1–3 (and those of other teams, if you have been presenting to each other), consider the desirability of CRM product offerings for a variety of businesses. Specifically, suppose you have been asked to recommend two of the CRM products you've explored for further research. For each of the following businesses, recommend two such products and justify your recommendation:
   a. An independent wedding planner who is working in her own business as a sole proprietor (like Anne Foster was before she joined Fox Lake)
   b. An online vendor, such as *www.sephora.com*
   c. A musical venue, such as *www.santafeopera.org*
   d. A vendor of consulting services, such as *www.crmsoftwaresolutions.ca*
   e. A vacation cruise ship line, such as *www.hollandamerica.com*

   Present your findings to the rest of the class.
5. Summarize what you have learned from this exercise about choosing a CRM product. Formulate your summary as an answer to a job interviewer's question about the difficulties that organizations face when choosing software products.

applications process a common customer database. This design eliminates duplicated customer data and removes the possibility of inconsistent data. It also means that each department knows what has been happening with the customer at other departments. Customer support, for example, will know not to provide $1000 worth of support labor to a customer that has generated $300 worth of business over time. They will also know to bend over backwards for the customers that have generated hundreds of thousands of dollars of business. The result of this integration to the customer is that he or she feels like they are dealing with one entity and not many.

CRM systems vary in the degree of functionality they provide. One of the primary tasks when selecting a CRM package is to determine the features you need and to find a package that meets that set of needs. You might be involved in just such a project during your career.

Enterprise Resource Planning (ERP)

Enterprise resource planning (ERP) is a suite of applications, a database, and a set of inherent processes for consolidating business operations into a single, consistent, computing platform. As shown in Figure 7-11, ERP includes the functions of CRM, but also incorporates accounting, manufacturing, inventory, and human resources applications.

Despite the clear benefits of inherent processes and ERP, there can be an unintended consequence. See the Ethics Guide on pages 172–173 and consider that risk.

ERP systems are used to forecast sales and to create manufacturing plans and schedules to meet those forecasts. Manufacturing schedules include the use of material, equipment, and personnel and thus need to incorporate inventory and human resources applications. Because ERP includes accounting, all of these activities are automatically posted in the general ledger and other accounting applications.

SAP is the worldwide leader of ERP vendors. In addition to its base ERP offering, SAP offers industry-specific packages that customize its product for particular uses. There is an SAP package for automobile manufacturing, for example, and for many other specialty industries as well.

Figure 7-11
ERP Applications

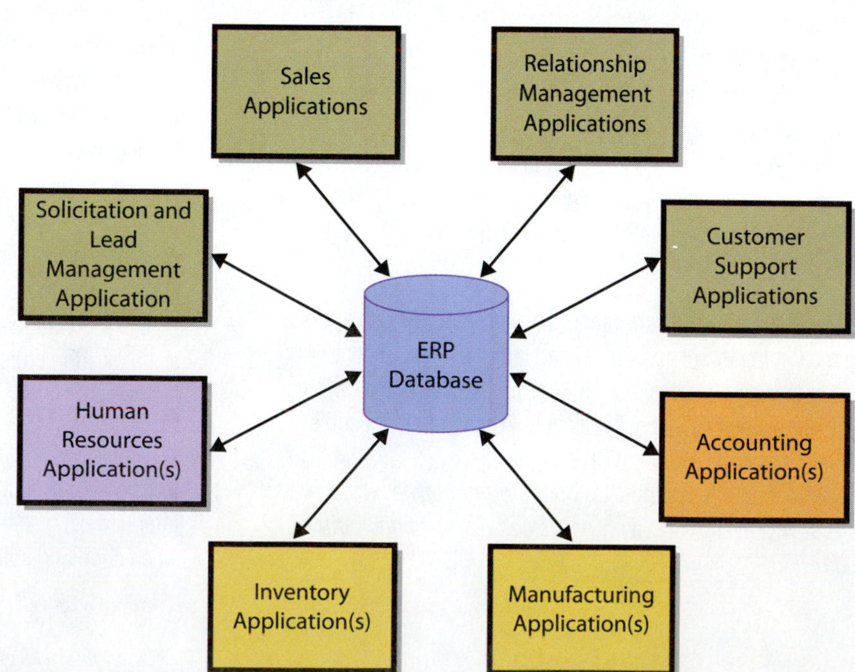

ERP originated in manufacturing and has a definite manufacturing flavor. However, it has been adapted for use in service organizations like hospitals as well as many other organizations.

You can learn more about ERP applications in Chapter Extension 12.

Enterprise Application Integration (EAI)

ERP systems are not for every organization. For example, some nonmanufacturing companies find the manufacturing orientation of ERP inappropriate. Even for manufacturing companies, some find the process of converting from their current system to an ERP system too daunting. Others are quite satisfied with their manufacturing application systems and do not wish to change them.

Companies for which ERP is inappropriate still have the problems of information silos, however, and some choose to use **enterprise application integration (EAI)** to solve those problems. EAI is a suite of software applications that integrates existing systems by providing layers of software that connect applications together. EAI does the following:

- It connects system "islands" via a new layer of software/system.
- It enables existing applications to communicate and share data.
- It provides integrated information.
- It leverages existing systems—leaving functional applications as is, but providing an integration layer over the top.
- It enables a gradual move to ERP.

The layers of EAI software shown in Figure 7-12 enable existing applications to communicate with each other and to share data. For example, EAI software can be configured to automatically make the data conversion required to automatically make data conversions among different systems. When the CRM applications send data to the manufacturing application system, for example, the CRM system sends its data to an EAI software program. That EAI program makes the conversion and then sends the converted data to the ERP system. The reverse action is taken to send data back from the ERP to the CRM.

Although there is no centralized EAI database, the EAI software keeps files of metadata that describe where data are located. Users can access the EAI system to find the data they need. In some cases, the EAI system provides services that provide a "virtual integrated database" for the user to process.

The major benefit of EAI is that it enables organizations to use existing applications while eliminating many of the serious problems of isolated systems. Converting to an EAI system is not nearly as disruptive as converting to ERP, and it provides many of the benefits of ERP. Some organizations develop EAI applications as a stepping-stone to complete ERP systems.

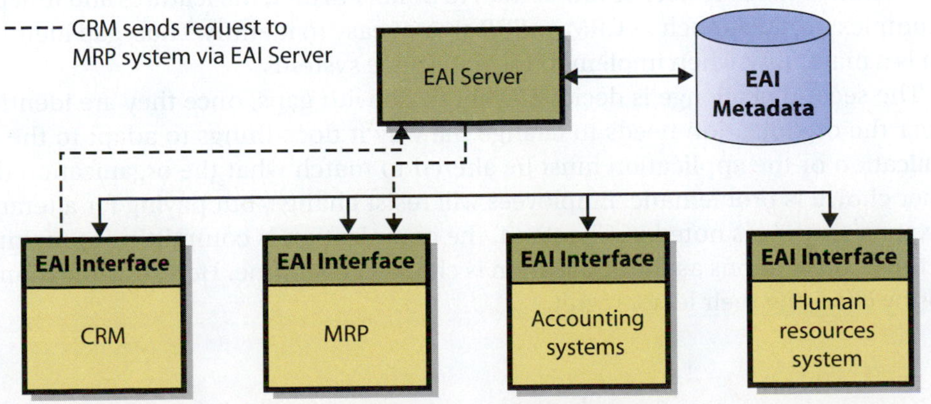

Figure 7-12 Enterprise Application Integration (EAI) Architecture

Q5 What Are the Challenges When Implementing New Enterprise Systems?

Implementing new enterprise systems is challenging, difficult, expensive, and risky. It is not unusual for enterprise system projects to be well over budget and a year or more late in delivery. The expense and risks arise from four primary factors:

- Collaborative management
- Requirements gaps
- Transition problems
- Employee resistance

Collaborative Management

Unlike departmental systems in which a single department manager is in charge, enterprise systems have no clear boss. Examine the discharge process in Figure 7-8; there is no manager of discharge. The discharge process is a collaborative effort among many departments (and customers).

With no single manager, who resolves disputes that inevitably arise? All of these departments ultimately report to the CEO, so there is a single boss over all of them, but employees can't go to the CEO with a problem about, say, coordinating discharge activities between nursing and housekeeping. The CEO would throw them out of his or her office. Instead, the organization needs to develop some sort of collaborative management for resolving process issues.

Usually this means that the enterprise develops committees and steering groups for providing enterprise process management. Although this can be an effective solution, and in fact may be the *only* solution, the work of such groups is both slow and expensive.

Requirements Gaps

As stated in Q3, few organizations today create their own enterprise systems from scratch. Instead, they license an enterprise product that provides specific functions and features and that includes inherent procedures. But, such licensed products are never a perfect fit. Almost always there are gaps between the requirements of the organization and the capabilities of the licensed application.

The first challenge is identifying the gaps. To specify a gap, an organization must know both what it needs and what the new product does. However, it can be very difficult for an organization to determine what it needs; that difficulty is one reason organizations chose to license rather than to build. Further, the features and functions of complex products such as CRM or ERP are not easy to identify. Thus, gap identification is a major task when implementing enterprise systems.

The second challenge is deciding what to do with gaps, once they are identified. Either the organization needs to change the way it does things to adapt to the new application or the application must be altered to match what the organization does. Either choice is problematic. Employees will resist change, but paying for alterations is expensive and, as noted in Chapter 4, the organization is committing to maintaining those alternations as the application is changed over time. Here, organizations fill gaps by choosing their lesser regret.

Transition Problems

Transitioning to a new enterprise system is also difficult. The organization must somehow change from using isolated departmental systems to using the new enterprise system, while continuing to run the business. It's like having heart surgery while running a 100-yard dash.

Such transitions require careful planning and substantial training. Inevitably, problems will develop. Knowing this will occur, senior management needs to communicate the need for the change to the employees and then stand behind the new system as the kinks are worked out. It is an incredibly stressful time for all involved employees. We will discuss development techniques and implementation strategies further in Chapter 10.

Employee Resistance

People resist change. Change requires effort and it engenders fear. Considerable research and literature exists about the reasons for change resistance and how organizations can deal with it. Here we will summarize the major principles.

First, senior-level management needs to communicate the need for the change to the organization and must reiterate that, as necessary, throughout the transition process. Second, employees fear change because it threatens **self-efficacy**, which is a person's belief that he or she can be successful at his or her job. To enhance confidence, employees need to be trained and coached on the successful use of the new system. Word-of-mouth is a very powerful factor, and, in some cases, key users are trained ahead of time to create positive buzz about the new system. Video demonstrations of employees successfully using the new system are also effective.

Some companies may change too often. See the Guide on pages 174–175 for a discussion on how management fads can grow tiresome for employees.

Third, employees may need to be given extra inducement to change to the new system. As one experienced change consultant said, "Nothing succeeds like praise or cash, especially cash." Straight-out pay for change is bribery, but contests with cash prizes among employees or groups can be very effective at inducing change.

Implementing new enterprise systems can solve many problems and bring great efficiency and cost savings to an organization, but it is not for the faint of heart.

How does the knowledge in this chapter help *Fox Lake* and you?

If key personnel at Fox Lake knew the problems of information silos, they would have been able to avoid the situation that occurred here. Specifically, when Jeff Stone created the wedding events business plan, he would have known to consider the need for enterprise systems for facility reservations. In fact, in addition to resource conflicts between wedding events and facilities, he should also have considered likely facility conflicts among wedding events, golf, and tennis, as well as facilities.

You can benefit from this knowledge because you have been forewarned about the consequences of information silos and data duplication. You also understand how enterprise systems can eliminate silos, but know that developing and implementing such systems is not easy. You also know the basic functions of the "big three" enterprise systems: CRM, ERP, and EAI. Finally, you know the major challenges of implementing enterprise systems and have some idea of how to deal with resistance to change.

Ethics Guide

Dialing for Dollars

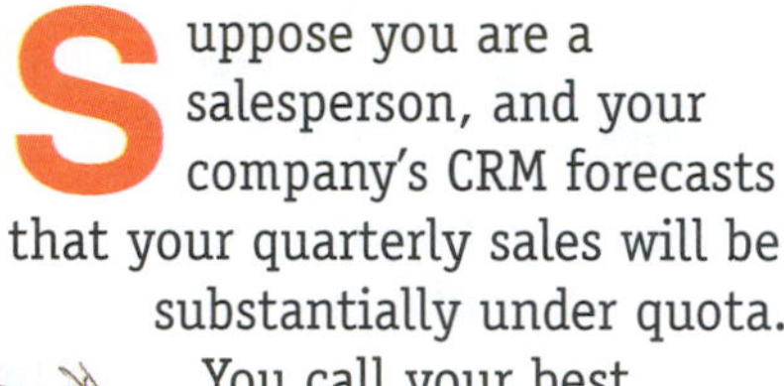

Suppose you are a salesperson, and your company's CRM forecasts that your quarterly sales will be substantially under quota. You call your best customers to increase sales, but no one is willing to buy more.

Your boss says that it has been a bad quarter for all of the salespeople. It's so bad, in fact, that the vice president of sales has authorized a 20-percent discount on new orders. The only stipulation is that customers must take delivery prior to the end of the quarter so that accounting can book the order. "Start dialing for dollars," she says, "and get what you can. Be creative."

Using your CRM, you identify your top customers and present the discount offer to them. The first customer balks at increasing her inventory, "I just don't think we can sell that much."

"Well," you respond, "how about if we agree to take back any inventory you don't sell next quarter?" (By doing this, you increase your current sales and commission, and you also help your company make its quarterly sales projections. The additional product is likely to come back next quarter, but you think, "Hey, that's then and this is now.")

"OK," she says, "but I want you to stipulate the return option on the purchase order."

You know that you cannot write that on the purchase order because accounting won't book all of the order if you do. So you tell her that you'll send her an email with that stipulation. She increases her order, and accounting books the full amount.

With another customer, you try a second strategy. Instead of offering the discount, you offer the product at full price, but agree to pay a 20-percent credit in the next quarter. That way you can book the full price now. You pitch this offer as follows: "Our marketing department analyzed past sales using our fancy new computer system, and we know that increasing advertising will cause additional sales. So, if you order more product now, next quarter we'll give you 20 percent of the order back to pay for advertising."

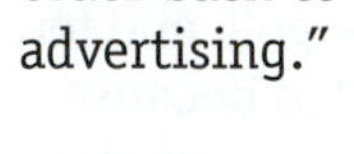

Discussion Questions

1. Is it ethical for you to write the email agreeing to take the product back? If that email comes to light later, what do you think your boss will say?
2. Is it ethical for you to offer the "advertising" discount? What effect does that discount have on your company's balance sheet?
3. Is it ethical for you to ship to the fictitious company? Is it legal?
4. Describe the impact of your activities on next quarter's inventories.
5. Setting aside the ethical issues, would you say the enterprise system is more a help or a hindrance in this example?

In truth, you doubt the customer will spend the money on advertising. Instead, they'll just take the credit and sit on a bigger inventory. That will kill your sales to them next quarter, but you'll solve that problem then.

Even with these additional orders, you're still under quota. In desperation, you decide to sell product to a fictitious company that is "owned" by your brother-in-law. You set up a new account, and when accounting calls your brother-in-law for a credit check, he cooperates with your scheme. You then sell $40,000 of product to the fictitious company and ship the product to your brother-in-law's garage. Accounting books the revenue in the quarter, and you have finally made quota. A week into the next quarter, your brother-in-law returns the merchandise.

Meanwhile, unknown to you, your company's ERP system is scheduling production. The program that creates the production schedule reads the sales from your activities (and those of the other salespeople) and finds a sharp increase in product demand. Accordingly, it generates a schedule that calls for substantial production increases and schedules workers for the production runs. The production system, in turn, schedules the material requirements with the inventory application, which increases raw materials purchases to meet the increased production schedule.

Guide

The Flavor-of-the-Month Club

"Oh, come on. I've been here 30 years and I've heard it all. All these management programs. . . . Years ago, we had Zero Defects. Then it was Total Quality Management, and after that, Six Sigma. We've had all the pet theories from every consultant in the Western Hemisphere. No, wait, we had consultants from Asia, too.

"Do you know what flavor we're having now? We're redesigning ourselves to be 'customer-centric.' We are going to integrate our functional systems into a CRM system to transform the entire company to be 'customer-centric.'

"You know how these programs go? First, we have a pronouncement at a 'kick-off meeting' where the CEO tells us what the new flavor is going to be and why it's so important. Then a swarm of consultants and 'change management' experts tell us how they're going to 'empower' us. Then HR adds some new item to our annual review, such as, 'Measures taken to achieve customer-centric company.'

"So, we all figure out some lame thing to do so that we have something to put in that category of our annual review. Then we forget about it because we know the next new flavor of the month will be along soon. Or worse, if they actually force us to use the new system, we comply, but viciously. You know, go out of our way to show that the new system can't work, that it really screws things up.

"You think I sound bitter, but I've seen this so many times before. The consultants and rising stars in our company get together and dream up one of these programs. Then they present it to the senior managers. That's when they make their first mistake: They think that if they can sell it to management, then it must be a good idea. They treat senior management like the customer. They should have to sell the idea to those of us who actually sell, support, or make things. Senior management is just the banker; the managers should let us decide if it's a good idea.

"If someone really wanted to empower me, she would listen rather than talk. Those of us who do the work have hundreds of ideas of how to do it better. Now it's customer-centric? As if we haven't been trying to do that for years!

"Anyway, after the CEO issues the pronouncements about the new system, he gets busy with other things and forgets about it for a while. Six months might go by, and then we're either told we're not doing enough to become customer-centric (or whatever the flavor is) or the company announces another new flavor.

"In manufacturing they talk about push versus pull. You know, with push style, you make things and push them onto the sales force and the customers. With pull style, you let the customers' demand pull the product out of manufacturing. You build when you have holes in inventory. Well, they should adapt those ideas to what they call 'change management.' I mean, does anybody need to manage real change? Did somebody have a 'Use the iPhone program'? Did some CEO announce, 'This year, we're all going to use the iPhone'? Did the HR department put a line into our annual evaluation form that asked how many times we'd used an iPhone? No, no, no, and no. Customers pulled the iPhone through. We wanted it, so we bought and used iPhones. Same with Kindle, iPad, Twitter, and Facebook.

"That's pull. You get a group of workers to form a network, and you get things going among the people who do the work. Then you build on that to obtain true organizational change. Why don't they figure it out?

"Anyway, I've got to run. We've got the kick-off meeting of our new initiative—something called business process management. Now they're going to empower me to manage my own activities, I suppose. Like, after 30 years, I don't know how to do that. Oh, well, I plan to retire soon.

"Oh, wait. Here, take my T-shirt from the knowledge management program 2 years ago. I never wore it. It says, 'Empowering You through Knowledge Management.' That one didn't last long."

Discussion Questions

1. Clearly, this person is cynical about new programs and new ideas. What do you think might have been the cause of her antagonism? What seems to be her principal concern?
2. What does she mean by "vicious" compliance? Give an example of an experience you've had that exemplifies such compliance.
3. Consider her point that the proponents of new programs treat senior managers as the customer. What does she mean? To a consultant, is senior management the customer? What do you think she's trying to say?
4. What does she mean when she says, "If someone wants to empower me, she would listen rather than talk"? How does listening to someone empower that person?
5. Her examples of "pull change" all involve the use of new products. To what extent do you think pull works for new management programs?
6. How do you think management could introduce new programs in a way that would cause them to be pulled through the organization? Consider the suggestion she makes, as well as your own ideas.
7. If you managed an employee who had an attitude like this, what could you do to make her more positive about organizational change and new programs and initiatives?

ACTIVE REVIEW

Use this Active Review to verify that you understand the ideas and concepts that answer the chapter's study questions.

Q1 How do information systems vary by scope?

Explain how information systems vary by scope. Provide an example of an information system's scope based on an organization similar to Fox Lake Country Club but different than the one in Figure 7-1. Describe characteristics of information systems of each type.

Q2 When are information silos a problem?

Define *information silo,* and explain how such silos come into existence. When do such silos become a problem? Name and describe five common functional applications. Describe data that are likely duplicated among those five applications. Summarize the problems that information silos cause.

Q3 How do enterprise information systems eliminate silos?

Explain how the information silo at Fox Lake led to the conflict between the wedding events and facilities departments at Fox Lake. Describe how the system in Figure 7-7 solves this problem. Describe a situation in which an enterprise system creates a burden for one department without any benefit to that department. Explain a key difference between the enterprise system at Fox Lake and the one at the hospital in Figure 7-8. Describe a key benefit to kitchen operations of the enterprise system to the hospital. Define *business process reengineering,* and explain why it is difficult and expensive.

Q4 How do CRM, ERP, and EAI support enterprise systems?

Explain two major reasons why it is expensive to develop enterprise information systems in-house. Explain the advantages of inherent processes. Define and differentiate among *CRM, ERP,* and *EAI.* Explain how CRM and ERP are more similar to one another than to EAI.

Q5 What are the challenges when implementing new enterprise systems?

Name and describe four sources of challenge when implementing enterprise systems. Describe why enterprise systems management must be collaborative. Explain two major tasks required to identify requirements gaps. Summarize challenges of transitioning to an enterprise system. Explain why employees resist change, and describe three ways of responding to that resistance.

How does the **knowledge** in this chapter help **Fox Lake** and **you?**

Explain how Jeff Stone would have benefited from the knowledge of this chapter. Describe how you can benefit as well. Suppose a job interviewer asked you, "What do you know about ERP?" How would you respond?

KEY TERMS AND CONCEPTS

USING YOUR KNOWLEDGE

1. Using the example of your university, give examples of information systems for each of the four levels of scope shown in Figure 7-1. Describe three workgroup information systems that are likely to duplicate data. Explain how the characteristics of information systems in Figure 7-1 relate to your examples.

2. In your answer to question 1, explain how the three workgroup information systems create information silos. Describe the kinds of problems that those silos are likely to cause. Use Figure 7-6 as a guide.

3. Using your answer to question 3, describe an enterprise information system that will eliminate the silos. Explain whether your information system is more like that in Figure 7-7 or more like the one in Figure 7-8. Would the implementation of your system require process reengineering? Explain why or why not.

4. Is the information system you proposed in your answer to question 3 an application of CRM, ERP, or EAI? If so, which one and why? If not, explain why not.

5. Explain how the four sources of challenge discussed in Q5 would pertain to the implementation of the information system you propose in your answer to question 3. Give specific examples of each.

COLLABORATION EXERCISE 7

Before you start this exercise, read Chapter Extensions 1 and 2, which describe collaboration techniques as well as tools for managing collaboration tasks. In particular, consider using Google Docs, Windows Live SkyDrive, Microsoft SharePoint, or some other collaboration tool.

The county planning office issues building permits, septic system permits, and county road access permits for all building projects in the county. The planning office issues permits to homeowners and builders for the construction of new homes and buildings and for any remodeling projects that involve electrical, gas, plumbing, and other utilities, as well as the conversion of unoccupied spaces such as garages into living or working space. The office also issues permits for new or upgraded septic systems and permits to provide driveway entrances to county roads.

Figure 7-13 shows the permit process that the county used for many years. Contractors and homeowners found this process to be slow and very frustrating. For one, they did not like its sequential nature. Only after a permit had been approved or rejected by the engineering review process would they find out that a health or highway review was also needed. Because each of these reviews could take 3 or 4 weeks, applicants requesting permits wanted the review processes to be concurrent rather than serial. Also, both the permit applicants and county personnel were frustrated because they never knew where a particular application was in the permit process. A contractor would call to ask how much longer, and it might take an hour or more just to find which desk the permits were on.

Accordingly, the county changed the permit process to that shown in Figure 7-14. In this second process, the permit office made three copies of the permit and distributed one to each department. The departments reviewed the permits in parallel; a clerk would analyze the results and, if there were no rejections, approve the permit.

Unfortunately, this process had a number of problems, too. For one, some of the permit applications were lengthy; some included as many as 40 to 50 pages of large architectural drawings. The labor and copy expense to the county was considerable.

Second, in some cases departments reviewed documents unnecessarily. If, for example, the highway department rejected an application, then neither the engineering nor health departments needed to continue their reviews. At first, the county responded to this problem by having the clerk who analyzed results cancel the reviews of other departments when he or she received a rejection. However, that policy was exceedingly unpopular with the permit applicants, because once an application was rejected and the problem corrected, the permit had to go back through the other departments. The permit would go to the end of the line and work its way back into the departments from which it had been pulled. Sometimes this resulted in a delay of 5 or 6 weeks.

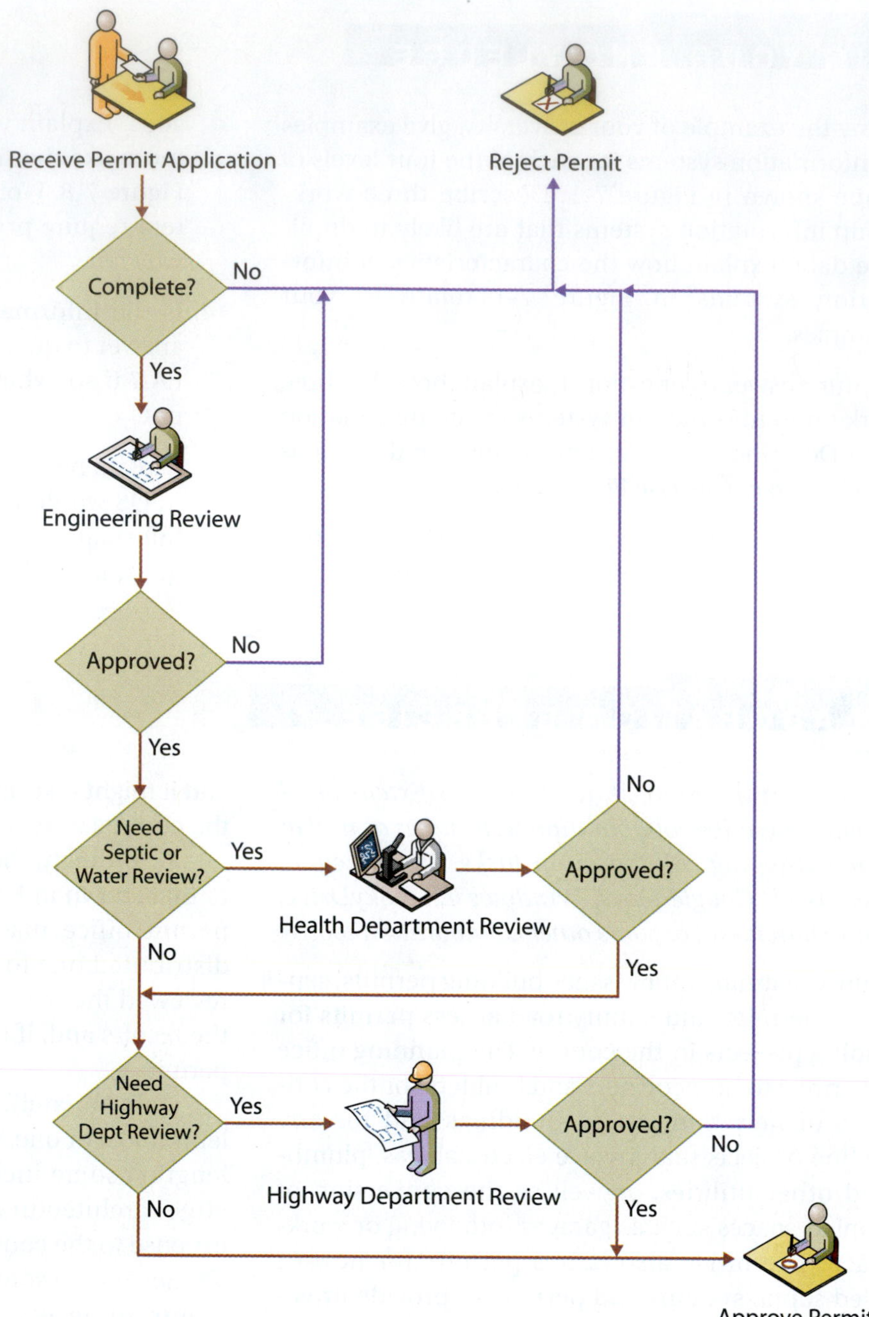

Figure 7-13
Sequential Permit-Review Process

Canceling reviews was unpopular with the departments as well, because permit-review work had to be repeated. An application might have been nearly completed when it was cancelled due to a rejection in another department. When the application came through again, the partial work results from the earlier review were lost.

1. Explain why the processes in Figures 7-13 and 7-14 are classified as enterprise processes rather than as departmental processes. Why are these processes not considered to be interorganizational processes?
2. Using Figure 7-8 as an example, redraw Figure 7-13 using an enterprise information system that processes a shared database. Explain the advantages of this system over the paper-based system in Figure 7-13.
3. Using Figure 7-8 as an example, redraw Figure 7-14 using an enterprise information system that processes a shared database. Explain the advantages of this system over the paper-based system in Figure 7-14.
4. Assuming that the county has just changed from the system in Figure 7-13 to 7-14, which of your answers

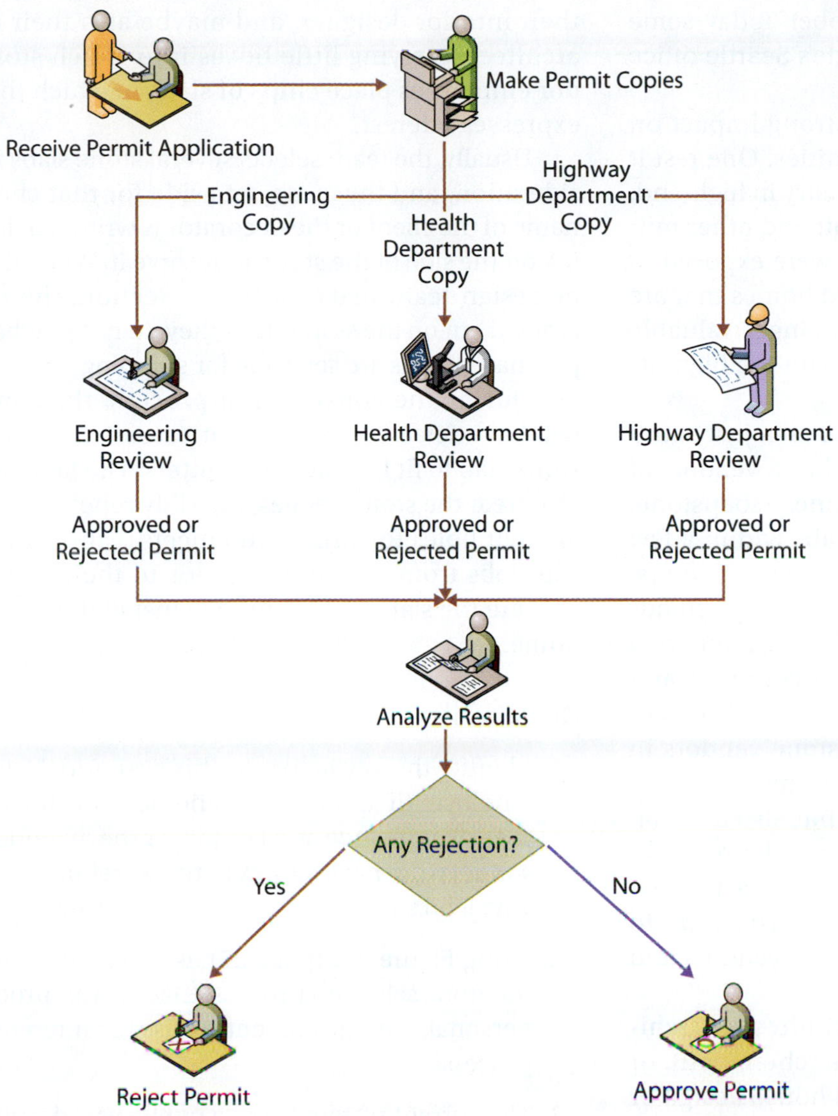

Figure 7-14
Parallel Permit-Review Process

in questions 2 and 3 do you think is better? Justify your answer.

5. Assume your team is in charge of the implementation of the system you recommend in your answer to question 4. Describe how each of the four challenges discussed in Q5 pertain to this implementation. Explain how your team will deal with those challenges. Read the Guide on pages 174–175, if you have not already done so. Assume that person is a key player in the implementation of the new system. How will your team deal with her?

CASE STUDY 7

Process Cast in Stone

Bill Gates and Microsoft were exceedingly generous in the allocation of stock options to Microsoft employees, especially during Microsoft's first 20 years. Because of that generosity, Microsoft created 4 billionaires and an estimated 12,000 millionaires as Microsoft succeeded and the value of employee stock options soared. Not all of those millionaires stayed in the Seattle/Redmond/Bellevue, Washington, area, but thousands did. These thousands of millionaires were joined by a lesser number who made their millions at Amazon.com and, to a lesser extent, at RealNetworks, Visio (acquired by

Microsoft), and Aldus (acquired by Adobe). Today, some Google employees who work at Google's Seattle office are joining these ranks.

The influx of this wealth had a strong impact on Seattle and the surrounding communities. One result has been the creation of a thriving industry in high-end, very expensive homes. These Microsoft and other millionaires are college educated; many were exposed to fine arts at the university. They created homes that are not just large and situated on exceedingly valuable property, but that also are appointed with the highest-quality components.

Today, if you drive through a small area just south of central Seattle, you will find a half dozen vendors of premium granite, marble, limestone, soapstone, quartzite, and other types of stone slabs within a few blocks of each other. These materials cover counters, bathrooms, and other surfaces in the new and remodeled homes of this millionaire class. The stone is quarried in Brazil, India, Italy, Turkey, and other countries and either cut at its origin or sent to Italy for cutting. Huge cut slabs, 6 feet by 10 feet, arrive at the stone vendors in south Seattle, who stock them in their warehouses. The stone slabs vary not only in material, but also in color, veining pattern, and overall beauty (see Figure 7-15). Choosing these slabs is like selecting fine art. (Visit *www.pentalonline.com* or *www.metamarble.com* to understand the premium quality of these vendors and products.)

Typically, the client (homeowner) hires an architect who either draws plans for the kitchen, bath, or other stone area as part of the overall house design or who hires a specialized kitchen architect who draws those plans. Most of these clients also hire interior decorators who help them select colors, fabrics, furniture, art, and other home furnishings. Because selecting a stone slab is like selecting art, clients usually visit the stone vendors' warehouses personally. They walk through the warehouses, often accompanied by their interior designer, and maybe also their kitchen architect, carrying little boxes into which stone vendor employees place chips of slabs in which the client expresses interest.

Usually, the team selects several stone slabs for consideration, and those are set aside for that client. The name of the client or the decorator is written in indelible ink on the side of the stone to reserve it. When the client or design team makes a final selection, the name is crossed out on the stone slabs they do not purchase. The purchased slabs are set aside for shipping.

During the construction process, the contractor will have selected a stone fabricator, who will cut the stone slab to fit the client's counters. The fabricator will also treat the stone's edges, possibly repolish the stone, and cut holes for sinks and faucets. Fabricators move the slabs from the stone vendor to their workshops, prepare the slab, and eventually install it in the client's home.

Questions

1. Identify the key actors in this scenario. Name their employer (if appropriate) and describe the role that they play. Include as a key player the operations personnel who move stones in the warehouse as well as who load stones on the fabricators' trucks.

2. Using Figure 2-2 (page 27) as an example, diagram the stone selection process. Classify this process as a personal, workgroup, enterprise, or interenterprise process.

3. The current system is not a paper-based system; it is a stone-based system. Explain why this is so.

4. Create an enterprise system that uses a shared database. Change the diagram you created in your answer to question 2 to include this database. (Assume every slab of stone and every location in the warehouse has a unique identifier.) Does the

Figure 7-15
High-End Countertops from Pental

Source: Used with permission of Pental Granite and Marble.

shared database system solve the problems of the stone-based system? Why or why not?

5. Do you think the customers, designers, and fabricators would prefer the stone-based system or the database system? Explain.

6. Suppose you manage the stone vendor company. If you implement the system in your answer to question 4, what problems can you expect? If you do not implement that system, what problems can you expect? What course of action would you take and why?

7. Explain how a knowledge of enterprise systems can help you become a stone slab client rather than a stone chipper.

CHAPTER 8

E-Commerce, Web 2.0, and Social Networking

This could happen to you

"I would totally recommend Fox Lake *Country Club for your wedding reception if you want to be told to disinvite your close friends and family. I dreamed my whole life about having my wedding reception there, and I was so excited . . . little did I know that they were TOTAL liars who planned ballroom renovations DURING my wedding reception—told me to cut 15 people from my guest list!! What is the point of having your dream wedding if the people you love aren't there to enjoy it with you!!?? They are just greedy businesspeople who want to get your money no matter what!!! Whatever you do, don't ever work with Fox Lake Country Club!!!!!"*

—Posting on Fox Lake's Facebook page

"She said WHAT?" asked Jeff Lloyd, general manager of Fox Lake Country Club.

"She said that we're a bunch of greedy businesspeople who want to get money, no matter what,'" Anne responded.

"On our Facebook page????" Jeff is incredulous.

"Yup."

"Well, delete it then. That shouldn't be too hard." Jeff turns to look out the window at the golfers headed to the first tee.

"Jeff, we can do that, but I think we should be careful here," Anne offers this opinion cautiously as she pushes back.

"No, of course, let's leave it out there. Let's tell the whole world that you and I are greedy businesspeople out to take advantage of our customers. What did she say, 'Don't ever work with Fox Lake?' Yeah, let's leave that there, too . . . maybe put a link to it on our Web site. That'll help at the next board meeting." Sarcasm drips from his voice.

STUDY QUESTIONS

Q1 What types of interorganizational systems exist?

Q2 How do companies use e-commerce?

Q3 Why is Web 2.0 important to business?

Q4 How does social capital benefit you and organizations?

Q5 How does social CRM empower customers?

How does the knowledge in this chapter help *Fox Lake* and you?

"Well, Jeff, here's the deal. You don't want to enrage the connected . . . they have power. Remember what happened to Nestlé?"

"No, what? Are they greedy businesspeople, too?"

"They got some bad PR on their site and just deleted it. Bingo, it came back, but a thousandfold. Worse, someone at Nestlé got high handed and posted criticism of the commenters; it was pouring gas on a raging fire."

"SHE SAID WHAT?—ON OUR FACEBOOK PAGE???"

"Anne, you're tedious. Tell me what we CAN do!"

"Be open. The key is open, honest communication. We fix the problem—get the maintenance done ahead of schedule or delay, I don't care. Then, we tell our upset and nervous bride that we fixed it . . . maybe ask her, gently, to write that on our page. Possibly we follow up with our side of the story, briefly and not defensively."

"Too passive for me. Let's sue her for defamation." Jeff's sarcasm turns to anger.

"No, Jeff. No. That's not the way. You have any idea of the comments we'd get?"

"A lot."

"Besides, we have another problem." Anne represses a smile as she thinks.

"What's that, Anne?"

"Her father. He's a partner in the club's law firm. You gonna hire him to sue his own daughter? Over her wedding plans?" Anne tries hard not to chuckle.

Jeff stares at the golfers out the window, "Weddings. Why did I think weddings were a good idea? What's the matter with golf? It's a good business . . . you water the grass, put out the flags, move the tees around . . . ."

Optional Extensions for this chapter are • CE13: Supply Chain Management 480 • CE14: Processing Social Capital: Facebook, Twitter, and User-Generated Content (UGC) 490

Q1 What Types of Interorganizational Systems Exist?

Chapter 7 presented information systems within organizations. In this chapter, we extend that discussion to address **interorganizational IS**, which we define as information systems used between or among organizations that are independently owned and managed. In this discussion, we include customers as organizations, even if they are only a sole individual. Figure 8-1 shows four types of interorganizational systems in use today. These types are presented in the order in which they developed.

Pre-Internet Systems

Prior to the general use of the Internet in the mid-1990s, interorganizational systems communicated via postal mail, telephone, and fax. As you would expect, by today's standards the pace was incredibly slow.

Because such systems are fading from use, we will not consider them in this text. However, note that in this pre-Internet age vendors were in control of the customer relationship. They controlled how their image was used through advertising and public relations. They decided when and how frequently they would contact the customer. Except for limited customer support, communication was one-way, from the vendor to the customer.

E-Commerce

E-commerce is the buying and selling of goods and services over public and private computer networks. E-commerce became feasible with the creation and widespread use of HTTP, HTML, and server applications such as Web storefronts that enabled browser-based transactions.

E-commerce was not only faster than pre-Internet commerce, it also brought vendors closer to their customers, and in the process changed market characteristics and dynamics. Amazon.com and eBay were two big winners in the e-commerce era. We discuss e-commerce in greater detail in Q2.

Web 2.0

The increased capabilities of browsers, together with browser extensions such as Flash, have enabled thin-client applications to have considerable functionality. Vendors can now perform sophisticated operations in a browser, with no program download or installation required. The collection of many of these new capabilities, and the new business models that have resulted, has come to be known as Web 2.0.

Figure 8-1
Types of Interorganizational Systems

Type	Supporting technologies	Characteristics
Pre-Internet	Postal mail, telephone, fax, EDI	Slow. Vendors in control of relationship. Primitive interorganizational IS.
E-commerce	HTTP, HTML, Web storefronts	Faster. Vendors and customers closer. New market dynamics.
Web 2.0	Thin clients, Flash	Even faster. Advertising revenue models; flexibility. Rise of user-generated content.
Enterprise 2.0	Facebook, Twitter, social CRM; service-oriented architecture (SOA)	Emergent relationships; customer selects relationship characteristics; vendors lose control of relationship. Dynamic interorganizational IS.

Google led the way when it developed a new business model that provided customized advertising (coupled with its superb search engine). Once customers received ads based on their recent searches, a new era was born. When Oracle places an Oracle CRM ad in the *Wall Street Journal,* it has only a very general idea of how many qualified prospects read that ad. However, run that same ad to customers who have just Googled "Oracle CRM," and Oracle knows that it has reached an interested reader, if not a qualified one. By using Web 2.0 technology, Oracle can determine how many customers the ad reached, how long they read the ad, what actions they took in response to the ad, and so forth. This shift in advertising has been the death knell for traditional newspapers and magazines, but it has taken a decade for that outcome to become apparent.

Around the same time that Google launched search with advertising, users began to employ their powerful browsers to provide feedback about products they had purchased. Amazon.com facilitated book reviews; eBay, seller reviews; CNET.com, electronics reviews; and so forth. Independent reviewer sites such as TripAdvisor (*www.tripadvisor.com*) also emerged. This user-generated content meant that vendors began to lose control of their messages and their image. We discuss Web 2.0 further in Q3.

Enterprise 2.0

The meaning of Enterprise 2.0 is emerging. At present, **Enterprise 2.0** is the application of Web 2.0 technologies, collaboration systems, social networking, and related technologies to facilitate the cooperative work of intellectual workers in organizations. The term was originated by Andrew McAfee in 2006[1] and has since taken on numerous interpretations and flavors.

Emergence is a key principle of Enterprise 2.0. Relationships are not predefined; ideas are not predefined; even projects are not predefined. Instead, they emerge as a result of collaboration via social networking. Whereas McAfee defined Enterprise 2.0 to encompass interactions both within and across organizations, the term so far has received the greatest attention in its application to vendor–customer relationships, where it is referred to as **Social CRM**.

The bottom line of these movements, however, is that the customer now controls his or her relationship with the company. Organizations offer many different customer touch points: the company's Web site, Facebook, Twitter, customer support sites, and others. Customers tailor their relationship with the vendor in the way they use those touch points, and, in Enterprise 2.0 fashion, the relationship emerges. This phenomenon will revolutionize marketing and possibly CRM; we investigate this further in Q5.

Enterprise 2.0 and Social CRM have also given a boost to **service-oriented architecture (SOA)**, which is a software design methodology and set of program communication standards that greatly improve the flexibility and adaptability of interorganizational program-to-program communication. SOA standards are meta, metadata. They are standards for defining how interprogram communication metadata are to be created.

You can learn more about SOA in Chapter Extension 18.

We begin the discussion with e-commerce.

Q2 How Do Companies Use E-Commerce?

As stated earlier, e-commerce is the buying and selling of goods and services over public and private computer networks. Notice that this definition restricts e-commerce to buying and selling transactions. Checking the weather at yahoo.com is not e-commerce,

[1] Andrew McAfee, "Enterprise 2.0: The Dawn of Emergent Collaboration," *MIT Sloan Management Review*, Spring 2006. Available at: *http://sloanreview.mit.edu/the-magazine/files/saleable-pdfs/47306.pdf* (accessed May 2010).

Figure 8-2
E-Commerce Categories

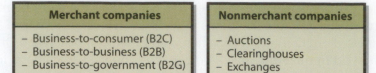

Merchant companies	Nonmerchant companies
– Business-to-consumer (B2C) – Business-to-business (B2B) – Business-to-government (B2G)	– Auctions – Clearinghouses – Exchanges

but buying a weather-service subscription that is paid for and delivered over the Internet is.

Figure 8-2 lists categories of e-commerce companies. The U.S. Census Bureau, which publishes statistics on e-commerce activity, defines **merchant companies** as those that take title to the goods they sell. They buy goods and resell them. It defines **nonmerchant companies** as those that arrange for the purchase and sale of goods without ever owning or taking title to those goods. Regarding services, merchant companies sell services that they provide; nonmerchant companies sell services provided by others. Of course, a company can be both a merchant and nonmerchant company.

E-Commerce Merchant Companies

The three main types of merchant companies are those that sell directly to consumers, those that sell to companies, and those that sell to government. Each uses slightly different information systems in the course of doing business. **B2C**, or **business-to-consumer e-commerce**, concerns sales between a supplier and a retail customer (the consumer). Traditional B2C information systems rely on a **Web storefront** that customers use to enter and manage their orders. Amazon.com, REI.com, and LLBean.com are examples of companies that use B2C information systems. More modern B2C systems integrate social networking functionality, as you will learn in Q5 of this chapter.[2]

You can learn more about information systems and supply chains in Chapter Extension 13.

The term **B2B**, or **business-to-business e-commerce**, refers to sales between companies. As Figure 8-3 shows, raw materials suppliers use B2B systems to sell to manufacturers, manufacturers use B2B systems to sell to distributors, and distributors uses B2B systems to sell to retailers.

B2G, or **business-to-government e-commerce**, refers to sales between companies and governmental organizations. In Figure 8-3, the manufacturer that uses an e-commerce site to sell computer hardware to the U.S. Department of State is engaging in B2G commerce. Suppliers, distributors, and retailers sell to the government as well.

B2C applications first captured the attention of mail-order and related businesses. However, companies in all sectors of the economy soon realized the enormous potential of B2B and B2G. The number of companies engaged in B2B and B2G commerce now far exceeds those engaged in B2C commerce.

Furthermore, today's B2B and B2G applications implement just a small portion of their potential capabilities. Their full utilization is some years away. Although most experts agree that these applications will involve SOA-designed systems that integrate supplier CRM systems with customer purchasing systems, the nature of that integration is being developed. Consequently, you can expect further progress and development in B2B and B2G applications during your career.

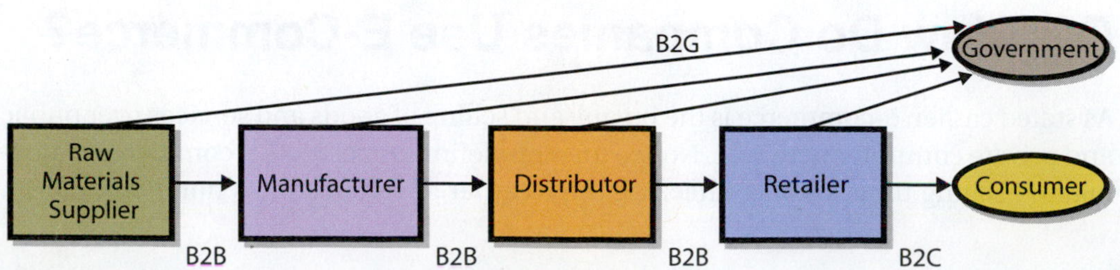

Figure 8-3
Example of Use of B2B, B2G, and B2C

[2] *Tourism Business Magazine*, November 2009, p. 20.

Nonmerchant E-Commerce

The most common nonmerchant e-commerce companies are auctions and clearinghouses. E-commerce **auctions** match buyers and sellers by using an e-commerce version of a standard auction. This e-commerce application enables the auction company to offer goods for sale and to support a competitive-bidding process. The best-known auction company is eBay, but many other auction companies exist; many serve particular industries.

Clearinghouses provide goods and services at a stated price and arrange for the delivery of the goods, but they never take title. One division of Amazon.com, for example, operates as a nonmerchant clearinghouse, allowing individuals and used bookstores to sell used books on the Amazon.com Web site. As a clearinghouse, Amazon.com matches the seller and the buyer and then takes payment from the buyer and transfers the payment to the seller, minus a commission. eBay operates in the same manner.

Another type of clearinghouse is an **electronic exchange** that matches buyers and sellers; the business process is similar to that of a stock exchange. Sellers offer goods at a given price through the electronic exchange, and buyers make offers to purchase over the same exchange. Price matches result in transactions from which the exchange takes a commission. Priceline.com is an example of an exchange used by consumers.

How Does E-Commerce Improve Market Efficiency?

E-commerce improves market efficiency in a number of different ways. For one, e-commerce leads to **disintermediation**, which is the elimination of middle layers of distributors and suppliers. You can buy a 3D TV from a typical "bricks-and-mortar" electronics store, or you can use e-commerce to buy it from the manufacturer. If you take the latter route, you eliminate the distributor, the retailer, and possibly more companies. The product is shipped directly from the manufacturer's finished goods inventory to you. You eliminate the distributor's and retailer's inventory-carrying costs, and you eliminate shipping overhead and handling activity. Because the distributor and associated inventories have become unnecessary waste, disintermediation increases market efficiency.

E-commerce also improves the flow of price information. As a consumer, you can go to any number of Web sites that offer product price comparisons. You can search for the 3D TV you want and sort the results by price and vendor reputation. You can find vendors that avoid your state sales tax or that omit or reduce shipping charges. The improved distribution of information about price and terms enables you to pay the lowest possible cost and serves ultimately to remove inefficient vendors. The market as a whole becomes more efficient.

From the seller's side, e-commerce produces information about **price elasticity** that has not been available before. Price elasticity measures the amount that demand rises or falls with changes in price. Using an auction, a company can learn not just what the top price for an item is, but also the second, third, and other prices from the losing bids. In this way, the company can determine the shape of the price elasticity curve.

Similarly, e-commerce companies can learn price elasticity directly from experiments on customers. For example, in one experiment, Amazon.com created three groups of similar books. It raised the price of one group 10 percent, lowered the price of the second group 10 percent, and left the price of the third group unchanged. Customers provided feedback to these changes by deciding whether to buy books at the offered prices. Amazon.com measured the total revenue (quantity times price) of each group and took the action (raise, lower, or maintain prices) on all books that maximized revenue. Amazon.com repeated the process until it reached the point at which the best action was to maintain current prices.

Managing prices by direct interaction with the customer yields better information than managing prices by watching competitors' pricing. By experimenting, companies

Figure 8-4
E-Commerce Market Efficiencies

Market Efficiencies
– Disintermediation – Increased information on price and terms – Knowledge of price elasticity • Losing-bidder auction prices • Price experimentation • More accurate information obtained directly from customer

learn how customers have internalized competitors' pricing, advertising, and messaging. It might be that customers do not know about a competitor's lower prices, in which case there is no need for a price reduction. Or, it may be that the competitor is using a price that, if lowered, would increase demand sufficiently to increase total revenue. Figure 8-4 summarizes the ways e-commerce generates market efficiencies.

What Economic Factors Disfavor E-Commerce?

Although there are tremendous advantages and opportunities for many organizations to engage in e-commerce, the economics of some industries may disfavor e-commerce activity. Companies need to consider the following economic factors:

- Channel conflict
- Price conflict
- Logistics expense
- Customer service expense

Consider the example of the manufacturer selling directly to the government agency shown in Figure 8-3. Before engaging in such e-commerce, the manufacturer must consider the unfavorable economic factors just listed. First, what **channel conflict** will develop? Suppose the manufacturer is a computer maker that is selling directly, B2G, to the State Department. When the manufacturer begins to sell goods B2G that State Department employees used to purchase from a retailer down the street, that retailer will resent the competition and might drop the manufacturer. If the value of the lost sales is greater than the value of the B2G sales, e-commerce is not a good solution, at least not on that basis.

Furthermore, when a business engages in e-commerce it may also cause **price conflict** with its traditional channels. Because of disintermediation, the manufacturer may be able to offer a lower price and still make a profit. However, as soon as the manufacturer offers the lower price, existing channels will object. Even if the manufacturer and the retailer are not competing for the same customers, the retailer still will not want a lower price to be readily known via the Web.

Also, the existing distribution and retailing partners do provide value; they are not just a cost. Without them, the manufacturer will have the increased *logistics expense* of entering and processing orders in small quantities. If the expense of processing a 1-unit order is the same as that for processing a 12-unit order (which it might be), the average logistics expense per item will be much higher for goods sold via e-commerce.

Similarly, *customer service expenses* are likely to increase for manufacturers that use e-commerce to sell directly to consumers. The manufacturer will be required to provide service to less sophisticated users and on a one-by-one basis. For example, instead of explaining to a single sales professional that the recent shipment of 100 Gizmo 3.0s requires a new bracket, the manufacturer will need to explain that 100 times to less knowledgeable, frustrated customers. Such service requires more training and more expense.

All four economic factors are important for organizations to consider when they contemplate e-commerce sales.

Q3 Why Is Web 2.0 Important to Business?

E-commerce sites duplicate the experience of shopping in a grocery store or other retail shop. The customer moves around the store, places items in a shopping cart, and then checks out. Shopping carts and other e-commerce techniques have been a boon to business, especially B2C commerce, but they do not take full advantage of the Web's potential.

Amazon.com was one of the first to recognize other possibilities when it added the "Customers Who Bought This Book Also Bought" feature to its Web site. With that feature, e-commerce broke new ground. No grocery store could or would have a sign that announced, "Customers who bought this tomato soup, also bought . . . ." That idea was the first step toward what has come to be known as Web 2.0.

What Is Web 2.0?

Although the specific meaning of **Web 2.0** is hard to pin down, it generally refers to a loose grouping of capabilities, technologies, business models, and philosophies. Figure 8-5 compares Web 2.0 to traditional processing. (For some reason, the term *Web 1.0* is not used.)

Software as a (Free) Service

Google, Amazon.com, and eBay exemplify Web 2.0. These companies do not sell software licenses, because software is not their product. Instead, they provide **software as a service (SAAS)**. You can search Google, run Google Docs, use Google Earth, process Gmail, and access Google Maps, all from a thin-client browser, with the bulk of the processing occurring in the cloud, somewhere on the Internet. Instead of software license fees, the Web 2.0 business model relies on advertising or other revenue that results as users employ the software as a service.

Web 2.0 applications are thin clients. As such, they do not require an installation on the users' computers. Web servers download Web 2.0 programs as code within HTML, as Flash, or as Silverlight code. Because this is so, they are readily (and frequently) updated. New features are added with little notice or fanfare. Web 2.0 users are accustomed to, and even expect, frequent updates to their license-free software.

Figure 8-6 shows new features that Google is considering adding to Google Maps (as of May 2010, that is). Notice the warning that they "may change, break, or disappear at

Web 2.0 Processing	Traditional Processing
Major winners: Google, Amazon.com, eBay	Major winners: Microsoft, Oracle, SAP
Software as a (free) service	Software as product
Frequent releases of thin-client applications	Infrequent, controlled releases
Business model relies on advertising or other revenue-from-use	Business model relies on sale of software licenses
Viral marketing	Extensive advertising
Product value increases with use and users	Product value fixed
Organic interfaces, mashups encouraged	Controlled, fixed interface
Participation	Publishing
Some rights reserved	All rights reserved

Figure 8-5
Comparison of Web 2.0 with Traditional Processing

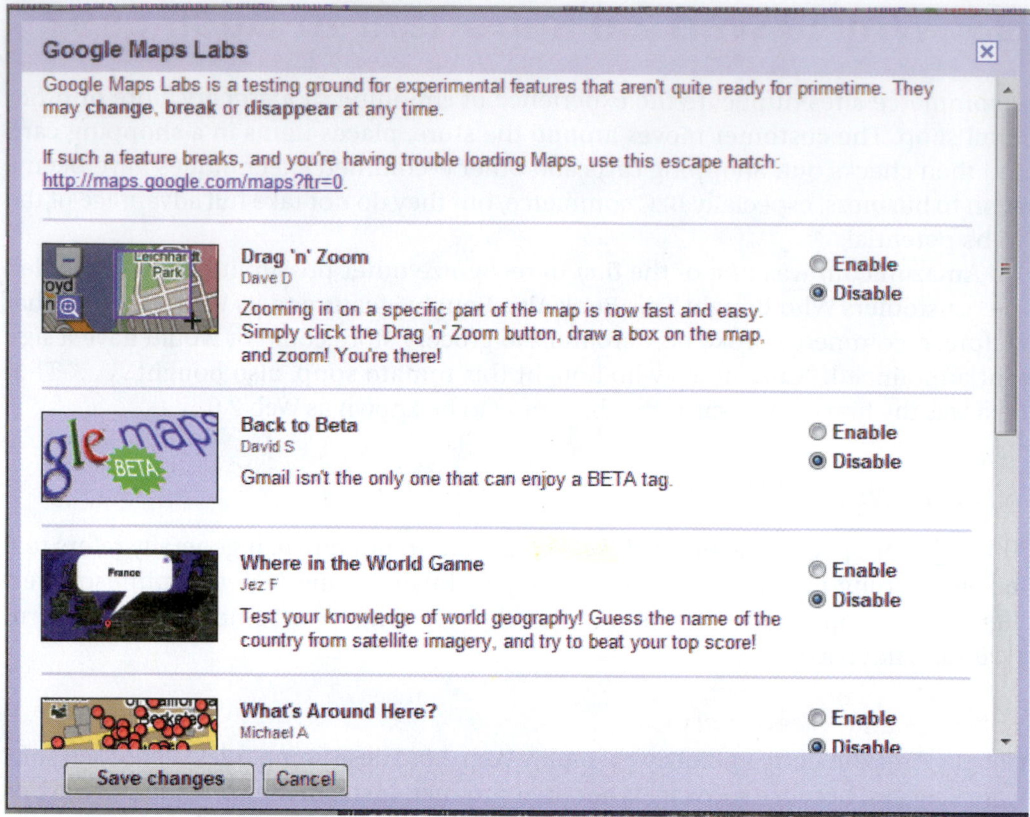

Figure 8-6
Potential New Features in Google Maps

Source: Used with permission from Google.

any time." By providing frequent updates this way, Google maintains its reputation as an innovative company while obtaining testing and usability feedback on new features.

Software as a service clashes with the software model used by traditional software vendors, such as Microsoft, Oracle, and SAP. Software is their product. They release new versions and new products infrequently. For example, 3 years separated the release of Microsoft Office 2007 from 2010. Releases are made in a very controlled fashion, and extensive testing and true beta programs precede every release.

Traditional software vendors depend on software license fees. If a large number of Office users switched to free word processing and spreadsheet applications, the hit on Microsoft's revenue would be catastrophic. Because of the importance of software licensing revenue, substantial marketing efforts are made to convert users to new releases.

In the Web 2.0 world, no such marketing is done; new features are released and vendors wait for users to spread the news to one another, one friend sending a message to many friends; most of whom send that message, in turn, to their friends; and so forth, in a process called **viral marketing**. Google has never announced any software in a formal marketing campaign. Users carry the message to one another. In fact, if a product requires advertising to be successful, then it is not a Web 2.0 product.

By the way, traditional software companies do use the term *software as a service*. However, they use it only to mean that they will provide their software products via the cloud rather than having customers install that software on their computers. Software licenses for their products still carry a sometimes hefty license fee. So, to be accurate, we should say that in the Web 2.0 world software is provided as a *free* service.

Use Increases Value

Another characteristic of Web 2.0 is that the value of the site increases with users and use. Amazon.com gains more value as more users write more reviews. Amazon.com becomes *the* place to go for information about books or other products. Similarly, the more people who buy or sell on eBay, the more eBay gains value as a site.

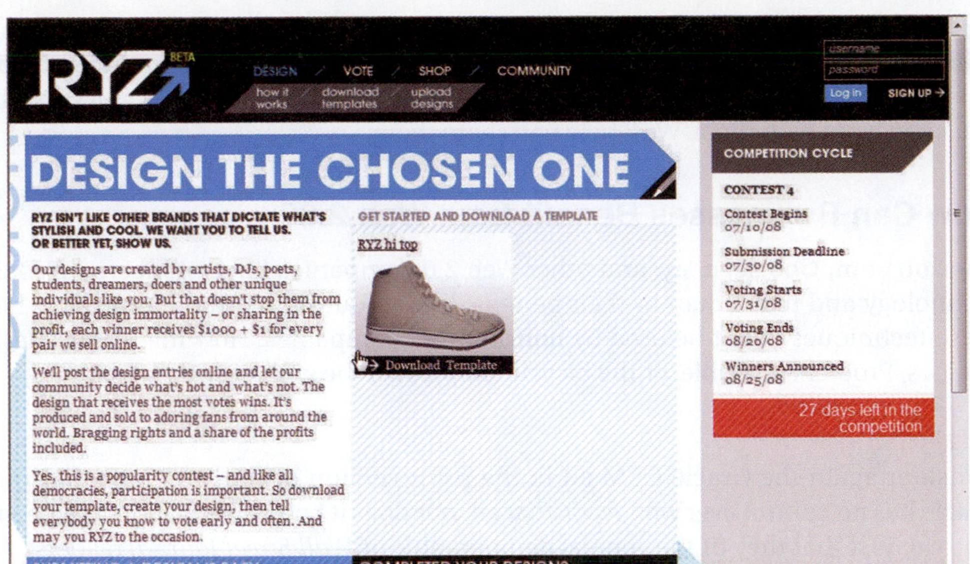

Figure 8-7
Design by Crowdsourcing

Source: Used with permission from RYZ.

The term **user-generated content (UGC)** refers to Web site content that is contributed by users. Although reviews are still the bulk of such content, some companies have created Web sites and tools that encourage users to contribute in other ways. On some sites, users can provide customer support to one another, or even participate in the creation of product specifications, designs, and complete products in a process called **crowdsourcing**. As shown in Figure 8-7, the shoe start-up company RYZ (*www.ryzwear.com*) sponsors shoe design contests to help it understand which shoes to create and how to market those designs.

When people contribute UGC, they have personal interests and biases. To reflect on ethics issues involved when contributing UGC, see the Ethics Guide on pages 200–201.

Crowdsourcing combines social networking, viral marketing, and open-source design, saving considerable cost while cultivating customers. With crowdsourcing, the crowd performs classic in-house market research and development and does so in such a way that customers are being set up to buy.

Organic User Interfaces and Mashups

The traditional software model carefully controls the users' experience. All Office programs share a common user interface; the ribbon (toolbar) in Word is similar to the ribbon in PowerPoint and in Excel. In contrast, Web 2.0 interfaces are organic. Users find their way around eBay and PayPal, and if the user interface changes from day to day, well, that is just the nature of Web 2.0. Further, Web 2.0 encourages **mashups**, which result when the output from two or more Web sites is combined into a single user experience.

Google's **My Maps** is an excellent mashup example. Google publishes Google Maps and provides tools for users to make custom modifications to those maps. Thus, users mash the Google map product with their own knowledge. One user demonstrated the growth of gang activity to the local police by mapping new graffiti sites on Google maps. Other users share their experiences or photos of hiking trips or other travel.

In Web 2.0 fashion, Google provides users a means for sharing their mashed-up map over the Internet and then indexes that map for Google search. If you publish a mashup of a Google map with your knowledge of a hiking trip on Mt. Pugh, anyone who performs a Google search for Mt. Pugh will find your map. Again, the more users who create My Maps, the greater the value of the My Maps site.

You can learn more about map mashups in Chapter Extension 17.

Participation and Ownership Differences

Mashups lead to another key difference. Traditional sites are about publishing; Web 2.0 is about participation. Users provide reviews, map content, discussion responses, blog entries, and so forth. A final difference, listed in Figure 8-5, concerns *ownership*.

Traditional vendors and Web sites lock down all the legal rights they can. For example, Oracle publishes content and demands that others obtain written permission before reusing it. Web 2.0 locks down only some rights. Google publishes maps and says, "Do what you want with them. We'll help you share them."

How Can Businesses Benefit from Web 2.0?

Amazon.com, Google, eBay, and other Web 2.0 companies have pioneered Web 2.0 technology and techniques to their benefit. A good question today, however, is how these techniques might be used by non-Internet companies. How might 3M, Alaska Airlines, Procter & Gamble, or the bicycle shop down the street use Web 2.0?

Advertising

Consider again the Oracle CRM ad in the print version of the *Wall Street Journal*. Oracle has no control over who reads that ad, nor does it know much about the people who do (just that they fit the general demographic of *Wall Street Journal* readers). On any particular day, 10,000 qualified buyers for Oracle products might happen to read the ad, or then again, perhaps only 1,000 qualified buyers read it. Neither Oracle nor the *Wall Street Journal* knows the number, but Oracle pays the same amount for the ad, regardless of the number of readers or who they are.

In the Web 2.0 world, advertising is specific to user interests. Someone who searches online for "customer relationship management" is likely an IT person (or a student) who has a strong interest in Oracle and its competing products. Oracle would like to advertise to that person.

As stated earlier, Google pioneered Web 2.0 advertising. With its **AdWords** software, vendors pay Google a certain amount for particular search words. For example, FlexTime (the opening vignette in Chapters 1 through 6) might agree to pay $2 for the word *workout*. When someone Googles that term, Google will display a link to FlexTime's Web site. If the user clicks that link (and *only* if the user clicks that link), Google charges FlexTime's account $2. FlexTime pays nothing if the user does not click. If it chooses, FlexTime, which is based in Indianapolis, can agree to pay only when users in the Indianapolis area click the ad.

The amount that a company pays per word can be changed from day to day, and even hour to hour. If FlexTime is about to start a new spinning class, it will be willing to pay more for the word *spinning* just before the class starts than it will afterward. The value of a click on *spinning* is low when the start of the next spinning class is a month away.

AdSense is another advertising alternative. Google searches an organization's Web site and inserts ads that match content on that site. When users click those ads, Google pays the organization a fee. Other Web 2.0 vendors offer services similar to AdWords and AdSense.

With Web 2.0, the cost of reaching a particular, qualified person is much smaller than in the traditional advertising model. As a consequence, many companies are switching to the new lower-cost medium, and newspapers and magazines are struggling with a sharp reduction in advertising revenue.

Mashups

How can two non-Internet companies mash the content of their products? Suppose you're watching a hit movie and you would like to buy the jewelry, dress, or watch worn by the leading actress. Suppose that Nordstrom sells all those items. With Web 2.0 technology, the movie's producer and Nordstrom can mash their content together so that you, watching the movie on a computer at home, can click on the item you like and be directed to a Nordstrom e-commerce site that will sell it to you. Or, perhaps Nordstrom is disintermediated out of the transaction, and you are taken to the e-commerce site of the item's manufacturer.

Not for All Applications

Before we get too carried away with the potential for Web 2.0, note that not all business information systems benefit from flexibility and organic growth. Any information system that deals with assets, whether financial or material, requires some level of control. You probably do not want to mash up your credit card transactions on My Maps and share that mashup with the world. As CFO, you probably do not want your accounts payable or general ledger system to have an organic user interface; in fact, the Sarbanes-Oxley Act prohibits that possibility.

Q4 How Does Social Capital Benefit You and Organizations?

You don't need this book to learn how to use Facebook or Twitter. You already know how to do that. But when you use such sites, there is more going on than you realize. If you are using such sites solely for entertainment or self-expression, then deeper understanding isn't too important. But, if, like many professionals, you use such sites for both self-expression and for professional purposes, then understanding how such sites contribute to your social capital and how such capital influences and benefits organizations is important.

Social capital is earned through social networking. A **social network** is a structure of individuals and organizations that are related to each other in some way. **Social networking** is the process by which individuals use relationships to communicate with others in a social network.

What Is Social Capital?

Business literature defines three types of capital. Karl Marx defined **capital** as the investment of resources for future profit. This traditional definition refers to investments into resources such as factories, machines, manufacturing equipment, and the like. **Human capital** is the investment in human knowledge and skills for future profit. By taking this class, you are investing in your own human capital. You are investing your money and time to obtain knowledge that you hope will differentiate you from other workers and ultimately give you a wage premium in the workforce.

According to Nan Lin, **social capital** is the investment in social relations with the expectation of returns in the marketplace.[3] When you attend a business function for the purpose of meeting people and reinforcing relationships, you are investing in your social capital. Similarly, when you join LinkedIn or contribute to Facebook, you are (or can be) investing in your social capital.

According to Lin, social capital adds value in four ways:

- Information
- Influence
- Social credentials
- Personal reinforcement

Relationships in social networks can provide *information* about opportunities, alternatives, problems, and other factors important to business professionals. They also provide an opportunity to *influence* decision makers in one's employer or in other organizations who are critical to your success. Such influence cuts across formal

[3] Nan Lin. *Social Capital: The Theory of Social Structure and Action* (Cambridge, UK: Cambridge University Press, 2001), Location 310 of the Kindle Edition.

In the preparation of this text, a number of Pearson (this textbook's publisher) employees joined a private Facebook group, and we used it to discuss the issues raised in the Guide on pages 202–203.

organizational structures such as reporting relationships. Third, being linked to a network of highly regarded contacts is a form of *social credential*. You can bask in the glory of those with whom you are related. Others will be more inclined to work with you if they believe critical personnel are standing with you and may provide resources to support you. Finally, being linked into social networks reinforces a professional's image and position in an organization or industry. It reinforces the way you define yourself to the world (and to yourself).

Social networks differ in value. The social network you maintain with your high school friends probably has less value than the network you have with your business associates, but not necessarily so. According to Henk Flap,[4] the **value of social capital** is determined by the number of relationships in a social network, by the strength of those relationships, and by the resources controlled by those related. If your high school friends happen to be Bill Gates and Paul Allen, and if you maintain strong relations with them via your high school network, then the value of that social network far exceeds any you'll have at work. For most of us, however, it is the network of our current professional contacts that provides social capital.

So, when you use social networking professionally, consider those three factors. You gain social capital by adding more friends and by strengthening the relationships you have with existing friends. Further, you gain more social capital by adding friends and strengthening relationships with people who control resources that are important to you. Such calculations may seem cold, impersonal, and possibly even phony. When applied to the recreational use of social networking, they may be. But when you use social networking for professional purposes, keep them in mind.

The Importance of Weak Relationships

Strong relationships create the most social capital in a social network, but ironically it is weak relationships that contribute the most to the growth of social networks. To understand why, consider the network diagram in Figure 8-8. Assume that each line represents a relationship between two people. Notice that the people in your department tend to know each other, and the people in the accounting department also tend to know each other. That's typical.

Now suppose you are at the weekly employee afterhours party and you have an opportunity to introduce yourself either to Linda or Eileen. Setting aside personal considerations, thinking just about network building, which person should you meet?

If you introduce yourself to Linda, you shorten your pathway to her from two steps to one and your pathway to Shawna from three to two. You do not open up any new channels because you already have them to the people in your department.

Figure 8-8
A Network Diagram

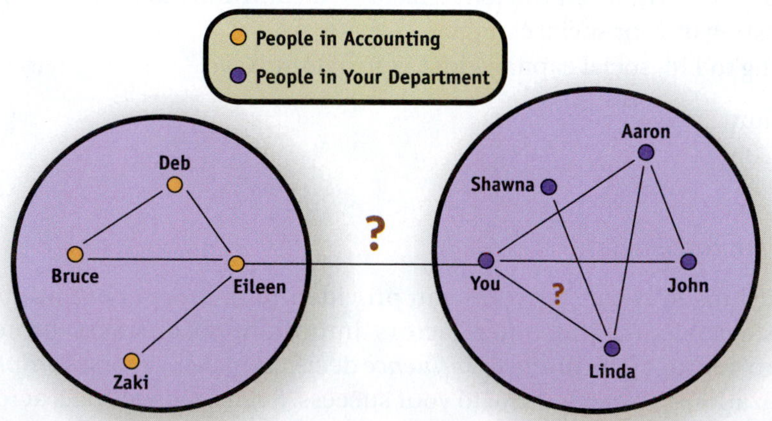

[4] Henk D. Flap, "Social Capital in the Reproduction of Inequality," *Comparative Sociology of Family, Health, and Education,* Vol. 20, pp. 6179–6202 (1991). Cited in Nan Lin, *Social Capital* (Cambridge, UK: Cambridge University Press, 2002), Kindle location 345.

However, if you introduce yourself to Eileen, you open up an entirely new network of acquaintances. So, considering just network building, you use your time better by meeting Eileen and other people who are not part of your current circle. It opens up many more possibilities. The connection from you to Eileen is called a weak tie in social network theory,[5] and such links are crucial in increasing the number of relationships in your network. *In general, the people you know the least contribute the most connections to your network.*

This concept is simple, but you'd be surprised by how few people pay attention to it. At most company events, everyone talks with the people they know, and, if the purpose of the function is to have fun, then that behavior makes sense. In truth, however, no business social function exists for having fun, regardless of what people say. Business functions exist for business reasons, and you can use them to create and expand networks. Given that time is always limited, you may as well use such functions efficiently.

The same comments apply to online social networking: Weak links add the greatest number of new connections to your social network.

How Do Social Networks Add Value to Business?

Organizations have social capital just as humans do. Their social capital is measured in the same way: number of relationships, strength of relationships, and resources controlled by "friends." Historically, organizations have created social capital via salespeople, via customer support, and via public relations. Endorsements by high-profile people are a traditional way of increasing social capital, but there are tigers in those woods.

Today, progressive organizations maintain a presence on Facebook, LinkedIn, Twitter, and possibly other sites. They include links to their social networking presence on their Web sites and make it easy for customers and interested parties to leave comments. In most cases, such connections are positive, but they can backfire, as you saw at Fox Lake in the opening of this chapter.

You can learn more about the use and management of user-generated content in Chapter Extension 14.

Consider organizational social networking from the standpoint of social capital. Figure 8-9(a) shows a portion of my Facebook page in April 2010. As shown, I'd just become a fan of Yo-Yo Ma (famous cellist), Microsoft PowerPoint, and Lie-Nielsen Toolworks (maker of high-quality woodworking tools). In Figure 8-9(b), you can see how my fan connection appears on the Facebook pages of my friends. By endorsing these companies or products, I've connected my social network to them.

Think about these endorsements as the exchange of social capital. If I have, say, 50 friends, unless they are people like Bill Gates or Warren Buffet (they aren't), I haven't contributed much social capital to any of these three. But, if I can connect the readers of this text to these sites, because there are tens of thousands of you, I am contributing considerable social capital.

However, that value varies to these organizations because they each have a different perception of your value. Few of you are likely to be woodworkers, and as college students you probably choose not to buy expensive saws, chisels, and planes, so the value of a large group of business students to Lie-Nielsen is low. Similarly, Yo-Yo Ma has something like 65,000 friends already, and the value of my social network, even augmented by readers of this text, is low to him.

Normally, the same would be true to Microsoft; they are huge and my social capital is small. Except that all of you, the readers of this book, are future business professionals, and the lifetime value of your future software purchases is huge. If I endorse PowerPoint (I actually think PowerPoint is an incredibly useful product, and I endorse it honestly and with enthusiasm), I have added considerably to PowerPoint's social capital—all at very low cost to Microsoft.

5. See Terry Granovetter, "The Strength of Weak Ties," *American Journal of Sociology*, May 1973.

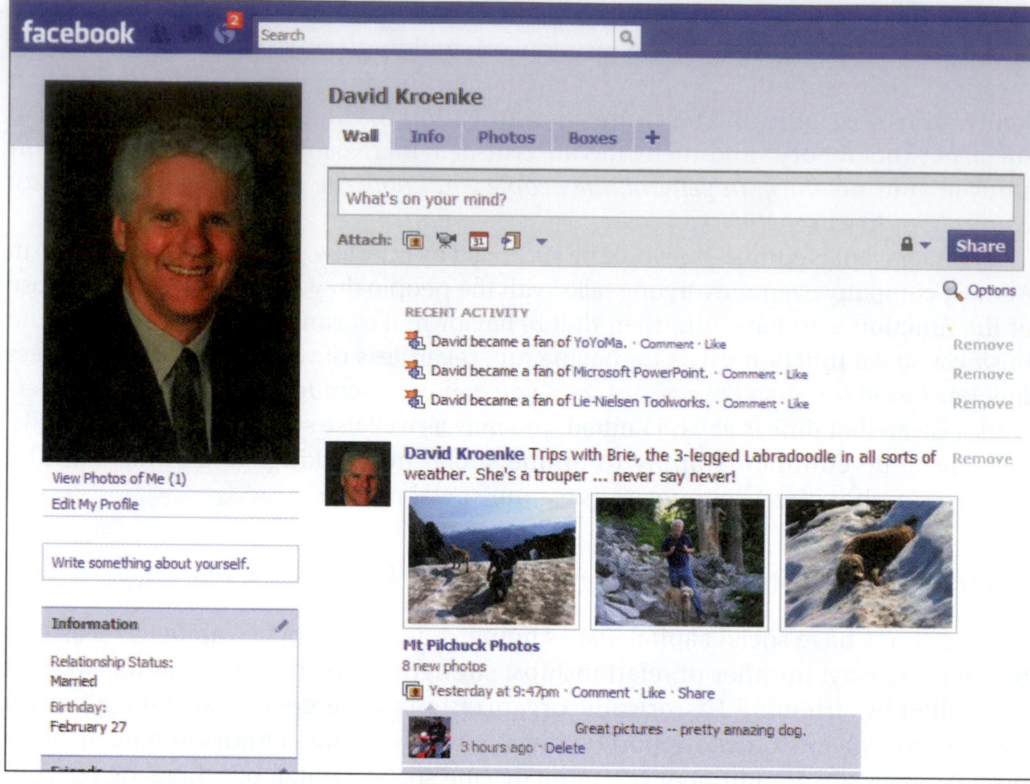

Figure 8-9(a)
Author's Facebook Page

Now look at the other side of that equation. My fan endorsements add those organization's social capital to me as well. By endorsing Yo-Yo Ma, I reinforce an image that I like fine music, am cultured enough to know about Yo-Yo Ma, like cello music, and so on. Endorsing PowerPoint is probably negative to my social capital. Open source software fans will be disappointed with me and being a fan of a Microsoft product doesn't impress anyone else positively. Unless you're a woodworker, my endorsing of Lie-Nielsen is probably neutral.

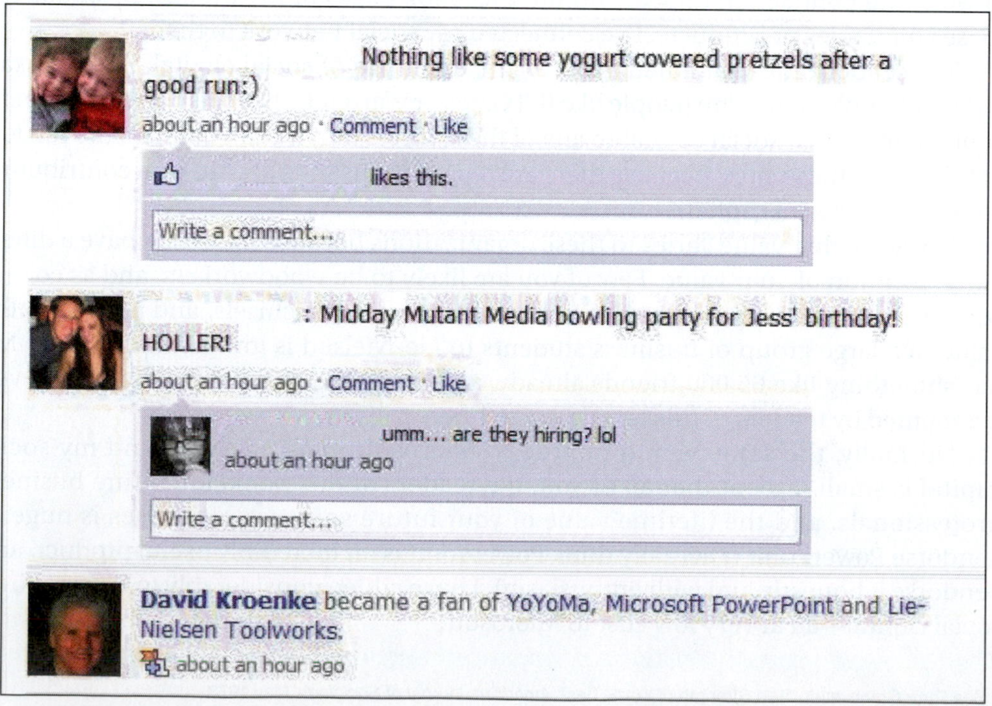

Figure 8-9(b)
Author's Fan Connections Appear on the Pages of Facebook Friends

Experiencing MIS InClass Exercise 8

Computing Your Social Capital

Social capital is not an abstract concept that applies only to organizations; it applies to you as well. You and your classmates are accumulating social capital now. What is the value of that capital? To see, form a group and answer the following questions:

1. Define *capital, human capital,* and *social capital.* Explain how these terms differ.
2. How does the expression "It's not what you know, but who you know that matters" pertain to the terms you defined in step 1?
3. Do you, personally, agree with the statement in item 2? Form your own opinion before discussing it with your fellow group members.
4. As a group, discuss the relative value of human and social capital. In what ways is social capital more valuable than human capital? Formulate a group consensus view on the validity of the statement in item 2.
5. Visit the Facebook, LinkedIn, Twitter, or other social networking presence site of each group member.
   a. Using the definition of social capital value in this chapter, assess the value of each group member's social networking presence.
   b. Recommend at least one way to add value to each group member's social capital at each site.
6. Suppose you each decide to feature your Facebook or other social networking page on your professional résumé.
   a. How would you change your presence that you evaluated in item 5 in order to make it more appropriate for that purpose?
   b. Describe three or four types of professionals that you could add to your social network that would facilitate your job search.
7. Imagine that you are the CEO of a company that has just one product to sell: You!
   a. Review the Enterprise 2.0 SLATES principles in Figure 8-10 and assess how each could pertain to the selling of your "product" (i.e., obtaining a quality job that you want). You can find the McAfee article at: *http://sloanreview.mit.edu/the-magazine/files/saleable-pdfs/47306.pdf.*
   b. Explain how you could use your social networking presence to facilitate Social CRM selling of your product.
   c. Devise a creative and interesting way to use this exercise as part of your Social CRM offering.
8. Present your answers to items 4 and 7 to the rest of the class.

In summary, endorsing Yo-Yo Ma was positive to my social capital, endorsing Microsoft PowerPoint was negative, and endorsing Lie-Nielsen was neutral. So why did I endorse PowerPoint? My enthusiasm for the product appears to have led me into a mistake. Give some thought to my mistake next time you contribute your (professional) social capital!

Q5 How Does Social CRM Empower Customers?

Prior to the Internet, organizations controlled their relationships with their customers. In fact, the primary purpose of CRM was to manage customer touches. Traditional CRM ensured that the organization spoke to customers with one voice and that it controlled the messages, offers, and even support that customers received based on the value of the customer. In 1990, if you wanted to know something about an IBM product, you'd contact their local sales office; that office would classify you as a prospect and then use that classification to control the literature and documentation you received and your access to IBM personnel.

Today, the vendor–customer relationship is far more complex and is not controlled by the vendor. Businesses offer many different customer touch points, and customers craft their own relationship with the business by their use of those touch points. Social CRM is the creation and use of the Enterprise 2.0 collaborative relationship between businesses and customers. Because Social CRM is a manifestation of Enterprise 2.0, we begin with it.

What Are the Characteristics of Enterprise 2.0?

As stated in Q1, Enterprise 2.0 is the application of Web 2.0 technologies, collaboration systems, social networking, and related technologies to facilitate the cooperative work of people in organizations. You can think of Enterprise 2.0 as the migration and use of Web 2.0 tools and techniques inside the organization. Enterprise 2.0 provides a set of capabilities that workers use to collaborate and that allows content to emerge, rather than be preplanned.

McAfee defined six characteristics of Enterprise 2.0, which he refers to by the acronym **SLATES** (see Figure 8-10). Workers want to be able to *search* for content inside the organization just like they do on the Web. Most workers find that searching is more effective than navigating content structures such as lists and tables of content. Workers want to access organizational content by *link,* just as they do on the Web. They also want to *author* organizational content using blogs, wikis, discussion groups, published presentations, and so forth.

Enterprise 2.0 content is *tagged,* just like content on the Web, and tags are organized into structures, as is done on the Web at sites such as Delicious (*http://delicious.com*). These structures organize tags as a taxonomy does, but, unlike taxonomies, they are not preplanned; they emerge. A **folksonomy** is a content structure that has emerged from the processing of many user tags. Additionally, Enterprise 2.0 workers want applications to enable them to rate tagged content and to use the tags to predict content that will be of interest to them (as with Pandora), a process McAfee refers to as *extensions.* Finally, Enterprise 2.0 workers want relevant content pushed to them; they want to be *signaled* when something of interest to them happens in organizational content.

Figure 8-10
McAffee's SLATES Enterprise 2.0 Model

Enterprise 2.0 Component	Remarks
Search	People have more success searching than they do in finding from structured content.
Links	Links to enterprise resources (like on the Web).
Authoring	Create enterprise content via blogs, wikis, discussion groups, presentations, etc.
Tags	Flexible tagging (e.g., Delicious) results in folksonomies of enterprise content.
Extensions	Using usage patterns to offer enterprise content via tag processing (e.g., Pandora).
Signals	Pushing enterprise content to users based on subscriptions and alerts.

Social CRM Is Enterprise 2.0 CRM

Social CRM is customer relationship management done in the style of Enterprise 2.0. The relationships between organizations and customers emerge as both parties create and process content. In addition to the traditional forms of promotion, employees in the organization create wikis, blogs, discussion lists, FAQs, sites for user reviews and commentary, and other dynamic content. Customers search this content, contribute reviews and commentary, tag content, ask more questions, create user groups, and so forth. With Social CRM, each customer crafts its own relationship with the company.

Social CRM flies in the face of the principles of traditional CRM. Because relationships emerge from joint activity, customers have as much control as companies. This characteristic is anathema to traditional sales managers who want control over what the customer is reading, seeing, and hearing about the company and its products. For example, the general manager at Fox Lake is incensed because a negative review was published on his organization's Facebook page. He wants to delete it but finds he has insufficient social power to do so.

Further, traditional CRM is centered on lifetime value; customers who are likely to generate the most business get the most attention and have the most impact on the organization. But, with Social CRM, the customer who spends 10 cents but who is an effective reviewer, commentator, or blogger can have more influence than the quiet customers who purchase $10 million a year. Such imbalance is incomprehensible to traditional sales managers.

This brings us to the leading edge of the use of Web 2.0, social networking, and Enterprise 2.0 in business. What happens next is yet to be told; you will have exciting opportunities to work with these technologies early in your career! But remember to tell the world you learned it here first: *www.facebook.com/david.kroenke!*

How does the knowledge of this chapter help *Fox Lake* and you?

The knowledge of this chapter would help Anne Foster increase wedding events revenue. Knowing the rudiments of Web 2.0, social networking in business, Enterprise 2.0, and Social CRM, she could craft a new marketing capability for her line of business (and you can, too, if you complete Collaboration Exercise 8). Knowledge of this chapter would help Jeff understand what Anne might do and would enable him to encourage the other members of his staff to consider new marketing efforts as well.

The knowledge of this chapter helps you in the same ways it helps Anne. Additionally, if you craft a short summary of what you've learned about Web 2.0, Enterprise 2.0, and Social CRM, you can use it in a job interview. You can also use new insights into social networking in business to help you find a job.

Ethics Guide

Hiding the Truth?

No one is going to publish their ugliest picture on their Facebook page, but how far should you go to create a positive impression? If your hips and legs are not your best features, is it unethical to stand behind your sexy car in your photo? If you've been to one event with someone very popular in your crowd, is it unethical to publish photos that imply you meet as an everyday occurrence? Surely there is no obligation to publish pictures of yourself at boring events with unpopular people just to balance the scale for those photos in which you appear unrealistically attractive and overly popular.

As long as all of this occurs on a Facebook or MySpace account that you use for personal relationships, well, what goes around comes around. But consider social networking in the business arena.

a. Suppose that a river rafting company starts a group on a social networking site for promoting rafting trips. Graham, a 15-year-old high school student who wants to be more grown up than he is, posts a picture of a handsome 22-year-old male as a picture of himself. He also writes witty and clever comments on the site photos and claims to play the guitar and be an accomplished masseuse. Are his actions unethical? Suppose someone decided to go on the rafting trip, in part, because of Graham's postings, and was disappointed with the truth about Graham. Would the rafting company have any responsibility to refund that person's fees?

b. Suppose you own and manage that same rafting company. Is it unethical for you to encourage your employees to write positive reviews about your company? Does your assessment change if you ask your employees to use an email address other than the one they have at work?

c. Again, suppose you own and manage the rafting company and that you pay your employees a bonus for every client they bring to a rafting trip. Without specifying any particular technique, you encourage your employees to be creative in how they obtain clients. One employee invites his MySpace friends to a party at which he shows photos of prior rafting trips. On the way to the party, one of the friends has an automobile accident and dies. His spouse sues your company. Should it be held accountable? Does it matter if you knew about the presentation? Would it matter if you had not encouraged your employees to be creative?

d. Suppose your rafting company has a Web site for customer reviews. In spite of your best efforts at camp cleanliness, on one trip (out of dozens) your staff accidentally serves contaminated food and everyone becomes ill with food poisoning. One of those clients writes a poor review because of that experience. Is it ethical for you to delete that review from your site?

e. Assume you have a professor who has written a popular textbook. You are upset with the grade you received in his class, so you write a

To get even, you use Facebook to spread rumors to your friends (many of whom are river guides) about the safety of the company's trips. Are your actions unethical? Are they illegal? Do you see any ethical distinctions between this situation and that in item d?

g. Again, suppose that you were at one time employed by the rafting company and were undeservedly terminated. You notice that the company's owner does not have a Facebook account, so you create one for her. You've known her for many years and have dozens of photos of her, some of which were taken at parties and are unflattering and revealing. You post those photos along with critical comments that she made about clients or employees. Most of the comments were made when she was tired or frustrated, and they are hurtful, but because of her wit, also humorous. You send friend invitations to people whom she knows, many of whom are the target of her biting and critical remarks. Are your actions unethical?

scandalously poor review of that professor's book on Amazon.com. Are your actions ethical?

f. Suppose you were at one time employed by the river rafting company and you were, undeservedly you think, terminated by the company.

Discussion Questions

1. Read the situations in items a through g and answer the questions contained in each.
2. Based on your answers in question 1, formulate ethical principles for creating or using social networks for business purposes.
3. Based on your answers in question 1, formulate ethical principles for creating or using user-generated content for business purposes.
4. Summarize the risks that a business assumes when it chooses to sponsor user-generated content.
5. Summarize the risks that a business assumes when it uses social networks for business purposes.

Guide

Blending the Personal and the Professional

Many businesses are beginning to use social networking sites such as Facebook and MySpace for professional purposes. It began with coworkers sharing their accounts with each other socially, just as they did in college. The first interactions concerned activities such as photos of the company softball team or photos at a cocktail party at a recent sales meeting. However, every business social function is a *business* function, so even sharing photos and pages with the work softball team began to blur the personal–professional boundary.

The employees of Pearson, the publisher of this textbook, are no exception. When I began work on this chapter, I started a Facebook group called "Experiencing MIS." I then queried Facebook for Pearson employees I guessed might have Facebook accounts and invited them to be "friends." Most accepted, and I asked them to join the Experiencing MIS group. The first day I checked my account, I found an entry from Anne, one of my new friends, who stated that she had been out too late the prior night. That day she happened to be working on the sales plan for this book, and I realized that I didn't want to know her current condition. So, in the group, I asked whether the blending of the personal and the professional is a good thing, and the following conversation resulted:

Anne: I think that for a lot of reasons it is a good thing . . . within reason. I think that people seeing a personal side of you can humanize you. For example, my "I was out too late last night" post didn't mean that I was not into work early and ready to go (which I was, just with a larger coffee than usual), just that I like to have a good time outside of my work life. Also, with all the time we spend at work, our social lives are intertwined with our work lives.

Also, 9–5 work hours are becoming more and more obsolete. I may be updating my Facebook page at noon on a Friday, but you will surely find me working at least part of my day on Saturday and Sunday.

Bob: I definitely see Anne's point of view. There is the temptation to believe that we are all family. I am too old to believe that, but corporate advancement is always going to be predicated to some degree on your willingness to surrender the personal for the professional and/or allow blur. Technology may give you the illusion that you can safely have it both ways.

I am skeptical of business applications for Facebook. My guess is most folks find them lame in the way that business blogs and Xmas cards from your insurance agent are.

Lisa: I actually think there is a place for Facebook in business . . . For example, think about how it's connected a team like ours—where everyone is located all over the country—to have a place where we actually get to know each other a little better. It's corny, perhaps, but reading people's status updates on my iPhone gives me a better sense of who they are in "real life," not just on the job. I'd get that if we all sat in the same office every day; given that we don't, it's a pretty decent substitute.

I totally agree with Anne's notion that, in many ways, the personal and the professional already do blur . . . but I think that's more to do with who we are and what we do, than any specific notion of "corporations." Our work is portable and always on—and judged by results, not hours logged (I think!). In a work universe like that, the lines sort of slowly and inevitably blur . . . PS: Anne, I was out too late too. :)

Clearly, I am the curmudgeon here. But, just as I was reflecting on these comments, I received a private email from another person who chose not to be identified:

Other person: A few weeks ago, Pearson started getting really into Facebook. I went from not really using it to getting tons of "friend requests" from coworkers. Then, I got a request from somebody in an executive position at Pearson. I was worried at first—I had heard so many stories of people who had lost their jobs due to social networking, blogging, or other information they posted on the Internet. When I received this request, I must have gone over my profile 10 times to ensure there was nothing that could any way be misconstrued as offensive or illegal. I think many people at the company already know a lot about me, but I . . . I think you would have to be more careful if you're in the introductory months of a new job.

Discussion Questions

1. Do you think Anne's post that she was "Out too late last night" was inappropriate, given that she knew that her professional colleagues were reading her page? Explain your answer.
2. Anne and Lisa contend that Facebook allows employees to get to know each other better in "real life" and not just on the job. Both of these women are very successful business professionals, and they believe such knowledge is important. Do you? Why or why not?
3. Bob is skeptical that Facebook has potential business applications. He thinks social networking sites will become as lame and as uninteresting as business blogs and corporate holiday cards. Do you agree? Why or why not?
4. In the olden days before social networking, instant messaging, email, and "free" long-distance phone calls, social networking was restricted to the people in your department, or maybe those who worked on your floor. You knew the people to whom you revealed personal data, and they were close to you in the organizational hierarchy. You would have had almost no contact with your manager's manager's manager, and what contact you did have would have been in the context of a formal meeting. How do you think management is affected when personal data is readily shared far up and down the organizational hierarchy?
5. Do you think it was appropriate for the senior manager to invite distant subordinates in the organization to be friends? Why did this action put the junior employees in a tight spot? What advantages accrue to the senior manager of having very junior friends? What advantages accrue to the junior professional of having a senior friend?
6. All of the people in this dialog update Facebook using iPhones that they purchased with their own money. Because they are not using a corporate asset, managers at Pearson would be unable to stop these employees from using Facebook, if they wanted to. How does this fact change the power structure within an organization? Consider, for example, what would happen if senior management announced an unpopular change in employee benefits or some other program.
7. As the lawyers say, "You cannot unring the bell." Once you've revealed something about yourself, you cannot take it back. Knowing that, what criteria will you use to decide what you will post on a social networking site that is read by your professional colleagues? How do those criteria differ from the criteria you use at school?

ACTIVE REVIEW

Use this Active Review to verify that you understand the ideas and concepts that answer the chapter's study questions.

Q1 What types of interorganizational systems exist?

Name four types of interorganizational systems and explain the characteristics of each. Compare and contrast these types.

Q2 How do companies use e-commerce?

Define *e-commerce.* Define *B2C, B2B,* and *B2G.* Distinguish among auctions, clearinghouses, and exchanges. How does e-commerce improve market efficiency? Define and explain *disintermediation,* and give an example other than one in this text. Explain how e-commerce improves the flow of price information. Define *price elasticity,* and explain how e-commerce companies can estimate it. List four factors that disfavor e-commerce. Explain the impact of each factor.

Q3 Why is Web 2.0 important to business?

How did Amazon.com usher in Web 2.0? Explain the term *software as a (free) service* and how it differs from traditional software licensing. Describe the difference in business models between Web 2.0 and traditional software companies. Explain the statement, "If a product requires advertising, then it is not Web 2.0." Explain how use increases value in Web 2.0. Define *mashup.* In what way are Web 2.0 interfaces organic? How does rights management differ between Web 2.0 and traditional software? Summarize the ways that businesses can benefit from Web 2.0.

Q4 How does social capital benefit you and organizations?

Summarize, in general terms, the importance of social networks in business. Define *capital, human capital,* and *social capital.* Name and explain four ways that social capital adds value. Name and explain three factors that determine the value of social capital. Using Figure 8-8 as a guide, explain how weak ties add value to your social networks. Describe how social networks add value to business. Explain how becoming a fan of a company changes social capital for both you and that company. With regards to business use of social networking, describe criteria you should use when linking your social network to an organization.

Q5 How does social CRM empower customers?

Characterize the differences between traditional and Social CRM. Define *Enterprise 2.0,* and explain the meaning of the SLATES acronym. Define *Social CRM.* Explain the statement "Social CRM is CRM done in the style of Enterprise 2.0." How does Social CRM conflict with the traditional view of CRM?

How does the knowledge of this chapter help *Fox Lake* and you?

Explain how Anne Foster and Jeff Lloyd could use the knowledge of this chapter. Summarize how it helps you. How can you use the knowledge of this chapter in a job interview?

KEY TERMS AND CONCEPTS

AdSense 192
AdWords 192
Auctions 187
Business-to-business (B2B) e-commerce 186
Business-to-consumer (B2C) e-commerce 186
Business-to-government (B2G) e-commerce 186
Capital 193
Channel conflict 188
Clearinghouses 187
Crowdsourcing 191
Disintermediation 187
E-commerce 184
Electronic exchange 187
Enterprise 2.0 185
Folksonomy 198
Human capital 193
Interorganizational IS 184
Mashup 191
Merchant companies 186
My Maps 191
Nonmerchant companies 186
Price conflict 188
Price elasticity 187
Service-oriented architecture (SOA) 185
SLATES 198
Social capital 193

USING YOUR KNOWLEDGE

1. Recall the process that you used when you applied for admission to your university. Classify that process in terms of the four interorganizational system types in Figure 8-1. Do you think a system of a type other than the one you used would be better? Why or why not?

2. Shop for a Sonos S5 audio system (or any other Sonos audio product). You can buy this product from Sonos itself, or you can buy it from online vendors of electronic equipment. Compare prices and terms. Describe how Sonos has channel conflict and explain how it appears to deal with that conflict.

3. Google or Bing "Chloé" and search for sites that offer Chloé fashion products. Identify companies that have purchased the Chloé AdWord. Follow three or four such links. Identify as many Web 2.0 features in the sites that you encounter as you can. Explain what you think the business rationale is for each site.

4. Visit either *www.lie-nielsen.com* or *www.sephora.com*. On the site you chose, find links to social networking sites. In what ways are those sites sharing their social capital with you? In what ways are they attempting to cause you to share your social capital with them? Describe the business value of social networking to the business you chose.

5. According to Paul Greenberg, Amazon.com is the master of the 2-minute relationship and Boeing is the master of the 10-year relationship.[6] Visit *www.boeing.com* and *www.amazon.com*. From Greenberg's statement and from the appearance of these Web sites, it appears that Boeing is committed to traditional CRM and Amazon.com to Social CRM. Give evidence from each site that this might be true. Explain why the products and business environment of each company cause this difference. Is there any justification for traditional CRM at Amazon.com? Why or why not? Is there any justification for Social CRM at Boeing? Why or why not? Based on these companies, is it possible that a company might endorse Enterprise 2.0, but not endorse Social CRM? Explain.

COLLABORATION EXERCISE 8

Before you start this exercise, read Chapter Extensions 1 and 2, which describe collaboration techniques as well as tools for managing collaboration tasks. In particular, consider using Google Docs, Windows Live SkyDrive, Microsoft SharePoint, or some other collaboration tool.

Suppose your team has been hired by Anne Foster to investigate the use of Web 2.0, social networking, and Social CRM for wedding events at Fox Lake. Work with your group to answer the following questions:

1. Describe the potential use of AdWords and AdSense by Fox Lake for advertising its wedding services. Which, if either, of these would you recommend for Fox Lake? Why?

2. Explain how to assess the social capital of a wedding party. Is it possible to compare the social capital of two different wedding parties? If so, how? If not, why not? In what ways is knowledge of the relative social value of two wedding parties useful to Fox Lake? Are such considerations tawdry? Why or why not?

3. Describe techniques that Fox Lake could use to encourage wedding parties to contribute their social capital to Fox Lake. On the surface, Fox Lake appears to be the primary beneficiary of such a contribution. What can Fox Lake do to increase the value of such contributions to wedding parties?

4. Describe ways that Fox Lake can make it easy for wedding parties to contribute their social capital to Fox Lake via Facebook and Twitter.

5. Traditional CRM, in which resources are allocated to customers on the basis of their lifetime value, makes no sense for weddings, unless Fox Lake wants to market to those most likely to divorce. Anne understands this and decides that Social CRM makes more

[6] Paul Greenberg, *CRM at the Speed of Light*, 4th ed. (New York: McGraw-Hill, 2010), p. 105.

sense. Suppose she wants to create a variety of touch points for those who are in the market for wedding venues. Using the SLATES model, specify how Fox Lake could create a Social CRM site with the following elements:

a. Search
b. Links
c. Author
d. Tags
e. Extensions
f. Signals

6. Summarize your recommendations for Anne in a one-page memo.

7. Prepare a 2-minute summary of what you have learned from this exercise that your group's members could use in a job interview. Give your presentation to the rest of the class.

CASE STUDY 8

Tourism Holdings Limited (THL)

Note: Because this case involves concepts from both this chapter and from Chapter 9, it is continued at the end of that chapter.

Tourism Holdings Limited (THL) is a publicly listed New Zealand corporation that owns multiple brands and businesses in the tourism industry. Principal holdings of THL include:

- New Zealand tourist attractions, including Waitomo Black Water Rafting and Waitomo Glowworm Caves
- Kiwi Experience and Feejee Experience, hop-on, hop-off tourist bus services
- Four brands of holiday rental vehicles
- Ci Munro, a van-customization manufacturing facility

In 2009, THL earned $5 million in profit before interest and taxes on $170 million in revenue. It operates in New Zealand, Australia, and Fiji and has sales offices in Germany and the United Kingdom as well.

THL originated as The Helicopter Line, which provided scenic helicopter flights over New Zealand. Over the years, THL sold the helicopter business and has since owned and operated numerous tourism organizations and brands. THL continues to frequently buy and sell tourism businesses. For the current list of businesses, visit *www.thlonline.com/THLBusinesses.*

According to Grant Webster, THL's CEO, "THL is a house of brands and not a branded house." Thus, in the holiday rental business, THL owns and operates four different van rental brands: Maui, Britz, Backpacker, and ExploreMore. These brands are differentiated on price; Maui is the most expensive line, whereas ExploreMore appeals to the most budget-conscious traveler. Britz is the next step down in price from Maui, and Backpacker falls between Britz and ExploreMore.

Tourism Market

In 2008, an estimated 866 million international visitors toured the world. That number is expected to grow to more than 1.6 billion visitors by 2020, according to *Tourism Business Magazine.* In 2008, travel and tourism was the world's largest business sector, accounting for 230 million jobs and over 10 percent of the world's GDP.

In spite of these long-term growth prospects, international tourism has contracted recently, following the financial crisis of Fall 2008. As of June 2009, an annual total of 1.15 million international travelers visited New Zealand, a decrease of 5 percent from the year before, and 5.5 million international travelers visited Australia, a decline of 2 percent.

According to Webster, "While we believe the long-term prospects of tourism in our traditional markets of New Zealand, Australia, and Fiji will remain strong, THL's substantial growth opportunities will be achieved by expanding to other countries, possibly the United States, or Europe."

Investment in Information Systems

THL considers information systems and technology as a core component of its business value and has invested in a variety of innovative information systems and Web 2.0 technologies. Webster speaks knowledgeably about information technologies, including SharePoint, Microsoft Office SharePoint Services (MOSS), Microsoft Report Server, OLAP, and data mining (discussed in Chapter 9).

Because of its acquisition of multiple brands and companies, THL accumulated a disparate set of information systems, based on a variety of different technologies. These disparate technologies created excessive software maintenance activity and costs. To reduce costs and simplify IS management, THL converted its customer-facing Web sites to use Microsoft SharePoint and MOSS. "Having a single development platform reduced our maintenance expenses and enabled us to focus management attention, development, and personnel training on a single set of technologies," according to Steve Pickering, Manager of Interactive Information Systems.

THL uses SharePoint not for collaboration, as discussed in Chapter 2, but rather as a development and

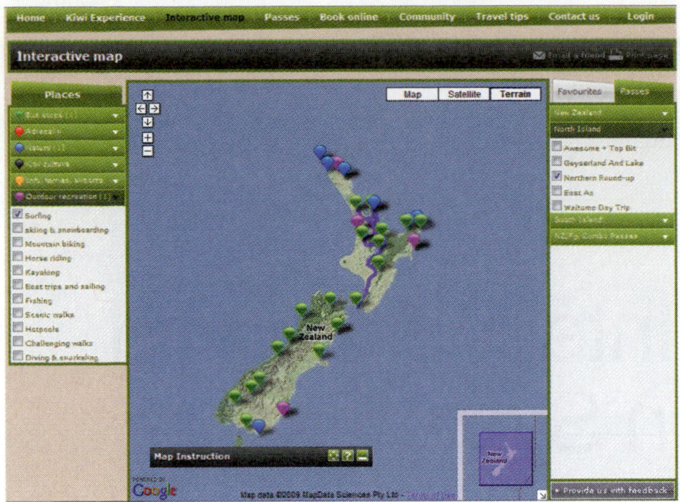

Figure 8-11
Interactive Map of New Zealand at *www.KiwiExperience.com.*
Source: Used with permission of Tourism Holdings Limited.

hosting platform for sophisticated, highly interactive Web sites. You can find an example of such sophisticated capability at *www.kiwiexperience.com.* Click "Design Your Own Trip . . ." and the Web site will display a map of New Zealand as well as a menu of instructions. You can then select different locations, experiences, and sites from a menu, and the Web site will recommend particular tours, as shown in the right-hand pane in Figure 8-11. Visit the site to get a sense of the interactivity and sophistication of processing.

Web 2.0 technologies enable the tourism industry to disintermediate sales channels. According to the New Zealand Ministry of Tourism, the Internet was used by 49 percent of international travelers to research travel options in 2006. That percentage has increased dramatically, and it is likely well over 50 percent today.

As with all disintermediation, when THL sells directly to the consumer, it saves substantial distribution costs. To facilitate direct sales, THL actively uses Google AdWords and Google Analytics, a Google-supplied information system that enables AdWords customers to better understand how their sites are processed. THL is also experimenting with online chat, both voice and video. "A camper rental can cost $5,000 to $10,000 or more, and we believe our customers want a trusted relationship with a salesperson in order to commit," according to Webster. "We think that video online chat might give us that relationship with our customers."

Sources: Tourism Business Magazine, November 2009, p. 20; *www.tourismbusinessmag.co.nz* (accessed July 2010); New Zealand Ministry of Tourism, *www.tourismresearch.govt.nz* (accessed July 2010); Tourism of Australia, *www.tourism.australia.com* (accessed July 2010).

Questions

1. This case implies that the frequent acquisition and disposition of tourism brands poses problems for information systems. Summarize what you think those problems might be. Consider all five components of an information system. To what extent does standardizing on a single development platform solve those problems? Which of the five components does such standardization help the most?

2. Using Figure 3-7 as a guide, summarize the ways in which IS gives THL a competitive advantage. Discuss each of the elements in Figure 3-7.

3. Visit *www.kiwiexperience.com* and click "Design Your Own Trip." Select a variety of locations in the Adrenalin, Nature, and Kiwi Culture menus. Select several locations in each category and then select a pass that fits your destinations.
   a. Evaluate this user interface. Describe its strengths and weaknesses.
   b. Evaluate the Map Instructions. Do you find these instructions to be adequate? Explain why or why not.
   c. Summarize the ways in which this site uses social networking.
   d. Explain why this site is an example of a mashup.

4. Consider the Kiwi Experience site in the context of Social CRM.
   a. Identify the customer touch points.
   b. Which of the elements of the SLATES model does this site contain?
   c. Consider the SLATES model elements that this site does not contain. Which ones do you think might be appropriate?
   d. Explain one way to implement each of the elements you identified in part c.
   e. Describe how your recommended Social CRM capabilities would help to generate a trusted relationship.

CHAPTER 9

Business Intelligence and Information Systems for Decision Making

This could happen to you

"I'm not sure." Jeff rocks back in his chair, looks out the window, and watches two sweaty tennis players come in from their match.

"Come on, Jeff, the data's there. Just let me have it." Anne is pleading about her need for information.

"Let me be sure I get this. You want to go into our membership database and extract the names of all the members who have daughters between 20 and 30 years of age?"

"Right."

"Why not older than 30?" Jeff asks out of curiosity.

"Because they'll be less influenced by their families. But, OK, let's say 35. And I want their email addresses, too." Anne's not letting up the pressure.

"You gonna send out a blanket email? 'Hey, you've got a daughter, how about a wedding right here at Fox Lake?'"

"No, I'm going to write something quite a bit more sophisticated than that."

"What if their daughter is already married?"

"Well, that's a problem. I've got two ways to go. I can either write the promotion in a general way . . . you know, "Fox Lake is a wonderful wedding site, blah, blah, and if your daughter or any of her friends are recently engaged, consider Fox . . .' Something like that."

"That's not too bad. I'm warming up to this idea."

"Or, I could be a lot more direct. We buy the marital data. My

STUDY QUESTIONS

Q1 Why do organizations need business intelligence?

Q2 How do business intelligence (BI) systems provide competitive advantages?

Q3 What problems do operational data pose for BI systems?

Q4 What are the purpose and components of a data warehouse?

Q5 What is a data mart, and how does it differ from a data warehouse?

Q6 What are the characteristics of data mining systems?

How does the knowledge in this chapter help *Fox Lake* and you?

brother-in-law was telling me it's amazing the data you can buy about people's personal lives."

"Oh, no. We're not spying on our membership."

"He says this isn't spying. All the data is from public records. They just put all this public data together and sell it."

"Two problems: One, members are going to feel like they're being spied on. And two, that data's got to be pricey."

"Ah, now we're just talking price!"

"No, I said two problems: *price* and I don't like the appearance of spying."

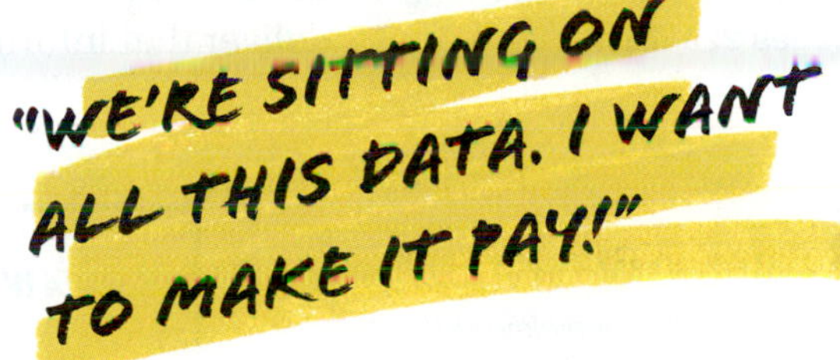

"WE'RE SITTING ON ALL THIS DATA. I WANT TO MAKE IT PAY!"

"Look, Jeff, how will they know? I'm not gonna say, 'Hey, our records indicate you've got a pregnant, unmarried daughter, better hurry in to set up the wedding.'"

"Like, you've got 60,000 miles on your car, time for an oil change?"

"Yeah, no, I mean, no, I'm not going to say that."

"What are you going to say?"

"I don't say anything about them. It's about us! It looks like the promo went out to everyone, but, in truth, it just goes to families that we learn have unmarried, 20-something daughters. If we do it that way, I can spend a lot more on each promo piece. Maybe send out a package by courier. That'd be classy . . . with a flower for the Mom? Or . . ."

"Hey, kid, stop dreaming and get back to this meeting. If I agree, can we do this? Does anyone know how to get qualified names from the database?"

"I talked to Mike. He's got this groundskeeper guy who's a techno-whiz. Anyway, that guy knows how to query our database. In fact, he already looked at the data; we've got nearly 450 families with daughters of the right age."

"And sons? What about sons?"

"Yeah, I know. Just because the daughter's family pays . . . Maybe. But, for now, let's start with daughters."

"I have a bad feeling about this."

"Jeff, you told me to increase the wedding revenue. Let's do it!"

"OK. Find out what data we can buy and how much it costs. Make sure it's all public data. And, all the expenses, including any data purchases, come out of your budget. Got it?"

"I have it. I'll get going. Thanks, Jeff!"

Optional Extensions for this chapter are • CE15: Database Marketing 505 • CE16: Reporting Systems and OLAP 515 • CE17: Geographic Information Systems 529

Q1 Why Do Organizations Need Business Intelligence?

Because data communications and data storage are essentially free, enormous amounts of data are created and stored every day. In 2007, Kevin Kelly estimated that 2 million emails, 31,000 text messages, and 162,000 instant messages are transmitted *every second.* He also estimated total online computer storage to be 246 exabytes and predicted that it will grow to 600 exabytes by 2010.[1]

The terms **petabyte** and **exabyte** are defined in Figure 9-1. As shown there, 200 petabytes is roughly the amount of all printed material ever written. So, one exabyte equals five times the amount of all printed material.

Somewhere in all that data is **business intelligence (BI)**—information containing patterns, relationships, and trends. But that information needs to be found and produced. For example, somewhere in the more than 300 million individual demographic records that Acxiom Corporation collects[2] is evidence that someone is going to default on a loan. Or, to bring it closer, somewhere in the cloud, maybe on an Axciom server, is data about the marital status of Fox Lake's members' daughters.

As useful as data mining and business intelligence can be for organizations, they are not without problems, as discussed in the Ethics Guide on pages 220–221.

Businesses use business intelligence systems to process this immense ocean of data; to produce patterns, relationships, and other forms of information; and to deliver that information on a timely basis to users who need it.

Figure 9-1
How Big Is an Exabyte?

Source: http://slms.berkeley.edu/researchprojects/how-much-info/datapowers.html, accessed May 2005. Used with the permission of Peter Lyman and Hal R. Varian, University of California at Berkeley.

Kilobyte (KB)	*1,000 bytes* or *10³ bytes* 2 Kilobytes: A typewritten page 100 Kilobytes: A low-resolution photograph
Megabyte (MB)	*1,000,000 bytes* or *10⁶ bytes* 2 Megabytes: A high-resolution photograph 5 Megabytes: The complete works of Shakespeare 10 Megabytes: A minute of high-fidelity sound 100 Megabytes: One meter of shelved books 500 Megabytes: A CD-ROM
Gigabyte (GB)	*1,000,000,000 bytes* or *10⁹ bytes* 1 Gigabyte: A pickup truck filled with books 20 Gigabytes: A good collection of the works of Beethoven 100 Gigabytes: A library floor of academic journals
Terabyte (TB)	*1,000,000,000,000 bytes* or *10¹² bytes* 1 Terabyte: 50,000 trees made into paper and printed 2 Terabytes: An academic research library 10 Terabytes: The print collections of the U.S. Library of Congress 400 Terabytes: National Climactic Data Center (NOAA) database
Petabyte (PB)	*1,000,000,000,000,000 bytes* or *10¹⁵ bytes* 2 Petabytes: All U.S. academic research libraries 200 Petabytes: All printed material
Exabyte (EB)	*1,000,000,000,000,000,000 bytes* or *10¹⁸ bytes* 2 Exabytes: Total volume of information generated in 1999 5 Exabytes: All words ever spoken by human beings

1. Kevin Kelly, *The Technium*, November 2, 2007, *www.kk.org/thetechnium/archives/2007/11/dimensions_of_t.php* (accessed August 2008).
2. *www.acxiom.com/about_us/Pages/AboutAcxiom.aspxm* (accessed July 2009).

Q2 How Do Business Intelligence (BI) Systems Provide Competitive Advantages?

A **business intelligence (BI) system** is an information system that provides information for improving decision making. BI systems vary in their characteristics and capabilities and in the way they foster competitive advantage.

Figure 9-2 summarizes the characteristics and competitive advantages of four categories of business intelligence systems. **Reporting systems** integrate data from multiple sources, and they process that data by sorting, grouping, summing, averaging, and comparing. Such systems format the results into reports and deliver those reports to users. Reporting systems improve decision making by providing the right information to the right user at the right time.

You can learn more about OLAP in Chapter Extension 16, "Reporting Systems and OLAP."

Data mining systems process data using sophisticated statistical techniques, such as regression analysis and decision tree analysis. Data mining systems find patterns and relationships that cannot be found by simpler reporting operations, such as sorting, grouping, and averaging. Data mining systems improve decision making by using the discovered patterns and relationships to *anticipate* events or to *predict* future outcomes. An example of a data mining system is one that predicts the likelihood that a prospect will donate to a cause or political campaign based on the prospect's characteristics, such as age, sex, and home zip code. **Market basket analysis** is another data mining system, which computes correlations of items on past orders to determine items that are frequently purchased together. We will discuss data mining in more detail at the end of this chapter.

Knowledge management (KM) systems create value from intellectual capital by collecting and sharing human knowledge of products, product uses, best practices, and other critical knowledge with employees, managers, customers, suppliers, and others who need it.

Business Intelligence System	Characteristics	Competitive Advantage
Reporting systems	Integrate and process data by sorting, grouping, summing, and formatting. Produce, administer, and deliver reports.	Improve decisions by providing relevant, accurate, and timely information to the right person.
Data mining systems	Use sophisticated statistical techniques to find patterns and relationships.	Improve decisions by discovering patterns and relationships in data to predict future outcomes.
Knowledge management systems	Share knowledge of products, product uses, best practices, etc., among employees, managers, customers, and others.	Improve decisions by publishing employee and others' knowledge. Create value from existing intellectual capital. Foster innovation, improve customer service, increase organizational responsiveness, and reduce costs.
Expert systems	Encode human knowledge in the form of If/Then rules and process those rules to make a diagnosis or recommendation.	Improve decision making by nonexperts by encoding, saving, and processing expert knowledge.

Figure 9-2 Characteristics and Competitive Advantage of BI Systems

Expert systems are the fourth category of BI system in Figure 9-2. Expert systems encapsulate the knowledge of human experts in the form of *If/Then* rules. In a medical diagnosis system, for example, an expert system might have a rule such as:

If Patient_Temperature > 103,
Then Initiate High_Fever–Procedure

Operational expert systems can have hundreds or even thousands of such rules. Although few expert systems have demonstrated a capability equivalent to a human expert, some are good enough to considerably improve the diagnosis and decision making of nonexperts.

As with all information systems, it is important to distinguish between business intelligence *tools* and business intelligence *systems*. Business Objects licenses the reporting tool Crystal Reports. SPSS licenses the data mining suite Clementine, and Microsoft offers SharePoint Server as, in part, a knowledge management system. All of these products are, however, just software. They represent just one of the five components.

To gain the promise of improved decision making, organizations must incorporate data mining products into complete information systems. A reporting tool can generate a report that shows a customer has cancelled an important order. It takes a reporting *system*, however, to alert the customer's salesperson to this unwanted news in time for the salesperson to attempt to reverse the decision. Similarly, a data mining tool can create an equation that computes the probability that a customer will default on a loan. A data mining *system*, however, uses that equation to enable banking personnel to approve or reject a loan on the spot.

Q3 What Problems Do Operational Data Pose for BI Systems?

Data from transaction processing and other operational systems can be processed to create basic reports without problem. If we want to know, for example, current sales and how those sales relate to sales projections, we simply process data in the order-entry database.

However, raw operational data is seldom suitable for more sophisticated reporting or data mining. Figure 9-3 lists the major problem categories. First, although data that are critical for successful operations must be complete and accurate, data that are only marginally necessary do not need to be. For example, some systems gather demographic data in the ordering process. But because such data are not needed to fill, ship, and bill orders, their quality suffers.

Problematic data are termed **dirty data**. Examples are values of *B* for customer gender and of *213* for customer age. Other examples are a value of *999-999-9999* for a U.S. phone number, a part color of *gren*, and an email address of *WhyMe@GuessWhoIAM.org*. All of these values can be problematic for data mining purposes.

Missing values are a second problem. A nonprofit organization can process a donation without knowing the donor's gender or age, but a data mining application will suffer if there are many such missing values.

Figure 9-3
Problems of Using Transaction Data for Analysis and Data Mining

- Dirty data
- Missing values
- Inconsistent data
- Data not integrated
- Wrong granularity
  - Too fine
  - Not fine enough
- Too much data
  - Too many attributes
  - Too many data points

Inconsistent data, the third problem in Figure 9-3, are particularly common for data that have been gathered over time. When an area code changes, for example, the phone number for a given customer before the change will not match the customer's number after the change. Likewise, part numbers can change, as can sales territories. Before such data can be used, they must be recoded for consistency over the period of the study.

Some data inconsistencies occur from the nature of the business activity. Consider a Web-based order-entry system used by customers worldwide. When the Web server records the time of order, which time zone does it use? The server's system clock time is irrelevant to an analysis of customer behavior. Coordinated Universal Time (formerly called Greenwich Mean Time) is also meaningless. Somehow, Web server time must be adjusted to the customer's time zone.

Another problem is nonintegrated data. Suppose, for example, that an organization wants to perform an analysis of customer purchase and payment behavior. Unfortunately, the organization records payment data in an Oracle financial management database that is separate from the Microsoft CRM database that has the order data. Before the organization can perform the analysis, the data must be integrated.

Data can also be too fine or too coarse. Data **granularity** refers to the degree of summarization or detail. Coarse data are highly summarized; fine data express precise details. For example, suppose we want to analyze the placement of graphics and controls on an order-entry Web page. It is possible to capture the customers' clicking behavior in what is termed **clickstream data**. Those data are very fine, however, including everything the customer does at the Web site. In the middle of the order stream are data for clicks on the news, email, instant chat, and a weather check. Although all of that data is needed for a study of consumer computer behavior, such data will be overwhelming if all we want to know is how customers respond to ad locations. Because the data are too fine, the data analysts must throw away millions and millions of clicks.

Data can also be too coarse. For example, a file of order totals cannot be used for a market-basket analysis. For market-basket analysis, we need to know which items were purchased with which others. This doesn't mean the order-total data are useless. They can be adequate for other purposes; they just won't do for a market-basket analysis.

Generally, it is better to have too fine a granularity than too coarse. If the granularity is too fine, the data can be made coarser by summing and combining. Only analysts' labor and computer processing are required. If the granularity is too coarse, however, there is no way to separate the data into constituent parts.

The final problem listed in Figure 9-3 concerns too much data. As shown in the figure, we can have either too many attributes or too many data points. Think of the tables in Chapter 5. We can have too many columns (attributes) or too many rows (columns).

Consider the first problem: too many attributes. Suppose we want to know the factors that influence how customers respond to a promotion. If we combine internal customer data with customer data that we can purchase, we could have more than a hundred different attributes to consider. How do we select among them? Because of a phenomenon called the **curse of dimensionality**, the more attributes there are, the easier it is to build a model that fits the sample data but that is worthless as a predictor. There are other good reasons for reducing the number of attributes, and one of the major activities in data mining concerns efficient and effective ways of selecting attributes.

The Guide on pages 222–223 discusses data sampling in more detail.

The second way to have too much data is to have too many data points—too many rows of data. Suppose we want to analyze clickstream data on the CNN Web site *(www.cnn.com)*. How many clicks does that site receive per month? Millions upon millions! In order to meaningfully analyze such data, we need to reduce the amount of data. There is a good solution to this problem: statistical sampling. Organizations should not be reluctant to sample data in such situations.

Experiencing MIS InClass Exercise 9

Do You Have a Club Card?

A **data aggregator** is a company that obtains data from public and private sources and stores, combines, and publishes it in sophisticated ways. When you use your grocery store club card, the data from your grocery shopping trip are sold to a data aggregator. Credit card data, credit data, public tax records, insurance records, product warranty card data, voter registration data, and hundreds of other types of data are sold to aggregators.

Not all of the data are identified in the same way (or, in terms of Chapter 5, not all of it has the same primary key). But, using a combination of phone number, address, email address, name, and other partially identifying data, such companies can integrate that disparate data into an integrated, coherent whole. They then query, report, and data mine the integrated data to form detailed descriptions about companies, communities, zip codes, households, and individuals.

As you will learn in Chapter 12, laws limit the types of data that federal and other governmental agencies can acquire and store. There are also some legal safeguards on data maintained by credit bureaus and medical facilities. However, no such laws limit data storage by most companies (nor are there laws that prohibit governmental agencies from buying results from data aggregators).

InClass Group Exercise:

Acxiom Corporation, a data aggregator with $1.2 billion in sales in 2009, has been described as the "biggest company you never heard of." Visit *www.acxiom.com* and complete the following tasks:

1. Navigate the Acxiom Web site and make a list of 10 different products that Acxiom provides.
2. Describe Acxiom's top customers.
3. Examine your answers to items 1 and 2 and describe, in general terms, the kinds of data that Acxiom must collect to be able to provide these products to its customers.
4. In what ways might companies like Acxiom need to limit their marketing so as to avoid a privacy outcry from the public?
5. According to the Web site, what is Acxiom's privacy policy? Are you reassured by its policy? Why or why not?
6. Should there be laws governing companies like Acxiom? Why or why not?
7. Prepare a 3-minute presentation of your answers to items 3–6. Give your presentation to the rest of the class.

Q4 What Are the Purpose and Components of a Data Warehouse?

The purpose of a **data warehouse** is to extract and clean data from operational systems and other sources and to store and catalog that data for processing by BI tools. Figure 9-4 shows the basic components of a data warehouse. Programs read operational data and extract, clean, and prepare that data for BI processing. The prepared data are stored in a data warehouse database using a data warehouse DBMS, which can be different from the organization's operational DBMS. For example, an organization might use Oracle for its operational processing, but use SQL Server for its data warehouse. Other organizations use SQL Server for

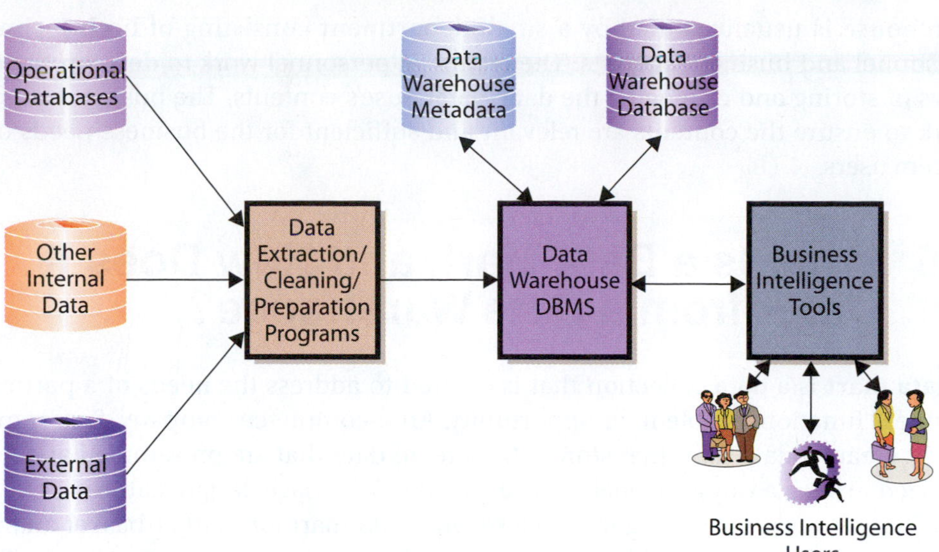

Figure 9-4
Components of a Data Warehouse

operational processing, but use DBMSs from statistical package vendors, such as SAS or SPSS, in the data warehouse.

Data warehouses can include external data purchased from outside sources. A typical example is customer credit data. Figure 9-5 lists some of the consumer data than can be purchased from commercial vendors. An amazing (and, from a privacy standpoint, frightening) amount of data is available.

Social networking and user-generated content applications generate potentially large amounts of data. Because the data come directly from the source (prospect or client), it will likely be more accurate than purchased data. Social networking and user-generated content are just now coming into use in business, and organizations have not yet compiled large amounts of that data. In the years to come, however, such data will play a key role in data warehouse applications. For example, if you brag about your new 3D TV on Facebook, the data aggregators will know you buy expensive, leading-edge electronics.

Metadata concerning the data—its source, its format, its assumptions and constraints, and other facts about the data—is kept in a data warehouse metadata database. The data warehouse DBMS extracts and provides data to BI tools, such as data mining programs.

By the way, do not interpret the term *warehouse* literally. It is a warehouse only in the sense that it is a facility for storing data for use by others. It is *not* a large building with shelves and forklifts buzzing through aisles loaded with pallets. Physically, a data warehouse consists of a few fast computers with very large storage devices. The data

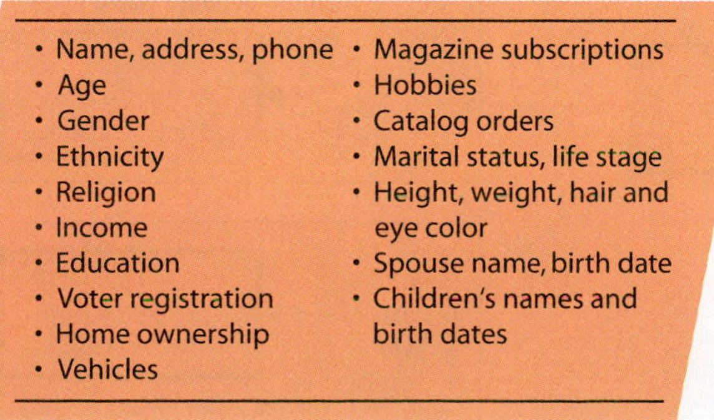

• Name, address, phone
• Age
• Gender
• Ethnicity
• Religion
• Income
• Education
• Voter registration
• Home ownership
• Vehicles
• Magazine subscriptions
• Hobbies
• Catalog orders
• Marital status, life stage
• Height, weight, hair and eye color
• Spouse name, birth date
• Children's names and birth dates

Figure 9-5
Consumer Data Available for Purchase from Data Vendors

warehouse is usually staffed by a small department consisting of both technical personnel and business analysts. The technical personnel work to develop the best ways of storing and cataloging the data warehouse's contents. The business analysts work to ensure the contents are relevant and sufficient for the business needs of BI system users.

Q5 What Is a Data Mart, and How Does It Differ from a Data Warehouse?

For additional information on database marketing, see Chapter Extension 15.

A **data mart** is a data collection that is created to address the needs of a particular business function, problem, or opportunity. An e-commerce company, for example, might create a data mart that stores clickstream data that are presampled and summarized in such a way as to enable the analysis of Web page design features.

That same company might have a second data mart for market-basket analysis. This second data mart would contain records of past sales data organized to facilitate the computation of item-purchase correlations. A third data mart could contain inventory data and be organized to support a BI system used to plan the layout of inventory.

So how is a data warehouse different from a data mart? In a way, you can think of a *data warehouse* as a distributor in a supply chain. The data warehouse takes data from the data manufacturers (operational systems, other internal systems, etc.), cleans and processes the data, and locates the data on its shelves, so to speak—that is, on the disks of the data warehouse computers. The people who work with a data warehouse are experts at data management, data cleaning, data transformation, metadata design, and the like. Data warehouse business analysts know the general needs of the business, but they are not experts in a given business function.

As stated, a *data mart* is a data collection, smaller than the data warehouse, that addresses a particular component or functional area of the business. If the data warehouse is the distributor in a supply chain, then a data mart is like a retail store in a supply chain. Users in the data mart obtain data that pertain to a particular business function from the data warehouse. Such users do not have the data management expertise that data warehouse employees have, but they are knowledgeable analysts for a given business function. Figure 9-6 illustrates these relationships.

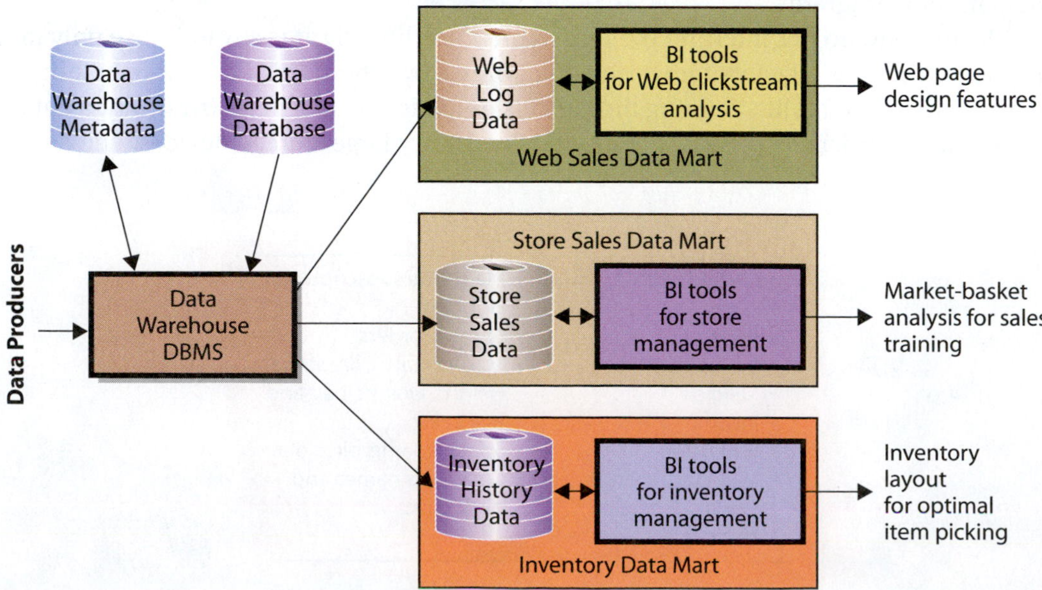

Figure 9-6
Data Mart Examples

As you can imagine, it is expensive to create, staff, and operate data warehouses and data marts. Only large organizations with deep pockets can afford to operate a system like that shown in Figure 9-6. Smaller organizations operate subsets of this system; they may have just a simple data mart for analyzing promotion data, for example.

Q6 What Are the Characteristics of Data Mining Systems?

We now return to the concept of data mining. **Data mining** is the application of statistical techniques to find patterns and relationships among data and to classify and predict. As shown in Figure 9-7, data mining represents a convergence of disciplines. Data mining techniques emerged from statistics and mathematics and from artificial intelligence and machine-learning fields in computer science. As a result, data mining terminology is an odd blend of terms from these different disciplines. Sometimes people use the term *knowledge discovery in databases* (*KDD*) as a synonym for *data mining.*

Data mining techniques take advantage of developments in data management for processing the enormous databases that have emerged in the last 10 years. Of course, these data would not have been generated were it not for fast and cheap computers, and, without such computers, the new techniques would be impossible to compute.

Most data mining techniques are sophisticated, and many are difficult to use. Such techniques are valuable to organizations, however, and some business professionals, especially those in finance and marketing, have become expert in their use. Today, in fact, there are many interesting and rewarding careers for business professionals who are knowledgeable about data mining techniques.

Data mining techniques fall into two broad categories: unsupervised and supervised. We explain both types in the following sections.

Unsupervised Data Mining

With **unsupervised data mining**, analysts do not create a model or hypothesis before running the analysis. Instead, they apply the data mining technique to the data and

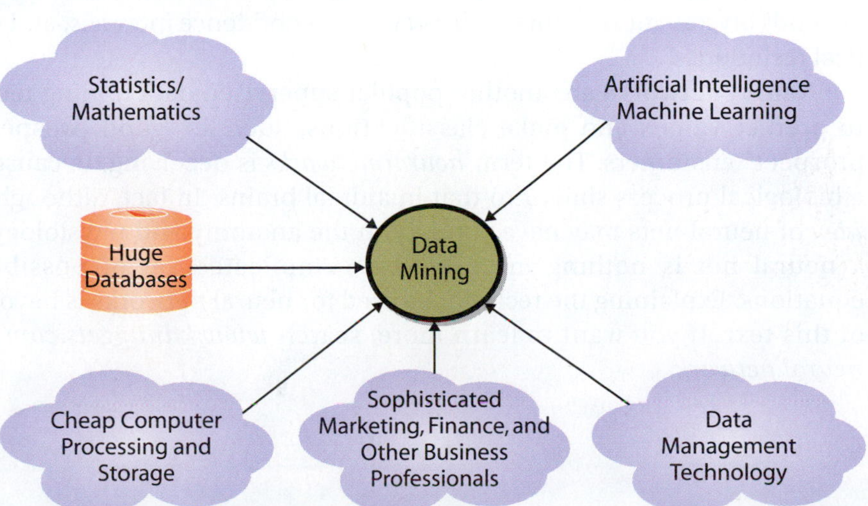

Figure 9-7
Convergence Disciplines for Data Mining

observe the results. With this method, analysts create hypotheses after the analysis to explain the patterns found.

One common unsupervised technique is **cluster analysis**. With it, statistical techniques identify groups of entities that have similar characteristics. A common use for cluster analysis is to find groups of similar customers from customer order and demographic data.

For example, suppose a cluster analysis finds two very different customer groups: One group has an average age of 33; owns at least one laptop, at least one cell phone, and one iPad; drives an expensive SUV; and tends to buy expensive children's play equipment. The second group has an average age of 64, owns vacation property, plays golf, and buys expensive wines. Suppose the analysis also finds that both groups buy designer children's clothing.

These findings are obtained solely by data analysis. There is no prior model about the patterns and relationship that exist. It is up to the analyst to form hypotheses, after the fact, to explain why two such different groups are both buying designer children's clothes.

Supervised Data Mining

With **supervised data mining**, data miners develop a model prior to the analysis and apply statistical techniques to data to estimate parameters of the model. For example, suppose marketing experts in a communications company believe that cell phone usage on weekends is determined by the age of the customer and the number of months the customer has had the cell phone account. A data mining analyst would then run an analysis that estimates the impact of customer and account age. One such analysis, which measures the impact of a set of variables on another variable, is called a **regression analysis**. A sample result for the cell phone example is:

$$\text{CellPhoneWeekendMinutes} = 12 + (17.5 \times \text{CustomerAge}) + (23.7 \times \text{NumberMonthsOfAccount})$$

Using this equation, analysts can predict the number of minutes of weekend cell phone use by summing 12, plus 17.5 times the customer's age, plus 23.7 times the number of months of the account.

As you will learn in your statistics classes, considerable skill is required to interpret the quality of such a model. The regression tool will create an equation, such as the one shown. Whether that equation is a good predictor of future cell phone usage depends on statistical factors such as *t* values, confidence intervals, and related statistical techniques.

Neural networks are another popular supervised data mining technique used to predict values and make classifications, such as "good prospect" or "poor prospect" customers. The term *neural networks* is deceiving, because it connotes a biological process similar to that in animal brains. In fact, although the original *idea* of neural nets may have come from the anatomy and physiology of neurons, a neural net is nothing more than a complicated set of possibly nonlinear equations. Explaining the techniques used for neural networks is beyond the scope of this text. If you want to learn more, search *www.kdnuggets.com* for the term *neural network*.

How does the knowledge of this chapter help Fox Lake and you?

Knowledge of this chapter would help Jeff understand the value of the data that Fox Lake has in its operational systems. Anne is pushing for using some of that data, but, undoubtedly, BI applications exist that can help Fox Lake market its golf and tennis services as well as its restaurant. Also, BI applications probably exist that would help the facilities department improve its efficiency. Fox Lake is too small to have a data warehouse, but it might want to create an informal data mart to support these possible BI applications.

You can benefit in the same way. At your future employer, remember the value of stored data. Whether in sales, marketing, manufacturing, accounting, or management, you will find potential BI applications to help you solve problems and work more effectively.

Ethics Guide

Data Mining in the Real World

"I'm not really against data mining. I believe in it. After all, it's my career. But data mining in the real world is a lot different from the way it's described in textbooks.

"There are many reasons it's different. One is that the data are always dirty, with missing values, values way out of the range of possibility, and time values that make no sense. Here's an example: Somebody sets the server system clock incorrectly and runs the server for a while with the wrong time. When they notice the mistake, they set the clock to the correct time. But all of the transactions that were running during that interval have an ending time before the starting time. When we run the data analysis, and compute elapsed time, the results are negative for those transactions.

"Missing values are a similar problem. Consider the records of just 10 purchases. Suppose that two of the records are missing the customer number and one is missing the year part of the transaction date. So you throw out three records, which is 30 percent of the data. You then notice that two more records have dirty data, and so you throw them out, too. Now you've lost half your data.

"Another problem is that you know the least when you start the study. So you work for a few months and learn that if you had another variable, say the customer's zip code, or age, or something else, you could do a much better analysis. But those other data just aren't available. Or, maybe they are available, but to get the data you have to reprocess millions of transactions, and you don't have the time or budget to do that.

"Overfitting is another problem, a huge one. I can build a model to fit any set of data you have. Give me 100 data points and in a few minutes, I can give you 100 different equations that will predict those 100 data points. With neural networks, you can create a model of any level of complexity you want, except that none of those equations will predict new cases with any accuracy at all. When using neural nets, you have to be very careful not to overfit the data.

"Then, too, data mining is about probabilities, not certainty. Bad luck happens. Say I build a model that predicts the probability that a customer will make a purchase. Using the model on new-customer data, I find three customers who have a .7 probability of buying something. That's a good number, well over a 50-50 chance, but it's still

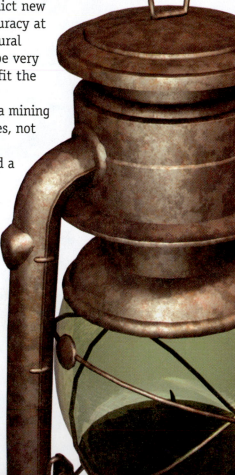

possible that none of them will buy. In fact, the probability that none of them will buy is $.3 \times .3 \times .3$, or .027, which is 2.7 percent.

"Now suppose I give the names of the three customers to a salesperson who calls on them, and sure enough, we have a stream of bad luck and none of them buys. This bad result doesn't mean the model is wrong. But what does the salesperson think? He thinks that the model is worthless and that he can do better on his own. He tells his manager who tells her associate, who tells the northeast regional manager, and sure enough, the model has a bad reputation across the company.

"Seasonality is another problem. Say all your training data are from the summer. Will your model be valid for the winter? Maybe, but maybe not. You might even know that it won't be valid for predicting winter sales, but if you don't have winter data, what do you do?

"When you start a data mining project, you never know how it will turn out. I worked on one project for 6 months, and when we finished, I didn't think our model was any good. We had too many problems with data: wrong, dirty, and missing. There was no way we could know ahead of time that it would happen, but it did.

"When the time came to present the results to senior management, what could we do? How could we say we took 6 months of our time and substantial computer resources to create a bad model? We had a model, but I just didn't think it would make accurate predictions. I was a junior member of the team, and it wasn't for me to decide. I kept my mouth shut, but I never felt good about it."

Discussion Questions

1. Did this employee have an ethical responsibility to speak up regarding his belief about the quality of the data mining model? Why or why not?
2. If you were this employee, what would you have done?
3. The case doesn't indicate how the data mining model was to be used. Suppose it was to be used at a hospital emergency room to predict the criticality of emergency cases. In this case, would you change your answers to questions 1 and 2? Why or why not?
4. Suppose the data mining model was to be used to predict the likelihood that sales prospects respond to a promotional postal mailing. Say the cost of the mailing is $10,000 and will be paid by a marketing department having an annual budget of $25 million. Do your answers to questions 1 and 2 change for this situation? Why or why not?
5. If your answers are different for questions 3 and 4, explain why. If they are not different, explain why not.
6. Suppose you were this employee and you spoke to your direct boss about your misgivings. Your boss said, "Forget about it, junior." How would you respond?
7. Suppose your boss told you to forget about it, but in a meeting with your boss and your boss's boss, the senior manager asks you what you think of the predictive ability of this model. How do you respond?

Guide

Counting and Counting and Counting

Not long ago, in a very large software company, a meeting occurred between a group of highly competent product managers and a group of equally competent data miners. The product managers wanted the data miners to analyze customer clicks on a Web page to determine customer preferences for particular product lines. The products were competing with one another for resources, and the results of the analysis were important in allocating those resources.

The meeting progressed well until one of the data miners started to explain the sampling scheme that they would use.

"Sampling?" asked the product managers in a chorus. "Sampling? No way. We want all the data. This is important, and we don't want a guess."

"But there are millions, literally, millions of ad clicks to analyze. If we don't sample, it will take hours, maybe even days, to perform the calculations. You won't see the results from each day's analysis until several days later if we don't sample." The data miners were squirming.

"We don't care," said the product managers. "We must have an accurate study. Don't sample!"

This leads us to a statistical concept you need to know: *There's nothing wrong with sampling.* Properly done, the results from a sample are just as accurate as results from the complete data set. Studies done from samples are also cheaper and faster. Sampling is a great way to save time and money.

Suppose you have a bag of randomly mixed blue and red balls. Let's say the bag is big enough to contain 100,000 balls. How many of those balls do you need to examine to calculate, accurately, the proportion of each color?

You go to the park on a sunny day, sit down with your bag, and start pulling balls out of the bag. After 100 balls, you conclude the ratio of blue to red is 4.1 to 5.9. After 1,000 balls, you conclude the ratio of blue to red balls is 4.02 to 5.98. After 5,000 balls, you conclude the ratio of blue to red balls is 4.002 to 5.998. After 10,000 balls, you conclude the ratio of blue to red balls is 4 to 6. Do you really need to sit there until next week, counting balls day and night, to examine every ball in the bag? And, if you're the manager who needs to know that ratio, do you really want to pay someone to count all those balls?

That's why the data miners were so depressed after their meeting with the product managers. They knew they had to count Web clicks long, long after there was any more information to be gained from continuing to count. To add to the pain of their situation, they had to do it only because of the product managers' ignorance.

In truth, skill is required to develop a good sample. The product managers should have listened

to the data miners' sampling plan and ensured that the sample would be appropriate, given the goals of the study. If they didn't have the knowledge to determine if the sampling plan was correct, they should have employed a knowledgeable third party to assess it. Hiring the third party would have been far cheaper and faster than buying all the computers necessary to process all the data. Unfortunately, this company bought the computers!

Understanding just this concept will save you and your organization substantial money!

Discussion Questions

1. In your own words, explain why a sample can give the same accuracy of results as the entire data set. Under what circumstances would it not give the same results?
2. Suppose you want to predict the demand for toothbrushes from past sales data. Suppose there are 5 colors and 10 styles. If you want to predict the sales for all types of toothbrushes, how should you sample? If you want to predict the sales for each color and style, would you sample differently? Why or why not?
3. The data miners tried to sell the idea of sampling based on the reduction of work. Suppose instead they had tried to sell the idea based on the idea of equal accuracy. Would the result have been different?

ACTIVE REVIEW

Use this Active Review to verify that you understand the ideas and concepts that answer this chapter's study questions.

Q1 Why do organizations need business intelligence?

Identify the economic factors that have caused so much data to be created. Define *petabyte* and *exabyte*. Explain the opportunities that all of this data presents to business.

Q2 How do business intelligence (BI) systems provide competitive advantages?

Define *business intelligence systems.* Name four categories of BI systems, and describe the basic characteristics of each. Explain how systems in each category contribute to competitive advantage.

Q3 What problems do operational data pose for BI systems?

List problems that occur when using operational data for BI systems. Briefly summarize each problem. Define *granularity.* Explain the problem posed by the *curse of dimensionality.*

Q4 What are the purpose and components of a data warehouse?

Define *data warehouse* and state its purpose. Explain the role of each component in Figure 9-4. Of the many different types of data that can be purchased, name five that you think are the most concerning from a privacy standpoint. State reasons why some businesses might want to purchase this data. Describe the impact that social networks and user-generated content will have on data warehouses. Explain why the term *warehouse* is misleading.

Q5 What is a data mart, and how does it differ from a data warehouse?

Define *data mart,* and give an example of one not described in this chapter. Explain how data warehouses and data marts are like components of a supply chain. Under what conditions does an organization staff a data warehouse with several data marts?

Q6 What are the characteristics of data-mining systems?

State the purpose of data mining systems. Explain how data mining emerged from the convergence of different disciplines. Describe the impact this history had on data mining terminology. Explain the characteristics and uses of unsupervised data mining. Explain the characteristics and uses of supervised data mining. Explain why the term *neural network* is a misnomer.

How does the knowledge of this chapter help Fox Lake and you?

Explain how knowledge of BI could help Anne and Jeff make better decisions at Fox Point. Summarize how this knowledge could help you in your career, in whatever field you choose to work.

KEY TERMS AND CONCEPTS

USING YOUR KNOWLEDGE

1. Explain why the knowledge that we are storing exabytes of data is important to decision making. Name and describe three decision-making applications of stored data not mentioned in this chapter. Use one example for each of the four types of BI system in Figure 9-2.

2. How does the data storage trend described in question 1 impact your university? What types of data do you think are growing the fastest? Of the fast-growing data, what percentage do you think is generated by students? By classroom activities? By administrators? By research? Explain your answer.

3. Suppose you work for the university and have access to student, class, professor, department, and grade data. Suppose you want to determine whether grade inflation exists, and, if so, where it seems to be the greatest. Describe a reporting system that would produce evidence of grade inflation. How would you structure the reports to determine where it is the greatest?

4. Suppose you work for the university and have access to student, class, professor, department, and grade data. Assume the student data includes students' home address, high school, and prior college performance (if any). Describe an unsupervised data mining technique that could be used to predict college applicants who are likely to succeed academically. Is it responsible or irresponsible to use an unsupervised technique for such a problem?

5. Same as question 4, but describe a supervised data mining technique that could be used to predict the success of applicants. Is using a supervised technique more justifiable than using an unsupervised technique? Explain.

6. Explain how a set of If/Then rules could be used to select facilities for wedding events. Give an example of five rules that would be pertinent to this problem. Given Fox Lake's size and culture, do you think it is likely that it would embrace an expert system? Explain. How could Anne use such rules in a more informal manner?

COLLABORATION EXERCISE 9

Before you start this exercise, read Chapter Extensions 1 and 2, which describe collaboration techniques as well as tools for managing collaboration tasks. In particular, consider using Google Docs, Windows Live SkyDrive, Microsoft SharePoint, or some other collaboration tool.

One of the consequences of free data communications and data storage is the collection and storage of vast amounts of data about individuals, families, and organizations. These data are gathered and aggregated by businesses, which then sell the resulting information to companies and governmental agencies. Is the use of such data ethical? Is it wise? What policies should exist for the use of such data by companies and governments?

You will have an opportunity to consider these issues as you answer the following questions.

1. At Fox Lake, Anne wants to buy data about the marital status of members' daughters.
   - **a.** Do you think this activity is ethical?
   - **b.** Do you think it is a wise business decision?
   - **c.** Does it matter that the data she needs is publicly accessible? Why or why not?

2. Data aggregators are companies that obtain publicly accessible data records and combine them into profiles about individuals, families, and organizations. To learn more about them, read:
   - **a.** Experiencing MIS InClass Exercise 9 (page 214)
   - **b.** *http://blog.fvsu.edu/2008/03/the-data-aggregator-and-you/*

3. Visit four of the following sites and answer the questions in item 4:
   - **a.** *www.acxiom.com/Pages/Home.aspx*
   - **b.** *http://atxp.choicepoint.com/default.htm*
   - **c.** *www.catalinamarketing.com/company/*
   - **d.** *https://schwabpt.com/providers/data/aggregators.htm*
   - **e.** *www.aristotle.com*
   - **f.** *http://donnellymsa.com/*

4. Choose two of the sites you visited in item 3 and provide the following information on each:
   - **a.** Describe the major products that organization provides.
   - **b.** Describe the organization's data sources.
   - **c.** Describe the organization's primary customers.
   - **d.** Describe the organization's pricing model.
   - **e.** Using your answers to a–d, summarize the organization's business model.

5. In addition to wedding events, Fox Lake offers golf and tennis activities; a restaurant; special events, such as golf and tennis tournaments; and golf, tennis, and swimming lessons.
   a. Describe three ways that Fox Lake could use its membership data (data that it stores in its own databases) to promote these activities.
   b. Describe three ways that Fox Lake could purchase data in addition to its own database data to promote these activities.
6. Among your team, discuss the role of data aggregators in commerce and formulate a policy for ethical use of data aggregation products.
7. Among your team, discuss the role of data aggregators in government and formulate a policy for ethical use of data aggregation products.
8. Prepare a 2-minute presentation for each of your answers to items 4, 5, 6, and 7. Provide your answers to the rest of the class.

CASE STUDY 9

THL (cont.)

Before proceeding, reread Case Study 8, page 206, which introduces THL, Tourism Holdings Limited, a New Zealand–based company that owns and operates multiple businesses. In this case, we will examine how THL uses information systems to support vehicle leasing in its four camper-leasing business lines.

Leasing camper vehicles to customers has three fundamental phases:

1. Matching customer requirements with vehicle availability
2. Reserving vehicles and informing operations
3. Billing and customer service

Online Reservations Systems

Customers access a Web site for whichever brand of vehicle they wish to rent. On that site, they specify the dates and locations from which they want to rent and return a vehicle. THL information systems access the vehicle inventory to determine which vehicles might be available.

That determination is complex. THL may not have the wanted vehicle in the desired location, but it might have a higher-priced vehicle available and choose to offer the customer a free upgrade. Or, it might have the desired vehicle in a different city and choose to move the vehicle to that location. However, moving the vehicle might impact prior reservations for that vehicle, making such movement infeasible. Finally, this complexity is compounded because certain vehicles are not to be rented from particular locations. (Two-wheel-drive standard vehicles cannot be rented for the Australian outback, for example). And, of course, vehicles undergo both scheduled and unscheduled maintenance.

Pricing is another complicated decision in the reservation process. Like hotels and airlines, THL engages in flex pricing, whereby prices are determined not only by the vehicle and rental period, but also by customer demand.

To accommodate this complexity, THL developed a rule-based availability information system known as Aurora. Business analysts create business rules like those shown in Figures 9-8 and Figure 9-9.

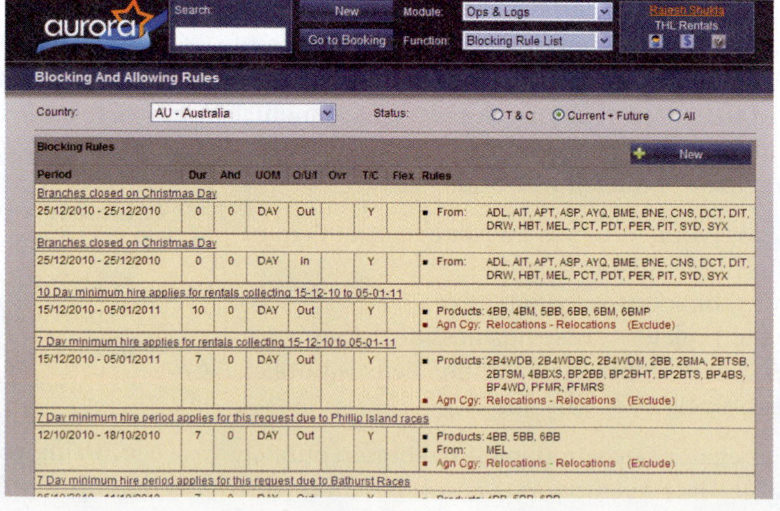

Figure 9-8
Example Rental Rules

Source: © Tourism Holdings Limited. Used with permission.

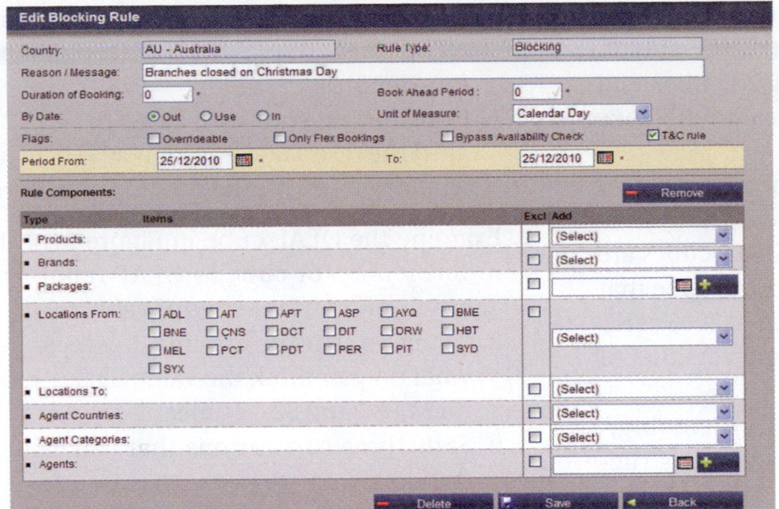

Figure 9-9
Setting Up a Blocking Rule

Source: © Tourism Holdings Limited. Used with permission.

Figure 9-8 shows an example of rules that block vehicles from rental; Figure 9-9 shows a screen that is used to setup or modify a rule. All rules are stored in a SQL Server database, a database that also contains all of the vehicle reservation data. Application programs in the Aurora system access and process the business rules when determining vehicle availability. Because rules are set up and managed with easy-to-use interfaces like that in Figure 9-9, nonprogrammer business analysts are able to change reservation policy without the assistance of technical personnel.

THL also operates information systems for vehicle check-in and customer billing.

The Aurora reservation system off-loads data to a second SQL Server database that operates a Report Server (see Figure 9-10). By off-loading the data, THL produces numerous sophisticated reports without impacting the performance of the online reservation system.

Reports from the guide show both operational and managerial activities. One report, for example, shows the vehicles that are to be checked out and returned to each rental location. Other reports show which vehicles need to be transferred to other locations, which vehicles are to be sent for maintenance, which vehicles are to be retired from the fleet, and so forth.

Business Intelligence Information Systems

"We know our operational data contains a wealth of information about our customers, their rental needs,

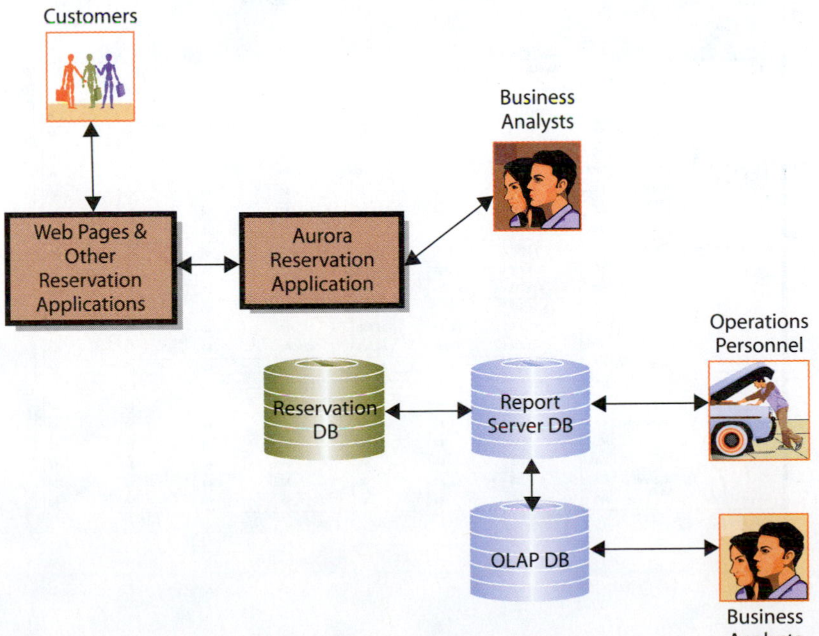

Figure 9-10
THL Information Systems

trends in rental activity and vehicle needs, and other key business drivers," Grant Webster, CEO, stated. "We've already developed numerous OLAP cubes and we're working on other types of business intelligence applications."

As shown in Figure 9-10, data from the report server is downloaded to a third server that provides OLAP services. Operational data is processed, and OLAP cubes are created on a weekly basis. Figure 9-11 shows a cube that displays revenue earned from vehicle sales in 2005 (THL is, naturally, reluctant to publish current versions of such private data).

OLAP stands for "online analytical processing," and it refers to the production of reports whose structure can be changed dynamically by the user. In Figure 9-10, the user could, for example, change the brand and geographic market columns, and the totals would be adjusted accordingly. Excel Pivot charts are an example of an OLAP report (or *cube,* as OLAP reports are called). The difference is that THL's report server produces reports based on thousands of transactions; such volume would be very difficult to process in Excel.

Questions

1. Considering the rule-based reservation system:
   a. Summarize the benefits of having policy determined by rules rather than by computer code.
   b. What are the consequences of someone entering an incorrect rule? Offer both mundane and drastic examples.
   c. Considering your answer to part b, if you managed the reservation system at THL, what process would you use for the modification of rules?

2. Examine the OLAP cube in Figure 9-11. The values in this report (or cube as OLAP reports are called) are sums of rental revenue of vehicles.
   a. Using your intuition and business knowledge, what do you think the value $3,697 means? What do $1,587 and $2,121 mean?
   b. State three conclusions that you can make from this data.
   c. The principal advantage of OLAP is that columns and rows can be switched and the report values will be recalculated automatically. Explain what would happen if the user of this report were to switch the first column (geographic area) with the third column (brand). You do not have sufficient data to compute values, but explain in words what will happen.

3. Considering customer reservation data, give an example of the use of each of the following:
   a. Reporting application (other than OLAP)
   b. Market-basket analysis
   c. Unsupervised data mining
   d. Supervised data mining

Figure 9-11
THL OLAP Report

Source: © Tourism Holdings Limited. Used with permission.

You can learn more about OLAP in Chapter Extension 16, "Reporting Systems and OLAP."

PowerPlay - [Monthly S & M Report.ppx of CombinedVehicleSales (Reporter)]
File Edit View Insert Explore Calculate Format Tools Window Help
Vehicle | Out City | Package | Relocation | To City | Brand | Inclusive | Oneway | Country | Cancelled | Cancelled | BookDate | OutDate | Hire Length | Flex

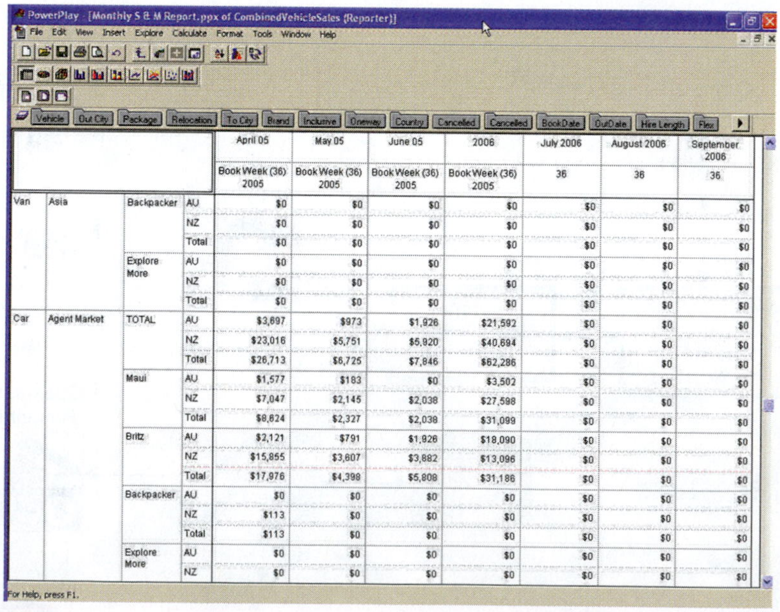

				April 05	May 05	June 05	2006	July 2006	August 2006	September 2006
				Book Week (36) 2005	Book Week (36) 2005	Book Week (36) 2005	Book Week (36) 2005	36	36	36
Van	Asia	Backpacker	AU	$0	$0	$0	$0	$0	$0	$0
			NZ	$0	$0	$0	$0	$0	$0	$0
			Total	$0	$0	$0	$0	$0	$0	$0
		Explore More	AU	$0	$0	$0	$0	$0	$0	$0
			NZ	$0	$0	$0	$0	$0	$0	$0
			Total	$0	$0	$0	$0	$0	$0	$0
Car	Agent Market	TOTAL	AU	$3,697	$973	$1,926	$21,592	$0	$0	$0
			NZ	$23,016	$5,751	$5,920	$40,694	$0	$0	$0
			Total	$26,713	$6,725	$7,846	$62,286	$0	$0	$0
		Maui	AU	$1,577	$183	$0	$3,502	$0	$0	$0
			NZ	$7,047	$2,145	$2,038	$27,598	$0	$0	$0
			Total	$8,624	$2,327	$2,038	$31,099	$0	$0	$0
		Britz	AU	$2,121	$791	$1,926	$18,090	$0	$0	$0
			NZ	$15,855	$3,607	$3,882	$13,096	$0	$0	$0
			Total	$17,976	$4,398	$5,808	$31,186	$0	$0	$0
		Backpacker	AU	$0	$0	$0	$0	$0	$0	$0
			NZ	$113	$0	$0	$0	$0	$0	$0
			Total	$113	$0	$0	$0	$0	$0	$0
		Explore More	AU	$0	$0	$0	$0	$0	$0	$0
			NZ	$0	$0	$0	$0	$0	$0	$0

For Help, press F1.

e. Rank your answers to parts a–d on the basis of their desirability. Justify your ranking.

4. Suppose that THL decides to start a van rental business in the United States. Suppose that it is considering opening operations in Alaska, California, Arizona, New Mexico, or Florida.

a. Given the nature of THL's current camper-vehicle rental activities, which of those states do you think would be best? Justify your decision. Consider potential competition, market size, applicability of THL's experience, and other factors you deem relevant.

b. Summarize THL's competitive strengths for this new operation.

c. Summarize THL's competitive vulnerabilities for this new operation.

d. Describe how its reservation system adds value to this new operation.

e. Summarize the problems that you think THL might have in running a business 7,500 miles (or more) from its headquarters.

5. Name and describe information systems and technologies that THL could use to mitigate the problems in your answer to part e in question 4.

Part 4

Information Systems Management

Part 4 addresses the management of information systems development, resources, and security in Chapters 10, 11, and 12, respectively. Even if you are not an IS major, you need to know about these functions so that you can be a successful and effective consumer of IS professionals' services. FlexTime and Fox Lake are small companies, each having well under $100 million a year in sales. Like most small companies, neither has a formal organization for managing information systems development, resources, and security. However, small organizations are not exempt from these responsibilities. In small businesses without professional IS personnel, these responsibilities often fall to business managers, like you will be. So, pay close attention to the user and management responsibilities in these three chapters. If you work for a medium-sized or large organization that does have the support of a professional staff, these chapters will help you understand the responsibilities and activities of IS professionals, which will enable you to work more effectively with them.

This could happen to you

In Chapter 10, we will examine how Fox Lake could proceed to develop an information system for facility scheduling. In Chapter 11, we will investigate what Fox Lake is and is not doing with regard to the management of IS resources. Finally, in Chapter 12, we will see why Fox Lake's information systems are particularly vulnerable to computer misuse and crime. It's not going to be pretty!

CHAPTER 10

Information Systems Development

This could happen to you

"Jeff, we clean the clubhouse restrooms twice a day . . . in the morning before 7 and again just before lunch. We've been doing that for years. Never been a problem." Mike Stone, the facilities manager, is defending his department in a meeting with Jeff Lloyd, Fox Lake's general manager, and Anne Foster, manager of the newly formed wedding events department.

"That's just great Mike. Just great." Anne raises her voice, "And what if, like on the PAST THREE SATURDAYS, we have two weddings in the afternoon? Do you think maybe guests at the second wedding would like clean bathrooms?" Anne is incredulous that she has to ask for clean bathrooms, of all things. "It's your friends and family at a wedding . . . at Fox Lake! You would hope the bathrooms will be clean!"

Jeff sits impatiently, he doesn't like the direction of this discussion, but he doesn't know where to take it.

Mike continues. "Look, Anne, I can hire staff to clean the bathrooms on whatever schedule you want. I DO have a budget to pay attention to, however, so I'm not going to hire people to clean bathrooms that are already clean because we DIDN'T have two weddings that day."

"Well, Mike, should we talk about our problem with the toilet in the Ladies room?"

"What do you mean?"

"I mean for one whole month, we've had a toilet that overflows . . ."

STUDY QUESTIONS

Q1 What is systems development?

Q2 Why is systems development difficult and risky?

Q3 What are the five phases of the SDLC?

Q4 How is system definition accomplished?

Q5 What is the users' role in the requirements phase?

Q6 How are the five components designed?

Q7 How is an information system implemented?

Q8 What are the tasks for system maintenance?

Q9 What are some of the problems with the SDLC?

How does the **knowledge** in this chapter help ***Fox Lake*** and **you?**

"Mike, is that right?" Jeff jumps in.

"Look. I don't have a plumber on staff. Steve's the weekend manager. He knows we watch our expenses, and he's not going to call a plumber on Saturday, weekend rates and all. So, he does the right thing. He goes over there and tries to fix it himself."

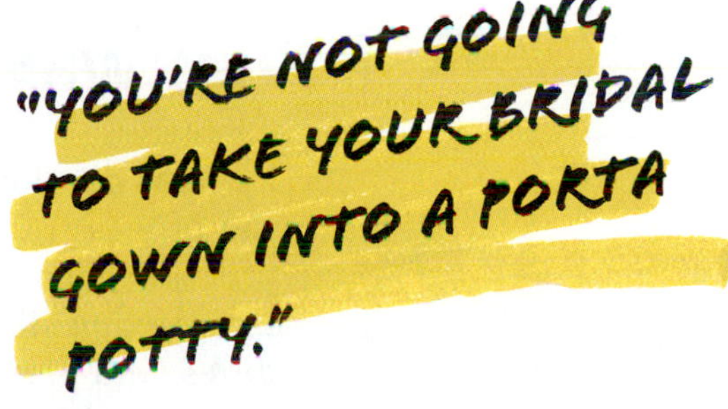
"YOU'RE NOT GOING
TO TAKE YOUR BRIDAL
GOWN INTO A PORTA
POTTY."

"Seems like a good response, doesn't it?" Jeff asks, wondering where this one is going.

"I thought so, too. Saves us money and solves the problem. Turns out that plumbing equipment was never designed to have 250 people at an event. It's designed for one or two people from the restaurant, maybe a party of four golfers. Anyway, he fixes the toilet with spare parts and whatnot and, with that heavy use, it breaks again, and Anne comes unglued! Besides, if I had notice, I could bring in some Porta Potties . . ."

"Mike!!! This is a wedding! You're not going to take your bridal gown into a Porta Potty. I CAN'T BELIEVE I'M HAVING THIS DISCUSSION!!!" Anne is stupefied at his comment.

Jeff steps in. "OK, you two. Clearly, we've got some work to do. We're almost at the end of the big wedding season. Take a break and then sit down together and schedule it out. Figure out what it will take to get us through this year. Mike, let me know if you need more money and I'll see what I can come up with. But, I don't mean a lot. Meanwhile, I'll start thinking about a longer-term solution."

Next week, Jeff meets in his office with Laura Shen, who'd been recommended to him as someone who could help solve the wedding events and facilities problems.

"Laura, I don't really know what you do. Margaret Silvester, one of our board members, said you'd helped with some computer problems at her company and she insisted I meet with you. This doesn't seem like a problem for a computer programmer, though."

"Jeff, I'm not a programmer. I'm what's called a 'business analyst.' I know technology, and while I have written computer programs, that's not what I do.

Optional Extensions for this chapter are • CE18: Business Process Management 549 • CE19: Systems Development Project Management 565

I specialize in understanding business needs, strategies, and goals and helping businesses implement systems to accomplish those goals. Often that involves computer-based systems, but not always."

"Well, what do you know about us?"

"Margaret gave me a quick rundown. You've recently acquired a wedding events business and you've had problems integrating it with the rest of Fox Lake."

"That's about right. But, we didn't acquire a business . . . we hired someone who owned a small business and she hoped to make it bigger working for Fox Lake. I was looking for a source of additional revenue."

"So, what's the problem?"

"Facilities, mostly. We had some issues about using membership data for marketing, but not serious ones. The big problems are sharing facilities, timely maintenance, and tracking repairs. And, these wedding events stress us in ways we're not used to. The crew at the restaurant can serve up a few burgers and fries to the club members, but when we start putting high-end caterers into their kitchen space, well, like I said, it's stressful . . . "

"I might be able to help. Did you see this coming when you started wedding events?"

"No, not really. We just thought we could use our buildings for weddings . . . I didn't understand how it would impact everything else."

"Well, let me talk with your key people for a bit, and I'll get back to you with some ideas and a proposal."

Q1 What Is Systems Development?

Systems development, or **systems analysis and design**, as it is sometimes called, is the process of creating and maintaining information systems. Notice that this process concerns *information systems*, not just computer programs. Developing an *information system* involves all five components: hardware, software, data, procedures, and people. Developing a *computer program* involves software programs, possibly with some focus on data and databases. Figure 10-1 shows that systems development has a broader scope than computer program development.

Because systems development addresses all five components, it requires more than just programming or technical expertise. Establishing the system's goals, setting up the project, and determining requirements require business knowledge and management skill. Tasks like building computer networks and writing computer programs require technical skills; developing the other components requires nontechnical, human relations skills. Creating data models requires the ability to interview users and understand their view of the business activities. Designing procedures, especially those involving group action, requires business knowledge and an understanding of group dynamics. Developing job descriptions, staffing, and training all require human resource and related expertise.

Therefore, do not suppose that systems development is exclusively a technical task undertaken by programmers and hardware specialists. Rather, it requires coordinated teamwork of both specialists and nonspecialists with business knowledge.

Figure 10-1
Systems Development Versus Program Development

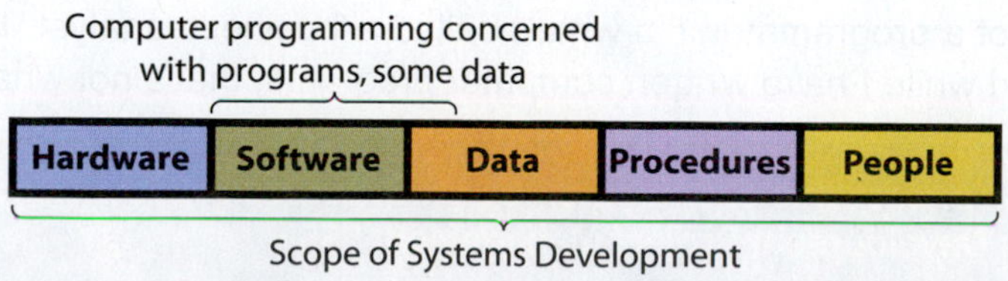

In Chapter 4, you learned that there are three sources for software: off-the-shelf, off-the-shelf with adaptation, and tailor-made. Although all three sources pertain to software, only two of them pertain to information systems. Unlike software, *information systems are never off-the-shelf.* Because information systems involve your company's people and procedures, you must construct or adapt procedures to fit your business and people, regardless of how you obtain the computer programs.

As a future business manager, you will have a key role in information systems development. In order to accomplish the goals of your department, you need to ensure that effective procedures exist for using the information system. You need to ensure that personnel are properly trained and are able to use the IS effectively. If your department does not have appropriate procedures and trained personnel, you must take corrective action. Although you might pass off hardware, program, or data problems to the IT department, you cannot pass off procedural or personnel problems to that department. Such problems are your problems. The single most important criterion for information systems success is for users to take ownership of their systems.

Q2 Why Is Systems Development Difficult and Risky?

Systems development is difficult and risky. Many projects are never finished. Of those that are finished, some are 200 or 300 percent over budget. Still other projects finish within budget and schedule, but never satisfactorily accomplish their goals.

You can learn more about project planning by reading Chapter Extension 19, "Systems Development Project Management."

You may be amazed to learn that systems development failures can be so dramatic. You might suppose that with all the computers and all the systems developed over the years that by now there must be some methodology for successful systems development. In fact, there *are* systems development methodologies that can result in success, and we will discuss the primary one in this chapter. But, even when competent people follow this or some other accepted methodology, the risk of failure is still high.

In the following sections, we will discuss the five major challenges to systems development displayed in Figure 10-2.

The Difficulty of Requirements Determination

First, requirements are difficult to determine. Suppose that Laura works with Fox Lake and together they determine that Fox Lake needs a facilities management information system for event and maintenance scheduling and for facility problem tracking and reporting. What specifically is that system to do? How does a wedding planner use the new system to reserve a room or a building? What does the data entry screen look like? How does a planner add or reduce the facilities needed once a wedding has been scheduled? What should the system do when a wedding is cancelled? How does the facility schedule system interface with accounting systems, if at all? Does the system need to reserve floor or refrigerator space in the restaurant kitchen? Should the wedding application be a thin or thick client? Is there a need for wedding planners to use the system from remote locations? What is the data model for the database content? Many, many details need to be identified and specified.

Believe it or not, the proposed Fox Lake system is simple. Consider, instead, the development of a new interorganizational system to be used by the suppliers of the Boeing 787 airplane. What features and functions should it have? What is to be

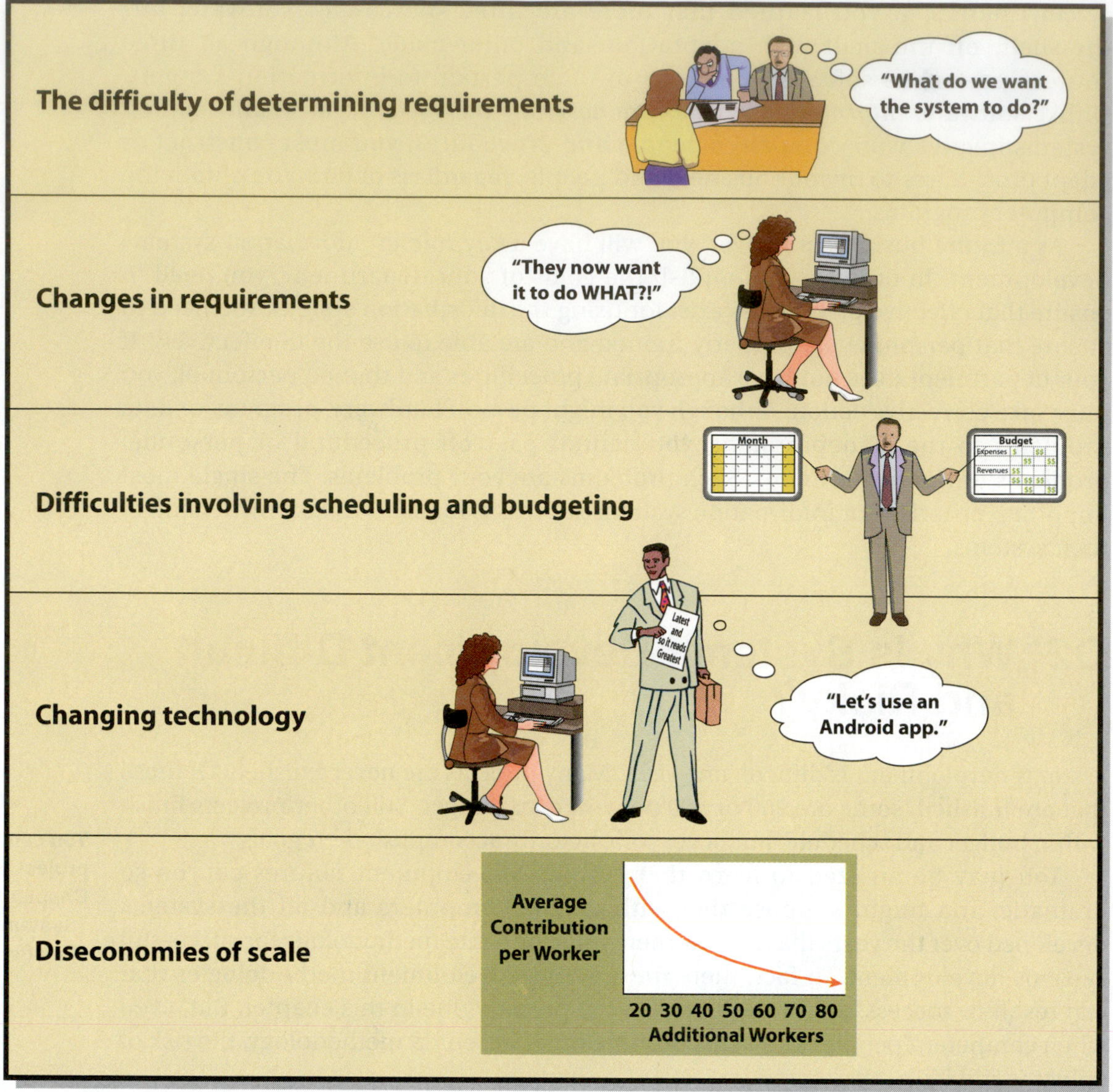

Figure 10-2
Major Challenges to Systems Development

done if different companies have different ideas about the IS features required? Companies may disagree about the data they are willing to share. How are those differences to be resolved? Hundreds of hours of labor will be required to determine the requirements.

The questions could go on and on. One of the major purposes of the systems development process is to create an environment in which such questions are both asked and answered.

Changes in Requirements

Even more difficult, systems development aims at a moving target. Requirements change as the system is developed, and, the bigger the system and the longer the project, the more the requirements change.

When requirements do change, what should the development team do? Stop work and rebuild the system in accordance with the new requirements? If they do that, the system will develop in fits and starts and may never be completed. Or, should the team finish the system, knowing that it will be unsatisfactory the day it is implemented and will, therefore, need immediate maintenance?

Scheduling and Budgeting Difficulties

Other challenges involve scheduling and budgeting. How long will it take to build a system? That question is not easy to answer. Suppose you are developing a new facilities maintenance database at Fox Lake. How long will it take to create the data model? Even if you know how long it takes to create the data model, others may disagree with you and with each other. How many times will you need to rebuild the data model until everyone agrees?

Again, the Fox Lake system is a simple problem. What if you are building the new database for the supply chain system? How many hours will it take to create the data model, review, and approve it? Consider database applications. How long will it take to build the forms, reports, queries, and application programs? How long will it take to test all of them? What about procedures and people? What procedures need to be developed, and how much time should be set aside to create and document them, develop training programs, and train the personnel?

Further, how much will all of this cost? Labor costs are a direct function of labor hours; if you cannot estimate labor hours, you cannot estimate labor costs. Moreover, if you cannot estimate how much a system costs, then how do you perform a financial analysis to determine if the system generates an appropriate rate of return?

Changing Technology

Yet another challenge is that while the project is underway, technology continues to change. For example, say that while you are developing your facilities maintenance application, Apple, Microsoft, and Google and their business partners all release new versions of smart phones. You know that with these new phones you can create a better facilities scheduling capability for wedding planners and maintenance workers, but using these phones means a major change in requirements.

Do you want to stop your development to switch to the new technology? Would it be better to finish developing according to the existing plan? Such decisions are tough. Why build an out-of-date system? But, can you afford to keep changing the project?

Diseconomies of Scale

Unfortunately, as development teams become larger, the average contribution per worker decreases. This is true because as staff size increases, more meetings and other coordinating activities are required to keep everyone in sync. There are economies of scale up to a point, but beyond a workgroup of, say, 20 employees, diseconomies of scale begin to take over.

A famous adage known as **Brooks' Law** points out a related problem: *Adding more people to a late project makes the project later.*[1] Brooks' Law is true not only because a larger staff requires increased coordination, but also because new people need training. The only people who can train the new employees are the existing team members, who are thus taken off productive tasks. The costs of training new people can overwhelm the benefit of their contribution.

In short, managers of software development projects face a dilemma: They can increase work per employee by keeping the team small, but in doing so they extend the project's timeline. Or, they can reduce the project's timeline by adding staff, but

1. Fred Brooks was a successful executive at IBM in the 1960s. After retiring from IBM, he wrote a classic book on IT project management called *The Mythical Man-Month.* Published by Addison-Wesley in 1975, the book is pertinent today and should be read by every IT or IS project manager. It's an enjoyable book, too.

because of diseconomies of scale they will have to add 150 or 200 hours of labor to gain 100 hours of work. And, due to Brooks' Law, once the project is late, both choices are bad.

Furthermore, schedules can be compressed only so far. According to one other popular adage, "Nine women cannot make a baby in one month."

Is It Really So Bleak?

Is systems development really as bleak as the list of challenges makes it sound? Yes and no. All of the challenges just described do exist, and they are all significant hurdles that every development project must overcome. As noted previously, once the project is late and over budget, no good choice exists. "I have to pick my regrets," said one beleaguered manager of a late project.

The IT industry has over 50 years of experience developing information systems; over those years, methodologies have emerged that successfully deal with these problems. In the next study question, we will consider the systems development life cycle (SDLC), the most common process for systems development.

Q3 What Are the Five Phases of the SDLC?

The **systems development life cycle (SDLC)** is the traditional process used to develop information systems. The IT industry developed the SDLC in the "school of hard knocks." Many early projects met with disaster, and companies and systems developers sifted through the ashes of those disasters to determine what went wrong. By the 1970s, most seasoned project managers agreed on the basic tasks that need to be performed to successfully build and maintain information systems. These basic tasks are combined into phases of systems development.

Different authors and organizations package the tasks into different numbers of phases. Some organizations use an eight-phase process, others use a seven-phase process, and still others use a five-phase process. In this book, we will use the following five-phase process:

1. **System definition**
2. **Requirements analysis**
3. **Component design**
4. **Implementation**
5. **Maintenance**

Figure 10-3 shows how these phases are related. Development begins when a business-planning process identifies a need for a new system. We address IS planning processes in Chapter 11. For now, suppose that management has determined, in some way, that the organization can best accomplish its goals and objectives by constructing a new information system.

Chapter Extension 18 discusses business process management, a modern approach for managing processes that often provides the impetus for new information systems development.

At Fox Lake, Laura, as a business analyst, will investigate the wedding events integration problems. She and the senior Fox Lake managers may determine that Fox Lake needs a new facilities management system. If so, that decision would kick off the SDLC for the development of that new system.

Developers in the first SDLC phase—system definition—use management's statement of the system needs in order to begin to define the new system. The resulting project plan is the input to the second phase—requirements analysis. Here, developers identify the particular features and functions of the new system. The output of that

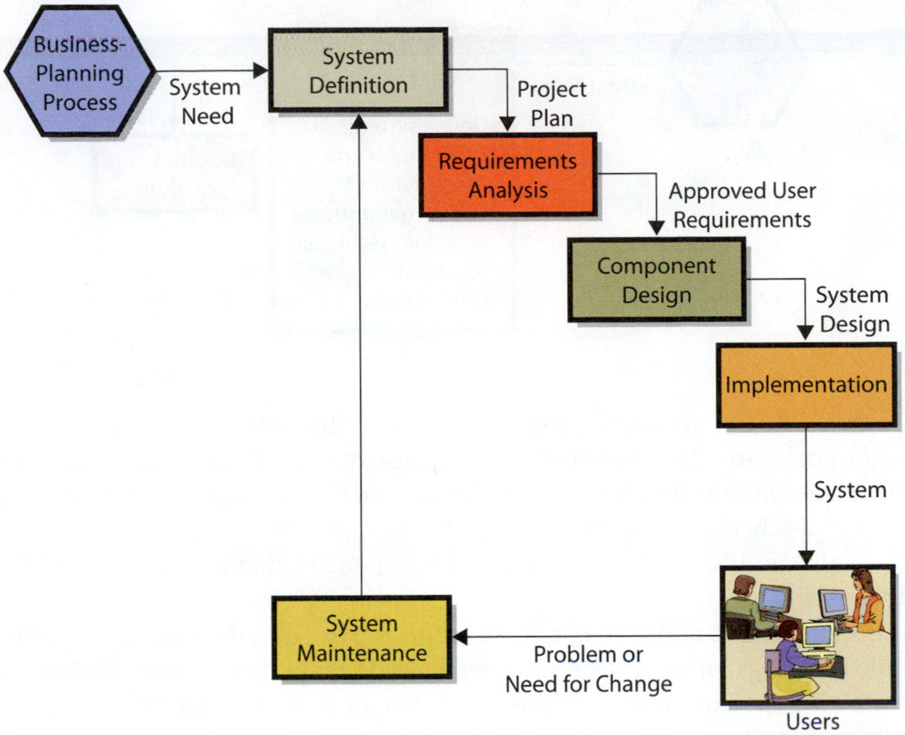

Figure 10-3
Phases in the SDLC

phase is a set of approved user requirements, which become the primary input used to design system components. In phase 4, developers implement, test, and install the new system.

Over time, users will find errors, mistakes, and problems. They will also develop new requirements. The description of fixes and new requirements is input into a system maintenance phase. The maintenance phase starts the process all over again, which is why the process is considered a cycle.

In the following sections, we will consider each phase of the SDLC in more detail.

Q4 How Is System Definition Accomplished?

In response to the need for the new system, the organization will assign a few employees, possibly on a part-time basis, to define the new system, to assess its feasibility, and to plan the project. Typically, someone from the IS department leads the initial team, but the members of that initial team are both users and IS professionals. In the case of a small company like Fox Lake, Jeff has hired Laura, an independent expert, to work with Mike, Anne, himself, and other key employees to define the system.

Define System Goals and Scope

As Figure 10-4 shows, the first step is to define the goals and scope of the new information system. Information systems exist to facilitate an organization's competitive strategy by supporting business processes or by improving decision making. At this step, the development team defines the goal and purpose of the new system in terms of these reasons.

Figure 10-4
SDLC: System Definition Phase

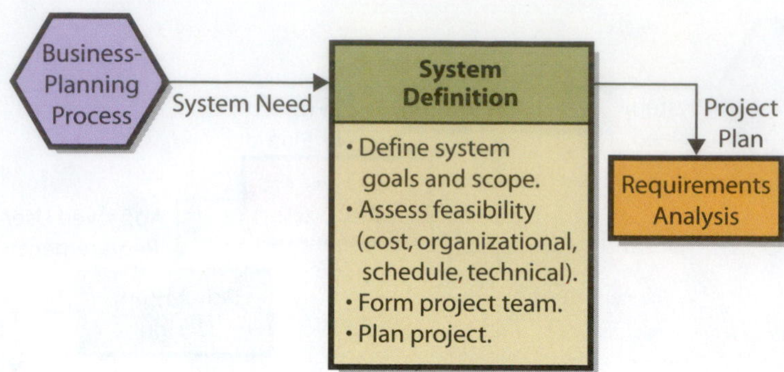

Consider the new facilities system at Fox Lake. What is the purpose of that system? Fox Lake's goal is to raise revenue from wedding events, but these events are stressing facilities scheduling and maintenance. The goals of the new system are to eliminate or at least reveal schedule conflicts and improve maintenance tracking. But the new system must also be affordable so that it is not so expensive that it creates a net loss from wedding events.

Another task is to define the project's scope. At Fox Lake, does the new system only schedule buildings for wedding events? Or, does it include golf, tennis, and swimming event scheduling? Does it include the scheduling of restaurant facilities, such as floor and refrigerator space? Is it just for building maintenance, or does it include golf course, tennis court, and swimming pool maintenance?

In other systems, the scope might be defined by specifying the users who will be involved, or the business processes that will be involved, or the plants, offices, and factories that will be involved.

Assess Feasibility

For a discussion of ethical issues relating to estimation, see the Ethics Guide on pages 252–253.

Once we have defined the project's goals and scope, the next step is to assess feasibility. This step answers the question, "Does this project make sense?" The aim here is to eliminate obviously nonsensible projects before forming a project development team and investing significant labor.

Feasibility has four dimensions: **cost**, **schedule**, **technical**, and **organizational**. Because IS development projects are difficult to budget and schedule, cost and schedule feasibility can be only an approximate, back-of-the-envelope analysis. The purpose is to eliminate any obviously infeasible ideas as soon as possible.

Cost feasibility involves an assessment of the cost of the project. At Fox Lake, Laura will investigate how much similar projects have cost in the past. She will think not only about development costs, but also about the operational costs of hosting the application and the cost of employee labor for maintaining the site. It is possible that the new system will cost more than an entire year's wedding revenue; if so, the cost is infeasible. In this case, Laura and the team would look for other solutions, such as a revision to manual procedures. Or, even if costs are substantially less than wedding revenue, the cost may be more than Fox Lake is willing to spend. In this case, for the project to be cost-feasible it will need to reduce the project's scope or find other solutions.

Like cost feasibility, *schedule feasibility* is difficult to determine because it is difficult to estimate the time it will take to build the system. However, if Laura determines that it will take, say, no less than 6 months to develop the system and put it into operation, Fox Lake can then decide if it can accept that minimum schedule. At this stage of the project, the company should not rely on either cost or schedule estimates; the purpose of these estimates is simply to rule out any obviously unacceptable projects.

Technical feasibility refers to whether existing information technology is likely to be able to meet the needs of the new system. At Fox Lake, the new system is most likely well within the capabilities of existing technology. For more advanced systems, this is not always the case. A system that requires data-intensive applications on an iPhone, an Android, and the Windows Series 7 phone might not (yet) be technically feasible.

Finally, *organizational feasibility* concerns whether the new system fits within the organization's customs, culture, charter, or legal requirements. For example, if the new Fox Lake system is used to schedule maintenance workers, does it violate any union rules or labor laws? Will existing business customs at Fox Lake make it impossible for workers to be scheduled by an automated system?

Form a Project Team

If the defined project is determined to be feasible, the next step is to form the project team. Normally the team consists of both IT personnel and user representatives. The project manager and IT personnel can be in-house personnel or outside contractors. In Chapter 11, we will describe various means of obtaining IT personnel using outside sources and the benefits and risks of outsourcing.

Typical personnel on a development team are a manager (or managers for larger projects), business analysts, system analysts, programmers, software testers, and users. As Laura explained at the start of this chapter, **business analysts** specialize in understanding business needs, strategies, and goals and helping businesses implement systems to accomplish their competitive strategies. **Systems analysts** are IT professionals who understand both business and technology.

Systems analysts are closer to IT and are a bit more technical, though there is considerable overlap in the duties and responsibilities of business and system analysts. Both are active throughout the systems development process and play a key role in moving the project through the systems development process. Business analysts work more with managers and executives; systems analysts integrate the work of the programmers, testers, and users. Depending on the nature of the project, the team may also include hardware and communications specialists, database designers and administrators, and other IT specialists.

The team composition changes over time. During requirements definition, the team will be heavy with business and systems analysts. During design and implementation, it will be heavy with programmers, testers, and database designers. During integrated testing and conversion, the team will be augmented with testers and business users.

User involvement is critical throughout the system development process. Depending on the size and nature of the project, users are assigned to the project either full or part time. Sometimes users are assigned to review and oversight committees that meet periodically, especially at the completion of project phases and other milestones. Users are involved in many different ways. *The important point is for users to have active involvement and to take ownership of the project throughout the entire development process.*

Fox Lake does not have an IT department, so the development team will consist, at least initially, of Laura, Jeff, Mike, and Anne. As the project progresses, Fox Lake will need to outsource for professional systems developers and programmers.

The first major task for the assembled project team is to plan the project. Members of the project team specify tasks to be accomplished, assign personnel, determine task dependencies, and set schedules.

Q5 What Is the Users' Role in the Requirements Phase?

The primary purpose of the requirements analysis phase is to determine and document the specific features and functions of the new system. For most development projects, this phase requires interviewing dozens of users and documenting potentially hundreds of requirements. Requirements definition is, thus, expensive. It is also difficult, as you will see.

Determine Requirements

Determining the system's requirements is the most important phase in the systems development process. If the requirements are wrong, the system will be wrong. If the requirements are determined completely and correctly, then design and implementation will be easier and more likely to result in success.

Examples of requirements are the contents and the format of Web pages and the functions of buttons on those pages, or the structure and content of a report, or the fields and menu choices in a data entry form. Requirements include not only what is to be produced, but also how frequently and how fast it is to be produced. Some requirements specify the volume of data to be stored and processed.

If you take a course in systems analysis and design, you will spend weeks on techniques for determining requirements. Here, we will just summarize that process. Typically, systems analysts interview users and record the results in some consistent manner. Good interviewing skills are crucial; users are notorious for being unable to describe what they want and need. Users also tend to focus on the tasks they are performing at the time of the interview. Tasks performed at the end of the quarter or end of the year are forgotten if the interview takes place mid-quarter. Seasoned and experienced systems analysts know how to conduct interviews to bring such requirements to light.

As listed in Figure 10-5, sources of requirements include existing systems as well as the Web pages, forms, reports, queries, and application features and functions desired in the new system. Security is another important category of requirements.

If the new system involves a new database or substantial changes to an existing database, then the development team will create a data model. As you learned in Chapter 5, that model must reflect the users' perspective on their business and business activities. Thus, the data model is constructed on the basis of user interviews and must be validated by those users.

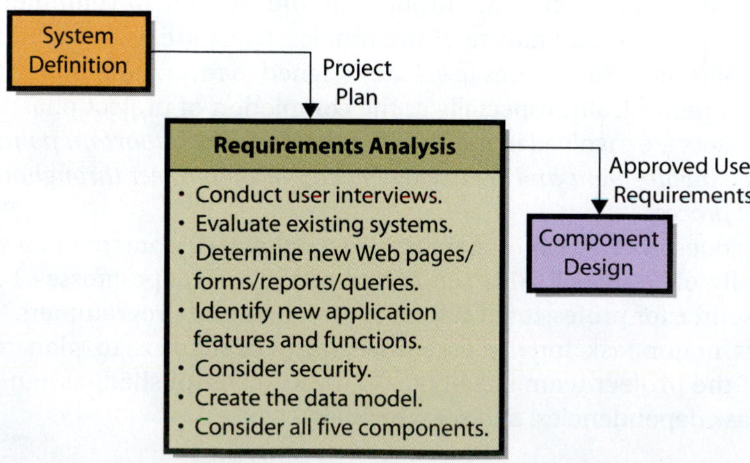

Figure 10-5
SDLC: Requirements Analysis Phase

Experiencing MIS InClass Exercise 10

Garden Traker

Suppose that you and two or three other students have been groundskeepers at Fox Lake, and you have decided to go out on your own and open a business that offers landscaping services. Your goal is to develop a list of clients for whom you provide regular and recurring services, such as mowing, weeding, and pool cleaning, as well as specialty services, such as pruning, garden preparation, tree removal, sprinkler installation and repair, and the like.

You know that it will be critical for your success to have an information system for tracking customers, services you have provided, and services you are scheduled to provide in the future. As a new small business, you want a simple and affordable system based on Excel or Access. You name your new system *Garden Tracker*.

Form a team of three or four students and, given what you know about lawn and garden maintenance and your intuition and business knowledge, complete the following tasks:

1. Explain how you would use the SDLC to develop GardenTraker.
2. Define the scope of your system.
3. Explain the process you would use to determine the feasibility of GardenTraker. List data you need for such an assessment, and explain how you might obtain or estimate that data.
4. Consider just the tracking of recurring services, and list all of the requirements that you can imagine for that functionality. Be specific and answer at least the following:
   - **a.** What data will you need?
   - **b.** How will you input that data? Show a mockup of a data entry screen, and describe how it will be used.
   - **c.** Using your mockup, describe how you will modify recurring service data.
   - **d.** Using your mockup, describe how you will cancel a recurring service.
   - **e.** Specify any other requirements you believe are important for tracking recurring services.
5. Present your answers to item 4 to the rest of the class and obtain feedback from your classmates.
6. Modify your answer to item 4 based upon feedback you received in item 5.
7. Considering just the recurring services functionality, do you think it would be better to use Excel or Access for this project? List the criteria you used to answer that question. Summarize the consequences of making a poor choice between these two products.
8. What does this short exercise tell you about information systems development? Answer this question in such a way that you could use your answer to demonstrate your critical-thinking skills in a job interview.

Sometimes, the requirements determination is so focused on the software and data components that other components are forgotten. Experienced project managers ensure consideration of requirements for all five IS components, not just for software and data. Regarding hardware, the team might ask: Are there special needs or restrictions on hardware? Is there an organizational standard governing what kinds of hardware may or may not be used? Must the new system use existing hardware? What requirements are there for communications and network hardware?

Similarly, the team should consider requirements for procedures and personnel: Do accounting controls require procedures that separate duties and authorities? Are there restrictions that some actions can be taken only by certain departments or specific personnel? Are there policy requirements or union rules that restrict activities to certain categories of employees? Will the system need to interface with information systems from other companies and organizations? In short, requirements need to be considered for all of the components of the new information system.

These questions are examples of the kinds of questions that must be asked and answered during requirements analysis.

Approve Requirements

Once the requirements have been specified, the users must review and approve them before the project continues. The easiest and cheapest time to alter the information system is in the requirements phase. Changing a requirement at this stage is simply a matter of changing a description. Changing a requirement in the implementation phase may require weeks of reworking applications components and the database.

Q6 How Are the Five Components Designed?

Each of the five components is designed in this stage. Typically, the team designs each component by developing alternatives, evaluating each of those alternatives against the requirements, and then selecting among those alternatives. Accurate requirements are critical here; if they are incomplete or wrong, then they will be poor guides for evaluation. Figure 10-6 shows that design tasks pertain to each of the five IS components.

Hardware Design

For hardware, the team determines specifications for the hardware they need and the source of that hardware. They can purchase the hardware, lease it, or lease time from a hosting service in the cloud. (The team is not designing hardware in the sense of building a CPU or a disk drive.)

At Fox Lake, Laura is the only person with knowledge of systems development, so she will work with the development contractor to help specify Fox Lake's needs. If Fox Lake is already operating its own computer network, it might choose to use it. Or, Fox

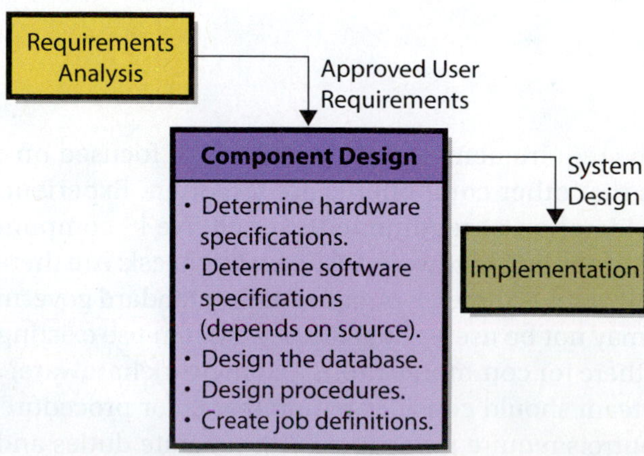

Figure 10-6
SDLC: Component Design Phase

Lake might place the application in the cloud and pay a cloud vendor for the time and resources it uses. Laura and the development team would make a recommendation for Fox Lake's approval.

Software Design

Software design depends on the source of the programs. For off-the-shelf software, the team must determine candidate products and evaluate them against the requirements. For off-the-shelf-with-alteration software, the team identifies products to be acquired off-the-shelf and then determines the alterations required. For custom-developed programs, the team produces design documentation for writing program code.

Database Design

If developers are constructing a database, then during this phase they convert the data model to a database design using techniques such as those described in Chapter 5. If developers are using off-the-shelf programs, then little database design needs to be done; the programs will handle their own database processing.

Procedure Design

For a business information system, the system developers and the organization must also design procedures for both users and operations personnel. Procedures need to be developed for normal, backup, and failure recovery operations, as summarized in Figure 10-7. Usually, teams of systems analysts and key users design the procedures.

Design of Job Descriptions

With regard to people, design involves developing job descriptions for both users and operations personnel. Sometimes new information systems require new jobs. If so, the duties and responsibilities for the new jobs need to be defined in accordance with the organization's human resources policies. More often, organizations add

	Users	Operations Personnel
Normal processing	• Procedures for using the system to accomplish business tasks.	• Procedures for starting, stopping, and operating the system.
Backup	• User procedures for backing up data and other resources.	• Operations procedures for backing up data and other resources.
Failure recovery	• Procedures to continue operations when the system fails. • Procedures to convert back to the system after recovery.	• Procedures to identify the source of failure and get it fixed. • Procedures to recover and restart the system.

Figure 10-7
Procedures to Be Designed

new duties and responsibilities to existing jobs. In this case, developers define these new tasks and responsibilities in this phase. Sometimes, the personnel design task is as simple as statements like, "Jason will be in charge of making backups." As with procedures, teams of systems analysts and users determine job descriptions and functions.

Q7 How Is an Information System Implemented?

Once the design is complete, the next phase in the SDLC is implementation. Tasks in this phase are to build, test, and convert the users to the new system (see Figure 10-8). Developers construct each of the components independently. They obtain, install, and test hardware. They license and install off-the-shelf programs; they write adaptations and custom programs, as necessary. They construct a database and fill it with data. They document, review, and test procedures, and they create training programs. Finally, the organization hires and trains needed personnel.

System Testing

Once developers have constructed and tested all of the components, they integrate the individual components and test the system. So far, we have glossed over testing as if there is nothing to it. In fact, software and system testing are difficult, time-consuming, and complex tasks. Developers need to design and develop test plans and record the results of tests. They need to devise a system to assign fixes to people and to verify that fixes are correct and complete.

A **test plan** consists of sequences of actions that users will take when using the new system. Test plans include not only the normal actions that users will take, but also incorrect actions. A comprehensive test plan should cause every line of program code to be executed. The test plan should cause every error message to be displayed. Testing, retesting, and re-retesting consume huge amounts of labor. Often, developers can reduce the labor cost of testing by writing programs that invoke system features automatically.

Today, many IT professionals work as testing specialists. Testing, or **product quality assurance (PQA)**, as it is often called, is an important career. PQA personnel

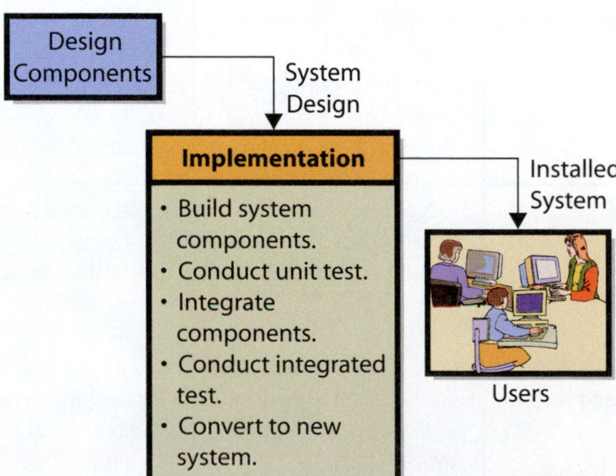

Figure 10-8
SDLC: Implementation Phase

usually construct the test plan with the advice and assistance of users. PQA test engineers perform testing, and they also supervise user test activity. Many PQA professionals are programmers who write automated test programs.

In addition to IT professionals, users should be involved in system testing. Users participate in the development of test plans and test cases. They also can be part of the test team, usually working under the direction of PQA personnel. Users have the final say on whether the system is ready for use. If you are invited to participate as a user tester, take that responsibly seriously. It will become much more difficult to fix problems after you have begun to use the system in production.

Beta testing is the process of allowing future system users to try out the new system on their own. Software vendors, such as Microsoft, often release beta versions of their products for users to try and to test. Such users report problems back to the vendor. Beta testing is the last stage of testing. Normally, products in the beta test phase are complete and fully functioning; they typically have few serious errors. Organizations that are developing large new information systems sometimes use a beta-testing process just as software vendors do.

System Conversion

Once the system has passed integrated testing, the organization installs the new system. The term **system conversion** is often used for this activity because it implies the process of *converting* business activity from the old system to the new.

Organizations can implement a system conversion in one of four ways:

- Pilot
- Phased
- Parallel
- Plunge

IS professionals recommend any of the first three, depending on the circumstances. In most cases, companies should avoid "taking the plunge!"

With **pilot installation**, the organization implements the entire system on a limited portion of the business. An example would be for Fox Lake to use the new system for a selected portion of its buildings; or for buildings, but not the restaurant; or for some other piece of the scope of the system. The advantage of pilot implementation is that if the system fails, the failure is contained within a limited boundary. This reduces exposure of the business and also protects the new system from developing a negative reputation throughout the organization.

As the name implies, with **phased installation** the new system is installed in phases across the organization. Once a given piece works, then the organization installs and tests another piece of the system, until the entire system has been installed. Some systems are so tightly integrated that they cannot be installed in phased pieces. Such systems must be installed using one of the other techniques.

With **parallel installation**, the new system runs in parallel with the old one until the new system is tested and fully operational. Parallel installation is expensive, because the organization incurs the costs of running both systems. Users must work double time, if you will, to run both systems. Then, considerable work is needed to determine if the results of the new system are consistent with those of the old system.

However, some organizations consider the costs of parallel installation to be a form of insurance. It is the slowest and most expensive style of installation, but it does provide an easy fallback position if the new system fails.

	Hardware	Software	Data	Procedures	People
Design	Determine hardware specifications.	Select off-the-shelf programs. Design alterations and custom programs as necessary.	Design database and related structures.	Design user and operations procedures.	Develop user and operations job descriptions.
Implementation	Obtain, install, and test hardware.	License and install off-the-shelf programs. Write alterations and custom programs. Test programs.	Create database. Fill with data. Test data.	Document procedures. Create training programs. Review and test procedures.	Hire and train personnel.
	Integrated Test and Conversion				

(Design and Implementation rows for each component: Unit test each component)

Figure 10-9
Design and Implementation for the Five Components

The final style of conversion is **plunge installation** (sometimes called *direct installation*). With it, the organization shuts off the old system and starts the new system. If the new system fails, the organization is in trouble: Nothing can be done until either the new system is fixed or the old system is reinstalled. Because of the risk, organizations should avoid this conversion style, if possible. The one exception is if the new system is providing a new capability that is not vital to the operation of the organization.

Figure 10-9 summarizes the tasks for each of the five components during the design and implementation phases. Use this figure to test your knowledge of the tasks in each phase.

Q8 What Are the Tasks for System Maintenance?

The last phase of the SDLC is maintenance. Maintenance is a misnomer; the work done during this phase is either to *fix* the system so that it works correctly or to *adapt* it to changes in requirements.

Figure 10-10 shows tasks during the maintenance phase. First, there needs to be a means for tracking both failures[2] and requests for enhancements to meet new requirements. For small systems, organizations can track failures and enhancements using word-processing documents. As systems become larger, however, and as the number of failure and enhancement requests increases, many organizations find it necessary to develop a failure-tracking database. Such a database contains a description of each failure or enhancement. It also records who reported the problem, who

[2] A *failure* is a difference between what the system does and what it is supposed to do. Sometimes, you will hear the term *bug* used instead of *failure.* As a future user, call failures *failures*, because that's what they are. Don't have a *bugs list*, have a *failures list.* Don't have an *unresolved bug*, have an *unresolved failure.* A few months of managing an organization that is coping with a serious failure will show you the importance of this difference in terms.

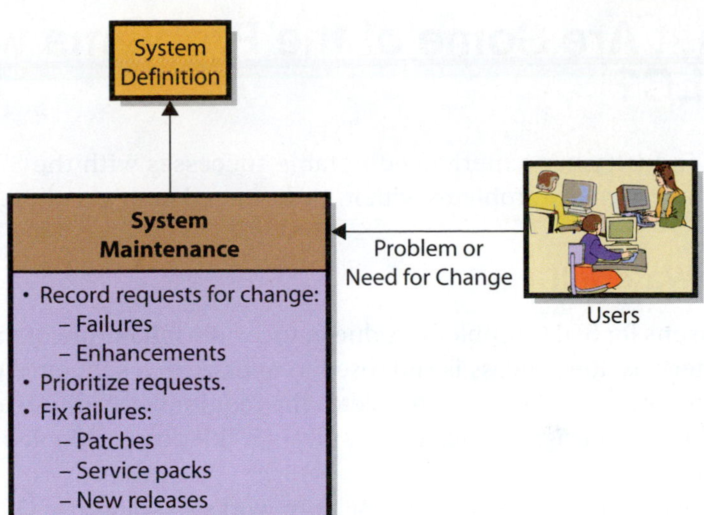

Figure 10-10
SDLC: System Maintenance Phase

will make the fix or enhancement, what the status of that work is, and whether the fix or enhancement has been tested and verified by the originator.

Typically, IS personnel prioritize system problems according to their severity. They fix high-priority items as soon as possible, and they fix low-priority items as time and resources become available.

With regard to the software component, software developers group fixes for high-priority failures into a **patch** that can be applied to all copies of a given product. As described in Chapter 4, software vendors supply patches to fix security and other critical problems. They usually bundle fixes of low-priority problems into larger groups called **service packs**. Users apply service packs in much the same way that they apply patches, except that service packs typically involve fixes to hundreds or thousands of problems.

By the way, you may be surprised to learn this, but all commercial software products are shipped with known failures. Usually vendors test their products and remove the most serious problems, but they seldom, if ever, remove all of the defects they know about. Shipping with defects is an industry practice; Microsoft, Adobe, Oracle, IBM, and many others ship products with known problems.

Because an enhancement is an adaptation to new requirements, developers usually prioritize enhancement requests separate from failures. The decision to make an enhancement includes a business decision that the enhancement will generate an acceptable rate of return. Although minor enhancements are made using service packs, major enhancement requests usually result in a new release of a product.

As you read this, keep in mind that although we usually think of failures and enhancements as applying to software they can apply to the other components as well. There can be hardware or database failures or enhancements. There can also be failures and enhancements in procedures and people, though the latter is usually expressed in more humane terms than *failure* or *enhancement*. The underlying idea is the same, however.

As stated earlier, note that the maintenance phase starts another cycle of the SDLC process. The decision to enhance a system is a decision to restart the systems development process. Even a simple failure fix goes through all of the phases of the SDLC; if it is a small fix, a single person may work through those phases in an abbreviated form. But each of those phases is repeated, nonetheless.

Q9 What Are Some of the Problems with the SDLC?

The Guide on pages 254–255 states the challenges and difficulties with project estimation in the real world.

Although the industry has experienced notable successes with the SDLC process, there have also been many problems with it, as discussed in this section.

The SDLC Waterfall

One of the reasons for SDLC problems is due to the **waterfall** nature of the SDLC. Like a series of waterfalls, the process is supposed to operate in a sequence of nonrepetitive phases. For example, the team completes the requirements phase and goes over the waterfall into the design phase, and on through the process (look back to Figure 10-3, page 239).

Unfortunately, systems development seldom works so smoothly. Often, there is a need to crawl back up the waterfall, if you will, and repeat work in a prior phase. Most commonly, when design work begins and the team evaluates alternatives, they learn that some requirements statements are incomplete or missing. At that point, the team needs to do more requirements work, yet that phase is supposedly finished. On some projects, the team goes back and forth between requirements and design so many times that the project seems to be out of control.

Requirements Documentation Difficulty

Another problem, especially on complicated systems, is the difficulty of documenting requirements in a usable way. I once managed the database portion of a software project at Boeing in which we invested more than 70 labor-years into a requirements statement. When printed, the requirements document was 20-some volumes that stood 7 feet tall when stacked on top of one another.

When we entered the design phase, no one really knew all the requirements that concerned a particular feature. We would begin to design a feature only to find that we had not considered a requirement buried somewhere in the documentation. In short, the requirements were so unwieldy as to be nearly useless. Additionally, during the requirements analysis interval, the airplane business moved on. By the time we entered the design phase, many requirements were incomplete and some were obsolete. Projects that spend so much time documenting requirements are sometimes said to be in **analysis paralysis**.

Scheduling and Budgeting Difficulties

For a new, large-scale system, schedule and budgeting estimates are so approximate as to become nearly laughable. Management attempts to put a serious face on the need for a schedule and a budget, but when you are developing a large multiyear, multimillion-dollar project estimates of labor hours and completion dates are approximate and fuzzy. The employees on the project, who are the source for the estimates, know little about how long something will take and about how much they had actually guessed. They know that the total budget and timeline is a summation of everyone's similar guesses. Many large projects live in a fantasy world of budgets and timelines.

In truth, the software community has done much work to improve software development forecasting. But for large projects with large SDLC phases, just too much is unknown for any technique to work well. So, development methodologies other than the SDLC have emerged for developing systems through a series of small, manageable chunks. Rapid application development, object-oriented development, and extreme programming are three such methodologies.

How does the knowledge in this chapter help Fox Lake and you?

All the critical people on this project at Fox Lake—Jeff, Mike, and Anne—can benefit from the knowledge in this chapter. They all need to know the basic process for creating an information system. They need to know the importance of defining scope, and then need to know to ask for a feasibility assessment up front. They also need to know the difficulty (and importance) of providing accurate requirements.

At some point in your career, you will need this knowledge. You will be running a business unit or a department or a project that needs an information system. You will need to know how to proceed, and the knowledge of this chapter will get you started on the right path.

Ethics Guide

Estimation Ethics

A *buy-in* occurs when a company agrees to produce a system or product for less than it knows the project will require. An example for Fox Lake would be if a consultant agreed to build the system for $15,000 when good estimating techniques indicate that it will take $35,000. If the contract for the system or product is written for "time and materials," the customer will ultimately pay the $35,000 for the finished system. Or the customer will cancel the project once the true cost is known. If the contract for the system or product is written for a fixed cost, then the developer will absorb the extra costs. The latter strategy is used if the contract opens up other business opportunities that are worth the $20,000 loss.

Buy-ins always involve deceit. Most would agree that buying in on a time-and-materials project, planning to stick the customer with the full cost later, is unethical and wrong. Opinions vary on buying in on a fixed-priced contract. Some would say buying in is always deceitful and should be avoided. Others say that it is just one of many different business strategies.

What about in-house projects? Do the ethics change if an in-house development team is building a system for use in-house? If team members know there is only $50,000 in the budget for some new system, should they start the project if they believe its true cost is $75,000? If they do start, at some point senior management will either have to admit a mistake and cancel the project or find the additional $25,000. Project sponsors can make all sorts of excuses for such a buy-in. For example, "I know the company needs this system. If management doesn't realize it and fund it appropriately, then we'll just force their hand."

These issues become even stickier if team members disagree about how much the project will cost. Suppose one faction of the team believes the new system will cost $35,000, another faction estimates $50,000, and a third thinks $65,000. Can the project sponsors justify taking the average? Or, should they describe the range of estimates?

Other buy-ins are more subtle. Suppose you are a project manager of an exciting new project that is possibly a career-maker for you. You are incredibly busy, working 6 days a week and long hours each day. Your team has developed an estimate for $50,000 for your project. A little voice in the back of your mind says that maybe not all costs for every aspect of the project are included in that estimate. You mean to follow up on that thought, but more pressing matters in your schedule take precedence. Soon you find yourself in front of management, presenting the $50,000 estimate. You probably should have found the time to investigate the estimate, but you didn't. Is your behavior unethical?

Or suppose you approach a more senior manager with your dilemma. You tell the senior manager, "I think there may be other costs, but

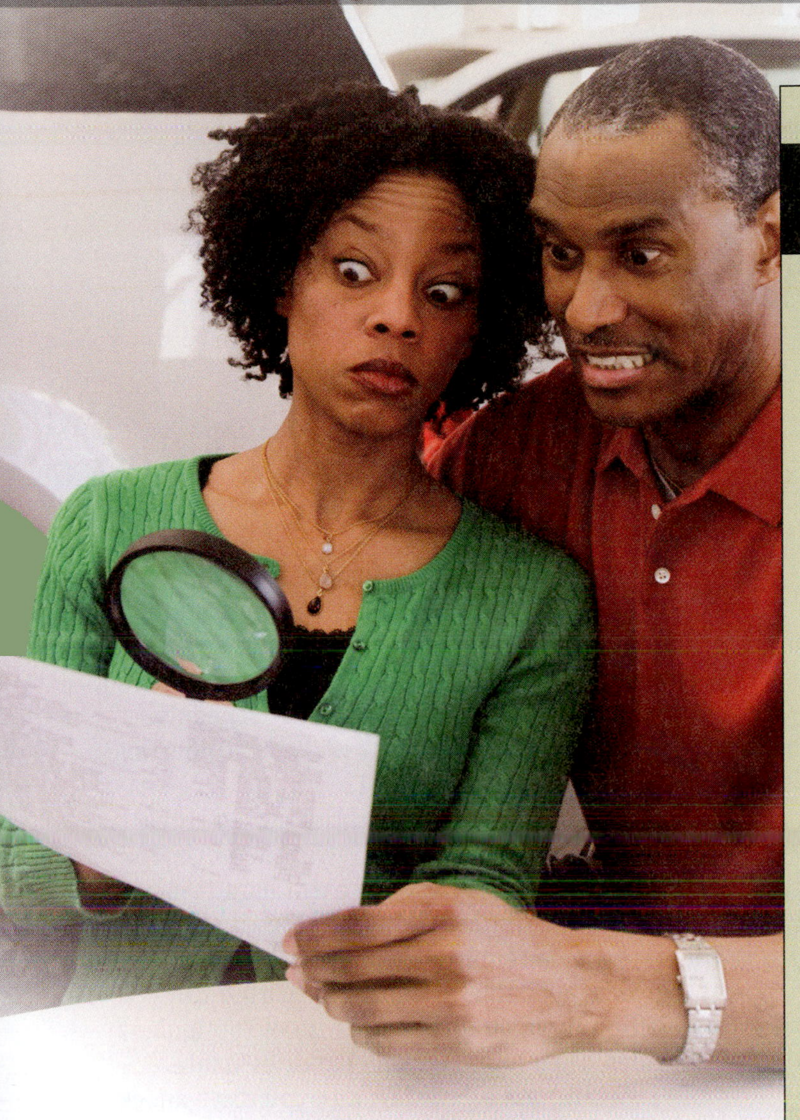

I know that $50,000 is all we've got. What should I do?" Suppose the senior manager says something like, "Well, let's go forward. You don't know of anything else, and we can always find more budget elsewhere if we have to." How do you respond?

You can buy in on schedule as well as cost. If the marketing department says, "We have to have the new product for the trade show," do you agree, even if you know it's highly unlikely? What if marketing says, "If we don't have it by then, we should just cancel the project"? Suppose it's not impossible to make that schedule, it's just highly unlikely. How do you respond?

Discussion Questions

1. Do you agree that buying in on a time-and-materials project is always unethical? Explain your reasoning. Are there circumstances in which it could be illegal?
2. Suppose you learn through the grapevine that your opponents in a competitive bid are buying in on a time-and-materials contract. Does this change your answer to question 1?
3. Suppose you are a project manager who is preparing a request for proposal on a time-and-materials systems development project. What can you do to prevent buy-ins?
4. Under what circumstances do you think buying in on a fixed-price contract is ethical? What are the dangers of this strategy?
5. Explain why in-house development projects are always time-and-materials projects.
6. Given your answer to question 5, is buying in on an in-house project always unethical? Under what circumstances do you think it is ethical? Under what circumstances do you think it is justifiable, even if it is unethical?
7. Suppose you ask a senior manager for advice, as described in the Ethics Guide. Does the manager's response absolve you of guilt? Suppose you ask the manager and then do not follow her guidance. What problems result?
8. Explain how you can buy in on schedule as well as costs.
9. For an in-house project, how do you respond to the marketing manager who says that the project should be cancelled if it will not be ready for the trade show? In your answer, suppose that you disagree with this opinion—suppose you know the system has value regardless of whether it is done by the trade show.

Guide

The Real Estimation Process

"I'm a software developer. I write programs in an object-oriented language called C# (pronounced 'C-sharp'). I'm a skilled object-oriented designer, too. I should be—I've been at it 12 years and worked on major projects for several software companies. For the last 4 years, I've been a team leader. I lived through the heyday of the dot-com era and now work in the development group at an iPad application vendor.

"All of this estimating theory is just that—theory. It's not really the way things work. Sure, I've been on projects in which we tried different estimation techniques. But here's what really happens: You develop an estimate using whatever technique you want. Your estimate goes in with the estimates of all the other team leaders. The project manager sums all those estimates together and produces an overall estimate for the project.

"By the way, in my projects, time has been a much bigger factor than money. At one software company I worked for, you could be 300 percent over your dollar budget and get no more than a slap on the wrist. Be 2 weeks late, however, and you were finished.

"Anyway, the project managers take the project schedule to senior management for approval, and what happens? Senior management thinks they are negotiating. 'Oh, no,' they say, 'that's way too long. You can surely take a month off that schedule. We'll approve the project, but we want it done by February 1 instead of March 1.'

"Now, what's their justification? They think that tight schedules make for efficient work. You know that everyone will work extra hard to meet the tighter timeframe. They know Parkinson's Law—'the time required to perform a task expands to the time available to do it.' So, fearing the possibility of wasting time because of too-lenient schedules, they lop a month off our estimate.

"Estimates are what they are; you can't knock off a month or two without some problem, somewhere. What does happen is that projects get behind, and then management expects us to work longer and longer hours. Like they said in the early years at Microsoft, 'We have flexible working hours. You can work any 65 hours per week you want.'

"Not that our estimation techniques are all that great, either. Most software developers are optimists. They schedule things as if everything will go as planned, and things seldom do. Also, schedulers usually don't allow for vacations, sick days, trips to the dentist, training on new technology, peer reviews, and all the other things we do in addition to writing software.

"So we start with optimistic schedules on our end, then management negotiates a month or two off, and voilà, we have a late project. After a while, management has been burned by late projects so much that they mentally add the month or even more back onto the official schedule. Then both sides work in a fantasy world, where no one believes the schedule, but everyone pretends they do.

"I like my job. I like software development. Management here is no better or worse than in other places. As long as I have interesting work to do, I'll stay here. But I'm not working myself silly to meet these fantasy deadlines."

Discussion Questions

1. What do you think of this developer's attitude? Do you think he's unduly pessimistic, or do you think there's merit to what he says?
2. What do you think of his idea that management thinks they're negotiating? Should management negotiate schedules? Why or why not?
3. Suppose a project actually requires 12 months to complete. Which do you think is likely to cost more: (a) having an official schedule of 11 months with at least a 1-month overrun or (b) having an official schedule of 13 months and, following Parkinson's Law, having the project take 13 months?
4. Suppose you are a business manager, and an information system is being developed for your use. You review the scheduling documents and see that little time has been allowed for vacations, sick leave, miscellaneous other work, and so forth. What do you do?
5. Describe the intangible costs of having an organizational belief that schedules are always unreasonable.
6. If this developer worked for you, how would you deal with his attitude about scheduling?
7. Do you think there is something different when scheduling information systems development projects than when scheduling other types of projects? What characteristics might make such projects unique? In what ways are they the same as other projects?
8. What do you think managers should do in light of your answer to question 7?

ACTIVE REVIEW

Use this Active Review to verify that you understand the ideas and concepts that answer this chapter's study questions.

Q1 What is systems development?

Define *systems development.* Explain how systems development differs from program development. Describe the types of expertise needed for systems development projects. Explain why Jeff needs the knowledge in this chapter.

Q2 Why is systems development difficult and risky?

Describe the risk in systems development. Summarize the difficulties posed by the following: requirements definition, requirements changes, scheduling and budgeting, changing technology, and diseconomies of scale.

Q3 What are the five phases of the SDLC?

Name the five phases in the systems development life cycle, and briefly describe each.

Q4 How is system definition accomplished?

Using Figure 10-4 as a guide, explain how you would describe to Jeff the systems definition task for his new system. Name and describe four elements of feasibility. (*Hint:* The four types of feasibility can be arranged as Cost, Operational, Schedule, Technical; arranged this way, the first letter of each makes the acronym *COST.*)

Q5 What is the users' role in the requirements phase?

Summarize the tasks in the requirements phase. Describe the role for users in this phase. Discuss what you believe will happen if users are not involved or if users do not take this work seriously. Describe the role users play in requirements approval.

Q6 How are the five components designed?

Summarize design activities for each of the five components of an information system. Explain six categories of procedure that need to be designed.

Q7 How is an information system implemented?

Name the two major tasks in systems implementation. Summarize the system testing process. Describe the difference between system and software testing. Explain testing tasks for each of the five components. Name four types of system conversion. Describe each way, and give an example of when each would be effective.

Q8 What are the tasks for system maintenance?

Explain why the term *maintenance* is a misnomer. Summarize tasks in the maintenance phase.

Q9 What are some of the problems with the SDLC?

Explain why the SDLC is considered a waterfall process, and describe why this characteristic can be a problem. Describe problems that occur when attempting to develop requirements using the SDLC. Summarize scheduling and budgeting difficulties that the SDLC presents.

How does the knowledge in this chapter help Fox Lake and you?

Summarize how Jeff, Mike, and Anne can use the knowledge of the SDLC. Explain how you can use it as well. Use the SDLC and the five components to explain the proper role for Laura, Jeff, and Anne.

KEY TERMS AND CONCEPTS

USING YOUR KNOWLEDGE

1. Assume that you are an intern working with Laura and that you are present at the initial conversations she has with Fox Lake. Assume that Laura asks you to help her investigate this new system.
   a. Develop a plan for this project using the SDLC.
   b. Specify in detail the tasks that must be accomplished during the system definition phase.
   c. Write a memo to Laura explaining how you think Fox Lake should proceed.
2. Consider the Fox Lake process problem discussed in Chapter 7. Laura has asked you to design a new process that reserves facilities for maintenance.
   a. Describe the tasks that need to be accomplished for each phase of the SDLC to build such a system.
   b. Specify in detail the tasks that must be accomplished during the systems definition phase.
3. Use Google or Bing to search for the phrase "what is a business analyst?" Investigate several of the links that you find and answer the following questions:
   a. What are the primary job responsibilities of a business analyst?
   b. What knowledge do business analysts need?
   c. What skills and personal traits do successful business analysts need?
   d. Would a career as a business analyst be interesting to you? Explain why or why not.

COLLABORATION EXERCISE 10

Before you start this exercise, read Chapter Extensions 1 and 2, which describe collaboration techniques as well as tools for managing collaboration tasks. In particular, consider using Google Docs, Windows Live SkyDrive, Microsoft SharePoint, or some other collaboration tool.

Many students do not appreciate the need for systems development processes. To help you relate to this need, suppose you work at Fox Lake and Anne gives you the task of defining a project to create a social networking application for wedding events. In particular, she has asked you to investigate the possibility of creating a Facebook application called "Plan Your Wedding."

She wants the application to have some compelling feature that will cause users to recommend it to each other and hence achieve viral distribution. She does not know what that feature is; she expects you to think of it and then create a plan that she can take to a Facebook application developer such as Infinistorm *(www.infinistorm.com)*. Anne does not know to say this, but she wants you to accomplish the tasks in the *systems definition* and *systems requirements* phases, as summarized in Figures 10-4 and 10-5.

Of course, to have any value, the application must not only have a strong viral hook, but it must also serve to increase wedding events revenue. Thus, your task has two major components. First, you must develop features for Plan Your Wedding that will make it viral and increase revenue. Second, you must create a plan that Anne can take to a developer that accomplishes as many of the steps as possible in the systems definition and requirements stage.

1. Ensure that everyone on your team understands the terms *viral marketing* and *viral hook.* Also ensure that everyone understands the purpose and functions of a social networking application. Using a wiki, document these terms on your team site.
2. Visit Facebook or MySpace and find an application that is similar to the one that Fox Lake wants to develop. Do not restrict your search to wedding-planning applications. Instead, look for applications that have a similar feel and that probably provide

their sponsors a similar value. Create a list of three such applications. Compare and contrast them with the goals you envision for Plan Your Wedding.

3. Brainstorm with your team possible viral hooks for Plan Your Wedding. Create a list of five alternatives. Establish criteria for evaluating those alternatives, and then as a team rank those alternatives. Justify your ranking.

4. Describe how the SDLC pertains to the development of this application. Describe the tasks that need to be accomplished in each phase. Indicate who should perform the tasks: Fox Lake, an outsourced development vendor, or both.

5. Develop a list of the top five to seven features of your application. Explain how those features pertain to your viral hook. Explain how those features will help increase wedding revenue. Evaluate the four dimensions of feasibility for each of your features. Make assumptions as necessary and justify your assumptions.

6. Visit the sites of three social networking application vendors (for example, *www.infinistorm.com*). Explain how you would use your answer to question 4 when you contact that vendor. Judging from the vendors' Web sites, which one do you think would be most amenable to working with you, given that you have some knowledge of the SDLC? Explain how you think your knowledge of the SDLC will improve your interaction and/or results.

7. Define criteria for success for your application. Assess how likely your application is to achieve success. Compare the potential benefit of your social networking application to the facilities management and scheduling application at the start of this chapter. If you managed Fox Lake, which application would you fund? Justify your answer.

CASE STUDY 10

Slow Learners, or What?

In 1974, when I was teaching at Colorado State University, we conducted a study of the causes of information systems failures. We interviewed personnel on several dozen projects and collected survey data on another 50 projects. Our analysis of the data revealed that the single most important factor in IS failure was a lack of user involvement. The second major factor was unclear, incomplete, and inconsistent requirements.

At the time, I was a devoted computer programmer and IT techie, and frankly I was surprised. I thought that the significant problems would have been technical issues.

I recall one interview in particular. A large sugar producer had attempted to implement a new system for paying sugar-beet farmers. The new system was to be implemented at some 20 different sugar-beet collection sites, which were located in small farming communities, adjacent to rail yards. One of the benefits of the new system was significant cost savings, and a major share of those savings occurred because the new system eliminated the need for local comptrollers. The new system was expected to eliminate the jobs of 20 or so senior people.

The comptrollers, however, had been paying local farmers for decades; they were popular leaders not just within the company, but in their communities as well. They were well liked, highly respected, important people. A system that caused the elimination of their jobs was, using a term from this chapter, *organizationally infeasible*, to say the least.

Nonetheless, the system was constructed, but an IS professional who was involved told me, "Somehow, that new system just never seemed to work. The data were not entered on a timely basis, or they were in error, or incomplete; sometimes the data were not entered at all. Our operations were falling apart during the key harvesting season, and we finally backed off and returned to the old system." Active involvement of system users would have identified this organizational infeasibility long before the system was implemented.

That's ancient history, you say. Maybe, but in 1994 the Standish Group published a now famous study on IS failures. Entitled "The CHAOS Report," the study indicated the leading causes of IS failure are, in descending order: (1) lack of user input, (2) incomplete requirements and specifications, and (3) changing requirements and specifications (*www.standishgroup.com*). That study was completed some 20 years after our study.

In 2004, Professor Joseph Kasser and his students at the University of Maryland analyzed 19 system failures to determine their cause. They then correlated their analysis of the cause with the opinions of the professionals involved in the failures. The correlated results indicated that the first-priority cause of system failure was "poor requirements"; the second-priority cause was "failure to communicate with the customer." Search the Web for "Joseph Kasser" to learn more.

In 2003, the IRS Oversight Board concluded the first cause of a massive, expensive failure in the development of a new information system for the IRS was "inadequate business unit ownership and sponsorship of projects. This resulted in unrealistic business cases and continuous project scope 'creep'" (*www.treas.gov/irsob/reports/special_report1203.pdf*).

For over 30 years, studies have consistently shown that leading causes of system failures are a lack of user involvement and incomplete and changing requirements. Yet failures from these very failures continue to mount.

Source: www.standishgroup.com.

Questions

1. Using the knowledge you have gained from this chapter, summarize the roles that you think users should take during an information systems development project. What responsibilities do users have? How closely should they work with the IS team? Who is responsible for stating requirements and constraints? Who is responsible for managing requirements?

2. If you ask users why they did not participate in requirements specification, some of the common responses are the following:
   - **a.** "I wasn't asked."
   - **b.** "I didn't have time."
   - **c.** "They were talking about a system that would be here in 18 months, and I'm just worried about getting the order out the door today."
   - **d.** "I didn't know what they wanted."
   - **e.** "I didn't know what they were talking about."
   - **f.** "I didn't work here when they started the project."
   - **g.** "The whole situation has changed since they were here; that was 18 months ago!"

   Comment on each of these statements. What strategies do they suggest to you as a future user and as a future manager of users?

3. If you ask IS professionals why they did not obtain a complete and accurate list of requirements, common responses are:
   - **a.** "It was nearly impossible to get on the users' calendars. They were always too busy."
   - **b.** "The users wouldn't regularly attend our meetings. As a result, one meeting would be dominated by the needs of one group, and another meeting would be dominated by the needs of another group."
   - **c.** "Users didn't take the requirement process seriously. They wouldn't thoroughly review the requirements statements before review meetings."
   - **d.** "Users kept changing. We'd meet with one person one time and another person a second time, and they'd want different things."
   - **e.** "We didn't have enough time."
   - **f.** "The requirements kept changing."

   Comment on each of these statements. What strategies do they suggest to you as a future user and a future manager of users?

4. If it is widely understood that one of the principal causes of IS failures is a lack of user involvement, and if this factor continues to be a problem after 30+ years of experience, does this mean that the problem cannot be solved? For example, everyone knows that you can maximize your gains by buying stocks at their annual low price and selling them at their annual high price, but doing so is very difficult. Is it equally true that although everyone knows that users should be involved in requirements specification, and that requirements should be complete, it just cannot be done? Why or why not?

CHAPTER 11

Information Systems Management

This could happen to you

"Jeff, want to talk about information systems?" Laura, a business analyst that Fox Lake hired to help solve process and systems problems, is proceeding cautiously with Jeff, Fox Lake's general manager.

"Sure, Laura, I've been wondering what you're up to."

"Well, I found some process problems that Mike, Anne, and I are working out. I think we're well on our way there." Laura's starting with the good news.

"Great."

"And, some of those processes use information systems, so I've been looking at them as well."

"Good."

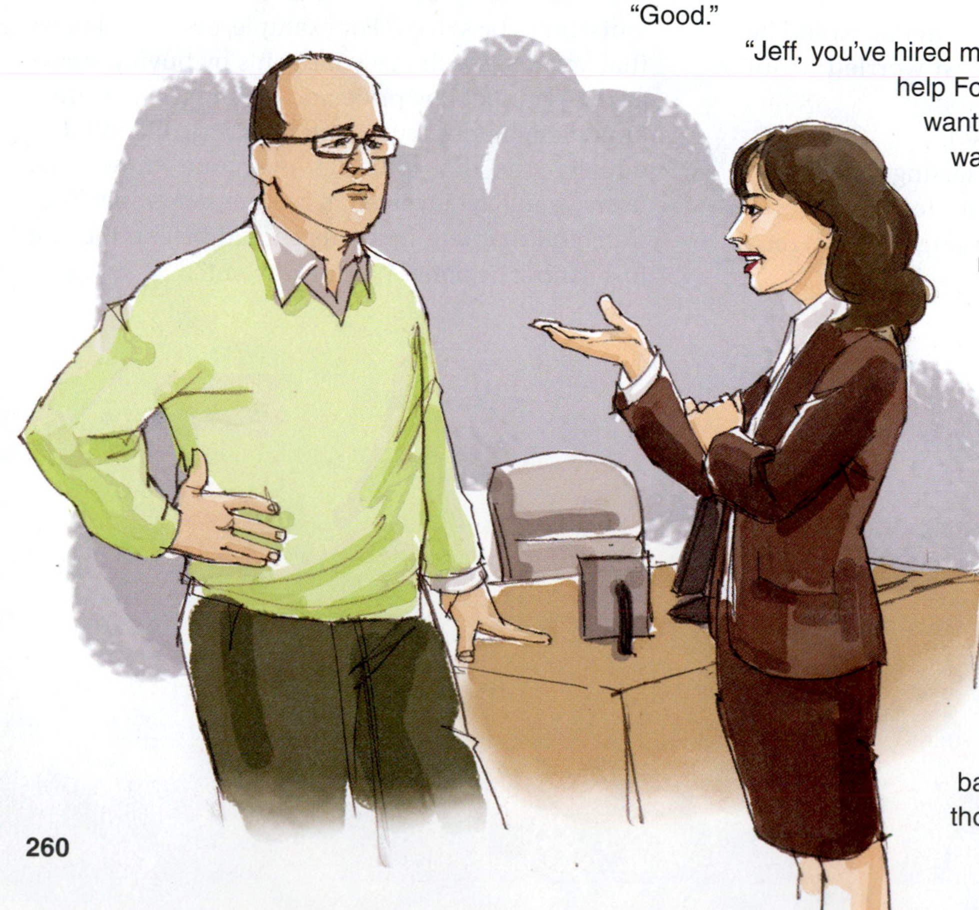

"Jeff, you've hired me to help resolve some problems and help Fox Lake with IS and IT, and I really want to do that," Laura continues, still warming up to her point.

"That's what we want, Laura."

"Well, OK, then, Jeff, I think you need to manage the IS function more directly."

"WHAT?"

"I see some problems, some lack of organization, some IS issues that need to be addressed, and you're the person to do it." Laura waits for that news to settle.

"Laura, I'm not an IT guy. I can barely do my email, or schedule a tee time on our Web site. I don't know anything about IT."

"I understand. That's not your background, and it's nothing you thought you'd be doing as a GM."

"You can bet on it."

STUDY QUESTIONS

Q1 Why do you need to know about the IS department?

Q2 What are the responsibilities of the IS department?

Q3 How is the IS department organized?

Q4 What IS-related job positions exist?

Q5 How do organizations decide how much to spend on IS?

Q6 What are your IS rights and responsibilities?

How does the knowledge in this chapter help Fox Lake and you?

"Well, in a larger company, you'd have a senior manager in charge. You'd have a chief information officer or at least an IS/IT manager to do it. You'd manage him . . . or her. But, you don't."

"You're right, Laura, we don't have anyone by that title. That's why I look to Mike to do it."

"Jeff, there are a couple of problems with that. For one, it's not Mike's background, and, as you know, Mike's a new manager. If he were more senior he might be able to handle it, but he's not. He's a hard-working maintenance supervisor who's struggling to manage all of Fox Lake's facilities."

"THE SECOND PROBLEM IS... YOU'VE GOT A FOX IN CHARGE OF A HEN HOUSE."

"And he's done a good job at it."

"OK, Jeff, but set that aside. The second problem of having Mike do it is that you've got the fox in charge of the hen house."

"What do you mean?"

"He's incentivized to stay within budget. Including all of the IT/IS that he's managing, he's also manager of facilities and needs some of the IT/IS budget for support to facilities. He has no incentive, other than professional courtesy, to provide any new IS capability to wedding events, or any other function."

"You think he's got a conflict of interest?" Jeff sits back in his chair reflecting.

"Like you said, 'You can bet on it.' Plus, Fox Lake is vulnerable." Laura finally brings up the issue that concerns her.

"Vulnerable? How?"

"Well, you're running servers and your network from the facilities building. They're in the backroom, but access to the servers is wide open. I'm not worried about someone running into them with a golf cart, though that could happen. I'm more worried that anyone with access to that building has access to all of the servers, the applications, and all of your data."

"I thought we moved some of those systems to the cloud, whatever that is. At least, I approved the budget to do that."

"That was for the new facilities scheduling system. The Fox Lake membership applications, all the accounting systems, and all the older systems still run on those servers." Laura thinks she's making some headway.

"Hmpf. I don't know. Maybe I should hire someone to manage it."

Optional Extension for this chapter is • CE20: Outsourcing 578

"You could. It would be expensive, and you may not need to. Why not get involved yourself, clean it up, and then hire someone if necessary?"

"OK, you've got my attention. Let's talk some more. I've got to run now, but put down your thoughts and let me take a look. Then, we'll see."

"Will do. Thanks, Jeff." Laura leaves, much relieved. She had deeper suspicions than she stated but not enough data to bring them up. "At least, we'll get him on track," she thinks as she walks to her car.

Q1 Why Do You Need to Know About the IS Department?

You need to know about the IS department for three principal reasons. First, like Jeff, you might someday be a manger of a business that is too small to hire a full-time IS manager. However, in 2010 and beyond, there will be very few businesses that do not use information systems in some capacity. Thus, like Jeff, you'll be forced into managing IS whether you want to or not. And, if you know that, you can avoid problems like those that Jeff will find he has in Chapter 12.

Second, in larger companies, you need to understand the responsibilities and duties of the IS department so you can be an effective consumer of the IS department's resources. If you understand what the IS department does and how it is organized, you'll know how better to obtain the equipment, services, or systems you (and organizations you manage) need.

Third, you need to know the functions of the IS department to be a better informed and effective business planner or innovator. For example, more than one merger or acquisition has been negotiated, signed, and planned without anyone thinking of the IS departments. As you can now understand, marrying the IT infrastructure and IS of two organizations requires extensive planning.

Less dramatic, you might have an idea for a new product line or service or a markedly different business process. If so, if you know the responsibilities of the IS department, you'll know if your idea impacts the IS department, and, if so, be better able to anticipate the needs of that department.

Information systems are a major element of nearly every organization today, and understanding the responsibilities and organization of the IS department is key knowledge for every business professional.

Q2 What Are the Responsibilities of the IS Department?

The IS department[1] has four primary responsibilities, as shown in Figure 11-1. We'll consider each.

Figure 11-1
Primary Responsibilities of the IS Department

1. Plan for information systems and IT infrastructure.
3. Develop and adapt information systems and IT infrastructure.
5. Maintain information systems and operate and manage infrastructure.
4. Protect infrastructure and data.

1. We use the term *IS department* and not *IT department* because this function has responsibility for information systems and not just information technology. However, the term *IT department* is often used in business (reflecting the general misunderstanding of the role of IS and IT in business). If, at work, you read or hear "IT department," think "IS department" instead.

Plan for Information Systems and IT Infrastructure

Information systems exist to further the organization's competitive strategy. They exist to facilitate business processes and to help improve decision making. Thus, there are no "IS projects"; instead, all projects involving IS are a part of some other business system or facilitate some business goal.

The IS department has the responsibility of aligning all of its activities with the organization's primary goals and objectives. As new technology emerges, the IS department is responsible for assessing that technology and determining if it can be used to advance the organization's goals. Furthermore, as the business changes, the IS department is responsible for adapting infrastructure and systems to the new business goals.

Several years ago, Microsoft began to use the term **agile enterprise** in its advertising. Today, many executives use the term to refer to an organization that can quickly adapt to changes in the market, industry, product, law, or other significant external factors. Microsoft used this term because IT infrastructure and systems are known to be particularly difficult to adapt to change, and it claimed its products would change this characteristic. This might be the case, but the one certain effect of its campaign was to alert IS managers and business executives to the need to be adaptable.

Develop and Adapt Information Systems and IT Infrastructure

Given a plan, the next task for the IS department is to create, develop, and adapt both information systems and IT infrastructure. We discussed systems development in Chapter 10; we need not say more about that topic here.

In addition to systems development, the IS department is responsible for creating and adapting IT infrastructure, such as computer networks, servers, data centers, data warehouses, data marts, and other IS resources. The IS department is also charged with creating systems infrastructures, such as email systems, VPNs, company blogs, SharePoint sites, and other IS-based infrastructure the company needs.

In most organizations, user departments pay for computers and related equipment out of their own budgets. However, because the IS department is responsible for maintaining that equipment and for connecting it to the organizational networks, the IS department will specify standard computer systems and configurations that it will support. The IS department is responsible for defining those specifications.

Maintain Information Systems and Operate and Manage Infrastructure

We discussed information systems maintenance in Chapter 10 and will not repeat that discussion here. Regarding the operation and management of infrastructure, realize that IT infrastructure is not like the building's plumbing or wiring. You cannot install a network or a server and then forget it. IT infrastructure must be operated and managed. Networks and servers need to be powered on, and they need to be monitored. From time to time, they need to be adjusted, or **tuned**, to changes in the workload. Components fail, and when they do, the IS department is called upon to repair the problem.

To understand the importance of this function, consider what happens when a network fails. Users cannot connect to their local servers; they cannot run the information systems they need to perform their jobs. Users cannot connect with the

Experiencing MIS InClass Exercise 11

What's That Humming Sound?

Green computing is environmentally conscious computing consisting of three major components: power management, virtualization, and e-waste management. In this exercise, we focus on power.

You know, of course, that computers (and related equipment, such as printers) consume electricity. That burden is light for any single computer or printer. But consider all of the computers and printers in the United States that will be running tonight, with no one in the office. Proponents of green computing encourage companies and employees to reduce power and water use (for air conditioning) by turning off devices when not in use.

Is this issue important? Is it just a concession to environmentalists to make computing professionals appear virtuous? Form a team and develop your own, informed opinion by considering computer use at your campus.

1. Search the Internet to determine the power requirements for typical computing and office equipment. Consider laptop computers, desktop computers, CRT monitors, LCD monitors, and printers. For this exercise, ignore server computers. As you search, be aware that a *watt* is a measure of electrical power. It is *watts* that the green computing movement wants to reduce.
2. Estimate the number of each type of device in use on your campus. Use your university's Web site to determine the number of colleges, departments, faculty, staff, and students. Make assumptions about the number of computers, copiers, and other types of equipment used by each.
3. Using the data from items 1 and 2, estimate the total power used by computing and related devices on your campus.
4. A computer that is in screensaver mode uses the same amount of power as one in regular mode. Computers that are in sleep mode, however, use much less power, say 6 watts per hour. Reflect on computer use on your campus and estimate the amount of time that computing devices are in sleep versus screensaver or use mode. Compute the savings in power that result from sleep mode.
5. Computers that are automatically updated by the IS department with software upgrades and patches cannot be allowed to go into sleep mode because if they are sleeping they will not be able to receive the upgrade. Hence, some universities prohibit sleep mode on university computers (sleep mode is never used on servers, by the way). Determine the cost, in watts, of such a policy.
6. Calculate the monthly cost, in watts, if:
   a. All user computers run full time night and day.
   b. All user computers run full time during work hours and in sleep mode during off-hours.
   c. All user computers are shut off during nonwork hours.
7. Given your answers to items 1–6, is computer power management during off-hours a significant concern? In comparison to the other costs of running a university, does this issue really matter? Discuss this question among your group and explain your answer.

Internet or send or receive email. Users may not even be able to reach their contact lists to find phone numbers to make telephone calls to explain why they are not responding. Truly, the business stops. In businesses like FlexTime and Fox Lake, customers will be standing in long lines as they attempt to make purchases!

Protect Infrastructure and Data

The IS department is responsible for protecting infrastructure and data from threats. We will discuss threats and safeguards against them in Chapter 12. For now, just understand that threats to IT infrastructure and data arise from three sources: human error and mistakes, malicious human activity, and natural events and disasters.

The IS department helps the organization manage risk. The department needs to identify potential threats, estimate both financial and other risks, and specify appropriate safeguards. Nothing is free, including safeguards, and, indeed, some safeguards are very expensive. The IS department works with the CFO and others in the organization to determine what safeguards to implement, or stated differently, what level of risk to assume. See Chapter 12 for more information.

Q3 How Is the IS Department Organized?

Figure 11-2 shows typical top-level reporting relationships. As you will learn in your management classes, organizational structure varies depending on the organization's size, culture, competitive environment, industry, and other factors. Larger organizations with independent divisions will have a group of senior executives like those shown here for each division. Smaller companies may combine some of these departments. Consider the structure in Figure 11-2 as a typical example.

The title of the principal manager of the IS department varies from organization to organization. A common title is **chief information officer (CIO)**. Other common titles are *vice president of information services, director of information services*, and, less commonly, *director of computer services*.

In Figure 11-2, the CIO, like other senior executives, reports to the chief executive officer (CEO), although sometimes these executives report to the chief operating officer (COO), who, in turn, reports to the CEO. In some companies, the CIO reports to the chief financial officer (CFO). That reporting arrangement may make sense if the primary information systems support accounting and finance activities. In organizations that operate significant nonaccounting information systems, such as manufacturers, the arrangement shown in Figure 11-2 is more common and effective.

The structure of the IS department also varies among organizations. Figure 11-2 shows a typical IS department with four groups and a data administration staff function.

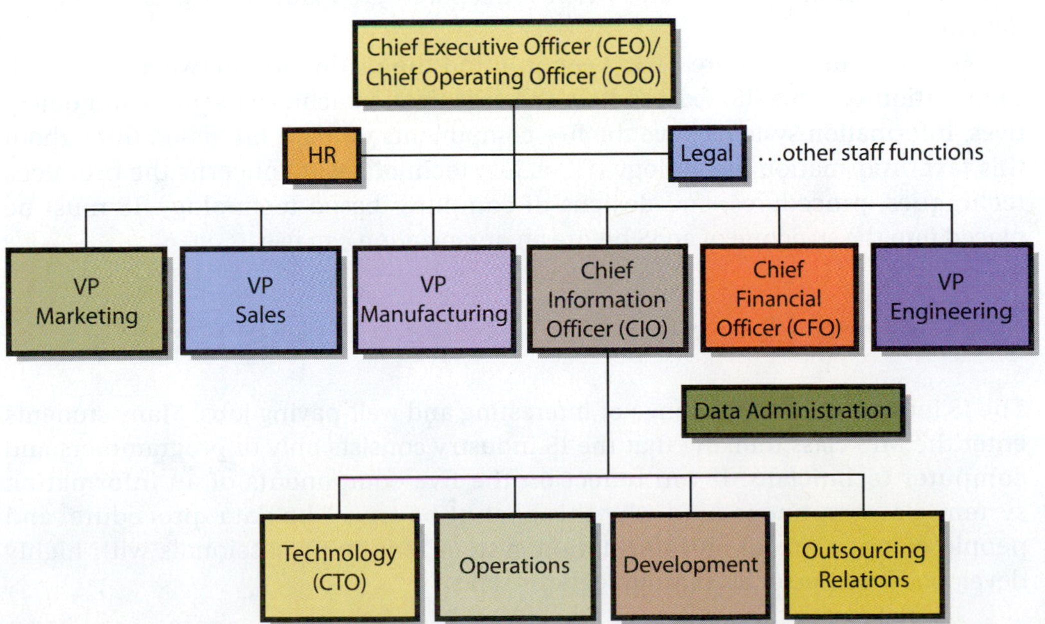

Figure 11-2
Typical Senior-Level Reporting Relationships

Most IS departments include a *technology* office that investigates new information systems technologies and determines how the organization can benefit from them. For example, today many organizations are investigating cloud computing, virtualization, SOA, social networking, and user-generated content and planning on how they can best use those technologies to accomplish their goals and objectives. An individual called the **chief technology officer (CTO)** often heads the technology group. The CTO sorts through new ideas and products to identify those that are most relevant to the organization. The CTO's job requires deep knowledge of information technology and the ability to envision how new IS will affect the organization over time.

The next group in Figure 11-2, *operations*, manages the computing infrastructure, including individual computers, computer centers, networks, and communications media. This group includes system and network administrators. As you will learn, an important function for this group is to monitor user experience and respond to user problems.

The third group in the IS department in Figure 11-2 is *development*. This group manages the process of creating new information systems as well as maintaining existing information systems. (Recall from Chapter 10 that in the context of information systems, *maintenance* means either removing problems or adapting existing information systems to support new features and functions.)

The size and structure of the development group depends on whether programs are developed in-house. If not, this department will be staffed primarily by systems analysts who work with users, operations, and vendors to acquire and install licensed software and to set up the system components around that software. If the organization develops programs in-house, then this department will include programmers, test engineers, technical writers, and other development personnel.

The last IS department group in Figure 11-2 is *outsourcing relations*. This group exists in organizations that have negotiated outsourcing agreements with other companies to provide equipment, applications, or other services.

You will learn more about outsourcing in Chapter Extension 20 on page 578.

Figure 11-2 also includes a *data administration* staff function. The purpose of this group is to protect data and information assets by establishing data standards and data management practices and policies.

There are many variations on the structure of the IS department shown in Figure 11-2. In larger organizations, the operations group may itself consist of several different departments. Sometimes, there is a separate group for data warehousing and data marts.

As you examine Figure 11-2, keep in mind the distinction between IS and IT. Information systems (IS) exist to help the organization achieve its goals and objectives. Information systems have the five components we have discussed throughout this text. Information technology (IT) is just technology. It concerns the products, techniques, procedures, and designs of computer-based technology. IS must be placed into the structure of an IS before an organization can use it.

Q4 What IS-Related Job Positions Exist?

The IS industry has a wide range of interesting and well-paying jobs. Many students enter the MIS class thinking that the IS industry consists only of programmers and computer technicians. If you reflect on the five components of an information system, you can understand why this cannot be true. The data, procedure, and people components of an information system require professionals with highly developed interpersonal communications skills.

Figure 11-3 summarizes the major job positions in the IS industry. With the exception of computer technician and possibly of PQA test engineer, all of these positions require a 4-year degree. Furthermore, with the exception of programmer and PQA test engineer, all of these positions require business knowledge. In most cases, successful professionals have a degree in business. Note, too, that most positions require good verbal and written communications skills. Business, including information systems, is a social activity.

Many of the positions in Figure 11-3 have a wide salary range. Lower salaries are for professionals with limited experience or for those who work in smaller companies or work on small projects. The larger salaries are for those with deep knowledge and experience who work for large companies on large projects. Do not expect to begin your career at the high end of these ranges. As noted, all salaries are for positions in the United States and are shown in U.S. dollars.

In the 40 years of my career, I have worked as a systems analyst, programmer, small- and large-scale project manager, consultant, and CTO. It's been great fun, and the industry becomes more and more interesting each year. Give these careers some thought.

By the way, for all but the most technical positions knowledge of a business specialty can add to your marketability. If you have the time, a dual major can be an excellent choice. Popular and successful dual majors are: accounting and information systems, marketing and information systems, and management and information systems.

Q5 How Do Organizations Decide How Much to Spend on IS?

Information systems and information technology are expensive. Consequently, organizations need to address the investment in IS and IT in the same way that they address investments in plant, inventories, or any other substantial project. Typically, decisions to invest in any business project involve an analysis of the costs and benefits.

All such analysis requires estimates of the costs and benefits of the project. However, to compare costs to benefits, both the costs and benefits need to be expressed in dollars or some other currency. Estimating dollar costs of IT or IS projects is no more difficult than estimating them for other projects. The difficulty arises when attempting to place a dollar value on benefits. For example, what is the dollar value of an email system? Employees require access to email in order to do any work. Asking the dollar value of the email system is like asking the dollar value of the restroom. How can you compute it?

Other value computations are difficult, but possible. For example, if a customer support information system reduces the likelihood of losing a customer, then the value of that system can be computed by multiplying the probability of loss times the lifetime value of that customer. Or, if an information system enables customer support representatives to service customers 10 percent faster, then the dollar value of that system is 10 percent of the anticipated customer support costs.

Most IS and IT investment analyses divide benefits into two categories: tangible and intangible. **Tangible benefits** are those for which a dollar value can be computed. Reducing customer support costs by 10 percent is a tangible benefit. **Intangible benefits** are those for which it is impossible to compute a dollar value. The benefits of the email system are intangible.

One common method for justifying IS and IT projects is to compute the costs and tangible benefits of the system and to perform a financial analysis. If the

Figure 11-3
Job Positions in the Information Systems Industry

Title	Responsibilities	Knowledge, Skill, and Characteristics Requirements	United States 2010 Salary Range (USD)
Business analyst	Work with business leaders and planners to develop processes and systems that implement business strategy and goals.	Knowledge of business planning, strategy, process management, and technology. Can deal with complexity. See big picture but work with details. Strong interpersonal and communication skills needed.	\$75,000–\$125,000
System analyst	Work with users to determine system requirements, design and develop job descriptions and procedures, help determine system test plans.	Strong interpersonal and communications skills. Knowledge of both business and technology. Adaptable.	\$65,000–\$125,000
Programmer	Design and write computer programs.	Logical thinking and design skills, knowledge of one or more programming languages.	\$50,000–\$150,000
PQA test engineer	Develop test plans, design and write automated test scripts, perform testing.	Logical thinking, basic programming, superb organizational skills, eye for detail.	\$40,000–\$95,000
Technical writer	Write program documentation, help-text, procedures, job descriptions, training materials.	Quick learner, clear writing skills, high verbal communications skills.	\$40,000–\$95,000
User support representative	Help users solve problems, provide training.	Communications and people skills. Product knowledge. Patience.	\$40,000–\$65,000
Computer technician	Install software, repair computer equipment and networks.	Associate degree, diagnostic skills.	\$30,000–\$65,000
Network administrator	Monitor, maintain, fix, and tune computer networks.	Diagnostic skills, in-depth knowledge of communications technologies and products.	\$75,000–\$200,000+
Consultant	Wide range of activities: programming, testing, database design, communications and networks, project management, security and risk management, strategic planning.	Quick learner, entrepreneurial attitude, communications and people skills. Respond well to pressure. Particular knowledge depends on work.	From \$35 per hour for a contract tester to more than \$500 per hour for strategic consulting to executive group.
Salesperson	Sell software, network, communications, and consulting services.	Quick learner, knowledge of product, superb professional sales skills.	\$65,000–\$200,000+
Small-scale project manager	Initiate, plan, manage, monitor, and close down projects.	Management and people skills, technology knowledge. Highly organized.	\$75,000–\$150,000
Large-scale project manager	Initiate, plan, monitor, and close down complex projects.	Executive and management skills. Deep project management knowledge.	\$150,000–\$250,000+
Database administrator	Manage and protect database (see Chapter 12).	Diplomatic skills, database technology knowledge.	\$75,000–\$250,000
Chief technology officer (CTO)	Advise CIO, executive group, and project managers on emerging technologies.	Quick learner, good communication skills, deep knowledge of IT.	\$125,000–\$300,000+
Chief information officer (CIO)	Manage IT department, communicate with executive staff on IT- and IS-related matters. Member of the executive group.	Superb management skills, deep knowledge of business, and good business judgment. Good communicator. Balanced and unflappable.	\$150,000–\$500,000, plus executive benefits and privileges.

project can be justified on tangible benefits alone, then the favorable decision is made. If it cannot be justified on the basis of tangible benefits, then the intangible benefits are considered, and a subjective decision is made as to whether the intangibles are sufficiently valuable to overcome the missing tangible benefits that would be required.

Keep in mind that the changing nature of technology—and of business generally—will demand that you remain agile, as discussed in the Guide on pages 274–275.

Q6 What Are Your IS Rights and Responsibilities?

We conclude this chapter with a summary of your rights and responsibilities with regard to the IS department. Figure 11-4 lists what you are entitled to receive and indicates what you are expected to contribute.

Your Rights

You have a right to have the computing resources you need to perform your work as proficiently as you want. You have a right to the computer hardware and programs that you need. If you process huge files for data mining applications, you have a right to the huge disks and the fast processor that you need. However, if you merely receive email and consult the corporate Web portal, then your right is for more modest requirements (leaving the more powerful resources for those in the organization who need them).

You have a right to reliable network and Internet services. Reliable means that you can process without problems almost all of the time. It means that you never go to work wondering, "Will the network be available today?" Network problems should be a rare occurrence.

You also have a right to a secure computing environment. The organization should protect your computer and its files, and you should not normally even need to think about security. From time to time, the organization may ask you to take particular actions to protect your computer and files, and you should take those actions. But such requests should be rare and related to specific outside threats.

You have a right to participate in requirements meetings for new applications that you will use and for major changes to applications that you currently use. You

Figure 11-4
User's IS Rights and Responsibilities

You have a right to:
- Computer hardware and programs that allow you to perform your job proficiently
- Reliable network and Internet connections
- A secure computing environment
- Protection from viruses, worms, and other threats
- Contribute to requirements for new system features and functions
- Reliable systems development and maintenance
- Prompt attention to problems, concerns, and complaints
- Properly prioritized problem fixes and resolutions
- Effective training

You have a responsibility to:
- Learn basic computer skills
- Learn standard techniques and procedures for the applications you use
- Follow security and backup procedures
- Protect your password(s)
- Use computer resources according to your employer's computer-use policy
- Make no unauthorized hardware modifications
- Install only authorized programs
- Apply software patches and fixes when directed to do so
- When asked, devote the time required to respond carefully and completely to requests for requirements for new system features and functions
- Avoid reporting trivial problems

may choose to delegate this right to others, or your department may delegate that right for you, but, if so, you have a right to contribute your thoughts through that delegate.

You have a right to reliable systems development and maintenance. Although schedule slippages of a month or two are common in many development projects, you should not have to endure schedule slippages of 6 months or more. Such slippages are evidence of incompetent systems development.

Additionally, you have a right to receive prompt attention to your problems, concerns, and complaints about information services. You have a right to have a means to report problems, and you have a right to know that your problem has been received and at least registered with the IS department. You have a right to have your problem resolved, consistent with established priorities. This means that an annoying problem that allows you to conduct your work will be prioritized below another's problem that interferes with his or her ability to do the job.

Finally, you have a right to effective training. It should be training that you can understand and that enables you to use systems to perform your particular job. The organization should provide training in a format and on a schedule that is convenient to you.

Your Responsibilities

You also have responsibilities toward the IS department and your organization. Specifically, you have a responsibility to learn basic computer skills and to learn the basic techniques and procedures for the applications you use. You should not expect hand-holding for basic operations. Nor should you expect to receive repetitive training and support for the same issue.

You have a responsibility to follow security and backup procedures. This is especially important because actions that you fail to take may cause problems for your fellow employees and your organization as well as for you. In particular, you are responsible for protecting your password(s). In the next chapter, you will learn that this is important not only to protect your computer, but, because of intersystem authentication, it is important to protect your organization's networks and databases as well.

You have a responsibility for using your computer resources in a manner that is consistent with your employer's policy. Many employers allow limited email for critical family matters while at work, but discourage frequent and long casual email. You have a responsibility to know your employer's policy and to follow it.

See the Ethics Guide on pages 272–273 for additional discussions on computer-use policy.

You also have a responsibility to make no unauthorized hardware modifications to your computer and to install only authorized programs. One reason for this policy is that your IS department constructs automated maintenance programs for upgrading your computer. Unauthorized hardware and programs may interfere with these programs. Additionally, the installation of unauthorized hardware or programs can cause you problems that the IS department will have to fix.

You have a responsibility to install computer patches and fixes when asked to do so. This is particularly important for patches that concern security and backup and recovery. When asked for input to requirements for new and adapted systems, you have a responsibility to take the time necessary to provide thoughtful and complete responses. If you do not have that time, you should delegate your input to someone else.

Finally, you have a responsibility to treat information systems professionals professionally. Everyone works for the same company, everyone wants to succeed, and professionalism and courtesy will go a long way on all sides. One form of professional behavior is to learn basic skills so that you avoid reporting trivial problems.

How does the knowledge in this chapter help *Fox Lake* and you?

Jeff needs the knowledge in this chapter to understand how he should be managing the IS and IT resources at Fox Lake. With this knowledge, he could direct Mike more effectively. With this knowledge, he could also have prevented the problem that you will learn about in Chapter 12.

You can use the knowledge of this chapter to be a more informed consumer of your IS department's services. In the case of a small company, you can use this knowledge to help your organization better manage and plan its information systems and IT infrastructure. Finally, with this knowledge you will be better able to work with the IS department on any innovative projects you envision that have an IS component.

Ethics Guide

Using the Corporate Computer

Suppose you work at a company that has the following computer-use policy:

Computers, email, and the Internet are to be used primarily for official company business. Small amounts of personal email can be exchanged with friends and family, and occasional usage of the Internet is permitted, but such usage should be limited and never interfere with your work.

Suppose you are a manager, and you learn that one of your employees has been engaged in the following activities:

1. Playing computer games during work hours
2. Playing computer games on the company computer before and after work hours
3. Responding to emails from an ill parent
4. Watching DVDs during lunch and other breaks
5. Sending emails to plan a party that involves mostly people from work
6. Sending emails to plan a party that involves no one from work
7. Updating your Facebook page
8. Reading the news on CNN.com
9. Checking the stock market over the Internet
10. Tweeting friends about your softball win last night on your work computer
11. Selling personal items on eBay
12. Paying personal bills online
13. Paying personal bills online when traveling on company business
14. Buying an airplane ticket for an ill parent over the Internet
15. Changing the content of a personal Web site
16. Changing the content of a personal business Web site
17. Buying an airplane ticket for a personal vacation over the Internet

Discussion Questions

1. Explain how you would respond to each situation.
2. Suppose someone from the IS department notifies you that one of your employees is spending 3 hours a day surfing the Web. How do you respond?
3. For question 2, suppose you ask how the IS department knows about your employee and you are told, "We secretly monitor computer usage." Do you object to such monitoring? Why or why not?
4. Suppose someone from the IS department notifies you that one of your employees is sending many personal emails. When you ask how they know the emails are personal, you are told that they measure account activity and that when suspicious email usage is suspected the IS department reads employees' email. Do you think such reading is legal? Is it ethical? How do you respond?
5. As an employee, if you know that your company occasionally reads emails, does that change your behavior? If so, does that justify the company reading your email? Does this situation differ from having someone read your personal postal mail that happens to be delivered to you at work? Why or why not?
6. Write what you think is the best corporate policy for personal computer usage at work.

Guide

Jumping Aboard the Bulldozer

The U.S. and global economies are struggling. As of 2010, a recovery appears to be underway, but unemployment hovers near 10 percent. The press talks about a "jobless recovery." Jobs that disappeared in the Fall of 2008 don't seem to be coming back. Something is going on, but what?

Some people blame the lack of new jobs on overseas outsourcing, but the numbers don't add up. Brainard and Litan (2004) cite research that indicates that organizations will move approximately 250,000 jobs per year overseas between now and 2015. Although that may sound like a lot, in the context of the 137 million U.S. workers, and in the context of the 15 million Americans who lose their jobs due to other factors, 250,000 jobs overseas is not much.

The culprit—if *culprit* is the right word—is not overseas outsourcing; it is productivity. Because of information technology, Moore's Law, and all the information systems that you have learned about in this book, worker productivity continues to increase, and it is possible to have an economic recovery without a binge of new hiring.

The Austrian economist Joseph Schumpeter (1975) called such processes "creative destruction" and said that they are the cleansers of the free market. Economic processes operate to remove unneeded jobs, companies, and even industries, thereby keeping the economy growing and prospering. In fact, the lack of such processes hindered the growth of Japan and some European nations in the 1990s.

(By the way, there's a historical irony here, because creative destruction gave rise to one of the first information systems. This system consisted of a group of human "calculators" who were employed by the French in the 1790s to compute scientific tables for the then-new metric system. According to Ken Alder (2002), the human calculators were wigmakers who had become unemployed due to the French Revolution. The guillotine not only reduced the size of the market for wigs, but also made aristocratic hairstyles less popular, and so wigmakers became human calculators.)

This idea of creative destruction is all well and good for an economic theory, but what do you, as a student in the first decade of the twenty-first century, do? How do you respond to the dynamics of shifting work and job movements? You can take a lesson from the railroads in the 1930s. They were blindsided by air transportation. In a now-classic marketing blunder, the railroads perceived themselves as purveyors of railroad transportation instead of purveyors of transportation more generally. The railroads were well positioned to take advantage of air transportation, but they did nothing and were overtaken by the new airline companies.

How does this apply to you? As you have learned, MIS is the development and use of information systems that enable organizations to achieve their goals and objectives. When you work with information systems, you are not a professional of a particular system or technology; rather, you are a developer or user of a system that helps your organization achieve its goals and objectives.

Suppose, for example, you work with an email-based purchasing system. If you view yourself as an expert in email-based purchasing, then you are doomed, because it will be supplanted by SOA systems. Are you better off to define yourself as an expert in some aspect of SOA, say XML coding? No, because SOA will someday be replaced with something else, and writing XML schemas is work that can easily be moved offshore. Instead, define yourself more generally as someone who specializes in the application of emerging technology to help your business achieve its goals and objectives. Going all the way back to Chapter 1, define yourself as an innovator.

From this perspective, the technology you learned in this class can help you start your career. If IS-based productivity is the bulldozer that is mowing down traditional jobs, then use what you have learned here to jump aboard that bulldozer. Not as a technologist, but as a business professional who can determine how best to use that bulldozer to enhance your career.

In the case of purchasing, learn something about SOA and XML and apply that knowledge to gain employment in a company that uses them to accomplish its goals and objectives. But realize that SOA/XML only helps you get that job; it just gets you started. Your long-term success depends not on your knowledge of those particular technologies, but rather on your ability to think, to solve problems, to collaborate, and to use technology and information systems to help your organization achieve its goals and objectives.

Sources: Lial Brainard and Robert Litan, "Services Offshoring Bane or Bone and What to Do?" *CESifo Forum*, Summer 2004, Vol. 5, Issue 2, p. 307; Joseph Schumpeter, *Capitalism, Socialism, and Democracy* (New York: Harper, 1975), pp. 82–85; Ken Alder, *The Measure of All Things* (New York: The Free Press, 2002), p. 142.

Discussion Questions

1. Describe several ways that the overseas outsourcing problem is overstated.
2. Summarize the argument that the "culprit" is not overseas outsourcing, but rather productivity.
3. Why is it incorrect to consider productivity as a culprit?
4. Explain the phenomenon of creative destruction.
5. Why are your career prospects limited if you define yourself as an expert in SOA and XML?
6. Apply the line of reasoning you used in your answer to question 5 to some other technology or system, such as CRM, ERP, OLAP, or RFM.
7. Explain how you can use one of the technologies in question 6 to help you start your career. To be successful, what perspective must you then maintain?

ACTIVE REVIEW

Use this Active Review to verify that you understand the ideas and concepts that answer the chapter's study questions.

Q1 Why do you need to know about the IS department?

List three reasons why you need to know about the IS department. Summarize why Jeff needed to know about it. Give an example of a business initiative that involves IS support. Explain why knowing the functions of IS will help you develop that initiative. Summarize why you need to know the responsibility of an IS department if you work in a small company.

Q2 What are the responsibilities of the IS department?

Identify four responsibilities of the IS department. Briefly describe each.

Q3 How is the IS department organized?

Draw an organization chart for a typical IS department. Explain the functions of the CIO and the CTO. State reporting relationships of the IS department and the CIO.

Q4 What IS-related job positions exist?

Identify the positions in the IS department that do not require a 4-year degree. Name positions that do not require substantial knowledge of business. State your conclusions from these observations. Select two positions in Figure 11-3 that interest you. Describe what you think you could do to prepare yourself for these positions. Explain why a joint major of IS and another functional discipline may make sense.

Q5 How do organizations decide how much to spend on IS?

Explain the general principles that organizations use for justifying investments in IS and IT. Explain the difference between tangible and intangible benefits. Describe the problem of intangible benefits, and offer one way of assessing projects that cannot be justified on their tangible benefits.

Q6 What are your IS rights and responsibilities?

Using Figure 11-4 as a guide, summarize the rights you have with regard to information systems and technology. Summarize the responsibilities that you have toward the IS department as well.

How does the **knowledge** in this chapter help *Fox Lake* and **you?**

Summarize the ways that Jeff could have used the knowledge in this chapter. Explain three ways that the knowledge in this chapter can benefit you.

KEY TERMS AND CONCEPTS

Agile enterprise 263
Chief information officer (CIO) 265
Chief technology officer (CTO) 266
Green computing 264
Intangible benefit 267
Tangible benefit 267
Tuned 263

USING YOUR KNOWLEDGE

1. Explain why Jeff needs to become involved with IS management at Fox Lake. To what extent do you think general managers of other small companies need to be involved in IS management?

2. Suppose you work for an organization that you believe does not adequately protect its data and IS assets. Assume you manage the telesales department and you have raised your concerns several times with your management, all to no avail. Describe how you would protect yourself and your department.

3. Suppose you represent an investor group that is acquiring hospitals across the nation and integrating them into a unified system. List five potential problems and risks concerning information systems. How do you think IS-related risks compare to other risks in such an acquisition program?

COLLABORATION EXERCISE 11

Before you start this exercise, read Chapter Extensions 1 and 2, which describe collaboration techniques as well as tools for managing collaboration tasks. In particular, consider using Google Docs, Windows Live SkyDrive, Microsoft SharePoint, or some other collaboration tool.

Suppose that you and a team of fellow students are interns working for Laura. She has asked you to gather information on Fox Lake's computing infrastructure and to write a one-page memo to Jeff outlining what he should be doing to manage IS at Fox Lake.

1. Reread the chapter introductions regarding Fox Lake in Chapters 7 through 11. List and briefly describe the information systems that are being used at Fox Lake. Although we have not considered accounting systems, add them to your list.

2. Describe the Fox Lake computing infrastructure. Assume that Fox Lake servers are located in the facilities building and that Fox Lake operates a local area network among its buildings and facilities. Portions of the network are wired and others are wireless. Assume that the network is supported by a third party. Use your knowledge of business to list other computing equipment that Fox Lake must have.

3. With the exception of the new facilities scheduling system that will be operated in the cloud, assume that Fox Lake's data are stored on servers in the facilities building. List major categories of data that must exist to support the golf, tennis, restaurant, pro shop, and wedding activities.

4. Using the answers you provided to questions 1–3, summarize the major activities for Fox Lake for each of the four responsibility categories in Figure 11-1.

5. Describe why Mike has a conflict of interest in the management of IS at Fox Lake (see the chapter introduction). Assuming that Jeff wants to continue to have Mike manage the IS facilities and resources, how can he reduce the impact of this conflict?

6. Given your answers to questions 1–6, write a one-page memo to Jeff explaining how he should be involved in management of the IS department.

7. Generalize the memo in your answer to question 6 to describe the responsibilities for IS management for owners of small businesses of any type. Write this memo in such a way that you might use it in a job interview with the owner of a small business.

CASE STUDY 11

Marriott International, Inc.

Marriott International, Inc., operates and franchises hotels and lodging facilities throughout the world. Its 2009 revenue was just over $10.91 billion. Marriott groups its business into segments according to lodging facility. Major business segments are full-service lodging, select-service lodging, extended-stay lodging, and timeshare properties. Marriott states that its three top corporate priorities are profitability, preference, and growth.

In the mid-1980s, the airlines developed the concept of *revenue management*, which adjusts prices in accordance with demand. The idea gained prominence in the airline industry, because an unoccupied seat represents revenue that is forever lost. Unlike a part in inventory, an unoccupied seat on today's flight cannot be sold tomorrow. Similarly, in the lodging industry today's unoccupied hotel room cannot be sold tomorrow. So, for hotels revenue management translates to raising prices on Monday when a convention is in town and lowering them on Saturday in the dead of winter when few travelers are in sight.

Marriott had developed two different revenue-management systems, one for its premium hotels and a second one for its lower-priced properties. It developed both of these systems using pre-Internet technology; systems upgrades required installing updates locally. The local updates were expensive and problematic. Also, the two systems required two separate interfaces for entering prices into the centralized reservation system.

In the late-1990s, Marriott embarked on a project to create a single revenue-management system that could be used by all of its properties. The new system, called OneSystem, was developed in-house, using a process similar to those you learned about in Chapter 10. The IS professionals understood the importance of user involvement, and they formed a joint IS–business user team that developed the business case for the new system and jointly managed its development. The team was careful to provide constant communication to the system's future users, and it used prototypes to identify problem areas early. Training is a continuing activity for all Marriott employees, and the company integrated training facilities into the new system.

OneSystem recommends prices for each room, given the day, date, current reservation levels, and history. Each hotel property has a revenue manager who can override these recommendations. Either way, the prices are communicated directly to the centralized reservation system. OneSystem uses Internet technology so that when the company makes upgrades to the system it makes them only at the Web servers, not at the individual hotels. This strategy saves considerable maintenance cost, activity, and frustration.

OneSystem computes the theoretical maximum revenue for each property and compares actual results to that maximum. Using OneSystem, the company has increased the ratio of actual to theoretical revenue from 83 to 91 percent. That increase of 8 percentage points has translated into a substantial increase in revenues.

Source: Case based on *www.cio.com/article/119209/The_Price_Is_Always_Right* (accessed June 2010).

Questions

1. How does OneSystem contribute to Marriott's objectives?
2. What are the advantages of having one revenue-management system instead of two? Consider both users and the IS department in your answer.

3. At the same time it was developing OneSystem in-house, Marriott chose to outsource its human relations information system. Why would it choose to develop one system in-house but outsource the other? Consider the following factors in your answer:

   - Marriott's objectives
   - The nature of the systems
   - The uniqueness of each system to Marriott
   - Marriott's in-house expertise

4. How did outsourcing HR contribute to the success of OneSystem?

CHAPTER 12

Information Security Management

This could happen to you

"It's weird, Jeff. I don't get it. Someone's stealing wedding presents . . . five times in the last month! I thought it was bad luck, but five times???" Anne Foster, manager of wedding events, is talking with Jeff, Fox Lake's general manager.

"We'd better assign someone for security, Anne."

"Yeah, I guess, but I hate to have a guard standing around. It doesn't happen all the time . . . we had 23 weddings this month."

"Do you remember which five?" Jeff asks.

"Maybe, let's see . . . the Kibby, the Horan, the Grant, the Yagan, the Svendson . . . hey, that's odd, those families are all members here. And, those could be the only member weddings we've had this month. How weird!" Anne looks puzzled.

"Any idea what was taken?" Jeff asks, feeling more and more uncomfortable about this conversation.

"That's odd, too. All expensive things. Sonos speakers, Bose radios, that kind of stuff."

"Anne, let me look into this. I'll get back to you. Meanwhile, move the presents out of the lobby . . . somewhere less public . . . back of the reception room or something."

"OK."

After Anne leaves, Jeff picks up his phone to call Laura.

"Laura, I think we've got a problem."

"What's up?"

"Someone's stealing wedding presents . . . but only from weddings of members."

"That *is* odd."

Laura sounds hesitant on the phone.

STUDY QUESTIONS

Q1 What are the sources and types of security threats?

Q2 What are the elements of a security program?

Q3 How can technical safeguards protect against security threats?

Q4 How can data safeguards protect against security threats?

Q5 How can human safeguards protect against security threats?

Q6 What is necessary for disaster preparedness?

Q7 How should organizations respond to security incidents?

How does the knowledge in this chapter help *Fox Lake* and you?

"Could someone be getting to our data? Finding out when members are having weddings?"

"Maybe, but why just steal gifts from members' weddings?" Laura asks.

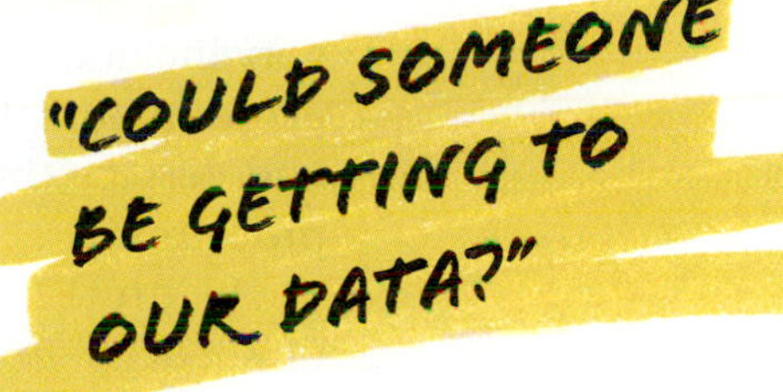

"Because members are well-to-do. Their presents are expensive." Jeff's not happy at all.

"Ah. Well, like I said last week, those servers are open to anyone with a key to the facilities building. If someone knew how to get into the system, how to access the database, maybe a little SQL . . . sure, it could be done."

"Laura, can you come over here for a meeting this afternoon? Say 1:30?"

That afternoon, Jeff and Laura walk into Mike's office. Laura looks over Mike's shoulder and sees little yellow sticky notes on the screen, the writing looks like passwords.

"That takes care of access," she says to herself.

"Mike, do you remember several months ago when Anne needed a report about members with daughters?"

"Yeah, I do . . . " Mike looks concerned. Why are Jeff and Laura popping in on him?

"Who created that report?" Jeff asks.

"Jason and Chris—they did a good job, too." Mike sounds defensive.

"Who are they?" Laura asks, although she's already figured it out.

"Groundskeepers. Chris took computer courses somewhere and knows a lot! Anne was really pleased with their results. Is she upset now?" Jeff looks worried.

"No, not at all." Jeff tries to reassure Mike.

"They have a key to the building?" Laura asks.

"Well, they did when they were working on that job. But I got the keys back."

"They could make a copy . . . Mike, I think you better call the police." Jeff looks down at his feet while Mike makes the call.

Optional Extension for this chapter is • CE21: International MIS 587

Q1 What Are the Sources and Types of Security Threats?

We begin by describing security threats. We will first summarize the sources of threats and then describe specific problems that arise from each source. Three sources of **security threats** are human error and mistakes, malicious human activity, and natural events and disasters.

Human errors and mistakes include accidental problems caused by both employees and nonemployees. An example is an employee who misunderstands operating procedures and accidentally deletes customer records. Another example is an employee who, in the course of backing up a database, inadvertently installs an old database on top of the current one. This category also includes poorly written application programs and poorly designed procedures. Finally, human errors and mistakes include physical accidents like driving a forklift through the wall of a computer room.

The second source of security problems is *malicious human activity*. This category includes employees and former employees who intentionally destroy data or other system components. It also includes both hackers who break into a system as well as malware (see Q3) writers who infect computer systems. Malicious human activity also includes outside criminals who break into a system to steal for financial gain; it also includes cyberterrorism.

Natural events and disasters are the third source of security problems. This category includes fires, floods, hurricanes, earthquakes, tsunamis, avalanches, and other acts of nature. Problems in this category include not only the initial loss of capability and service, but also losses stemming from actions to recover from the initial problem.

Figure 12-1 summarizes threats by type of problem and source. Five types of security problems are listed: unauthorized data disclosure, incorrect data

Figure 12-1
Security Threats

		Source		
		Human Error	**Malicious Activity**	**Natural Disasters**
Problem	**Unauthorized data disclosure**	Procedural mistakes	Pretexting Phishing Spoofing Sniffing Computer crime	Disclosure during recovery
	Incorrect data modification	Procedural mistakes Incorrect procedures Ineffective accounting controls System errors	Hacking Computer crime	Incorrect data recovery
	Faulty service	Procedural mistakes Development and installation errors	Computer crime Usurpation	Service improperly restored
	Denial of service (DOS)	Accidents	DOS attacks	Service interruption
	Loss of infrastructure	Accidents	Theft Terrorist activity	Property loss

modification, faulty service, denial of service, and loss of infrastructure. We will consider each type.

Unauthorized Data Disclosure

Unauthorized data disclosure can occur by human error when someone inadvertently releases data in violation of policy. An example at a university would be a new department administrator who posts student names, numbers, and grades in a public place, when the releasing of names and grades violates state law. Another example is employees who unknowingly or carelessly release proprietary data to competitors or to the media.

The popularity and efficacy of search engines has created another source of inadvertent disclosure. Employees who place restricted data on Web sites that can be reached by search engines may mistakenly publish proprietary or restricted data over the Web.

Of course, proprietary and personal data can also be released maliciously. **Pretexting** occurs when someone deceives by pretending to be someone else. A common scam involves a telephone caller who pretends to be from a credit card company and claims to be checking the validity of credit card numbers: "I'm checking your MasterCard number; it begins 5491. Can you verify the rest of the number?" MasterCard numbers commonly start with 5491; the caller is attempting to steal a valid number.

Phishing is a similar technique for obtaining unauthorized data that uses pretexting via email. The *phisher* pretends to be a legitimate company and sends an email requesting confidential data, such as account numbers or passwords, Social Security numbers, and so forth. Phishing compromises legitimate brands and trademarks.

Spoofing is another term for someone pretending to be someone else. If you pretend to be your professor, you are spoofing your professor. **IP spoofing** occurs when an intruder uses another site's IP address as if it were that other site. **Email spoofing** is a synonym for phishing.

Sniffing is a technique for intercepting computer communications. With wired networks, sniffing requires a physical connection to the network. With wireless networks, no such connection is required: **Drive-by sniffers** simply take computers with wireless connections through an area and search for unprotected wireless networks. They can monitor and intercept wireless traffic at will. Even protected wireless networks are vulnerable, as you will learn. Spyware and adware are two other sniffing techniques discussed later in this chapter. Other forms of computer crime include breaking into networks to steal data such as customer lists, product inventory data, employee data, and other proprietary and confidential data.

Finally, people may inadvertently disclose data during recovery from a natural disaster. Usually, during a recovery, everyone is so focused on restoring system capability that they ignore normal security safeguards. A request like "I need a copy of the customer database backup" will receive far less scrutiny during disaster recovery than at other times.

Incorrect Data Modification

The second problem category in Figure 12-1 is *incorrect data modification*. Examples include incorrectly increasing a customer's discount or incorrectly modifying an employee's salary, earned days of vacation, or annual bonus. Other examples include placing incorrect information, such as incorrect price changes, on the company's Web site or company portal.

Incorrect data modification can occur through human error when employees follow procedures incorrectly or when procedures have been incorrectly designed. For proper internal control on systems that process financial data or that control inventories of assets, such as products and equipment, companies should ensure separation of duties and authorities and have multiple checks and balances in place.

A final type of incorrect data modification caused by human error includes *system errors*. An example is the lost-update problem discussed in Chapter 5 (page 110).

Hacking occurs when a person gains unauthorized access to a computer system. Although some people hack for the sheer joy of doing it, other hackers invade systems for the malicious purpose of stealing or modifying data. Criminals invade computer networks to obtain critical data or to manipulate the system for financial gain. Examples are reducing account balances or causing the shipment of goods to unauthorized locations and customers.

Finally, faulty recovery actions after a disaster can result in incorrect data changes. The faulty actions can be unintentional or malicious.

Faulty Service

The third problem category, *faulty service*, includes problems that result because of incorrect system operation. Faulty service could include incorrect data modification, as just described. It also could include systems that work incorrectly by sending the wrong goods to the customer or the ordered goods to the wrong customer, incorrectly billing customers, or sending the wrong information to employees. Humans can inadvertently cause faulty service by making procedural mistakes. System developers can write programs incorrectly or make errors during the installation of hardware, software programs, and data.

Usurpation occurs when unauthorized programs invade a computer system and replace legitimate programs. Such unauthorized programs typically shut down the legitimate system and substitute their own processing. Faulty service can also result from mistakes made during the recovery from natural disasters.

Denial of Service

Human error in following procedures or a lack of procedures can result in **denial of service (DOS)**. For example, humans can inadvertently shut down a Web server or corporate gateway router by starting a computationally intensive application. An OLAP application that uses the operational DBMS can consume so many DBMS resources that order-entry transactions cannot get through.

Denial-of-service attacks can be launched maliciously. A malicious hacker can flood a Web server, for example, with millions of bogus service requests that so occupy the server that it cannot service legitimate requests. As you will learn in Q3, computer worms can infiltrate a network with so much artificial traffic that legitimate traffic cannot get through. Finally, natural disasters may cause systems to fail, resulting in denial of service.

Loss of Infrastructure

Human accidents can cause *loss of infrastructure*. Examples include a bulldozer cutting a conduit of fiber-optic cables and the floor buffer crashing into a rack of Web servers.

Theft and terrorist events also cause loss of infrastructure. A disgruntled, terminated employee can walk off with corporate data servers, routers, or other crucial

Experiencing MIS InClass Exercise 12

Phishing for Credit Cards, Identifying Numbers, Bank Accounts

A **phisher** is an individual or organization that spoofs legitimate companies in an attempt to illegally capture personal data such as credit card numbers, email accounts, and driver's license numbers. Some phishers install malicious program code on users' computers as well.

Phishing is usually initiated via email. Phishers steal legitimate logos and trademarks and use official sounding words in an attempt to fools users into revealing personal data or clicking a link. Phishers do not bother with laws about trademark use. They place names and logos like Visa, MasterCard, Discover, and American Express on their Web pages and use them as bait. In some cases, phishers copy the entire look and feel of a legitimate company's Web site.

In this exercise, you and a group of your fellow students will be asked to investigate phishing attacks. If you search the Web for phishing, be aware that your search may bring the attention of an active phisher. Therefore, do not give any data to any site that you visit as part of this exercise!

1. To learn the fundamentals of phishing, visit the following site: *www.microsoft.com/protect/fraud/phishing/symptoms.aspx.* To see recent examples of phishing attacks, visit *www.fraudwatchinternational.com/phishing/.*
   a. Using examples from these Web sites, describe how phishing works.
   b. Explain why a link that appears to be legitimate, such as *www.microsoft.mysite.com* may, in fact, be a link to a phisher's site.
   c. List five indicators of a phishing attack.
   d. Write an email that you could send to a friend or relative who is not well versed in technical matters that explains what phishing is and how your friend or relative can avoid it.

Your Order ID: "17152492"
Order Date: "09/07/10"
Product Purchased: "Two First Class Tickets to Cozumel"
Your card type: "CREDIT"
Total Price: "$349.00"

Hello, when you purchased your tickets you provided an incorrect mailing address.
See more details here
Please follow the link and modify your mailing address or cancel your order. If you have questions, feel free to contact us account@usefulbill.com

Figure 1
Fake Phishing Email

2. Suppose you received the email in Figure 1 and mistakenly clicked See more details here. When you did so, you were taken to the Web page shown in Figure 2. List every phishing symptom that you find in these two figures and explain why it is a symptom.
3. Suppose you work for an organization that is being phished.
   a. How would you learn that your organization is being attacked?
   b. What steps should your organization take in response to the attack?
   c. What liability, if any, do you think your organization has for damages to customers that result from a phishing attack that carries your brand and trademarks?
4. Summarize why phishing is a serious problem to commerce today.
5. Describe actions that industry organizations, companies, governments, or individuals can take to help to reduce phishing.

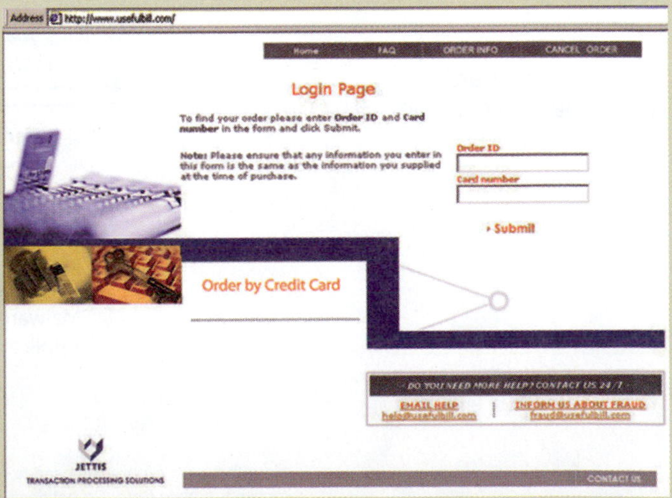

Figure 2
Fake Phishing Screen

equipment. Terrorist events can also cause the loss of physical plants and equipment.

Because of their severity, natural disasters present the largest risk for infrastructure loss. A fire, flood, earthquake, or similar event can destroy data centers and all they contain. The devastation of hurricanes Katrina and Rita in the fall of 2005 and the earthquake in Haiti are potent examples of the risks to infrastructure from natural causes.

Q2 What Are the Elements of a Security Program?

All of the problems listed in Figure 12-1 are real and as serious as they sound. Accordingly, organizations must address security in a systematic way. A security program[1] has three components: senior management involvement, safeguards of various kinds, and incident response.

Effective security requires balanced attention to all five components! Senior management has two critical security functions: overall policy and risk management. Considering the first, senior management must establish the security policy that governs personal use of company computers, employee data privacy, whether the organization will inspect employee emails, and other broad issues. The security policy also includes specific systems issues such as whether customer data is to be shared with third parties.

The second senior management security function is to manage risk. Security can be expensive. How much is enough? Because no security program is perfect, regardless of the investment, there is always risk of a bad outcome. Management manages risk by deciding how much to spend on security and therefore how much risk to take.

Safeguards are protections against security threats. A good way to view safeguards is in terms of the five components of an information system, as shown in Figure 12-2. Some of the safeguards involve computer hardware and software. Some involve data; others involve procedures and people. In addition to these safeguards, organizations must also consider disaster recovery safeguards. An effective security program consists of a balance of safeguards of all these types.

The final component of a security program consists of the organization's planned response to security incidents. Clearly, the time to think about what to do is not when

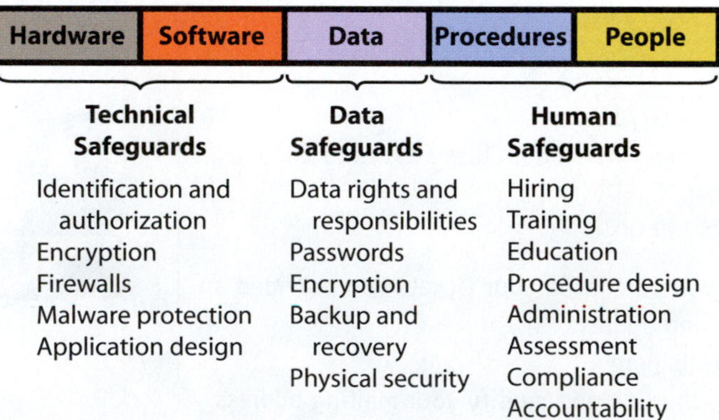

Figure 12-2
Security Safeguards as They Relate to the Five Components

1. Note the word *program* is used here in the sense of a management program that includes objectives, policies, procedures, directives, and so forth. Do not confuse this term with a *computer program.*

the computers are crashing all around the organization. We will discuss incident response in the last section of this chapter.

Q3 How Can Technical Safeguards Protect Against Security Threats?

Technical safeguards involve the hardware and software components of an information system. Figure 12-3 lists primary technical safeguards. Consider each.

Identification and Authentication

Every information system today should require users to sign on with a user name and password. The user name *identifies* the user (the process of **identification**), and the password *authenticates* that user (the process of **authentication**). Review the material on strong passwords and password etiquette in Chapter 1 (pages 14–15) if you have forgotten that discussion.

Passwords have important weaknesses. For one, users tend to be careless in their use. Despite repeated warnings to the contrary, yellow sticky notes holding written passwords adorn many computers. In addition, users tend to be free in sharing their passwords with others. Finally, many users choose ineffective, simple passwords. With such passwords, intrusion systems can very effectively guess passwords.

These deficiencies can be reduced or eliminated using smart cards and biometric authentication.

Smart Cards

A **smart card** is a plastic card similar to a credit card. Unlike credit, debit, and ATM cards, which have a magnetic strip, smart cards have a microchip. The microchip, which holds far more data than a magnetic strip, is loaded with identifying data. Users of smart cards are required to enter a **personal identification number (PIN)** to be authenticated.

Biometric Authentication

Biometric authentication uses personal physical characteristics such as fingerprints, facial features, and retinal scans to authenticate users. Biometric authentication provides strong authentication, but the required equipment is expensive. Often, too, users resist biometric identification because they feel it is invasive.

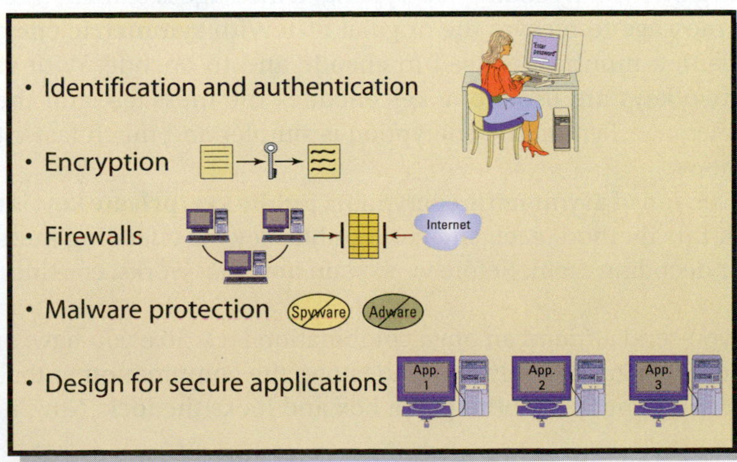

Figure 12-3
Technical Safeguards

Biometric authentication is in the early stages of adoption. Because of its strength, it likely will see increased usage in the future. It is also likely that legislators will pass laws governing the use, storage, and protection requirements for biometric data. For more on biometrics, search for *biometrics* at *http://searchsecurity.techtarget.com.*

Note that authentication methods fall into three categories: what you know (password or PIN), what you have (smart card), and what you are (biometric).

Single Sign-on for Multiple Systems

Information systems often require multiple sources of authentication. For example, when you sign on to your personal computer, you need to be authenticated. When you access the LAN in your department, you need to be authenticated again. When you traverse your organization's WAN, you will need to be authenticated to even more networks. Also, if your request requires database data, the DBMS server that manages that database will authenticate you yet again.

It would be annoying to enter a name and password for every one of these resources. You might have to use and remember five or six different passwords just to access the data you need to perform your job. It would be equally undesirable to send your password across all of these networks. The further your password travels, the greater the risk it can be compromised.

Instead, today's operating systems have the capability to authenticate you to networks and other servers. You sign on to your local computer and provide authentication data; from that point on your operating system authenticates you to another network or server, which can authenticate you to yet another network and server, and so forth.

Encryption

Encryption is the process of transforming clear text into coded, unintelligible text for secure storage or communication. Considerable research has gone into developing **encryption algorithms** (procedures for encrypting data) that are difficult to break. Commonly used methods are DES, 3DES, and AES; search the Web for these terms if you want to know more about them.

A **key** is a number used to encrypt the data. It is called a *key* because it unlocks a message, but it is a number used with an encryption algorithm and not a physical thing like the key to your apartment.

To encode a message, a computer program uses the encryption method with the key to convert a noncoded message into a coded message. The resulting coded message looks like gibberish. Decoding (decrypting) a message is similar; a key is applied to the coded message to recover the original text. With **symmetric encryption**, the same key (again, a number) is used to encode and to decode. With **asymmetric encryption**, two keys are used; one key encodes the message, and the other key decodes the message. Symmetric encryption is simpler and much faster than asymmetric encryption.

A special version of asymmetric encryption, **public key/private key**, is used on the Internet. With this method, each site has a public key for encoding messages and a private key for decoding them. Before we explain how that works, consider the following analogy.

Suppose you send a friend an open combination lock (like you have on your gym locker). Suppose you are the only one who knows the combination to that lock. Now, suppose your friend puts something in a box and locks the lock. Now, neither your friend nor anyone else can open that box. They send the locked box to you, and you apply the combination to open the box.

A public key is like the combination lock, and the private key is like the combination. Your friend uses the public key to code the message (lock the box), and you use the private key to decode the message (use the combination to open the lock).

Now, suppose we have two generic computers, A and B. Suppose A wants to send an encrypted message to B. To do so, A sends B its public key (in our analogy, A sends B an open combination lock). Now B applies A's public key to the message and sends the resulting coded message back to A. At that point, neither B nor anyone other than A can decode that message. It is like the box with a locked combination lock. When A receives the coded message, A applies its private key (the combination in our analogy) to unlock or decrypt the message.

Again, public keys are like open combination locks. Computer A will send a lock to anyone who asks for one. But A never sends its private key (the combination) to anyone. Private keys stay private.

Most secure communication over the Internet uses a protocol called **HTTPS**. With HTTPS, data are encrypted using a protocol called the **Secure Socket Layer (SSL)**, which is also known as **Transport Layer Security (TLS)**. SSL/TLS uses a combination of public key/private key and symmetric encryption.

The basic idea is this: Symmetric encryption is fast and is preferred. But, the two parties (say you and a Web site) don't share a symmetric key. So, the two of you use public/private encryption to share the same symmetric key. Once you both have that key, you use symmetric encryption.

Figure 12-4 summarizes how SSL/TLS works when you communicate securely with a Web site:

1. Your computer obtains the public key of the Web site to which it will connect.
2. Your computer generates a key for symmetric encryption.
3. Your computer encodes that key using the Web site's public key. It sends the encrypted symmetric key to the Web site.
4. The Web site then decodes the symmetric key using its private key.
5. From that point forward, your computer and the Web site communicate using symmetric encryption.

At the end of the session, your computer and the secure site discard the keys. Using this strategy, the bulk of the secure communication occurs using the faster

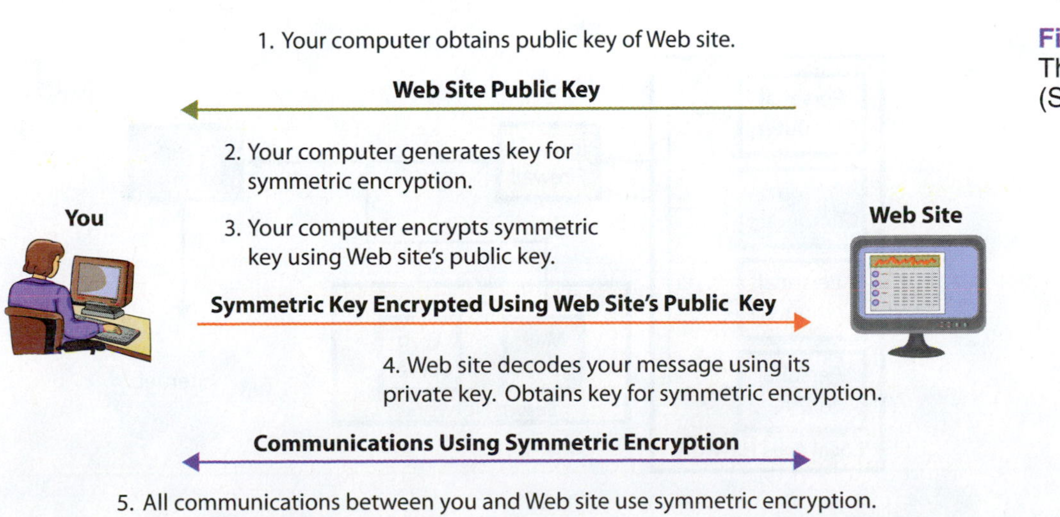
1. Your computer obtains public key of Web site.
Web Site Public Key
2. Your computer generates key for symmetric encryption.
You
3. Your computer encrypts symmetric key using Web site's public key.
Web Site
Symmetric Key Encrypted Using Web Site's Public Key
4. Web site decodes your message using its private key. Obtains key for symmetric encryption.
Communications Using Symmetric Encryption
5. All communications between you and Web site use symmetric encryption.

Figure 12-4
The Essence of HTTPS (SSL or TLS)

symmetric encryption. Also, because keys are used for short intervals, there is less likelihood they can be discovered.

Use of SSL/TLS makes it safe to send sensitive data such as credit card numbers and bank balances. Just be certain that you see *https://* in your browser and not just *http://*.

Warning: Under normal circumstances, neither email nor instant messaging (IM) uses encryption. It would be quite easy for one of your classmates or your professor to read any email or IM that you send over a wireless network in your classroom, in the student lounge, at a coffee shop, or in any other wireless setting. Let the sender beware!

Firewalls

A **firewall** is a computing device that prevents unauthorized network access. A firewall can be a special-purpose computer or it can be a program on a general-purpose computer or on a router.

Organizations normally use multiple firewalls. A **perimeter firewall** sits outside the organizational network; it is the first device that Internet traffic encounters. In addition to perimeter firewalls, some organizations employ **internal firewalls** inside the organizational network. Figure 12-5 shows the use of a perimeter firewall that protects all of an organization's computers and a second internal firewall that protects a LAN.

A **packet-filtering firewall** examines each part of a message and determines whether to let that part pass. To make this decision, it examines the source address, the destination address(es), and other data.

Packet-filtering firewalls can prohibit outsiders from starting a session with any user behind the firewall. They can also disallow traffic from particular sites, such as known hacker addresses. They also can prohibit traffic from legitimate, but unwanted, addresses, such as competitors' computers. Firewalls can filter outbound traffic as well. They can keep employees from accessing specific sites, such as competitors' sites, sites with pornographic material, or popular news sites. As a future manager, if you have particular sites with which you do not want your employees to communicate, you can ask your IS department to enforce that limit via the firewall.

Packet-filtering firewalls are the simplest type of firewall. Other firewalls filter on a more sophisticated basis. If you take a data communications class, you will learn about them. For now, just understand that firewalls help to protect organizational computers from unauthorized network access.

Figure 12-5
Use of Multiple Firewalls

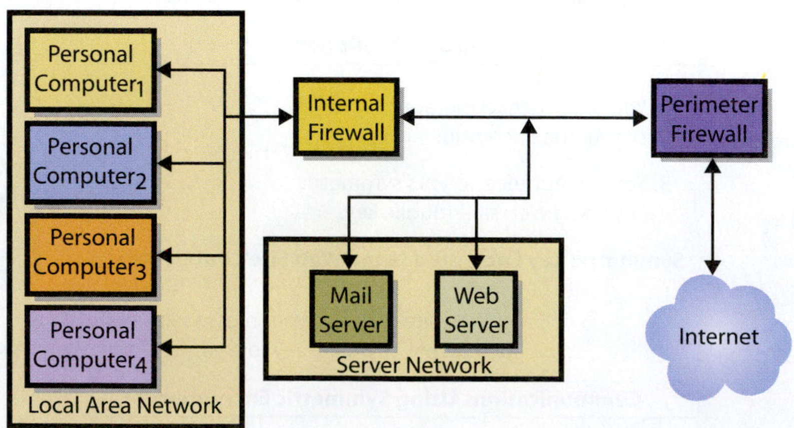

No computer should connect to the Internet without firewall protection. Many ISPs provide firewalls for their customers. By nature, these firewalls are generic. Large organizations supplement such generic firewalls with their own. Most home routers include firewalls, and Microsoft Windows 7 has a built-in firewall as well. Third parties also license firewall products.

Malware Protection

The next technical safeguard in our list in Figure 12-3 is malware. The term **malware** has several definitions. Here we will use the broadest one: *Malware* is viruses, worms, Trojan horses, spyware, and adware.

A **virus** is a computer program that replicates itself. Unchecked replication is like computer cancer; ultimately, the virus consumes the computer's resources. Furthermore, many viruses also take unwanted and harmful actions.

The program code that causes unwanted activity is called the **payload**. The payload can delete programs or data—or, even worse, modify data in undetected ways. Imagine the impact of a virus that changed the credit rating of all customers. Some viruses publish data in harmful ways—for example, sending out files of credit card data to unauthorized sites.

There are many different types of viruses. **Trojan horses** are viruses that masquerade as useful programs or files. The name refers to the gigantic mock-up of a horse that was filled with soldiers and moved into Troy during the Trojan War. A typical Trojan horse appears to be a computer game, an MP3 music file, or some other useful, innocuous program.

Macro viruses attach themselves to Word, Excel, or other types of documents. When the infected document is opened, the virus places itself in the start-up files of the application. After that, the virus infects every file that the application creates or processes.

A **worm** is a virus that propagates using the Internet or other computer network. Worms spread faster than other virus types because they are specifically programmed to spread. Unlike nonworm viruses, which must wait for the user to share a file with a second computer, worms actively use the network to spread. Sometimes, worms so choke a network that it becomes unusable.

Spyware programs are installed on the user's computer without the user's knowledge or permission. Spyware resides in the background and, unknown to the user, observes the user's actions and keystrokes, monitors computer activity, and reports the user's activities to sponsoring organizations. Some malicious spyware captures keystrokes to obtain user names, passwords, account numbers, and other sensitive information. Other spyware supports marketing analyses, observing what users do, Web sites visited, products examined and purchased, and so forth.

Adware is similar to spyware in that it is installed without the user's permission and it also resides in the background and observes user behavior. Most adware is benign in that it does not perform malicious acts or steal data. It does, however, watch user activity and produce pop-up ads. Adware can also change the user's default window or modify search results and switch the user's search engine. For the most part, it is just annoying, but users should be concerned any time they have unknown programs on their computers that perform unrequested functions.

Figure 12-6 lists some of the symptoms of adware and spyware. Sometimes these symptoms develop slowly over time as more malware components are installed. Should these symptoms occur on your computer, remove the spyware or adware using antimalware programs.

Figure 12-6
Spyware and Adware Symptoms

- Slow system start up
- Sluggish system performance
- Many pop-up advertisements
- Suspicious browser homepage changes
- Suspicious changes to the taskbar and other system interfaces
- Unusual hard-disk activity

Malware Safeguards

Fortunately, it is possible to avoid most malware using the following malware safeguards:

1. *Install antivirus and antispyware programs on your computer.* Your IT department will have a list of recommended (perhaps required) programs for this purpose. If you choose a program for yourself, choose one from a reputable vendor. Check reviews of antimalware software on the Web before purchasing.
2. *Set up your antimalware programs to scan your computer frequently.* You should scan your computer at least once a week and possibly more often. When you detect malware code, use the antimalware software to remove it. If the code cannot be removed, contact your IT department or antimalware vendor.
3. *Update malware definitions.* **Malware definitions**—patterns that exist in malware code—should be downloaded frequently. Antimalware vendors update these definitions continuously, and you should install these updates as they become available.
4. *Open email attachments only from known sources.* Also, even when opening attachments from known sources, do so with great care. According to professor and security expert Ray Panko, about 90 percent of all viruses are spread by email attachments.[2] This statistic is not surprising, because most organizations are protected by firewalls. With a properly configured firewall, email is the only outside-initiated traffic that can reach user computers.

   Most antimalware programs check email attachments for malware code. However, all users should form the habit of *never* opening an email attachment from an unknown source. Also, if you receive an unexpected email from a known source or an email from a known source that has a suspicious subject, odd spelling, or poor grammar, do not open the attachment without first verifying with the known source that the attachment is legitimate.
5. *Promptly install software updates from legitimate sources.* Unfortunately, all programs are chock full of security holes; vendors are fixing them as rapidly as they are discovered, but the practice is inexact. Install patches to the operating system and application programs promptly.
6. *Browse only in reputable Internet neighborhoods.* It is possible for some malware to install itself when you do nothing more than open a Web page. Don't go there!

Design for Secure Applications

The final technical safeguard in Figure 12-3 concerns the design of applications. As a future IS user, you will not design programs yourself. However, you should ensure that

2. Ray Panko, *Corporate Computer and Network Security* (Upper Saddle River, NJ: Prentice Hall, 2004), p. 165.

any information system developed for you and your department includes security as one of the application requirements.

Q4 How Can Data Safeguards Protect Against Security Threats?

Data safeguards protect databases and other organizational data. Two organizational units are responsible for data safeguards. **Data administration** refers to an organization-wide function that is in charge of developing data policies and enforcing data standards. Data administration is a staff function to the CIO, as discussed in Chapter 11.

Database administration refers to a function that pertains to a particular database. ERP, CRM, and MRP databases each have a database administration function. Database administration ensures that procedures exist to ensure orderly multiuser processing of the database, to control changes to the database structure, and to protect the database.

Both data and database administration are involved in establishing the data safeguards in Figure 12-7. First, data administration should define data policies such as "We will not share identifying customer data with any other organization" and the like. Then, data administration and database administration(s) work together to specify user data rights and responsibilities. Third, those rights should be enforced by user accounts that are authenticated at least by passwords.

The organization should protect sensitive data by storing it in encrypted form. Such encryption uses one or more keys in ways similar to that described for data communication encryption. One potential problem with stored data, however, is that the key might be lost or that disgruntled or terminated employees might destroy it. Because of this possibility, when data are encrypted, a trusted party should have a copy of the encryption key. This safety procedure is sometimes called **key escrow**.

Another data safeguard is to periodically create backup copies of database contents. The organization should store at least some of these backups off premises, possibly in a remote location. Additionally, IT personnel should periodically practice recovery to ensure that the backups are valid and that effective recovery procedures exist. Do not assume that just because a backup is made that the database is protected.

Physical security is another data safeguard. The computers that run the DBMS and all devices that store database data should reside in locked, controlled-access facilities. If not, they are subject not only to theft, but also to damage. For better security, the organization should keep a log showing who entered the facility, when, and for what purpose.

In some cases, organizations contract with other companies to manage their databases. If so, all of the safeguards in Figure 12-7 should be part of the service contract. Also, the contract should give the owners of the data permission to inspect the premises of the database operator and to interview its personnel on a reasonable schedule.

- Define data policies
- Data rights and responsibilities
- Rights enforced by user accounts authenticated by passwords
- Data encryption
- Backup and recovery procedures
- Physical security

Figure 12-7
Data Safeguards

Q5 How Can Human Safeguards Protect Against Security Threats?

Human safeguards involve the people and procedure components of information systems. In general, human safeguards result when authorized users follow appropriate procedures for system use and recovery. Restricting access to authorized users requires effective authentication methods and careful user account management. In addition, appropriate security procedures must be designed as part of every information system, and users should be trained on the importance and use of those procedures. In this section, we will consider the development of human safeguards for employees.

Human safeguards are even more important for employees who manage the security system, as discussed in the Ethics Guide on pages 302–303.

Human Safeguards for Employees

Figure 12-8 lists security considerations for employees. The first is position definitions.

Position Definitions

Effective human safeguards begin with definitions of job tasks and responsibilities. In general, job descriptions should provide a separation of duties and authorities. For example, no single individual should be allowed both to approve expenses and write checks. Instead, one person should approve expenses, another pay them, and a third should account for the payment. Similarly, in inventory, no single person should be

Figure 12-8
Security Policy for In-House Staff

- Position definition
  - Separate duties and authorities.
  - Determine least privilege.
  - Document position sensitivity.

- Hiring and screening

- Dissemination and enforcement (responsibility, accountability, compliance)

- Termination
  - Friendly

  - Unfriendly

allowed to authorize an inventory withdrawal and also to remove the items from inventory.

Given appropriate job descriptions, user accounts should be defined to give users the *least possible privilege* needed to perform their jobs. For example, users whose job description does not include modifying data should be given accounts with read-only privilege. Similarly, user accounts should prohibit users from accessing data their job description does not require. Because of the problem of semantic security, even access to seemingly innocuous data may need to be limited.

For more on semantic security, see Chapter Extension 16, "Reporting Systems and OLAP," on page 515.

Finally, the security sensitivity should be documented for each position. Some jobs involve highly sensitive data (e.g., employee compensation, salesperson quotas, and proprietary marketing or technical data). Other positions involve no sensitive data. Documenting *position sensitivity* enables security personnel to prioritize their activities in accordance with the possible risk and loss.

Hiring and Screening

Security considerations should be part of the hiring process. Of course, if the position involves no sensitive data and no access to information systems, then screening for information systems security purposes will be minimal. When hiring for high-sensitivity positions, however, extensive interviews, references, and background investigations are appropriate. Note, too, that security screening applies not only to new employees, but also to employees who are promoted into sensitive positions.

Dissemination and Enforcement

Employees cannot be expected to follow security policies and procedures that they do not know about. Therefore, employees need to be made aware of the security policies, procedures, and responsibilities they will have.

Employee security training begins during new-employee training, with the explanation of general security policies and procedures. That general training must be amplified in accordance with the position's sensitivity and responsibilities. Promoted employees should receive security training that is appropriate to their new positions. The company should not provide user accounts and passwords until employees have completed required security training.

Enforcement consists of three interdependent factors: responsibility, accountability, and compliance. First, the company should clearly define the security *responsibilities* of each position. The design of the security program should be such that employees can be held *accountable* for security violations. Procedures should exist so that when critical data are lost, it is possible to determine how the loss occurred and who is accountable. Finally, the security program should encourage security *compliance*. Employee activities should regularly be monitored for compliance, and management should specify disciplinary action to be taken in light of noncompliance.

Management attitude is crucial: Employee compliance is greater when management demonstrates, both in word and deed, a serious concern for security. If managers write passwords on staff bulletin boards, shout passwords down hallways, or ignore physical security procedures, then employee security attitudes and employee security compliance will suffer. Note, too, that effective security is a continuing management responsibility. Regular reminders about security are essential.

Termination

Companies also must establish security policies and procedures for the termination of employees. Most employee terminations are friendly, and occur as the result of promotion, retirement, or when the employee resigns to take another position. Standard human resources policies should ensure that system administrators receive notification in advance of the employee's last day, so that they can remove accounts and passwords. The need to recover keys for encrypted data and any other special security requirements should be part of the employee's out-processing.

Unfriendly termination is more difficult, because employees may be tempted to take malicious or harmful actions. In such a case, system administrators may need to remove user accounts and passwords prior to notifying the employee of his or her termination. Other actions may be needed to protect the company's information assets. A terminated sales employee, for example, may attempt to take the company's confidential customer and sales-prospect data for future use at another company. The terminating employer should take steps to protect those data prior to the termination.

The human resources department should be aware of the importance of giving IS administrators early notification of employee termination. No blanket policy exists; the information systems department must assess each case on an individual basis.

Account Administration

The administration of user accounts, passwords, and help-desk policies and procedures is another important human safeguard.

Account Management

Account management concerns the creation of new user accounts, the modification of existing account permissions, and the removal of unneeded accounts. Information system administrators perform all of these tasks, but account users have the responsibility to notify the administrators of the need for these actions. The IT department should create standard procedures for this purpose. As a future user, you can improve your relationship with IS personnel by providing early and timely notification of the need for account changes.

The existence of accounts that are no longer necessary is a serious security threat. IS administrators cannot know when an account should be removed; it is up to users and managers to give such notification.

Password Management

Passwords are the primary means of authentication. They are important not just for access to the user's computer, but also for authentication to other networks and servers to which the user may have access. Because of the importance of passwords, the National Institute of Standards and Technology (NIST) recommends that employees be required to sign statements similar to that shown in Figure 12-9.

Figure 12-9
Sample Account Acknowledgment Form

Source: National Institute of Standards and Technology, *Introduction to Computer Security: The NIST Handbook*, Publication 800–812, p. 114.

I hereby acknowledge personal receipt of the system password(s) associated with the user IDs listed below. I understand that I am responsible for protecting the password(s), will comply with all applicable system security standards, and will not divulge my password(s) to any person. I further understand that I must report to the Information Systems Security Officer any problem I encounter in the use of the password(s) or when I have reason to believe that the private nature of my password(s) has been compromised.

When an account is created, users should immediately change the password they are given to a password of their own. In fact, well-constructed systems require the user to change the password on first use.

Additionally, users should change passwords frequently thereafter. Some systems will require a password change every 3 months or perhaps more frequently. Users grumble at the nuisance of making such changes, but frequent password changes reduce not only the risk of password loss, but also the extent of damage if an existing password is compromised.

Some users create two passwords and switch back and forth between those two. This strategy results in poor security, and some password systems do not allow the user to reuse recently used passwords. Again, users may view this policy as a nuisance, but it is important.

Help-Desk Policies

In the past, help desks have been a serious security risk. A user who had forgotten his password would call the help desk and plead for the help-desk representative to tell him his password or to reset the password to something else. "I can't get this report out without it!" was (and is) a common lament.

The problem for help-desk representatives is, of course, that they have no way of determining that they are talking with the true user and not someone spoofing a true user. But, they are in a bind: If they do not help in some way, the help desk is perceived to be the "unhelpful desk."

To resolve such problems, many systems give the help-desk representative a means of authenticating the user. Typically, the help-desk information system has answers to questions that only the true user would know, such as the user's birthplace, mother's maiden name, or last four digits of an important account number. Usually, when a password is changed, notification of that change is sent to the user in an email. Email, as you learned, is sent as plaintext, however, so the new password itself ought not to be emailed. If you ever receive notification that your password was reset when you did not request such a reset, immediately contact IT security. Someone has compromised your account.

All such help-desk measures reduce the strength of the security system, and, if the employee's position is sufficiently sensitive, they may create too large a vulnerability. In such a case, the user may just be out of luck. The account will be deleted, and the user must repeat the account-application process.

Systems Procedures

Figure 12-10 shows a grid of procedure types—normal operation, backup, and recovery. Procedures of each type should exist for each information system. For example, the order-entry system will have procedures of each of these types, as will the Web storefront, the inventory system, and so forth. The definition and use of standardized procedures reduces the likelihood of computer crime and other malicious activity by insiders. It also ensures that the system's security policy is enforced.

Procedures exist for both users and operations personnel. For each type of user, the company should develop procedures for normal, backup, and recovery operations. As a future user, you will be primarily concerned with user procedures. Normal-use procedures should provide safeguards appropriate to the sensitivity of the information system.

Backup procedures concern the creation of backup data to be used in the event of failure. Whereas operations personnel have the responsibility for backing up system

Figure 12-10
System Procedure

	System Users	Operations Personnel
Normal operation	Use the system to perform job tasks, with security appropriate to sensitivity.	Operate data center equipment, manage networks, run Web servers, and do related operational tasks.
Backup	Prepare for loss of system functionality.	Back up Web site resources, databases, administrative data, account and password data, and other data.
Recovery	Accomplish job tasks during failure. Know tasks to do during system recovery.	Recover systems from backed up data. Perform role of help desk during recovery.

databases and other systems data, departmental personnel have the need to back up data on their own computers. Good questions to ponder are, "What would happen if I lost my computer (or PDA) tomorrow?" "What would happen if someone dropped my computer during an airport security inspection?" "What would happen if my computer were stolen?" Employees should ensure that they back up critical business data on their computers. The IT department may help in this effort by designing backup procedures and making backup facilities available.

Finally, systems analysts should develop procedures for system recovery. First, how will the department manage its affairs when a critical system is unavailable? Customers will want to order and manufacturing will want to remove items from inventory even though a critical information system is unavailable. How will the department respond? Once the system is returned to service, how will records of business activities during the outage be entered into the system? How will service be resumed? The system developers should ask and answer these questions and others like them and develop procedures accordingly.

Security Monitoring

Security monitoring is the last of the human safeguards we will consider. Important monitoring functions are activity log analyses, security testing, and investigating and learning from security incidents.

Many information system programs produce *activity logs.* Firewalls produce logs of their activities, including lists of all dropped packets, infiltration attempts, and unauthorized access attempts from within the firewall. DBMS products produce logs of successful and failed log-ins. Web servers produce voluminous logs of Web activities. The operating systems in personal computers can produce logs of log-ins and firewall activities.

None of these logs adds any value to an organization unless someone looks at them. Accordingly, an important security function is to analyze these logs for threat patterns, successful and unsuccessful attacks, and evidence of security vulnerabilities.

Additionally, companies should test their security programs. Both in-house personnel and outside security consultants should conduct such testing.

Another important monitoring function is to investigate security incidents. How did the problem occur? Have safeguards been created to prevent a recurrence of such problems? Does the incident indicate vulnerabilities in other portions of the security system? What else can be learned from the incident?

Security systems reside in a dynamic environment. Organization structures change. Companies are acquired or sold; mergers occur. New systems require new security measures. New technology changes the security landscape, and new threats arise. Security personnel must constantly monitor the situation and determine if the existing security policy and safeguards are adequate. If changes are needed, security personnel need to take appropriate action.

Security, like quality, is an ongoing process. There is no final state that represents a secure system or company. Instead, companies must monitor security on a continuing basis.

Q6 What Is Necessary for Disaster Preparedness?

A disaster is a substantial loss of computing infrastructure caused by acts of nature, crime, or terrorist activity. As has been stated several times, the best way to solve a problem is not to have it. The best safeguard against a disaster is appropriate location. If possible, place computing centers, Web farms, and other computer facilities in locations not prone to floods, earthquakes, hurricanes, tornados, or avalanches. Even in those locations, place infrastructure in unobtrusive buildings, basements, backrooms, and similar locations well within the physical perimeter of the organization. Also, locate computing infrastructure in fire-resistant buildings designed to house expensive and critical equipment.

However, sometimes business requirements necessitate locating the computing infrastructure in undesirable locations. Also, even at a good location, disasters do occur. Therefore, some businesses prepare backup processing centers in locations geographically removed from the primary processing site.

Figure 12-11 lists major disaster preparedness tasks. After choosing a safe location for the computing infrastructure, the organization should identify all mission-critical applications. These are applications without which the organization cannot carry on and which if lost for any period of time could cause the organization's failure. The next step is to identify all resources necessary to run those systems. Such resources include computers, operating systems, application programs, databases, administrative data, procedure documentation, and trained personnel.

Next, the organization creates backups for the critical resources at the remote processing center. So-called **hot sites** are remote processing centers run by commercial disaster-recovery services. For a monthly fee, they provide all the equipment needed to continue operations following a disaster. See *www.ragingwire.com/services* for information about services provided by a typical vendor. **Cold sites**, in contrast, provide office space, but customers themselves provide and install the equipment needed to continue operations.

Once the organization has backups in place, it must train and rehearse cutover of operations from the primary center to the backup. Periodic refresher rehearsals are mandatory.

- Locate infrastructure in safe location.
- Identify mission-critical systems.
- Identify resources needed to run those systems.
- Prepare remote backup facilities.
- Train and rehearse.

Figure 12-11
Disaster Preparedness Guidelines

Preparing a backup facility is very expensive; however, the costs of establishing and maintaining that facility are a form of insurance. Senior management must make the decision to prepare such a facility by balancing the risks, benefits, and costs.

Q7 How Should Organizations Respond to Security Incidents?

The last component of a security plan that we will consider is incident response. Figure 12-12 lists the major factors. First, every organization should have an incident-response plan as part of the security program. No organization should wait until some asset has been lost or compromised before deciding what to do. The plan should include how employees are to respond to security problems, whom they should contact, the reports they should make, and steps they can take to reduce further loss.

Consider, for example, a virus. An incident-response plan will stipulate what an employee should do when he notices the virus. It should specify whom to contact and what to do. It may stipulate that the employee should turn off his computer and physically disconnect from the network. The plan should also indicate what users with wireless computers should do.

The plan should provide centralized reporting of all security incidents. Such reporting will enable an organization to determine if it is under systematic attack or whether an incident is isolated. Centralized reporting also allows the organization to learn about security threats, take consistent actions in response, and apply specialized expertise to all security problems.

When an incident does occur, speed is of the essence. Viruses and worms can spread very quickly across an organization's networks, and a fast response will help to mitigate the consequences. Because of the need for speed, preparation pays. The incident-response plan should identify critical personnel and their off-hours contact information. These personnel should be trained on where to go and what to do when they get there. Without adequate preparation, there is substantial risk that the actions of well-meaning people will make the problem worse. Also, the rumor mill will be alive with all sorts of nutty ideas about what to do. A cadre of well-informed, trained personnel will serve to dampen such rumors.

Finally, organizations should periodically practice incident response. Without such practice, personnel will be poorly informed on the response plan, and the plan itself may have flaws that only become apparent during a drill.

Figure 12-12
Factors in Incident Response

- Have plan in place
- Centralized reporting
- Specific responses
  - Speed
  - Preparation pays
  - Don't make problem worse
- Practice!

How does the knowledge in this chapter help *Fox Lake* and you?

The knowledge in both Chapter 11 and in this chapter would have helped Jeff and Mike better protect Fox Lake's computing infrastructure. Mike would have known to protect his passwords better. Both he and Jeff would have known the dangers of having someone like Jason or Chris producing reports for Anne. Mike would have known at least to give him a temporary account and password and to remove it after Jason and Chris finished their work.

In truth, Fox Lake does a poor job of managing and protecting its infrastructure. Unfortunately, such situations are common among small businesses. If you work in a small business, take the example of Fox Lake to heart. Remembering these problems can help you do a better job of protecting your computing assets.

That's it! You've reached the end of the book. Take a moment to reflect on how you will use what you will learn, as described in the Guide on pages 304–305.

Ethics Guide

Metasecurity

Recall from Chapter 5 that metadata is data about data. In a similar vein, metasecurity is security about security. In other words, it asks the question, "How do we secure the security system?"

Consider an obvious problem: What is a secure way to store a file of accounts and passwords? Such files must exist, otherwise operating systems would be unable to authenticate users. But, how should one store such a file? It cannot be stored as plaintext, because anyone who reads the file gains unlimited access to the computer, the network, and other assets. So, it must be stored in encrypted form, but how? And who should know the encryption key?

Consider another problem. Suppose you work at the help desk at Vanguard Funds, and part of your job is to reset user passwords when users forget them. Clearly, this is an essential job that needs to be done, but what keeps you from resetting the passwords of accounts held by elderly people who never look at their statements? What keeps you from accessing those accounts with your reset password and moving funds to the accounts of your friends?

The accounting profession has dealt with some of these problems for decades and has developed a set of procedures and standards known as *accounting controls*. In general, these controls involve procedures that provide checks and balances, independent reviews of activity logs, control of critical assets, and so forth. Properly designed and implemented, such controls will catch the help-desk representative performing unauthorized account transfers. But many computer network threats are new, proper safeguards are under development, and some threats are not yet known.

The safeguards for some problems have unexpected consequences. For example, suppose you give one of your employees the task of finding security flaws in your network and financial applications (an activity called *white-hat hacking*). Assume that your employee finds ways to crack into your system and, say, schedule undetectable, unauthorized shipments of goods from inventory to any address she wants. Your employee reports the flaws, and you fix them. Except, how do you know she reported all the flaws she found?

Further, when she's finished, what do you do with your white-hat hacker? You are afraid to fire her, because you have no idea what she'll do with the information she has. But what job can she safely perform now that she knows the holes in your security system? Do you want her, ever again, to have an account and password in your corporate computer network? Even if you fix all the problems she reports, which is doubtful, you suspect that she can always find more.

Or consider Microsoft's problem. If you were a computer criminal, where is the ultimate place to lodge a Trojan horse or trapdoor? In Windows code. Microsoft hires hundreds of people to write its operating system; people who work all over the world. Of course, Microsoft performs background screening on everyone it can, but did it get a

Clearly, hardware and software are only part of the problem. Metasecurity extends to the data, procedures, and people components as well. It's a fascinating field, one that is continually developing, and one of great importance. It would make an interesting career choice—but be careful what you learn!

complete and accurate background report on every Windows programmer in India, France, Ireland, China, and so on? Microsoft uses careful procedures for controlling what code gets into its products, but even still, somebody at Microsoft must lose sleep over the possibilities.

Ironically, the answers for many metasecurity problems lie in openness. Encryption experts generally agree that any encryption algorithm that relies on secrecy is ultimately doomed, because the secret will get out. Secrecy with encryption must lie only with the (temporary) keys that are used, and not with a secret method. Thus, encryption algorithms are published openly, and anyone with a mathematical bent is encouraged to find (and report) flaws. An algorithm is safe to deploy only when thousands of people have tested and retested it. One very common wireless security protocol, Wired Equivalency Protocol, or WEP, was unwisely deployed before it was tested, and thousands upon thousands of wireless networks are vulnerable as a result.

Discussion Questions

1. Explain the term *metasecurity.* Describe two metasecurity problems not mentioned in this guide.
2. Explain the control problem that exists when personnel can reset customer passwords. Describe a way to reduce this threat using an audit log and at least two independent employees.
3. Describe the dilemma posed by an in-house hacker. Describe the problem of using an outside company for white-hat hacking. If you were asked to manage a project to test your computer network security, would you use in-house or outsourced personnel? Why?
4. A typical corporate computer has software from Microsoft, SAP, Siebel, Oracle, and possibly dozens of smaller vendors. How do users know that none of the software from these companies contains a Trojan horse?
5. Explain why part of the security solution lies in openness. Describe how openness applies to accounting controls like the one you designed in your answer to question 2. Explain the danger of procedural controls that rely on secrecy.

Guide

The Final, Final Word

Congratulations! You've made it through the entire book. With this knowledge you are well prepared to be an effective user of information systems. And with work and imagination, you can be much more than that. Many interesting opportunities are available to those who can apply information in innovative ways. Your professor has done what she can do, and the rest, as they say, is up to you.

So what's next? Back in Chapter 1 we claimed that Introduction to MIS is the most important course in the business curriculum today. That claim was based on the availability of nearly free data communications and data storage. By now, you've learned many of the ways that businesses and organizations use these resources and information systems based upon those resources. You've also seen how businesses like FlexTime and Fox Lake use information systems to solve problems and to further their competitive strategies. In some cases, particularly with Fox Lake, they *struggled* to use information systems for those purposes.

How can you use this knowledge? Chapter 1 claimed that future business professionals must be able "to assess, evaluate, and apply emerging information technology to business." Have you learned how to do that? At least, are you better able to do that than you were prior to this class? You probably know the meaning of many more terms than you did when you started this class, and such knowledge is important. But, even more important is the ability to use that knowledge to apply MIS to your business interests.

Chapter 1 also reviewed the work of the RAND Corporation and that of Robert Reich on what professional workers in the twenty-first century need to know. Those sources state that such workers need to know how to innovate the use of technology and how to "collaborate, reason abstractly, think in terms of systems, and experiment." Have you learned those behaviors? Or, at least, are you better at them than when you started this course?

As of August 2010, the national unemployment rate was about 9.5 percent. Under these circumstances, good jobs will be difficult to obtain. You need to apply every asset you have. One of those assets is the knowledge you've gained in this class. Take the time to do the exercises at the end of this guide, and then use those answers in your job interviews!

Look for the job you truly want to do, get that job, and work hard. In the movie *Phillip Glass in 12 Acts,* the composer Phillip Glass claimed he knew the secret to success. It was, he said, "Get up early and work hard all day." That quotation seems obvious and hardly worth stating. Except that it has the ring of truth. And, if you can find a job you truly love, it isn't even hard. Actually, it's fun, most of the time. So, use what you've learned in this class to obtain the job you truly want!

Discussion Questions

1. Reflect on what you have learned from this course. Write two paragraphs on how the knowledge you have gained will help you to "assess, evaluate, and apply emerging information technology to business." Shape your writing around the kind of job that you want to obtain upon graduation.
2. Write two paragraphs on how the knowledge and experiences you've had in this class will help you to "collaborate, reason abstractly, think in terms of systems, and experiment." Again, shape your writing around the kind of job you wish to obtain.
3. Using your answer to question 1, extract three or four sentences about yourself that you could use in a job interview.
4. Using your answer to question 2, extract three or four sentences about yourself that you could use in a job interview.
5. Practice using your answers to questions 3 and 4 in a job interview with a classmate, roommate, or friend.

ACTIVE REVIEW

Use this Active Review to verify that you understand the ideas and concepts that answer the chapter's study questions.

Q1 What are the sources and types of security threats?

Explain the difference among security threats, threat sources, and threat types. Give one example of a security threat for each cell in the grid in Figure 12-1. Describe a phishing attack. Explain the threat of phishing to individuals. Explain the threat of phishing to company and product brands.

Q2 What are the elements of a security program?

Define *technical, data,* and *human safeguards.* Show how these safeguards relate to the five components of an information system.

Q3 How can technical safeguards protect against security threats?

List five technical safeguards. Define *identification* and *authentication.* Describe three types of authentication. Explain how SSL/TLS works. Define *firewall,* and explain its purpose. Define *malware,* and name five types of malware. Describe six ways to protect against malware. Summarize why malware is a serious problem.

Q4 How can data safeguards protect against security threats?

Define *data administration* and *database administration,* and explain their difference. List data safeguards.

Q5 How can human safeguards protect against security threats?

Summarize human safeguards for each activity in Figure 12-8. Summarize safeguards that pertain to nonemployee personnel. Describe three dimensions of safeguards for account administration. Explain how system procedures can serve as human safeguards. Describe security monitoring techniques.

Q6 What is necessary for disaster preparedness?

Define *disaster.* List major considerations for disaster preparedness. Explain the difference between a hot site and a cold site.

Q7 How should organizations respond to security incidents?

Summarize the actions that an organization should take when dealing with a security incident.

How does the **knowledge** in this chapter help **Fox Lake** and **you?**

Describe the ways Fox Lake can use the knowledge from this chapter. Explain how you can use the knowledge of security threats and safeguards to become a better business professional.

KEY TERMS AND CONCEPTS

USING YOUR KNOWLEDGE

1. Credit reporting agencies are required to provide you with a free credit report each year. Most such reports do not include your credit score, but they do provide the details on which your credit score is based. Use one of the following companies to obtain your free report: *www.equifax.com*, *www.experion.com*, and *www.transunion.com*.
   a. You should review your credit report for obvious errors. However, other checks are appropriate. Search the Web for guidance on how best to review your credit records. Summarize what you learn.
   b. What actions can you take if you find errors in your credit report?
   c. Define *identity theft*. Search the Web and determine the best course of action if someone thinks he has been the victim of identity theft.

2. Suppose you lose your company laptop at an airport. What should you do? Does it matter what data are stored on your disk drive? If the computer contained sensitive or proprietary data, are you necessarily in trouble? Under what circumstances should you now focus on updating your resume?

3. Suppose you alert your boss to the security threats in Figure 12-1 and to the safeguards in Figure 12-2. Suppose he says, "Very interesting. Tell me more." In preparing for the meeting, you decide to create a list of talking points.
   a. Write a brief explanation of each threat in Figure 12-1.
   b. Explain how the five components relate to safeguards.
   c. Describe two to three technical, two to three data, and two to three human safeguards.
   d. Write a brief description about the safeguards in Figure 12-8.
   e. List security procedures that pertain to you, a temporary employee.
   f. List procedures that your department should have with regard to disaster planning.

4. Suppose you need to terminate an employee who works in your department. Summarize security protections you must take. How would you behave differently if this termination were a friendly one?

COLLABORATION EXERCISE 12

Before you start this exercise, read Chapter Extensions 1 and 2, which describe collaboration techniques as well as tools for managing collaboration tasks. In particular, consider using Google Docs, Windows Live SkyDrive, Microsoft SharePoint, or some other collaboration tool.

Suppose that Chris and Jason, the groundskeepers at Fox Lake, are the same Chris and Jason that appeared in the Ethics Guide on pages 112–113. After Chris was fired from his job, he wandered around, couldn't find professional work, and settled for cutting the grass at Fox Lake. He happened to tell Mike about his computer knowledge the day before Anne made her request for a report on membership data (see Chapter 9, pages 208–209). Mike thought giving Chris that task would possibly help Chris's professional job prospects as well as solve a problem for Fox Lake. Jason was working at Fox Lake part time, and it was he who hatched the scheme to steal expensive wedding presents. Chris provided the data and Jason did the stealing.

Assume that the wedding event data and the membership data are stored in separate databases on the server in the facilities building. Access to both is protected via user account and password, but Mike leaves his passwords on his desktop computer monitor. The machines themselves are located in a backroom of the facilities building.

Meeting with your group, answer the following questions:

1. In what ways did weaknesses in technical safeguards allow this situation to occur?

2. In what ways did weaknesses in data safeguards allow this situation to occur?

3. In what ways did weaknesses in human safeguards allow this situation to occur?
4. How should Fox Lake respond to this incident?
5. What security mistakes, if any, did each of the following make:
   a. Anne
   b. Mike
   c. Jeff
   d. Laura
6. If you were Jeff, how would you remedy the weaknesses you identified in your answers to questions 1–3?
7. Suppose you were in a job interview with the owner of a small business, with IS and IT infrastructure similar to that at Fox Lake. If that owner were to ask you what the top three issues for IS security in a small business are, how would you respond?

CASE STUDY 12

ChoicePoint, a Georgia-based corporation, is a data aggregator that specializes in risk-management and fraud-prevention data. Traditionally, ChoicePoint provided motor vehicle reports, claims histories, and similar data to the automobile insurance industry; in recent years, it broadened its customer base to include general business and government agencies. Today, it also offers data for volunteer and job-applicant screening and data to assist in the location of missing children. ChoicePoint has over 4,000 employees, and its 2007 revenue was $982 million. It was acquired by Reed Elsevier in 2008 and financial results have not been made public since.

In the fall of 2004, ChoicePoint was the victim of a fraudulent spoofing attack in which unauthorized individuals posed as legitimate customers and obtained personal data on more than 145,000 individuals. According to the company's Web site:

> **These criminals were able to pass our customer authentication due-diligence processes by using stolen identities to create and produce the documents needed to appear legitimate. As small business customers of ChoicePoint, these fraudsters accessed products that contained basic telephone directory-type data (name and address information) as well as a combination of Social Security numbers and/or driver's license numbers and, at times, abbreviated credit reports. They were also able to obtain other public record information including, but not limited to bankruptcies, liens, and judgments; professional licenses; and real property data.**

ChoicePoint became aware of the problem in November 2004, when it noticed unusual processing activity on some accounts in Los Angeles. Accordingly, the company contacted the Los Angeles Police Department, which requested that ChoicePoint not reveal the activity until the department could conduct an investigation. In January, the LAPD notified ChoicePoint that it could contact the customers whose data had been compromised.

This crime is an example of a failure of authentication, not a network break-in. ChoicePoint's firewalls and other safeguards were not overcome. Instead, the criminals spoofed legitimate businesses. The infiltrators obtained valid California business licenses, and until their unusual processing activity was detected they appeared to be legitimate users.

In response to this problem, ChoicePoint established a hotline for customers whose data had been compromised. It also purchased a credit report for each victim and paid for a credit-report-monitoring service for 1 year. In February 2005, attorneys initiated a class-action lawsuit for all 145,000 customers, with an initial loss claim of $75,000 each. At the same time, the U.S. Senate announced that it would conduct an investigation.

Ironically, ChoicePoint exposed itself to a public relations nightmare, considerable expense, a class-action lawsuit, a Senate investigation, and a 20 percent drop in its share price because it contacted the police and cooperated in the attempt to apprehend the criminals. When ChoicePoint noticed the unusual account activity, had it simply shut down data access for the illegitimate businesses, no one would have known. Of course, the 145,000 customers whose identities had been compromised would have unknowingly been subject to identity theft, but it is unlikely that such thefts could have been tracked back to ChoicePoint.

As a data utility, ChoicePoint maintains relationships with many different entities. It obtains its data from both public and private sources. It then sells access to this data to its customers. Much of the data, by the way, can be obtained directly from the data vendor. ChoicePoint adds value by providing a centralized access point for many data needs. In addition to data sources and customers, ChoicePoint maintains relationships with partners such as the vital records departments in major cities. Finally, ChoicePoint also has relationships with the people and organizations on which it maintains data.

Questions

1. ChoicePoint exposed itself to considerable expense, many problems, and a possible loss of brand confidence because it notified the Los Angeles Police Department, cooperated in the investigation, and notified the individuals whose records had been compromised. It could have buried the theft and possibly avoided any responsibility. Comment on the ethical issues and ChoicePoint's response. Did ChoicePoint choose wisely? Consider that question from the viewpoint of customers, law enforcement personnel, investors, and management.

2. Given ChoicePoint's experience, what is the likely action of similar companies whose records are compromised in this way? Given your answer, do you think federal regulation and additional laws are required? What other steps could be taken to ensure that data vendors notify people harmed by data theft?

3. Visit *www.choicepoint.com.* Summarize the products that ChoicePoint provides. What seems to be the central theme of this business?

4. Suppose that ChoicePoint decides to establish a formal security policy on the issue of inappropriate release of personal data. Summarize the issues that ChoicePoint should address in this policy.

STUDY QUESTIONS

CHAPTER EXTENSION 1

Chapter 1 provides the background for this Extension.

Improving Your Collaboration Skills

Q1 Why Learn Collaboration Skills?

Chapter 1 described why collaboration is important for workers in the twenty-first century, and you probably have a team project in every one of your business school classes. Besides the work of experts such as Robert Reich, you might personally know professionals like Lily Shen, an information systems project manager at Hitachi Systems. Lily works in Houston, Texas, but her major client is located in China; and her team is scattered all over the world. She manages a distributed collaborative team. According to the RAND Corporation,[1] jobs like Lily's will become increasingly common, important, and remunerative for workers in this century.

Ho, hum, you may be thinking. I've heard this all before. Well, have you thought, seriously, that collaboration requires skill? Do you realize that collaboration is like tennis or golf—you start with a certain native ability but you can improve that ability with coaching and practice? It is likely that you've been going to team meetings since grade school. Do you just show up, offer your thoughts, do something toward a common goal, and just turn it in? Ever wonder how you could collaborate better? How your team could work better together? Whether you might have created a better product with less work? Have you asked yourself if it is possible to create a team that has conflict yet is still a productive group? One that you looked forward to meeting with? Or, one that produced a product that was better than anything any one of you could have done individually?

Learning effective collaboration skills is a lifelong project. Start now. Think about the ways that you interact with your teammates; think about the structure of your team; think about how you handle conflict. When you become a skilled collaborator, you can help your team to do better work, faster.

This textbook can help you improve your collaboration skills in two ways. In this chapter extension, we consider collaboration *behaviors*; in Chapter Extension 2 we consider information systems *tools* that your team can use to collaborate more efficiently, and maybe even more effectively.

Q2 What Is Collaboration?

Collaboration occurs when two or more people work together to achieve a common goal, result, or work product. When collaboration is effective, the results of the group are greater than could be produced by any of the individuals working alone. Collaboration involves coordination and communication, but it is greater than either of those.

[1] Lynn A. Karoly and Constantijn W. A. Panis, *The 21st Century at Work* (Santa Monica, CA: RAND Corporation, 2004), p. xiv.

Consider an example of a student team that is assigned a term project. Suppose the team meets and divides the work into sections, and then team members work independently on their individual pieces. An hour before the project is due the team members meet again to assemble their independent pieces into a whole. Such a process is *not* collaboration. Although the members of such a team are *cooperating*, they are not *collaborating*.

The Importance of Feedback and Iteration

Collaboration involves *feedback* and *iteration*. In a collaborative team, group members review each others' work product and revise that product as a result. The effort proceeds in a series of steps, or iterations, in which one person produces something, others comment on what was produced, a revised version is produced, and so forth. Further, in the process of reviewing others' work, team members learn from each other and change the way they work and what they produce. The feedback and iteration enable the group to produce something greater than any single person could accomplish working independently.

It is not possible to collaborate at the last minute. You cannot produce a document at midnight the day before the project is due and expect your teammates to review it in time for you or someone else to revise. In most student teams, collaboration proceeds over a period of weeks, not hours.

Critical Collaboration Drivers

The effectiveness of a collaborative effort is driven by three critical factors:

- Communication
- Content management
- Workflow control

Communication has two key elements. The first is the communication skills and abilities of the group members. The ability to give and receive critical feedback is particularly important, as you will see. The product can improve only when group members can criticize each others' work without creating rancor and resentment and can improve their contributions based on criticism received.

The second key communication element is the availability of effective communication systems. Today, few collaborative meetings are conducted face-to-face. Group members may be geographically distributed, or they may be unable to meet at the same time, or both. In such cases, the availability of email and more sophisticated and effective communications systems is crucial.

Most students today should give up on face-to-face meetings. It is too difficult to get everyone together in one place at one time. Instead, use information systems to meet virtually and maybe not all at the same time. Chapter Extension 2 describes the use of several such systems.

The second driver of effective collaboration is *content management*. When multiple users are contributing and changing documents, schedules, task lists, assignments, and so forth, one user's work might interfere with another's. Users need to manage content so that such conflict does not occur. Also, it is important to know who made what changes, when, and why. Content management systems track and report such data. Finally, in some collaborations members have different rights and privileges. Some team members have full permissions to create, edit, and delete content, others are restricted to editing, and still others are restricted to a read-only status. Information systems play a key role in enforcing such restrictions.

Workflow control is the third key driver of effective collaboration. A *workflow* is a process or procedure by which content is created, edited, used, and disposed. For a team that supports a Web site, for example, a workflow design might specify that certain members create Web pages, others review those pages, and still others post the reviewed and approved pages to the Web site. The workflow specifies particular ordering of tasks and includes processes for handling rejected changes as well as for dealing with exceptions.

The three collaboration drivers are not equally important for all collaborations. For one-time, *ad hoc* workgroups, it is seldom worthwhile to create and formalize workflows. For such groups, communication is the most important driver. However, for a team of engineers designing a new airplane a formally defined workflow is crucial.

In Chapter Extension 2, you can learn about information systems tools that will facilitate collaboration in your team projects at school as well as later as a working professional.

Q3 What Is an Effective Team?

Some teams are more effective than others, and considerable research has been done to determine why. Before we address that question, first consider what we mean by **team**. Katzenbach and Smith[2] define a *team* as:

> A small number of people with complementary skills who are committed to a common purpose, performance goals, and approach for which they hold themselves mutually accountable. (p. 45)

The authors define *small* as fewer than 25, but their book was published in the 1990s, prior to the emergence of information systems collaboration technology. Today, a small team might be fewer than 50, or maybe even 75. Notice the key phrases in this definition:

- "Complementary skills"
- "Committed to a common purpose, goals, and approach"
- "Hold themselves mutually accountable"

As stated earlier, some teams are more effective than others. Richard Hackman, a Harvard professor who has been conducting research on teams for more than 30 years, identifies three characteristics of an **effective team**:[3]

1. The team accomplishes its goals and objectives in a way that satisfies the team's sponsors and clients.
2. Over time, the team increases in capability. Working together becomes easier and more effective.
3. Team members learn and feel fulfilled as a result of working on the team.

Consider each of these elements in turn.

Accomplishing Goals and Objectives

Your situation for teams at school is different than for the industry teams that Hackman studies. In school, your professor is the sponsor of your team, and he or she will determine the official assessment of your team's work. If you are like many students, you prefer projects with clearly defined goals and definite answers. Unfortunately, in the business world goals and objectives are seldom so cut-and-dried.

For example, in industry a team might be given a goal such as, "Find the best possible use for Microsoft Surface for accomplishing our competitive strategy." The team might not even know what Microsoft Surface is (*www.Microsoft.com/surface*). How will the team ever be able to determine if they have found the *best possible use*?

2. Jon Katzenbach and Douglas Smith, *The Wisdom of Teams* (New York: Harper Business, 1999), p. 45.
3. Richard Hackman, *Leading Teams* (Boston: Harvard University Press, 2002), p. 213.

If your professor gives you fuzzy goals like this one, be grateful, not critical. It isn't that he or she doesn't care or is poorly organized. Rather, your professor knows that in business, the only questions that have definite answers are those that are not worth asking.

However, in such situations it is critical that your team have a common understanding of the goals and objectives of the project. Invest the time to ensure that everyone is working toward the same end. If not, considerable team energy will be wasted.

Improve the Ability for the Team to Work Together

Most students stop right there, after the first element. Their one and only concern is to earn a high grade for the project. But Hackman defines two other measures of team effectiveness. One such measure concerns the team itself: Did the team become more effective as time went on? Did team members learn each others' strengths and how to use them wisely? Did team members learn each others' weaknesses and hot buttons and learn how to work around or otherwise manage them?

As stated, collaboration always involves feedback and iteration. Did team members learn how to give and receive critical feedback to one another? Did team members gain in their proficiency at using that critical feedback?

When teams improve their ability to work together, team members often come to like and enjoy each other more. But, such enjoyment is not essential to teamwork. Sometimes team members are just too different in personal perspective. What is essential, however, is that team members come to respect and trust each other.

Learning and Fulfillment

According to Hackman, teams have much to offer their members in terms of gaining new knowledge and skills from one another and learning from the different world perspectives of members on the team. Teams can provide a sense of belonging and serve to facilitate the development of new friendships.[4]

For a group to be considered successful, the group should enable members to do what they want and need to do, it should foster members' personal learning, and membership on the team should generate positive emotions about having worked with the group.

Q4 What Skills Are Important for Effective Collaboration?

The behavior of people in groups varies tremendously. Some people have a natural ability to collaborate, whereas others find it difficult, frustrating, or inefficient. Most people, though, with coaching and experience, can improve their collaboration skills. Before addressing specific skills, consider the factors that influence team member behaviors.

Factors That Influence Team Member Behavior

Psychologists and social scientists who have devoted considerable research to teamwork generally agree that team members' behavior is influenced by:

- Natural skills and abilities
- Childhood formative environment
- Past team experiences
- Attitude (and skill) of the team leader
- Nature of the work

4. *Ibid.*, pp. 28, 29.

People are born with different social abilities. Some people are naturally empathetic. Some are born leaders. Some people are shy and do not like to be in the center of activities. Beyond natural ability, the team members' formative environment influences their ability to collaborate. Team members who were born as the middle child in a family with nine children will have learned collaboration skills that someone raised as an only child will not know. Further, team members bring memories of their past experiences, and those memories determine their initial expectations for the team.

Team leaders have a major impact on team members' behavior. A team leader who is actively involved, who encourages participation, and who expects (and welcomes) conflict creates an environment that fosters collaboration. Finally, the nature of the work and its relationship to the interests and abilities of the team influence team behavior. Most people find it hard to collaborate on a project they find unimportant or boring."

Key Skills for Collaborators

Ditkoff, Allen, Moore, and Pollard[5] surveyed 108 business professionals on the qualities, attitudes, and skills that make a good collaborator. Their results found no significant differences in response to the top 10 qualities with regard to the respondents' age, gender, experience, or occupation. All respondents seemed to agree on the top 10.

The table in Figure CE1-1 lists the most and least important characteristics reported in the survey. Three of the top seven characteristics involve disagreement: speaking an unpopular viewpoint (3), willingness to engage in difficult conversations (5), and skill at giving and receiving critical feedback (7). Note, too, that these three fall *after* enthusiasm for the subject (1) and being curious and open-minded (2). The respondents seem to be saying, "You need to care, you need to be open-minded, but you need to be able to deal with conflict, effectively disagree, and receive opinions that are different from your own."

These results are not surprising when we think about collaboration as an iterative process in which team members give and receive feedback. During collaboration, team members learn from each other, and it will be difficult to learn if no one is willing to express unpopular or contentious ideas. The respondents also seem to be saying, "You can, even should, be negative, as long as you care about what we're doing." These collaboration skills do not come naturally to people who have been taught to "play well with others," and that may be why they were ranked so highly in the survey.

The characteristics rated as not relevant also are revealing. Experience as a collaborator or in business does not seem to matter. Being popular also is not important. A big surprise, however, is that being well organized was rated 31st out of 39 characteristics. Perhaps collaboration itself is not a very well-organized process.

Q5 What Characterizes Productive Conflict?

All of the research on collaboration indicates that conflict is common and, when properly conducted and managed, is a productive and positive factor for the team's performance. Student teams often fail because of an unwillingness to engage in conflict. Students might not want to be seen as unpopular or as not fitting in with the group, or perhaps students do not yet understand the importance of raising contrary or unpopular opinions. For whatever reason, many students will remain silent and walk away rather than express ideas that run counter to the rest of the group.

(There are some students whose standard behavior is to be negative and contrarian. They do not have problems avoiding conflict; they revel in it. But there are many

5. Mitch Ditkoff, Tim Moore, Carolyn Allen, and Dave Pollard, "What Qualities, Attitudes, and Skills Help Make a Good Collaborator?" *http://blogs.salon.com* (accessed November 2005).

Rankings of Individual Collaboration Characteristics:
Essential:
Enthusiastic (1)
Curious and open-minded (2)
Says what they think, even if an unpopular perspective (3)
Highly Appreciated:
Responds promptly (4)
Can engage in difficult conversations (5)
Good listener (6)
Good with critical feedback (giving & receiving) (7)
Will voice unpopular ideas (8)
Easy to work with (9)
Does what commits to do (10)
Enthusiastic learner (11)
Provides different perspectives (12)
Not Important:
Well organized (31)
Similar personality (32)
Trust based on past experience (33)
Experienced with collaboration (34)
Effective presentation skills (35)
Outgoing and social (36)
Someone I already know (37)
Reputation as experienced collaborator (38)
Seasoned business experience (39)

Figure CE1-1
The Most and Least Important Characteristics Reported in a Survey of Collaboration Skills

other students, normally pleasant and anxious to please, who cannot bring themselves to express negative or opposing thoughts. If you are such a student, you will have greater success in business if you learn to behave differently.)

Among rational people, conflict occurs because of differences in perspective. One person understands the task differently from another, one person views a nuance in the situation that others do not see, or perhaps someone has experience that other team members do not have. When conflict occurs, it is important to understand the idea of differences in perspective and to use empathetic thinking to elicit the differences in behavior.

When differences in perspective are identified, the team must decide if those differences are consequential. Will those differences make a difference to the team's effectiveness? Note, too, that if you subscribe to Hackman's definition of team effectiveness, this means asking two additional questions: Will the difference matter to accomplishing team goals? Will the difference hamper the team's ability to grow as a team or inhibit the individual growth of the team members?

If the differences are consequential, then the team needs to keep communicating. Team members should strive to hear, learn, and adapt, when appropriate. The understanding of differences and their resolution can be frustrating. But team members must avoid personal attacks. *All of the literature on team performance indicates that attacks on a team member's personality, appearance, intelligence, or any other personal characteristic does **irreparable** harm to the team.* Never engage in such behavior. Instead, focus on the task at hand and on the differences that you have with regard to the team's work.

See the "Understanding Perspectives" Guide on page 38 and the "Egocentric vs. Empathetic Thinking" Guide on page 36.

Sometimes when teams are stuck in seemingly unending conflict, the problem is caused by team members unknowingly using different criteria. As a simple example, one team member might believe that cost is the most important factor for judging an alternative, whereas another team member might believe that the delivery schedule is more important. They may not know that they are using different criteria. In such cases, no progress can be made until the difference is made explicit and the team agrees on a common set of criteria. This sometimes leads to a discussion of what criteria should be used to select the criteria. If so, carry the discussion through until the team has arrived at a common set of "criteria for criteria" and then a common set of criteria.

To repeat, all of the literature on teamwork indicates that conflict is inevitable and, when properly managed, results in better team performance. Do not shy away from productive conflict.

Q6 How Can You Improve Your Collaboration Skills?

As stated, collaboration skills are like any other skills; they can be improved by practice. Important behaviors to practice are listed in Figure CE1-2. The first requirement for improving your collaboration skills is to show up and get involved. You need to play tennis to improve tennis, and you need to collaborate to improve your collaboration skills. You need to believe that you can be better at collaboration and make a conscious and active effort to do so.

Assess yourself. Go through the list of behaviors in Figure CE1-1 and score yourself on the first 10 items in the list. Find the two or three items on which you score yourself the worst and identify ways to improve. There is an old management that says, "If you always do what you've always done, then you'll always get what you've always gotten." As the saying suggests, in order to improve your collaboration skills you must try some new behavior(s), no matter how awkward or uncomfortable you feel. If you have difficulty expressing contrary opinions, make a goal of expressing at least one in a future meeting.

Keep Hackman's three criteria in mind as you practice new skills. An effective team is one that not only accomplishes the given task, but one that also grows as a team and fosters the individual growth of team members. What new behaviors can you engage in to foster the second two?

It is very difficult for any of us to assess our own social skills. We're just too biased an observer. Ask your teammates for feedback. Or, if that is too personal, create a policy in your team for team members to provide feedback for everyone. Do this for your own growth, even if your instructor does not require it.

Finally, keep at it. Acquiring strong collaboration skills is a lifelong process. It may also be the single most important skill in business, because business is a social activity; people do business with people. When you are 60 years old and a vice president of whatever, you will still be collaborating, and you will still be perfecting your collaboration skills. Start now.

Figure CE1-2
Ways to Improve Your Collaboration Skills

- Show up...get involved.
- Assess yourself.
- Try new behaviors...and watch what happens.
- Keep Hackman's three goals of an effective team in mind.
- Engage in productive conflict.
- Ask for feedback and listen to it.
- Keep at it.

ACTIVE REVIEW

Use this Active Review to verify that you understand the material in the chapter extension. You can read the entire chapter extension and then perform the tasks in this review, or you can read the text material for just one question and perform the tasks in this review for that question before moving on to the next one.

Q1 Why learn collaboration skills?

In your own words, explain why collaboration is important and how collaboration is like tennis or golf. Identify reasons for improving your collaboration skills. Name your best collaboration skill and your worst collaboration skill. Explain your selection.

Q2 What is collaboration?

Define *collaboration*. Explain why collaboration is more than just cooperation. Identify the two critical characteristics of collaboration and explain them. Explain why you cannot collaborate at the last minute. Identify three critical collaboration drivers and summarize each. Explain why the textbook discourages face-to-face meetings.

Q3 What is an effective team?

Define *team*. Name and explain the key terms in the definition. List Hackman's three characteristics of an effective team. Explain each characteristic. Besides accomplishing the goal of the project, do you agree with the effectiveness criteria? Why or why not? Do differences between teams in school and teams in business mean that Hackman's effectiveness criteria are inappropriate for school teams? Why or why not?

Q4 What skills are important for effective collaboration?

Summarize the factors that influence a team member's collaborative behavior. Describe which, if any, of those factors are within the control of the team. Explain how the team might accommodate factors that are not within its control. Summarize the indispensible and very important behaviors that Ditkoff et al. found for collaboration. Summarize the not-relevant factors. Describe what you believe are the three most surprising behaviors in this survey and explain why you find them surprising.

Q5 What characterizes productive conflict?

Explain why it is naïve and incorrect to not expect conflict in collaboration teams. Describe why you think students tend to avoid conflict in team meetings. Explain the role of perspectives in group conflict. Identify a situation in which a difference in perspective is consequential and one in which it is not. Describe the role of criteria in assessing how consequential a difference might be. Describe behavior in conflict situations that must be avoided at all costs. Give an example of criteria and of "criteria for criteria."

Q6 How can you improve your collaboration skills?

Summarize techniques for improving your collaboration skills. Assess your skills in terms of Figure CE1-1. Describe your three weakest skills. Develop tasks for you to accomplish to address correcting those three weakest skills.

KEY TERMS AND CONCEPTS

USING YOUR KNOWLEDGE

1. Explain why collaboration will be important to you as a business professional.
2. What is the relationship between collaboration and teams? Are all teams collaborative? Does every collaborative activity involve a team? Consider a team of five students painting a house. Is that team collaborative? Does it proceed via a sequence of steps using feedback and iteration? Are teams that are cooperative but not collaborative bad?
3. Consider a team of students given the task of recommending ways to improve campus security. Explain why such a team is likely to be collaborative. Identify three issues that such a team might address, and explain why those issues would need feedback and iteration.
4. Consider the following statement: "In business, the only questions that have definite answers are those that are not worth asking." What do you think this means? Do you agree or disagree? Explain.
5. The text states that if your professor gives you an ambiguous problem statement, you should be grateful, not critical. Why do you think the author wrote that sentence? Do you agree or disagree? How common do you think ambiguous problems are in business?
6. The number one characteristic in the Ditkoff et al. survey is enthusiasm for the subject of the collaboration. Suppose you are assigned to a collaborative team that has been given a task that you find tedious and boring. Besides resigning yourself to failing in a horrible experience, describe three creative ways you can respond to this challenge. How might this situation differ at work from that at school?
7. Consider the following statement: "All of the literature on team performance indicates that attacks on a team member's personality, appearance, intelligence, or any other personal characteristic does *irreparable* harm to the team." Define the term *irreparable*. If, in a moment of frustration and anger, you tell someone that he or she is stupid, what can you do to repair the damage? What can your teammates do? Suppose in that moment of anger and frustration you have the thought that the person with whom you are conversing is stupid. What can you do that will increase the effectiveness of your team? Keep Hackman's three criteria in mind as you answer. Explain the statement, "The easiest way to solve a problem is not to have it."

CHAPTER EXTENSION 2

Chapter 1 provides the background for this Extension.

Using Collaboration Information Systems

STUDY QUESTIONS

Q1 Why use information systems for collaboration?

Q2 How can you use collaboration systems to improve team communication?

Q3 How can you use collaboration systems to manage content?

Q4 How can you use Microsoft SharePoint for team projects?

Q1 Why Use Information Systems for Collaboration?

Collaboration is critical in business, and numerous software vendors and open-source developers have created computer programs to facilitate various collaborative tasks. Note that they have created *computer programs*, not information systems. If you choose to use one or more of these tools, it will be up to you to create the *information system*, especially the procedure and personnel (training) components.

Why should you do that? Why should your team choose to use a collaboration information system? For one, it will make your life easier. Once you and your team learn how to use the tools, and have developed procedures for using them, teamwork will be easier. You will no longer need to get everyone together face-to-face. You will no longer lose documents; you will be able to determine who is contributing and who is not.

By the way, in some cases you will be applying skills you already possess. If you use multiparty text chat (discussed in Q2, next), you are applying texting skills that you already know. Similarly, you may already know how to participate in a discussion group or read or contribute to a wiki; if so, using a collaboration IS will give you a forum to apply those skills to your group work.

Another reason for using collaboration tools is that you will create better results. Such systems facilitate true collaboration, which, as discussed in Chapter Extension 1, means feedback and iteration. Each team member can produce documents, and others can comment and make revisions to them. Your work can evolve into something much better than you'd originally planned.

Additionally, collaboration skills are highly marketable. Take the example of Microsoft SharePoint. SharePoint is the fastest-growing product in Microsoft history. It reached $1 billion in sales faster than any other Microsoft product. With this success, Microsoft increased its investment in SharePoint and has added features and functions to its latest version, SharePoint 2010. Because many organizations use SharePoint, SharePoint skills are highly marketable.

In this chapter, we will first consider how to use collaboration systems to improve communication. Then we will discuss sharing documents and files with Google Docs and with Windows Live SkyDrive. Finally, we will illustrate how you can use SharePoint for student projects.

Q2 How Can You Use Collaboration Systems to Improve Team Communication?

If you truly are going to *collaborate* on your team projects, if you are going to create work products (such as documents), encourage others to criticize those products, and revise those products, then you will need to communicate. Similarly, if you are going to review others' work, make critical comments, and help them improve their product, then you will also need to communicate. So, improving communication capabilities is key to collaboration success.

Figure CE2-1 summarizes technology available to facilitate communication. **Synchronous communication** occurs when all team members meet at the same time, such as with face-to-face meetings or conference calls. **Asynchronous communication** occurs when team members do not meet at the same time. Employees who work different shifts at the same location or team members who work in different time zones around the world must meet asynchronously.

Most student teams attempt to meet face-to-face, at least at first. Arranging such meetings is always difficult, however, because student schedules and responsibilities differ. If you are going to arrange such meetings, consider creating an online group calendar in which team members post their availability, week by week. Also, use the meeting facilities in Microsoft Outlook to issue invitations and gather RSVPs. If you don't have Outlook, use an Internet site such as Evite (*www.evite.com*) for this purpose. For face-to-face meetings, you will need little other technology beyond standard Office applications such as Word and PowerPoint.

However, given today's communication technology and collaboration applications, most students should forgo face-to-face meetings. They are too difficult to arrange and seldom worth the trouble. Instead, learn to use **virtual meetings** in which participants do not meet in the same place and possibly not at the same time.

If your virtual meeting is synchronous (all meet at the same time), you can use **conference calls**, **Webinars**, or **multiparty text chat**. A Webinar is a virtual meeting in which attendees view on the attendee's computer screens. **WebEx** (*www.webex.com*) is a popular commercial Webinar application used for sales presentations. **SharedView** is a free, downloadable product from Microsoft for sharing a computer screen among several people. Find the current link by searching the Web for "SharedView download."

Some students find it weird to use text chat for school projects, but why not? You can attend meetings wherever you are, silently. Google Text supports multiparty text chat, as does **Microsoft Office SharePoint Workspace** (a thick client application that

Figure CE2-1 Information Technology for Communication

Synchronous		Asynchronous
Shared calendars Invitation and attendance		
Single location	Multiple locations	Single or multiple locations
Office applications such as Word and PowerPoint	Conference calls Webinars Multiparty text chat Microsoft SharePoint Workspaces Videoconferencing	Email Discussion forums Team surveys Windows Live SkyDrive Google Docs Microsoft SharePoint
	Virtual meetings	

Figure CE2-2
User Participating in NetMeeting

Source: Courtesy of Zigy Kaluzny, Getty Images/Getty Images, Inc.

was formerly known as Microsoft Groove). Google or Bing "multiparty text chat" to find other, similar products.

If everyone on your team has a camera on his or her computer, you can also do **videoconferencing**, like that shown in Figure CE2-2. Google Talk supports video conversations, as does Microsoft NetMeeting. You can find many such applications on the Internet. Videoconferencing is more intrusive than text chat; you have to comb your hair, but it does have a more personal touch. Sometime during your student career you should use it to see what you think.

In some (most?) classes and situations, synchronous meetings, even virtual ones, are impossible to arrange. You just cannot get everyone together at the same time. In this circumstance, when the team must meet asynchronously, most students try to communicate via **email**. The problem with email is that there is too much freedom. Not everyone will participate, because it is easy to hide from email. Discussion threads become disorganized and disconnected. After the fact, it is difficult to find particular emails, comments, or attachments.

Discussion forums are an alternative. Here, one group member posts an entry, perhaps an idea, a comment, or a question, and other group members respond. Figure CE2-3 shows an example. Such forums are better than email because it is harder for the discussion to get off track. Still, however, it remains easy for some team members not to participate.

Team surveys are another form of communication technology. With these, one team member creates a list of questions and other team members respond. Surveys are an effective way to obtain team opinions; they are generally easy to complete, so most team members will participate. Also, it is easy to determine who has not yet responded. Figure CE2-4 shows the results of one team survey. Confirmit (*www.confirmit.com*) is one common survey application program. You can find others on the Internet. Microsoft SharePoint has a built-in survey capability, as you'll see in Q4. Other products shown in the last column of Figure 2-1 will be discussed later in this chapter extension.

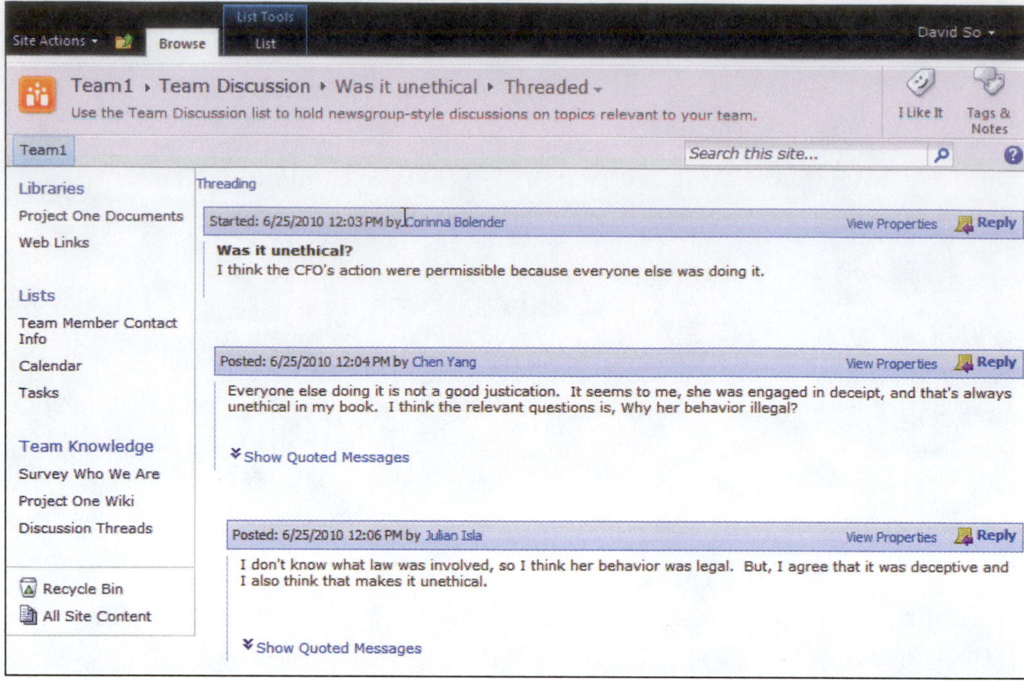

Figure CE2-3 Example of a Discussion Forum

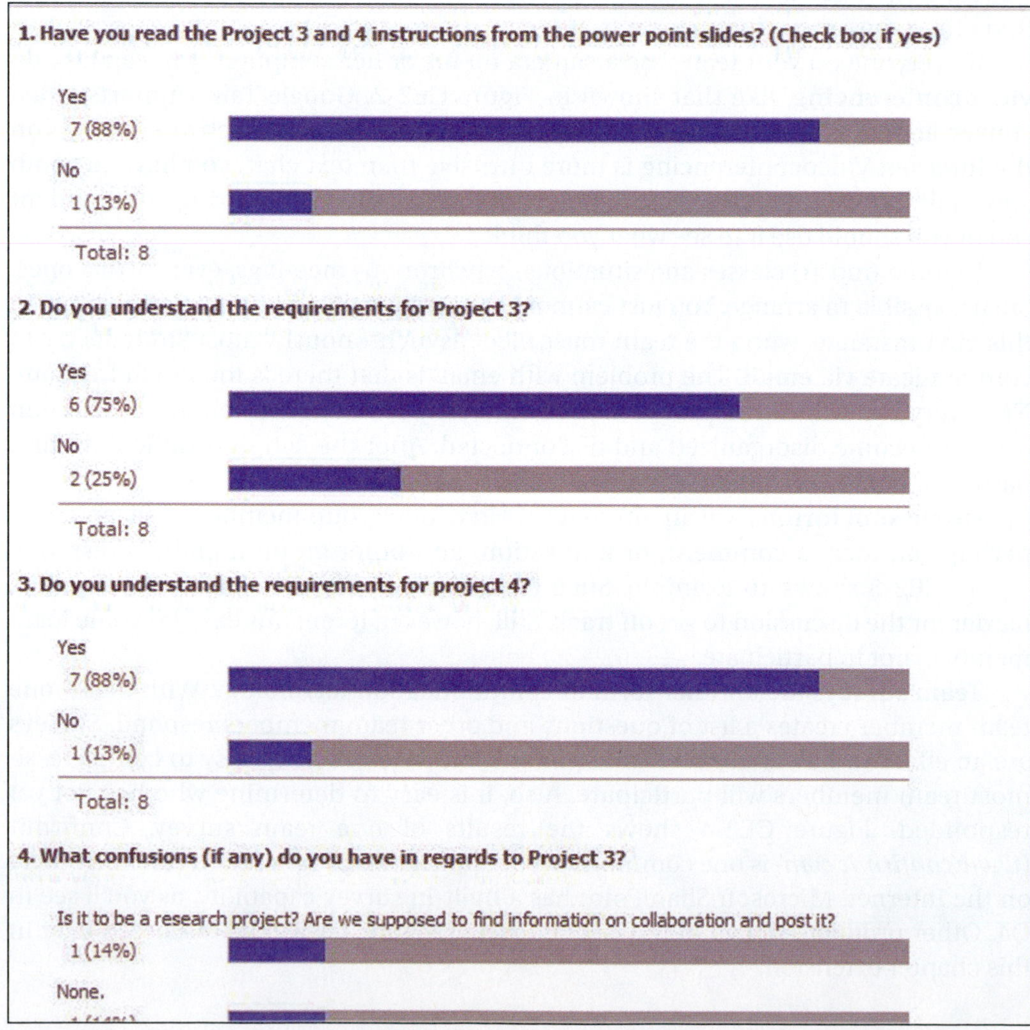

Figure CE2-4 Portion of a Sample Team Survey

Q3 How Can You Use Collaboration Systems to Manage Content?

Every collaborative project involves the sharing of content. At school, you and your teammates will need to share documents, illustrations, spreadsheets, and other data. The products you use for sharing content depend on the degree of control that you want. Figure CE2-5 lists three categories of content management control: no control, version tracking, and version management. Consider each.

Shared Content with No Control

The most primitive way to share content is via email attachments. It is easy to share content this way, but email attachments have numerous problems. For one, there is always the danger that someone does not receive an email, does not notice it in his or her inbox, or does not bother to save the attachments. Then, too, if three users obtain the same document as an email attachment, each user changes it, and each sends back the changed documents via email, different, incompatible versions of that document will be floating around. So, although email is simple, easy, and readily available, it will not suffice for collaborations in which there are many document versions or for which there is a desire for content control.

Another way to share content is to place it on a file server. As you learned in Chapter 4, a server is a computer that provides a service, in this case, content storage. If your team has access to a file server, you can put documents on the server and others can download them, make changes, and upload them back onto the server. **FTP** often is used to get and place documents (discussed in Chapter 6).

Storing documents on servers is better than using email attachments because documents have a single storage location. They are not scattered in different team members' email boxes. Team members have a known location for finding documents.

However, without any additional control it is possible for team members to interfere with one another's work. For example, suppose team members A and B download a document and edit it, but without knowing about the other's edits. Person A stores his version back on the server and then person B stores her version back on the server. In this scenario, person A's changes will be lost.

Furthermore, without any version management it will be impossible to know who changed the document and when. Neither person A nor person B will know whose version of the document is on the server. To avoid such problems, some form of version management is recommended.

Shared Content with Version Management

Systems that provide **version management** track changes to documents and provide features and functions to accommodate concurrent work. The means by which this is

Figure CE2-5
Information Technology for Sharing Content

Alternatives for Sharing Content		
No Control	Version Management	Version Control
Email with attachments Shared files on a server	Wikis Google Docs Windows Live SkyDrive	Microsoft SharePoint

Increasing degree of content control

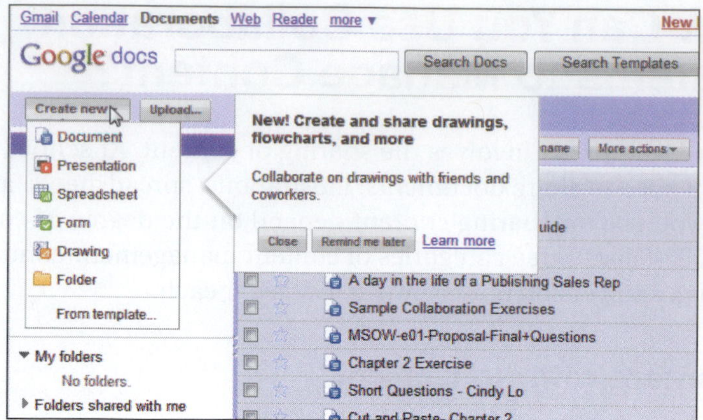

Figure CE2-6
Types of Google Docs

Source: Google Docs & Spreadsheets™. Google is a trademark of Google Inc.

done depends on the particular system used. In this section, we consider two free and readily available tools: Google Docs and Windows Live SkyDrive.

Google Docs

Google Docs is a free thin-client application for sharing documents, spreadsheets, presentations, drawings, and other types of data, as shown in Figure CE2-6. (Google Docs is evolving; by the time you read this, Google may have added additional file types or changed the system from what is described here. Google the name "Google Docs" to obtain the latest information about it.)

With Google Docs, anyone who edits a document must have a Google account, which is not the same as a Gmail account. You can establish a Google account using an email address from Hotmail, a university, or any other email service. Your Google account will be affiliated with whatever email account you enter.

To create a Google document, go to *http://docs.google.com* (note that there is no *www* in this address). Sign in with (or create) your Google account. From that point on, you can create, upload, process, save, and download documents. You can also save most of those documents to PDF and Microsoft Office formats, such as Word, Excel, and PowerPoint.

With Google Docs, you can make documents available to others by entering their email addresses or Google accounts. Those users are notified that the document exists and are given a link by which they can access it. If they have a Google account, they can edit the document; otherwise they can just view the document.

Documents are stored on a Google server. Users can access the documents from Google and simultaneously see and edit documents. In the background, Google merges the users' activities into a single document. You are notified that another user is editing a document at the same time as you are, and you can refresh the document to see their latest changes. Google tracks document revisions, with brief summaries of changes made. Figure CE2-7 shows a sample revision for a sample document that has been shared among three users.

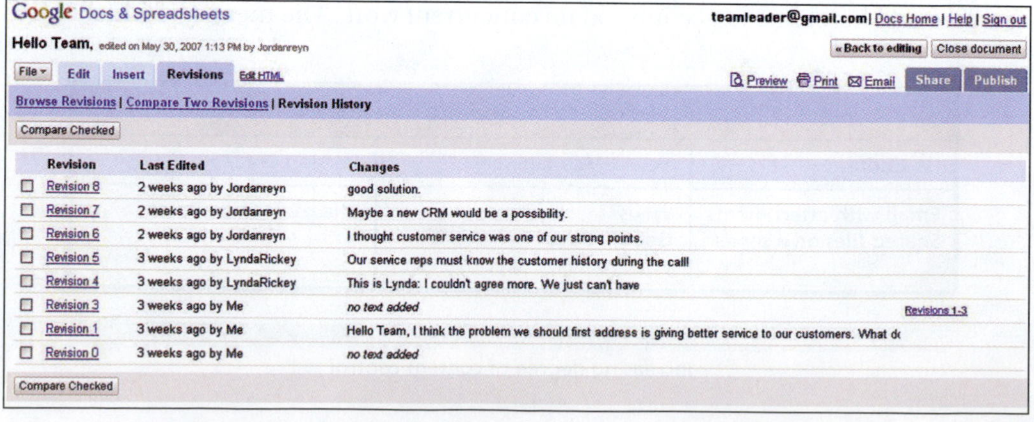

Figure CE2-7
Sample Google Docs & Spreadsheet Document Version

Source: Google Docs & Spreadsheets™. Google is a trademark of Google Inc.

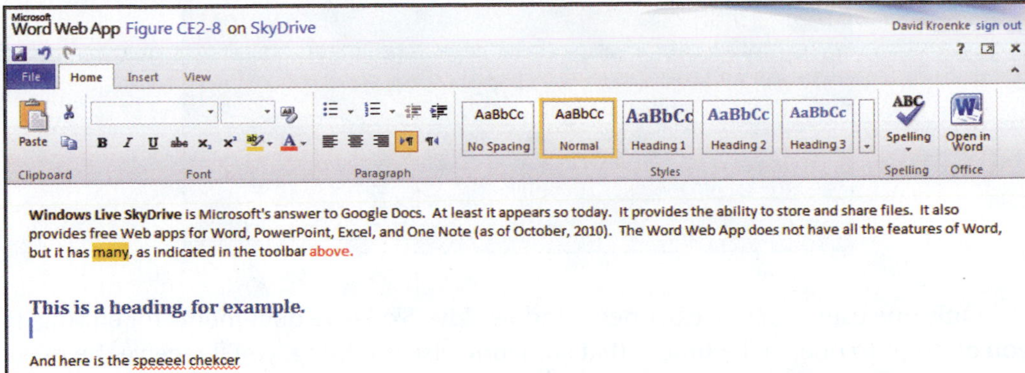

Figure CE2-8
Example Use of Word Web App

Windows Live SkyDrive

Windows Live SkyDrive is Microsoft's answer to Google Docs. It provides the ability to store and share Office documents and other files and offers free storage of up to 25 GB. Additionally, Windows Live SkyDrive includes license-free Web application versions of Word, Excel, PowerPoint, and OneNote, called **Office Web Apps**. These applications run in the browser and are quite easy to use. Figure CE2-8 shows an instance of the Word Web App. These programs have less functionality than desktop Office programs, but they are free and readily accessed on the Web.

In addition to Office Web Apps, the desktop Office 2010 applications are tightly integrated with Windows Live SkyDrive. You can open and save documents directly from and to SkyDrive from inside Microsoft Office products, as shown in Figure CE2-9.

To set up a Windows Live SkyDrive, you need a Windows Live ID. If you have either a Hotmail or MSN email account, that account is your Windows Live ID. If you do not have a Hotmail or MSN email account, you can create a Windows Live ID with some other email account, or you can create a new Hotmail account, which is free.

Once you have a Windows Live ID, go to *www.skydrive.com* and sign in. You will be given 25GB of storage. You can create file folders and files and use either Office or Web Apps as well.

Like Google accounts, you can share folders with others by entering their Office Live IDs or their email accounts. Users who have an Office Live ID can view and edit documents; users who do not have an Office Live ID can only view documents.

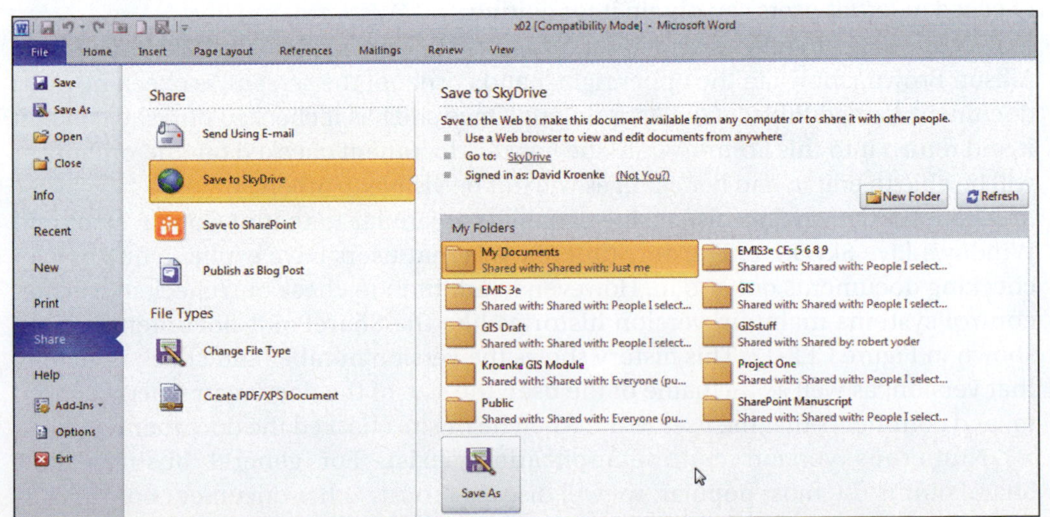

Figure CE2-9
Saving a Word 2010 Document to a SkyDrive Account

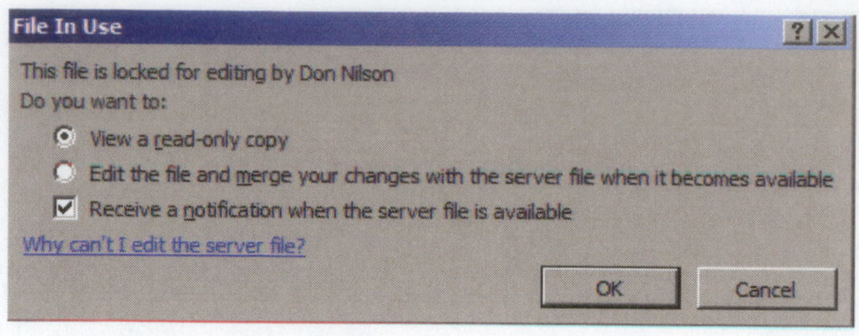

Figure CE2-10
SkyDrive Options When Opening a Document Locked by Another User

Only one user at a time can open Windows Live SkyDrive documents for editing. If you attempt to open a document that someone else is editing, you'll receive the message shown in Figure CE2-10.

As shown, you can open the document in read-only mode, you can have your changes merged with the document when it is available, or you can simply be notified when the document is available.

Microsoft has developed a Facebook application for processing Windows Live SkyDrive documents. That application, called Docs (not to be confused with Google Docs), works just as described here, it has just been given the look and feel of a Facebook application.

Both Google Docs and Windows Live SkyDrive are free and very easy to use. They are both far superior to exchanging documents via email or via a file server. If you are not using one of these two products, you should. Go to *http://docs.google.com* and *www.skydrive.com* and check them out. You'll find easy-to-understand demos if you need additional instruction.

Shared Content with Version Control

Version management systems improve the tracking of shared content and potentially eliminate problems caused by concurrent document access. They do not, however, provide **version control**. They do not limit the actions that can be taken by any particular user, and they do not give control over the changes to documents to particular users.

With version control systems, each team member is given an account with a set of permissions. Shared documents are placed into shared directories, sometimes called **libraries**. For example, on a shared site with four libraries, a particular user might be given read-only permission for library 1; read and edit permission for library 2; read, edit, and delete permission for library 3; and no permission even to see library 4.

Furthermore, document directories can be set up so that users are required to check out documents before they can modify them. When a document is checked out, no other user can obtain it for the purpose of editing it. Once the document has been checked in, other users can obtain it for editing.

Figure CE2-11 shows a screen for a user of Microsoft SharePoint 2010. The user, Allison Brown (shown in the upper right-hand corner of the screen), is checking out a document named Project One Assignment. Once she has it checked out, she can edit it and return it to this library. While she has the document checked out, no other user will be able to edit it, and her changes will not be visible to others.

As described so far, this locking capability is similar to that of Google Docs and Windows Live SkyDrive. The only difference is that users have explicit control over checking documents out and in. However, in addition to check out/check in, version control systems maintain version histories like the SharePoint document history shown in Figure CE2-12. This history shows the version number and check-in date of that version, as well as the name of the user, the size of the document when checked in, and comments that the user wrote when he or she checked the document in.

Numerous version control applications exist. For general business use, SharePoint is the most popular; we will discuss it next. Other document control systems include MasterControl (*www.mastercontrol.com*) and Document Locator

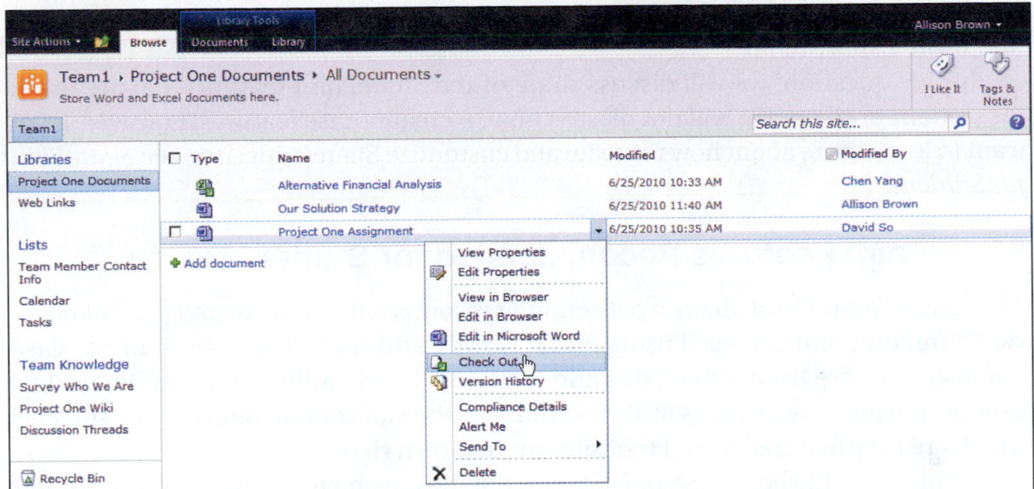

Figure CE2-11
Checking Out a Document

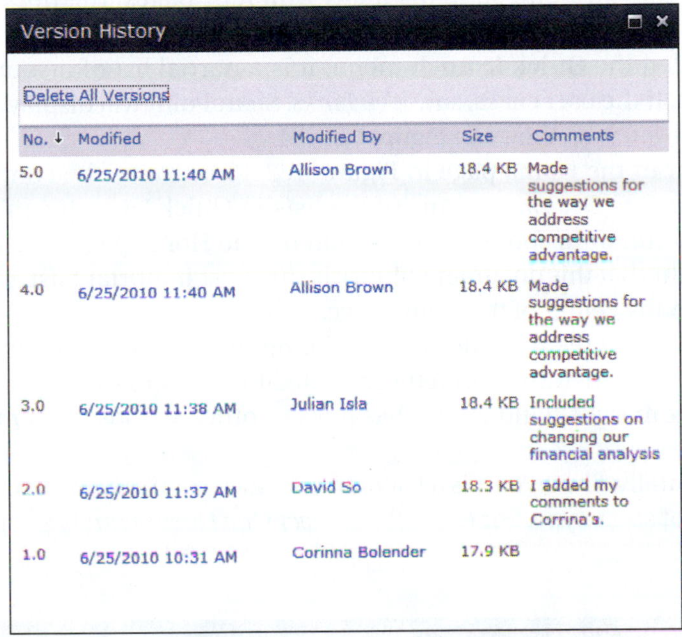

Figure CE2-12
Document Version History

(*www.documentlocator.com*). Software development teams use applications such as CVS (*www.nongnu.org/cvs*) or Subversion (*http://subversion.tigris.org*) to control versions of software code, test plans, and product documentation.

Q4 How Can You Use Microsoft SharePoint for Student Team Projects?

Microsoft SharePoint is a comprehensive platform for creating, operating, and administrating Web sites. It is most widely known as a platform for creating and managing collaboration sites, and we will consider it in the collaboration context here. However, SharePoint can also be used as the backbone of more general purpose Web sites. For example, the site *www.kiwiexperience.com* is based on SharePoint.

With a few basic skills, it is quite easy to create a SharePoint collaboration site and to set it up for use on student projects. That site can then be customized using SharePoint tools in your browser. For additional customization, you can use **Microsoft Office SharePoint Designer**, a tool specifically designed to tailor the look and feel of

SharePoint sites. For even greater customization and control, developers can use Microsoft Visual Studio.

In this question, we will discuss some of the SharePoint features that are useful for student projects. We will not discuss how to create those features, however. If you want to learn more about how to create and customize SharePoint sites, see *SharePoint for Students*.[1]

SharePoint Features Recommended for Student Teams

To begin, a **SharePoint site** is a collection of resources that are created and managed via SharePoint and accessed using HTTP, HTML, and related protocols. In our case, the resources are used for collaboration, but, as noted earlier, they can be used for general-purpose Web sites as well. A SharePoint site can contain one or more subsites, which are fully featured SharePoint sites in their own right.

Figure CE2-13 shows a SharePoint site that has been created for use by a student team. The name of the site is *Team 1*, as you can tell from the upper left-hand corner of the figure. The Team 1 site contains many different pages; the notation Team 1 ▶ Home means this figure is showing the Home page of the Team 1 site. The left-hand column is called the **Quick Launch** menu; it is a partial list of resources contained within the site. If the user clicks, say, *Web Links*, SharePoint will display a list of links to additional Web sites, as shown in Figure CE2-14.

The center of the Home page in Figure CE2-13 contains the contents of the list named *Project One Documents*. Any of the lists in Quick Launch could be shown in this same position or in some other position on the Home page. The team that uses this site thought that this document library is the most important list, so they chose to place it here in the center of the Home page.

In most cases, a team would replace the picture of the flower with a picture of team members or a picture of something related to the team's assignment. Finally, the list in the bottom right-hand corner has links to other actions team members might take on this site.

Fundamentally, SharePoint is a list manager. Each of the items in Quick Launch is a list of items of some type. For example, *Project One Documents* is a list of documents

Figure CE2-13
Example Student Team Site

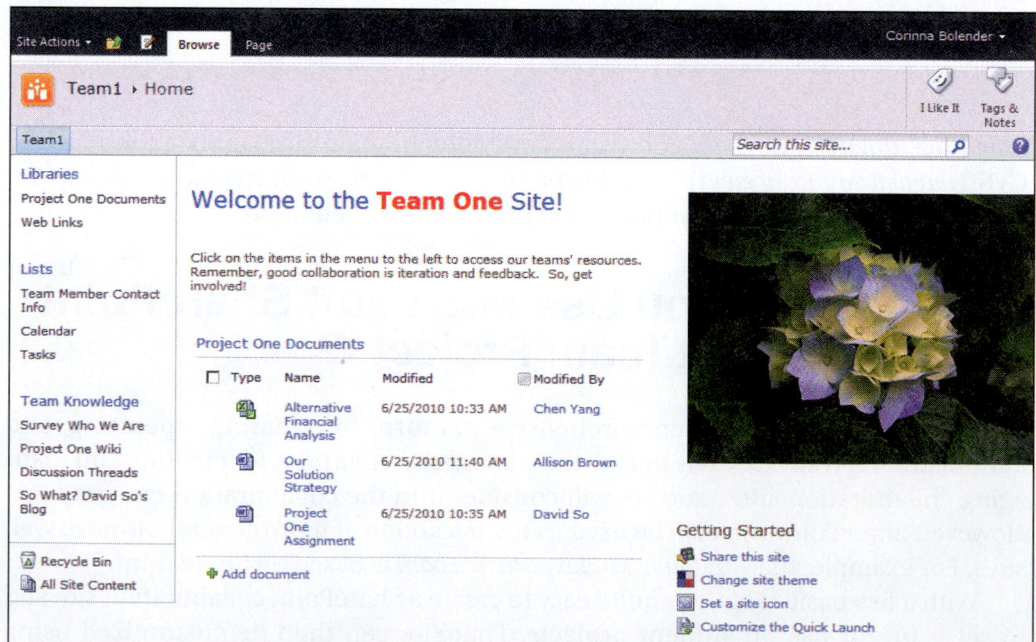

1. Steve Fox, Carey Cole, and David Kroenke, *SharePoint for Students* (Upper Saddle River, NJ: Pearson Education, 2012).

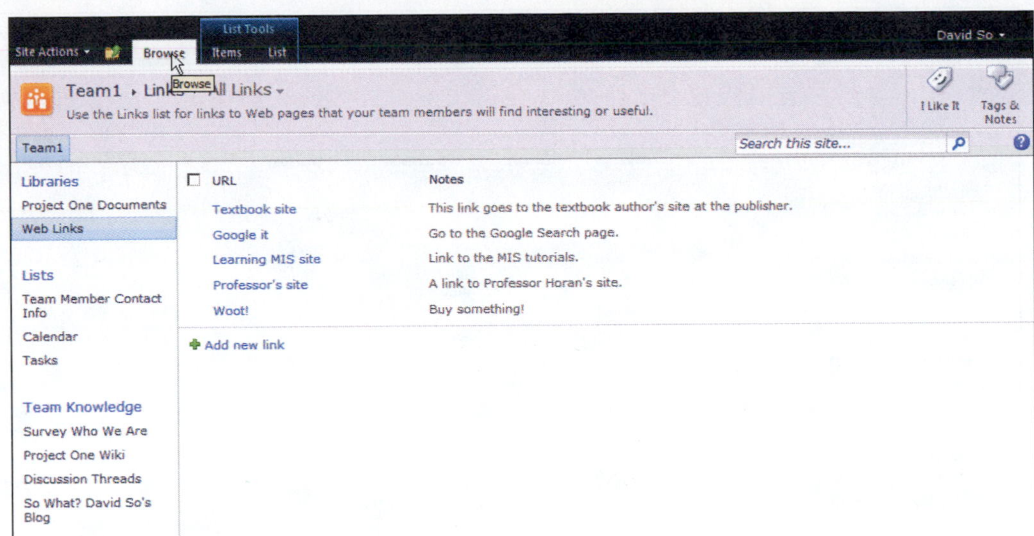

Figure CE2-14
Example Web Links Library

for team members to share. *Web Links* is a list of Web links, as shown in Figure CE2-14. *Team Member Contact Info* is a list of team members, their email addresses, phone numbers, and so forth. *Calendar* is a list of events shown in a calendar; *Tasks* is a list of team tasks, and so forth.

The actions that can be taken on the elements in a list depend on the list type. *Project One Documents* is a document list; the actions available for documents are shown in Figure CE2-15. If the user clicks *View in Browser* or *Edit in Browser*, SharePoint will open the document in the Microsoft Word Web App (discussed under Windows Live SkyDrive). Other options include checking out and checking in, producing a version history, and other options, including *Delete*.

One option is particularly useful for team work. If you click *Alert Me*, SharePoint will send you an email any time anyone changes the document. This is particularly useful for lists that have the latest-breaking news, such as an announcement list (not shown here).

Figure CE2-16 shows a calendar list. An event has already been scheduled for November 10, and the user is in the process of adding a new event on November 8. You can change the calendar to different formats such as weekly and daily as well.

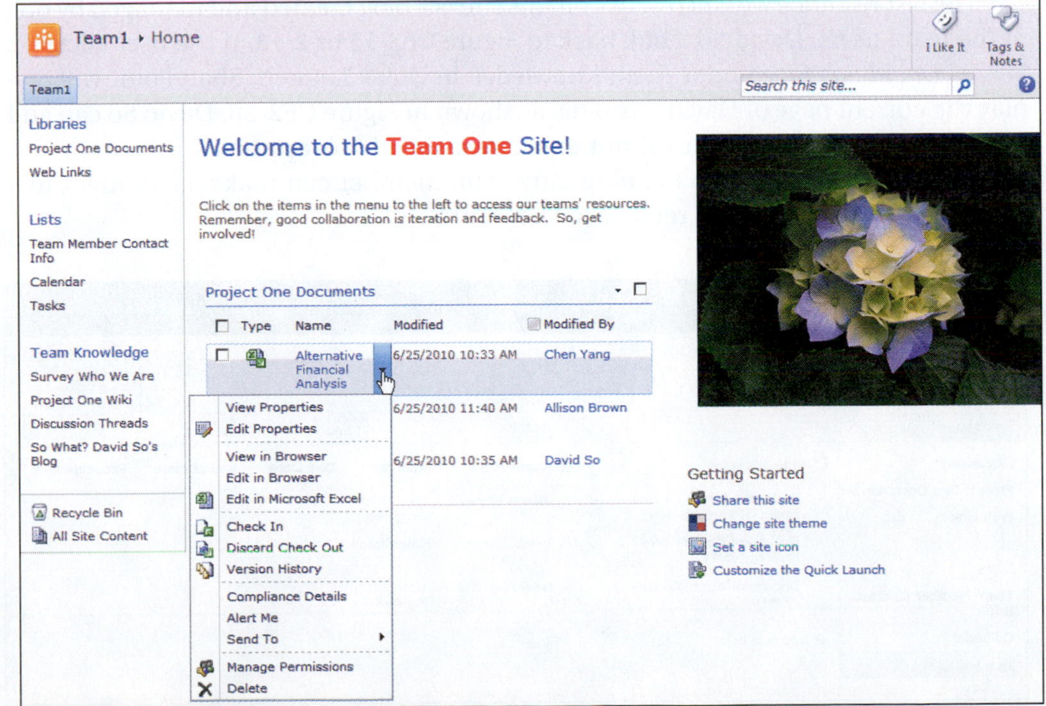

Figure CE2-15
Document Actions

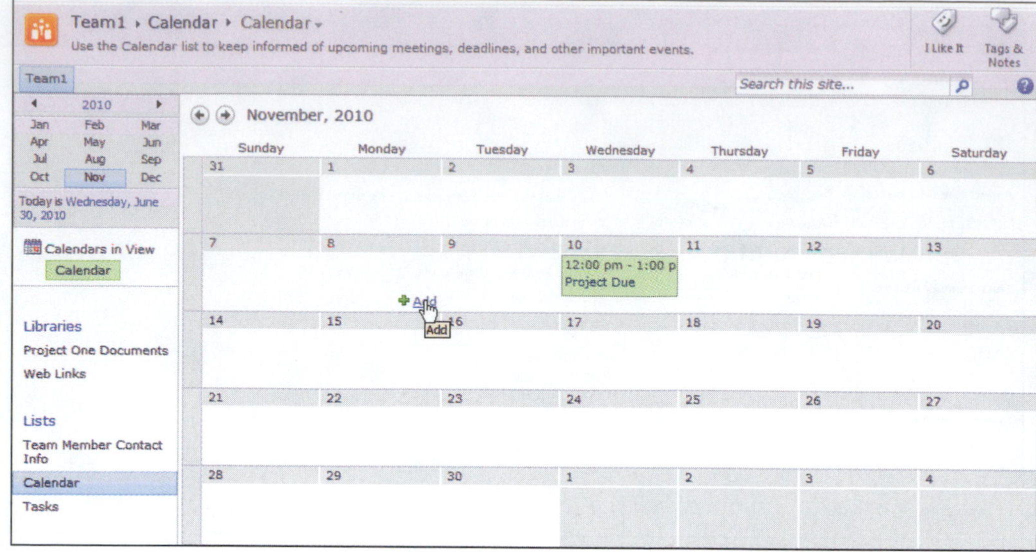

Figure CE2-16
SharePoint Team Calendar

SharePoint provides a special type of list called a task list. Figure CE2-17 shows an example task list with three tasks. Notice that the task is assigned to a particular person and that each task has Status, Due Date, and % Complete metadata. If the task has predecessor tasks that must be completed before that task, those predecessors can also be added to the task list. SharePoint can produce a Gantt diagram of tasks, if desired (not shown).

SharePoint surveys are easy to use. Figure CE2-18 shows a page for completing an example survey. Creating a survey is also quite simple, but it involves multiple steps that are beyond the scope of this discussion. See *SharePoint for Students* to learn how.

Teams can readily create Wiki libraries using SharePoint. Figure CE2-19 shows the top-level page called *Project One Wiki.* By default, team members easily change the text on each page, but SharePoint permissions can be set to allow only certain members to edit entries, if desired. Note in this figure that Project 1 and Project 1 Grade are links to other Wiki pages, as are the three phrases at the bottom of this figure. The links Project 2 and Project 3 have been entered into this page, but underlining of the link names indicates that those pages have not yet been created.

The last resource we will discuss on this site is a blog created and managed by one of the team users, David So. Look back to Figure CE2-15 or 2-13. If the user clicks *So What? David So's Blog* under Team Knowledge in Quick Launch, SharePoint will display the current page of David So's blog, as shown in Figure CE2-20. David So can add entries. Team members can submit entries for David So's approval. If he approves them, they will be added to the blog. Any team member can make a comment to a blog entry, but David So can remove it if he wants.

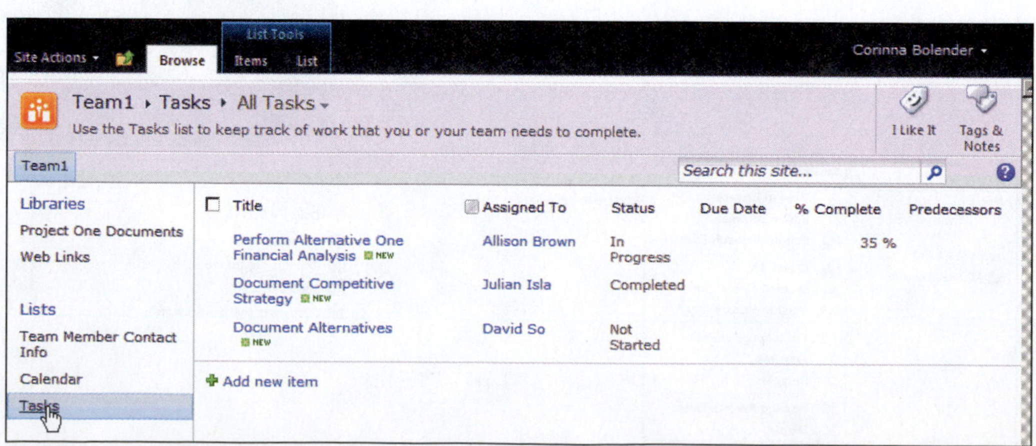

Figure CE2-17
SharePoint Task List

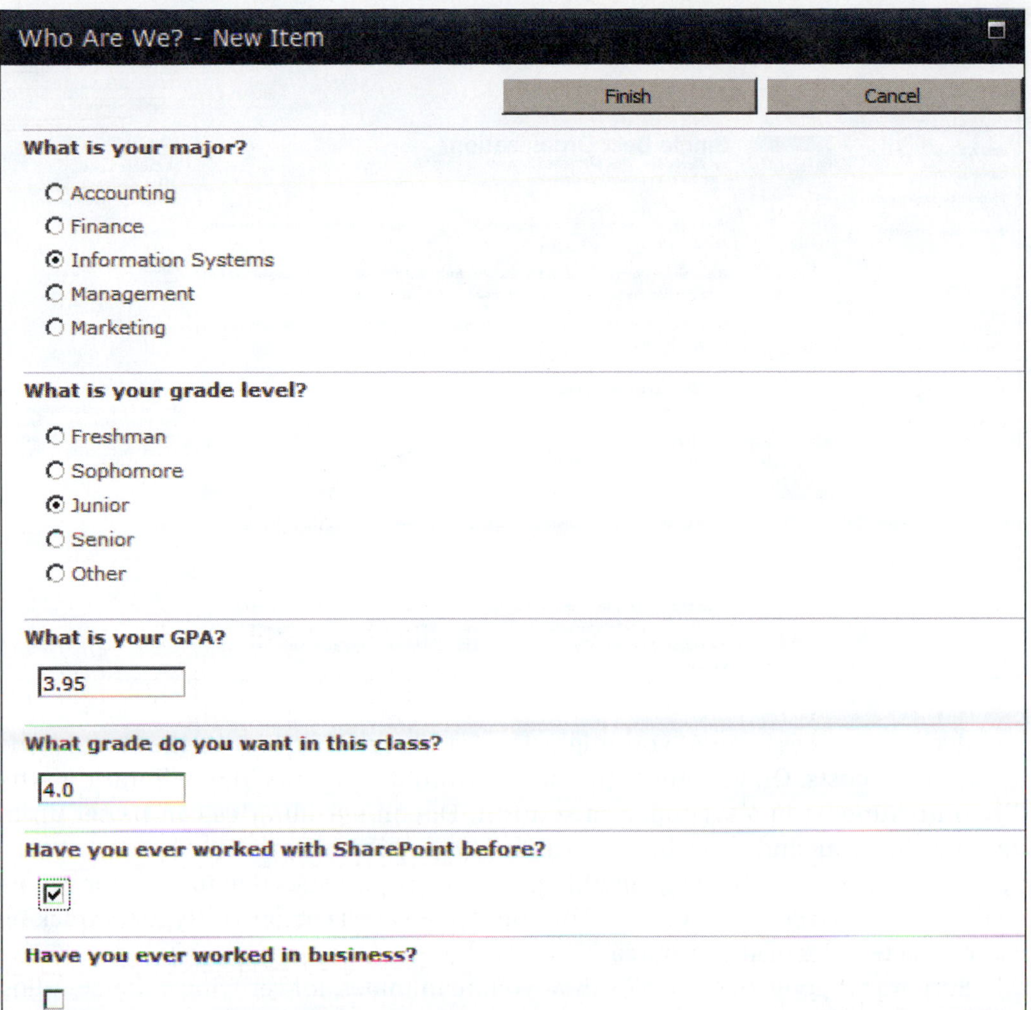

Figure CE2-18
Taking a SharePoint Survey

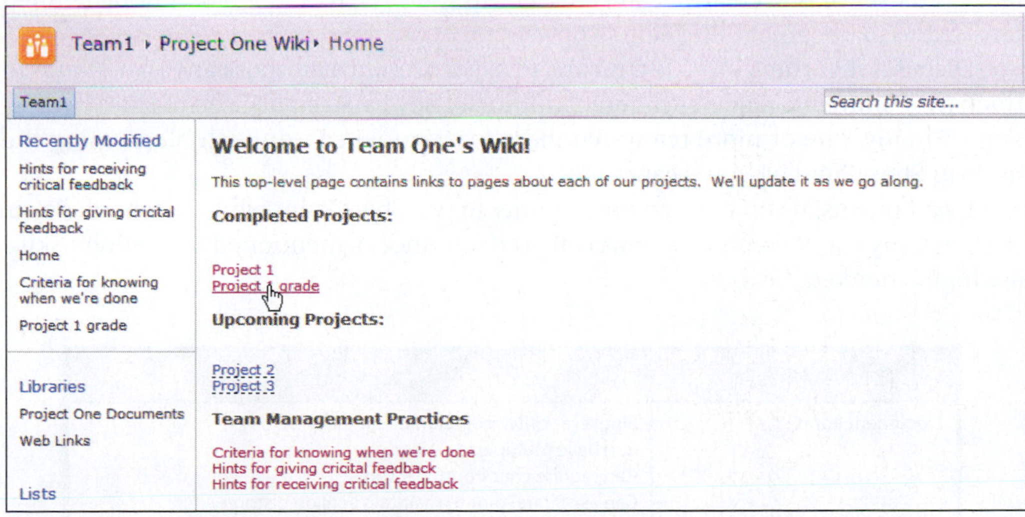

Figure CE2-19
Example SharePoint Wiki Page

What Are Recommended Uses for Particular SharePoint Tools?

SharePoint provides many different tools for teams to use. To decide which might be appropriate for you, consider Figure CE2-21, which lists common SharePoint collaboration tools and recommends potential applications for them.

Document libraries serve as a repository for team documents. You might have different libraries for different aspects of the project. For example, if your project

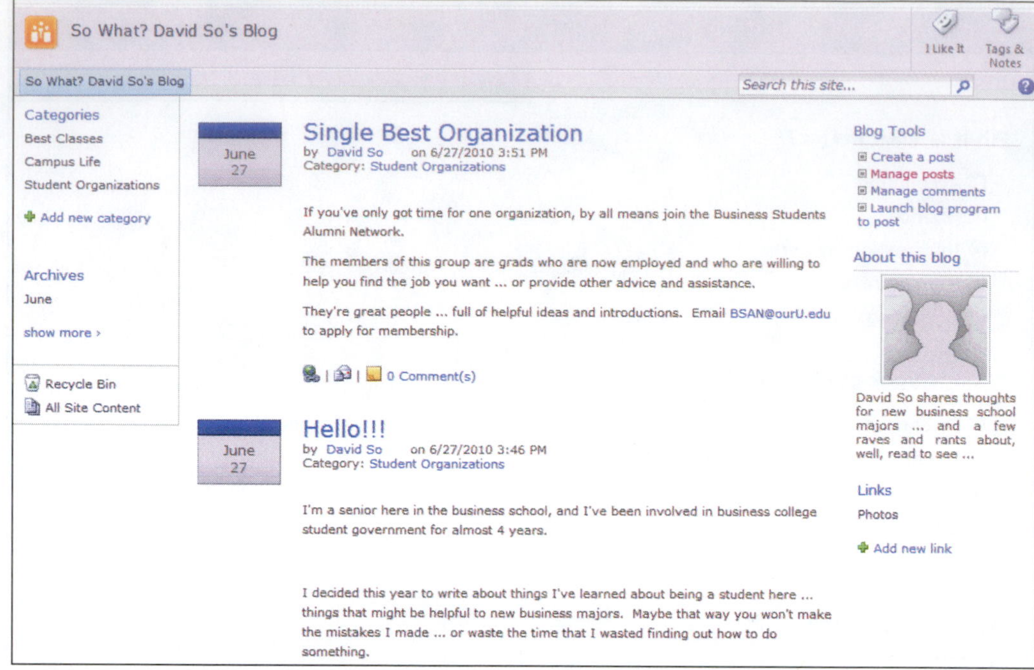

Figure CE2-20
Example SharePoint Blog

involves cost assessments, you might have a library that has all the documents concerning costs. Or, you might put all the Word documents in one library, all the Excel documents in a second, and so forth. Document libraries can be set up to require check out and check in as well as to have version histories.

Lists are good for tracking anything. SharePoint provides default lists for events (calendar lists), tasks, and contacts. You can also create a custom list type for tracking the characteristics of any resource.

Surveys are good for getting to know your teammates, for verifying understanding of project goals and other topics, and for deciding when to wrap up the project. The team can use wikis to create a team glossary, to show the relationships among defined terms, and to document the team's knowledge.

Discussion forums provide a means to asynchronously discuss any issue—and to track the comments made by different authors. They can also be used to share knowledge. Finally, one or more team members (or groups) can publish blogs using the built-in SharePoint blogging capability.

By all means, if you have an opportunity to use SharePoint while in school, do so. It is an easily learned and very powerful product. And, as mentioned, SharePoint skills are highly marketable today.

Figure CE2-21
Potential Uses of SharePoint Features

SharePoint Feature	Use
Document library	Single repository of team documents Can have multiple libraries Can require check out/check in Can ask SharePoint to maintain version history
Lists	Track events, tasks, contacts Create a general-purpose list for tracking any resource
Survey	Introduce team members Verify understanding of goals and other topics Wrap up project
Wiki	Share and document team knowledge
Discussion forums	Discuss one or more topics
Blog	Publish opinions and get feedback on them

ACTIVE REVIEW

Use this Active Review to verify that you understand the material in the chapter extension. You can read the entire chapter extension and then perform the tasks in this review, or you can read the text material for just one question and perform the tasks in this review for that question before moving on to the next one.

Q1 Why use information systems for collaboration?

Explain the difference between a collaboration program and a collaboration information system. Summarize the reasons that your team might want to use a collaboration system for its work. Explain how you can use skills you already possess, and give an example of how knowledge of one collaboration tool can give you a competitive advantage.

Q2 How can you use collaboration systems to improve team communication?

Explain why communication is important to student collaborations. Define *synchronous* and *asynchronous communication*, and explain when each is used. Name two collaboration tools that can be used to help set up synchronous meetings. Describe collaboration tools that can be used for face-to-face meetings. Describe tools that can be used for virtual, synchronous meetings. Describe tools that can be used for virtual, asynchronous meetings. Compare and contrast the advantages of email, discussion forums, and team surveys.

Q3 How can you use collaboration systems to manage content?

Describe three categories of document sharing control. Explain one potential use for each. Summarize the problems of using email and file servers to share content. Describe the types of documents you can share when using Google Docs. Explain what you need to do to obtain access to Google Docs and what you need to do to be able to edit Google Docs. Summarize how Office documents can be created from Google Docs.

Describe the types of documents you can share when using Windows Live SkyDrive. Explain the purpose and functionality of Office Web Apps. Describe how desktop Office programs are tightly integrated with SharePoint. Summarize what you need to do to obtain access to a Windows Live SkyDrive and what you need to do to be able to edit documents on SkyDrive. Explain what Microsoft Docs is. Summarize version control and explain the role of document check out and check in.

Q4 How can you use Microsoft SharePoint for student team projects?

Describe SharePoint, and explain its broader role as well as the role discussed here. Summarize three ways of customizing a SharePoint site. Define *SharePoint site*, and explain what a subsite is. Explain the role of Quick Launch. Describe what happens when the user clicks each of the items in the Quick Launch menu shown in Figure CE2-13. Summarize the features, functions, and roles for SharePoint: document libraries, Web link libraries, contact, calendar, and task lists, surveys, wikis, discussion boards, and blogs.

KEY TERMS AND CONCEPTS

USING YOUR KNOWLEDGE

1. This exercise requires you to experiment with Google Docs. You will need two Google accounts to complete this exercise. If you have two different email addresses, then set up two Google accounts using those addresses. Otherwise, use your school email address and set up a Google Gmail account. A Gmail account will automatically give you a Google account.
   a. In the memo, explain the role of communication in collaboration. Go to *http://docs.google.com* and sign in with one of your Google accounts. Upload your memo using Google Docs. Save your uploaded document and share it with the email in your second Google account. Sign out of your first Google account.

      (If you have access to two computers situated close to each other, use both of them for this exercise. You will see more of the Google Docs functionality by using two computers. If you have two computers, do not sign out of your Google account. Perform step b and all actions for the second account on that second computer. If you are using two computers, ignore the instructions in the following steps to sign out of the Google accounts.)
   b. Open a new window in your browser. Access *http://docs.google.com* from that second window and sign in using your second Google account. Open the document that you shared in step a.
   c. Change the memo by adding a brief description of the need to manage the content in many collaboration projects. Save the document from your second account. If you are using just one computer, sign out from your second account.
   d. Sign in on your first account. Open the most recent version of the memo and add a description of the role of version histories. Save the document. (If you are using two computers, notice how Google warns you that another user is editing the document at the same time. Click *Refresh* to see what happens.) If you are using just one computer, sign out from your first account.
   e. Sign in on your second account. Re-open the shared document. From the File menu, save the document as a Word document. Describe how Google processed the changes to your document.
2. This exercise requires you to experiment with Windows Live SkyDrive. You will need two Office Live IDs to complete this exercise. The easiest way to do it is to work with a classmate. If that is not possible, set up two OfficeLive accounts, using two different Hotmail addresses.
   a. Go to *www.skydrive.com* and sign in with one of your accounts. Create a memo about collaboration tools using the Word Web App. Save your memo. Share your document with the email in your second Office Live account. Sign out of your first account.

      (If you have access to two computers situated close to each other, use both of them for this exercise. If you have two computers, do not sign out of your Office Live account. Perform step b and all actions for the second account on that second computer. If you are using two computers, ignore the instructions in the following steps to sign out of the Office Live accounts.)
   b. Open a new window in your browser. Access *www.skydrive.com* from that second window and sign in using your second Office Live account. Open the document that you shared in step a.
   c. Change the memo by adding a brief description of content management. Do not save the document yet. If you are using just one computer, sign out from your second account.
   d. Sign in on your first account. Attempt to open the memo and note what occurs. Sign out of your first account and sign back in with your second account. Save the document. Now, sign out of your second account and sign back in with the first account. Now attempt to open the memo. (If you are using two computers, perform these same actions on the two different computers.)
   e. Sign in on your second account. Re-open the shared document. From the File menu, save the document as a Word document. Describe how Google processed the changes to your document.
3. Repeat exercise 2, but use Facebook Docs rather than Windows Live SkyDrive.
4. If your instructor has enabled a Microsoft SharePoint site for your class, you can perform exercises using SharePoint. Go to *www.pearsonhighered.com/kroenke* and find the file *Chapter 2 SharePoint Exercise.* Perform the exercises shown there.
5. Reflect on your experience working on teams in previous classes as well as on collaborative teams in other settings, such as a campus committee. To what extent was your team collaborative? Did it involve feedback and iteration? If so, how? How did you use collaborative information systems, if at all? If you did not use collaborative information systems, describe how you think such systems might have improved your work methods and results. If you did use collaborative information systems, explain how you could improve on that use, given the knowledge you have gained from this chapter extension.

CHAPTER EXTENSION 3

STUDY QUESTIONS

Chapter 2 provides the background for this Extension.

Q1 How do decisions vary by level?

Q2 What is the difference between structured and unstructured decisions?

Q3 How do decision level and decision process relate?

Q4 What is the difference between automation and augmentation?

Q5 How does IS support decision steps?

Information Systems and Decision Making

Chapters 2 and 3 described how information systems support business processes and how organizations use such systems to implement organizational strategy. This chapter extension presents a third perspective: how information systems support decision making.

Decision making in organizations is varied and complex, and so before discussing the role of information systems in support of decision making we need to investigate the characteristics and dimensions of decision making itself.

Q1 How Do Decisions Vary by Level?

As shown in Figure CE3-1, in organizations decisions occur at three levels: *operational, managerial,* and *strategic*. The types of decisions vary depending on the level. **Operational decisions** concern day-to-day activities. Typical operational decisions are: How many widgets should we order from vendor A? Should we extend credit to vendor B? Which invoices should we pay today? Information systems that support operational decision making are called **transaction processing systems (TPS)**.

Managerial decisions concern the allocation and utilization of resources. Typical managerial decisions are: How much should we budget for computer hardware and programs for department A next year? How many engineers should we assign to project B? How many square feet of warehouse space do we need for the coming year? Information systems that support managerial decision making are called **management information systems (MIS)**. (Notice that the term *MIS* can be used in two ways: broadly, to mean the subjects in this entire book, and narrowly, to mean information systems that support managerial-level decision making. Context will make the meaning of the term clear.)

Strategic decisions concern broader-scope, organizational issues. Typical decisions at the strategic level are: Should we start a new product line? Should we open a

- Decision Level
  - Operational
  - Managerial
  - Strategic
- Decision Process
  - Structured
  - Unstructured

Figure CE3-1
Decision-Making Dimensions

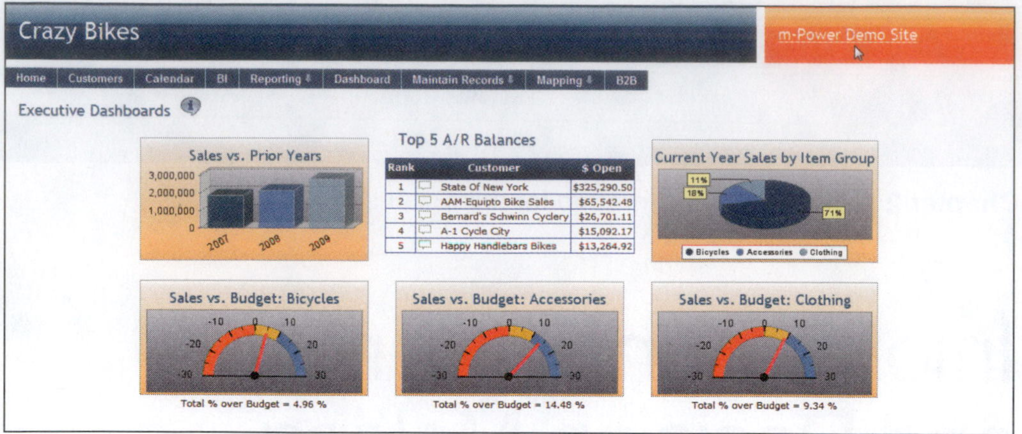

Figure CE3-2
An Example of an Executive Information System (EIS)

centralized warehouse in Tennessee? Should we acquire company A? Information systems that support strategic decision making are called **executive information systems (EIS)**. A hypothetical example is shown in Figure CE3-2.

Notice that, in general, the decision time frame increases as we move from operational to managerial to strategic decisions. Operational decisions normally involve actions in the short term: What should we do today or this week? Managerial decisions involve longer time frames: What is appropriate for the next quarter or year? Strategic decisions involve the long term; their consequences are not realized for years.

Q2 What Is the Difference Between Structured and Unstructured Decisions?

Figure CE3-3 shows levels of information systems with two decision processes: *structured* and *unstructured*. These terms refer to the method by which the decision is to be made, not to the nature of the underlying problem. A **structured decision** is one for which there is an understood and accepted method for making the decision. A formula for computing the reorder quantity of an item in inventory is an example of a structured decision process. A standard method for allocating furniture and equipment to employees is another structured decision process.

An **unstructured decision** process is one for which there is no agreed-on decision-making method. Predicting the future direction of the economy or the stock market is a famous example. The prediction method varies from person to person; it is neither standardized nor broadly accepted. (As one wit put it, "If you laid all the

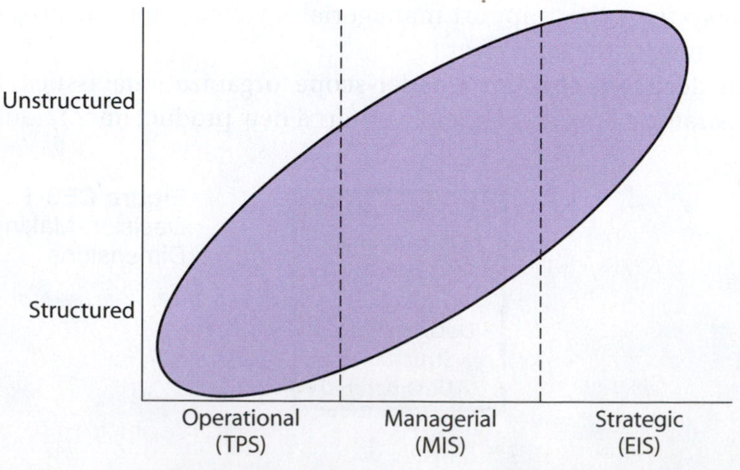

Figure CE3-3
Relationship of Decision Level and Decision Process

economists in the world end to end, they still would not reach a conclusion.") Another example of an unstructured decision process is assessing how well suited an employee is for performing a particular job. Managers vary in the manner in which they make such assessments.

Again, keep in mind that the terms *structured* and *unstructured* refer to the decision process, not to the underlying subject. Weather forecasting is a structured decision because the process used to make the decision is standardized among forecasters. Weather itself, however, is an unstructured phenomenon, as tornadoes and hurricanes demonstrate every year.

Q3 How Do Decision Level and Decision Process Relate?

The decision type and decision process are loosely related. As shown by the gray oval in Figure CE3-3, decisions at the operational level tend to be structured, whereas decisions at the strategic level tend to be unstructured. Managerial decisions tend to be both structured and unstructured.

We use the words *tend to be* because there are exceptions to the relationship illustrated in Figure CE3-3. Some operational decisions are unstructured (e.g., "How many taxicab drivers do we need on the night before the homecoming game?"), and some strategic decisions can be structured (e.g., "How should we assign sales quotas for a new product?"). In general, however, the relationship shown in Figure CE3-3 holds.

Q4 What Is the Difference Between Automation and Augmentation?

Figure CE3-4 contrasts two types of information system. **Automated information systems** are those in which the hardware and software components do most of the work. An information system that computes the quantity of items to order for inventory is an example of an automated system. Humans start the software and use the results, but hardware and software do most of the work.

Augmentation information systems are those in which humans do the bulk of the work. The information system exists to augment, support, or supplement the work done by people. An information system that uses email, instant messaging, and videoconferencing to assist the decision of whether to buy a competing company is an augmentation system. In contrast to the order-quantity computation system, the users look for support rather than answers.

Figure CE3-5 shows the relationship between the decision type and the IS type. In general, structured decisions can be supported by automated information systems, and they are generally applied at the operational and managerial levels of decision making. In contrast, unstructured decisions are supported by augmentation information systems, and they are generally applied at the managerial and strategic levels.

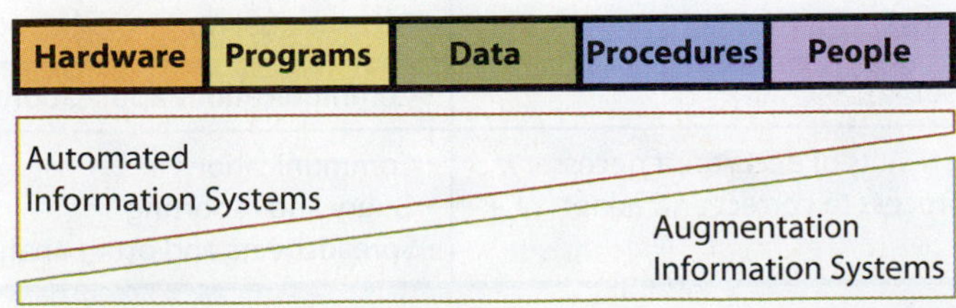

Figure CE3-4
Automated vs. Augmentation Information Systems

Figure CE3-5
How Decision Level, Decision Type, and IS Type Are Related

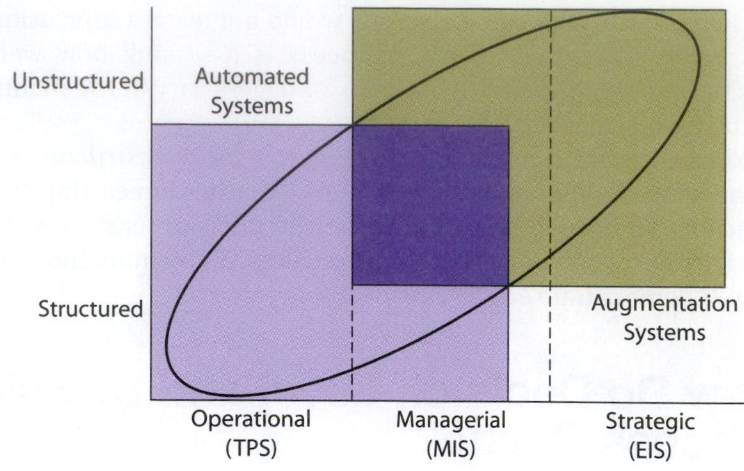

At this point, you may be wondering, "Why does all this matter?" One of the goals of this class is to help you become a better consumer of information systems and information technology. When you think about a new information system, you will be a better IT consumer if you ask yourself, "What is the nature of the underlying decision process?" If you can identify the type of process, you will know what type of information system may be helpful. Additionally, you will know not to invest in automated information systems for unstructured problems or in augmentation information systems for structured problems. This point may seem obvious, but organizations have wasted millions of dollars by not understanding the basic relationships shown in Figure CE3-5.

Q5 How Does IS Support Decision Steps?

Another way to examine the relationship between information systems and decision making is to consider how an information system is used during the steps of the decision-making process. The first two columns of Figure CE3-6 show the typical steps in the decision-making process: intelligence gathering, formulation of alternatives, choice, implementation, and review. During **intelligence gathering**, the decision makers determine what is to be decided, what the criteria for the decision will be, and what data are available. **Alternatives formulation** is the stage in which

Figure CE3-6
Decision-Making Steps

Decision Step	Description	Examples of Possible Information Systems
Intelligence gathering	• What is to be decided? • What are the decision criteria? • Obtain relevant data	• Communications applications (email, video-conferencing, word processing, presentation) • Query and reporting systems • Data analysis applications
Alternatives formulation	• What are the choices?	• Communications applications
Choice	• Analyze choices against criteria using data • Select alternative	• Spreadsheets • Financial modeling • Other modeling
Implementation	• Make it so!	• Communications applications
Review	• Evaluate results of decision; if necessary, repeat process to correct and adapt	• Communications • Query and reporting • Spreadsheets and other analysis

decision makers lay out various alternatives. They analyze the alternatives and select one during the **choice step**, and then they implement the decision in the **implementation step**. Finally, the organization reviews the results of the decision. The **review step** may lead to another decision and another iteration through the decision process.

As summarized in the right column of Figure CE3-6, each of these decision-making steps needs a different type of information system. During intelligence gathering, email and videoconferencing facilitate communication among the decision makers. Also, during the first phase, decision makers use query and reporting systems as well as other types of data analysis applications to obtain relevant data. Decision makers use email and videoconferencing systems for communication during the alternatives-formulation step. During the choice step, analysis applications such as spreadsheets and financial and other modeling applications help decision makers to analyze alternatives. The implementation stage again involves the use of communications applications, and all types of information systems can be used during review.

ACTIVE REVIEW

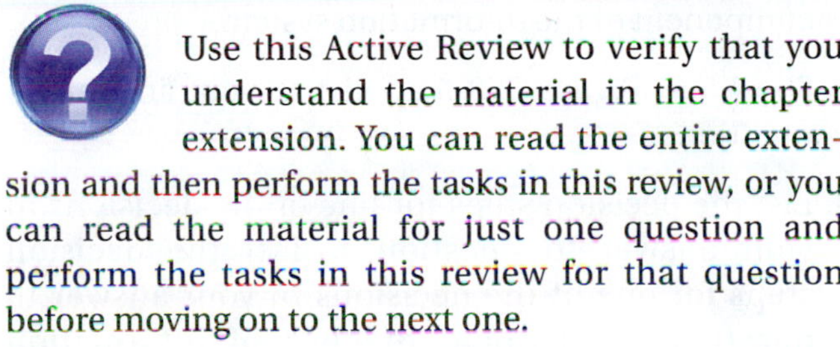

Use this Active Review to verify that you understand the material in the chapter extension. You can read the entire extension and then perform the tasks in this review, or you can read the material for just one question and perform the tasks in this review for that question before moving on to the next one.

Q1 How do decisions vary by level?

Describe the differences among operational, managerial, and strategic decision making. Give an example, other than one in this book, of each. Explain how TPS, MIS, and EIS relate to these levels. Describe two different meanings for the term *MIS*.

Q2 What is the difference between structured and unstructured decisions?

Describe the difference between a structured decision and an unstructured decision. Explain why these terms do not rely on the underlying problem, but rather pertain to the process used.

Q3 How do decision level and decision process relate?

Explain the blue oval in Figure CE3-3.

Q4 What is the difference between automation and augmentation?

Describe the difference between an automated system and an augmentation system. Explain which components do the work for each. Give an example of automated and augmentation versions of a customer service application. Describe the practical application to you of the information illustrated in Figure CE3-5.

Q5 How does IS support decision steps?

List and describe the steps in a decision process. Give an example of an information system that supports each step.

KEY TERMS AND CONCEPTS

USING YOUR KNOWLEDGE

Singing Valley Resort is a top-end (rooms cost from $400 to $2,500 per night), 50-unit resort located high in the mountains of Colorado. Singing Valley prides itself on its beautiful location, its relaxing setting, and its superb service. The resort's restaurant is highly rated and has an extensive list of exceptional wines. The well-heeled clients are accustomed to the highest levels of service.

1. Give an example of three different operational decisions that Singing Valley personnel make each day. Describe an information system that could be used to facilitate those decisions.
2. Give an example of three different managerial decisions that Singing Valley managers make each week. Describe an information system that could be used to facilitate those decisions.
3. Give an example of three different strategic decisions that Singing Valley's owners might make in a year. Describe an information system for each.
4. Which of the decisions in your answers to questions 1–3 are structured? Which, if any, are unstructured?
5. Give an example of an automated system that would support one of the decisions in your answer to question 1. Describe work performed by each component of the information system.
6. Give an example of an augmentation system that would support one of the decisions in your answer to question 1. Describe work performed by each component of the information system.
7. Show how Figure CE3-5 applies to your answers to questions 1–6.
8. List the decision steps for one of the decisions in your answer to question 1. List the decision steps for one of the decisions in your answer to question 3. Compare the use of information systems to support each of the decision steps for these two decisions.

CHAPTER EXTENSION 4

STUDY QUESTIONS

Chapter 3 provides the background for this Extension.

Knowledge Management and Expert Systems

Q1 What are the benefits of knowledge management?

Q2 What are content management systems?

Q3 What are the challenges of content management?

Q4 How do people share knowledge via collaboration?

Q5 What are expert systems?

Q1 What Are the Benefits of Knowledge Management?

Knowledge management (KM) is the process of creating value from intellectual capital and sharing that knowledge with employees, managers, suppliers, customers, and others who need that capital. Although KM is supported by IS technology, KM is not technology. It is a *process* supported by the five components of an information system. Its emphasis is on people, their knowledge, and effective means for sharing that knowledge with others.

The benefits of KM accrue by managing and delivering organizational knowledge so as to enable employees and others to work smarter. Santosus and Surmacz[1] cite the following as the primary benefits of KM:

1. KM fosters innovation by encouraging the free flow of ideas.
2. KM improves customer service by streamlining response time.
3. KM boosts revenues by getting products and services to market faster.
4. KM enhances employee retention rates by recognizing the value of employees' knowledge and rewarding them for it.
5. KM streamlines operations and reduces costs by eliminating redundant or unnecessary processes.

In addition, KM preserves organizational memory by capturing and storing the lessons learned and best practices of key employees.

For example, consider the help desk at any organization, say, one that provides support for electronic components . . . maybe iPhones. When a user has a problem with an iPhone, he or she might contact Apple support for help. The customer service department has, collectively, seen just about any problem that can ever occur with an iPhone. The organization, as a whole, knows how to solve the user's problem. However, that is no guarantee that a particular support representative knows how to solve that problem. The goal of KM is to enable employees to be able to use knowledge possessed collectively by the organization.

People can share their knowledge in three different ways. First, people can share knowledge via books, papers, memos, Web pages, and other documents. Organizational

[1] Megan Santosus and John Surmacz, "The ABCs of Knowledge Management," *CIO Magazine*, May 23, 2001, *http://cio.com/research/knowledge/edit/kmabcs.html*(accessed July 2005).

information systems that store, manage, and deliver documents are called *content management systems*. Second, with the advent of modern communications technology, people can share their knowledge via *collaborative KM systems*. Finally, in addition to content management and collaboration, people can also share knowledge via *expert systems*. Such systems codify human knowledge into rules and process those rules to give advice or guidance. We will consider each type of KM system in the remainder of this chapter extension.

Q2 What Are Content Management Systems?

Content management systems are information systems that track organizational documents, Web pages, graphics, and related materials. Such systems differ from operational document systems in that they do not directly support business operations. An insurance company, for example, scans every document it receives and stores those documents as part of its client-processing application. This is not an example of a KM system, because it is part of an operational, transaction-processing application. KM content management systems are not concerned with operational documents. Instead, they are concerned with the creation, management, and delivery of documents that exist for the purpose of imparting knowledge.

The largest collection of documents ever assembled exists on the Internet, and the world's best-known document search engine is Google. When you search for a term, or "Google it," you are tapping into the world's largest content management system. This system, however, was not designed for a particular KM purpose; it just emerged. Here, we are concerned with content management systems that are created and used by organizations for a specific KM purpose.

Typical users of content management systems are companies that sell complicated products and want to share their knowledge of those products with employees and customers. Someone at Toyota, for example, knows how to change the timing belt on the four-cylinder 2011 Toyota Camry. Toyota wants to share that knowledge with car owners, mechanics, and Toyota employees. Cisco wants to share with network administrators its knowledge about how to determine if a Cisco router is malfunctioning. Microsoft wants to share with the data miners of the world its knowledge about how to use its Data Transformation Services product to move data from an Oracle database into Excel.

The basic functions of content management systems are documents. Usually, the authoring of documents is considered to be outside the domain of the content manager. Documents arise from some source, and the goal of the content management system is to manage and deliver them. Documents and other resources have been prepared using Word, FrontPage, Acrobat, or some other document product. The only requirement that content managers place on document authoring is that the document has been created in a standardized format.

Q3 What Are the Challenges of Content Management?

Content management functions are, however, exceedingly complicated. First, most content databases are huge; some have thousands of individual documents, pages, and graphics. Figure CE4-1 shows the scale of the content management problem at Microsoft.com (*www.microsoft.com*). Although the size of the content store is impressive (10GB is equivalent to 110 pickup trucks of books), the more critical number is the amount of new or changed content per day: 5GB. This means that

- 110GB of content
- 3.2 million files
- Content created/changed 24/7 at a rate of 5GB per day
- 1,100 databases
- Multiple languages
- 125 million unique users per month
- 999 million page views per month

Figure CE4-1
Document Management at Microsoft.com (as of December 2003)

Source: http://microsoft.com/backstage/inside.htm (accessed February 2004). ©2003 Microsoft Corporation. All rights reserved.

roughly 5 percent of the content of Microsoft.com changes *every day.* (This example is 7 years old. Unfortunately, Microsoft no longer makes such data available. We can only surmise that their problem has grown considerably larger in those intervening years . . . most likely, exponentially larger.)

Another complication for content management systems is that documents do not exist in isolation from each other. Documents may refer to one another or multiple documents may refer to the same product or procedure. When one of them changes, others must change as well. Some content management systems maintain linkages among documents so that content dependencies are known and used to maintain document consistency.

A third complication is that document contents are perishable. Documents become obsolete and need to be altered, removed, or replaced. Consider, for example, what happens when a new product is announced. October 14, 2008, Microsoft shipped an important new Web development product called Silverlight. Prior to that date, Microsoft had been promoting prerelease and beta versions of this product. When the production version of Silverlight shipped, all the existing promotional materials had to be replaced by materials such as the Web page in Figure CE4-2.

Finally, consider the content management problem for multinational companies. Microsoft publishes Microsoft.com in over 40 languages. In fact, at Microsoft.com, English is just another language. Every document, in whatever language it was authored, must be translated into all languages before it can be published on Microsoft.com. Figure CE4-3 shows the Spanish version of the Web page announcing Silverlight. On that same date, versions of this page were published in French, German, Chinese, Korean, and many other languages.

Users cannot pull content if they do not know it exists. So the content must be arranged and indexed, and a facility for searching the content devised. Here, however, organizations get a break, at least for their publicly accessible content.

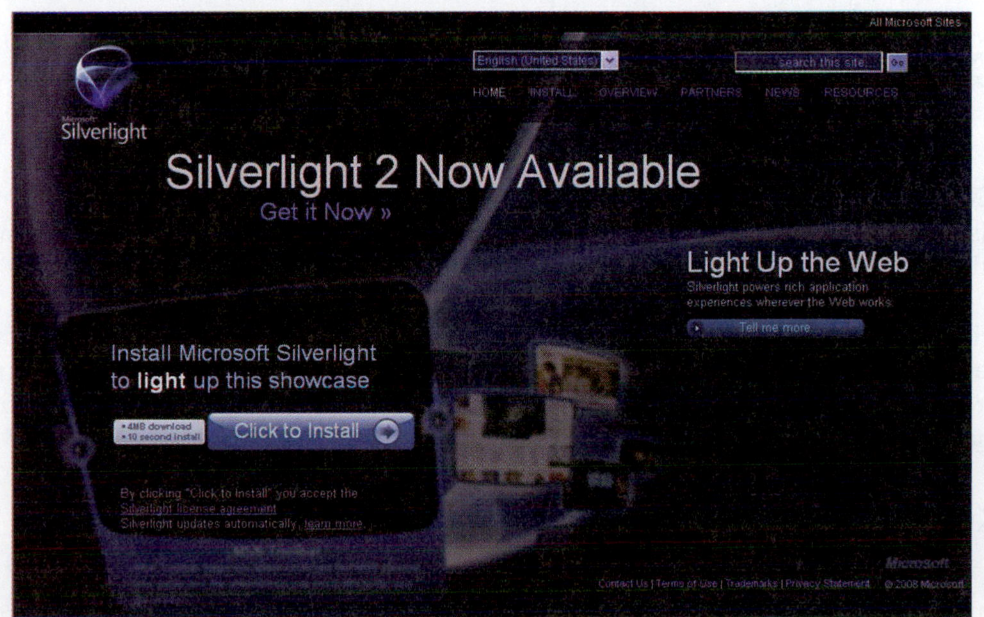

Figure CE4-2
Microsoft Silverlight: English

Source: http://www.microsoft.com/silverlight.

Figure CE4-3
Microsoft Silverlight: Spanish

Source: http://www.microsoft.com/silverlight.

As stated, the world's largest and most popular search engine is Google. Google searches through all public sites of all organizations. This means that Google is usually the fastest and easiest way to find a document. This often is true even within an organization. It may be easier, for example, for a General Motors employee to find a General Motors document using Google than using an in-house search engine. Google will have crawled through the General Motors site and will have indexed all documents using its superior technology.

Documents that reside behind a corporate firewall, however, are not publicly accessible and will not be reachable by Google or other search engines. Organizations must index their own proprietary documents and provide their own search capability for them.

One last consideration concerns the formatting of documents when they are delivered. Web browsers and other programs can readily format content expressed in HTML, PDF, or another standard format. Also, XML documents often contain their own formatting rules that browsers can interpret. The content management system will have to determine an appropriate format for content expressed in other ways.

Q4 How Do People Share Knowledge via Collaboration?

KM systems are concerned with the sharing not only of content, as just described, but also with the sharing of knowledge among people. How can one person share knowledge with another? How can one person learn of another person's great idea?

Nothing is more frustrating for a manager to contemplate than the situation in which one employee struggles with a problem that another employee knows how to solve easily. Similarly, it would be frustrating to learn of a customer who returns a large order because the customer could not perform a basic operation with the product that many employees (and other customers) can readily perform.

Knowledge Management Alternatives

A variety of different information systems can be used to facilitate the sharing of human knowledge. In this section, we will consider several of the major alternatives.

Portals, Discussion Groups, and Email

Consider the following story:

> Around the holidays in 2000, a Giant Eagle deli manager thought of a way to display the seafood delicacy that proved irresistible to harried shoppers, accounting for an extra \$200 in 1-week sales. But uncertain of his strategy, he first posted the idea on the KnowAsis portal. Other deli managers ribbed him a bit, but one tried the idea in his store and saw a similar boost in sales. The total payoff to the company, for this one tiny chunk of information, was about \$20,000 in increased sales in the two stores. The company estimates that if it had implemented the display idea across all its stores during this period, the payoff might have been \$350,000. Previously, "there was no tradition of sharing ideas in the store environment," says Jack Flanagan, executive vice president of Giant Eagle business systems.[2]

An employee may have a good idea, a novel approach, or a better way to solve a problem, and KM systems enable that employee to share that knowledge with others. Notice in this example that the employee shared the idea gratuitously; no one asked him about how to arrange the seafood delicacy, the employee just posted the good idea on the team **portal**. It was up to other managers and employees to pull that knowledge down from the portal.

Discussion groups are another form of organizational KM. They allow employees or customers to post questions and queries seeking solutions to problems they have. Most large organizations that have complicated product families support product discussion groups where users can post questions and where employees, vendors, and other users can answer them. Later, the organization can edit and summarize the questions from such discussion groups into **frequently asked questions (FAQs)**, another form of knowledge-sharing. For examples, search Google for the Web sites of Oracle, IBM, and 3M and locate FAQs and discussion groups on those sites.

Basic email can also be used for knowledge-sharing, especially if email lists have been constructed with KM in mind. For example, an email list of all product-quality engineers, across all plants, across the organization, can facilitate communication among those employees.

Blogs and Podcasts

A **blog** is a personal journal that is accessible on the Web, usually publicly so. Many employees enjoy authoring opinions, product information, support documentation, and other elements of their knowledge. As you will learn in Chapter 8, blogs are not only important for knowledge sharing, they also serve a key role in social CRM.

Social networking sites such as Facebook and microblogging sites such as Twitter are increasingly being used to share employee knowledge. See Chapter 8 and Chapter Extension 15 for more about this important new development.

Both video and audio **podcasts** can be used to share knowledge as well. An expert in, say, database design can publish a podcast on a particular design problem—for example, the representation of N:M relationships in the relational model. (See Chapter Extension 7, "Database Design," for a description of this problem and a method for solving it.) Expert salespeople can describe the secrets to their sales success in an audio podcast; similarly, experts in particular manufacturing techniques, such as welding stainless steel, can demonstrate in a video podcast how to perform that operation.

Both blogs and podcasts can be effective forms of knowledge sharing, but their characteristics are different. Whereas a blog is open-ended, can take many formats, and can address many dimensions of a situation, podcasts are usually short and focused on a particular problem. A blog can be an effective way of publishing podcasts.

Resistance to Knowledge-Sharing

Two human factors inhibit knowledge-sharing. The first is that employees can be reluctant to exhibit their ignorance. Out of fear of appearing incompetent, employees

2. Lauren Gibbons Paul, "Why Three Heads Are Better Than One" *CIO Magazine*, December 1, 2003, *http://cio.com/archive/20103/km.html*.

may not post their queries on bulletin boards or use email groups. Such reluctance can sometimes be reduced by the attitude and posture of the managers of such groups. One strategy for employees in this situation is to use email lists to identify a smaller group of people who have an interest in a specific problem. Members of that smaller group can then discuss the issue in a less-inhibiting forum.

The other inhibiting human factor is employee competition. "Look," says the top salesperson. "I earn a substantial bonus from being the top salesperson. Why would I want to share my sales techniques with others? I'd just be strengthening the competition." This understandable perspective may not be changeable. A KM application may be ill-suited to a competitive group. Or, the company may be able to restructure rewards and incentives to foster sharing of ideas among employees (e.g., giving a bonus to the group that develops the best idea).

Even in situations where there is no direct competition, employees may be reluctant to share ideas out of shyness, fear of ridicule, or inertia. In these cases, a strong management endorsement for knowledge-sharing can be effective, especially if that endorsement is followed by strong positive feedback. As one senior manager said, "There is nothing wrong with praise or cash, and especially cash."

Q5 What Are Expert Systems?

Expert systems, the last form of KM we will consider, are rule-based systems that encode human knowledge in the form of **If/Then rules**, which are statements that indicate if a particular condition exists, then some action should be taken. Figure CE4-4 shows an example of a few rules that could be part of a medical expert system for diagnosing heart disease. In this set of rules, the system examines various factors for heart disease and computes a *CardiacRiskFactor.* Depending on the value of that risk factor, other variables are given values. Unlike this example, an operational expert system may consist of hundreds, if not thousands, of rules. The set of rules shown here may need to be processed many times because it is possible that *CardiacRiskFactor* is used on the If side of a rule occurring before these rules.

The programs that process a set of rules are called **expert systems shells**. Typically, the shell processes rules until no value changes. At that point, the values of all the variables are reported as results.

To create the system of rules, the development team interviews human experts in the domain of interest. The rules in Figure CE4-4 would have been obtained by interviewing cardiologists who are known to be particularly adept at diagnosing cardiac disease. Such a system encodes the knowledge of those highly skilled experts and makes it available to less-skilled or less-knowledgeable professionals.

Many expert systems were created in the late 1980s and early 1990s; some have been successful. They suffer from three major disadvantages, however. First, they are

Figure CE4-4
Example of If/Then Rules

```
Other rules here...

IF CardiacRiskFactor = 'Null' THEN Set CardiacRiskFactor = 0
IF PatientSex = 'Male' THEN Add 3 to CardiacRiskFactor
IF PatientAge >55 THEN Add 2 to CardiacRiskFactor
IF FamilyHeartHistory = 'True' THEN Add 5 to CardiacRiskFactor
IF CholesterolScore = 'Problematic' THEN Add 4 to CardiacRiskFactor
IF BloodPressure = 'Problematic' THEN Add 3 to CardiacRiskFactor
IF CardiacRiskFactor >15 THEN Set EchoCardiagramTest = 'Schedule'
...
Other rules here...
```

difficult and expensive to develop. They require many labor hours from both experts in the domain under study and designers of expert systems. This expense is compounded by the high opportunity cost of tying up domain experts. Such experts are normally some of the most sought-after employees in an organization.

Second, expert systems are difficult to maintain. Because of the nature of rule-based systems, the introduction of a new rule in the middle of hundreds of others can have unexpected consequences. A small change can cause very different outcomes. Unfortunately, such side effects cannot be predicted or eliminated. They are the nature of complex rule-based systems.

Finally, expert systems were unable to live up to the high expectations set by their name. Initially, proponents of expert systems hoped to be able to duplicate the performance of highly trained experts, like doctors. It turned out, however, that no expert system has the same diagnostic ability as knowledgeable, skilled, and experienced doctors. Even when expert systems were developed that came close in ability, changes in medical technology required constant changing of the expert system, and the problems caused by unexpected consequences made such changes very expensive.

Today, however, there are successful, less ambitious expert systems. Typically these systems address more restricted problems than duplicating a doctor's diagnostic ability.

ACTIVE REVIEW

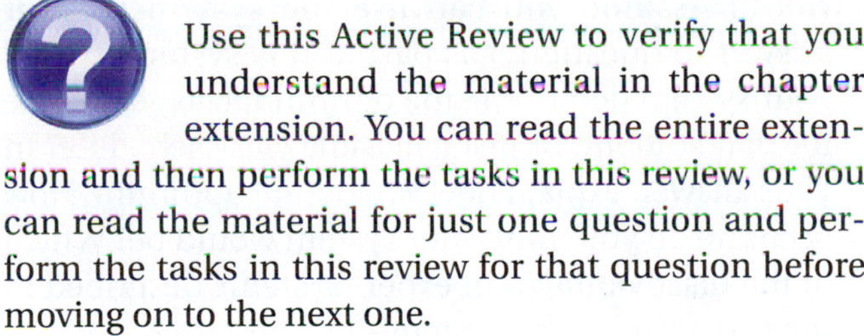

Use this Active Review to verify that you understand the material in the chapter extension. You can read the entire extension and then perform the tasks in this review, or you can read the material for just one question and perform the tasks in this review for that question before moving on to the next one.

Q1 What are the benefits of knowledge management?

Define *knowledge management.* Explain five key benefits of KM. Briefly describe three types of KM system.

Q2 What are content management systems?

Explain the purpose of a content management system. Describe how the Internet could be considered a content management system. Describe a more typical use of a content management system. Name and describe two functions of content management.

Q3 What are the challenges of content management?

Describe why size, dependencies, currency, and multinational factors make content management difficult. Explain two ways that organizations can index their documents.

Q4 How do people share knowledge via collaboration?

Describe a need, other than one in this book, for a collaborative KM. Explain how portals, discussion groups, and email can be used for collaborative KM. Explain how FAQs can be used. Explain how blogs and podcasts be used for collaborative KM. Explain the difference in focus of a blog and a podcast. Describe two human factors that inhibit collaborative knowledge sharing.

Q5 What are expert systems?

Define *expert systems.* Explain the meaning of the rules in Figure CE4-4. Explain why a given set of rules might be evaluated more than once. Define *expert system shell.* Sketch the history of expert systems use. Describe three problems in developing and using expert systems. Describe the kinds of expert systems that are successful today.

KEY TERMS AND CONCEPTS

USING YOUR KNOWLEDGE

1. Consider the test bank that students in a fraternity, sorority, or other organization maintain. Is such a test bank an example of a content management system? Is it a computer-based system? Does it need to be computer-based to be considered a content management system? If it is not computer-based, describe advantages of having it be computer-based. What features and functions would you want in such a system? How could such a test bank be indexed? By professor? By class? What other dimensions might be used for indexing?
2. Assume you developed the system in question 1. Is it legal to use such a system? Is it ethical? Assume that your system is unavailable to all students. Is it unfair? How could you apply the skills and knowledge you obtained in developing such a system to your future career?
3. Explain how the challenges for content management systems described in this chapter extension would apply to the test bank system in your answer to question 1.
4. Explain how you use collaborative knowledge-sharing in your MIS class. Differentiate between techniques that are sponsored by your professor and techniques that you and your classmates have evolved on your own. Are there techniques described in this extension that you do not use? If so, describe how you might use them.
5. Develop the If/Then rules for an expert system that determines whether a particular student can enroll in a class. For your system, is there a need for multiple passes through the rule set? How accurate do you think your system would be? Which of the disadvantages of expert systems described in the text apply to this system?
6. Develop the If/Then rules for an expert system that selects a term class schedule for a particular student. (*Warning:* This can require a large number of rules.) Assume you can use the system in your answer to question 5 as part of this system. Would your system determine the optimum class schedule for that student, or just a feasible class schedule? In your answer, explain how you define optimum. How accurate do you think your system would be? Which of the disadvantages of expert systems described in the text apply to this system?

CHAPTER EXTENSION 5

Chapter 4 provides the background for this Extension.

Introduction to Microsoft Excel 2010

This chapter extension teaches basic skills with Microsoft Excel, a product for creating and processing spreadsheets. If you already know how to use Excel, use this chapter extension for review. Otherwise, use this chapter extension to gain essential knowledge, which every businessperson needs today.

STUDY QUESTIONS

- **Q1** What is a spreadsheet?
- **Q2** How do you get started with Excel?
- **Q3** How can you enter data?
- **Q4** How can you insert and delete rows and columns and change their size?
- **Q5** How can you format data?
- **Q6** How can you create a (simple) formula?
- **Q7** How can you print results?

Q1 What Is a Spreadsheet?

A **spreadsheet** is a table of data having rows and columns. Long before the advent of the computer, accountants and financial planners used paper spreadsheets to make financial calculations. Today, the term *spreadsheet* almost always refers to an *electronic* spreadsheet, and most frequently to a spreadsheet that is processed by Microsoft Excel. Electronic spreadsheets provide incredible labor savings over paper spreadsheets and were a major factor in the early adoption of personal computers.

As shown in Figure CE5-1, Excel spreadsheets have rows and columns. The rows are identified by numbers, and the columns are identified by letters. Because there are only 26 letters in the alphabet, the following scheme is used to label columns: The letters A through Z identify the first 26 columns; the letters AA through AZ identify the next 26; BA through BZ the next 26; and so forth.

Figure CE5-1
Excel Spreadsheet Showing Rows and Columns

In Excel, the term **worksheet** refers to a spreadsheet. One or more worksheets are combined to form a **workbook**. In the lower left-hand corner of Figure CE5-1, notice three tabs. The current tab is named *Sheet1*; two other tabs are named *Sheet2* and *Sheet3*. Each sheet is a separate spreadsheet (or equivalently, worksheet), and the collection of the three sheets comprises the workbook.

Figure CE5-1 shows a spreadsheet processed by Excel 2010, the current version of Excel. You can process spreadsheets in earlier versions of Excel, but the structure of commands and menu items will be different from that described here. If you are just starting to learn Excel, learn Excel 2010 rather than an earlier version.

The intersection of a row and a column is called a **cell**. Each cell is identified by the name of its row and column. In Figure CE5-1, the cell named A1 is highlighted. The cell K5 is the cell in the K column, row number 5. The cell AB1207 (not visible in Figure CE5-1) is the cell located in column AB and row 1207.

You may be asking, "Row 1207? How many rows and columns can I have?" Don't bother asking . . . you can have more than you will ever need or want. And, if you should ever run out of rows and columns, you're using the wrong tool. In that case, you probably should be using Microsoft Access or another DBMS (see Chapter 5) instead.

Q2 How Do You Get Started with Excel?

When you first start Excel 2010, it will create a workbook exactly like that in Figure CE5-1. Even though you haven't done anything yet, your first task should be to save your workbook under an appropriate name. Life is uncertain; you never know when a computer might fail or power might be cut off or some other unplanned event might occur. Get in the habit of saving your work initially and then frequently after that.

To save your workbook, click *File* with your left mouse button (in the following text, unless otherwise specified, the term *click* means to click with the left mouse button), ignore the big green banner that says Info, and click *Save*, as shown in Figure CE5-2.

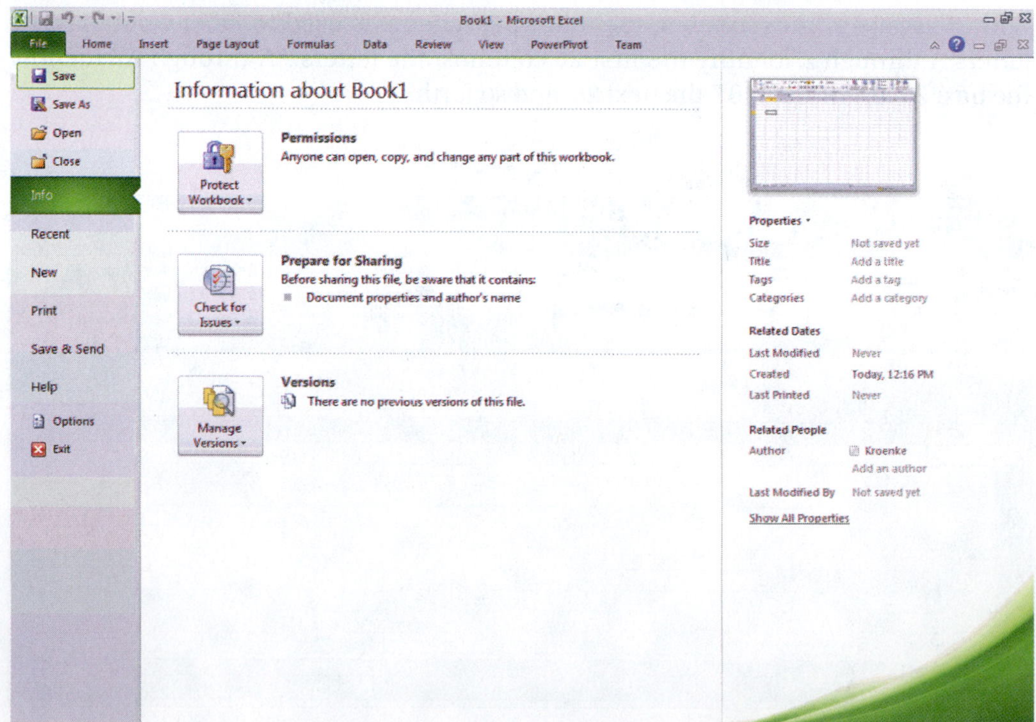

Figure CE5-2
Saving Your Workbook in Excel

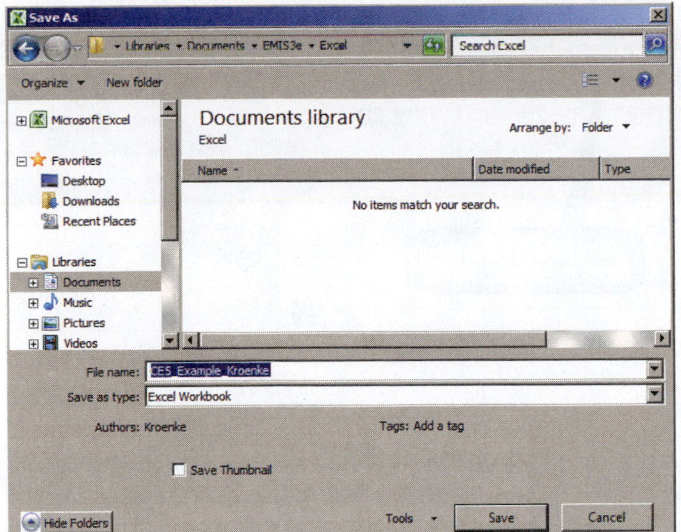

Figure CE5-3
Entering a File Name in Excel

The display in Figure CE5-3 will appear. In the lower center, find the label *File name:* and to the right of that label enter a name for this file. In Figure CE5-3, I have entered the name *CE5_Example_Kroenke*. Your instructor may have given you instructions for creating file names; if so, follow them. Otherwise, follow this example or use some other scheme. Click the *Save* button to save your workbook. Once you have saved your workbook, you can perform subsequent saves by clicking the small disk icon located next to the Office button.

Figure CE5-4 shows the workbook after it has been named; note that the name of the file appears in the top of the window. A sequence of tabs appears just below the top, dark window border in Figure CE5-4. These tabs control the contents of the **ribbon**, which is the wide bar of tools and selections that appears just under the tabs. In Figure CE5-4, the *Home* tab has been selected, and the contents of the ribbon concern fonts, alignment, and so forth. Figure CE5-5 shows the appearance of the ribbon when the *Page Layout* tab is selected.

In general, you choose a tab depending on the task at hand. For general work, the tools and selection under the *Home* tab are most useful. If you are inserting pictures, graphs, hyperlinks, or other items into your spreadsheet, click the *Insert* tab. You would use *Page Layout* to format your page, often for printing. The *Formulas* tab is

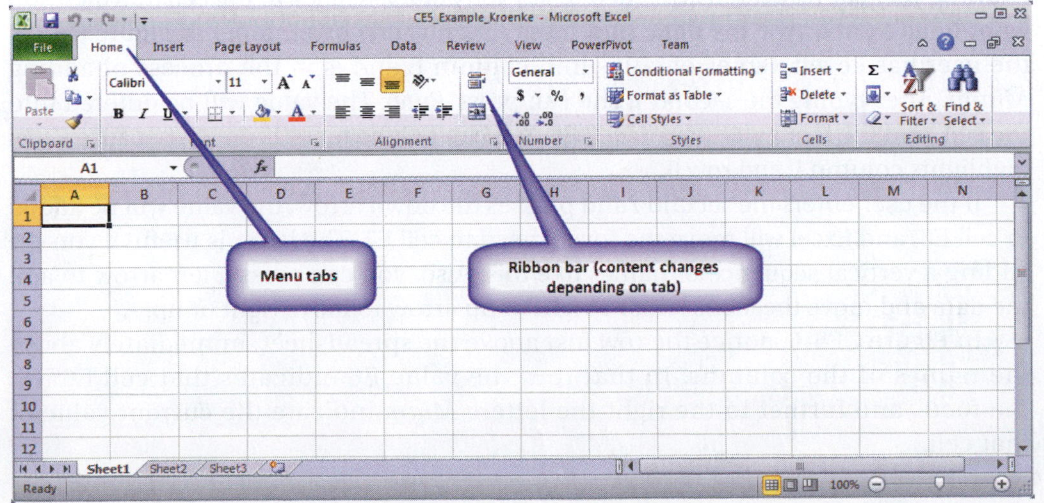

Figure CE5-4
Excel Menu Tabs and Ribbon Bar

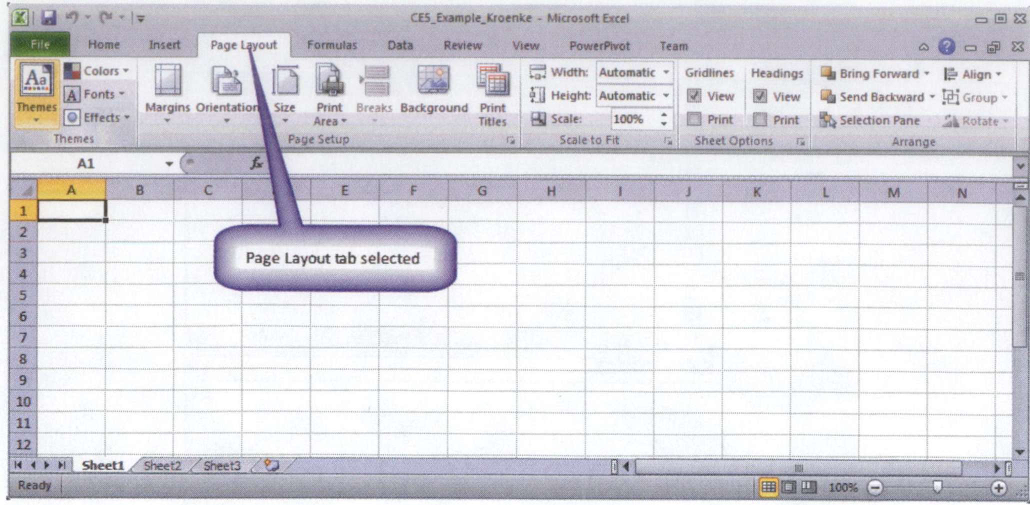

Figure CE5-5
Ribbon with Page Layout Tab Selected

used for creating more complex formulas, the *Data* tab for filtering and sorting data in your spreadsheet, the *Review* tab for tracking changes and making comments, the *View* tab for configuring the appearance of Excel, and the *Add-Ins* tab for using nonstandard features that have been added to Excel.

At this point, don't worry about which tab to choose; just click around to see the tools and selections available. If in doubt, click on the *Home* tab, because it holds the most frequently used tools and selections.

Q3 How Can You Enter Data?

Data can be entered into an Excel worksheet in three ways:

- Key in the data.
- Let Excel add data based on a pattern.
- Import data from another program.

Here we will illustrate the first two options. Chapter Extension 9 discusses how to import data from Microsoft Access into Excel.

Key in the Data

Nothing very sophisticated is needed to key the data. Just click in the cell in which you want to add data, type the data, and press *Enter* when you're done. In Figure CE5-6, the user has keyed names of cities into column E and is in the process of adding *Miami*. After typing the second *i*, she can press *Enter*. The value will be entered into the cell, and the focus will stay on cell E6. You can tell the focus is on E6, because Excel highlights column E and row 6.

If the user enters the second *i* and presses the down arrow, the value will be added to cell E6, and Excel will move the focus down to cell E7. The latter is useful if you are adding a vertical sequence of names like this. Also, you can press a left arrow to add the data and move the focus left or a right or up arrow to move right or up.

In Figure CE5-6, notice the row just above the spreadsheet, immediately above the names of the columns. In that row, the value E6 indicates that cell E6 has the focus and further to the right the letters *Miam* indicate the current value of that cell.

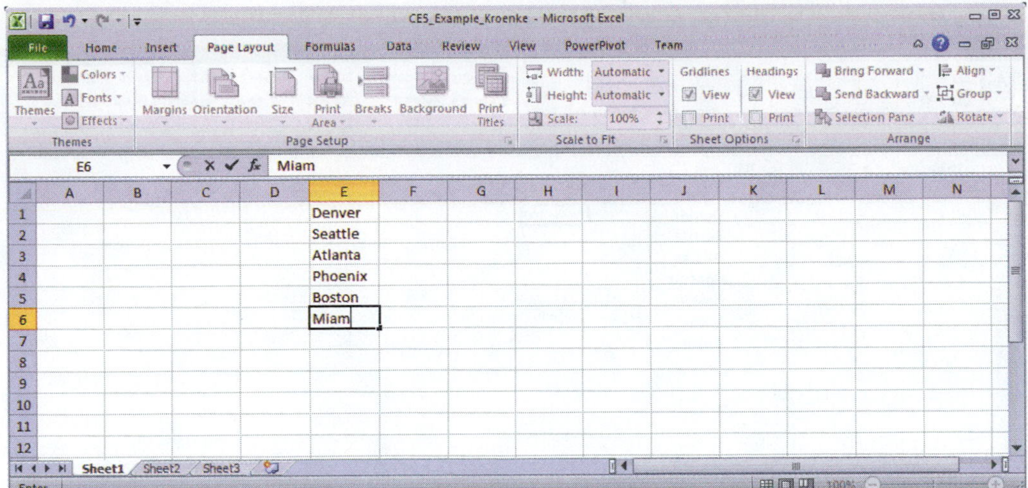

Figure CE5-6
Entering City Names in Column E

Figure CE5-7 shows a sequence of seven city names. But, notice that the user never entered the second *i* in Miami. To correct this, she can go back to that cell and retype the entire word *Miami* or she can go to the cell and press the <F2> function key. In the latter case, she can just add the missing *i* to the word and press Enter (or down or up, etc.). Using the F2 key is recommended when you have a long value in a cell and you just want to fix a letter or two without retyping the whole entry. (If nothing happens when you press F2, press the F Lock key on your keyboard. Then press F2 again.)

Let Excel Add the Data Using a Pattern

Suppose that for some reason for each of the cities we want to have the number 100 in column G of the spreadsheet in Figure CE5-7. Another way of saying this is that we want the value 100 to be entered into cells G1 through G7. One way of proceeding is to type the value 100 in each of the seven rows. There's a better way, however.

If our user types the value 100 into cell G1, presses Enter, and then clicks cell G1, a rectangle will be drawn around the cell with a little black box in the lower right-hand

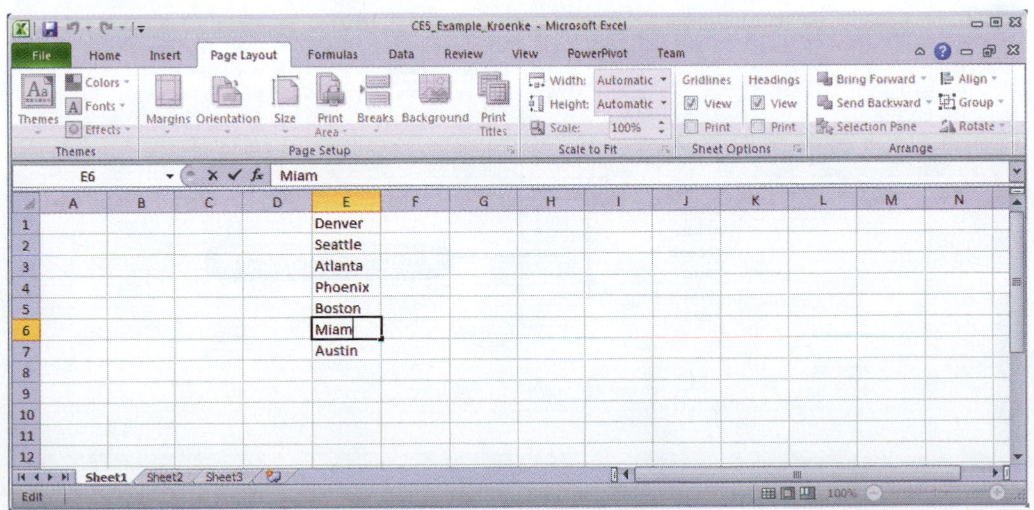

Figure CE5-7
Using a Function Key to Make Entry Corrections

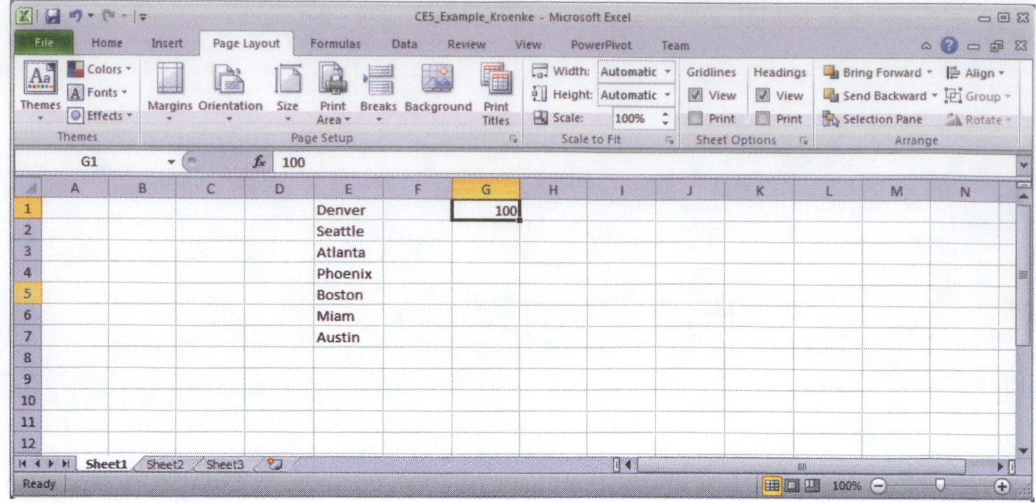

Figure CE5-8
Entering Identical Data in Multiple Cells, Step 1

corner, as shown in Figure CE5-8. Now if the user drags (left-click and hold the mouse button down as you move the mouse) that little black box down to cell G7, Excel will fill in the value 100 into all of those cells. Figure CE5-9 shows the user dragging the cells, and Figure CE5-10 shows the result.

But it gets much better! Suppose we want the numbers in column G to identify the cities. Say we want the first city, Denver, to have the number 100, the second city, Seattle, to have the number 200, the third city, Atlanta, to have the number 300, and so forth.

Excel will fill in the values we want if we give it an indication of the pattern to follow. So, if our user types 100 in cell G1, 200 in cell G2, and then *selects both cells G1 and G2,* Excel will draw a rectangle around the two cells, and again show the small black box, as shown in Figure CE5-11. If the user drags the small black box, Excel will fill in the numbers in a sequence, as shown in Figure CE5-12.

Excel is sophisticated in its interpretation of the patterns. If you key *January* and *February* into cells C1 and C2 and then select both cells and drag down, Excel will fill in with March, April, May, and so on. Or, if in column A you key in the sequence *Q1, Q2, Q3,* and *Q4* and then select all four values and drag the small black box, Excel will

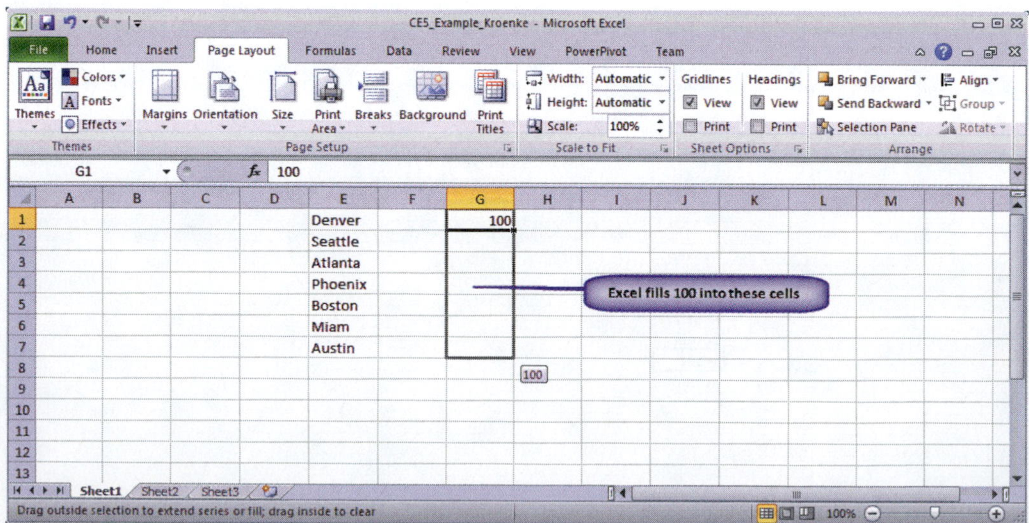

Figure CE5-9
Entering Identical Data in Multiple Cells, Step 2

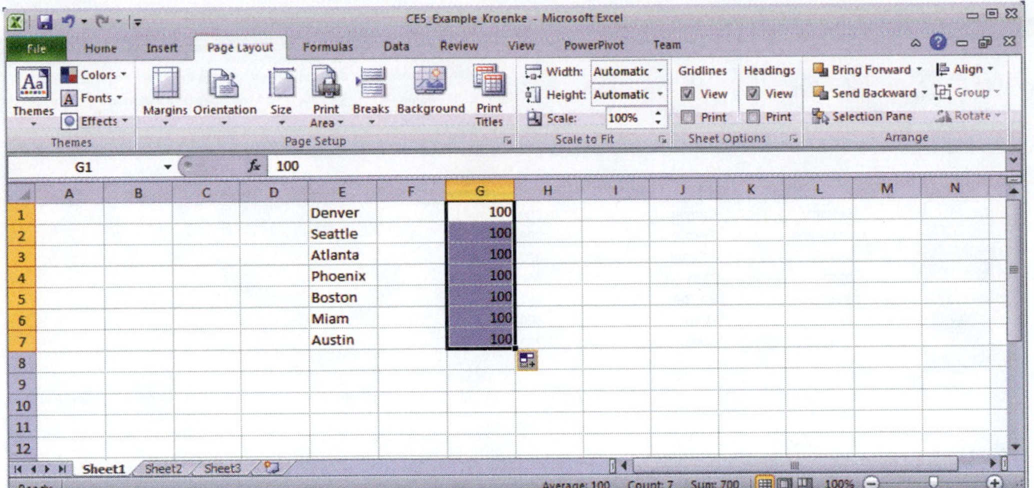

Figure CE5-10
Identical Data Entered in Multiple Cells

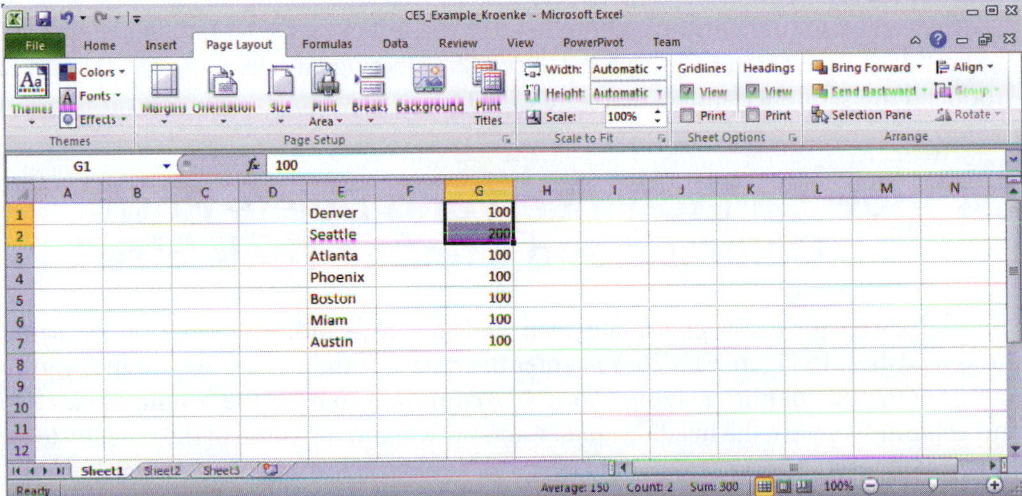

Figure CE5-11
Entering Patterned Data in Multiple Cells

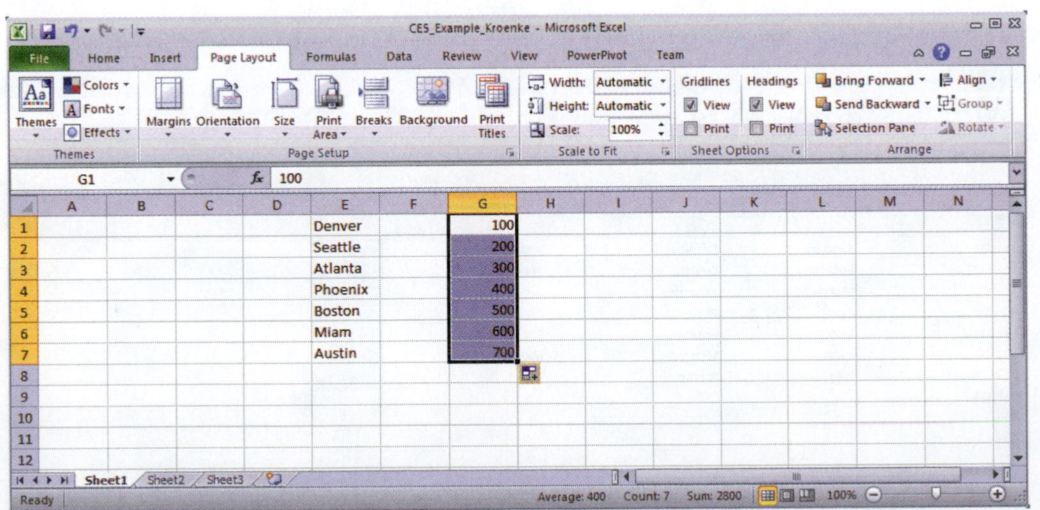

Figure CE5-12
Patterned Data Entered in Multiple Cells

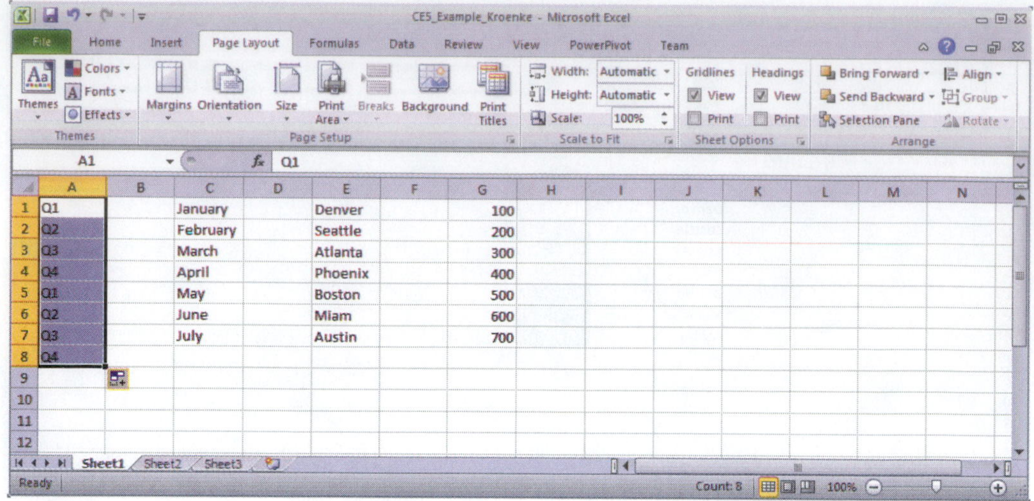

Figure CE5-13
Sophisticated Entry of Patterned Data in Multiple Cells

repeat the sequence Q1 through Q4. Figure CE5-13 shows the results of these last two operations.

Excel will also find patterns within text values. In Figure CE5-14, the user entered *Figure 1-1* into cell J1, and *Figure 1-2* into cell J2. Selecting and dragging cells J1 and J2 produced the sequence shown in Figure CE5-14.

Q4 How Can You Insert and Delete Rows and Columns and Change Their Size?

Suppose you are the manager of a sales team and you are recording this month's sales into the spreadsheet in Figure CE5-15. You enter the data shown but then realize that you've forgotten to add column headings. You'd like column A to have the heading *Sales Rep* and column B to have the heading *Sales*. You don't want to retype all of the data; instead, you want to insert two new rows so that you can add the labels as well as a blank line.

To insert new rows, click the number of the row above which you want new rows, and select as many rows as you want to insert. In Figure CE5-16, the user has clicked row 1 and selected two rows. Now, using the right mouse button, click the selection.

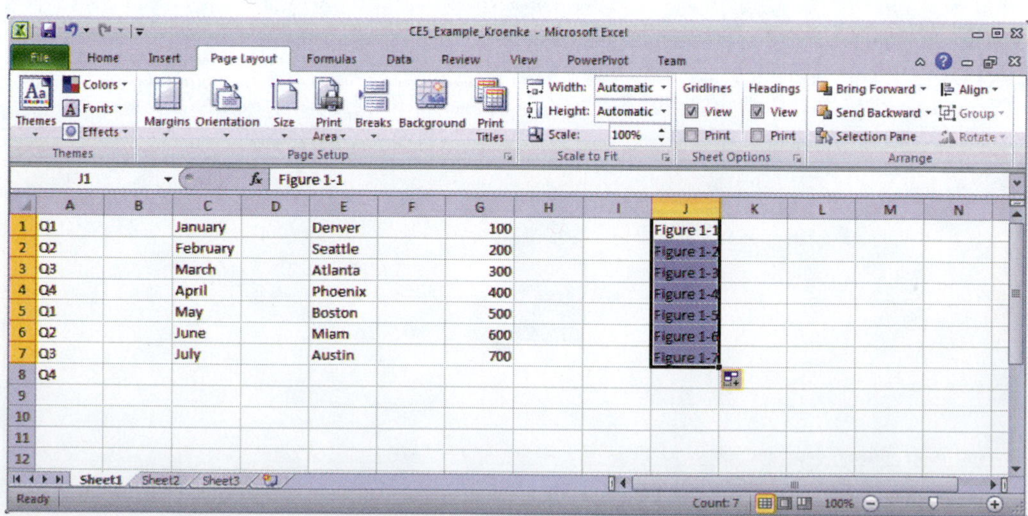

Figure CE5-14
Patterned Data Within Text Values

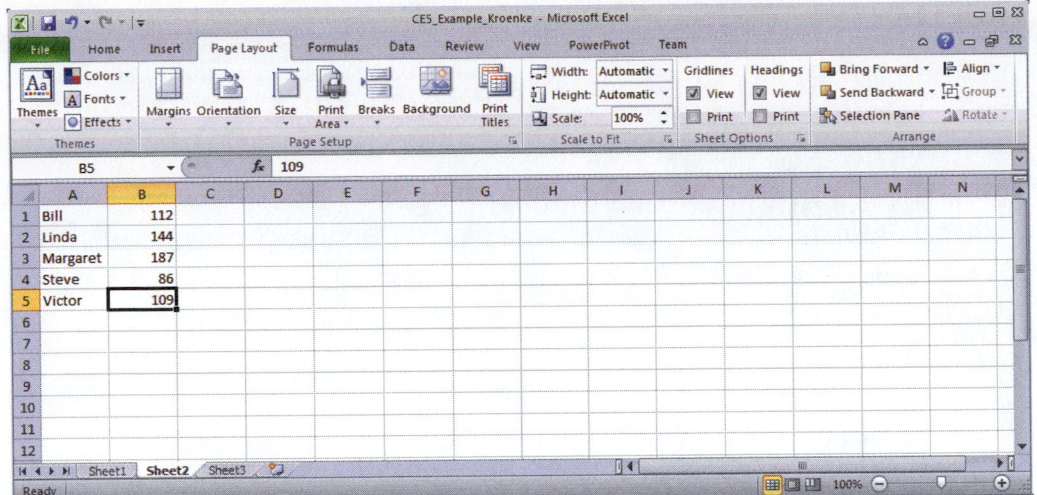

Figure CE5-15
Spreadsheet to Which User Wants to Add New Rows for Column Headings

The menu shown in Figure CE5-16 will appear. Using your mouse, left-click the word *Insert* and two rows will be inserted, as shown in Figure CE5-17. If you had selected only one row, then only one row would be added. If you had selected five rows, then five rows would be added.

Notice that when you click the name of a row (or column) you are selecting the *entire* row (or column). Thus, when you click the 1 of row 1, you are selecting the entire row, even if it has 1,000 or more columns.

You can use a similar approach to delete rows. Click the name of the row (or rows) you want to delete and then right-click. Then, left-click the word *Delete.* Those rows will be deleted and any remaining rows moved up.

Adding and deleting columns is similar. To add a column, click the name of the column before which you want to insert columns, select as many columns to the right of that as you want to add, right-click, and then select *Insert.* To delete, click the name of the columns you want to delete, right-click, and then select *Delete.*

Changing the width of a column or the height of a row is easy. Suppose in Figure CE5-17 that you want to include both first and last names in column A. At present, column A is not large enough to show both names. To make it larger, in the column headings click the line between the A and the B. Your cursor changes to a vertical bar

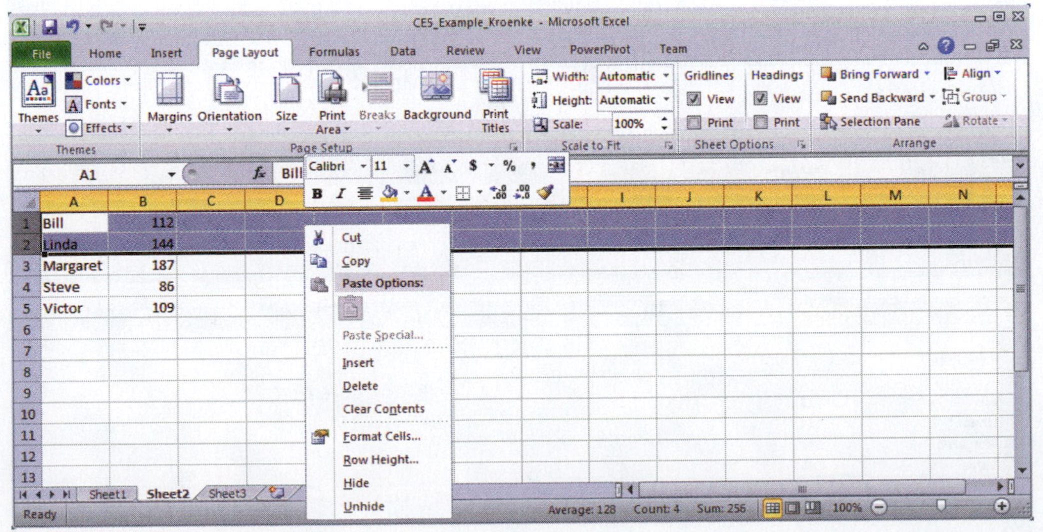

Figure CE5-16
Menu for Adding Inserts Such as New Rows

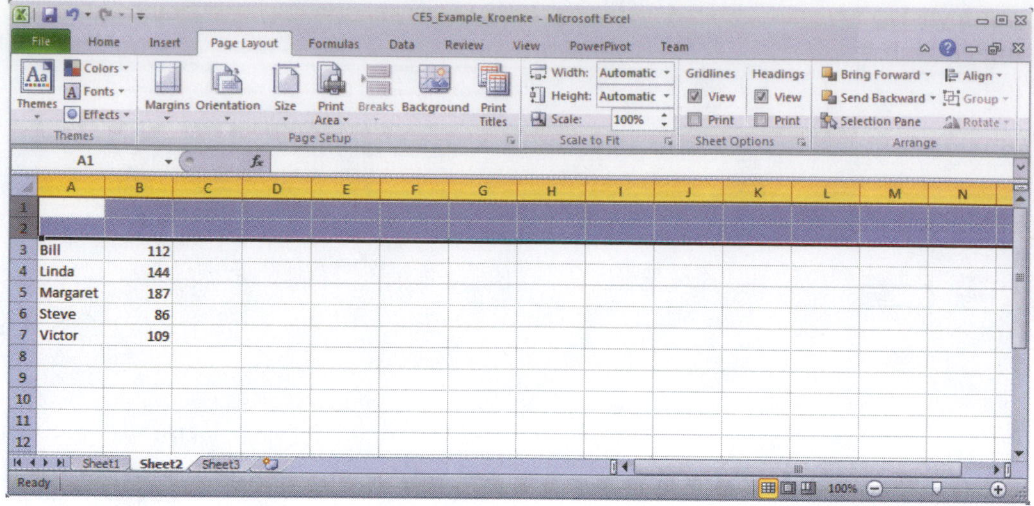

Figure CE5-17 Spreadsheet to Which User Has Added New Rows for Column Headings

with an arrow on each side, as shown in Figure CE5-18. Move the cursor to the right to increase the size of the column and to the left to decrease it. Similarly, to increase or decrease the height of a row click the line between the line numbers and drag up to decrease the row height and down to increase it.

Figure CE5-19 shows the spreadsheet after column A has been made wider and row 1 has been increased in height. *Sales Rep* has been entered as the heading for column A, and *Sales* has been entered as the name for column B.

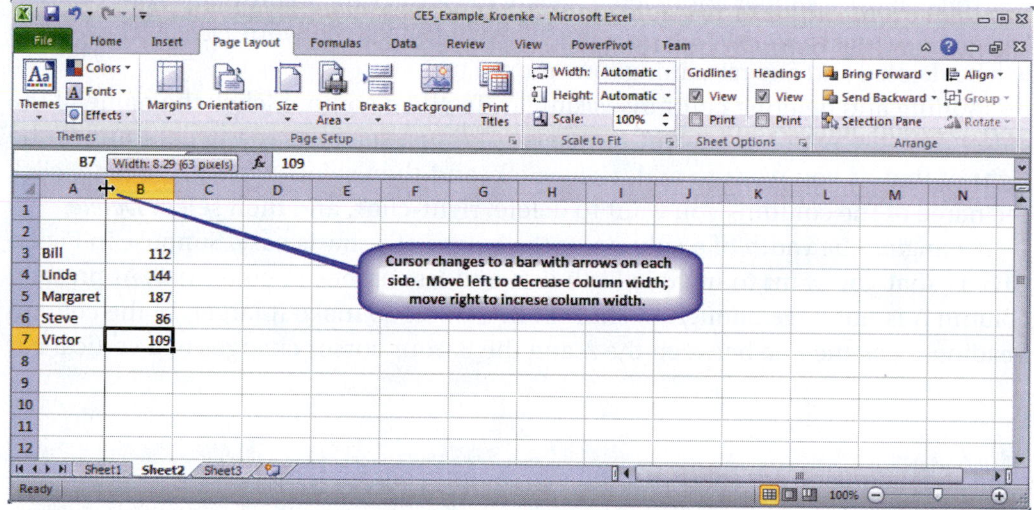

Figure CE5-18 Changing Cursor to a Vertical Bar to Change Column Widths

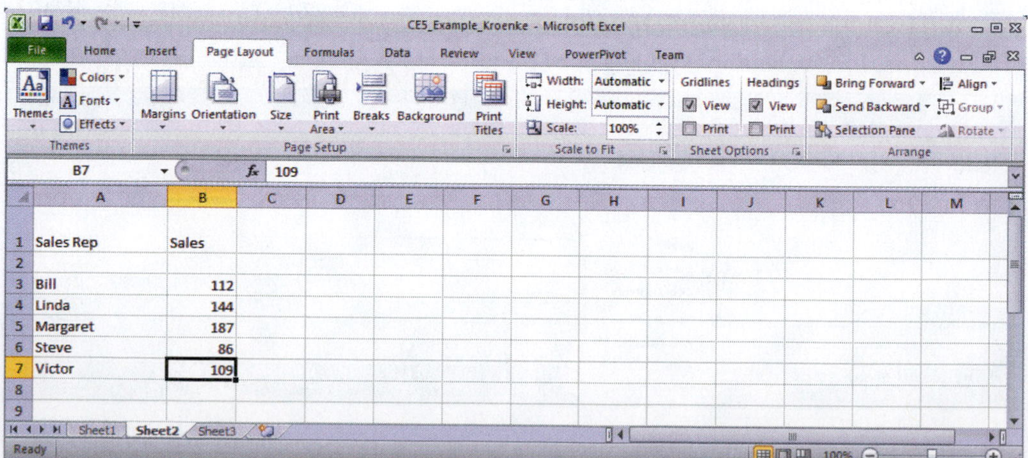

Figure CE5-19 Spreadsheet with Rows Added and Sizes of Columns Changed

Q5 How Can You Format Data?

Excel has a powerful and complicated set of tools for formatting spreadsheets. Here we will just scratch the surface with a few of the hundreds of possibilities.

The spreadsheet in Figure CE5-19 is boring and misleading. It would be better if the headings were centered over the columns and if they looked like headings. Also, are the sales in dollars or some other currency? If in dollars, they should have a dollar sign and maybe two decimal points.

To make the headings more interesting, highlight cells A1 and B1 (to do this, click A1 and hold the mouse button down as you move the mouse pointer to B1) and in the *Font* section of the ribbon select 16 rather than 11. This action increases the font size of the labels. In the same *Font* section of the ribbon, with A1 and B1 selected, click the bucket of paint. Select a medium blue. Now, still with cells A1 and B1 selected, in the *Alignment* section of the ribbon click the center icons, as shown in Figure CE5-20. Your labels will appear centered both horizontally and vertically in the cell.

The sales figures are actually in dollars, but they are formatted incorrectly. To place dollar signs in front of them, select cells B3 to B7 and in the *Number* section of the ribbon click the down arrow next to the dollar sign. Select $ English (United States), and your spreadsheet will be formatted like that in Figure CE5-21.

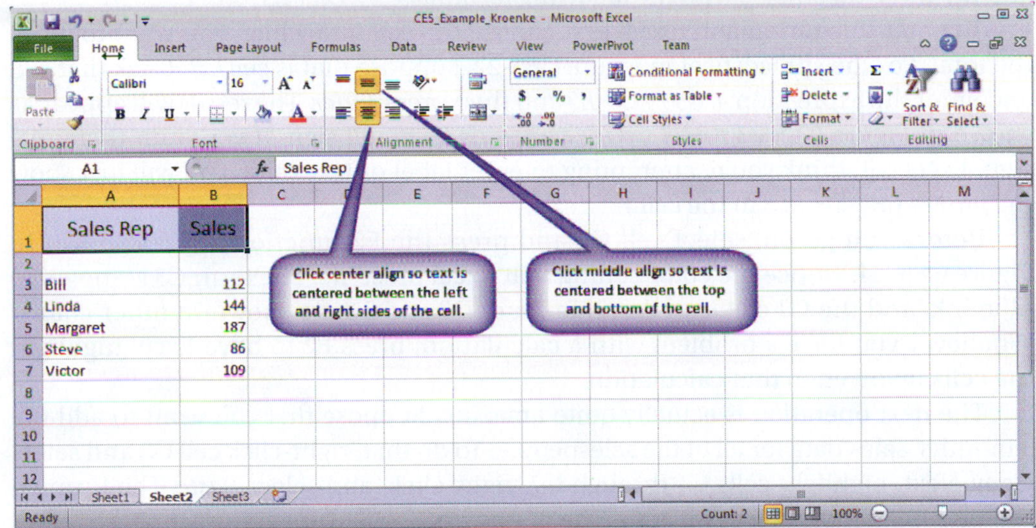

Figure CE5-20
Centering Labels in Cells

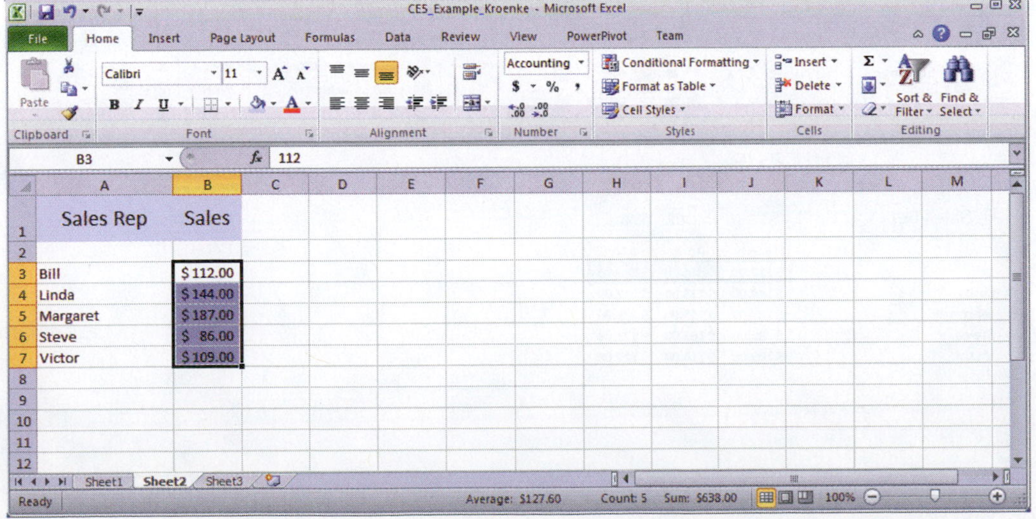

Figure CE5-21
Adding Dollar Signs in Cells

As stated, Excel provides hundreds of options for formatting your spreadsheet. You can add lines and borders, you can change the color of font, and you can even add conditional formatting so that large sales numbers appear in bold, red type. There is insufficient room in this short introduction to explain such capabilities, but explore on your own using Excel Help (the question mark in the upper right-hand corner).

Q6 How Can You Create a (Simple) Formula?

In spite of how it might appear to you at this point, the power of Excel is not the ease by which you can enter data or change the form of the spreadsheet, nor is it in the flexible ways you can format your data. The real power of Excel lies in its amazing computational capability. In this section, we will introduce a few simple formulas. We will expand on this introductory discussion in Chapter Extension 6, where we will use Excel to develop a computer budget.

For now, consider the spreadsheet in Figure CE5-22. Suppose that we want to add Bill's sales numbers together to obtain his total sales for the months of March, April, and May. Those sales are located in cells C3, D3, and E3, respectively. A logical way to add the three together is with the following formula: *C3+D3+E3.*

To enter this formula in Excel, first choose the cell into which you want to place the total. For the spreadsheet in Figure CE5-22, suppose that is cell G3. Click that cell and enter the expression *=C3+D3+E3* and then press *Enter.* The result will appear as shown in Figure CE5-23. (Be sure to start with an equal sign. If you omit the equal sign, Excel will think you're attempting to enter label or text value and will just show the letters *C3+D3+E3* in the cell.)

Before you go on, select cell G3 and press the F2 function key, as shown in Figure CE5-24. Notice the color coding that Excel presents. The term *C3* is shown in blue ink, and the C3 cell is outlined in blue; *D3* and *E3* are shown in other colors. Whenever you have a problem with a calculation, press F2 to have Excel highlight the cells involved in that calculation.

The next operation is actually quite amazing. Suppose that you want to add the 3 months' sales data for all of the salespeople. To do that, right-click cell G3 and select *Copy.* Next, highlight cells G4 through G7, right-click, and select *Paste.* The formula will be copied into each of the cells. The correct totals will appear in each row.

Figure CE5-22 Selecting Cells to Be Summed

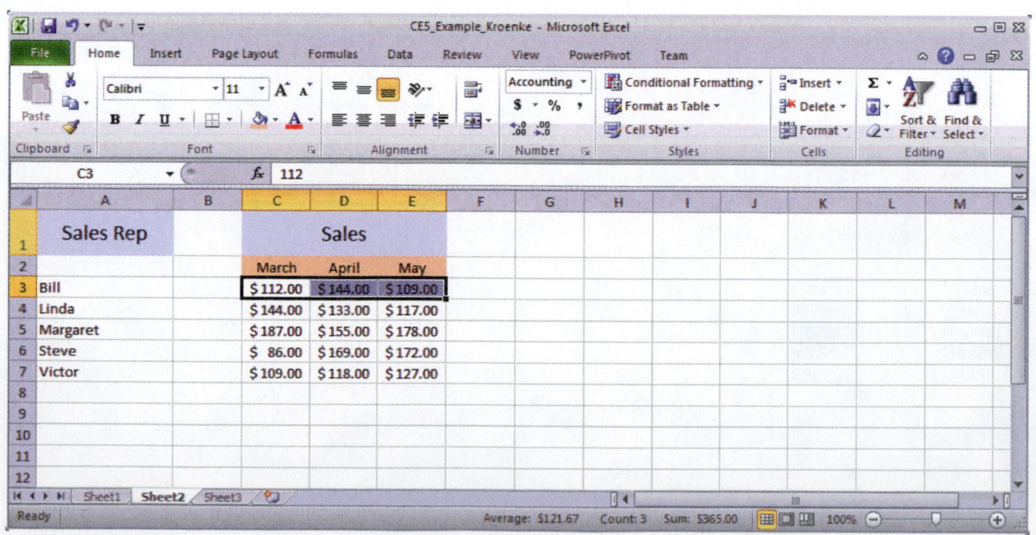

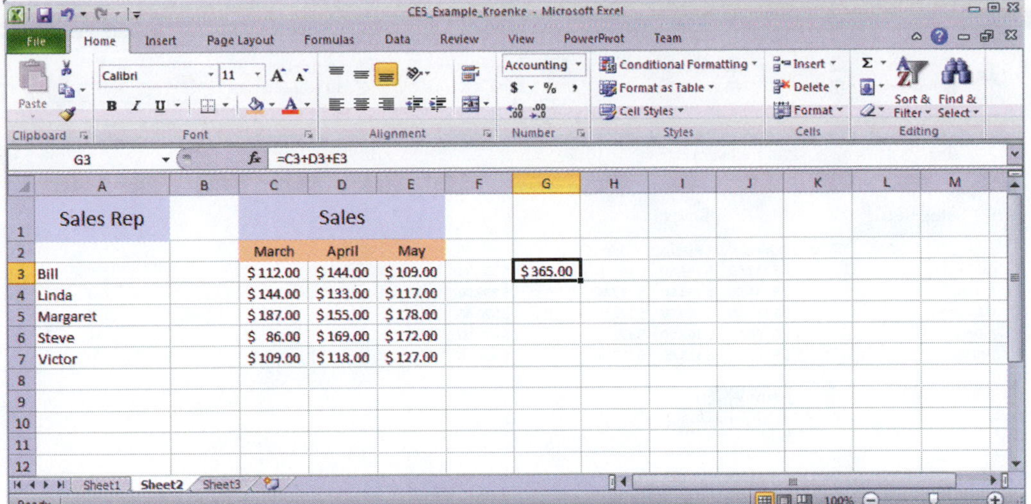

Figure CE5-23
The Result of Applying a Formula That Summed Cells C3, D3, and E3

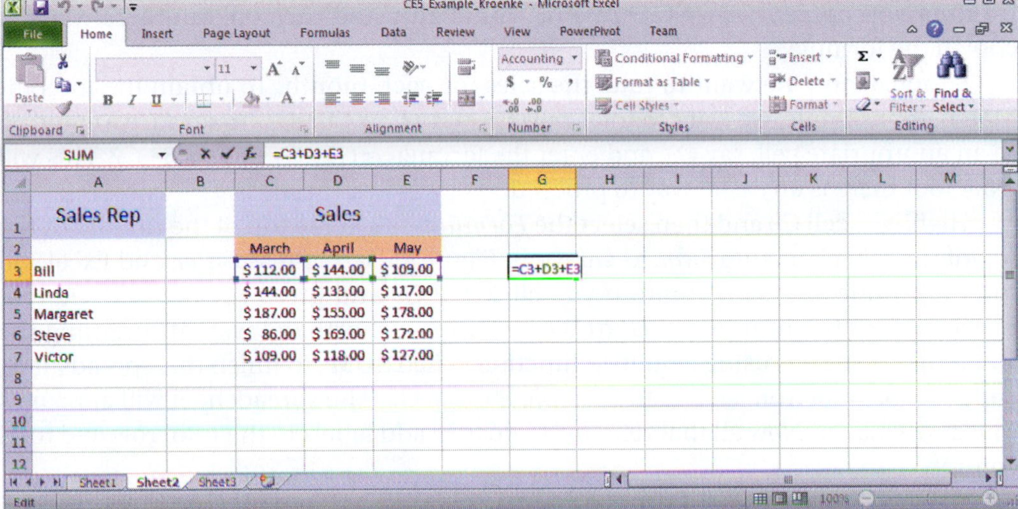

Figure CE5-24
Using the F2 Function Key to Show Color Coding of Cells Involved in a Calculation

Here's the amazing part: When Excel copied the formula, it did not blindly do so. Instead, it adjusted the terms of the formula so that each would refer to cells in the row to which it was copied. To verify this, highlight cell G5, for example, and press F2, as shown in Figure CE5-25. Notice that the formula in this cell is *=C5+D5+E5*. The

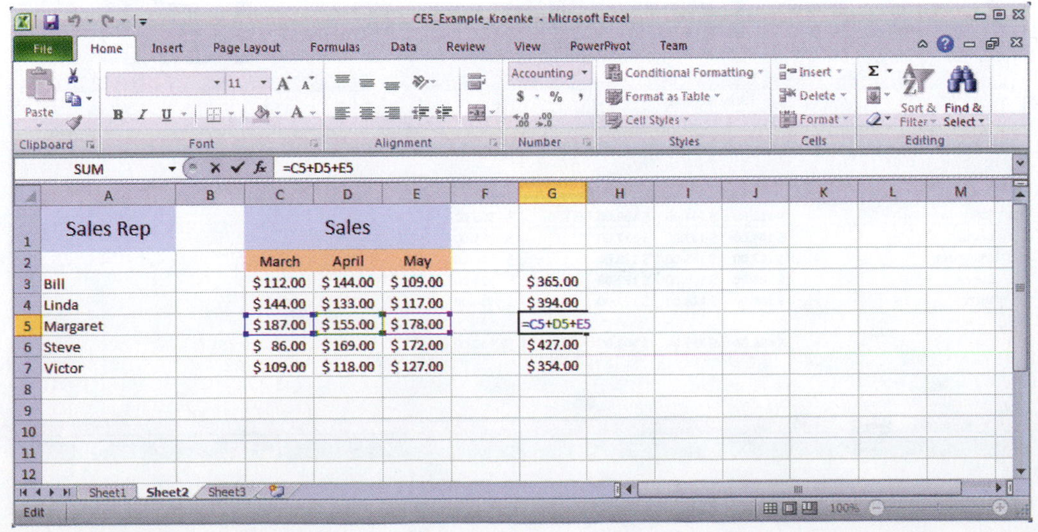

Figure CE5-25
Using the F2 Function Key to Confirm That a Formula Was Correctly Copied into Multiple Cells

Figure CE5-26
Auto Sum Function

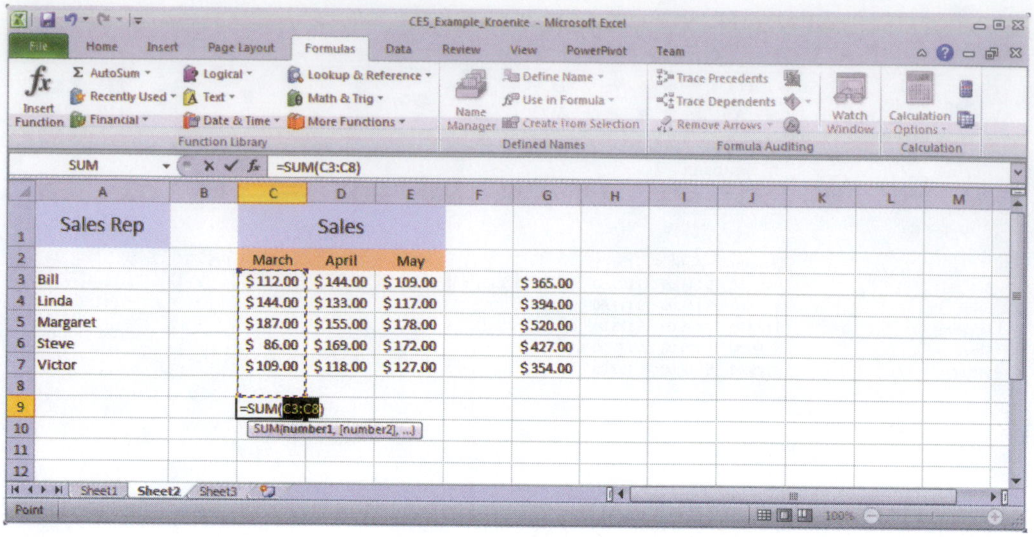

formula you copied was =*C3+D3+E3*. Excel adjusted the row numbers when it copied the formula!

Suppose now we want to total the sales for each month. To obtain the total for March, for example, we want to total cells C3+C4+C5+C6+C7. To do so, we could go to an appropriate cell, say C9, and enter the formula =*C3+C4+C5+C6+C7*. This will work, but there is an easier way to proceed.

Highlight cell C9 and then select the *Formulas* tab at the top of the ribbon. At the top of the tab, click *Auto Sum*, as shown in Figure CE5-26. Press *Enter*, and Excel will total the values in the column. If you click cell C9 and press F2, you will see that Excel entered the formula =*SUM(C3:C8)*. This is a shorthand way of summing the values in those cells using a built-in function called **SUM**. To finish this spreadsheet, copy the formula from cell C9 to cells D9, E9, and G9. The spreadsheet will appear as in Figure CE5-27. Now all that remains to do is to add labels to the total row and total column.

You can use an Excel formula to create just about any algebraic expression. However, when you create a formula, remember the rules of high school algebra. For example, =*(B2+B3)/7* will add the contents of cell B2 to those of B3 and divide the sum by 7. In contrast, =*B2+B3/7* will first divide B3 by 7 and then add the result to the

Figure CE5-27
Summing Sales by Month

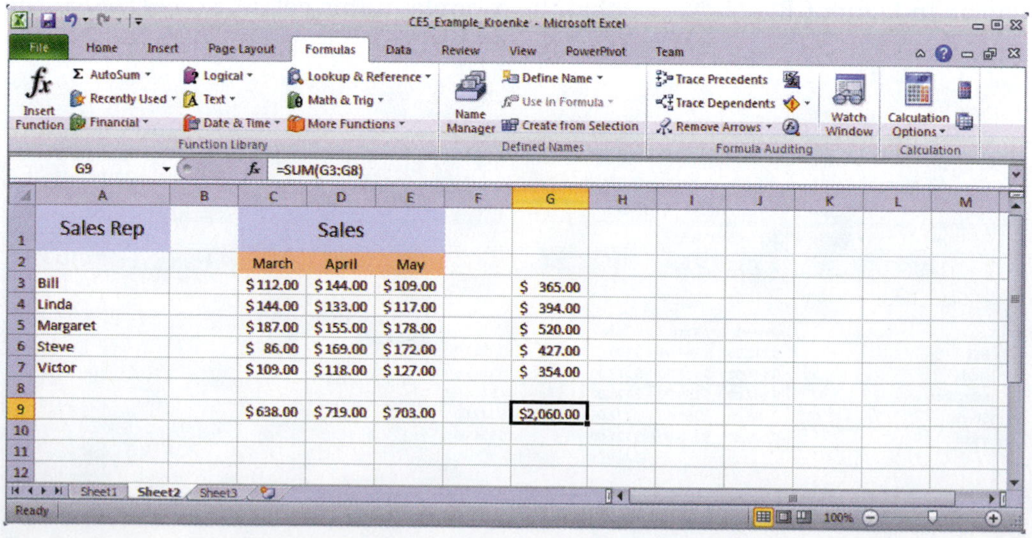

contents of B2. When in doubt, just key in a formula you think might work and experiment until you get the results you want.

Q7 How Can You Print Results?

Excel provides a wide variety of tools and settings for printing worksheets. Here we will illustrate several features that will give you an idea of the possibilities. After you have read this section, you can experiment on your own.

Before you start printing, you can save paper and ink if you make use of Excel's Print Preview feature. To do so, click *File* and then *Print,* as shown in Figure CE5-28. Before you click the large Print button (next to Copies), examine the Print Preview thumbnail of your printout to see if you like it. If you do, press *Print,* and Excel will print your document. For now, however, select the *Page Layout* tab in the Excel ribbon.

The tools and selections in the Page Layout ribbon determine how the document will be arranged as a printed document. In this ribbon, the next to last group is *Sheet Options*; in that group notice that you have the option of viewing and printing gridlines as well as column and row headings.

If you now select *Print* under *Gridlines* and *Headings,* and then select *Print Preview,* you can see that your worksheet will be printed with guidelines and headings, as shown in Figure CE5-29. Most people prefer to see gridlines and headings in the screen display but not see them, or at least not see the headings, in the printed display. Click *Close Print Preview* to return to the spreadsheet view. For now, check *View* and *Print Guidelines,* but under *Headings* check only *View.*

As you can see, you have many other options in the *Page Layout* ribbon. Use *Margins* to set the size of the page margins. *Orientation* refers to whether the worksheet is printed normally (upright) on the page (called *Portrait*) or sideways on the page (called *Landscape*). Try each and preview your print to see the impact they have.

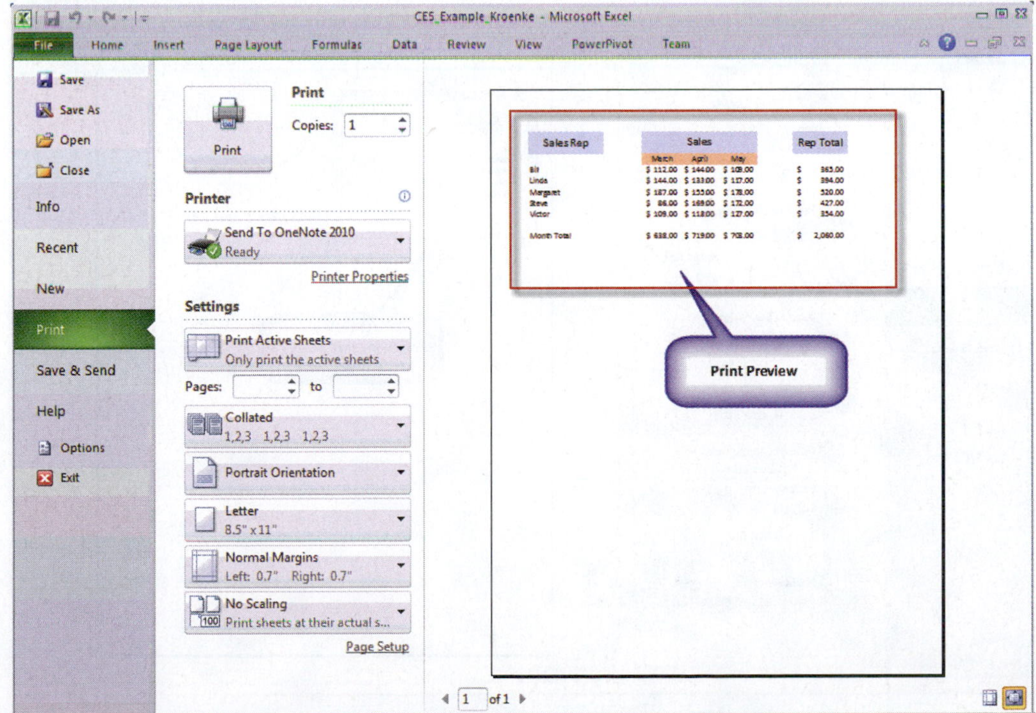

Figure CE5-28
The Print Preview Screen in Excel

Figure CE5-29
Using Print Preview to View the Spreadsheet with Gridlines and Headings

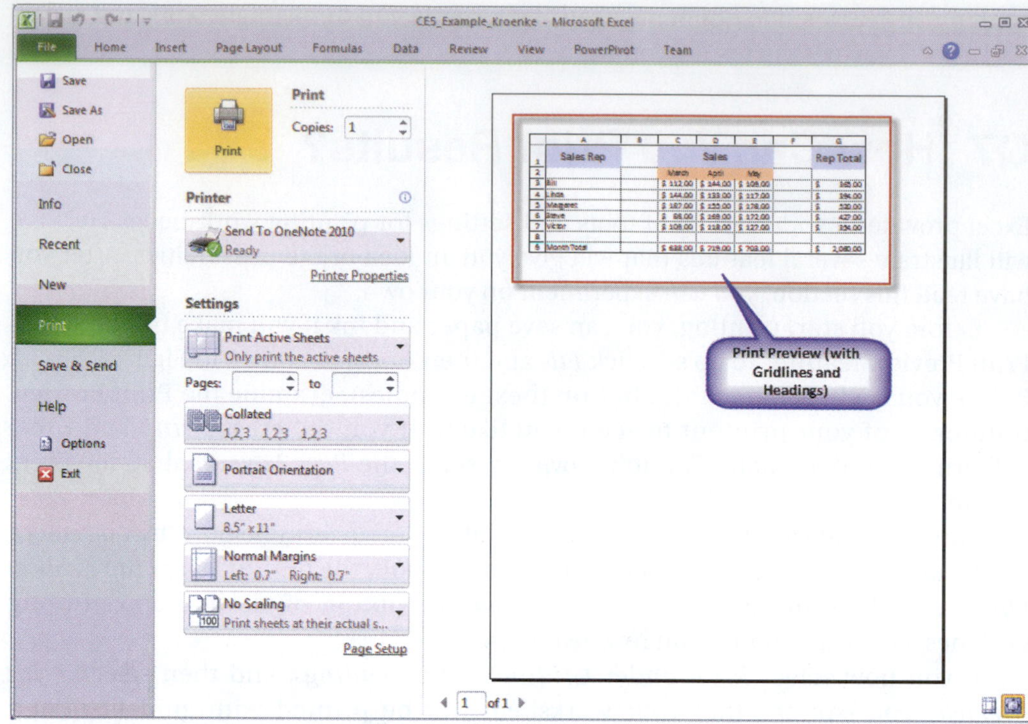

You can use print area to specify the portion of the spreadsheet that you want to print. If for some reason you want to list only the name of the sales reps, you can highlight cells A1 through A7 and then click *Print Area* and then click *Set Print Area.* If you do this, your print preview will appear as in Figure CE5-30.

These commands should be enough for you to print basic assignments. Of course, Excel offers many more options for you to explore. Experiment with them!

Figure CE5-30
Using Print Preview to Select Only a Portion of the Spreadsheet

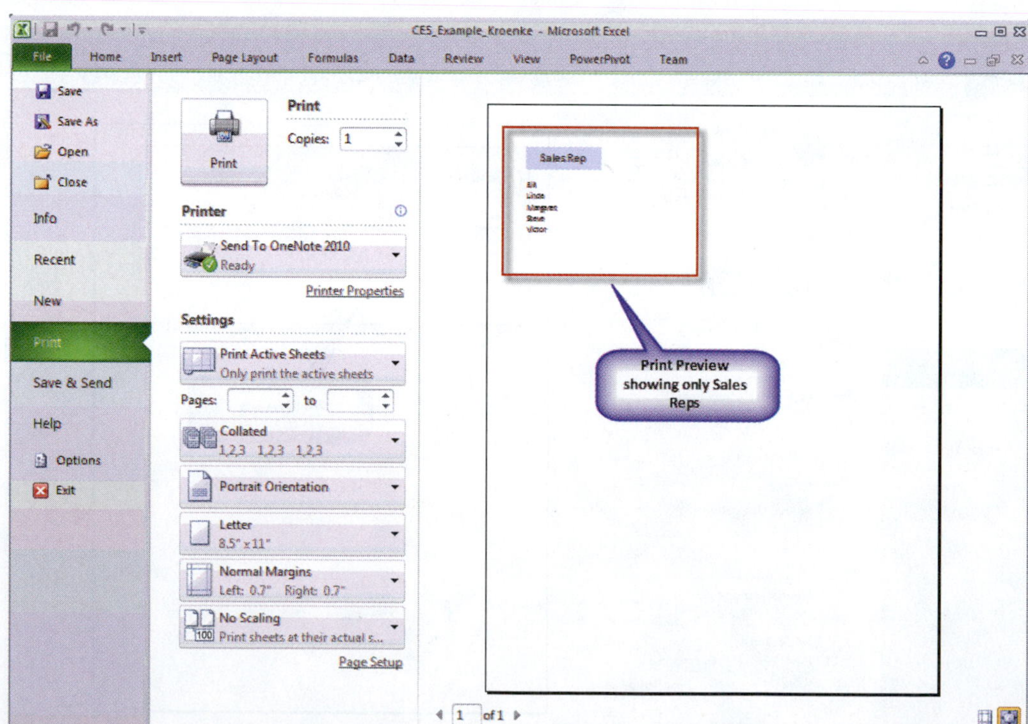

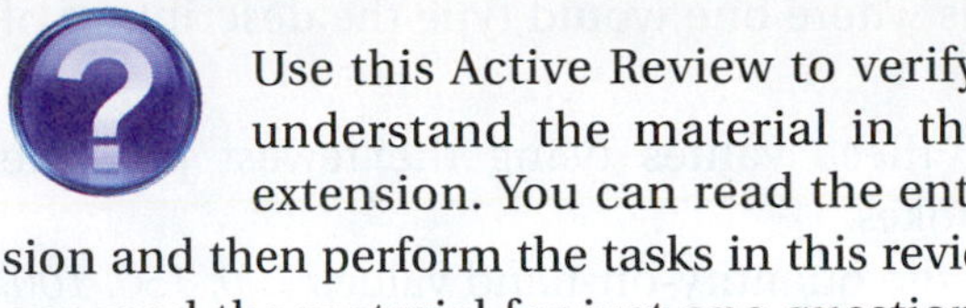

ACTIVE REVIEW

Use this Active Review to verify that you understand the material in the chapter extension. You can read the entire extension and then perform the tasks in this review, or you can read the material for just one question and perform the tasks in this review for that question before moving on to the next one.

Q1 What is a spreadsheet?

Explain how the following terms are related: *spreadsheet, electronic spreadsheet, Microsoft Excel, worksheet,* and *workbook*. Explain how spreadsheet cells are addressed. Where would you find cell Q54?

Q2 How do you get started with Excel?

Describe the first task you should do when creating a spreadsheet. Open a new workbook and give it the name *My_Sample_WB*. Explain the relationship of tabs and tools and selections. Which tab is the most likely one to have the tools and selections you need?

Q3 How can you enter data?

List three ways of entering data into Excel. Describe the advantage of using the F2 key to edit data. Explain two ways that Excel uses a pattern to enter data.

Q4 How can you insert and delete rows and columns and change their size?

Describe how to insert and delete rows. Describe a circumstance in which you would need to insert rows. Describe how to make a row taller or shorter. Describe how to change the width of a column.

Q5 How can you format data?

Open Excel and explain the purpose of each of the icons in the *Font* section of the *Home* tab of the ribbon. Explain the purpose of the *Alignment* and *Number* sections.

Q6 How can you create a (simple) formula?

Write the expression you would need to add the content of cell B2 to the content of cell B7. Write the expression to multiply the content of cell C4 by 7.3. Write the expression to find the average of the values in cells D7, D8, and D9. Use a built-in formula to total the values in cells E2, E3, E4, E5, E6, and E7.

Q7 How can you print results?

Explain the purpose and use of *Print Preview.* Open Excel, go to the *Page Layout* tab, and explain the purpose of the *Margins, Orientation,* and *Print Area* tools in the *Page Setup* section. Also, explain the function of the *View* and *Print* checkboxes in the *Gridlines* and *Headings* portion of the *Sheet Options* section.

KEY TERMS AND CONCEPTS

Cell 350
Ribbon 351
Spreadsheet 349
SUM 362
Workbook 350
Worksheet 350

USING YOUR KNOWLEDGE

1. Open Excel and duplicate each of the actions in this chapter extension.
2. Create a new workbook and take the following actions:
   a. Name and save your workbook using a name of your own choosing.
   b. Enter the value *This is the content of cell C7* into cell C7.
   c. Use F2 to change the value in cell C7 to *This is part of the content of cell C7.*
   d. Add the value *January* to cells B2 through B14. Key the data just once.
   e. Add the value *January* to cell C2 and the value *February* to cell C3. Highlight both cells C2 and C3 and drag the small black box down to cell C14. Explain what happens.

f. Create a list of odd numbers from 1 to 11 in cells C3 through C8. Key only the values 1 and 3.
g. Enter the value *MIS-1* in cell D2 and the value *MIS-2* in cell D3. Highlight cells D2 and D3 and drag the small black box down to cell D14. Explain what happens.

3. Click the tab named *Sheet2* in the workbook you used for question 2.
   a. Place the labels *Part Description, Quantity on Hand, Cost,* and *Total Value* in cells A2, A3, A4, and A5, respectively. Center each label in its cell and make the labels bold. (Do this by highlighting the labels and clicking the bold **B** in the *Font* section of the *Home* tab.) Make each column large enough to show the entire label after formatting.
   b. In cells B3, B4, B5, B6, and B7, respectively, enter the following values:

      This is where one would type the description of Part 1
      This is where one would type the description of Part 2
      This is where one would type the description of Part 3
      This is where one would type the description of Part 4
      This is where one would type the description of Part 5

      Enter these values using the fewest possible keystrokes.
   c. Enter the quantity-on-hand values *100, 150, 100, 175,* and *200* in cells C3 through C7, respectively. Enter these values using the fewest possible keystrokes.
   d. Enter the values *$100, $178, $87, $195,* and *$117* in cells D3 through D7, respectively. Do not enter the dollar signs. Instead, enter only the numbers and then reformat the cells so that Excel will place them.
   e. In cell E3, enter a formula that will multiply the quantity on hand (C3) by the cost (D3).
   f. Create the same formula in cells E4 through E7. Use select and copy operations.
   g. Explain what is magic about the operation in part f.
   h. Print the result of your activities in parts a–f. Print your document in landscape mode, showing cell boundaries and row and column names.

CHAPTER EXTENSION 6

STUDY QUESTIONS

Chapters 4 and 6 provide the background for this Extension.

Preparing a Computer Budget Using Excel

Q1 Is $80,000 enough?
Q2 What process should you use for establishing a budget?
Q3 What hardware do we need?
Q4 What software do we need?
Q5 What is the role of the IT department?
Q6 Is $80,000 enough? (continued)

This chapter extension applies the knowledge you gained from Chapters 4 and 6 to the problem of establishing a hardware and software budget. We will use Excel to build a tool for computing the budget based on various assumptions of organizational growth. To understand why this knowledge is relevant, consider the first question.

Q1 Is $80,000 Enough?

Suppose that you manage the customer service department at a company that generates $100 million in sales—say, a manufacturer of fireplaces and related equipment. Assume that you just started the job and that at the end of your second day your boss sticks her head in your office and announces, "I'm in a rush and have to go, but I wanted to let you know that I put $80,000 in the budget for computers for your department next year. Is that okay? Unfortunately, I've got to know by the day after tomorrow. Thanks."

How do you respond? You have 2 days to decide. If you agree to $80,000 and it turns out to be insufficient, then sometime next year your department will lack computing resources, and you will have a management problem. If that happens, you may have to spend over your budget. You know that effective cost control is important to your new company, so you dread overspending. However, if you ask for more than $80,000, you will need to justify why you need it. How do you proceed?

The goal of this chapter extension is to prepare you to ask the right questions so you can respond effectively to your boss's question. You will learn how to address this question as well as how to use Excel to create a budget analysis tool.

Q2 What Process Should You Use for Establishing a Budget?

The steps for preparing a departmental hardware budget are summarized in Figure CE6-1. First you need to determine the base requirements. This involves assessing the work your employees perform, creating job categories, and determining the computer workload requirements for each category.

Figure CE6-1
A Process for Preparing a Departmental IT Budget

Determine base requirements:
- The types of workload your employees perform
- The hardware requirements for each type
- The software requirements for each type

Forecast requirement changes during the budget period:
- Changes in the number of employees
- Changes in workload—new job tasks or information systems
- Mandatory changes in hardware or software

Prepare the budget:
- Using guidance from the IT department and accounting, price the hardware and software
- Determine if your department will be charged for networks, servers, communications, or other overhead expenses
- Add overhead charges as necessary

What Are Hardware and Software Needs for Job Categories?

In your customer service department, suppose you determine that you have three categories of employees: first-line service reps, senior reps, and managers (including yourself). You further determine that the first-line reps need hardware and software to access the company's Web portal, to process email, to perform minimal word processing, and to access the company's help documentation. Senior reps handle calls that are escalated (referred up the chain of command) by the first-line reps. Calls are typically escalated for two reasons: the first-line rep cannot solve the customer's problem or the resolution of the problem requires returning equipment or refunding payments in excess of a $400 limit established by management. Senior reps need all of the computer capability of the first-line reps, plus they need access to customer account data and to the help sites of your three principal suppliers.

Finally, the managers, who are the shift managers, and you, need all of the capability of the senior managers. The managers need to be able to process budgets and other financial-planning documents in Excel. Managers also need to be able to access the company's human resource system.

Once you have identified the job categories and the computer workload requirements for each, you can apply the knowledge from Chapters 4 and 6 and from the rest of this chapter extension to determine hardware and software requirements for each type. You can also use past departmental experience as a guide. If employees complain about computer performance with the equipment they have, you can determine if more is needed. If there are no bottlenecks or performance problems, you know the current equipment will do.

Given the base requirements, the next step is to forecast changes. Will you be adding or losing employees during the year? Will the workload change? Will your department be given new tasks that will necessitate additional hardware or software? Finally, during the year, will your organization mandate changes in hardware or software? Will you be required to upgrade your operating system or applications software? If so, will your budget be charged for those upgrades?

Once you have the base requirements and your change forecasts, you can prepare the budget. The first task is to price the hardware and software. As you learned in Chapter 11, your IT department will most likely have established standards for hardware and software from which you will select. They will probably have negotiated prices on your behalf. If not, the accounting department can probably help you estimate costs based on their prior experience. You can also learn from the past experience of your own department.

Your organization may have a policy of charging the department's overhead fees for support, networks, servers, and communications. If so, you will need to add those charges to the budget as well.

Given the number of workers in each category and the price of hardware and software for each, you can then use Excel to forecast your budgetary needs.

Estimating Headcount

Figure CE6-2 shows an Excel spreadsheet that the customer support department can use to plan its headcount. Column B has the current headcount; columns C and D project that headcount for 10 percent and 25 percent growth, respectively. In this figure, the focus is on cell D6, and you can see in the row just above the column names that the formula used is to multiply cell B6 by 1 plus the growth factor (thus, by 1.1). The cells in column E are multiplied by 1.25 because that column assumes 25 percent growth.

The problem with this spreadsheet is that it shows *fractions* of employees. Of course, the department does not have 40.7 first-line reps. We can force Excel to round the numbers using the built-in ROUND function as follows:

```
= ROUND (B7 * 1.1, 0)
```

The numbers inside the parentheses are passed to the ROUND function. The first is the number to be rounded, and the second is the number of places to round to. Because we want only whole numbers, the second number is zero.

Figure CE6-3 shows the results when using ROUND for columns D and E. Notice the formula used for cell D6.

The results so far are acceptable, but what if you or the other managers want to analyze growth factors other than 10 and 25 percent? The spreadsheet in Figure CE6-4 shows one way to do this. Examine rows 14 and 15. Cell B14 contains a value of the

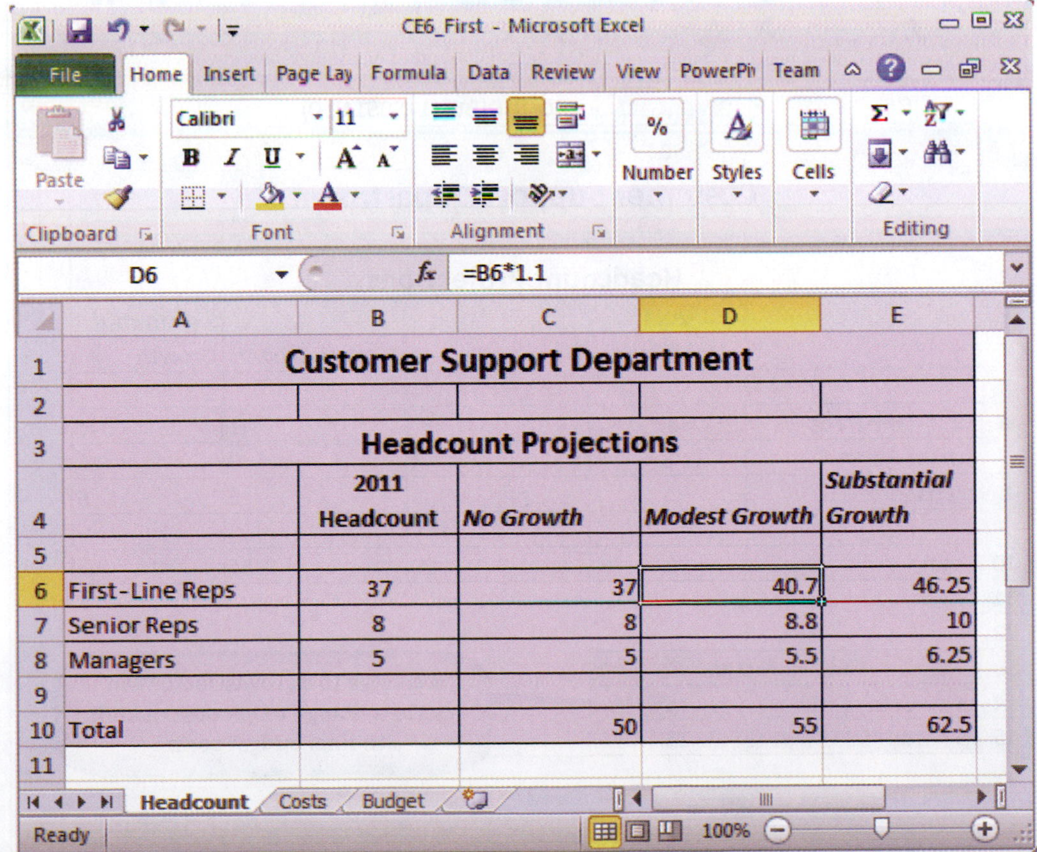

Figure CE6-2
Excel Spreadsheet for Planning Headcount of Customer Support Department

Figure CE6-3
Results of Using the Rounding Function in Excel

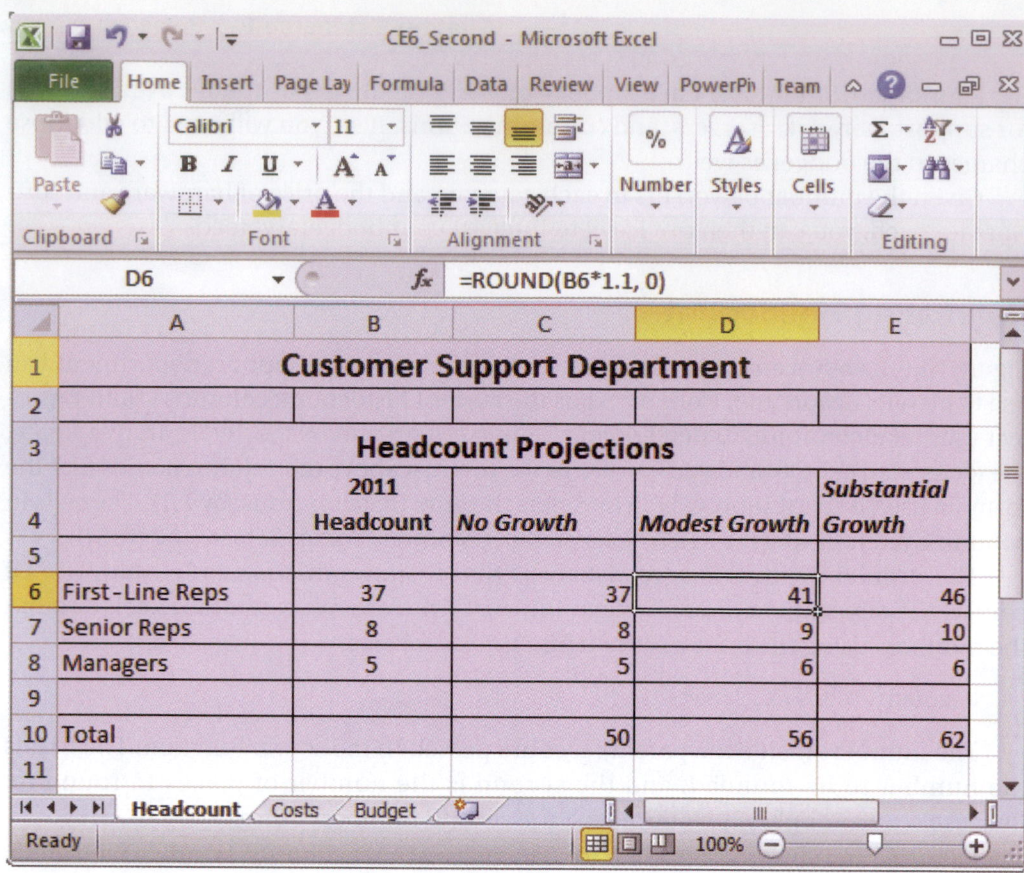

Figure CE6-4
Spreadsheet Showing Assumed Growth Factors of 10 and 25 Percent

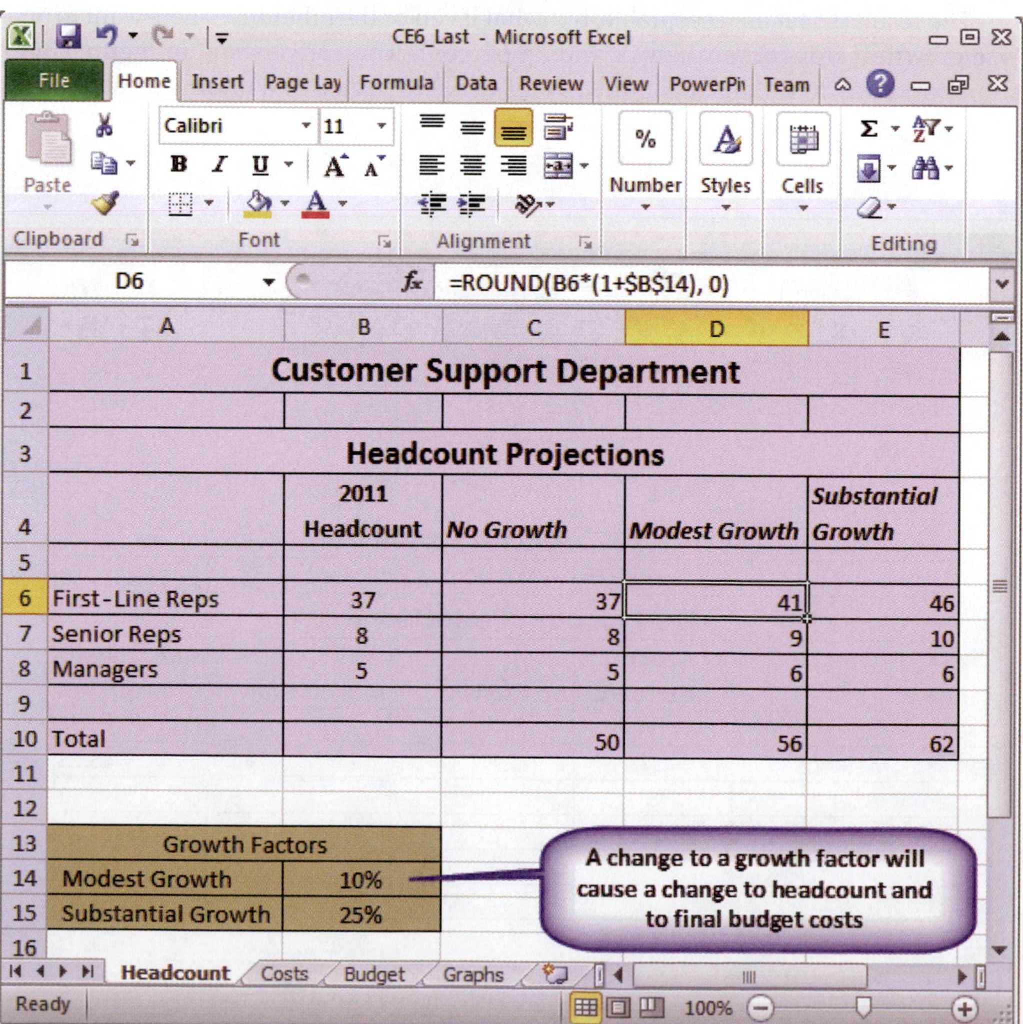

assumed modest growth rate (here, 10%), and cell B15 contains a value of the assumed substantial growth rate (here, 25%). The formulas in cells D6, D7, and D8 use the value in B14, and those in cells E6, E7, and E8 use the value in B15. Now, if the user changes the value in cell B14 or B15 (or both), the headcounts will be recomputed using those new values. Further, as we continue to develop this spreadsheet, we will take headcount numbers from this worksheet. Therefore, changes made here will propagate through the whole budget. Figure CE6-5 shows the results if the user enters 20 for B14 and 40 for B15.

However, one important alteration is needed. Consider the formula for cell D6. It is tempting to write the formula as = ROUND (B6 * (1 + B14), 0), which will add the value of B14 to 1, multiply that sum by the value in B6, and then round to zero decimal points. That's OK, but consider what happens when we copy that formula to cell D7. Excel will note that the formula has been moved down one cell, and so it will move both B6 and B14 down one cell. The result will be: = ROUND (B7 * (1 + B15), 0). B7 is correct, but B15 is wrong. We did not want Excel to alter B14.

Excel provides **absolute addresses** for this situation. If, instead of coding B14, we place a dollar sign in front of the B and in front of the 14, Excel will interpret B14 as an absolute address that should not be changed when the formula is copied or moved. And, in Figures CE6-4 and Figures CE6-5, that is exactly what we did. Verify the contents of cell D6.

At this point, we have a tool for projecting headcounts for the three types of employee for two different growth factors—and we can readily alter the growth factors. We will continue developing this budgetary tool as this chapter extension unfolds.

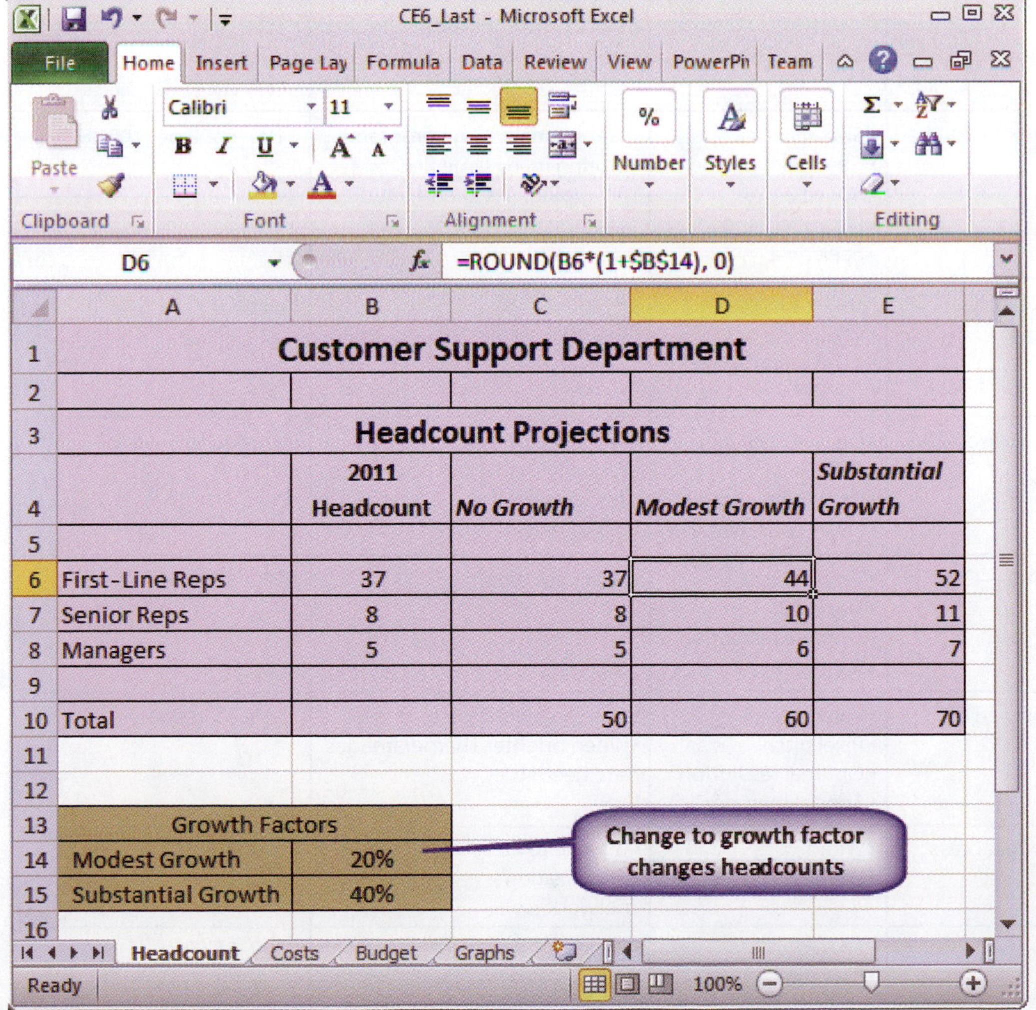

Figure CE6-5 Spreadsheet Showing Changes to Assumed Growth Factors of 20 and 40 Percent

Q3 What Hardware Do We Need?

We discussed the basic features and functions of hardware in Chapters 4 and 6. Figure CE6-6 is based on Figure 4-1 with the addition of a column showing typical prices. In this section, we discuss the characteristics of the elements in this table in more detail.

Today, most computers are sold as packages to which the buyer can optionally upgrade and add equipment. You might choose a certain base package and add another 512MB of memory or a larger disk. However, if you find that you are adding substantial equipment to a standard package, you are usually better off to back up and begin with a higher-grade standard package.

Laptop or Desktop?

To understand the computer-buying process, visit *www.dell.com* (or another hardware vendor site). You first will be given a choice of computer type: laptop or desktop.

Figure CE6-6 Hardware Components, Performance Factors, and Prices

Component	Performance Factors	Beneficial For:	Typical 2010 Price
CPU and data bus	• CPU speed • Cache memory • Data bus speed • Data bus width	• Fast processing of data once the data reside in main memory	Laptop: $500 (1GHz) $2,500 (3GHz) Workstation: $300 (1GHz) $2,000 (3GHz)
Main memory	• Size • Speed	• Holding multiple programs at one time • Processing very large amounts of data	$250–$400 per 500MB
Magnetic disk	• Size • Channel type and speed • Rotational speed • Seek time	• Storing many large programs • Storing many large files • Swapping files in and out of memory	$100–$400 per 100GB
Optical disc—CD	• Up to 700MB • CD-ROM • CD-R (recordable) • CD-RW (rewritable)	• Reading CDs • Writable media can be used to back up files	Included with system
Optical disc—DVD	• Up to 4.7GB • DVD-ROM • DVD-R (recordable) • DVD-RW (rewritable)	• Process both DVDs and CDs • Writable media can be used to back up files	Included to $400 for DVD-RW
Monitor—CRT	• Viewing size • Dot pitch • Optimal resolution • Special memory?	• Small budgets	$100–$500
Monitor—LCD	• Viewing size • Pixel pitch • Optimal resolution • Special memory?	• Crowded workspaces • When brighter, sharper images are needed	$100–$11,000+
Network access	• Wired • Wireless	• Choose to fit organization's network	Included
Printers	• Shared • Personal	• Reports	$200–$5,000+

In general, desktops are cheaper, so unless employees have a need to travel or take their computers to meetings, select desktop. Also, desktops tend to be more reliable than laptops: They are neither bashed around at airport security check-ins nor dropped in the snow on the street. Furthermore, laptop designs force many components into a small shell and can have heat-dissipation problems that lead to failure.

When preparing the budget for your department, you need to make the laptop/desktop decision for each job category. Next, you need to select the CPU speed and size of main memory. We consider these components next.

The CPU and Memory

As stated in Chapter 4, a fast CPU and data bus are most useful when processing data that already reside in main memory. Once you download a large spreadsheet, for example, a fast CPU will rapidly perform complicated, formula-based what-if analyses. A fast CPU also is useful for processing large graphics files. If, for example, you are manipulating the brightness of the elements of a large picture, a fast CPU will enable that manipulation to proceed quickly.

If the applications that you or your employees use do not involve millions of calculations or manipulations on data in main memory, then buying the fastest CPU is probably not worthwhile. In fact, a lot of the excitement about CPU speed is just industry "hype." Speed is an easily marketed and understood idea, but for most business processing having a very fast CPU is often not as important as other factors, such as main memory.

Main Memory

According to the second row of Figure CE6-6, the two key performance factors for main memory are speed and size. Normally, a particular computer make and model is designed to use a given memory type, and the speed for that type is fixed. Once you buy the computer, there is nothing you can do to increase memory *speed.*

You can, however, increase the *amount* of main memory, up to the maximum size of memory that your computer brand and model can hold. In 2010, the maximum amount of memory for new 32-bit personal computers ranged from 3.0 to 4.0GB; the maximum for a 64-bit personal computer ranged from 8 to 12GB.

By the way, if budget is a consideration, you can sometimes buy memory from third parties more economically than from the computer manufacturer. However, you must make sure that you buy the correct memory type. Installing more memory is easy; low-skill technicians can perform that task or, if no vendor support is available, someone in your IT department can do it.

As shown in Figure CE6-6, installing more memory is beneficial for situations in which you run many different applications at the same time or if you process many large files (several megabytes or more, each). If your computer is constantly swapping files, installing more memory will dramatically improve performance. In truth, memory is cheap and is often the best way to get more performance out of a computer.

The operating system has tools and utilities that measure main memory utilization and file swapping. A computer technician can use these tools to determine, quite easily, whether more memory would be helpful.

Magnetic Disks

As stated in Chapter 4, magnetic and optical disks provide long-term, nonvolatile data storage. The types and sizes of such storage devices will affect computer performance. First, understand that data are recorded on magnetic disks in concentric circles

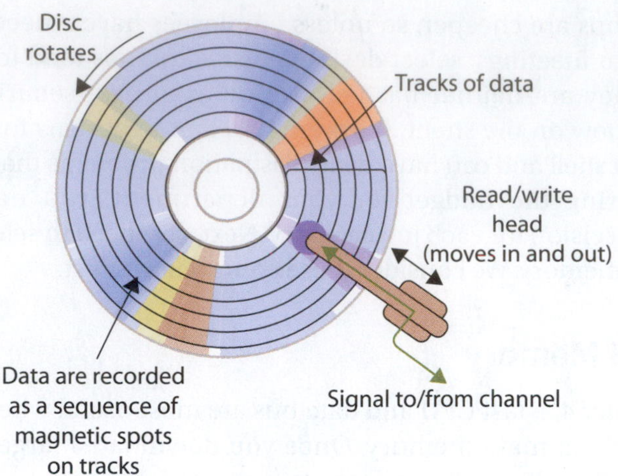

Figure CE6-7
Magnetic Disc Components

(Figure CE6-7). The disks spin inside the disk unit, and as they spin magnetic spots on the disk are read or written by the *read/write head.*

The time required to read data from a disk depends on two measures: The first measure, called the **rotational delay**, is the time it takes the data to rotate under the read/write head. The second, called **seek time**, is the time it takes the read/write arm to position the head over the correct circle. The faster the disk spins, the shorter the rotational delay. Seek time is determined by the make and model of the disk device.

Once the read/write head is positioned over the correct spot on the disk, data can flow over the channel to or from main memory. Like the data bus, the rate of data transfer depends on the width and speed of the channel. A number of different standards govern channel characteristics. As of 2008, a common standard is the **ATA-100 (Advanced Technology Attachment) standard**. The number 100 indicates that the maximum transfer rate is 100MB per second.

When you buy a computer, you generally have just a few disk-type choices. You may be able to choose one or two different channel standards (e.g., ATA-66 or ATA-100), and you may be able to choose disks with different rotational speeds.

You will always, however, be offered a number of choices in disk size. For most business users, 50GB is more than enough disk space. Large disks are cheap to manufacture, however, and you will be offered disks much larger than this (400GB or more). If you need to store a detailed map of every county in the United States or if you need to store huge downloads from your organization's server computers, then you may need such a large disk. Otherwise, don't fall prey to the hype; buy better monitors or something else, instead.

As stated in Figure CE6-6, you can use a fast disk to compensate, to some extent, for too little memory. Recall that if you have too little memory, your computer will be swapping files in and out; a fast disk will speed this process. You might attempt to compensate with a fast disk if you have installed the maximum memory your computer can take and you still have a swapping problem. In that case, however, you would probably also benefit from a faster processor, and you might just as well buy a new computer.

Optical Disks

The two kinds of optical disks are compact discs (CDs) and digital versatile discs (DVDs). Both are made of plastic and are coated with a photosensitive material. As stated in Chapter 4, bits are recorded by burning a pit into the photosensitive material using a low-power laser. The presence of a pit causes light to reflect and signifies a one; the absence of reflection signifies a zero. Like magnetic disks, optical disks are nonvolatile; they maintain their contents even when not powered.

The major difference between CDs and DVDs is how they store data; that difference is unimportant to this discussion, however. The *practical* differences between CDs and DVDs are capacity and speed. A typical CD has a maximum capacity of 700MB, whereas a DVD can store up to 4.7GB. Additionally, DVD transfer rates are about 10 times faster than those for CDs.

As shown in Figure CE6-6, some optical discs are *read only*; they cannot record data. These discs are abbreviated as **CD-ROM** and **DVD-ROM**. (*ROM* stands for *read-only memory.*) Other optical discs, denoted **CD-R** and **DVD-R**, can record data once. (The *R* stands for *recordable.*) A third group, denoted **CD-RW** and **DVD-RW**, can write data hundreds of times. (The *RW* stands for *rewritable.*)

CDs and DVDs see their greatest use in the entertainment industry for playing music and videos. DVDs are used widely in commerce for distributing programs and other large files. Operating systems and programs, such as Windows and Microsoft Office, are distributed and installed from DVDs, for example. Also, writable media can be used to back up magnetic disk files.

Today, every computer should have at least a DVD-ROM for installing programs. Most computers should also have some version of a writable optical disk for backing up data. Beyond those purposes, the major reason for having a CD or DVD is entertainment, and that reason may not be the best use of your organization's resources.

Video Displays

There are two types of video display monitors: CRTs and LCDs. **CRT monitors** use *cathode-ray tubes*, the same devices used in traditional TV screens. Because they use a large tube, CRTs are big and bulky, about as deep as they are wide. **LCD monitors** use a technology called *liquid crystal display* (LCD). With LCD monitors, no tube is required, so they are much slimmer, around 2 inches or so deep.

Both types of monitors display images by illuminating small spots on the screen called **pixels**. Pixels are arranged in a rectangular grid. An inexpensive monitor might display an image 800 pixels wide and 600 pixels high. A higher-quality monitor would display a grid of 1,024 × 768 pixels, and some display as many as 1,600 × 1,200 pixels.

The number of pixels displayed depends not only on the size of the monitor, but also on the design of the mechanism that creates the image. For a CRT monitor, the **dot pitch** of the monitor is the distance between pixels. The smaller the dot pitch, the sharper and brighter the screen image will be. For an LCD monitor, the **pixel pitch** is the distance between pixels on the screen. As with CRT monitors, the smaller the pixel pitch, the sharper and brighter the image will be.

Each monitor has an **optimal resolution**, which is the size of the pixel grid (e.g., 1,024 × 768) that will give the best sharpness and clarity. This optimal resolution depends on the size of the screen, the dot or pixel pitch, and other factors. More expensive monitors have higher optimal resolution than others.

Each pixel on the monitor is represented in main memory. If the resolution of the monitor is 1,024 × 768, then there will be a table in memory with 1,024 rows and 768 columns. Each cell of this table has a numeric value that represents the color of the pixel that it represents. Programs change the display on the monitor by instructing the operating system to change values in this image table.

The amount of memory used for each cell in the pixel grid depends on the number of colors that each pixel is to display. For a black-and-white image, the cells can consist of a single bit: zero for white and one for black. To represent 16 colors, each pixel is represented by four bits. (Four bits can hold the numbers from 0 to 15—each number signifies a particular color.) Today, most monitors use a large color palette that necessitates 32 bits for each pixel and allows for 8,589,934,591 colors.

Substantial main memory is needed for this large palette. To represent an image in 1,024 × 768 resolution, a total of 3,145,728 bytes of memory (1,024 × 768 × 4 bytes) is needed. For reasons beyond the scope of this text, sometimes several versions of this pixel table are in memory.

Because these tables occupy a large amount of memory, some computers dedicate a separate memory cache just to the video display. The design of such memory is optimized for video use as well. Such special-purpose video memory is particularly important for multimedia applications where large images change rapidly. It is also important for 3D video in computer games.

For monitors of equivalent quality, the initial cost of CRT monitors is less than that for LCD monitors. LCD monitors have a longer life, however, so they may actually cost less over time. Because of the speed at which technology improvements take place, most people upgrade to a better computer before they ever wear out their monitor, so this extra life may not matter.

The big advantage of LCD monitors is, of course, their smaller footprint, which means they take up less desk space. They are especially desirable when work requires viewing more than one monitor at a time. Stock traders on Wall Street, for example, need three or four monitors, and these monitors are always LCDs.

Today, CRTs have almost disappeared from the workplace. You might see them in poorly funded organizations, or you might find one in highly specialized situations where CRTs have an advantage, but for the most part they are no longer used.

Network Access

As you learned in Chapter 6, every networked computer must have a network interface card (NIC). NICs support either wired or wireless connections, and the decision about which to choose will be dictated by the type of network your department has. Today, most computers ship with both types as standard equipment. Otherwise, you'll need to add the proper NIC to the computers you specify. Note, too, that wired computers can be readily upgraded to wireless by the installation of a wireless NIC.

Printers

Printers are available in many different types, sizes, and qualities. The discussion of those options is not within the scope of an MIS book. Visit *www.cnet.com/printers* or other similar Web sites if you want to know more about printer options.

We will be concerned here only with whether you want employees to share the printer. If you do, there are two options: A printer can be attached to a computer and others can access the printer via that computer, or the printer can be equipped with its own NIC and users can access it directly. For most purposes, the latter is preferred because it frees up a computer.

Hardware for the Customer Support Budget

Figure CE6-8 shows the same workbook that was shown in Figures CE6-2 through CE6-5, but a different worksheet is activated. The bottom left-hand corner of this figure shows three tabs: Headcount, Costs, and Budget. The Headcount worksheet shown earlier can be viewed by clicking the Headcount tab. In Figure CE6-8, the Costs tab is activated.

The team that prepared the budget for this department analyzed the work that needed to be done and, with help from the IT department, determined that the first-line reps could do their work with a workstation that costs $1,200 and a $300 monitor (cells C7 and C8). The senior reps need a workstation that is somewhat faster and has a larger disk that costs $1,800. They, too, can work with a $300 monitor. Finally, the managers need a laptop (they attend meetings where they need to make PowerPoint presentations from their computers) that costs $2,000.

We will discuss the rest of this worksheet in the sections that follow.

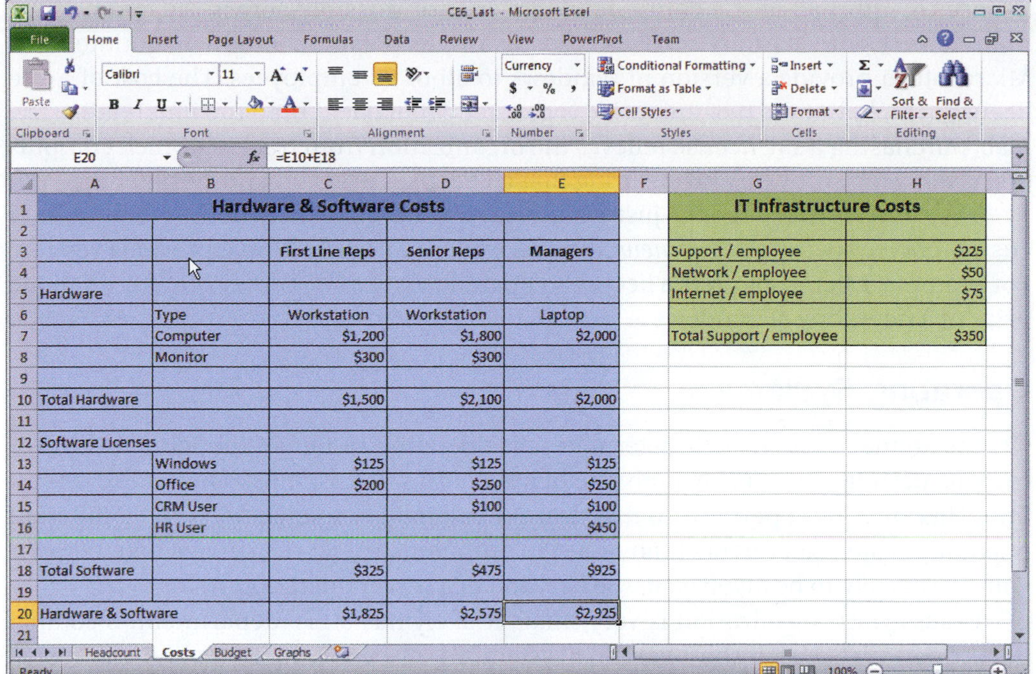

	A	B	C	D	E	F	G	H
1	Hardware & Software Costs						IT Infrastructure Costs	
2								
3			First Line Reps	Senior Reps	Managers		Support / employee	$225
4							Network / employee	$50
5	Hardware						Internet / employee	$75
6		Type	Workstation	Workstation	Laptop			
7		Computer	$1,200	$1,800	$2,000		Total Support / employee	$350
8		Monitor	$300	$300				
9								
10	Total Hardware		$1,500	$2,100	$2,000			
11								
12	Software Licenses							
13		Windows	$125	$125	$125			
14		Office	$200	$250	$250			
15		CRM User		$100	$100			
16		HR User			$450			
17								
18	Total Software		$325	$475	$925			
19								
20	Hardware & Software		$1,825	$2,575	$2,925			

Figure CE6-8 The Costs Worksheet of the Computer Budget Workbook, Showing IT Infrastructure Costs for Different Types of Employees

Q4 What Software Do We Need?

We discussed the features and functions of software in Chapter 4. Figure CE6-9 shows categories of software, the decisions you'll need to make, and the approximate prices. Note in the *Price* column that software is sometimes included with the purchase of hardware. Also, the term **site license** means that an organization has purchased a

Figure CE6-9 Software Components and Prices

Category	Decisions to Make	Typical 2010 Prices
Operating system (Windows, Mac OS, Linux)	• Usually determined by organizational policy. • May need to select version.	• Possibly included with hardware. • Possibly paid for by site license. • Otherwise, $100–$300 for upgrade. • $300–$700 new.
Standard horizontal application, such as Microsoft Office or Open Office	• May be determined by organizational policy. • Choose package with components you need: word processing, spreadsheet, presentation, email client, or personal DBMS.	• Usually only the very minimum included with hardware. • Possibly paid for by site license. • Otherwise, $100–$300 for upgrade. • $300–$700 new.
Other horizontal applications	Document creation (Adobe Acrobat), photo processing (Adobe Photoshop, Jasc Paint Shop Pro), illustration (Adobe Illustrator), etc.	• Possibly minimum feature "teaser" versions included with hardware. • Possibly paid for by site license. • Otherwise, $100–$300 for upgrade. • $300–$1000 new.
Vertical package software (Goldmine, Act!, AutoCad)	Determined by job category needs.	• Seldom included with hardware. • Possibly paid for by site license. • Otherwise, $100–$500 for upgrade. • $300–$1,500 new.
Vertical applications (CRM, ERP, etc.)	Determined by job category needs.	• Not included with hardware. • Possibly paid for by site license, or a license for a certain number of seats (users). • Otherwise, $500–$1,000 per user or more.

license to equip all of the computers on a site (or possibly across the company at many sites) with certain software. For example, Pearson might negotiate with Microsoft to provide a version of Windows to all of its employees. The cost of a site license is high, but the per-unit price is generally much less than the unit retail price. Also, purchasing a site license relieves the organization from tracking which computers have which software and ensuring that all licenses are paid appropriately.

The term **upgrade** means just what it says: Vendors usually do not require their customers to pay the price of *new* software when upgrading from a previous version. For example, Microsoft offers a license to upgrade Vista to Windows 7 for less than the price of a new copy of Windows 7.

Operating Systems

Organizational policy usually determines the operating system. Although some organizations permit users to run a mixture of operating systems, most standardize on just one. This statement pertains to user computers; many organizations run a different operating system on servers than on user computers. We ignore servers here because you are unlikely to be involved in the decision of a server operating system.

Unless your organization is very small, it likely has an IT department. If so, that department will install the operating system on all new computers and will install upgrades on existing computers as well. In a small organization, you will likely buy a computer from a vendor such as Dell that has done the operating system installation for you.

Horizontal Market Software

Most organizations today use Microsoft Office for their standard applications such as word processing and spreadsheets. Office licenses are sold in a number of different configurations. Some include just Word and Excel; others include Word, Excel, PowerPoint, Access, Outlook, and possibly other applications. Your organization may have a site license for a particular version.

OpenOffice.org (*www.openoffice.org*) is an alternative to Office that is supported by the open-source community and is license-free in most cases. OpenOffice.org is slowly gaining in popularity, especially in organizations that are very conscious of costs. OpenOffice.org can process most documents prepared by Office, and vice versa. One exception to this is that OpenOffice.org does not have a personal DBMS that is compatible with Access.

Your employees may require other types of horizontal software. Designers and other document preparers may need software for document preparation, photo processing, desktop publishing, or illustrations. Software vendors often provide free teaser versions (products with limited functionality) of their products with new computers. Sometimes these limited versions provide sufficient capability for a given job. Additionally, vendors sometimes offer license-free software that allows the user to read or view a file but not to work with it. Adobe, for example, offers the Acrobat Reader for free, and Microsoft offers the Silverlight runtime license for free as well.

Vertical Market Software

Examples of vertical market software are contact managers such as Goldmine and Act! and engineering software such as AutoCad. Such products are almost never included in the price of a new computer. Your organization may have negotiated a site license for such software or even a restricted site license to provide it to the employees of certain departments.

Licenses for some of this software can be surprisingly expensive, and some small organizations elect to install the software without licenses. **This practice is both illegal and highly unethical**. Some small companies believe they are too small to be worth the cost of a lawsuit and use the software anyway. Such practice is dishonest, disreputable, and entirely reprehensible.

As you will read in Chapter 7, customer relationship management (CRM) and enterprise resource planning (ERP) systems are used widely throughout an organization. They can have hundreds or even thousands of users. The vendors of these products usually charge a license for each user or for a certain number of users (sometimes expressed in **seats**). Your organization might buy a license for, say, up to 500 seats of a particular application. If your department is using any of these systems, you need to check with your IT department to determine what costs apply to you.

Software for the Customer Support Budget

The software costs for the customer support department are shown in Figure CE6-8 (page 377). The company has negotiated a company-wide license fee with Microsoft. The fee for Windows 7 for each computer is $125. Two versions of Office exist: one includes Word and PowerPoint and costs $200; the second includes Word, PowerPoint, Excel, and Access and costs $250. First-line reps need the first version, and senior reps and managers need the second.

The company uses a CRM system that has a per-user, or seat-license, fee of $100. Both senior reps and managers need that software. Additionally, managers need a license to use a human resources (HR) system that has a per-user license fee of $450. All of the software costs are entered into the spreadsheet in Figure CE6-8 in rows 12–18. The total hardware and software costs are shown in line 20.

Q5 What Is the Role of the IT Department?

As you will learn in Chapter 11, the IT department normally provides a help desk or other facility to assist users. Unknown to most users, however, is that the IT department has many other responsibilities, including maintaining networks and servers, administering databases, planning IT, developing and installing new systems, and so forth. Its responsibilities are compounded because it must do all of this while providing a secure computing environment.

To meet these many responsibilities, most IT departments set standards on the hardware and software that users can employ. In some cases, the IT department will specify a menu of different computer systems, from very powerful computers for, say, high-performance graphics computation, down to less-powerful ones for email and Internet access only. Additionally, the IT department may specify a particular operating system, and particular versions of both horizontal and vertical applications software.

As the manager of an end-user department, you are strongly advised to work within these standards. Even if they seem objectionable, overly restrictive, or excessively costly to you or your employees, you will be better off in the long run by staying within the IT department's guidelines. By following their standards, you will make it easier and cheaper for them to provide high-quality, secure computing service to your department. If you cannot live within those standards, then raise the issue with the IT department manager, but do not work around them.

IT Infrastructure Costs for the Customer Support Budget

The IT department charges a per-computer cost for the IT infrastructure used by the customer support department. Columns G and H in Figure CE6-8 show the annual costs: $225 for general support, another $50 for internal network servers and services, and $75 for Internet access. The total cost is $350 per employee.

Q6 Is $80,000 Enough? (Continued)

At this point, we can bring together the spreadsheets shown earlier to compute your departmental budget. The Headcount worksheet contains the current and projected headcount for two levels of growth. The Costs worksheet contains costs for hardware, software, and infrastructure. Data from those worksheets are input into the Budget worksheet shown in Figure CE6-10.

The department need not purchase new equipment for all of its existing employees. However, some of the equipment will need to be replaced. For this budget, assume that 40 percent of the existing computers will need to be replaced.

The top section of the worksheet shows the current headcount and the costs that were computed for new systems. This data came from the other, supporting worksheets. For example, notice the formula in cell B5: Costs!C20. (If you want to sound like a techie, you can pronounce the exclamation point as "Bang." Thus, the formula in cell B5 is read, "Costs bang C20.") This syntax tells Excel to go to the worksheet named Costs and extract the value from the C20 cell. Examine cell C20 in Figure CE6-8 and you

Figure CE6-10
Completed Departmental Budget Worksheet

CE6_Last - Microsoft Excel

File | Home | Insert | Page Layout | Formulas | Data | Review | View | PowerPiv | Team

B5 | =Costs!C20

	A	B	C	D	E
1		First-Line Reps	Senior Reps	Managers	Totals
2					
3	Current Headcount	37	8	5	
4					
5	Cost of New System	$1,825	$2,575	$2,925	
6					
7	Number to replace (40 percent)	15	3	2	
9					
10	No Growth				
11	New Employees	0	0	0	
12	Total New Systems	15	3	2	
13	New System Costs	$27,375	$7,725	$5,850	$40,950
14	Total Headcount				50
15	Infrastructure costs				$17,500
16	Total Budget				$58,450
17					
18	Modest Growth				
19	New Employees	4	1	1	
20	Total New Systems	19	4	3	
21	New System Costs	$34,675	$10,300	$8,775	$53,750
22	Total Headcount				56
23	Infrastructure Costs				$19,600
24	Total Budget				$73,350
25					
26	Substantial Growth				
27	New Employees	9	2	1	
28	Total New Systems	24	5	3	
29	New System Costs	$43,800	$12,875	$8,775	$65,450
30	Total Headcount				62
31	Infrastructure Costs				$21,700
32	Total Budget				$87,150

Headcount | Costs | Budget | Graphs

Ready 90%

will see that it has the cost of a new system for first-line reps as $1,825, the same figure shown here. A similar approach is used for data values for cells B3, B19, and B27. In the case of B19, the formula is Headcount!D6 – Headcount!B6. The same technique is used to obtain values for these rows in columns C and D. It is also used to obtain the Total Headcount and infrastructure costs values in column E.

The rest of the spreadsheet should be self-explanatory. The number of new systems is multiplied by the cost of new systems in rows 13, 21, and 29. The total headcount is multiplied by the infrastructure costs from the Costs worksheet in rows 15, 23, and 31.

So, is $80,000 enough? It *is* enough for the current and modest growth headcounts. It is *not* enough for the substantial growth (25%) headcount. Given this data, you, as a manager, now know how to respond to your new boss. And, knowing one way to approach such questions should be useful to you throughout your business career.

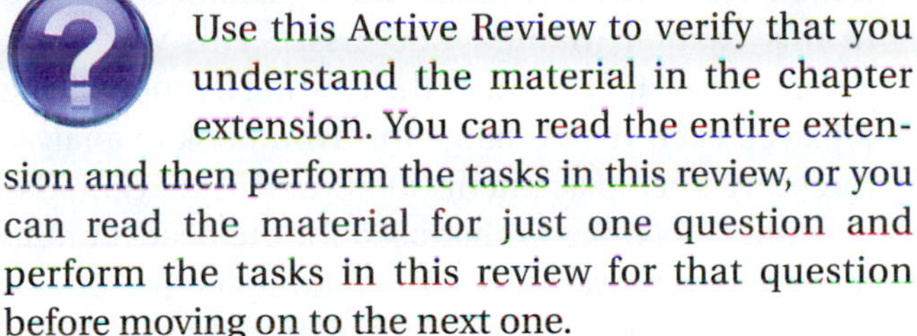

ACTIVE REVIEW

Use this Active Review to verify that you understand the material in the chapter extension. You can read the entire extension and then perform the tasks in this review, or you can read the material for just one question and perform the tasks in this review for that question before moving on to the next one.

Q1 Is $80,000 enough?

Summarize the task that you have been given. Explain the consequences if you do not budget enough. Explain the consequences if you ask for more budget than you need. Explain how you would proceed. Describe why this task is more difficult and also more important because you are new to your job.

Q2 What process should you use for establishing a budget?

List the tasks of the process in Figure CE6-1. Explain the work to be done for each task. Describe why the order of the tasks is important. Describe the purpose of the spreadsheet in Figure CE6-2. Explain the syntax of the ROUND function. Describe how you can use this spreadsheet to evaluate the headcount for different levels of growth. Define absolute address, give an example, and explain why such addresses are necessary.

Q3 What hardware do we need?

Describe how you would use the table in Figure CE6-6. Explain how this table relates to the process in Figure CE6-1. Ensure you understand each row and column of this table. Explain how the hardware choices in Figure CE6-8 relate to the job functions for each category of employee described in Q2.

Q4 What software do we need?

Describe how you would use the table in Figure CE6-9. Explain how this table relates to the process in Figure CE6-1. Ensure that you understand each row and column of this table. Explain the term *site license.* Characterize the behavior of a company that chooses to install software without licenses, assuming they are too small to sue. Explain how the software costs in Figure CE6-8 relate to the job functions for each category of employee described in Q2.

Q5 What is the role of the IT department?

Summarize the responsibilities of the IT department as described in this chapter extension. (You will learn more about these and other responsibilities in Chapter 11.) Describe the importance of standards in light of these responsibilities. Explain each of the IT infrastructure costs in Figure CE6-8. Do you think $350 per employee is excessive? Why or why not?

Q6 Is $80,000 enough? (continued)

Describe how you would use the spreadsheet in Figure CE6-10 to answer the following questions: Under what circumstances would $80,000 be enough? Under what circumstances would it be insufficient? Write a one-paragraph email to your boss explaining your results. Suppose your manager returns to you in a week saying that you have only $70,000 in your budget. Explain how you could use the workbook developed in this chapter to plan your response as a manager.

KEY TERMS AND CONCEPTS

USING YOUR KNOWLEDGE

1. As Moore's Law describes, computer price/performance data are continually falling. Suppose that you have been given the task of updating the price data in Figure CE6-6. Visit *www.dell.com* and *www.cnet.com*, and any other site you wish, and verify or change the data in the *Price* column in Figure CE6-6.

2. Software prices also change, but not as dramatically as hardware prices. Nonetheless, visit *www.amazon.com* or other Web sites and verify the data in Figure CE6-7. For prices on particular products, such as Goldmine, Acrobat, PaintShop Pro, and so forth, your best strategy might be to Google these products, using the product name and price; thus, Google "Goldmine license prices" or a similar term.

3. Many site licenses are negotiated on a one-on-one basis, and it may be difficult to find the actual price and other terms of a site license for a particular product. Search the Internet, though, for terms like "Windows site license program" or "Acrobat site license program," and determine the terms of the site licenses, even if you cannot obtain the specific price.

4. Why does Adobe provide licenses to Acrobat Reader for free? Do you think a better strategy would be to charge a modest license fee, say $50, for Acrobat Reader? What are the consequences of that action? How can Adobe verify the wisdom of this pricing decision?

5. Go to this text's support site at *www.pearsonhighered.com/kroenke* and download the workbook developed in this chapter (named **CE6_Last**). Using the spreadsheet, determine what level of growth will require exactly $80,000 (or as close as you can come to $80,000 without going over that amount.) Change the spreadsheet so that everyone has the same hardware as the managers (do not change the software). What budget is required to support the decision to give everyone a laptop? Suppose everyone in the department is given access to the CRM system. How much cost would such a requirement add to the budget?

6. Go to this text's support site at *www.pearsonhighered.com/kroenke* and download the workbook developed in this chapter (named **CE6_Last**). This workbook assumes that 40 percent of the existing laptops will be replaced each year. Change this workbook to analyze three levels of replacement: 30, 40, and 50 percent. Use a technique similar to that used for the headcount in the Headcount worksheet. What level of replacement would reduce the budgetary requirement to $70,000?

7. Regarding the $80,000 question, you, a new employee, have only 2 days to answer, and you probably had already scheduled meetings for those 2 days when your boss dropped this in your lap.
   - **a.** Can you complain? Would it be wise to do so?
   - **b.** Often, students will answer this question by specifying a complex, time-consuming, and *totally schedule-infeasible* process. You don't have time for a complex analysis. Still, an answer must be provided, and the answer is important. Explain how you can delegate aspects of this task.
   - **c.** Do you think your boss already knows the answer to this question? If so, why would she ask you?
   - **d.** Is it possible your boss is using this exercise as a way of learning how you manage? If you think this is possible, how does that realization change your response to this question?
   - **e.** You've been managing your department for only 2 days. How does the way you respond to this challenge influence the perception that your employees will have of you? Is this an important consideration? Would you consider having a lower-quality answer if it meant a higher-quality process? Is such a trade-off necessary?

CHAPTER EXTENSION 7

Chapter 5 provides the background for this Extension.

Database Design

STUDY QUESTIONS

Q1 Who will volunteer?

Q2 How are database application systems developed?

Q3 What are the components of the entity-relationship data model?

Q4 How is a data model transformed into a database design?

Q5 What is the users' role?

Q6 Who will volunteer? (continued)

In this chapter extension, you will learn about data modeling and how data models are transformed into database designs. You'll also learn the important role that business professionals have in the development of a database application system.

Q1 Who Will Volunteer?

Suppose you are the manager of fund-raising for a local public television station. Twice a year you conduct fund drives during which the station runs commercials that ask viewers to donate. These drives are important; they provide nearly 40 percent of the station's operating budget.

One of your job functions is to find volunteers to staff the phones during these drives. You need 10 volunteers per night for six nights, or 60 people, twice per year. The volunteers' job is exhausting, and normally a volunteer will work only one night during a drive.

Finding volunteers for each drive is a perpetual headache. Two months before a drive begins, you and your staff start calling potential volunteers. You first call volunteers from prior drives, using a roster that your administrative assistant prepares for each drive. Some volunteers have been helping for years; you'd like to know that information before you call them so that you can tell them how much you appreciate their continuing support. Unfortunately, the roster does not have that data.

Additionally, some volunteers are more effective than others. Some have a particular knack for increasing the callers' donations. Although those data are available, the information is not in a format that you can use when calling for volunteers. You think you could better staff the fund-raising drives if you had that missing information.

You know that you can use a computer database to keep better track of prior volunteers' service and performance, but you are not sure how to proceed. By the end of this chapter extension, when we return to this fund-raising situation, you will know what to do.

Q2 How Are Database Application Systems Developed?

You learned in Chapter 5 that a database application system consists of a database, a DBMS, and one or more database applications. A database application, in turn, consists of forms, reports, queries, and possibly application programs. The question

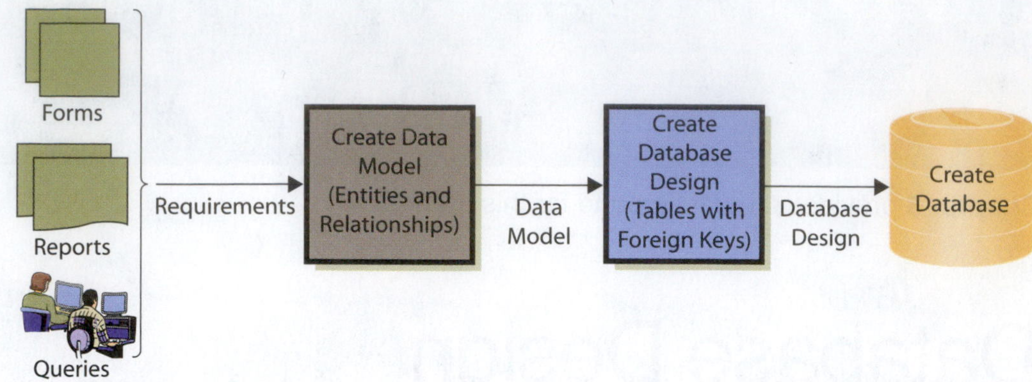

Figure CE7-1 Database Development Process

then becomes: How are such systems developed? And, even more important to you, what is the users' role? We will address these questions in this chapter extension.

Figure CE7-1 summarizes the database application system development process. First, the developers interview users and develop the requirements for the new system. During this process, the developers analyze existing forms, reports, queries, and other user activities. The requirements for the database are then summarized in something called a **data model**, which is a logical representation of the structure of the data. The data model contains a description of both the data and the relationships among the data. It is akin to a blueprint. Just as building architects create a blueprint before they start construction, so, too, database developers create a data model before they start designing the database.

Once the users have validated and approved the data model, it is transformed into a database design. After that, the design is implemented in a database, and that database is then filled with user data.

You will learn much more about systems development in Chapter 10 and its related extensions. We discuss data modeling here because users have a crucial role in the success of any database development: They must validate and approve the data model. Only the users know what should be in the database.

Consider, for example, a database of students that an adviser uses for his or her advisees. What should be in it? Students? Classes? Records of emails from students? Records of meetings with students? Majors? Student Organizations? Even when we know what themes should be in the database, we must ask, how detailed should the records be? Should the database include campus addresses? Home addresses? Billing addresses?

In fact, there are many possibilities, and the database developers do not and cannot know what to include. They do know, however, that a database must include all the data necessary for the users to perform their jobs. Ideally, it contains that amount of data and no more. So during database development, the developers must rely on the users to tell them what they need in the database. They will rely on the users to check the data model and to verify it for correctness, completeness, and appropriate level of detail. That verification will be your job. We begin with a discussion of the entity-relationship data model—the most common tool to use to construct data models.

Q3 What Are the Components of the Entity-Relationship Data Model?

The most popular technique for creating a data model is the **entity-relationship (E-R) data model**. With it, developers describe the content of a database by defining the things (*entities*) that will be stored in the database and the *relationships* among those entities. A second, less popular tool for data modeling is the **Unified Modeling Language (UML)**. We will not describe that tool here. However, if you learn how to interpret E-R models, with a bit of study you will be able to understand UML models as well.

Entities

An **entity** is some thing that the users want to track. Examples of entities are *Order, Customer, Salesperson,* and *Item.* Some entities represent a physical object, such as *Item* or *Salesperson*; others represent a logical construct or transaction, such as *Order* or *Contract.* For reasons beyond this discussion, entity names are always singular. We use *Order*, not *Orders*; *Salesperson*, not *Salespersons*.

Entities have **attributes** that describe characteristics of the entity. Example attributes of *Order* are *OrderNumber, OrderDate, SubTotal, Tax, Total,* and so forth. Example attributes of *Salesperson* are *SalespersonName, Email, Phone,* and so forth.

Entities have an **identifier**, which is an attribute (or group of attributes) whose value is associated with one and only one entity instance. For example, *OrderNumber* is an identifier of *Order,* because only one *Order* instance has a given value of *OrderNumber.* For the same reason, *CustomerNumber* is an identifier of *Customer.* If each member of the sales staff has a unique name, then *SalespersonName* is an identifier of *Salesperson.*

Before we continue, consider that last sentence. Is the salesperson's name unique among the sales staff? Both now and in the future? Who decides the answer to such a question? Only the users know whether this is true; the database developers cannot know. This example underlines why it is important for you to be able to interpret data models, because only users like yourself will know for sure.

Figure CE7-2 shows examples of entities for the Student database. Each entity is shown in a rectangle. The name of the entity is just above the rectangle, and the identifier is shown in a section at the top of the entity. Entity attributes are shown in the remainder of the rectangle. In Figure CE7-2, the *Adviser* entity has an identifier called *AdviserName* and the attributes *Phone, CampusAddress,* and *EmailAddress.*

Observe that the entities *Email* and *Office_Visit* do not have an identifier. Unlike *Student* or *Adviser,* the users do not have an attribute that identifies a particular email. In fact, *Email* and *Office_Visit* are identified, in part, by their relationship to Student. For now, we need not worry about that. The data model needs only to show how users view their world. When it comes to database design, the designer will deal with the missing identifiers by adding columns, possibly using hidden identifiers, to implement the users' view. You can learn about the modeling and representation of such entities if you enroll in a database class.

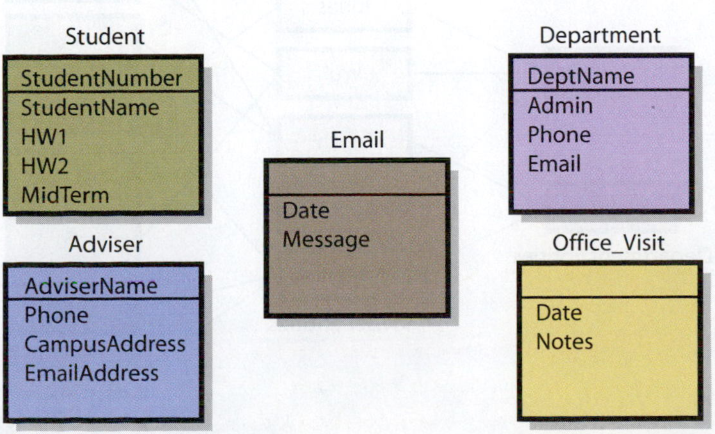

Figure CE7-2
Student Data Model Entities

Relationships

Entities have **relationships** to each other. An *Order*, for example, has a relationship to a *Customer* entity and also to a *Salesperson* entity. In the Student database, a *Student* has a relationship to an *Adviser*, and an *Adviser* has a relationship to a *Department*.

Figure CE7-3 shows sample *Department, Adviser*, and *Student* entities and their relationships. For simplicity, this figure shows just the identifier of the entities and not the other attributes. For this sample data, *Accounting* has three professors, Jones, Wu, and Lopez, and *Finance* has two professors, Smith and Greene.

The relationship between *Advisers* and *Students* is a bit more complicated, because in this example an adviser is allowed to advise many students and a student is allowed to have many advisers. Perhaps this happens because students can have multiple majors. In any case, note that Professor Jones advises students 100 and 400 and that student 100 is advised by both Professors Jones and Smith.

Diagrams like the one in Figure CE7-3 are too cumbersome for use in database design discussions. Instead, database designers use diagrams called **entity-relationship (E-R) diagrams**. Figure CE7-4 shows an E-R diagram for the data in Figure CE7-3. In this figure, all of the entities of one type are represented by a single rectangle. Thus, there are rectangles for the *Department, Adviser*, and *Student* entities. Attributes are shown as before in Figure CE7-2.

Additionally, a line is used to represent a relationship between two entities. Notice the line between *Department* and *Adviser*, for example. The forked lines on the right side of that line signify that a department may have more than one adviser. The little lines, which are referred to as a **crow's foot**, are shorthand for the multiple lines between *Department* and *Adviser* in Figure CE7-3. Relationships like this one are called **one-to-many (1:N)** relationships because one department can have many advisers.

Now examine the line between *Adviser* and *Student*. Here, a crow's foot appears at each end of the line. This notation signifies that an adviser can be related to many students and that a student can be related to many advisers, which is the situation in Figure CE7-3. Relationships like this one are called **many-to-many (N:M)** relationships, because one adviser can have many students and one student can have many advisers.

Students sometimes find the notation N:M confusing. Interpret the *N* and *M* to mean that a variable number, greater than one, is allowed on each side of the relationship. Such a relationship is not written *N:N*, because that notation would imply that there are the same number of entities on each side of the relationship, which is not

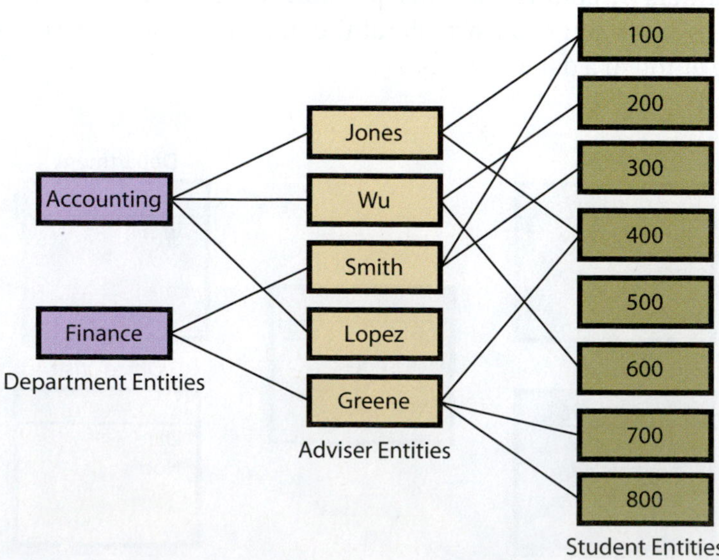

Figure CE7-3
Example of *Department, Adviser*, and *Student* Entities and Relationships

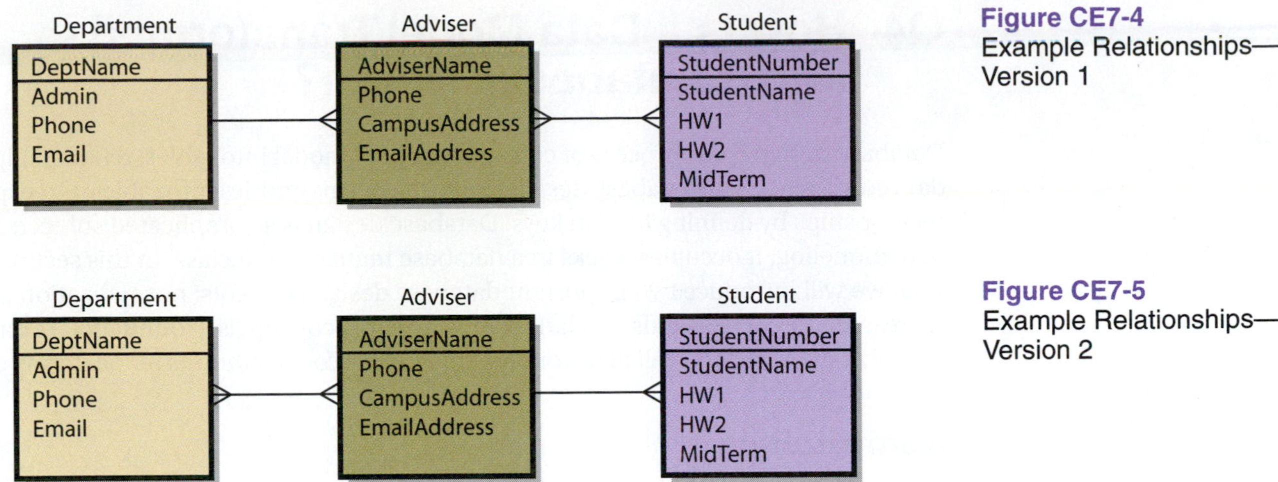

Figure CE7-4
Example Relationships—Version 1

Figure CE7-5
Example Relationships—Version 2

necessarily true. *N:M* means that more than one entity is allowed on each side of the relationship and that the number of entities on each side can be different.

Figure CE7-4 is an example of an entity-relationship diagram. Unfortunately, there are several different styles of entity-relationship diagrams. This one is called, not surprisingly, a **crow's-foot diagram** version. You may learn other versions if you take a database management class.

Figure CE7-5 shows the same entities with different assumptions. Here, advisers may advise in more than one department, but a student may have only one adviser, representing a policy that students may not have multiple majors.

Which, if either of these versions—Figure CE7-4 or Figure CE7-5—is correct? Only the users know. These alternatives illustrate the kinds of questions you will need to answer when a database designer asks you to check a data model for correctness.

The crow's-foot notation shows the maximum number of entities that can be involved in a relationship. Accordingly, they are called the relationship's **maximum cardinality**. Common examples of maximum cardinality are 1:N, N:M, and 1:1 (not shown).

Another important question is, "What is the minimum number of entities required in the relationship?" Must an adviser have a student to advise, and must a student have an adviser? Constraints on minimum requirements are called **minimum cardinalities**.

Figure CE7-6 presents a third version of this E-R diagram that shows both maximum and minimum cardinalities. The vertical bar on a line means that at least one entity of that type is required. The small oval means that the entity is optional; the relationship need not have an entity of that type.

Thus, in Figure CE7-6, a department is not required to have a relationship to any adviser, but an adviser is required to belong to a department. Similarly, an adviser is not required to have a relationship to a student, but a student is required to have a relationship to an adviser. Note, also, that the maximum cardinalities in Figure CE7-6 have been changed so that both are 1:N.

Is the model in Figure CE7-6 a good one? It depends on the rules of the university. Again, only the users know for sure.

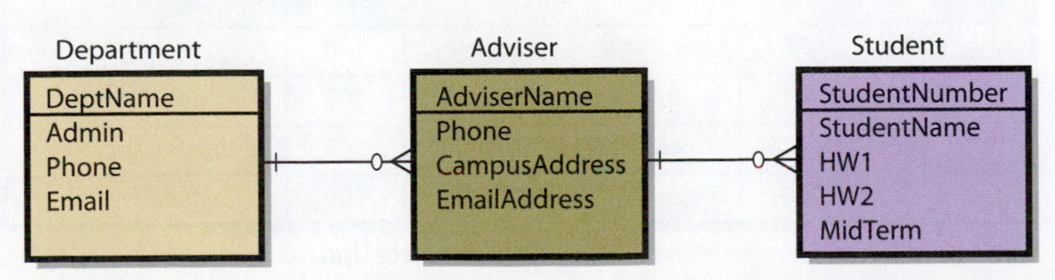

Figure CE7-6
Example of Relationships Showing Minimum Cardinalities

Q4 How Is a Data Model Transformed into a Database Design?

Database design is the process of converting a data model into tables, relationships, and data constraints. The database design team transforms entities into tables and expresses relationships by defining foreign keys. Database design is a complicated subject; as with data modeling, it occupies weeks in a database management class. In this section, however, we will introduce two important database design concepts: normalization and the representation of two kinds of relationships. The first concept is a foundation of database design, and the second will help you understand key considerations made during design.

Normalization

Normalization is the process of converting poorly structured tables into two or more well-structured tables. A table is such a simple construct that you may wonder how one could possibly be poorly structured. In truth, there are many ways that tables can be malformed—so many, in fact, that researchers have published hundreds of papers on this topic alone.

Consider the *Employee* table in Figure CE7-7. It lists employee names, hire dates, email addresses, and the name and number of the department in which the employee works. This table seems innocent enough. But consider what happens when the Accounting department changes its name to Accounting and Finance. Because department names are duplicated in this table, every row that has a value of "Accounting" must be changed to "Accounting and Finance."

Data Integrity Problems

Suppose the Accounting name change is correctly made in two rows, but not in the third. The result is shown in Figure CE7-7. This table has what is called a **data integrity problem**: Some rows indicate that the name of Department 100 is Accounting and Finance, and another row indicates that the name of Department 100 is Accounting.

This problem is easy to spot in this small table. But consider a table in a large database that has over 300,000 rows. Once a table that large develops serious data integrity problems, months of labor will be required to remove them.

Figure CE7-7
A Poorly Designed *Employee* Table

Employee

Name	HireDate	Email	DeptNo	DeptName
Jones	Feb 1, 2007	Jones@ourcompany.com	100	Accounting
Smith	Dec 3, 2004	Smith@ourcompany.com	200	Marketing
Chau	March 7, 2004	Chau@ourcompany.com	100	Accounting
Greene	July 17, 2007	Greene@ourcompany.com	100	Accounting

a. Table Before Update

Employee

Name	HireDate	Email	DeptNo	DeptName
Jones	Feb 1, 2007	Jones@ourcompany.com	100	Accounting and Finance
Smith	Dec 3, 2004	Smith@ourcompany.com	200	Marketing
Chau	March 7, 2004	Chau@ourcompany.com	100	Accounting and Finance
Greene	July 17, 2007	Greene@ourcompany.com	100	Accounting

b. Table with Incomplete Update

Data integrity problems are serious. A table that has data integrity problems will produce incorrect and inconsistent information. Users will lose confidence in the information, and the system will develop a poor reputation. Information systems with poor reputations become heavy burdens to the organizations that use them.

Normalizing for Data Integrity

The data integrity problem can occur only if data are duplicated. Because of this, one easy way to eliminate the problem is to eliminate the duplicated data. We can do this by transforming the table in Figure CE7-7 into two tables, as shown in Figure CE7-8. Here, the name of the department is stored just once, therefore no data inconsistencies can occur.

Of course, to produce an employee report that includes the department name, the two tables in Figure CE7-8 will need to be joined back together. Because such joining of tables is common, DBMS products have been programmed to perform it efficiently, but it still requires work. From this example, you can see a trade-off in database design: Normalized tables eliminate data duplication, but they can be slower to process. Dealing with such trade-offs is an important consideration in database design.

The general goal of normalization is to construct tables such that every table has a *single* topic or theme. In good writing, every paragraph should have a single theme. This is true of databases as well; every table should have a single theme. The problem with the table in Figure CE7-7 is that it has two independent themes: employees and departments. The way to correct the problem is to split the table into two tables, each with its own theme. In this case, we create an *Employee* table and a *Department* table, as shown in Figure CE7-8.

As mentioned, there are dozens of ways that tables can be poorly formed. Database practitioners classify tables into various **normal forms** according to the kinds of problems they have. Transforming a table into a normal form to remove duplicated data and other problems is called *normalizing* the table.[1] Thus, when you hear a database designer say, "Those tables are not normalized," she does not mean that the tables have irregular, not-normal data. Instead, she means that the tables have a format that could cause data integrity problems.

Summary of Normalization

As a future user of databases, you do not need to know the details of normalization. Instead, understand the general principle that every normalized (well-formed) table

Employee

Name	HireDate	Email	DeptNo
Jones	Feb 1, 2010	Jones@ourcompany.com	100
Smith	Dec 3, 2008	Smith@ourcompany.com	200
Chau	March 7, 2004	Chau@ourcompany.com	100
Greene	July 17, 2007	Greene@ourcompany.com	100

Department

DeptNo	DeptName
100	Accounting
200	Marketing
300	Information Systems

Figure CE7-8
Two Normalized Tables

1. See David Kroenke and David Auer, *Database Processing*, 11th ed. (Upper Saddle River, NJ: Prentice Hall, 2010) for more information.

has one and only one theme. Further, tables that are not normalized are subject to data integrity problems.

Be aware, too, that normalization is just one criterion for evaluating database designs. Because normalized designs can be slower to process, database designers sometimes choose to accept non-normalized tables. The best design depends on the users' requirements.

Representing Relationships

Figure CE7-9 shows the steps involved in transforming a data model into a relational database design. First, the database designer creates a table for each entity. The identifier of the entity becomes the key of the table. Each attribute of the entity becomes a column of the table. Next, the resulting tables are normalized so that each table has a single theme. Once that has been done, the next step is to represent the relationship among those tables.

For example, consider the E-R diagram in Figure CE7-10 (a). The *Adviser* entity has a 1:N relationship to the *Student* entity. To create the database design, we construct a table for *Adviser* and a second table for *Student*, as shown in Figure CE7-10 (b). The key of the *Adviser* table is *AdviserName*, and the key of the *Student* table is *StudentNumber.*

Further, the *EmailAddress* attribute of the *Adviser* entity becomes the *EmailAddress* column of the *Adviser* table, and the *StudentName* and *MidTerm* attributes of the *Student* entity become the *StudentName* and *MidTerm* columns of the *Student* table.

The next task is to represent the relationship. Because we are using the relational model, we know that we must add a foreign key to one of the two tables. The possibilities are: (1) place the foreign key *StudentNumber* in the *Adviser* table or (2) place the foreign key *AdviserName* in the *Student* table.

The correct choice is to place *AdviserName* in the *Student* table, as shown in Figure CE7-10 (c). To determine a student's adviser, we just look into the *AdviserName* column of that student's row. To determine the adviser's students, we search the *AdviserName* column in the *Student* table to determine which rows have that adviser's name. If a student changes advisers, we simply change the value in the *AdviserName* column. Changing *Jackson* to *Jones* in the first row, for example, will assign student 100 to Professor Jones.

For this data model, placing *StudentNumber* in *Adviser* would be incorrect. If we were to do that, we could assign only one student to an adviser. There is no place to assign a second adviser.

This strategy for placing foreign keys will not work for N:M relationships, however. Consider the data model in Figure CE7-11 (a); here, there is an N:M relationship between advisers and students. An adviser may have many students, and a student may have multiple advisers (for multiple majors). The strategy we used for

Figure CE7-9
Transforming a Data Model into a Database Design

- Represent each entity with a table
  - Entity identifier becomes table key
  - Entity attributes become table columns
- Normalize tables as necessary
- Represent relationships
  - Use foreign keys
  - Add additional tables for N:M relationships

Figure CE7-10
Representing a 1:N Relationship

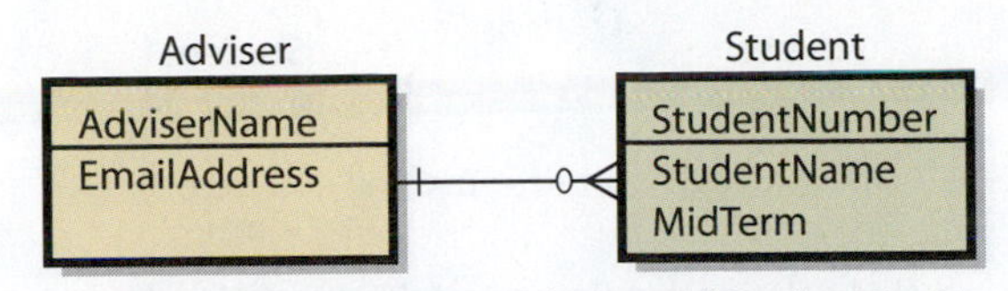

a. 1:N Relationship Between Adviser and Student Entities

Adviser Table—Key is AdviserName

AdviserName	EmailAddress
Jones	Jones@myuniv.edu
Choi	Choi@myuniv.edu
Jackson	Jackson@myuniv.edu

Student Table—Key is StudentNumber

StudentNumber	StudentName	MidTerm
100	Lisa	90
200	Jennie	85
300	Jason	82
400	Terry	95

b. Creating a Table for Each Entity

Adviser Table—Key is AdviserName

AdviserName	EmailAddress
Jones	Jones@myuniv.edu
Choi	Choi@myuniv.edu
Jackson	Jackson@myuniv.edu

Student—Key is StudentNumber

StudentNumber	StudentName	MidTerm	AdviserName
100	Lisa	90	Jackson
200	Jennie	85	Jackson
300	Jason	82	Choi
400	Terry	95	Jackson

Foreign Key Column Represents Relationship

c. Using the AdviserName Foreign Key to Represent the 1:N Relationship

the 1:N data model will not work here. To see why, examine Figure CE7-11 (b). If student 100 has more than one adviser, there is no place to record second or subsequent advisers.

It turns out that to represent an N:M relationship, we need to create a third table, as shown in Figure CE7-11 (c). The third table has two columns, *AdviserName* and *StudentNumber*. Each row of the table means that the given adviser advises the student with the given number.

As you can imagine, there is a great deal more to database design than we have presented here. Still, this section should give you an idea of the tasks that need to be accomplished to create a database. You should also realize that the database design is a direct consequence of decisions made in the data model. If the data model is wrong, the database design will be wrong as well.

Figure CE7-11
Representing an N:M Relationship

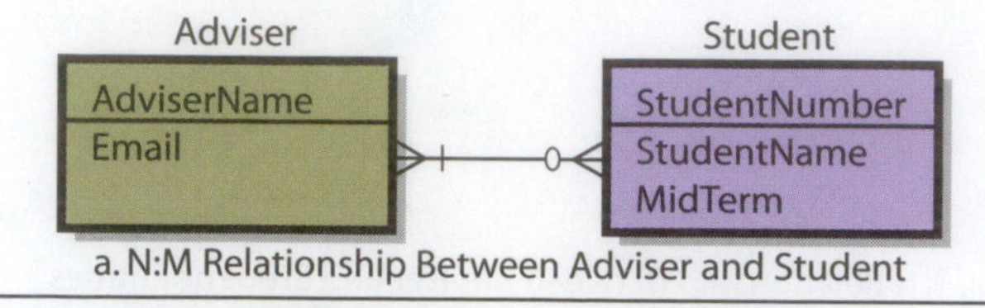

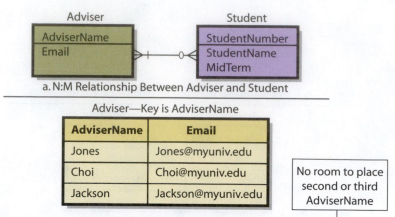

a. N:M Relationship Between Adviser and Student

Adviser—Key is AdviserName

AdviserName	Email
Jones	Jones@myuniv.edu
Choi	Choi@myuniv.edu
Jackson	Jackson@myuniv.edu

No room to place second or third AdviserName

Student—Key is StudentNumber

StudentNumber	StudentName	MidTerm	AdviserName
100	Lisa	90	Jackson
200	Jennie	85	Jackson
300	Jason	82	Choi
400	Terry	95	Jackson

b. Incorrect Representation of N:M Relationship

Adviser—Key is AdviserName

AdviserName	Email
Jones	Jones@myuniv.edu
Choi	Choi@myuniv.edu
Jackson	Jackson@myuniv.edu

Student—Key is StudentNumber

StudentNumber	StudentName	MidTerm
100	Lisa	90
200	Jennie	85
300	Jason	82
400	Terry	95

Adviser_Student_Intersection

AdviserName	StudentNumber
Jackson	100
Jackson	200
Choi	300
Jackson	400
Choi	100
Jones	100

Student 100 has three advisers.

c. Adviser_Student_Intersection Table Represents the N:M Relationship

Q5 What Is the Users' Role?

As stated, a database is a model of how the users view their business world. This means that the users are the final judges as to what data the database should contain and how the records in that database should be related to one another.

The easiest time to change the database structure is during the data modeling stage. Changing a relationship from 1:N to N:M in a data model is simply a matter of changing the 1:N notation to N:M. However, once the database has been constructed, loaded with data, and application forms, reports, queries, and application programs created, changing a 1:N relationship to N:M means weeks of work.

You can glean some idea of why this might be true by contrasting Figure CE7-10 (c) with Figure CE7-11 (c). Suppose that instead of having just a few rows, each table has thousands of rows; in that case, transforming the database from one format to the other involves considerable work. Even worse, however, is that application components will need to be changed as well. For example, if students have at most one adviser, then a single text box can be used to enter *AdviserName.* If students can have multiple advisers, then a multiple-row table will need to be used to enter *AdviserName,* and a program will need to be written to store the values of *AdviserName* into the *Adviser_Student_Intersection* table. There are dozens of other consequences as well, consequences that will translate into wasted labor and wasted expense.

The conclusion from this discussion is that user review of a data model is crucial. When a database is developed for your use, you must carefully review the data model. If you do not understand any aspect of it, you should ask for clarification until you do. The data model must accurately reflect your view of the business. If it does not, the database will be designed incorrectly, and the applications will be difficult to use, if not worthless. Do not proceed unless the data model is accurate.

As a corollary, when asked to review a data model, take that review seriously. Devote the time necessary to perform a thorough review. Any mistakes you miss will come back to haunt you, and by then the cost of correction may be very high with regard to both time and expense. This brief introduction to data modeling shows why databases can be more difficult to develop than spreadsheets.

Q6 Who Will Volunteer? (Continued)

Knowing what you know now, if you were the manager of fund-raising at the TV station, you would hire a consultant and expect the consultant to interview all of the key users. From those interviews, the consultant would then construct a data model.

You now know that the structure of the database must reflect the way the users think about their activities. If the consultant did not take the time to interview you and your staff or did not construct a data model and ask you to review it, you would know that you are not receiving good service and would take corrective action.

Suppose you found a consultant who interviewed your staff for several hours and then constructed the data model shown in Figure CE7-12. This data model has an entity for *Prospect*, an entity for *Employee*, and three additional entities for *Contact, Phone,* and *Work*. The *Contact* entity records contacts that you or other employees have made with the prospective volunteer. This record is necessary so that you know what has been said to whom. The *Phone* entity is used to record multiple phone

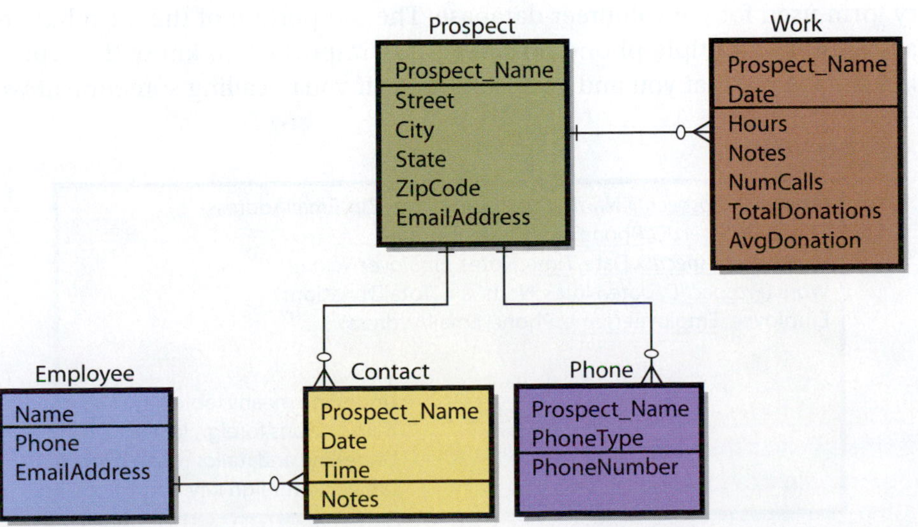

Figure CE7-12
Data Model for Volunteer Database

Figure CE7-13
First Table Design for Volunteer Database

Prospect (Name, Street, City, State, Zip, EmailAddress)
Phone (*Name*, PhoneType, PhoneNumber)
Contact (*Name*, Date, Time, Notes, *EmployeeName*)
Work (*Name*, Date, Notes, NumCalls, TotalDonations)
Employee (EmployeeName, Phone, EmailAddress)

Note:
Underline means table key.
Italics means foreign key.
Underline and italics mean both table and foreign key.

numbers for each prospective volunteer, and the *Work* entity records work that the prospect has performed for the station.

After you reviewed and approved this data model, the consultant constructed the database design shown in Figure CE7-13. In this design, table keys are underlined, foreign keys are shown in italics, and columns that are both table and foreign keys are underlined and italicized. Observe that the *Name* column is the table key of *Prospect*, and it is both part of the table key and a foreign key in *Phone*, *Contact*, and *Work*.

The consultant did not like having the *Name* column used as a key or as part of a key in so many tables. Based on her interviews, she suspected that prospect names are fluid—and that sometimes the same prospect name is recorded in different ways (e.g., sometimes with a middle initial and sometimes without). If that were to happen, phone, contact, and work data could be misallocated to prospect names. Accordingly, the consultant added a new column, *ProspectID* to the prospect table and created the design shown in Figure CE7-14. Values of this ID will have no meaning to the users, but the ID will be used to ensure that each prospect obtains a unique record in the Volunteer database. Because this ID has no meaning to the users, the consultant will hide it on forms and reports that users see.

There is one difference between the data model and the table designs. In the data model, the *Work* entity has an attribute, *AvgDonation*, but there is no corresponding *AvgDonation* column in the *Work* table. The consultant decided that there was no need to store this value in the database because it could readily be computed on forms and reports using the values in the *NumCalls* and *TotalDonations* columns.

Once the tables had been designed, the consultant created a Microsoft Access 2007 database. She defined the tables in Access, created relationships among the tables, and constructed forms and reports. Figure CE7-15 shows the primary data entry form used for the Volunteer database. The top portion of the form has contact data, including multiple phone numbers. It is important to know the type of the phone number so that you and your staff know if you're calling someone at work or

Figure CE7-14
Second Table Design for Volunteer Database

Prospect (*ProspectID*, Name, Street, City, State, Zip, EmailAddress)
Phone (*ProspectID*, PhoneType, PhoneNumber)
Contact (*ProspectID*, Date, Time, Notes, *EmployeeName*)
Work (*ProspectID*, Date, Notes, NumCalls, TotalDonations)
Employee (EmployeeName, Phone, EmailAddress)

Note:
Underline means table key.
Italics means foreign key.
Underline and italics mean both table and foreign key.

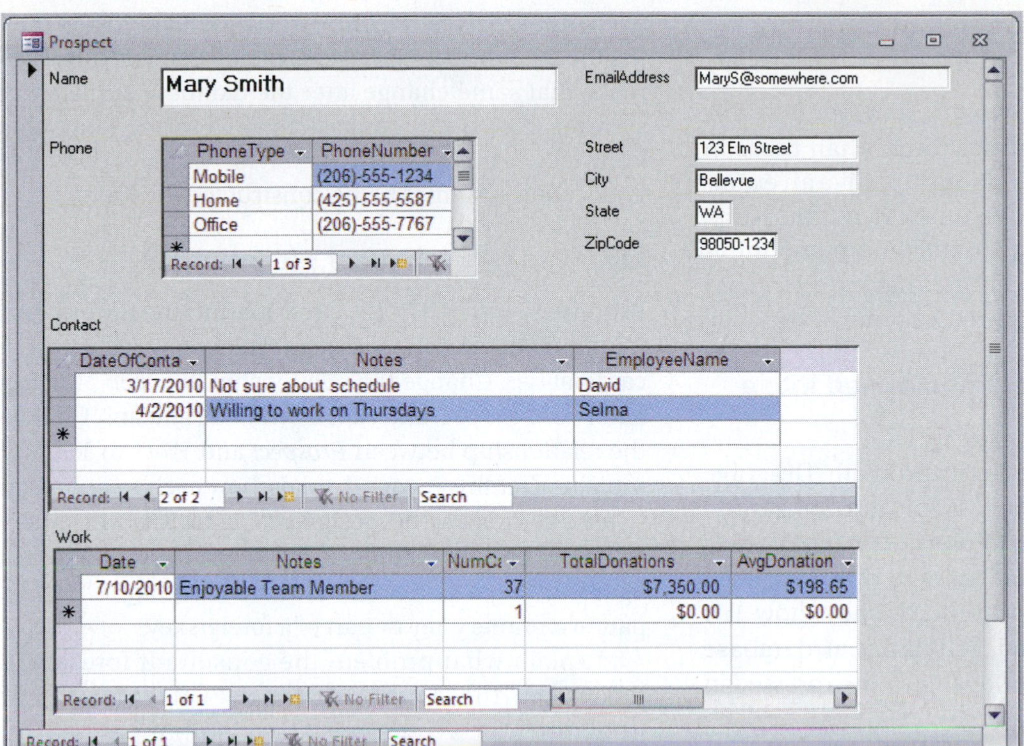

Figure CE7-15
Volunteer Prospect Data Entry Form

another setting. The middle and bottom sections of this form have contact and prior work data. Observe that *AvgDonation* has been computed from the *NumCalls* and *Total Donations* columns.

You were quite pleased with this database application, and you're certain that it helped you to improve the volunteer staffing at the station. Of course, over time, you thought of several new requirements, and you already have changes in mind for next year.

ACTIVE REVIEW

Use this Active Review to verify that you understand the material in the chapter extension. You can read the entire extension and then perform the tasks in this review, or you can read the material for just one question and perform the tasks in this review for that question before moving on to the next one.

Q1 Who will volunteer?

Summarize the problem that the fund-raising manager must solve. Explain how a database can help solve this problem. Describe the missing information. In your own words, what data must be available to construct the missing information?

Q2 How are database application systems developed?

Name and briefly describe the components of a database application system. Explain the difference between a database application system and a database application program. Using Figure CE7-1 as a guide, describe the major steps in the process of developing a database application system. Explain what role is crucial for users and why that role is so important.

Q3 What are the components of the entity-relationship data model?

Define the terms *entity*, *attributes*, and *relationship*. Give an example of two entities (other than those in this book) that have a 1:N relationship. Give an example of two entities that have an N:M relationship. Explain the difference between maximum and minimum cardinality. Show two entities having a 1:N relationship in which one is required and one is optional.

Q4 How is a data model transformed into a database design?

Give an example of a data integrity problem. Describe, in general terms, the process of normalization. Explain how normalizing data prevents data integrity problems. Explain the disadvantage of normalized data. Using your examples from Q3, show how 1:N relationships are expressed in relational database designs. Show how N:M relationships are expressed in relational database designs.

Q5 What is the users' role?

Describe the major role for users in the development of a database application system. Explain what is required to change a 1:N relationship to an N:M relationship during the data modeling stage. Explain what is required to make that same change after the database application systems has been constructed. Describe how this knowledge impacts your behavior when a database application system is being constructed for your use.

Q6 Who will volunteer? (continued)

Examine Figure CE7-12. Describe the maximum and minimum cardinality for each relationship. Justify these cardinalities. Change the relationship between *Prospect* and *Phone* to N:M, and explain what this means. Change the relationship between *Prospect* and *Work* to 1:1, and explain what this means. Explain how each relationship is represented in the design in Figure CE7-14. Show examples of both primary keys and foreign keys in this figure. In *Contact*, determine whether *EmployeeName* is part of a primary key or part of a foreign key.

Explain what problem the consultant foresaw in the use of the *Name* attribute. Explain how that problem was avoided. The consultant added an attribute to the data model that was not part of the users' world. Explain why that attribute will not add unnecessary complication to the users' work experiences.

KEY TERMS AND CONCEPTS

Attribute 385
Crow's foot 387
Crow's foot diagram 388
Data integrity problem 387
Data model 384
Entity 385
Entity-relationship (E-R) diagram 386
Entity-relationship (E-R model) data model 384
Identifier 385
Many-to-many (N:M) relationship 386
Maximum cardinality 387
Minimum cardinality 387
Normal form 389
Normalization 388
One-to-many (1:N) relationship 386
Relationship 386
Unified Modeling Language (UML) 385

USING YOUR KNOWLEDGE

1. Explain how you could use a spreadsheet to solve the volunteer problem at the television station. What data would you place in each column and row of your spreadsheet? Name each column and row of your spreadsheet. What advantages does a database have over a spreadsheet for this problem? Compare and contrast your spreadsheet solution to the database solution shown in the design in Figure CE7-14 and the data entry form in Figure CE7-15.
2. Suppose you are asked to build a database application for a sports league. Assume that your application is to keep track of teams and equipment that is checked out to teams. Explain the steps that need to be taken to develop this application. Specify entities and their relationships. Build an E-R diagram. Ensure your diagram shows both minimum and maximum cardinalities. Transform your E-R diagram into a relational design.

3. Suppose you are asked to build a database application for a bicycle rental shop. Assume your database is to track customers, bicycles, and rentals. Explain the steps that need to be taken to develop this application. Specify entities and their relationships. Build an entity-relationship diagram. Ensure your diagram shows both minimum and maximum cardinalities. Transform your E-R diagram into a relational design.

4. Assume you work at the television station and are asked to evaluate the data model in Figure CE7-12. Suppose that you want to differentiate between prospects who have worked in the past and those who have never worked, but who are prospects for future work. Say that one of the data modelers tells you, "No problem. We'll know that because any *Prospect* entity that has no relationship to a *Work* entity is a prospect who has never worked." Restate the data modeler's response in your own words. Does this seem like a satisfactory solution? What if you want to keep *Prospect* data that pertains only to prospects who have worked? (No such attributes are shown in *Prospect* in Figure CE7-12, but say there is an attribute such as *YearFirstVolunteered* or some other attribute that pertains to prospects who have worked in the past.) Show an alternative E-R diagram that would differentiate between prospects who have worked in the past and those who have not. Compare and contrast your alternative to the one shown in Figure CE7-12.

5. Suppose you manage a department that is developing a database application. The IT professionals who are developing the system ask you to identify two employees to evaluate data models. What criteria would you use in selecting those employees? What instructions would you give them? Suppose one of the employees says to you, "I go to those meetings, but I just don't understand what they're talking about." How would you respond? Suppose that you go to one of those meetings and don't understand what they're talking about. What would you do? Describe a role for a prototype in this situation. How would you justify the request for a prototype?

CHAPTER EXTENSION 8

STUDY QUESTIONS

Q1 How do you create tables?

Q2 How do you create relationships?

Q3 How do you create a data entry form?

Q4 How can you create queries using the query design tool?

Q5 How do you create a report?

Chapter 5 provides the background for this Extension.

Using Microsoft Access 2010

In this chapter extension, you will learn fundamental techniques for creating a database and a database application with Microsoft Access.

Q1 How Do You Create Tables?

Before using Access or any other DBMS, you should have created a data model from the users' requirements, and you must transform that data model into a database design. For the purpose of this chapter extension, we will use a portion of the database design created in Chapter Extension 7. Specifically, we will create a database with the following two tables:

PROSPECT (<u>ProspectID</u>, Name, Street, City, State, Zip, Email Address)

and

WORK (<u>*ProspectID*</u>, <u>Date</u>, <u>Hour</u>, NumCalls, TotalDonations)

As in Chapter Extension 7, an underlined attribute is the primary key and an italicized attribute is a foreign key. Thus, <u>ProspectID</u> is the primary key of PROSPECT, and the combination (<u>ProspectID</u>, <u>Date</u>, <u>Hour</u>) is the primary key of WORK. *ProspectID* is also a foreign key in WORK, hence it is shown both underlined and in italics. The data model and database design in Chapter Extension 7 specified that the key of WORK is the combination (<u>*ProspectID*</u>, <u>Date</u>). Upon review, the users stated that prospects will sometimes work more than one time during the day. For scheduling and other purposes, the users want to record both the date and the hour that someone worked. Accordingly, the database designer added the Hour attribute and made it part of the key of WORK.

The assumption in this design is that each row of WORK represents an hour's work. If a prospect works for consecutive hours, say from 7 to 9 PM, then he or she would have two rows, one with an Hour value of 1900 and a second with an Hour value of 2000. Figure CE8-1 further documents the attributes of the design. Sample data for this table are shown in Figure CE8-2 on page 400.

Note the ambiguity in the name *PROSPECT.* Before someone has become a volunteer, he is a prospect, and the term is fine. However, once that person has actually done work, he is no longer merely a prospect. This ambiguity occurs because the database is used both for finding volunteers and for recording their experiences once

Table	Attribute (Column)	Remarks	Data Type	Example Value
PROSPECT	ProspectID	An identifying number provided by Access when a row is created. The value has no meaning to the user.	AutoNumber	55
PROSPECT	Name	A prospect's name.	Text (50)	Emily Jones
PROSPECT	Street	Prospect's contact street address.	Text (50)	123 West Elm
PROSPECT	City	Prospect's contact city.	Text (40)	Miami
PROSPECT	State	Prospect's contact state.	Text (2)	FL
PROSPECT	Zip	Prospect's contact zip code.	Text (10)	30210-4567 or 30210
PROSPECT	EmailAddress	Prospect's contact email address.	Text (65)	ExamplePerson@somewhere.com
WORK	ProspectID	Foreign key to PROSPECT. Value provided when relationship is created.	Number (Long Integer)	55
WORK	Date	The date of work.	Date	9/15/2007
WORK	Hour	The hour at which work is started.	Number (Integer)	0800 or 1900 (7 PM)
WORK	NumCalls	The number of calls taken.	Number (Integer)	25
WORK	TotalDonations	The total of donations generated.	Currency	$10,575
WORK	AvgDonations	The average donation.	Currency	To be computed in queries and reports

Figure CE8-1
Attributes of the Database

they have joined. We could rename PROSPECT as VOLUNTEER, but then we'd still have a problem. The person is not a volunteer until he has actually agreed to become one. So, for now, just assume that a PROSPECT who has one or more WORK records is no longer a prospect but has become a volunteer.

Starting Access

Figure CE8-3 shows the opening screen for Microsoft Access 2010. (If you use another version of Access, your screen will appear differently, but the essentials will be the same.) To create a new database, select Blank database under *Available Templates* in the center of the screen. Then, type the name of your new database under *File Name* (here we use *Volunteer*). Access will suggest a directory; change it if you want to use another one, and then click *Create*. You will see the screen shown in Figure CE8-4 on page 401.

Creating Tables

Access opens the new database by creating a default table named Table 1. We want to modify the design of this table, so in the upper left-hand corner, where you see a pencil and a right angle square, click *View* and select *Design View*. Access will ask you to name your table. Enter *PROSPECT* and click *OK*. Your screen will appear as in Figure CE8-5 on page 402.

Example of PROSPECT Data

Prospect ID	Name	Street	City	State	Zip	EmailAddress
1	Carson Wu	123 Elm	Los Angeles	CA	98007	Carson@somewhere.com
2	Emily Jackson	2234 17th	Pasadena	CA	97005	JacksonE@elsewhere.com
3	Peter Lopez	331 Moses Drive	Fullerton	CA	97330	PeterL@ourcompany.com
4	Lynda Dennison	54 Strand	Manhattan Beach	CA	97881	Lynda@somewhere.com
5	Carter Fillmore III	Restricted	Brentwood	CA	98220	Carter@BigBucks.com
6	CJ Greene	77 Sunset Strip	Hollywood	CA	97330	CJ@HollywoodProducers.com
7	Jolisa Jackson	2234 17th	Pasadena	CA	97005	JacksonJ@elsewhere.com

Example of WORK Data

ProspectID	Date	Hour	NumCalls	TotalDonations
3	9/15/2009	1600	17	8755
3	9/15/2009	1700	28	11578
5	9/15/2009	1700	25	15588
5	9/20/2009	1800	37	29887
5	9/10/2010	1700	30	21440
5	9/10/2010	1800	39	37050
6	9/15/2009	1700	33	21445
6	9/16/2009	1700	27	17558
6	9/10/2010	1700	31	22550
6	9/10/2010	1800	37	36700

Figure CE8-2
Sample Data

The screen shown in Figure CE8-5 has three parts. The left-hand pane lists all of the tables in your database. At this point, you should see only the PROSPECT table in this list. We will use the upper part of the right-hand pane to enter the name of each attribute (which Access calls *Fields*) and its *Data Type*. We can optionally enter a *Description* of that field. The Description is used for documentation; as you will see, Access displays any text you enter as help text on forms. In the bottom part of the screen, we set the properties of each field (or attribute, using our term). To start designing the table, replace the *Field Name* ID with *ProspectID*. Access has already set its type to *AutoNumber*, so you can leave that alone.

To create the rest of the table, enter the *Field Names* and *Data Types* according to our design.[1] Figure CE8-6 shows how to set the length of a Text Data Type. In this

[1] When you enter the Name field, Access will give you an error message. Ignore the message and click OK. The fact that you are using a reserved word for this example will not be a problem. If you want to be safe, you could enter *PName* or *ProspectName* (rather than *Name*) and avoid this issue. Many people, including me, believe that Access 2010 is poorly designed. This restriction is a case in point; you ought to be able to enter any value for Field Name the way you want. Access 2010 should stay out of your way; you shouldn't have to stay out of its way!

Figure CE8-3 Opening Screen for Microsoft Access 2010

figure, the user has set City to *Text* and then has moved down into the bottom part of this form and entered 40 under *Field Size*. You will do the same thing to set the length of all of the Text Field Names. The complete table is shown in Figure CE8-7.

ProspectID is the primary key of this table, and the little key icon next to the ProspectID *Field Name* means Access has already made it so. If we wanted to make

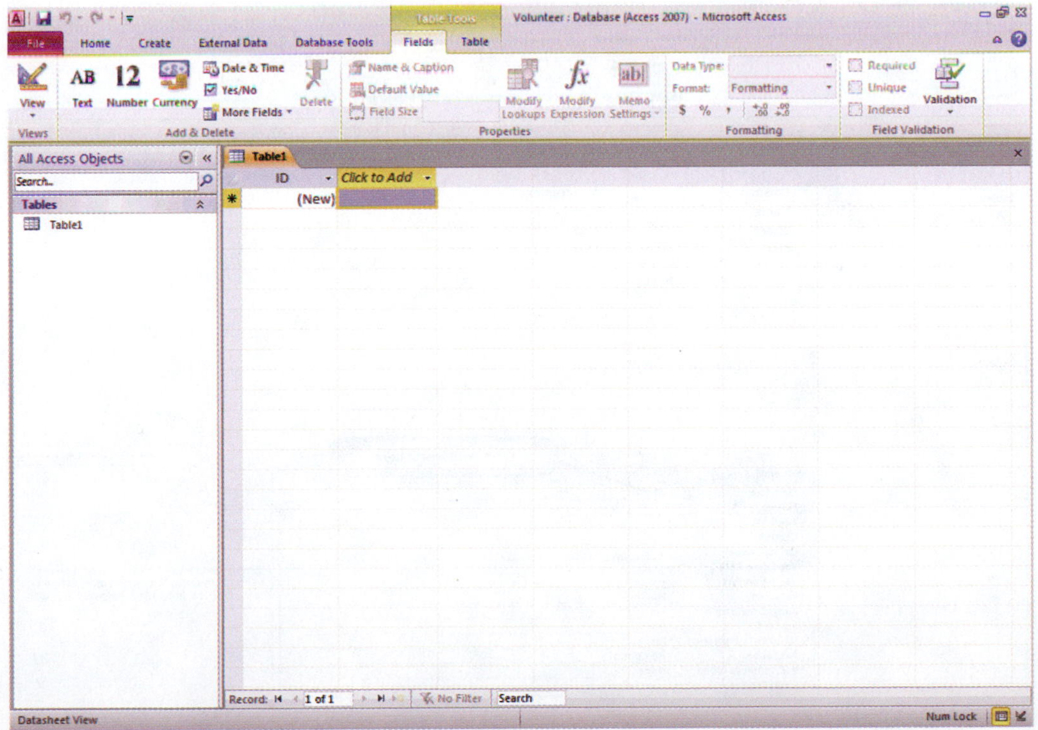

Figure CE8-4 Access Opens with a Start on a Table Definition

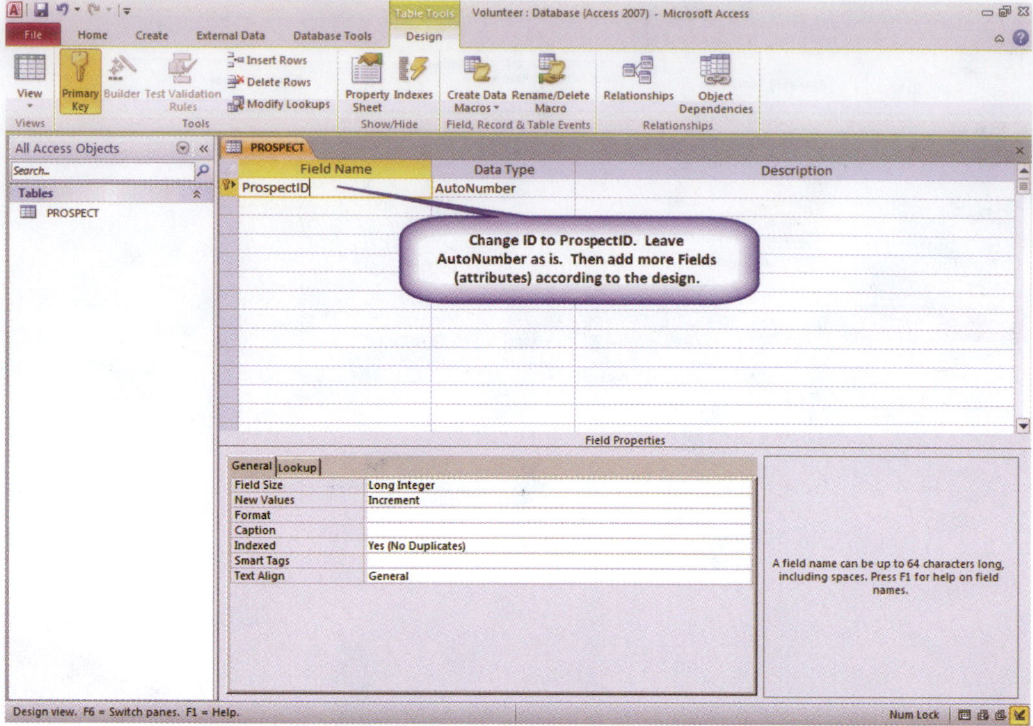

Figure CE8-5
Creating Tables in Access, Step 1

another field the primary key, we would highlight that field and then click the *Primary Key* icon in the left-hand portion of the *Design* ribbon.

Follow similar steps to create the WORK table. The only difference is that you will need to create a key of the three columns (ProspectID, Date, Hour). To create that key, highlight all three rows by dragging the three squares to the left of the names of ProspectID, Date, and Hour. Then click the *Key* icon in the *Design* ribbon. Also, change

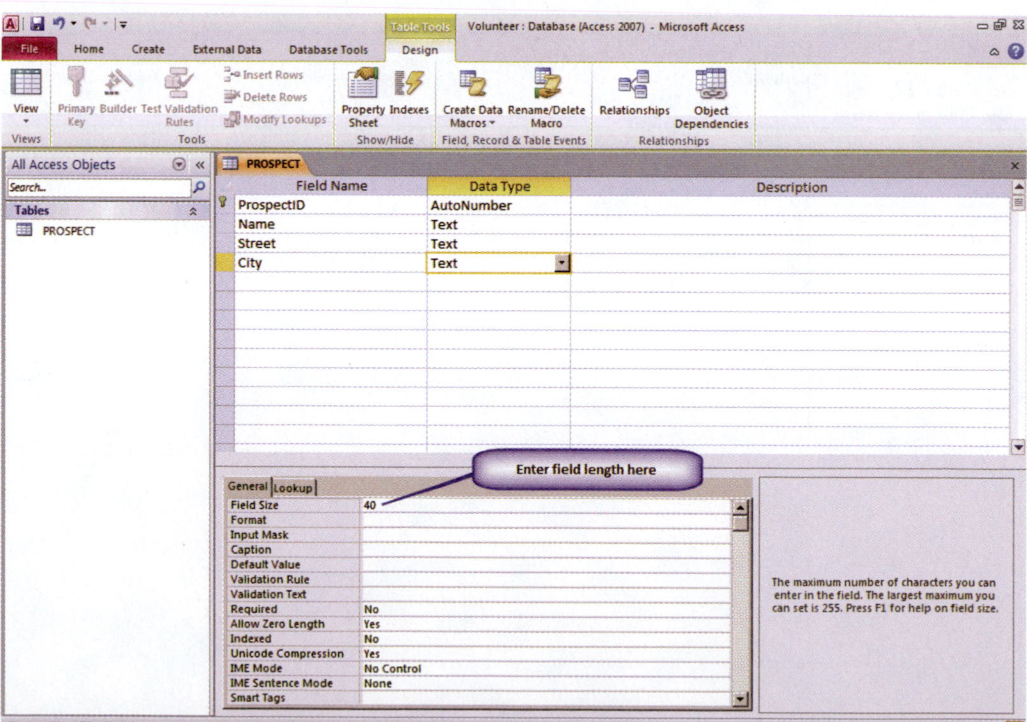

Figure CE8-6
Creating Tables in Access, Step 2

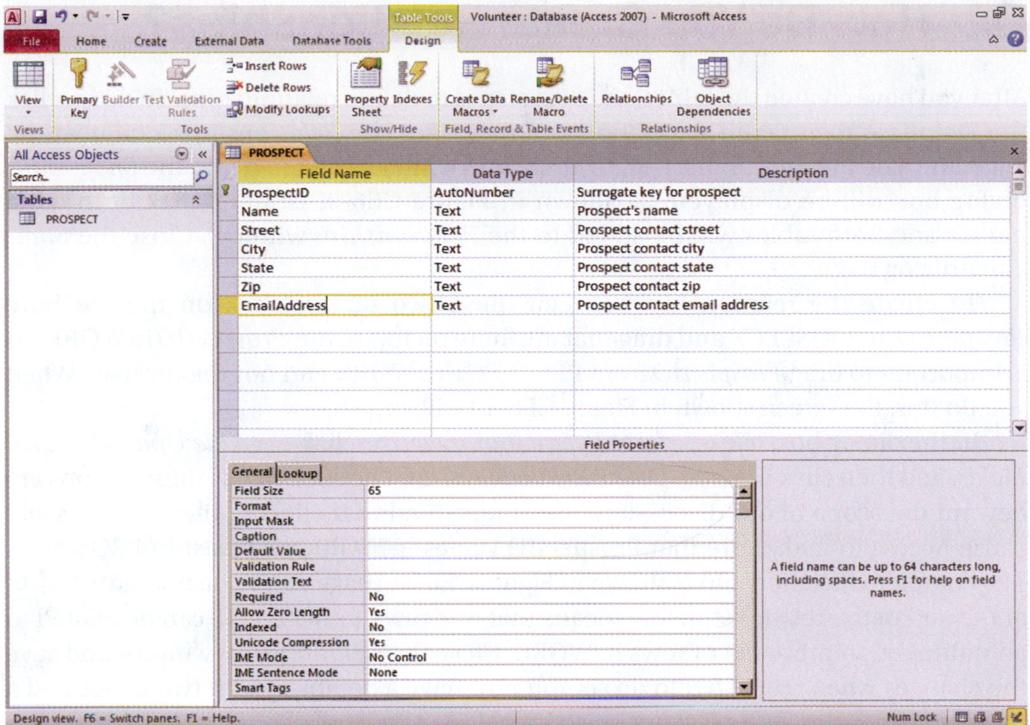

Figure CE8-7
Complete Sample PROSPECT Table

the *Required Field Property* for each of these columns to *Yes*. The finished WORK table is shown in Figure CE8-8. This figure also shows that the user selected *Number* for the *Data Type* of *NumCalls* and then set its *Field Size* (lower pane) to *Integer*. This same technique was used to set the *Data Type* of ProspectID (in WORK) to *Number* (*Field Size* of *Long Integer*) and that of *Hour* to *Number* (*Field Size* of *Integer*).

At this point, close both tables and save your work. You have created your first database!

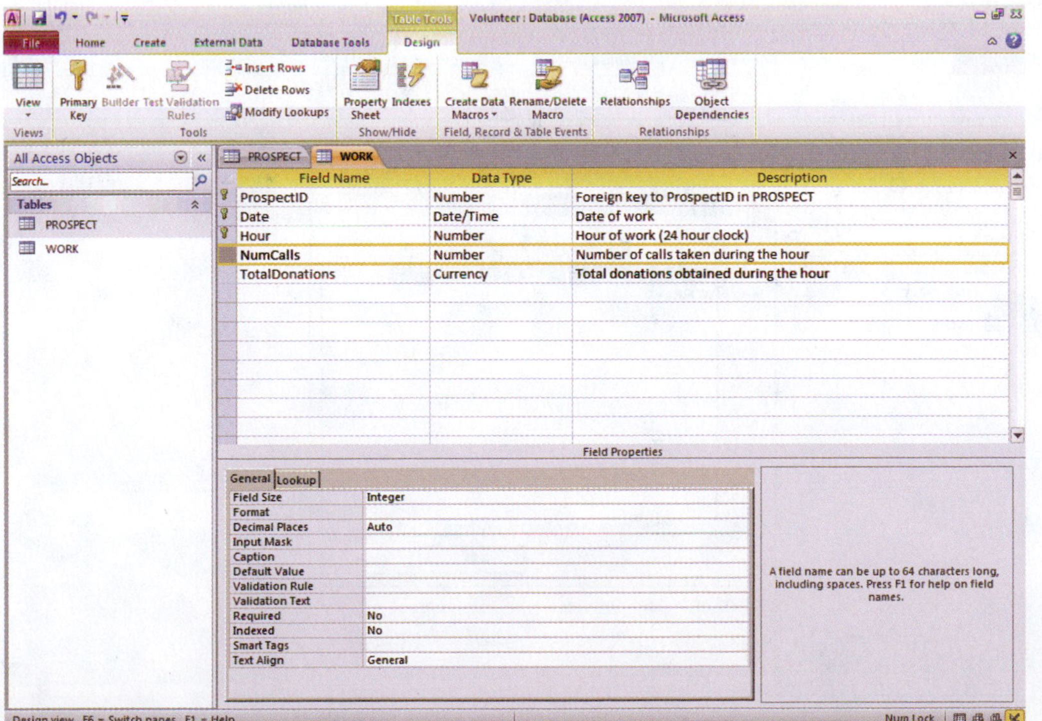

Figure CE8-8
Finished WORK Table

Q2 How Do You Create Relationships?

After you have created the tables, the next step is to define relationships. To do so, click the *Database Tools* tab in the ribbon and then click the *Relationships* icon near the left-hand side of that ribbon. The *Relationships* window will open and the *Show Table* dialog box will be displayed, as shown in Figure CE8-9. Double-click both table names and both tables will be added to the *Relationships* window. Close the *Show Table* dialog box.

To create the relationship between these two tables, click on the attribute *ProspectID* in PROSPECT and drag that attribute on top of the *ProspectID* in WORK. (It is important to drag *ProspectID* from PROSPECT to WORK and not the reverse.) When you do this, the screen shown in Figure CE8-10 will appear.

In the dialog box, click *Enforce Referential Integrity*, click *Cascade Update Related Fields*, and then click *Cascade Delete Related Records*. The specifics of these actions are beyond the scope of our discussion. Just understand that clicking these options will cause Access to make sure that ProspectID values in WORK also exist in PROSPECT. The completed relationship is shown in Figure CE8-11 (page 405). The notation *1 . . .* ∞ at the end of the relationship line means that one row of PROSPECT can be related to an unlimited number (*N*) of rows in WORK. Close the *Relationships* window and save the changes when requested to do so. You now have a database with two tables and a relationship.

The next step is to enter data. To enter data, double-click the table name in the *All Tables* pane. The table will appear, and you can enter values into each cell. You cannot and need not enter values for the *ProspectID* field. Access will create those values for you.

Enter the data in Figure CE8-2 for both PROSPECT and WORK, and you will see a display like that in Figures CE8-12a and CE8-12b. Examine the lower left-hand corner of Figure CE8-12b. The text *Total donations obtained during the hour* is the

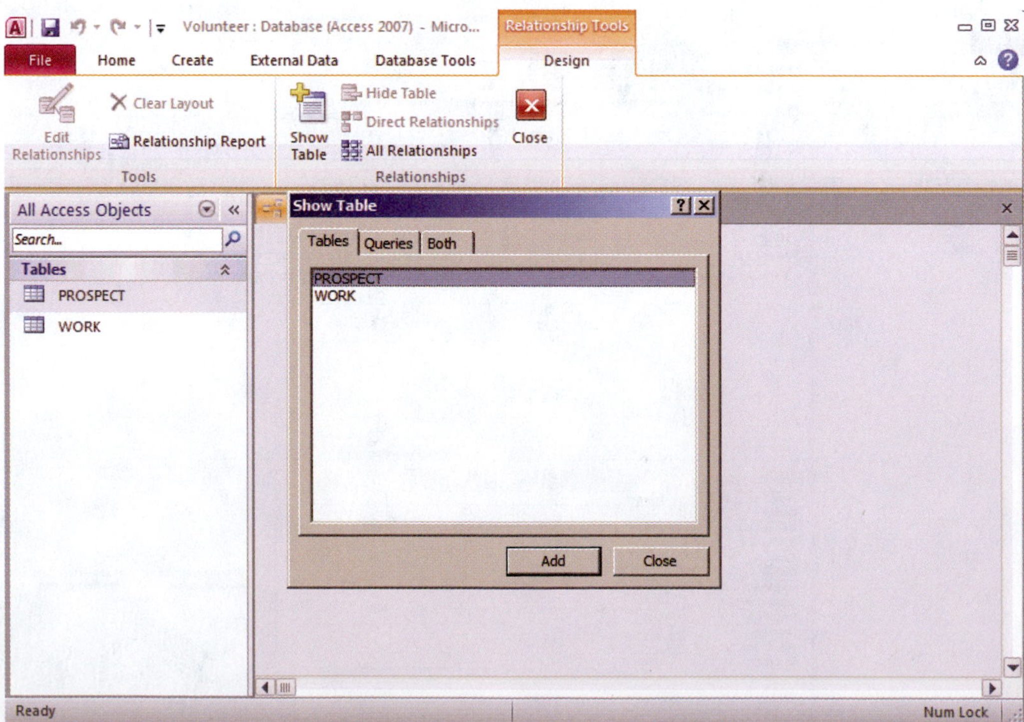

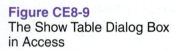

Figure CE8-9
The Show Table Dialog Box in Access

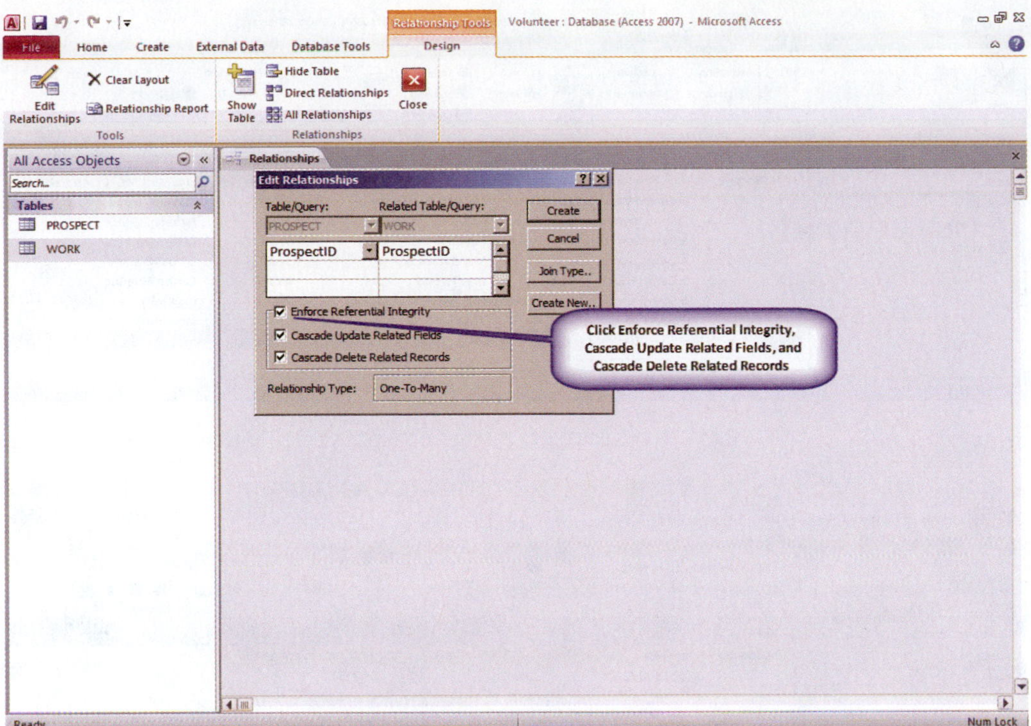

Figure CE8-10
Creating a Relationship Between Two Tables

Description that you provided when you defined the TotalDonations column when the WORK table was created. (You can see this in the TotalDonations column in Figure CE8-8.) Access displays this text because the focus is on the TotalDonations column in the active table window (WORK). Move your cursor from field to field and watch this text change.

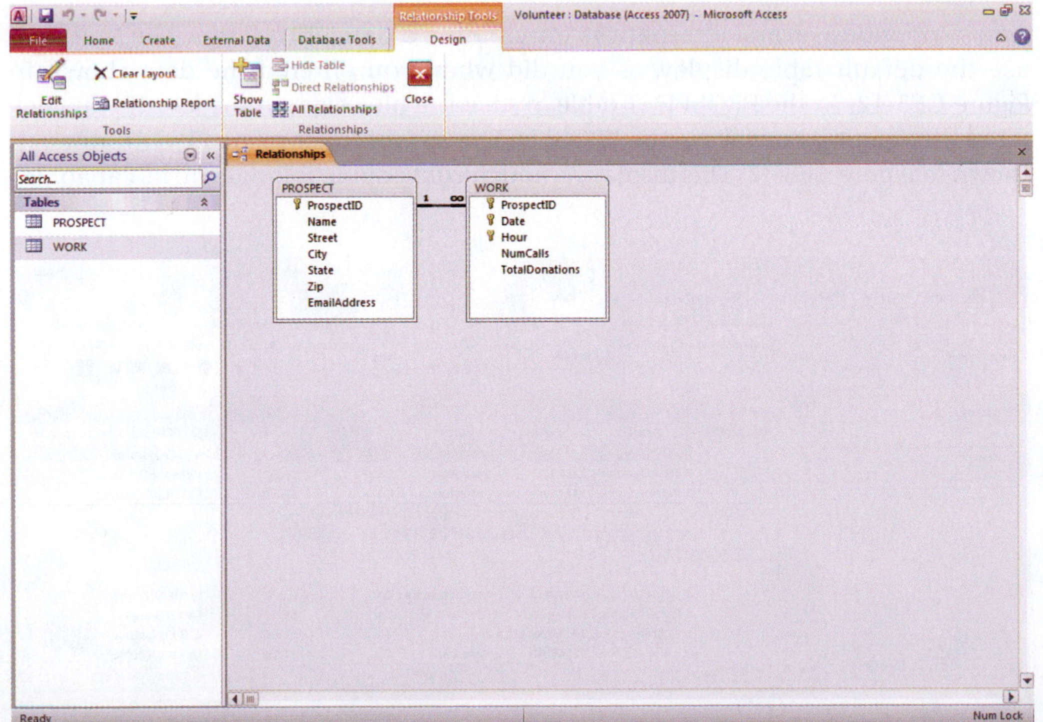

Figure CE8-11
Completed Relationship Between PROSPECT and WORK Tables

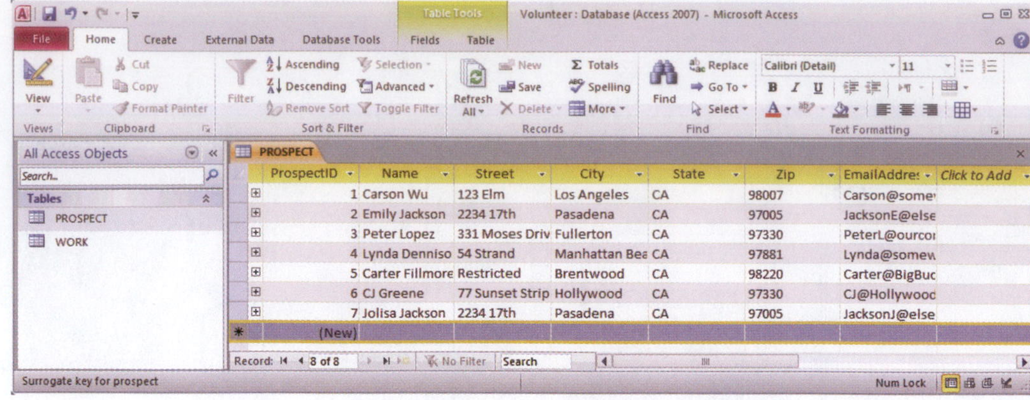

Figure CE8-12a
Tables with Data Entered for PROSPECT

ProspectID	Name	Street	City	State	Zip	EmailAddres	Click to Add
1	Carson Wu	123 Elm	Los Angeles	CA	98007	Carson@some	
2	Emily Jackson	2234 17th	Pasadena	CA	97005	JacksonE@else	
3	Peter Lopez	331 Moses Driv	Fullerton	CA	97330	PeterL@ourcoi	
4	Lynda Denniso	54 Strand	Manhattan Bea	CA	97881	Lynda@somew	
5	Carter Fillmore	Restricted	Brentwood	CA	98220	Carter@BigBuc	
6	CJ Greene	77 Sunset Strip	Hollywood	CA	97330	CJ@Hollywooc	
7	Jolisa Jackson	2234 17th	Pasadena	CA	97005	JacksonJ@else	
(New)							

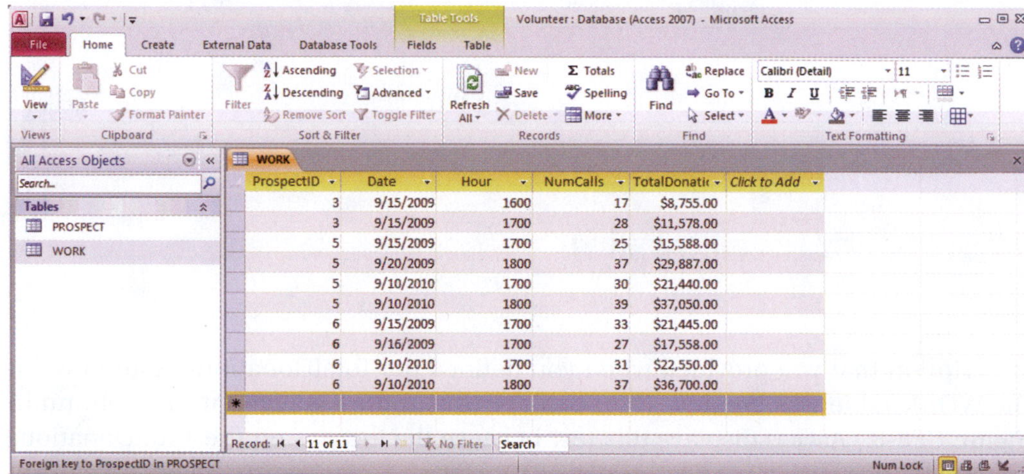

Figure CE8-12b
Tables with Data Entered for WORK

ProspectID	Date	Hour	NumCalls	TotalDonatic	Click to Add
3	9/15/2009	1600	17	$8,755.00	
3	9/15/2009	1700	28	$11,578.00	
5	9/15/2009	1700	25	$15,588.00	
5	9/20/2009	1800	37	$29,887.00	
5	9/10/2010	1700	30	$21,440.00	
5	9/10/2010	1800	39	$37,050.00	
6	9/15/2009	1700	33	$21,445.00	
6	9/16/2009	1700	27	$17,558.00	
6	9/10/2010	1700	31	$22,550.00	
6	9/10/2010	1800	37	$36,700.00	

Q3 How Do You Create a Data Entry Form?

Access provides several alternatives for creating a data entry form. The first is to use the default table display, as you did when you entered the data shown in Figure CE8-12. In the PROSPECT table, notice the plus sign on the left. If you click those plus signs, you will see the PROSPECT rows with their related WORK rows, as shown in Figure CE8-13. This display, although convenient, is limited in its capability.

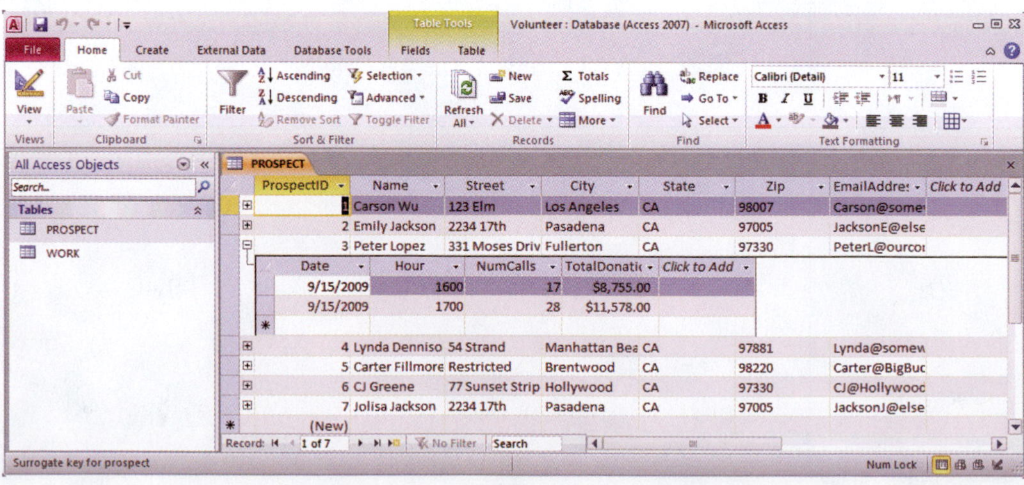

Figure CE8-13
Default Table Display

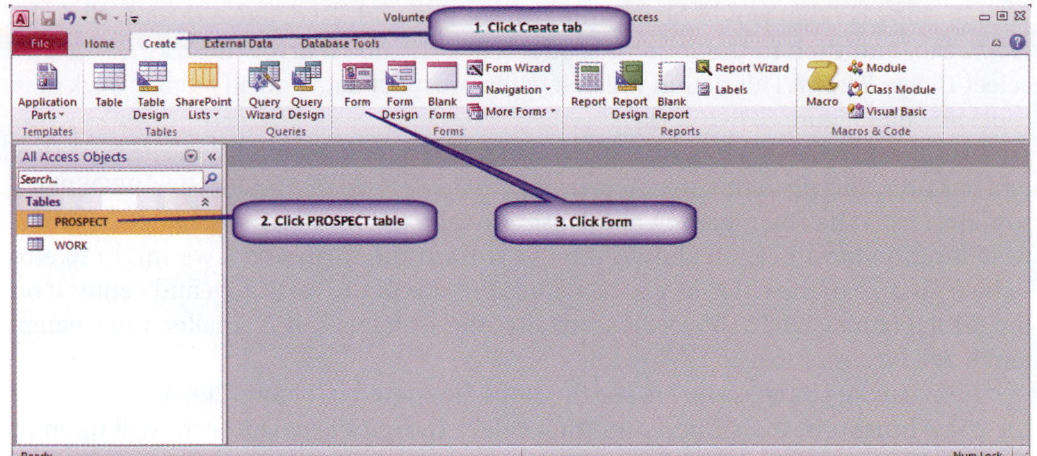

Figure CE8-14
Starting the Form Generator

It also does not provide a very pleasing user interface. For more generality and better design, you can use the Access form generator.

Access can generate a data entry form that is more pleasing to view and easier to use than that in Figure CE8-13. The process is shown in Figure CE8-14. First, click the *Create tab* to open the *Create ribbon*. Next, click the PROSPECT table (this causes Access to create a form for PROSPECT). Finally, click *Form*. Access uses metadata about the tables and their relationship to create the data entry form in Figure CE8-15.

The data about a prospect is shown in the top portion of this form, and data about that person's work sessions is shown in the bottom portion. The user of this form has clicked the arrow at the bottom of the form to bring up the third Prospect record, the one for Peter Lopez. Notice that he has two work sessions. If you click the arrow in the next-to-last row of this form, you will change the focus of the work record.

You can use this form to modify data; just type over any data that you wish to change. You can also add data. To add work data, just click in the last row of the work

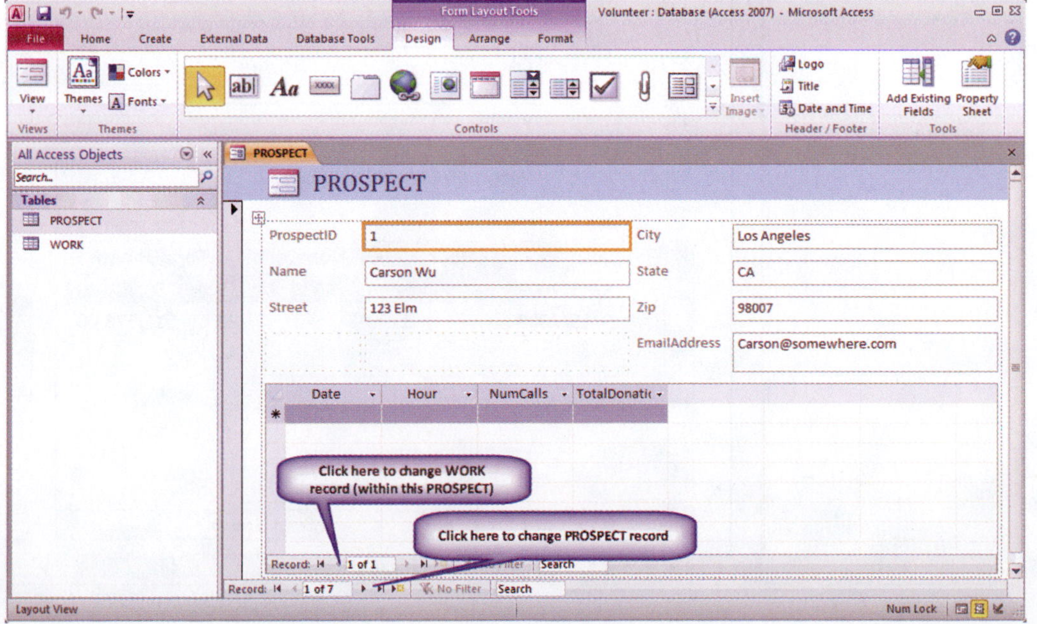

Figure CE8-15
Resulting Data Entry Form

grid; in this case that would be the third row of this grid. To delete a record, click the *Home* tab, and then in the *Records* section click the down arrow next to *Delete* and select *Delete Record*. This action will delete the prospect data and all related work data (not shown in Figure CE8-15).

This form is fine, but we can make it better. For one, ProspectID is a surrogate key and has no meaning to the user. Access uses that key to keep track of each PROSPECT row. Because it has no meaning to the user (in fact, the user cannot change or otherwise modify its value), we should remove it from the form. Also, we might like to reduce the size of the fields as well as reduce the size of the work area and center it on the form. Figure CE8-16 shows the form after these changes. It is smaller and cleaner, and it will be easier to use.

To make the changes shown, see the steps illustrated in Figure CE8-17. First, click the *View* button in the ribbon and then select *Design View*. The form will open in Design mode; click the right edge of the rightmost rectangle, and, holding your mouse down, drag to the left. Access will reduce the width of each of these fields.

Third, to resize the work subform, click within the area labeled *Table.WORK*. Next, click that table area's right edge and drag to the left. Access will reduce the size of this subform. Lift up on your mouse and then click again and you can move the area to center it under the PROSPECT fields.

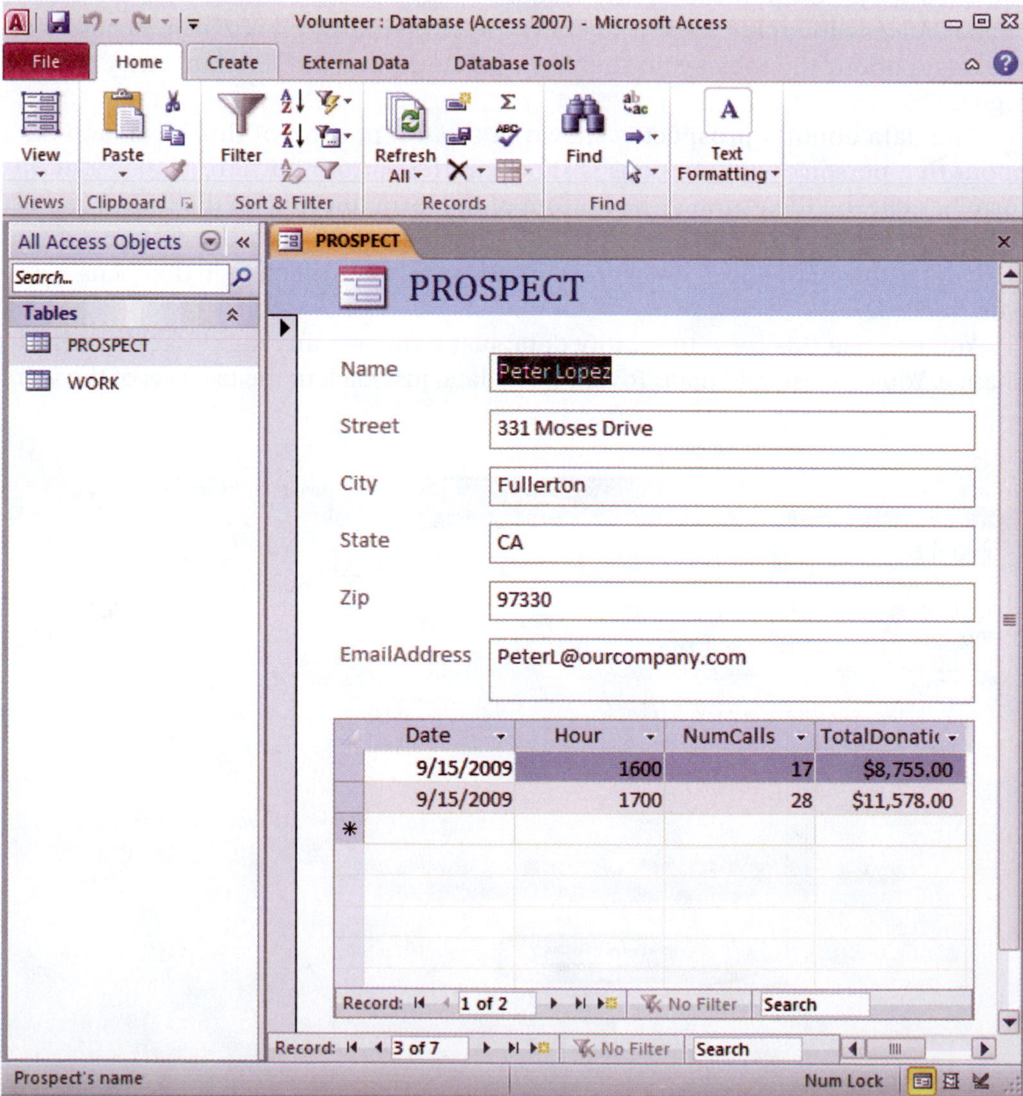

Figure CE8-16
Reformatted Data Entry Form

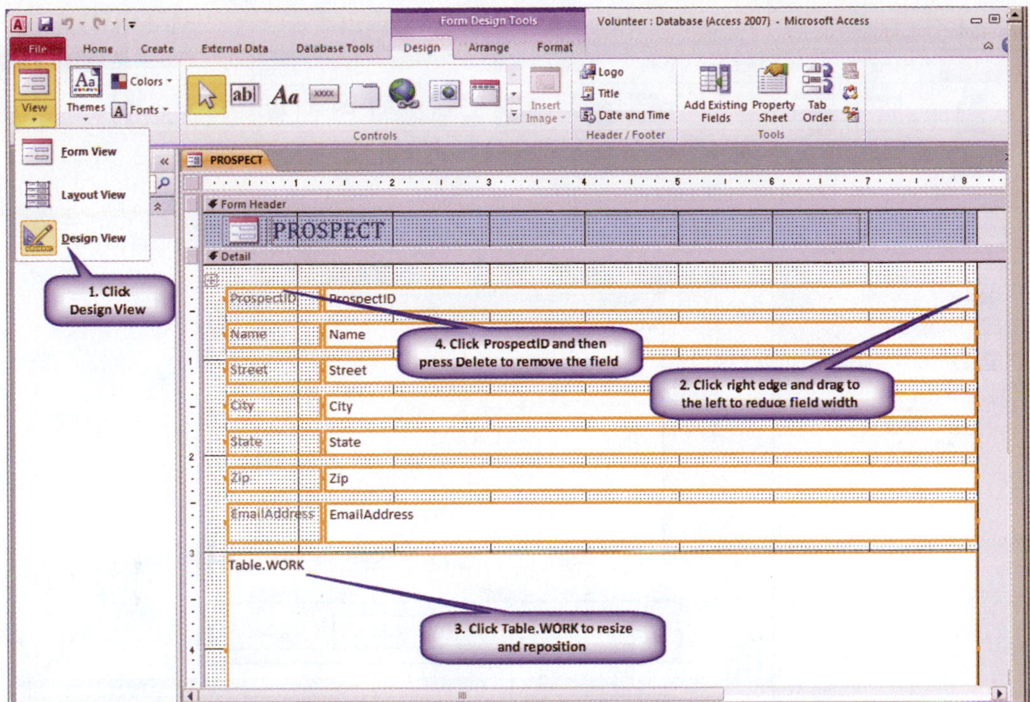

Figure CE8-17
Process for Reformatting Data Entry Form

Finally, click *ProspectID*, as shown in step 4. Press the *Delete* key, and the ProspectID field will be removed from the form. Click *View/Form View*, and your form should look like that in Figure CE8-16. You can go back to *Design View* to make more adjustments, if necessary.

To save your form, either close it and Access will give you the chance to save it or click the *Office* button and select *Save*. Save with an informative file name, such as PROSPECT Data Entry Form.

There are many options for customizing Access forms. You can learn about them if you take a database processing class after you complete this MIS class.

Q4 How Can You Create Queries Using the Query Design Tool?

Like all modern DBMS products, Access can process the SQL query language. Learning that language, however, is beyond the scope of this textbook. However, Access does provide a graphical interface that we can use to create and process queries, and that graphical interface will generate SQL statements for us.

To begin, first clean up your screen by closing the PROSPECT Data Entry Form. Click the *Create* tab in the ribbon, and in the *Queries* section click the *Query Design* button. You should see the display shown in Figure CE8-18. Double-click the names of both the PROSPECT and WORK tables, and close the *Show Table* window. Access will have placed both tables into the query design form, as shown in Figure CE8-19. Notice that Access remembers the relationship between the two tables (shown by the line connecting ProspectID in PROSPECT to the same attribute in WORK).

To create a query, drag columns out of the PROSPECT and WORK tables into the grid in the lower part of the query definition form. In Figure CE8-20, the *Name*,

Figure CE8-18
Creating a Query, Step 1

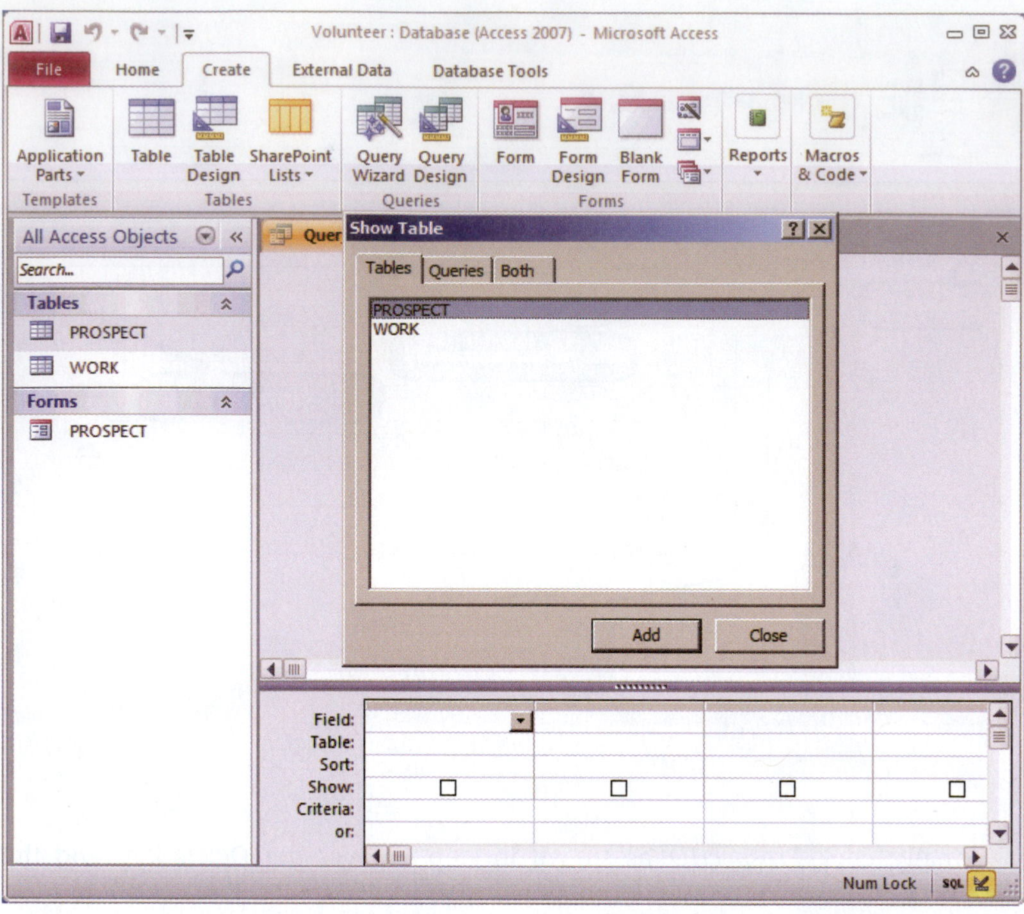

Figure CE8-19
Creating a Query, Step 2

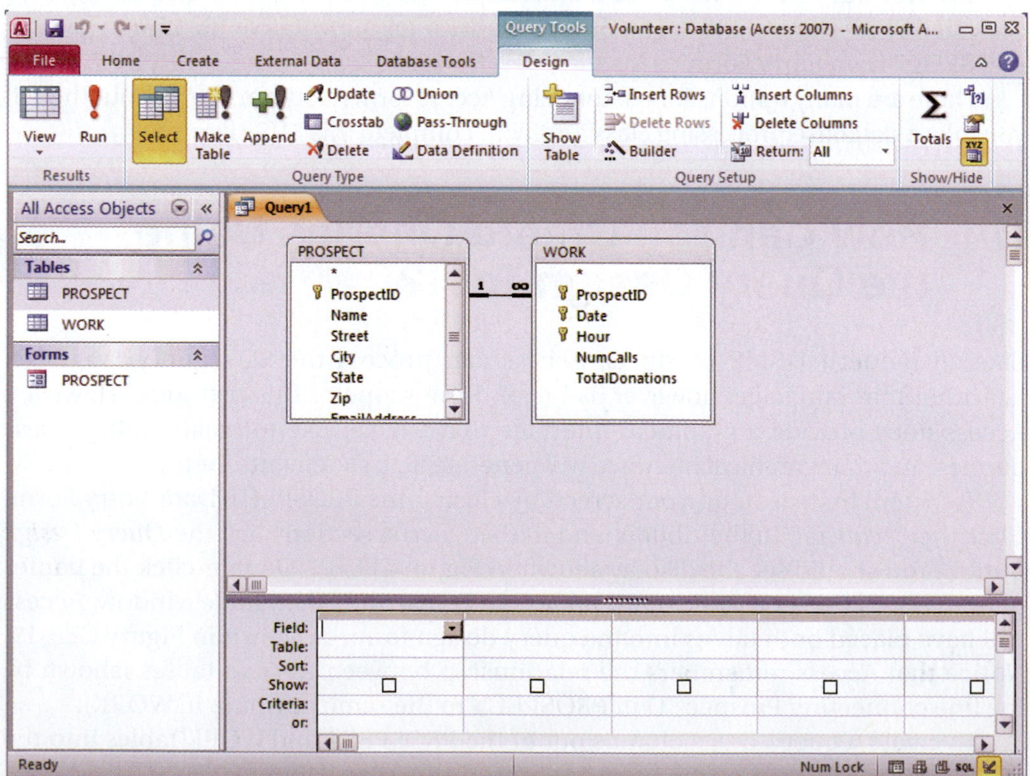

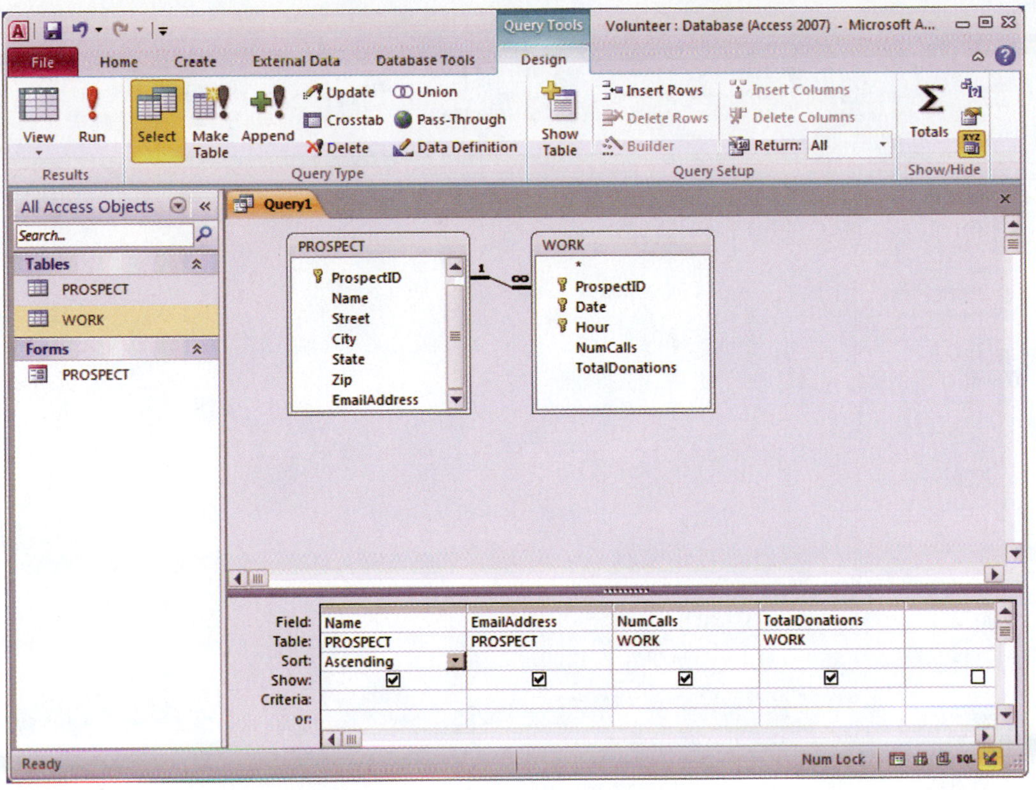

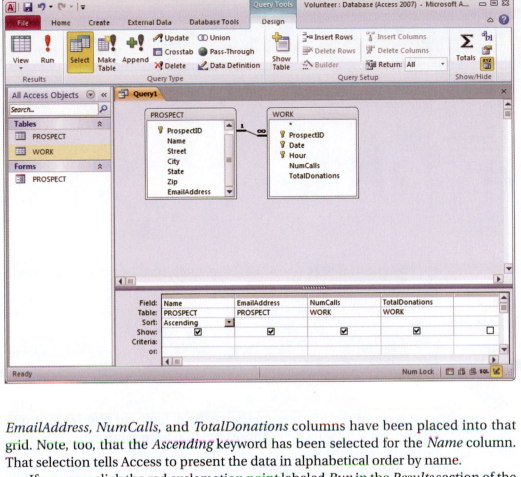

Figure CE8-20
Creating a Query, Step 3

EmailAddress, *NumCalls*, and *TotalDonations* columns have been placed into that grid. Note, too, that the *Ascending* keyword has been selected for the *Name* column. That selection tells Access to present the data in alphabetical order by name.

If you now click the red exclamation point labeled *Run* in the *Results* section of the ribbon, the result shown in Figure CE8-21 will appear. Notice that only PROSPECT

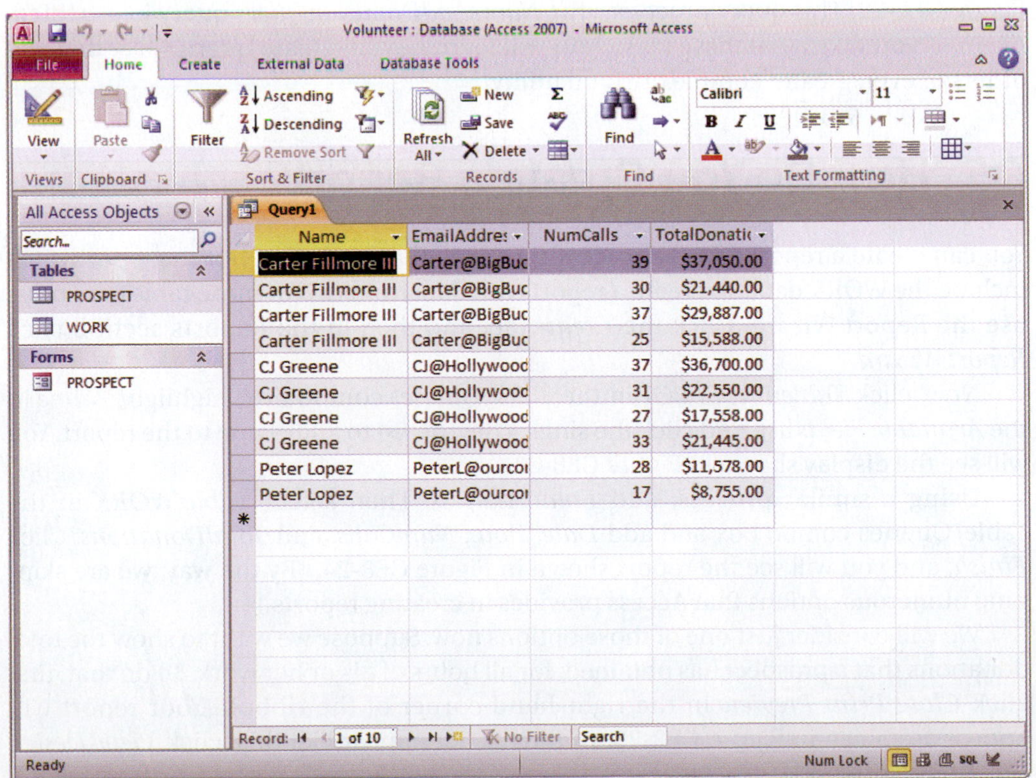

Figure CE8-21
Results of *TotalDonations* Query

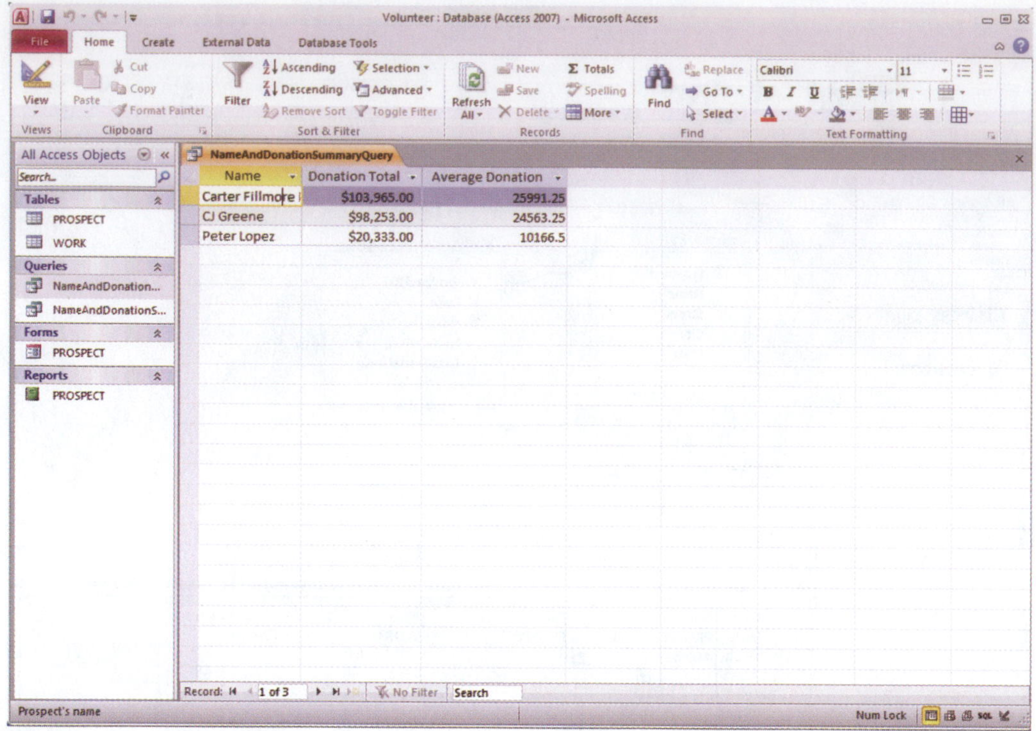

Figure CE8-22
Result of More Advanced Query

rows that have at least one WORK row are shown. By default, for queries of two or more tables Access (and SQL) shows only those rows that have value matches in both tables. Save the query under the name *NameAndDonationQuery.*

Queries have many useful purposes. For example, suppose we want to see the average dollar value of donation generated per hour of work. This query, which is just slightly beyond the scope of this chapter extension, can readily be created using either the Access graphical tool or SQL. The results of such a query are shown in Figure CE8-22. This query processes the *NameAndDonationQuery* query just created. Again, if you take a database class, you will learn how to create queries like this and others of even greater complexity (and utility).

Q5 How Do You Create a Report?

You can create a report using a process similar to that for forms, but the report won't include the WORK data. To create a report with data from two or more tables, we must use the Report Wizard. Click the *Create* tab, and then in the Reports section click *Report Wizard.*

Now, click *Table:PROSPECT* in the *Table/Queries* combo box, highlight *Name* in the *Available Fields* list, and click the single chevron (>) to add Name to the report. You will see the display shown in Figure CE8-23.

Using a similar process, add *EmailAddress.* Then select *Table:WORK* in the Table/Queries combo box and add *Date, Hour, NumCalls,* and *TotalDonations.* Click *Finish,* and you will see the report shown in Figure CE8-24. (By the way, we are skipping numerous options that Access provides in creating reports.)

We will consider just one of those options now. Suppose we want to show the total donations that a prospect has obtained, for all hours of his or her work. To do that, first click *Close Print Preview* in the right-hand corner of the ribbon. Your report will appear as shown in Figure CE8-25. (If it does not appear like this, click *View, Design View* in the ribbon.)

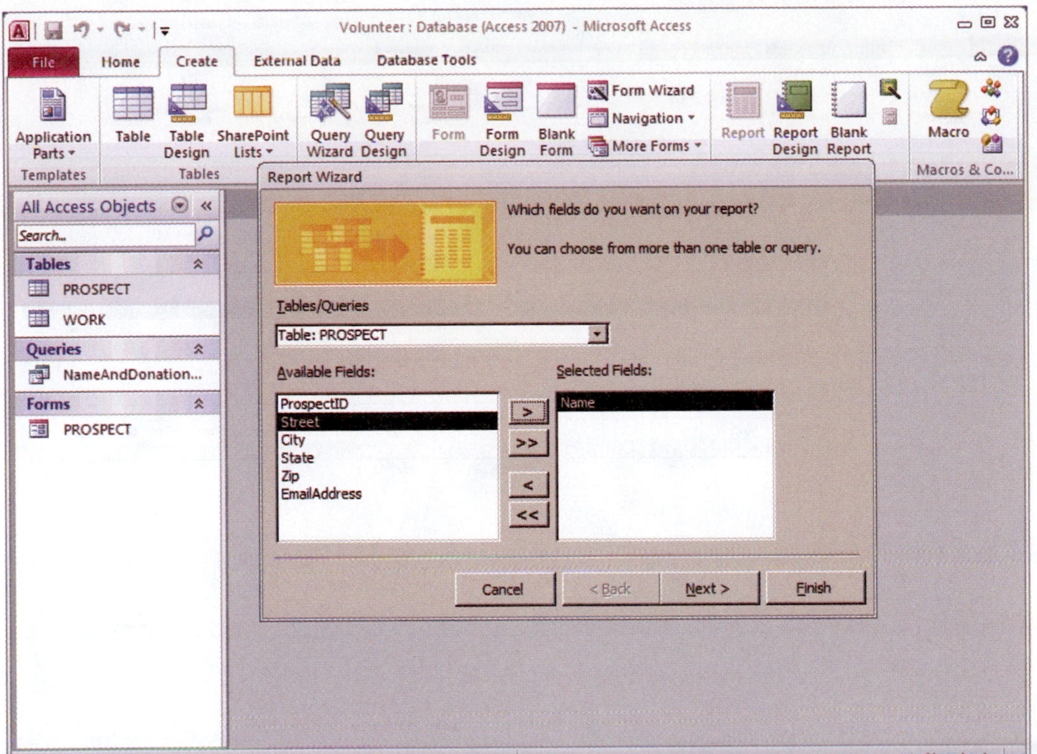

Figure CE8-23
Selecting Data to Show in a Report

In the ribbon, click *Group and Sort* in the *Grouping & Totals* section. In the bottom of the form, click *More*, and then click the down arrow next to the phrase *with no totals*. Next, select *TotalDonations* from the *TotalOn* box, and then check *Show Grand Total* and *Show subtotal in group footer*, as illustrated in Figure CE8-26.

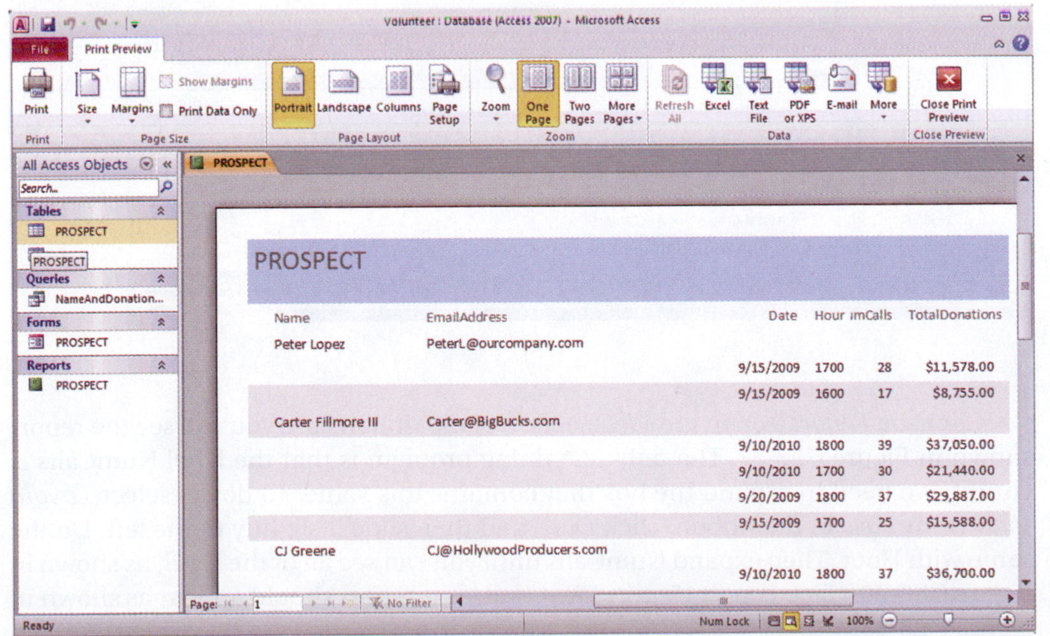

Figure CE8-24
Report on Donations, by Prospect

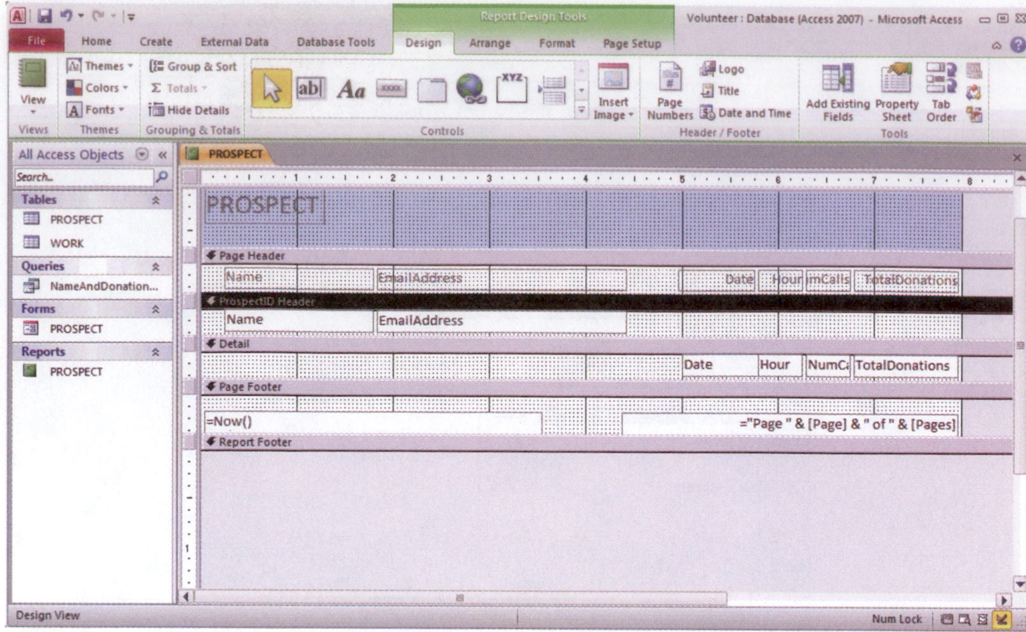

Figure CE8-25
Report Design View

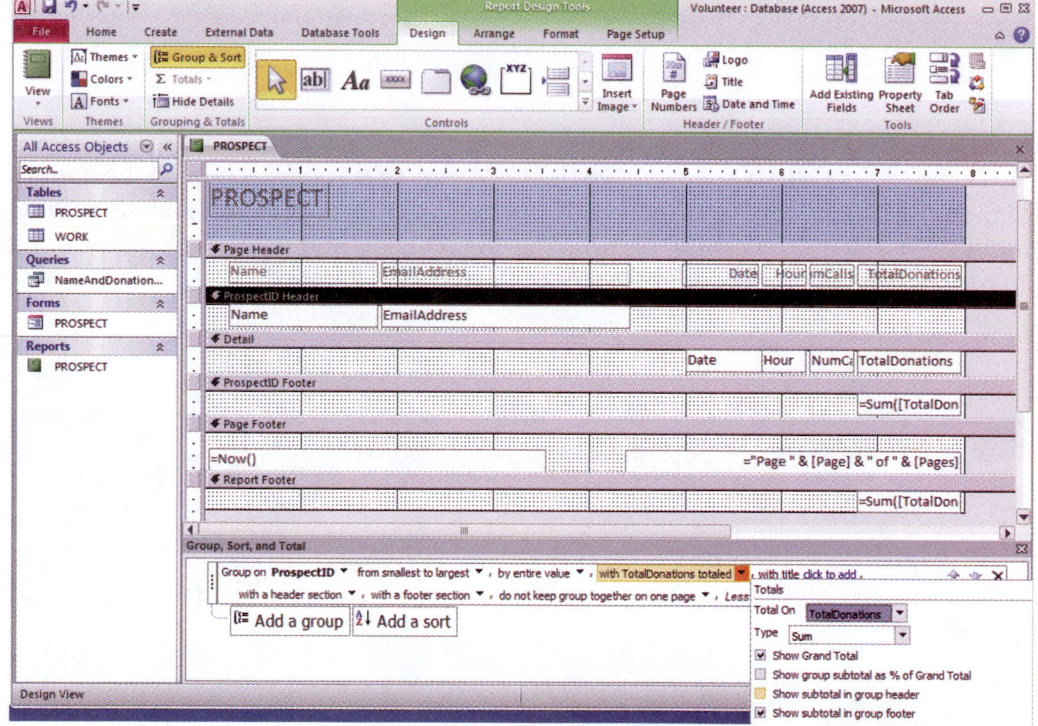

Figure CE8-26
Creating a Sum of *TotalDonations* for Each Prospect

Click the *Report* icon in the *View* section of the ribbon, and you will see the report shown in Figure CE8-27. The only remaining problem is that the label NumCalls is cut off. We need to expand the box that contains this value. To do so, select *Layout View* from *View* in the ribbon, click *Date,* and then slide it slightly to the left. Do the same with Hour. Then expand NumCalls until you can see all of the label, as shown in Figure CE8-28. Click *Report View* in *View,* and your report should appear as shown in Figure CE8-29.

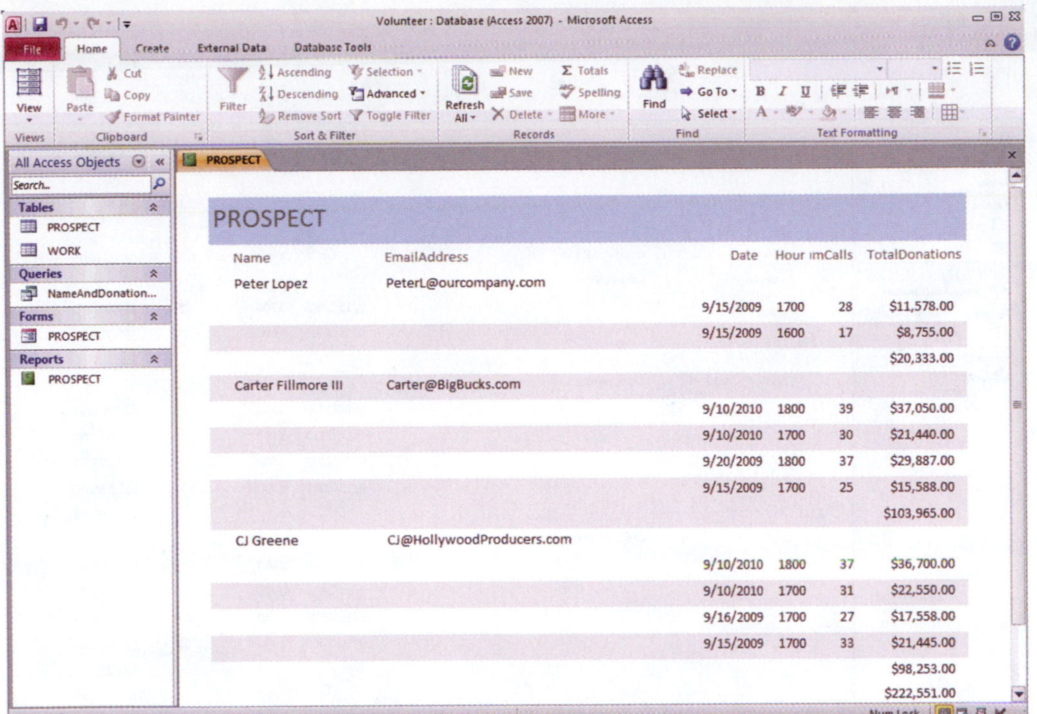

Figure CE8-27
Report with Sum of *TotalDonations*

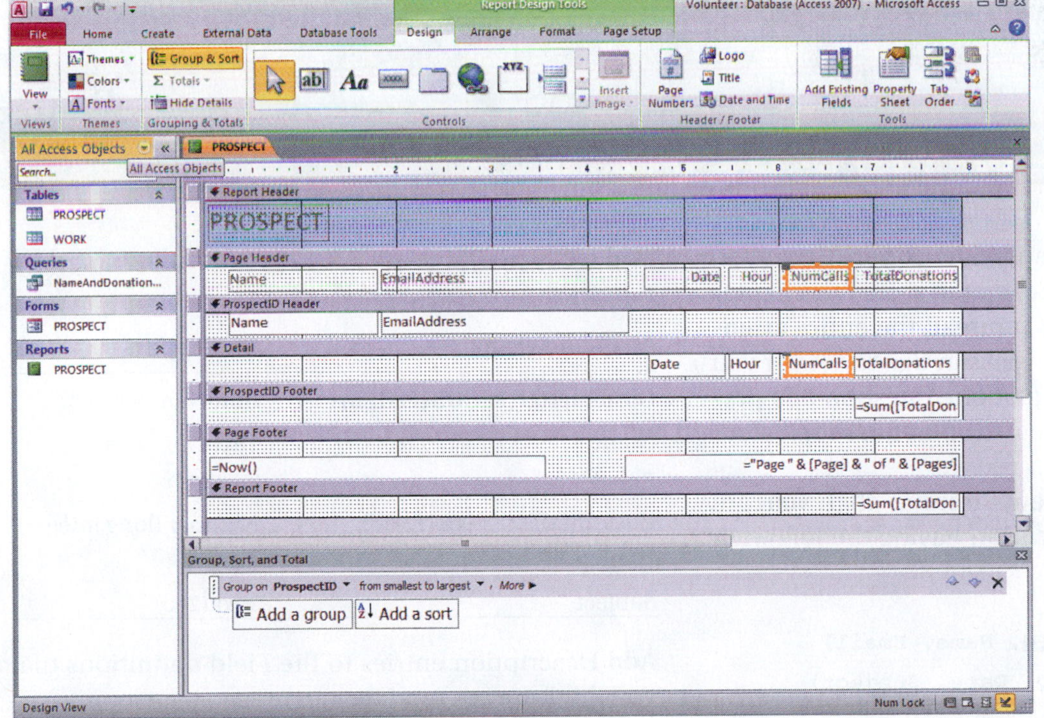

Figure CE8-28
Reducing the Size of the *EmailAddress* Field

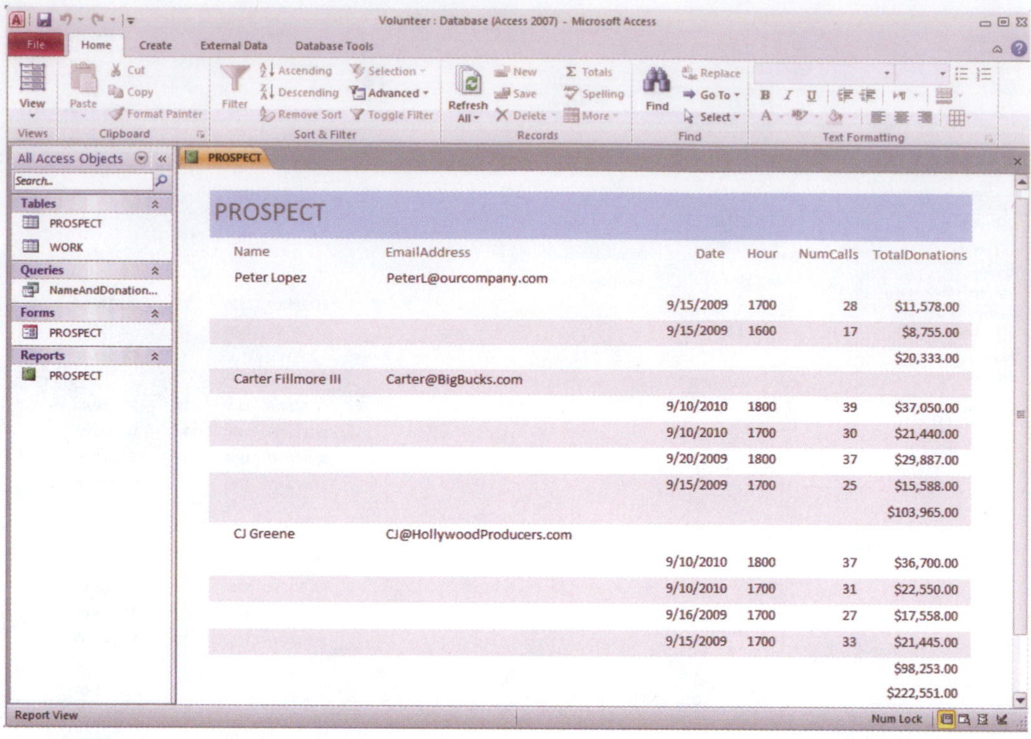

Figure CE8-29
Final Version of Report

ACTIVE REVIEW

Use this Active Review to verify that you understand the material in the chapter extension. You can read the entire extension and then perform the tasks in this review, or you can read the material for just one question and perform the tasks in this review for that question before moving on to the next one.

For this Active Review, assume that you are creating a database application having the following two tables:

CUSTOMER (<u>CustomerID</u>, Name, Email)

CONTACT (<u>*CustomerID*</u>, <u>Date</u>, Subject)

Q1 How do you create tables?

Open Access and create a new database having a name of your choosing. Create the CUSTOMER and CONTACT tables. Assume the following data types:

Attribute (Field)	Data Type
CustomerID (in CUSTOMER)	AutoNumber
Name	Text (50)
Email	Text (75)
CustomerID (in CONTACT)	Number (long integer)
Date	Date
Subject	Text (200)

Add Description entries to the Field definitions that you think are appropriate.

Q2 How do you create relationships?

Open the *Relationships* window and create a relationship from CUSTOMER to CONTACT using the

CustomerID attribute. Click all of the checkboxes. Enter sample data. Add at least five rows to CUSTOMER and at least seven rows to CONTACT. Ensure that some CUSTOMER rows have no matching CONTACT rows.

Q3 How do you create a data entry form?

Open the default data entry form for the CUSTOMER table. Click the CUSTOMER rows to display the related CONTACT data. Now use the *Form* tool to create a data entry form. Navigate through that form to see that the CONTACT rows are correctly connected to the CUSTOMER rows. Adjust spacing as you deem appropriate; remove the CustomerID field from the CUSTOMER section.

Q4 How can you create queries using the query design tool?

Create a query that displays Name, Email, Date, and Subject. Sort the results of Name in alphabetical order.

Q5 How do you create a report?

Use the Report Wizard to create a report that has Name, Email, Date, and Subject. View that report. Add a group total for each CUSTOMER that counts the number of contacts for each customer. Follow the procedure shown, except instead of selecting Sum for Type choose *Count Records* instead.

USING YOUR KNOWLEDGE

1. Answer question 2 at the end of Chapter Extension 7 (page 396). Use Access to implement your database design. Create the tables and add sample data. Create a data entry form that shows teams and the equipment they have checked out. Verify that the form correctly processes new checkouts, changes to checkouts, and equipment returns. Create a report that shows each team, the items they have checked out, and the number of items they have checked out. (Use the Records selection as explained in Active Review Q5.)

2. Answer question 3 at the end of Chapter Extension 7 (page 397). Create an Access database for the CUSTOMER and RENTAL tables only. Create the tables and add sample data. Create a data entry form that shows customers and all of their rentals (assume customers rent bicycles more than once). Verify that the form correctly processes new rentals, changes to rentals, and rental returns. Create a report that shows each customer, the rentals they have made, and the total rental fee for all of their rentals.

CHAPTER EXTENSION 9

STUDY QUESTIONS

Q1 Why use Excel and Access together?

Q2 What is import/export?

Q3 How can you create graphs with Excel?

Q4 How can you create group totals in Access?

Q5 How can you use Excel to graph Access data?

Q6 How can you use Access to report Excel data?

Q7 How can you combine Excel and Access to analyze data?

Chapters 4 and **5** provide the background for this Extension.

Using Excel and Access Together

Excel and Access are two different products with two different purposes. In this chapter extension, you will learn how to use them together to analyze data in ways that neither can do alone. You will also learn how to create graphs in Excel and group totals in Access queries.

Q1 Why Use Excel and Access Together?

As you learned in Chapter Extension 5, Excel is superb at processing interrelated formulas. Because of this strength, business users often select Excel for processing financial statements, creating budgets, and performing financial analyses. As you will learn in this chapter extension, you can use Excel to create sophisticated and stylish graphics with very little work on your part (Excel has a lot of work to do, though!).

Access is a DBMS, and as you learned in Chapter 5 the primary purpose of a DBMS is to keep track of things. Access is superior for tracking orders, inventory, equipment, people, and so forth. As you learned in Chapter Extension 8, you can readily create data entry forms, queries, and sophisticated and professional reports with Access. In this chapter extension, you will learn how to create more sophisticated queries.

But, what if you want to use Excel to process data stored in Access? What if you want, for example, to create graphs of Access data? Or what if you want to include Access data in a financial analysis? You could rekey all of the Access data into Excel, but that process is not only labor-intensive (and therefore expensive), but also error-prone. Similarly, what if you want to use Access to summarize data and produce sophisticated reports? Again, you could rekey the data into Access, but with the same disadvantages.

In both cases, a better approach than rekeying is to import or export the data to or from Excel or Access. We begin with a discussion of import/export in the next question.

Q2 What Is Import/Export?

Import/export is the process of transferring data from one computer system to another. We can say that system A imports data from system B or, equivalently, that system B exports data to system A.

In almost all cases, including Excel and Access, import/export does not maintain an active connection to the source of the data. For example, when you import Access data into Excel, the data are current at the time of the import. If users subsequently change the Access data, the imported data in Excel will be out-of-date until you re-import it. Because imported data can become out-of-date, you should develop procedures (either manual or automated) to ensure that data are refreshed on a timely basis.

Import/Export of Text Data

A common way for systems to exchange data is to create files of text. One system will export text data, and another will import it. Consider, for example, a professor who wants to track students' in-class comments using Microsoft Access. Most university enrollment systems can export class enrollment data into text files. Figure CE9-1 shows a typical export.

This file contains students' names, numbers, majors, and grade levels. Notice that the field values are separated by commas. Accordingly, such a file is called a **comma-delimited file**. Sometimes, however, the data itself contains commas, and so commas cannot be used to separate field data. In that case, some other character is used to delimit the fields. The tab character is frequently used, in which case the export file is called a **tab-delimited file**.

Delimited text files are easy to import into either Excel or Access. In Access, just create (or open a database) and click the *External Data* tab, as shown in Figure CE9-2. Next, as shown in Figure CE9-3, select the file that contains the data, and check *Import*. (Ignore the other option, it's not very useful and is beyond the scope of our discussion.) When you click *OK*, a multiple-panel wizard opens.

In Figure CE9-4a, you specify that your file is delimited. To assist you, Access shows the first rows of the file. Click *Next* to specify the delimiter; here we are using the comma, as shown in Figure CE9-4b on page 421. Click *Next* again and you will be given a chance to name the fields as well as to specify their data type. Ignore Indexed. In Figure CE9-4c on page 422, we have renamed the first three columns and are about to rename the fourth. In the next screen (not shown), you have a chance to name the table into which Access will import the data. At this point, click *Finish*, and Access will import the data into a new table, as shown in Figure CE9-5 on page 422.

Access will process the new table just like any other table. You can create data entry forms, reports, queries, and even relationships to other tables. Note, too, that although we have imported only five rows in this example, it would be no more work for us to import 50, 5,000, or 50,000 rows.

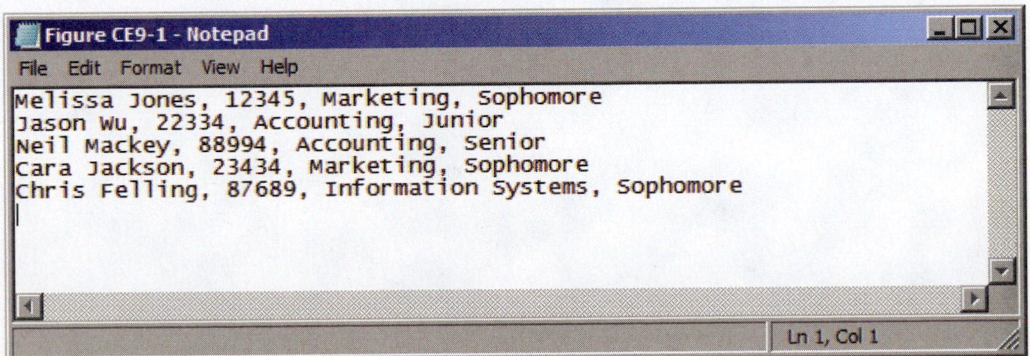

Figure CE9-1
Example of Data Exported from University Enrollment System

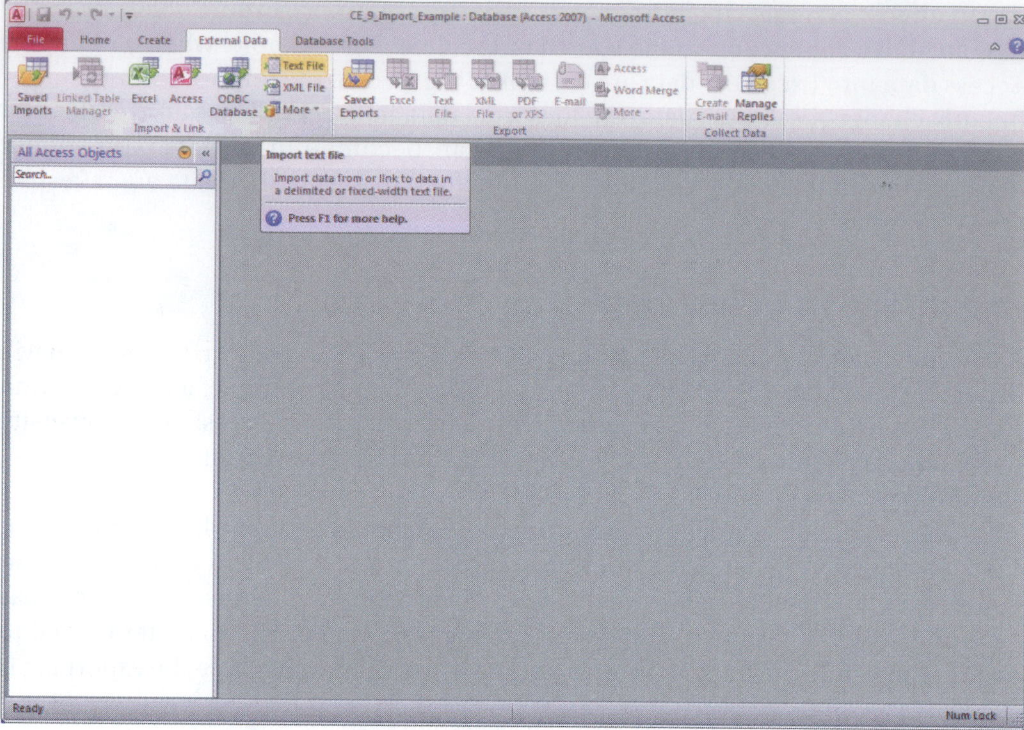

Figure CE9-2
External Data Menu Choice

You can follow an almost identical process to import data into Excel. (Memo to Microsoft: Why isn't it *exactly* the same process?) Open Excel, click the *Data* tab, and in the *Get External Data* section of that ribbon click *From Text*. You will need to specify a comma delimiter and indicate where in the worksheet you want the data placed. This process is easy, as you will see when you do question 1 of Using Your Knowledge at the end of this extension.

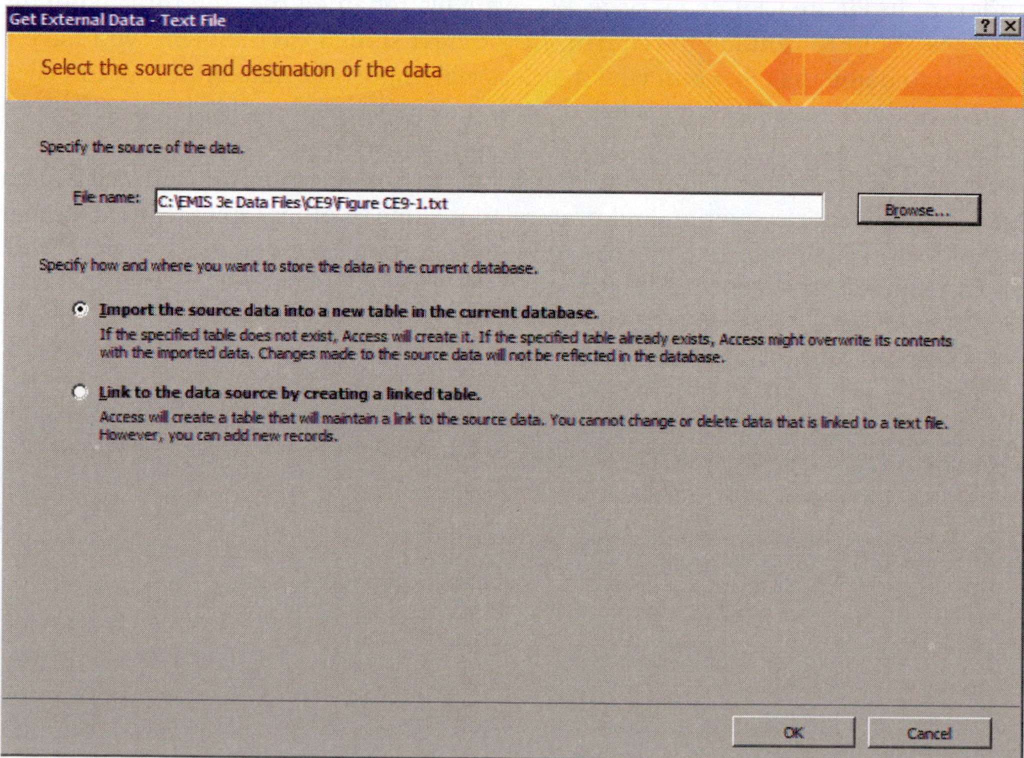

Figure CE9-3
Specifying the Source File and Destination

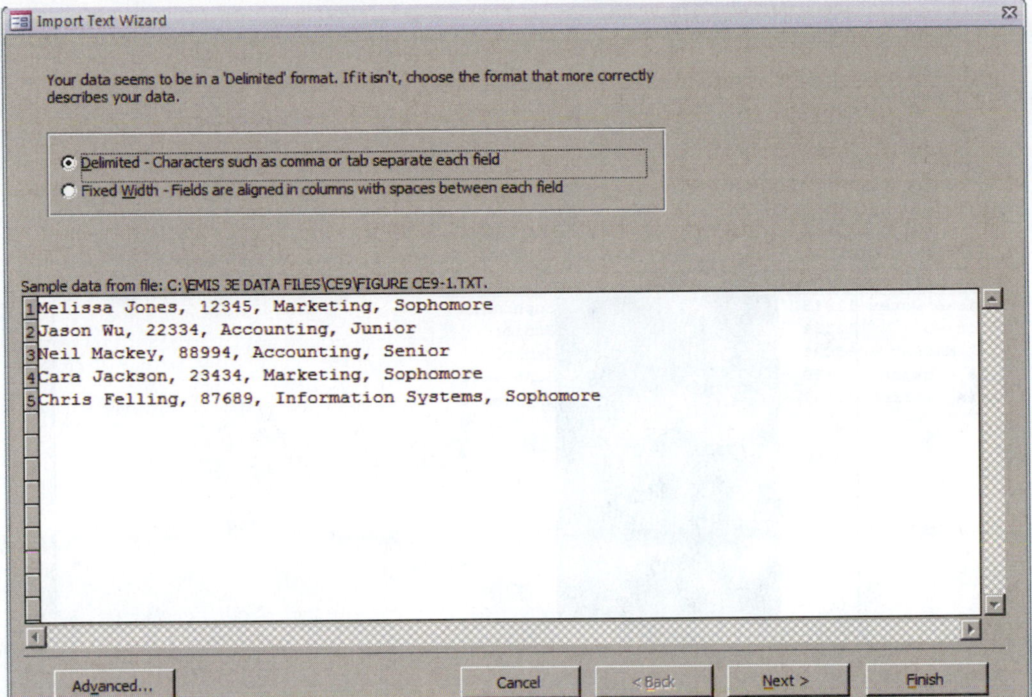

Figure CE9-4a
Importing Text Data into Access: Specifying a Delimited File

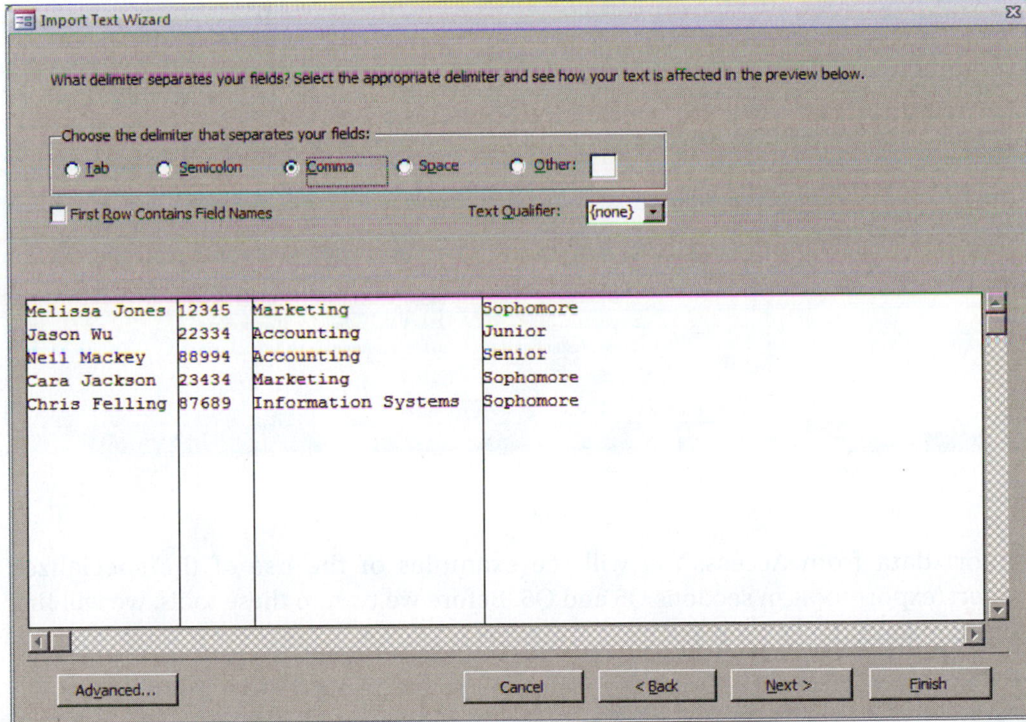

Figure CE9-4b
Importing Text Data into Access: Specifying a Comma-Delimited File

Import/Export of Excel and Access Data

One way you could exchange data between Excel and Access would be to export the data into a text file and then import that text data. However, because many users want to transfer data between Excel and Access, Microsoft has created special tools for that purpose. You can use Access to both export and import data. You can use Excel to

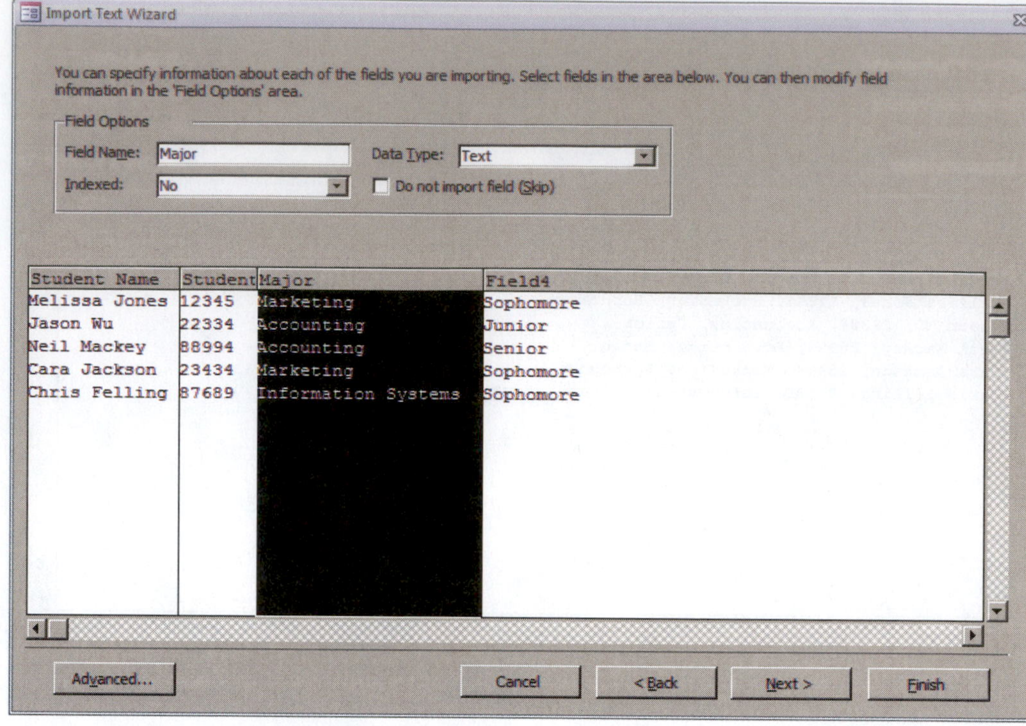

Figure CE9-4c
Importing Text Data into Access: Naming and Describing Columns During Import

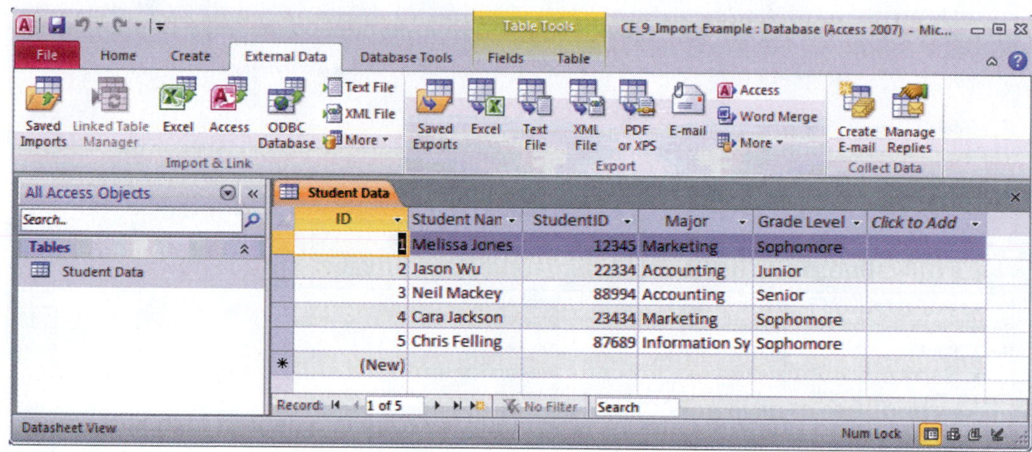

Figure CE9-5
Data After Import

import data from Access. You will see examples of the use of the specialized import/export tools in sections Q5 and Q6. Before we turn to these tools, we will first consider additional features of Excel and Access.

Q3 How Can You Create Graphs with Excel?

Microsoft Excel includes comprehensive tools for graphing data. You can use it to construct column and bar charts, pie charts, line and scatter plots, and other graphs. Here you will learn how to construct pie and column charts. Follow the discussion in this section to learn the gist of the process, and then learn more by experimenting with Excel. You can make custom charts quite easily; like the rest of Office 2010, however, it's a matter of finding the ribbon that has the tool you want.

In this section, we will use the computer budget workbook we created in Chapter Extension 6. In that extension, we created a budget for three different levels of growth, as shown in Figure CE6-10 (page 380). In the Budget worksheet, line 13 shows the New System Costs for each job function for the no-growth alternative. Figure CE9-6 shows that workbook with the addition of a worksheet named Graphs. Cells D4 through D6 of the Graphs worksheet pick up the data from the Budget worksheet. In this figure, note, for example, that cell D4 contains the formula *Budget!B13*. This notation means to copy the value of cell B13 from the Budget worksheet.

Creating a Pie Chart

Figure CE9-6 shows a pie chart of the new system cost data. This chart, which is very easy to create, is one example of the kind of graph that Excel can produce. To create this pie chart, we highlight cells C4 through D6 (shown in Figure CE9-7), click the *Insert* tab in the ribbon, and in the *Charts* section of that ribbon select the *Pie* icon. As shown, Excel can create several different versions of pie charts; here, we have selected the first choice.

Excel provides many different tools to customize a graph. To access them, click the graph you want to change. Excel will show a special tab called *Chart Tools* at the top of the window. Click *Chart Tools* to make them available, as shown in Figure CE9-8.

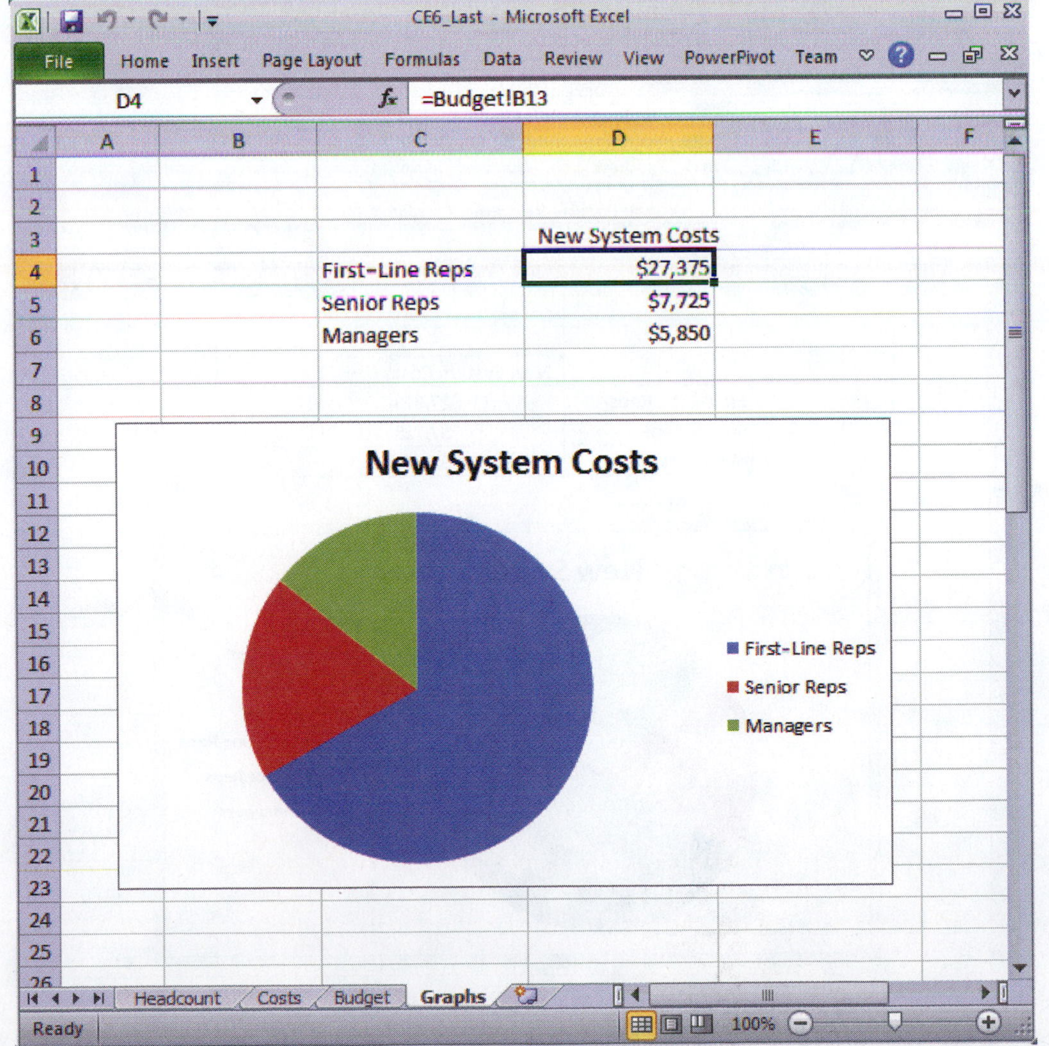

Figure CE9-6
Pie Chart

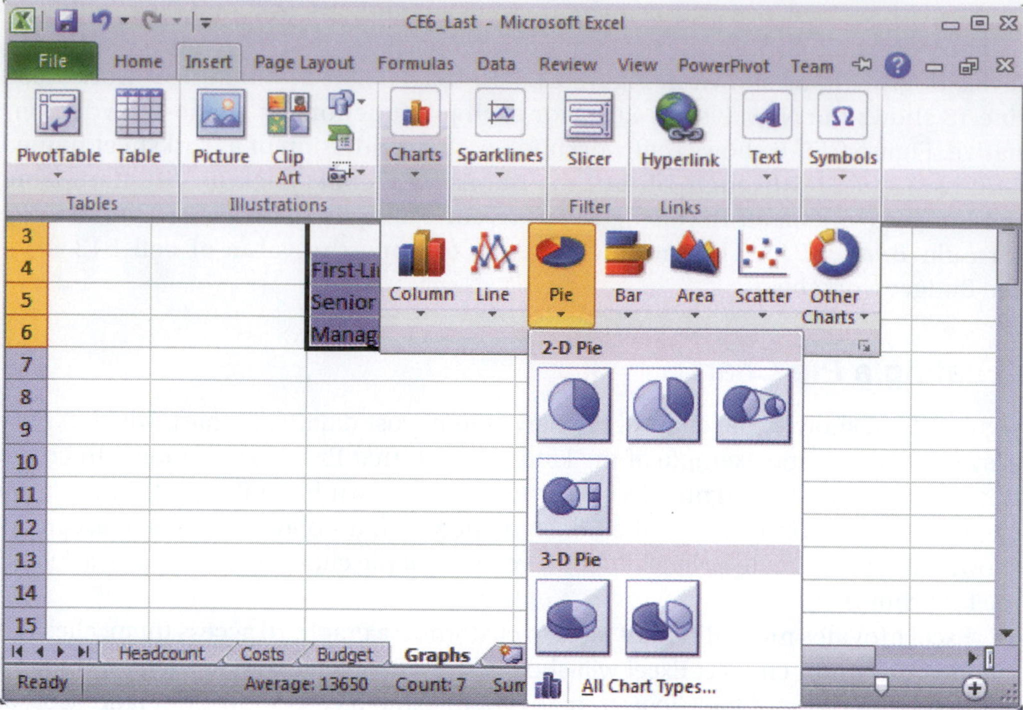

Figure CE9-7
Creating the Pie Chart

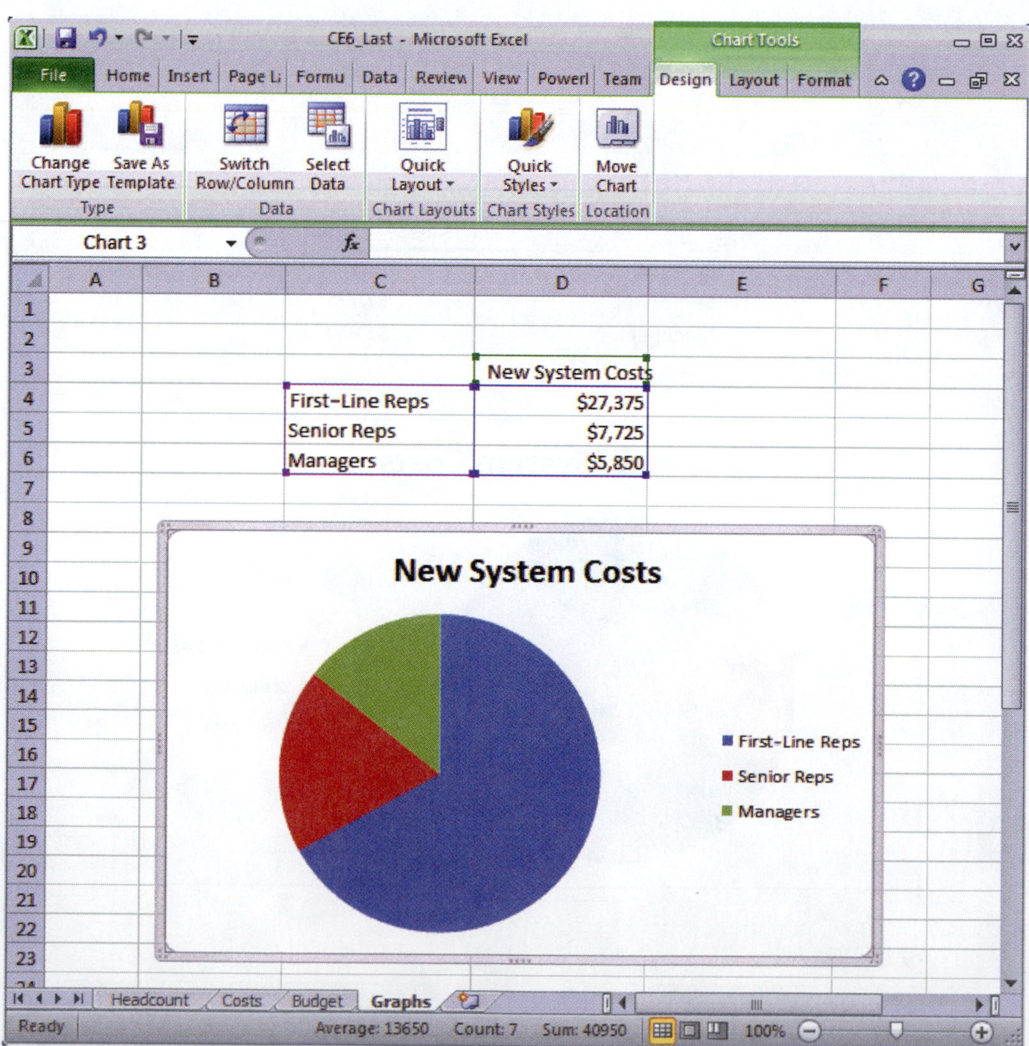

Figure CE9-8
Selecting the Chart Tools

The discussion of these tools is beyond the scope of this chapter extension. But, they are intuitive, and you can learn much about their use by experimenting with them.

Creating a Column Chart

The pie chart in Figure CE9-6 shows only the data for the no-growth scenario. If we want to compare the various growth alternatives, we can do so with a column or a bar chart. Figure CE9-9 shows a column chart.

As shown in that figure, we have copied the data from the Budget worksheet into this worksheet, named Graphs. Notice in Figure CE9-9 that cell D37 contains the formula *=Budget!C21*. That cell contains the value of new systems costs for Senior Reps in the moderate-growth scenario, as shown in Figure CE6-10 (page 380). Other cost values are taken from appropriate cells in the Budget worksheet.

To create the column chart, we highlighted the data and selected *Column* in the *Charts* section of the *Insert* tab, as shown in Figure CE9-10. With one exception, Excel created the chart shown in Figure CE9-9 with no further work on our part.

The exception concerns the title. Notice that the data on which the graph is based do not include any text that would make a suitable title. Hence, when Excel first

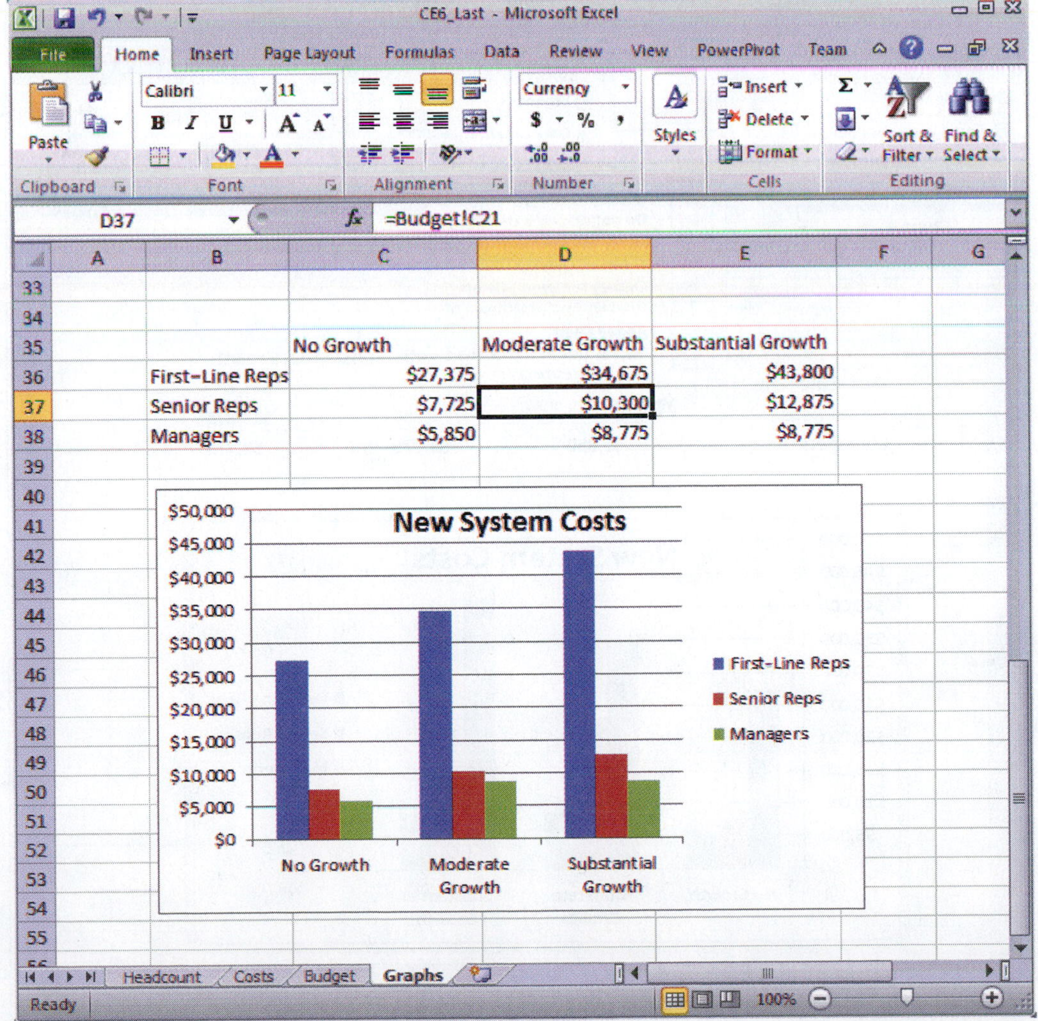

Figure CE9-9
Sample Column Chart

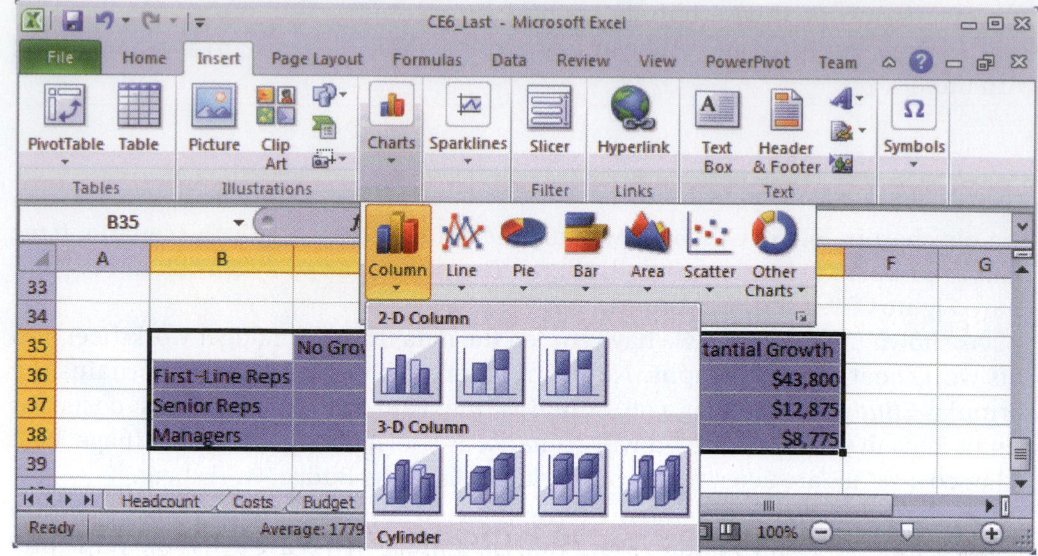

Figure CE9-10
Creating the Column Chart

produced the graph shown in Figure CE9-9, the graph had no title. To insert a title, we click the column chart, select *Chart Tools*, click the *Layout* tab, click *Chart Title*, and select *Center Overlay Title*. Excel has placed a textbox for the title on the graph, and we enter *New System Costs* into that textbox, as shown in Figure CE9-11.

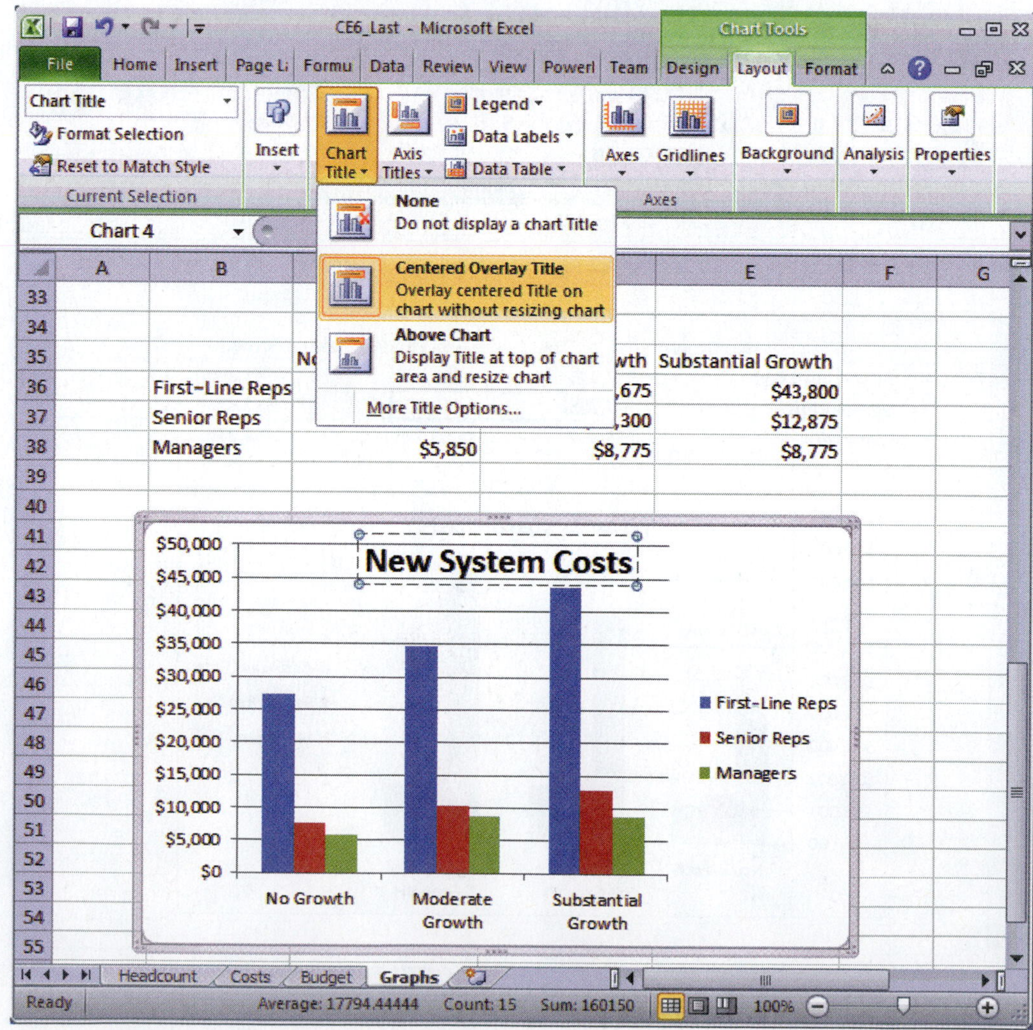

Figure CE9-11
Creating the Chart Title

As you can guess, Excel has many, many options for creating interesting and informative graphs. As stated, one good way to learn more is to create some data and experiment. You can also find many resources for learning Excel on the Web.

Q4 How Can You Create Group Totals in Access?

In Chapter Extension 8, you learned how to create basic queries in Access. With more advanced queries, you can create considerably more information from the same amount of data. To learn some of the possibilities, consider the Volunteer database that we created in Chapter Extension 8.

Suppose a manager of the station wants to know the total of TotalDonations[1] for each date of fundraising effort. Maybe she thinks that certain dates are more advantageous than others. To create this information, we can query the WORK table, group all donations for a given date, and then sum the TotalDonations for each group.

To do that, we need to open the Volunteer database, click the *Create* tab, click *Query Design*, and then, as shown in Figure CE9-12, select the WORK table for the query. After adding that table, click *Close*.

Now, to add Date and TotalDonations to the query output, double-click *Date* and *TotalDonations* in the WORK table diagram. Access adds them to the query contents table at the bottom of the query, as shown in Figure CE9-13. To group the WORK rows according to date, we click the *Totals* button in the *Show/Hide* section of the *Design* tab. When we do this, Access adds a row labeled *Total* to the query contents table, as shown in Figure CE9-14.

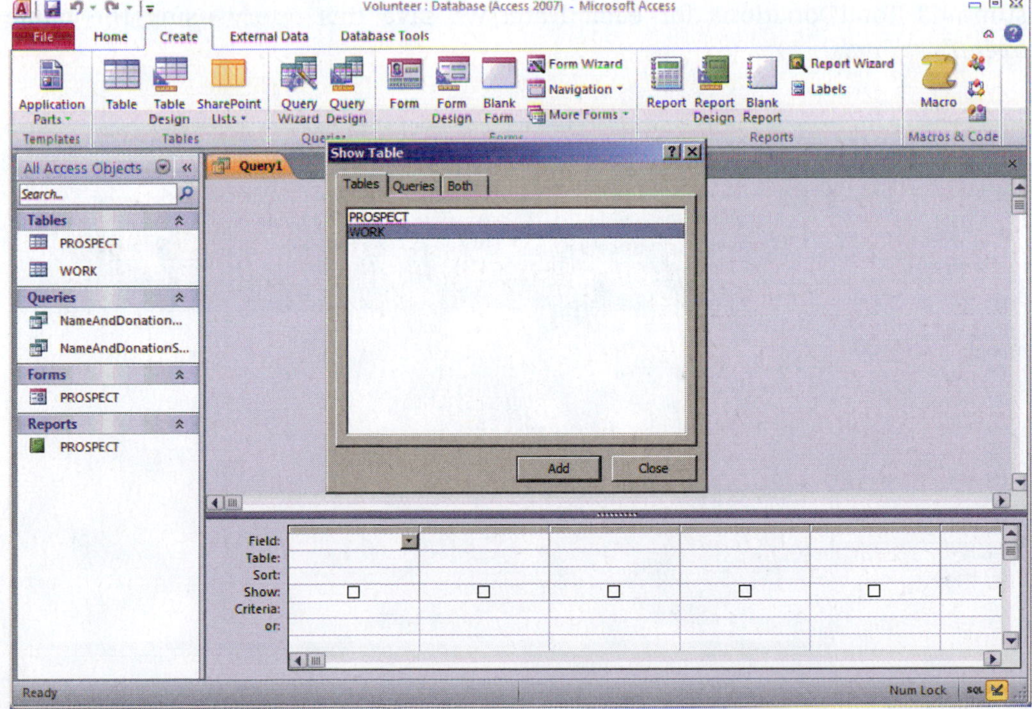

Figure CE9-12
Selecting the WORK Table for the Query

1. The terminology may be confusing. The value in TotalDonations is the total of all donations received by a particular volunteer in a particular hour on a particular date. Here, the manager wants to know the total of all donations for all volunteers for all hours on a given date.

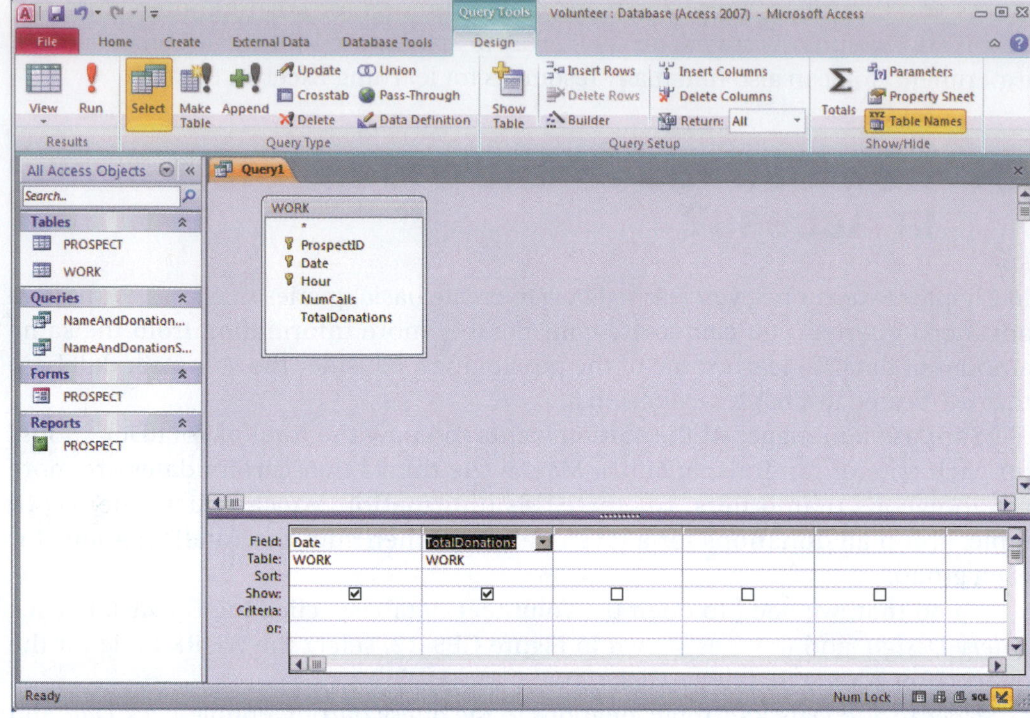

Figure CE9-13 Adding Data and TotalDonations to the Query

To group the rows by date, we need to select the keyword *Group By* in the Total row under *Date*. To sum TotalDonations for each group, we need to select the keyword *Sum* under the TotalDonations column, in that same Total row. Figure CE9-14 shows this last action.

We run the query by clicking the large exclamation point in the *Results* section of the *Design* ribbon, and the results shown in Figure CE9-15 are generated. Access has summed TotalDonations for each Date. We save this query using the name *EventDateTotals*.

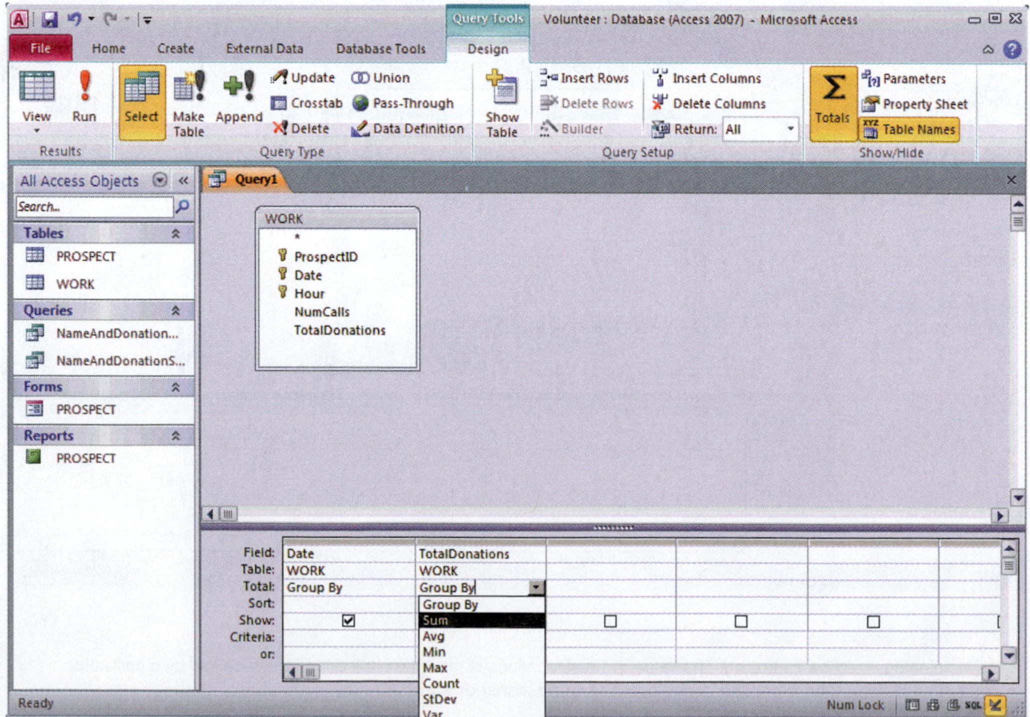

Figure CE9-14 Selecting Sum in the Total Row for TotalDonations

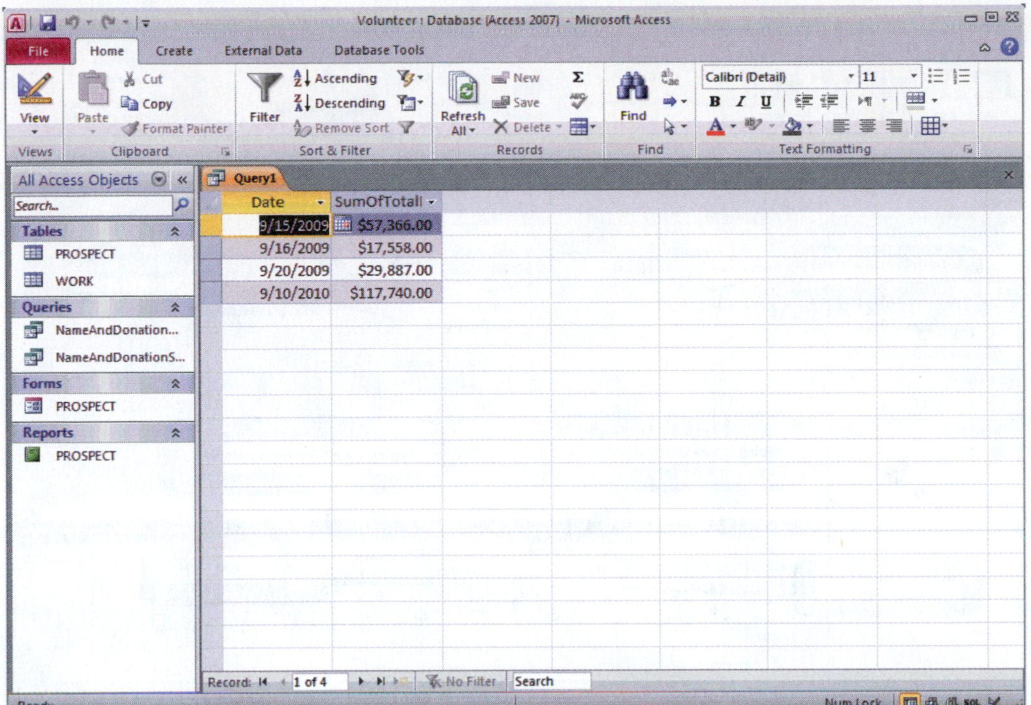

Figure CE9-15
Results of Query with Group by Date

Suppose we want to perform another, similar query, but for a more complicated example. Say we want to show the name of each volunteer (called PROSPECT in this database), the total number of hours each has worked, and the total donations obtained. Recall that each row of WORK details the results from one hour's activity. Therefore, we can compute the total number of hours a prospect worked by counting the number of rows for that prospect's ID.

The process is summarized in Figure CE9-16. To begin, we open *Query Design* and add both the PROSPECT and WORK tables. Now, we just need to complete the following seven steps:

1. In the PROSPECT table, double-click *Name* to insert it into the query results.
2. In the WORK table, double-click *ProspectID* and *TotalDonations* to insert them into the query.
3. In the ribbon, click the *Totals* icon to cause Access to insert the Total row into the query contents table.
4. In the *Total* row under ProspectID, select *Count.* This informs Access to count the number of times each value of ProspectID occurred in the table.
5. In the *Total* row under TotalDonations, select *Sum.*
6. Create a column heading for the ProspectID column by typing the heading *Hours Worked,* followed by a colon in front of ProspectID.
7. Create a column heading for the TotalDonations column by typing the heading *Total Obtained,* followed by a colon in front of TotalDonations.

Running the query produces the results shown in Figure CE9-17.

We could use this query to compute the average donation total per hour for each worker. We would just divide Total Obtained by Hours Worked. However, Access provides an average function, and it is easier to use it.

To obtain the average, add TotalDonations again to the query (in column 4 of Figure CE9-18) and, under this copy of TotalDonations, in the *Total* row, we select *Avg.*

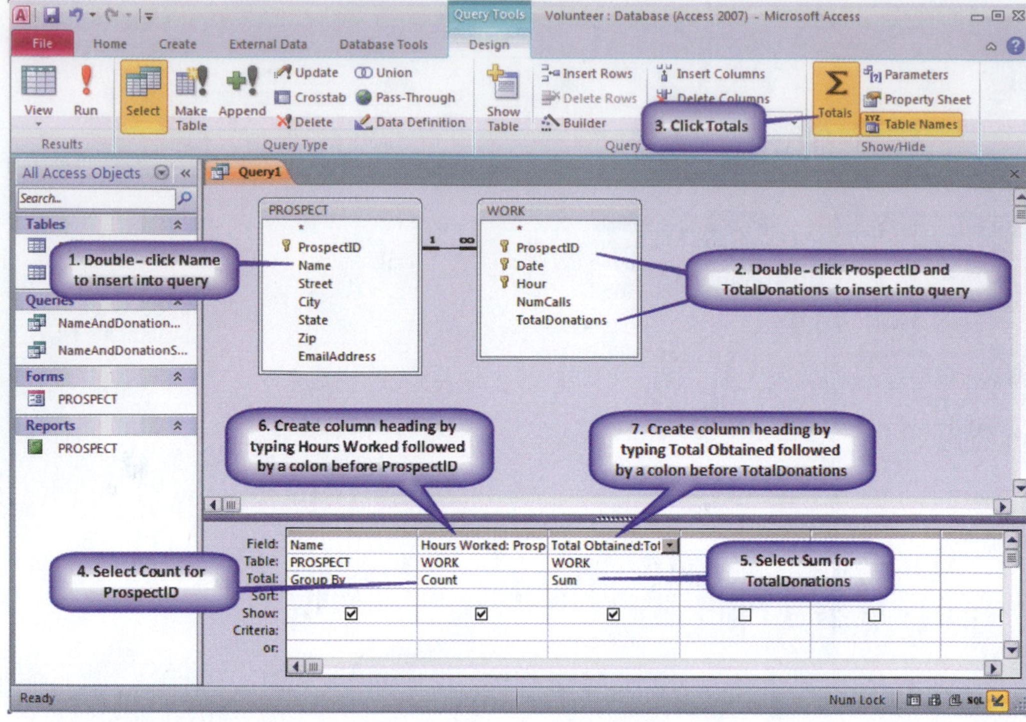

Figure CE9-16
Process for Creating a Query to Compute Total Hours and Donations for Each Prospect

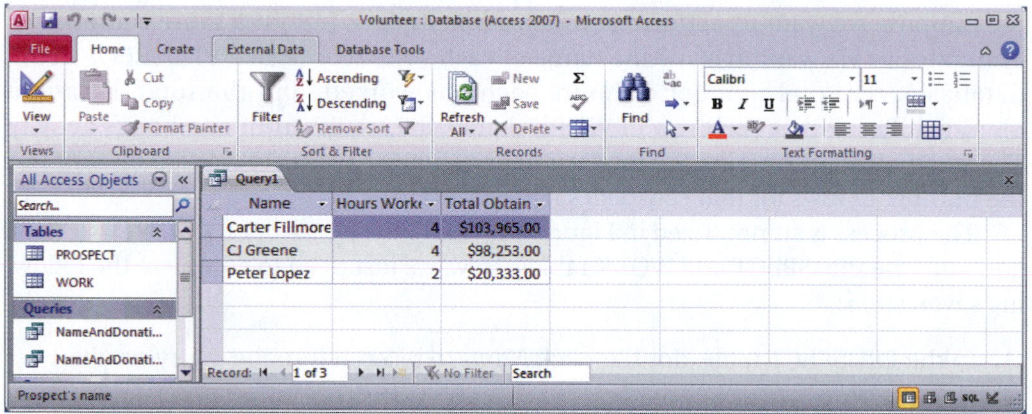

Name	Hours Worke	Total Obtain
Carter Fillmore	4	$103,965.00
CJ Greene	4	$98,253.00
Peter Lopez	2	$20,333.00

Figure CE9-17
Results of the Query in Figure CE9-16

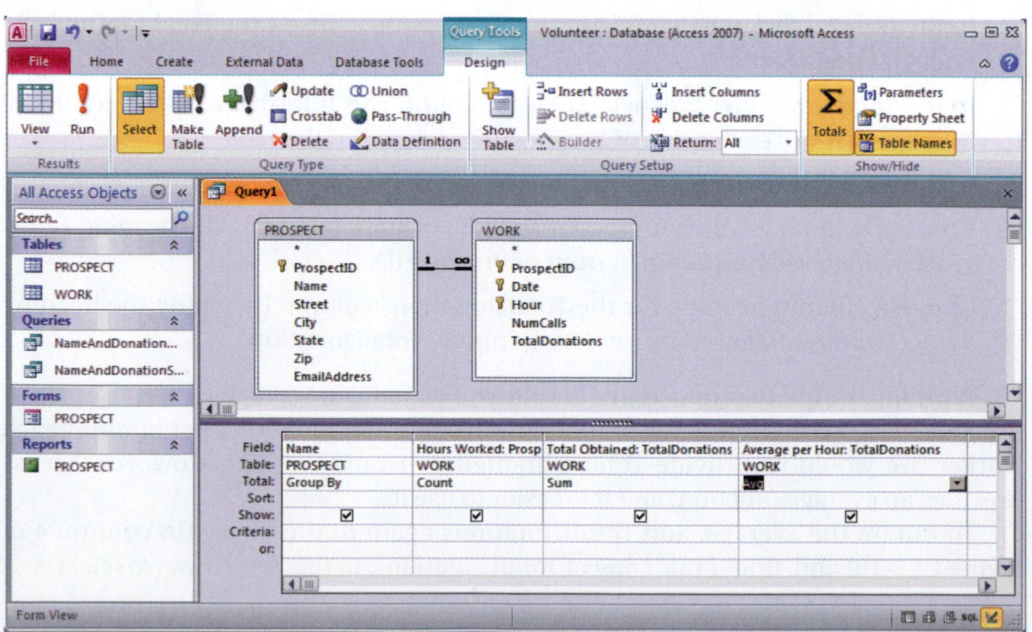

Figure CE9-18
Adding Average Donations per Hour

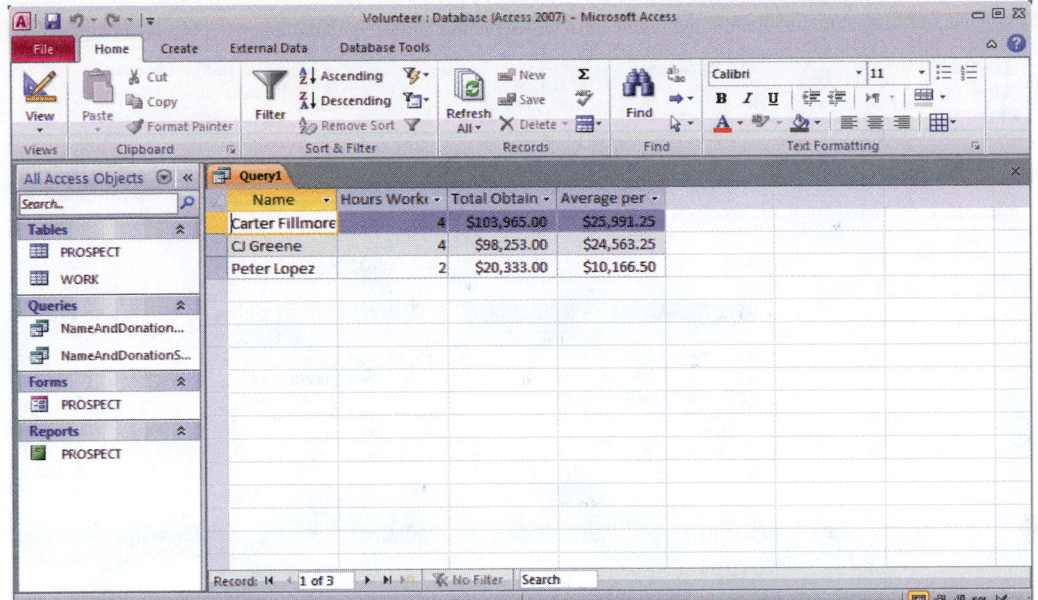

Figure CE9-19
Results of the Query in Figure CE9-17

Insert the column heading *Average per Hour.* Running this query generates the results in Figure CE9-19. Use a calculator to verify the averages are what you would expect. Save this query using the name *AvgDonationQuery.*

Again, to learn more about queries and Access create a table, enter some data, and experiment!

Q5 How Can You Use Excel to Graph Access Data?

We can produce interesting information by combining the results of the discussions in the last two sections. In particular, we can import the Access query created in Q4 into Excel and then use Excel's graphing capability to display the results.

To import data into Excel, open Excel, click the *Data* tab in the ribbon and then, in the *Get External Data* section, select *From Access,* as shown in Figure CE9-20. After you

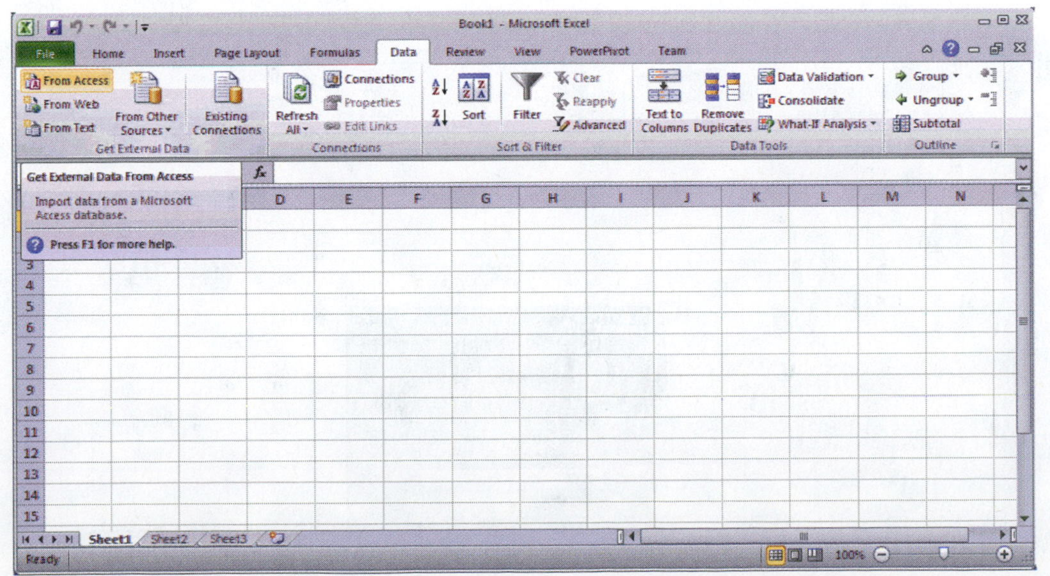

Figure CE9-20
Menu to Import Data from Access into Excel

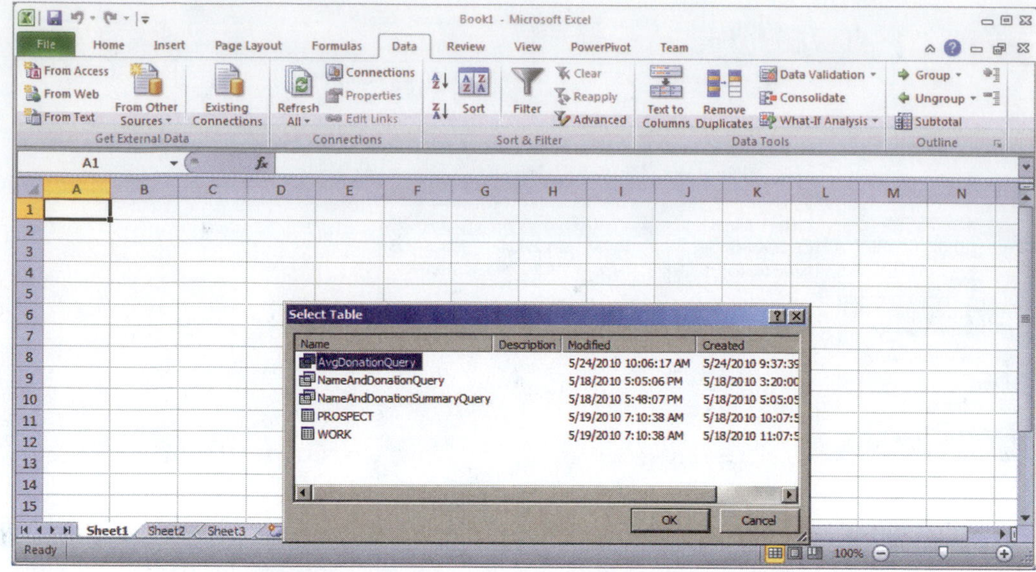

Figure CE9-21
Selecting the Query to Import

select the Volunteer database (not shown), Excel will query Access to determine the tables and queries that exist in that database. Excel will display the results, as shown in Figure CE9-21. Select *AvgDonationQuery* and click *OK*.

Next, Excel will ask how you want the data displayed. Choose *Table* and *Existing worksheet*, and enter an absolute address for the top, left-hand corner of the table. In Figure CE9-22, cell C3 (*C3*) was chosen. Click *OK*.

Excel will cause Access to run this query and will place the results into the worksheet in the location you specified. The results are shown in Figure CE9-23. Notice that Excel does not format the currency values as currency. To overcome this deficiency, highlight the cells containing the currency amounts and click *Currency* in the *Number* section of the *Home* ribbon. Next, click the *small arrow* in the bottom-right corner of the *Number* section, and select *zero decimal points*. The spreadsheet will appear as in Figure CE9-24.

To create the bar chart, follow the procedure explained in the discussion of Q3. To simplify the chart, delete the Hours Worked column. To do so, right-click the *D* in the Hours Worked column heading and then select Delete.

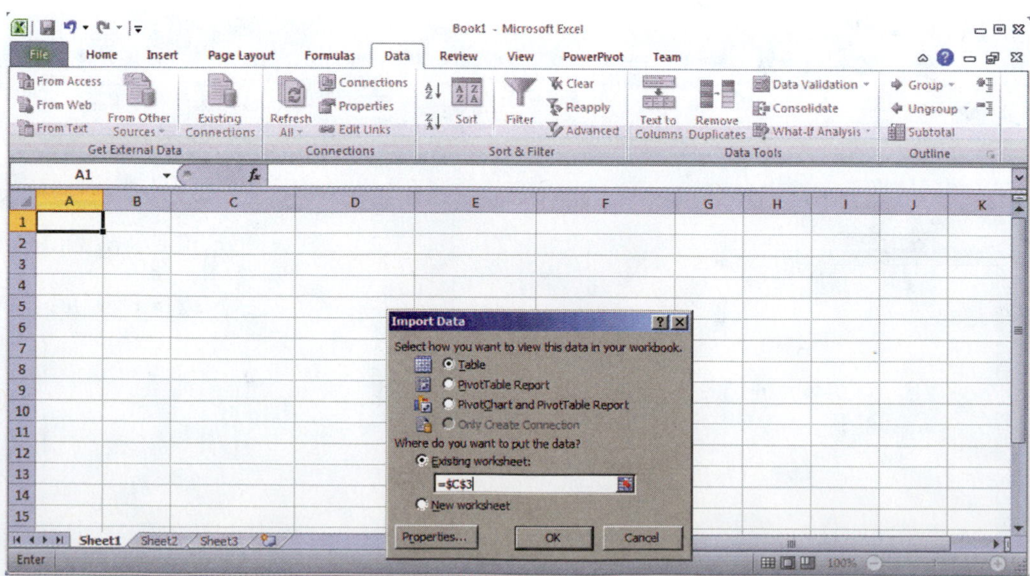

Figure CE9-22
Placing the Imported Data in the Spreadsheet

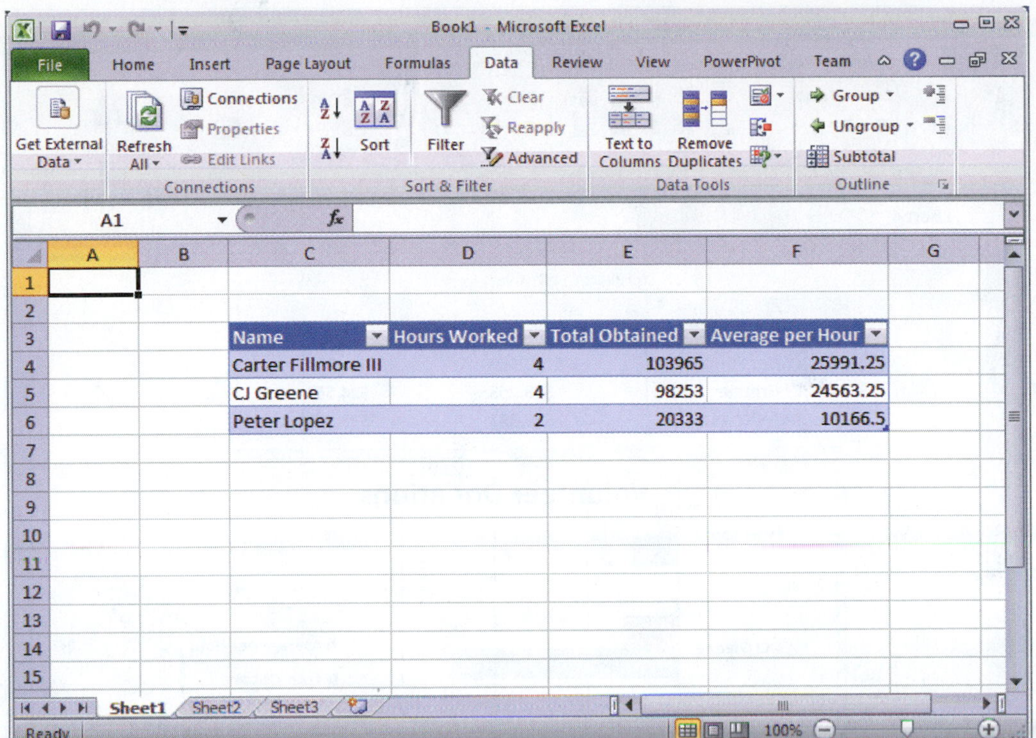

Figure CE9-23 Spreadsheet with Imported Data

Now, to make the chart, highlight cells C3 through E6, click the *Insert* tab, and select *bar chart*. Next, to insert a title, click *Chart Tools, Layout, Chart Title,* and then *Centered Overlay Title*. Then type the chart's title. In Figure CE9-25, we entered *Volunteer Donations* as the title.

Reflect a moment on what we have done. We used Access to keep track of volunteers and their received donations and to query and group data, all tasks for which Access is ideally suited. However, we then imported that data into Excel and used Excel's easy graphing capability to create the bar chart. Cool!

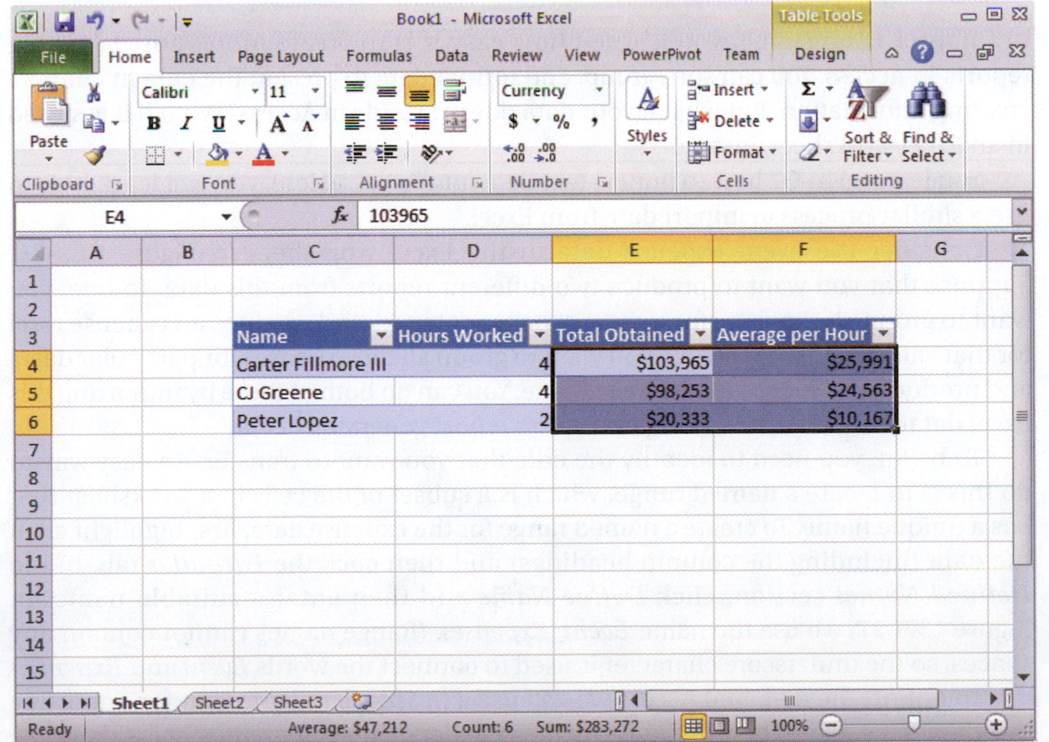

Figure CE9-24 Formatted Imported Data

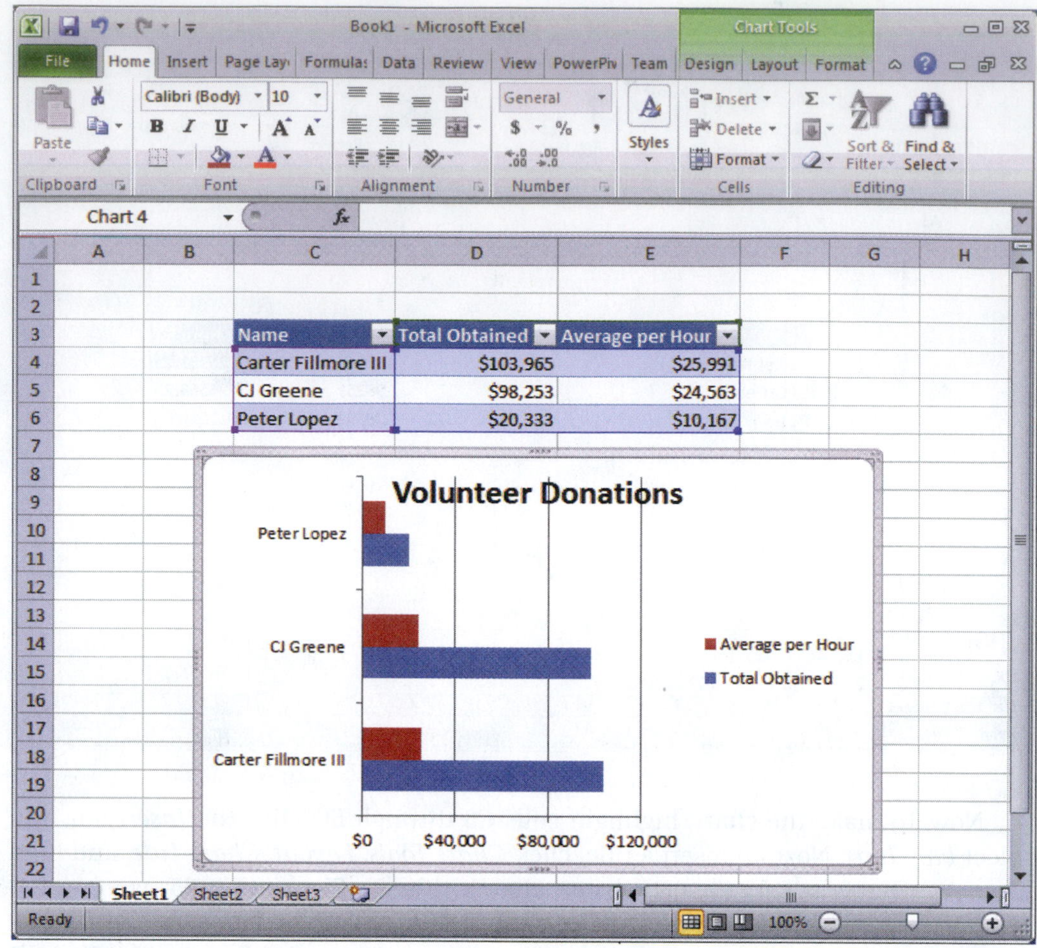

Figure CE9-25
A Bar Chart of the Imported Data

Q6 How Can You Use Access to Report Excel Data?

In Chapter Extension 8, you learned how easy it is to create professional-looking reports in Access. You can sort, group, and format data to present the data in context, creating information. But what if your data doesn't reside in Access? What if it is stored in an Excel worksheet, instead?

You learned in Q2 how to import text data into Access. Here, you will learn how to use a similar process to import data from Excel.

Consider the event expense data in the Excel worksheet in Figure CE9-26. Suppose that you want to produce two different reports from this data. In one, you want to group all expenses for a given expense category and produce an expense total for that category. In the second, you want to group all the expenses for particular dates and produce an expense total for each date. You can do both of these by importing this Excel data into Access and using the Access report generator.

To begin, you need to identify the data that you want to transfer. An easy way to do this is to create a **named range**, which is a subset of the cells in a worksheet that has a unique name. To create a named range for the expense data, first highlight all of the data (including the column headings) and then click the *Formulas* tab. In the *Defined Names* section, click *Define Name* and then enter a suitable name. In Figure CE9-27, we use the name *Event_Expenses.* (Range names cannot contain any spaces, so the underscore character is used to connect the words *Event* and *Expense.*)

To import the data into Access we will use a process similar to that for importing text data. First, close the workbook that has the data. Then, open the Access database

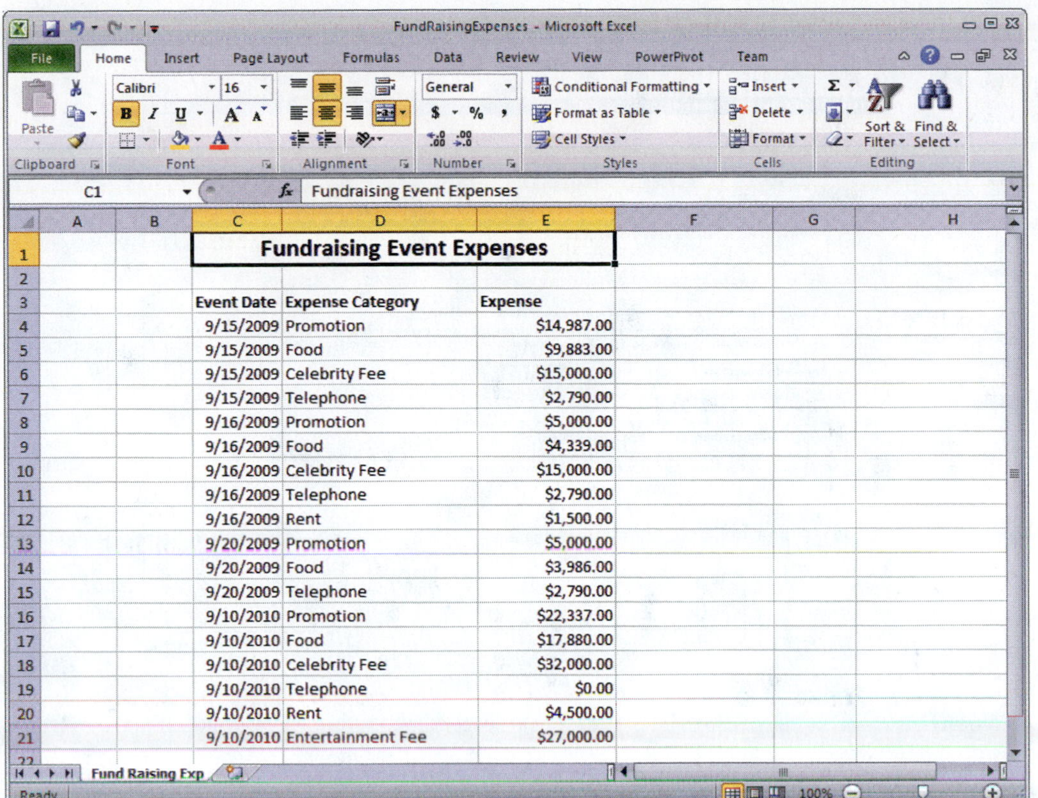

Fundraising Event Expenses

Event Date	Expense Category	Expense
9/15/2009	Promotion	$14,987.00
9/15/2009	Food	$9,883.00
9/15/2009	Celebrity Fee	$15,000.00
9/15/2009	Telephone	$2,790.00
9/16/2009	Promotion	$5,000.00
9/16/2009	Food	$4,339.00
9/16/2009	Celebrity Fee	$15,000.00
9/16/2009	Telephone	$2,790.00
9/16/2009	Rent	$1,500.00
9/20/2009	Promotion	$5,000.00
9/20/2009	Food	$3,986.00
9/20/2009	Telephone	$2,790.00
9/10/2010	Promotion	$22,337.00
9/10/2010	Food	$17,880.00
9/10/2010	Celebrity Fee	$32,000.00
9/10/2010	Telephone	$0.00
9/10/2010	Rent	$4,500.00
9/10/2010	Entertainment Fee	$27,000.00

Figure CE9-26
Sample Expense Data

into which you want to import the data, click the *External Data* tab, and, in the *Import* section, click *Excel*. In the screen that appears, select the spreadsheet that has the data and click *Import the source data into a new table in the current database*, as shown in Figure CE9-28. Click *OK* to continue.

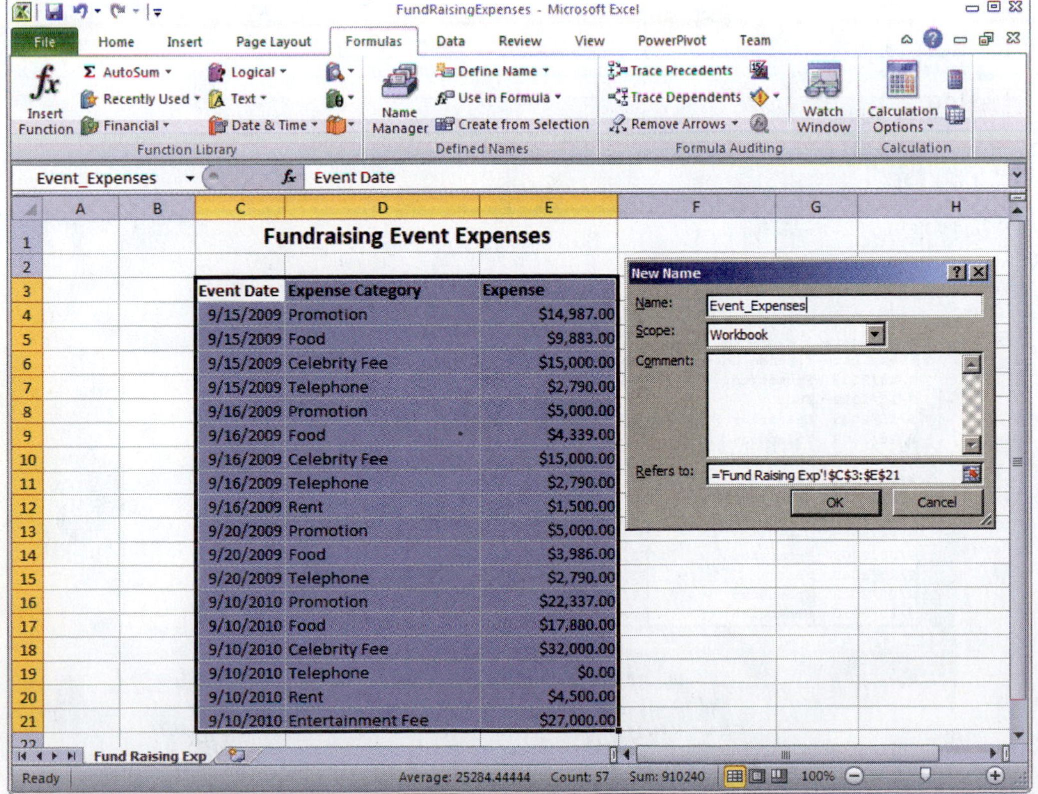

Figure CE9-27
Creating a Named Range

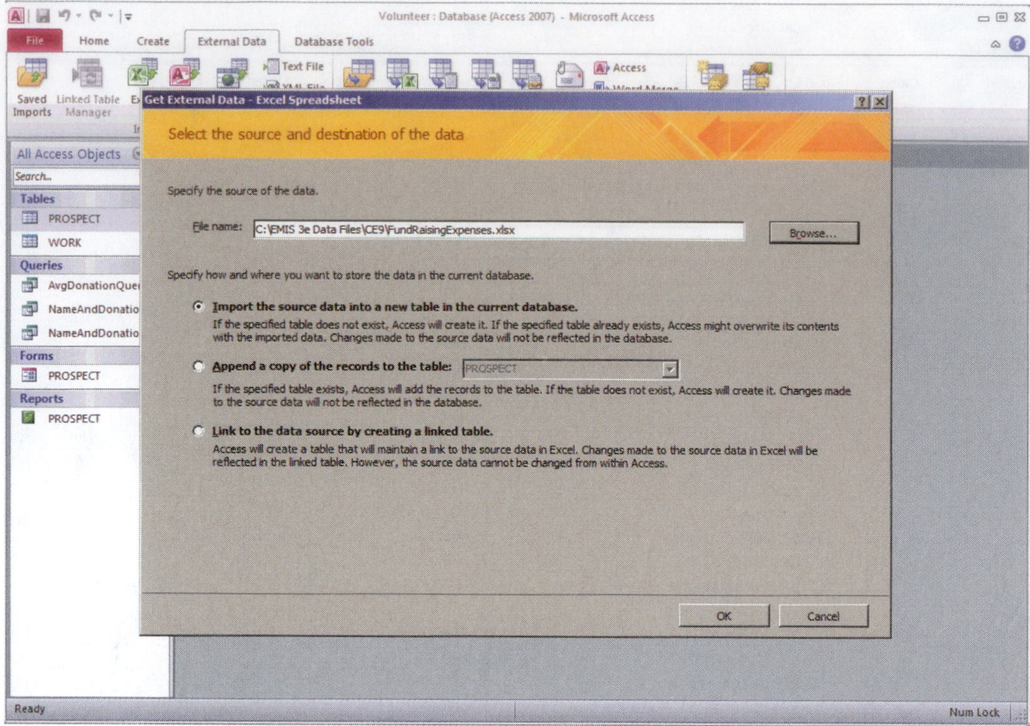

Figure CE9-28
Importing an Excel File

In the next form that appears, click *Show Name Ranges* and select the *Event_Expenses* range, as shown in Figure CE9-29a. Click *Next*. Check *First Row Contains Column Names* if it is not already checked. Your screen should look like that in Figure CE9-29b. At this point, Access has enough metadata to perform the import correctly, so you can click *Finish*. If you're curious, just click *Next* to see the default import values that Access will use. When asked if you want to save the import steps, ignore the instructions and just click *Close*.

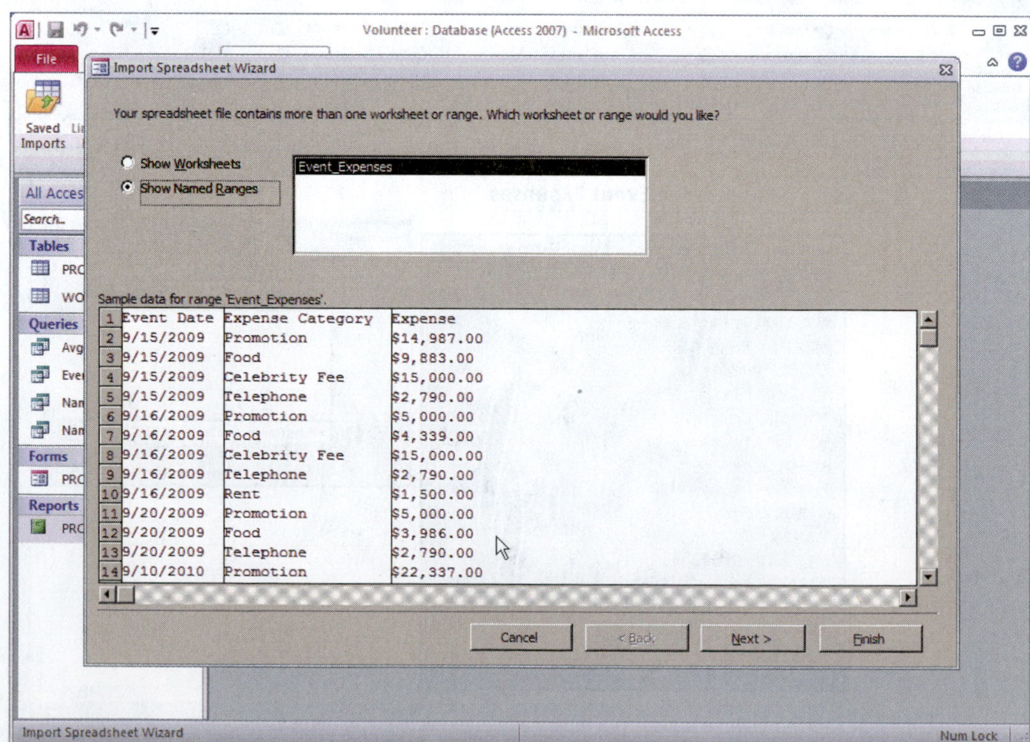

Figure CE9-29a
Importing Excel Data into Access: Importing the Data in the Named Range

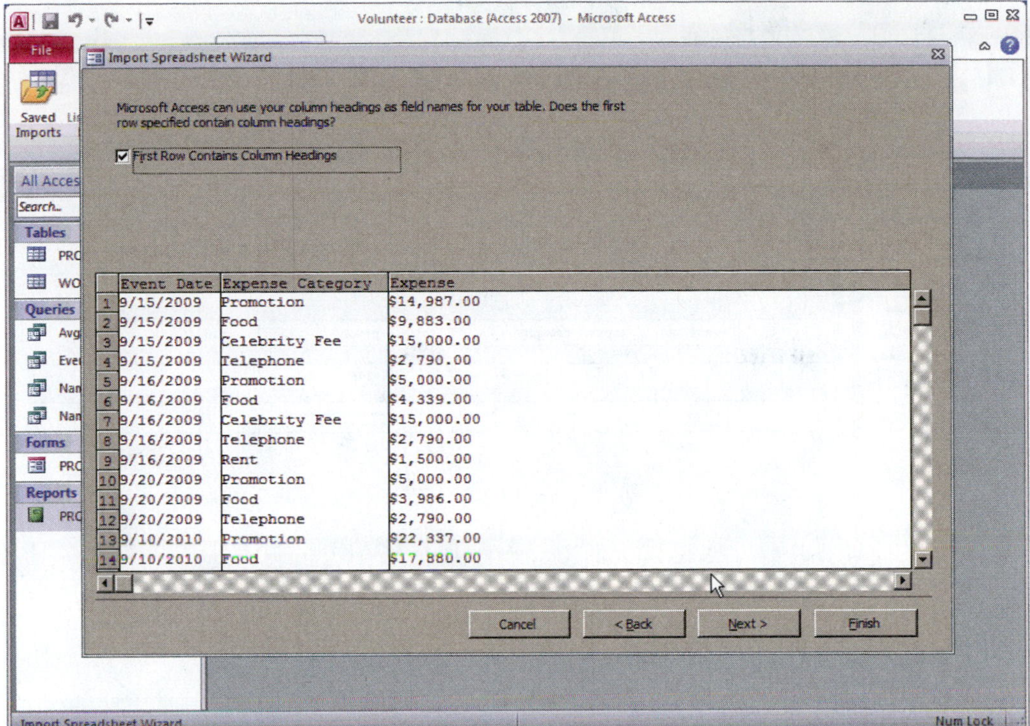

Figure CE9-29b
Importing Excel Data into Access: Access Has Metadata to Guide Import

At this point, Access has imported the data and placed it into a table named Event_Expenses. Open that table to ensure that the data has been imported as you would expect. Observe that Access added a surrogate key named ID. We will ignore this field in this example.

With the Event_Expenses table highlighted, click *Create* and, in the *Reports* section of the ribbon, click *Report*. Access creates a report that we will modify to obtain the format we want.

First, in the *Views section*, click the down arrow and select *Design View*. Click in an unused part of this screen to deselect all of the columns (those outlined in a heavy yellow/brown line). Once everything has been deselected, click *ID* in the *Page Header* to give it the focus and then press *Delete*. Do the same for ID in the Detail section. The ID column will be removed from the report. (If you don't deselect everything before you press delete, you will delete all of the report's contents. If you do this, just close the report without saving it and start over.)

In the *Grouping & Totals* section of the *Design* ribbon, click *Group & Sort*, if it is not already clicked. Then, at the bottom of the report design window, click *Add a group*. Then click *Expense Category*, as shown in Figure CE9-30. At the bottom of the design window, click *More* and then click *with Expense totaled*. As shown in Figure CE9-31, select *Expense* for *Total On* and click *Show Grand Total* and *Show subtotal in group footer*. At this point your report is finished. In Views, click the report icon and you will see a report like that in Figure CE9-32.

You can perform a similar series of steps to create a report that is grouped by Event Date rather than Expense Category.

Q7 How Can You Combine Excel and Access to Analyze Data?

In Q5, you learned how to use Excel to graph Access data. In this section, you will learn how to use Excel to perform calculations on data imported from Access. We will use the Event_Expense data imported from Excel in the last section.

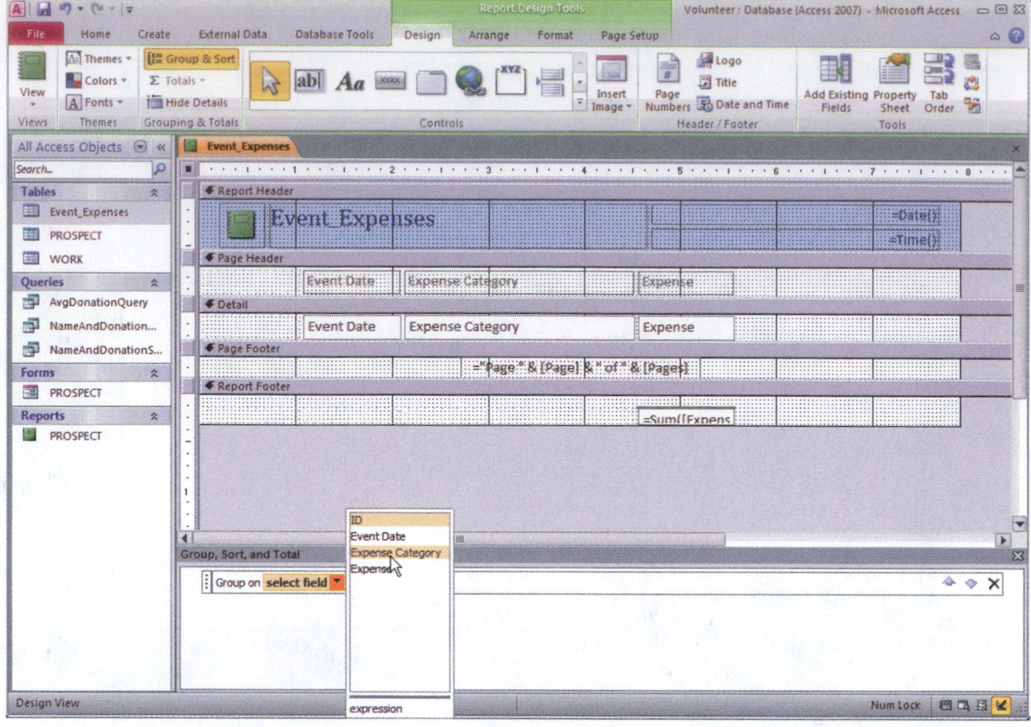

Figure CE9-30 Grouping Report Data by Expense Category

We begin by creating a query to sum all of the expenses for a given date. As shown in Figure CE9-33, open the database with the Event_Expense data and click *Create/Query Design* in the *Other* section. Now add Event Date and Expense to the query, click *Totals* to create the Total row in the query contents grid, and select *Group By* under *Event Date* and *Sum* under *Expense*. The heading *Total Event Expense* is also shown in Figure CE9-33. Save this query with the name *EventExpenseTotals*.

Now we are going to create a query that combines the results of two other queries. Specifically, we are going to merge EventExpenseTotals (the query we just created) with the EventDateTotals query we created in Q4. To do this, click *Create/Query Design*, but

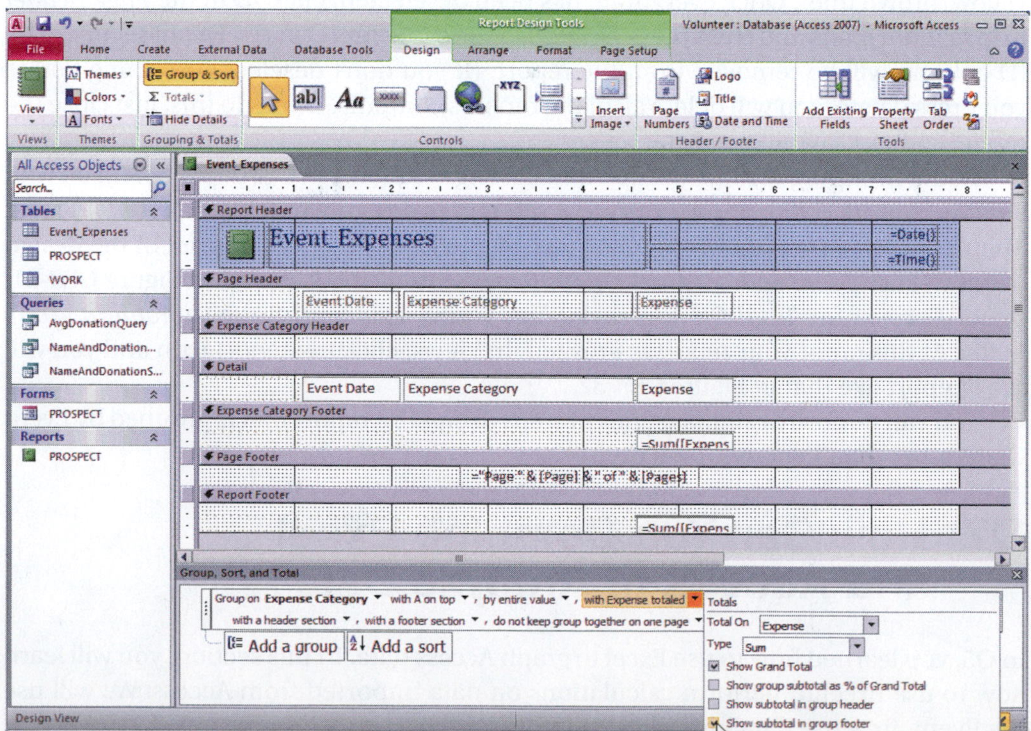

Figure CE9-31 Creating Group Totals

Event_Expenses

Monday, May 24, 2010
2:18:18 PM

Event Date	Expense Category	Expense
9/15/2009	Celebrity Fee	$15,000.00
9/10/2010	Celebrity Fee	$32,000.00
9/16/2009	Celebrity Fee	$15,000.00
		$62,000.00
9/10/2010	Entertainment Fee	$27,000.00
		$27,000.00
9/15/2009	Food	$9,883.00
9/10/2010	Food	$17,880.00
9/20/2009	Food	$3,986.00
9/16/2009	Food	$4,339.00
		$36,088.00
9/20/2009	Promotion	$5,000.00
9/10/2010	Promotion	$22,337.00
9/16/2009	Promotion	$5,000.00
9/15/2009	Promotion	$14,987.00
		$47,324.00
9/16/2009	Rent	$1,500.00
9/10/2010	Rent	$4,500.00
		$6,000.00
9/20/2009	Telephone	$2,790.00
9/15/2009	Telephone	$2,790.00

Figure CE9-32
Resulting Report

this time click the *Queries* tab in the *Show Table* window, as shown in Figure CE9-34. Now add both EventDateTotals and EventExpenseTotals to the query.

We need to inform Access that the Date values in the two queries are the same. To do so, drag the Date field in EventDateTotals and drop it on top of Event Date in the EventExpenseTotals query. The result is shown in Figure CE9-35. Now add Date,

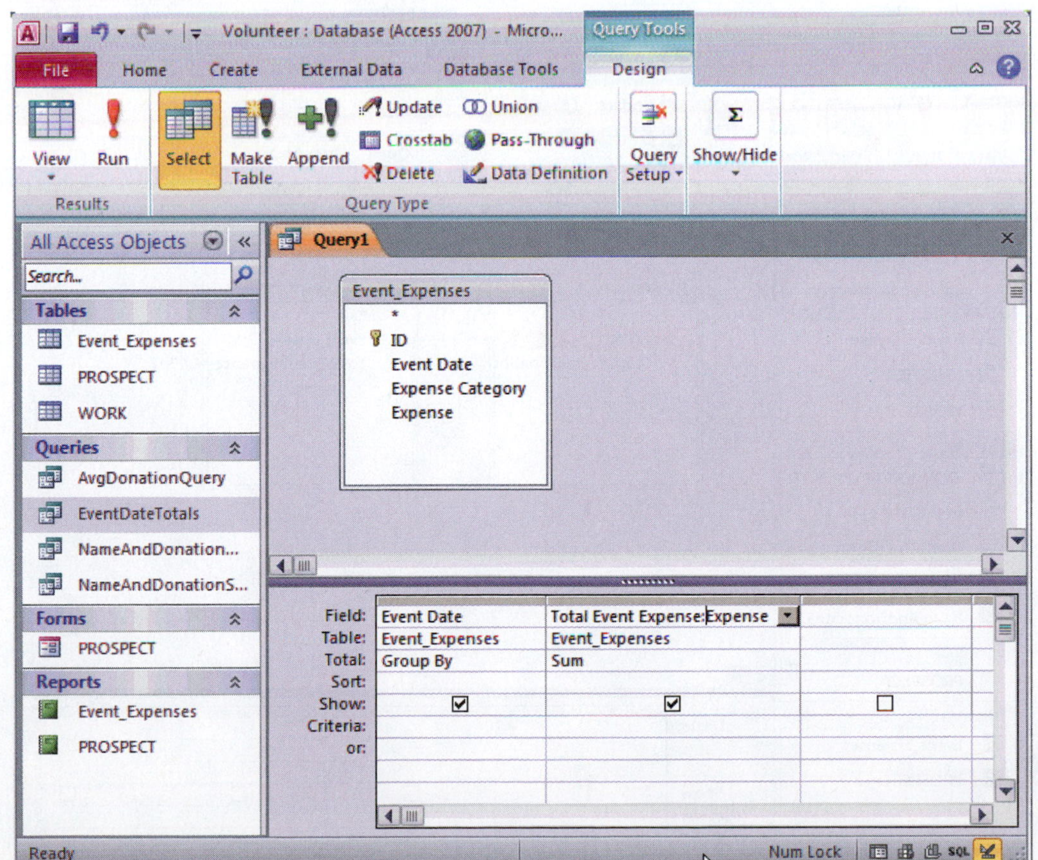

Figure CE9-33
Creating a Query to Sum Expenses by Date

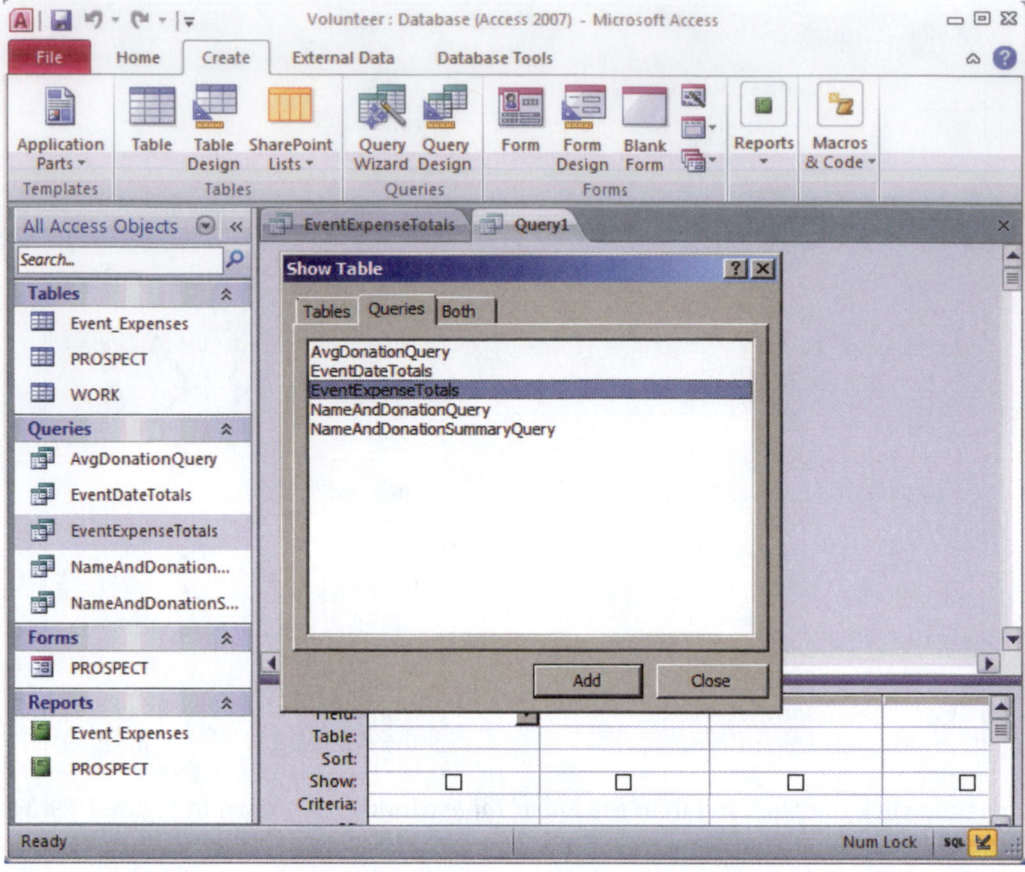

Figure CE9-34 Combining the Results of Two Queries

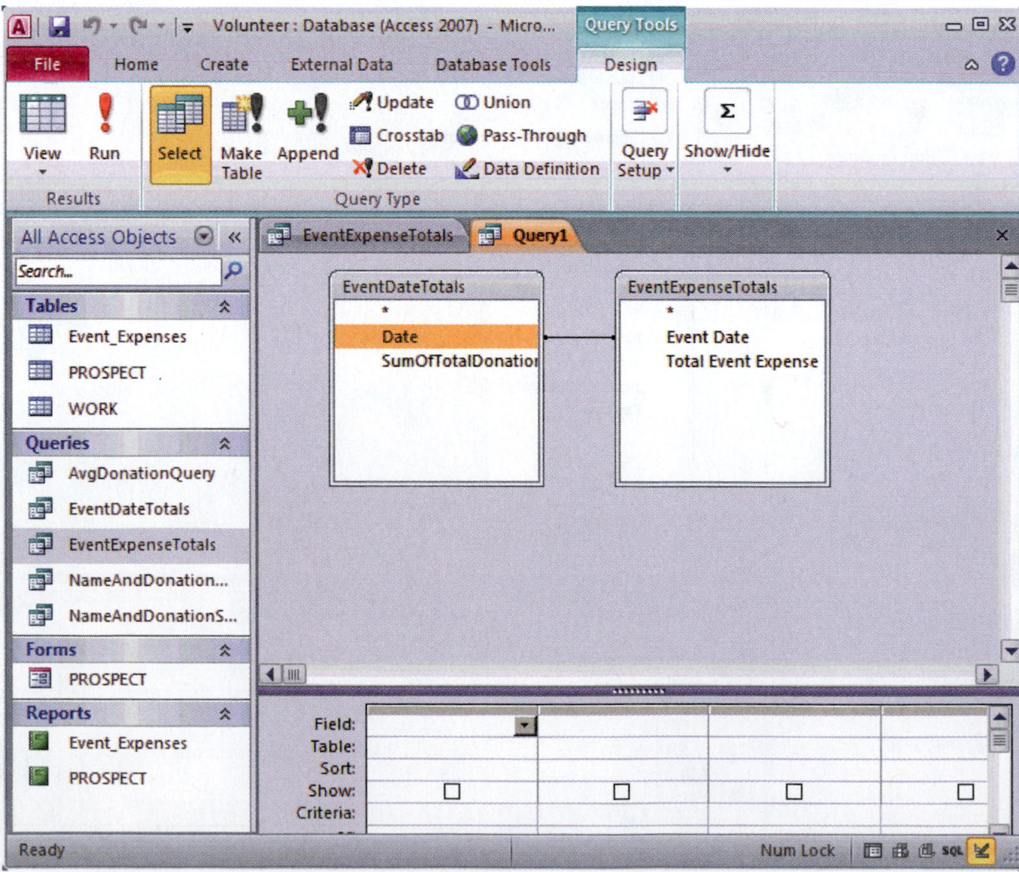

Figure CE9-35 Matching Date Values in the Two Queries

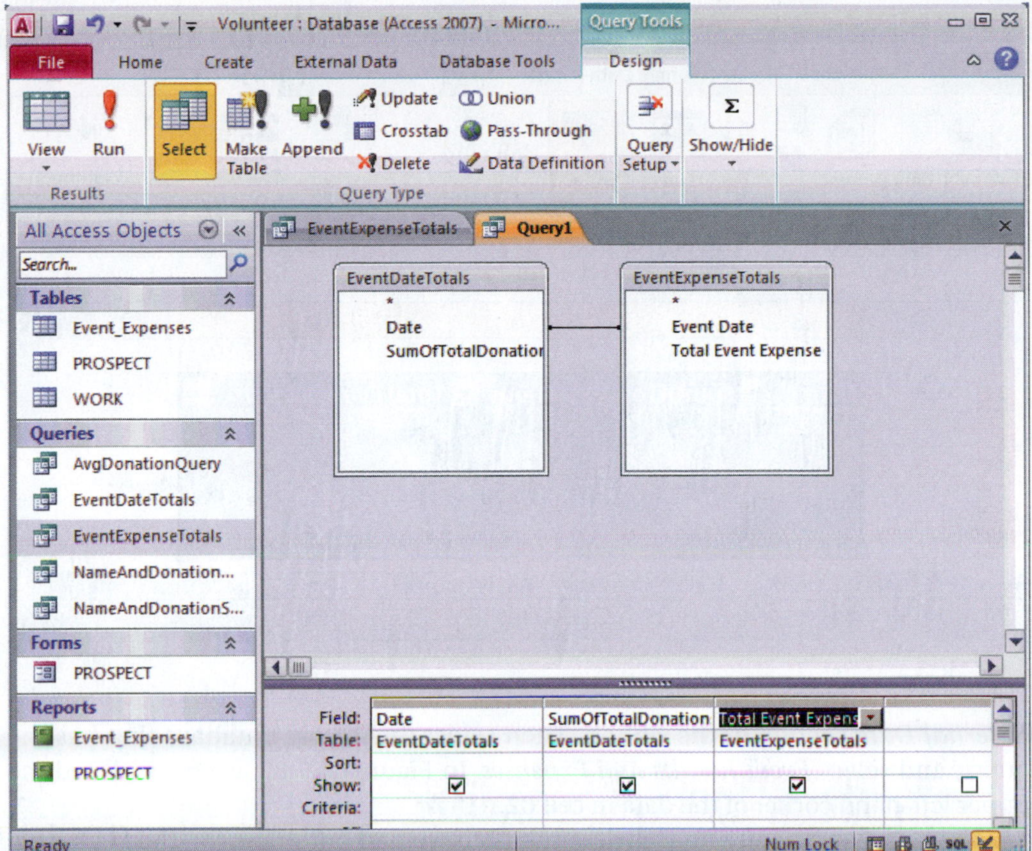

Figure CE9-36
Query with Columns Added

SumOfTotalDonation, and Total Event Expense to the query, as shown in Figure CE9-36. Run the query, and you will see the result, as shown in Figure CE9-37. Save your query with the name *Event Results and Expenses.*

Now, open a workbook in Excel and import the Event Results and Expenses query. Use the same process used in the discussion of Q5. Click *Data From Access* in the *Get*

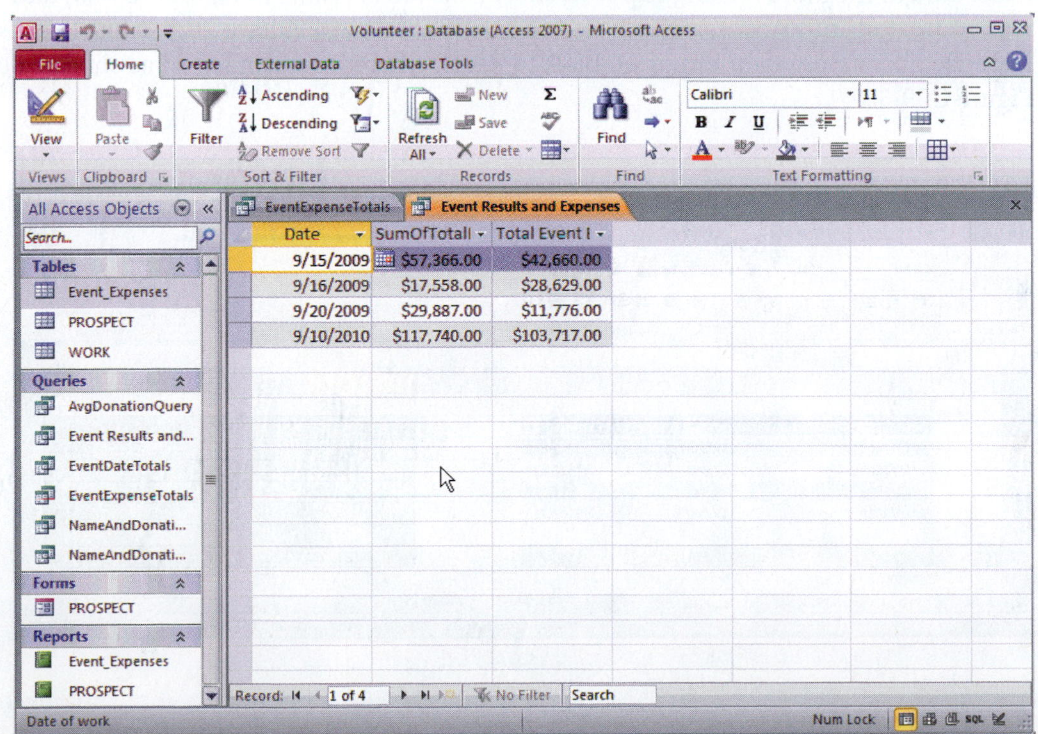

Figure CE9-37
Result of Query in Figure CE9-36

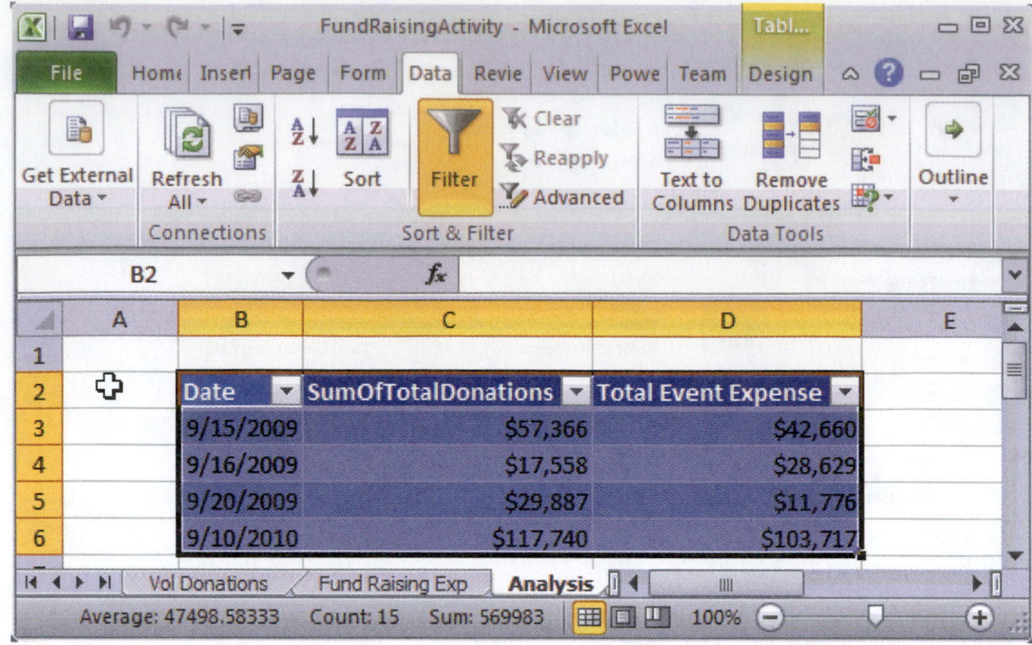

Figure CE9-38
Query in Figure CE9-36 Imported to Excel

External Data section of the ribbon. Then select the Access database that has the query, and select *Event Results and Expenses.* In Figure CE9-38, we have placed the upper left-hand corner of the data in cell B2.

Now, we can operate on this data just as if we had entered it via the keyboard. We can graph it as described in Q5. Or, we can analyze it as shown in Figure CE9-39. Here, the user is computing the Net Gain, Net Gain as a Percent of Expense, and Totals for donations and expenses. The focus is on cell F3; notice that this cell contains the formula = *C3–D3*, which computes the difference between two imported numbers.

Reflect for a moment on the history of this data. The Total Donation data originated in Access and was summed using an Access query. The expense data began as Excel data in the Fund Raising Exp worksheet (this tab is visible in Figure CE9-39) and was imported into Access, where it was summed. The results of the Total Event Expense query were then imported back to Excel, where it was analyzed as shown in Figure CE9-39!

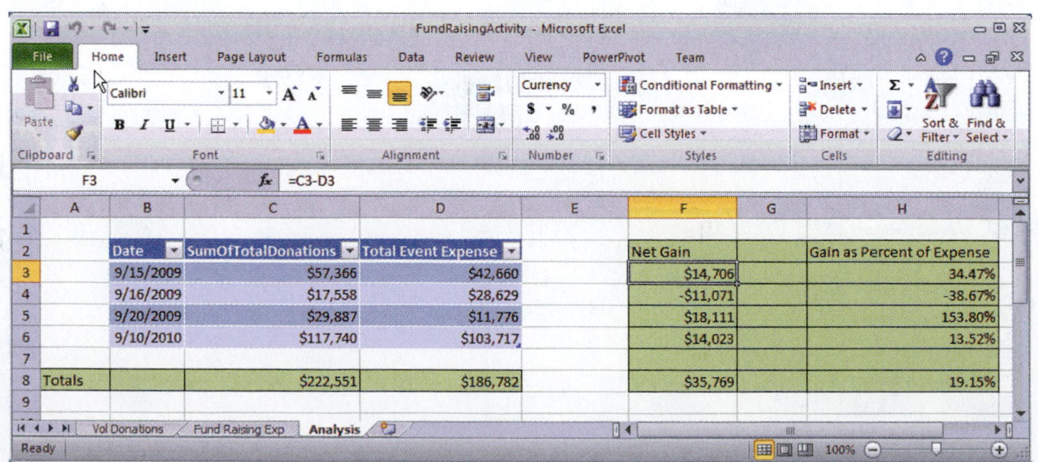

Figure CE9-39
Imported to Excel

ACTIVE REVIEW

Use this Active Review to verify that you understand the material in the chapter extension. You can read the entire extension and then perform the tasks in this review, or you can read the material for just one question and perform the tasks in this review for that question before moving on to the next one.

Q1 Why use Excel and Access together?

Describe the chief strengths of both Excel and Access. Summarize the primary purposes of Excel and Access. Give an example of why you might want to process Access data in Excel and another example of why you might want to process Excel data in Access.

Q2 What is import/export?

Define *import/export.* Explain how data can become out-of-date when using import/export and describe a solution to this problem. Explain the difference between comma-delimited and tab-delimited data. Go to the text's Web site at *www.pearsonhighered.com/kroenke* and obtain the text file **CE 9-1.txt**. Follow the process described in Q2 to import the data into Access. Explain how you could use a text file to transfer data from Access to Excel. Describe tools that Microsoft provides that make this unnecessary.

Q3 How can you create graphs with Excel?

Go to this text's Web site at *www.pearsonhighered.com/kroenke* and download the file **CE6_Last.xlsx**, the computer budget workbook developed in Chapter Extension 6. Follow the steps explained in Q3 to create the graphics shown in Figures CE9-6 and CE9-9.

Q4 How can you create group totals in Access?

Explain the term *day's total of TotalDonations.* Explain what the *Group By* function does. Go to the text's Web site at *www.pearsonhighered.com/kroenke* and download the Access database file **Volunteer.accdb**. Follow the instructions in this question to duplicate the query shown in Figures CE9-15, CE9-17, and CE9-19.

Q5 How can you use Excel to graph Access data?

Follow the instructions in this section to use Excel to graph the results of the query you generated in your review for Q4. Your graph should look like that in Figure CE9-25. Explain how this exercise takes advantage of some of the relative strengths of these two products.

Q6 How can you use Access to report Excel data?

Explain why you might want to use Access to create reports on Excel data. Go to the text's Web site at *www.pearsonhighered.com/kroenke* and download the Excel file **FundRaisingExpenses.xslx**. Follow the instructions in discussion of this question to create a report like that in Figure CE9-32. Use the same Access database that you used for your review of Q4.

Q7 How can you combine Excel and Access to analyze data?

Open the database with the Event_Expense query that you created in your review of Q6. Follow the procedures described in this section to create an Excel worksheet that looks like that shown in Figure CE9-39. Explain how some of this data made a roundtrip from Excel to Access and back to Excel. Does this make sense? Why or why not?

KEY TERMS AND CONCEPTS

Comma-delimited file 419
Import/export 418
Named range 434
Tab-delimited file 419

USING YOUR KNOWLEDGE

1. Go to the text's Web site at *www.pearsonhighered.com/kroenke* and download the text file **CE 9-1.txt**. Import this data into an Excel workbook.

2. Create a spreadsheet of sample college expenses. Place a grid in your spreadsheet that has three rows—*Rent, Food, Entertainment*—and three columns—*2007, 2008, 2009.* Enter realistic, but hypothetical, data. Create a pie chart showing the expenses for 2007. Create a column chart for expenses for all 3 years. Create a bar chart for expenses for all 3 years. Do you prefer the column chart or the bar chart? Explain.

3. Create an Access database with a table called *My_Expenses* that has the fields Date, Expense Category, and Amount. Fill the table with 12 rows of hypothetical student expense data. Ensure that you have several expenses for each date and for each expense category. Create a query that shows the total expenses for each date. Create a query that shows the total and average expenses for each category.

4. Export the data that you created in question 3 to an Excel spreadsheet. Create a pie chart of the data for expenses by category. Create a bar chart for expenses by category and date (one bar of each date within a category).

5. Open the database you created in question 3. Import the data from Excel that you created for question 4 into this database. (Yes, you are re-importing the same data from Excel that you previously exported to Excel. You should have the original copy of the data as well.) Compare the values for the original data to the values of the export/import data. They should be the same. Using the imported data, construct a report similar to that in Figure CE9-32.

6. Using the workbook that you created in your answer to question 4, add a budgeted amount column for each expense category. Enter values for each budgeted amount. Add a column showing the difference between the budgeted amount and the actual amount. Generalize this example. Describe a business scenario in which a financial analyst would obtain data from a database and compare it to data in a spreadsheet.

Chapter 6 provides the background for this extension.

Remote, Nomadic, and Mobile Systems

STUDY QUESTIONS

Q1 What are the differences among remote, nomadic, and mobile access?

Q2 How will remote, nomadic, and mobile access be delivered?

Q3 What is the role of the cloud and client virtualization?

Q4 What are the implications for business professionals?

Q5 What about privacy?

Q1 What Are the Differences Among Remote, Nomadic, and Mobile Access?

Nearly free data communications and data storage have enabled the development and use of information systems beyond the traditional personal computer and local area network. Remote, nomadic, and mobile access are common; we consider each in this chapter extension.

Remotely Accessed Systems

Remote access is the ability to provide computer-based activity or action at a distance. By enabling action at a distance, remote access systems save time and travel expense and make the skills and abilities of an expert available in places where he or she is not physically located.

Chapter Extension 1 presented some of the systems that use remote access, such as teleconferencing, Webinars, and videoconferencing, to facilitate collaboration. Other remote access systems include **telediagnosis**, which is used by health care professionals to provide expertise in rural or remote areas. Surgeons can perform **telesurgery** by operating robotic equipment from distant locations. In 2001, Dr. Jacques Marescaux, located in New York City, performed the first trans-Atlantic surgery when he successfully operated on a patient in Strasbourg, France.[1] Figure CE10-1 shows a medical robot that can be operated remotely to perform heart surgeries.

Other uses for remote systems include **telelaw enforcement**, such as the REDFLEX system offered by the Redflex Holding Group that uses cameras and motion-sensing equipment to issue tickets for red light and speeding violations. Redflex Holding Group, headquartered in South Melbourne, Victoria, Australia, earns 87 percent of its revenue from traffic violations in the United States. It offers a turnkey traffic-citation information system that includes all five information system components.[2]

Many remote systems are designed to provide services in dangerous locations, such as robots that clean nuclear reactors or biologically contaminated sites. Drones and other unoccupied military equipment are examples of remote systems used in war zones.

1. Sharon Kay, "Remote Surgery," *www.pbs.org/wnet/innovation/episode7_essay1.html* (accessed May 2010).
2. Redflex Holdings Group, *www.redflex.com* (accessed February 2010) and CameraFRAUD, "Why Oppose Automatic Ticketing?" *http://camerafraud.wordpress.com/why/* (accessed February 2010).

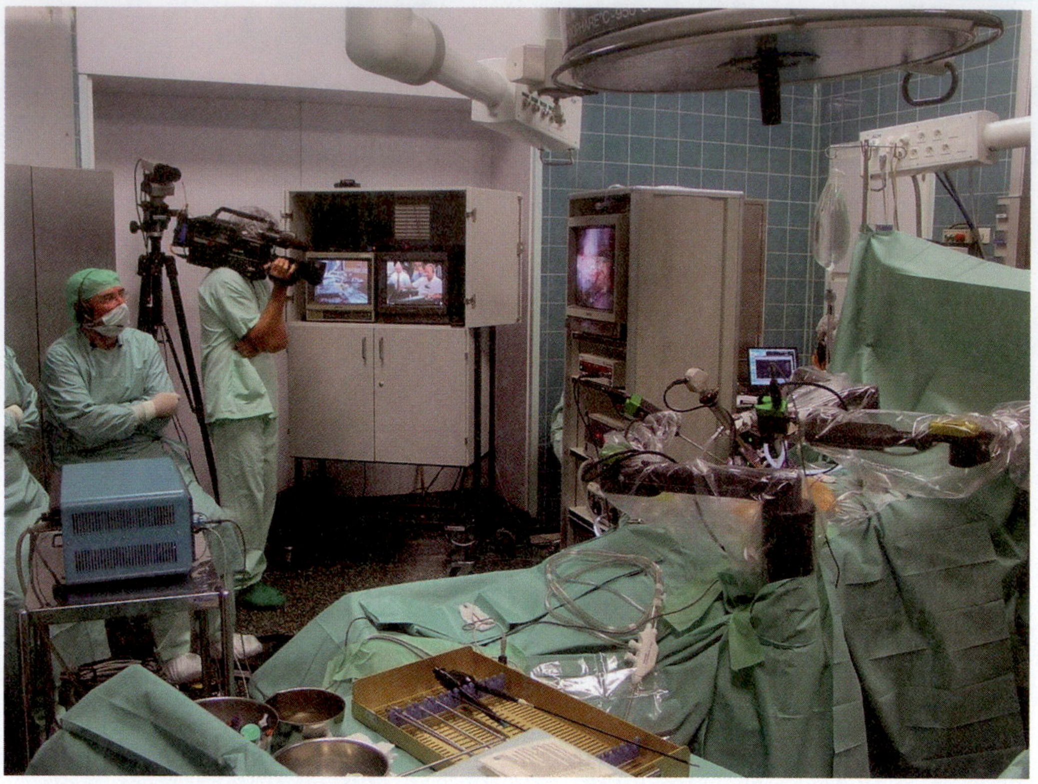

Figure CE10-1
Heart Surgery Robot Can Be Operated Remotely

Nomadic Access Systems

With **nomadic access**, users access networks from different locations, but not while in motion from site to site. The classic nomadic application is a business traveler who accesses networks at work from a hotel, an airport lobby, or from some other travel locations. Another common example is accessing a network at work while at home or on vacation. In the past, the user would carry a laptop from one location to another, but that habit is changing, as we discuss in Q2.

Wireless hotspot hubs are devices that wirelessly connect to a WAN using cell phone technology and provide wireless connectivity to computers located in close proximity to the hub. Dodge offers this capability in its Ram trucks for contractors who need a nomadic office at construction sites. You can also buy such devices as stand-alone units, without the truck (but not from Dodge).

A superb example of nomadic access occurred when the Israeli Home Front Command moved a full field hospital to Haiti to provide medical treatment to victims of the 2010 earthquake. Within 48 hours, the agency had set up a temporary LAN in the field among its medical tents and facilities. The facility could serve up to 500 patients a day. To keep track of these patients, an injured person's name, family data, address, and photo were stored in a database that was accessed over the LAN. All medical images were stored as well. The LAN was connected to a WAN that had access to medical systems and facilities in Israel. When the temporary hospital closed after providing emergency treatment for several weeks, all of the equipment was packed up and returned for use in the next medical emergency. See Figure CE10-2.[3]

Mobile Access

Mobile access refers to the use of networked computers while in motion. Typical examples are accessing the Web or email while riding in a train or on an airplane.

3. Noam Barkam, "Israelis Rescue Earthquake Survivors in Haiti," *Ynetnews.com*, January 17, 2010, *www.ynetnews.com/articles/0,7340,L-3835262,00.html* (accessed May 2010).

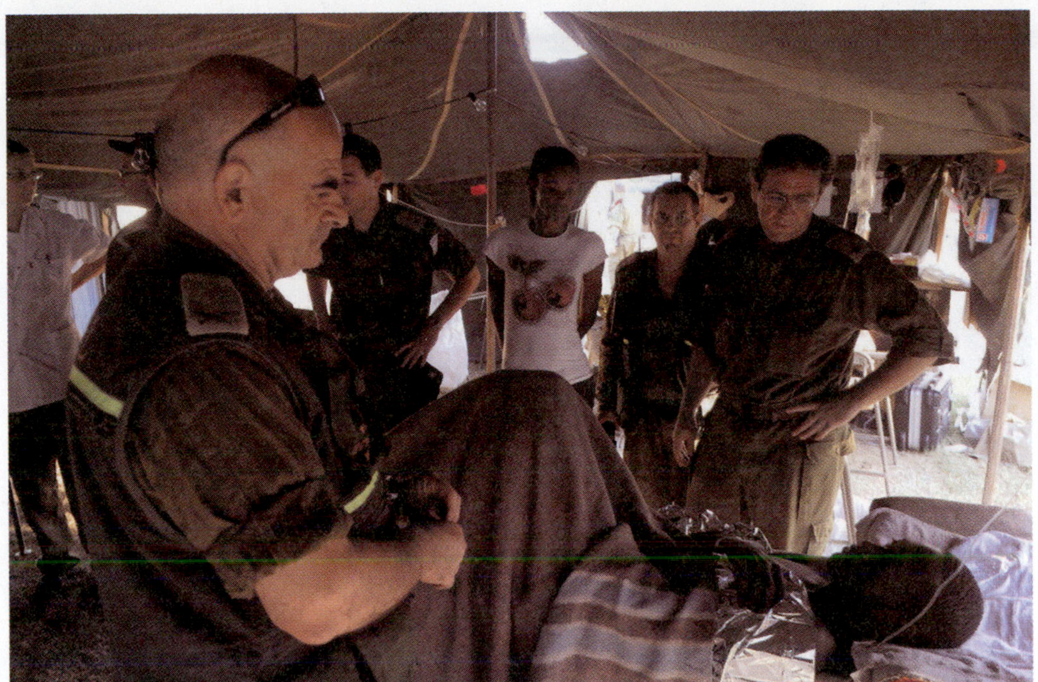

Figure CE10-2
Israeli IDF Used Nomadic Access as Part of Haitian Earthquake Relief

Source: Newscom.

Google, Microsoft, Genentech, and Yahoo! all operate private bus systems for their employees to travel to and from work. Microsoft provides the Connector system, which operates more than 50 buses on 19 routes throughout the Seattle/Redmond metropolitan area. In 2009, it provided transportation for over 3,000 employees per day.[4] The Connector buses have power and mobile wireless network connections. Riders connect their laptops to the network and get to work, processing email and performing other tasks during their commute (Figure CE10-3). Riding the bus not only saves employees the hassle of driving, it enables Microsoft employees to extend their workday. In addition, the Connector reduces Seattle traffic congestion and pollution by taking nearly 3,000 vehicles off the Seattle streets each day.

Q2 How Will Remote, Nomadic, and Mobile Access Be Delivered?

As of 2010, two diverse schools of thought exist about how users will access their remote, nomadic, or mobile (RNM) applications. Microsoft is the champion of one direction, and Apple and Amazon.com are the leaders of the other.

As of 2010, Microsoft is building momentum for its Windows Series 7 operating system for phones. Part of its marketing campaign claims that users want access to networks and applications on their "three screens," which to Microsoft means computer screen, phone screen, and television screen. Microsoft encourages those who build applications with its development tools to construct their applications to function well on all three screens.

Apple, meanwhile, is investing in completely new screen devices with touch and other interface innovations. The iPod, iPhone, and iPad all broke new ground. Amazon.com has done something similar, though less spectacular, with its Kindle devices. None of these devices fit into the Microsoft three-screen model.

The market seems to be voting between these two alternatives in favor of Apple and Amazon.com. iPhone sales were up 5,000 percent in 2009, and the Kindle is currently

4. Katherine Long, "Microsoft Connector: 19 Routes, 53 Buses Later," *Seattle Times,* April 12, 2009, *http://seattletimes.nwsource.com/html/microsoft/2009025535_msshuttle12m.html* (accessed May 2010).

Figure CE10-3
Microsoft Connector Mobile Workforce Example
Source: David M. Kroenke.

(2010) the fastest-selling item at Amazon.com. It would appear that people prefer new devices that don't fit into the established three-screen categories. Thus, it would seem that the future belongs to new device types that provide innovative RNM access. And, as of May 26, 2010, Apple's enterprise value exceeded Microsoft's for the first time.

Don't count Microsoft down and out, however. The current product situation may replay similar situations in Microsoft's history. Apple led the way with graphical user interfaces; Netscape led the way on the Internet, and, again, Apple seems to be leading the way with RNM access. However, once the direction becomes clear, Microsoft will likely invest heavily and eventually compete very successfully. One industry wag once wrote that Microsoft is superior at finding a parade that is underway and then getting in front of it.

Another aspect of RNM access may also be about to change. Today, everyone takes their PC or other device wherever they go. Every day, business professionals, working like **PC mules**, carry their devices wherever they go. At airport security, you can see them unpacking and packing their computer loads, every day (see Figure CE10-4).

Figure CE10-4
A PC Mule at the Airport
Source: Photolibrary/Peter Arnold, Inc.

Will that model continue? Will users carry their iPads or other RNM connectivity devices? If the devices are small enough, probably so. But for large screen access, for devices that are used for heavy-duty computing work, it is doubtful. More likely is that large screen computing/connectivity devices will be available everywhere like pay telephones once were. Instead of carrying your computer, you'll simply access a public RNM device and connect to your data in the cloud.

Q3 What Is the Role of the Cloud and Client Virtualization?

Today, professionals carry their computers because those computers store data and provide thick-client applications that they need. But, if all applications become thin-client, or at least if every important application has a thin-client version, and if organizations store their data in the cloud, why carry your computer?

Office 2010 seems to signal such a change. It provides thin-client versions of Word, Excel, PowerPoint, and OneNote. As you learned in Chapter Extension 2, all Office 2010 applications can store data on SkyDrive devices. Google provides similar free online storage of Google Docs as well. With these capabilities, you can access your data and applications (at least popular applications) from any computer. This trend will accelerate with thin-client versions of CRM, ERP, and functional applications. Because any computer will provide access to those applications and your data, why carry one? We PC mules will be the first to agree.

However, there is a limitation. My personal computer provides more than just data and thick-client applications. It has my personal organization. It has my screen saver, it has my desktop, it has my files arranged just the way I want them. I need my computer to provide my personal world in a familiar way.

Chapter 4 discussed server virtualization, in which one operating system acts as a host to other operating systems. Each hosted operating system is called a **virtual machine** and each such machine has complete control of the assets it is assigned, such as disk space, devices, network connections, and so forth. To the user of the virtual machine, it appears as if that operating system is the only one on the computer.

Client virtualization, or as it is sometimes called, **desktop virtualization**, enables users to run their desktop on different computers. A server provides many different desktops that can be accessed via other computers. Instead of hosting multiple operating systems, with client virtualization the virtual machine hosts multiple instances of a client, say Windows 7 or Macintosh.

Using client virtualization, you can access any public computer, connect to your personal virtual client, and, voilà, you are running what you now think to be *your computer*. In fact, it is your computer, except that it is running on a public machine that is connected to your virtual client on the server.

If that is the case, why haul any hardware anywhere? At least why haul any hardware that weighs more than a few ounces? In this world, your hotel room comes with a computer, your airplane seat comes with a computer, your bus seat comes with a computer, your convention center is full of computers. With all of these devices, you need only access your virtual client, somewhere in the cloud, and you are up and running on "your machine."

This mode of access solves another aggravating problem. Many professionals use several different computers and have different sets of data on each. This situation creates data synchronization problems. If you work on your computer at home, when you get to work you have to synchronize (or **synch**) your computer at work with any changes you've made on the computer you took home. But, if your machine is a virtual client in the cloud, everything is always synchronized because there's only one version.

Q4 What Are the Implications for Business Professionals?

The emergence of always-on, always-connected commerce will have dramatic consequences for business professionals, but what are they? No one knows for sure, but asking that question and continuing to ask that question for the next 5 to 10 years will be worthwhile to anyone seeking innovation opportunities. Let's consider the implications for remote access first.

What Does Remote Access Mean for Business Professionals?

We can divide remote access into two categories: communication at a distance and action at a distance. The first category includes teleconferencing, Webinars, YouTube videos, and the like. The second includes services such as telesurgery.

Communication at a Distance

Possible consequences of communication at a distance are summarized in Figure CE10-5. One likely consequence of communication at a distance is a reduction in business travel. Webinars, for example, may replace a good portion of in-person sales presentations. Recreational travel is likely to occupy a larger proportion of the travel industry.

Another consequence relates to Robert Reich's point, which was discussed in Chapter 1; with ever-increasing communication at a distance, more and more routine work will flow to the lowest bidder. That low bidder is not likely to be those who work in the United States or in another advanced economy. So, again, you need to become an expert in some type of nonroutine work if you want to work in an advanced economy.

Yet another consequence is that experts can communicate their expertise to larger audiences more cheaply. Robert Feynman was a superb physicist and teacher; lectures that he gave in the early 1960s are popular on YouTube today. Closer to home that means your professor need not be an expert lecturer in every subject, and that has other consequences you can explore in exercise 5 in Using Your Knowledge.

Management changes, too. Rather than manage a team of 7 to 10 employees who work closely together in the same office, who share the same culture, values, and language, new managers may manage teams of 30 to 40 people who work in disbursed offices in different countries and who have different values, languages, expectations, and goals. Team members may never meet face-to-face. Management will be more challenging not only because of the larger span of control, but also because it will require cultural sensitivity and adaptability with relative strangers. It will also require the willingness to attend meetings at midnight, local time.

Figure CE10-5
Possible Consequences of Remote Access

- Communication at a distance
  - Reduced business travel
  - Recreational travel larger proportion of travel industry
  - Routine work moves to lowest bidder
  - Experts have larger audience
  - Management becomes multicultural
- Action at a distance
  - Increased value for superior skills
  - Local mediocrity challenged
  - Need for local support
  - Robotics important

Action at a Distance

Tele-action, or action at a distance, increases the value of superior skills. With telesurgery, a heart surgeon who is highly skilled in a particular type of heart surgery can provides those skills to patients all over the world.

So far, such tele-action has been used in high-value industries like medicine. But, as the cost of teledistance technology decreases, tele-action will benefit other industries as well. Why does the world's best figure skating coach need to be physically present at a skater's practice? Why can't the world's best ski instructor provide high-value instruction to skiers on mountains all over the world?

Tele-action also reduces the value of local mediocrity. The claim "Well, I'm not the best, but at least I'm the best here" loses value in a tele-action world. *Lame but local* no longer works. In 1990, when Reich wrote *The Work of Nations*, he could sensibly claim that those who provide routine face-to-face services are exempt from the dangers of offshoring. That claim loses validity in the tele-action world.

However, the need for local support staff increases with tele-action. The remote hospital may not need its own mediocre heart surgeon, but it will need staff who can prepare the patient for surgery; it will need a local anesthesiologist, and it will need local nursing. Similar comments pertain to the world's best figure skating coach. Someone needs to be on-scene.

Finally, tele-action increases the value of robotics. Someone needs to design, build, market, sell, and support the machines that are on the other end of the expert's action. If the value of the expert increases, so, too, does the value of the robot.

What Does Nomadic and Mobile Access Mean for Business Professionals?

The widespread availability of affordable nomadic and mobile network access, using a variety of existing and yet-to-come iSomethings, has implications for the structure of every industry. Such access also has consequences for work styles as well, as summarized in Figure CE10-6.

Consequences on Industry Structure

We see some of the consequences of nomadic and mobile access in the example of talking shoes in the FlexTime case. Felix wants to connect his talking shoes to the FlexTime network. In a broader sense, FlexTime clients want to be able to connect all of their exercise activities into a profile that is stored somewhere, possibly on a FlexTime server in the cloud.

The FlexTime example serves as a marker for a larger issue. In all industries, rivalry will intensify as innovative organizations find ways to improve their products and services using nomadic and mobile access.

- Industry Structure Consequences
  - Increased rivalry pressure
  - Barriers to entry up (and down)
  - New substitutes
- Work Style Consequences
  - 9 to 5 is quaint
  - Presence important
  - Blend of personal and professional
  - Farm not factory
  - No weekends off
  - Segmented careers?

Figure CE10-6
Possible Consequences of Nomadic and Mobile Access

Nomadic and mobile access both raises and lowers barriers to entry. It raises them because companies that find ways to incorporate such access will set the bar higher for rivals who will need similar capabilities to compete. However, such access creates the potential of lowering barriers to entry for new substitutes. With regards to FlexTime, trainers like Felix might be able to provide services to clients at home. If so, trainers become a substitute for club memberships.

The credit card industry is feeling that pinch from substitutes right now. With mobile access, customers can use PayPal to pay for goods and services instead of credit and debit cards. Customers who routinely pay off their credit card balance will be happy to do so if the retailer provides some financial incentive to do so.

In truth, no one knows the impact of widely available nomadic and mobile access on any industry's structure. Such access will certainly create many opportunities for innovation during the early years of your career, and taking time to think about how the new iSomethings impact your industry will be a good investment. It's also a good exercise when preparing for job interviews as well.

Consequences on Work Style

Figure CE10-6 summarizes some of the impacts of widely available nomadic and remote access on work, and the news isn't good. The notion of 9 to 5 seems quaint in this environment. Workplace presence matters and is readily detectable by systems that report who is online, when, and for how long. You may or may not like that feature on Facebook; if you enjoy texting with friends, you'll probably like it. But, if you're telecommuting from home, do you want your boss to know when you started or stopped work?

For most professionals, such detectable presence isn't so much a matter of hiding work hours. Instead, the problem is that professionals in this environment are never off. Personal and professional life become blended because you're always reachable.

During the industrial revolution, factory workers went to work at 6 and were off at 3, with an hour break for lunch. That work style contrasted dramatically with the work style on the farm. A farmer is never off; farmers have no weekends. The cows always need to be fed and milked. Widely available nomadic and mobile access turns us all into farmers.

Can newly emerging business professionals stand a lifetime career with no weekends off? Will you become accustomed to it because you never knew anything any different? Or, will careers become segmented? Will you work intensely for a number of years, achieve success that you put in the bank, and take a few years off for recuperation? Whatever ensues, you and your classmates will be in the vanguard.

Q5 What About Privacy?

Every time we do something with an automated system, a record is kept, somewhere, often in several different databases. As someone gets on the bus, they scan their employee ID. A mobile application verifies their employment and, well, does what? With that data, Microsoft knows where everyone got on the bus and where everyone got off. They also know how long these people were at work. Undoubtedly, Microsoft is very careful with such data. But, that picture raises a question about what will happen with all the data we generate with remote, nomadic, and mobile applications.

Government intelligence agencies use cell phone data to track suspects. Data aggregators already digest our purchases, travel patterns, tax payments, and so on. Will such organizations now seek records of where we were at every moment of every day? What if a private investigator wants to know why an employee who lives in Maple Valley gets on the company bus every Thursday morning in Wallingford (25 miles apart)?

Figure CE10-7
Why Are You Taking the Bus from Wallingford When You Live in Maple Valley?
Source: David M. Kroenke.

Redflex, the Australian company that remotely generates traffic citations in the United States, also operates in the People's Republic of China. Reflex knows which cars and drivers are at which locations on particular dates and times. Where is that data stored? Where is it backed up? In the United States? In Australia? In China? Who knows?

And, taking a paranoid perspective, what if some agency doesn't want an employee to get on that bus? Or buy an airplane ticket? Or order a pizza? Or buy blood pressure medication? If you haven't read George Orwell's book *1984*, do so.

ACTIVE REVIEW

Use this Active Review to verify that you understand the material in the chapter extension. You can read the entire chapter extension and then perform the tasks in this review, or you can read the material for just one question and perform the tasks in this review for that question before moving on to the next one.

Q1 What are the differences among remote, nomadic, and mobile access?

Define *remote access,* and name and describe three remote access applications. Define *nomadic access,* and give two examples, one involving a truck. *Define mobile* access, and give two examples.

Q2 How will remote, nomadic, and mobile access be delivered?

Summarize the two schools of thought about the hardware that will be used to access RMN applications. Name and describe the three screens. If this situation replays similar situations with Microsoft in the past, what will happen next? (Or, what has happened since this text was written?) Describe possible relief for PC mules.

Q3 What is the role of the cloud and client virtualization?

How will thin clients and the cloud free business professionals? Explain how Office 2010 signals this change. Define *virtual client,* and explain the advantages that the role that such technology could play for nomadic and mobile applications. Describe the synchronization problem, and explain how virtual clients solve it.

Q4 What are the implications for business professionals?

Summarize the implication of communication at a distance for businesses and business professionals. How does communication at a distance reinforce Reich's theory, as discussed in Chapter 1. Summarize management changes that will ensue. Describe two opportunities for action at a distance that are not described in this text. Explain how action at a distance challenges some professionals while it increases the need for local support. Name an industry that will benefit from action at a distance. Explain the consequences of nomadic and mobile access on industry structure. Summarize how nomadic and mobile access change work styles.

Q5 What about privacy?

Summarize the kinds of data that RNM access generates. Describe how that data could be used to invade privacy. Explain how RNM access could be used by a government agency to control citizen activity.

KEY TERMS AND CONCEPTS

Client virtualization 449
Desktop virtualization 449
Mobile access 446
Nomadic access 446
PC mule 448
Remote access 445
Synch 449
Telediagnosis 445
Telelaw enforcement 445
Telesurgery 445
Virtual machine 449
Wireless hotspot hubs 446

USING YOUR KNOWLEDGE

1. Using your imagination to come up with an innovative application for each of the following: remote access, nomadic access, and mobile access. Describe applications that, as far as you know, do not exist but that have true value to some set of customers.
2. What do you think is Microsoft's real plan regarding the three-screens versus iSomething differences? Was Microsoft caught flat-footed? Did it underestimate the value of the iPod, iPhone, and iPad? Read recent news on this topic and summarize what you think Microsoft's current strategy must be.
3. As of this writing (June 2010), Apple has closed the development environment for the iSomethings. If you want to build an application for these devices, you must use Apple technology, Apple tools, and Macintosh computers. This move, which has been highly unpopular in the application development community, places developers who are committed to Microsoft technology out in the cold. Summarize what you think the consequences are to Apple. To Microsoft. To Microsoft developers. What do you think happens next?
4. Explain the advantages of a virtual client. Describe three potential applications of virtual clients at your university. Explain the benefits to students of each of your applications.
5. Suppose that you could view every topic in this course in a video that is presented by the world's best lecturer on that topic. If that were possible, what is the role of your professor? If you could watch lectures from the world's best professor of every subject you study, what is the role of your university? Do you need your professor or your university for anything other than monitoring tests and issuing credentials? Explain.

CHAPTER EXTENSION 11

Chapter 7 provides the background for this Extension.

Functional Processes, Applications, and Systems

STUDY QUESTIONS

Q1 How Do Functional Processes Relate to Functional Applications and Systems?

Functional processes are business processes that support a single organizational function. Examples are the accounts payable business process, the sales lead-tracking business process, and the customer support business process. As stated in Chapter 7, management of functional processes is easier than for cross-functional or interorganizational processes, because the activities and resources involved fall under the direction of a single functional manager. Functional processes do not cross departmental or organizational boundaries.

A **functional application** is a computer program that supports or possibly automates the major activities in a functional process. Few organizations develop their own functional applications. Instead, most license functional application software from a vendor and then adapt. Adaptation is necessary because organizations differ in the way they structure their functional processes; almost never does an off-the-shelf functional application provide a perfect fit.

Creating Functional Information Systems

To create a functional information systems, organizations first determine the requirements of the business function (see Chapter 10 for more on this important topic). They then evaluate functional applications and select one that provides the closest fit. Next, the organization implements the functional application in the context of its particular functional process. During implementation, either the business processes are altered to match the software or the software is altered to meet the organization's process. For many reasons, most organizations choose to adapt their process to match the software.

During implementation, the functional application is transformed into an information system. As licensed, the functional application will have software, a database design, and some default procedures. During implementation, the organization will build the remaining components of an information system. It will acquire and install hardware, fill the database with data, adapt standard procedures, and train staff. Thus, the organization acquires the functional application software and adapts it to support functional processes by creating functional information systems.

Example of a Functional Application at Fox Lake

Suppose, for example, that Fox Lake wants to provide a thin-client application to its members for reserving golf tee times and tennis courts. Fox Lake wants members to be able to use browsers as well as mobile devices such as iPhones to make these reservations. The first step would be to model that process (see Chapter Extension 12 for information on business process modeling) and to determine specific requirements. It would then identify potential off-the-shelf applications and select the one that best meets its requirements.

The vendor developed an application to manage typical country club facility reservations and to produce typical reports about reservation data. It also created default procedures for using that software in the typical situation. However, Fox Lake, like most organizations, will want to store nontypical data that the off-the-shelf reservation application does not include. For example, suppose no vendor has an iPhone application that works with its software. In this case, Fox Lake will either need to change its requirements or hire a firm to create an iPhone application that connects to its reservation application.

Either way, Fox Lake will create an information system around the reservation application. It will acquire hardware (maybe in the form of a cloud computing contract), fill the database with data, modify procedures to fit its particular reservation process, and train personnel and members.

Why is this important? In the following sections, we will describe features and functions of functional applications that organizations can license. Be aware, however, that acquiring such applications is just the tip of the iceberg. Once organizations have licensed the software, they need to create information systems around that software in such a way that they implement their own, unique functional processes. As a future manager, understand that the bulk of the work for you and your organization occurs *after* the software acquisition.

Q2 What Are the Functions of Sales and Marketing Applications?

The primary purpose of the sales process is to find prospects and transform them into customers by selling them something. Sales processes also *manage customers*, which is a euphemism for selling existing customers more product. Other functional sales processes forecast future sales.

In marketing, processes exist to manage products and brands. Companies use such processes to assess the effectiveness of marketing messages, advertising, and promotions and to determine product demand among various market segments.

Figure CE11-1 shows specific functions for sales and marketing applications. **Lead-generation applications** (also called *prospect-generation* applications) include those used to send both postal mail and email. Web sites are commonly used to generate leads as well. Some Web sites feature just product information; other sites offer to send the prospect white papers or other documents of value in exchange for the prospect's contact information.

Lead-tracking applications record lead data and product interests and keep records of customer contacts. Figure CE11-2 shows a form used by a small company that sells classic 1960s muscle cars (fast cars with large engines and underdesigned brakes). The company uses this form for both lead tracking and customer management. (Note that the company uses the term *customer* rather than *lead* or *prospect*.) As you can see, the application maintains customer name and contact data, the customer's product interests, past purchases, and a history of all contacts with the customer.

It is not clear from this form whether *Autos Currently Owned* represents autos purchased just from Bainbridge or autos the customer has purchased from any source.

- **Prospect (or lead) generation**
  - Mailings
  - Emailings
  - Web site

- **Lead tracking**
  - Record leads
  - Track product interests
  - Maintain history of contacts

- **Customer management**
  - Maintain customer contact and order history
  - Maintain and report credit status
  - Track product interests

- **Sales forecasting**
  - Record individual sales projections
  - Roll up sales projections into district, region, national, and international
  - Track variances over time

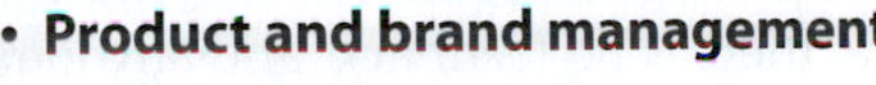

- **Product and brand management**
  - Obtain sales results from order processing or receivables applications
  - Compare results to projections
  - Assess promotions, advertising, and sales channels
  - Assess product success in market segments
  - Manage product life cycle

Figure CE11-1
Functions of Sales and Marketing Applications

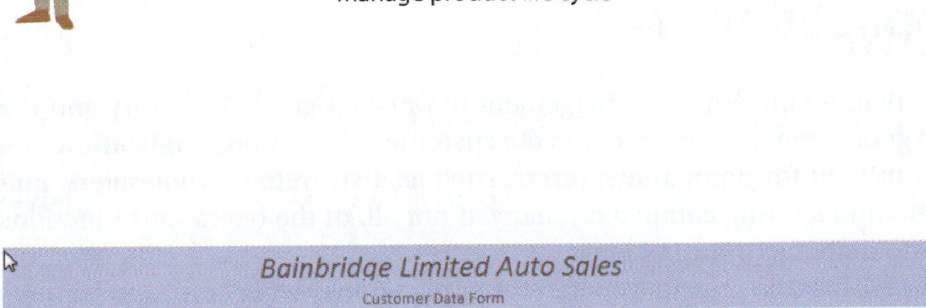

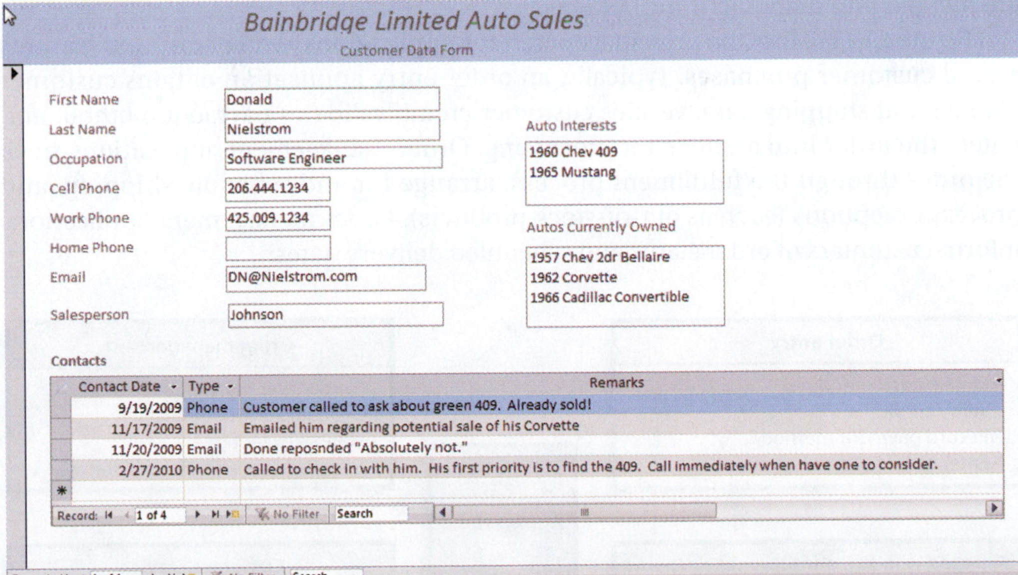

Bainbridge Limited Auto Sales

Customer Data Form

First Name: Donald
Last Name: Nielstrom
Occupation: Software Engineer
Cell Phone: 206.444.1234
Work Phone: 425.009.1234
Home Phone:
Email: DN@Nielstrom.com
Salesperson: Johnson

Auto Interests:
1960 Chev 409
1965 Mustang

Autos Currently Owned:
1957 Chev 2dr Bellaire
1962 Corvette
1966 Cadillac Convertible

Contacts

Contact Date	Type	Remarks
9/19/2009	Phone	Customer called to ask about green 409. Already sold!
11/17/2009	Email	Emailed him regarding potential sale of his Corvette
11/20/2009	Email	Done reposnded "Absolutely not."
2/27/2010	Phone	Called to check in with him. His first priority is to find the 409. Call immediately when have one to consider.

Record: 1 of 4 No Filter Search

Record: 1 of 1 No Filter Search

Figure CE11-2
Form Used for Lead Tracking and Customer Management

This ambiguity illustrates the need for procedures and employee training. If Bainbridge has five salespeople, and if two salespeople record only autos purchased from Bainbridge while the three other salespeople record autos purchased from any source, the data will be inconsistent. Subsequent reports or analyses based on this data will be hampered by this discrepancy. Again, applications (programs) are not information systems!

Companies use **customer management applications** to obtain additional sales from existing customers. As Figure CE11-1 showed, such applications maintain customer contact and order-history data and track product interests, and some maintain information about the customer's credit status with the organization. The latter data are used to prevent salespeople from generating orders that the accounts receivable department will later refuse due to poor customer credit.

The most common functional applications in marketing are **product and brand management applications**. With these, records of past sales are imported from order processing or accounts receivable systems and compared to projections and other sales estimates. The company uses the comparisons to assess the effectiveness of promotions and advertising as well as sales channels. It also can use such systems to assess the desirability of the product to different market segments. Finally, the company uses such applications to manage the product through its life cycle. Sales trends may indicate the need for new versions of the product or may help to determine when it is time to remove a product from the market.

In truth, it is impossible to manage a product or a brand without these kinds of information. Without the data, there is no feedback, and anyone's guess is as good as any other's with regard to the effectiveness of the marketing messaging, promotions, advertising, and other marketing activities.

Q3 What Are the Functions of Operations Applications?

Operations activities concern the management of finished-goods inventory and the movement of goods from that inventory to the customer. **Operations applications** are especially prominent for nonmanufacturers, such as distributors, wholesalers, and retailers. For manufacturing companies, many, if not all, of the operations functions are merged into manufacturing systems.

Figure CE11-3 lists the principal operations applications. Order entry applications record customer purchases. Typically, an order entry application obtains customer contact and shipping data, verifies customer credit, validates payment method, and enters the order into a queue for processing. Order management applications track the order through the fulfillment process, arrange for and schedule shipping, and process exceptions (such as out-of-stock products). Order management applications inform customers of order status and scheduled delivery dates.

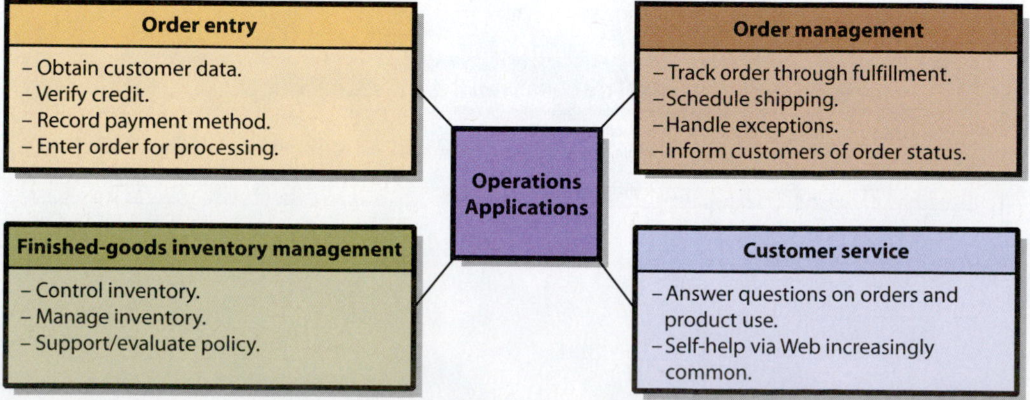

Figure CE11-3
Functions of Operations Applications

In nonmanufacturing organizations, operations applications include features to manage finished-goods inventory. We will not address those applications here; see the discussion of inventory applications in the next section. As you read that discussion, just realize that nonmanufacturers do not have raw materials or goods-in-process inventories. They have only finished-goods inventories.

Customer service is the last operations application in Figure CE11-3. Customers call customer service to ask questions about products, order status, and problems and to make complaints. Today, many organizations are placing as much of the customer service function on Web pages as they can. Many organizations allow customers direct access to order status and delivery information. Also, organizations are increasingly providing product-use support using Enterprise 2.0 techniques.

Q4 What Are the Functions of Manufacturing Applications?

Manufacturing applications facilitate the production of goods. As shown in Figure CE11-4, manufacturing applications include inventory, planning, scheduling, and manufacturing operations. We begin with inventory.

Inventory Applications

Inventory applications support inventory control, management, and policy. In terms of inventory control, inventory applications track goods and materials into, out of, and between inventories. Inventory tracking requires that items be identified by a number. In the least sophisticated systems, employees must enter inventory numbers manually. Today, however, most applications use UPC bar codes (the familiar bar code you find on items at the grocery store) or RFIDs (radio frequency identification tags) to track items as they move in, around, and out of inventories.

Inventory management applications use past data to compute stocking levels, reorder levels, and reorder quantities in accordance with inventory policy. They also have features for assisting inventory counts and for computing inventory losses from those counts and from inventory-processing data.

With regard to inventory policy, there are two schools of thought in modern operations management. Some companies view inventories primarily as assets. In this view, large inventories are beneficial. Their cost is justified, because large inventories minimize disruptions in operations or sales due to outages. Large finished-goods inventories increase sales by offering greater product selection and availability to the customer.

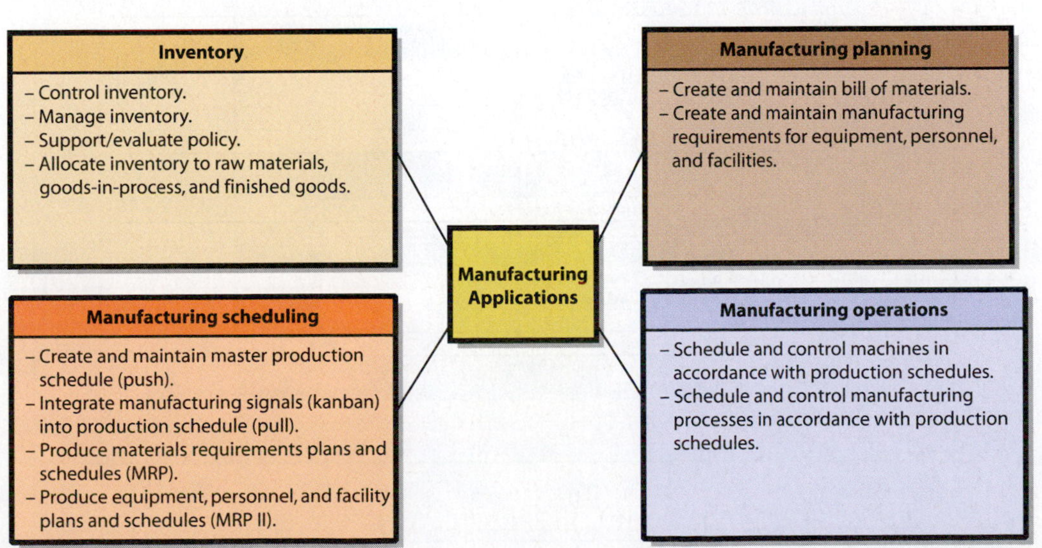

Figure CE11-4
Functions of Manufacturing Applications

Other companies, such as Dell, view inventories primarily as liabilities. In this view, companies seek to keep inventories as small as possible and to eliminate them completely if possible. The ultimate expression of this view is demonstrated in the **just-in-time (JIT) inventory policy**. This policy seeks to have production inputs (both raw materials and work-in-process) delivered to the manufacturing site just as they are needed. By scheduling delivery of inputs in this way, companies are able to reduce inventories to a minimum.

Still others use both philosophies: Wal-Mart, for example, has large inventories in its stores, but minimizes all other inventories in its warehouses and distribution centers.

Inventory applications help an organization implement its particular philosophy and determine the appropriate balance between inventory cost and item availability, given that philosophy. Features include computing the inventory's return on investment (ROI), reports on the effectiveness of current inventory policy, and some means of evaluating alternative inventory policies by performing what-if analyses.

Manufacturing-Planning Applications

In order to plan materials for manufacturing, it is first necessary to record the components of the manufactured items. A **bill of materials (BOM)** is a list of the materials that comprise a product. This list is more complicated than it might sound, because the materials that comprise a product can be subassemblies that need to be manufactured. Thus, the BOM is a list of materials, and materials within materials, and materials within materials within materials, and so forth.

In addition to the BOM, if the manufacturing application schedules equipment, people, and facilities, then a record of those resources for each manufactured product is required as well. The company may augment the BOM to show labor and equipment requirements or it may create a separate nonmaterial requirements file.

Figure CE11-5 shows a sample BOM for a child's red wagon having four components: handle bar, wagon body, front-wheel assembly, and rear-wheel assembly. Three of these have the subcomponent parts shown. Of course, each of these subcomponents could have sub-subcomponents, and so forth, but these are not shown. Altogether, the

Figure CE11-5
Bill of Materials Example

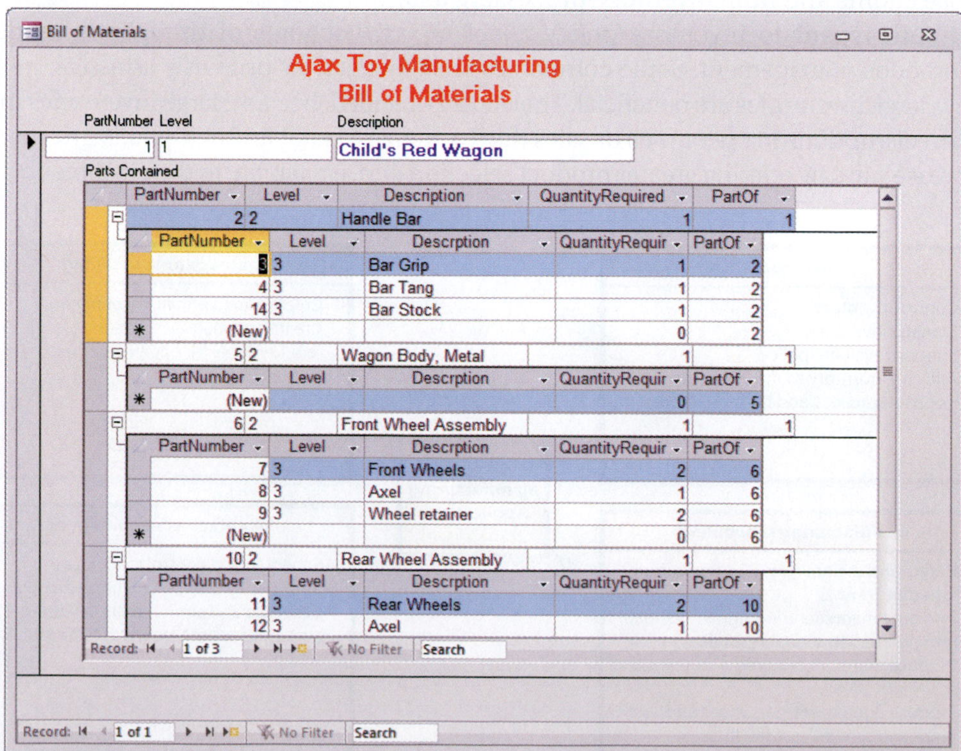

BOM shows all of the parts needed to make the wagon and the relationships of those parts to each other.

Manufacturing-Scheduling Applications

Companies use three philosophies to create a manufacturing schedule. One is to generate a **master production schedule (MPS)**, which is a plan for producing products. To create the MPS, the company analyzes past sales levels and makes estimates of future sales. This process is called a **push manufacturing process**, because the company pushes the products into sales (and customers) according to the MPS.

Figure CE11-6 shows a manufacturing schedule for wagon production at a toy company. This plan includes three colors of wagons and shows subtle production increases prior to the summer months and prior to the holiday season. Again, the company obtains these production levels by analyzing past sales. The MPS for an actual manufacturer would, of course, be more complicated.

A second philosophy is not to use a preplanned, forecasted schedule, but rather to plan manufacturing in response to signals from customers or downstream production processes that products or components are currently needed. The Japanese word *kanban*, which means "card," is sometimes used to refer to the signal to build something. Manufacturing processes that respond to kanbans must be more flexible than those that are MPS-based. A process based on such signals is sometimes called a **pull manufacturing process**, because the products are pulled through manufacturing by demand.

Finally, a third philosophy is a combination of the two. The company creates an MPS and plans manufacturing according to the MPS, but it uses kanban-like signals to modify the schedule. For example, if the company receives signals that indicate increased customer demand, it might add an extra production shift for a while in order to build inventory to meet the increased demand. This combination approach requires sophisticated information systems for implementation.

Two acronyms are common in the manufacturing domain: **Materials requirements planning (MRP)** is an application that plans the need for materials and inventories of materials used in the manufacturing process. MRP does not include the planning of personnel, equipment, or facilities requirements.

Manufacturing resource planning (MRP II) is a follow-up to MRP that includes the planning of materials, personnel, and machinery. MRP II supports many linkages across the organization, including linkages with sales and marketing via the development of a master production schedule. MRP II also includes the capability to perform what-if analyses on variances in schedules, raw materials availabilities, personnel, and other resources.[1]

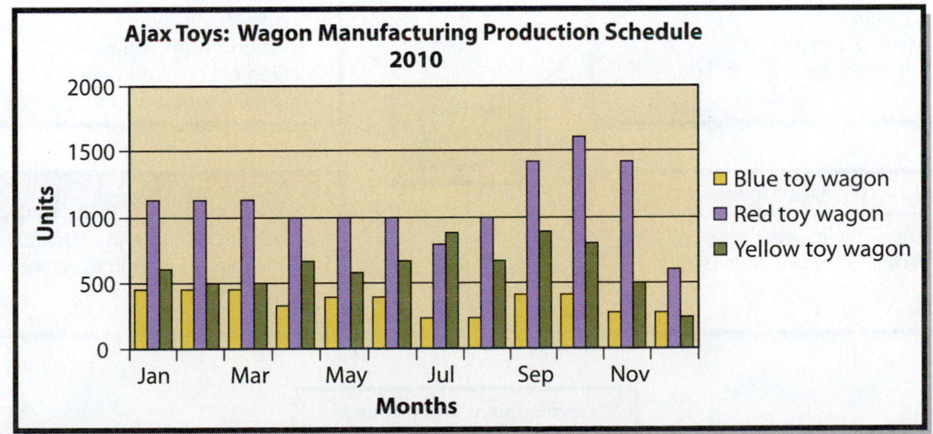

Figure CE11-6
Sample Manufacturing Plan

1. To add even more complication to this subject, some in the operations management field use the terms *MRP Type I* and *MRP Type II* instead of *MRP* and *MRP II*. *MRP Type I* refers to material requirements planning; *MRP Type II* refers to manufacturing resource planning. When used in this way, the different interpretations of the letters *MRP* are ignored, as if *MRP* were not an acronym. Unfortunately, such sets of confusing terminology cannot be avoided in a growing field.

Manufacturing Operations

A fourth category of IS in manufacturing is the control of machinery and production processes. Computer programs operate lathes, mills, and robots, and even entire production lines. In a modern facility, these programs have linkages to the manufacturing-scheduling applications. Because they run machines rather than support business processes, we will not consider them further.

Q5 What Are the Functions of Human Resources Applications?

Human resources applications support recruitment, compensation, assessment, development and training, and planning. The first-era human resources (HR) applications did little more than compute payroll. Modern HR applications concern all dimensions of HR activity, as listed in Figure CE11-7.

Depending on the size and sophistication of the company, recruiting methods may be simple or very complex. In a small company, posting a job may be a simple task requiring one or two approvals. In a larger, more formal organization, posting a new job may involve multiple levels of approval requiring use of tightly controlled and standardized procedures.

Compensation includes payroll for both salaried employees and hourly employees. It may also include pay to consultants and permanent, but nonemployee, workers, such as contractors and consultants. Compensation refers not only to pay, but also to the processing and tracking of vacation, sick leave, and health care and other benefits. Compensation activities also support retirement plans, company stock purchases, and stock options and grants. They can also include transferring employee contribution payments to organizations such as the United Way and others.

Employee assessment includes the publication of standard job and skill descriptions as well as support for employee performance evaluations. Such support may include applications that allow employees to create self-evaluations and to evaluate peers and subordinates. Employee assessment is used for the basis of compensation increases as well as promotion.

Development and training activities vary widely from firm to firm. Some organizations define career paths formally, with specific jobs, skills, experience, and training

Figure CE11-7
Functions of Human Resources Applications

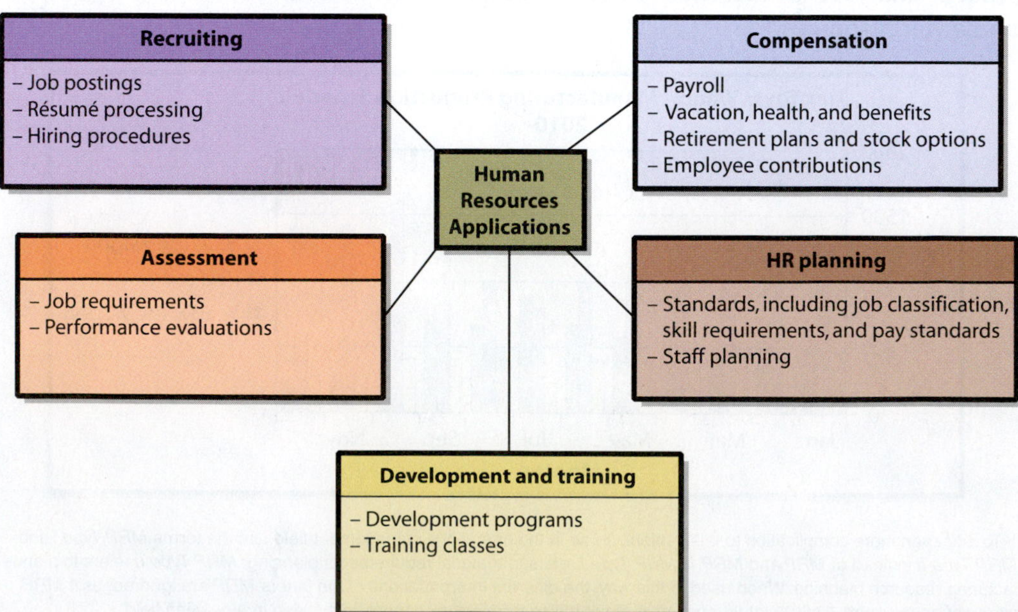

requirements. HR applications have features and functions to support the publication of these paths. Some HR applications track training classes, instructors, and students.

Finally, HR applications must support planning functions. These include the creation and publication of organizational standards, job classifications, and compensation ranges for those classifications. Planning also includes determining future requirements for employees by level, experience, skill, and other factors.

Q6 What Are the Functions of Accounting Applications?

Typical **accounting applications** are listed in Figure CE11-8. You know what a general ledger is from your accounting classes. Financial reporting applications use the general ledger data to produce financial statements and other reports for management, investors, and federal reporting agencies like the Securities and Exchange Commission (SEC).

Cost-accounting applications determine the marginal cost and relative profitability of products and product families. Budgeting applications allocate and schedule revenues and expenses and compare actual financial results to the plan.

Accounts receivable includes not just recording receivables and the payments against receivables, but also account aging and collections management. Accounts payable applications include features to reconcile payments against purchases and to schedule payments according to the organization's payment policy.

Cash management is the process of scheduling payments and receivables and planning the use of cash so as to balance the organization's cash needs against cash availability. Other financial management applications concern checking account reconciliation, as well as managing electronic funds transfer throughout the organization. Finally, treasury applications concern the management and investment of the organization's cash and payment of cash dividends.

Figure CE11-8
Functions of Accounting Applications

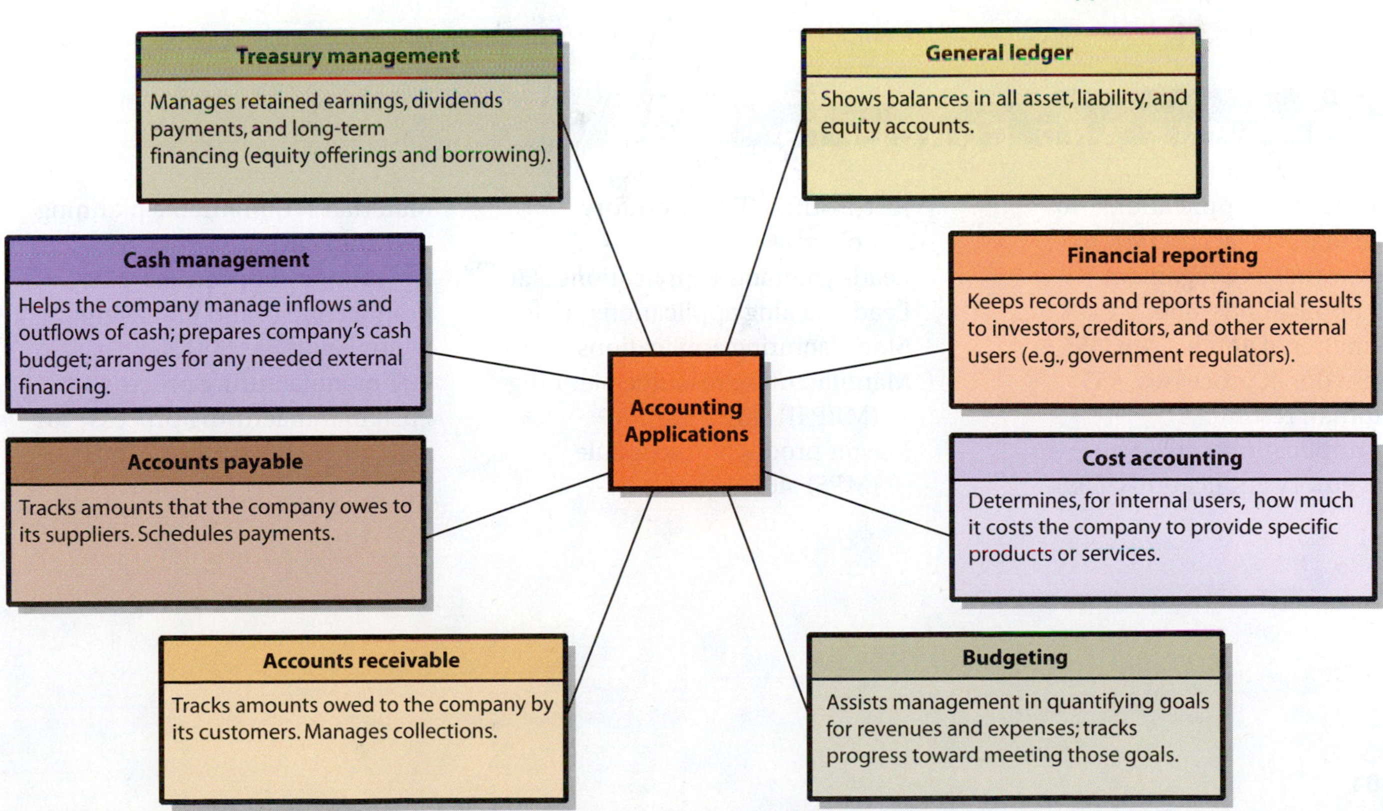

Treasury management
Manages retained earnings, dividends payments, and long-term financing (equity offerings and borrowing).
General ledger
Shows balances in all asset, liability, and equity accounts.
Cash management
Helps the company manage inflows and outflows of cash; prepares company's cash budget; arranges for any needed external financing.
Financial reporting
Keeps records and reports financial results to investors, creditors, and other external users (e.g., government regulators).
Accounting Applications
Accounts payable
Tracks amounts that the company owes to its suppliers. Schedules payments.
Cost accounting
Determines, for internal users, how much it costs the company to provide specific products or services.
Accounts receivable
Tracks amounts owed to the company by its customers. Manages collections.
Budgeting
Assists management in quantifying goals for revenues and expenses; tracks progress toward meeting those goals.

ACTIVE REVIEW

Use this Active Review to verify that you understand the material in the chapter extension. You can read the entire extension and then perform the tasks in this review, or you can read the material for just one question and perform the tasks in this review for that question before moving on to the next one.

Q1 How do functional processes relate to functional applications and systems?

Define *functional process* and *functional application,* and distinguish between them. Explain why adaptation is usually required when licensing functional applications. Differentiate functional applications from functional information systems. Explain the statement, "To support business processes, functional applications must be converted to information systems." Explain why acquiring a functional application is just the tip of the iceberg.

Q2 What are the functions of sales and marketing applications?

List the functional categories of sales and marketing applications and describe the primary functions of each.

Q3 What are the functions of operations applications?

List the functional categories of operations applications and describe the primary functions of each.

Q4 What are the functions of manufacturing applications?

List the functional categories of manufacturing applications and describe the primary functions of each. Explain just-in-time inventory policy. Describe a bill of materials and give a brief example. Describe push manufacturing and explain the role of the MPS. Describe pull manufacturing systems and explain the term *kanban.* Decode the acronyms *MRP* and *MRP II,* and explain the functions of each.

Q5 What are the functions of human resources applications?

List the functional categories of human resource applications and describe the primary functions of each.

Q6 What are the functions of accounting applications?

List the functional categories of accounting applications and describe the primary functions of each.

KEY TERMS AND CONCEPTS

Accounting applications 463
Bill of materials (BOM) 460
Customer-management applications 458
Functional application 455
Functional processes 455
Human resources applications 462
Inventory applications 459
Just-in-time (JIT) inventory policy 460
Lead-generation applications 456
Lead-tracking applications 456
Manufacturing applications 459
Manufacturing resource planning (MRP II) 461
Master production schedule (MPS) 461
Materials requirements planning (MRP) 461
Operations applications 458
Product and brand management applications 458
Pull manufacturing process 461
Push manufacturing process 461

USING YOUR KNOWLEDGE

1. The text uses the example of a reservation system as a functional application. However, Fox Lake's requirements indicate the need for reservations for both golf and tennis. Because two activities are involved, is it really a functional application? Is it better considered a cross-functional application? Explain your answer. If you need further information, describe what information you need and explain why that information would be pertinent to your answer.
2. In your own words, explain the differences among functional processes, applications, and systems. Suppose you manage golf and tennis operations activities at Fox Lake, and you've just been informed that Fox Lake is going to implement a new reservation system. Write a one-page memo to Jeff Lloyd (the general manager) explaining the role that you think you should have in this process. Justify your statements.
3. The text indicates that when a new customer-facing application is implemented, both employees and customers need to be trained. It is easy to envision employee training, but how do you train your customers? Identify three techniques that you could use to train customers. Employees are paid for training; to customers, it's a nuisance. Describe techniques you could use to incentivize your customers to use the three customer training techniques you identified.
4. Based on this chapter extension, choose the category of functional application that is closest to your major. Select one application from the list of applications described for that category. For that application:
   a. Google or Bing your application and identify five possible off-the-shelf applications.
   b. Characterize the differences among those five applications.
   c. Describe, in general terms, how you would go about evaluating those five applications.
   d. List criteria you would use to select one of those applications.
   e. Summarize the risks of choosing the wrong application.

STUDY QUESTIONS

CHAPTER EXTENSION 12

Chapter 7 provides the background for this Extension.

- **Q1** What is the purpose of ERP systems?
- **Q2** What are the elements of an ERP solution?
- **Q3** How are ERP systems implemented?
- **Q4** What types of organizations use ERP?
- **Q5** How do the major ERP vendors compare?

Enterprise Resource Planning (ERP) Systems

Q1 What Is the Purpose of ERP Systems?

As stated in Chapter 7, **enterprise resource planning (ERP)** is a suite of applications, called **modules**; a database; and a set of inherent processes for consolidating business operations into a single, consistent, computing platform. An **ERP system** is an information system based on ERP technology. ERP systems integrate all of an organization's purchasing, human resources, production, sales, and accounting data into a single system.

The primary purpose of an ERP system is integration; an ERP system allows the left hand of the organization to know what the right hand is doing. This integration allows real-time updates, globally, whenever and wherever a transaction takes place. Critical business decisions can then be made on a timely basis using the latest data.

To understand the utility of this integration, consider the pre-ERP systems shown in Figure CE12-1. This diagram of the processes used by a bicycle manufacturer includes five different databases, one each for vendors, raw materials, finished goods, manufacturing plan, and CRM. Consider the problems that appear with such separated data when the sales department closes a large order, say for 1,000 bicycles.

First, should the company take the order? Can it meet the schedule requirements for such a large order? Suppose one of the primary parts vendors recently lost capacity due to an earthquake, and the manufacturer cannot obtain parts for the order in time. If so, the order schedule ought not to be approved. However, with such separated systems, this situation is unknown.

Even if parts can be obtained, until the order is entered into the finished-goods database, purchasing is unaware of the need to buy new parts. The same comment applies to manufacturing. Until the new order is entered into the manufacturing plan, the production department doesn't know that it needs to increase manufacturing. And, as with parts, does the company have sufficient machine and floor capacity to fill the order on a timely basis? Does it have sufficient personnel with the correct skill sets? Should it be hiring? Can production meet the order schedule? No one knows before the order is approved.

Figure CE12-1 does not show accounting. We can assume, however, that the company has a separate accounting system that is similarly isolated. Eventually, records of business activity find their way to the accounting department and will be posted into the general ledger. With such a pre-ERP system, financial statements are always dated, becoming available several weeks after the close of the quarter or other accounting period.

Contrast this situation with the ERP system in Figure CE12-2. Here, all activity is processed by ERP application programs and consolidated data are stored in a centralized ERP database. When sales is confronted with the opportunity to sell 1,000

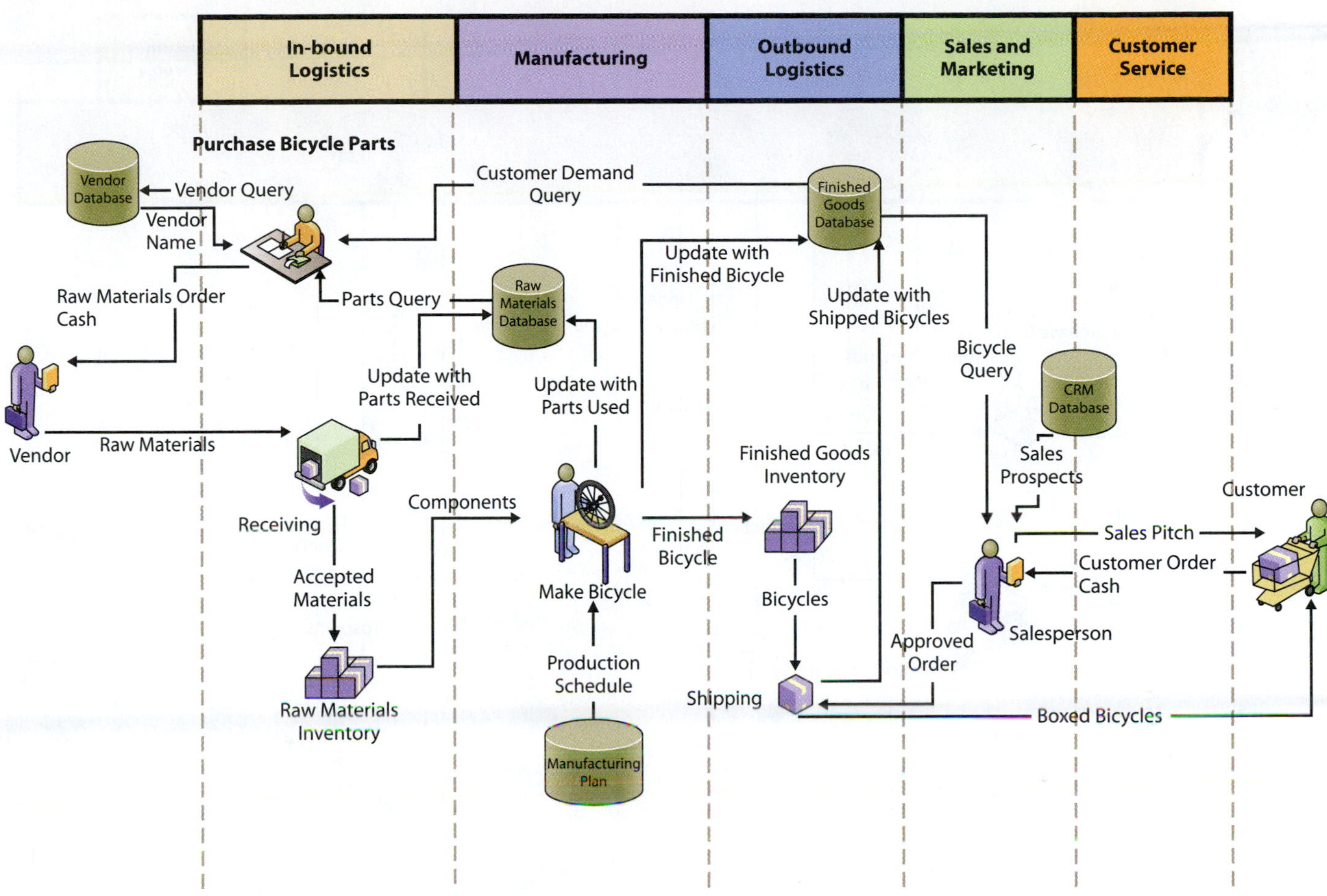

Figure CE12-1
Pre-ERP Information Systems

bicycles, the information that it needs to confirm that the order, schedule, and terms are feasible can be obtained from the ERP system immediately. Once the order is accepted, all departments, including purchasing, manufacturing, human resources, and accounting, are notified. Further, transactions are posted to the ERP database as they occur; the result is that financial statements are available quickly, and in most cases correct financial statements can be produced in real time. With such integration, ERP systems can display the current status of critical business factors to managers and executives, as shown in the sales dashboard in Figure CE12-3.

Of course, the devil is in the details. It's one thing to draw a rectangle on a chart, label it "ERP application programs," and then assume that data integration takes all the problems away. It is far more difficult to write those application programs and to design the database to store that integrated data. Even more problematic, what procedures should employees and others use to process those application programs? Specifically, what actions should salespeople take before they approve a large order? The following are some of the questions that procedures need to answer or resolve:

- How does the sales department determine that an order is large? By dollars? By volume?
- Who approves customer credit (and how)?
- Who approves production capacity (and how)?
- Who approves schedule and terms (and how)?
- What actions need to be taken if the customer modifies the order?
- How does management obtain oversight on sales activity?

As you can imagine, many other questions must be answered as well.

ERP Database

In-bound Logistics
Manufacturing
Outbound Logistics
Sales and Marketing
Customer Service

Purchasing Module
Materials Management Module
Production & Manufacturing Module
Sales & Distribution Module
Customer Relationship Module
Financial & Cost Module

Vendor Query
Purchase Bicycle Parts
Vendor Name
Customer Demand Query
Parts Query
Update with Parts Received
Raw Materials Order
Cash
Vendor
Raw Materials
Receiving
Accepted Materials
Raw Materials Inventory
Components
Production Schedule
Update with Finished Bicycle
Update with Parts Used
Make Bicycle
Finished Bicycle
Finished Goods Inventory
Bicycles
Shipping
Update with Shipped Bicycles
Update with Sale
Bicycle Query
Sales Prospects
Approved Order
Salesperson
Sales Pitch
Customer Order
Cash
Customer
Boxed Bicycles

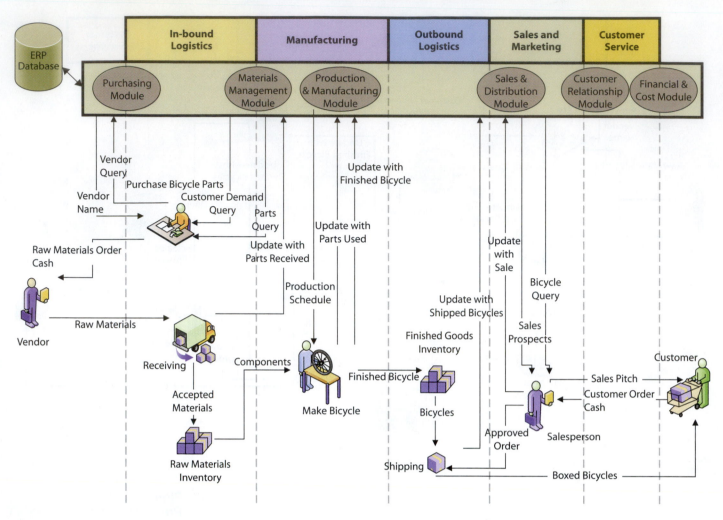

Figure CE12-2
ERP Information Systems

Figure CE12-3
Sales Dashboard

Source: Microsoft Corporation.

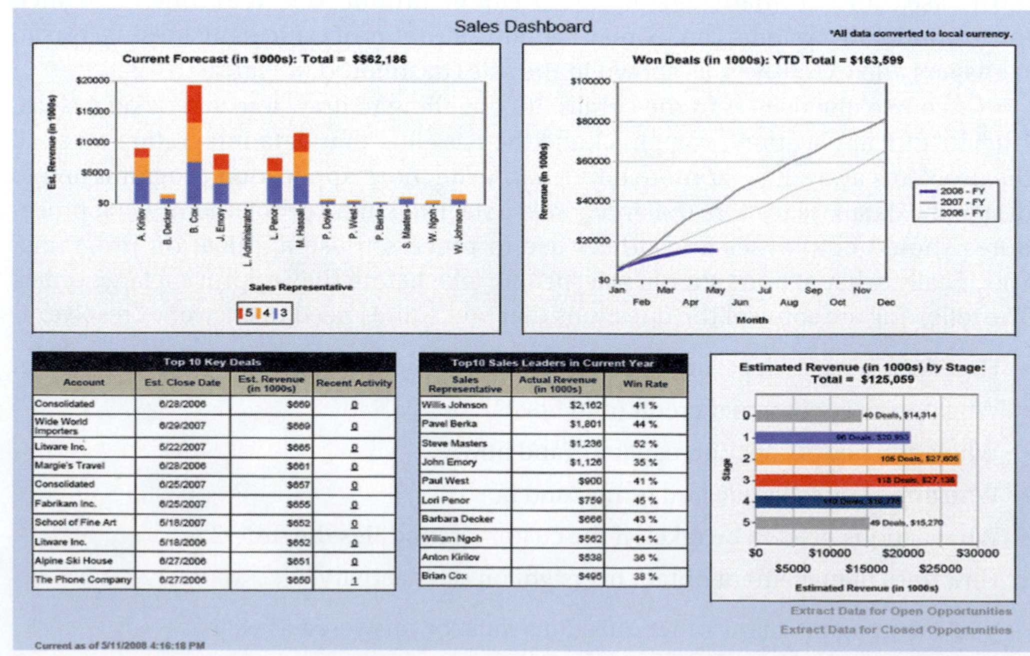

Top 10 Key Deals			
Account	Est. Close Date	Est. Revenue (in 1000s)	Recent Activity
Consolidated	6/28/2006	$669	0
Wide World Importers	6/29/2007	$669	0
Litware Inc.	5/22/2007	$665	0
Margie's Travel	6/28/2006	$661	0
Consolidated	6/25/2007	$657	0
Fabrikam Inc.	6/25/2007	$655	0
School of Fine Art	5/18/2007	$652	0
Litware Inc.	5/18/2006	$652	0
Alpine Ski House	6/27/2006	$651	0
The Phone Company	6/27/2006	$650	1

Top10 Sales Leaders in Current Year		
Sales Representative	Actual Revenue (in 1000s)	Win Rate
Willis Johnson	$2,162	41 %
Pavel Berka	$1,801	44 %
Steve Masters	$1,236	52 %
John Emory	$1,126	35 %
Paul West	$900	41 %
Lori Penor	$759	45 %
Barbara Decker	$666	43 %
William Ngoh	$562	44 %
Anton Kirilov	$538	36 %
Brian Cox	$495	38 %

As stated in Chapter 7, in the late 1980s and early 1990s some organizations attempted to develop their own ERP applications and procedures. The process was too difficult and expensive for most to succeed. During that era, ERP software vendors developed ERP applications that included program code, databases, and inherent processes that addressed issues such as those just listed. Today, almost no organization develops its own ERP software; such systems are licensed from vendors such as those described in Q4.

Even with solutions provided by ERP vendors, however, the process of converting an organization from systems like those in Figure CE12-1 to an ERP system like that in Figure CE12-2 is daunting and expensive. For most organizations, it is a multiyear project that involves millions of dollars and hundreds of employees, consultants, and vendor personnel.

Q2 What Are the Elements of an ERP Solution?

The term *ERP* has been applied to a wide array of application solutions. Some vendors attempted to catch the buzz for ERP by misapplying the term to applications that were nothing more than one or two integrated functional applications.

The organization ERPSoftware360 publishes a wealth of information about ERP vendors, products, solutions, and applications. According to its Web site (*www.erpsoftware360.com/erp-101.htm*), for a product to be considered a true ERP product, it must include applications that integrate the following:

- Supply chain (procurement, sales order processing, inventory management, supplier management, and related activities)
- Manufacturing (scheduling, capacity planning, quality control, bill of materials, and related activities)
- CRM (sales prospecting, customer management, marketing, customer support, call center support)
- Human resources (payroll, time and attendance, HR management, commission calculations, benefits administration, and related activities)
- Accounting (general ledger, accounts receivable, accounts payable, cash management, fixed-asset accounting)

An ERP solution consists of application programs, databases, business process procedures, and training and consulting. We consider each, in turn.

ERP Application Programs

ERP vendors design application programs to be configurable so that development teams can alter them to meet customer requirements without changing program code. Accordingly, during the ERP development process, the development team sets configuration parameters that specify how ERP application programs will operate. For example, an hourly payroll application is configured to specify the number of hours in the standard workweek, hourly wages for different job categories, wage adjustments for overtime and holiday work, and so forth.

Of course, there are limits to how much configuration can be done. If a new ERP customer has requirements that cannot be met via program configuration, then it either needs to adapt its business to what the software can do or write (or pay another vendor to write) application code to meet its requirement. As stated in Chapter 4, such custom programming is expensive both initially and in long-term maintenance costs. Thus, choosing an ERP solution that has applications that function close to the organization's requirements is critically important to success.

ERP Databases

An ERP solution includes a database design as well as initial configuration data. It does not, of course, contain the company's operational data. During development, the team must enter the initial values for that data as part of the development effort.

If your only experience with databases is creating a few tables in Microsoft Access, then you probably underestimate the value and importance of ERP database designs. SAP, the leading vendor of ERP solutions, provides ERP databases that contain over 15,000 tables. The design includes the metadata for those tables, as well as their relationships to each other and rules and constraints about how the data in some tables must relate to data in other tables. As stated, the ERP solution also contains tables filled with initial configuration data.

Furthermore, although we did not discuss this database feature in Chapter 5, large organizational databases contain two types of program code. The first, called a **trigger**, is a computer program stored within the database that runs to keep the database consistent when certain conditions arise. The second, called a **stored procedure**, is a computer program stored in the database that is used to enforce business rules. An example of such a rule would be never to sell certain items at a discount. Triggers and stored procedures are also part of the ERP solution.

Reflect on the difficulty of creating and validating data models (as discussed in Chapter Extension 5), and you will have some idea of the amount of intellectual capital invested in a database design of 15,000 tables. Also, consider the magnitude of the task of filling such a database with users' data!

Business Process Procedures

The third component of an ERP solution is a set of inherent procedures that implement standard business processes. ERP vendors develop hundreds, or even thousands, of procedures that enable the ERP customer organization to accomplish its work using the applications provided by the vendor. Figure CE12-4 shows a part of the SAP ordering business process; this process implements a portion of the activities shown on the left-hand side of Figure CE12-2. Some ERP vendors call the inherent processes that are defined in the ERP solution **process blueprints**.

Without delving into the details, you should be able to understand the flow of work outlined in this process. Every function (rounded rectangle) consists of a set of procedures for accomplishing that function. Typically, these procedures require an ERP user to use application menus, screens, and reports to accomplish the activity.

As with application programs, ERP users must either adapt to the predefined, inherent processes and procedures or design new ones. In the latter case, the design of new procedures may necessitate changes to application programs and to database structures as well. Perhaps you can begin to understand why organizations attempt to conform to vendor standards.

Training and Consulting

Because of the complexity and difficulty of implementing and using ERP solutions, ERP vendors have developed training curricula and classes. SAP operates universities, in which customers and potential customers receive training both before and after the ERP implementation. In addition, ERP vendors typically conduct classes on

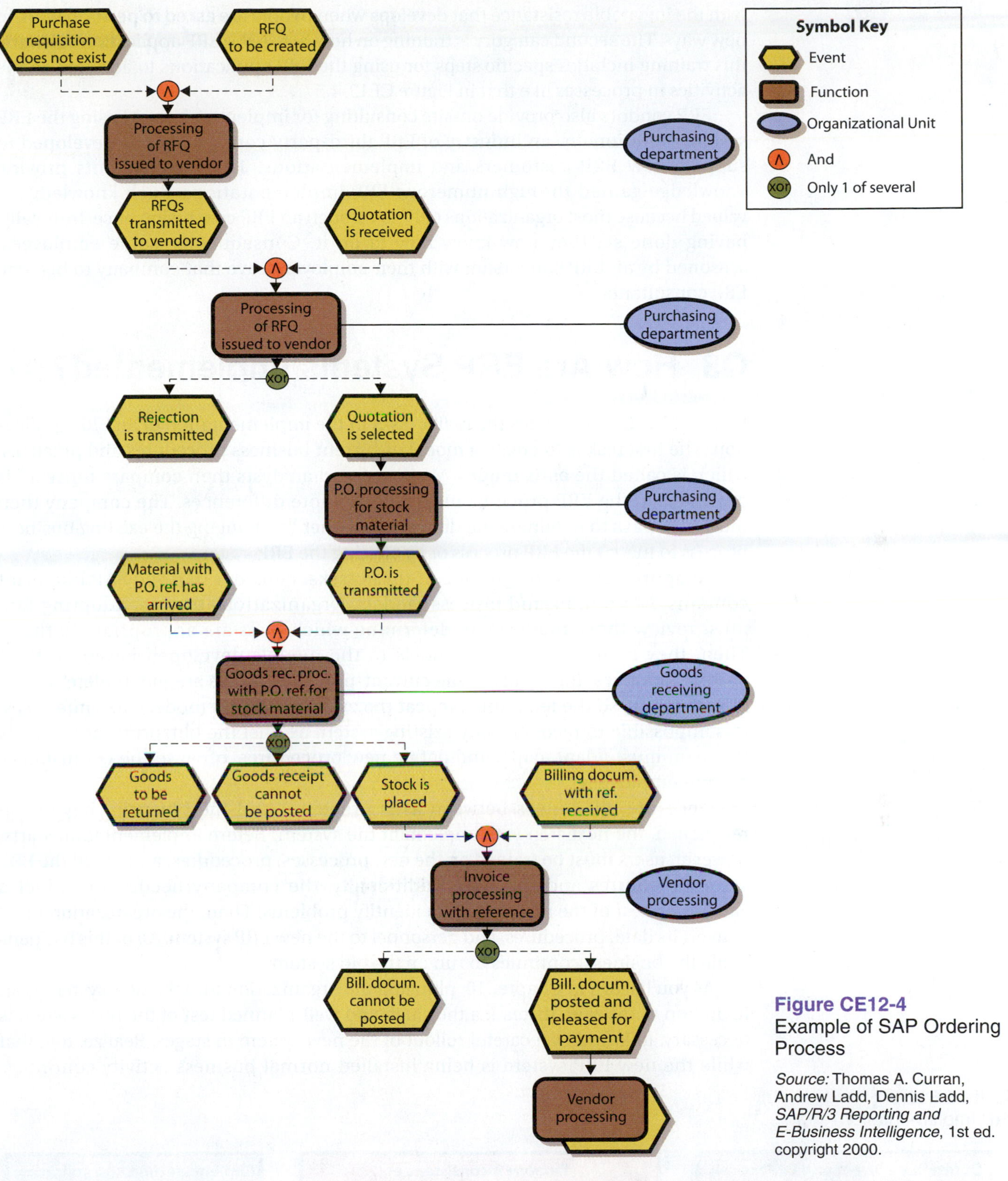

Figure CE12-4
Example of SAP Ordering Process

Source: Thomas A. Curran, Andrew Ladd, Dennis Ladd, *SAP/R/3 Reporting and E-Business Intelligence*, 1st ed. copyright 2000.

site. To reduce expenses, the vendors sometimes train some of the organization's employees, called Super Users, to become in-house trainers, in training sessions called **train the trainer**.

ERP training falls into two broad categories. The first category is training about how to implement the ERP solution. This training includes topics such as obtaining top-level management support, preparing the organization for change, and dealing with the inevitable resistance that develops when people are asked to perform work in new ways. The second category is training on how to use the ERP application software; this training includes specific steps for using the ERP applications to accomplish the activities in processes like that in Figure CE12-4.

ERP vendors also provide on-site consulting for implementing and using the ERP system. Additionally, an industry of ERP third-party consultants has developed to support new ERP customers and implementations. These consultants provide knowledge gained through numerous ERP implementations. Such knowledge is valued because most organizations only go through an ERP conversion once. Ironically, having done so, they now know how to do it. Consequently, some employees, seasoned by an ERP conversion with their employer, leave that company to become ERP consultants.

Q3 How Are ERP Systems Implemented?

Figure CE12-5 summarizes the major tasks in the implementation of an ERP application. The first task is to create a model of current business procedures and practices, which is called the **as-is model**. Managers and analysts then compare those as-is processes to the ERP process blueprints and note differences. The company then must find ways to eliminate the differences, either by changing the existing business process to match the ERP process or by altering the ERP system.

To appreciate the magnitude of these tasks, consider that the SAP blueprint contains over a thousand process models. Organizations that are adopting ERP must review those models and determine which ones are appropriate to them. Then, they compare the ERP models to the models developed based on their current practices. Inevitably, some current-practice models are incomplete, vague, or inaccurate, so the team must repeat the existing process models. In some cases, it is impossible to reconcile any existing system against the blueprint model. If so, the team must adapt, cope, and define new procedures, often to the confusion of current employees.

Once the differences between as-is processes and the blueprint have been reconciled, the next step is to implement the system. Before implementation starts, however, users must be trained on the new processes, procedures, and use of the ERP system's features and function. Additionally, the company needs to conduct a simulation test of the new system to identify problems. Then, the organization must convert its data, procedures, and personnel to the new ERP system. All of this happens while the business continues to run on the old system.

As you'll learn in Chapter 10, plunging the organization into the new system is an invitation to disaster. Instead, a thorough and well-planned test of the new system is necessary, followed by a careful rollout of the new system in stages. Realize, too, that while the new ERP system is being installed normal business activity continues.

Figure CE12-5
ERP Implementation

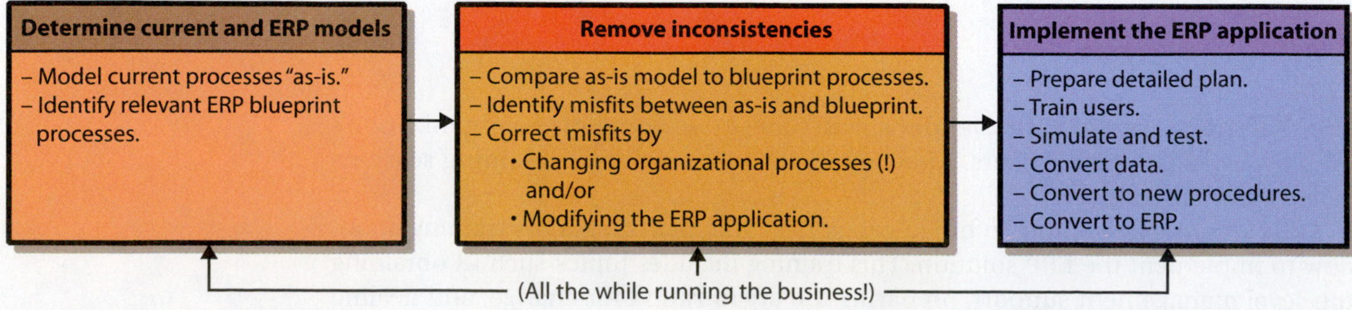

Somehow the employees of the organization must continue to run the company while the rollout is underway. It is a difficult and challenging time for any organization that undergoes this process.

Implementing an ERP system is not for the faint of heart. Because so much organizational change is required, all ERP projects must have the full support of the CEO and executive staff. Like all cross-functional processes, ERP crosses departmental boundaries, and no single departmental manager has the authority to force an ERP implementation. Instead, full support for the task must come from the top of the organization. Even with such support there is bound to be concern and second-guessing.

Q4 What Types of Organizations Use ERP?

ERP originated as an outgrowth of MRP II manufacturing functional applications (see Chapter Extension 10). ERP extended MRP II from just the planning and scheduling of manufacturing to include the planning and use of facilities, people, equipment, materials flow, orders, customers, and accounting, encompassing the scope described in Q2.

ERP by Industry Type

Because of its origins, the first major ERP customers were large manufacturers. Manufacturers in the aerospace, automotive, and industrial equipment industries led the way. SAP, currently the market leader, spurred ERP growth by providing industry-specific implementations. For example, as SAP assisted one auto manufacturer in using its product, it learned process patterns that were typical of auto manufacturers. Over time, it constructed an auto–manufacturing-specific ERP solution as a product offering. These **industry-specific solutions** became popular, and today SAP and other ERP vendors offer dozens of them. SAP, for example, has 24 industry-specific versions of its ERP products.

Given their success with manufacturers, it was natural for ERP vendors to go up the supply chain and sell ERP solutions to distributors, raw materials extractors and processors, and the petroleum industry. At the same time, health care was becoming more complex, and hospitals were changing from a service to a profit orientation. As you learned in Chapter 7, hospital systems are incredibly complex, and they were ripe candidates for ERP sales and solutions. Over time, ERP use spread to companies and organizations in other industries, as shown in Figure CE12-6.

ERP by Organization Size

ERP, as stated, was initially adopted by large manufacturing organizations that had complex process problems that needed ERP solutions. Those large organizations also had the resources and skilled personnel needed to accomplish and manage an ERP implementation. Over time, ERP use spread downward from large companies with

- Manufacturing
- Distribution
- Mining, materials extraction, petroleum
- Medical care
- Government & public service
- Utilities
- Retail
- Education

Figure CE12-6
ERP Use by Industry

billions of dollars in sales to midsized companies with $100 million in sales. Today, ERP is used in small organizations with $5 million to $100 million in sales.

The value chains and basic business processes are similar for small and large organizations. To quote F. Scott Fitzgerald, "The rich are no different from you and me, they just have more money." The steps required to check credit, verify product availability, and approve terms are no different for order processing at Amazon.com than they are at Phil's muffler shop. They differ in scale, but not in character.

However, companies of different sizes have one very important difference that has a major impact on ERP: the availability of skilled IT personnel. Small organizations employ only one or two IT specialists who not only manage the ERP system, but the entire IS department as well (see Chapter 11 for a discussion of these responsibilities). They are spread very thin and often are in over their heads during an ERP implementation. Smaller, simpler ERP solutions are common among these companies, as discussed in Q5.

Midsized organizations expand IT from one person to a small staff, but frequently this staff is isolated from senior management. Such isolation creates misunderstanding and distrust. As stated in Q3, because of the expense, organizational disruption, and length of ERP projects, senior management must be committed to the ERP solution. When IT management is isolated, such commitment is difficult to obtain and may not be strong. This issue is so prevalent that many ERP consultants say the first step in moving toward ERP is to obtain deep senior-level management commitment to the project.

Large organizations have a full IT staff that is headed by the chief information officer (CIO), who is a business and IT professional who sits on the executive board and is an active participant in organizational strategic planning. ERP implementation will be part of that strategic process and, once begun, will have the full backing of the entire executive group. See *www.erpsoftware360.com/software-markets.htm* for more information about the role and use of ERP by size of business.

International ERP

Another way that the ERP needs of large organizations differ from those of small organizations is international presence. Most billion-dollar companies operate in multiple countries, and the ERP application programs must be available in several languages. Inherent ERP procedures must be adaptable to different cultures. Some companies can declare a single "company language" and force all company business to be transacted in that language (usually English). Other companies must accommodate multiple languages in their ERP solution. We discuss IS internationalization in Chapter Extension 21.

Once implemented, ERP brings huge benefits to multinational organizations. International ERP solutions are designed to support multiple currencies and languages, manage international transfers of goods in inventories, and work effectively with international supply chains. Even more important, ERP solutions provide a worldwide consolidation of financial statements on a timely basis. See *http://advice.cio.com/puneesh/deploy_erp_to_improve_globalization_efficiency_of_your_organization* for more details on the advantages of ERP to international organizations.

Q5 How Do the Major ERP Vendors Compare?

Although more than 100 different companies advertise ERP products, not all of those products meet the minimal ERP criteria listed in Q2. Even of those that do, the bulk of the market is held by the five vendors described in Figure CE12-7.

Company	ERP Market Rank	Remarks	Future
Epicor	5	Strong, industry-specific solutions, especially retail.	Epicor 9 designed for flexibility (SOA). Highly configurable ERP. Lower cost.
Microsoft Dynamics	4	Four products acquired AX, Nav, GP, and Solomon. AX and Nav more comprehensive. Solomon on the way out? Large VAR channel.	Products not well integrated with Office. Not integrated at all with Microsoft development languages. Product direction uncertain. Watch for Microsoft ERP announcement on the cloud (Azure).
Infor	3	Privately held corporation that has acquired an ERP product named Baan, along with more than 20 others.	Spans larger small companies to smaller large companies. Offers many solutions.
Oracle	2	Combination of in-house and acquired (PeopleSoft, Siebel) products.	Intensely competitive company with strong technology base. Large customer base. Flexible SOA architecture. Expensive. Oracle CEO Ellison owns 70% of NetSuite.
SAP	1	Led ERP success. Largest vendor, most comprehensive solution. Largest customers.	Technology older. Expensive and seriously challenged by less expensive alternatives. Huge customer base. Future growth uncertain.

Figure CE12-7
Characteristics of Top ERP Vendors

ERP Vendor Market Ranking

Figure CE12-7 presents the ERP vendors by market rank rather than by market share because it is difficult to obtain comparable revenue numbers. Infor is owned by private-equity investors and does not publish financial data. Microsoft's ERP revenue is combined with its CRM revenue, thus its true ERP revenue is unknown. Similarly, Oracle and SAP combine ERP revenue with revenue generated by other products.

The rankings were obtained as follows:

- Epicor, a publicly traded company, reported 2009 revenue of $410 million.
- Microsoft Dynamics revenue is reported to be in the range of $1.3 billion, but that revenue includes general ledger accounting system sales. Still, even though Dynamic's ERP-only revenue is uncertain, it is most likely greater than Epicor's $410 million.
- Industry estimates for Infor's revenue are in the range of $2 billion.
- Oracle's ERP revenue is known to be more than $2 billion, but, judging by the number of installations and the size of the company's customers, Oracle's ERP revenue is considerably less than SAP's.

In 2005,[1] AMR Research reported that SAP had 42 percent of the market, Oracle 20 percent, Microsoft 4 percent, Infor 2 percent, and Epicor 1 percent. However, Infor has substantially increased its market position since 2005, and its revenues have surpassed Microsoft's.

ERP Products

Figure CE12-8 shows how the ERP products from each of these companies relate to the size of their customers. Both Epicor and Microsoft Dynamics address the

1. Marianne Bradford, *Modern ERP* (Lulu.com, 2008), p. 11.

needs of small and midsized organizations. Infor has a product for almost everyone, as you'll see. Oracle and SAP serve the largest organizations. Specific product details follow.

Epicor

Epicor is known primarily for its retail-oriented ERP software, although it is broadening its penetration in other industry segments. Its lead ERP product, Epicor 9, is based on a modern software development design pattern called *service-oriented architecture (SOA)*. You can learn about this pattern in Chapter Extension 18. For now, understand that SOA enables cost-effective application flexibility and allows organizations to connect their application programs with Epicor 9 in highly customizable ways. Epicor's products are lower in cost than those from other companies.

Microsoft Dynamics

Microsoft offers five ERP products, all obtained via acquisition: AX (pronounced "A and X," not "axe"), Nav, GP, Solomon, and Dynamics CRM. AX and Nav have the most capabilities, GP is more limited and easier to use. The future of Solomon is cloudy; supposedly Microsoft outsources the maintenance of the code to provide continuing support to existing customers. To add to the confusion, although Dynamics CRM is primarily a CRM product, it is extensible in ways that enable customers to use it for ERP as well as CRM.

Microsoft is in the process of consolidating its offerings. Most likely AX will continue going forward as a true ERP product for larger organizations. Dynamics CRM will serve as both a CRM product as well as a platform for custom ERP solutions. Dynamics GP, which is the easiest of the products to install, will continue as a general-ledger program that can also be used as a platform for simpler ERP solutions.

Microsoft relies heavily on its network of independent software vendors to create customer solutions using the Dynamics platform. These vendors take off-the-shelf Dynamics products and adapt and customize them for particular situations. Further developments in the Dynamics product line are likely. Search www.microsoft.com for the keyword *dynamics* to learn more.

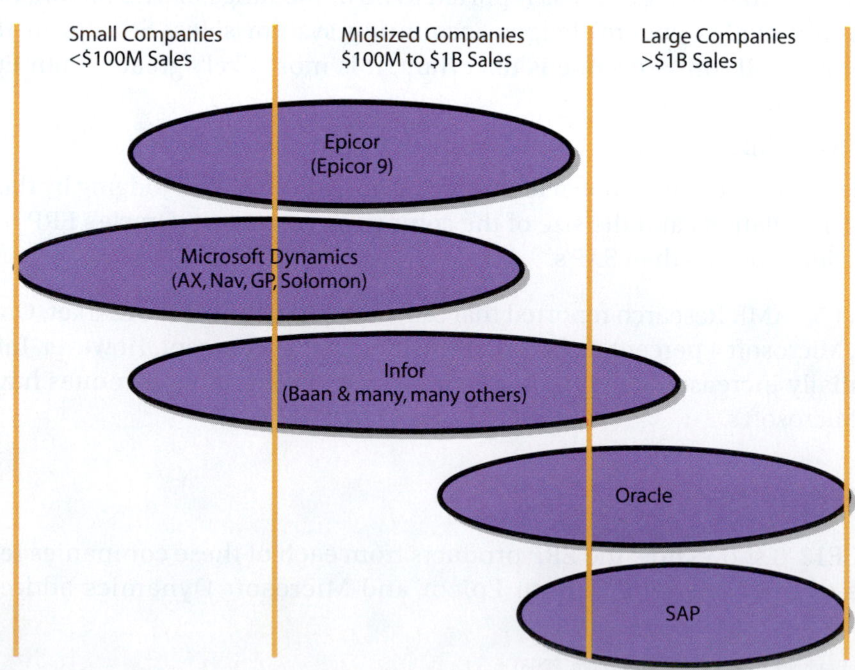

Figure CE12-8
Top ERP Vendors and Customer Size

Infor

Infor was purchased in 2002 by private-equity investors, primarily Golden Gate Partners. The company then went on an acquisition binge to consolidate multiple product offerings under one sales and marketing organization. It purchased Baan, a well-known and successful ERP company, along with more than 20 other companies. Today, Infor sells many ERP products for many different industries.

As you might imagine, the products vary in purpose, scope, and quality. They span the midrange, serving higher-end small companies and lower-end large companies. The Infor story is still being written; the company remains little known, despite its sizable revenue and expansive product portfolio.

Oracle

Oracle is an intensely competitive company with a deep base of technology and high-quality technical staff. Oracle developed some of its ERP products in-house, and complemented those products with the acquisition of PeopleSoft (high-quality HR products) and Siebel (high-quality CRM products).

Oracle's ERP products are designed according to SOA principles and hence are adaptable and customizable. Beginning with its first DMBS product release, Oracle has never been known to create easy-to-use products. It is known, however, for producing fully featured products with superior performance. They are also expensive.

Oracle CEO Larry Ellison owns 70 percent of NetSuite, a company that offers a cloud-based solution for integrated financial reporting for large, international organizations. It would not be unexpected for Oracle to acquire that company as the part of a future ERP product in the cloud.

SAP

SAP is the gold standard of ERP products. It led the direction of the ERP industry in the 1990s and the first decade of the twenty-first century. SAP sells to the largest companies and offers the most expensive of the ERP products.

Ironically, SAP's past success creates a problem today. SAP uses classic, thick-client, client-server architecture. Because of its installed base, SAP cannot make a rapid move to thin client, SOA, or cloud-based solutions. Instead, it must focus resources and attention on the needs of its current customers (and the attendant, large revenue stream from their maintenance contracts).

In 2003, SAP announced Netweaver, which is an SOA-based system that serves as the backbone for integrating existing SAP applications. Netweaver is believed to be the way in which SAP will gradually move its products and installed base toward a more flexible and modern product architecture. As of 2010, Netweaver has not achieved prominence in the SAP installed base.

The Future: ERP in the Cloud

As of 2010, there is no true ERP product in the cloud. Workday, started by the founder of PeopleSoft, offers hosted HR applications. Ellison's NetSuite offers accounting and financial systems for large, international organizations in the cloud. SAP's Netweaver also provides a hosted solution, and SAP may be able to gradually move its large installed base to it.

The ERP industry appears to be entering a new phase. Traditional vendors cannot ignore SOA, thin-client technologies, HTML 5, Enterprise 2.0, social CRM, ERP on mobile devices, and other recent developments. One possibility is that established companies like SAP and Oracle will maintain control of traditional ERP functionality, but that smaller vendors will create complementary products that incorporate newer technologies. The SOA architecture makes it easier for ERP customers to integrate their applications with ERP functionality, but it also makes it easier for vendors of specialty software to connect their programs with ERP programs and data.

Interesting times are ahead for the ERP industry as it determines what to do with all this new technology!

ACTIVE REVIEW

Use this Active Review to verify that you understand the material in the chapter extension. You can read the entire extension and then perform the tasks in this review, or you can read the material for just one question and perform the tasks in this review for that question before moving on to the next one.

Q1 What is the purpose of ERP systems?

Define *ERP* and *ERP system*. Identify the primary purpose of an ERP system. Summarize the problems that the bicycle manufacturer in Figure CE12-1 has. Explain how the ERP system in Figure CE12-2 overcomes those problems. Explain why "the devil is in the details." Describe the reasons that organizations find it next to impossible to create their own ERP solutions.

Q2 What are the elements of an ERP solution?

List the requirements that a system must meet to be considered a legitimate ERP solution. Name four components of an ERP solution. Explain how and why ERP applications are configurable. Describe the components of an ERP database design. Define *trigger* and *stored procedure*. How do such designs differ from the design of the typical Access database? Explain the importance of process blueprints. Interpret Figure CE12-4. Explain the term *train the trainer*, and summarize two categories of training. Explain the role of consultants in ERP implementations.

Q3 How are ERP systems implemented?

Summarize the process shown in Figure CE12-5. Explain why it is expensive and time consuming. Explain why it is necessary for the project to have the full support of senior management.

Q4 What types of organizations use ERP?

Describe the origins of ERP, and explain how those origins led to the initial ERP implementations in industry. Define *industry-specific solution*. Summarize the three categories of business size defined in this chapter extension. Explain how the fundamental ERP processes are the same for different sized organizations and how the IT departments differ. Describe the value of ERP systems for international organizations.

Q5 How do the major ERP vendors compare?

Name the five primary ERP vendors and rank them according to market size. Name and describe the primary product(s) of each of those five vendors. Explain how the vendors' products relate to customer size. Describe the status of ERP in the cloud, and summarize the author's concept of one possibility for the future of ERP.

KEY TERMS AND CONCEPTS

USING YOUR KNOWLEDGE

1. Using the patient discharge process in Figure 7-5 (page 161), explain how the hospital benefits from an ERP solution. Describe why integration of patient records in one system is better than spreading patient records across separated databases. Explain the value of an industry-specific ERP solution to the hospital.

2. Consider the problem at Fox Lake at the start of Chapter 7. A wedding was scheduled at the same time a large maintenance project was. Explain why this problem was caused by a lack of integration. In what ways would ERP help Fox Lake? If Fox Lake decided to implement ERP, which vendors are likely to have suitable products? Do you think you would recommend ERP to Fox Lake? Why or why not?

3. Google or Bing each of the five vendors in Figure CE12-7. In what ways have their product offerings changed since this text was written? Do those vendors have new products? Have they made important acquisitions? Have they been acquired? Have any new companies made important inroads into their market share? Update Figure CE12-7 with any important late-breaking news.

4. Read the explanation of SOA in Chapter Extension 18. In your own words, explain how a SOA-designed ERP system enables ERP customers to better integrate existing and new company applications into the vendor's ERP package. Explain how SOA creates an opportunity for smaller companies to develop and sell ERP-related applications.

5. Go to *www.microsoft.com* and search for "Microsoft Dynamics." Ignore Dynamics CRM. Have any important changes occurred in Microsoft's ERP product offerings since this text was written? Has Microsoft brought a cloud-based ERP solution to market? Have any of the four ERP systems described in the chapter extension been better integrated with Office or the Microsoft Developer's platform? Using your knowledge guided by experience, what do you think are Microsoft's intentions with regard to ERP?

STUDY QUESTIONS

CHAPTER EXTENSION 13

Q1 What are typical interorganizational processes?

Q2 What is a supply chain?

Q3 What factors affect supply chain performance?

Q4 How does supply chain profitability differ from organizational profitability?

Q5 What is the bullwhip effect?

Q6 How do information systems affect supply chain performance?

Chapter 8 provides the background for this Extension.

Supply Chain Management

Q1 What Are Typical Interorganizational Processes?

As stated in Chapter 8, an **interorganizational process** is one in which process activities occur in two or more independent organizations. Interorganizational process management is more difficult than for other types of processes, because cooperation is governed by negotiation and contract, and conflict resolution is done by negotiation, arbitration, and litigation.

Interorganizational processes vary in scope and complexity. An example of a simple interorganizational process is a sales process at a small retailer in which the retailer processes customers' credit card transactions. The retailer, customer, and credit card company (and possibly the bank that issued the card) are all part of the business process that processes the payment. Such a process is common, standardized, and relatively simple; few businesses give it much thought. Processing of checks using the **Automated Clearing House (ACH)** system among banks is another example of a standardized interorganizational process, though one that is more complicated than that for processing credit card transactions.

At the other end of the spectrum are customized interorganizational processes among large companies. Consider, for example, the interorganizational process that exists among Boeing, General Electric, and other companies for supplying engines to the 787 aircraft, whose production Boeing has largely outsourced. The complexity of the interactions among the supplying organizations, as well as the number of supplying organizations, meant that new, customized interorganizational processes had to be designed and agreed upon. Use of a service-oriented architecture and SOA standards is crucial.

This chapter extension considers a sample interorganizational process of supply chain management among distributors and retailers. We will consider supply chain management from a generic standpoint using examples that are much simpler than the Boeing/GE process. Understanding the principles in this chapter extension will serve as a good basis if you work in more complicated supply chain situations during your career.

Q2 What Is a Supply Chain?

A **supply chain** is a network of organizations and facilities that transforms raw materials into products delivered to customers. Figure CE13-1 shows a generic supply chain. Customers order from retailers, who, in turn, order from distributors, who, in turn,

Figure CE13-1
Supply Chain Relationships

order from manufacturers, who, in turn, order from suppliers. In addition to the organizations shown here, the supply chain also includes transportation companies, warehouses, and inventories and some means for transmitting messages and information among the organizations involved.

Because of disintermediation, not every supply chain has all of these organizations. Dell, for example, sells directly to the customer. Both the distributor and retailer organizations are omitted from its supply chain. In other supply chains, manufacturers sell directly to retailers and omit the distribution level.

The term *chain* is misleading. *Chain* implies that each organization is connected to just one company up (toward the supplier) and down (toward the customer) the chain. That is not the case. Instead, at each level, an organization can work with many organizations both up and down the supply chain. Thus, a supply chain and the processes that support it are networks.

To understand the operation of a supply chain, consider Figure CE13-2. Suppose you decide to take up cross-country skiing. You go to REI (either by visiting one of its stores or its Web site) and purchase skis, bindings, boots, and poles. To fill your order, REI removes those items from its inventory of goods. Those goods have been purchased, in turn, from distributors. According to Figure CE13-2, REI purchases the skis, bindings, and poles from one distributor and boots from a second. The distributors, in turn, purchase the required items from the manufacturers, which, in turn, buy raw materials from their suppliers.

The only source of revenue in a supply chain is the customer. In the REI example, you spend your money on the ski equipment. From that point all the way back up the

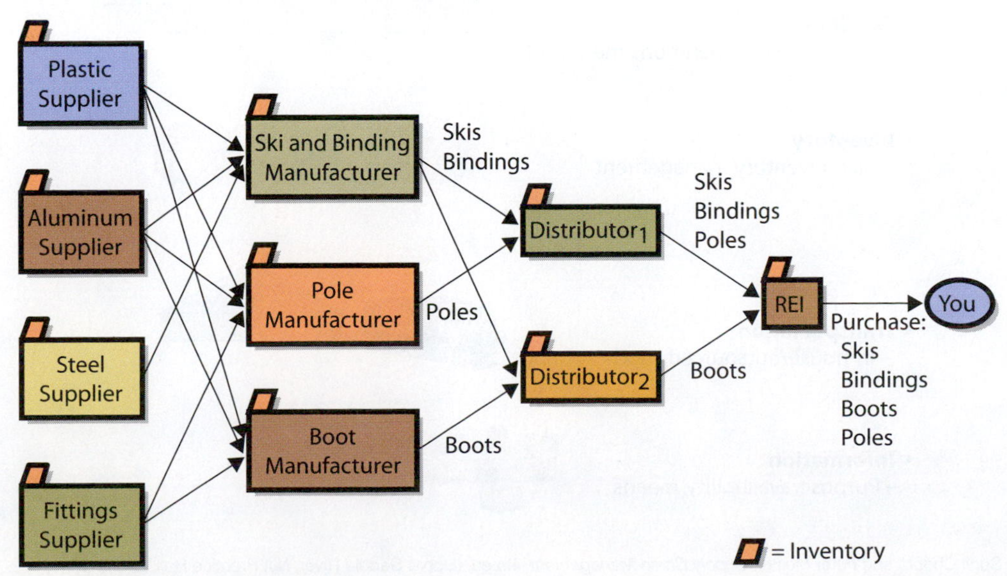

Figure CE13-2
Supply Chain Example

supply chain to the raw material suppliers, there is no further injection of cash. The money you spend on the ski equipment is passed back up the supply chain as payments for goods or raw materials. Again, the customer is the only source of revenue.

Q3 What Factors Affect Supply Chain Performance?

Four major factors, or *drivers*, affect supply chain performance: facilities, inventory, transportation, and information.[1] Figure CE13-3 lists these drivers of supply chain performance. We will summarize the first three factors in this text and focus our attention on the fourth factor, information. (You can learn in detail about the first three factors in operations management classes.)

As Figure CE13-3 indicates, *facilities* concern the location, size, and operations methodology of the places where products are fabricated, assembled, or stored. The optimal design of facilities is a complicated subject. For example, given all of REI's stores and its e-commerce site, where should it locate its warehouses? How large should they be? How should items be stored and retrieved from the inventories? If one considers facilities for the entire supply chain, these decisions become even more complicated.

Inventory includes all of the materials in the supply chain, including raw materials, in-process work, and finished goods. Each company in Figure CE13-2 maintains one or more inventories. When you and others purchase items from REI, its inventory is reduced, and at some point REI reorders from its distributors. The distributors, in turn, maintain their inventories, and at some point they reorder from the manufacturers, and so forth.

Managing an inventory requires balancing between availability and cost. Inventory managers can increase product availability by increasing inventory size. Doing so, however, increases the cost of the inventory and, thus, reduces the company's profitability. However, decreasing the size of the inventory increases the odds that an item will be unavailable for purchase. If that happens, the customer may order from a different source, which will reduce the company's revenue and profit. Inventory management is always a balance between availability and cost.

Figure CE13-3
Drivers of Supply Chain Performance

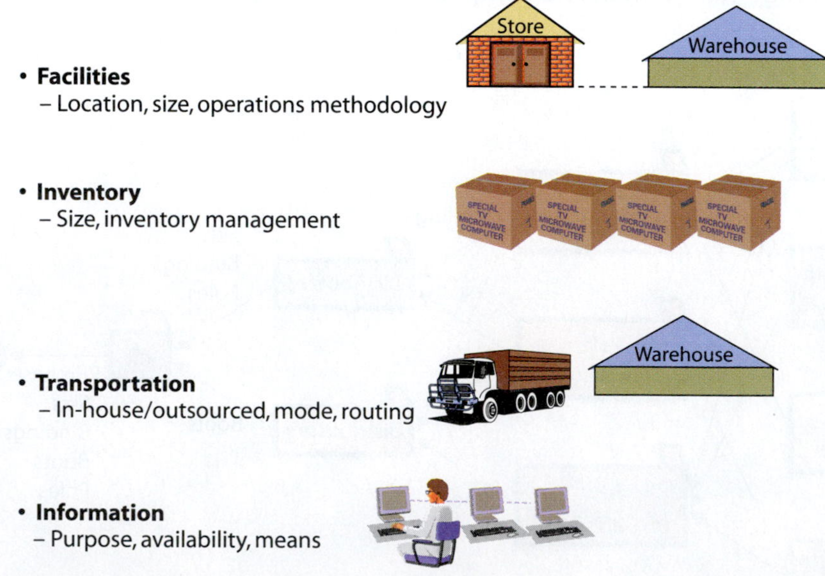

• Facilities
– Location, size, operations methodology
Store
Warehouse
• Inventory
– Size, inventory management
• Transportation
– In-house/outsourced, mode, routing
Warehouse
• Information
– Purpose, availability, means

1. Sunil Chopra and Peter Meindl, *Supply Chain Management*, 4th ed. (Upper Saddle River, NJ: Prentice Hall, 2004), pp. 41–43.

Inventory management decisions include not only the size of the inventory, but also the frequency with which items are reordered and the size of reorders. For example, assume that REI determines that it needs an inventory of 1,000 boots per month. It can order the full 1,000 at the start of the month or it can order 250 four times per month. Decisions like this and other inventory management decisions have a major impact on supply chain performance.

Transportation, the third driver in Figure CE13-3, concerns the movement of materials in the supply chain. Some organizations have their own transportation facilities; others use outsourced vendors such as Roadway, UPS, and FedEx; still others use a combination. The transportation mode (such as surface versus air) influences both speed and cost. Routing decisions affect how goods are moved from stage to stage throughout the supply chain.

The fourth driver, *information*, is the factor that most concerns us. Information influences supply chain performance by affecting the ways that organizations in the supply chain request, respond, and inform one another. Figure CE13-3 lists three factors of information: purpose, availability, and means. The *purpose* of the information can be transactional, such as orders and order returns, or it can be informational, such as the sharing of inventory and customer order data. *Availability* refers to the ways in which organizations share their information; that is, which organizations have access to which information and when. Finally, *means* refers to the methods by which the information is transmitted. Modern organizations use some version of the SOA standards for exchanging information.

We will expand on the role of information in the supply chain throughout this chapter extension. For now, however, we consider two of the ways that information can affect supply chain performance: supply chain profitability and the bullwhip effect.

Q4 How Does Supply Chain Profitability Differ from Organizational Profitability?

Each of the organizations in Figures CE13-1 and CE13-2 is an independent company, with its own goals and objectives. Each has a competitive strategy that may differ from the competitive strategies of the other organizations in the supply chain. Left alone, each organization will maximize its own profit, regardless of the consequences of its actions on the profitability of the others.

Supply chain profitability is the difference between the sum of the revenue generated by the supply chain and the sum of the costs that all organizations in the supply chain incur to obtain that revenue. In general, the maximum profit to the supply chain *will not* occur if each organization in the supply chain maximizes its own profits in isolation. Usually, the profitability of the supply chain increases if one or more of the organizations operates at less than its own maximum profitability.

To see why this is so, consider your purchase of the ski equipment from REI. Assume that you purchase either the complete package of skis, bindings, boots, and poles or you purchase nothing. If you cannot obtain boots, for example, the utility of skis, bindings, and poles is nil. In this situation, an outage of boots causes a loss of revenue not just for the boots, but also for the entire ski package.

According to Figure CE13-2, REI buys boots from distributor 2 and the rest of the package from distributor 1. If boots are unavailable, distributor 2 loses the revenue of selling boots, but does not suffer any of the revenue loss from the nonsale of skis, bindings, and poles. Thus, distributor 2 will carry an inventory of boots that is optimized considering only the loss of boot revenue—not considering the loss of revenue for the entire package. In this case, the profitability to the supply chain will increase if distributor 2 carries an inventory of boots that is larger than optimal for it.

In theory, the way to solve this problem is to use some form of transfer payment to induce distributor 2 to carry a larger boot inventory. For example, REI could pay distributor 2 a premium for the sale of boots in packages and recover a portion of this premium from distributor 1, who would recover a portion of it from the manufacturers, and so forth, up the supply chain. In truth, such a solution is difficult to implement. For higher-priced items or for items with very high volume, there can be an economic benefit for creating an information system to identify such a situation. If the dynamic is long-lasting, it will be worthwhile to negotiate the transfer-payment agreements. All of this requires a comprehensive supply-chain-wide information system, as you will see.

Q5 What Is the Bullwhip Effect?

The **bullwhip effect** is a phenomenon in which the variability in the size and timing of orders increases at each stage up the supply chain, from customer to supplier (in Figure CE13-2, from *You* all the way back to the suppliers). Figure CE13-4 summarizes the situation. In a famous study,[2] the bullwhip effect was observed in Procter & Gamble's supply chain for diapers.

The Ethics Guide on pages 486–487 discusses some of the ethical issues that occur in supply chain information sharing.

As you can imagine, except for random variation, diaper demand is constant. Diaper use is not seasonal; the requirement for diapers doesn't change with fashion or anything else. The number of babies determines diaper demand, and that number is constant or possibly slowly changing.

Retailers do not order from the distributor with the sale of every diaper package. The retailer waits until the diaper inventory falls below a certain level, called the *reorder quantity*. Then the retailer orders a supply of diapers, perhaps ordering a few more than it expects to sell to ensure that it does not have an outage.

The distributor receives the retailer's orders and follows the same process. It waits until its supply falls below the reorder quantity, and then it reorders from the

Figure CE13-4
The Bullwhip Effect

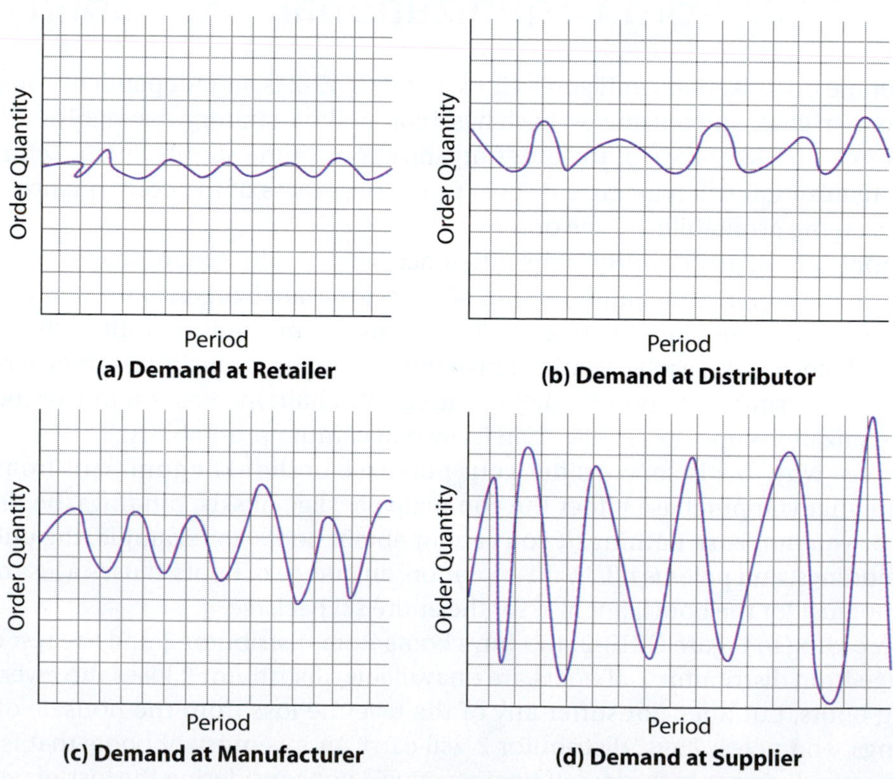

[2] Hau L. Lee, V. Padmanabhan, and S. Whang, "The Bullwhip Effect in Supply Chains," *Sloan Management Review*, Spring 1997, pp. 93–102.

manufacturer, with perhaps an increased amount to prevent outages. The manufacturer, in turn, uses a similar process with the raw-materials suppliers.

Because of the nature of this process, small changes in demand at the retailer are amplified at each stage of the supply chain. As shown in Figure CE13-4, those small changes become quite large variations on the supplier end.

The bullwhip effect is a natural dynamic that occurs because of the multistage nature of the supply chain. It is not related to erratic consumer demand, as the study of diapers indicated. You may have seen a similar effect while driving on the freeway. One car slows down, the car just behind it slows down a bit more abruptly, which causes the third car in line to slow down even more abruptly, and so forth, until the thirtieth car or so is slamming on its brakes.

The large fluctuations of the bullwhip effect force distributors, manufacturers, and suppliers to carry larger inventories than should be necessary to meet the real consumer demand. Thus, the bullwhip effect reduces the overall profitability of the supply chain.

One way to eliminate the bullwhip effect is to give all participants in the supply chain access to consumer-demand information from the retailer. Each organization can plan its inventory or manufacturing based on the true demand (the demand from the only party that introduces money into the system) and not on the observed demand from the next organization up the supply chain. Of course, an *interorganizational information system* is necessary to share such data.

Q6 How Do Information Systems Affect Supply Chain Performance?

Information systems have had an exceedingly positive impact on supply chain performance. CRM and less-integrated functional systems, such as e-commerce sales systems, have dramatically reduced the costs of buying and selling. Sourcing, buying, and selling have all become faster, easier, more effective, and less costly. The emergence of SOA and the SOA standards have enabled businesses to integrate their information systems with less cost and greater speed and agility then ever before.

The presence of information systems has expanded supply chain **speed**, which is the dollar value of goods exchanged in a given period of time. Without information systems, Amazon.com would not have been able to process an average of 41 items per second for 24 hours on December 14, 2005. And, without information systems, it would not have been able to deliver 99 percent of those items on time.

As shown in Figure CE13-5, a third factor is that information systems have enabled both suppliers and customers to reduce the size of their inventories and, thus, reduce their inventory costs. This reduction is possible because the speed and efficiency provided by information systems enables the processing of small orders, quickly.

Information systems also improve delivery scheduling. Using information systems, suppliers can deliver materials and components at the time and in the sequence needed. Such delivery enables just-in-time inventory, and it allows manufacturers to reduce raw materials inventory size as well as the handling of raw materials.

- Reduce costs of buying and selling.
- Increase supply chain speed.
- Reduce size and cost of inventories.
- Improve delivery scheduling—enable JIT.
- Fix bullwhip effect.
- Do not optimize supply chain profitability.

Figure CE13-5
Benefits of Information Systems on Supply Chain Performance

Ethics Guide

The Ethics of Supply Chain Information Sharing

Suppose that you work for a distributor that has developed information systems to read inventory data both up and down the supply chain. You can query the finished goods inventories of your manufacturers and the store inventories of your retailers. These systems were developed to increase supply chain efficiency and profitability. Consider the following situations:

Situation A: You notice that the store inventories of all retailers are running low on items in a particular product family. You know the retailers will soon send rush orders for some of those items, and, in anticipation, you accumulate an oversupply of those items. You query the manufacturers' inventory data, and you find that the manufacturers' finished goods inventories are low. Because you believe you have the only supply of those items, you increase their price by 15 percent. When the retailers ask why, you claim extra transportation costs. In fact, all of the increase is going straight to your bottom line.

Situation B: Unknown to you, one of your competitors has also accumulated a large inventory of those same items. Your competitor does not increase prices on those items, and consequently you sell none at your increased price. You decide you need to keep better track of your competitors' inventories in the future.

You have no direct way to read your competitors' inventories, but you can infer their inventories by watching the decrease of inventory levels on the manufacturer side and comparing that decrease to the sales on the retail side. You know what's been produced, and you know what's been sold. You also know how much resides in your inventory. The difference must be held in your competitor's inventories. Using that process, you now can estimate your competitors' inventories.

Situation C: Assume that the agreement that you have with the retailers is that you are able to query all of their current inventory levels but only the orders they have with you. You are not supposed to be able to query orders they have with your competitors. However, the information system contains a flaw, and by mistake you are able to query everyone's orders, your own as well as your competitors.

Situation D: Assume the same agreement with your retailers as in situation C. One of your developers, however, notices a hole in the retailer's security system and writes a program to exploit that hole. You now have access to all of the retailer's sales, inventory, and order data.

Discussion Questions

1. Is the price increase in situation A legal? Is it ethical? Is it smart? Why or why not? Is it ethical to claim transportation costs have caused the increase? What are some of the long-term consequences of this action?
2. In situation B, is it legal for you to query and analyze the data to estimate your competitor's inventory levels? Is it ethical? Would you recommend this kind of analysis?
3. Do you have a responsibility to reveal the hole in the information system in situation C? What are the consequences if you do not reveal this problem? Is it illegal or ethical for you to benefit from this mistake?
4. Do you have a responsibility to reveal the hole in the information system in situation D? What are the consequences if you do not reveal this problem? Is it illegal or ethical for you to benefit from this mistake? Is your response different between situations C and D? Why or why not?
5. In a supply chain, it is likely that other organizations can query your data as well as you querying theirs. What steps do you think you need to take to ensure that your own systems are not being misused and do not have errors or security holes?

Information systems have the capability to eliminate the bullwhip effect, though doing so requires retailers to be willing to share sales data with the entire supply chain. Such sharing entails some risk, and many retailers refuse to release such data. Part of the problem is that the benefit of releasing such data accrues to the supply chain and not to the retailer. Although there is some possibility that eliminating the bullwhip effect will reduce prices, many retailers view it only as a *potential* possibility. In their view, it is more likely that the savings will be kept by upstream companies.

This doubt brings us to the last factor in Figure CE13-5. Information systems do not optimize supply chain profitability. They benefit the companies that actively participate in a particular information system. However, as noted, maximizing individual company profitability does not necessarily maximize supply chain profitability. Perhaps some system of transfer payments will someday be worked out, but not during my career, and I doubt during yours either.

ACTIVE REVIEW

Use this Active Review to verify that you understand the material in the chapter extension. You can read the entire extension and then perform the tasks in this review, or you can read the material for just one question and perform the tasks in this review for that question before moving on to the next one.

Q1 What are typical interorganizational processes?

Define *interorganizational process,* and explain why process management is more difficult for such processes than for functional or cross-functional processes. Give examples, other than ones in this book, of simple, standardized interorganizational processes and of complex, customized interorganizational processes.

Q2 What is a supply chain?

Define *supply chain.* Explain how disintermediation affects supply chain structure. Explain why the term *chain* is misleading. Give an example of a supply chain different from the one in Figure CE13-2.

Q3 What factors affect supply chain performance?

Name the four factors that influence supply chain performance. Briefly explain each.

Q4 How does supply chain profitability differ from organizational profitability?

Explain the difference between supply chain profitability and organizational profitability. Give an example that demonstrates why maximizing organizational profitability does not necessarily lead to the maximization of supply chain profitability. Explain how, in theory, these two can be made the same.

Q5 What is the bullwhip effect?

Define the *bullwhip effect,* and explain how it occurs. Describe why the bullwhip effect is undesirable. Explain how information systems can eliminate this effect.

Q6 How do information systems affect supply chain performance?

List the ways in which information systems affect supply chain performance. Define *speed* as it pertains to supply chains. Explain why information systems cannot, today, maximize supply chain profit.

KEY TERMS AND CONCEPTS

Automated Clearing House (ACH) 480
Bullwhip effect 484
Interorganizational process 480
Speed 485
Supply chain 480
Supply chain profitability 483

USING YOUR KNOWLEDGE

1. Create a process diagram for the interorganizational process that exists to process debit card payments at a grocery store. Create separate swim lanes for the customer, the store, and the customer's bank. Make necessary assumptions and state them. Include sufficient detail so that your process includes the processing of a PIN.

2. So far we have ignored the restaurant at Fox Lake. However, it is supposed to be a profit center, even though it has not been profitable in the past year. With restaurant traffic down, wastage of ingredients has been a problem, but the restaurant must keep high-quality ingredients on hand for the customers it does have.
   a. Describe, in words, the process involved in ordering ingredients. In your answer, explain why this is an interorganizational process.
   b. Diagram, to the level of detail shown in Figure CE13-1, the enterprises involved in providing dairy products to the restaurant.
   c. Describe the role that information plays in the ingredient supply chain in your answer in part b.
   d. How does the bullwhip effect pertain to the supply chain in your answer to part b?
   e. Describe three ways in which a supplier to the restaurant could use information systems to obtain a competitive advantage over other suppliers.

3. Consider the supply chain for Amazon.com. Assume that Amazon.com buys books directly from publishers and also buys from book distributors. Ignore used book sales.
   a. Diagram this supply chain. Use Figure CE13-2 as an example. Because shippers are so important to Amazon.com, include them in your diagram.
   b. Explain how the four factors described in Q3 affect this supply chain's performance. Describe how these factors affect Amazon.com's profitability.
   c. Do you think the bullwhip effect is a problem for this supply chain? Why or why not?
   d. Explain how Amazon.com could use interorganizational information systems to obtain time and cost savings for Amazon.com.

CHAPTER EXTENSION 14

STUDY QUESTIONS

Chapter 8 provides the background for this Extension.

Q1 How do organizations use information systems to increase the value of their social capital?

Q2 How can organizations use Facebook?

Q3 How can organizations use Twitter?

Q4 What are business applications for User-Generated Content?

Q5 What are the risks of using social networking and UGC?

Processing Social Capital: Facebook, Twitter, and User-Generated Content (UGC)

Q1 How Do Organizations Use Information Systems to Increase the Value of Their Social Capital?

According to Chapter 8, the value of social capital is a function of the number of relationships, the strength of those relationships, and the assets controlled by those to whom the organization is connected. Organizations have been using advertising, public relations, events, contests, and the like to increase these factors for years. What's different today is their use of social networking information systems.

Using Social Networking (SN) to Increase the Number of Relationships

The term **social networking (SN)** refers to any activity that an entity (individual, project, or organization) takes with entities with which it is related. As shown in Figure CE14-1, in a traditional business relationship you (the client) have some experience with a business, such as the restaurant at Fox Lake. Traditionally, you may express your opinions about that experience by word-of-mouth to your social network (here denoted by friends F1, F2, etc.). However, such communication is unreliable and brief: You are more likely to say something to your friends if the experience was particularly good or bad; but, even then, you are likely only to say something to those friends whom you encounter while the experience is still recent. And once you have said something, that's it; your words don't live on for days or weeks.

A **social networking information system** is an information system that facilitates interactions on a social network. Social networking information systems have numerous characteristics, one of which is that they make the transmission of your opinions more reliable and longer lasting. For example, suppose the Fox Lake restaurant establishes a presence on a social network, maybe it has a page on Facebook. The nature of the presence is unimportant here.

When you mention the Fox Lake restaurant on your social network, something about that business will be broadcast to your friends, as shown in Figure CE14-2. That messaging is automatic; "I just had the Sunday night lobster dinner at Fox Lake, Yummm!" will be

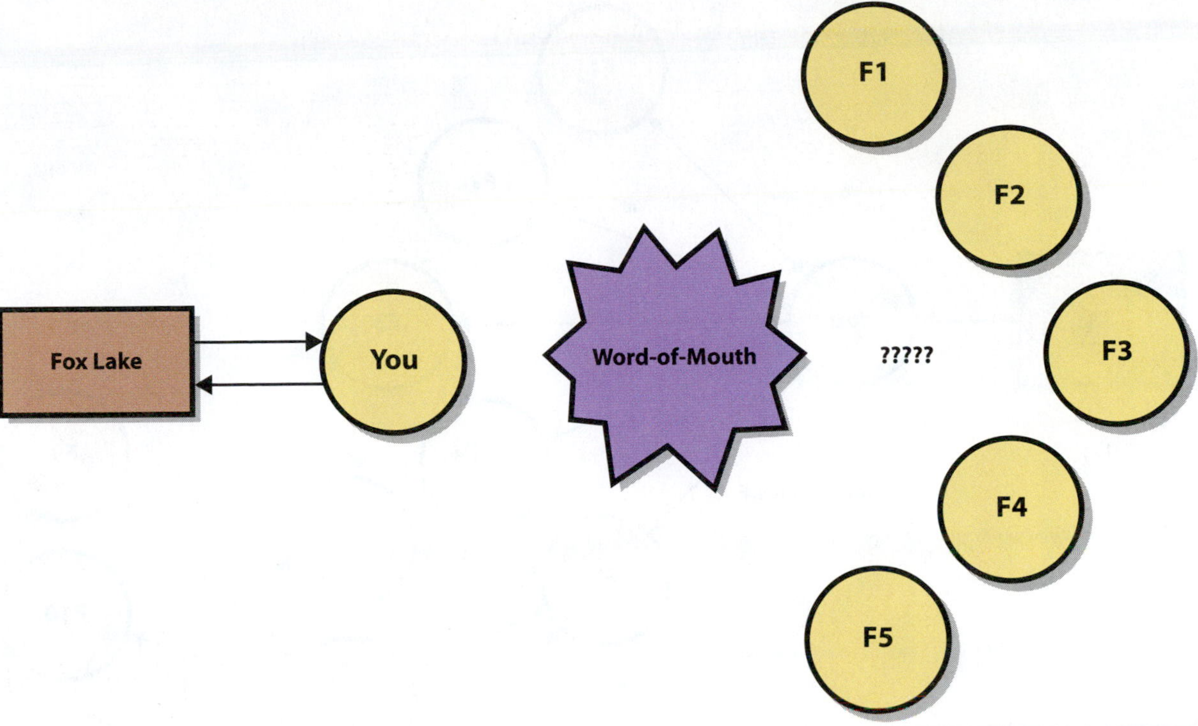

Figure CE14-1
Word-of-Mouth Marketing

reliably broadcast to all of your friends, and, unlike word-of-mouth, that message will last for hours, even days. That, in itself, is a powerful marketing program.

However, SN provides even greater possibilities. As shown in Figure CE14-3, you have friends (OK, you have more than five friends, but space is limited), and your friends have friends, and those friends have friends. If something about your message, induces F5 (for example) to broadcast about Fox Lake to her friends, and if that message induces F7 to broadcast about Fox Lake to his friends, and so forth, the messaging will be viral. The something that induces people to share your message is called a **viral hook**.

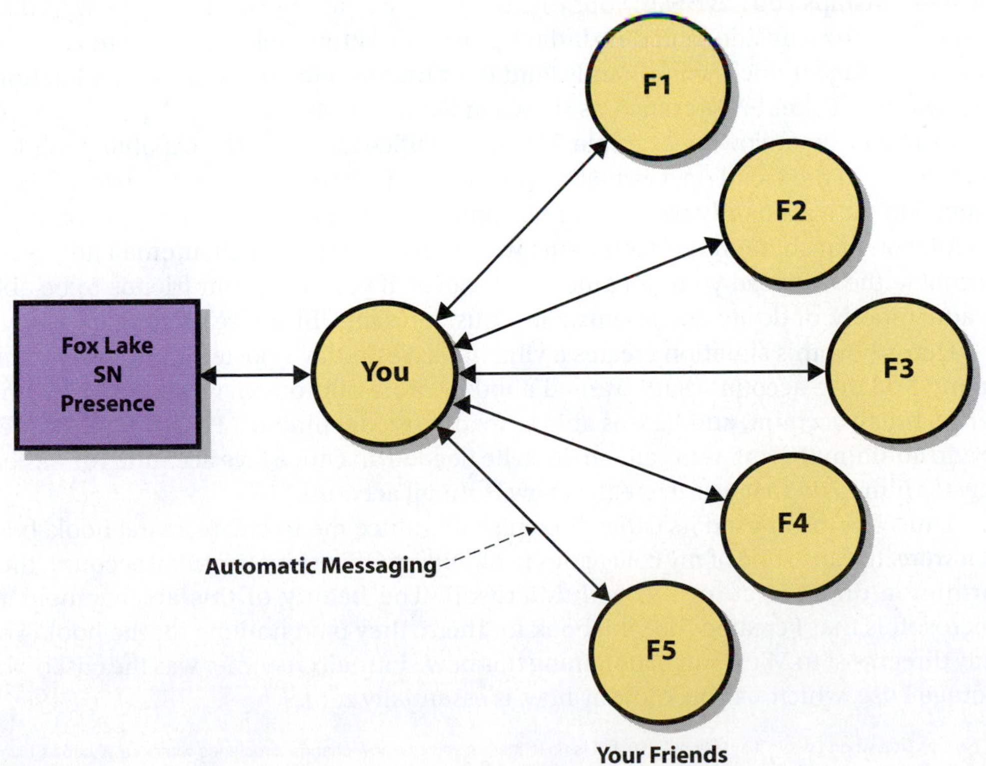

Figure CE14-2
Social Network Marketing at Fox Lake

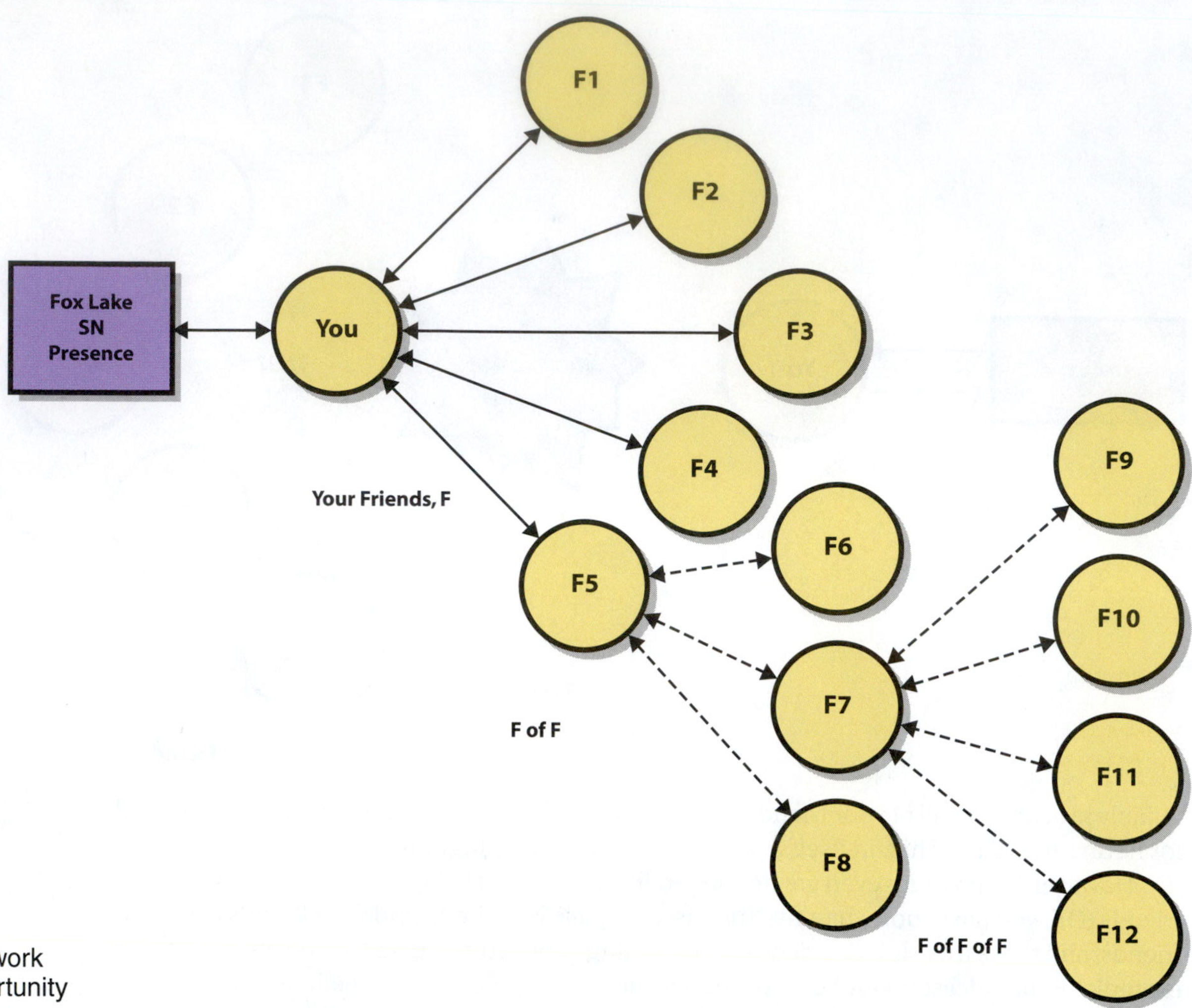

Figure CE14-3
Viral Social Network Marketing Opportunity

As shown in Figure CE14-3, some of the social capital you contribute to Fox Lake is the relationships you have with your friends, and the relationships they have with their friends. But those relationships are indirect. Viral marketing will be even more powerful if your message induces your friends (and their friends, etc.) to form a direct relationship with Fox Lake's SN presence, as shown in Figure CE14-4.

Consider the following example. Microsoft Office 2010 has the capability to store documents in the cloud on a virtual server called Windows Live SkyDrive (see Chapter Extension 2). It's a handy way to store backup copies of documents, but, even more useful, you can share those documents with friends. You enter their email addresses to enable them to read your documents. However, if you want your friends to be able to add, modify, or delete documents, they must have an Office Live account.

Here's how this situation creates a viral hook: Yesterday I posted some documents on my SkyDrive account that I wanted another professor to review. I entered his university email account, and he was able to read those documents. However, he wanted to add additional documents and to do so he needed an Office Live account; the easiest way for him to do that was to create a new Hotmail account.

Thus, Microsoft used its Office franchise to induce me to create a viral hook, bait, as it were, to cause one of my colleagues to obtain an Office Live/Hotmail account, thus forming a direct relationship with Microsoft. The beauty of this arrangement to Microsoft is that I created the viral hook for them; they paid nothing for the hook. The only direct cost to Microsoft of obtaining this new Hotmail customer was the cost of the storage I use, which, as you know by now, is essentially zero.[1]

1. This was true when I wrote it in May of 2010, but is no longer as you can now change directories without a Windows Live account. This is just another example of how quickly technology changes.

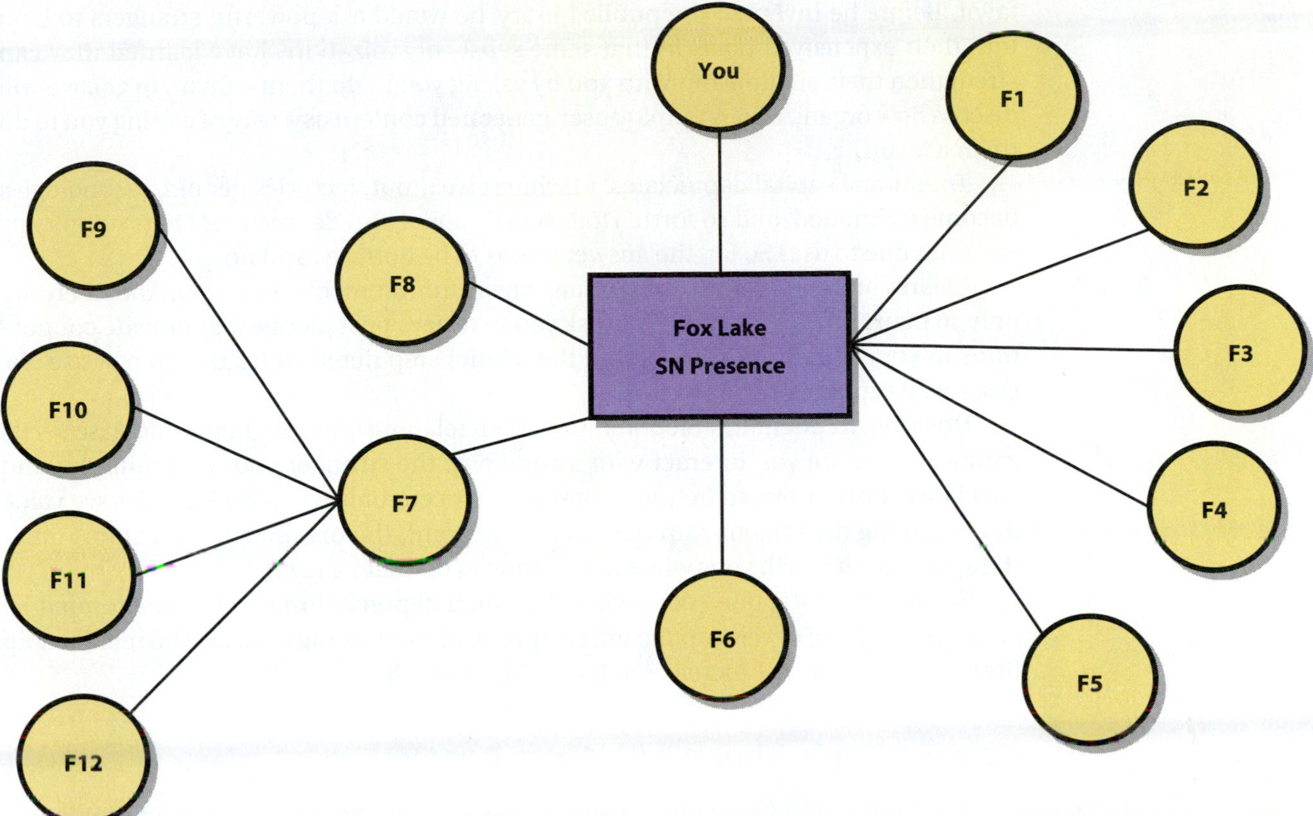

Figure CE14-4
Viral Message Causes Your Friends (and Theirs) to Connect with Fox Lake

Fox Lake has a waiting list for new memberships, so it is unlikely to use social networking to induce people to become members. However, brides need not be club members to have their weddings at Fox Lake, so Fox Lake would be interested in inducing one Fox Lake bride to convince a friend to have her wedding at Fox Lake as well. You'll learn how they can do that using groups and applications in Q2.

Increasing the Strength of Relationships

To an organization, the **strength of a relationship** is the likelihood that the entity (person or other organization) in the relationship will do something that benefits the organization. An organization has a strong relationship with you if you buy its products, write positive reviews about it, post pictures of your use of the organization's products or services, and so on.

RFM analysis (see Chapter Extension 15) measures how recently, how frequently, and how much money a customer spends with an organization. It is a standard measure of the strength of the purchasing relationship a company has with its customers. But, as you learned in the discussion of social CRM in Chapter 8, customers provide value to an organization not only by the amount of money they spend, but also by their relationship in a social network.

As stated in Chapter 8, social networks provide four forms of value: influence, information, social credentials, and reinforcement. If an organization can induce those in its relationships to provide more of any of those factors, it has strengthened that relationship.

In his autobiography, Benjamin Franklin[2] provided a key insight. He said that if you want to strengthen your relationship with someone in power, ask them to do you a

[2] Founding father of the United States. Author of *Poor Richard's Almanac*. Successful businessman; owner of a chain of print shops. Discoverer of ground-breaking principles in the theory of electricity. Inventor of bifocals, the potbelly stove, the lightning rod, and much more; founder of the public library and the postal service. Darling of the French court and salons, and, now, contributor to social network theory!

favor. Before he invented the public library, he would ask powerful strangers to lend him their expensive books. In that same sense, organizations have learned they can strengthen their relationship with you by asking you to do them a favor. In Q5, we will discuss how organizations employ user-generated content as a way of getting you to do them a favor.

Traditional capital depreciates. Machines wear out, factories get old, technologies become outmoded, and so forth. Does social capital also depreciate? Do relationships wear out due to use? So far, the answer seems to be both yes and no.

Clearly, one can only ask for so many favors from someone in power. And, there are only so many times a company can ask you to review, post pictures, or provide connections to your friends. At some point, the relationship deteriorates due to overuse. So, yes, social capital does depreciate.

However, frequent interactions strengthen relationships and hence increase social capital. The more you interact with a company, the stronger your commitment and allegiance. But continued frequent interactions occur only when both parties see value in continuing the relationship. Thus, at some point, the organization must do something to make it worth your while to continue to do them a favor.

So, social capital does depreciate, but such depreciation can be ameliorated by adding something of value to the interaction. And, continuing a successful relationship over time substantially increases relationship strength.

Connecting to Those with More Assets

The third measure of the value of social capital is the size of the assets controlled by those in the relationships. An organization's social capital is thus partly a function of the social capital of those to whom it relates. The most visible measure is number of relationships. Someone with 1,000 loyal Twitter followers is usually more valuable than someone with 10. But the calculation is more subtle than that; if those 1,000 followers are college students, and if the organization's product is adult diapers, the value of relationships to the followers is low. A relationship with 10 Twitter followers who are in retirement homes would be more valuable.

There is no formula for computing social capital, but the three factors would seem to be more multiplicative than additive. Or, stated in other terms, the value of social capital is more in the form of:

$$\text{SocialCapital} = \text{NumberRelationship} \times \text{RelationshipStrength} \times \text{EntityResources}$$

Than it is:

$$\text{SocialCapital} = \text{NumberRelationship} + \text{RelationshipStrength} + \text{EntityResources}$$

Again, do not take these equations literally; take them in the sense of the interaction of the three factors.

The multiplicative nature of social capital means that a huge network of relationships to people who have few resources may be lower than that of a smaller network with people with substantial resources. Furthermore, those resources must be relevant to the organization. Students with pocket change are relevant to Pizza Hut; they are irrelevant to a BMW dealership.

This discussion brings us to the brink of social networking practice. Most organizations today (2010) ignore the value of entity assets and simply try to connect to more people with stronger relationships. This area is ripe for innovation. Companies such as ChoicePoint and Acxiom maintain detailed data about people, worldwide. It would seem that such data could be used by information systems to calculate the potential value of a relationship to a particular individual. This possibility would enable organizations to better understand the value of their social networks as well as guide their behavior with regard to particular individuals.

Stay tuned; many possibilities exist and some will be very successful. But for the remainder of this extension, we'll confine ourselves to the ways that organizations use Facebook, Twitter, and User-Generated Content.

Q2 How Can Organizations Use Facebook?

The easiest way for an organization to use Facebook is to create a page and manage that page for business purposes using the same techniques that you use to manage your page. Organizations can build the number of relationships by inducing Facebook members to "Like" them, as discussed in Chapter 7. Here, we will consider how organizations use groups and applications.

Using Facebook Groups

A **social networking group** is an association of SN members related to a particular topic, event, activity, or other collective interest. In addition to members, SN groups have resources such as photos, videos, documents, discussion threads, a wallboard, and features. In some cases, groups have one or more events.

Three types of groups are possible:

- **Public**. Anyone can find the group by searching and anyone can join it.
- **Invitation**. Anyone can find the group by searching, but he or she must be invited to join.
- **Private**. The group cannot be found by searching, and members must be invited to join.

Businesses can use groups to strengthen relationships among customers and to create the possibility of a viral hook. For example, Fox Lake could create an invitation group for each wedding to use as its wedding Web site. Like all such sites, the bride invites everyone on the guest list to join the group. Prior to the wedding, members place photos and videos of their relationship and engagement on the group site; the site could also feature links to gift registries, directions to Fox Lake, weather forecasts, and any other information of interest to the wedding attendees. It also could start a discussion list about the bride and groom.

If Fox Lake can convince wedding parties to use its groups, it can form relationships with the wedding invitees, as shown for the two weddings in Figure CE14-5.

Additionally, at some point, Fox Lake may ask brides if it can create a public version of the wedding as part of its club news site. Club members who see wedding pictures of members' families will be more likely to consider Fox Lake for themselves or their friends.

Notice that SN groups can be used for more than marketing. To help plan weddings, Anne might create a private group for just the wedding party. That group could have information about the rehearsal, rehearsal dinner, logistics, other planning, and so forth. Brides might be more willing to share the email addresses of these people with Fox Lake than they would be willing to share email addresses of all invitees. Of course, once the wedding is over, Fox Lake has the email addresses of the wedding party, and we're back to . . . marketing!

Using Facebook Applications

A **social networking application** is a computer program that interacts with and processes information in a social network. For example, consider Survey Hurricane, a Facebook application created by Infinistorm (*www.infinistorm.com*). Users who install the Survey Hurricane application on their page can survey their friends on topics of

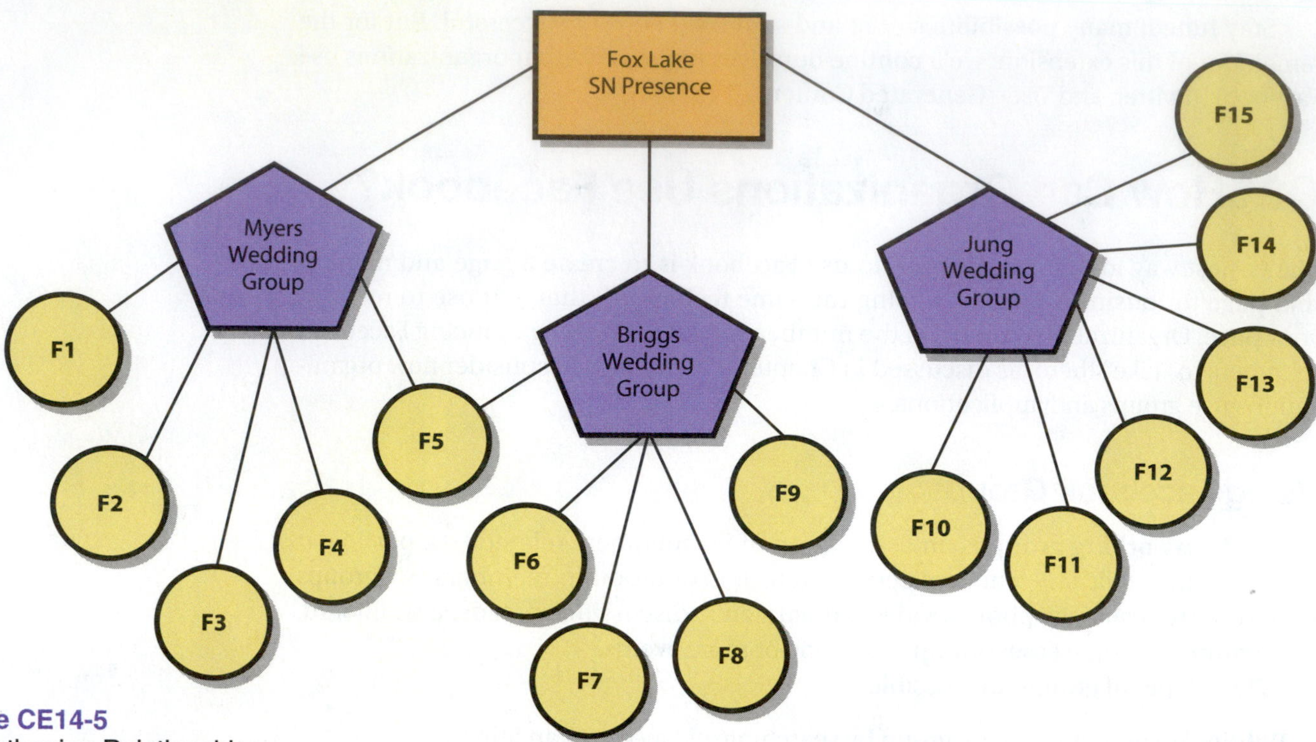

Figure CE14-5
Strengthening Relationships with Wedding Groups

interest. The *New York Times* quiz is another application, as are applications for buying and selling items, comparing movies, and so on.

SN applications run on servers provided by the application creator. When someone accesses the application on the SN vendor's site (e.g., Facebook or MySpace), the request for that service is passed to the application provider's server. That application can call back to the SN vendor to create friend requests, find your existing friends, generate email, make requests, poke your friends, or take other actions. In the process, it can collect data about you and your friends for individualized marketing or for data mining (see Chapter 9).

Organizations can use social networking applications to increase their competitive advantage as well as to increase the value of their social networks. For example, Fox Lake could create an application called "Plan Your Fox Lake Wedding" and make it part of its product offerings. If the application has features that greatly simplify and facilitate wedding planning and includes ideas, dos and don'ts, recommended vendors, and other resources of interest to wedding planners, it would be one more reason for brides to choose Fox Lake. Figure CE14-6 shows this application supporting three different weddings. Friend 5 is an attendant at two weddings. By creating this application, Fox Lake will obtain at least the name and email address and possibly the geographic address of all attendants. Using this data, Fox Lake can begin to build stronger relationships with each person.

Applications give the application vendor more control over the users' experience than groups do. An application can be developed to require passwords and user accounts. Fox Lake would need to implement user accounts to be able to ensure that only members of the wedding party can access the planning application. That application would probably also have rules and restrictions about who could add, edit, or delete content.

The key to success is, of course, to make the application compelling. Facebook publishes considerable documentation and advice to its developers, including advice on application design. Facebook's four principles for a meaningful application are as follows:

- **Social**. *Meaningful applications use information in the social graph.* A **social graph** is a network of relationships; Figure CE14-6 shows a portion of the social graph among three different wedding parties. A survey application uses information from

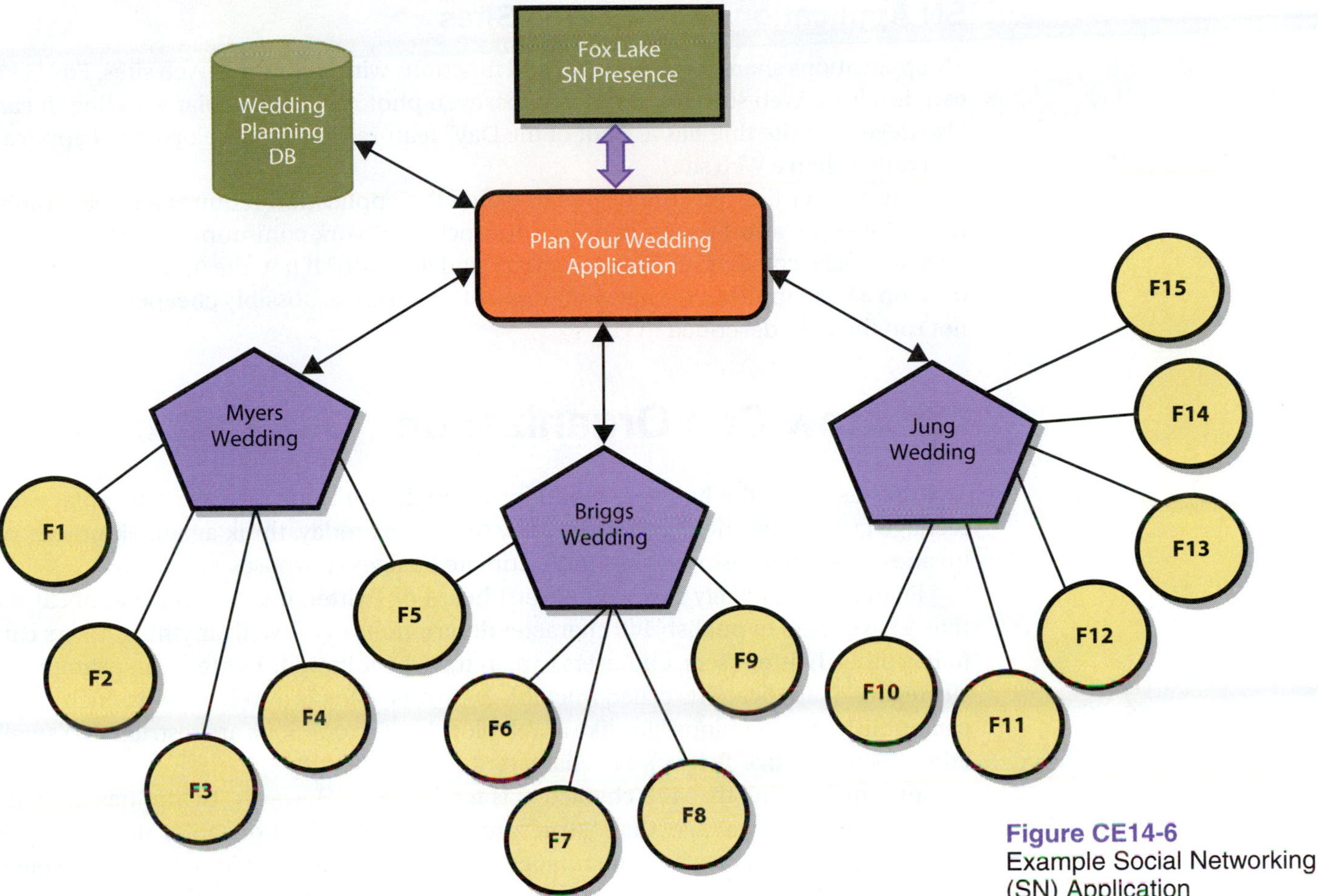

Figure CE14-6
Example Social Networking (SN) Application

the social graph because it uses the links to your friends to ask the survey questions. If "Plan Your Wedding" asks friends to label photos of the groom in amusing situations, it is using the social graph in a compelling way. Both you and your friends will find it far more meaningful than an application that just shows wedding pictures.

- **Useful**. *Meaningful applications address real needs, from entertainment to practical tasks.* In a business setting, no one cares what you had for breakfast or where you put your toothbrush this morning. They might, however, be interested in what cities you'll be visiting on your next business trip. Similarly, "Plan Your Wedding" could have features to enable the wedding party to plan ride sharing.
- **Expressive**. *Meaningful applications share a personal perspective on the world.* People participate in SN activities because they want to share something about themselves. An SN application that publishes generic photos, or even personal photos in a generic way, does not allow the user to express his or her individuality. Instead, Fox Lake would make "Plan You Wedding" more expressive if it allowed members of the wedding party to describe how they first met the bride or groom, or what they thought when they heard about the wedding, or any other expressive perspective. Such personal reflections induce clients to author more comments and their friends to read them more frequently.
- **Engaging**. *Meaningful applications compel users to come back again, and again, and again.* Engaging applications are dynamic; they give participants a reason to come back. A dynamic application slowly reveals more of its contents, changes its contents, or alters the actions that participants can take. This principle is less appropriate to weddings because weddings are a one-time event. Fox Lake, however, might have a golfing application that includes a feature like "Shot of the Day," "Duffer of the Day," or something similar.

SN Applications Versus Web Sites

SN applications share many features and functions with traditional Web sites. Fox Lake can develop a Web site with many photos, even photos of a particular wedding. It can also develop a site that has a "Shot of the Day" feature. So why develop an SN application rather than a Web site?

The answer lies with the degree to which the application requires a social graph. Does the application use or benefit from social network communication? Is there a need for social collaboration? For feedback and iteration? If not, the organization could develop a Web application that would be just as effective, possibly cheaper, and would not run the risks described in Q5.

Q3 How Can Organizations Use Twitter?

Twitter has taken the business world by storm. If you think of Twitter as a place for teenage girls to describe the lipstick they're wearing today, think again. Hundreds of businesses are now using Twitter for legitimate business purposes.

First, in the unlikely case you haven't heard of Twitter, it is a Web 2.0 application that allows users to publish 140 character descriptions of . . . well, anything. Users can follow other Twitter users, and users can, in turn, be followed. Twitter is an example of a category of applications called *microblogs.* A **microblog** is a Web site on which users can publish their opinions, just like a Web blog, but the opinions are restricted to small amounts of text, like Twitter's 140 characters.

You might think that 140 characters is too limiting. However, Twitter has demonstrated the design adage that "structure is liberating." Thousands more people microblog than blog because microblogging is less intimidating. You don't have space to write a well-constructed paragraph; in fact, the character limitation forces you to abbreviate words and grammar. It isn't necessary to spell correctly or to know that sentences need a subject and a verb, either. Microbloggers just have to be (barely) comprehensible to their audience. And, it is easy to fit a headline and a link to a Web site that provides more information.

Microblog competitors to Twitter are emerging, and it is possible that by the time you read this Twitter will be old news. If so, as you read, replace Twitter with the name of whatever microblog application is currently the rage.

We Are All Publishers Now

Microblogs like Twitter make everyone a publisher. Anyone can join, for free, and immediately publish his or her ideas, worldwide. If you happen to be the world's expert on making pine-bark tea, and if you have developed innovative techniques for harvesting pine bark, you have a free, worldwide platform for publishing those techniques.

Before we continue, think about that statement. As recently as 10 years ago, worldwide publishing was expensive and restricted to the very few. The *New York Times,* the *Wall Street Journal,* and a few other newspapers and large television networks were the only worldwide publishing venues in the United States. Publishing was a one-way street. They published and we consumed.

Microblogging enables two-way publishing, worldwide. You publish your ideas on pine-bark harvesting and others can publish you back. Notice that, unlike email, you are both *publishing,* not just communicating to each other. Your interchange, your conversation, is available for others to read, worldwide.

By the way, microblogging would be far less important if it lacked search features. Unfortunately for you, only four other people, worldwide, care about pine-bark harvesting. Were it not for the ability to search microblogs, they and you would never find one another. So, microblogging is important not just because it turns us all into publishers—by itself, that would not be very useful. Equally important is that microblogging enables users with similar interests to find each other.

How Can Businesses Benefit from Microblogging?

As of June 2010, businesses are actively experimenting with microblogging. Three obvious applications have emerged so far:

- Public relations
- Relationship sales
- Market research

We'll examine each of these, in turn, but stay tuned! Newer innovative applications are in the works.

Public Relations

Microblogging enables any employee or business owner to communicate with the world. No longer is it necessary to meet with editors and writers at newspapers and magazines and attempt to influence them to publish something positive about your product or other news. Instead, write it yourself and click Update. The only requirements are having something to say that your customers want to read and using keywords on which your customers are likely to search.

Possible examples are a product manager who's excited about a new use for his product. He can publish the idea and a summary of instructions. If the concept is longer than 140 words, he can include a link to a blog or Web site that has the rest of the description. Or, a customer service representative can publish warnings about possible misuse of a product or provide instructions for a new way of performing product maintenance, again with a link to a Web site, if necessary.

Pete Carroll, former coach of the University of Southern California football team, introduced microblogging by college football coaches. Coaches can increase fan awareness by blogging with insider details, how the practice went, comments about the recent game, and so forth. Coaches no longer have to depend on sportswriters and sportscasters for team public relations. Furthermore, microblogging means that coaches can control the content that is published.

By the way, these new public relations capabilities are stressing existing institutions. The NCAA has many rules and regulations about how and when coaches can contact potential recruits. How does a coach's microblogging fit into this scheme? The NCAA and others are scrambling to figure it out.

Relationship Sales

Social networking in general and microblogging in particular are all about relationships—forming new relationships and strengthening existing ones. Such relationships can serve as an ideal channel for sales. For example, suppose you are the owner of a plant nursery and you've just received a shipment of 100 hard-to-get plants. If you've formed Twitter relationships with your customers, you can Tweet the arrival of the plants and include a link to a Web site with pictures of how gorgeous these plants can be.

However, experience has shown that pure sales pitches are ineffective when microblogging. People stop following sources that only publish ads and sales pitches. Instead, people look for Tweeters who offer something they value, such as advice, links to resources, and interesting and thought-provoking opinions. So you, as the plant nursery owner, should offer advice and assistance, such as reminders that it's time to prune the roses or fertilize the azaleas.

From time to time, you can publish an ad, but, even then, it should be written to resemble communication to a friend. Hard come ons won't work; instead, make the pitch in terms of "I thought you might want to know about the arrival of the. . . . " just as you would pass advice on to a friend. You can find many other sales ideas in books such as *Twitter Revolution: How Social Media and Mobile Marketing Is Changing the Way We Do Business and Market Online.*[2]

Market Research

Market research is the third promising business use of microblogging. Want to know what people think of your product? Search Twitter to find out. Office 2010 is an interesting example. Office 2010 was released to a limited set of expert users as a beta in the fall of 2008 and to a larger group of experienced users as a release candidate in the spring of 2009. Users of both these releases used Twitter to comment about their experiences as well as to ask for help or provide assistance to each other. Meanwhile, Microsoft product managers were searching the Twitter traffic to learn the buzz about the new product. They used knowledge of what users especially liked to craft the launch of the actual product in 2010. Product developers and technical writers also learned about features that were hard to understand and use.

Of course, such research is only useful if the product has a large following of users who employ Twitter to make comments. As of May 2010, a Twitter search for *Experiencing MIS* (the title of this book) revealed no Tweets. Maybe you can change that?

Q4 What Are Business Applications for User-Generated Content?

Users have been generating content on the Internet since its beginning. However, with Web 2.0, many companies have found (and are finding) innovative ways of using user-generated content (UGC) for business functions. This section surveys common types of UGC and discusses their business applications.

Types of UGC

Figure CE14-7 lists the common types of UGC. You are undoubtedly familiar with most, if not all, of these. Product ratings and surveys have been used for years. Product opinions are also common. Recent research indicates that ratings and opinions of fellow customers are far more trusted than any advertising. In March 2007, Jupiter Research found that social network users were three times more likely to trust their peers' opinions over advertising when making purchase decisions.[3]

Some companies find it advantageous to facilitate customers' storytelling about the use of the company's products. According to Bazaarvoice (*www.bazaarvoice.com*), "Giving visitors a place to share their stories will increase brand involvement, interaction, intimacy and influence. Far beyond just increasing time on site, personal

Figure CE14-7
Types of User-Generated Content

- **Ratings and surveys**
- **Opinions**
- **Customer stories**
- **Discussion groups**
- **Wikis**
- **Blogs**
- **Video**

2. Warren Whitlock and Deborah Micek, *Twitter Revolution: How Social Media and Mobile Marketing Is Changing the Way We Do Business and Market Online* (Las Vegas, NV: Xeno Press, 2008).
3. Jupiter Research, "Social Networking Sites: Defining Advertising Opportunities in a Competitive Landscape," March 2007.

stories engage visitors and writers alike, all increasing overall loyalty to your site—and your brand."[4]

Still other companies sponsor discussion groups for customers to offer advice and assistance to one another. In addition to customer support, those sites provide the company with useful information for product marketing and development. Wikis and blogs are another form of UGC in which customers and partners can offer advice and assistance regarding products.

Video is increasingly used to tell stories, offer product demonstrations, and apply products to specific needs and problems. The amount of UGC video is staggering. According to YouTube, 10 hours of UGC video are uploaded to its site *every minute.* That video is equivalent to 57,000 feature-length movies every week.[5]

UGC Applications

Figure CE14-8 lists the most common applications for UGC. In sales, the presence of ratings, reviews, and recommendations increases conversion rates—in some cases, doubling the rate of purchase. Interestingly, conversion rates are higher for products with less-than-perfect reviews than for products with no reviews at all.[6] Furthermore, return rates fall dramatically as the number of product reviews increases.[7] Marketing via crowdsourcing is another UGC application, as described in Chapter 8.

For years, Microsoft has supported its software, database, and other developers on its MSDN Web site (*www.msdn.com*; MSDN stands for "Microsoft Developer Network"). Developers post answers to questions, articles, best practices, blogs, code samples, and other resources for developing Microsoft applications.

Yet another UGC business application is product development. Electronic Arts involved game developers worldwide in the development of spore creatures for Spore, its universe-simulation game. Ryz uses UGC to design footwear; if the strategy is successful, it plans to use it to design other clothing items as well.

YouTube is famous for hosting UGC videos provided as bait for advertising. Finally, some sites include UGC as part of the product. The magazines *Fine Woodworking* and *Wooden Boat* both include UGC video as part of their product offerings.

The use of UGC has been increasing with the growth of e-commerce and Web 2.0. Undoubtedly, many successful applications are yet to be invented. UGC for business will be an exciting field during the early years of your career.

Figure CE14-8
UGC Applications

Application	Example
Sale (ratings, reviews, recommendations, stories)	*www.amazon.com*
Marketing (crowdsourcing)	*www.ryzwear.com*
Product support (problem solving, Q&A, advice, applications)	*www.msdn.com*
Product development (research and development)	*www.spore.com* *www.ryzwear.com*
UGC as bait for advertising	*www.youtube.com* *www.funnyordie.com*
UGC as part of product	*www.finewoodworking.com* *www.woodenboat.com*

4. Quote from *www.bazaarvoice.com/stories.html* (accessed August 2008).
5. N'Gai Croal, "The Internet Is the New Sweatshop," *Newsweek*, July 7–14, 2008, *www.newsweek.com/id/143740* (accessed July 2008).
6. Bazaarvoice, "Industry Statistics, July 2008," *www.bazaarvoice.com/industryStats.html* (accessed August 2008).
7. Matt Hawkings, "PETCO.com Significantly Reduces Return Rates," *Marketing Data Analyst*, June 27, 2006, *www.bazaarvoice.com/cs_rr_returns_petco.html* (accessed August 2008).

Q5 What Are the Risks of Using Social Networking and UGC?

Before any business plunges full-bore into the world of social networking and UGC, it should be aware of the risks that these tools entail. Some of the major risks are:

- Junk and crackpots
- Inappropriate content
- Unfavorable reviews
- Mutinous movements
- Dependency on SN vendor

When a business participates in a social network or opens its site to UGC, it opens itself to misguided people who post junk unrelated to the purpose of the site. Crackpots may also use the network or UGC site as a way of expressing passionately held views about unrelated topics, such as UFOs, government cover-ups, weird conspiracy theories, and so forth. Because of the possibility of such content, employees of the hosting business must regularly monitor the site and remove objectionable material immediately. Companies like Bazaarvoice offer services not only to collect and manage ratings and reviews, but also to monitor the site for irrelevant content.

Unfavorable reviews are another risk. Research does indicate that customers are sophisticated enough to know that few, if any, products are perfect. Most customers want to know the disadvantages of a product before purchasing so they can determine if those disadvantages are important for their application. However, if every review is bad, if the product is rated 1 star out of 5, then the company is using Web 2.0 technology to publish its problems. In this case, corrective action must be taken.

Mutinous movements are an extension of bad reviews. The campaign Web site *www.my.barackobama.com* had a strong social networking component, and when then-Senator Obama changed his position on immunity for telecoms engaged in national security work, 22,000 members of his site joined a spontaneous group to object. Hundreds of members posted very critical comments of Obama, on his own site! This was an unexpected backlash to a campaign that had enjoyed unprecedented success raising money from small donors via social networking.

Although it is possible for organizations to develop their own social networking capability (as the Obama campaign did), many organizations use social networking vendors such as Facebook and MySpace. Those organizations are vulnerable to the success and policies of Facebook, MySpace, and others. These SN vendors are new companies with unproven business models; they may not survive. Also, using a social networking vendor for a business purpose makes the business vulnerable to the reliability and performance the SN vendor provides.

The license agreements of SN vendors are strongly biased in favor of the vendor. In some cases, the vendor owns the content that is developed; in other cases, the vendor can remove social networking applications at its discretion. In July 2008, for example, under pressure from Hasbro, the owner of Scrabble, Facebook required the creators of "Scrabulous" to redesign its game into "Wordscraper."[8]

The vulnerability is real, but the choices are limited. As stated, companies can create their own social networking capability, but doing so is expensive and requires highly skilled employees. And, having developed its own capability, no company will have the popularity and mindshare of Facebook or MySpace.

We have reached the leading edge of social networking technology in business. What happens next will be, in some measure, up to you!

8. Caroline McCarthy, "Why Facebook Left 'Scrabulous' Alone," *CNET News*, August 1, 2008, *http://news.cnet.com/8301-13577_3-10003821-36.html?part=rss&subj=news&tag=2547-1_3-0-5* (accessed August 2008).

ACTIVE REVIEW

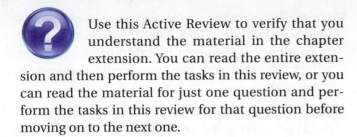

Use this Active Review to verify that you understand the material in the chapter extension. You can read the entire extension and then perform the tasks in this review, or you can read the material for just one question and perform the tasks in this review for that question before moving on to the next one.

Q1 How do organizations use information systems to increase the value of their social capital?

Name the three factors that determine social capital. Explain two ways social networks improve on word-of-mouth. Define *viral hook,* and give an example. Define *strength of relationship.* Describe Franklin's principle of increasing the strength of a relationship. Explain factors that determine the depreciation of social capital. Explain how value controlled by those in relationships contributes to social capital. Give an example in which a network with few people has more value than one with many. Explain the importance of the multiplicative nature of social capital. Explain the innovation in the computation of social capital that is described in Q1.

Q2 How can organizations use Facebook?

Define *social networking group,* and give an example from your own experience. Name and define three types of groups. Explain how Fox Lake might use groups. Define *social networking application.* How can businesses utilize social networking applications? Explain the role of services in an SN application. Name and explain four characteristics of a meaningful application and give an example of each, other than ones in this book.

Q3 How can organizations use Twitter?

Summarize how Twitter works. Define *microblog.* Explain why the 140-character limit is liberating. Describe how microblogging makes everyone a publisher. Explain how Twitter publishes conversations. Explain the role and importance of being able to search microblogs. Identify and describe three applications for microblogging in business.

Q4 What are business applications for User-Generated Content?

Give an example of each of the types of UGC in Figure CE14-8. Do not use examples in this textbook.

Q5 What are the risks of using social networking and UGC?

Summarize the risks of social networking. Show how those risks apply to Fox Lake's use of groups for wedding events, as described in this chapter extension.

KEY TERMS AND CONCEPTS

USING YOUR KNOWLEDGE

1. Go to your own Facebook or MySpace account and make a sketch (or partial sketch) of your social network. Include at least some friends of friends with whom you have no relationship. Assess your social capital and describe three ways you could increase it. One of those ways should involve a group.
2. Choose an activity or school organization in which you have an interest. Explain how you could use social networking to create a viral marketing campaign for your group. Identify three feasible viral hooks.
3. Create a group for the organization you chose in question 2. Explain how you would use it to bring

students (or other clients) closer to your organization's presence. Describe the type of group and the group's features that you would create. Explain steps you would take to make your group viral.

4. For the organization you chose in question 2, describe an application that you could hire someone to develop. Describe the features of the application and explain how those features will make the application meaningful.

5. For the organization you chose in question 2, describe five different types of UGC that you could use, and explain how they would add value to your organization's presence.

6. For the organization you chose in question 2, summarize the risks to which your presence, as defined in your answer to questions 3 through 5, would be vulnerable. Describe how you would respond to those risks.

7. Visit *www.my.barackobama.com*, and explain how social networking is used on this site.

CHAPTER EXTENSION 15

STUDY QUESTIONS

Chapter 9 provides the background for this Extension.

Database Marketing

Q1 What is a database marketing opportunity?

Q2 How does RFM analysis classify customers?

Q3 How does market-basket analysis identify cross-selling opportunities?

Q4 How do decision trees identify market segments?

Q1 What Is a Database Marketing Opportunity?

Database marketing is the application of business intelligence systems to the planning and execution of marketing programs. The term is broader than it sounds. Databases are a key component of database marketing, but, as you'll see, data mining techniques are also very important. To understand the need for database marketing, consider the following scenario:

> Mary Keeling owns and operates Carbon Creek Gardens, a retailer of trees, garden plants, perennial and annual flowers, and bulbs. "The Gardens," as her customers call it, also sells bags of soil, fertilizer, small garden tools, and garden sculptures. Mary started the business 10 years ago when she bought a section of land that, because of water drainage, was unsuited for residential development. With hard work and perseverance, Mary has created a warm and inviting environment with a unique and carefully selected inventory of plants. The Gardens has become a favorite nursery for serious gardeners in her community.
>
> "The problem," she says, "is that I've grown so large, I've lost track of my customers. The other day, I ran into Tootsie Swan at the grocery store, and I realized I hadn't seen her in ages. I said something like, 'Hi, Tootsie, I haven't seen you for a while,' and that statement unleashed an angry torrent from her. It turns out that she'd been in over a year ago and wanted to return a plant. One of my part-time employees waited on her and had apparently insulted her or at least didn't give her the service she wanted. So she decided not to come back to the Gardens.
>
> "Tootsie was one of my best customers. I'd lost her, and I didn't even know it! That really frustrates me. Is it inevitable that as I get bigger, I lose track of my customers? I don't think so. Somehow, I have to find out when regular customers aren't coming around. Had I known Tootsie had stopped shopping with us, I'd have called her to see what was going on. I need customers like her.
>
> "I've got all sorts of data in my sales database. It seems like the information I need is in there, but how do I get it out?"
>
> Mary needs database marketing.

CE15

Figure CE15-1
Example of RFM Score Data

Customer	RFM Score
Ajax	1 1 3
Bloominghams	5 1 1
Caruthers	5 4 5
Davidson	3 3 3

Q2 How Does RFM Analysis Classify Customers?

RFM analysis is a way of analyzing and ranking customers according to their purchasing patterns.[1] It is a simple technique that considers how *recently* (R) a customer has ordered, how *frequently* (F) a customer orders, and how much *money* (M) the customer spends per order. We consider this technique here because it is a useful analysis that can be easily implemented.

To produce an RFM score, the program first sorts customer purchase records by the date of most recent (R) purchase. In a common form of this analysis, the program then divides the customers into five groups and gives customers in each group a score of 1 to 5. Thus, the 20 percent of the customers having the most recent orders are given an **R score** of 1, the 20 percent of the customers having the next most recent orders are given an R score of 2, and so forth, down to the last 20 percent, who are given an R score of 5.

The program then re-sorts the customers on the basis of how frequently they order. The 20 percent of the customers who order most frequently are given an **F score** of 1, the next 20 percent of most frequently ordering customers are given a score of 2, and so forth, down to the least frequently ordering customers, who are given an F score of 5.

Finally, the program sorts the customers again according to the amount spent on their orders. The 20 percent who have ordered the most expensive items are given an **M score** of 1, the next 20 percent are given an M score of 2, and so forth, down to the 20 percent who spend the least, who are given an M score of 5.

Figure CE15-1 shows sample RFM data. The first customer, Ajax, has ordered recently and orders frequently. The company's M score of 3 indicates, however, that it does not order the most expensive goods. From these scores, the sales team members can surmise that Ajax is a good and regular customer but that they should attempt to up-sell more expensive goods to Ajax.

The second customer in Figure CE15-1 could be a problem. Bloominghams has not ordered in some time, but when it did order in the past, it ordered frequently, and its orders were of the highest monetary value. This data suggests that Bloominghams may have taken its business to another vendor. Someone from the sales team should contact this customer immediately.

No one on the sales team should be talking to the third customer, Caruthers. This company has not ordered for some time; it did not order frequently; and, when it did order, it bought the least-expensive items, and not many of them. The sales team should not waste any time on this customer; if Caruthers goes to the competition, the loss would be minimal.

The last customer, Davidson, is right in the middle. Davidson is an OK customer, but probably no one in sales should spend much time with it. Perhaps sales can set up an automated contact system or use the Davidson account as a training exercise for an eager departmental assistant or intern.

A reporting system can generate the RFM data and deliver it in many ways. For example, a report of RFM scores for all customers can be pushed to the vice president

[1] Arthur Middleton Hughes, "Boosting Response with RFM," *Marketing Tools*, May 1996. See also *www.dbmarketing.com*.

of sales; reports with scores for particular regions can be pushed to regional sales managers; and reports of scores for particular accounts can be pushed to the account salespeople. All of this reporting can be automated.

Q3 How Does Market-Basket Analysis Identify Cross-Selling Opportunities?

Suppose you run a dive shop, and one day you realize that one of your salespeople is much better at up-selling to your customers. Any of your sales associates can fill a customer's order, but this one salesperson is especially good at selling customers items *in addition to* those for which they ask. One day, you ask him how he does it.

"It's simple," he says. "I just ask myself what is the next product they would want to buy. If someone buys a dive computer, I don't try to sell her fins. If she's buying a dive computer, she's already a diver and she already has fins. But, these dive computer displays are hard to read. A better mask makes it easier to read the display and get the full benefit from the dive computer."

A **market-basket analysis** is a data mining technique for determining sales patterns. A market-basket analysis shows the products that customers tend to buy together. In marketing transactions, the fact that customers who buy product *X* also buy product *Y* creates a **cross-selling** opportunity; that is, "If they're buying *X*, sell them *Y*" or "If they're buying *Y*, sell them *X*."

Figure CE15-2 shows hypothetical sales data from 400 sales transactions at a dive shop. The first row of numbers under each column is the total number of times an item was sold. For example, the 270 in the first row of *Mask* means that 270 of the 400 transactions included masks. The 90 under *Dive Computer* means that 90 of the 400 transactions included dive computers.

	Mask	Tank	Fins	Weights	Dive Computer
Mask	270	10	250	10	90
Tank	10	200	40	130	30
Fins	250	40	280	20	20
Weights	10	130	20	130	10
Dive Computer	90	30	20	10	120
	Support				
Num Trans	400				
Mask	0.675	0.025	0.625	0.025	0.225
Tank	0.025	0.5	0.1	0.325	0.075
Fins	0.625	0.1	0.7	0.05	0.05
Weights	0.025	0.325	0.05	0.325	0.025
Dive Computer	0.225	0.075	0.05	0.025	0.3
	Confidence				
Mask	1	0.05	0.892857143	0.076923077	0.75
Tank	0.037037037	1	0.142857143	1	0.25
Fins	0.925925926	0.2	1	0.153846154	0.166666667
Weights	0.037037037	0.65	0.071428571	1	0.083333333
Dive Computer	0.333333333	0.15	0.071428571	0.076923077	1
	Lift (Improvement)				
Mask		0.074074074	1.322751323	0.113960114	1.111111111
Tank	0.074074074		0.285714286	2	0.5
Fins	1.322751323	0.285714286		0.21978022	0.238095238
Weights	0.113960114	2	0.21978022		0.256410256
Dive Computer	1.111111111	0.5	0.238095238	0.256410256	

Figure CE15-2
Market-Basket Example

We can use the numbers in the first row to estimate the probability that a customer will purchase an item. Because 270 of the 400 transactions were masks, we can estimate the probability that a customer will buy a mask to be 270/400, or .675.

In market-basket terminology, **support** is the probability that two items will be purchased together. To estimate that probability, we examine sales transactions and count the number of times that two items occurred in the same transaction. For the data in Figure CE15-2, fins and masks appeared together 250 times, and thus the support for fins and a mask is 250/400, or .625. Similarly, the support for fins and weights is 20/400, or .05.

These data are interesting by themselves, but we can refine the analysis by taking another step and considering additional probabilities. For example, what proportion of the customers who bought a mask also bought fins? Masks were purchased 270 times, and of those individuals who bought masks, 250 also bought fins. Thus, given that a customer bought a mask, we can estimate the probability that he or she will buy fins to be 250/270, or .926. In market-basket terminology, such a conditional probability estimate is called the **confidence**.

Reflect on the meaning of this confidence value. The likelihood of someone walking in the door and buying fins is 250/400, or .625. But the likelihood of someone buying fins, given that he or she bought a mask, is .926. Thus, if someone buys a mask, the likelihood that he or she will also buy fins increases substantially, from .625 to .926. Thus, all sales personnel should be trained to try to sell fins to anyone buying a mask.

Now consider dive computers and fins. Of the 400 transactions, fins were sold 250 times, so the probability that someone walks into the store and buys fins is .625. But of the 90 purchases of dive computers, only 20 appeared with fins. So the likelihood of someone buying fins, given he or she bought a dive computer, is 20/90 or .1666. Thus, when someone buys a dive computer, the likelihood that she will also buy fins falls from .625 to .1666.

The ratio of confidence to the base probability of buying an item is called **lift**. Lift shows how much the base probability increases or decreases when other products are purchased. The lift of fins and a mask is the confidence of fins given a mask, divided by the base probability of fins. In Figure CE15-2, the lift of fins and a mask is .926/.625, or 1.32. Thus, the likelihood that people buy fins when they buy a mask increases by 32 percent. Surprisingly, it turns out that the lift of fins and a mask is the same as the lift of a mask and fins. Both are 1.32.

We need to be careful here, though, because this analysis only shows shopping carts with two items. We cannot say from this data what the likelihood is that customers, given that they bought a mask, will buy both weights and fins. To assess that probability, we need to analyze shopping carts with three items. This statement illustrates, once again, that we need to know what problem we're solving before we start to build the information system to mine the data. The problem definition will help us decide if we need to analyze three-item, four-item, or some other sized shopping cart.

Many organizations are benefiting from market-basket analysis today. You can expect that this technique will become a standard CRM analysis during your career.

By the way, one famous market-basket analysis shows a high correlation of the purchase of beer and diapers.[2] That correlation was strongest on Thursdays. Interviews indicated that customers were buying goods for the weekend, goods which included both beer and diapers.

2. Michael J. A. Berry and Gordon Linoff, *Data Mining Techniques for Marketing, Sales, and Customer Support* (New York: John Wiley, 1997).

Q4 How Do Decision Trees Identify Market Segments?

A **decision tree** is a hierarchical arrangement of criteria that predict a classification or a value. Here, we will consider decision trees that predict classifications. Decision tree analyses are an unsupervised data mining technique: The analyst sets up the computer program and provides the data to analyze, and the decision tree program produces the tree.

A Decision Tree for Student Performance

The basic idea of a decision tree is to select attributes that are most useful for classifying entities on some criterion. Suppose, for example, that we want to classify students according to the grades they earn in the MIS class. To create a decision tree, we first gather data about grades and attributes of students in past classes.

We then input that data into the decision tree program. The program analyzes all of the attributes and selects an attribute that creates the most disparate groups. The logic is that the more different the groups, the better the classification will be. For example, if every student who lived off campus earned a grade higher than 3.0 and if every student who lived on campus earned a grade lower than 3.0, then the program would use the variable *live-off-campus* or *live-on-campus* to classify students. In this unrealistic example, the program would be a perfect classifier, because each group is pure, with no misclassifications.

More realistically, consider Figure CE15-3, which shows a hypothetical decision tree analysis of MIS class grades. Again, assume we are classifying students depending on whether their GPA was greater than 3.0 or less than or equal to 3.0.

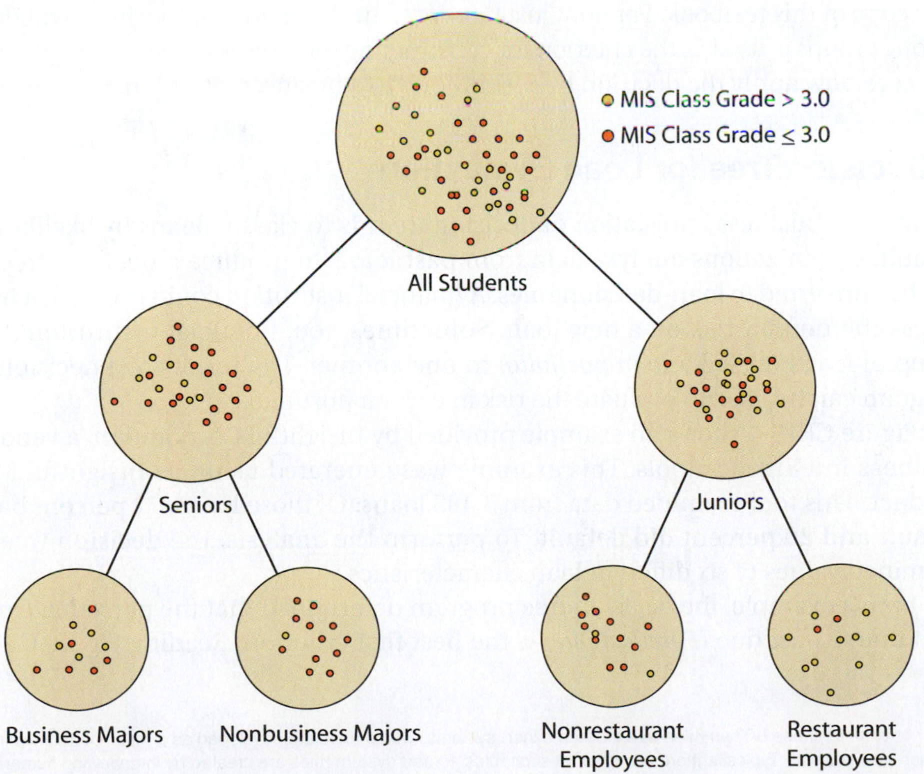

Figure CE15-3
GPAs of Students from Past MIS Class (Hypothetical Data)

The decision tree tool that created this tree examined students' characteristics, such as their class (junior or senior), their major, their employment, their age, their club affiliations, and other student characteristics. It then used values of those characteristics to create groups that were as different as possible on the classification GPA above or below 3.0.

For the results shown here, the decision tree program determined that the best first criterion is whether the students are juniors or seniors. In this case, the classification was imperfect, as shown by the fact that neither of the senior nor the junior groups consisted only of students with GPAs above or below 3.0. Still, it did create groups that were less mixed than in the *All Students* group.

Many problems exist with classification schemes, especially those that classify people. The Ethics Guide on page 512–513 examines some of them.

Next, the program examined other criteria to further subdivide *Seniors* and *Juniors* so as to create even more pure groups. The program divided the senior group into subgroups: those who are business majors and those who are not. The program's analysis of the junior data, however, determined that the difference between majors is not significant. Instead, the best classifier (the one that generated the most different groups) is whether the junior worked in a restaurant.

Examining this data, we see that junior restaurant employees do well in the class, but junior nonrestaurant employees and senior nonbusiness majors do poorly. Performance in the other senior group is mixed. (Remember, these data are hypothetical.)

A decision tree like the one in Figure CE15-3 can be transformed into a set of decision rules having the format, **If/Then**. Decision rules for this example are:

- If student is a junior and works in a restaurant, then predict grade > 3.0.
- If student is a senior and is a nonbusiness major, then predict grade < 3.0.
- If student is a junior and does not work in a restaurant, then predict grade < 3.0.
- If student is a senior and is a business major, then make no prediction.[3]

As stated, decision tree algorithms create groups that are as pure as possible, or stated otherwise, as different from each other as possible. The algorithms use several metrics for measuring difference among groups. Further explanation of those techniques is beyond the scope of this textbook. For now, just be sure to understand that maximum difference among groups is used as the criterion for constructing the decision tree.

Let's now apply the decision tree technique to a business situation.

A Decision Tree for Loan Evaluation

A common business application of decision trees is to classify loans by likelihood of default. Organizations analyze data from past loans to produce a decision tree that can be converted to loan-decision rules. A financial institution could use such a tree to assess the default risk on a new loan. Sometimes, too, financial institutions sell a group of loans (called a *loan portfolio*) to one another. The results of a decision tree program can be used to evaluate the risk in a given portfolio.

Figure CE15-4 shows an example provided by Insightful Corporation, a vendor of business intelligence tools. This example was generated using its Insightful Miner product. This tool examined data from 3,485 loans. Of those loans, 72 percent had no default and 28 percent did default. To perform the analysis, the decision tree tool examined values of six different loan characteristics.

In this example, the decision tree program determined that the percentage of the loan that is past due (*PercPastDue*) is the best first criterion. Reading Figure CE15-4,

[3] Do not confuse these If/Then rules with those in expert systems. These rules are developed as a result of data mining via decision tree analysis. Typically, there are 10 or 12 such rules. Expert system rules are created by interviewing human experts. Typically, there are hundreds, or even thousands, of such rules.

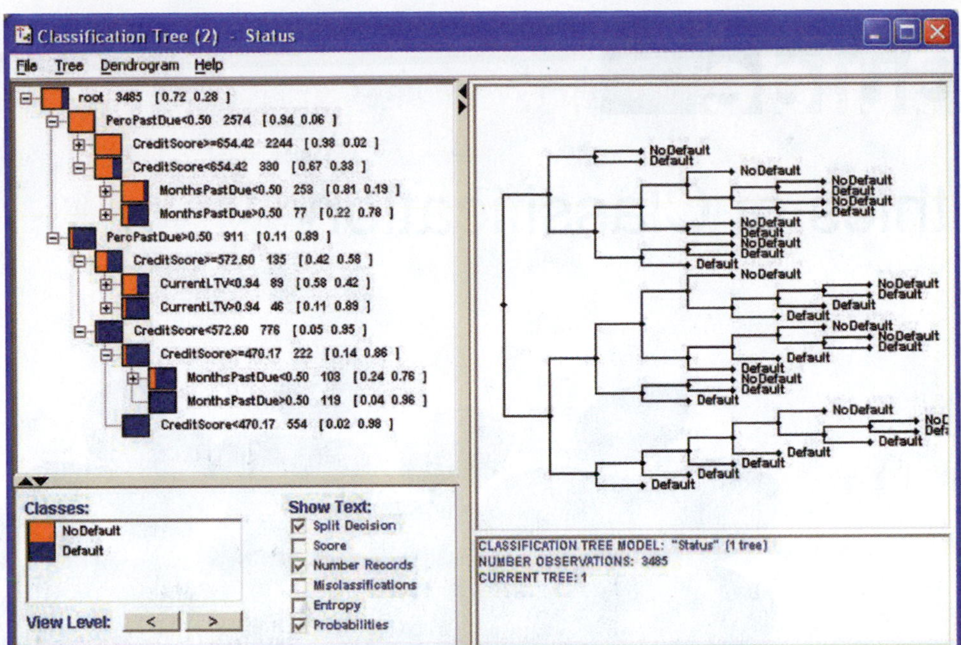

Figure CE15-4
Credit Score Decision Tree

Source: Used with permission of Insightful Corporation.

you can see that of the 2,574 loans with a *PercPastDue* value of .5 or less (more than half paid off), 94 percent were not in default. Hence, any loan that is more than half paid off has little risk of default.

Reading down several lines in this tree, 911 loans had a value of *PercPastDue* greater than .5; of those loans, 89 percent were in default.

These two major categories are then further subdivided into three classifications: *CreditScore* is a creditworthiness score obtained from a credit agency; *MonthsPastDue* is the number of months since a payment; and *CurrentLTV* is the current ratio of outstanding balance of the loan to the value of the loan's collateral.

With a decision tree like this, the financial institution can structure a marketing program for "instant approval" refinancing. For example, from Figure CE15-4, the bank can deduce the following rules:

- If the loan is more than half paid, then accept the loan.
- If the loan is less than half paid and
  - If *CreditScore* is greater than 572.6 and
  - If *CurrentLTV* is less than .94, then accept the loan.
- Otherwise, reject the loan.

These rules identify loans the bank will approve, and they also specify characteristics that identify a particular market segment. On the basis of this analysis, the bank can structure a marketing campaign to appeal to that segment.

We have shown here how decision trees can identify a market segment, but realize that they can be used for numerous other classification and prediction problems as well. They are easy to understand and—even better—easy to implement using decision rules. They also can work with many types of variables, and they deal well with missing values. Organizations can use decision trees by themselves or combine them with other techniques. In some cases, organizations use decision trees to select variables that are then used by other types of data mining tools.

Ethics Guide

The Ethics of Classification

Classification is a useful human skill. Imagine walking into your favorite clothing store and seeing all of the clothes piled together on a center table. T-shirts, pants, and socks intermingle, with the sizes mixed up. Retail stores organized like this would not survive, nor would distributors or manufacturers who managed their inventories this way. Sorting and classifying are necessary, important, and essential activities. But those activities can also be dangerous.

Serious ethical issues arise when we classify people. What makes someone a good or bad "prospect"? If we're talking about classifying customers in order to prioritize our sales calls, then the ethical issue may not be too serious. What about classifying applicants for college? As long as there are more applicants than positions, some sort of classification and selection process must be done. But what kind?

Suppose a university collects data on the demographics and the performance of all of its students. The admissions committee then processes these data using a decision tree data mining program. Assume the analysis is conducted properly and the tool uses statistically valid measures to obtain statistically valid results. Thus, the following resulting decision tree accurately represents and explains variances found in the data; no human judgment (or prejudice) was involved.

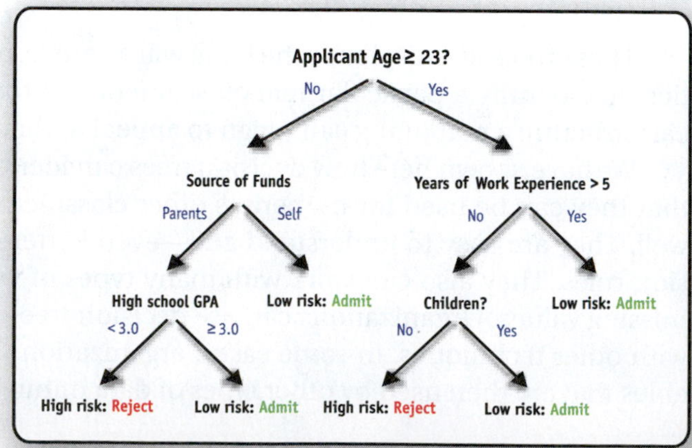

Discussion Questions

1. Explain what conditions in the data could have caused this particular structure to emerge. For example, what conditions may have existed for self-funding students under the age of 23 to be classified as low risk? Explain how you think the three other branches in this tree may have come about.
2. Consider this tree from the standpoint of:
   a. A 23-year-old woman whose job experience is 3 years as a successful Wall Street financial analyst.
   b. A 28-year-old gay male with 4 years' job experience who has no children and pays his own college education.
   c. The university fund-raising committee that wants to raise money from parent donations.
   d. A student who was seriously ill while attending a top-notch high school but managed to graduate with a GPA of 2.9 by working independently on her classes from her hospital room.
3. Suppose you work in admissions and your university's public relations department asks you to meet with the local press for an article it is preparing regarding your admittance policy. How do you prepare for the press meeting?
4. Would your answer to question 3 change if you work at a private rather than public institution? Would it change if you work at a small liberal arts college rather than a large engineering-oriented university?
5. What conclusions do you make regarding the use of decision trees for categorizing student applicants?
6. What conclusions do you make regarding the use of decision trees for categorizing prospects in general?

ACTIVE REVIEW

Use this Active Review to verify that you understand the material in the chapter extension. You can read the entire extension and then perform the tasks in this review, or you can read the material for just one question and perform the tasks in this review for that question before moving on to the next one.

Q1 What is a database marketing opportunity?

Define *database marketing.* Explain why the term is a misnomer. Give an example of the need for database marketing other than ones described in this chapter extension.

Q2 How does RFM analysis classify customers?

Explain the meaning of *R, F,* and *M scores.* Describe how each score is computed. State the action(s) that should be taken for customers having the following RFM scores: [1, 1, 3], [5, 4, 5], [2, 2, 2], [3, 1, 1], [1, 3, 1], and [1, 1, 1].

Q3 How does market-basket analysis identify cross-selling opportunities?

Define *cross-selling.* Define *support, confidence,* and *lift.* In Figure CE15-2, state the probability that someone walks into the store and buys fins. Compute the support for fins and a dive computer. Explain what it means if the value of lift is greater than 1. Explain what it means if the value of lift is less than 1. Compute the lift for fins and a dive computer.

Q4 How do decision trees identify market segments?

Define *decision tree,* and explain the basic idea of decision trees. For the hypothetical data in Figure CE15-3, state the grade you would predict for senior, nonbusiness students. State the grade you would predict for junior, restaurant employees. State the grade you would predict for senior, business majors. Explain how a decision tree could be used to identify a desirable market segment for loan refinancing.

KEY TERMS AND CONCEPTS

USING YOUR KNOWLEDGE

1. Of the three database marketing techniques described in this chapter extension, which best solves the problem at Carbon Creek Gardens? Explain how Mary could have used that technique to identify Tootsie as a lost customer.
2. Describe a use for RFM analysis for Fox Lake. Consider golf, tennis, the restaurant, or the pro shop as candidates. Which do you think is best suited to RFM? Explain your rationale. For your application, explain what you would do for customers that have the following scores: [1, 1, 1], [3,1,1], [1, 4, 1], [3, 3, 1], and [1, 1, 3].
3. Describe an application for market-basket analysis other than for a dive shop. Explain how you would use the knowledge that two products have a lift of 7. Explain how you would use the knowledge that two products have a lift of .003. If they have a lift of 1.03? If they have a lift of 2.1?
4. Describe an application for decision tree analysis for customer service and support at a computer vendor like Dell. Assume your decision tree analysis considered customer name, company, number of employees at that company, job title, and number and type of computer systems purchased. How could you use the results of your analysis to classify the knowledge and experience of your customers? How could you use those results to structure the buying experience for each of those customers? What other uses can you think of for the results of this decision tree analysis?

CHAPTER EXTENSION 16

STUDY QUESTIONS

Chapter 9 provides the background for this Extension.

Reporting Systems and OLAP

Q1 How Do Reporting Systems Create Information?

A **reporting system** is an information system that creates information by processing data from disparate sources and delivering that information to the proper users on a timely basis. Before we describe the components of a reporting system, first consider how reporting operations can be used to construct meaningful information.

Chapter 1 explained the difference between data and information. Data are recorded facts or figures; information is knowledge derived from data. Alternatively, information is data presented in a meaningful context. Reporting systems generate information from data as a result of four operations:

1. Filtering data
2. Sorting data
3. Grouping data
4. Making simple calculations on the data

Consider the sales data shown in Figure CE16-1. This list of raw data contains little or no information; it is just data. We can create information from this data by *sorting* by customer name, as shown in Figure CE16-2. In this format, we can see that some customers have ordered more than once, and we can readily find their orders.

This is a step forward, but we can produce even more information by *grouping* the orders, as shown in Figure CE16-3 on page 517. Notice that the reporting tool not only grouped the orders, but it also *computed* the number of orders for each customer and the total purchase amount per customer.

Suppose we are interested in repeat customers. If so, we can *filter* the groups of orders to select only those customers that have two or more orders. The results of these operations are shown in Figure CE16-4 on page 517. The report in this figure not only has filtered the results, but it also has *formatted* them for easier understanding. Compare Figure CE16-4 to Figure CE16-1. If your goal is to identify your best customers, the report in Figure CE16-4 is far more useful and will save you considerable work.

Figure CE16-1
Raw Sales Data

CustomerName	CustomerEmail	DateOfSale	Amount
Ashley, Jane	JA@somewhere.com	5 /5 /2010	$110
Corning,Sandra	KD@somewhereelse.com	7 /7 /2010	$375
Ching, Kam Hoong	KHC@somewhere.com	5 /17/2010	$55
Rikki, Nicole	GC@righthere.com	6 /19/2008	$155
Corning,Sandra	SC@somewhereelse.com	2 /4 /2009	$195
Scott, Rex	RS@somewhere.com	7 /15/2010	$56
Corovic,Jose	JC@somewhere.com	11/12/2010	$55
McGovern, Adrian	BL@righthere.com	11/12/2008	$47
Wei, Guang	GW@ourcompany.com	11/28/2009	$385
Dixon,Eleonor	ED@somewhere.com	5 /17/2010	$108
Lee,Brandon	BL@somewhereelse.com	5 /5 /2008	$74
Duong,Linda	LD@righthere.com	5 /17/2009	$485
Dixon, James T	JTD@somewhere.com	4 /3 /2009	$285
La Pierre,Anna	SG@righthere.com	9 /22/2010	$120
La Pierre,Anna	WS@somewhere.com	3 /14/2010	$48
La Pierre,Anna	TR@righthere.com	9 /22/2010	$580
Ryan, Mark	MR@somewhereelse.com	11/3 /2010	$42
Rikki, Nicole	MR@righthere.com	3 /14/2010	$175
Scott, Bryan	BS@somewhere.com	3 /17/2009	$145
Warrem, Jason	JW@ourcompany.com	5 /12/2010	$160
La Pierre,Anna	ALP@somewhereelse.com	3 /15/2009	$52
Angel, Kathy	KA@righthere.com	9 /15/2010	$195
La Pierre,Anna	JQ@somewhere.com	4 /12/2010	$44
Casimiro, Amanda	AC@somewhere.com	12/7 /2009	$52
McGovern, Adrian	AM@ourcompany.com	3 /17/2009	$52
Menstell,Lori Lee	LLM@ourcompany.com	10/18/2010	$72
La Pierre,Anna	DJ@righthere.com	12/7 /2009	$175
Nurul,Nicole	NN@somewhere.com	10/12/2010	$84
Menstell,Lori Lee	VB@ourcompany.com	9 /24/2010	$120
Pham,Mary	MP@somewhere.com	3 /14/2010	$38

Figure CE16-2
Sales Data Sorted by Customer Name

CustomerName	CustomerEmail	DateOfSale	Amount
Adams, James	JA3@somewhere.com	1 /15/2010	$145
Angel, Kathy	KA@righthere.com	9 /15/2010	$195
Ashley, Jane	JA@somewhere.com	5 /5 /2010	$110
Austin, James	JA7@somewhere.com	1 /15/2009	$55
Bernard, Steven	SB@ourcompany.com	9 /17/2010	$78
Casimiro, Amanda	AC@somewhere.com	12/7 /2009	$52
Ching, Kam Hoong	KHC@somewhere.com	5 /17/2010	$55
Corning,Sandra	KD@somewhereelse.com	7 /7 /2010	$375
Corning,Sandra	SC@somewhereelse.com	2 /4 /2009	$195
Corovic,Jose	JC@somewhere.com	11/12/2010	$55
Daniel, James	JD@somewhere.com	1 /18/2010	$52
Dixon, James T	JTD@somewhere.com	4 /3 /2009	$285
Dixon,Eleonor	ED@somewhere.com	5 /17/2010	$108
Drew, Richard	RD@righthere.com	10/3 /2009	$42
Duong,Linda	LD@righthere.com	5 /17/2009	$485
Garrett, James	JG@ourcompany.com	3 /14/2010	$38
Jordan, Matthew	MJ@righthere.com	3 /14/2009	$645
La Pierre,Anna	DJ@righthere.com	12/7 /2009	$175
La Pierre,Anna	SG@righthere.com	9 /22/2010	$120
La Pierre,Anna	TR@righthere.com	9 /22/2010	$580
La Pierre,Anna	ALP@somewhereelse.com	3 /15/2009	$52
La Pierre,Anna	JQ@somewhere.com	4 /12/2010	$44
La Pierre,Anna	WS@somewhere.com	3 /14/2010	$48
Lee,Brandon	BL@somewhereelse.com	5 /5 /2008	$74
Lunden,Haley	HL@somewhere.com	11/17/2007	$52
McGovern, Adrian	BL@righthere.com	11/12/2008	$47
McGovern, Adrian	AM@ourcompany.com	3 /17/2009	$52
Menstell,Lori Lee	LLM@ourcompany.com	10/18/2010	$72
Menstell,Lori Lee	VB@ourcompany.com	9 /24/2010	$120
Nurul,Nicole	NN@somewhere.com	10/12/2010	$84

CustomerName	NumOrders	TotalPurcha:
Adams, James	1	$145.00
Angel, Kathy	1	$195.00
Ashley, Jane	1	$110.00
Austin, James	1	$55.00
Bernard, Steven	1	$78.00
Casimiro, Amanda	1	$52.00
Ching, Kam Hoong	1	$55.00
Corning,Sandra	2	$570.00
Corovic,Jose	1	$55.00
Daniel, James	1	$52.00
Dixon, James T	1	$285.00
Dixon,Eleonor	1	$108.00
Drew, Richard	1	$42.00
Duong,Linda	1	$485.00
Garrett, James	1	$38.00
Jordan, Matthew	1	$645.00
La Pierre,Anna	6	$1,018.50
Lee,Brandon	1	$74.00
Lunden,Haley	1	$52.00
McGovern, Adrian	2	$99.00
Menstell,Lori Lee	2	$192.00
Nurul,Nicole	1	$84.00
Pham,Mary	1	$38.00
Redmond, Louise	1	$140.00
Rikki, Nicole	2	$330.00
Ryan, Mark	1	$42.00
Scott, Bryan	1	$145.00
Scott, Rex	1	$56.00
UTran,Diem Thi	1	$275.00
Warrem, Jason	1	$160.00

Figure CE16-3
Sales Data Sorted by Customer Name and Grouped by Number of Orders and Purchase Amount

Repeat Customers

NumOrders	CustomerName	TotalPurchases
6	La Pierre,Anna	$1,018.50
2	Corning,Sandra	$570.00
2	Rikki, Nicole	$330.00
2	Menstell,Lori Lee	$192.00
2	McGovern, Adrian	$99.00

Figure CE16-4
Sales Data Filtered to Show Repeat Customers

In the remainder of this chapter extension, we will consider the components and functions of these reporting systems, as well as some examples.

Q2 What Are the Components and Characteristics of Reporting Systems?

Figure CE16-5 shows the major components of a reporting system. Data from disparate data sources are read and combined, using filtering, sorting, grouping, and simple calculating, to produce information. Figure CE16-5 combines data from an

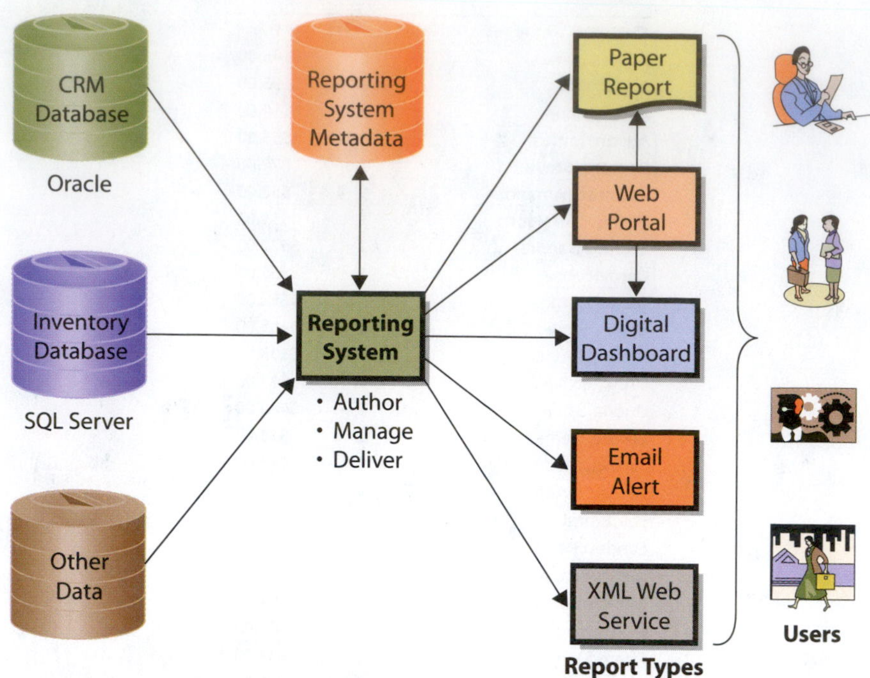

Figure CE16-5 Components of a Reporting System

Oracle database, a SQL Server database, and other nondatabase data. Some data are generated within the organization, other data are obtained from public sources, and still other data may be purchased from data utilities.

A reporting system maintains a database of reporting metadata. The metadata describe reports, users, groups, roles, events, and other entities involved in the reporting activity. The reporting system uses the metadata to prepare and deliver reports to the proper users on a timely basis.

As shown in Figure CE16-5, organizations can prepare reports in a variety of formats. Figure CE16-6 lists report characteristics by type, media, and mode, which we discuss next.

Report Type

In terms of **report type**, reports can be *static* or *dynamic*. **Static reports** are prepared once from the underlying data, and they do not change. A report of past year's sales, for example, is a static report. Other reports are **dynamic**; at the time of creation, the

Figure CE16-6 Summary of Report Characteristics

Type	Media	Mode
Static	Paper and PDF file	Push
Dynamic	Computer screen via application	Pull
Query	Web site	
Online analytical processing (OLAP)	Digital dashboard	
	Alerts via email or cell phone	
	Export to Excel, Quicken, TurboTax, QuickBooks, or other application	
	XML Web service	

reporting system reads the most current data and generates the report using that fresh data. A report on sales today and a report on current stock prices are both dynamic reports.

Query reports are prepared in response to data entered by users. Google provides a handy example of a query report: You enter the keywords you want to search on, and the reporting system within Google searches its database and generates a response that is particular to your query. Within an organization, a query report could be generated to show current inventory levels. The user enters item numbers, and the reporting system responds with inventory levels of those items at various stores and warehouses.

Online analytical processing (*OLAP*) is a fourth type of report. OLAP reports allow the user to dynamically change the report grouping structures. An OLAP reporting application is illustrated later in this chapter extension.

Report Media

Today, reports are delivered via many different **report media**, or channels. Some reports are printed on paper; others are created in formats, such as PDF, that can be printed or viewed electronically. Other reports are delivered to computer screens. Applications for CRM and ERP systems, for example, include dozens of different reports that users view online. Additionally, companies sometimes place reports on internal corporate Web sites for employees to access. For example, an organization might place a report of its latest sales on the sales department's Web site or a report on customers serviced on the customer service department's Web site.

Another report medium is a **digital dashboard**, which is an electronic display that is customized for a particular user. Vendors like Yahoo! and MSN provide common examples. Users of these services can define content they want—say, a local weather forecast, a list of stock prices, or a list of news sources—and the vendor constructs the display customized for each user. Figure CE16-7 shows an example.

Other dashboards are particular to an organization. Executives at a manufacturing organization, for example, might have a dashboard that shows up-to-the-minute production and sales activities.

Alerts are another form of report. Users can declare that they wish to receive notification of events, say, via email or on their cell phones. Of course, some cell phones are capable of displaying Web pages, and digital dashboards can be delivered to them as well.

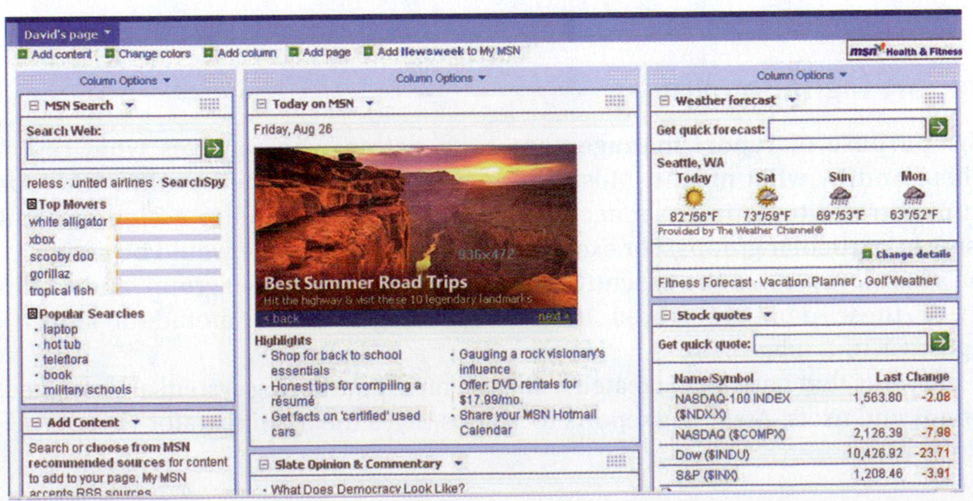

Figure CE16-7
Digital Dashboard Example

Some reports are exported from the report generator to another program, such as Excel, Quicken, QuickBooks, and so forth. For example, application programs at many banks can export customer checking account transactions into Excel, Quicken, or Money.

Finally, reports can be published via a Web service. The Web service produces the report in response to requests from the service-consuming application. This style of reporting is particularly useful for interorganizational information systems like supply chain management.

Report Mode

The final report characteristic in Figure CE16-6 is the **report mode**, a term which refers to the way a report is initiated. Organizations send a **push report** to users according to a preset schedule. Users receive the report without any activity on their part. In contrast, users must request a **pull report**. To obtain a pull report, a user goes to a Web portal or digital dashboard and clicks a link or button to cause the reporting system to produce and deliver the report.

Q3 How Are Reports Authored, Managed, and Delivered?

In the middle of Figure CE16-5, under the drawing of the reporting system, three functions of a reporting system are listed: author, manage, and deliver. Consider each.

Report Authoring

Report authoring involves connecting to data sources, creating the report structure, and formatting the report. You can learn how to create a report for Microsoft Access in Chapter Extension 8, question 5 (starting on page 417).

Of course, much organizational data resides in databases other than Access. One common way that organizations author reports is to use a developer tool like Microsoft's Visual Studio that can connect to many different data sources. For example, in Figure CE16-8 a report author is using Visual Studio to connect to a database that contains source data and has just entered a SQL statement, shown in the lower-center portion of this display, to generate a report. Visual Studio can be used to format the report as well.

Report Management

The purpose of **report management** is to define who receives what reports, when, and by what means. Most report management systems allow the report administrator to define user accounts and user groups and to assign particular users to particular groups. For example, all of the salespeople would be assigned to the sales group, all of the executives assigned to the executive group, and so forth. All of these data are stored in the reporting system's metadata shown in Figure CE16-5 (page 518).

Reports that have been created using the report authoring system are assigned to groups and users. Assigning reports to groups saves the administrator work: When a

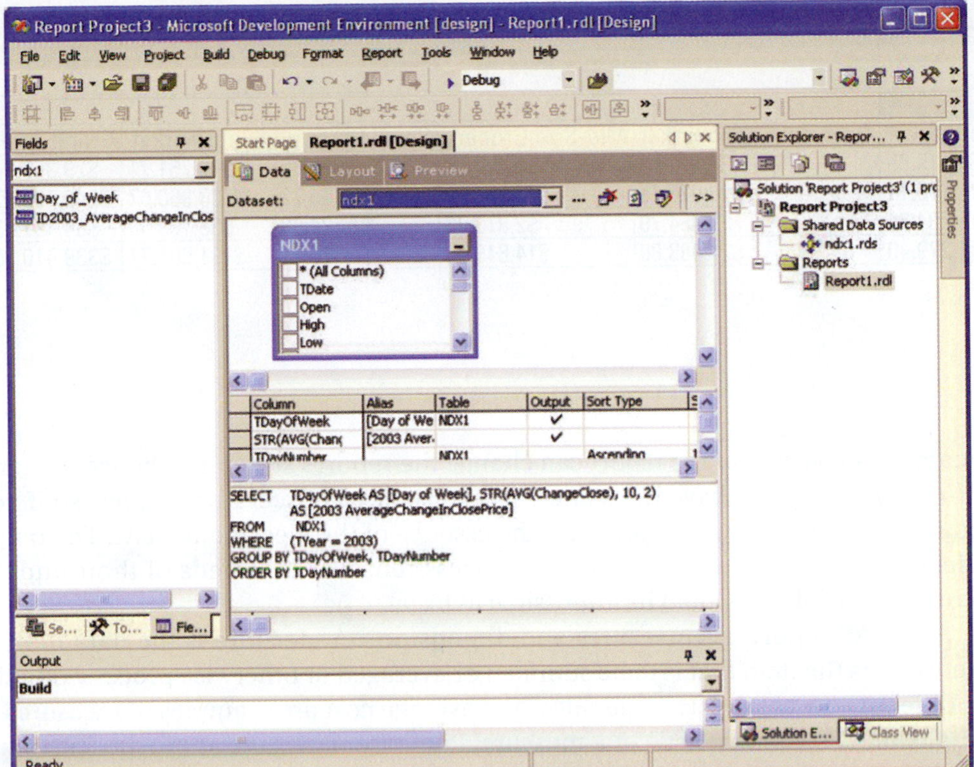

Figure CE16-8
Connecting to a Report Data Source Using Visual Studio

Source: Microsoft product screenshot reprinted with permission from Microsoft Corporation.

report is created, changed, or removed, the administrator need only change the report assignments to the group. All of the users in the group will inherit the changes.

As stated, the report management metadata indicate which format of this report is to be sent to which user. The metadata also indicate what channel is to be used and whether the report is to be pushed or pulled. If the report is to be pushed, the administrator declares whether the report is to be generated on a regular schedule or as an alert.

Report Delivery

The **report delivery** function of a reporting system pushes reports or allows them to be pulled according to report management metadata. Reports can be delivered via an email server, via a Web site, via SOA services, or by other program-specific means. The report delivery system uses the operating system and other program security components to ensure that only authorized users receive authorized reports. It also ensures that push reports are produced at appropriate times.

For query reports, the report delivery system serves as an intermediary between the user and the report generator. It receives user query data, such as the item numbers in an inventory query, passes the query data to the report generator, receives the resulting report, and delivers the report to the user.

For a discussion of security issues relating to reporting systems, see the Guide on pages 524–525.

Q4 How Are OLAP Reports Dynamic?

Online analytical processing (OLAP) is a reporting technology that provides the ability to sum, count, average, and perform other simple arithmetic operations on groups of data. The remarkable characteristic of OLAP reports is that their format is

	A	B	C	D	E	F	G
1							
2							
3	Store Sales Net	Store Type					
4	Product Family	Deluxe Supermarket	Gourmet Supermarket	Mid-Size Grocery	Small Grocery	Supermarket	Grand Total
5	Drink	$8,119.05	$2,392.83	$1,409.50	$685.89	$16,751.71	$29,358.98
6	Food	$70,276.11	$20,026.18	$10,392.19	$6,109.72	$138,960.67	$245,764.87
7	Nonconsumable	$18,884.24	$5,064.79	$2,813.73	$1,534.90	$36,189.40	$64,487.05
8	Grand Total	$97,279.40	$27,483.80	$14,615.42	$8,330.51	$191,901.77	$339,610.90

Figure CE16-9
OLAP Product Family by Store Type

dynamic. The viewer of the report can change the report's structure—hence the term *online*. OLAP reports have the same characteristics as Excel Pivot tables, so if you know how such tables work, you have the essence of the idea about OLAP. The major difference is that OLAP is designed to process tens and hundreds of thousands of records; such volume would be impossible in Excel.

An OLAP report has measures and dimensions. A **measure** is the data item of interest. It is the item that is to be summed or averaged or otherwise processed in the OLAP report. Total sales, average sales, and average cost are examples of measures. A **dimension** is a characteristic of a measure. Purchase date, customer type, customer location, and sales region are all examples of dimensions.

Figure CE16-9 shows a typical OLAP report. Here, the measure is *Store Sales Net*, and the dimensions are *Product Family* and *Store Type*. This report shows how net store sales vary by product family and store type. Stores of type *Supermarket*, for example, sold a net of $36,189 worth of nonconsumable goods.

A presentation of a measure with associated dimensions like that in Figure CE16-9 is often called an **OLAP cube**, or sometimes simply a *cube*. The reason for this term is that some products show these displays using three axes, like a cube in geometry. The origin of the term is unimportant here, however. Just know that an *OLAP cube* and an *OLAP report* are the same thing.

The OLAP report in Figure CE16-9 was generated by SQL Server Analysis Services and is displayed in an Excel Pivot table. The data were taken from a sample instructional database, called Food Mart, that is provided with SQL Server. It is possible to display OLAP cubes in many ways besides with Excel. Some third-party vendors provide more extensive graphical displays. For more information about such products, check for OLAP vendors and products at the Data Warehousing Review at *www.dwreview.com/OLAP/index.html*. Note, too, that OLAP reports can be delivered just like any of the other reports described for report management systems.

As stated earlier, the distinguishing characteristic of an OLAP report is that the user can alter the format of the report. Figure CE16-10 shows such an alteration. Here, the user added another dimension, *Store Country and State*, to the horizontal display. Product-family sales are now broken out by the location of the stores. Observe that the sample data include only stores in the United States and only in the western states of California, Oregon, and Washington.

With an OLAP report, it is possible to **drill down** into the data. This term means to further divide the data into more detail. In Figure CE16-11, for example, the user has

	A	B	C	D	E	F	G	H	I
1									
2									
3	Store Sales Net			Store Type					
4	Product Family	Store	Store State	Deluxe Supermarket	Gourmet Supermarket	Mid-Size Grocery	Small Grocery	Supermarket	Grand Total
5	Drink	USA	CA		$2,392.83		$227.38	$5,920.76	$8,540.97
6			OR	$4,438.49				$2,862.45	$7,300.94
7			WA	$3,680.56		$1,409.50	$458.51	$7,968.50	$13,517.07
8		USA Total		$8,119.05	$2,392.83	$1,409.50	$685.89	$16,751.71	$29,358.98
9	Drink Total			$8,119.05	$2,392.83	$1,409.50	$685.89	$16,751.71	$29,358.98
10	Food	USA	CA		$20,026.18		$1,960.53	$47,226.11	$69,212.82
11			OR	$37,778.35				$23,818.87	$61,597.22
12			WA	$32,497.76		$10,392.19	$4,149.19	$67,915.69	$114,954.83
13		USA Total		$70,276.11	$20,026.18	$10,392.19	$6,109.72	$138,960.67	$245,764.87
14	Food Total			$70,276.11	$20,026.18	$10,392.19	$6,109.72	$138,960.67	$245,764.87
15	Nonconsumable	USA	CA		$5,064.79		$474.35	$12,344.49	$17,883.63
16			OR	$10,177.89				$6,428.53	$16,606.41
17			WA	$8,706.36		$2,813.73	$1,060.54	$17,416.38	$29,997.01
18		USA Total		$18,884.24	$5,064.79	$2,813.73	$1,534.90	$36,189.40	$64,487.05
19	Nonconsumable Total			$18,884.24	$5,064.79	$2,813.73	$1,534.90	$36,189.40	$64,487.05
20	Grand Total			$97,279.40	$27,483.80	$14,615.42	$8,330.51	$191,901.77	$339,610.90

Figure CE16-10
OLAP Product Family and Store Location by Store Type

drilled down into the stores located in California; the OLAP report now shows sales data for the four cities in California that have stores.

Notice another difference between Figures CE16-10 and CE16-11 (page 526). The user has not only drilled down, but she has also changed the order of the dimensions. Figure CE16-10 shows *Product Family* and then store location within *Product Family*. Figure CE16-11 shows store location and then *Product Family* within store location.

Both displays are valid and useful, depending on the user's perspective. A product manager might like to see product families first and then store location data. A sales manager might like to see store locations first and then product data. OLAP reports provide both perspectives, and the user can switch between them while viewing the report.

Unfortunately, all of this flexibility comes at a cost. If the database is large, doing the necessary calculating, grouping, and sorting for such dynamic displays will require substantial computing power. Although standard, commercial DBMS products do have the features and functions required to create OLAP reports, they are not designed for such work. They are designed, instead, to provide rapid response to transaction processing applications, such as order entry or manufacturing operations.

Accordingly, special-purpose products called **OLAP servers** have been developed to perform OLAP analysis. As shown in Figure CE16-12 (page 527), an OLAP server reads data from an operational database, performs preliminary calculations, and stores the results of those calculations in an OLAP database. (Databases that are structured to support OLAP processing are called **dimensional databases**.) Several different schemes are used for this storage, but the particulars of those schemes are beyond this discussion. Normally, for performance and security reasons the OLAP server and the DBMS run on separate computers.

Guide

Semantic Security

Security is a very difficult problem—and it gets worse every year. Not only do we have cheaper, faster computers (remember Moore's Law), we also have more data, more systems for reporting and querying that data, and easier, faster, and broader communication. All of these combine to increase the chances that we inadvertently divulge private or proprietary information.

Physical security is hard enough: How do we know that the person (or program) that signs on as Megan Cho really is Megan Cho? We use passwords, but files of passwords can be stolen. Setting that issue aside, we need to know that Megan Cho's permissions are set appropriately. Suppose that Megan works in the human resources department, so she has access to personal and private data of other employees. We need to design the reporting system so that Megan can access all of the data she needs to do her job, and no more.

Also, the report delivery system must be secure. A reporting server is an obvious and juicy target for any would-be intruder. Someone can break in and change access permissions. Or a hacker could pose as someone else to obtain reports. Reporting servers help the authorized user, resulting in faster access to more information. But without proper security, reporting servers also ease the intrusion task for unauthorized users.

All of these issues relate to physical security. Another dimension to security is equally serious and far more problematic: semantic security. **Semantic security** concerns the unintended release of protected information through the release of a combination of reports or documents that are independently not protected.

Take an example from class. Suppose I assign a group project, and I post a list of groups and the names of students assigned to each group. Later, after the assignments have been completed and graded, I post a list of grades on the Web site. Because of university privacy policy, I cannot post the grades by student name or identifier; so instead, I post the grades for each group. If you want to get the grades for each student, all you have to do is combine the list from Lecture 5 with the list from Lecture 10. You might say that the release of grades in this example does no real harm—after all, it is a list of grades from one assignment.

But go back to Megan Cho in human resources. Suppose Megan evaluates the employee compensation program. The chief operating officer (COO) believes that salary offers have been inconsistent over time and that they vary too widely by department. Accordingly, the COO authorizes Megan to receive a report that lists *SalaryOfferAmount* and *OfferDate* and a second report that lists *Department* and *AverageSalary*.

Those reports are relevant to Cho's task and seem innocuous enough. But Megan realizes that she could use the information they contain to determine individual salaries—information she does not have and is not authorized to receive. She proceeds as follows.

Like all employees, Megan has access to the employee directory on the Web portal. Using the directory, she can obtain a list of employees in each department, and using the facilities of her ever-so-helpful report-authoring system, she combines that list with the department and average-salary report. Now she has a list of the names of employees in a group and the average salary for that group.

Megan's employer likes to welcome new employees to the company. Accordingly, each week the company publishes an article about new employees who have been hired. The article makes pleasant comments about each person and encourages employees to meet and greet them.

Megan, however, has other ideas. Because the report is published on the Web portal, she can obtain an electronic copy of it. The report is in Adobe Acrobat, and using Acrobat's handy Search feature, she soon has a list of employees and the week they were hired.

She now examines the report she received for her study, the one that has *SalaryOfferAmount* and the offer date, and she does some interpretation. During the week of July 21, three offers were extended: one for $35,000, one for $53,000, and one for $110,000. She also notices from the "New Employees" report that a director of marketing programs, a product test engineer, and a receptionist were hired that same week. It's unlikely that they paid the receptionist $110,000; that sounds more like the director of marketing programs. So she now "knows" (infers) that person's salary.

Next, going back to the department report and using the employee directory, she sees that the marketing director is in the marketing programs department. There are just three people in that department, and their average salary is $105,000. Doing the arithmetic, she now knows that the average salary for the other two people is $102,500. If she can find the hire week for one of those other two people, she can find out both the second and third person's salaries.

You get the idea. Megan was given just two reports to do her job. Yet she combined the information in those reports with publicly available information and is able to deduce salaries, for at least some employees. These salaries are much more than she is supposed to know. This is a semantic security problem.

SALARY INFORMATION

Discussion Questions

1. In your own words, explain the difference between physical security and semantic security.
2. Why do reporting systems increase the risk of semantic security problems?
3. What can an organization do to protect itself against accidental losses due to semantic security problems?
4. What legal responsibility does an organization have to protect against semantic security problems?
5. Suppose semantic security problems are inevitable. Do you see an opportunity for new products from insurance companies? If so, describe such an insurance product. If not, explain why not.

	A	B	C	D	E	F	G	H	I	J
1										
2										
3	Store Sales Net				Store Type					
4	Store Country	Store Sta	Store City	Product Family	Deluxe Super	Gourmet Supermarket	Mid-Size Grocery	Small Grocery	Supermarket	Grand Total
5	USA	CA	Beverly Hills	Drink		$2,392.83				$2,392.83
6				Food		$20,026.18				$20,026.18
7				Nonconsumable		$5,064.79				$5,064.79
8			Beverly Hills Total			$27,483.80				$27,483.80
9			Los Angeles	Drink					$2,870.33	$2,870.33
10				Food					$23,598.28	$23,598.28
11				Nonconsumable					$6,305.14	$6,305.14
12			Los Angeles Total						$32,773.74	$32,773.74
13			San Diego	Drink					$3,050.43	$3,050.43
14				Food					$23,627.83	$23,627.83
15				Nonconsumable					$6,039.34	$6,039.34
16			San Diego Total						$32,717.61	$32,717.61
17			San Francisco	Drink				$227.38		$227.38
18				Food				$1,960.53		$1,960.53
19				Nonconsumable				$474.35		$474.35
20			San Francisco Total					$2,662.26		$2,662.26
21		CA Total				$27,483.80		$2,662.26	$65,491.35	$95,637.41
22		OR		Drink	$4,438.49				$2,862.45	$7,300.94
23				Food	$37,778.35				$23,818.87	$61,597.22
24				Nonconsumable	$10,177.89				$6,428.53	$16,606.41
25		OR Total			$52,394.72				$33,109.85	$85,504.57
26		WA		Drink	$3,680.56		$1,409.50	$458.51	$7,968.50	$13,517.07
27				Food	$32,497.76		$10,392.19	$4,149.19	$67,915.69	$114,954.83
28				Nonconsumable	$8,706.36		$2,813.73	$1,060.54	$17,416.38	$29,997.01
29		WA Total			$44,884.68		$14,615.42	$5,668.24	$93,300.57	$158,468.91
30	USA Total				$97,279.40	$27,483.80	$14,615.42	$8,330.51	$191,901.77	$339,610.90
31	Grand Total				$97,279.40	$27,483.80	$14,615.42	$8,330.51	$191,901.77	$339,610.90

Figure CE16-11
OLAP Product Family and Store Location by Store Type, Showing Sales Data for Four Cities

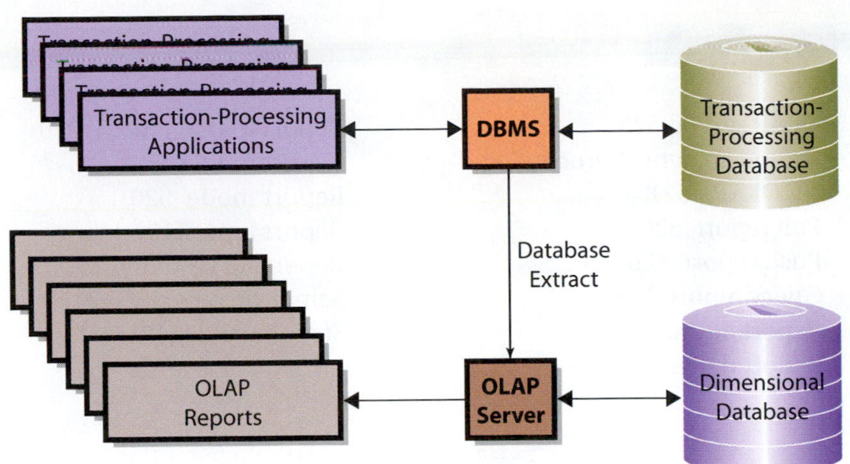

Figure CE16-12
Role of OLAP Server and Dimensional Database

Case 9, on page 226 shows an example of an OLAP report that is used by a camper-vehicle rental company.

ACTIVE REVIEW

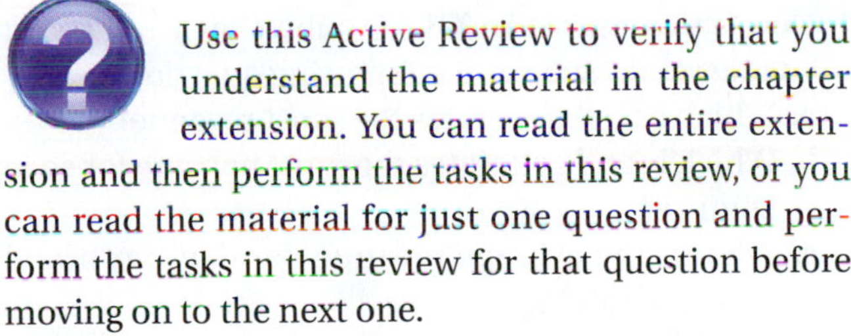

Use this Active Review to verify that you understand the material in the chapter extension. You can read the entire extension and then perform the tasks in this review, or you can read the material for just one question and perform the tasks in this review for that question before moving on to the next one.

Q1 How do reporting systems create information?

Describe the purpose of a reporting system. Give two definitions of *information*. List four basic reporting operations. Using Figures CE16-1 and CE16-4, explain the difference between data and information.

Q2 What are the components and characteristics of reporting systems?

Describe the role of each of the components in Figure CE16-5. Explain what reporting metadata describes. Name four types of reports, and give an example of each. Name seven different report media. Explain the difference between push and pull reports.

Q3 How are reports authored, managed, and delivered?

Name the three functions of report authoring. Explain the purpose of report management. Describe the role of metadata for report management. Describe the report delivery function. Explain the role of report delivery for security and for query reports.

Q4 How are OLAP reports dynamic?

Describe the basic operation of an OLAP report. Define *measure*, and give an example. Define *dimension*, and give at least two examples. Using hypothetical data and Figure CE16-9 as a guide, show how your measure and dimensions would appear in an OLAP report. Show how the structure of the report changes if you switch the two dimensions. Using your sample data, explain why OLAP reports are considered more dynamic than standard reports. Describe the circumstances under which an OLAP server is required.

KEY TERMS AND CONCEPTS

USING YOUR KNOWLEDGE

1. Suppose you work for Fox Lake, and Anne asks you to design a report that she could use as the basis of her campaign to market to members having daughters of a suitable age. Draw a mockup of a report that would enable her to do so. Explain how you would filter, group, and sort rows in the report.

2. Same as question 1, except mock up two reports regarding members and golfing activities (for use by the golf pros) and members and tennis activities (for use by the tennis pros). Assume that the purpose of your report is to identify prospects for golf and tennis lessons. Explain how you would filter, group, and sort rows in the report.

3. Suppose Fox Lake wants to analyze member charges using an OLAP cube. Thinking about all of the club's activities (tennis, golf, swimming, restaurant, lessons, and pro shop), answer the following questions.

   a. Define appropriate measures for this cube.

   b. Suppose Fox Lake defines Year, Quarter, Month, and DayOfWeek dimensions (the OLAP server can construct these using the date of the expense). Explain the meaning of the measures you identified in part a if the columns of the cube are ordered as DayOfWeek, Quarter, Year. What is the meaning if the columns are ordered Year, DayOfWeek, Quarter?

   c. Create a mockup of an OLAP cube that Fox Lake could use to assess which club activities generate the most business in the early spring and late fall. Assume you are interested in determining whether weekday specials are a good idea. How would you use the cube to determine whether the desirability of weekday specials differs among activities or times of the year?

4. Read about RFM analysis in Q2 of Chapter Extension 15, if you have not already done so. Explain how you can use the basic reporting functions to generate an RFM analysis. Include in your explanation the sequence of sorting and grouping operations that would be needed to create an RFM report.

5. Read the THL case at the end of Chapters 8 and 9. Describe a report or OLAP cube that would best enable you to answer the following questions:

   a. Which brand generates the most revenue?

   b. Which brand generates the most revenue for each country?

   c. What is the average revenue per day, per brand for all rentals?

   d. What is the average revenue per day, per brand for each month for all rentals in each country?

   e. Which locations (rental offices in cities in the countries in which THL is active) generate the most business? Assume a rental office rents just one brand of vehicle (i.e., Britz offices only rent Britz vehicles).

   f. Which locations generate the most business per season?

   g. Which locations generate the most business per season and year?

   h. Examine your answers to parts a–g and explain the criteria you used in determining whether you needed a report or an OLAP cube.

CHAPTER EXTENSION 17

Chapter 9 provides the background for this Extension.

Geographic Information Systems

STUDY QUESTIONS

Q1 What are the components of a geographic information system?

Q2 How are GIS maps constructed?

Q3 How do organizations use GIS?

Q4 How do maps deceive?

Q1 What Are the Components of a Geographic Information System?

A **geographic information system (GIS)** is an information system that captures, stores, analyzes, and displays geospatial data. As an information system, a GIS has the five components that all such systems have. It is the term *geospatial data* that makes GIS unique among IS. The root *geo* refers to the earth, and *spatial data* are data that can be ordered in some space. Thus, **geospatial data** means that data that can be ordered in reference to the earth. GIS are sometimes used for mapping the Moon, Mars, and other planets, but, in general, when people say GIS, they are referring to a system for processing earth's geographic data.

Of the four definitions of information discussed in Chapter 1, the one that best fits GIS is *data presented in a meaningful context.* Consider Figure CE17-1, which shows census tracts that have primary care physician shortages in the state of Indiana. Because few of us keep the boundaries of census tracts in our minds, data in this format are not informative. However, consider that same data as presented in

Find Shortage Areas: HPSA by State & County

- Shortage Designation Home
- **Find Shortage Areas**
- HPSA & MUA/P by Address
- HPSA Eligible for the Medicare Physician Bonus Payment
- MUA/P by State & County

Criteria:

State: Indiana
County: All Counties
Date of Last Update: All Dates
HPSA Score (lower limit): 0
Discipline: Primary Medical Care
Metro: All
Status: Designated
Type: All

Results: 273 records found.
(Satellite sites of Comprehensive Health Centers automatically assume the HPSA score of the affiliated grantee. They are not listed separately.)

HPSA Name	ID	Type	FTE	# Short	Score
001 - Adams County					
No HPSAs in this county.					
003 - Allen County					
Fort Wayne Inner City	1189991855	Geographical Area	13	4	9
C.T. 0011.00		Census Tract			
C.T. 0012.00		Census Tract			
C.T. 0013.00		Census Tract			
C.T. 0014.00		Census Tract			
C.T. 0015.00		Census Tract			
C.T. 0016.00		Census Tract			
C.T. 0017.00		Census Tract			
C.T. 0018.00		Census Tract			
C.T. 0020.00		Census Tract			
C.T. 0021.00		Census Tract			
C.T. 0023.00		Census Tract			
C.T. 0025.00		Census Tract			
C.T. 0026.00		Census Tract			
C.T. 0027.00		Census Tract			

Figure CE17-1
Listing of Geographic Data

Source: U.S. Department of Health and Human Services, Health Resources and Services Administration.

Figure CE17-2. Health care planners who are familiar with the geography of Indiana will find this map, along with a key to the meanings of the color-coded census tracts, to be much more informative than the list in Figure CE17-1. Hence, GIS create information by manipulating and displaying data in a geospatial context.

GIS are subject to the same trends as other information systems. As of 1990, most GIS were stand-alone desktop applications. Throughout the 1990s, some of this capability was moved to thick-client, client-server applications, and in the first part of this century some GIS applications, notably graphical viewers such as Google Maps and Bing Maps, moved to cloud-based, thin-client applications. Undoubtedly, GIS applications that use HTML 5 are in development now. Today, we see GIS operating on all of these platforms, from stand-alone computers to thin clients accessing data in the cloud.

Let's consider each of the five components of a GIS.

Hardware

Like all IS, GIS hardware includes client and server computers and network equipment. As stated, GIS run the gamut of hardware, from stand-alone applications, to classic client-server applications, to the three-tier architecture described in Chapter 6. However, GIS also employ special-purpose hardware for capturing geospatial data. Such hardware includes surveying equipment, cameras, satellite devices, GPS devices, map scanners, and additional specialized input hardware. That specialized equipment is outside the scope of this discussion.

Software

In addition to operating systems, GIS software includes application-specific programs, a GIS, and a DBMS. Figure CE17-3 shows the relationship of these programs. Notice the ambiguity in use of the term *GIS*. We have defined a GIS as an information system with all five components. However, and unfortunately, the term *GIS* is

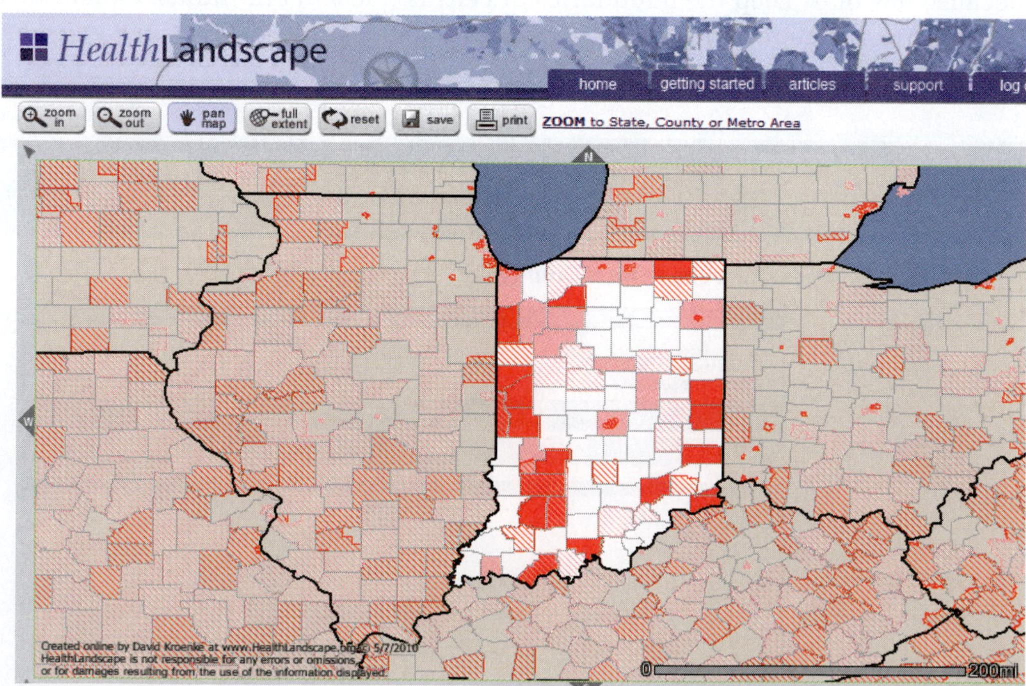

Figure CE17-2
Map of Data in Figure CE17-1

Source: Used with permission of HealthLandscape, LLC.

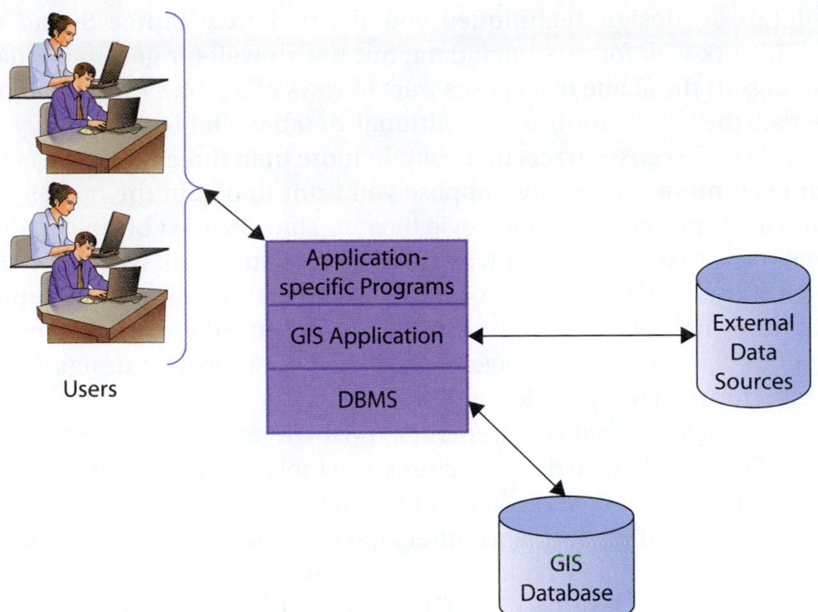

Figure CE17-3
Structure of GIS Application Components

also used to refer to a computer program, the **GIS application**, that manages geospatial data.

Application-specific programs are akin to application programs for database systems. They are created to add special-purpose features and functions on top of the raw GIS mapping capability. The map in Figure CE17-2 was produced using a medical-specific application developed by HealthLandscape, a corporation that provides GIS solutions for health care and other industries. The application uses ArcGIS, a generic GIS, which is a program that provides tools for importing and exporting, storing, analyzing, and displaying geospatial data. ArcGIS, in turn, calls upon a DBMS for the storage and retrieval of data.

In addition to ArcGIS, other popular commercial GIS programs include Autodesk, MapInfo, Bentley GIS, and many others. Open-source GIS include GRASS and uDig. Search the Web to learn more about any of these products.

A common scenario for business use of GIS is for the GIS application to obtain base geospatial data from a service like Google Earth or Bing Maps, add organizational-specific data from its own database, and display that data to clientsin browsers. In Q3, you'll see an example of how Harley-Davidson implements this scenario.

GIS applications vary in their ease of use. Some GIS viewer applications like Google Earth are intended for the public user, and its intuitive interface is easy to employ. However, tools for inputting, manipulating, and structuring GIS outputs can be complicated and difficult to use. Most GIS provide a set of tools and expect the geospatial analyst to know how to use those tools to accomplish particular tasks.

Data

GIS consist of a blend of external geospatial and relational database data. Some of the data in the map in Figure CE17-2 came from external government data sources. Some of it is geospatial data stored in the GIS database, and some of it is relational (table) data concerning physicians, population characteristics, community medical needs, and so forth.

The database design techniques you learned in Chapter 5 and Chapter Extension 5, work well for relational data, but not so well for geospatial data. How can you represent the shape of a census tract in rows of a table? Even more problematic, how can the application use traditional database tables to rapidly perform queries like "List the census tracts that contain more than three hospitals"?

Or, for even more complexity, suppose you want to obtain the names of restaurants within a 10-minute drive of a movie theater. The GIS must be able to determine the optimal route to each restaurant, and the design of data storage for the computation of such routes is challenging. To add another layer of complexity, suppose you want to know the names of restaurants within a 10-minute drive of that theater *for the current traffic conditions*. The storage of geospatial data must be designed to readily integrate external data from traffic sources.

Because of these special requirements, most GIS applications extend the base capabilities of the DBMS with data structures and tools that provide unique functions for processing geospatial data. Because of the importance of GIS today, DBMS vendors such as Oracle, Microsoft, and others have augmented their standard DBMS products to provide geospatial database capabilities.

Like the map in Figure CE17-2, GIS frequently combine data from several sources. Some is purchased from Google, Microsoft, or other sources, and much is available for free from national and local governments. The U.S. Government provides hundreds of different types of free geospatial data; Figure CE17-4 shows a few examples. Go to *http://viewer.nationalmap.gov/viewer* to learn more. (Don't be misled by the Add to Cart button. The data are free; you add what you want to your cart, input your email address, and the site mails you the data for you to input to your GIS application. That data will be useless to you, however, unless you have a GIS program and know how to use it.)

Procedures

Figure CE17-5 shows procedures necessary for using a GIS. For sites like Google Maps/Earth and Bing Maps, the user interface is designed to be intuitive and easy to use. For more complicated sites with more domain-specific capabilities, procedures

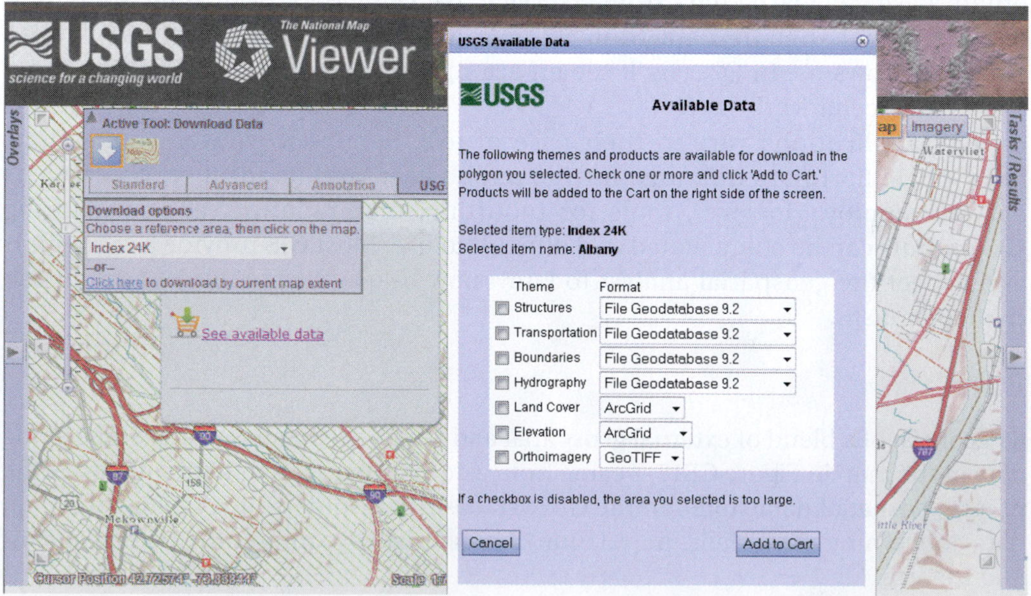

Figure CE17-4
Example Geospatial Data Available from the U.S. Government

Source: The National Map Viewer, USGS, *http://viewer.nationalmap.gov/viewer.*

- Find a map
- Search (point, near, include) features
- Zoom in/out
- Navigate the map
- Change the views
- Add, edit, and delete user data
- Import/export bulk data
- Manage map libraries

Figure CE17-5
Typical Procedures for GIS Use

are needed to help users obtain and process the data they need. We will discuss this further in Q4, when we discuss GIS for business intelligence.

Procedures are also needed for importing and exporting bulk data. This task can be complex and is important, especially for GIS sites that have multiple users whose analyses can be invalidated by incorrect or unexpected data imports. Finally, many, perhaps hundreds, of maps are produced for various purposes and studies, and these maps are often shared among a group. Consequently, procedures for managing large map libraries are important.

People

The following are common types of users for GIS applications:

- Casual users
- BI users
- Developers
- Operations personnel
- Field personnel

A casual user is someone like you who wants to use Google Maps to find directions to a friend's house, a business that wants to view a map of a customer's location, or a house hunter looking for all the houses in a neighborhood for sale in a given price range.

Business intelligence users employ GIS to help solve a problem. For example, a city may want to know how best to deploy its ambulances to fire stations, a company may want to determine how best to locate retail stores, or a police department may want to know if the locations of particular crimes in a city are changing. Such users need to know how best to employ the GIS to solve their problem.

By the way, do not be misled by one of the terms in the definition of GIS. We said that a GIS is an IS for capturing, storing, analyzing, and displaying geospatial data. GIS application programs can capture, store, and display geospatial data in an automated fashion. However, few GIS applications *analyze* data. Few GIS programs are sophisticated enough to state where the city should put its ambulances, for example. Instead, people, working with the GIS application's tools, analyze the geospatial data. Thus, it is the IS, including people, that analyze geospatial data. The GIS system augments human intuition for solving unstructured problems.

Developers create GIS systems in response to requirements, as described in Chapter 10. Operations personnel run and maintain the system; a major responsibility for GIS operations personnel is maintaining the currency of database data. Field personnel are involved in the capture of geospatial data.

Before we turn to examples of the use of GIS in business, you need to understand the composition of computer-based maps and a few related issues and problems.

Q2 How Are GIS Maps Constructed?

A GIS map typically consists of layers of individual maps that are placed over one another. One layer might, for example, portray the terrain such as mountains and valleys and slopes. Another layer might portray vegetation, another layer portray streets and highways, another layer buildings, and so forth. Each layer is placed on top of the others. The map that is shown to the user is a composite of several maps. The GIS display manager can add, remove, or reorder layers according to the users' needs.

The construction and management of these layers, although easy to describe, is filled with challenges. To understand some of those challenges, you need to know basic map characteristics.

Raster Versus Vector Maps

Each map layer is constructed in one of two formats: raster or vector. A **raster map** consists of pixels, each of which has some value; often that value is a color, but it could also be a data value, such as elevation or temperature. Pictures that you take with your camera are recorded in color raster format. Figure CE17-6(a) shows the outline of two shapes in raster format.

A **vector map** consists of points, lines, and shapes. Figure CE17-6(b) shows the outline of the same two shapes in vector format. Here, each shape is an ordered list of points and, because these shapes are closed, the first and last points are the same.

Each format has strengths and weaknesses and both are used in GIS. Raster maps are easy to create from pictures and scanners and, at the scale in which they were created, they show details well. However, raster maps become blurry when enlarged, as you have probably noticed when you zoom too far into a photo. Also, when raster maps are shrunk, features disappear. For example, the small triangular shape will disappear if that raster image is reduced beyond a certain point.

Because raster maps are made of pixels, straight lines can appear irregular, like the right edge of the triangle in Figure CE17-6(a). Finally, GIS applications cannot readily identify features on a raster map. You can look at a raster map of the United States and find the Mississippi River, but a computer program cannot.

Vector maps overcome the deficiencies of raster maps, but are difficult to create. In most cases, some human involvement is required to construct a vector map.

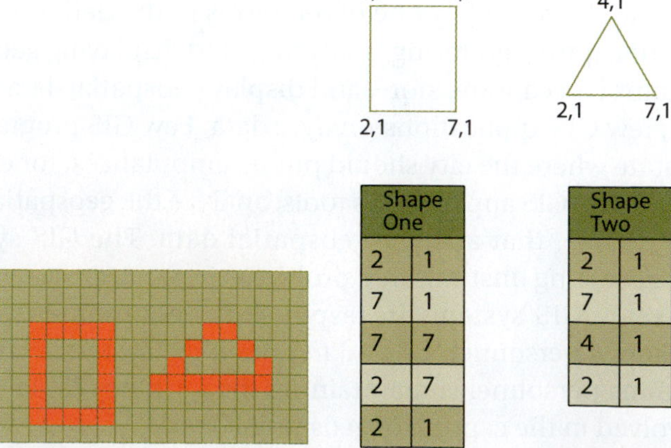

Figure CE17-6
Raster Versus Vector Format

Programs for converting raster maps to vector maps exist, but the results are seldom satisfying.

Once created, however, vector maps scale perfectly. You can double or halve the size of a vector map as many times as you want without loss of fidelity. Straight lines are always straight lines. (By the way, although not shown in Figure CE17-6(b), vector maps include many types of curved lines and shapes; with enough points, any curved shape can be represented in a vector map.) Because vector features are named, they are readily identifiable by programs. A user who searched the vector map in Figure CE17-6(b) for "Shape One" will readily find it, and a user who searches for "Shape Three" will know for certain that it does not exist on the map.

The layers in most GIS maps are a combination of raster and vector layers. In Google Maps and Bing Maps, you can turn layers on and off. In Bing, if you select *Aerial*, you'll see a raster map; if you select *Road*, you'll see a vector map. If you select both, you'll see a raster map with a vector map on top of it. In Figure CE17-7, the left-hand section of the map is in vector format and the right-hand section is a raster image with vector features added on top of it.

When combining layers of different types, map alignment is important. If the alignment is poor, you'll see roads in places where they are not, for example. Techniques for aligning layers exist but are beyond the scope of our discussion.

Mapping the Earth

Constructing a map of the earth requires answers to three difficult questions:

- How big is the earth?
- What is the shape of the earth?
- How can the curved surface of the earth be shown flat?

How Big Is the Earth?

In order to compute map elevations, we need to know what sea level is. But, because of tides, the sea level constantly changes. At what point, worldwide, are all the tides at

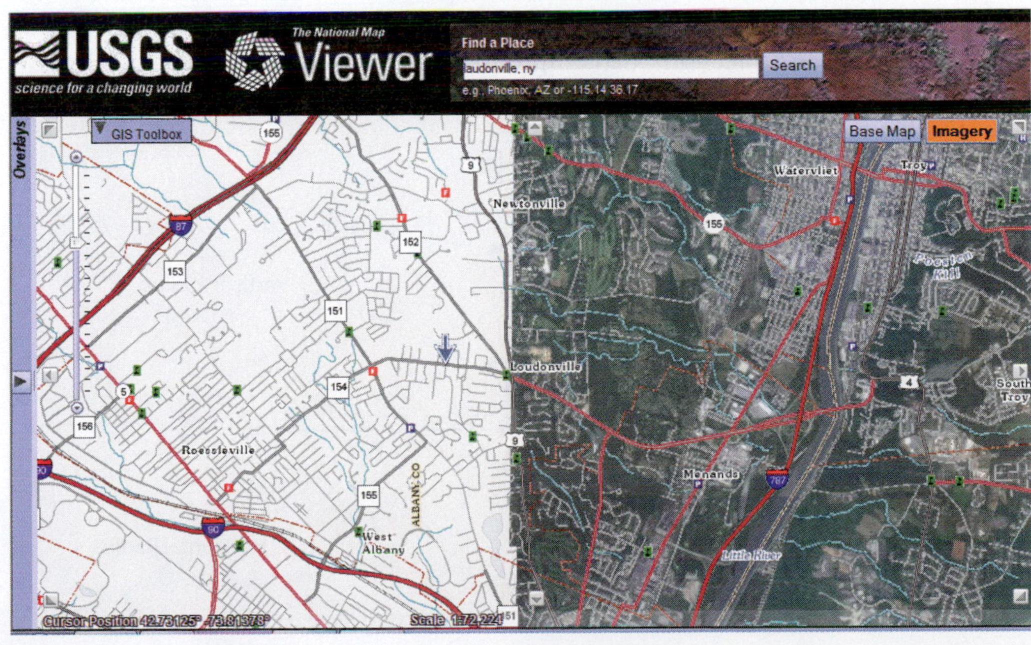

Figure CE17-7
Vector and Raster Image Examples

Source: The National Map Viewer, USGS, *http://viewer.nationalmap.gov/viewer.*

sea level? This question has no satisfying answer, and so cartographers (map makers) ask another question. What is the radius of the earth? An answer to that question determines a sensible value for sea level, worldwide. However, to use that approach for computing elevations, we must answer the second question.

What Is the Shape of the Earth?

The earth is not a perfect sphere; in fact, it is not a sphere at all. The best geometric model for the surface of the earth is an ellipsoid, which is a three-dimensional ellipse. Think of the earth as having the shape of an orange that you are squeezing on the top and bottom so that is it fatter than it is tall.

Because the earth is an ellipsoid, the question of how big the earth is requires not just a single radius, as for a sphere, but two radii. One radius is needed for the vertical dimension and one for the horizontal dimension. See Figure CE17-8.

Given values for these radii, elevations for points on the earth can be determined. A **datum** is a set of elevations based on particular values of the earth's radii. Over the years, different radii values have been used, and the result is numerous datums. WGS84 is a worldwide datum; NAD83 is a datum for North America, GRS80 is yet a third worldwide datum. The differences (and the explanation of the names) of these datums are unimportant to us, except that when importing data from different sources the data must arise from the same datum or the data must be converted to a single datum. Most GIS applications include tools for such conversions.

How Can the Curved Surface of the Earth Be Shown Flat?

It can't, at least not without error. You cannot accurately portray the surface of an ellipsoid on a flat piece of paper or flat computer screen. Every flat map of the earth has significant distortions; the trick with GIS is to choose a mapping technique with distortions that are the least important for the application.

A **map projection** is a technique for placing locations on the surface on the earth onto a flat surface. Over the centuries, cartographers have devised numerous map projections that result in different types of distortion. Some of these projections are accurate in the way they portray area; they are said to preserve area. Others, which are used for local navigation, preserve angles between map features. Other projections show the shortest distance between two points on the surface of the earth as a straight line on the map. And some projections are compromises of all of these. Figure CE17-9 shows two common map projections: a Mercator projection, which is good for navigation but

Figure CE17-8
Earth Modeled as an Ellipsoid

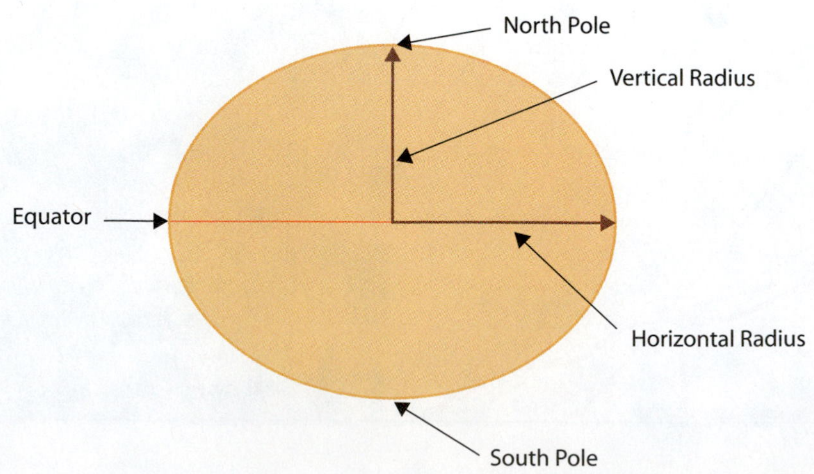

Figure CE17-9
Mercator and Peters Map Projections

Source: © 2009, Akademische Verlagsanstalt.

distorts areas, and a Peters projection, which preserves areas but distorts angles and cannot be used for navigation.

When composing layered maps, it is important that the maps be based on the same map projection. Combining layers that use different projections produces nonsense. Most GIS applications have tools for converting commonly used projections.

Where Is It?

A GIS application needs a means for placing features on maps. Buildings are identified by addresses and legal descriptions, natural features are identified by latitude and longitude, population characteristics are identified by census tract, and physical features are identified by other means. To construct a map, the GIS application needs to convert all of these location identifiers to a common scheme, a process called **geocoding**.

Many different schemes are used. The two most common for GIS are geographic coordinates and the Military Grid Coordinate System. **Geographic coordinates** are based on latitude and longitude. Zero latitude is the equator; the North Pole is 90 degrees north latitude and the South Pole is 90 degrees south latitude. By convention, north latitudes are shown with a positive sign and south latitudes are shown with a negative sign. Geographic coordinates (arbitrarily) set zero longitude at Greenwich, England. Locations west of Greenwich and east of 180 degrees are called *west longitudes* and are denoted with a negative sign. Locations east of Greenwich but west of 180 degrees are called *east longitudes* and are denoted with a positive sign.

Each degree is divided into 60 minutes, and fractions of minutes are normally shown as decimals. For example, the geographic coordinates of Loudonville, New York, are 42 degrees 42.6 minutes north (+) and 71 degrees 45.6 minutes west (–).

The **Military Grid Coordinate System (MGRS)** was developed by the U.S. military in 1947 and is used in GIS applications, worldwide. It was created before GPS, when longitudes were difficult to determine and always suspect. It divides the earth into 60 north-south segments, like segments in an orange. The segments are called **zones**. Zones are divided into squares that are 6 degrees east/west and 8 degrees north/south. Each square has a two-letter identifier. Within a square, distances are measured in meters from the east boundary and from the north boundary. In MGRS, the coordinates of Loudonville, New York, are 18T XN 01957 28809. Thus, it is located in the zone 18T block XN of that zone and is 1,957 meters east of the right-hand border of that block and 28,809 meters north of the southern border of that block. (Well, not quite. This location identifies a 1-meter square. The entire town of Loudonville is not located in that square!)

Numerous additional coordinate systems based upon the MGRS are in use today. In fact, if you go to the USGS National Map Viewer, you'll be offered a choice of four different coordinate systems.

The bottom line is that many alternatives exist for creating maps and for expressing locations on maps. When combining data from different sources, the GIS application must convert that data into consistent formats.

Q3 How Do Organizations Use GIS?

Organizations use GIS for the same reasons they do any information system; namely, to achieve their goals and objectives, which for competitive organizations means to obtain a competitive advantage. The ways in which GIS are used are as varied as there are different competitive strategies. In this section, we will examine GIS use on Web sites, for asset tracking, and as a BI tool.

How Do Organizations Use GIS on Their Web Sites?

The motorcycle manufacturer Harley-Davidson provides an excellent example of GIS use in its Ride Planner application. Figure CE17-10 shows the introductory screen. This display shows a vector-based map of the United States as well as public user procedures (and the location of the Harley-Davidson museum!). Suppose a rider wants to plan a motorcycle trip through the Capitol Reef National Park in Utah. To do so, the user would zoom into Utah by clicking repeatedly until he or she obtained a map with a scale that is useful for planning that trip. This site uses Microsoft Bing to provide zooming and map display, so the map quality is high and the user interface is already familiar to many users.

Figure CE17-10
Harley-Davidson Ride Planner

Source: http://rideplanner.harley-davidson.com/rideplanner/ridePlanner.jsp?locale=en_US&bmLocale=en_US. Courtesy of Harley-Davidson Motor Company.

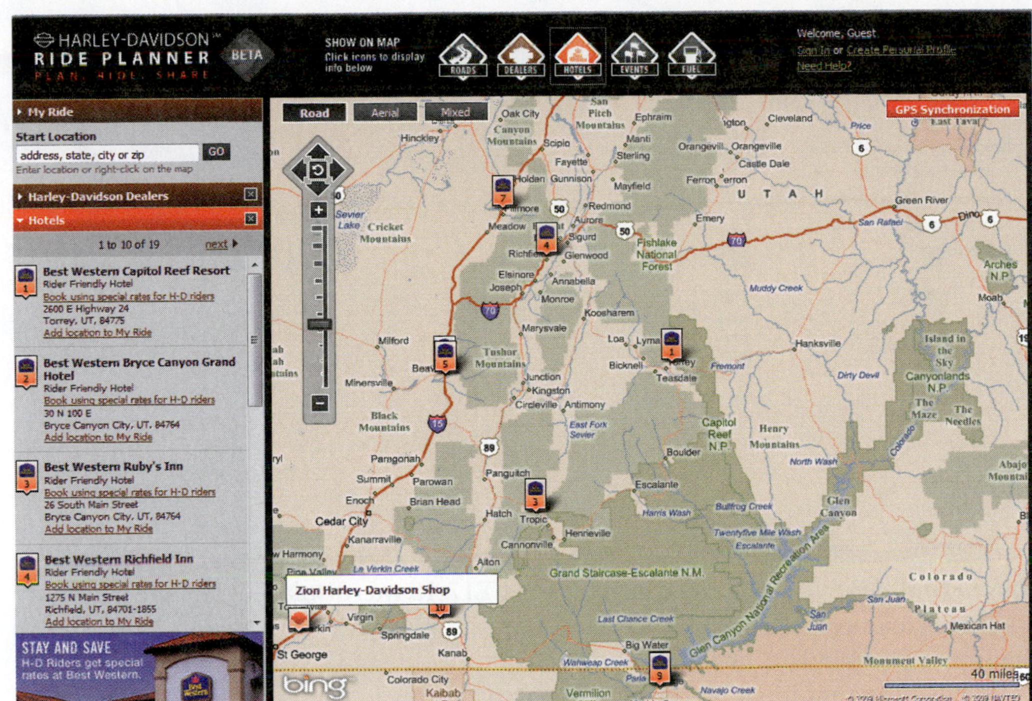

Figure CE17-11
Planning a Capitol Reef Ride: Roads

Source: http://rideplanner.harley-davidson.com/rideplanner/ridePlanner.jsp?locale=en_US&bmLocale=en_US. Courtesy of Harley-Davidson Motor Company.

Harley-Davidson adds its own GIS data on top of the Bing-provided maps, as shown in Figure CE17-11. This map shows the location of the nearest Harley-Davidson franchise (dealer) in St. George, Utah. If the user clicks that symbol, the GIS will display additional data about the dealership, its facilities, hours, phone number, location, and so forth. Further, by clicking *Hotels*, the ride planner learns locations of Best Western Hotels that have agreed to provide discounts to Harley-Davidson riders.

Figure CE17-12 shows another option. When the user clicked *Roads*, the GIS displayed trip reports that had been submitted by Harley-Davidson riders. When the user

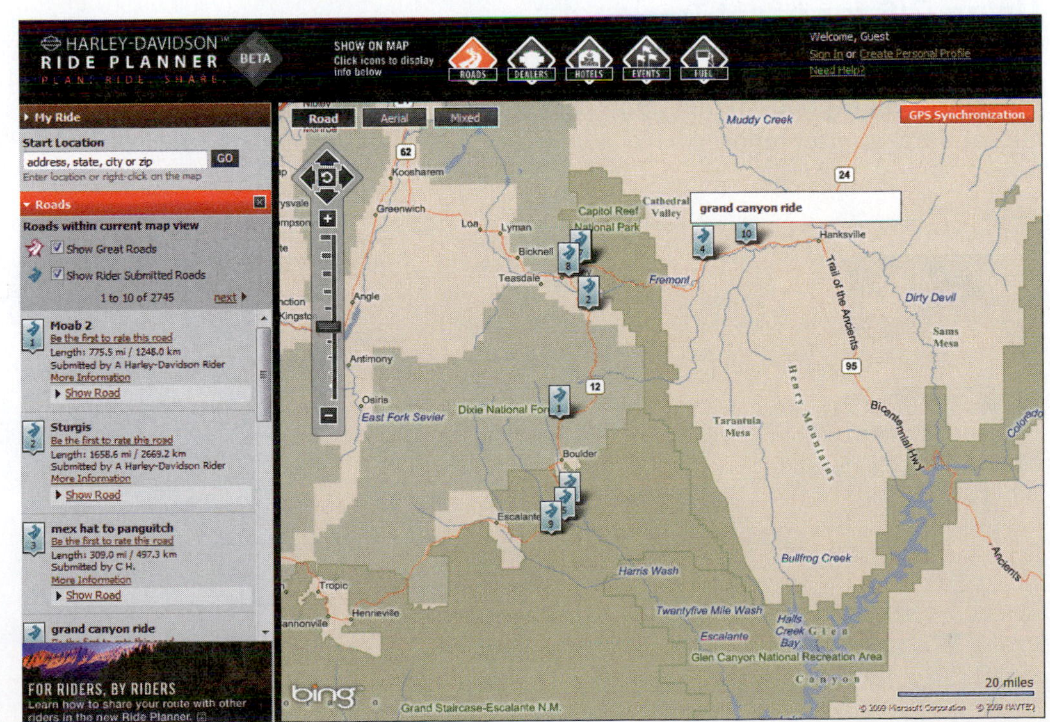

Figure CE17-12
User-Generated Content via GIS

Source:http://rideplanner.harley-davidson.com/rideplanner/ridePlanner.jsp?locale=en_US&bmLocale=en_US. Courtesy of Harley-Davidson Motor Company.

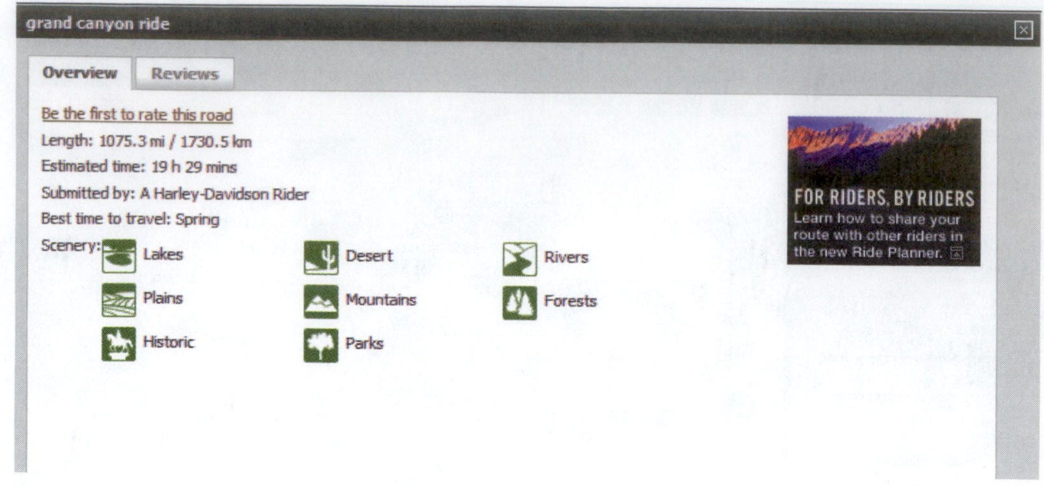

Figure CE17-13
User Contributed Data

Source:http://rideplanner.harley-davidson.com/rideplanner/ridePlanner.jsp?locale=en_US&bmLocale=en_US. Courtesy of Harley-Davidson Motor Company.

clicked *Grand Canyon ride*, the data in Figure CE17-13 was displayed. The site has many additional features, which you can explore by visiting *www.harley-davidson.com*. Under the *Experience* menu, click *Ride Planner*.

Reflect for a moment on how this site contributes to Harley-Davidson's competitive strengths. It promotes its museum. It raises the barrier to entry for other motorcycle manufactures and creates brand loyalty among customers. It reinforces alliances between the manufacturer and its franchises. It also reinforces alliances with cooperating hotels. Finally, it provides users an opportunity to contribute content and to form social networks with each other.

Because these tools are built on Microsoft Bing, Harley-Davidson was able to bring it to market much faster and at far less expense than if it had developed the base mapping capability itself.

GIS are used on the Web sites of nonprofit organizations as well as government agencies. Figure CE17-14 shows another Bing-based application developed by the City of Miami for displaying 311-call (government services) data.

Using GIS for Asset Tracking

Asset tracking is another organizational use of GIS. One common example is to track the movement of goods in the supply chain using a GPS device and a GIS. An onboard GPS and transmitter reports the location of the asset, say a pallet of goods, a truck, a

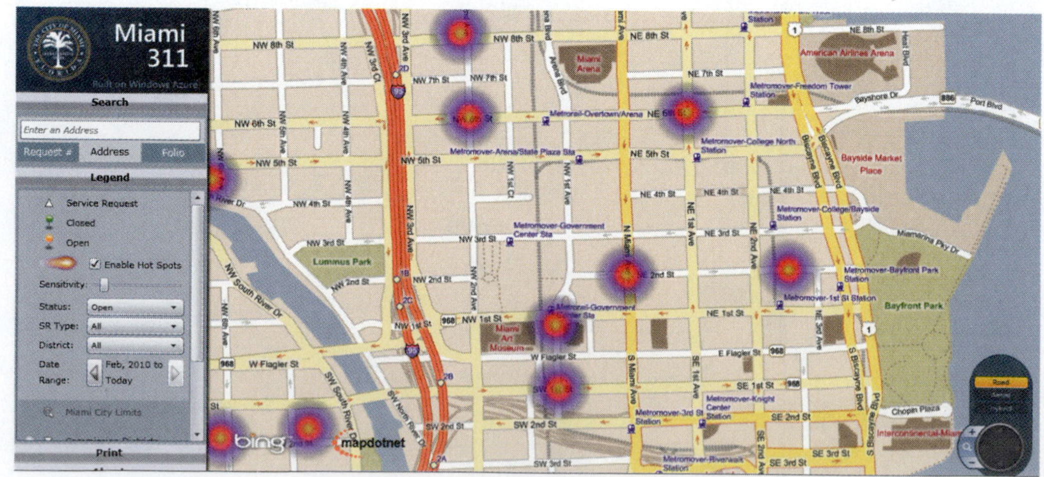

Figure CE17-14
Miami, Florida, 311-Call Patterns

Source: http://miami311.cloudapp.net.

container, or even a single item within a container. The reported locations are input to a GIS, and the locations of all such assets can be plotted on a GIS display.

A **geofence** is a geographic boundary set up within a GIS. One application for such boundaries is to notify personnel when trucks or other containers are nearing their destination. In this way, organizations can assemble the crew necessary to deal with the arrival of goods on a just-in-time basis.

One intriguing use of a geofence is to protect company personnel when they operate in politically dangerous locations. A geofence is established for safe zones. Any time an employee moves into an unsafe zone, as would happen in a kidnapping, the GIS notifies security personnel. Blue CRM is a risk management firm that provides just this capability. Visit *www.bluecrm.co.uk* to learn more.

GIS for Business Intelligence

GIS have become important for BI systems that involve geospatial data. A common application for GIS is to inform decisions about the location of resources and facilities. In this section, we will consider a typical example.

Community Health Network is a nonprofit organization that employs more than 10,000 people in the greater Indianapolis, Indiana, metropolitan area. It owns and operates four hospitals, many clinics, and a behavioral care pavilion. Community Health's primary charter is to provide access to health care services to a broad spectrum of people, particularly those who live in medically underserved neighborhoods.

Community Health Network endeavors to place facilities and medical professionals close to the point of need. As you can see in Figure CE17-15, it has placed its Health Centers in locations (census tracts) that have professional shortages or that are underserved in some other way.

Because populations are dynamic, the client needs of the Community Health Network change over time. Economic conditions change the number of people who

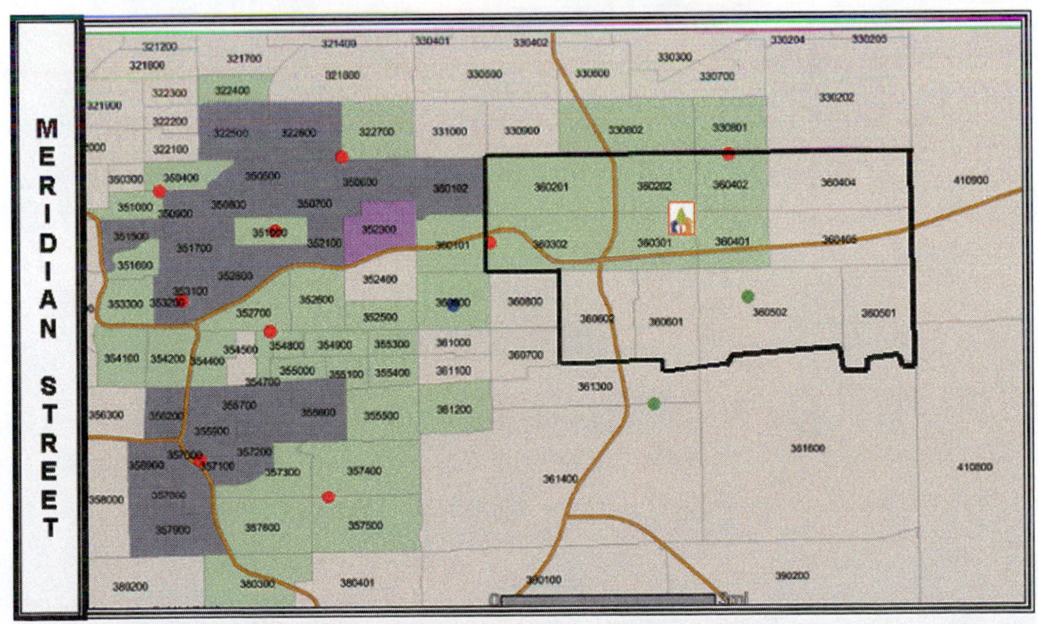

Legend:

Jane Pauley Community Health Center
Tracts with Health Profession Shortage Areas
Tracts with Medically Underserved Area / Population
Community Health Centers
Hospitals
School Based Health Clinics

Figure CE17-15
Community Health Network Facilities

Source: Used with permission of HealthLandscape, LLC.

need assistance, and people move in, out, and within the areas served by Community Health Network. For example, in recent years the Fall Creek Place neighborhood, which had been economically blighted, has become gentrified as part of Indianapolis' urban renewal. With this gentrification, many of the poor who had lived in that neighborhood were displaced. Those who moved still need medical services, however, and Community Health Services needs to know how this displacement impacted needs at other locations.

Community Health uses GIS to investigate such changes in population and economic conditions. The number of vacant residences in a neighborhood is correlated with poverty, and so changes in medical needs are correlated with changes in number of vacant residences. Figure CE17-16 shows maps of vacant residences for the first and last quarters of 2008. By comparing these maps, Community Health gains visibility on how medical needs may have changed during this year. Its analyses include not only maps, but other data sources as well. For example, if the map analysis indicates a possible increase in the number of disadvantaged people, analysts check for other evidence of poverty, such as an increase in free/reduced lunch

Figure CE17-16
Maps Used to Assess Change in Need for Medical Access

Source: Used with permission of HealthLandscape, LLC.

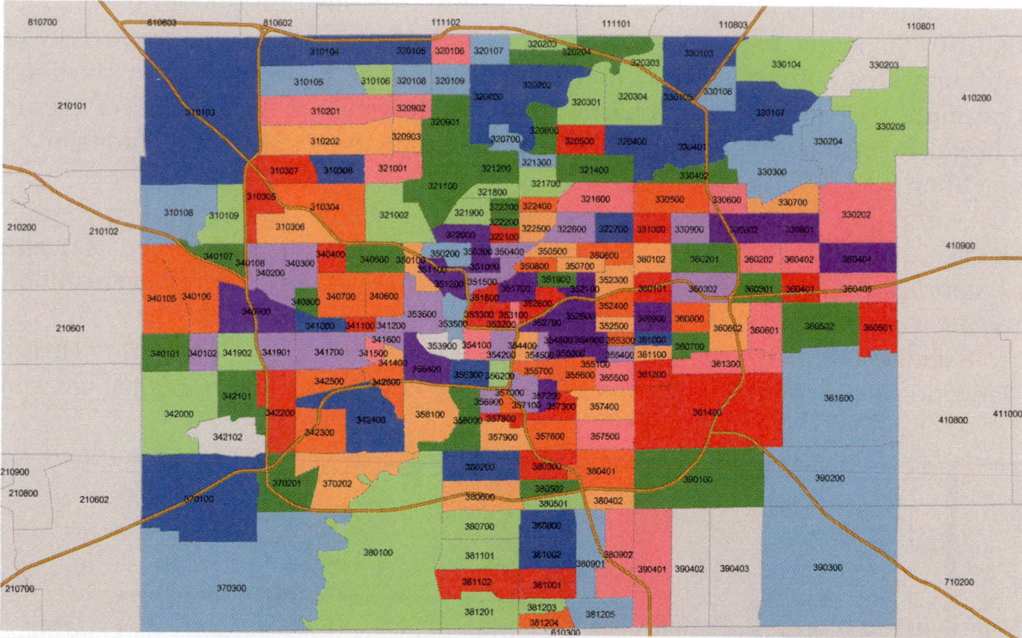

a. Total Vacant Residences, Q1 2008

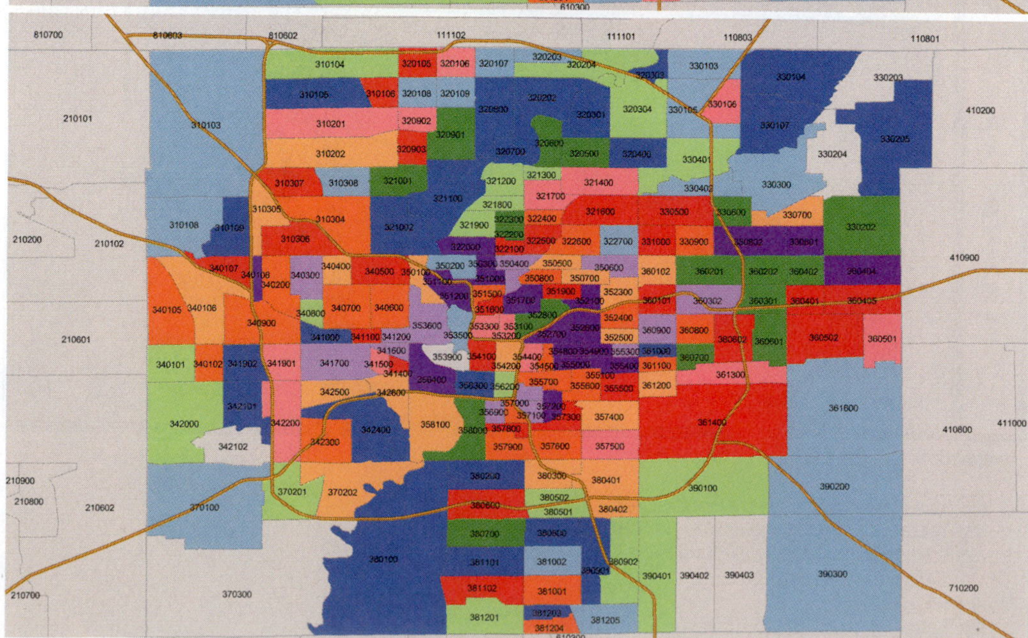

b. Total Vacant Residences, Q4 2008

requirements in schools. Combining maps and other data help Community Health to decide when and where to open new community health clinics. Such information also helps them to obtain funding for those clinics.

Community Health Network specializes in providing access to health care services; they do not specialize in GIS. Consequently, they contract with HealthLandscape, a for-profit organization that operates specialized GIS for medical applications, worldwide. HealthLandscape uses ArcGIS as its GIS application and adds data about medical needs that it obtains from a variety of sources, chiefly government agencies. Go to *www.healthlandscape.org* to learn about HealthLandscape's products. Also, see Using Your Knowledge, exercise 5, on page 548.

Q4 How Do Maps Deceive?

As you have learned, GIS maps create information by placing geospatial data into a meaningful context. Unfortunately, maps are also effective at deception. For some reason, perhaps the way humans process visual data, we tend to be less critical of maps and other graphic displays than we are of prose. Perhaps signals in the visual cortex bypass our critical apparatus.

Recall that all flat maps require distortion of some type. The judicious use of this distortion can lead map viewers into unwarranted conclusions. Accordingly, maps are used for propaganda, for advertising, and for biased reporting and analysis. In this question, we will discuss how maps are biased, how they seem to communicate more than they do, and how they can be structured to deceive.

Map Bias

Every human being is embedded in a culture and holds unconscious, or at least unrecognized, cultural biases. Like fish that are unaware of water, we swim in our culture and seldom challenge cultural values, including those embedded in maps. For example, examine Figure CE17-17 and pay close attention to your thinking as you do so.

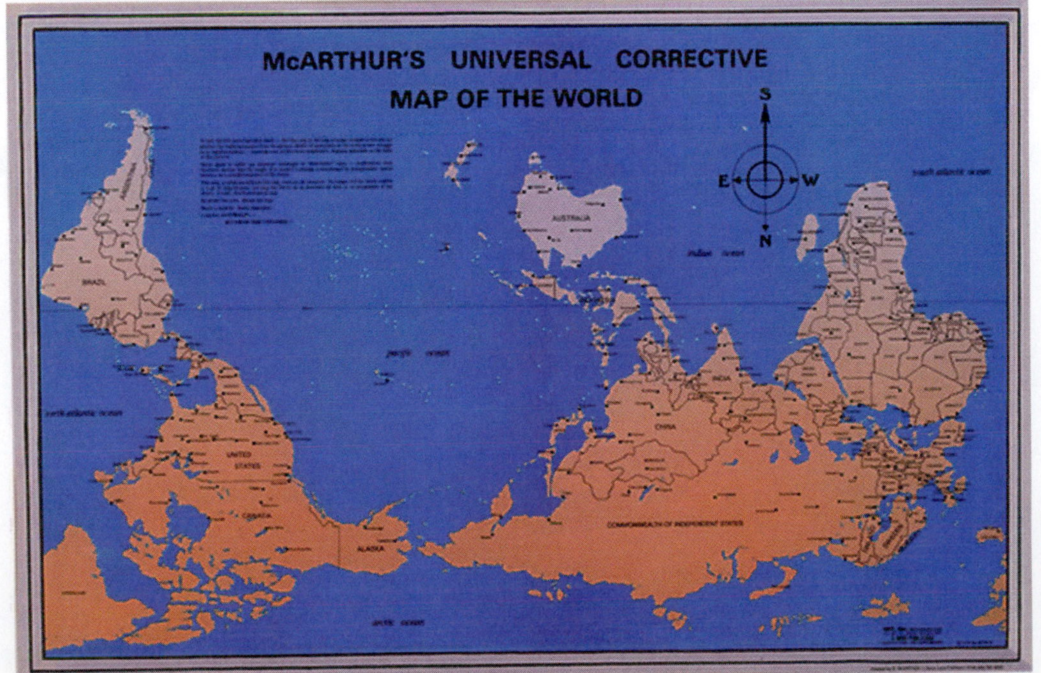

Figure CE17-17
A Proper (or Improper?) Map of the World

Source: McArthur's Universal Corrective Map of the World. © 1979 McArthur. Available world-wide from ODT, Inc. (1-800-736-1293; *www.ODTmaps.com*; Fax: 413-549-3503; E-mail: *odtstore@odt.org*). Also available in Australia from McArthur Maps, 208 Queens Parade, North Fitzroy, 3068, Australia. ODTmaps.com publishes a variety of alternative world maps including other south-on-top maps, equal area maps, and world population maps.

There is no reason that south cannot be up, nor is there any reason that Australia and New Zealand cannot be in the top or center of a map. Doing so places Mexico above the United States and the United States above Canada. If you live in any of these countries, something will seem wrong with the implications of this map, but only your cultural biases cause you to think so.

Some direction has to be up, and other than the fact that North is *always* up, cartographers can be forgiven for standard world maps. However, because all flat maps involve distortion, cartographers (or today, any GIS user) can create maps that use distortion to artificially reinforce a position. Someone who wants to emphasize world hunger could use a projection that would make Africa much larger in proportion to other continents. Or, someone who wants to de-emphasize world hunger could use a projection that would make Africa much smaller. Similarly, maps can be constructed that show two features much closer together than they are in proportion to the distances of other features. And, with modern GIS, it is possible for the untrained person to unknowingly create a great looking map that is full of distortions that appear to be meaningful. So, the first guide to map use is to pay attention to map orientation, projection, scale, and source.

Problems with Choropleth Maps

The map in Figure CE17-18 is an instance of a **thematic map**, or a map that shows themes about geographic locations. It is also an instance of a **choropleth map**, which is a map that displays colors, shades, or patterns in accordance with category values of underlying data.

Chorpleth maps have numerous problems (or opportunities if you're looking for deception possibilities). First, they convey homogeneity that seldom exists. The map in Figure CE17-18 makes it appear that everyone who lives in the Midwest voted Republican in 2004. If you are a Democrat, you can use this map to reconfirm whatever bias you have about people who live in the Midwest. If you are a Republican, you can use it to reconfirm whatever bias you have about people on the West Coast, etc.

Reality is, of course, much more complicated. In the state of Washington, for example, the eastern half of the state voted heavily Republican in the 2004 election;

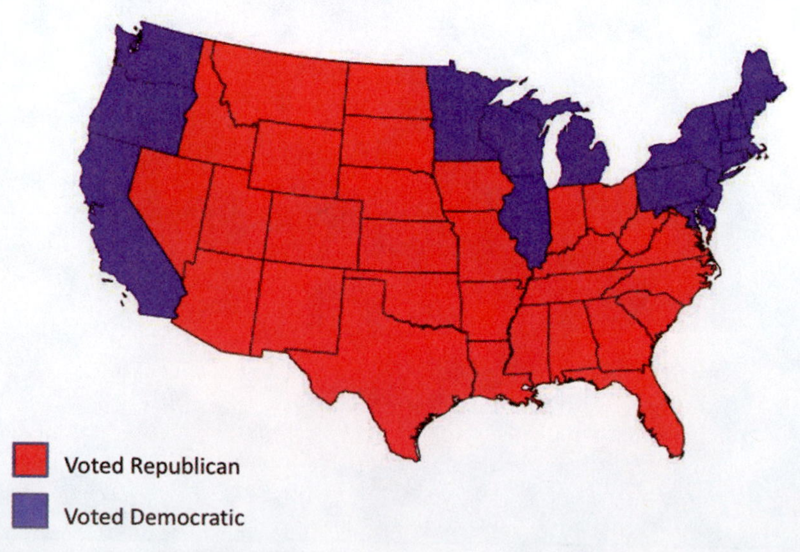

Figure CE17-18
Thematic, Choropleth Map Example

Source: Bob Yoder.

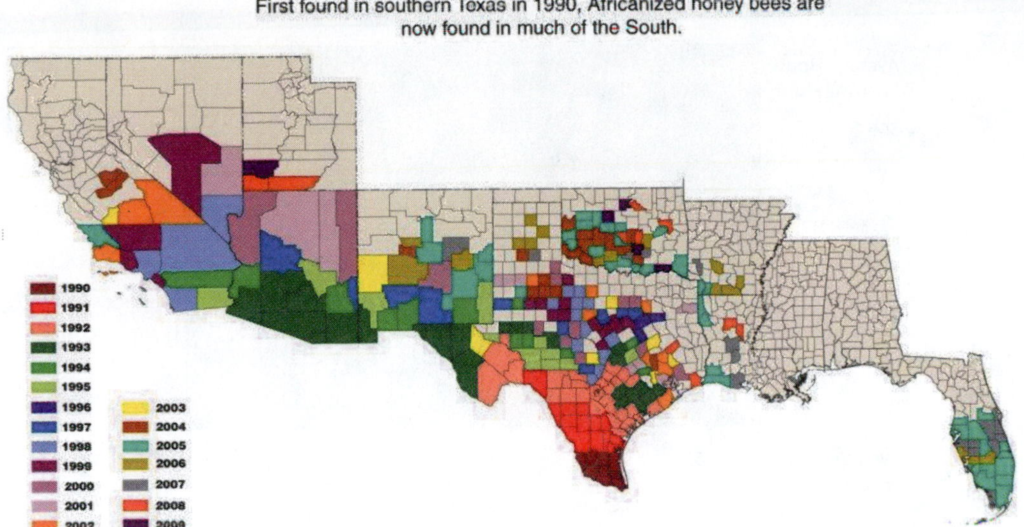

Figure CE17-19
What Is the Information in This Map?

Source: http://www.ars.usda.gov/Research/docs.htm?docid=11059&page=6.

but this fact is not visible in this map. Furthermore, the election was close in some states and not at all close in others. It is impossible to discern these differences on a choropleth map.

Figure CE17-19 demonstrates other interpretation problems of choropleth maps. A first look at this map would cause you to conclude that Africanized honey bees (so-called killer bees) are a growing menace. Perhaps such bees are a menace, but we can't conclude that from this map.

What, actually, does this map communicate? The large county in Nevada apparently had one or more Africanized bees in 1999. But because the entire county is colored, the map visually implies that the bees visited every part of that county. Furthermore, was the county visited by one bee or thousands? And, are the bees still there? Or did they move on? In fact, in spite of appearances, this map only communicates that at least one bee was found somewhere in a county in the year indicated. The results in the entire map could have been created by one very busy bee. But, by its structure, it seems to communicate more. It is also poorly designed; it has too many colors that are difficult to interpret.

It's unfair to criticize this map without reading the article that goes with it. But, use it as a caution to think carefully before unconsciously accepting what maps seem to say to our visual cortex.

Modifiable Areal Unit Problem

The **modifiable areal unit problem (MAUP)** is a condition that occurs when point-based spatial data are aggregated into regions and the results depend on how the regions are defined.[1]

For GIS, it occurs when geospatial point data are grouped into geographic regions. It is a problem because the results obtained depend on the definition of the regions, and thus different region definitions can give very different results.

Consider the housing price data in Figure CE17-20. Suppose that each square represents a city block, and the number represents the average price of houses on that block. Notice that if we group the data into three vertical columns, the average

[1] See Mark Monmonier, *How to Lie with Maps*, 2nd ed. (Chicago: University of Chicago Press, 1996).

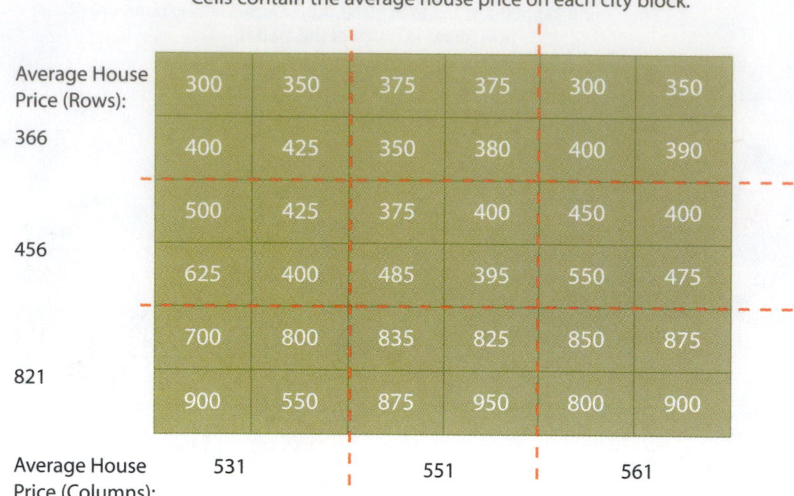

Cells contain the average house price on each city block.
Average House Price (Rows):
366
456
821
300 350 375 375 300 350
400 425 350 380 400 390
500 425 375 400 450 400
625 400 485 395 550 475
700 800 835 825 850 875
900 550 875 950 800 900
Average House Price (Columns):
531
551
561

Figure CE17-20
Average Housing Prices by City Block

house prices are 531, 551, and 561; all values are about the same. However, if we group the data into three horizontal columns, the average values are 366, 456, and 821. In this form, it is not too difficult to see that these differences are due only to grouping.

However, suppose we want to show that our city is a homogenous, middle-class one, so we construct the choropleth map shown in Figure CE17-21. We can use soft shades of a neutral color like green to reinforce our position.

But, grouping the same data in rows, as in Figure CE17-22, we can also show that this city (no longer ours!) is highly segregated. The poor live in the north and the rich in the south. We can also use emotional colors like red for poor and the princely purple for the rich.

Which is it? Is it a homogenous or segregated neighborhood? The only difference between Figures CE17-21 and CE17-22 is MAUP. By the way, in politics, they call MAUP *gerrymandering.*

The bottom line: Don't jump to conclusions when viewing maps, especially choropleth maps. Take the time to understand the bias of the map, the required distortion, the false homogeneity of choropleth maps, the use of emotional colors, and MAUP.

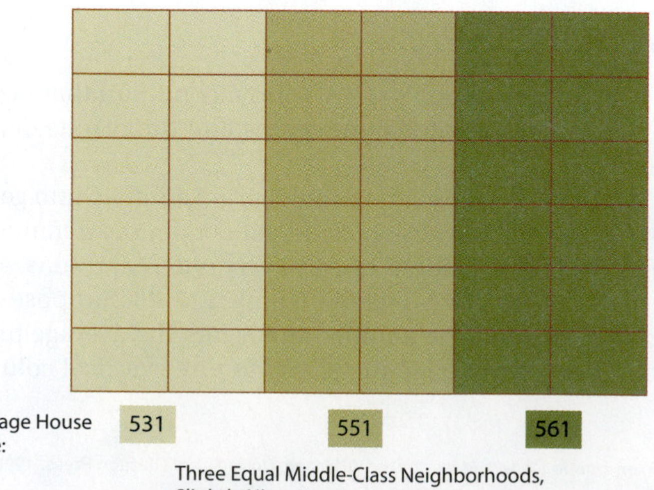

Figure CE17-21
First Grouping of Data in Figure CE17-20

Figure CE17-22
Second Grouping of Data in Figure CE17-20

ACTIVE REVIEW

Use this Active Review to verify that you understand the material in the chapter extension. You can read the entire extension and then perform the tasks in this review, or you can read the material for just one question and perform the tasks in this review for that question before moving on to the next one.

Q1 What are the components of a geographic information system?

Define *GIS* and *geospatial data.* Identify the type of information that is most appropriate for GIS, and explain why it is most appropriate. Summarize each of the five components of a GIS. Explain the role of application-specific programs and a GIS application. Name two GIS applications. Describe challenges for storing geospatial data. List three types of geospatial data available from the U.S. government. Name and describe the five types of GIS users.

Q2 How are GIS maps constructed?

Explain how maps are layered. Define *raster* and *vector maps,* and compare and contrast their advantages and disadvantages. Explain how sea level is determined, and describe the shape of the earth. Define *datum.* Explain why all flat maps of the earth involve distortion. Define *map projection.* Name and briefly describe two techniques that GIS use for locating features on maps.

Q3 How do organizations use GIS?

Summarize features of the Harley-Davidson map planner application. Explain how this application contributes to Harley-Davidson's competitive strength. Summarize the ways organizations use GIS for asset tracking. Describe the challenges faced by Community Health Network when it tries to use GIS to determine where to place its clinics. Summarize the role of GIS in making location decisions.

Q4 How do maps deceive?

Explain why maps are good candidates for creating deception. Describe the bias in maps and summarize your reaction to the map in Figure CE17-17. Describe thematic and choropleth maps. Summarize interpretation problems for the maps in Figures CE17-18 and CE17-19. What does the map in Figure CE17-19 actually convey? What does it appear to convey? Define *MAUP,* and explain how it is illustrated in Figures CE17-21 and CE17-22.

KEY TERMS AND CONCEPTS

Choropleth map 544
Datum 536
Geocoding 537
Geofence 541
Geographic coordinates 537
Geographic information system (GIS) 529
Geospatial data 529
GIS application 531
Map projection 536
Military Grid Coordinate System (MGRS) 537
Modifiable areal unit problem (MAUP) 545
Raster map 534
Thematic map 544
Vector map 534
Zone 537

USING YOUR KNOWLEDGE

1. Visit *www.harley-davidson.com* and plan a trip. Explain the roles played by the software components in Figure CE17-3 as you do so. Keep in mind that the base map data are coming from Microsoft Bing.

2. Use the Harley-Davidson trip planner to find a dealer in Grand Junction, Colorado. Use either Google Maps or Microsoft Bing to locate a nearby Mexican restaurant. Summarize the geospatial and structured database data that are required to produce these results. Is the phone number of the restaurant you found data or information to you? Explain.

3. Compare and contrast Google Maps and Google Earth. Summarize the disadvantages of a thick client to both you and Google. Install Google Earth. Find the restaurant you identified in your answer to question 2 in both Google Maps and Google Earth. Do you think Google Earth is worth installing? Why or why not?

4. Visit *http://udig.refractions.net*. Summarize the capability of the products offered at this site. Find and describe two interesting maps in the uDig gallery. Visit *http://grass.osgeo.org*. Summarize the capability of the products offered at this site. Go to the GRASS gallery and find and describe one interesting vector map and one interesting raster map. (Look in the Screenshots category in the left-hand menu on the homepage.) Summarize the process you would use to choose one of these products if you were looking for an open-source GIS product.

5. Visit *www.healthlandscape.org* and navigate to *My HealthLandscape*. Summarize the capability and benefits of this site. Create an account as a public user. Zoom to the county of your home town. Using the menu on the right, go to *Health Workforce Data*. Produce a map of Health Center Locations in your home county.

6. Use the knowledge you gained from Q4 of this chapter extension to construct a personal guide to map interpretation. List rules and reminders that you should use when interpreting maps, especially choropleth maps.

CHAPTER EXTENSION 18

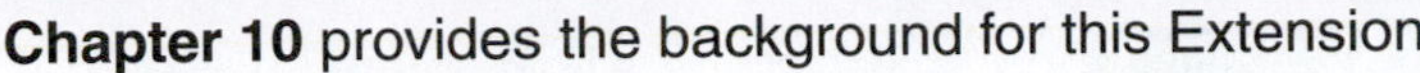
Chapter 10 provides the background for this Extension.

Business Process Management

STUDY QUESTIONS

Q1 Why do organizations need to manage business processes?

Q2 How does Business Process Modeling Notation (BPMN) document business processes?

Q3 How can business processes be improved?

Q4 How are SOA principles used to design business processes?

Q5 Why are XML and other SOA standards important?

Q1 Why Do Organizations Need to Manage Business Processes?

Chapter 2 defined a *business process* as a network of activities, roles, resources, repositories, and data flows that interact to accomplish a business function. To review, *activities* are collections of related tasks that receive inputs and produce outputs. *Roles* are collections of procedures, and *resources* are people, facilities, or computer applications assigned to roles. A *repository* is a collection of business records, and a *data flow* is a movement of data from one activity to another, from an activity to a repository, or the reverse. In that chapter, we also said that common roles for information system are to implement activities, to manage data repositories, and to control the flow of data. In this chapter extension, we refine and clarify these definitions. Before we do so, however, we will discuss the reasons why organizations need to manage business processes. To do that, consider a sample ordering business process.

A Sample Ordering Business Process

Suppose that you work in sales for a company that sells equipment and supplies to the hotel industry. Your products include hotel furniture, cleaning equipment, and supplies, such as towels and linens and staff uniforms. Processing an order involves five steps, as shown in Figure CE18-1.

As a salesperson, you do not perform all of the activities shown; rather, you orchestrate their performance. You are the customer's representative within the firm. You ensure that the operations department verifies that the product is available and can be delivered to the customer on the requested schedule. You check with accounting to verify credit required to process the order, and you check with your boss, a sales manager, to approve any special terms the customer might have requested (discounts, free shipping, extended return policy, etc.). We will document this process further in Q2.

Why Does this Process Need to Be Managed?

When you joined the firm, they taught you to follow this process, and you've been using it for two years. It seems to work, so why does it need to be managed? The fundamental answer to this question is that processes are dynamic and often need to be changed. This need can arise because a process doesn't work very well, because of a change in technology, or because of a change in some business fundamental.

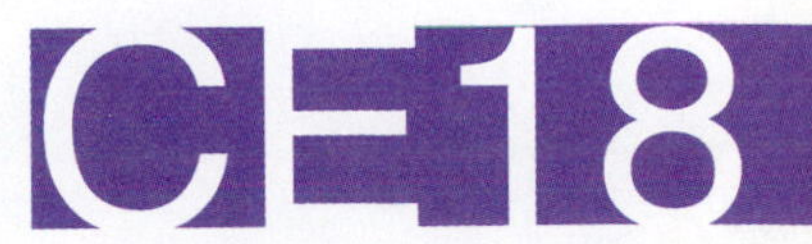

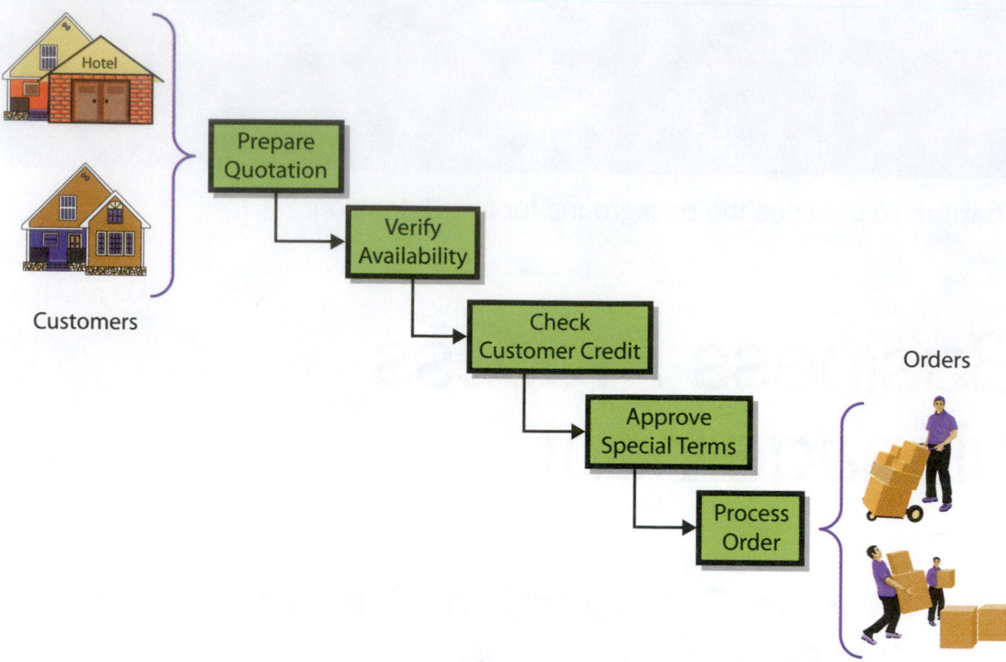

Figure CE18-1
Steps in Processing an Order

Processes That Don't Work (Well)

The most obvious reason for changing a process is that it doesn't work. The process does not produce the desired result or it is so confused, with everyone following their own personal way of getting things done, that it is only good fortune when desired outputs are produced. Businesses with such broken processes cannot survive; consequently, few processes are such complete failures. More common are processes that work, but not very well.

For example, according to Figure CE18-1, salespeople verify product availability before checking customer credit. If checking availability means nothing more than querying an information system for inventory levels, that sequence makes sense. But, suppose that checking availability means that someone in operations needs not only to verify inventory levels, but also to verify that the goods can be shipped to arrive on time. If the order delivery is complex, say, the order is for a large number of beds that have to be shipped from three different warehouses, then 1 or 2 hours of labor may be required to verify shipping schedules.

After verifying shipping, the next step is to verify credit. If it turns out the customer has insufficient credit and the order is refused, the shipping-verification labor will have been wasted. So, it might make sense to check credit before checking availability.

Similarly, if the customer's request for special terms is disapproved, the cost of checking availability and credit is wasted. If the customer has requested special terms that are not normally approved, it might make sense to obtain approval of special terms before checking availability or credit. However, your boss might not appreciate being asked to consider special terms for orders in which the items are not available or for customers with bad credit.

Another reason that processes don't work well is that they are misaligned with the organization's goals, objectives, or competitive strategy. If, for example, the vendor has chosen a low-cost strategy, then taking the time to verify shipping dates might be at odds with that competitive strategy. The labor to verify shipping dates will raise sales costs and may prohibit the vendor from providing the lowest possible prices to its customers.

As you can see, it's not easy to determine what process structure is best. The need to monitor process effectiveness and adjust process design as appropriate is one reason that processes need to be managed.

Change in Technology

Changing technology is a second reason for managing processes. For example, suppose the equipment supplier in Figure CE18-1 invests in a new geographic information system (see Chapter Extension 17) that enables it to track the location of trucks in real time. Suppose that with this capability the company can provide next-day availability of goods to customers. That capability will be of limited value, however, if the existing credit-checking process requires 2 days. "I can get the goods to you tomorrow, but I can't verify your credit until next Monday" will not be satisfying to either customers or salespeople. Thus, when new technology changes any of a process's activities in a significant way, the entire process needs to be evaluated. That evaluation is another reason for managing processes.

Change in Business Fundamentals

A third reason for managing business processes is a change in business fundamentals. A substantial change in any of the following can indicate a need to modify business processes:

- Market (e.g., new customer category, change in customer demographics)
- Product lines
- Supply chain
- Company policy
- Company organization (e.g., merger or acquisition)
- Globalization
- Business environment

To understand the implications of such changes, consider just the sequence of verifying availability and checking credit in Figure CE18-1. A new category of customers could mean that the credit-checking process needs to be modified; perhaps a certain category of customers is too risky to be extended credit. All sales to customers in this category must be cash. Or, a change in product lines might require different ways of checking availability. A change in the supply chain might mean that the company no longer stocks some items in inventory, but ships directly from the manufacturer instead.

Or, the company might make broad changes to its credit policy. It might, for example, decide to accept more risk and sell to companies with lower credit scores. In this case, most customers will pass the credit check, so special terms approval becomes more of a factor in choosing whether to accept an order. If so, the company might choose to first check special terms and then check credit.

Of course a merger or acquisition will mean substantial change in the organization and its products and markets, as will the moving of portions of the business offshore or engaging in international commerce. Finally, a substantial change in the business environment, say, the onset of a recession, might mean that checking credit becomes vitally important and needs to be moved to first in this process.

Business Process Management

The factors just discussed will necessitate business process changes, whether the organization recognizes that need or not. Organizations can either plan to develop and modify business processes or they can wait and let the need for change just happen to them. In the latter case, the business will continually be in crisis, dealing with one process emergency after another.

Figure CE18-2 shows the basic activities in **business process management (BPM)**, a cyclical (recurring) process for systematically creating, assessing, and altering business processes. This cycle begins by creating models of business processes. The business users who have expertise and are involved in the particular process (this could be you!) adjust and evaluate those models. Usually teams build an **as-is model**

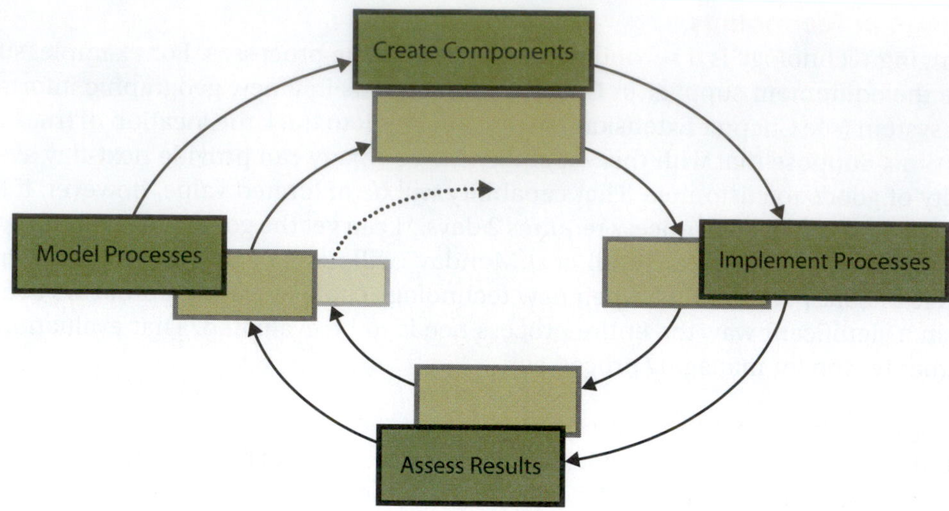

Figure CE18-2
The BPM Cycle

that documents the current situation and then changes that model to make adjustments necessary to solve process problems.

Given the model, the next step is to create system components. Those components have the five elements of every information system, although some are entirely automated (no people or procedures) and some are entirely manual (no hardware or software). Next, needed business processes or changes to existing business processes are implemented. Well-managed organizations don't stop there. Instead, they create policies, procedures, and committees to continually assess business process effectiveness. When a need for change arises, the company models a new, adjusted business process, and the cycle is repeated.

Effective BPM enables organizations to attain continuous process improvement. Like quality improvement, process improvement is never finished. Process effectiveness is constantly monitored and processes are adjusted as required.

Business process management has the same scope as discussed for information systems in Chapter 7: functional, cross-functional, and interorganizational. As shown in Figure CE18-3, BPM becomes more difficult as the scope of the underlying processes increases.

The Information Systems Audit and Control Association has created a set of standard practices called **COBIT (Control Objectives for Information and related Technology)** that are often used in the assessment stage of the BPM cycle. Explaining these standards is beyond the scope of this discussion, but you should know that they exist. See *www.isaca.org/cobit* for more information.

Figure CE18-3
Scope of Business Process Management

Scope	Description	Example	BPM Role
Functional	Business process resides within a single business function.	Accounts payable	BPM authority belongs to a single departmental manager who has authority to resolve BPM issues.
Cross-functional	Business process crosses into multiple departments within a single company.	Customer relationship management (CRM) Enterprise resource management (ERP)	BPM authority shared across several or many departments. Problem resolution via committee and policy.
Interorganizational	Business process crosses into multiple companies.	Supply chain management (SCM)	BPM authority shared by multiple companies. Problem resolution via negotiation and contract.

Finally, do not assume that BPM applies only to commercial, profit-making organizations. Nonprofit and government organizations have all three types of processes shown in Figure CE18-3, but most of these processes are service-oriented, rather than revenue-oriented. Your state's Department of Labor, for example, has a need to manage its processes, as does the Girl Scouts of America. BPM applies to all types of organizations.

How Does BPM Relate to the SDLC?

Chapter 10 discussed the phases of the System Development Life Cycle (SDLC), and you may be wondering how BPM differs from or relates to the SDLC. In brief, the scope of BPM is *processes;* BPM is concerned with all business processes, whether or not they involve information systems. SDLC, in contrast, is only concerned with the development of *information systems*. Thus, BPM is broader in scope than SDLC. Further, BPM precedes SDLC; the management of business processes may indicate the need for a new information system. If so, the results of BPM will be the impetus to start the SDLC for that system.

Q2 How Does Business Process Modeling Notation (BPMN) Document Business Processes?

A key BPM task is to document models of business processes. Both the as-is model and the models that incorporate changes to processes must be documented. In this section, you will learn standard notation for creating process documentation using the sales order process introduced in Q1.

Need for Standard for Business Processing Notation

As stated earlier, we define a *business process* as a network of activities, roles, resources, repositories, and data flows that interact to accomplish a business function. This definition is commonly accepted, but unfortunately dozens of other definitions are used by other authors, industry analysts, and software products. For example, IBM, a key leader in business process management, has a product called WebSphere Business Modeler that uses a different set of terms. It has activities and resources, but it uses the term *repository* more broadly than we do and it uses the term *business item* for *data flow*. Other business-modeling software products use still other definitions and terms. These differences and inconsistencies can be problematic, especially when two different organizations with two different sets of definitions must work together.

Accordingly, a software-industry standards organization called the **Object Management Group (OMG)** created a standard set of terms and graphical notations for documenting business processes. That standard, called **Business Process Modeling Notation (BPMN)**, is documented at *www.bpmn.org*. A complete description of BPMN is beyond the scope of this text. However, the basic symbols are easy to understand, and they work naturally with our definition of business process. Hence, we will use the BPMN symbols in the illustrations in the chapter. Be aware, however, that the companies you work for may use a different set of terms and symbols. The essence of the ideas you learn here will help you, however, regardless of the tools, symbols, and terms your company uses.

Documenting the As-Is Business Order Process

Figure CE18-4 shows the as-is, or existing, order process. First, note that this process is a model, and, as such, it shows the essential elements of the process but omits many details. If it did not, it would be as large as the business itself. This diagram is shown in **swim-lane layout**. Like swim lanes in a swimming pool, each role is shown in its own

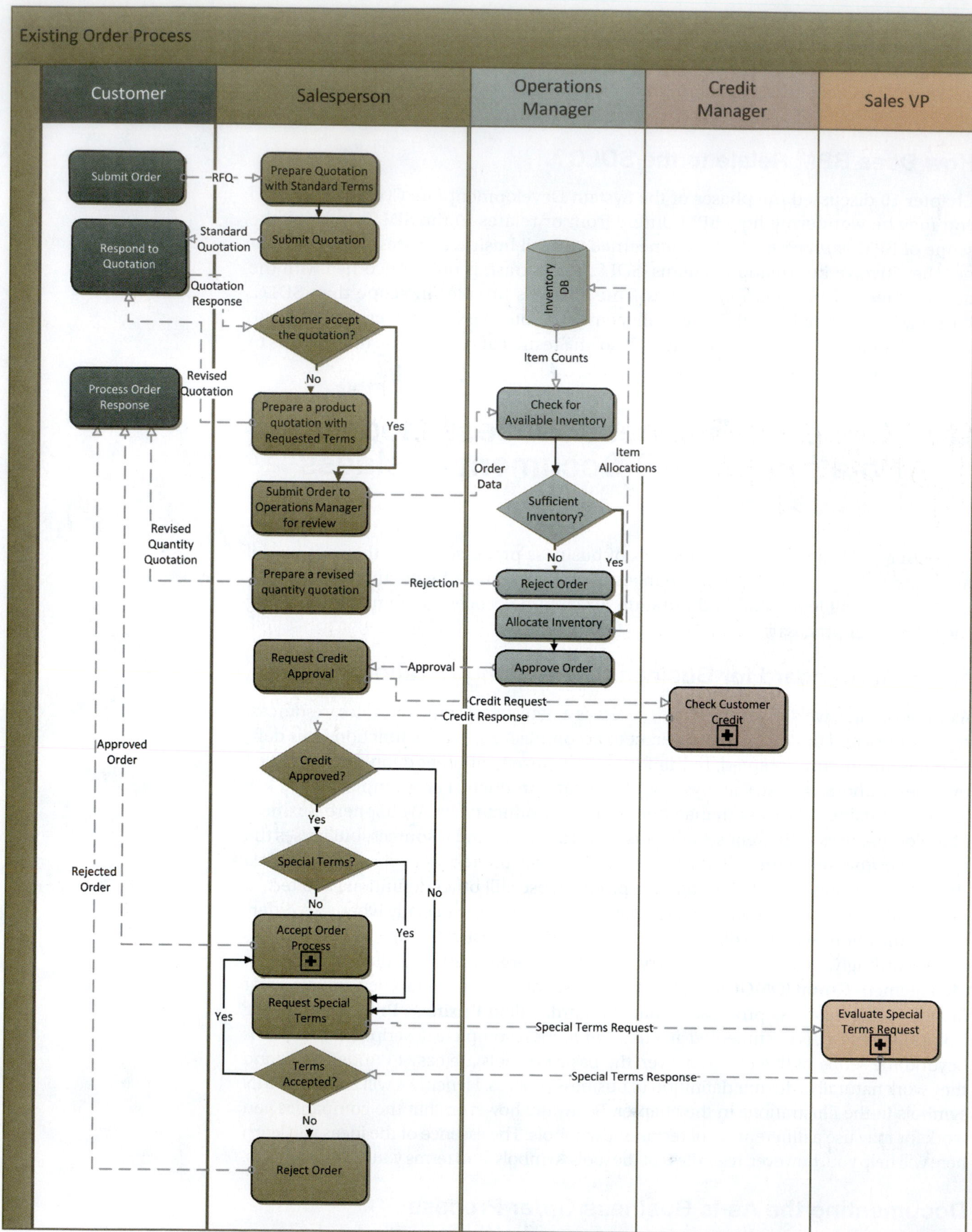

Figure CE18-4
Existing Ordering Process

vertical lane. Swim-lane layout simplifies process diagrams and draws attention to interactions among components of the diagram.

Two kinds of arrows are shown. Dotted arrows depict the flow of messages and data flows. Solid arrows depict the flow or sequence of the activities in the process. Thus, in Figure CE18-4, the customer sends an RFQ (request for quotation) to a salesperson (dotted arrow). That salesperson prepares a quotation in the first activity and then (solid arrow) submits the quotation back to the customer. You can follow the rest of the process in this diagram. *Allocate inventory* means that if the items are available, they are allocated to the customer so that they will not be sold to someone else. Figure CE18-5 summarizes the basic BPMN symbols.

Diamonds represent decisions and usually contain a question that can be answered with yes or no. Process arrows labeled Yes and No exit two of the points of the diamond. Three of the activities in the as-is diagram contain a square with a plus (+) sign. This notation means that the activity is considered to be independent of this process and that it is defined in greater detail in another diagram. We will explain further implications of the + symbol in Q4.

The Check Customer Credit Process is shown in Figure CE18-6. Note the role named *CRM*. In fact, this role is performed entirely by an information system, although we cannot determine that fact from this diagram. It is common to model information systems in this way.

Using Process Diagrams to Identify Process Problems

The processes shown in Figures CE18-4 and CE18-6 have problems. Before you continue, examine these figures and see if you can determine what the problems are.

The problems with these processes involve allocation. In Figure CE18-4, the Operations Manager role allocates inventory to the orders as they are processed, and in Figure CE18-6 the Credit Manager role allocates credit to the customer of orders

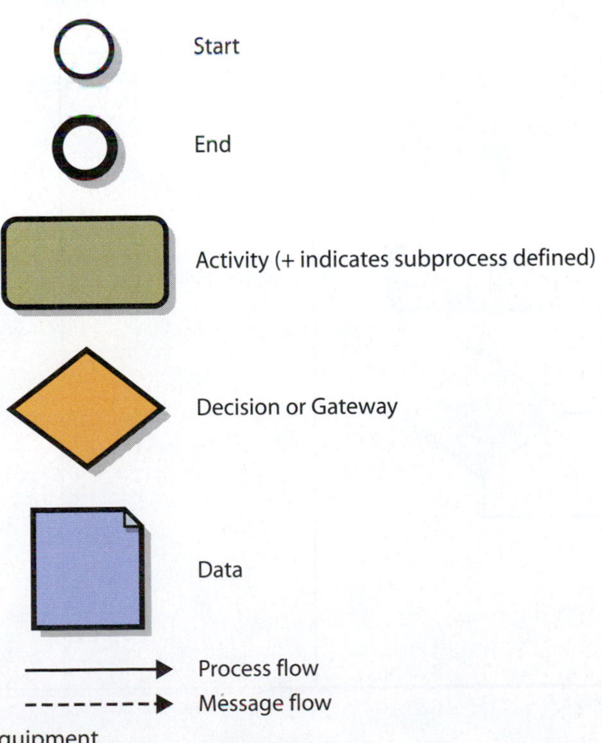

Figure CE18-5
Business Process Management Notation (BMPN Symbols)

Source: www.bpmn.org.

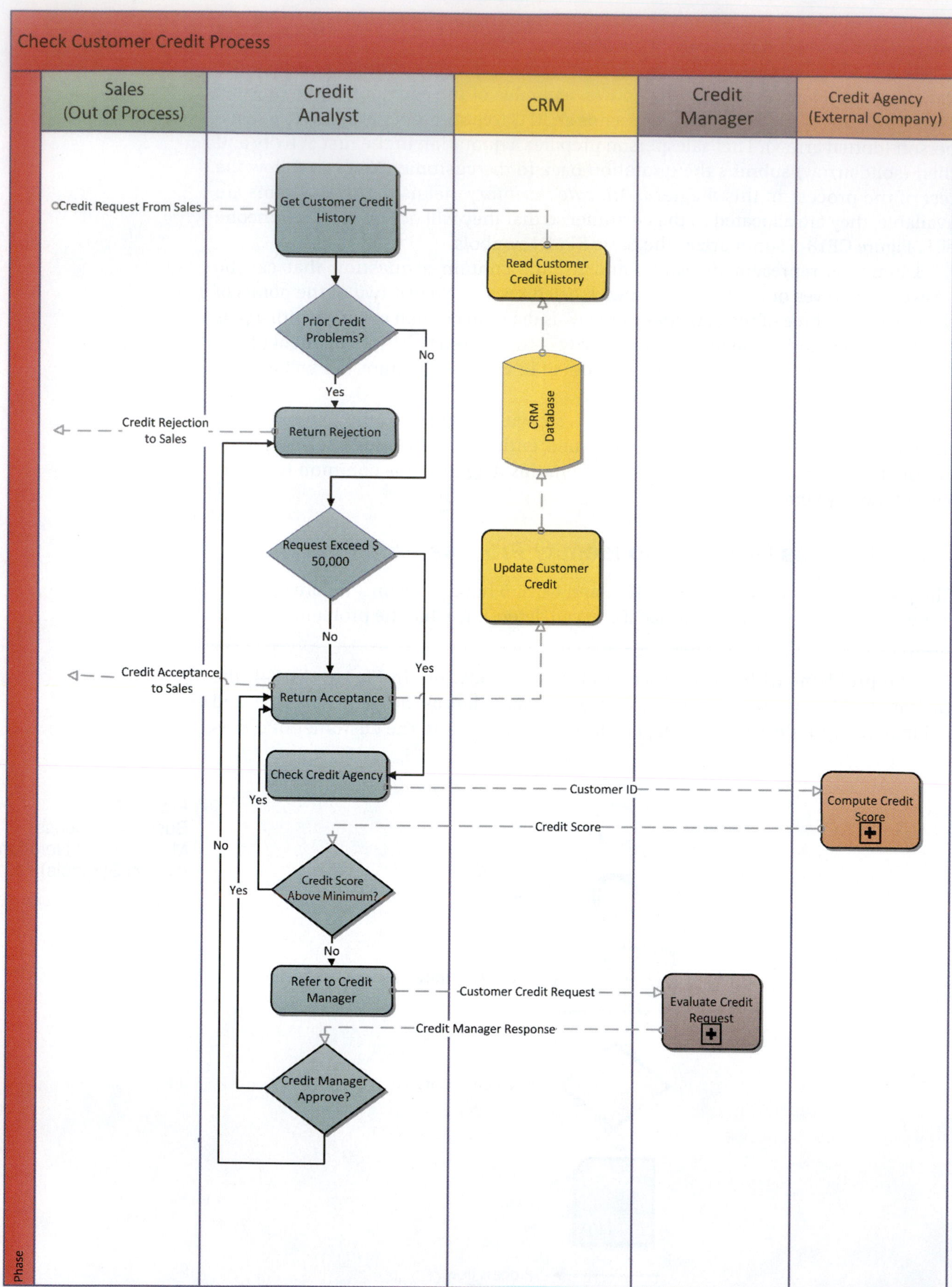

Figure CE18-6
Check Customer Credit Process

in process. These allocations are correct as long as the order is approved. However, if the order is rejected, these allocations are not freed. Thus, inventory is allocated that will not be ordered and credit is extended for orders that will not be processed.

One fix (several are possible) is to define an independent process for Reject Order (in Figure CE18-4 that would mean placing a box with a + in the Reject Order activity) and then designing the Reject Order subprocess to free allocations. Creating such a diagram is left as exercise 3 in Using Your Knowledge (page 395).

Q3 How Can Business Processes Be Improved?

The two major dimensions of business process effectiveness are performance and cost. Process designers can increase the performance of a business process in three fundamental ways. First, they can add more resources to a given process without changing its structure. This is the *brute-force approach:* Add more people or equipment to the existing way of doing business. Such a change always adds to the cost. Second, designers can change the *structure* of a process without changing resource allocations. In some cases, if the change is particularly effective, it can result in the same or even greater performance at no additional cost. Finally, designers can do both by changing the structure and adding resources.

To better understand these alternatives, suppose the supplier in Figure CE18-4 finds that its inventory costs are greater than expected. Investigation of the causes determines that inventory is being held for excessive amounts of time because orders are delayed due to the time required to check credit. To solve this problem, the company could speed up the credit-checking process by adding more people (resources) to the Credit Analyst role shown in Figure CE18-6. By the way, the company needn't necessarily add people as the resource to the credit-checking process. It might add resources by investing in an information system to augment or replace the humans who perform the credit-checking role.

Alternatively, the company could address this problem by changing the structure of the process to perform credit checks before checking inventory availability. Such a change is shown in Figure CE18-7. Another option is for the company to add resources to the credit-checking process and to change the sequence of inventory and credit checking.

Q4 How Are SOA Principles Used to Design Business Processes?

Many different process designs can fulfill a given business need. Some of those designs are easily understood and are readily modified and updated as business needs change. Other designs are confused and contorted and result in high expense when they are modified. In this question, we introduce a design methodology that has been shown to result in simpler, cleaner process designs that are easy to adapt. This methodology, called **service-oriented architecture (SOA)**, constructs processes so that primary activities are modeled as *independent, encapsulated services* and so that processes communicate only by requesting and responding to *service requests*.

SOA was originally used to design the interaction of computer programs. More recently, systems designers have applied SOA principles to business process activities, whether those activities are manual, partly automated, or fully automated.

Consider each of the italicized terms in the definition of SOA, starting with *service.* A **service** is a repeatable task that a business needs to perform. Using SOA, a BPMN

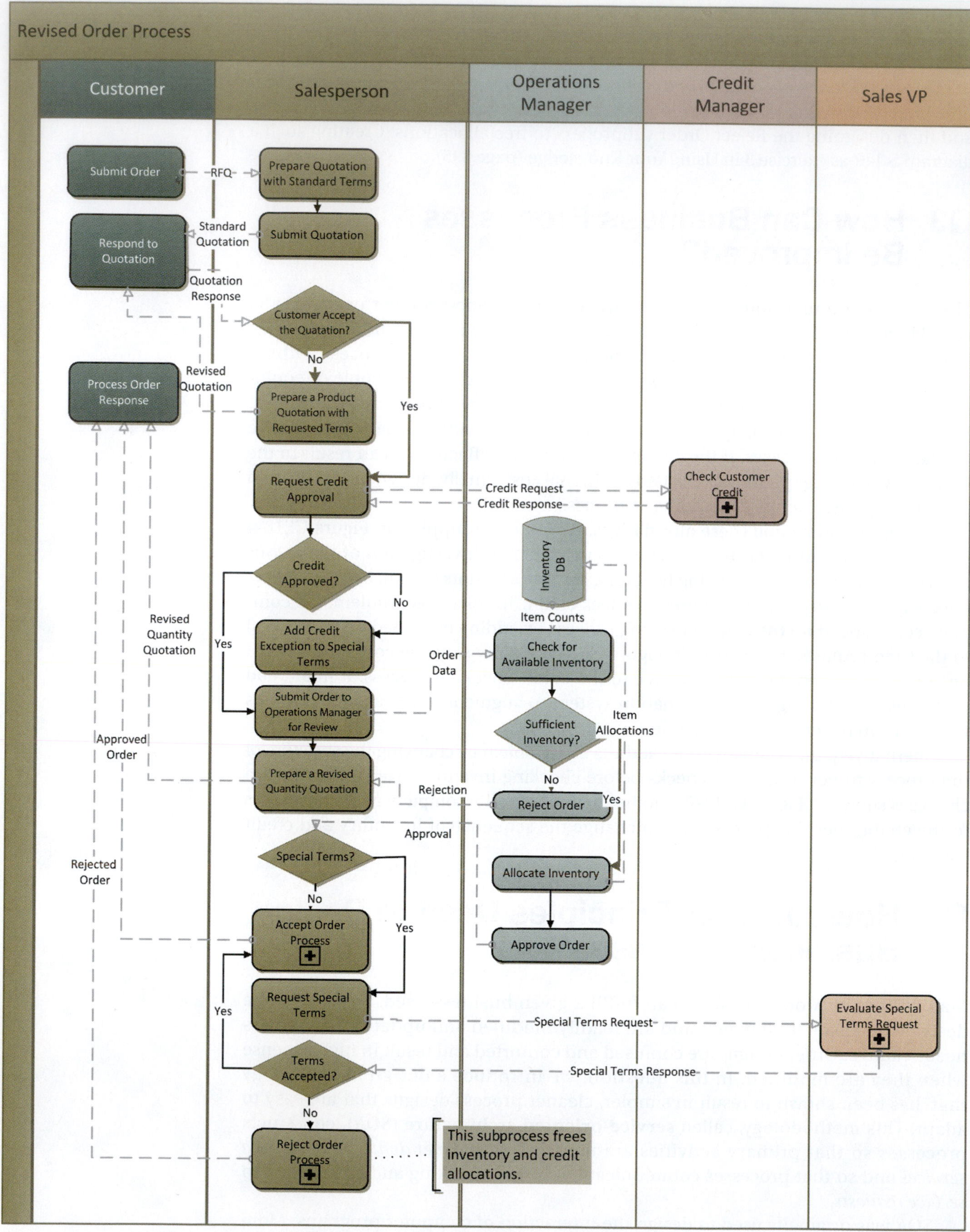

Figure CE18-7
Revised Order Process

activity accomplishes its function by providing one or more services. Examples of services for the order process we have been considering are:

- Check customer credit
- Evaluate special terms request
- Accept order
- Reject order

An activity that conforms to SOA principles is called a **service provider**. With SOA, the services provided by each activity are formally defined, and the only interaction among activities is to request or to provide one of these predefined services. Figures CE18-4, CE18-6, and CE18-7 show service providers as activities with plus signs.

Activities Modeled as Independent and Encapsulated

To understand the terms *independent* and *encapsulated*, consider an example. In Figures CE18-4 and CE18-7, the operations manager determines product availability by checking inventory levels. If inventory is sufficient, the order is approved. Let's suppose, however, that another element of availability, one not shown in either of these figures, is whether the vendor can ship the items to arrive on time. A new hotel cannot open without beds, for example, so knowing that goods will make their scheduled delivery date is critical to customers.

The salespeople are the closest to the customer and will be the first to learn the importance of delivery times. Professional salespeople are superb at removing impediments to sales, and let's suppose that each salesperson takes it upon him- or herself to verify shipping schedules. Most likely, if there are 15 salespeople, they will invent 15 different ways of making this check, all of which will vary in efficiency.

Furthermore, it will be difficult to implement a change in shipping methods or alternatives. Suppose the vendor contracts with a new shipping company that can provide shipments more quickly. With 15 different ways of verifying shipping dates, this knowledge of this new shipper will need to be incorporated into 15 different, personal processes.

A company that is engaged in BPM would notice this inefficiency as part of its BPM assessment. In response, it would replace these duplicated checks with a new activity, called, say, Verify Shipping Date, which would verify the shipping terms of an order. Consolidating shipping verification into a single activity will standardize that process. If designed correctly, it will also make that process more efficient. Thus, instead of 15 different versions of varying degrees of efficiency, there will be just one efficient process, independent of the salespeople.

Further, all of the activity involved in verifying shipping dates will be isolated in a single process. Logic that is so isolated is said to be encapsulated in the service. **Encapsulation** is a design practice that places the logic in one place; all other services go to that one place for that service. Figure CE18-8 shows the first part of the Revised Order Process with both the Check Inventory and Check Shipping Date activities modeled as independent, encapsulated services.

Because of encapsulation, when the Verify Shipping Date activity needs to be changed, when there is another alternative for shipper, for example, then only the Verify Shipping Date process needs to be modified. The change will be implemented more consistently than it would be if 15 salespeople each had their own, different process.

Finally, with encapsulation, it does not matter who performs a service or where that service is performed. That service could be performed by a human being, or it could be performed by a computer system. It could be done in the operations department, or it could be done by a third party in India, or anywhere else, worldwide.

Figure CE18-8
Portion of Revised Order Process with Shipment Schedule Checking

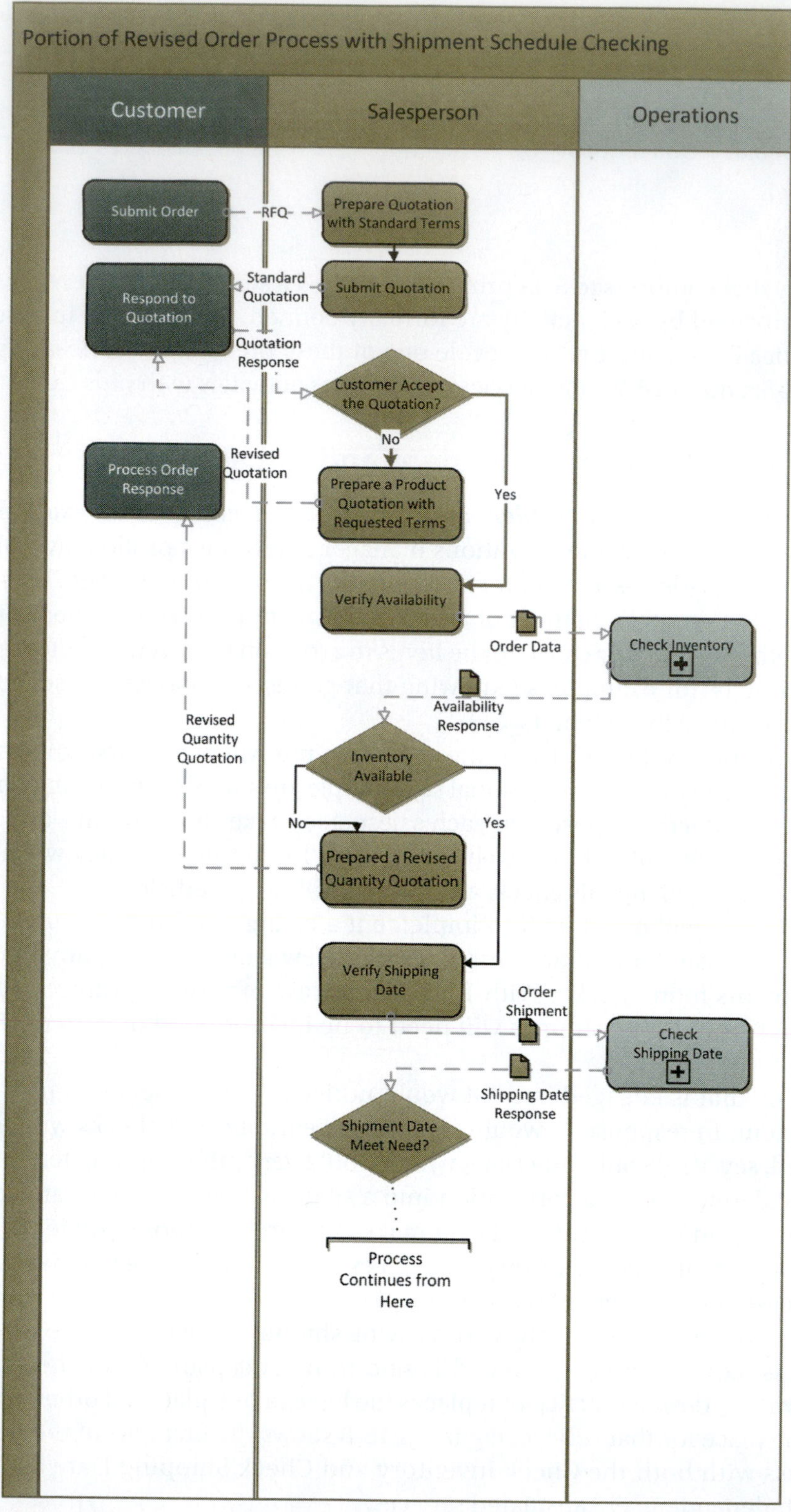

To summarize, constructing processes as assemblies of independent and encapsulated service providers promotes standardization, makes it easier to change processes, and makes those processes more adaptable.

Defined Service

In SOA, services are defined by the data that they request and provide. In essence, a service provider declares that it will accept data of a particular format and it will return data in another format. A service provider at Amazon.com, for example, declares that it will receive queries for products in a particular format, and it will return products that meet the parameters of the query in a second format. In SOA terms, those declarations are the definition of the service that the service provider offers.

For our example in Figure CE18-8, the Check Shipping Date service receives the Order Shipment document and returns a Shipping Date Response document. The content of both of these documents is documented and serves as the definition of the Check Shipping Date service.

In Figure CE18-8, the small rectangles with the folded corners represent data documents that are formally defined. We examine how such documents are coded in a standard language called XML in Q5.

According to SOA principles, service providers reject improperly formatted service requests and provide only properly formatted service responses. This principle is important, because many service requestors and service providers are not people, but computer programs.

As stated, SOA was originally developed for use by computer systems. However, the general principles can be used for designing business activities, regardless of who performs that activity. In fact, if you look back at Figure CE18-7, you'll see that Check Customer Credit, Evaluate Special Terms Request, Accept Order Process, and Reject Order Process are designed just that way. All of these activities are independent and encapsulated, and all receive a service request and respond to it. (By the way, the data that flows to and from all of these services should be formally defined and should be represented with data symbols as well. Those symbols were omitted from the first few process diagrams for simplicity.)

Humans are more flexible than computer-based systems, and, for humans, the interface between a service requestor and a service provider need not be more formal than just described. If, however, either the service requestor or the provider is a computer program, more is needed. As a result, the computer industry developed a set of SOA standards that govern how SOA-based applications will interact. We consider them next.

Q5 Why Are XML and Other SOA Standards Important?

SOA has become quite important for information systems. When a Facebook application connects to Facebook, it does so via an SOA interface. Or, when a vendor wishes to connect programmatically to Amazon.com, it does so via an SOA interface. Or, when Harley-Davidson wants to mash up its content with maps from Microsoft Bing (see Chapter Extension 17), it does so via an SOA interface. Because of the widespread use of SOA, you should understand the nature of these standards.

Numerous SOA standards have been developed, but the most important ones, and the ones you should be able to recognize, are XML, SOAP, and WSDL. As explained in Chapter 6, **XML (eXtensible Markup Language)** is a markup language like HTML, but it solves several important HTML problems. XML is important for many reasons beyond SOA; in fact, Bill Gates once called XML "the *lingua franca*" of the Internet. Here we will discuss just a few of the important features of XML as they pertain to SOA.

Using SOA, documents like the Order Shipment document in Figure CE18-8 will be coded in XML. Figure CE18-9 shows such a document with two example orders. Like HTML, XML includes **tags**, which are metadata that name and identify data items. Tags occur in pairs. <OrderNumber> signifies the start of the *OrderNumber* and </OrderNumber> signifies the end. The value of the tag is contained between the <OrderNumber> and the </OrderNumber>. Thus, <OrderNumber>12345 </OrderNumber> specifies that the value for *OrderNumber* is 12345.

The value of an XML element can either be a value, like 12345, or it can be a set of one or more contained XML elements. For example, consider *OrderItem*. After the opening <OrderItem> tag, the document contains tag pairs for values of *ItemNumber, ItemDescription, Quantity, ShipperName, ShipmentDate,* and *ArrivalDate.* Then *OrderItem* is closed with the </OrderItem> tag.

Similarly, the value for *OrderShipment* is a value of *OrderNumber* together with two sets of *OrderItems.* The complete set of XML tags and data is referred to as an **XML document**.

XML has many important features, most of which are beyond the scope of this text. You should know, however, that the purpose of some XML documents is to describe the structure of other XML documents. In particular, an **XML schema** is an XML document whose content describes the structure of other XML documents. An XML schema document for *OrderShipment* would indicate that the *OrderShipment* consists of *OrderNumber* followed by a variable number of *OrderItem* groups. The schema would also indicate that *OrderItem* must have *ItemNumber, ItemDescription, Quantity, ShipperName, ShipmentDate,* and *ArrivalDate* elements as well.

The importance of a schema document is that any program (or human, for that matter) can read the schema to determine the structure of an XML document for processing. For example, as shown in Figure CE18-10, the Verify Shipping Date activity reads the XML schema for Order Shipment documents to prepare the Order Shipment document. It then sends that document to the Check Shipping Data service. That service, in turn, reads the XML schema for Order Shipment documents and uses it to verify that it received a complete document, properly formatted.

XML is important for SOA because it enables programs to share data in a standardized way. As long as all services create and maintain XML data in conformance with that data's schema, XML data can be passed from one service to another without problem.

The SOAP and WSDL Standards

Two other standards are important for SOA. **SOAP** (which, oddly enough, is not an acronym) is a protocol for exchanging messages encoded in XML. When the Verify Shipping Date activity in Figure CE18-10 sends customer credit data to the Check Shipping Date service; it formats the data in accordance with the XML schema for Order Shipment documents, as just described; and then sends that data as a message using SOAP. SOAP sits on top of the transport protocol and can use any available protocol. SOAP messages can be exchanged using HTTP, HTTPS, FTP, or other transport protocol.

Figure CE18-9
Example XML Document

```
<OrderShipment>
  <OrderNumber>12345</OrderNumber>
  <OrderItem>
    <ItemNumber>1000</ItemNumber>
    <ItemDescription>King Size Bedframe</ItemDescription>
    <Quantity>35</Quantity>
    <ShipperName>Amalgamted Shipping</ShipperName>
    <ShipmentDate>10/12/2010</ShipmentDate>
    <ArrivalDate>11/5/2010</ArrivalDate>
  </OrderItem>
  <OrderItem>
    <ItemNumber>2000</ItemNumber>
    <ItemDescription>Night Stand</ItemDescription>
    <Quantity>155</Quantity>
    <ShipperName>NextDay Wonder Shipping</ShipperName>
    <ShipmentDate>10/12/2010</ShipmentDate>
    <ArrivalDate>11/17/2010</ArrivalDate>
  </OrderItem>
</OrderShipment>
```

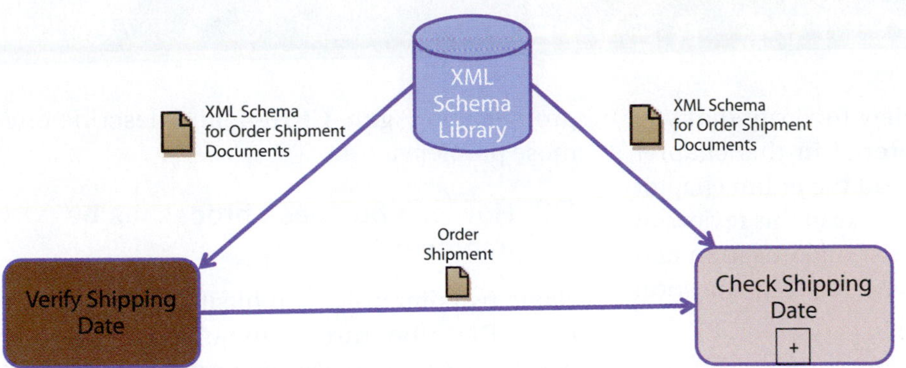

Figure CE18-10
Use of XML Schema Document

A SOAP message can include metadata that specifies how the message is to be routed, what services need to process it, how security and encryption are to be handled, and so forth. SOAP is independent of any device, network, vendor, or product. By the way, although SOAP is commonly used, other messaging protocols also exist.[1]

The last important SOA standard that you should know about is the **Web Services Description Language (WSDL)**. To understand the need for WSDL, suppose you are a computer programmer assigned the task of writing a program to implement the Verify Shipping Date activity in Figure CE18-10. You know that you want to use the Check Shipping Date service, but you do not know how to do that. Suppose that the Check Shipping Date service provides five different features about five different shipment options. As a computer programmer, how do you learn how to interface with those features?

The answer is WSDL. To expose a service or services to the world, the designer of the service creates a WSDL document that describes, in a standard way, the particular features that the service provides and the data that need to be sent or that will be returned from the service. Microsoft, IBM, and other interested companies create developer tools for creating SOA service programs. Those developer tools are created to read a service's WSDL and to provide seamless integration with that service to the programmer. Additionally, when you, as a programmer, create a service, those developer tools will write the WSDL for your service for you.

In short, WSDL is a language that services can use to describe what they do and how other computer programs can access their features. To understand this more deeply, you need to know quite a bit about computer programming.

The bottom line is that XML, SOAP, and WSDL eliminate the need for proprietary SOA services designs and make it much easier for programs to interact with one another, whether on the same machine, the same network, or just somewhere off in the cloud. Figure CE18-11 summarizes the key features of these three important SOA standards.

Figure CE18-11
Important SOA Standards

Standard	Purpose	Remarks
XML (eXtensible Markup Language)	Provide structure to data exchanges among SOA services. Schema documents used to ensure documents comply with defined data structures.	*Lingua franca* of the Internet. Very important. No significant challengers for SOA.
SOAP	A protocol for message exchange. Sits on top of transport protocols such as HTTP, HTTPS, and FTP. Allows for description of message routing, processing, security, and encryption.	Other protocols, such as REST, are also used.
WSDL (Web Services Description Language)	Languages for describing the programmatic interface to a service. Makes service-to-service programming much easier.	Microsoft, IBM, and others build WSDL into their programming development tools.

[1] Another messaging protocol called REST (Representational State Transfer) is also very popular. We will not discuss REST here, however.

ACTIVE REVIEW

Use this Active Review to verify that you understand the material in this chapter extension. You can read the entire chapter extension and then perform the tasks in this review, or you can read the material for just one question and perform the tasks in this review for that question before moving on to the next one.

Q1 Why do organizations need to manage business processes?

Define *business process,* explain the nature of each of the elements of your definition, and discuss the role of information systems in business processes. Summarize three reasons why business processes don't work well. Give examples of each. Define *BPM,* and name and describe four basic activities in the BPM process. Describe the three different scopes for BPM. Explain the purpose of COBIT. Compare and contrast BPM and SDLC.

Q2 How does Business Process Modeling Notation (BPMN) document business processes?

Describe the need for a standard set of process symbols. Define *BPMN.* Explain the meaning of each of the symbols in Figure CE18-4. Define *swim-lane layout,* and explain its advantages in your own words. Explain the meaning of each of the symbols in Figure CE18-6, and describe the relationship of this process diagram to that in Figure CE18-4. Explain the process problems in Figure CE18-4, and describe one fix to those problems.

Q3 How can business processes be improved?

Name two dimensions of business process effectiveness. Describe three fundamental ways process designers can increase the performance of business processes. Explain three ways of reducing the time required to perform credit checking in Figures CE18-4 and CE18-6.

Q4 How are SOA principles used to design business processes?

Summarize the advantages of SOA designs. Explain two ways SOA principles are used. Define *service, service provider, encapsulated,* and *encapsulation.* Summarize the advantages of independent, encapsulated service-providers. Explain how services are defined.

Q5 Why are XML and other SOA standards important?

Name the three SOA standards described in this chapter and explain the purpose of each. Give an example of a four-line XML document different from the one in this chapter. If you do not know the meaning of the term *lingua franca,* learn it and explain what it means to say that XML is the *lingua franca* of the Internet. Explain the purpose and use of an XML schema document. Explain how SOAP and WSDL are used in an SOA system.

KEY TERMS AND CONCEPTS

USING YOUR KNOWLEDGE

1. In your own words, explain why organizations need to manage business processes. Choose a business process at your university and identify the principle components of that process. Explain how each of the change factors discussed in Q1 might apply to this process. Summarize how the stages of BPM would apply to the management of the process you selected.

2. Use BPMN to document the process you identified in your answer to question 1. Use Figures CE18-4 and CE18-6 as a guide to the level of detail you should provide. If possible, use Visio to document your process. Visio 2010 includes standard BPMN shapes in the Flowchart shape category. Use them in a way that is similar to their use in this text.

3. Using your own experience and knowledge, create a process diagram for a Reject Order activity that would fix the allocation problem in Figure CE18-4. Use Figure CE18-6 as an example. Use Visio 2010 and the standard BPMN shapes, if possible. Explain how your process fixes the allocation problem.

4. Assume that the activity you created in your answer to question 3 is to be designed according to SOA principles so that it can be automated. Explain what those principles are and show how you have followed them. Give an example of an XML document that could be used to share data needed to free inventory allocations.

5. Explain why XML is meta, metadata. Use Figure CE18-11 in your answer. Is an XML schema meta, meta metadata? Explain your answer.

CHAPTER EXTENSION 19

STUDY QUESTIONS

Q1 Why is formalized project management necessary?

Q2 What are the trade-offs in requirements, cost, and time?

Q3 What are the dimensions of project management?

Q4 How does a work-breakdown structure drive project management?

Q5 What is the biggest challenge for planning a systems development project?

Q6 What are the biggest challenges for managing a systems development project?

Q7 What is the single most important task for users on a systems development project?

Chapter 10 provides the background for this Extension.

Systems Development Project Management

Q1 Why Is Formalized Project Management Necessary?

FlexTime and Fox Lake are small companies, and thus their projects to develop their information systems will be modest in scale. They might be able to apply the systems development life cycle (SDLC) to create an information system without formalized project management. Small companies can sometimes get along by implementing small IS projects on an informal, catch-as-catch-can basis. Of course, good project management would be beneficial, but it might not be required.

The situation is very different for projects at medium and large companies, however. Here, IS projects are large and complex, and strong, formalized project management is mandatory. Information systems at such companies have many features and functions. They require substantial server farms and necessitate the creation of multifaceted, complicated computer programs. They process databases with hundreds of tables; dozens, possibly hundreds, of relationships; and terabytes of data. Such large-scale systems affect many business processes and support hundreds, possibly thousands, of concurrent users.

Because of their size, such systems require a large development team, often comprising 50 to 100 or more business and systems analysts, programmers, PQA engineers, and managers. To add further complexity, large-scale systems are often simultaneously developed at multiple sites. A project might involve teams in the United States, India, China, and other countries. Additionally, the development of large-scale systems can involve integrating products and services from different companies. In these development projects, some companies provide licensed software; others provide particular expertise, such as database design; and others provide development labor. Large-scale systems are frequently localized for different languages. Finally, large-scale systems development requires extended development intervals, sometimes as long as 5 or 6 years. Figure CE19-1 summarizes the characteristics of large-scale systems.

The Internal Revenue Service provides a good example of a large-scale IS project. The IRS employs more than 100,000 people in 1,000 different sites and processes over 200 million tax returns a year. Starting in 1995, it set out to modernize the information systems for processing tax returns. Today, more than 15 years and several billion dollars later, it has not completed that project.

Formalized project management is a necessity for such large-scale projects. Without it, millions, even billions, of dollars will be wasted, projects will run late, and

- Many features and functions
- Large, complex computer programs
- Databases with hundreds of tables, dozens to hundreds of relationships, and terabytes of data
- Affect many business processes
- Support hundreds or thousands of concurrent users
- Large development team
- Multiple sites
- International development
- Integration of work from several companies
- Localization necessary
- Extended development intervals

Figure CE19-1
Characteristics of Large-Scale Systems Development Projects

team morale will be low. In this chapter extension, we will consider the major components of IS project management. We begin the discussion of IS project management by discussing project trade-offs.

Q2 What Are the Trade-offs in Requirements, Cost, and Time?

Systems development projects require the balancing of three critical drivers: **requirements** (scope),[1] **cost**, and **time**. To understand this balancing challenge, consider the construction of something relatively simple—say, a piece of jewelry like a necklace or the deck on the side of a house. The more elaborate the necklace or the deck, the more time it will take. The less elaborate, the less time it will take. Further, if we embellish the necklace with diamonds and precious gems, it will cost more. Similarly, if we construct the deck from old crates it will be cheaper than if we construct it of clear-grained, prime Port Orford cedar.

We can summarize this situation as shown in Figure CE19-2. We can *trade off* requirements against time and against cost. If we make the necklace simpler, it will take less time. If we eliminate the diamonds and gems, it will be cheaper. The same **trade-offs** exist in the construction of anything: houses, airplanes, buildings, ships, furniture, *and* information systems.

The relationship between time and cost is more complicated. Normally, we can reduce time by increasing cost, but *only to a point*. For example, we can reduce the time it takes to produce a deck by hiring more laborers. At some point, however, there will be so many laborers working on the deck that they will get in one another's way, and the time to finish the deck will actually increase. Thus, at some point, adding more people creates **diseconomies of scale** (recall Brooks' Law in Chapter 10).

In some projects, we can reduce costs by increasing time. If, for example, we are required to pay laborers time-and-a-half for overtime, we can reduce costs by eliminating overtime. If finishing the deck—by, say, Friday—requires overtime, then it may be cheaper to avoid overtime by completing the deck sometime next week. This trade-off is not always true, however. By extending the project interval, we will need to pay labor and overhead for a longer period of time. Adding more time can increase cost.

Consider how these trade-offs pertain to information systems. We specify a set of requirements for the new information system, and we schedule labor over a period of time. Suppose the initial schedule indicates the system will be finished in 3 years. If business requirements necessitate the project be finished in 2 years, we must shorten

[1] When we speak of information systems, we usually refer to the characteristics of the system to be constructed as *requirements.* The discipline of project management refers to those characteristics as project *scope.* If you read literature from the Project Management Institute, for example, it will use the term *scope* in the same sense that we use *requirements.* For the purposes of this chapter extension, consider *scope* and *requirements* to be the same.

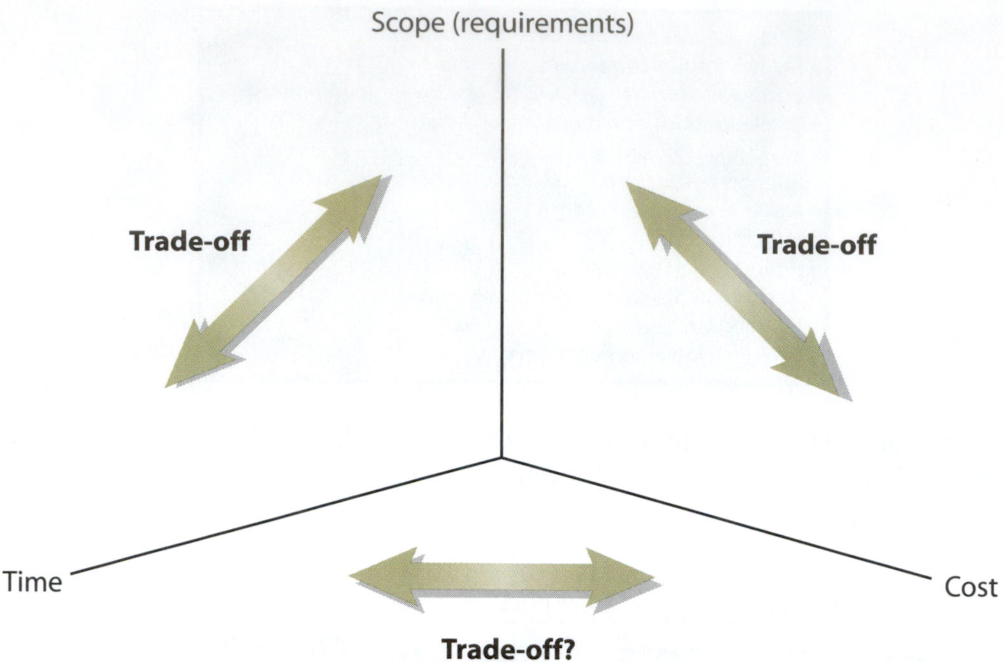

Figure CE19-2
Primary Drivers of Systems Development

the schedule. We can proceed in two ways: reduce the requirements or add labor. For the former, we eliminate functions and features. For the latter, we hire more staff or contract with other vendors for development services. Deciding which course to take will be difficult and risky.

Furthermore, in most projects, we cannot make these decisions once and for all. We begin with a plan, called the **baseline**. It stipulates the tasks to be accomplished, the labor and other resources assigned to those tasks, and the schedule for completion. However, nothing ever goes according to plan, and the larger the project and the longer the development interval, the more things will violate the plan. Critical people may leave the company; a hurricane may destroy an office; the company may have a bad quarter and freeze hiring just as the project is staffing up; technology will change; competitors may do something that makes the project more (or less) important; or the company may be sold and new management may change requirements and priorities. When these events occur, project managers must reassess the trade-offs between requirements, cost, and time. It is a balancing act undertaken in the presence of continual change and substantial risk and uncertainty.

Q3 What Are the Dimensions of Project Management?

Many methods exist for developing information systems. Chapter 10 described the SDLC, the workhorse of the industry for years. This technique stipulates phases and processes for constructing information systems, but it does not address the management of projects, particularly large-scale projects. The systems definition phase of the SDLC, for example, stipulates that the project should be planned, but it does not indicate how. It stipulates that components need to be designed, but it does not address the management of the design activity, nor the communications among employees, groups, and sites. And so forth.

Large-scale projects require formalized project management. Although Jeff, the general manager at Fox Lake, can get by with informal meetings with his business analyst consultant, Alaska Airlines cannot deliver a new thin-client reservation system that way. A formalized project management process is needed.

Over the years, people have proposed dozens of different project management methodologies and processes. In recent years, the process promulgated by the **Project Management Institute (PMI)** has achieved prominence. PMI is an international organization focused on disseminating best practices in project management. Both the American National Standards Institute (ANSI) and International Standards Organization (ISO) have endorsed PMI's work.

PMI publishes project management documents and offers project management training. It also offers the **Project Management Professional (PMP)** certification. Professionals who have 4,500 hours of project work experience can earn the certification by passing PMI's examination. Once you have the required work experience, the PMP is a worthwhile certification for any professional involved in project management work of any type. (The PMP certification pertains to project management in general and not only to information systems project management. See *www.pmi.org* for more information.)

Since its origin in 1969, PMI has evaluated many project management concepts and techniques and brought the best of them together under the umbrella of a document entitled the *Project Management Body of Knowledge (PMBOK®) Guide*. This document contains what many believe are the best project management processes, practices, and techniques. The document does not describe the details of each practice or technique, but instead identifies those practices that are known to be effective for different situations and briefly describes their use. Versions of this document are denoted by the year in which they are published. As of 2010, the current version is *A Guide to the Project Management Body of Knowledge* (*PMBOK® Guide*), Fourth Edition.

The *PMBOK® Guide* is organized according to the grid in Figure CE19-3, which shows five *process groups* and nine *knowledge areas*. The process groups refer to different stages in the life of a project; the nine knowledge areas refer to factors to be managed throughout the life of the project.

You can surmise the meanings of the process groups from their titles. The knowledge areas provide an excellent summary of project management dimensions. *Project integration* refers to the management of the overall project and the construction of the final product. We have already discussed the trade-offs among *scope* (*requirements*), *time*, and *cost*. *Quality* management refers to quality assurance; for an IS project, it concerns planning and managing the product quality-assurance function.

The nature of *human resources* management is clear from its name. *Communications* management concerns the methods, media, and schedules for communicating with the project's sponsors, within the team itself, and with others having an interest in the

Project Management Processes

Knowledge Areas	Initiating	Planning	Executing	Monitoring and Controlling	Closing
Project integration					
Scope (requirements)					
Time					
Cost					
Quality					
Human resources					
Communications					
Risk					
Procurement					

Figure CE19-3
Dimensions of Project Management

progress of the project. The decision to use a team SharePoint site, for example, would be part of communications management. Risk is inherent in all projects, and especially so for projects that involve new technology or the innovative application of existing technology. The purpose of *risk* management is to ensure that managers understand project risks and balance risk factors—or that they take other appropriate action to mitigate unwanted outcomes. Finally, *procurement* management concerns contracts with outside vendors for services, materials, and outsourcing of functions.

The *PMBOK® Guide* specifies practices, documents, techniques, and methods to be used for most of the cells of the grid in Figure CE19-3. For specific guidance on particular practices for process groups or knowledge areas, see the *PMBOK® Guide*. The particular contents of each cell are beyond the scope of this text; to learn more, take a project management class. However, you can consider the elements in Figure CE19-3 as a summary of the dimensions or factors that large-scale information systems development projects must address.

Q4 How Does a Work-Breakdown Structure Drive Project Management?

The key strategy for large-scale systems development—and, indeed, the key strategy for any project—is to divide and conquer. Break up large tasks into smaller tasks and continue breaking up the tasks until they are small enough to manage, thus enabling you to estimate time and costs. Each task should culminate in one or more **deliverables**. Examples of deliverables are documents, designs, prototypes, data models, database designs, working data-entry screens, and the like. Without a deliverable, it is impossible to know if the task was accomplished.

A **work-breakdown structure (WBS)** is a hierarchy of the tasks required to complete a project. The WBS for a large project is huge; it might entail hundreds or even thousands of tasks. Figure CE19-4 shows the WBS for the system definition phase of the Fox Lake facilities scheduling system. The overall task, *System definition*, is divided into *Define goals and scope*, *Assess feasibility*, *Plan project*, and *Form project team*. Each of those tasks is broken into smaller tasks, until the work has been divided into small tasks that can be managed and estimated.

Note, by the way, that the term **scope** is being used here in two different ways. As used in this WBS example, *scope* means to define the system boundaries, which is the sense in which it is used in the SDLC. As noted in Q3, *scope* for the *PMBOK® Guide* means to define the requirements. That use of scope does not appear in Figure CE19-4.

Once the project is decomposed into small tasks, the next step is to define task dependencies and to estimate task durations. Regarding dependencies, some tasks must begin at the same time, some tasks must end at the same time, and some tasks cannot start until other tasks have finished. Task dependencies are normally input to planning software such as Microsoft Project. Figure CE19-5 shows the WBS as input to Microsoft Project, with task dependencies and durations defined. The display on the right, called a **Gantt chart**, shows tasks, dates, and dependencies.

All of the tasks from the WBS have been entered, and each task has been assigned a duration. Task dependencies have also been specified, although the means used to do so is beyond our discussion. The two red arrows emerging from task 4, *Define system boundaries*, indicate that neither the *Review results* task nor the *Assess feasibility task* can begin until *Define system boundaries* is completed. Other task dependencies are also shown; you can learn about them in a project management class.

The **critical path** is the sequence of activities that determine the earliest date by which the project can be completed. Reflect for a moment on that statement: The earliest date is the date determined by considering the *longest path* through the

System definition			
1.1	Define goals and scope		
	1.1.1	Define goals	
	1.1.2	Define system boundaries	
	1.1.3	Review results	
	1.1.4	Document results	
1.2	Assess feasibility		
	1.2.1	Cost	
	1.2.2	Schedule	
	1.2.3	Technical	
	1.2.4	Organizational	
	1.2.5	Document feasibility	
	1.2.6	Management review and go/no go decision	
1.3	Plan project		
	1.3.1	Establish milestones	
	1.3.2	Create WBS	
		1.3.2.1	Levels 1 and 2
		1.3.2.2	Levels 3+
	1.3.3	Document WBS	
		1.3.3.1	Create WBS baseline
		1.3.3.2	Input to Project
	1.3.4	Determine resource requirements	
		1.3.4.1	Personnel
		1.3.4.2	Computing
		1.3.4.3	Office space
		1.3.4.4	Travel and Meeting Expense
	1.3.5	Management review	
		1.3.5.1	Prepare presentation
		1.3.5.2	Prepare background documents
		1.3.5.3	Give presentation
		1.3.5.4	Incorporate feedback into plan
		1.3.5.5	Approve project
1.4	Form project team		
	1.4.1	Meet with HR	
	1.4.2	Meet with IT Director	
	1.4.3	Develop job descriptions	
	1.4.4	Meet with available personnel	
	1.4.5	Hire personnel	

Figure CE19-4 Sample WBS for the Definition Phase of a Thin-Client Order-Entry System

network of activities. Paying attention to task dependencies, the planner will compress the tasks as much as possible. Those tasks that cannot be further compressed lie on the critical path. Microsoft Project and other project-planning applications can readily identify critical path tasks.

Figure CE19-5 shows the tasks on the critical path in red. Consider the first part of the WBS. The project planner specified that task 4 cannot begin until 2 days before task 3 starts. (That's the meaning of the red arrow emerging from task 3.) Neither task 5 nor task 8 can begin until task 4 is completed. Task 8 will take longer than tasks 5 and 6, and so task 8—not tasks 5 or 6—is on the critical path. Thus, the critical path to this point is tasks 3, 4, and 8. You can trace the critical path through the rest of the WBS by following the tasks shown in red, though the entire WBS and critical path are not shown.

Figure CE19-5 Gantt Chart of WBS for Definition Phase of a Thin-Client System

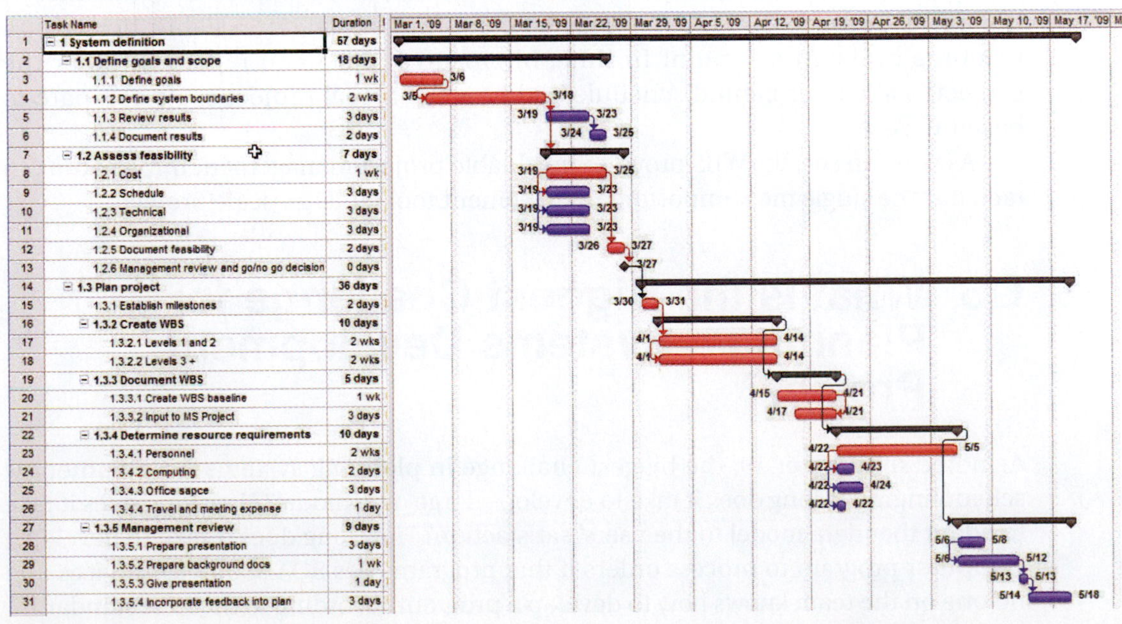

	Task Name	Duration
1	1 System definition	57 days
2	1.1 Define goals and scope	18 days
3	1.1.1 Define goals	1 wk
4	1.1.2 Define system boundaries	2 wks
5	1.1.3 Review results	3 days
6	1.1.4 Document results	2 days
7	1.2 Assess feasibility	7 days
8	1.2.1 Cost	1 wk
9	1.2.2 Schedule	3 days
10	1.2.3 Technical	3 days
11	1.2.4 Organizational	3 days
12	1.2.5 Document feasibility	2 days
13	1.2.6 Management review and go/no go decision	0 days
14	1.3 Plan project	36 days
15	1.3.1 Establish milestones	2 days
16	1.3.2 Create WBS	10 days
17	1.3.2.1 Levels 1 and 2	2 wks
18	1.3.2.2 Levels 3+	2 wks
19	1.3.3 Document WBS	5 days
20	1.3.3.1 Create WBS baseline	1 wk
21	1.3.3.2 Input to MS Project	3 days
22	1.3.4 Determine resource requirements	10 days
23	1.3.4.1 Personnel	2 wks
24	1.3.4.2 Computing	2 days
25	1.3.4.3 Office sapce	3 days
26	1.3.4.4 Travel and meeting expense	1 day
27	1.3.5 Management review	9 days
28	1.3.5.1 Prepare presentation	3 days
29	1.3.5.2 Prepare background docs	1 wk
30	1.3.5.3 Give presentation	1 day
31	1.3.5.4 Incorporate feedback into plan	3 days

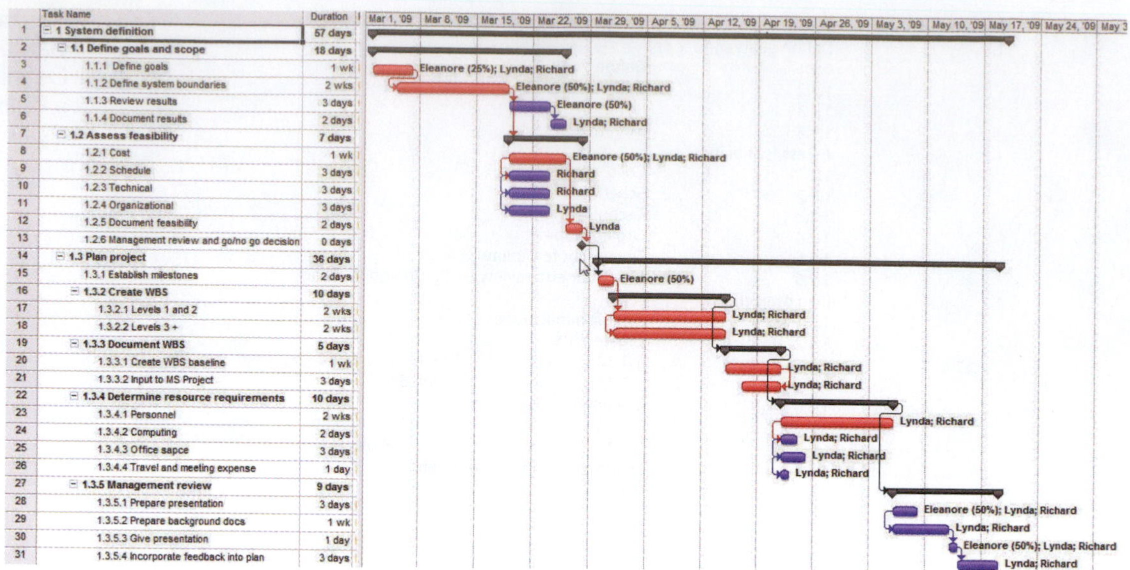

Figure CE19-6
Gannt Chart with Resources Assigned

Using Microsoft Project or a similar product, it is possible to assign personnel to tasks and to stipulate the percentage of time that each person devotes to a task. Figure CE19-6 shows a Gantt chart for which this has been done. The notation means that Eleanore works only 25 percent of the time on task 3; Lynda and Richard work full time. Additionally, one can assign costs to personnel and compute a labor budget for each task and for the WBS overall. One can assign resources to tasks and use Microsoft Project to detect and prevent two tasks from using the same resources. Resource costs can be assigned and summed as well.

Managers can use the critical path to perform **critical path analysis**. First, note that if a task is on the critical path, and if that task runs late, the project will be late. Hence, tasks on the critical path cannot be allowed to run late if the project is to be delivered on time. Second, tasks not on the critical path can run late to the point at which they would become part of the critical path. Hence, up to a point, resources can be taken from noncritical path tasks to shorten tasks on the critical path. Using critical path analysis, managers can move resources among tasks so as to compress the schedule.

So far, we have discussed the role of the WBS for planning. It can be used for monitoring as well. The final WBS plan is denoted the **baseline WBS**. This baseline shows the planned tasks, dependencies, durations, and resource assignments. As the project proceeds, project managers can input actual dates, labor hours, and resource costs. At any point in time, Microsoft Project can report whether the project is ahead or behind schedule and how the actual project costs compare to baseline costs.

As you can see, the WBS provides invaluable project management information. In fact, it is the single most important management tool for large-scale projects.

Q5 What Is the Biggest Challenge for Planning a Systems Development Project?

As noted in Chapter 10, the biggest challenge in planning systems development is scheduling. How long does it take to develop a large data model? How long does it take to adapt that data model to the users' satisfaction? How long does it take to develop a computer program to process orders if that program uses SOA standard services and no one on the team knows how to develop a program according to the SOA standards?

Fred Brooks defined software as "logical poetry." It is pure thought-stuff. Some years ago, when I pressed a seasoned software developer for a schedule, he responded by asking me, "What would Shakespeare have said if someone asked him how long it would take him to write *Hamlet*?" Another common rejoinder is, "What would a fisherman say if you ask him how long will it take to catch three fish? He doesn't know, and neither do I."

No company should know better how to estimate software schedules than Microsoft. It has more experience developing software than any other company; it is loaded with smart, even brilliant, developers; it can draw from enormous financial resources, and it has strong incentives to schedule projects accurately. However, Microsoft Vista was delivered 2 years late. It was supposed to take 3 years, and it took 5. That's a 67 percent schedule overrun from the largest software developer in the world on what is arguably the world's most important computer program. And this is not just one project that ran awry. SQL Server 2008 barely made it into 2008. Office 2007 was late, and so on.

Part of the problem is that errors accumulate. If scheduling a single task is difficult, then scheduling a large-scale project becomes a nightmare. Suppose you have a WBS with thousands of tasks, and any one of those tasks can be 67 percent over schedule. It is impossible to do any credible planning. The term *critical path* loses meaning when there is that much doubt about task duration. In that setting, every task has some chance of being on the critical path.

Organizations take three approaches to this challenge. The first is to avoid the major schedule risks and never develop software in-house. Instead, they license software from vendors. For example, few companies choose to develop their own ERP or CRM software. ERP or CRM systems still have the substantial schedule risks of adapting procedures and training personnel, but those risks are much smaller than the schedule risks of developing complex software and databases.

But what if no suitable software exists? In that case, companies take one of two remaining approaches. They can admit the impossibility of systems development scheduling and plan accordingly. They abandon the SDLC and decide to invest a certain level of resources into a project, manage it as best they can, and take the schedule that results. Only loose commitments are made regarding the completion date and final system functionality. Project sponsors dislike this approach because they feel they are signing a blank check. But sometimes it is just a matter of admitting the reality that exists: "We don't know, and it's worse to pretend that we do."

The third approach is to attempt to schedule the development project in spite of all the difficulties. Several different estimation techniques can be used. If the project is similar to a past project, the schedule data from that past project can be used for planning. When such similar past projects exist, this technique can produce quality schedule estimates. If there is no such past project, managers can estimate the number of **lines of code** that will need to be written. Then they can use industry or company averages to estimate the time required. Another technique is to estimate the **function points** in a program, use each function point to determine the number of lines of code, and use that number to estimate schedules. A function point is simply a feature or function of the new program. Updating a customer record is an example. For more information on the use of lines of code and function points for software scheduling, visit *http://sunset.usc.edu/csse/research/COCOMOII/cocomo_main.html*. Of course, lines of code and function point techniques estimate schedules only for software components. The schedules for creating databases and the other system components must be estimated using other techniques.

During your career, be aware of the challenges and difficulties of scheduling large-scale information systems development. As a user or manager, do not take schedules as guarantees. Plan for schedule slippage, and if it does *not* occur, be pleasantly surprised.

Q6 What Are the Biggest Challenges for Managing a Systems Development Project?

The challenges of managing large-scale systems development projects arise from four different factors:

- Coordination
- Diseconomies of scale
- Configuration control
- Unexpected events

Larger IS development projects are usually organized into a variety of development groups that work independently. Coordinating the work of these independent groups can be difficult, particularly if the groups reside in different geographic locations or different countries. An accurate and complete WBS facilitates coordination, but no project ever proceeds exactly in accordance with the WBS. Delays occur, and unknown or unexpected dependencies develop among tasks.

The coordination problem is increased because software is pure thought-stuff. When constructing a new house, electricians install wiring in the walls as they exist; it is impossible to do otherwise. No electrician can install wiring in the wall as designed 6 months ago, before a change. In software, such physical constraints do not exist. It is entirely possible for a team to develop a set of application programs to process a database using an obsolete database design. When the database design was changed, all involved parties should have been notified, but this may not have occurred. Wasted hours, increased cost, and poor morale are the result.

As mentioned in Chapter 10, another problem is diseconomies of scale. Adding more people to a project increases coordination requirements. The number of possible interactions among team members rises exponentially with the number of team members. Ultimately, no matter how well managed a project is, diseconomies of scale will set in. According to Brooks' Law, adding more people to a late software project makes it later.

As the project proceeds, controlling the configuration of the work product becomes difficult. Consider requirements, for example. The development team produces an initial statement of requirements. Meetings with users produce an adjusted set of requirements. Suppose an event then occurs that necessitates a change to requirements. After deliberation, assume the team decides to ignore a large portion of the requirements changes resulting from the event. At this point, there are four different versions of the requirements. If the changes to requirements are not carefully managed, changes from the four versions will be mixed up, and confusion and disorder will result. No one will know which requirements are the correct, current requirements.

Similar problems occur with designs, program code, database data, and other system components. The term **configuration control** refers to a set of management policies, practices, and tools that developers use to maintain control over the project's resources. Such resources include documents, schedules, designs, program code, test suites, and any other shared resource needed to complete the project. Configuration control is vital; a loss of control over a project's configuration is so expensive and disruptive that it can result in termination for senior project managers.

The last major challenge to IS project management is unexpected events. The larger and longer the project, the greater the chance of disruption due to an unanticipated event. Critical people can change companies; even whole teams have been known to pack up and join a competitor. The organization can be acquired, and new management may have different priorities. Congress can change applicable law; Sarbanes-Oxley is a good example of a law that affected not only financial systems, but also other systems whose resources were taken to comply with the new law. Natural disasters like hurricanes can destroy offices or significantly affect employees' lives.

Because software is thought-stuff, team morale is crucial. I once managed two strong-headed software developers who engaged in a heated argument over the design of a program feature. The argument ended when one threw a chair at the other. The rest of the team divided its loyalties between the two developers, and work came to a standstill as subgroups sneered and argued with one another when they met in hallways or at the coffee pot. How do you schedule that event in your WBS? As a project manager, you never know what strange event is heading your way. Such unanticipated events make project management challenging, but also incredibly fascinating!

Q7 What Is the Single Most Important Task for Users on a Systems Development Project?

Taking responsibility for requirements is the single most important task you, a future user or manager of users, can perform for a large-scale development project. Taking responsibility goes beyond participating in requirements meetings and stating your opinion on how things should work. Taking responsibility means understanding that the information system is built for your business function and managing requirements accordingly.

"There are no IT projects," says Kaiser-Permanente CIO Cliff Dodd. Rather, he says, "Some business projects have an IT component."[2] Dodd is right. Information systems exist to help organizations achieve their goals and objectives. Information systems exist to facilitate business processes and to improve decision making. Every information system is simply a part of some larger business project.

When investigating the problems in the IRS modernization program, the IRS Oversight Board stated, "The IRS business units must take direct leadership and ownership of the Modernization program and its projects. In particular this must include defining the scope of each project, preparing realistic and attainable business cases, and controlling scope changes throughout each project's life cycle."[3]

Users cannot be passive recipients of the IT department's services. Instead, users are responsible for ensuring that requirements are complete and accurate. Users must ask only for what they need and must avoid creating requirements that cannot possibly be constructed within the available budget. Because users may not know what is difficult or unrealistic, requirements definition can occur only through an extended conversation among the users and the development team.

Once the requirements are known, the development team will create a project WBS and will initiate management activities for each of the nine knowledge areas in Figure CE19-3. It will staff positions, begin the design process, and, later, implement the stated requirements. If users subsequently change their minds about what is needed, considerable rework and waste will occur. **Requirements creep** is the process by which users agree to one set of requirements, then add a bit more ("It won't take too much extra work"), then add a bit more, and so forth. Over time, the requirements creep so much that they describe a completely new project, but the development team is left with the budget and plan of the original project.

Users must take responsibility for managing requirements changes and for avoiding requirements creep. Some requirements change is inevitable; but if changes become extensive, if requirements creep cannot be avoided, start a new project. Don't

[2] Quoted in Steve Ulfelder, "How to Talk to Business," *www.computerworld.com/managementtopics/management/story/0,10801,109403,00.html*, March 13, 2006 (accessed June 2010).

[3] IRS Oversight Board, "Independent Analysis of IRS Business Systems Modernization Special Report," *www.irsoversightboard.treas.gov* (accessed June 2010).

try to turn a doghouse into a skyscraper, one small change at a time. In that course of action, disaster is the only outcome.

A final part of the users' responsibility for requirements concerns *testing*. You and those who work for you may be asked to help in several different ways. You may be asked to specify testing criteria. If so, you need to help define testable conditions that determine whether a feature or function is complete and operational. Testing may occur in several stages during the project. For example, you may be asked to test design components; evaluating a data model is a good example. Or you may be asked to provide sample data and sample scenarios for program and systems testing. You may be asked to participate in the testing of beta versions. Because only the users can know if a feature works correctly, testing is part of requirements management.

Once more: Taking responsibility for system requirements is the single most important task you can perform on a large-scale development project!

ACTIVE REVIEW

Use this Active Review to verify that you understand the material in the chapter extension. You can read the entire extension and then perform the tasks in this review, or you can read the material for just one question and perform the tasks in this review for that question before moving on to the next one.

Q1 Why is formalized project management necessary?

Summarize the characteristics of large-scale information systems development projects. Explain why these characteristics make large-scale projects hard to manage. Give two examples of large-scale systems development projects.

Q2 What are the trade-offs in requirements, cost, and time?

Describe two meanings for the term *scope*. Describe how requirements affect cost and time. Describe the trade-offs that exist between requirements and time. Explain the trade-offs that exist between time and cost. Describe circumstances in which increasing cost reduces time. Explain circumstances in which increasing cost increases time. Describe circumstance in which time extensions reduce costs.

Q3 What are the dimensions of project management?

Describe the difference between development processes like the SDLC and project management. Summarize the activities of the PMI. Describe the contents of the *PMBOK® Guide*. Name the five process groups and the nine knowledge areas. Briefly explain the focus of each management area. Explain how you can use Figure CE19-3.

Q4 How does a work-breakdown structure drive project management?

State the key strategy for large-scale systems development. Explain why each task needs to produce one or more deliverables. Define *work-breakdown structure,* and give an example. In Figure CE19-4, explain the numeric notation under task 1.3. Define *Gantt chart,* and describe its contents. Explain how task dependencies influence project work. Define *critical path analysis,* and, using your own words, explain what it means. Describe two ways managers can use critical path analysis. Summarize how the WBS can be used to estimate costs. Define *baseline WBS,* and explain how the baseline can be used to monitor a project.

Q5 What is the biggest challenge for planning a systems development project?

Name the biggest challenge for systems development planning. Explain why this is so. Describe how the logical-poetry nature of software development affects scheduling. Summarize the three approaches that organizations can take to the systems development scheduling challenge. Describe two ways of estimating time to write computer programs. Describe how you can use the knowledge you have about systems development scheduling.

Q6 What are the biggest challenges for managing a systems development project?

Name four factors that create challenges for managing systems development. Give an example of each factor. Define *configuration control.*

Q7 What is the single most important task for users on a systems development project?

State and describe the single most important task for users on a systems development project. Explain why, as Dodd put it, there are no IT projects. Summarize user responsibilities for managing requirements. Define *requirements creep.* Describe the action that should occur if requirements creep cannot be stopped. Summarize the users' role for systems testing.

KEY TERMS AND CONCEPTS

USING YOUR KNOWLEDGE

1. Consider two projects: one to track the use of facilities at Fox Lake and the second to upgrade the reservations system for Alaska Airlines. Explain how the general characteristics of these two systems development projects differ.
2. Consider the facilities tracking system at Fox Lake. Suppose the system is to be used to track rooms, equipment, tennis courts, golf course tee times, and reservations at the restaurant. Explain the trade-offs that can be made among requirements, cost, and schedule. For a given set of requirements, explain how cost and schedule can be traded off.
3. Consider the process of an election campaign—say, a campaign to elect one of your fellow students for the position of student government president (or similar office at your university):
   - **a.** Develop a WBS for the election campaign.
   - **b.** Explain how knowledge of the critical path could help you plan the campaign.
   - **c.** Explain two ways you can use critical path analysis for planning the campaign.
   - **d.** Explain how you can use critical path analysis for executing and monitoring the campaign progress.
   - **e.** If you have access to Microsoft Project (or other planning software):
     - i. Input your WPS to Microsoft Project.
     - ii. Assign durations to tasks in your project.
     - iii. Specify task dependencies.
     - iv. Identify the critical path.
4. Suppose you have a computer virus that is so severe you must reformat your hard drive:
   - **a.** Develop a WBS for the process for recovering your computer.
   - **b.** Estimate the time it will take you to perform each task.
   - **c.** Neither lines of code nor function point estimation pertain to this task. Explain one other way you can improve the quality of your estimate.
   - **d.** Suppose you suspect that your estimate for the time of recovery could be low by as much as 200 percent. How could you use this knowledge?
5. What is the single most important task for users on a systems development project? Do you agree? Why or why not? Why must requirements emerge as a result of a conversation between users and IT professionals?

STUDY QUESTIONS

CHAPTER EXTENSION 20

Chapter 11 provides the background for this Extension.

Outsourcing

Q1 What Is Outsourcing?

Outsourcing is the hiring of another organization to perform a service. Just about any business activity in the value chain can be outsourced, from marketing and sales to logistics, manufacturing, and customer service. Support functions, such as accounting and human resources, can be outsourced as well. In this chapter extension, we will focus on the outsourcing of IS and IT services, but realize that companies also outsource most other business activities.

The outsourced vendor can be domestic or international. Some companies choose to outsource overseas to access cheaper labor and to take advantage of time differences. International outsourcing is addressed in Chapter Extension 21, "International MIS," on page 589.

Peter Drucker, the father of modern management theory, is reputed to have said, "Your back room is someone else's front room." For example, in most companies the employee cafeteria is a "back room"—running the cafeteria is not an essential service. Google does not want to be known for the quality of its employee cafeteria. Using Drucker's sentiment, Google would be better off hiring a company that specializes in food service. That company *does* want to be known for the quality (or low cost, depending on its competitive strategy) of its food.

Because food service is that company's "front room," it will be better able to provide a given quality of food at an appropriate price. Hiring that company frees Google management from thinking about the cafeteria at all. Food quality, chef scheduling, silverware acquisition, kitchen cleanliness, waste disposal, and so on will be the concern of the outsource company. Google management can focus on the creation of innovative Web 2.0 software.

Q2 Why Do Organizations Outsource IS and IT?

Many companies have chosen to outsource portions of their information systems activities. Figure CE20-1 lists popular reasons for doing so. Consider each major group of reasons.

Management Advantages

First, outsourcing can be an easy way to gain expertise. Suppose, for example, that an organization wants to upgrade its thousands of user computers on a cost-effective basis. To do so, the organization would need to develop expertise in automated

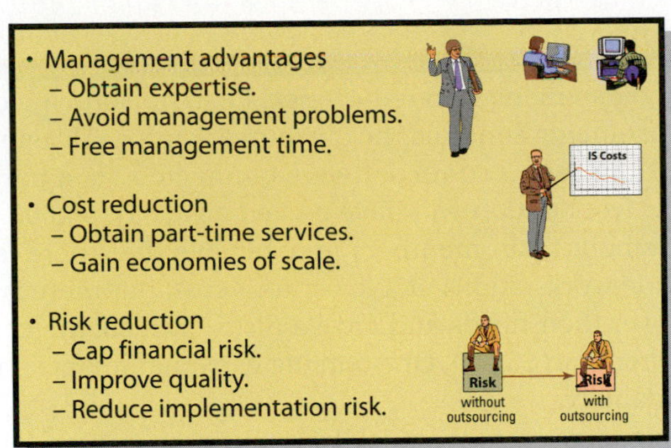

Figure CE20-1
Popular Reasons for Outsourcing IS Services

software installation, unattended installations, remote support, and other measures that can be used to improve the efficiency of software management. Developing such expertise is expensive, and it is not in the company's strategic direction. Efficient installation of software to thousands of computers is not in the "front room." Consequently, the organization might choose to hire a specialist company to perform this service.

Another reason for outsourcing is to avoid management problems. Suppose Fox Lake were larger and could afford to staff a full IS department. Would the company want to? How would it hire the appropriate staff? Suppose Fox Lake decided to build a Facebook application in-house. What kind of programmers does it need? Would it hire C# programmers, F# programmers, or HTML programmers? And, even if the company could find and hire the right staff, how would it manage them? How does Fox Lake create a good work environment for a C# programmer, when it doesn't even know what such a person does? Consequently Fox Lake will hire an outside firm to develop and maintain any custom applications that it needs.

Similarly, some companies choose to outsource to save management time and attention. Suppose FlexTime expands and processes so many customer transactions over the Web, using thin-client customer applications, that it needs a Web farm to process the workload. Even if FlexTime knew how to manage a Web farm, acquiring the appropriate computers, installing the necessary software, tuning the software for better performance, and hiring and managing the staff will all require significant management time. FlexTime will be better off buying time in the cloud.

Note, too, that the management time required is not just that of the direct manager of the activity. It is also time from more senior managers who approve the purchase and hiring requisitions for that activity. And those senior managers will need to devote the time necessary to understand enough about Web farms to approve or reject the requisitions. Outsourcing saves both direct and indirect management time.

Not everyone agrees on the desirability of outsourcing, as described in the Guide on pages 582–583.

Cost Reduction

Other common reasons for choosing to outsource concern cost reductions. With outsourcing, organizations can obtain part-time services. An office of 25 attorneys does not need a full-time network administrator. It does need network administration, but only in small amounts. By outsourcing that function, the office of attorneys can obtain network administration in the small amounts needed.

Another benefit of outsourcing is to gain economies of scale. If 25 organizations develop their own payroll applications in-house, then, when the tax law changes, 25 different groups will have to learn the new law, change their software to meet the law, test the changes, and write the documentation explaining the changes. However, if those same 25 organizations outsource to the same payroll vendor, then that vendor can make all of the adjustments once, and the cost of the change can be amortized over all of them (thus lowering the cost that the vendor can charge).

Risk Reduction

Another reason for outsourcing is to reduce risk. First, outsourcing can cap financial risk. In a typical outsourcing contract, the outsource vendor will agree to provide, say, computer workstations with certain software connected via a particular network. Typically, each new workstation will have a fixed cost, say, $3,500 per station. The company's management team members may believe that there is a good chance that they can provide workstations at a lower unit cost, but there is also the chance that they'll get in over their heads and have a disaster. If so, the cost per computer could be much higher than $3,500. Outsourcing caps that financial risk and leads to greater budgetary stability.

Second, outsourcing can reduce risk by ensuring a certain level of quality, or avoiding the risk of having substandard quality. A company that specializes in food service knows what to do to provide a certain level of quality. It has the expertise to ensure, for example, that only healthy food is served. So, too, a company that specializes in, say, Web-server hosting knows what to do to provide a certain level of service for a given workload.

Note that there is no guarantee that outsourcing will provide a certain level of quality or quality better than could be achieved in-house. But, in general, a professional outsourcing firm knows how to prepare cafeteria food to avoid giving everyone food poisoning or to avoid 2 days of downtime on the Web servers. And if that minimum level of quality is not provided, it is easier to hire another vendor than it is to fire and rehire internal staff.

Finally, organizations choose to outsource IS in order to reduce implementation risk. Hiring an outside vendor reduces the risk of picking the wrong hardware or the wrong software, using the wrong network protocol, or implementing tax law changes incorrectly. Outsourcing gathers all of these risks into the risk of choosing the right vendor. Once the company has chosen the vendor, further risk management is up to that vendor.

Q3 What Are Popular Outsourcing Alternatives?

Organizations have found hundreds of different ways to outsource information systems and portions of information systems. Figure CE20-2 organizes the major categories of alternatives according to information systems components.

Some organizations outsource the acquisition and operation of computer hardware. Electronic Data Systems (EDS) has been successful for more than 20 years as an outsource vendor of hardware infrastructure. Figure CE20-2 shows another alternative, outsourcing the computers by leasing time from a cloud vendor.

Acquiring licensed software, as discussed in Chapters 4 and 10, is a form of outsourcing. Rather than develop the software in-house, an organization licenses it from another vendor. Such licensing allows the software vendor to amortize the cost of software maintenance over all of the users, thus reducing that cost for all users.

Another possible outsourcing alternative is to outsource an entire application. PeopleSoft (now Oracle) attained prominence by outsourcing the entire payroll application. In such a solution, as the arrow in Figure CE20-2 implies, the vendor provides hardware, software, data, and some procedures. The company needs to provide only employee and work information; the payroll outsource vendor does the rest.

A Web storefront is another form of application outsourcing. Amazon.com, for example, provides a Web storefront for product vendors and distributors who choose not to develop their own Web presence. In this case, rather than pay a fixed fee for the storefront service, the product vendors and distributors pay Amazon.com a portion of

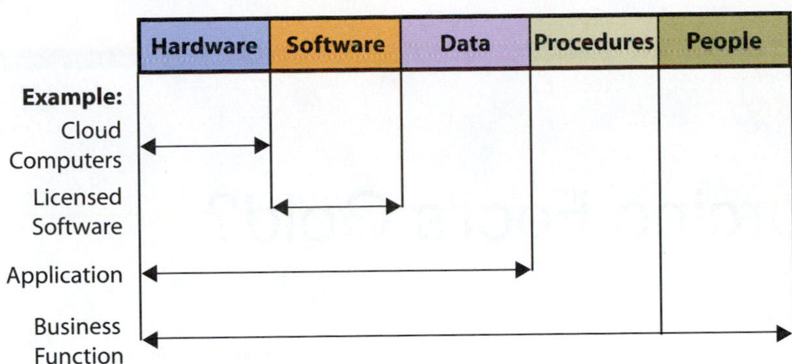

Figure CE20-2
IS/IT Outsourcing Alternatives

the revenue generated. Such Web service hosting has become a major profit center for Amazon.com.

Finally, some organizations choose to outsource an entire business function. For years, many companies have outsourced to travel agencies the function of arranging for employee travel. Some of these outsource vendors even operate offices within the company facilities. More recently, companies have been outsourcing even larger and more important functions. In 2005, for example, Marriott International chose Hewitt Associates to handle its HR needs for the next 7 years. Such agreements are much broader than outsourcing IS, but information systems are key components of the applications that are outsourced.

Q4 What Are the Risks of Outsourcing?

With so many advantages and with so many different outsourcing alternatives, you may wonder why any company has any in-house IS/IT functions. In fact, outsourcing presents significant risks, as listed in Figure CE20-3.

Loss of Control

The first risk of outsourcing is a loss of control. Outsourcing puts the vendor in the driver's seat. Each outsource vendor has methods and procedures for its service. Your organization and employees will have to conform to those procedures. For example, a hardware infrastructure vendor will have standard forms and procedures for requesting a computer, for recording and processing a computer problem, or for providing

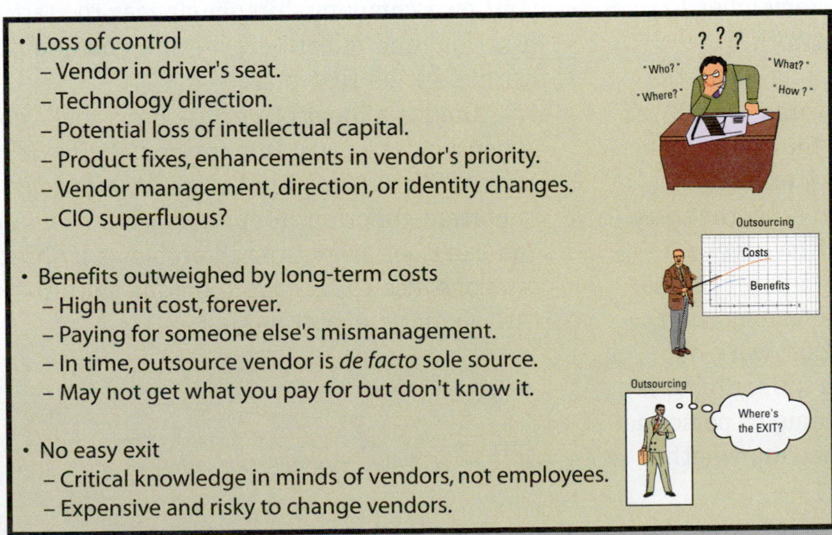

Figure CE20-3
Outsourcing Risks

Guide

Is Outsourcing Fool's Gold?

"People are kidding themselves. It sounds so good—just pay a fixed, known amount to some vendor, and all your problems go away. Everyone has the computers they need, the network never goes down, and you never have to endure another horrible meeting about network protocols, HTTPs, and the latest worm. You're off into information systems nirvana. . . .

"Except it doesn't work that way. You trade one set of problems for another. Consider the outsourcing of computer infrastructure. What's the first thing the outsource vendor does? It hires all of the employees who were doing the work for you. Remember that lazy, incompetent network administrator that the company had—the one who never seemed to get anything done? Well, he's baaaaack, as an employee of your outsource company. Only this time, he has an excuse, 'Company policy won't allow me to do it that way.'

"So the outsourcers get their first-level employees by hiring the ones you had. Of course, the outsourcer says it will provide management oversight, and if the employees don't work out they'll be gone. What you're really outsourcing is middle-level management of the same IT personnel you had. But there's no way of knowing whether the managers they supply are any better than the ones you had.

"Also, you think you had bureaucratic problems before? Every vendor has a set of forms, procedures, committees, reports, and other management 'tools.' They will tell you that you have to do things according to the standard blueprint. They have to say that because if they allowed every company to be different, they'd never be able to gain any leverage themselves, and they'd never be profitable.

"So now you're paying a premium for the services of your former employees, who are now managed by strangers who are paid by the outsource vendor, who evaluates those managers on how well they follow the outsource vendor's profit-generating procedures. How quickly can they turn your operation into a clone of all their other clients? Do you really want to do that?

"Suppose you figure all this out and decide to get out of it. Now what? How do you undo an outsource agreement? All the critical knowledge is in the minds of the outsource vendor's employees, who have no incentive to work for you. In fact, their employment contract probably prohibits it. So now you have to take an existing operation within your own company, hire employees to staff that function, and relearn everything you ought to have learned in the first place.

"Gimme a break. Outsourcing is fool's gold, an expensive leap away from responsibility. It's like saying, 'We can't figure out how to manage an important function in our company, so you do it!' You can't get away from IS problems by hiring someone else to manage them for you. At least you care about *your* bottom line."

Discussion Questions

1. Hiring an organization's existing IS staff is common practice when starting a new outsourcing arrangement. What are the advantages of this practice to the outsource vendor? What are the advantages to the organization?

2. Suppose you work for an outsource vendor. How do you respond to the charge that your managers care only about how they appear to their employer (the outsource vendor), not how they actually perform for the organization?

3. Consider the statement, "We can't figure out how to manage an important function in our company, so you do it!" Do you agree with the sentiment of this statement? If this is true, is it necessarily bad? Why or why not?

4. Explain how it is possible for an outsource vendor to achieve economies of scale that are not possible for the hiring organization. Does this phenomenon justify outsourcing? Why or why not?

5. In what ways is outsourcing IS infrastructure like outsourcing the company cafeteria? In what ways is it different? What general conclusions can you make about infrastructure outsourcing?

routine maintenance on computers. Once the vendor is in charge, your employees must conform.

When outsourcing the cafeteria, employees have only those food choices that the vendor cooks. Similarly, when obtaining computer hardware and services, the employees will need to take what the vendor supports. Employees who want equipment that is not on the vendor's list will be out of luck.

The outsource vendor chooses the technology that it wants to implement. If the vendor, for some reason, is slow to pick up on a significant new technology, then the hiring organization will be slow to attain benefits from that technology. An organization can find itself at a competitive disadvantage because it cannot offer the same IS services as its competitors.

Another concern is a potential loss of intellectual capital. The company may need to reveal proprietary trade secrets, methods, or procedures to the outsource vendor's employees. As part of its normal operations, that vendor may move employees to competing organizations, and the company may lose intellectual capital as that happens. The loss may not be intellectual theft; it may simply be that the vendor's employees learned to work in a new and better way at your company, and then they take that learning to your competitor.

Similarly, all software has failures and problems. Quality vendors track those failures and problems and fix them according to a set of priorities. When a company outsources a system, it no longer has control over prioritizing those fixes. Such control belongs to the vendor. A fix that may be critical to an organization may be of low priority to the outsource vendor.

Other problems are that the outsource vendor may change management, adopt a different strategic direction, or be acquired. When any of those changes occurs, priorities may change, and an outsource vendor that was a good choice at one time may be a bad fit after it changes direction. It can be difficult and expensive to change an outsource vendor when this occurs.

The final loss-of-control risk is that the company's chief information officer (CIO) can become superfluous. When users need a critical service that is outsourced, the CIO must turn to the vendor for a response. In time, users learn that it is quicker to deal directly with the outsource vendor, and the CIO is soon out of the communication loop. At that point, the vendor has essentially replaced the CIO, who has become a figurehead. However, employees of the outsource vendor work for a different company, with a bias toward their employer. Critical managers will not share the same goals and objectives as the rest of the management team. Biased, bad decisions can result.

Benefits Outweighed by Long-Term Costs

The initial benefits of outsourcing can appear huge. A cap on financial exposure, a reduction of management time and attention, and freedom from many management and staffing problems are all possible. (Most likely, outsource vendors promise these very benefits.) Outsourcing can appear too good to be true.

In fact, it *can* be too good to be true. For one, although a fixed cost does indeed cap exposure, it also removes the benefits of economies of scale. If the Web storefront takes off—and suddenly the organization needs 200 servers instead of 20—the using organization will pay 200 times the fixed cost of supporting one server. It is likely, however, that because of economies of scale, the costs of supporting 200 servers are far less than 10 times the costs of supporting 20 servers.

Also, the outsource vendor may change its pricing strategy over time. Initially, an organization obtains a competitive bid from several outsource vendors. However, as the winning vendor learns more about the business and as relationships develop between the organization's employees and those of the vendor, it becomes difficult for other firms to compete for subsequent contracts. The vendor becomes the *de facto* sole source and, with little competitive pressure, may increase its prices.

Another problem is that an organization can find itself paying for another organization's mismanagement, with little recourse. Over time, if the outsource vendor is mismanaged or suffers setbacks in other arenas, costs will increase. When this occurs, an outsourcing arrangement that initially made sense no longer makes sense. But the cost and risk of switching to another vendor are high.

Don Gray, a consultant who specializes in managing offshore development projects, warns that a common problem (at least for offshore projects) is the vendor's lack of management expertise: "If you contracted for 200 hours of programmer time, you will probably get that time. What you may not get, however, is the expertise required to manage that time well."[1] By choosing to employ an outsource vendor, the organization loses all visibility into the management effectiveness of the outsource vendor. The organization contracting with the outsource vendor may be paying for gross inefficiency and may not know it. Ultimately, such a situation will result in a competitive disadvantage with organizations that are not subsidizing such inefficiency.

No Easy Exit

The final category of outsourcing risk concerns ending the agreement. There is no easy exit. For one, the outsource vendor's employees have gained significant knowledge of the company. They know the server requirements in customer support, they know the patterns of usage, and they know the best procedures for downloading operational data into the data warehouse. Consequently, lack of knowledge will make it difficult to bring the outsourced service back in-house.

Also, because the vendor has become so tightly integrated into the business, parting company can be exceedingly risky. Closing down the employee cafeteria for a few weeks while finding another food vendor would be unpopular, but employees would survive. Shutting down the enterprise network for a few weeks would be impossible; the business would not survive. Because of such risk, the company must invest considerable work, duplication of effort, management time, and expense to change to another vendor. In truth, choosing an outsource vendor can be a one-way street.

1. Don Gray, personal communication, May 2010.

ACTIVE REVIEW

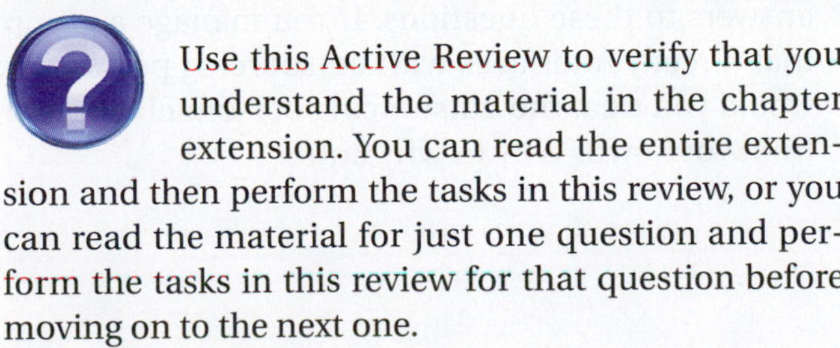

Use this Active Review to verify that you understand the material in the chapter extension. You can read the entire extension and then perform the tasks in this review, or you can read the material for just one question and perform the tasks in this review for that question before moving on to the next one.

Q1 What is outsourcing?

Define *outsourcing*. Explain the implications of Drucker's statement, "Your back room is someone else's front room." Give an example of an outsourcing opportunity at your university.

Q2 Why do organizations outsource IS and IT?

Name three categories of advantages of outsourcing. Describe two to three specific advantages of each.

Q3 What are popular outsourcing alternatives?

Explain how you can use the five components to organize outsourcing alternatives. Explain how the outsourcing of Web farms, licensed software, applications, and business functions pertains to the five components.

Q4 What are the risks of outsourcing?

Explain how outsourcing results in a loss of control. Describe why the long-term costs of outsourcing may outweigh the short-term benefits. Explain why there is no easy exit from outsourcing, and describe some of the challenges of ending an outsourcing agreement.

KEY TERMS AND CONCEPTS

Outsourcing 578

USING YOUR KNOWLEDGE

1. Consider the following statement: "In many ways, choosing an outsource vendor is a one-way street." Explain what this statement means. Do you agree with this statement? Why or why not?

2. Consider the outsourcing of the following business functions:
   - Employee cafeteria
   - General ledger accounting
   - Corporate IT infrastructure (networks, servers, and infrastructure applications, such as email)

   a. Compare the benefits of outsourcing for each business function.

   b. Compare the risks of outsourcing for each business function.

   c. Do you believe the decision to outsource is easier for some of these functions than for others? Why or why not?

3. Read Case Study 11, about Marriott International, on page 278. As stated in question 3, Marriott chose to outsource its human relations information system.

   a. List the advantages of outsourcing the HR function.

   b. List the risks of outsourcing the HR function.

   c. How did outsourcing HR reduce the risk in developing OneSystem?

   d. Think of all of the systems and IT infrastructure that a company like Marriott has. List five or six information systems that Marriott is likely to have, and list two or three items of IT infrastructure it is likely to need. Consider your two lists as the elements of a portfolio. Explain how outsourcing can be used to balance the risk in the total portfolio. Explain the advantages and disadvantages of outsourcing to the same or different vendors.

4. Suppose you are offered two jobs as a systems analyst. One is for a sizable, quality company like Marriott, and you will work on its in-house information systems. The second job is to work for a quality outsourcing company like EDS (*www.eds.com*). What do you expect your professional life would be like for the two different jobs? Which job do you think is more secure? Which job do you think has greater career prospects? Can you imagine that one job would be more fulfilling than the other? If so, which one? Assuming pay and benefits were equal, which job would you choose? Reflect on your answers to these questions. If you manage a group that directly interfaces with outsourcing personnel, would you treat the outsourcing personnel different from your own? Why or why not?

CHAPTER EXTENSION 21

STUDY QUESTIONS

This chapter extension is a capstone of all 12 chapters of this book.

International MIS

Q1 How does the global economy impact organizations and processes?

Q2 What are the characteristics of international IS components?

Q3 What are the challenges of international cross-functional applications?

Q4 How do interorganizational IS facilitate globalization?

Q5 What are the challenges of international IS management?

Q1 How Does the Global Economy Impact Organizations and Processes?

Businesses compete today in a global market. International business has been increasing at a rapid pace since the middle of the twentieth century. After World War II, the Japanese and other Asian economies exploded when those countries began to manufacture and sell goods to the West. The rise of the Japanese auto industry and the semiconductor industry in southeastern Asia greatly expanded international trade. At the same time, the economies of North America and Europe became more closely integrated.

Since then, a number of other factors have caused international business to skyrocket. The fall of the Soviet Union opened the economies of Russia and Eastern Europe to the world market. More important, the telecommunications boom during the dot-com heyday caused the world to be encircled many times over by optical fiber that can be used for data and voice communications.

After the dot-com bust, optical fiber was largely underutilized and could be purchased for pennies on the dollar. Plentiful, cheap telecommunications enabled people worldwide to participate in the global economy. Prior to the advent of the Internet, for a young Indian professional to participate in the Western economy, he or she had to migrate to the West—a process that was politicized and limited. Today, that same young Indian professional can sell his or her goods or services over the Internet without leaving home. During this same period, the Chinese economy became more open to the world, and it, too, benefits from plentiful, cheap telecommunications.

Columnist and author Thomas Friedman estimates that from 1991 until 2007, some 3 billion people were added to the world economy.[1]

Not all of those people speak English, and not all of them are well enough educated (or equipped) to participate in the world economy. But even if just 10 percent are, then 300 million people have been added to the world economy in the last 15 years!

How Does the Global Economy Change the Competitive Environment?

To understand the impact of globalization, consider each of the elements in Figure CE21-1 (page 588). The enlarged and Internet-supported world economy has altered every one of the five competitive forces. Suppliers have to reach a

CE21

1. Thomas L. Friedman, *The World Is Flat: A Brief History of the Twenty-First Century 3.0* (New York: Farrar, Strauss and Giroux, 2007).

wider range of customers, and customers have to consider a wider range of vendors. Suppliers and customers benefit not just from the greater size of the economy, but also by the ease with which businesses can learn of each other using tools such as Google and Bing.

Because of the information available on the Internet, customers can more easily learn of substitutions. The Internet has made it easier for new market entrants, although not in all cases. Amazon.com, Yahoo!, and Google, for example, have garnered such a large market share that it would be difficult for any new entrant to challenge them. Still, in other industries the global economy facilitates new entrants. Finally, the global economy has intensified rivalry by increasing product and vendor choices and by accelerating the flow of information about price, product, availability, and service.

How Does the Global Economy Change Competitive Strategy?

Today's global economy changes thinking about competitive strategies in two major ways. First, the sheer size and complexity of the global economy means that any organization that chooses a strategy allowing it to compete industry-wide is taking a very big bite! Competing in many different countries, with products localized to the language and culture of those countries, is an enormous and expensive task.

For example, to promote Windows worldwide Microsoft must produce a version of Windows in dozens of different languages. Even in English, Microsoft produces a U.K. version, a U.S. version, an Australian version, and so forth. The problem for Microsoft is even greater, because different countries use different character sets. In some languages, writing flows from left to right. In other languages, it flows from right to left. When Microsoft set out to sell Windows worldwide, it embarked on an enormous project.

The second major way today's world economy changes competitive strategies is that its size, combined with the Internet, enables unprecedented product differentiation. If you choose to produce the world's highest quality and most exotic oatmeal—and if your production costs require you to sell that oatmeal for $350 a pound—your target market might contain only 200 people worldwide. The Internet allows you to find them—and them to find you.

The decision involving a global competitive strategy requires the consideration of these two changing factors.

How Does the Global Economy Change Value Chains and Business Processes?

Because of information systems, any or all of the value chain activities in Figure CE21-1 can be performed anywhere in the world. An international company can conduct sales and marketing efforts locally, for every market in which it sells. 3M divisions, for

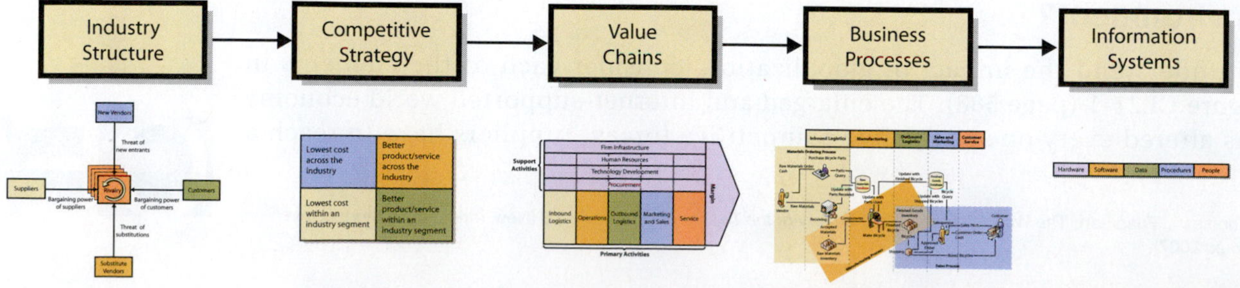

Figure CE21-1
Organizational Strategy Determines Information Systems

example, sell in the United States with a U.S. sales force, in France with a French sales force, and in Argentina with an Argentinean sales force. Depending on local laws and customs, those sales offices may be owned by 3M, or they may be locally owned entities with which 3M contracts for sales and marketing services. 3M can coordinate all of the sales efforts of these entities using the same CRM system. When 3M managers need to roll up sales totals for a sales projection, they can do so using an integrated, worldwide system.

Manufacturing of a final product is frequently distributed throughout the world. Components of the Boeing 787 are manufactured in Italy, China, England, and numerous other countries and delivered to Washington and South Carolina for final assembly. Each manufacturing facility has its own inbound logistics, manufacturing, and outbound logistics activities, but those activities are linked together via information systems.

For example, Rolls-Royce manufactures an engine and delivers that engine to Boeing via its outbound logistics activity. Boeing receives the engine using its inbound logistics activity. All of this activity is coordinated via shared, interorganizational information systems. Rolls-Royce's CRM is connected with Boeing's supply processes, using techniques such as CRM and enterprise resource planning (ERP).

Because of the abundance of low-cost, well-educated, English-speaking professionals in India, many organizations have chosen to outsource their service and support functions to India. Some accounting functions are outsourced to India as well.

World time differences enable global virtual companies to operate 24/7. Boeing engineers in Los Angeles can develop a design for an engine support strut and send that design to Roll-Royce in England at the end of their day. The design will be waiting for Roll-Royce engineers at the start of their day. They review the design, make needed adjustments, and send it back to Boeing in Los Angeles, where the reviewed, adjusted design arrives at the start of the workday in Los Angeles. The ability to work around the clock by moving work into other time zones increases productivity.

Q2 What Are the Characteristics of International IS Components?

To understand the impact of internationalization on information systems, consider the five components. Computer hardware is sold worldwide, and most vendors provide documentation in at least the major languages, so internationalization has little impact on that component. The remaining components of an information system, however, are markedly affected.

To begin, consider the user interface for an international information system. Does it include a local-language version of Windows? What about the software application itself? Does an inventory system used worldwide by Boeing suppose that each user speaks English? If so, at what level of proficiency? If not, what languages must the user interface support?

Next, consider the data component. Suppose that the inventory database has a table for parts data and that table contains a column named Remarks. Suppose Boeing needs to integrate parts data from three different vendors: one in China, one in India, and one in Canada. What language is to be used for recording Remarks? Does someone need to translate all of the Remarks into one language? Into three languages?

The human components—procedures and people—are obviously affected by language and culture. As with business processes, information systems procedures need to reflect local cultural values and norms. For systems users, job descriptions and reporting relationships must be appropriate for the setting in which the system is used. We will say more about this in Q5.

What's Required to Localize Software?

The process of making a computer program work in a second language is called **localizing**. It turns out to be surprisingly hard to do. To localize a document or a Web page, all you need to do is hire a translator to convert your document or page from one language to another. The situation is much more difficult for a computer program, however.

Consider a program you use frequently—say, Microsoft Word—and ask what would need to be done to translate it to a different language. The entire user interface will need to be translated. The menu bar and the commands on the menu bar will need to be translated. It is possible that some of the icons (the small graphics on a menu bar) will need to be changed, because some graphic symbols that are harmless in one culture are confusing or offensive in another.

What about a CRM application program that includes forms, reports, and queries? The labels on each of these will need to be translated. Of course, not all labels translate into words of the same length, and so the forms and reports may need to be redesigned. The questions and prompts for queries, such as "Enter part number for back order," must also be translated.

All of the documentation will need to be translated. That should be just a matter of hiring a translator, except that all of the illustrations in the documentation will need to be redrawn in the second language.

Think, too, about error messages. When someone attempts to order more items than there are in inventory, your application produces an error message. All of those messages will need to be translated. There are other issues as well. Sorting order is one. Spanish uses accents on certain letters, and it turns out that an accented *ó* will sort after *z* when you use the computer's default sort ordering. Figure CE21-2 summarizes the factors to address when localizing software.

Programming techniques can be used to simplify and reduce the cost of localization. However, those techniques must be used in the beginning. For example, suppose that when a certain condition occurs, the program is to display the message "Insufficient quantity in stock." If the programmer codes all such messages into the computer program, then, to localize that program, the programmer will have to find every such message in the code and then ask a translator to change that code. A preferred technique is to give every error message a number and to place the number and text of the error message into a separate file. Then, the code is written to display a particular error number from that file. During localization, translators simply translate the file of error messages into the second language.

The bottom line for you, as a future manager, is to understand two points: (1) Localizing computer programs is much more difficult, expensive, and time consuming than translating documents. (2) If a computer program is likely to be

Figure CE21-2
Issues to Address When Localizing a Computer Ptogram

- Translate the user interface, including menu bars and commands.
- Translate, and possibly redesign, labels in forms, reports, and query prompts.
- Translate all documentation and help text.
- Redraw and translate diagrams and examples in help text.
- Translate all error messages.
- Translate text in all message boxes.
- Adjust sorting order for different character set.
- Fix special problems in Asian character sets and in languages that read and write from right to left.

localized, then plan for that localization from the beginning. In addition, when considering the acquisition of a company in a foreign country, be sure to budget time and expense for the localization of information systems.

What Are the Problems and Issues of Global Databases?

When we discussed CRM and ERP in Chapter 7 and Chapter Extension 12, you learned of the advantage of having all data stored in a single database. In brief, a single database reduces data integrity problems and makes it possible to have an integrated view of the customer or the organization's operations.

International companies that have a single database must, however, declare a single language for the company. Every Remark or Comment or other text field needs to be in a single language. If not, the advantages of a single database disappear. This is not a problem for companies that commit to a single company language. For example, Thomas Keidel, CEO of the Mahr Group (*www.mahr.com*), states, "We standardized on English as the official company language; we use English in our meetings, in our emails, and in other correspondence. We have to do this because we have factories in 14 countries, and it would be impossible to make any decision otherwise. We chose English because it is a language that most business professionals have in common."[2] For a company like this, standardizing on a language for database contents is not a problem.

A single database is not possible, however, for companies that use multiple languages. Such companies often decide to give up on the benefits of a single database to let divisions in different countries use different databases, with data in local languages. For example, an international manufacturer might allow a component manufacturing division in South Korea to have a database in Korean and a final assembly division in Brazil to have a different database in Portuguese. In this scenario, the company needs applications to export and import data among the separated databases.

Besides language, performance is a second issue that confronts global databases. Oftentimes, data transmission speeds are too slow to process data from a single geographic location. If so, companies sometimes distribute their database in locations around the world.

Distributed database processing refers to the processing of a single database that resides in multiple locations. If the distributed database contains the same data, it is called a **replicated database**. If the distributed database does not contain copies of the same data, but rather divides the database into nonoverlapping segments, it is called a **partitioned database**. In most cases, querying either type of distributed database can improve performance without too much development work. However, updating a replicated database so that changes are correctly made to all copies of the data is full of challenges that require highly skilled personnel to solve. Still, companies like Amazon.com, which operates call centers in the United States, India, and Ireland, have invested in applications that are able to successfully update distributed databases, worldwide.

Q3 What Are the Challenges of International Cross-Functional Applications?

As you learned in Chapter 7 and Chapter Extension 18, functional business processes and applications support particular activities within a single department or business activity. Because the systems operate independently, the organization suffers from islands of automation. Sales and marketing data, for example, are not integrated with operations or manufacturing data.

2. Private correspondence with the author, May 2010.

You learned that many organizations eliminate the problems of information silos by creating cross-functional systems. With international IS, however, such systems may not be worthwhile.

Advantages of Functional Systems

Lack of integration is disadvantageous in many situations, but it has *advantages*, however, for international organizations and international systems. Because an order-processing functional system located in, say, the United States is separate from and independent of the manufacturing systems located in, say, Taiwan, it is unnecessary to accommodate language, business, and cultural differences in a single system. U.S. order-processing systems can operate in English and reflect the practices and culture of the United States. Taiwanese manufacturing information systems can operate in Chinese and reflect the business practices and culture of Taiwan. As long as there is an adequate data interface between the two systems, they can operate independently, sharing data when necessary.

Cross-functional, integrated systems, such as ERP, solve the problems of data isolation by integrating data into a database that provides a comprehensive and organization-wide view. However, as discussed in Q2, that advantage requires that the company standardize on a single language. Otherwise, separate functional databases are needed.

Problems of Inherent Processes

Inherent processes are even more problematic. Each software product assumes that the software will be used by people filling particular roles and performing their actions in a certain way. ERP vendors justify this standardization by saying that their procedures are based on industry-wide best practices and that the organization will benefit by following these standard processes. That statement may be true, but some inherent processes may conflict with cultural norms. If they do, it will be very difficult for management to convince the employees to follow those inherent processes. Or at least it will be difficult in some cultures to do so.

Differences in language, culture, norms, and expectations compound the difficulties of international process management. Just creating an accurate as-is model is difficult and expensive; developing alternative international processes and evaluating them can be incredibly challenging. With cultural differences, it can be difficult just to determine what criteria should be used for evaluating the alternatives, let alone performing the evaluation.

Because of these challenges, in the future it is likely that international business processes will be developed more like interorganizational business processes. A high-level process will be defined to document the service responsibilities of each international unit. Then SOA standards will be used to connect those services into an integrated, cross-functional, international system. Because of encapsulation, the only obligation of an international unit will be to deliver its defined service. One service can be delivered using procedures based on autocratic management policies, and another can be delivered using procedures based on collaborative management policies. The differences will not matter to a SOA-based cross-functional system.

Q4 How Do Interorganizational IS Facilitate Globalization?

As stated, the Internet played a major role in facilitating international commerce. Along with the Internet, however, another major factor has been the rise of international interorganizaitonal systems. Two examples are supply chain and manufacturing systems, as we discuss next. At some point, Web 2.0 systems may have a positive impact as well, although it is not yet clear how.

How Do Global Information Systems Affect Supply Chain Profitability?

In short, global information systems increase supply chain profitability. As you learned in Chapter Extension 13, supply chain performance is driven by four factors: facilities, inventories, transportation, and information. Every one of these drivers is positively affected by global information systems. Because of global information systems, facilities can be located anywhere in the world. If Amazon.com finds it economically advantageous to warehouse books in Iceland, it can do so. If Rolls-Royce can more cheaply manufacture its engine turbine blades in Poland, it can do so.

Furthermore, information systems reduce inventories and hence save costs. They can be used to reduce or eliminate the **bullwhip effect**, a phenomenon in which the variability in the size and timing of orders increases at each stage of the supply chain. They also support just-in-time (JIT) inventory techniques worldwide. Using information systems, the order of a Dell computer from a user in Bolivia triggers a manufacturing system at Dell, which, in turn, triggers the order of a component from a warehouse in Taiwan—all automatically.

To underscore this point, consider the inventories that exist at this moment in time, worldwide. Every component in one of those inventories represents a waste of the world's resources. Any product or component sitting on a shelf is not being used and is adding no value to the global economy. In the perfect world, a customer would think, "I want a new computer," and that thought would trigger systems all over the world to produce and assemble necessary components, instantly. Given that we live in a world bound by time and space, instantaneous production is forever unreachable. But the goal of worldwide information systems for supply chain inventory management is to come as close to instantaneous as possible.

Consider transportation, the third driver. When you order a book from Amazon.com, you are presented with at least four shipping options. You can choose the speed and attendant price that is appropriate for your needs. Similar systems for businesses allow them to choose the delivery option that optimizes the value they generate. Further, automated systems enable suppliers and customers to track the shipment's location, 24/7, worldwide.

Finally, global information systems produce comprehensive, accurate, and timely information. As you learned in Chapter 9, information systems produce data at prodigious rates, worldwide. That data facilitates operations as just discussed, but it also produces information for planning, organizing, deciding, and other analyses.

What Is the Economic Impact of Global Manufacturing?

Henry Ford pioneered modern manufacturing methods, and in the process he reduced the price of automobiles to the point they were no longer the playthings of the very rich but were affordable to the general population. In 1914, Ford took the unprecedented step of unilaterally increasing his workers' pay from $2.50 per day for 10 hours' work to $5 per day for 8 hours' work. As a consequence, many of his workers could soon afford to purchase an automobile. By paying his workers more, Ford increased demand.

The increase in demand was not due only to purchases by his workers, of course. Because of what economists call the **accelerator effect**, a dollar spent will contribute two or three dollars of activity to the economy. Ford's workers spent their increased pay not just on autos, but also on goods and services in their local community, which benefited via the accelerator effect. That benefit enabled non–Ford workers also to

afford an auto. Further, because of the positive publicity he achieved with the pay increase, the community was strongly disposed to purchase a Ford automobile.

Consider those events in light of global manufacturing. For example, if Boeing manufactures airplanes entirely in the United States, the U.S. economy will be the sole beneficiary of that economic activity. If an Italian airline chooses to buy a Boeing plane, the transaction will be a cost to the Italian economy. There will be no accelerator effect, and the transaction will have no consequence on Italians' propensity to fly.

However, if Boeing purchases major components for its airplanes from Italian companies, then that purchase will generate an accelerator effect for the Italian economy. By buying in Italy, Boeing contributes to Italy's economy, and ultimately increases Italians' propensity to fly. That foreign-component purchase will, of course, reduce economic activity in the United States, but if it induces Italians to purchase sufficiently more Boeing airplanes, then it is possible that the loss will be compensated by the increase in airplane sales volume. That purchase will also benefit Boeing's image among Italians and increase the likelihood of sales to the Italian government.

The same phenomenon pertains to Dell computers, Cisco routers, and Microsoft programmers.

How Does Web 2.0 Affect International Business?

In truth, we do not know, at least not yet, how Web 2.0 affects international business. We do know that Web 2.0 technologies are used internationally: For example, Google AdWords is available in the Japanese and Indian markets, and social networks are popular in any culture with sufficient connectivity.

We do not know, however, how Web 2.0 affects international business, nor do we know the effectiveness of Enterprise 2.0 in multinational companies. It is possible that Web 2.0 technologies are so culturally biased that they work only in the culture in which they originate. A Facebook social graph of a young college woman in Japan is unlikely to connect in any meaningful way with a similar graph of a male business student in India. Each will have his or her own social network, but they will be domestic, not international.

Similar comments can be made about user-generated content. Teenagers in Chicago are unlikely to be influenced by user-generated tennis shoe designs that are popular in Hanover, Germany. Or are they? Is there a business opportunity for some innovative company to foster user-generated designs in one culture with the express purpose of marketing those designs in another culture? As of June 2010, we do not know.

Opportunities like this will exist for you and your classmates to explore early in your careers. As you use Facebook or MySpace and as you consume or create UGC, think about the international aspects of your activity. Both international Web 2.0 and international Enterprise 2.0 seem to be ripe for innovation.

Q5 What Are the Challenges of International IS Management?

Size and complexity make international IT management challenging. International information systems are larger and more complex. Projects to develop them are larger and more complicated to manage. International IT departments are bigger and composed of people from many cultures with many different native languages. International organizations have more IS and IT assets, and those assets are exposed to more risk and greater uncertainty. Because of the complexity of international law, security incidents are more complicated to investigate.

Why Is International Information Systems Development More Challenging?

The factors that affect international information systems development are more challenging than those that affect international software development. If the *system* is truly international, if many people from many different countries will be using the system, then the development project is exceedingly complicated.

To see why, consider the five components. Running hardware in different countries is not a problem, and localizing software is manageable, assuming programs were designed to be localized. Databases pose more difficulties. First, is a single database to be used, and if so, is it to be distributed? If so, how will updates be processed? Also, what language, currency, and units of measure will be used to store data? If multiple databases are to be used, how are data going to be transported among them? Some of these problems are difficult, but they are solvable with technical solutions.

The same cannot be said for the procedure and people components. An international system is used by people who live and work in cultures that are vastly different from one another. The way that customers are treated in Japan differs substantially from the way that customers are treated in Spain, which differs substantially from the way that customers are treated in the United States. The procedures for using a CRM will be correspondingly different.

Consider the phases of the SDLC as shown in Figure CE21-3. During systems definition, we are supposed to determine the purpose and scope of the system. As you know by now, information systems should facilitate the organization's competitive

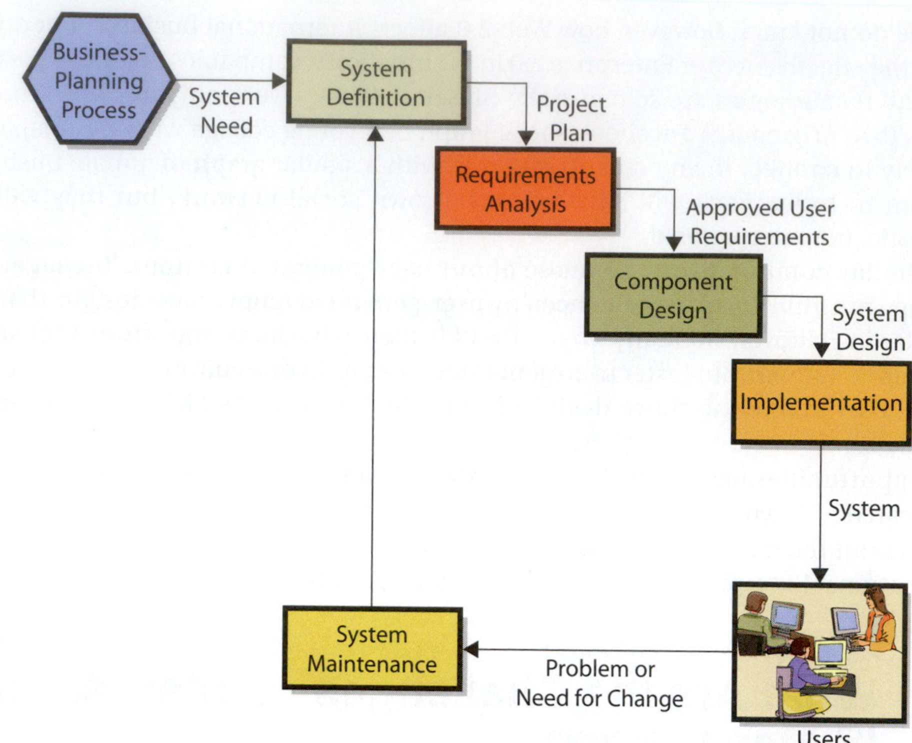

Figure CE21-3
Phases in the SDLC

strategy by supporting business processes. But what if the underlying processes differ? Again, customer support in Japan and customer support in Spain may involve completely different processes and activities.

Even if the purpose and scope can be defined in some unified way, how are requirements to be determined? Again, if the underlying business processes differ, then the specific requirements for the information system will differ. Managing requirements for a system in one culture is difficult, but managing requirements for international systems can be many times more difficult.

There are two responses to such challenges: (1) either define a set of standard business processes or (2) develop alternative versions of the system that support different processes in different countries. Both responses are problematic. The first response requires conversion of the organization to different work processes, and, as you learned in Chapter Extension 12, such conversion can be exceedingly difficult. People resist change, and they will do so with vehemence if the change violates cultural norms.

The second response is easier to implement, but it creates system design challenges. It also means that, in truth, there is not one system, but many.

In spite of the problems, both responses are used. For example, SAP, Oracle, and other ERP vendors define standard business processes via the inherent procedures in their software products. Many organizations attempt to enforce those standard procedures. When it becomes organizationally infeasible to do so, organizations develop exceptions to those inherent procedures and develop programs to handle the exceptions. This choice means high maintenance expense.

What Are the Challenges of International Project Management?

Managing a global information systems development project is difficult because of project size and complexity. Requirements are complex, many resources are required, and numerous people are involved. Team members speak different languages, live in different cultures, work in different time zones, and seldom meet face-to-face.

One way to understand how these factors impact global project management is to consider each of the project management knowledge areas as set out by the international Project Management Institute's document, the *PMBOK® Guide* (*www.pmi.org/Marketplace/Pages/ProductDetail.aspx?GMProduct=00100035801*). Figure CE21-4 summarizes challenges for each knowledge area. Project integration is more difficult because international development projects require the complex integration of results from distributed workgroups. Also, task dependencies can span teams working in different countries, increasing the difficulty of task management.

The scope and requirements definition for international IS is more difficult, as just discussed. Time management is more difficult because teams in different cultures and countries work at different rates. Some cultures have a 35-hour workweek, and some have a 60-hour workweek. Some cultures expect 6-week vacations, and some expect 2 weeks. Some cultures thrive on efficiency of labor, and others thrive on considerate working relationships. There is no standard rate of development for an international project.

In terms of cost, different countries and cultures pay vastly different labor rates. Using critical path analysis, managers may choose to move a task from one team to another. Doing so, however, may substantially increase costs. Thus, management may choose to accept a delay rather than move work to an available (but more expensive) team. The complex trade-offs that exist between time and cost become even more complex for international projects.

Quality and human resources are also more complicated for international projects. Quality standards vary among countries. The IT industry in some nations, like India, has invested heavily in development techniques that increase program quality. Other countries, like the United States, have been less willing to invest in quality. In any case, the integration of programs of varying quality results in an inconsistent system.

Worker expectations vary among cultures and nations. Compensation, rewards, and worker conditions vary, and these differences can lead to misunderstandings, poor morale, and project delays.

Knowledge Areas	Challenge
Project integration	Complex integration of results from distributed work groups. Management of dependencies of tasks from physically and culturally different work groups.
Scope (requirements)	Need to support multiple versions of underlying business processes. Possibly substantial differences in requirements and procedures.
Time	Development rates vary among cultures and countries.
Cost	Cost of development varies widely among countries. Two members performing the same work in different countries may be paid substantially different rates. Moving work among teams may dramatically change costs.
Quality	Quality standards vary among cultures. Different expectations of quality may result in an inconsistent system.
Human resources	Worker expectations differ. Compensation, rewards, work conditions vary widely.
Communications	Geographic, language, and cultural distance among team members impedes effective communication.
Risk	Development risk is higher. Easy to lose control.
Procurement	Complications of international trade.

Figure CE21-4
Challenges for International IS Project Management

Because of these factors, effective team communication is exceedingly important for international projects, but because of language and culture differences and geographic separation, such communication is difficult. Effective communication is also more expensive. Consider, for example, just the additional expense of maintaining a team portal in three or four languages.

If you consider all of the factors in Figure CE21-4, it is easy to understand why project risk is high for international IS development projects. So many things can go wrong. Project integration is complex; requirements are difficult to determine; cost, time, and quality are difficult to manage; worker conditions vary widely; and communication is difficult. Finally, project procurement is complicated by the normal challenges of international commerce.

What Are the Challenges of International IT Management?

Chapter 11 defined the four primary responsibilities of the IT department: plan, operate, develop, and protect information systems and IT infrastructure. Each of these responsibilities becomes more challenging for international IT organizations.

Regarding planning, the principal task is to align IT and IS resources with the organization's competitive strategy. The task does not change character for international companies; it just becomes more complex and difficult. Multinational organizations and operations are complicated, and the business processes that support their competitive strategies tend also to be complicated. Further, changes in global economic factors can mean dramatic changes in processes and necessitate changes in IS and IT support. Technology adoption can also cause remarkable change. The increasing use of cell phones in developing countries, for example, changes the requirements for local information systems. The rising price of oil will also change international business processes. Thus, planning tasks for international IT are larger and more complex.

Three factors create challenges for international IT operations. First, conducting operations in different countries, cultures, and languages adds complexity. Go to the Web site of any multinational corporation, say *www.3m.com* or *www.dell.com*, and you'll be asked to click on the country in which you reside. When you click, you are likely to be directed to a Web server running in some other country. Those Web servers need to be managed consistently, even though they are operated by people living in different cultures and speaking different languages.

The second operational challenge of international IS is the integration of similar, but different, systems. Consider inventory. A multinational corporation might have dozens of different inventory systems in use throughout the world. To enable the movement of goods, many of these systems need to be coordinated and integrated.

Or consider customer support that operates from three different support centers in three different countries. Each support center may have its own information system, but the data among those systems will need to be exported or otherwise shared. If not, then a customer who contacts one center will be unknown to the others.

The third complication for operations is outsourcing. Many organizations have chosen to outsource customer support, training, logistics, and other backroom activities. International outsourcing is particularly advantageous for customer support and other functions that must be operational 24/7. Many companies outsource logistics to UPS, because doing so offers comprehensive, worldwide shipping and logistical support. The organization's information systems usually need to be integrated with outsource vendors' information systems, and this may need to be done for different systems, all over the world.

The fourth IT department responsibility is protecting IS and IT infrastructure. We consider that function in the next question.

How Does the International Dimension Affect Computer Security Risk Management?

Computer security risk management is more difficult and complicated for international information systems. First, IT assets are subject to more threats. Infrastructure will be located in sites all over the world, and those sites differ in the threats to which they are exposed. Some will be subject to political threats, others to the threat of civil unrest, others to terrorists, and still others will be subject to threats of natural disasters of every conceivable type. Place your data center in Kansas, and it's subject to tornados. Place your data center internationally, and it's potentially subject to typhoons/hurricanes, earthquakes, floods, volcanic eruption, or mudslides. And don't forget epidemics that will affect the data center employees.

Second, the likelihood of a threat is more difficult to estimate for international systems. What is the likelihood that the death of Fidel Castro will cause civil unrest and threaten your data center in Havana? How does an organization assess that risk? What is the likelihood that a computer programmer in India will insert a Trojan horse into code that she writes on an outsourcing contract?

In addition to risk, international information systems are subject to far greater uncertainty. Uncertainty reflects the likelihood that something that "we don't know what we don't know" will cause an adverse outcome. Because of the multitudinous cultures, religions, nations, beliefs, political views, and crazy people in the world, uncertainty about risks to IS and IT infrastructure is high. Again, if you place your data center in Kansas, you have some idea of the magnitude of the uncertainty to which you are exposed, even if you don't know exactly what it is. Place a server in a country on every continent of the world, and you have no idea of the potential risks to which they are exposed.

Technical and data safeguards do not change for international information systems. Because of greater complexity there may be a need for more safeguards or for more complex ones, but the technical and data safeguards described in Chapter 12 all work for international systems. Human safeguards are another matter. For example, can an organization depend on the control of separation of duties and authorities in a culture for which graft is an accepted norm? Or, what is the utility of a personal reference in a culture in which it is considered exceedingly rude to talk about someone when they are not present? Because of these differences, human safeguards need to be chosen and evaluated on a culture-by-culture basis.

In short, risk management for both international information systems and IT infrastructure is more complicated, more difficult, and subject to greater uncertainty.

ACTIVE REVIEW

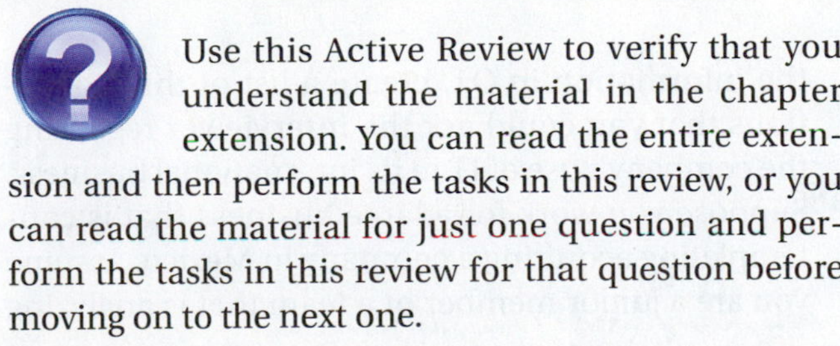

Use this Active Review to verify that you understand the material in the chapter extension. You can read the entire extension and then perform the tasks in this review, or you can read the material for just one question and perform the tasks in this review for that question before moving on to the next one.

Q1 How does the global economy impact organizations and processes?

Describe how the global economy has changed since the mid-twentieth century. Explain how the dot-com bust influenced the global economy and changed the number of workers worldwide. Summarize the ways in which today's global economy influences the five competitive forces. Explain how the global economy changes the way organizations assess industry structure. How does the global economy change competitive strategy? How do global information systems benefit the value chain? Using Figure 3-5 (page 52) as a guide, explain how each primary value chain activity can be performed anywhere in the world.

Q2 What are the characteristics of international IS components?

Explain how internationalization impacts the five components of an IS. What does it mean to localize software? Summarize the work required to localize a computer program. In your own words, explain why it is better to design a program to be localized rather than attempt to adapt an existing single-language program to a second language. Explain the problems of having a single database for an international IS. Define *distributed database, replicated database,* and *partitioned database.* State a source of problems for processing replicated databases.

Q3 What are the challenges of international cross-functional applications?

Summarize the advantages of functional systems for international companies. Summarize the issues of inherent processes for multinational ERP. Explain how SOA services could be used to address the problems of international cross-functional applications.

Q4 How do interorganizational IS facilitate globalization?

State the short answer to this question. Name the four drivers of supply chain profitability. Discuss how global information systems affect each driver. Explain how inventories represent waste. Summarize the impact that Henry Ford's act of increasing his workers' pay had on Ford auto sales. Explain how this same phenomenon pertains to Boeing acquiring major subsystems from manufacturers in Italy or to Toyota building autos in the United States. Explain how Web 2.0 and Enterprise 2.0 affect international companies. Explain the meaning of the following sentence: "It's possible that Web 2.0 technologies are so culturally biased that they work only in the culture in which they originate." Describe how this situation may create opportunities for businesses.

Q5 What are the challenges of international IS management?

State the two characteristics that make international IT management challenging. Explain the difference between international systems development and international software development. Using the five-component framework, explain why international systems development is more difficult. Give an example of one complication for each knowledge area in Figure CE21-4. State the four responsibilities for IT departments. Explain how each of these responsibilities is more challenging for international IT organizations. Describe three factors that create challenges for international IT operations. Explain why international IT assets are subject to more threats. Give three examples. Explain why the likelihood of international threats is more difficult to determine. Describe uncertainty, and explain why it is higher for international IT organizations. Explain how technical, data, and human safeguards differ for international IT organizations. Give two examples of problematic international human safeguards.

KEY TERMS AND CONCEPTS

Accelerator effect 593
Bullwhip effect 593
Distributed database processing 591
Localizing 590
Partitioned database 591
Replicated database 591

USING YOUR KNOWLEDGE

1. Suppose that you are about to have a job interview with a multinational company, such as 3M, Starbucks, or Coca-Cola. Further suppose that you wish to demonstrate an awareness of the changes for international commerce that the Internet and modern information technology have made. Using the information in Q1, create a list of three questions that you could ask the interviewer regarding the company's use of IT in its international business.
2. Suppose you work for a large business that is contemplating acquiring a company in Mexico. Assume you are a junior member of a team that is analyzing

the desirability of this acquisition. Your boss, who is not technically savvy, has asked you to prepare a summary of the issues that she should be aware of regarding the merging of the two companies' information systems. She wants your summary to include a list of questions that she should ask of both your IS department and the IS department personnel in the propsective acquistion. Prepare that summary.

3. Using the information in this chapter extenstion as well as in Chapter 7, summarize the strengths and weaknesses of functional systems, CRM, ERP, and EAI. How do the advantages and disadvantages of each change in an international setting? For your answer, create a table with strength and weakness columns and a row for each of the four system types.

4. Suppose that you are a junior member of a newly formed, international team that will meet regularly for the next year. You have team members in Europe, North and South America, Japan, Hong Kong, Singapore, Australia, and India. All of your team meetings will be virtual; some will be synchronous, but many will be asynchronous. The team leader has asked you to help prepare the environment for these meetings. In particular, he asked you to summarize the challenges that will occur in conducting these team meetings. He also wants you to assess the strengths and weaknesses of the following collaboration tools: email, Google Docs, Windows Live SkyDrive, Microsoft SharedView, WebEx, and Microsoft SharePoint. Use this chapter extension, as well as information in Chapter Extensions 1 and 2, in your assessment.

Application Exercises

PART 1

Chapter 1: Quality of Information with Excel

1. The spreadsheet in Microsoft Excel file **Ex01** contains records of employee activity on special projects. Open this workbook and examine the data that you find in the three spreadsheets it contains. Assess the accuracy, relevancy, and sufficiency of this data to the following people and problems.

    a. You manage the Denver plant, and you want to know how much time your employees are spending on special projects.

    b. You manage the Reno plant, and you want to know how much time your employees are spending on special projects.

    c. You manage the Quota Computation project in Chicago, and you want to know how much time your employees have spent on that project.

    d. You manage the Quota Computation project for all three plants, and you want to know the total time employees have spent on your project.

    e. You manage the Quota Computation project for all three plants, and you want to know the total labor cost for all employees on your project.

    f. You manage the Quota Computation project for all three plants, and you want to know how the labor-hour total for your project compares to the labor-hour totals for the other special projects.

    g. What conclusions can you make from this exercise?

Chapter 1: Comparing Information from Excel and Access

2. The database in the Microsoft Access file **Ex02** contains the same records of employee activity on special projects as in Application Exercise 1. Before proceeding, open that database and view the records in the Employee Hours table.

    a. Seven queries have been created that process this data in different ways. Using the criteria of accuracy, relevancy, and sufficiency, select the one query that is most appropriate for the information requirements in Application Exercise 1, parts a–f. If no query meets the need, explain why.

    b. What conclusions can you make from this exercise?

    c. Comparing your experiences on these two projects, what are the advantages and disadvantages of spreadsheets and databases?

Chapter 2: Use PowerPoint to Diagram Business Process

3. PowerPoint file **Ex03** contains a copy of Figure 2-2 as well as a collection of spare shapes. Using these shapes, create a business process for the Solicit Membership Process. Use your own knowledge and expertise to do this. Assume that the input to the process is the name and email address of a prospect and the output is either a new membership and a credit to Accounts Receivable or a record to a file that indicates that the person was contacted and declined buying a membership.

Chapter 3: Use Excel to Compute Inventory Value

4. Figure AE-1 shows an Excel spreadsheet that the resort bicycle rental business uses to value and analyze its bicycle inventory.

    Examine this figure to understand the meaning of the data. Now use Excel to create a similar spreadsheet. Note the following:

    - The top heading is in 20-point Calibri font. It is centered in the spreadsheet. Cells A1 through H1 have been merged.
    - The second heading, Bicycle Inventory Valuation, is in 18-point Calibri, italics. It is centered in Cells A2 through H2, which have been merged.
    - The column headings are set in 11-point Calibri, bold. They are centered in their cells, and the text wraps in the cells.

	A	B	C	D	E	F	G	H
1	Resort Bicycle Rental							
2	*Bicycle Inventory Valuation*							
3			Monday, October 29, 2007					
4	Make of Bike	Bike Cost	Number on Hand	Cost of Current Inventory	Number of Rentals	Total Rental Revenue	Revenue per Bike	Revenue as percent of Cost of Inventory
5	Wonder Bike	$325	12	$3,900	85	$6,375	$531	163.5%
6	Wonder Bike II	$385	4	$1,540	34	$4,570	$1,143	296.8%
7	Wonder Bike Supreme	$475	8	$3,800	44	$5,200	$650	136.8%
8	LiteLift Pro	$655	8	$5,240	25	$2,480	$310	47.3%
9	LiteLift Ladies	$655	4	$2,620	40	$6,710	$1,678	256.1%
10	LiteLift Racer	$795	3	$2,385	37	$5,900	$1,967	247.4%

Figure AE-1
Worksheet

a. Make the first two rows of your spreadsheet similar to that in Figure AE-1. Choose your own colors for background and type, however.
b. Place the current date so that it is centered in cells C3, C4, and C5, which must be merged.
c. Outline the cells as shown in the figure.
d. Figure AE-1 uses the following formulas:

Cost of Current Inventory = Bike Cost × Number on Hand

Revenue per Bike = Total Rental Revenue/Number on Hand

Revenue as a Percent of Cost of Inventory = Total Rental Revenue/Cost of Current Inventory

Please use these formulas in your spreadsheet, as shown in Figure AE-1.
e. Format the cells in the columns, as shown.
f. Give three examples of decisions that management of the bike rental agency might make from this data.
g. What other calculation could you make from this data that would be useful to the bike rental management? Create a second version of this spreadsheet in your worksheet document that has this calculation.

Chapter 3: Using Parameterized Queries

5. In this exercise, you will learn how to create a query based on data that a user enters and how to use that query to create a data entry form.

a. Download the Microsoft Access file **Ex05**. Open the file and familiarize yourself with the data in the Customer table.
b. Click *Create* in the Access ribbon. On the far right, select *Query Design*. Select the Customer table as the basis for the query. Drag Customer Name, Customer Email, Date Of Last Rental, Bike Last Rented, Total Number Of Rentals, and Total Rental Revenue into the columns of the query results pane (the table at the bottom of the query design window).
c. In the CustomerName column, in the row labeled Criteria, place the following text:

[Enter Name of Customer:]

Type this exactly as shown, including the square brackets. This notation tells Access to ask you for a customer name to query.
d. In the ribbon, click the red exclamation mark labeled *Run*. Access will display a dialog box with the text "Enter Name of Customer:" (the text you entered in the query Criteria row). Enter the value *Scott, Rex* and click OK.
e. Save your query with the name *Parameter Query*.
f. Click the Home tab on the ribbon and click the Design View (upper left-hand button on the Home ribbon). Replace the text in the Criteria column of the CustomerName column with the following text. Type it exactly as shown:

Like "*" & [Enter part of Customer Name to search by:] & "*"

g. Run the query by clicking *Run* in the ribbon. Enter *Scott* when prompted *Enter part of Customer Name to search by*. Notice that the two customers who have the name Scott are displayed. If you have any problems, ensure that you have typed the phrase previous shown *exactly* as shown into the Criteria row of the CustomerName column of your query.
h. Save your query again under the name *Parameter Query*. Close the query window.
i. Click *Create* in the Access ribbon. Under the Forms group, select the down arrow to the right of More Forms. Choose *Form Wizard*. In the dialog that opens, in the Tables/Queries box, click the down arrow. Select *Parameter Query*. Click the double chevron (>>) symbol and all of the columns in the query will move to the Selected Fields area.
j. Click *Next* three times. In the box under *What title do you want for your form?* enter *Customer Query Form* and click *Finish*.
k. Enter *Scott* in the dialog box that appears. Access will open a form with the values for Scott, Rex. At the bottom of the form, click the right-facing arrow and the data for Scott, Bryan will appear.
l. Close the form. Select *Object Type* and *Forms* in the Access Navigation Pane. Double-click *Customer Query Form* and enter the value *James*. Access will display data for all six-customers having the value James in their name.

Chapter Extensions 1 and 2: Free and Easy Collaboration Tools

6. Google Docs, see Exercise 1, page 334.

7. Windows Live SkyDrive, see Exercise 2, page 334.

8. Facebook Docs, see Exercise 3, page 334.

Chapter Extension 3: Managerial Decision Making with Excel

9. Suppose that you have been asked to assist in the managerial decision about how much to increase pay in the next year. Assume you are given a list of the departments in your company, along with the average salary for employees in that department for major companies in your industry. Additionally, you are given the names and salaries of 10 people in each of three departments in your company.

   Assume you have been asked to create a spreadsheet that shows the names of the 10 employees in each department, their current salary, the difference between their current salary and the industry average salary for their department, and the percent their salary would need to be increased to meet the industry average. Your spreadsheet should also compute the average increase needed to meet the industry average for each department and the average increase, company-wide, to meet industry averages.

   a. Use the data in the Word file **Ex9** and create the spreadsheet.
   b. How can you use this analysis to contribute to the employee salary decision? Based on this data, what conclusions can you make?
   c. Suppose other team members want to use your spreadsheet. Name three ways you can share it with them and describe the advantages and disadvantages of each.

Chapter Extension 3: Managerial Decision Making with Access

10. Suppose that you have been asked to assist in the managerial decision about how much to increase pay in the next year. Specifically, you are tasked to determine if there are significant salary differences among departments in your company.

    You are given an Access database with a table of employee data with the following structure:

    EMPLOYEE (Name, Department, Specialty, Salary)

    where *Name* is the name of an employee who works in a department, *Department* is the department name, *Specialty* is the name of the employee's primary skill, and *Salary* is the employee's current salary. Assume that no two employees have the same name. You have been asked to answer the following queries:

    (1) List the names, department, and salary of all employees earning more than $100,000.
    (2) List the names and specialties of all employees in the Marketing department.
    (3) Compute the average, maximum, and minimum salary of employees in your company.

(4) Compute the average, minimum, and maximum salary of employees in the Marketing department.

(5) Compute the average, minimum, and maximum salary of employees in the Information Systems department.

(6) *Extra credit:* Compute the average salary for employees in every department. Use *Group By.*

a. Design and run Access queries to obtain the answers to these questions, using the data in the Access file **Ex10**.

b. Explain how the data in your answer contributes to the salary increase decision.

c. Suppose other team members want to use your Access application. Name three ways you can share it with them, and describe the advantages and disadvantages of each.

PART 2

Note: The exercises for the chapter extensions are basically tutorials. Therefore, they are presented first, followed by exercises for Chapters 4–6.

Chapter Extension 5: Learning Excel

11. See Chapter Extension 5, Exercise 1, page 365.

12. See Chapter Extension 5, Exercise 2, page 365.

13. See Chapter Extension 5, Exercise 3, page 366.

Chapter Extension 6: Use Excel to Prepare a Computer Budget

14. See Chapter Extension 6, Exercise 5, page 382.

15. See Chapter Extension 6, Exercise 6, page 382.

Chapter Extension 7: Data Modeling with Visio

16. See Chapter Extension 7, Exercise 2, page 396. Use Microsoft Visio to document your entity-relationship design.

17. See Chapter Extension 7, Exercise 3, page 397. Use Microsoft Visio to document your entity-relationship design.

Chapter Extension 8: Apply Access Skills

18. See Chapter Extension 8, Exercise 1, page 417. Requires you to complete Exercise 17, above, first.

19. See Chapter Extension 8, Exercise 2, page 417 Requires you to complete Exercise 18 first.

Chapter Extension 9: Getting the Best Features from Excel and Access

20. See Chapter Extension 9, Exercises 1–6, page 459. Do all six of these Exercises; they are a set that will teach you how to import and export data to and from Excel and Access.

Chapter 4: Using Excel and Access to Inform Computer Upgrade Decisions

21. You have been asked to help your department decide how to upgrade computers. Let's say, for example, that you want to upgrade all of the computers' operating systems to Windows 7. Furthermore, you want to first upgrade the computers that most need upgrading, but suppose you have a limited budget. To address this situation, you would like to query the data in Figure AE-2, find all computers that do not have Windows 7, and then select those with slower CPUs or smaller memory as candidates for upgrading. To do this, you need to move the data from Excel and into Access.

Once you have analyzed the data and determined the computers to upgrade, you want to produce a report. In that case, you may want to move the data from Access and back to Excel, or perhaps into Word. In this exercise, you will learn how to perform these tasks.

a. To begin, download the Excel file **Ex21** from *www.pearsonhighered.com/kroenke* into one of your directories. We will import the data in this file into Access, but before we do so familiarize yourself with the data by opening it in Excel. Notice that there are three worksheets in this workbook. Close the Excel file.

b. Create a blank Access database. Name the database *Ex21_Answer*. Place it in some directory; it may be the same directory into which you have placed the Excel file, but it need not be. Close the default table that Access creates and delete it.

c. Now we will import the data from the three worksheets in the Excel file **Ex21** into a single table in your Access database. In the ribbon, select *External Data* and *Import from Excel.*

Figure AE-2
Data

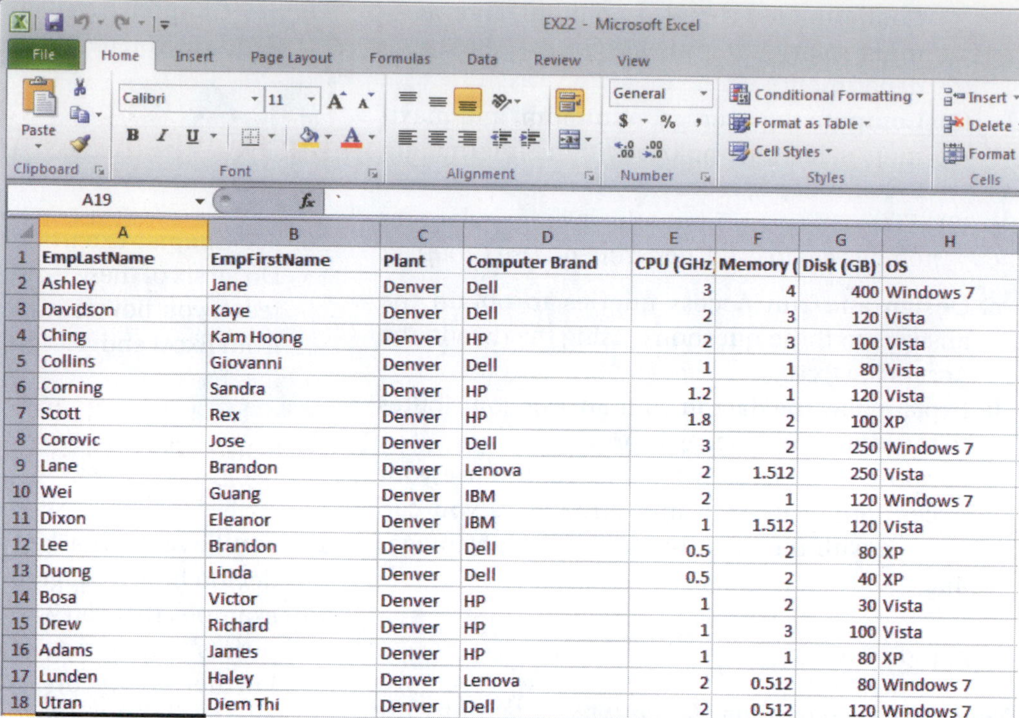

	A	B	C	D	E	F	G	H
1	EmpLastName	EmpFirstName	Plant	Computer Brand	CPU (GHz	Memory (	Disk (GB)	OS
2	Ashley	Jane	Denver	Dell	3	4	400	Windows 7
3	Davidson	Kaye	Denver	Dell	2	3	120	Vista
4	Ching	Kam Hoong	Denver	HP	2	3	100	Vista
5	Collins	Giovanni	Denver	Dell	1	1	80	Vista
6	Corning	Sandra	Denver	HP	1.2	1	120	Vista
7	Scott	Rex	Denver	HP	1.8	2	100	XP
8	Corovic	Jose	Denver	Dell	3	2	250	Windows 7
9	Lane	Brandon	Denver	Lenova	2	1.512	250	Vista
10	Wei	Guang	Denver	IBM	2	1	120	Windows 7
11	Dixon	Eleanor	Denver	IBM	1	1.512	120	Vista
12	Lee	Brandon	Denver	Dell	0.5	2	80	XP
13	Duong	Linda	Denver	Dell	0.5	2	40	XP
14	Bosa	Victor	Denver	HP	1	2	30	Vista
15	Drew	Richard	Denver	HP	1	3	100	Vista
16	Adams	James	Denver	HP	1	1	80	XP
17	Lunden	Haley	Denver	Lenova	2	0.512	80	Windows 7
18	Utran	Diem Thi	Denver	Dell	2	0.512	120	Windows 7

Start the import. For the first worksheet (Denver), you should select *Import the source data into a new table in the current database.* Be sure to click *First Row Contains Column Headings* when Access presents your data. You can use the default Field types and let Access add the primary key. Name your table *Employees* and click *Finish.* There is no need to save your import script.

For the second and third worksheets, again click *External Data, Import Excel,* but this time select *Append a copy of the records to the table Employees.* Import all data.

d. Open the *Employee* table and examine the data. Notice that Access has erroneously imported a blank line and the *Primary Contact* data into rows at the end of each data set. This data is not part of the employee records, and you should delete it (in three places—once for each worksheet). The *Employee* table should have a total of 40 records.

e. Now, create a parameterized query on this data. Place all of the columns except *ID* into the query. In the *OS* column, set the criteria to select rows for which the value is not *Windows 7.* In the *CPU* (GHz) column, enter the criterion: *<=[Enter cutoff value for CPU]* and in the *Memory* (GB) column enter the criterion: *<=[Enter cutoff value for Memory].* Test your query. For example, run your query and enter a value of *2* for both CPU and memory. Verify that the correct rows are produced.

f. Use your query to find values of CPU and memory that give you as close to a maximum of 15 computers to upgrade as possible.

g. When you have found values of CPU and memory that give you 15, or nearly 15, computers to upgrade, leave your query open. Now click *External data, Word,* and create a Word document that contains the results of your query. Adjust the column widths of the created table so that it fits on the page. Write a memo around this table explaining that these are the computers that you believe should be upgraded.

Chapter 5: Query Like Neil at FlexTime!

22. Neil at FlexTime used his studio database with Excel to obtain the data that he needs. A more common scenario is to use Microsoft Access with Excel: Users process relational data with Access, import some of the data into Excel, and use Excel's tools for creating professional looking charts and graphs. You will do exactly that in this exercise.

Download the Access file **Ex22** from *www.pearsonhighered.com/kroenke.* Open the database, select *Database Tools/Relationships.* As you can see, there are three tables: *Product, VendorProductInventory*, and *Vendor.* Open each table individually to familiarize yourself with the data.

For this problem, we will define *InventoryCost* as the product of *IndustryStandardCost* and *QuantityOnHand*. The query *InventoryCost* computes these values for every item in inventory for every vendor. Open that query and view the data to be certain you understand this computation. Open the other queries as well so that you understand the data they produce.

a. Sum this data by vendor and display it in a pie chart. Proceed as follows:
   (1) Open Excel and create a new spreadsheet.
   (2) Click *Data* on the ribbon and select *Access* in the *Get External Data* ribbon category.
   (3) Navigate to the location in which you have stored the Access file **Ex22**.
   (4) Select the query that contains the data you need for this pie chart.
   (5) Import the data into a table.
   (6) Format the appropriate data as currency.
   (7) Select the range that contains the data, press the function key, and proceed from there to create the pie chart. Name the data and pie chart worksheets appropriately.

b. Follow a similar procedure to create a bar chart. Place the data and the chart in separate worksheets and name them appropriately.

Chapter 5: Clean Up the Mess in the Salesperson's Spreadsheet

23. Reread the Guide on pages 114–115. Suppose you are given the task of converting the salesperson's data into a database. Because his data are so poorly structured, it will be a challenge, as you will see.

a. Download the Excel file named **Ex23** from *www.pearsonhighered.com/kroenke*. This spreadsheet contains data that fit the salesperson's description in the Guide. Open the spreadsheet and view the data.

b. Download the Access file with the same name, **Ex23**. Open the database, select *Database Tools*, and click *Relationships*. Examine the four tables and their relationships.

c. Somehow, you have to transform the data in the spreadsheet into the table structure in the database. Because so little discipline was shown when creating the spreadsheet, this will be a labor-intensive task. To begin, import the spreadsheet data into a new table in the database; call that table *Sheet1* or some other name.

d. Copy the *Name* data in *Sheet1* onto the clipboard. Then, open the *Customer* table and paste the column of name data into that table.

e. Unfortunately, the task becomes messy at this point. You can copy the *Car Interests* column into *Make or Model of Auto*, but then you will need to straighten out the values by hand. Phone numbers will need to be copied one at a time.

f. Open the *Customer* form and manually add any remaining data from the spreadsheet into each customer record. Connect the customer to his or her auto interests.

g. The data in the finished database are much more structured than the data in the spreadsheet. Explain why this is both an advantage and a disadvantage. Under what circumstances is the database more appropriate? Less appropriate?

Chapter 5: Allocate Computers to Employees with Access

24. In this exercise, you will create a two-table database, define relationships, create a form and a report, and use them to enter data and view results.

a. Download the Excel file **Ex24** from *www.pearsonhighered.com/kroenke*. Open the spreadsheet and review the data in the *Employee* and *Computer* worksheets.

b. Create a new Access database with the name *Ch05Ex24_Solution*. Close the table that Access automatically creates and delete it.

c. Import the data from the Excel spreadsheet into your database. Import the *Employee* worksheet into a table named *Employee*. Be sure to check *First Row Contains Column Headings*. Select *Choose my own primary key* and use the ID field as that key.

d. Import the *Computer* worksheet into a table named *Computer*. Check *First Row Contains Column Headings*, but let Access create the primary key.

e. Open the relationships window and add both *Employee* and *Computer* to the design space. Drag ID from *Employee* and drop it on *EmployeeID* in *Computer*. Check *Enforce Referential Integrity* and the two checkmarks below. Ensure you know what these actions mean.

f. Open the Form Wizard dialog box (under *Create, More Forms*) and add all of the columns for each of your tables to your form. Select *View your data by Customer*. Title your form *Employee* and your subform *Computer*.

g. Open the *Computer* subform and delete *EmployeeID* and *ComputerID*. These values are maintained by Access, and it is just a distraction to keep them. Your form should appear like the one shown in Figure AE-3.

h. Use your form to add two new computers to *Jane Ashley*. Both computers are Dells, and both use Vista; one costs $750, and the second costs $1,400.

i. Delete the Lenovo computer for Rex Scott.

j. Use the Report Wizard (under *Create*) to create a report having all data from both the *Employee* and *Computer* tables. Play with the report design until you find a design you like. Correct the label alignment if you need to.

Chapter 6: Internet Speed: Getting What You Pay For?

25. Numerous Web sites are available that will test your Internet data communications speed. You can find a good one at *www.speakeasy.net/speedtest/*. (If that site is no longer active, Google or Bing "What is my Internet speed?" to find another speed-testing site. Use it.)

a. While connected to your university's network, go to Speakeasy and test your speed against servers in Seattle, New York City, and Atlanta. Compute your average upload and download speeds.

b. Run the Speakeasy test again from your home or a public wireless site. Compute your average upload and download speeds. Compare your speed to those listed in Figure 6-4. If you are performing this test at home, are you getting the performance you are paying for?

c. Contact a friend or relative in another state. Ask him or her to run the Speakeasy test against those same three cities.

d. Compare the results in parts a, b, and c. What conclusion, if any, can you make from these tests?

Chapter 6: Budget Network Projects with Excel

26. Suppose you work for a company that will install the FlexTime network. Assume that you have been given the task of creating spreadsheets to generate cost estimates, not just for FlexTime, but for many different clients.

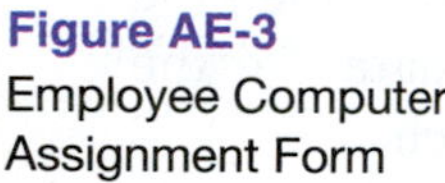

Figure AE-3
Employee Computer Assignment Form

a. Create a spreadsheet to estimate hardware costs. Assume that the user of the spreadsheet will enter the number of pieces of equipment and the standard cost for each type of equipment. Assume that the networks can include the following components: NIC cards; WNIC cards; wireless access points; switches of two types, one faster, one slower, at two different prices; and routers. Also assume that the company will use both UTP and optical fiber cable and that prices for cable are stated as per foot. Use the network in Figure 6-2 as an example.

b. Modify your spreadsheet to include labor costs. Assume there is a fixed cost for the installation of each type of equipment and a per foot cost for the installation of cable.

c. Give an example of how you might use this spreadsheet for planning network installations. Explain how you could adapt this spreadsheet for project tracking and billing purposes.

Chapter 6: Web Farm Buy-Versus-Lease Analysis with Excel

27. Assume you have been asked to create a spreadsheet to help make a buy-versus-lease decision for the servers on your organization's Web farm. Assume that you are considering the servers for a 5-year period, but you do not know exactly how many servers you will need. Initially, you know you will need 5 servers, but you might need as many as 50, depending on the success of your organization's e-commerce activity.

    a. For the buy-alternative calculations, set up your spreadsheet so that you can enter the base price of the server hardware, the price of all software, and a maintenance expense that is some percentage of the hardware price. Assume that the percent you enter covers both hardware and software maintenance. Also assume that each server has a 3-year life, after which it has no value. Assume straight-line depreciation for computers used fewer than 3 years, and that at the end of the 5 years you can sell the computers you have used for fewer than 3 years for their depreciated value. Also assume that your organization pays 2 percent interest on capital expenses. Assume the servers cost $5,000 each, and the needed software costs $750. Assume that the maintenance expense varies from 2 to 7 percent.

    b. For the lease-alternative calculations, assume that the leasing vendor will lease the same computer hardware as you can purchase. The lease includes all the software you need as well as all maintenance. Set up your spreadsheet so that you can enter various lease costs, which vary according to the number of years of the lease (1, 2, or 3). Assume the cost of a 3-year lease is $285 per machine per month, a 2-year lease is $335 per machine per month, and a 1-year lease is $415 per machine per month. Also, the lessor offers a 5 percent discount if you lease from 20 to 30 computers and a 10 percent discount if you lease from 31 to 50 computers.

    c. Using your spreadsheet, compare the costs of buy versus lease under the following situations. (Assume you either buy or lease. You cannot lease some and buy some.) Make assumptions as necessary and state those assumptions.

        (1) Your organization requires 20 servers for 5 years.

        (2) Your organization requires 20 servers for the first 2 years and 40 servers for the next 3 years.

        (3) Your organization requires 20 servers for the first 2 years, 40 servers for the next 2 years, and 50 servers for the last year.

        (4) Your organization requires 10 servers the first year, 20 servers the second year, 30 servers the third year, 40 servers the fourth year, and 50 servers the last year.

        (5) For the previous case, does the cheaper alternative change if the cost of the servers is $4,000? If it is $8,000?

PART 3

Chapter 7: Production Planning with Excel

28. Suppose your manager asks you to create a spreadsheet to compute a production schedule. Your schedule should stipulate a production quantity for seven products that is based on sales projections made by three regional managers at your company's three sales regions.

    a. Create a separate worksheet for each sales region. Use the data in the Word file **Ex28**, which you can download from the text's Web site. This file contains each manager's monthly sales projections for the past year, actual sales results for those same months, and projections for sales for each month in the coming quarter.

b. Create a separate worksheet for each manager's data. Import the data from Word into Excel.

c. On each of the worksheets, use the data from the prior four quarters to compute the discrepancy between the actual sales and the sale projections. This discrepancy can be computed in several ways: You could calculate an overall average, or you could calculate an average per quarter or per month. You could also weight recent discrepancies more heavily than earlier ones. Choose a method that you think is most appropriate. Explain why you chose the method you did.

d. Modify your worksheets to use the discrepancy factors to compute an adjusted forecast for the coming quarter. Thus, each of your spreadsheets will show the raw forecast and the adjusted forecast for each month in the coming quarter.

e. Create a fourth worksheet that totals sales projections for all of the regions. Show both the unadjusted forecast and the adjusted forecast for each region and for the company overall. Show month and quarter totals.

f. Create a bar graph showing total monthly production. Display the unadjusted and adjusted forecasts using different colored bars.

Chapter 8: Microsoft Docs: Delivering Value or Hype?

29. Microsoft created Windows Live SkyDrive and the Office Web applications as part of the Office 2010 launch. Somewhere in the middle of that launch, Microsoft Fuse realized that it would be a simple matter to put Facebook trappings (in tech parlance, Facebook Chrome) on top of SkyDrive, call it Docs, and enable SkyDrive to take advantage of Facebook's momentum. The question is, does Docs deliver value or hype?

a. Go to the Windows Live SkyDrive Web site (*www.skydrive.com*) and create a presentation having a few slides using the Microsoft PowerPoint Web App, as described in Chapter Extension 2. For the purpose of this exercise, it doesn't matter what is in your presentation; choose a presentation for another class if you want. Save that presentation and share it with several friends or team members.

b. Ask one or two of your friends to make several changes to the presentation.

c. Repeat part a, but this time, go to Docs (*docs.com*) and join. Add a Profile tab for Docs to your Facebook account. Share the PowerPoint presentation as in part a.

d. Ask one or two of your friends to make several changes to the presentation.

e. Reflect on your experience using SkyDrive and Docs. Does Docs add value or is it just hype? Explain you answer.

Chapter Extension 11: Make Your Own BOM with Access

30. Figure CE11-5, the sample bill of materials, is a form produced using Microsoft Access. Producing such a form is a bit tricky, so this exercise will guide you through the steps required. You can then apply what you learn to produce a similar report. You can also use Access to experiment on extensions of this form.

a. Create a table named *PART* with columns *Part Number, Level, Description, QuantityRequired,* and *PartOf. Description* and *Level* should be text, *PartNumber* should be AutoNumber, and *Quantity Required* and *PartOf* should be numeric, long integer. Add the *PART* data shown in Figure CE11-5 to your table.

b. Create a query that has all columns of *PART*. Restrict the view to rows having a value of 1 for *Level*. Name your query *Level1*.

c. Create two more queries that are restricted to rows having values of 2 or 3 for *Level*. Name your queries *Level2* and *Level3*, respectively.

d. Create a form that contains *PartNumber, Level,* and *Description* from *Level1*. You can use a wizard for this if you want. Name the form *Bill of Materials*.

e. Using the subform tool in the Toolbox, create a subform in your form in part d. Set the data on this form to be all of the columns of *Level2*. After you have created the subform, ensure that the Link Child Fields property is set to *PartOf* and that the Link Master Fields property is set to *PartNumber*. Close the *Bill of Materials* form.

f. Open the subform created in part e and create a subform on it. Set the data on this subform to be all of the columns of *Level3*. After you have created the subform, ensure that the Link Child Fields property is set to *PartOf* and that the Link Master Fields property is set to *PartNumber*. Close the *Bill of Materials* form.

g. Open the *Bill of Materials* form. It should appear as in Figure CE11-5. Open and close the form and add new data. Using this form, add sample BOM data for a product of your own choosing.

h. Following the process similar to that just described, create a *Bill of Materials Report* that lists the data for all of your products.

i. **(Optional, challenging extension)** Each part in the BOM in Figure CE11-5 can be used in at most one assembly (there is space to show just one *PartOf* value). You can change your design to allow a part to be used in more than one assembly as follows: First, remove *PartOf* from PART. Next, create a second table that has two columns: *AssemblyPartNumber* and *ComponentPartNumber*. The first contains a part number of an assembly and the second a part number of a component. Every component of a part will have a row in this table. Extend the views described above to use this second table and to produce a display similar to Figure CE11-5.

Chapter Extension 13: Evaluate Vendors with Access

31. Assume that you have been given the task of compiling evaluations that your company's purchasing agents make of their vendors. Each month, every purchasing agent evaluates all of the vendors that he or she has worked with in the past month on three factors: price, quality, and responsiveness. Assume the ratings are from 1 to 5, with 5 being the best. Because your company has hundreds of vendors and dozens of purchasing agents, you decide to use Access to compile the results.

a. Create a database with three tables: VENDOR (*VendorNumber, Name, Contact*), PURCHASER (*EmpNumber, Name, Email*), and RATING (*EmpNumber, VendorNumber, Month, Year, PriceRating, QualityRating, ResponsivenessRating*). Assume that *VendorNumber* and *EmpNumber* are the keys of VENDOR and PURCHASER, respectively. Decide what you think is the appropriate key for RATING.

b. Create appropriate relationships.

c. Go to this text's companion Web site and import the data in the Excel file **Ex31**. Note that data for VENDOR, PURCHASER, and RATING are stored in three separate worksheets.

d. Create a query that shows the names of all vendors and their average scores.

e. Create a query that shows the names of all employees and their average scores. *Hint:* In this and in part f, you will need to use the *Group By* function in your query.

f. Create a parameterized query that you can use to obtain the minimum, maximum, and average ratings on each criterion for a particular vendor. Assume you will enter *VendorName* as the parameter.

g. Using the information created by your queries, what conclusions can you make about vendors or purchasers?

Chapter Extension 15: Make Your Own Market-Basket Analysis with Access

32. It is surprisingly easy to create a market-basket report using table data in Access. To do so, however, you will need to enter SQL expressions into the Access query builder. Here, you can just copy SQL statements to type them in. If you take a database class, you will learn how to code SQL statements like those you will use here.

a. Create an Access database with a table named *Order_Data* having columns *OrderNumber, ItemName,* and *Quantity*, with data types Number (*LongInteger*), Text (50), and Number (*LongInteger*), respectively. Define the key as the composite (*OrderNumber, ItemName*).

b. Import the data from the Excel file **Ex32** into the *Order_Data* table.

c. Now, to perform the market-basket analysis, you will need to enter several SQL statements into Access. To do so, click the queries tab and select *Create Query* in Design view. Click *Close* when the Show Table dialog box appears. Right-click in the gray section above the grid in the *Select Query* window. Select *SQL View*. Enter the following expression exactly as it appears here:

```
SELECT  T1.ItemName as FirstItem,
        T2.ItemName as SecondItem
FROM    Order_Data T1, Order_Data T2
WHERE   T1.OrderNumber =
        T2.OrderNumber
AND     T1.ItemName <> T2.ItemName;
```

Click the red exclamation point in the toolbar to run the query. Correct any typing mistakes and, once it works, save the query using the name *TwoItemBasket.*

d. Now enter a second SQL statement. Again, click the queries tab and select *Create Query* in Design view. Click *Close* when the Show Table dialog box appears. Right-click in the gray section above the grid in the *Select Query* window. Select *SQL View.* Enter the following expression exactly as it appears here:

```
SELECT   TwoItemBasket.FirstItem,
         TwoItemBasket.SecondItem,
         Count(*) AS SupportCount
FROM     TwoItemBasket
GROUP BY  TwoItemBasket.FirstItem,
          TwoItemBasket.SecondItem;
```

Correct any typing mistakes and, once it works, save the query using the name *SupportCount.*

e. Examine the results of the second query and verify that the two query statements have correctly calculated the number of times that two items have appeared together. Explain further calculations you need to make to compute support.

f. Explain the calculations you need to make to compute lift. Although you can make those calculations using SQL, you need more SQL knowledge to do it, and we will skip that here.

g. Explain, in your own words, what the query in part c seems to be doing. What does the query in part d seem to be doing? Again, you will need to take a database class to learn how to code such expressions, but this exercise should give you a sense of the kinds of calculations that are possible with SQL.

Chapter Extension 16: Reporting with Access

33. In this exercise, you'll have an opportunity to practice creating reports in Access using the data shown in Figure CE16-1.

a. Open Access, create a new database, and import the data in the text file **Ex33**. Notice that the data includes an identifier; the four fields in Figure CE16-1; and a sixth field, called Quarter, that represents the calendar quarter in which the sale was made.

b. Use Access to create a report that sorts the data and presents it as shown in Figure CE16-2, except exclude sales less than $75. To do so, first create a query that has this data and then create a report based on that query. Format your report professionally.

c. Modify your report in part b to include subtotals for each customer.

d. Create a query to present the data as shown in Figure CE16-3. Produce a professionally formatted report of this data.

e. Create a query to compute the average of Amount for each Quarter.

f. Create a second table named QUARTER_DATA with fields *QuarterNumber* and *Average_Amount.* Place four rows in this table, one for each quarter and average amount.

g. Create a report that lists the sale data in ascending order of *CustomerName.* In your report, include the date and amount of each sale, as well as the amount of the sale divided by the average amount of a sale for that quarter.

h. Explain how all of the work you have done has been as a result of the simple operations of filtering, sorting, grouping, and calculating.

Chapter Extension 16: OLAP and Pivot with Excel

34. OLAP cubes are very similar to Microsoft Excel pivot tables. For this exercise, assume that your organization's purchasing agents rate vendors, similar to the situation described in Application Exercise 31.

a. Open Excel and import the data in the worksheet named *Vendors* from the Excel file **Ex34**, which you can find on the text's Web site. The spreadsheet will have the following column names: *VendorName, EmployeeName, Date, Year*, and *Rating.*

b. Under the *Insert* ribbon in Excel, click *Pivot Table.* A wizard will open. Select *Excel* and *Pivot Table* in the first screen. Click *Next.*

c. When asked to provide a data range, drag your mouse over the data you imported so as to select all of the data. Be sure to include the column headings. Excel will fill in the range values in the open dialog box. Place your pivot table in a separate spreadsheet.

d. Excel will create a field list on the right-hand side of your spreadsheet. Drag and drop the field named *VendorName* onto the words "Drop Row Fields Here." Drag and drop *EmployeeName* onto the words "Drop Column Fields Here." Now drag and drop the field named *Rating* onto the words "Drop Data Items Here." Voilà! You have a pivot table.

e. To see how the table works, drag and drop more fields on the various sections of your pivot table. For example, drop *Year* on top of *Employee*. Then move *Year* below *Employee*. Now move *Year* below *Vendor*. All of this action is just like an OLAP cube, and, in fact, OLAP cubes are readily displayed in Excel pivot tables. The major difference is that OLAP cubes are usually based on thousands or more rows of data.

Chapter Extension 18: Process Modeling with Visio

35. In this exercise, you will use Visio to create process diagrams in BPMN notation.

a. Download the Visio file **Ex35** from this text's support site. Open the file and familiarize yourself with this diagram. Match the diagram to the correct figure in Chapter Extension 18.

b. Notice that Visio includes the BPMN shapes. Go to the Shape organizer to see other types of flowchart shapes that Visio supports.

c. Create a new Visio diagram. Add BPMN shapes that you may want to use.

d. Model the customer process Respond to Quotation. Make sure your process accepts the inputs shown in **Ex35** and produces the outputs shown in that figure. Create your process so that your company checks prices and delivery dates and requests changes, if appropriate. Include other logic, if necessary.

e. Show your work by saving your document as a PDF file.

PART 4

Chapter 10: Planning Project Costs with Excel

36. Suppose you are given the task of keeping track of the number of labor hours invested in meetings for systems development projects. Assume your company uses the traditional SDLC and that each phase requires two types of meetings: working meetings and review meetings. *Working meetings* involve users, systems analysts, programmers, and PQA test engineers. *Review meetings* involve all of those people, plus level-1 and level-2 managers of both user departments and the IS department.

a. Import the data in the Word file **Ex36** from this text's Web site into a spreadsheet.

b. Modify your spreadsheet to compute the total labor hours invested in each phase of a project. When a meeting occurs, assume you enter the project phase, the meeting type, the start time, the end time, and the number of each type of personnel attending. Your spreadsheet should calculate the number of labor hours and should add the meeting's hours to the totals for that phase and for the project overall.

c. Modify your spreadsheet to include the budgeted number (in the source data) of labor hours for each type of employee for each phase. In your spreadsheet, show the difference between the number of hours budgeted and the number actually consumed.

d. Change your spreadsheet to include the budgeted cost and actual cost of labor. Assume that you enter, once, the average labor cost for each type of employee, as stipulated in the source data.

Chapter 10: Tracking Systems Failures with Access

37. Use Access to develop a failure-tracking database application. Use the data in the Excel file **Ex37** for this exercise. The file includes columns for the following:

FailureNumber
DateReported
FailureDescription
ReportedBy (the name of the PQA engineer reporting the failure)
ReportedBy_email (the email address of the PQA engineer reporting the failure)
FixedBy (the name of the programmer who is assigned to fix the failure)
FixedBy_email (the email address of the programmer assigned to fix the failure)
DateFailureFixed
FixDescription
DateFixVerified
VerifiedBy (the name of the PQA engineer verifying the fix)
VerifiedBy_email (the email address of the PQA engineer verifying the fix)

a. The data in the spreadsheet have not been normalized. Normalize the data by creating a *Failure* table, a *PQA Engineer* table, and a *Programmer* table. Add other appropriate columns to each table. Create appropriate relationships.

b. Create one or more forms that can be used to report a failure, to report a failure fix, and to report a failure verification. Create the form(s) so that the user can just pull down the name of a PQA engineer or programmer from the appropriate table to fill in the *ReportedBy, FixedBy*, and *VerifiedBy* fields.

c. Construct a report that shows all failures sorted by *ReportedBy* and then by *Date Reported.*

d. Construct a report that shows only fixed and verified failures.

e. Construct a report that shows only fixed but unverified failures.

Chapters 10 and 11: Keeping Track of Requests

38. At Fox Lake, the wedding events and facilities departments are having problems with repeated maintenance requests. They need to keep better track of requests so that management can get involved when requests are repeatedly made for the same problem or when too many problems are being reported for the same facility or piece of equipment.

This need is typical; any service organization needs to track requests. In this exercise, you will create such a system for an IS department that wants to track system problems and responses. Fox Lake could readily adapt this system for its facility maintenance tracking.

Suppose an organization keeps the following data about requests:

Ticket#
Date_Submitted
Date_Opened
Date_Closed
Type (new or repeat)
Reporting_ Employee_Name
Reporting_Employee_Division
Technician_Name Problem_System
Problem_Description

You can find sample ticket data in the Excel file **Ex38** on this text's Web site.

However, managers often need more information. Among their needs are information that will help them learn who are their best- and worst-performing technicians, how different systems compare in terms of number of problems reported and the time required to fix those problems, how different divisions compare in terms of problems reported and the time required to fix them, which technicians are the best and worst at solving problems with particular systems, and which technicians are best and worst at solving problems from particular divisions.

a. Use either Access or Excel, or a combination of the two, to produce the information listed above from the data in the Excel file **Ex38**. In your answer, you may use queries, formulas, reports, forms, graphs, pivot tables, pivot charts, or any other type of Access or Excel display. Choose the best display for the type of information you are producing.

b. Explain how you would use these different types of information to manage your department.

c. Specify any additional information that you would like to have produced from this data to help you manage your department.

d. Use either Access or Excel or a combination to produce the information in part c.

Chapter 12: How Easy Is Phishing?

39. This is an easy exercise with a major lesson!

a. Open any HTML editor, such as Dreamweaver or Expression Web.

b. Create a Web page with the title "Phishing Examples" and the subtitle "Go to These Sites."

c. Under the subtitle, create a hyperlink that will display the text "*www.msn.com.*" However, set the target of this link to be *www.yahoo.com.*

d. Create a second hyperlink that will display the text "*www.Google.com.*" However, set the target of this link to *www.bing.com.*

e. Test your Web page. Click each link and observe where your browser goes.

f. Explain how this exercise pertains to phishing.

Chapter 12: Computing the Cost of a Virus

40. Develop a spreadsheet model of the cost of a virus attack in an organization that has three types of computers: employee workstations, data servers, and Web servers. Assume that the number of computers affected by the virus depends on the severity of the virus. For the purposes of your model, assume that there are three levels of virus severity: *Low-severity* incidents affect fewer than 30 percent of the user workstations and none of the data or Web servers. *Medium-severity* incidents affect up to 70 percent of the user workstations, up to half of the Web servers, and none of the data servers. *High-severity* incidents can affect all organizational computers.

Assume that 50 percent of the incidents are low severity, 30 percent are medium severity, and 20 percent are high severity.

Assume that employees can remove viruses from workstations themselves, but that specially trained technicians are required to repair the servers. The time to eliminate a virus from an infected computer depends on the computer type. Let the time to remove the virus from each type be an input into your model. Assume that when users eliminate the virus themselves, they are unproductive for twice the time required for the removal. Let the average employee hourly labor cost be an input to your model. Let the average cost of a technician also be an input into your model. Finally, let the total number of user computers, data servers, and Web servers be inputs into your model.

Run your simulation 10 times. Use the same inputs for each run, but draw a random number (assume a uniform distribution for all random numbers) to determine the severity type. Then, draw random numbers to determine the percentage of computers of each type affected, using the constraints detailed earlier. For example, if the attack is of medium severity, draw a random number between 0 and 70 to indicate the percentage of infected user workstations and a random number between 0 and 50 to indicate the percentage of infected Web servers.

For each run, calculate the total of lost employee hours, the total dollar cost of lost employee labor hours, the total hours of technicians to fix the servers, and the total cost of technician labor. Finally, compute the total overall cost. Show the results of each run. Show the average costs and hours for the 10 runs.

41. In the Fox Lake case at the start of Chapter 12, Chris was able to use Mike's computer in the middle of the night, when no one was around. And, Fox Lake is about to discover that Jason, Chris's accomplice, stole more than $2,500 worth of equipment. Jason will be living in another state by the time this is discovered.

Suppose that Fox Lake has asked you to develop an Access database that tracks keys, equipment, and user accounts that have been issued to employees and contractors. Assume your database has four tables: *Person, Equipment, Key,* and *Account. Person* has data about employees and contractors, *Equipment* has data about equipment that has been allocated to individuals in the *Person* table, *Key* has data about keys that have been allocated to individuals in *Person,* and *Account* has data about accounts that have been created for individuals in *Person.* (This last table is needed because Fox Lake is about to start a policy that every user of every computer has his or her own account for using that computer. Thus, an account name is an asset, just like a building key or a paddle.)

a. Using your knowledge, experience, and intuition design the *Person, Equipment, Key,* and *Account* tables. Name and describe the columns of each table and indicate which columns are the primary key.

b. Specify the maximum cardinality of the relationships between:

   (1) *Person* and *Equipment*

   (2) *Person* and *Key*

   (3) *Person* and *Account*

c. Modify your design in part a to include the foreign keys necessary to support the relationships you specified in part b.

d. Create your database in Access and fill it with sample data.

e. Create a form for adding a new person and the equipment assigned to that person.

f. Create a form for allocating a key to an existing person.

g. Create a report suitable for use when an employee quits Fox Lake. Your report should include all resources that need to be recovered as well as computer accounts that need to be removed.

h. Create a parameterized query that accepts a person's name and generates the report in part g for that person.

10/100/1000 Ethernet A type of Ethernet that conforms to the IEEE 802.3 protocol and allows for transmission at a rate of 10, 100, or 1,000 Mbps (megabits per second). p. 127

32-bit CPU A processor that can effectively utilize up to 4GB of main memory. p. 78

64-bit CPU A processor that can use more than 4GB of memory; in fact, for all practical purposes, it can use an almost unlimited amount of main memory. p. 78

Absolute address In Excel, a cell address that includes one or two dollar signs that indicates to Excel that the value of a row, a column, or both should not be changed when a formula including the absolute address is moved. Example: for $B4, Excel will not change the value of B, even if the formula is moved to another column. For B4, Excel will not change the value of B or 4, even if the formula is moved to another column or row. p. 371

Abstract reasoning The ability to make and manipulate models. p. 8

Accelerator effect An economic theory that states that a dollar spent will contribute more than a dollar of activity to the economy. p. 593

Access A popular personal and small workgroup DBMS product from Microsoft. p. 106

Access point (AP) A point in a wireless network that facilitates communication among wireless devices and serves as a point of interconnection between wireless and wired networks. The AP must be able to process messages according to both the 802.3 and 802.11 standards, because it sends and receives wireless traffic using the 802.11 protocol and communicates with wired networks using the 802.3 protocol. p. 127

Accounting applications Applications that support accounting functions, such as budgeting, cash management, accounts payable and receivable, and financial reporting. p. 463

Accurate information Information that is based on correct and complete data and that has been processed correctly as expected. p. 32

Activity The part of a business process that transforms resources and information of one type into resources and information of another type; can be manual or automated. p. 27

AdSense A Web 2.0 product from Google. Google searches an organization's Web site and inserts ads that match content on that site; when users click those ads, Google pays the organization a fee. p. 192

Adware Programs installed on the user's computer without the user's knowledge or permission that reside in the background and, unknown to the user, observe the user's actions and keystrokes, modify computer activity, and report the user's activities to sponsoring organizations. Most adware is benign in that it does not perform malicious acts or steal data. It does, however, watch user activity and produce pop-up ads. p. 291

AdWords A Web 2.0 advertising product from Google. Vendors agree to pay a certain amount to Google for use of particular search words, which link to the vendor's site. p. 192

Agile enterprise An organization that can quickly adapt to changes in the market, industry, product, law, or other significant external factors; the term was coined by Microsoft. p. 263

Alert A form of report, often requested by recipients, that tells them some piece of usually time-related information, such as notification of the time for a meeting. p. 519

Alternatives formulation step A step in the decision-making process in which decision makers lay out various alternatives. p. 338

Analog signal A wavy signal. A modem converts the computer's digital data into analog signals that can be transmitted over dial-up Internet connections. p. 129

Analysis paralysis When too much time is spent documenting project requirements. p. 250

Application software Programs that perform a business function. Some application programs are general purpose, such as Excel or Word. Other application programs are specific to a business function, such as accounts payable. p. 83

As-is model A business process model that documents the current business process; teams then change that model to make adjustments necessary to solve process problems. p. 472, p. 551

Asymmetric digital subscriber lines (ADSL) DSL lines that have different upload and download speeds. p. 129

Asymmetric encryption An encryption method whereby different keys are used to encode and to decode the message; one key encodes the message, and the other key decodes the message. Symmetric encryption is simpler and much faster than asymmetric encryption. p. 288

Asynchronous communication Information exchange that occurs when all members of a work team do not meet at the same time, such as those who work different shifts or at different locations. p. 320

ATA-100 standard Within a computer, a standard type of channel connecting the CPU to main memory. The number 100 indicates that the maximum transfer rate is 100MB per second. p. 374

Attribute (1) A variable that provides properties for an HTML tag. Each attribute has a standard name. For example, the attribute for a hyperlink is *href*, and its value indicates which Web page is to be displayed when the user clicks the link. (2) Characteristics of an entity. Example attributes of *Order* would be *OrderNumber, OrderDate, SubTotal, Tax, Total,* and so forth. Example attributes of *Salesperson* would be *SalespersonName, Email, Phone,* and so forth. p. 140, p. 385

Auctions Applications that match buyers and sellers by using an e-commerce version of a standard, competitive-bidding auction process. p. 187

Augmentation information system An information system in which humans do the bulk of the work but are assisted by the information system. p. 337

Authentication The process whereby an information system approves (authenticates) a user by checking the user's password. p. 287

Automated Clearing House (ACH) A network of information systems that provides for the interbank clearing of electronic payments. p. 480

Automated information system An information system in which the hardware and software components do most of the work. p. 337

Baseline An initial plan for the development of an information system. p. 568

Baseline WBS The final work breakdown structure plan that shows the planned tasks, dependencies, durations, and resource assignments of a large-scale development project. p. 572

Beta testing The process of allowing future system users to try out the new system on their own. Used to locate program failures just prior to program shipment. p. 247

Bill of materials (BOM) A list of the materials that comprise a product. p. 460

Binary digits The means by which computers represent data; also called *bits*. A binary digit is either a zero or a one. p. 76

Biometric authentication The use of personal physical characteristics, such as fingerprints, facial features, and retinal scans, to authenticate users. p. 287

Bit The means by which computers represent data; also called *binary digit*. A bit is either a zero or a one. p. 76

Blog (Web-log) An online journal, which uses technology to publish information over the Internet. p. 345

Bluetooth A common wireless protocol designed for transmitting data over short distances; used to replace cables. p. 128

Broadband Internet communication lines that have speeds in excess of 256 kbps. DSL and cable modems provide broadband access. p. 130

Brooks' Law The famous adage that states: *Adding more people to a late project makes the project later.* Brooks' Law is true not only because a larger staff requires increased coordination, but also because new people need training. The only people who can train the new employees are the existing team members, who are thus taken off productive tasks. The costs of training new people can overwhelm the benefit of their contribution. p. 237

Bullwhip effect Phenomenon in which the variability in the size and timing of orders increases at each stage up the supply chain, from customer to supplier. p. 593

Bus Means by which the CPU reads instructions and data from main memory and writes data to main memory. p. 77

Business analysts People who specialize in understanding business needs, strategies, and goals and who help businesses use IT and implement systems to accomplish organizational strategies. p. 241

Business intelligence (BI) Information that results from the processing of operational data to create information that exposes patterns, relationships, and trends of importance to the organization. p. 210

Business intelligence (BI) system A system that provides the right information, to the right user, at the right time. A tool produces the information, but the system ensures that the right information is delivered to the right user at the right time. p. 211

Business process A network of activities, resources, facilities, and information that interact to achieve some business function; sometimes called a business system. p. 26

Business process management (BPM) The systematic process of creating, assessing, and altering business processes. p. 551

Business Process Modeling Notation (BPMN) A standard set of terms and graphical notations for documenting business processes, created by the Object Management Group (OMG). p. 553

Business process reengineering The activity of altering and designing business processes to take advantage of new information systems. p. 165

Business-to-business (B2B) E-commerce sales between companies. p. 186

Business-to-consumer (B2C) E-commerce sales between a supplier and a retail customer (the consumer). p. 186

Business-to-government (B2G) E-commerce sales between companies and governmental organizations. p. 186

Byte (1) A character of data. (2) An 8-bit chunk. p. 76, p. 101

Cable modem A type of modem that provides high-speed data transmission using cable television lines. The cable company installs a fast, high-capacity optical-fiber cable to a distribution center in each neighborhood that it serves. At the distribution center, the optical-fiber cable connects to regular cable-television cables that run to subscribers' homes or businesses. Cable modems modulate in such a way that their signals do not interfere with TV signals. Like DSL lines, they are always on. p. 130

Cache A file on a domain name resolver that stores domain names and IP addresses that have been resolved. Then, when someone else needs to resolve that same domain name, there is no need to go through the entire resolution process. Instead, the resolver can supply the IP address from the local file. p. 77

Capital The investment of resources with the expectation of future returns in the marketplace. p. 193

CD-R An optical disk that can record data once. p. 375

CD-ROM A read-only optical disk. p. 375

CD-RW A rewritable optical disk. p. 375

Cell In a spreadsheet, the intersection of a row and a column. p. 350

Central processing unit (CPU) The CPU selects instructions, processes them, performs arithmetic and logical comparisons, and stores results of operations in memory. p. 75

Channel conflict In e-commerce, a conflict that may result between a manufacturer that wants to sell products directly to consumers and the retailers in the existing sales channels. p. 188

Chief information officer (CIO) The title of the principal manager of the IT department. Other common titles are *vice president of information services, director of information services*, and, less commonly, *director of computer services*. p. 265

Chief technology officer (CTO) The head of the technology group. The CTO sorts through new ideas and products to identify those that are most relevant to the organization. The CTO's job requires deep knowledge of information technology and the ability to envision how new IT will affect the organization over time. p. 266

Choice step A step in the decision-making process in which decision makers analyze their alternatives and select one. p. 339

Choropleth map A map that displays colors, shades, or patterns in accordance with category values of underlying data. p. 544

Clearinghouse Entity that provides goods and services at a stated price, prices and arranges for the delivery of the goods, but never takes title to the goods. p. 187

Clickstream data E-commerce data that describes a customer's clicking behavior. Such data includes everything the customer does at the Web site. p. 213

Client A computer that provides word processing, spreadsheets, database access, and usually a network connection. p. 78

Client-server applications Applications that process code on both the client and the server. p. 86

Client virtualization (also **desktop virtualization**) The process of storing a user's desktop on a remote server. It enables users to run their desktops from many different client computers. p. 449

Closed source A project in which the source code is highly protected and only available to trusted employees and carefully vetted contractors. p. 88

Cloud computing Computing services that provide processing, data storage, and specific application functions over the Internet. p. 82

Cluster analysis An unsupervised data mining technique whereby statistical techniques are used to identify groups of entities that have similar characteristics. A common use for cluster analysis is to find groups of similar customers in data about customer orders and customer demographics. p. 218

Cold site A remote processing center that provides office space, but no computer equipment, for use by a company that needs to continue operations after a natural disaster. p. 299

Collaboration The situation in which two or more people work together toward a common goal, result, or product; information systems facilitate collaboration. p. 8, p. 310

Columns Also called *fields*, or groups of bytes. A database table has multiple columns that are used to represent the attributes of an entity. Examples are *PartNumber*, *EmployeeName*, and *SalesDate*. p. 101

Comma-delimited file An exported data file in which field values are separated by commas. p. 419

Commerce server A computer that operates Web-based programs that display products, support online ordering, record and process payments, and interface with inventory-management applications. p. 138

Competitive strategy The strategy an organization chooses as the way it will succeed in its industry. According to Porter, the four fundamental competitive strategies are: cost leadership across an industry or within a particular industry segment and product differentiation across an industry or within a particular industry segment. p. 51

Component design phase The third phase in the SDLC, in which developers determine hardware and software specifications, design the database (if applicable), design procedures, and create job descriptions for users and operations personnel. p. 238

Computer-based information system An information system that includes a computer. p. 10

Conference call A synchronous virtual meeting, in which participants meet at the same time via a voice-communication channel. p. 320

Confidence In market-basket terminology, the probability estimate that two items will be purchased together. p. 508

Configuration control Use by developers of a set of management policies, practices, and tools to maintain control over a project's resources. p. 574

Content management systems Information systems that track organizational documents, Web pages, graphics, and related materials. p. 342

Control Objectives for Information and related Technology (COBIT) A set of standard practices created by the Information Systems Audit and Control Association that are used in the assessment stage of the BPM cycle to determine how well an information system complies with an organization's strategy. p. 552

Cost The dollar amount required to develop an information system from start to finish; one of the critical drivers in large-scale IS development, which typically involves trade-offs with requirements and time. p. 567

Cost feasibility One of four dimensions of feasibility. p. 240

Critical path The sequence of activities that determine the earliest date by which a project can be completed; takes into account task dependencies. p. 570

Critical path analysis The planning and management of the tasks on the critical path. Tasks on the critical path cannot be allowed to run late; those not on the critical path can run late to the point at which they become part of the critical path. p. 572

Cross-selling The sale of related products; salespeople try to get customers who buy product *X* to also buy product *Y*. p. 507

Crow's foot A line on an entity-relationship diagram that indicates a 1:N relationship between two entities. p. 386

Crow's-foot diagram A type of entity-relationship diagram that uses a crow's foot symbol to designate a 1:N relationship. p. 387

Crowdsourcing The process by which organizations use Web 2.0 technologies such as user-generated content to involve their users in the design and marketing of their products. p. 191

CRT monitor A type of video display monitor that uses *cathode-ray tubes*, the same devices used in traditional TV screens. Because they use a large tube, CRTs are big and bulky, and about as deep as they are wide. p. 375

Curse of dimensionality The more attributes there are, the easier it is to build a data model that fits the sample data but that is worthless as a predictor. p. 213

Custom-developed software Tailor-made software. p. 84

Customer life cycle Taken as a whole, the processes of marketing, customer acquisition, relationship management, and loss/churn that must be managed by CRM systems. p. 166

Customer-management applications Sales and marketing applications that store data on customer contact, product interests, order history, and credit status, and use that data to provide information for obtaining new sales or additional sales from existing customers. p. 458

Customer relationship management (CRM) The set of business processes for attracting, selling, managing, and supporting customers. p. 166

Data administration A staff function that pertains to *all* of an organization's data assets. Typical data administration tasks are setting data standards, developing data policies, and providing for data security. p. 293

Data aggregator A company that obtains data from public and private sources and stores, combines, and processes it in sophisticated ways to produce information that is sold to customers. p. 214

Data channel Means by which the CPU reads instructions and data from main memory and writes data to main memory. p. 77

Data flow Movement of a data item from one activity to another activity or to or from a repository. p. 28

Data integrity problem In a database, the situation that exists when data items disagree with one another. An example is two different names for the same customer. p. 387

Data marts Facilities that prepare, store, and manage data for reporting and data mining for specific business functions. p. 216

Data mining The application of statistical techniques to find patterns and relationships among data and to classify and predict. p. 217

Data mining system Information system that processes data using sophisticated statistical techniques, such as regression analysis and decision-tree analysis, to find patterns and relationships that cannot be found by simpler operations, such as sorting, grouping, and averaging. p. 211

Data model A logical representation of the data in a database that describes the data and relationships that will be stored in the database. Akin to a blueprint. p. 384

Data safeguards Steps taken to protect databases and other organizational data by means of data administration and database administration. p. 293

Data warehouses Facilities that prepare, store, and manage data specifically for reporting and data mining. p. 214

Database A self-describing collection of integrated records. p. 101

Database administration A staff function that refers to the protection and effective use of a particular database and its related applications. (Contrast with data administration). Database administration responsibilities include protecting the data, controlling changes to database structure as well as to the supporting DBMS, monitoring and improving performance, and ensuring effective procedures for using the database exist. p. 293

Database application A collection of forms, reports, queries, and application programs that process a database. p. 107

Database application system Applications, having the standard five components, that make database data more accessible and useful. Users employ a database application that consists of forms, formatted reports, queries, and application programs. Each of these, in turn, calls on the database management system (DBMS) to process the database tables. p. 104

Database management system (DBMS) A program used to create, process, and administer a database. p. 106

Database marketing The application of data business intelligence systems to the planning and execution of marketing programs. p. 505

Database tier In the three-tier architecture, the tier that runs the DBMS and receives and processes SQL requests to retrieve and store data. p. 137

Datum A set of elevations based on particular values of the earth's radii. p. 536

DB2 A popular, enterprise-class DBMS product from IBM. p. 106

Decision In BPMN notation, a question that can be answered Yes or No. p. 28

Decision tree A hierarchical arrangement of criteria for classifying customers, items, and other business objects. p. 509

Deliverable A task that is one of many measurable or observable steps in a development project. p. 570

Denial of service (DOS) Security problem in which users are not able to access an information system; can be caused by human errors, natural disaster, or malicious activity. p. 284

Departmental information system Workgroup information systems that support a particular department. p. 157

Desktop programs Client applications, such as Word, Excel, or Acrobat, that run on a personal computer and do not require a connection to a server. p. 85

Desktop virtualization (also called **client virtualization**) The process of storing a user's desktop on a remote server. It enables users to run their desktops from many different client computers. p. 449

Digital dashboard An electronic display that is customized for a particular user. p. 519

Digital subscriber line (DSL) A data transmission line that runs that shares telephone lines with voice communication. Used primarily in homes and small businesses. Provides download speeds up to 6.5 Mbps and slower upload speeds, in the neighborhood of 512 Kbps. p. 129

Dimension A characteristic of an OLAP measure; purchase date, customer type, customer location, and sales region are examples of dimensions. p. 522

Dimensional database A database structured to support OLAP processing. p. 523

Dirty data Problematic data. Examples are a value of *B* for customer gender and a value of *213* for customer age. Other examples are a value of *999-999-9999* for a U.S. phone number, a part color of *gren*, and an email address of *WhyMe@GuessWhoIAM-Hah-Hah.org*. Such values are problematic when data mining. p. 212

Discussion forum A form of asynchronous communication in which one group member posts an entry and other group members respond. A better form of group communication than email, because it is more difficult for the discussion to go off track. p. 321

Discussion groups A form of organizational knowledge management that enables employees or customers to post questions and replies to those questions for the purposes of exploring topics and sharing knowledge. p. 345

Diseconomies of scale The added cost that will eventually occur as more people are added to an IS development project. p. 568

Disintermediation Elimination of one or more middle layers in the supply chain. p. 187

Distributed database processing The processing of a database that resides in whole, or in part, in multiple locations. p. 591

Domain name The registered, human-friendly valid name in the domain name system (DNS). The process of changing a name into its IP address is called *resolving the domain name*. p. 134

Dot pitch The distance between pixels on a CRT monitor; the smaller the dot pitch, the sharper and brighter the screen image will be. p. 375

Drill down With an OLAP report, to further divide the data into more detail. p. 522

Drive-by sniffers People who take computers with wireless connections through an area and search for unprotected wireless networks in an attempt to gain free Internet access or to gather unauthorized data. p. 283

DSL modem A type of modem. DSL modems operate on the same lines as voice telephones and dial-up modems, but they operate so that their signals do not interfere with voice telephone service. DSL modems provide much faster data transmission speeds than dial-up modems. Additionally, DSL modems always maintain a connection, so there is no need to dial in; the Internet connection is available immediately. p. 129

Dual processor A computer with two CPUs. p. 75

DVD-R A digital versatile disk that can record data once. p. 375

DVD-ROM A read-only digital versatile disk. p. 375

DVD-RW A rewritable digital versatile disk. p. 375

Dynamic report Report that is generated at the time of request; the reporting system reads the most current data and generates the report using that fresh data. A report on sales today and a report on current stock prices are both dynamic reports. p. 518

E-commerce The buying and selling of goods and services over public and private computer networks. p. 184

Effective team A group of people committed to a common purpose or goal such that a) the team's objective is accomplished; b) Over time, the team increase in capability; and c) team members fell fulfilled as a result of working on the team. p. 312

Electronic exchanges Sites that facilitate the matching of buyers and sellers; the business process is similar to that of a stock exchange. Sellers offer goods at a given price through the electronic exchange, and buyers make offers to purchase over the same exchange. Price matches result in transactions from which the exchange takes a commission. p. 187

Email A form of asynchronous communication in which participants send comments and attachments electronically. As a form of group communication, it can be disorganized, disconnected, and easy to hide from. p. 321

Email spoofing A synonym for *phishing*. A technique for obtaining unauthorized data that uses pretexting via email. The *phisher* pretends to be a legitimate company and sends email requests for confidential data, such as account numbers, Social Security numbers, account passwords, and so forth. Phishers direct traffic to their sites under the guise of a legitimate business. p. 283

Encapsulated Logic that is isolated in a service. p. 559

Encapsulation Isolating all of the logic for a given business process within a particular service. The logic is hidden from service users and thus can be changed as long as the data to and from the service remain the same. p. 559

Encryption The process of transforming clear text into coded, unintelligible text for secure storage or communication. p. 288

Encryption algorithms Algorithms used to transform clear text into coded, unintelligible text for secure storage or communication. Commonly used methods are DES, 3DES, and AES. p. 288

Enterprise 2.0 The application of Web 2.0 technologies, collaboration systems, social networking, and related technologies to facilitate the cooperative work in organizations. p. 185

Enterprise application integration (EAI) applications Applications that support cross-functional business processes by integrating existing functional applications. Unlike CRM or ERP, the organization need not replace existing applications; instead layers of software are created to integrate those applications. p. 169

Enterprise DBMS A product that processes large organizational and workgroup databases. These products support many users, perhaps thousands, and many different database applications. Such DBMS products support 24/7 operations and can manage databases that span dozens of different magnetic disks with hundreds of gigabytes or more of data. IBM's DB2, Microsoft's SQL Server, and Oracle's Oracle are examples of enterprise DBMS products. p. 110

Enterprise information system Information systems that support activities in multiple departments. p. 157

Enterprise resource planning (ERP) applications Cross-functional, enterprise-wide applications that integrate the primary value-chain activities with the functions of human resources and accounting. p. 168

Enterprise resource planning (ERP) system An information system based on ERP technology. p. 466

Entity In the E-R data model, a representation of some thing that users want to track. Some entities represent a physical object; others represent a logical construct or transaction. p. 385

Entity-relationship data model (E-R model) Popular technique for creating a data model, in which developers define the things that will be stored and the relationships among them. p. 384

Entity-relationship (E-R) diagrams A type of diagram used by database designers to document entities and their relationships to each other. p. 386

ERP System A suite of applications or modules, a database, and set of inherent processes for consolidating business operations into a single, consistent, computing platform. p. 466

Ethernet Another name for the IEEE 802.3 protocol, Ethernet is a network protocol that operates at Layers 1 and 2 of the TCP/IP–OSI architecture. Ethernet, the world's most popular LAN protocol, is used on WANs as well. p. 127

EVDO A WAN wireless protocol. p. 130

Exabyte 10^{18} bytes. p. 210

Executive information system (EIS) An information system that supports strategic decision making. p. 336

Experimentation Making a reasoned analysis of an opportunity, envisioning potential solutions, evaluating those possibilities, and developing the most promising ones, consistent with the resources you have. p. 9

Expert system Knowledge-sharing system that is created by interviewing experts in a given business domain and codifying the rules used by those experts. p. 212, p. 346

Expert system shell A program in an expert system that processes a set of rules, typically many times, until the values of the variables no longer change, at which point the system reports the results. p. 346

eXtensible Markup Language (XML) A document standard that separates document content, structure, and presentation; eliminates problems in HTML. p. 140, p. 561

F score In RFM analysis, a number rating that indicates in which fifth a customer ranks in terms of ordering *frequency*. p. 506

Fields Also called *columns*, groups of bytes in a database table. A database table has multiple columns that are used to represent the attributes of an entity. Examples are *partNumber*, *EmployeeName*, and *SalesDate*. p. 101

File A group of similar rows or records. In a database, sometimes called a *table*. p. 101

File Transfer Protocol (FTP) A Layer-5 protocol used to copy files from one computer to another. In interorganizational transaction processing, FTP enables users to easily exchange large files. p. 133, p. 323

Firewall A computing device located between a firm's internal and external networks that prevents unauthorized access to or from the internal network. A firewall can be a special-purpose computer or it can be a program on a general-purpose computer or on a router. p. 290

Firmware Computer software that is installed into devices such as printers, print services, and various types of communication devices. The software is coded just like other software, but it is installed into special, programmable memory of the printer or other device. p. 84

Five-component framework The five fundamental components of an information system—computer hardware, software, data, procedures, and people—that are present in every information system, from the simplest to the most complex. p. 10

Five forces model Model proposed by Michael Porter that assesses industry characteristics and profitability by means of five competitive forces—bargaining power of suppliers, threat of substitution, bargaining power of customers, rivalry among firms, and threat of new entrants. p. 48

Flash An add-on to browsers that was developed by Adobe and is useful for providing animation, movies, and other advanced graphics inside a browser. p. 140

Folksonomy Content structure that has emerged from the processing of many user tags. p. 198

Foreign keys A column or group of columns used to represent relationships. Values of the foreign key match values of the primary key in a different (foreign) table. p. 103

Form Data entry forms are used to read, insert, modify, and delete database data. p. 108

Frequently asked questions (FAQs) A form of knowledge-sharing in which the organization edits, prioritizes, and summarizes questions generated from discussion groups. p. 345

FTP See *File Transfer Protocol*. p. 323

Function point Estimating technique that attempts to schedule a development project by the number of function points in a project, using each function point to determine the number of lines of code and the time for the project. p. 573

Functional application Software that provides features and functions necessary to support a particular business activity (function). p. 455

Functional information system Workgroup information systems that support a particular business function. p. 157

Functional processes Processes that involve activities within a single department or business function, such as accounts payable or inventory management. p. 455

Gantt chart A project management chart that shows tasks and their dependencies on each other and schedules them in an optimal way so as to reduce the time it takes to complete them. p. 570

General Public License (GPL) agreement One of the standard license agreements for open source software. p. 86

Geocoding A process by which the GIS application needs to convert all of the location identifiers to a common scheme. p. 537

Geofence A geographic boundary set up within a GIS. p. 541

Geographic coordinates Coordinates based on latitude and longitude. p. 537

Geographic information system (GIS) An information system that captures, stores, analyzes, and displays geospatial data. p. 529

Geospatial data Data that can be ordered in reference to the earth. p. 529

Gigabyte (GB) 1,024 MB. p. 76

GIS application Term used to refer to a computer program that manages geospatial data. p. 531

Google Docs Version management system for sharing documents and spreadsheet data. Documents are stored on a Google server, from which users can access and simultaneously see and edit the documents. p. 326

GNU A self-referential acronym meaning GNU not Unix, originally a set of tools for developing and open-source version of UNIX. Used today primarily in conjunction with the GNU public license agreement (which see). p. 86

Granularity The level of detail in data. Customer name and account balance is large granularity data. Customer name, balance, and the order details and payment history of every customer order is smaller granularity. p. 213

Green computing Environmentally conscious computing consisting of three major components: power management, virtualization, and e-waste management. p. 264

Hacking Occurs when a person gains unauthorized access to a computer system. Although some people hack for the sheer joy of doing it, other hackers invade systems for the malicious purpose of stealing or modifying data. p. 284

Hardware Electronic components and related gadgetry that input, process, output, store, and communicate data according to instructions encoded in computer programs or software. p. 74

Horizontal-market application Software that provides capabilities common across all organizations and industries; examples include word processors, graphics programs, spreadsheets, and presentation programs. p. 83

Hot site A remote processing center run by a commercial disaster-recovery service that provides equipment a company would need to continue operations after a natural disaster. p. 299

HSDPA A WAN wireless protocol. p. 130

HTTPS An indication that a Web browser is using the SSL/TLS protocol to ensure secure communications. p. 133, p. 289

Human capital The investment in human knowledge and skills with the expectation of future returns in the marketplace. p. 193

Human resources applications Applications that support recruitment, compensation, evaluation, and professional development of employees and affiliated personnel. p. 462

Human safeguards Steps taken to protect against security threats by establishing appropriate procedures for users to follow for system use. p. 294

Hyperlink A pointer on a Web page to another Web page. A hyperlink contains the URL of the Web page to access when the user clicks the hyperlink. The URL can reference a page on the Web server that generated the page containing the hyperlink, or it can reference a page on another server. p. 139

Hypertext Markup Language (HTML) A language that defines the structure and layout of Web page content. An HTML tag is a notation used to define a data element for display or other purposes. p. 139

Hypertext Transport Protocol (HTTP) A Layer-5 protocol used to process Web pages. p. 132

ICANN Internet Corporation for Assigned Names and Numbers. A public agency that establishes procedures and authorizes organizations to association names with public IP addresses. p. 134

Identification The process whereby an information system identifies a user by requiring the user to sign on with a user name and password. p. 287

Identifier An attribute (or group of attributes) whose value is associated with one and only one entity instance. p. 385

IEEE 802.3 protocol This standard, also called *Ethernet*, is a network protocol that operates at Layers 1 and 2 of the TCP/IP–OSI architecture. Ethernet, the world's most popular LAN protocol, is used on WANs as well. p. 127

IEEE 802.11 protocol A wireless communications standard, widely used today, that enables access within a few hundred feet. The most popular version of this standard is IEEE 802.11g, which allows wireless transmissions of up to 54 Mbps. p. 127

IEE 802.16 protocol An emerging wireless communications standard, also known as *WiMax*, that enables broadband wireless access for fixed, nomadic, and portable applications. In fixed mode, it enables access across a several-mile or larger region. See also *WiMax*. p. 151

If/then rule Format for rules derived from a decision tree (data mining) or by interviewing a human expert (expert systems). p. 346, p. 510

Implementation phase The fourth phase in the SDLC, in which developers build and integrate system components, test the system, and convert to the new system. p. 238

Implementation step A step in the decision-making process in which decision makers implement the alternative they have selected. p. 339

Import/export The process of transferring data from one computer application to another. p. 418

Industry-specific solutions An ERP template that is designed to serve the needs of companies or organizations in specific industries. Such solutions save time and decrease risk; their existence has spurred ERP growth. p. 473

Information (1) Knowledge derived from data, where *data* is defined as recorded facts or figures. (2) Data presented in a meaningful context. (3) Data processed by summing, ordering, averaging, grouping, comparing, or other similar operations. (4) A difference that makes a difference. p. 30

Information silos A condition that exists when data are isolated in separated information systems. p. 156

Information system (IS) A group of components that interact to produce information. p. 10

Information technology (IT) The products, methods, inventions, and standards that are used for the purpose of producing information. p. 13

Inherent processes The procedures that must be followed to effectively use licensed software. For example, the processes inherent in MRP systems assume that certain users will take specified actions in a particular order. In most cases, the organization must conform to the processes inherent in the software. p. 165

Input hardware Hardware devices that attach to a computer; includes keyboards, mouse, document scanners, and bar-code (Universal Product Code) scanners. p. 74

Instruction set The collection of instructions that a computer can process. p. 80

Intangible benefit A benefit of an information system for which it is impossible to compute a dollar value. p. 267

Intelligence gathering step A step where decision makers determine what is to be decided, what the criteria for the decision will be, and what data are available. p. 338

Interenterprise information system Information system that is shared by two or more independent organizations. p. 158

Internal firewall A firewall that sits inside the organizational network. p. 290

Internet When spelled with a small *i*, as in *internet*, a private network of networks. When spelled with a capital *I*, as in *Internet*, the public internet known as the Internet. p. 124

Internet Corporation for Assigned Names and Numbers (ICANN) The organization responsible for managing the assignment of public IP addresses and domain names for use on the Internet. Each public IP address is unique across all computers on the Internet. p. 134

Internet Protocol (IP) A Layer-3 protocol. As the name implies, IP is used on the Internet, but it is used on many other internets as well. The chief purpose of IP is to route packets across an internet. p. 133

Internet service provider (ISP) An ISP provides users with Internet access. An ISP provides a user with a legitimate Internet address; it serves as the user's gateway to the Internet; and it passes communications back and forth between the user and the Internet. ISPs also pay for the Internet. They collect money from their customers and pay access fees and other charges on the users' behalf. p. 128

Interorganizational IS Information systems used between or among organizations that are independently owned and managed. p. 184

Interorganizational processes Business processes that cross not only departmental boundaries, but organizational boundaries as well. Such processes involve activities among organizations having different owners. p. 480

Inventory applications Applications that help control and manage inventory and support inventory policy. p. 459

IP address A series of dotted decimals in a format like 192.168.2.28 that identifies a unique device on a network or internet. With the *IPv4* standard, IP addresses have 32 bits. With the *IPv6* standard, IP addresses have 128 bits. Today, IPv4 is more common but will likely be supplanted by IPv6 in the future. With IPv4, the decimal between the dots can never exceed 255. p. 134

IP spoofing A type of spoofing whereby an intruder uses another site's IP address as if it were that other site. p. 283

IPv4 A standard for internet addressing that uses a four decimal digit notation like 65.193.123.253. Gradually being replaced by Ipv6. p. 134

IPv6 A standard for internet addressing that uses a long (128 bit) scheme for internet addresses and provides other benefits over IPv4 as well. Gradually overtaking IPv4. p. 134

Island of automation The structure that results when functional applications work independently in isolation from one another. Usually problematic because data are duplicated, integration is difficult, and results can be inconsistent. p. 159

Just barely sufficient information Information that meets the purpose for which it is generated, but just barely so. p. 32

Just-in-time (JIT) inventory policy A policy that seeks to have production inputs (both raw materials and work-in-process) delivered to the manufacturing site just as they are needed. By scheduling delivery of inputs in this way, companies are able to reduce inventories to a minimum. p. 460

Key (1) A column or group of columns that identifies a unique row in a table. (2) A number used to encrypt data. The encryption algorithm applies the key to the original message to produce the coded message. Decoding (decrypting) a message is similar; a key is applied to the coded message to recover the original text. p. 102, p. 288

Key escrow A control procedure whereby a trusted party is given a copy of a key used to encrypt database data. p. 293

Kilobyte (K) 1,024 bytes. p. 76

Knowledge management (KM) The process of creating value from intellectual capital and sharing that knowledge with employees, managers, suppliers, customers, and others who need that capital. p. 341

Knowledge management system (KMS) An information system for storing and retrieving organizational knowledge, whether that knowledge is in the form of data, documents, or employee know-how. p. 211

LAN device A computing device that includes important networking components, including a switch, a router, a DHCP server, and other elements. p. 126

LCD monitor A type of video display monitor that uses a technology called *liquid crystal display*. LCD monitors are flat and require much less space than CRT monitors. p. 375

Lead-generation applications Sales and marketing applications that send mailings (postal or email) for the purpose of generating sales prospects. Also called *prospect-generation* applications. p. 456

Lead-tracking applications Sales and marketing applications that record data on sales prospects and keep records of customer contacts. p. 456

Library In version-control collaboration systems, a shared directory that allows access to various documents by means of *permissions*. p. 326

License Agreement that stipulates how a program can be used. Most specify the number of computers on which the program can be installed and sometimes the number of users that can connect to and use the program remotely. Such agreements also stipulate limitations on the liability of the software vendor for the consequences of errors in the software. p. 82

Lift In market-basket terminology, the ratio of confidence to the base probability of buying an item. Lift shows how much the base probability changes when other products are purchased. If the lift is greater than 1, the change is positive; if it is less than 1, the change is negative. p. 508

Lines of code Estimating technique that attempts to schedule a development project by the number of lines of code developers must write for the project. p. 573

Linkages Process interactions across value chains. Linkages are important sources of efficiencies and are readily supported by information systems. p. 53

Linux A version of Unix that was developed by the open-source community. The open-source community owns Linux, and there is no fee to use it. Linux is a popular operating system for Web servers. p. 82

Local area network (LAN) A network that connects computers that reside in a single geographic location on the premises of the company that operates the LAN. The number of connected computers can range from two to several hundred. p. 124

Localizing The process of making a computer program work in a second language. p. 590

Lost-update problem An issue in multi-user database processing in which two or more users try to make changes to the data but the database cannot make the changes because it was not designed to process changes from multiple users. p. 110

M score In RFM analysis, a number rating that indicates in which fifth a customer ranks in terms of *amount spent* per order. p. 506

Mac OS An operating system developed by Apple Computer, Inc., for the Macintosh. The current version is Mac OS X. Macintosh computers are used primarily by graphic artists and workers in the arts community. Mac OS was developed for the Power PC, but as of 2006 will run on Intel processors as well. p. 81

Macro virus Virus that attaches itself to a Word, Excel, PowerPoint, or other type of document. When the infected document is opened, the virus places itself in the startup files of the application. After that, the virus infects every file that the application creates or processes. p. 291

Machine code A sequence of bits that represent computer instructions and data that can be processed by a computer. p. 88

Main memory A set of cells in which each cell holds a byte of data or instruction; each cell has an address, and the CPU uses the addresses to identify particular data items. p. 75

Maintenance phase A phase of the systems development lifecycle in which the information systems is either a) made to function as it was supposed to in the first place (failure fixing) or b) adapted to changes in requirements. p. 238

Malware Viruses, worms, Trojan horses, spyware, and adware. p. 291

Malware definitions Patterns that exist in malware code. Antimalware vendors update these definitions continuously and incorporate them into their products in order to better fight against malware. p. 292

Management information system (MIS) An information system that helps businesses achieve their goals and objectives. p. 10, p. 335

Managerial decision Decision that concerns the allocation and use of resources. p. 335

Manufacturing applications Applications that support one or more aspects of manufacturing processes, including planning, scheduling, inventory integration, quality control, and related processes. p. 459

Manufacturing resource planning (MRP II) A follow-on to MRP that includes the planning of materials, personnel, and machinery. It supports many linkages across the organization, including linkages with sales and marketing via the development of a master production schedule. It also includes the capability to perform what-if analyses on variances in schedules, raw materials availabilities, personnel, and other resources. p. 461

Many-to-many (N:M) relationship Relationships involving two entity types in which an instance of one type can relate to many instances of the second type, and an instance of the second type can relate to many instances of the first. For example, the relationship between Student and Class is N:M. One student may enroll in many classes and one class may have many students. Contrast with *one-to-many relationships*. p. 386

Map projection A technique for placing locations on the surface on the earth onto a flat surface. p. 536

Margin The difference between value and cost. p. 51

Market-basket analysis A data mining technique for determining sales patterns. A market-basket analysis shows the products that customers tend to buy together. p. 211, p. 507

Mashup The combination of output from two or more Web sites into a single user experience. p. 191

Master production schedule (MPS) A plan for producing products. To create the MPS, the company analyzes past sales levels and makes estimates of future sales. This process is sometimes called a *push manufacturing process,* because the company pushes the products into sales (and customers) according to the MPS. p. 461

Materials requirements planning (MRP) An information system that plans the need for materials and inventories of materials used in the manufacturing process. Unlike MRP II, MRP does not include the planning of personnel, equipment, or facilities requirements. p. 461

Maximum cardinality The maximum number of entities that can be involved in a relationship. Common examples of maximum cardinality are 1:N, N:M, and 1:1. p. 387

Measure The data item of interest on an OLAP report. It is the item that is to be summed, averaged, or otherwise processed in the OLAP cube. Total sales, average sales, and average cost are examples of measures. p. 522

Megabyte (MB) 1,024 KB. p. 76

Memory swapping The movement of programs and data into and out of memory. If a computer has insufficient memory for its workload, such swapping will degrade system performance. p. 77

Merchant companies In e-commerce, companies that take title to the goods they sell. They buy goods and resell them. p. 186

Metadata Data that describe data. p. 104

Microblog Web site on which users can publish opinions, just like a Web blog, but the opinions are restricted to small amounts of text, such as Twitter's 140 characters. p. 498

Microsoft Office SharePoint Designer A thick client application available license-free from Microsoft. It is used to customize SharePoint pages in more advanced ways than are possible in a browser. p. 327

Microsoft Office SharePoint Workspace A thick-client application that was formerly known as Microsoft Groove. p. 320

Microsoft SharePoint A Web page processing application that is primarily used for collaboration. SharePoint provides support for document libraries, lists, discussion forums, surveys, Wikis, blogs, and other collaboration tools. p. 327

Military grid coordinate system (MGRS) Coordinate system that divides the earth into 60 north-south segments, like segments in an orange and provides a means for specifying locations within those segments. p. 537

Minimum cardinality The minimum number of entities that must be involved in a relationship. p. 387

Mobile access The use of networked computers while in motion. p. 446

Modem Short for *modulator/demodulator,* a modem converts the computer's digital data into signals that can be transmitted over telephone or cable lines. p. 129

Modifiable areal unit problem (MAUP) A condition that occurs when point-based spatial data is aggregated into regions and the results depend on how the regions are defined. p. 545

Modules A suite of applications. p. 545

Moore's Law A law, created by Gordon Moore, stating that the number of transistors per square inch on an integrated chip doubles every 18 months. Moore's prediction has proved generally accurate in the 40 years since it was made. Sometimes this law is stated that the performance of a computer doubles every 18 months. Although not strictly true, this version gives the gist of the idea. p. 6

Multiparty text chat A synchronous virtual meeting, in which participants meet at the same time and communicate by typing comments over a communication network. p. 320

Multiuser processing When multiple users process the database at the same time. p. 110

My Maps A Web 2.0 product that provides tools with which users can make custom modifications to maps provided by Google; My Maps is an example of a mashup. p. 191

MySQL A popular open-source DBMS product that is license-free for most applications. p. 106

Named range A subset of the cells in a worksheet that has a unique name. p. 434

Narrowband Internet communication lines that have transmission speeds of 56 kbps or less. A dial-up modem provides narrowband access. p. 130

Network A collection of computers that communicate with one another over transmission lines. p. 124

Network interface card (NIC) A hardware component on each device on a network (computer, printer, etc.) that connects the device's circuitry to the communications line. The NIC works together with programs in each device to implement Layers 1 and 2 of the TCP/IP–OSI hybrid protocol. p. 126

Neural network A popular supervised data mining technique used to predict values and make classifications, such as "good prospect" or "poor prospect." p. 218

Nomadic access Application with which users access networks from different locations, but not while in motion from site to site. p. 446

Nonmerchant companies E-commerce companies that arrange for the purchase and sale of goods without ever owning or taking title to those goods. p. 186

Nonvolatile Memory that preserves data even when not powered (e.g., magnetic and optical disks). With such devices, you can turn the computer off and back on, and the contents will be unchanged. p. 78

Normal forms A classification of tables according to their characteristics and the kinds of problems they have. p. 389

Normalization The process of converting poorly structured tables into two or more well-structured tables. p. 388

Object Management Group (OMG) A software-industry standards organization that has sponsored the creation of many technology standards including the Business Process Modeling Notation (BPMN), a standard set of terms and graphical notations for documenting business processes. p. 553

Object-relational database A type of database that stores both OOP objects and relational data. Rarely used in commercial applications. p. 103

Off-the-shelf software Software that can be used without having to make any changes. p. 84

Off-the-shelf with alterations software Software bought off-the-shelf but altered to fit the organization's specific needs. p. 84

Office Web Apps License-free, Web-based versions of Word, Excel, PowerPoint, and OneNote available on SkyDrive. p. 325

OLAP See *Online analytical processing.* p. 228

OLAP cube A presentation of an OLAP measure with associated dimensions. The reason for this term is that some products show these displays using three axes, like a cube in geometry. Same as *OLAP report.* p. 522

OLAP servers Computer servers running software that performs OLAP analyses. An OLAP server reads data from an operational database, performs preliminary calculations, and stores the results of those calculations in an OLAP database. p. 523

Onboard NIC A built-in NIC. p. 126

One-of-a-kind application Software that is developed for a specific, unique need, usually for a particular company's operations. p. 83

One-to-many (1:N) relationship Relationships involving two entity types in which an instance of one type can relate to many instances of the second type, but an instance of the second type can relate to at most one instance of the first. For example, the relationship between Department and Employee is 1:N. A department may relate to many employees, but an employee relates to at most one department. p. 386

Online analytical processing (OLAP) A dynamic type of reporting system that provides the ability to sum, count, average, and perform other simple arithmetic operations on groups of data. Such reports are dynamic because users can change the format of the reports while viewing them. p. 228, p. 521

Open-source community A loosely coupled group of programmers who mostly volunteer their time to contribute code to develop and maintain common software. Linux and MySQL are two prominent products developed by such a community. p. 82

Operations applications Applications that maintain data on finished goods inventory and the movements of goods from inventory to the customer. p. 458

Operating system (OS) A computer program that controls the computer's resources: It manages the contents of main memory, processes keystrokes and mouse movements, sends signals to the display monitor, reads and writes disk files, and controls the processing of other programs. p. 77

Operational decisions Decisions that concern the day-to-day activities of an organization. p. 335

Optical-fiber cable A type of cable used to connect the computers, printers, switches, and other devices on a LAN. The signals on such cables are light rays, and they are reflected inside the glass core of the optical-fiber cable. The core is surrounded by a *cladding* to contain the light signals, and the cladding, in turn, is wrapped with an outer layer to protect it. p. 127

Optimal resolution The size of the pixel grid (e.g., 1,024 × 768) on a video display monitor that will give the best sharpness and clarity. This optimal resolution depends on the size of the screen, the dot or pixel pitch, and other factors. p. 375

Oracle A popular, enterprise-class DBMS product from Oracle Corporation. p. 106

Organizational feasibility One of four dimensions of feasibility. p. 240

Output hardware Hardware that displays the results of the computer's processing. Consists of video displays, printers, audio speakers, overhead projectors, and other special-purpose devices, such as large flatbed plotters. p. 75

Outsourcing The process of hiring another organization to perform a service. Outsourcing is done to save costs, to gain expertise, and to free up management time. p. 578

Packet A small piece of an electronic message that has been divided into chunks; these chunks are sent separately and then reassembled at their destination. p. 133

Packet-filtering firewall A firewall that examines each packet and determines whether to let the packet pass. To make this decision, it examines the source address, the destination addresses, and other data. p. 290

Parallel installation A type of system conversion in which the new system runs in parallel with the old one for a while. Parallel installation is expensive because the organization incurs the costs of running both systems. p. 247

Partitioned database A database that is divided into nonoverlapping segments, and two or more segments are distributed into different geographic locations. p. 591

Patch A group of fixes for high-priority failures that can be applied to existing copies of a particular product. Software vendors supply patches to fix security and other critical problems. p. 249

Payload The program code of a virus that causes unwanted or hurtful actions, such as deleting programs or data, or, even worse, modifying data in ways that are undetected by the user. p. 291

PC mules Business professionals who carry their devices wherever they go. p. 448

Personal DBMS DBMS products designed for smaller, simpler database applications. Such products are used for personal or small workgroup applications that involve fewer than 100 users, and normally fewer than 15. Today, Microsoft Access is the only prominent personal DBMS. p. 110

Personal identification number (PIN) A form of authentication whereby the user supplies a number that only he or she knows. p. 287

Personal information system Information systems used by a single individual. p. 156

Petabyte 10^{15} bytes. p. 210

Phased installation A type of system conversion in which the new system is installed in pieces across the organization(s). Once a given piece works, then the organization installs and tests another piece of the system, until the entire system has been installed. p. 247

Phisher An individual or organization that spoofs legitimate companies in an attempt to illegally capture personal data, such as credit card numbers, email accounts, and driver's license numbers. p. 285

Phishing A technique for obtaining unauthorized data that uses pretexting via email. The *phisher* pretends to be a legitimate company and sends an email requesting confidential data, such as account numbers, Social Security numbers, account passwords, and so forth. p. 283

Pilot installation A type of system conversion in which the organization implements the entire system on a limited portion of the business. The advantage of pilot implementation is that if the system fails, the failure is contained within a limited boundary. This reduces exposure of the business and also protects the new system from developing a negative reputation throughout the organization(s). p. 247

Pixel pitch The distance between pixels on the screen of an LCD monitor; the smaller the pixel pitch, the sharper and brighter the image will be. p. 375

Pixels Small spots on the screen of a video display monitor arranged in a rectangular grid. The number of pixels displayed depends not only on the size of the monitor, but also on the design of the computer's video card. p. 375

Plunge installation Sometimes called *direct installation,* a type of system conversion in which the organization shuts off the old system and starts the new system. If the new system fails, the organization is in trouble: Nothing can be done until either the new system is fixed or the old system is reinstalled. Because of the risk, organizations should avoid this conversion style if possible. p. 248

Podcast A digital file that can be downloaded and played; can be audio or video. p. 345

Portal A Web site that publishes information for users; can be public (such as Yahoo!) or private (such as for a company's employees or a specific work team). p. 345

Pretexting A technique for gathering unauthorized information in which someone pretends to be someone else. A common scam involves a telephone caller who pretends to be from a credit card company and claims to be checking the validity of credit card numbers. Phishing is also a form of pretexting. p. 283

Price conflict In e-commerce, a conflict that may result when manufacturers offer products at prices lower than those available through existing sales channels. p. 188

Price elasticity A measure of the sensitivity in demand to changes in price. It is the ratio of the percentage change in quantity divided by the percentage change in price. p. 187

Primary activities In Porter's value chain model, the fundamental activities that create value—inbound logistics, operations, outbound logistics, marketing/sales, and service. p. 51

Private IP address A type of IP address used within private networks and internets. Private IP addresses are assigned and managed by the company that operates the private network or internet. p. 134

Problem of the last mile The bottleneck on data communications into homes and into smaller businesses. p. 151

Process blueprint In an ERP product, a comprehensive set of inherent processes for organizational activities. p. 470

Product and brand management applications Marketing applications that import records of past sales from order processing or accounts receivable systems and compare those data to projections and sales estimates, in order to assess the effectiveness of promotions, advertising, and general success of a product brand. p. 458

Product quality assurance (PQA) The testing of a system. PQA personnel usually construct a test plan with the advice and assistance of users. PQA test engineers perform testing, and they also supervise user-test activity. Many PQA professionals are programmers who write automated test programs. p. 246

Project Management Institute (PMI) International organization focused on disseminating best practices in project management. p. 569

Project Management Professional (PMP) Certification awarded by the Project Management Institute to IT professionals who meet the organization's standards of practice and pass an examination. p. 568

Protocol A standardized means for coordinating an activity between two or more entities. p. 125

Public IP address An IP address used on the Internet. Such IP addresses are assigned to major institutions in blocks by the Internet Corporation for Assigned Names and Numbers (ICANN). Each IP address is unique across all computers on the Internet. p. 134

Pull manufacturing process A manufacturing process whereby products are pulled through manufacturing by demand. Items are manufactured in response to signals from customers or other production processes that products or components are needed. p. 461

Pull report A report that the user must request. To obtain a pull report, a user goes to a Web portal or digital dashboard and clicks a link or button to cause the reporting system to produce and deliver the report. p. 520

Push manufacturing process A plan for producing products whereby the company analyzes past sales levels, makes estimates of future sales, and creates a master production schedule. Products are produced according to that schedule and pushed into sales (and customers). p. 461

Push report Reports sent to users according to a preset schedule. Users receive the report without any activity on their part. p. 520

Quad processor A computer with four CPUs. p. 75

Query A request for data from a database. p. 108

Query report Report that is prepared in response to data entered by users. p. 519

Quick launch A partial list of resources contained within the site. p. 328

R score In RFM analysis, a number rating that indicates in which fifth a customer ranks in terms of *most recent* order. p. 506

RAM Stands for *random access memory*, which is main memory consisting of cells that hold data or instructions. Each cell has an address that the CPU uses to read or write data. Memory locations can be read or written in any order, hence the term *random access*. RAM memory is almost always volatile. p. 75

Raster map A map image that consists of pixels, each of which has some value, often that value is a color, but it could also be a data value like elevation or temperature. Contrast with vector map. p. 534

Records Also called *rows*, groups of columns in a database table. p. 101

Regression analysis A type of supervised data mining that estimates the values of parameters in a linear equation. Used to determine the relative influence of variables on an outcome and also to predict future values of that outcome. p. 218

Relation The more formal name for a database table. p. 103

Relational database Database that carries its data in the form of tables and that represents relationships using foreign keys. p. 103

Relationship An association among entities or entity instances in an E-R model or an association among rows of a table in a relational database. p. 386

Relevant information Information that is appropriate to both the context and the subject. p. 32

Remote access Using information systems to provide activity or action at a distance. p. 445

Replicated databases Databases that contain duplicated records. Processing of such databases is complex if users want to be able to update the same items at the same time without experiencing *lost-update problems*. p. 591

Report A presentation of data in a structured, meaningful context. p. 108

Report authoring The process of connecting to data sources, creating the report structure, and formatting the report. p. 520

Report delivery The function of reporting systems that determines that reports are pushed or pulled, in the right form, and to the right people at the right time. p. 520

Report management The function of reporting systems that defines who receives what reports, when, and by what means. p. 520

Report media In reporting systems, the channels by which reports are delivered, such as in paper form or electronically. p. 519

Report mode In reporting systems, the categorization of reports into either *push reports* or *pull reports*. p. 520

Report type In reporting systems, the categorization of reports as either *static* or *dynamic.* p. 518

Reporting system A system that creates information from disparate data sources and delivers that information to the proper users on a timely basis. p. 211, p. 515

Repository A collection of business records, usually implemented as a database. p. 28

Requirements The characteristics of an information system; one of the critical drivers in large-scale IS development, which typically involves trade-offs with cost and time. p. 567

Requirements analysis phase The second phase in the SDLC, in which developers conduct user interviews; evaluate existing systems; determine new forms/reports/queries; identify new features and functions, including security; and create the data model. p. 238

Requirements creep The process in which users agree to one set of requirements, and then add more over time. p. 575

Resources Items of value, such as inventory or funds, that are part of a business process. p. 28

Review step The final step in the decision-making process, in which decision makers evaluate results of their decision and, if necessary, repeat the process to correct or adapt the decision. p. 339

RFM analysis A way of analyzing and ranking customers according to the recency, frequency, and monetary value of their purchases. p. 506

Ribbon The wide bar of tools and selections that appears just under the tabs in an Excel workbook. p. 351

Roles In a business process, sets of procedures. p. 28

Rotational delay On a disk, the time it takes the data to rotate under the read/write head. The faster the disk spins, the shorter the rotational delay. p. 374

Router A special-purpose computer that moves network traffic from one node on a network to another. p. 133

Row In the relational model, a collection of columns or attribute values that refers to a single entity instance. Also called record or tuple. Just think of a row of a table and you'll be fine! p. 101

Schedule feasibility One of four dimensions of feasibility. p. 240

Scope In the discipline of project management, the characteristics needed to be built into an information system; same as the term *requirements.* In the Systems Development Life Cycle (SDLC), *scope* means to define the system boundaries. p. 570

Seats A measure of the number of users of a software product for licensing purposes. p. 379

Secure Socket Layer (SSL) A protocol that uses both asymmetric and symmetric encryption. SSL is a protocol layer that works between Levels 4 (transport) and 5 (application) of the TCP–OSI protocol architecture. When SSL is in use, the browser address will begin with *https://.* The most recent version of SSI is called TLS. p. 289

Security threat A problem with the security of an information system or the data therein caused by human error, malicious activity, or natural disasters. p. 282

Seek time On a disk, the time it takes the read/write arm to position the head over the correct circle. Seek time is determined by the make and model of the disk device. p. 374

Self-efficacy A person's belief that he or she can be successful at his or her job. p. 171

Semantic security Concerns the unintended release of protected information through the release of a combination of reports or documents that are independently not protected. p. 524

Server A computer that provides some type of service, such as hosting a database, running a blog, publishing a Web site, or selling goods. Server computers are faster, larger, and more powerful than client computers. p. 78

Server farm A large collection of server computers that coordinates the activities of the servers, usually for commercial purposes. p. 79

Server tier In the three-tier architecture, the tier that consists of computers that run Web servers to generate Web pages and other data in response to requests from browsers. Web servers also process application programs. p. 137

Service A repeatable task that a business needs to perform. p. 557

Service pack A large group of fixes that solve low-priority software problems. Users apply service packs in much the same way that they apply patches, except that service packs typically involve fixes to hundreds or thousands of problems. p. 249

Service provider An activity that conforms to SOA principles. p. 559

Service-oriented architecture (SOA) Processing philosophy that advocates that computing systems use a *standard method* to declare the services they provide and the interface by which those services can be requested and used. Web services are an implementation of SOA. p. 185, p. 557

SharedView A free, downloadable product from Microsoft for sharing a computer screen among several people. p. 320

SharePoint site A facility constructed and shared by Microsoft SharePoint, a component of Windows Server. A SharePoint site is a collection of libraries, lists, discussion boards, surveys, Wikis, and other collaboration tools. SharePoint sites support workflows, which are important for content management. A SharePoint site can have multiple subsites, and those subsites can have multiple subsites as well. p. 328

Silverlight A browser add-on that was developed by Microsoft to enhance browser features to improve the user interface, include movies, audio, and animation, and provide greater programmer control of user activity. p. 140

Simple Mail Transfer Protocol (SMTP) A Layer-5 architecture used to send email. Normally used in conjunction with other Layer-5 protocols (POP3, IMAP) for receiving email. p. 133

Site license A license purchased by an organization to equip all the computers on a site with certain software. p. 82, p. 377

SLATES An acronym for Enterprise 2.0 that refers to Search, Links, Authoring, Tags, Extensions, and Signals. See Figure 8-10. p. 198

Small office/home office (SOHO) A business office with usually fewer than 10 employees, often located in the business professional's home. p. 125

Smart card A plastic card similar to a credit card that has a microchip. The microchip, which holds much more data than a magnetic strip, is loaded with identifying data. Normally requires a PIN. p. 287

Sniffing A technique for intercepting computer communications. With wired networks, sniffing requires a physical connection to the network. With wireless networks, no such connection is required. p. 283

SOAP A protocol for exchanging messages encoded in XML. SOAP sits on top of any available transport protocol, such as HTTP, HTTPS, or FTP. SOAP is independent of any device, network, vendor, or product. p. 562

Social capital The investment in social relations with expectation of future returns in the marketplace. p. 193

Social CRM CRM that includes social networking elements and gives the customer much more power and control in the customer–vendor relationship. p. 185

Social graph A network of relationships. p. 496

Social network Connections of people with similar interests. Today, social networks typically are supported by Web 2.0 technology. p. 193

Social networking (SN) Any activity that an entity like an individual, project, or organization takes with the entities to which it is related. p. 193, p. 490

Social networking application A computer program that interacts with and processes information in a social network. p. 495

Social networking group An association of social networking members related to a particular topic, event, activity, or other collective interest. In addition to members, SN groups have resources such as photos, videos, documents, discussion threads, a wallboard, and features. p. 495

Social networking information system An information system that facilitates interactions on a social network. p. 490

Software as a service (SAAS) Business model whereby companies (such as Google, Amazon.com, and eBay) provide services based on their software, rather than providing software as a product (by means of software-usage licenses). Software as a service is an example of Web 2.0. p. 189

Source code Computer code as written by humans and that is understandable by humans. p. 88

Special function cards Cards that can be added to the computer to augment the computer's basic capabilities. p. 75

Speed The dollar-value rate at which goods are exchanged in a given period of time within a supply chain. p. 485

Spoofing When someone pretends to be someone else with the intent of obtaining unauthorized data. If you pretend to be your professor, you are spoofing your professor. p. 283

Spreadsheet A table of data having rows and columns. Computer-based spreadsheets, such as those processed by Excel, include formulas and sophisticated graphics and offer other capabilities. p. 349

Spyware Programs installed on the user's computer without the user's knowledge or permission that reside in the background and, unknown to the user, observe the user's actions and keystrokes, modify computer activity, and report the user's activities to sponsoring organizations. Malicious spyware captures keystrokes to obtain user names, passwords, account numbers, and other sensitive information. Other spyware is used for marketing analyses, observing what users do, Web sites visited, products examined and purchased, and so forth. p. 291

SQL Server A popular enterprise-class DBMS product from Microsoft. p. 106

Static report Report that is prepared once from the underlying data and that does not change. A report of the past year's sales, for example, is a static report. p. 518

Storage hardware Hardware that saves data and programs. Magnetic disk is by far the most common storage device, although optical disks, such as CDs and DVDs, also are popular. p. 75

Stored procedure A computer program stored in the database that is used to enforce business rules. p. 470

Strategic decision Decision that concerns broader-scope, organizational issues. p. 335

Strength of a relationship The likelihood that the entity (person or other organization) in a relationship will do something that benefits entities in the relationship. p. 493

Strong password A password with the following characteristics: seven or more characters; does not contain the user's user name, real name, or company name; does not contain a complete dictionary word, in any language; is different from the user's previous passwords; and contains both upper- and lowercase letters, numbers, and special characters. p. 14

Structured decision A type of decision for which there is a formalized and accepted method for making the decision. p. 336

Structured Query Language (SQL) An international standard language for processing database data. p. 107

SUM A built-in arithmetic function in Excel that sums the values in a row or column. p. 362

Supervised data mining A form of data mining in which data miners develop a model prior to the analysis and apply statistical techniques to data to estimate values of the parameters of the model. p. 218

Supply chain A network of organizations and facilities that transforms raw materials into products delivered to customers. p. 480

Supply chain profitability The difference between the sum of the revenue generated by the supply chain and the sum of the costs that all organizations in the supply chain incur to obtain that revenue. p. 483

Support In market-basket terminology, the probability that two items will be purchased together. p. 508

Support activities In Porter's value chain model, the activities that contribute indirectly to value creation—procurement, technology, human resources, and the firm's infrastructure. p. 51

Surface A new Microsoft hardware–software product that enables people to interact with data on the surface of a table. p. 95

Swim-lane layout A type of business process diagram. Like swim lanes in a swimming pool, each role is shown in its own horizontal rectangle. Swim-lane layout can be used to simplify process diagrams and to draw attention to interactions among components of the diagram. p. 553

Switch A special-purpose computer that receives and transmits data across a network. p. 126

Switching costs Business strategy of locking in customers by making it difficult or expensive to change to another product or supplier. p. 56

Symmetric encryption An encryption method whereby the same key is used to encode and to decode the message. p. 288

Symmetrical digital subscriber lines (SDSL) DSL lines that have the same upload and download speeds. p. 129

Synch The process of synchronizing the data on two or more computers. For example, if you work on your computer at home, when you get to work, you have to synchronize (or synch)your computer at work with any changes you've made on the computer at home. p. 449

Synchronous communication Information exchange that occurs when all members of a work team meet at the same time, such as face-to-face meetings or conference calls. p. 320

System A group of components that interact to achieve some purpose. p. 10

System conversion The process of *converting* business activity from the old system to the new. p. 247

System definition phase The first phase in the SDLC, in which developers, with the help of eventual users, define the new system's goals and scope, assess its feasibility, form a project team, and plan the project. p. 238

Systems analysis and design The process of creating and maintaining information systems. It is sometimes called *systems development.* p. 234

Systems analysts IS professionals who understand both business and technology. They are active throughout the systems development process and play a key role in moving the project from conception to conversion and, ultimately, maintenance. Systems analysts integrate the work of the programmers, testers, and users. p. 241

Systems development The process of creating and maintaining information systems. It is sometimes called *systems analysis and design.* p. 234

Systems development life cycle (SDLC) The classical process used to develop information systems. These basic tasks of systems development are combined into the following phases: system definition, requirements analysis, component design, implementation, and system maintenance (fix or enhance). p. 238

Systems thinking The ability to model the components of the system, to connect the inputs and outputs among those components into a sensible whole that reflects the structure and dynamics of the phenomenon observed. p. 8

Tab-delimited file An exported file in which data values are separated by tab characters. p. 419

Table Also called a *file*, a group of similar rows or records in a database. p. 101

Tag In markup languages such as HTML and XML, notation used to define a data element for display or other purposes. p. 139, p. 561

Tangible benefit A benefit of an IS that can be measured as a dollar value. p. 267

TCP/IP–OSI (protocol) architecture A protocol architecture having five layers that evolved as a hybrid of the TCP/IP and the OSI architecture. This architecture is used on the Internet and on most internets. p. 132

Team A small group of people with complementary skills who are committed to a common purpose, goals, and work approach. p. 312

Team survey A form of asynchronous communication in which one team member creates a list of questions and other team members respond. Microsoft SharePoint has built-in survey capability. p. 321

Technical feasibility One of four dimensions of feasibility. p. 240

Technical safeguards Safeguards that involve the hardware and software components of an information system. p. 287

Telediagnosis A remote access system used by health care professionals to provide expertise in rural or remote areas. p. 445

Telelaw enforcement A remote access system that provides law enforcement capability, such as the RedFlex system that uses cameras and motion-sensing equipment to issue tickets for red-light and speeding violations. p. 445

Telesurgery A remote access system that links surgeons to robotic equipment and patients at a distance. p. 445

Terabyte (TB) 1,024 GB. p. 76

Test plan Groups of sequences of actions that users will take when using the new system. p. 246

The Internet The public internet that you use when you send email or access a Web site. p. 124

Thematic map A map that shows themes about geographic locations. p. 544

Thick client A software application that requires programs other than just the browser on a user's computer; that is, it requires code on both a client and a server computer. p. 86

Thin client A software application that requires nothing more than a browser and can be run on only the user's computer. p. 86

Three-tier architecture Architecture used by most e-commerce server applications. The tiers refer to three different classes of computers. The user tier consists of users' computers that have browsers that request and process Web pages. The server tier consists of computers that run Web servers and in the process generate Web pages and other data in response to requests from browsers. Web servers also process application programs. The third tier is the database tier, which runs the DBMS that processes the database. p. 137

Time The duration from start to finish to develop an IS; one of the critical drivers in large-scale IS development, which typically involves trade-offs with cost and requirements. p. 567

Timely information Information that is produced in time for its intended use. p. 32

Trade-off A decision that must be made to favor one thing over another; in project development, a company might choose a trade-off of cost over scope. p. 568

Train the trainer Training sessions in which vendors train the organization's employees, called Super Users, to become in-house trainers in order to improve training quality and reduce training expenses. p. 471

Transaction processing system (TPS) An information system that supports operational decision making. p. 335

Transmission Control Protocol (TCP) TCP operates at Layer 4 of the TCP/IP–OSI architecture. TCP is used in two ways: as the name of a Layer 4 protocol and as part of the name of the TCP/IP–OSI protocol architecture. The architecture gets its name because it usually includes the TCP protocol. TCP receives messages from Layer-5 protocols (like HTTP) and breaks those messages up into segments that it sends to a Layer-3 protocol (like IP). p. 133

Transmission Control Protocol/Internet Protocol (TCP/IP) architecture A protocol architecture having four layers, developed by the Internet Engineering Task Force (IETF). TCP/IP is part of the TCP/IP–OSI protocol architecture that is used on the Internet and most internets today. p. 132

Transport Layer Security (TLS) A protocol, using both asymmetric and symmetric encryption, that works between Levels 4 (transport) and 5 (application) of the TCP–OSI protocol architecture. TLS is the new name for a later version of SSL. p. 289

Trigger A computer program stored within the database that runs to keep the database consistent. p. 470

Trojan horse Virus that masquerades as a useful program or file. The name refers to the gigantic mock-up of a horse that was filled with soldiers and moved into Troy during the Peloponnesian Wars. A typical Trojan horse appears to be a computer game, an MP3 music file, or some other useful, innocuous program. p. 291

Tuned Adjusting information systems from time to time to accommodate changes in workload. p. 264

Tunnel A virtual, private pathway over a public or shared network from the VPN client to the VPN server. p. 142

Twitter If you don't know, you need to spend less time reading textbooks and get out and have some fun. p. 498

Unauthorized data disclosure When a person inadvertently releases data in violation of policy. p. 283

Unified Modeling Language (UML) A series of diagramming techniques that facilitates OOP development. UML has dozens of different diagrams for all phases of system development. UML does not require or promote any particular development process. p. 385

Uniform resource locator (URL) A document's address on the Web. URLs begin on the right with a top level domain, and, moving left, include a domain name and then are followed by optional data that locates a document within that domain. p. 135

Unix An operating system developed at Bell Labs in the 1970s. It has been the workhorse of the scientific and engineering communities since then. p. 81

Unshielded twisted pair (UTP) cable A type of cable used to connect the computers, printers, switches, and other devices on a LAN. A UTP cable has four pairs of twisted wire. A device called an RJ-45 connector is used to connect the UTP cable into NIC devices. p. 126

Unstructured decision A type of decision for which there is no agreed-on decision-making method. p. 336

Unsupervised data mining A form of data mining whereby the analysts do not create a model or hypothesis before running the analysis. Instead, they apply the data mining technique to the data and observe the results. With this method, analysts create hypotheses after the analysis to explain the patterns found. p. 218

Upgrade A license offered by software vendors in the initial purchase of a product that allows users to obtain an updated version of the product for far less than the price of a new copy. p. 378

User-generated content (UGC) In Web 2.0, data and information that is provided by users. Examples are product ratings, product problem solutions, product designs, and marketing data. p. 191

User tier In the three-tier architecture, the tier that consists of computers that have browsers that request and process Web pages. p. 135

Usurpation Occurs when unauthorized programs invade a computer system and replace legitimate programs. Such unauthorized programs typically shut down the legitimate system and substitute their own processing. p. 284

Value The amount of money that a customer is willing to pay for a resource, product, or service. p. 51

Value chain A network of value-creating activities. p. 51

Value of social capital Value of a social network, which is determined by the number of relationships in a social network, by the strength of those relationships, and by the resources controlled by those related. p. 194

Vector map Map with features that consist of points, lines, and shapes. Vector maps can be scaled up and down without loss of fidelity. Contrast with *raster map*. p. 534

Version control Use of software to control access to and configuration of documents, designs, and other electronic versions of products. p. 326

Version management Use of software to control configuration of documents, designs, and other electronic versions of products. p. 323

Vertical-market application Software that serves the needs of a specific industry. Examples of such programs are those used by dental offices to schedule appointments and bill patients, those used by auto mechanics to keep track of customer data and customers' automobile repairs, and those used by parts warehouses to track inventory, purchases, and sales. p. 83

Videoconferencing Technology that combines a conference call with video cameras. p. 321

Viral hook A characteristic of a marketing program that causes one person to pass a marketing message on to others. The viral hook might be a humorous or outrageous video or story, or something of value to be exchanged. p. 491

Viral marketing A marketing method used in the Web 2.0 world in which *users* spread news about products and services to one another. p. 190

Virtual machine A computer program that presents the appearance of an independent operating system within a second, host operating system. The host can support multiple virtual machines, each of which is assigned assets such as disk space, devices, network connections, over which it has control. p. 449

Virtual meeting A meeting in which participants do not meet in the same place and possibly not at the same time. p. 320

Virtual private network (VPN) A WAN connection alternative that uses the Internet or a private internet to create the appearance of private point-to-point connections. In the IT world, the term *virtual* means something that appears to exist that does not exist in fact. Here, a VPN uses the public Internet to create the appearance of a private connection. p. 141

Virtualization The process whereby multiple operating systems share the same hardware. p. 82

Virus A computer program that replicates itself. p. 291

Volatile Data that will be lost when the computer or device is not powered. p. 78

WAN wireless A wide area network that provides network connections for computing devices such as smartphones, Kindles, or iPads using cell phone technology. p. 130

Waterfall The fiction that one phase of the SDLC can be completed in its entirety and the project can progress, without any backtracking, to the next phase of the SDLC. Projects seldom are that simple; backtracking is normally required. p. 250

Web The Internet-based network of browsers and servers that process HTTP or HTTPS. p. 133

Web 2.0 Generally, a loose cloud of capabilities, technologies, business models, and philosophies that characterize the new and emerging business uses of the Internet. p. 189

Web farm A facility that runs multiple Web servers. Work is distributed among the computers in a Web farm so as to maximize throughput. p. 138

Web pages Documents encoded in HTML that are created, transmitted, and consumed using the World Wide Web. p. 138

Web server A program that processes the HTTP protocol and transmits Web pages on demand. Web servers also process application programs. p. 138

Web Services Description Language (WSDL) A language that services can use to describe what they do and how other computer programs can access their features. p. 563

Web storefront In e-commerce, a Web-based application that enables customers to enter and manage their orders. p. 186

WebEx A popular commercial Webinar application used primarily for sales presentations. p. 320

Webinars A virtual meeting in which attendees can view the same computer desktop and communicate via phone and possibly via camera. p. 320

Web-log See *Blog*. p. 345

Wide area network (WAN) A network that connects computers located at different geographic locations. p. 124

WiMax An emerging technology based on the IEEE 802.16 standard. WiMax is designed to deliver the "last mile" of wireless broadband access and could ultimately replace cable and DSL for fixed applications and replace cell phones for nomadic and portable applications. See also *IEEE 802.16*. p. 130

Windows An operating system designed and sold by Microsoft. It is the most widely used operating system. p. 80

Windows Live SkyDrive A cloud-based facility that provides for the storage and sharing of Office documents and other files. SkyDrive offers free storage of up to 25GB and provides ready access to Office Web Applications for Word, Excel, PowerPoint, and OneNote. p. 325

Wireless hotspot hubs Devices that wirelessly connect to a WAN using cell phone technology and provide wireless connectivity to computers located in close proximity to the hub. p. 446

Wireless NIC (WNIC) Devices that enable wireless networks by communicating with wireless access points. Such devices can be cards that slide into the PCMA slot or they can be built-in, onboard devices. WNICs operate according to the 802.11 protocol. p. 127

Work breakdown structure (WBS) A hierarchy of the tasks required to complete a project; for a large project, it might involve hundreds or thousands of tasks. p. 570

Workbook In Microsoft Excel, one or more worksheets. p. 350

Workgroup information system An information system that is shared by a group of people for a particular purpose. p. 157

Worksheet A spreadsheet in Microsoft Excel. p. 350

Worm A virus that propagates itself using the Internet or some other computer network. Worm code is written specifically to infect another computer as quickly as possible. p. 291

Worth-its-cost information Information in which an appropriate relationship exists between the value of the information and the cost of creating it. p. 33

XML document A file of XML tags and data. p. 562

XML schema An XML document that specifies the structure of other XML documents. An XML schema is metadata for other XML documents. For example, a SalesOrder XML schema specifies the structure of SalesOrder documents. p. 562

Zones North-south segments in the Military Grid Coordinate System (MGRS). p. 537

PHOTO CREDITS

Chapter 1
Pages 2–3: Courtesy of *www.istockphoto.com*; Page 11: iStockphoto; Pages 16–17: Superstock Royalty Free; Pages 18–19: Sharon Dominick/iStockphoto.com.

Chapter 2
Page 31: *www.woot.com*; Pages 36–37: Eric Isselee/Shutterstock and Clover/Alamy Images Royalty Free. Pages 38–39 iStockphoto.com and sdominck/iStockphoto.com.

Chapter 3
Page 55: Superstock Royalty Free; Pages 60–61: Petr Nad/ Shutterstock and Steve Beer/Shutterstock; Pages 62–63: Sourabh/Shutterstock.

Chapter 4
Pages 70–71: Courtesy of *www.istockphoto.com*; Page 85: Newscom; Pages 90–91: iStockphoto.com; Pages 92–93: Beth Perkins/Stone/Getty Images.

Chapter 5
Page 105: iStockphoto.com and Superstock Royalty Free; Pages 112–113: PeskyMonkey/iStockphoto.com and Superstock Royalty Free; Pages 114–115: Skip ODonnell/ iStockphoto.com and Superstock Royalty Free.

Chapter 6
Page 136: Superstock Royalty Free; Pages 144–145: PhotoDisc/Getty Images; Pages 146–147: Maxx-Studio/Shutterstock.

Chapter 7
Pages 152–153: Courtesy of *www.istockphoto.com* and Michiel de Wit/Shutterstock; Page 167: Newscom; Pages 172–173: Gregory Gerber/Shutterstock.

Chapter 8
Page 182: © PhotoEdit/Alamy; Page 197: Superstock Royalty Free; Pages 200–201: RubberBall/Superstock Royalty Free; Pages 202–203: Christopher Pattberg/iStockphoto.com and Cultura/Corbis RF.

Chapter 9
Page 214: Shutterstock and Superstock Royalty Free; Pages 220–221: Allen Dellinger/iStockphoto.com and kkymek/Shutterstock; Pages 222–223: Andy Piatt/Shutterstock.

Chapter 10
Pages 230–231: Courtesy of *www.istockphoto.com* and Michiel de Wit/Shutterstock; Page 243: Superstock Royalty Free; Pages 252–253: Blend Images/Superstock Royalty Free; Pages 254–255: John Lund/Getty Images/Digital Vision.

Chapter 11
Page 264: Shutterstock; Pages 272–273: Superstock Royalty Free; Pages 274–275: filonmar/iStockphoto.com.

Chapter 12
Page 285: iStockphoto.com; Pages 302–303: Linda & Colin Mckie/iStockphoto.com; Pages 304–305: Masterfile Royalty Free Division.

Chapter Extension 13
Pages 486–487: Superstock Royalty Free.

Chapter Extension 15
Pages 512–513: Andrew Johnson/iStockphoto.com.

Chapter Extension 16
Pages 524–525: Courtesy of *www.istockphoto.com* and iStockphoto.com.

Chapter Extension 20
Pages 582–583: Tom McNemar/iStockphoto.com and Matthew Benolt/Shutterstock.

INDEX

Note: Page numbers with f indicate figures.

I

N

O

T

X

Y

Z